WORLD WAR II

in

BROOKLYN, N. Y.

WORLD WAR II

In Brooklyn, New York

1939-1945

Developed by **Historical Briefs, Inc.**, Box 629, Sixth Street & Madalyn Ave., Verplanck, NY 10596.

Printed by:
Monument Printers & Lithographers, Inc.
Sixth Street & Madalyn Ave., Verplanck, NY 10596

A WORD BEFORE YOU START

My Paternal Grandfather left Abruzzi, Italy knowing full well that he would never again see his mother or father or the place where he was born and raised. He was quite a young man in 1898 and he had ambition and courage and a deep desire to make a good life for himself in America. My maternal grandfather was born on the ship that made its way from Italy to New York with his parents aboard. They were from Napoli and were also looking to America for what they could not have in Italy. Both of them were fortunate to have their life in America begin in Brooklyn.

In Brooklyn they met and married my grandmothers, found work and raised their families. What a wonderful place Brooklyn was for them. In Brooklyn you could find every ethnic group. All the races were represented and every religion was to be found here.

This book, with its simply magnificent pages from the days of World War II will entertain you. You can reminisce, or perhaps take a look at a place, in a time you have not seen. You can check the movie schedule, see what and who is playing at the Paramount, be amazed at the prices in the ads, read the funnies and cartoons from that great era. You can check the national and international goings on from a Brooklyn point of view.

If you remember the times you can relive your youth in Brooklyn. You may find a bowling score of a friend from 'back then'. You'll find little articles on the bottom of the pages of *The Brooklyn Eagle* which will remind you of things you thought you had forgotten all about. The way we dressed in the forties will surely bring a warm smile to you lips. The cars we drove will surely bring you back.

As you read the war news you will probably have a serious moment to reflect on the greatest struggle in modern times. From Hitler invading Poland to Pearl Harbor to "D" Day to VE and VJ Days you will read about the war. You'll read about it just as though you were there again. Just as though it was happening now.

I know that you will completely enjoy the experience. So get to it because you will need a hundred (maybe two hundred) hours to complete the odyssey of World War II in Brooklyn, New York.

Tom Antonucci
-born in Bay Ridge-

Roosevelt Demands Arms to Meet 'Lawlessness'

President's Message

Washington, Jan. 4 (AP)—To the Congress of the United States:

In reporting on the state of the nation, I have felt it necessary on previous occasions to advise the Congress of disturbance abroad and of the need of putting our own house in order in the face of storm signals from across the seas.

As this 76th Congress opens there is need for further warning.

A war which threatened to envelop the world in flames has been averted; but it has become increasingly clear that peace is not assured.

All about us rage undeclared wars—military and economic. All about us grow more deadly armaments—military and economic. All about us are threats of new aggression—military and economic.

Storms from abroad directly challenge three institutions indispensable to Americans, now as always. The first is religion. It is the source of the other two—democracy and international good faith.

Religion, by teaching man his relationship to God, gives the individual a sense of his own dignity and teaches him to respect himself by respecting his neighbors.

Democracy, the practice of self-government, is a covenant among free men to respect the rights and liberties of their fellows.

International good faith, a sister of democracy, springs from the will of civilized nations of men to respect the rights and liberties of other nations of men.

In a modern civilization all three—religion, democracy and international good faith—complement each other.

Where freedom of religion has been attacked, the attack has come from sources opposed to democracy. Where democracy has been overthrown, the spirit of free worship has disappeared. And where religion and democracy have vanished, good faith and reason in international affairs have given way to strident ambition and brute force.

An ordering of society which relegates religion, democracy and good faith among nations to the background can find no place within it for the ideals of the Prince of Peace. The United States rejects such an ordering, and retains its ancient faith.

There comes a time in the affairs of men when they must prepare to defend not their homes alone but the tenets of faith and humanity on which their churches, their governments and their very civilization are founded. The defense of religion, *(continued on page 10)*

Weather Forecast
By U. S. Weather Bureau
Rain, Slowly Rising Temperature Tonight and Tomorrow.

BROOKLYN EAGLE
DAILY AND SUNDAY

Wall Street Closing Racing Extra
★★★★★★

98th YEAR—No. 3 | Entered in the Brooklyn Postoffice as 2d Class Mail Matter | BROOKLYN, N. Y., WEDNESDAY, JANUARY 4, 1939 | (Copyright 1939 The Brooklyn Daily Eagle) | THREE CENTS

Defy Aggressors--F. D.

Continued Spending Urged to Achieve Unity

Taxicab Strikers Agree to Return To Work Friday

Walkout to Continue Until Then, Leaders Say—Mayor's Parley Sets Poll Tomorrow

The general strike which crippled the city's $35,000,000 taxicab industry today will end Friday morning when hackmen return to work after an election to determine their collective bargaining agency.

This announcement was made by Mayor LaGuardia at 12:15 p.m. at the close of a half-hour conference in City Hall between representatives of the taxi companies and 11,000 striking drivers.

The election will be held tomorrow night at the 71st Regiment Armory, Manhattan, at an hour still to be fixed. Pending the vote, however, the strike will continue, according to leaders of the Transport Workers Union. The State Labor Relations Board will conduct the balloting.

New Contract to Be Negotiated

After the men return to their cabs their collective bargaining representatives and the flet owners will negotiate a new contract to replace the one which expired at midnight last Saturday. The State Mediation Board will participate in these negotiations, it was said.

The conference at City Hall got under way at 11:45 a.m., with the Mayor assisted in his peace-making rol eby Arthur S. Meyer, chairman of the State Mediation Board; City Councilman Robert K. Straus, Nathan Frankel, the Mayor's labor adviser, and Burton A. ZZorn, counsel

Continued on Page 2

INDEX

	Page
Books	25
Brain Teaser	24
Bridge	25
Broadway, by Hy Gardner	7
Building the Fair	4
By the Way	1st Page, 2d Section
Comics	24 and 25
Crossword Puzzle	23
Doc Rankin's Cartoon	12
Dr. Brady	25
Edgar Guest	12
Ed Hughes Column	16
Editorial	12
Ernest K. Lindley	1st Page, 2d Section
Events Tonight	22
Fact About Brooklyn	12
Financial	19 to 22
Grin and Bear It	12
Helen Worth	9
H. H. Clarke on Wall St.	19
Jimmy Wood's Sportopics	17
John A. Heffersan	1st Page, 2d Section
Line on Liners	22
Lost and Found, Personals	2
Novel	25
Obituaries	13
Radio	24
Ray Tucker	12
Real Estate	23
Referees	22
Robert Quillen	24
Ships	22
Shopping With Susan	5
Society	9
Sports	16 to 18
Theaters	8
Want Ads	22 and 23
Woman's Page	6

Succeeds Finegan

Joseph C. H. Flynn

Appointed as City Magistrate to fill the unexpired term of Special Sessions Justice James E. Finegan

Flynn Named As Magistrate

Horn of Queens Also Appointed To Bench by Mayor

Mayor LaGuardia announced today the appointment as magistrates of Joseph C. H. Flynn, former Republican leader of the 5th A.D. and protege of Supreme Court Justice Charles C. Lockwood, and Peter Maynard Horn, an independent Democrat and civic leader in Queens.

The new magistrates will be sworn in tomorrow morning at City Hall. Flynn's appointment is for the unexpired term of James E. Finegan, now a Special Sessions Justice, and Horn's for the unexpired term of Gustav W. M. Wieboldt, who also left the lower court for Special Sessions. Flynn's term runs to May 1, 1941 and Horn's to Apr. 30, 1947. The salary is $10,000.

Was Secretary to Faber

Mr. Flynn, who was married in 1925 to Hope Virginia Boyle, a niece of Justice Lockwood, lives with his

Continued on Page 10

Man Plunges to Death

Norman Penney, a son of the late District Attorney Thomas Penney of Buffalo, jumped or fell to his death yesterday a few minutes after he had ordered a double whisky sour sent to his room on the eighth floor of the Alpha Delta Phi Club, 136 W. 44th St., Manhattan. He was 47.

Lehman Urges Social Statutes Be Bolstered

Calls on Legislature To Consolidate Gains And Correct Errors

Eagle Bureau, Capitol Building.

By JOSEPH H. SCHMALACKER

Albany, Jan. 4—In a comprehensive annual message dealing with the serious problems confronting the State, Governor Lehman called upon the Legislature at the opening of its new session today to work for the perfection and consolidation of social gains achieved in behalf of New York's inhabitants.

Admitting there was no question that the efficiency of some of the statutes enacted needed improvement and recalling it was necessary often to formulate them under pressure of emergency conditions, the Governor urged their re-examination to strengthen the "processes" of their administration, "smooth out any rough edges" and "correct any mistakes disclosed by experience."

The Chief Executive cited the unemployment insurance law and announced that amendments would be submitted to the Legislature.

In the section of his message deal-

Continued on Page 11

Asks Relief Probe

Eagle Bureau, Capitol Building.

Albany, Jan. 4—An investigation of State and local relief financing by a joint legislative committee was proposed this afternoon by Senator Thomas C. Desmond (R., Newburgh).

Desmond, asserting relief financing was one of the most serious problems facing the State and its municipalities, drafted a resolution calling for appointment of a committee of three Senators and three Assemblymen. The committee would be required to submit its report no later than Feb. 15.

Chapereau Admits Bringing in Finery

Attorneys for Albert N. Chapereau, who was indicted for smuggling for Mrs. Elma N. Lauer, wife of Supreme Court Justice Edgar Lauer, admitted the facts today in Manhattan Federal Court, but said he was entitled to diplomatic immunity.

Chapereau, according to Charles L. Sylvester, one of his attorneys, as commercial attache for the Nicaraguan Government, had authority to bring in duty free the $1,933 worth of Parisian finery cited in the indictment. Mrs. Lauer has pleaded guilty to her share in the proceeding.

Federal Judge Murray Hulbert thereupon adjourned the trial scheduled to open today, until Monday, directing both sides to file briefs on the defense motion by Friday.

Should the court rule that Noel Pallais, consul of the Nicaraguan Government, was not qualified to sign a certificate granting immunity to Chapereau, as Assistant United State Attorney Joseph L. Delaney contends, Chapereau will in effect have pleaded guilty.

End of Labor Strife, Strong Defense Asked

Washington, Jan. 4 (AP)—President Roosevelt laid before Congress today the following broad program:

National Defense—Provide armed forces and defenses strong enough to ward off sudden attack against key positions; provide "key facilities essential to ensure sustained resistance and ultimate victory"; organize and locate those facilities for immediate use and rapid expansion "without danger of serious interruption by enemy attack."

Spending—Continue expenditures at the present level in anticipation of raising national income to $80,000,000,000, when present taxes would produce budget balancing revenue.

Taxes—Adjust inequalities through "relatively small" increases in some taxes and revamp tax relationship between Federal, State and local governments.

Labor—Find ways to end factional labor strife and employer-employee disputes.

Reorganization—Revamp the executive processes of government in the interest of more efficient administration.

Farm—Perfect the farm program "to protect farmers' income and consumers' purchasing power from alternate risks of crop gluts and crop shortages."

Railroads—Reconcile the "enormous, antagonistic interests" in the railroad and general transportation field.

Social Security—Make "better provision for our older people" and provide better care for the medically needy.

Neutrality—Revise neutrality laws so they may not "actually give aid to an aggressor and deny it to the victim."

Walker to Get Pension Credit

Estimate Board Acts To Let Ex-Mayor Withdraw $20,738

Former Mayor James J. Walker has been given permission by the Board of Estimate to withdraw the $20,738.09 which had accumulated to his credit in the city retirement system up to the time he quit as Mayor and sailed for Europe in September, 1932.

The board's approval of the withdrawal was learned today through publication in the City Record of the minutes of the Dec. 1 meeting at which the applications of the ex-Mayor and 64 other former city employes were passed as an added item to the calendar.

The sum which Walker receives represents his payments into the system from June 26, 1928, to Sept. 1, 1932, plus interest. Although he became Mayor on Jan. 1, 1926, the

Continued on Page 10

Crash Shakes 25 on Trolley

Oil Truck Overturns, Spills 1,200 Gallons—Motorman Badly Hurt

The intersection at 7th Ave. and 3d St. became a river of oil today when a fuel truck and a trolley collided shortly before noon, seriously injuring the motorman and shaking up the trolley's 25 passengers.

Robert Carini, 28, driver of the truck owned by the Carba Transportation Corporation, 1372 Flatbush Ave., was treated for laceration of the left ankle. His helper, Victor Casaliggi, 35, of 85 E. 31st St., was treated for shock.

The motorman, James Donough, 55, of 112 Windsor Place, was removed to Jewish Hospital.

The truck, transporting 1,200 gallons of oil, was tossed on its side, pinning the driver and his helper in the cab. It was going east on 3d St. The front part of the trolley,

Continued on Page 10

Tropical Park Results

FIRST RACE—Four-year-olds and up; ¾-mile.

Laddie Stone, 110 (J. Richard)	9.00	5.10	3.70
Rock High, 106 (Pariso)	—	4.70	3.50
Aunt Flor, 103 (Ashcroft)	—	—	6.30

Time, 1:12. Aftermath, Two Tricks, Flying Lance, Dark Prince, Hypo, Combatant, Imperial Maryan, Blakeen, Many Moons also ran. (Off time, 2:05.)

SECOND RACE—Three-year-olds. Three-fourths of a mile.

Persuasive (Stout)	8.60	5.50	4.00
Cupid's Arrow (Smock)	—	32.10	9.80
Black Crusade (Balaski)	—	—	4.10

Time, 1:12 3-5. Art Cooper, Saxonby, Midnight Star, Istanbul, Chatmin, Cross Badge, Wise Attorney also ran. (Off time, 2:32½).

THIRD RACE—Candy Hero, first; Jolyon, second; Espinaca, third.

He Tells Congress

President Roosevelt

Nazis Nervous As F. D. Talks

Watching Congress For Remarks Which Might Bring Break

Berlin, Jan. 4 (U.P.) — Responsible Nazi quarters today asserted that utterances before the United States Congress might determine the future of relations—already close to the breaking point—between the United States and Germany.

The implication in Nazi circles was that hostile remarks by President Roosevelt in his address to Congress and remarks by members of that body might "force" a break in relations, unless the United States Government should disavow any violent attacks on the Reich.

"We would not break relations unless the United States forces us," a Nazi spokesman said.

Nazi officials summed up their attitude with "it is up to the United States not us," admitting that German-American relations were close to the breaking point.

Responsible Foreign Office quarters again emphasized that Germany has no desire to break relations, but from a political and particularly an economic point of view desires to improve them.

Foreign Office quarters admitted, however, that any direct attack on the Reich by President Roosevelt might bring a drastic German response.

Foreign Office quarters summed up the German viewpoint as follows:

The United States Government, either through a spokesman for Congress or through an official announcement should disavow any violent attacks on the Reich which might be made in the Senate or House.

Germany officially draws a distinction between "politicians" and "responsible officials," but it is held here that the Government should in some way indicate its lack of connection with all violent anti-German attacks either in speeches or in the press.

Vice Consul Ends Life

Algiers, Jan. 4 (AP)—Juan Tirado, Spanish vice consul at Oran, committed suicide today by shooting himself after refusing to reply to an order of recall from the Barcelona Government. Tirado's wife and son are in insurgent Spain.

Tax Rise Hinted, New Deal Laws To Be Polished

Message to Congress Advocates Government Reform, Railroad Aid

Washington, Jan. 4 (AP)—President Roosevelt summoned the nation today to arm—economically, socially and with military force—to meet a world challenge of dictatorial aggression.

Before both houses of Congress, the Chief Executive solemnly asserted:

"A war which threatened to envelop the world has been averted; but it has become increasingly clear that peace is not assured."

To meet the challenge, Mr. Roosevelt laid down a program of action, both foreign and domestic, for meeting the troubles of the world "as one people."

To achieve domestic solidarity, the President urged:

Continued efforts to bolster national income through Federal spending.

Hinted at revision of the Labor Relations Act by urging peace in labor's strife and between capital and labor.

Asked perfection of the farm program.

Suggested tax readjustments with possible small increases.

Recommended the general polishing of New Deal laws and added two new enactments, Government reorganization and aid for the railroads.

To meet "international lawlessness" abroad, the President projected a program of rearmament suf-

Continued on Page 10

F. D. Message Boosts Stocks

Gains Up to 3 Points Recorded as Market Spurts After Talk

Reflecting the generally favorable impression placed on the President's message to Congress, the stock market today went into new high ground for its current advancing movement. Gains in individual issues ranged from fractions to about 3 points. Trading, quiet in early dealings, picked up during the afternoon.

Steel shares were leaders on the advance, with Bethlehem especially strong. Rails were also in good demand, many going into new high ground. Chrysler was a strong spot in the motors, rising about 2 points in late dealings. Numerous individual specialties scored gains running to 3 points. Aviations were inclined to lag behind the general market.

Response Cheerful

Initial response to the President's address in professional Wall Street quarters was more cheerful than otherwise. It was observed with interest that no attack was made on business and that a generally con-

Continued on Page 19

Rainy Weather Looms Tonight And Tomorrow

The weather man today promised—or threatened—rain and slowly rising temperatures for tonight and tomorrow. At no time, said the forecaster, would the temperature drop below 32, the freezing point.

In upstate New York a freezing rain left dangerously slippery roads in the vicinity of Albany, while farther north heavy snow fell to the depth of more than a foot at Saranac Lake, where the temperature dropped below zero. In Newtown Falls, St. Lawrence County, the mercury registered 16 below zero.

Duce Gets F. D.'s View on Refugees

Washington, Jan. 4 (U.P.)—Acting Secretary of State Sumner Welles revealed today that President Roosevelt's views on the political refugee problem were conveyed to Premier Benito Mussolini last night by U. S. Ambassador William Phillips.

Welles, explaining the nature of Phillips conversation with Il Duce, said he was instructed to inform Mussolini of this Government's attitude and at the same time to seek Mussolini's views.

Welles said Phillips' conversation with Mussolini, which lasted for 40 minutes, was devoted to the political refugee problem only and that no other matters were taken up. Welles did not reveal any details of the conversation.

Celler Urges U. S. Fund To Combat Nazi Spies

Washington, Jan. 4 (AP)—Representative Celler (D., N.Y.) urged Congress today to grant increased appropriations for counter-espionage to combat activities of "spies and devilish agents of Nazi Germany," who, he said, endangered security of the United States.

He said German agents were "hidden in Government bureaus, business offices, armories, ships, munition factories, airship plants" and "carry off to Hitler highly important secrets and information."

First Official View With a Directory Of World's Fair

Visitors coming to New York for the World's Fair, which opens April 30, will see two shows for the price of one—the world's largest city and the world's largest fair, both the most modern examples of their kind. The painting above, drawn by H. M. Pettit, is the first official painting of the Fair, showing the $155,000,000 "World of Tomorrow" exposition and the spires of New York City, "World of Today," beyond. The painting shows the exhibits and the major arterial, subway and railroad lines which tie the 1,216½-acre Fair to the mainland. The key below corresponds to the painting. Its numbers show:

(1) Fountain Lake Gate.
(2) Corona Gate.
(3) Administration Gate.
(4) Long Island R. R. Gate
(5) I. R. T.-B. M. T. Subway Gate
(6) Flushing Gate
(7) Horace Harding Gate
(8) Independent Subway Gate
(9) South Gate
(10) Focal Food Building
(11) U. S. Army Camp
(12) Florida Building
(13) Fountain Lake
(14) N. Y. State Marine Amphitheater
(15) Marine Transportation Building
(16) Firestone
(17) Aviation
(18) Chrysler
(19) Ford
(20) General Motors
(21) Railroads
(22) Goodrich
(23) Terrace Club
(24) Production and Distribution
(25) Westinghouse
(26) Electrical Products
(27) Pharmacy
(28) New York City Building
(29) Trylon
(30) Perisphere
(31) Helicline
(32) Business Systems and Insurance
(33) Administration
(34) Postoffice, Press and Promotion
(35) Communications
(36) Cosmetics
(37) Long Island Railroad Station
(38) Textiles and Women's Apparel
(39) General Electric
(40) Electrical Utilities
(41) American Tel. & Tel.
(42) U. S. Steel
(43) Consolidated Edison
(44) Metals and Mining
(45) Consumers Interests
(46) Medicine and Public Health
(47) Science and Education
(48) Radio Corporation of America
(49) Johns Manville
(50) B. M. T. and I. R. T. Subway Stations
(51) Building Materials
(52) Community Interests
(53) Contemporary Arts
(54) Tomorrow Town
(55) Works Progress Administration
(56) American Radiator
(57) Temple of Religion
(58) Flushing Creek
(59) American Gas Association
(60) Christian Science
(61) Y. M. C. A.
(62) House of Jewels
(63) Food Building
(64) Jewish Palestine
(65) Beechnut
(66) Carrier Igloo
(67) DuPont
(68) Petroleum Industry
(69) Glass Center
(70) Wonder Bakery
(71) Borden Rotolactor
(72) Industrial Science
(73) Men's Apparel
(74) Swift & Co.
(75) Lucky Strike
(76) General Cigar
(77) Turkey
(78) Academy of Sports
(79) Heinz
(80) Eastman Kodak
(81) Home Town Restaurant
(82) National Dairy Products
(83) Distilled Spirits
(84) Court of States
(85) New England Exhibit
(86) Belgium
(87) France
(88) Brazil
(89) Chile
(90) League of Nations
(91) Portugal
(92) Venezuela
(93) Poland
(94) Gardens on Parade
(95) British Empire
(96) Italy
(97) Netherlands
(98) Switzerland
(99) U. S. Federal Building
(100) Court of Peace and Halls of Nations
(101) Pan-American Wing
(102) Canada
(103) Argentina
(104) Ireland
(105) Norway
(106) Soviet Russia
(107) Czechoslovakia
(108) Japan
(109) Lagoon of Nations
(110) Constitution Mall
(111) Washington Square
(112) National Advisory Committees
(113) Children's World
(114) Independent Subway Station
(115) Music Hall and Auditorium
(116) Three Ring Restaurant
(117) Parachute Jumping Tower
(118) Amusement Zone
(119) Elgin Observatory

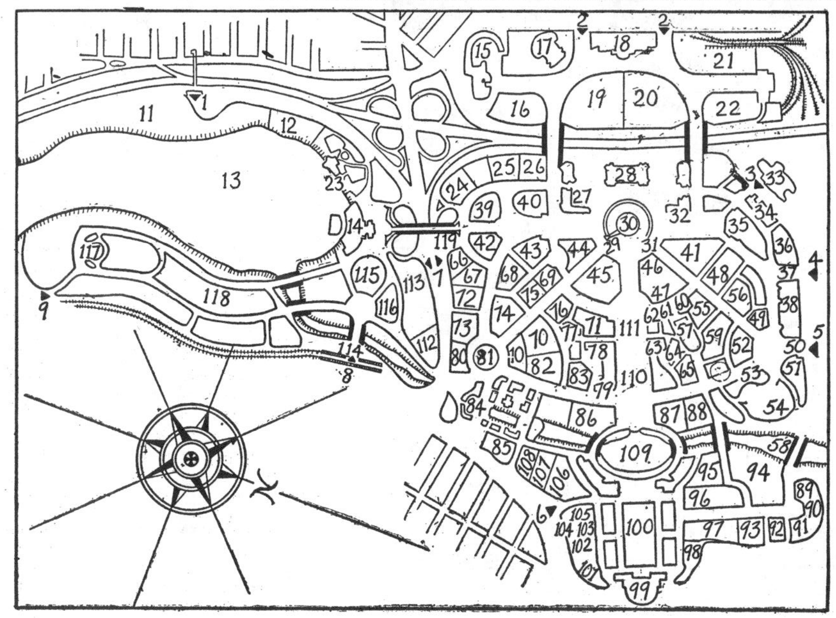

Herlands Subpenas Tax Jury Head for Quiz

Weather Forecast
By U. S. Weather Bureau
Partly Cloudy, Colder Tonight. Continued Cold Tomorrow.

BROOKLYN EAGLE

DAILY AND SUNDAY

Wall Street Closing Racing Extra
★★★★★★

98th YEAR—No. 75 | Entered in the Brooklyn Postoffice as 2d Class Mail Matter | BROOKLYN, N. Y., FRIDAY, MARCH 17, 1939 | THREE CENTS

U. S. Condemns Nazis

London Orders Envoy Home in Rebuff to Reich

Herlands Hales Sales Tax Jury Head to Quiz

Calls on Friedman To Bring Auto Firm's Records to Inquiry

Now facing an inquiry into his past by Assistant Attorney General Amen, Laurence J. Friedman, foreman of the "sales tax grand jury," today was served with a subpena to appear at the office of Commissioner of Investigation Herlands for questioning about his business affairs and the activities of the jury he headed for more than a year.

The subpena is returnable tomorrow at 10 a.m., with Abraham M. Block, Herlands' assistant, in charge of the preliminary probe.

Friedman was asked to bring with him the books and stock certificates of the Ace Automobile Company, Inc., of 366 Flatbush Ave. Extension, a firm now in tax difficulties with the city. The grand jury foreman claims he is a salesman for that company.

Herlands Non-Committal

It was learned that Commissioner Herlands wants to find out if Friedman holds any stock in the company. The subpena was served on the latter at the downtown office of the auto firm. Herlands refused to comment on the matter.

Affidavits now in the possession of Assistant Attorney General Amen charge that Friedman, 41, of 537 Crown St., was arrested on a grand larceny charge in the Ralph Ave. precinct on Nov. 30, 1932. The charge was subsequently dismissed by Magistrate Mark Rudich. Mr. Amen is seeking to learn if Friedman was asked if he had ever been in trouble with the law at the time he qualified for service on the December,

Continued on Page 25

Rudich Witnesses To Be Surprises

A number of surprise witnesses will be called when Magistrate Mark Rudich goes before the Appellate Division on Monday to answer charges of conduct unbecoming a judicial officer, it was revealed today by Assistant Attorney General Amen.

None of the witnesses will be public officials, Amen said. Asked if Magistrate Anthony F. Burke would be one of the witnesses against Magistrate Rudich, Amen said he did not know, that he had not yet been subpenaed. Magistrate Burke was mentioned in the charges as being a fellow magistrate to whom Rudich appealed in the interest of leniency for a prostitute. Magistrate Burke, according to the charges, refused to be influenced.

INDEX

	Page
Books	29
Brain Teaser	28
Bridge	29
Broadway, by Hy Gardner	10
Building the Fair	1st Page, 2d Section
By the Way	1st Page, 2d Section
Cassel's Cartoon	14
Comics	28 and 29
Crossword Puzzle	27
Dr. Brady	29
Edgar Guest	14
Ed Hughes' Column	20
Editorial	14
Events Tonight	26
Fact About Brooklyn	14
Financial	23 to 25
Garden Corner	27
Going Places	10
Grin and Bear It	14
Helen Worth	12
H. H. Clarke on Wall St.	23
Jimmy Wood's Sportopics	20
John A. Heffernan	1st Page, 2d Section
Line on Liners	26
Lost and Found, Personals	2
Novel	29
Obituaries	15
Radio	28
Ray Tucker	14
Real Estate	27
Referees	26
Robert Quillen Says	28
Shipping	26
Society	12
Sports	20 to 22
Theaters	11
Want Ads	26 and 27
Woman's Page	13

Half Million Cheer Paraders On Fifth Ave. After Boro March

Among the most ardent and interested spectators of today's parade of Ancient Order of Hibernian units through the Borough Hall and downtown sections, before they joined the Manhattan parade, were the youngsters in the picture at right. Billy Chambers, 2½, of 296 Warren St., reserves himself a seat on the curb, but both he and his sister, Marie Ann, 4, show their enthusiasm by carrying Irish flags. At the right are two of the pretty girl drum majors who led the more than a score of bands and bugle corps in the Brooklyn line of march, Evedyn Kuffner and Ella Houser, both of the band of the Charles Heissler Post, 179, American Legion. (Eagle Staff photos.)

McGuinness Spurns Mercy

Refuses Amen Offer For His Testimony In Probe of Geoghan

Assistant Attorney General Amen said today he did not intend to issue a subpena for William F. McGuinness, suspended Assistant District Attorney, to appear before the grand jury, inasmuch as McGuinness had refused to sign a waiver of immunity.

McGuinness and George Murphy, elevator starter in the Central Courts Building, are awaiting trial on an alleged attempt to "fix" a perjury case.

Amen said he did not expect to question McGuinness again, but that the offer to go before the grand jury still holds, if he wants to waive immunity.

Nor did Amen know why men from his office were studying records of the old Adams St. Court,

Continued on Page 25

Man Dies as He Seeks Place to Watch Parade

Thomas Kirk, 56, of 2040 E. 26th St., dropped dead today on 5th Ave., between 60th and 61st Sts, Manhattan, as he sought a spot from which t owatch the St. Patrick's day parade.

Kirk had traveled to Manhattan by subway and as he turned into 5th Ave. met his nephew, Police Sgt. Francis Kelly of the 63d Precinct, who had been assigned to duty along the line of march. As uncle and nephew greeted each other, the elder man collapsed to the sidewalk. He was pronounced dead by Dr. Heffernan, called from Bellevue Hospital.

Sons of Erin, 85,000 Strong, Honor Their Patron Saint

Brave in the green of their ancestral sod and stepping briskly to the lilting tunes of Ireland's triumphs and tragedies, 1,000 members of the Brooklyn divisions of the Ancient Order of Hibernians marched through the downtown and Borough Hall sections of the borough today before they took specially chartered trains of the Independent subway system to midtown Manhattan to take their places with 1,500 other Brooklyn Irish-Americans for the 5th Ave parade.

The marchers gathered at Court and Kane Sts., opposite St. Paul's R. C. Church, and formed into three divisions—Division 1, led by its president, Joseph De Cantillon; Division 2, led by President William A. Condon, and Division 3, led by President John W. Fletcher. Members of the Celtic Circle, headed by Deputy County Clerk James A. Kelly, also marched as members of the three divisions.

Green Was Everywhere

At 12:30 more than a score of boys and girls bands and fife and drum corps from Brooklyn church organizations swung into the "Wearing of the Green," "Come Back to Erin" and other Irish airs, and the parade got under way, with John J.

Continued on Page 3

F. D. Wears Green—Suit, Tie, Shamrock

Washington, March 17 (AP)—President Roosevelt, whose wedding anniversary, like St. Patrick's Day, is March 17, turned out for his press conference today in a green ensemble—green tweeds, green tie and shamrock.

He opened his conference by inspecting the front row of reporters, and noticing no green except on one newsman, inquired where all the Irishmen were.

Tropical Park Results

FIRST RACE—Three-year-olds; ¾-mile.

Cambreeze, 107 (Ensor)	43,00	19.60	10.60
Town League, 112 (I. Hanford)	—	69.40	24.90
Saxonby, 112 (Meade)	—	—	3.50

Time, 1:14. Jacopobelle, Gibby's Tornado, Welsh Star, Prudent Miss, Dongy, Mr. Jersey, Bert W., Amercup, Bolis also ran. (Off time, 2:04½)

SECOND RACE—Three-year-olds; ¾-mile.

Lady Wo, 109 (Peters)	38.50	12.80	7.20
Nanahcub, 111 (Peters)	—	6.20	3.50
Henryel's Pick, 109 (Ashcroft)	—	—	3.70

Time, 1:13 4-5. Phenomenal, Honeymaid, Maisco, Cream Cheese, Idle Zelda, Goodness Sake, Peachypie, Parking Ticket, Arabic also ran. (Off time, 2:33.)

Wild Firetruck Snags Traffic

Water Tower Rams One Car, Crushes Another Here

Have you ever envied the "tiller man," who breezes by on the tailend of one of those long pieces of fire apparatus that trails the regular fire truck?

Well, envy the tiller man no longer, because here's one who breezed right into an accident this morning when the trailing water tower he was steering swerved and sidewiped an automobile, crushed a second and tied up traffic for 20 minutes near the Flatbush Ave. Long Island Railroad depot.

The tiller man and his water tower were bound for an exhibition at Jacob Riis Park when the accident occurred.

Hits Car Waiting to Turn

Everything was fine as the procession shot up Flatbush Ave. Then at Pacific St. the trailing water tower struck a car owned by Peter Karros of 112 Highlawn Ave., waiting to make a left turn into Pacific St.

Arthur McCauley, the tiller man who was operating the trailer of the huge water tower, apparently misjudged his distance and the trailer swerved into the Karros automobile. Karros' car was thrown against a pillar of the elevated structure.

The water tower continued without slackening speed, the chauffeur, Fireman James Deegan, way up front, not knowing that the trailer had hit the car.

Rams Second Auto

The trailer, which had swung into a right angle with the truck proper, then rammed a second automobile operated by Nathan Klinger, 59, of 1611 Quentin Road.

Klinger's car was crushed like an accordion between the two sections of the water tower. He was treated for lacerations of the scalp and sent home.

Both automobile drivers received summons for failing to give right-of-way to fire apparatus—the fate of the "innocent bystander."

Upsets Mischief Case

Magistrate Folwell in Bridge Plaza Court today ruled that the accidental destruction of city property by an individual is not malicious mischief. He dismissed a charge of malicious mischief made against Daniel Mulligan, 25, of 148 Noll St., accused of breaking the glass in the door of a police radio car.

U. S. Indicts Manton Again, Fallon Also

Boyhood Briend Called Intermediary In $62,000 Bribe

For the second time within the month former Senior Circuit Court Judge Martin T. Manton, who resigned under fire, was indicted by the judiciary Federal grand jury in Manhattan, on three conspiracy charges today.

Indicted with him was William J. Fallon, described by United States Attorney John T. Cahill as the intermediary in accepting a $62,000 bribe in an infringement suit involving a chicken incubator. Fallon at present is in the Tombs serving an indeterminate term for commercial bribery.

The indictment was handed up to Judge John W. Clancy.

Mr. Fallon is 49, a boyhood friend of Manton and formerly was an investigator for the Prudence Company.

Gets Warrant for Fallon

Mr. Cahill asked Judge Clancy for a bench warrant for Fallon to serve as a detainer in the event he should be released from the Tombs. The court issued the warrant.

The indictment charged that "said William J. Fallon would obtain from Almon B. Hall various sums of money for the purpose of causing and permitting said Fallon to pay and deliver said sums of money or portions thereof to said Forest Hills Terrace Corporation or to said Martin T. Manton directly and otherwise to dispose of said sums of money for the use and benefit of the conspirators."

Manton, who underwent an operation on March 3, the day after his first indictment, left St. Vincent's Hospital, Manhattan, on Wednesday and is recuperating in his home, the Hotel Madison. He will be arraigned on the first indictment early next week.

As in the first indictment, the new indictment charged conspiracy to obstruct justice, conspiracy to defraud the United States Government of the impartial services of an officer and conspiracy involving the bribery of a judicial officer.

Reversed by Circuit Court

In the first instance he was indicted with George Spector in the Shick razor case.

The present indictment is based on the case of Samuel B. Smith, a Cleveland inventor, who in 1934 instituted a suit in the Connecticut District Court against Almon B. Hall and L. C. Hall of Wallingford, Conn., claiming infringement on his patent for a chicken hatching machine.

Smith, who had won numerous similar suits in the lower courts and the Supreme Court, was the victor in the Connecticut case. The Hall brothers appealed to the Circuit Court, which on April 6, 1936, handed down a decision, written by Judge Manton, reversing the lower court. The United States Supreme Court later upheld the Hall brothers, also.

Manton's opinion stated that the favorable opinion was based on the fact that in the case on which he ruled more complete and satisfactory evidence had been presented than in previous cases.

Checks Are Listed

The indictment set forth that payments were made by the Hall brothers to the Allied Rediscount Corporation, which was controlled by Fallon, as follows: $5,000 by check on Nov. 23, 1935; $5,000 by check on Dec. 16, 1935; $5,000 by check on Dec. 27, 1935; $10,000 by check on Feb. 14, 1936; $37,000 in cash on April 6, 1936; $5,000 by check on April 7, 1936.

The large cash payment was made on the day of the favorable decision to the Hall brothers.

On Dec. 17, 1935, the day after one of the $5,000 checks was paid to the Allied Rediscount Corporation, Fallon gave a $5,000 check to the order of the Forest Hills Terrace Corporation, which Mr. Cahill contends, is wholly owned or controlled by Judge Manton.

Navy Job to Boro Firm

Washington, March 17 (AP)—The Navy awarded yesterday a $12,838 contract to the Fred L. Lavanburg Company, Brooklyn, N. Y., for green chrome and red toluidine.

Britain Confers With France On Dual Protest

Kennedy Visits Halifax—Daladier Demands Free Hand

London, March 17 (AP)—Britain ordered her Ambassador home from Berlin today in a rebuff paralleling United States action last November and consulted with France on a possible protest to the Nazi government over her absorption of most of Czechoslovakia.

Sir Nevile Henderson was called back from the German capital "to report" on the moves which ended the existence of the war-born Czechoslovak republic this week.

While British and French Governments were in close contact on policy, sources close to the French Foreign Office said the question of summoning the French Ambassador in Berlin to Paris was not being considered at the present time.

Extend Daladier's Powers

Meanwhile in Paris Premier Daladier called on Parliament for a free hand to govern France by decree until Nov. 30 to bolster the nation's defense in view of the collapse of Czechoslovakia.

The bill to strengthen France against any menace from expanding Germany contained only the one article authorizing decree powers

Continued on Page 2

Fuehrer Rides Into Vienna

Avoids Bratislava On Way From Prague After Conquest

Berlin, March 17 (AP)—Adolph Hitler rode into Vienna today, completing a triumphant 24-hour journey between the two once-proud capitals which have fallen to his bloodless conquest within little more than a year.

The Nazi Fuehrer reached flag-decked Vienna after a short halt at Bruenn, where he reviewed German military detachments in his newly won Moravian protectorate.

Benes 'Protests'

Chicago, March 17 (U.P.)—Dr. Eduard Benes today telegraphed a "solemn protest" to President Roosevelt, Foreign Minister Litvinoff of Russia, Premier Daladier of France and Prime Minister Chamberlain of Great Britain against the "great international crime" of abandoning Czechoslovakia to Germany.

Under heavy guard Hitler left Prague late yesterday and spent the night at an undisclosed spot on the way to Bruenn.

Avoiding Bratislava, the Slovakian capital where crowds had gathered to greet him, Hitler swept on from Bruenn to Vienna, where Nazis were still celebrating the first anni-

Continued on Page 2

Cops' Stiff Fair Shift Brings Boycott Threat

"The policeman's lot is not a happy one," particularly when he thinks of the forthcoming World's Fair, it was stated officially today by the Patrolmen's Benevolent Association, which represents the city's 19,000 cops.

A statement issued by the association threatened a police boycott of the Flushing exhibition if the Police Commissioner adheres to his plan of putting the men on an emergency schedule which will give them only one day off in 27.

"The proposed working conditions will make impossible, or at least improbable visits to the Fair by members of the force and their families," the association declared.

'Wanton' Grab Called Threat To Civilization

F. D. Backs Welles Charge Hitler Crushes Liberty of Free People

Washington, March 17 (AP)—The United States Government expressed today its "condemnation" of Germany's "wanton lawlessness" and "arbitrary force" in occupying Czechoslovakia.

Lashes Hitler

Sumner Welles

With the approval of President Roosevelt, Acting Secretary of State Welles issued a formal statement in which he spoke of Germany's absorption of most of Czechoslovakia as a "temporary extinguishment of the liberties of a free and independent people with whom, from the day when the republic of Czechoslovakia attained its independence, the people of the United States have maintained specially close and friendly relations."

Welles declared: "It is manifest that acts of wanton lawlessness and of arbitrary force are threatening world peace and the very structure of modern civilization."

The acting Secretary of State made his statement after conferring with the President and he said his statement had received the Chief Executive's approval.

[Secretary of State Cordell Hull is vacationing in the South.]

Nazi Acts Condemned

"This Government," Welles said, "founded upon and dedicated to the principles of human liberty and of democracy, cannot refrain from making known this country's condemnation of the acts" of Germany.

Earlier, the President told a press conference that European developments demonstrated the need for a revision of the American neutrality act, at this session of Congress.

Mr. Roosevelt would not go into detail. Heretofore, there have been reports that the administration would prefer greater freedom or

Continued on Page 2

Czech Defies Orders to Quit Legation Here

Washington, March 17 (AP)—Czechoslovakia's defiant Minister rejected today orders from Prague to surrender the Czech Legation and Consulates to German representatives.

The Minister, Col. Vladimir's S. Hurban, said in a statement he had informed the Prague Foreign Affairs Ministry h edid not recognize President Hacha's capitulation as valid, "inasmuch as it is unconstitutional."

"According to the Constitution of the Czecho-Slovak Republic," Hurban said, "any territorial changes of the State must be approved by the Czecho-Slovak National Assembly with a three-fifth majority of all its members."

"The President or the Government is not empowered by the Constitution to cede any part of Czech-Slovak territory. The agreement signed in Berlin on March 15, therefore, is not valid.

"I took the oath to obey the laws of the Czecho-Slovak Republic; no one has power to force me to act against the law."

Hurban showed in his attitude something of the firmness he exhibited in the World War as a leader of the famous Czech legion which fought against the Russians.

He refused yesterday to agree to an evacuation demand from German representatives who visited his offices with an order from Berlin. He said then he must have written orders from his own government.

Mr. and Mrs. F.D. Mark 34th Wedding Milestone

Washington, March 17 (AP)—Memories of a St. Patrick's Day wedding in 1905 spanned more than 1,000 miles today for a greeting between the President and Mrs. Roosevelt on their 34th wedding anniversary.

It is their custom to exchange telegrams or talk by long distance telephone when they are apart on the anniversary. Mrs. Roosevelt, in the Southwest on a lecture tour, had a speaking engagement in San Antonio, Texas. The President was busy at his desk here.

Crisis Pulls Stocks Down 1 to 5 Points

Apprehensive selling swept the stock market today on receipt of European news dispatches. Prices went generally downward, with losses ranging form one to five points. Some individual issues lost even more than this. Greater part of the losses were incurred during heavy liquidation in the early part of the third hour, with the tickers running behind floor trading by several minutes.

Details on Financial Pages

Seek Prudence Co. Plan Okay Apr. 14

William R. Palmer, attorney for the RFC, notified Federal Judge Moscowitz today in Federal Court that he would submit an order asking for confirmation of the reorganization plan for the Prudence Company, Inc., by April 14.

Mr. Palmer said that creditors holding claims against the company amounting to $94,800,000 have consented to the plan and that they constitute more than the two-thirds acceptances required by law.

The Prudence Company, listing assets of $125,000,000, asked permission to reorganize under Section 77B on Feb. 1, 1935.

Judge Moscowitz was told today by Mr. Palmer that creditors will have elected a director by April 14, that the RFC will have named two more directors, and that it was up to the court to appoint four others, making a total of seven called for under the reorganization plan.

See Page 9 for Boys,' Girls' Week Contest Details

FANNED BY A FEM!

Harry Heilmann prefers to forget his farewell appearance at bat. Famous Detroit slugger of yesteryear now broadcasting baseball appeared with a team of announcers against a girls' softball outfit. Harry came up with the bases loaded and was fanned—by a fem!

Four Power Pact

It has been written that any first-division N. L. club can win the pennant. We have our 4-Power Pacts on the sports pages, too.

This being true, it seems the answer to the 1939 race is as simple as doping out the probable results of any World Series.

All one has to do is to determine (1) which team has the better pitching, (2) which has the better catching, (3) which has the better infield and outfield, (4) which is most improved over last season's statistics.

There's even a more simple solution, applied by several veteran observers. They base their calculations on the strength of a club "down the middle," or on a line from the catcher's box through pitcher and the second-base sector to center field.

Of course, getting down to cases—or brass tacks, if preferred—it might be advisable to probe for signs of added strength in second-division clubs. What if one or two of them show enough punch to push one of the four powers out of a first-division pact?

For example, St. Louis supporters expect the Cards to be stronger with Tom Sunkel and Morton Cooper, minor-league pitchers of promise. The Bees, with Al Simmons and Buddy Hassett, may give Casey Stengel the punch he has needed. Dodger pitching is a big question in Brooklyn with a certain anxiety evident over Stainback's ability to stand up over the schedule and Sington's chances to hit big-league pitching.

Any of these second-division nominees may caus trouble, if not enough to land on the elect side of the standing then at least enough to bother those thereon.

Giant's Chances

The Giants are favored by a few New York writers. They've picked up power since their last pennant outing in 1937.

But what of Hubbell and Whitehead, two big question marks?

Perhaps Giant followers underestimate the great climb they made to win in 1936. They rode in on Hub's remarkable winning streak of 16 straight. They got off flying on his zippy start of eight straight in 1937.

In 1936, Hub not only led both circuits with a 2.41 earned run mark but led his loop with 26 won and six lost for an .813 average. He was seventh in N. L. history to attain this distinction since 1912. And to gain this honor he worked through 303 innings in 42 games, 25 of them complete performances. The Giants, it might be added, were on their best defensive behavior that year.

Hub wasn't quite as effective in 1937, but was good enough. Last season he suffered his worst year since becoming a Giant.

Now comes the question of his arm, a question that can only be answered by his record through the season ahead, not on Spring training performances.

Smart baseball men still feel that the Giants' chances hang on Hubbell's southpaw wing. Perhaps the Terrymen's pennant hopes hinge more on a Hubbell comeback than on their own comeback off 1937.

Wager Angle

Now that Two-Ton Tony Galento has been officially okayed for slaughter against Joe Louis, gentlemen who like to speculate on their heavyweight judgment may be up against it for a wager.

There has been little enthusiasm over Louis wagers in his last few starts. Betting on the round in which darkness is expected to fall, or trying to pick No. 1 round in the pool has been the best diversion.

Out West, however, the speculative gents have worked out a new angle for Louis wagers. They're betting that Jack Roper lasts longer than old Two-Ton, and vice-versa.

They're quoting against both going more than two rounds, against both lasting one round on combined times.

Of course, this innovation in the betting mart also gives a slight idea of the low estate of the heavyweight situation. When odds are laid on two challengers not lasting one round it's a very sad state of affairs, to put it mildly.

BOTH SIDES

By HAROLD PARROTT

'Round and About—

Boston, March 25.

Memo for Commissioner Landis: Frank Frisch's salary for broadcasting in Boston will be $4,000 more than Casey Stengel gets for managing the Bees . . . 'Tain't right . . . Are you going to let radio overshadow the game itself? . . . Frisch is to get $500 a week for 24 weeks on the air . . . But it will be worth that, and more, if he starts describing the umpires as luridly as he used to on the field! . . . Wednesday night, after his basketball team's great national title victory, Clare Bee climbed a trunk in the Long Island U. dressing room, simply said: "The greatest team I ever coached!" . . . Strange to see Buck Freeman, who had so many great teams of his own at St. John's (though never an unbeaten one), grinning and joining in the general L. I. U. hallooing . . . The Cubs are counting on Charley Root again, and did you know that he was 40 years old March 17?

Groucho's Son a Star

Indignant New York hockey fans mimeographed petitions and picketed the Garden, because Colonel Kilpatrick arranged for the circus to move in April 7 . . . they feared that the Stanley Cup playoffs would be crowded out . . . Now it seems the Rangers and A's are the only ones being crowded out . . . They're being evicted from the playoffs so fast you'd think they were gatecrashers . . . The Arthur Marx who upset so many stars as he moved into the final of the Los Angeles metropolitan tennis championship this month (where Ronald Lubin beat him), is Groucho's son . . . They say Art Ross isn't squawking as usual during these playoff games because the Bruin chief wants to be elected president of the league, and can't afford to make enemies . . . At least not any more than he already has.

Colonel on Horseback

Col. John Reed Kilpatrick, who heads Madison Square Garden and wears Y-11 on his license plate to denote he escaped from Yale in 1911, lives in the same Park Ave. apartment house as his ousted predecessor, Colonel Hammond . . . They haven't collided yet, but may explode when they do . . . Colonel Kilpatrick has made the Garden click in the past half dozen years, and hops all over the landscape "scouting" attractions before they're booked into his arena . . . He was in Boston Thursday to watch his beloved Rangers, sent Red Dutton a wire of condolence, hopped back to New York yesterday, is due back to the Bruin-Ranger ringside tomorrow night . . . Joe Lapchick will be in Glens Falls, N. Y., next week scouting high school basketball players in the annual tournament there . . . The Basketball Writers' annual dinner will unfold Thursday . . . Australia is still in a dither about Adrian Quist's foot-faults . . . Plenty of squawking over there about naming him on their team, because he apparently hasn't corrected the failing that raised such a rumpus in the Davis Cup challenge round at Germantown last year.

Frisch's Strip Act

Oldest baseball writer still active is Jim O'Leary of the Boston Globe . . . At 77, his fondest boast is that he went on the water wagon 46 years ago, and never toppled off . . . Columbus Casey's membership drive is netting heavy results . . . Johnny Vandermeer, a Dodger at 19, made $20,000 at 24 (last season with the Reds) . . . It was Johnny's first full year in the big show, and his double no-hitter jacked up his expected $5,000 salary check with a raise, indorsements, etc. . . . Casey Stengel, Boston baseball writers Tell you, has the town by the ears, and is becoming one of the most popular baseball figures in its history . . . Frank Frisch says the funniest experience he ever had was in a football game against Holy Cross . . . Playing halfback for Fordham, Frankie was running back a punt when a Crusader end hooked a loop of his pants, with a flying index-finger tackle . . . Frankie was denuded and stood like a startled fawn until he was covered (by tacklers) . . . When Fresco Thompson was captain of those Phillies, the starting lineup he handed the umpires always included, after the name of the starting pitcher, the printed warning ". . . and others!"

Roper's Manager Balks at Encore

Los Angeles, March 25 (AP)—All is not serene on the Joe Louis-Jack Roper fight front.

Dick Donald, Roper's manager, has balked at demands of Mike Jacobs that his fighter sign a contract to give Louis an immediate return bout if Roper wins the heavyweight title from Louis here April 17.

"Anything can happen in a heavyweight fight," said Donald, "and if Jack is lucky enough to knock Louis out, we think we are entitled to at least one crack at the gravy before giving Louis a return match."

Donald said Roper's share of the fight proceeds "wasn't much."

McKalip 3 Sport Coach

Portland, Ore., March 25 — Bill McKalip, former star end on the Detroit Lions National Football League team, has signed a new contract to act as freshmen football, basketball and baseball coach at Oregon State College.

Irony Enters Reiser's Happy-Accident Career

Les Patrick Maps Plans to Stop Bruins

Ranger Chief Believes Main Hope Is to Check Bill Cowley

By HAROLD PARROTT
Brooklyn Eagle Staff Correspondent

Boston, March 25—Boss Lester Patrick planned like a draughtsman into the wee hours this morning, sketching ways and means of cracking the dread Maginot line of the Bruins, which has twice repulsed the Rangers.

The Maginot line, of course, consists of Bomber Bill Cowley, flanked by Snipers Roy Conacher on the left and Mel Hill on the right.

Patrick was making his plans without backing-up from Dave Kerr, who won't be in the Ranger nets tomorrow night when the two top teams of hockey meet in the third duel of their three-out-of-seven series. The Bruins won the first two games by 2 to 1 and 3 to 2.

Stanley Cup Log

Series A
(Best four out of seven)
March 21—Boston, 2; N. Y. Rangers, 1.
March 23—Boston, 3; N. Y. Rangers, 2.
March 26—N. Y. Rangers at Boston.
March 28—Boston at N. Y. Rangers.
March 30—(If necessary) at Boston.
April 1—(If necessary) at New York.
April 2—(If necessary) at Boston.

Series B
(Best two out of three)
March 21—Toronto, 4; N. Y. Americans, 0.
March 23—Toronto, 2; N. Y. Americans, 0.

Series C
(Best two out of three)
March 21—Canadiens, 2; Detroit, 0.
March 23—Detroit, 7; Canadiens, 3.
March 26—Canadiens at Detroit.

Series D
(Best two out of three)
Winners of Series B and C with dates and sites to be determined.

Series E
(Best four out of seven)
Championship and Stanley Cup between winners of Series A and D with dates and sites to be determined.

X-rays taken yesterday revealed that there was an eighth of an inch separation in the bones of Kerr's shoulder from the wallop Conacher handed him Tuesday night. This eighth of an inch does more than separate Kerr's shoulder—it separates him from the Rangers.

Patrick does not seem to mind that so much, for he has a very high opinion of Bert Gardiner, his substitute from Philadelphia. Gardiner is back in Philadelphia today with Bill Carse, battling the Hershey team for the Philly Ramblers in the minor league play-offs. He will hop right back here tomorrow.

Patrick today planned to have his defensemen muss Cowley up in tomorrow night's game even more than they've been doing. It is the Blueshirt chief's contention that Bomber Bill sets up the plays for his two rookie wings in a manner that makes them click. "Stop Cowley and you stop all," he says. This line has produced all five goals against the Rangers.

Patrick says that there are only two or three centers in the league capable of making Conacher and Hill look as good as they do with Cowley.

Patrick today admitted he once had Mel Hill, who has beaten his team twice with overtime goals in these playoffs. It was in 1934, when Lester decided to abandon his Crescent A. C. and start a hockey school. Twenty-four fine prospects came to him in Winnipeg. All he could take was five—the two Colvilles, Joe Cooper, Alex Shibicky and Gardiner, the goaler.

He had to "fire" the other 18. One of 'em was Hill, then a slight wisp of a youngster. And is Hill now happy because he's beating the "favored five" and Patrick? Well, I guess!

All-Star Team Picked

Toronto, March 25 (Canadian Press)—The pick of Boston's brick-wall defense and a Toronto-Montreal forward line heads the ninth annual all-star National Hockey League team announced today by the Canadian Press. The selection was made by 34 hockey writers in the major league cities.

The verdict was nearly unanimous for the first-team forward line of Sylvanus Apps and Gordon Drillon of the Toronto Maple Leafs and Hector (Toe) Blake of the Montreal Canadiens. Eddie Shore, driving force of the Bruins, led two of his mates to positions in the rear guard.

FIRST TEAM	Pos.
Brimsek, Boston	C.
Shore, Boston	R. D.
Clapper, Boston	L. D.
Apps, Toronto	C.
Drillo, Toronto	R. W.
Blake, Montreal	L. W.
Ross, Boston	Coach

ALTERNATE TEAM
Robertson, N. Y. Americans
Seibert, Chicago
Coulter, N. Y. Rangers
N. Colville, Rangers
Bauer, Boston
Gottselif, Chicago
Dutton, Americans

Italy's Tax Disbursements

Special to the Brooklyn Eagle

ROME—Tax disbursements for the eight provinces of Italy for the week ending March 25 were as follows, with figures representing thousands:

Naples	33	79	74	6	22
Bari	88	1	19	11	36
Florence	75	89	61	41	22
Milan	22	30	46	75	6
Palermo	5	13	29	41	67
Rome	43	47	70	15	58
Turin	2	31	34	61	55
Venice	21	10	71	76	4

Battle for Brooklyn Outfield Berths

Ernie Koy, Gene Moore and Fred Sington (top, left to right), and Tuck Stainback (bottom left) and Oral Hockett are leading candidates for regular jobs in Brooklyn outfield.

Charley-Horse Proper Touch At This Stage

Sensational Recruit Halted With String Of Eight for Eight

By TOMMY HOLMES
Brooklyn Eagle Staff Correspondent

Bradenton, Fla., March 25—Harold (Pete) Reiser finally has been stopped. Seven American and National League pitchers couldn't do it, but a lowly charlie horse hobbled Brooklyn's Spring training hero at Lakeland yesterday.

It was in the second inning against the Tigers that Reiser, who cost the Dodgers only $100, batted against equally young Fred Hutchinson, for whom the Tigers spent $100,000 in players and cash last Winter. Pete picked a change of pace pitch and pasted it to centerfield for his eighth straight hit since climbing into Dodger livery. It scored Lavagetto.

Dugout too Close to Plate

Reiser, who can outspeed a frightened thief, sprinted round the circuit on Stainback's double and scored standing up. But in pulling up to a sharp halt before the dugout, built much too close to home plate, Reiser strained a leg muscle. Manager Leo Durocher immediately withdrew him from the game.

The quirk of an injury instead of an opposing player temporarily breaking Reiser's spell is typical of the 19-year-old rookie's career. Everything about the kid's success has an accidental angle.

In the first place, it is accidental the Dodgers own him at all. Branch Rickey failed to cover Reiser in the Cardinal chain gang. He was declared a free agent last Spring along with a hundred-odd other ball players in the Card chain gang by Commissioner Landis. When the white-maned baseball czar issued his edict, the shortstop of the footloose Athletes sought by the Dodgers was Jimmy Webb, now a member of the Cleveland Indians. John McDonald, Larry MacPhail's assistant, kept the telegraph wires hot trying to reach Webb, and was authorized to go as high as $20,000 for Webb's signature to a Brooklyn contract.

And so Ted McGrew picked up Reiser for the Dodgers for $100 bonus and Pete is now the sensation of the Grapefruit circuit, while Webb is just another ball player with Cleveland.

Secondly, it is an accident Reiser is even in Brooklyn camp today. When optioned to Elmira last Fall, he was told to report to their Spring training base at Macon, Ga. Since he lives in St. Louis, he visited Leo Durocher and asked permission to work out wth the Montreal Royals at Lake Wales, Fla. He said he'd like to see Florida.

MacPhail had Better Idea

Leo promised to speak to MacPhail for him. Larry thought it would be a better idea to have Pete with the Dodgers so he could occasionally spell Durocher, who would be plenty busy with his managerial duties.

As every Flatbush fan knows by now Reiser can bat either right-handed or left-handed and throw hard with either hand. This, too, is an accident. Naturally, he is right-handed, but he acquired his ambidexterity because of an older brother, now dead, who, Pete modestly asserts was a far better ball player than he will ever be. Pete's brother was left-handed at bat or afield and Pete as a youngster fell into the habit, as he was prone to imitate him.

The elder Reiser was Yankee property, but died before he accomplished much in the big league scheme.

Our accidental hero's explanation for his astonishing success is almost as surprising as his success.

"It may seem funny but I'm more confident swinging against major league pitching than I was last Summer trying to hit what the flingers in the Class B Northern League," said Reiser. "Down here major league pitchers have real control and up in Superior, Wis., last year, they had me skipping the rope from the start to the finish of the season. I was hit by pitched balls 18 times last year, but I think it's a draw because I hit 18 home runs.

Wigglesworth Commodore

Frank Wigglesworth, Boston motorboat official and former inboard racing driver, has been elected commodore of the Central New England Regatta Association.

Giants, Tribe Renew Rivalry

By the Associated Press

New Orleans—The Indians and the Giants started out again today to settle their six-year-old exhibition feud. Annual touring companions since 1934, the two clubs have played 70 games, with the Indians winning 34, the Giants 33 and three contests ending in ties.

Los Angeles—Resuming their Chicago city series, Coast version, the managers of the Cubs and the White Sox could contemplate with pleasure today the development of a couple of their pitchers. Rookie Ed Carnett virtually clinched a spot on the Bruins' staff by holding Pittsburgh to two hits in four frames yesterday, while Bill Dietrich of the Sox showed signs of his old form in holding Los Angeles to four hits in five innings.

San Francisco—Worried by the inability of his pitching mainstays to show anything resembling winning form, Manager Pie Traynor decided to start Joe Bowman against San Francisco today. Bowman, used mainly in relief last season, won three and lost four. The Pirates broke camp at San Bernardino yesterday and will head eastward March 30.

Tripped by Tigers

Brooklyn (N. L.)	ab	r	h	o	a	Detroit (A. L.)	ab	r	h	o	a
S'nback,cf	4	0	1	1	0	Crucher,ss	4	1	0	3	2
Co'art,2b	2	0	0	2	3	Walker,lf	5	1	1	3	0
Moore,cf	2	0	1	2	0	Gehringer,2b	3	0	2	4	5
Koy,cf	2	0	0	0	0	Gr'nberg,1b	4	0	0	10	1
Phelps,c	3	0	0	4	0	Fox,rf	3	1	1	1	0
Hayworth,c	2	0	0	0	0	C'nbine,cf	4	1	1	4	0
Camilli,1b	3	2	2	7	1	Tebbetts,c	2	0	1	2	1
Sington,lf	4	0	3	1	0	York,c	2	1	1	0	0
Lavagetto,3b	4	1	2	3	1	Rogell,3b	4	0	3	0	4
Reiser,ss	1	1	1	0	0	F.H'nson,p	0	0	0	0	0
Hudson,ss	3	0	0	3	2	Harris,p	1	0	0	0	1
Tamulis,p	2	0	1	0	1	†Christman	1	1	1	0	0
*Haas	1	0	0	0	0	Eisenstat,p	2	0	0	0	0
F. Hu'ins'n,p	1	0	0	1	0						
Totals	34	4	11	24	8	Totals	35	6	11	27	14

*Batted for Tamulis in sixth inning.
†Batted for Harris in fifth inning.

Brooklyn ———— 0 3 0 0 0 0 1 0 0—4
Detroit ———— 0 0 0 2 2 0 0 2 x—6

Errors—Croucher, Hudson. Runs batted in—Lavagetto, Reiser, Stinback, Fox, Tebbetts, Christman, Gehringer, Sington, Rogell, Eisenstat. Two-base hit—Stinback. Three-base hits—Lavagetto, Walker, Camilli. Home run—Christman. Stolen base—Croucher. Sacrifice—Coscarart. Double plays—Coscarart and Camilli; Rogell, Gehringer and Greenberg. Left on bases—Brooklyn, 11; Detroit, 9. Bases on balls—Off Tamulis, 1; off F. Hutchinson, 4; off Harris, 1; off Eisenstat, 1; off I. Hutchinson, 2. Struck out—By Tamulis, 3; by Harris, 1. Hits—Off Tamulis, 8 in 5 innings; off I. Hutchinson, 3 in 3; off F. Hutchinson, 4 in 1 2-3; off Harris, 3 in 3 1-3; off Eisenstat, 4 in 4. Wild pitch—F. Hutchinson. Balks—Harris (3), Eisenstat. Winning pitcher—Eisenstat. Losing pitcher—I. Hutchinson. Umpires—Ormsby and Goetz. Time—2:35.

Moe's French Slays High School Misses

By TOMMY HOLMES
Staff Correspondent of the Brooklyn Eagle

Bradenton, Fla., March 25—Scene in a Sarasota soda shop:—Moe Berg, outstanding linguist in the major leagues, wanders in and sees three high school girls busy on nut sundaes, their school books on the table . . . Noticing a French grammar in each collection, Moe politely inquires how they are getting along with the language . . . "Terrible," chorus the youngsters . . . It winds up with Moe sitting down, ordering another round of sundaes and rehearsing the next day's lesson until each girl has it letter perfect . . . They think he is wonderful.

Why Lazzeri No Likes

Tony Lazzeri is not particularly fond of Bill Werber . . . A few years ago, when Lazzeri was still a Yank and Werber was with the A's, the Yanks won the first game of a doubleheader, were way ahead in the second . . . It was a hot afternoon and Tony, whose stoic exterior hides a hell-raising streak, was having no fun until he thought of an idea . . . He got the oldest, blackest ball he could find, substituted it for the white, shiny one he received as the infield threw it around and handed the old ball to Kemp Wicker, who was pitching . . . Wicker threw it to the hitter and with the first pitch a near riot broke loose . . . Tony would have got away with his trick except for Werber, the only man in the park who saw what happened . . . Werber insisted that the umpires search Lazzeri . . . In his hip pocket they found the ball intended for play . . . The result was that the American League fined Tony $400.

The Dodger quartet has become a quintet, the added starter being Red Evans . . . The boys are good too . . . Fat Stuff Tamulis sings the lead, with Stainback the high tenor, Rosen the second tenor and Bert Haas harmonizing in a beautiful baritone . . . Evans sings bass.

Fred Fitzsimmons, nearing 38, can't be expected to pitch successfully much longer . . . But he says he wishes to remain in baseball as long as he lives, because it's the life he loves best . . . And there is a good chance that he will . . . "I know that as long as I'm connected with the Brooklyn club," said Larry MacPhail recently, "there always will be room in the organization for a fellow of Fitz' hustle and intelligence."

Ross Another Walters?

Don Ross, stylish third baseman who, for the time being at least, has little chance of sticking with the Dodgers, slings that ball so hard and accurately across the diamond that many wonder how he'd do as a pitcher, a la Bucky Walters . . .

Yanks Again Spread Terror

By the Associated Press

St. Petersburg, Fla.—The American League opponents of the Yankees should be full of fear and trembling by the time you read this. The world champions have clouted five home runs in the last two days and Joe DiMaggio, who never hit a homer in Spring training before, has collected three of them.

Ocala, Fla.—Fearing the spread of influenza, Owner Clark Griffith of the Washington Senators today ordered the squad to stay away from Cecil Travis, the club's stricken shortstop, who has been confined to bed for five days.

San Benito, Texas—Note to Don Heffner and Ralph Kress, St. Louis Browns holdouts, somewhere in California: They don't even mention you any more in the Browns' section of the citrus circuit. Sig Gryska and Johnny Berardino have lighted up that old double play corner like a couple of floodlights.

An impressive thing about Pete Coscarart down here is that the errors he committed in early games have not discouraged him in the least.

The most popular idle-hour diversion of the Dodgers is pool on the Fort Harrison Hotel's one and only table . . . Some of the lads are pretty good, but not good enough to challenge the manager .

It's as DiMaggio Goes So Go Yanks—If Gehrig Goes

By BILL McCULLOUGH

They used to say "as Babe Ruth goes, so go the Yankees." And when the immortal Babe called it quits the slogan was "as Gehrig goes."

We hope that reports from the Southland to the effect that Gehrig is ready for the rocking chair are premature—that the Iron Horse will be exploding long hits again when the bell rings next month.

But it seems certain that Gehrig soon is about to go with the wind, else Marse Joe McCarthy wouldn't be experimenting with several new first basemen. Therefore, Joe DiMaggio today looms as the new hub of the world champions' machine and from now on it'll be "as DiMaggio goes, so go the Yankees."

DiMaggio is generally regarded as the best player in the game. A wonderful fielder (undoubtedly the best since Tris Speaker), he is likewise one of the best hitters who has come across the baseball horizon.

In the American League three years, DiMaggio has driven in 432 runs and turned in batting averages of .323, .346 and .342. Although his batting was only ordinary during the first half of the last season he was hitting .341 in early September and threatened to win the league championship.

Then the Yankees, having cleared the field, began to take things easy with the result that the brilliant Italian from Fisherman's Wharf in Frisco coasted along with Charley Ruffing, Monte Pearson, Bill Dickey and Tom Henrich. The boys didn't have to bear down and all of their averages suffered.

Still DiMaggio drove in 140 runs, a tremendous total when one considers that the Athletics' entire outfield hammered in only 153! And playing in any other park but the Stadium, where his 400-foot drives are glover, Joe would have had a higher total.

DiMaggio is 25 years old. He has been in the league three years and has yet to play a full season because of illness and holdoutitis. His record is remarkable. Joe has never had the benefit of a training season. The guy just steps in there and powders the ball.

DiMaggio is far from his peak, Connie Mack told the scribes at the last World Series, and there is no telling how far Joe will go. He may knock Speaker out of the all-time outfield, which also includes Ty Cobb and Ruth. How are they going to keep him out if Joe continues to move at his present pace?

At the St. Petersburg camp they are hailing him as a new DiMaggio. No longer is he egotistical and arrogant. That booing he received during the early weeks of the last race from Boston to St. Louis took a lot of wind out of his sails. Sound advice from his freshman professor, Frank (Lefty) O'Doul, during the Winter has made Joe more tolerable.

"Shake off the mob and stick with the ball players," Lefty warned DiMaggio. "Treat the fans like human beings. They are paying your salary. Follow this advice and when you return to the Coast next Fall you'll find that you had the goodwill of everybody—something Ruth, Matty, Wagner and the rest always had."

President Sits in to Smash Coal Deadlock

Weather Forecast
By U. S. Weather Bureau
Showers Tonight. Cloudy and Slightly Warmer Tomorrow.

BROOKLYN EAGLE
DAILY AND SUNDAY

Wall Street Closing
Racing Extra
★★★★★★

98th YEAR—No. 128 | Entered in the Brooklyn Postoffice as 2d Class Mail Matter | BROOKLYN, N. Y., TUESDAY, MAY 9, 1939 | (Copyright 1939 The Brooklyn Daily Eagle) | THREE CENTS

Amen Indicts Baldwin

Congress Gets F. D's Second Merger Plan

Proposal to Effect 14 Bureau Transfers At Estimated Saving Of $1,250,000

Washington, May 9 (AP)—President Roosevelt proposed his second government reorganization plan to Congress today involving 14 interdepartmental bureau transfers and consolidations estimated to save $1,250,000 a year.

The President in a lengthy message declared this would be his final reorganization proposal to Congress this session under the recently enacted reorganization law.

"In view of the fact that it is now May 9," he said, "and that any reorganization plan must lie before the Congress for 60 calendar days and because the reorganizations of an intradepartmental character require a great deal of research and careful, painstaking, detailed work, I do not propose to send any further general reorganization plans to the Congress at this session."

PROVISIONS OF PLAN

The first plan, involving merger of a score of independent lending, welfare and public works agencies into three new Federal agencies, becomes effective June 24 because the veto resolution failed of passage in the House last week.

His second plan today proposes:

1. Abolition of the National Bituminous Coal Commission and transfer of its functions to the Secretary of the Interior.

"The Congress," the President said, "placed this commission in the Department of the Interior, but experience has shown that direct administration will be cheaper, better and more effective than through the cumbersome medium of an unnecessary commission.

BUREAUS AFFECTED

2. Transfer the foreign commerce service of the Commerce Department and the foreign agricultural service of the Agriculture Department to the Department of State for consolidation with that department's foreign service.

3. Transfer of the Foreign Service Buildings Commission, now independent, to the State Department.

4. Transfer of the Bureau of Lighthouses, Commerce Department, to the Treasury Department for merger with the Coast Guard.

5. Abolition of the office of Director General of Railroads and War Finance Corporation, World War-born agencies, and transfer of their functions to the Treasury "to be wound up" as rapidly as possible; the latter corporation to be finally dissolved not later than Dec. 31, 1939.

6. Transfer to the Department of Justice of the Federal Prison Industries, Inc., and National Training School for Boys, now independent,

Continued on Page 19

Bottoms Up For $46,000 Illegal Hootch

Police Officials Rid City of Contraband

Down the hatch, but not the way you like it, goes $46,000 worth of contraband giglewater—hard likker, wines and beer—seized by the Police Department in various raids. Above Fifth Deputy Police Commissioner Martin Meaney (bending over) and Lt. Joseph Brawley of the police property clerk's office, start pouring the illegal hooch into the waters of the bay at the foot of 36th St. At the left is shown another way of disposing of it by smashing the bottles against a brick wall. And yet they can smile! (Eagle Staff Photos.)

Pope Proposes 5-Power Peace Talk on Danzig

Vatican Mediation Of French-Italian Dispute Is Offered

Paris, May 9 (U.P.)—Pope Pius has proposed a five-Power conference to settle Polish-German differences and has offered direct Vatican mediation of the French-Italian dispute, it was learned today.

News came from a high diplomatic source that the Pope had:

1. Invited the governments of France, Great Britain, Poland, Germany and Italy to a conference at the Vatican to seek a settlement of the dispute between Germany and Poland, centering on Danzig.
2. Offered his own good offices and those of Cardinal Maglione, his secretary of state, to mediate in the French-Italian dispute arising from Benito Mussolini's "aspirations" in the Mediterranean.

Negotiations were proceeding among the Powers concerned—between France and Great Britain and between them jointly and Poland; and between Germany and Italy, the "axis" Powers, now committed to a definite military pact.

For the moment, the position was said to be as follows:

1. France and Great Britain were not particularly favorable to the conference on Polish-German differences. But it was understood that negotiations had now turned toward the idea of direct Vatican mediation between Poland and Germany. The British and French were agreeable to that and Germany and Italy were reported to be agreeable provided Poland's consent could be obtained.
2. France was inclined to decline the offer of mediation in the

Continued on Page 2

Brief Session On Coal Crisis Ends at Capital

Negotiators Will Resume Talks Here After Seeing F. D. R.

BULLETIN

Washington, May 9 (AP)—The soft coal operators and miners conference at the White House ended today with only a statement by John L. Lewis that the negotiators would meet again tomorrow, in New York.

Washington, May 9 (AP)—The soft coal operators-miners conference with President Roosevelt broke up at 1:15 p.m. (E. S. T.) today after a discussion lasting more than an hour.

Washington, May 9 (AP)—Negotiators in the soft coal crisis walked silently into the White House today to discuss with President Roosevelt the wage contract dispute which has left 450,000 miners idle.

Joint negotiating committees, invited here by Mr. Roosevelt after he became increasingly concerned with the almost complete shutdown of the industry, declined to speculate beforehand on prospect of an agreement.

The Administration was particularly worried over a possibly serious shortage of coal for industry and transportation.

Sitting in on the conference was

Continued on Page 13

3d Geoghan Aide Charged With Accepting Bribes

Accused of Taking $800 From Juffe, Fur Racketeer, for Neglect of Duty --Weisman Thanks Troy for His Help

Assistant District Attorney Alexander A. R. Baldwin was indicted today on a charge of accepting $800 in bribes from Isidore Juffe, Brooklyn fur racketeer, who is himself in jail awaiting trial on grand larceny and bribery accusations in the fur racket.

In Probe Net

Alexander A. R. Baldwin

Latest in Amen probe net, Mr. Baldwin faces bribery charges. (Eagle Staff photo.)

The first extraordinary grand jury handed up the two-count indictment, which charged receiving a bribe and accepting a gratuity for neglecting his duty as a prosecutor, to Supreme Court Justice Francis D. McCurn.

Baldwin surrendered in the office of Assistant Attorney General Amen in Borough Hall, was arrested on a bench warrant and was taken to the Poplar St. station for formal booking.

From the Poplar St. station Baldwin was taken to Manhattan police headquarters where he was fingerprinted and photographed. Then he was returned to Brooklyn for arraignment before Justice McCurn.

3D AD TO BE INDICTED

Baldwin was the third of District Attorney Geoghan's assistants to be indicted since Mr. Amen, on orders of Governor Lehman, launched his investigation into law enforcement corruption in Brooklyn. The other two were William A. McGuinness, who was indicted for bribery on Sept. 20 and has since pleaded guilty, and Francis A. Madden, indicted on April 21. They were charged with taking bribes in the abortion and other rackets.

Baldwin is 42, married, the father of three children, and lives at 57 Downing St. He is the son of the late Police Inspector Sylvestre D. Baldwin and a brother of Dr. Joseph Baldwin, personal friend of Mr. Geoghan and for many years a Police Department surgeon. He has been an assistant district attorney for six years.

FOLLOWS BRIBE RUMORS

Rumors that a bribe had been paid to prevent a fur racket indictment were publicly aired on Aug. 15 last, and the next day Mr. Geoghan's office obtained the first fur racket indictment, in which, however, Juffe was not named. A later Geoghan indictment also named Sam Davis and Nathan Krapes and on March 2 an Amen grand jury handed up a superseding indictment including Juffe.

The Baldwin indictment charged that the assistant prosecutor received the $800 bribe in two installments, $500 on Aug. 11 and $300 on Aug. 22. If convicted on both counts he would face a maximum sentence of ten years in jail and a $5,000 fine.

THANKS TROY FOR AID

Assistant Attorney General Herman L. Weisman of Mr. Amen's staff, who obtained the indictment, expressed his appreciatoin of the aid given in the fur racket investigation by Magistrate Mathew J. Troy, Inspector Michael F. McDermott and Commissioner of Investigation William E. Herlands.

"Today's indictment of Assistant District Attorney Baldwin," he declared, "represents the high point thus far in the investigation of the Brooklyn fur racket, which was

Continued on Page 2

Deny Subway Coal Shortage

Industry's Official Paper Says Plenty Of Fuel Is on Hand

By TOM STEUTEL

While B. M. T. and I. R. T. subways because of the announced fears of a shortage resulting from the coal stoppage, were operating today on reduced schedules, the current issue of the Black Diamond, official organ of the coal industry, asserted that "there is not now nor has there been what could be classified as an acute shortage of steam coal."

Reports that the two privately operated subway systems had turned down sales offers of coal were denied by William G. Fullen, Transit Commissioner, as "not so at all; the B. M. T. and I. R. T. are not well supplied."

Despite Fullen's denial it has been authoritatively learned by the Brooklyn Eagle that officials of the B. M. T. told a Brooklyn coal broker the company "was not interested at this time" in his proffer of coal.

SHORTAGE DENIED

The Black Diamond article pointed out that "in spite of numerous alarmist statements made by Mayor LaGuardia concerning the coal supply available for essential utilities and other important industries in New York City, there is not now, nor has there been, what could be classified as an acute shortage of steam coal. It is true that many consumers have been handicapped by having to purchase at high prices some very poor qualities.

"Such large users as Consolidated Edison, Interboro, Brooklyn Edison and others, have been able to get their supplies," the article continued, "from central Pennsylvania and Virginia ports without reaching the panic stage in spite of the attempts of municipal authorities to make pro-labor capital out of the suspension."

Several other large industrial coal consumers in Brooklyn revealed

Continued on Page 13

Mayor Hissed At Fascist Fete

Opens Italian Exhibit At Fair—Ignores Mussolini Salute

Mayor LaGuardia's welcoming speech at the dedication of the Italian Building in the World's Fair today was marked by some hissing, cries of "Viva Mussolini," playing of the Fascist anthem and the Fascist salute.

The Mayor spoke in both English and Italian, praising Italy's culture and industrial aims and expressing the hope that she would "continue to be devoted to world peace." He paid no mind to the booing nor the playing of the Fascist anthem and made no move to return the Fascist salute given him and Grover Whalen by guards in the building.

Two thousand members of Italian-American societies took part in the ceremonies held in the three-story building occupying 100,000 square feet, just off the Court of Peace. A tower surmounts the building and atop the tower is a replica of the ancient statue, the Goddess of

Continued on Page 3

Gem Theft Fizzles

It looked for a few minutes as if there might be some big excitement at the World's Fair today. The burglar alarm went off in the House of Jewels, wherein are exhibited some $8,000,000 in gems. But it was just a false alarm. An offcial said there was no robbery. A newsreel was being taken at the time.

Fall Off Car Kills Noted Aviatrix

London, May 9 (AP)—The body of Mrs. G. A. R. Williams, once widely known as an aviatrix when she was Lady Mary Heath, was identified today by relatives at a hospital, where she died of head injuries suffered in falling down the steps of a double-deck street car.

The flier, who had not appeared in public much recently, was 43.

At the height of her aviation career she was injured in 1929 when her plane crashed at the Cleveland air races. In 1930 she obtained a divorce in Reno from Sir James Heath, British iron-master and colliery owner. She subsequently married George Anthony Reginald Williams, also a well-known British flier, at Lexington, Ky.

1,701,576 Attend Fair In First Nine Days

Visitors to the World's Fair totaled 1,701,576 for the first nine days ending this morning, according to President Grover A. Whalen. There were 1,387,301 the first week, 222,423 Sunday and 91,852 yesterday.

Burglaries Increase In Livingston St. Area

Shopkeepers Up in Arms as 2-Year-Old Crime Wave Flares With New Vigor

Shopkeepers along Livingston St. and on side streets between Flatbush Ave. and Smith St. leading into Livingston St. are up in arms about the epidemic of burglaries that has raged through the section with varying intensity for the past two years and which broke out with redoubled vigor in the last few days.

A survey by The Brooklyn Eagle of only a portion of the neighborhood brought to light 19 stores that have been burglarized, three of them within the past week. A number of stores were visited more than once by marauders. One store, in fact, was broken into last Friday for the fifth time in two years.

The businessmen said they had complained frequently to the Police Department and special patrols had been assigned sporadically to the district but that there had been no

Continued on Page 13

Workmen's Union Pickets Fair Gates

A number of men, who identified themselves as members of Local 1420, of the International Union of Hod Carriers, Builders and Common Laborers, an A. F. of L. affiliate, were picketing entrances to the World's Fair grounds today. They were protesting, they said, their discharge by the Fair Corporation, and they charged that non-union men were hired in their stead.

There were three pickets at the World's Fair Boulevard gate and two each at the Corona gates, north and south. They carried placards which stated that the "World's Fair Corporation is unfair to Fair ground workers."

The union has offices at 40-03 National Ave., Corona. Norman Rothman, president of the local, refused to make any statement concerning the picketing. He referred all inquiries to James Bove, international vice president of the union. He said Bove was in Manhattan but would return to the local headquarters later today.

Payroll Theft Suspect Captured in Suffolk

Special to the Brooklyn Eagle

Patchogue, May 9—Facing a grand larceny charge in the theft of a $357 payroll on April 7 Anthony Kosloiski, 26, a laborer, of Eastport was turned over to Linden, N. J., police today after his arrest yesterday in Center Moriches when he disembarked from a ferry which carried county highway department workers to the mainland from the barrier beach.

The complainant is Frank A. Baraclough, president of the Atkinson Freight Company, Brooklyn, who charges that Kosloiski begged a ride on April 7 on an Atkinson truck bound for Philadelphia. The driver left the truck to enter a restaurant and his passenger remained behind, but when he returned both the passenger and the payroll, addressed to the Philadelphia office of the trucking firm, were gone, Baraclough charged.

In the Eagle Today

	Page		Page
Books	25	Let's Go to Fair	6
Brain Teaser	24	Line on Liners	22
Bridge	25	Lost and Found	2
Brooklyn Fact	12	Obituaries	13
Cassel's Cartoon	12	Quillen	24
Clifford Evans	15	Radio	24
Comics	24-25	Real Estate	23
Crossword	23	Referees	22
Dr. Brady	25	Serial	25
Ed Hughes	16	Shipping	22
Editorial	12	Society	11
Events	22	Sports	16-18
Financial	19-21	Theaters	9
Garden Corner	23	Tommy Holmes	16
Grin and Bear It	12	Tucker	12
Heffernan	15	Want Ads	22-23
Helen Worth	11	Washington	15
Tommy Wood	16	Women	10

Narragansett Pk. Results

FIRST RACE—Three-year-olds and up; three-quarters mile.

Ground Oak (Van Tas'l)	94.90	83.10	35.90
Bright Spot (Wilson)	—	7.50	5.40
Mr. Hyland (McCombs)	—	—	9.10

Time, 1:13 2-5. Cambreeze, Lady Weaver, Pribaby, Circus Night, Dona Montez, Cordate, My Gracious, Way Yonder, Lilting also ran. (Off time, 2:24½.)

Jamaica Results

FIRST RACE—Three-year-olds and up; three-quarters mile.

JaZck Fly (Balaski)	10-1	3-1	8-5
Ritorno (Longden)	—	1-3	Out
St. Anna (Meade)	—	—	1-3

Time, 1:13 2-5. Ease-M-Up, Rocky Margot, Speed Limit, Hello Stranger, Salavina also ran. (Off time, 2:32½.)

Hammer Slayer, Aged Mother Weep in Reunion at His Trial

Mineola, May 9 — There was a tearful reunion in County Court here today between Vernon Elmer Oldaker, handyman on trial for first degree murder, and his 80-year-old mother, Mrs. Eva Oldaker, a respected resident of Iowa City, Iowa.

Oldaker has confessed the hammer slaying of Anna Louise McKee, a spinster, in her Mineola home on March 6.

Two jurors were selected at he morning session, bringing the total number in the box up to 11. Since the trial started yesterday 90 prospective talesmen were examined, a record in a case of this kind.

Picked today were Oscar E. Kelly, New York Telephone Company engineer, of Baldwin, and Arthur Allgeier, salesman, of Malverne, who became jurors 10 and 11.

The elderly Mrs. Oldaker, dressed plainly in black, came into court with Mrs. Doris Brown of Westbury, his first wife, from whom he never was divorced. Mrs. Brown comforted the old lady and held her hand during the morning. Mrs. Oldaker embraced her son in the courtroom and both were weeping.

District Attorney Edward T. Neary asked prospective jurors if they would be influenced by the appearance of the defendant's mother.

Wife Defends Husband In Son's Mercy Killing

A sorrowful mother, whose boy "wasn't just right" went on the witness stand today in Bronx County Court to defend her husband on trial for the mercy slaying of their son.

Mrs. Anna Greenfield, a slight, pathetic figure in black, under the gentle guidance of Samuel Leibowitz, defense counsel, recited the unhappy story of her 16-year-old son's unnatural development and his death from chloroform administered by his father, Lous Greenfield, a few months ago.

Before the tragedy of their mentally undeveloped son, Greenfield was a happy-go-lucky fellow, always laughing and cheerful, Mrs. Greenfield testified. As the unhappy years piled up, he grew more and more depressed, she said, and they spent all their money on their unfortunate child.

Lauer, Quitting, Cleans Up Work

Justice Edgar J. Lauer, whose resignation from the Manhattan Supreme Court bench as the aftermath of the smuggling activities of his wife, Elma, takes effect June 15, worked busily in his chambers today to dispose of the remaining court business pending before him.

Reported ill yesterday at his home, 570 Park Ave., Manhattan, Justice Lauer arrived at the Manhattan Supreme Court building early this morning and went immediately to his chambers. Through his secretary, he said he would make no statement on the letter of resignation which he transmitted last night to Governor Lehman.

Mrs. Lauer pleaded guilty to smuggling $1,833 worth of Parisian-made wearing apparel into this country, paid a $2,500 fine and is now serving a three-month sentence.

Court Frees Davis As Torrio Witness

Federal Judge Muray Hulbert in Manhattan dismissed today a warrant under which Richard J. (Dixie) Davis was held as a material witness in the case of John Torrio, on motion of Assistant United States Attorney Seymour Klein. This leaves Davis a free man, except for the remaining five months he must serve for his part in the lottery case in which former Tammany Leader James J. Hines was convicted.

Senate Passes Bill To End Lunacy Boards

Albany, May 9—The Desmond bill, designed to abolish lunacy commissions, was passed by a vote of 31 to 16 in the Senate this afternoon. The measure now goes to the Assembly.

Future sanity examinations of persons charged with crime would be made by qualified psychiatrists on the public hospital staffs.

The vote on the measure cut across party lines and seven Democrats joined with the Republican majority in voting for the bill sponsored by Senator Thomas C. Desmond, up-State Republican.

Oust Jewish Refugees

San Jose, Costa Rica, May 9 (AP)—A government decree today ordered the immediate departure from Costa Rica of all Jewish refugee families who had arrived in the past [illegible] months [illegible] tourists.

[illegible]

Baldwin Expected to Resign Under Fire Today

Weather Forecast
By U. S. Weather Bureau
Cloudy and Warm Today and Tomorrow

BROOKLYN EAGLE
DAILY AND SUNDAY

Wall Street Closing
Racing Extra
★★★★★★

98th YEAR—No. 129 | Entered in the Brooklyn Postoffice as 2d Class Mail Matter | BROOKLYN, N. Y., WEDNESDAY, MAY 10, 1939 | THREE CENTS

Coal Peace Held Sure Tonight

Baldwin Due To Quit Under Fire Today

Geoghan Declares He's Disillusioned But Not Set to Resign

Assistant District Attorney Alexander R. Baldwin, indicted yesterday, intends to resign late this afternoon, it was learned by the Brooklyn Eagle on the best authority.

Meanwhile Baldwin's superior, District Attorney Geoghan, declared he was disillusioned about holding public office and commented wearily:

"I wish I never had entered public life."

Geoghan announced that later in the day he would hold a press conference at which it was expected he would announce receipt of Baldwin's resignation. Two other Geoghan assistants also are under indictment.

One of them, William F. McGuinness, already has pleaded guilty to bribery charges. Observers said that Geoghan's decision as to resigning himself may depend on the case against the other, Francis A. Madden.

Friends of both declared the prosecutor might step out of office to act as counsel in Madden's trial—thus at the same time fighting for Madden, a personal appointee, and for vindication of his own conduct in office.

It was expected that Baldwin's defense would be based on discrepancies between the indictment handed up yesterday and testimony given by a principal in the fur racket case and his sister. Nathan Krapes, a defendant, and Mrs. Mollie Rosenthal were believed to have quoted Isidore Juffe, key Amen witness, as having spoken of bribes paid in July, 1938. The indictment, on the other hand, alleged Baldwin received $800 in bribes the following month.

"Public office is not worth the heartaches it entails," Mr. Geoghan said in an interview today and when

Continued on Page 2

Girl's Plea That Father Be Jailed Bares Fight to Care for 6 Tots

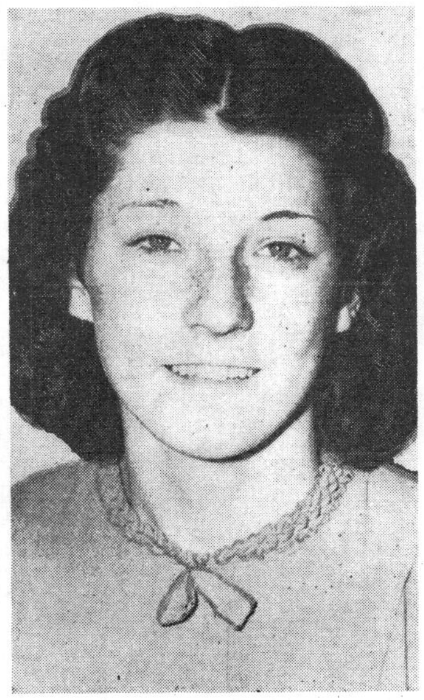

Frances Hartman

By VIOLET J. BROWN

The other day Frances Hartman, 17, appeared in Pennsylvania Avenue Court to ask that her father be jailed. She said that he beat her.

But in the forgotten cubbyholes at 230 Georgia Ave. there are more cogent reasons.

They are all under seven years of age: Robert, who chops wood for the wood-stove which is the sole heating and cooking apparatus of the cubbyholes; Charles, 6; Henry, 4; Edward, 2 and crippled—she says her father ran after her with an ax when she insisted that the child be put to sleep late Saturday night; Raymond, 1½, who eats very little but looks, in his sister's words, "as though he ate chicken," and Arlene, 7 months old, who is very good but can't keep her milk down because it is canned, the only kind of milk Frances can get on credit.

Frances herself is a tall, slim, unusually pretty girl, who was brought up in an orphan asylum and left a year ago to join her parents. Five other Hartman children are still in orphanages and homes.

What she found "at home" made her sick. But, she said today over her dishes, "No matter what your home is, it's your ma and pa. That's something."

She found her family on relief and her father a drunkard.

"He drinks 'smoke,' gets a pint or a quart for about 15 cents. He hasn't been sober this month."

She found a flat that looks as though it had been spewed out of "Tobacco Road." "I have to meet my boy friends outside, it's so terrible. For crying out loud, what kind of girl can they think I am?"

'CURSED LIKE TROOPERS'

She found that the five little boys cursed like troopers. "In the orphanage I never even heard those words. But they're good little boys. They don't curse now, I tanned them so much when they

Continued on Page 12

Chamberlain Explains Stand On Soviet Pact

Russian Armed Aid Sought After England Had Taken Field

London, May 10 (AP)—Prime Minister Chamberlain told the House of Commons today that Britain sought Soviet Russia's promise of military aid in Eastern Europe only after Britain and France themselves had taken the field.

Breaking his silence on the government's security alliance proposals to remove what he said appeared to be a misunderstanding of them in Soviet Russia, Chamberlain said the proposals "made it plain it was not a part of their (the British) intention that the Soviet Government should commit themselves to intervene irrespective of whether Great Britain and France had already, in discharge of their obligations, done so."

REASSURES RUSSIA

Asked whether, in view of the delay in the negotiations, Foreign Secretary Viscount Halifax would "proceed to Moscow and have straightforward discussions" with the new Soviet Foreign Minister, Vyacheslaff Molotoff, the Prime Minister replied:

"We had better await the reply of the Soviet Government."

Chamberlain sought to allay any Soviet suspicion that Russia might be left alone in intervening in behalf of smaller States in some circumstances. He said Russia could make her intervention contingent on that of Britain.

Russia's position in regard to Poland or Rumania, to whom Britain and France already have given separate guarantees, thus would be the same as in the Soviet-French pact with the old Czechoslovakia, where Russia was obligated to aid only if France did so.

SPEED CONSCRIPTION

Answering a question, Chamberlain said the mutual assistance pact between Britain and Poland did not exclude the possibility of an alliance between Britain and Russia.

After answering questions, the Prime Minister moved a resolution designed to eliminate red tape and enable the government to rush

Continued on Page 3

Mayor Tells Critics He Builds for Future

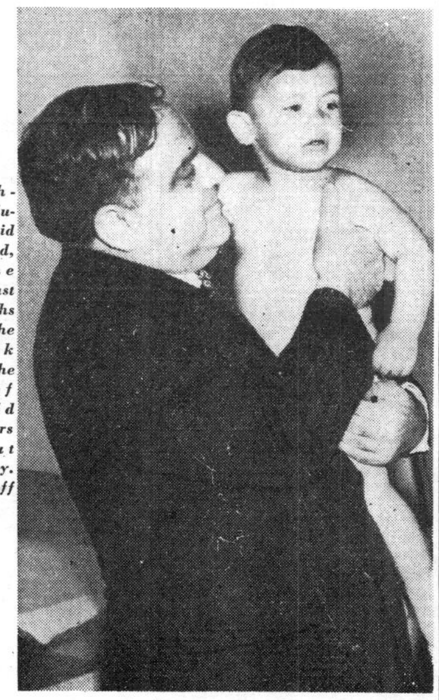

Sixteen - month - old Patsy Molluco, with the aid of his friend, Hizzoner the Mayor, has just found he weighs 25 pounds. The weighing took place during the dedication of three child health centers throughout Brooklyn today. (Eagle Staff photo.)

Speaks at Dedication Of Three New Boro Child Health Centers

Mayor LaGuardia, dedicating three new child health stations in Brooklyn today with other city officials, inspected the premises, shook hands with dozens of children, weighed a few, was photographed with some and seized the opportunity to answer "prominent people" who have assailed his "spending for the future" policies.

Commenting that the three health units were part of a chain throughout the city, the Mayor said, "This is the kind of work prominent people, or people who think they are prominent, have criticized at Albany. They said if I spent less money for the future I wouldn't have to ask for slashes in the salaries of idle, useless politicians.

BUILDING FOR TOMORROW

"These prominent people criticize the construction of parks, playgrounds and health centers of this sort. My answer is that I am building for tomorrow. These children are my proof. When they are 8 years old they will have more sense than to criticize agencies building for tomorrow. Dr. Rice (Health Commissioner John L. Rice) deserves great praise for the extension of the Health Department and I want to thank the WPA for its assistance."

The three centers, each costing approximately $50,000, are at 130 Nostrand Ave., 62 2d Place and 8658 16th Ave. They replace rented structures with inadequate facilities at 583 Park Ave., 82 Luquer St. and 218 Throop Ave. They are one-story brick buildings, constructed with WPA labor, under the supervision

Continued on Page 2

Conciliator Confers With Two Groups

Utilities Called To Bare Shortage—Central Cuts Trains

Prospects of reaching a coal strike settlement today are "reassuring," Dr. John R. Steelman, chief Federal labor conciliator, said this afternoon.

Dr. Steelman conferred for 2½ hours with representatives of the bituminous coal operators and the United Mine Workers of America, who returned from Washington with President Roosevelt's demand that an agreement to reopen the mines be reached by midnight.

When the conference recessed for luncheon at the Biltmore Hotel, Manhattan, Dr. Steelman issued this brief statement:

"In accordance with the President's statement to the joint conferees yesterday, my position today is one of imperatively demanding a solution of the situation within the time limit as set."

WON'T COMMENT

Pressed by questioners, he chose to answer only one query. That was: "Can we reassure the country of chances of the success of the conferees in complying with the President's request?"

"I think you can," he answered, and quickly added, "That's my assumption."

Spokesmen for both the union and the operators declined to comment, but unofficially several operators revealed that a formula for settlement had not yet been reached.

Dr. Steelman expected to confer again briefly with the operator representatives and then to meet both sides in a joint conference.

Meanwhile the increasing coal shortage extended its deadening influence.

UTILITIES CALLED

The New York Central Railroad cut its schedule in anticipation of a continuing deadlock and the Transit Commission summoned the utilities in the Metropolitan area to a hearing to determine the extent of their fuel shortage and the steps to be taken to meet it. Later hearings,

Continued on Page 15

Clergymen Stand 5-1 For Flatbush Cabaret

Go on Record Favoring Issuance of License To Cafe Over Lone Opposition of Dr. Berg

Against the opposition of the Rev. Dr. J. Frederic Berg, pastor of the famous Reformed Protestant Dutch Church at Flatbush and Church Aves., five other Flatbush clergymen, as well as leaders of religious organizations, have filed recommendations favoring issuance of a cabaret license to the neighborhood's most ornate cafe and restaurant, the Morillon, at Church Ave. and E. 21st St.

The letters of the clergymen, who have sponsored social functions held in the cafe's banquet hall, are part of the record filed in Supreme Court in an appeal from a decision of the Police Department refusing the petition of Charles E. Anderson, president and general manager of the company, for such a license. Jacob A. Freedman, attorney for Anderson, declared that it is not the purpose of the desired license to have a show or night club effects but to permit orchestral or band music for dancing at the banquets, dinners and luncheons held in the place. The appeal is scheduled for a hearing May 16 before Justice Charles C. Lockwood, who will be asked to issue a mandamus to compel the Police Department to issue the license.

The cafe is across the street from the ancient burial ground in the rear of the Reformed Protestant Dutch Church on land owned by the Y. M. C. A., which in 1936 leased it to the Kenchurch Corporation for

Continued on Page 2

Ex-Justice Dike Sued for Divorce

Special to the Brooklyn Eagle

Reno, May 10—Mrs. Evelyn Biddle Dike today brought suit for divorce from former Supreme Court Justice Norman S. Dike of Brooklyn, now an official referee there. They were married June 30, 1917, and have one son, now a student at Brown University. The charge given was cruelty.

Narragansett Park Results

FIRST RACE—Three-year-olds and upward; three-quarters of a mile.

Sunabell (Taylor)	8.40	4.40	3.20
Whiskbriar (McCombs)	—	15.10	7.60
Star Pupil (Sena)	—	—	3.70

Time, 1:14 1-5. Selmajack, Joe's Mary, Melva D., Cona Dara, Justify, Country Jim, Night Princess, Ah-Mi also ran. (Off time, 2:18.)

SECOND RACE—Count Rae, first; Primer, second; Erech, third.

Jamaica Results

FIRST RACE — Two-year-olds; five-eighths of a mile.

Updo (Nash)	3-1	4-5	1-4
Pirate Ship (Longden)		7-5	2-5
Milltea (James)			4-5

Time—1:01. Running Cedar, Mess, Colored Post also ran. (Off time, 2:33.)

SECOND RACE—Count Edward, first; Devil's Mate, second; Highscope, third.

Assembly Votes Liquor Boost

Bill Providing 50% Increase in Levy Is Sent to Senate

Eagle Bureau, Capitol Building.

Albany, May 10—Governor Lehman's bill providing for a 50 percent increase in the tax on hard liquor was passed in the Assembly today and was sent to the Senate immediately for final approval. The vote was 104 to 34.

The provision in the bill which makes the tax effective as of today caused a sharp debate on the Assembly floor and Minority Leader Irwin Steingut of Brooklyn warned that unless the liquor industry was given adequate time to adjust itself to the new tax the industry's representatives were fearful that it would cause a chaotic condition and possibly lead to a destructive price war.

Steingut warned that the full responsibility would have to rest with the Republicans because of their insistence upon passing the bill today without revising the date when the tax would become effective. He made an unsuccessful plea to have the date when the tax would go into effect changed to June 1.

WARNS OF BOOTLEGGING

Assemblyman Michael J. Gillen, Brooklyn Democrat, took the floor also and warned that the imposition of the heavier taxes on hard liquor would cause a renewal of bootlegging.

"The more you encourage bootlegging," Gillen told the House, "the more you encourage the advocates of prohibition."

The measure increases the tax from $1 to $1.50 per gallon. Floor stock up to 250 gallons is exempt from the increased levy. The tax, to be collected from the retailer, is expected to yield about $8,000,000 more in revenue for the State.

SEEK NEW REVENUE

Republicans in the Legislature, in a surprise move today, decided to tap a new source of revenue for the State.

A bill requiring unclaimed funds of life insurance companies to be handed over to the State was reported out of the Assembly Rules Committee and ordered acted upon before final adjournment of the Legislature. Leaders said the measure was expected to produce about $7,000,000 in the next fiscal year.

The bill was reported out of the Rules Committee after being drafted by Assemblyman R. Foster Piper, Erie Republican, and Nathan R. Sobel of Brooklyn, Governor Lehman's counsel.

France Is Cool To Pope's Plea

Paris, May 10 (AP)—France reacted coolly today to soundings by Vatican envoys which diplomats believed looked toward a settlement of the Danzig problem and other issues disturbing the peace of Europe.

A suggestion in the Paris press that Premier Mussolini of Italy had at least approved the initiative taken by Pope Pius XII caused an unfavorable impression here.

Informed circles contended that the Pontiff could not have made his soundings without Mussolini's approval because of the 1929 Lateran accord between Italy and the Vatican by which the latter undertook not to intervene in political issues except under special circumstances.

RUSSIA HELD FACTOR

Paris, May 10 (U.P.)—Pope Pius' failure to include Russia among interested nations was an important factor in the coldness shown by France and Great Britain to his offer to mediate in the Polish-German and French-Italian disputes, it was understood today.

It was said here that Russia had made it plain that if its co-operation in the French-British "security front" was expected it must not naturally be included in any negotiations which the great powers undertook.

Curran to Go Back on Bench

Passes Up Higher Salary to Become Magistrate Again

Deputy Mayor Henry H. Curran will return to the Magistrates' bench on July 1, Mayor LaGuardia announced today during a luncheon at the Sulgrave Club in the Merrie England Pavilion at the World's Fair, at which he was a guest.

Curran, it was learned, was given his choice, at a conference with the Mayor earlier in the day at the Summer City Hall at the Arrowbrook Country Club, of a job on the Magistrates' bench or the Special Sessions bench, and took the $10,000 a year magistracy because he thought he "could do more good there."

Curran, therefore, not only loses the $15,000 deputy mayor salary, cut down to $1 a year by the Mayor in the 1939-40 budget, but passed up the extra $2,000 he would get on the Special Sessions bench.

REPLACES BROUGH

Appointed for the full 10-year term, Curran will take the place of Magistrate Alexander Brough, Manhattan Republican, who retired because of the age limit on July 1. There will be a vacancy at the same time in Special Sessions when Justice William A. Walling, Manhattan Democrat and former assistant corporation counsel, retires.

Curran was a magistrate when he was appointed New York's first deputy mayor in 1937. He is a Republican and was formerly United States commissioner of immigration, Manhattan Borough President and vice chairman of the Board of Aldermen.

Curran's place as deputy mayor will be filled by Rufus C. McGahen of the Board of Water Supply, who has already announced he will waive the $1-a-year salary.

Earlier today Mayor LaGuardia said he had visited three new baby health stations in Brooklyn. He also received a visit at the Summer City Hall from Mrs. Genevieve B. Earle, Brooklyn Councilwoman.

Teacher Plunges 5 Stories to Death At Queens School

Mrs. Margaret Collery, 52, of 97-22 Sanders Place, a teacher for the last ten years at Public School 121, 126-12 109th Ave., Richmond Hill, was killed at 11:40 a.m. today when she plunged from the ledge of a fifth-floor window of the school to the yard.

Two witnesses told police that they saw Mrs. Collery climb out from a vacant classroom and walk about 20 to 25 feet along the ledge. She then hurtled to the courtyard. She had arrived at the school shortly after 11 a.m. and was to have conducted a late session class at 11:4[illegible] a.m. on the third floor.

Herbert R. Rex of 148-19 90th Ave., Jamaica, a surveyor for the Board of Education, who was working in front of the school, said that he was attracted by screams of pedestrians who saw the woman and immediately ran inside and summoned Vincent Fisher, assistant principal.

He said they ran up the five flights of stairs but when they reached the classroom window Mrs Collery had already plunged. She landed on an iron grating and then rolled into a grass plot. An ambulance surgeon from Jamaica Hospital pronounced her dead.

The classroom window from which the teacher gained the ledge is immediately above the school entrance which is covered by a high roo[illegible] supported by Colonial columns.

Mrs. Collery had recently bee[illegible] attended for a nervous breakdown it was learned at the principal's office. A school teacher since 190[illegible] she was a widow and the mother of two grown children.

Pari-Mutuel Bill Debated in Senate

BULLETIN

Albany, May 10—The Dunnigan resolution proposing an amendment to the State Constitution to permit pari-mutuel betting on horse races at the New York tracks was passed in the Senate this afternoon.

Eagle Bureau, Capitol Building.

Albany, May 10—The State Senate this afternoon opened debate on the Dunnigan resolution proposing amendment of the State Constitution to authorize pari-mutuel betting on horse racing at the New York tracks.

Indications were that the proposal would be adopted and sent to the Assembly immediately for concurrence to permit the measure to be submitted to the voters at the coming general election.

Senate Minority Leader John J. Dunnigan, sponsor of the resolution which was first approved by the Legislature last year, told the chamber that the amendment, if approved, would yield $10,000,000 in additional revenue for the State's treasury.

He pointed out that in less than two months New Jersey voters would go to the polls in their State in a referendum to permit pari-mutuel wagering.

"If it is approved there and not submitted in New York State," he said, "then, as far as horse racing is concerned, the Hudson River will become an imaginary boundary.

"Our people will crowd the tunnels, ferry boats and bridges for a chance to bet under the preferred system. The race courses which will be constructed on the west bank of the river will flourish and our own will become deserted."

New Job for Amlie

Washington, May 10 (U.P.)—Thomas R. Amlie, whose nomination to the Interstate Commerce Commission was withdrawn by President Roosevelt, probably will be named a special assistant to the Attorney General, Justice Department officials said today.

'Will of God' Made Him Slay Helpless Son, Father Testifies

The morning he held a chloroform-saturated handkerchief to the nostrils of his imbecile son, until the overgrown youth was dead, he was carrying out "the will of God," Louis Greenfield testified today in Bronx County Court where he is being tried for the slaying of the youth.

A grey-haired man of 46, charged with manslaughter, Greenfield sobbed as he took the witness stand in his own defense. He told of the agony he and his wife suffered during the 16 years their son, Jerome, was growing to be six feet tall but with a mind so unformed he was unable to care for his simplest wants.

A voice came to him in his dreams, Greenfield said, and whispered: "Stop his suffering. Stop his suffering. If you love him, stop his suffering."

"I tried to put it off as long as I could," he continued. "Then I decided to let him sleep so that he no longer would be tortured by doctors."

Samuel Leibowitz of Brooklyn, his attorney, pointed a finger at him and demanded brusquely:

"You killed him. Why did you do it?"

"Because," Greenfield said, "I loved him."

"My first thought," he said, telling of his son's birth in 1922, "was that I would give him the education I had missed. I was so happy. I thought, then, that he would be a normal, healthy boy. I planned for him."

But within three months came the realization that something was amiss. Greenfield suddenly let his head sag to illustrate how the baby would lie in its crib.

"He couldn't grasp," he continued, "he couldn't hold his head up. He lay there like a lump of pudding."

F. D. Has Nose Irritation

Washington, May 10 (U.P.)—President Roosevelt, suffering from a slight nose irritation, stayed away from his executive office today and carried on his work in the second floor study of the White House.

Hitler, Franco Agree To Push Trade Pact

London, May 10 (U.P.)—Adolf Hitler and Gen. Francisco Franco, leader of Nationalist Spain, have agreed to negotiate an important trade agreement which Germany hopes will give her a predominant economic position in Spain, it was learned today.

Dr. Helmuth Wohltat, expert of the German Ministry of Economics, who negotiated the German-Rumanian accord at the end of March, will go to Burgos shortly to conduct the Reich's negotiations with Spain.

U. S. Needn't Fear Attack by Reich or Japan, Singly or Together, Admiral Declares at Fair

Neither Germany nor Japan could successfully attack the United States and if they tried it, singly or together, we have no reason to fear them, Rear Admiral Albert W. Johnson, commandant of the Atlantic Squadron, now berthed in New York harbor, declared today.

The Admiral was the guest of honor, in the absence of Mayor LaGuardia, at a luncheon in Perylon Hall, at the World's Fair, in celebration of the 164th anniversary of the capture of Fort Ticonderoga by the "Green Mountain Boys" of Revolutionary fame. Stephen H. P. Pell, director of the Fort Ticonderoga Museum, and Mrs. Pell, were the hosts.

"The United States might get involved in trouble," the admiral remarked, as the luncheon started, "possibly because of our sea trade, as was the case in the World War." And he added:

'WHY SHOULD WE FEAR?'

"But why should we be afraid of war at the present time? Who will attack us? Certainly not Japan. Why the hell should we be afraid of Japan—or any of the aggressor nations? They could not even get to the shores of our country. And anyway, we would wait until the Japs got here and rang us up on the telephone before we got in a fight with them."

Still looking at the world situation through a navy man's eyes, he concluded:

"The United States has no need to worry, even if Germany and Japan both attacked us at the same time. We are sitting pretty and afraid of nobody."

In his formal address at the luncheon, the admiral said:

"The peaceful visit of the Atlantic Squadron to New York stands out in

Continued on Page 3

Nice, Comfy Today But It Won't Last

Pleasant, seasonable May is in store for today, the Bureau's report indicate[illegible] morrow is expected to [illegible]

Partly cloudy an[illegible] warm is forecast f[illegible] night. The ther[illegible] is keeping [illegible] mal ave[illegible] date, 5[illegible] ture low[illegible]

In the Eagle Today

	Page		Page
Books	27	Hy Gardner	8
Brain Teaser	26	Jimmy Wood	18
Bridge	27	Lindley	17
Brooklyn Fact	14	Line on Liners	24
By the Way	17	Lost and Found	2
Cassel's Cartoon	14	Obituaries	15
Comics	26-27	Quillen	26
Crossword	25	Radio	26
Dr. Brady	27	Real Estate	25
Ed Hughes	18	Serial	27
Editorial	14	Shipping	24
Events	24	Society	10
Financial	21-23	Sports	18-20
Garden Corner	25	Theaters	13
[illegible]in and Bear It	14	Tucker	14
[illegible]ernan	17	Want Ads	24-25
Worth	10	Women	11

Flow of Small Gifts Cheers Fusion Party

Shows Average Man Is Being Won Over, Boro Chairman Says

A flow of quarter, half-dollar and dollar contributions to the City Fusion party campaign fund since the start of its reorganization for the 1939 election was hailed today by Leon D. Sachter, now Brooklyn chairman, as indicating that "current political disclosures are winning the man in the street to the independent fold."

Mr. Sachter reported the successful launching of a drive for funds following last night's reorganization committee meeting in the Towers Hotel. J. Charles Totten, Fusion veteran, is fund treasurer.

"We have adopted an unusual fund-raising policy for a political organization," Mr. Sachter said. "A campaign must have money to be successful, but Fusian has no politically appointed office-holders to blackjack, no special interests to shake down with promises. Nor are we going to use blackjack methods on any one.

"We feel confident that the public consciousness of the community is being awakened by the Amen disclosures to the need of replacement of some of our judicial and law enforcement officers. The first signs of this awakening are financial support for Fusion."

Mr. Sachter contended that the treasury of the City Fusion party should be "the conscience fund of a community whose citizens have allowed inept, inattentive and corrupt officials to win election after election, virtually by default."

He named temporary committees for organizational functions and initiated plans for opening of new Brooklyn headquarters.

Talks on Peru

Godfrey Macdonald

Mr. Macdonald will be the speaker at tonight's meeting of the Tuesday Club of the Church of the Saviour, 50 Monroe Place. He is also assistant passenger manager of the Grace Line. "A Trip to Peru—Ancient and Modern" will be his subject

Boro Pupils Visit Fair

Fourteen children from Mrs. Babcock's Play School, 9515 Shore Road, spent yesterday at the World's Fair. Accompanying the group were Mrs. Carolyn Babcock and Miss Dorothy Birdsall of the faculty and Mrs. Florence Holly and Mr. and Mrs. E. S. Armstrong.

Foremen's Club Elects Archbold

Sperry Firm Employe Installed President At Meeting in 'Y'

Thomas M. Archbold of the Sperry Gyroscope Company, temporary president of the Kings County Foremen's Club, was elected and installed head of the group at a meeting last night in the Central Branch Y. M. C. A., 55 Hanson Place.

N. D. Hoff, director of the National Association of Foremen's Clubs, was installing officer. The organization is composed of foremen, executives and supervisors in Brooklyn industrial plants.

M. D. Griffith, executive vice president of the New York Board of Trade, addressed the group.

Other officers elected and inducted were: Joseph J. Markart of the Eberhard Faber Pencil Company, first vice president; James Reed of the American Manufacturing Company, second vice president; George Walker of the National Meter Company, third vice president; W. Kronenberger of the Sperry Gyroscope Company, fourth vice president; Ferdinand G. Tuero of A. Schrader's Son Division, secretary, and John Rolff of A. Schrader's Son Division, treasurer.

Brooklyn Man Held In Hoboken Holdup

Special to the Brooklyn Eagle

Hoboken, May 23—Roy Harrington, 37, of Brooklyn was under arrest here today on charges of having participated in a holdup April 17 in which $1,500 in cash and $5,000 in jewelry were taken from a safe in the home of Armando Castellini at 1002 Bloomfield St., Hoboken. Police said Harrington, sought in an eight-State alarm, was picked up in Bayonne yesterday for speeding.

Couple Mark Golden Wedding In Congregational Home

A wedding march staged in 1889 was re-enacted as Mr. and Mrs. Charles A. Belknap of the Congregational Home for Aged observed their 50th wedding anniversary at a reception last night in the home, 123 Linden Boulevard.

Mr. Belknap, 85, and his wife, 81, are natives of Wooster, Ohio, and were married in that city. They came to Brooklyn many years ago and are members of the Tompkins Avenue Congregational Church.

At the start of the reception the couple marched down a broad stairway and into the reception room as 73 members of the home arose and applauded.

Mr. and Mrs. Belknap were then presented to the group, Mrs. J. J. Pearsall, president of the home board of managers, heading the reception line. Miss Mollie Stryker, home superintendent, was also present.

The assemblage sang "You've Gone a Long Way Together" to feature a program of entertainment. Among the messages of congratulation received was a letter from William L. Long, mayor of Wooster.

Boy Scouts Take Part In Playground Drive

Seven thousand signers of a petition requesting a playground and recreation center within the boundaries of Vernon Ave., Flushing Ave., Broadway and Nostrand Ave. will be sought by Boy Scouts of Troop 167 and others acting as solicitors, according to Samuel S. Serra of 61 Floyd St., Navy Yard employe, who is acting as chairman of the drive. The petition will be presented to Mayor LaGuardia.

Members of the Parent-Teachers Association of P. S. 55 were to meet this afternoon to plan their part in the solicitation of signers among parents and residents of the neighborhood.

Legion Post Holds Memorial Service

Thirteenth Post, 13, American Legion, honored the memory of its 77 deceased members at a memorial service attended by 200 relatives and friends of former comrades last night in the 245th Coast Artillery Armory, 357 Sumner Ave.

Supreme Court Justice Frank E. Johnson urged the Legionnaires to take a "highly active interest" in communal work in order to promote democratic harmony." Other speakers were Mons. J. Jerome Reddy, director of Catholic Charities of the Roman Catholic Diocese of Brooklyn, and Howard Anderson, State detachment commander of the Sons of the Legion.

Milton Schellens, member of the post, sang "My Buddy." John F. McGrath, post commander, presided.

Chief Battery Span Foe Approves Changes Made in Plan by Moses

Objections Met By Revisions, Moran Asserts

Touring Executive Doubts Navigation Interests Can Oppose

Continued from Page 1

gation requirements under which local Army officials had "agreed in principle," according to Mr. Moses, to recommend issuance of a permit.

Colonel Hall, asserting that a public hearing on the new design will not be necessary, immediately plunged into a consideration of the modifications, which he is expected to rule on within a week.

"Things are going to move pretty fast now," he declared. "Mr. Moses is a good accelerator."

Commissioner Moses' estimate that the alterations would add only $2,800,000 to the $41,200,000 cost of the originally planned bridge threw into confusion Manhattan opponents who were heralding the defeat of the project on the supposition that Army requirements could only be met at excessive high cost.

In a letter to Colonel Hall which accompanied the modified plans, Commissioner Moses pointed out that the new total estimated cost is within the amount of money which the Triborough Bridge Authority is empowered to borrow through the sale of special revenue bonds.

The revisions were designed by Commissioner Moses and his staff of experts to answer War Department objections that the Manhattan or East River Channel under the old plan, for which a 1,450-foot waterway had been provided, was too narrow to permit free flow of the congested harbor traffic. Under the modified plan the waterway is increased to 2,210 feet.

TO BE BUILT AT ANGLE

To provide for this clearance two suspension bridges are to be built at a slight angle to each other in place of the straightline series of suspension spans called for originally. The apex is to be at a joint anchorage on the tip of Governors Island and the two central piers of the old design are moved closer together, well out of the East River and Buttermilk Channels.

The distance between piers on the Manhattan side is to be increased from 1,600 feet to 2,400 feet and the second span, on the Brooklyn side of Governors Island, is to stretch almost from the Red Hook shore to the island, precluding all interference with navigation in Buttermilk Channel.

Commenting on the revised application for a permit, Commissioner Moses expressed confidence today that the specifications will now meet with the War Department's approval and that work will go forward and the span completed by July, 1941, as he had originally stated.

CONFIDENT FROM OUTSET

"There has never been any question in my mind as to the final success of the project," he said.

In his memorandum to Colonel Hall, Mr. Moses emphasized that "no changes are required in the plan for Battery Park or in plans for the Manhattan and Brooklyn approaches."

Writing as chairman of the Triborough Bridge Authority, which under the span enabling act is to finance and build the proposed structure, he told Colonel Hall:

"Supplementing our communication to you of April 25 in support of the original application for approval of plans to construct the Brooklyn-Battery Bridge and pursuant to other communications, including the letter dated May 17 1939, from Maj. Gen. Julian L. Schley, Chief of Engineers, we submit herewith a revised application which we believe will meet all the objections raised by the War Department to the bridge as originally planned.

MEETS THE OBJECTIONS'

"Our conference with you and Col. Francis Wilby, division engineer, held at the suggestion of General Schley, have indicated that the War Department has come to the conclusion that the two main piers and the joint anchorage in the waters of the East River in the location originally planned would create an additional hazard and obstruction to free navigation in that vicinity and that this was the basis for the denial of the original application.

"The new application meets the objections outlined at the conferences with you and Colonel Wilby."

The commissioner asserted that, while he does not advocate it, the Authority is prepared to meet a request from the War Department to construct an elevator at Governors Island so that motor vehicles can make use of the bridge between the island and the two boroughs "as a substitute for the present inadequate ferry system with its delays and congestion."

ASKS 'EARLY DECISION'

Mr. Moses concluded his memorandum by requesting "an early decision on this revised application."

The same procedure is to be followed by Army officials in deciding whether to grant a permit as in the previous plan. Colonel Hall is to submit a ruling to Colonel Wilby, who is to act on it and forward his decision to Major General Schley, who in turn will recommend that the office of the Secretary of War either approve or deny the application.

Hutton Resigns From Zonite Post

Edward F. Hutton has resigned as chairman of the board of Zonite Products Corporation, it was learned today. Hutton is understood to be gradually retiring from active business. He is still a director of the Zonite company.

Army Receives Altered Plans for Battery Span

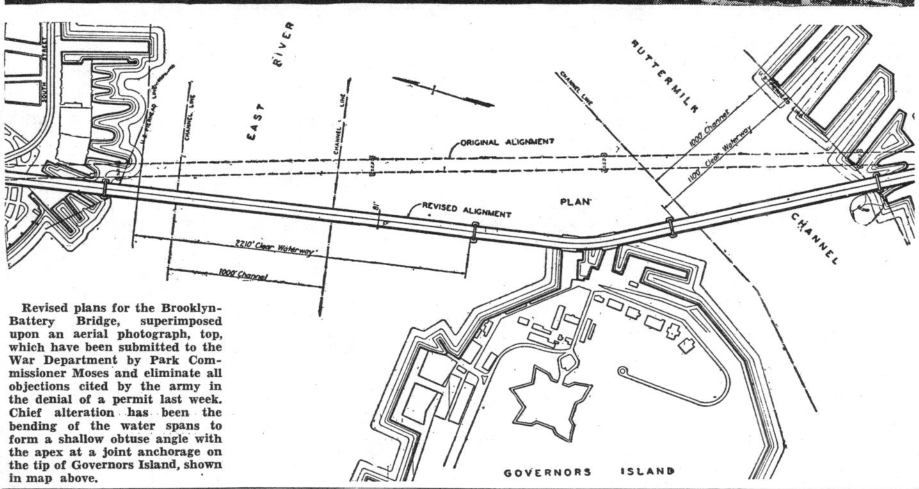

Revised plans for the Brooklyn-Battery Bridge, superimposed upon an aerial photograph, top, which have been submitted to the War Department by Park Commissioner Moses and eliminate all objections cited by the army in the denial of a permit last week. Chief alteration has been the bending of the water spans to form a shallow obtuse angle with the apex at a joint anchorage on the tip of Governors Island, shown in map above.

Boro Woman Wins on Derby

Continued from Page 1

money, so it's a lucky break for them." Their ticket was signed with the nom-de-plume "28 Try Again."

Jenikovsky is the owner of the Sully Press, 158 Spruce St., Manhattan, a commerical printing concern. He and his wife and three children listened to the race on the radio today.

The half interest, he said, was sold for $6,016. The group purchased 15 tickets, each one contributing a small sum. They bought them on the 28th of the month, thus the "28 Try Again," signature, he said.

Miss Mulcahy had also sold half share in her ticket to a syndicate, she told the Brooklyn Eagle today.

"I thought it was too risky with so many horses running," she said, "but I don't regret doing it. I'm not greedy."

She had stayed home from her job today just to listen to the radio, she said, and had her ear glued to the instrument when the good news came. Other boarders in the boarding house where she has occupied a $12-a-week room for 17 years clustered about her with congratulations. And Battle, whom she named after last year's sweeps winner, Battleship, and in whose name she took the ticket, chirped merrily away.

WON'T GO TO IRELAND

"It certainly feels wonderful," she admitted. "But I won't go to Ireland to collect the money. I'll stay right here where I belong."

Miss Mulcahy was born in Fort Hamilton and is a "real Brooklynite," she said, "one of the farmers of Brooklyn."

Miss Mulcahy enjoyed a slight foretaste of her good fortune last week, she said, when she won $2 playing Screeno. "That was the first and only thing I had ever won," she declared.

As for marriage, Miss Mulcahy is going to enjoy her single blessedness and her money and keep both. Asked if she contemplated marriage, she patted her gray hair and laughed: "Indeed I don't. They'd only want me for my money now. In fact, I had a proposal this morning from one of the roomers here, but it was only a joke and we both knew it.

THINKS BIRD INTUITIVE

"Last Saturday I bought a dollar's worth of birdseed for Battle," she said. "He's been singing since last Thursday, when I drew the ticket on the horse, and today when I was listening to the race on the radio he sang so loudly I had to put him in another room. I think the little rascal has intuition and knew I was going to win."

She doesn't need a vacation, she feels, since she has only averaged about five days work a month for nearly seven years—she gets $4.40 a day—but she doesn't think she'll work any more.

Twelve United States holders of tickets on the first three horses in the Derby won $865,800 in prize money from the Irish Hospitals Sweepstakes, according to the Associated Press.

Two Americans held tickets on Blue Peter, the winner, for a total of $280,800; five ticket holders on Fox Cub, second, get a total of $351,-000, and five on Heliopolis, third, receive $234,000.

American winnings total $2,031,573 as there were 389 American ticket-holders on non-starters and unplaced horses, each of whom receives $1,957, a total of $761,273.

Thirty-four Americans drew residual prizes of $5,250 each and 483 drew consolation prizes of $468 each, a total of $404,500.

Luckiest people in the Metropolitan area were two who held tickets on the winning horse, the favorite Blue Peter, which brought prize money of about $140,400 for each ticket-holder.

One of these was George McGowan, manager of a chain grocery at 1838 Nereid Ave., the Bronx, who lives at 3055 Decatur Ave., the Bronx. He signed his ticket "Donegal Girl" because his wife comes from County Donegal in Ireland. The other holder in the Metropolitan area was known only as "Come to Papa, 508 W. 132d St.

Fox Cub, a long shot at 100 to 9 just before the race, came in second and brings approximately $70,000 to the only holder of a ticket on him in the Metropolitan area, one signed only "Two Friends," Riverside Hospital, North Brothers Island, N. Y."

Blue Peter Wins

Epsom, England, May 24 (AP)—Blue Peter, Lord Rosebery's 7 to 2 favorite, burst from the melee of 27 3-year-olds at Tattenham Corner and dashed down the home stretch to win the 155th Derby by four lengths today.

Edward Esmond's Fox Cub, 100 to 6, was second and Lord Derby's Heliopolis, at 100 to 9, third as William Woodward's Hypnotist, only American-owned horse in the field, wound up seventh.

While close to a half-million people shrieked his name the husky son of Fairway out of Fancy Free gave the lie to those who had said he was not a stayer. Touched by the whip two and a half furlongs from home, Blue Peter ran right away from the field. He was clocked in 2 minutes 36 4-5 seconds, well behind the stake record of 2:32 3-5, established in 1916.

Nazi Driver Fired Upon In Danzig, He Declares

Danzig, May 24 (U.P.)—A German chauffeur, driving into Danzig from Elbing, in East Prussia, asserted today that he was fired at but not struck after having passed Polish customs officials.

The Nazi Danzig Senate sent a strong protest to the Polish diplomatic representative as soon as it heard of the allegation. At the same time it handed in a new note in answer to Polish protests against disorders during the weekend, as the result of which a Polish official chauffeur killed a Danzig German.

Skimpy Pickins This Trip, Laments Sweeps Investor

Sidney Freeman, the English speculator who follows closely on the heels of telegraph messengers with lucky tidings for ticket holders in the Irish Sweepstakes, sailed for home today on the Queen Mary, a disappointed man.

He "only" held a half interest in three tickets on Blue Peter, the winner, and "made only a small amount, after expenses were deducted"—$30,000. Of the three persons with whom he shared tickets, one was from New York, and two from Canada.

Lamenting that he had arrived with $1,000,000 to invest and used only half the sum and that the sale of tickets had been only half the usual amount, the speculator explained that international politics have affected even the sport of kings.

"People, these days," he said, "don't feel much like sending money out of their own country, particularly Americans. They don't know what's going to happen next."

For the past seven years he has made three trips annually to buy all or part of lucky tickets and the past trip brought the poorest pickings, he said.

Others aboard the Cunard White Star liner, which left with 1,655 passengers, were Beatrice Lillie, the comedienne; Mr. and Mrs. Douglas Fairbanks and Lauritz Melchior, opera star.

Mexican Ace Speeds On Flight to New York

Mexico City, May 24 (AP)—Francisco Sarabia, Mexico's ace civilian pilot, took off from Mexico City today on a non-stop flight to New York which he hoped would break the existing record by five hours.

Flying a low-winged, 1,000 horsepower monoplane, Sarabia expected to reach New York nine hours after his takeoff at 7:50 a.m. The established Mexico City-New York record, set by Amelia Earhart in 1935, is 14 hours 19 minutes.

The aviator's flight plan would take him over the Gulf of Mexico to New Orleans, thence near Atlanta and Washington to Floyd Bennett Field.

Settlement Players In Costume Play

A play entitled "The Tenth Word," contrasting life in a school for "elegant females" in the year 1812 with that lived by students in the same school more than a century later, was presented last night in the Willoughby House Settlement, 97 Lawrence St. The scenes were laid in the walled garden of the school. Attractive old-fashioned costumes were worn by the players in the early part of the piece.

Appearing in the cast were members of the Willoughby House Players, including Gertrude Clouse, Anna Clouse, Irene Connelly, Beulah Osofsky and Gertrude Caitano. Sue Carrington Smith directed the play.

British Rulers Visit Winnipeg

Winnipeg, May 24 (AP) — King George VI came today to the center of his great Canadian dominion to speak to the 500,000,000 people of his realm on Empire Day, British worldwide holiday.

His Empire Day broadcast, the first message ever spoken on a world hookup by a British king away from England, was awaited as the high point of the royal visit to Winnipeg, although the city has been celebrating the coming of King George and Queen Elizabeth for several days and last night staged a two-mile parade of 40 floats tracing the romantic history of the Canadian West.

In view of King George's previous utterances of significance since he arrived in Canada, first in regards to British relations with the United States and later in what was interpreted as a warning to the dictators of Europe as he unveiled the Canadian National War Memorial at Ottawa on Sunday, his Winnipeg address was awaited with much interest.

Queen Mary's Eye Injured in Crash

London, May 24 (AP)—Queen Mary suffered injury to one eye when her automobile overturned yesterday and spent a restless night, her doctors said today.

The physicians' bulletin said:

"Her Majesty Queen Mary has passed a restless night partly due to injury to one eye which, although painful, is not a source of anxiety. Her Majesty's general condition is satisfactory."

Queen Mary will be 72 years old on Friday.

Sir Richard Cruise, a famed specialist who is surgeon-occulist to the Queen, called on her last night and again today with other physicians.

Doctors attending the Queen Mother remained at her residence, Marlborough House, for more than an hour before issuing the bulletin. No other bulletin was expected today.

In addition to Sir Stanley Hewett and Lord Dawson of Penn, who signed last night's bulletin saying the Queen had suffered bruises and shock, the physicians in attendance were increased by the visit of Sir John Weir, the first homeopathist to be appointed to the royal family.

Scouts Open Drive For Playground

One hundred members of Boy Scout Troop 167 today began distribution of petitions in a drive for 7,000 signatures indorsing the campaign for a playground and recreation center in the area bounded by Vernon Ave., Flushing Ave., Broadway and Nostrand Ave.

The petitions were given to patrol leaders last night at a meeting in the clubrooms of Williamsburg Post, V. F. W., 87 Tompkins Ave. Samuel S. Serra, campaign chairman, presided.

Rush Selection Of Martin Jury; Nine in Box

Lengthy Questions On Testimony Law Ordered Boiled Down

Continued from Page 1

tails to find out whether the jurors would abide by the law on the testimony of accomplices and self-confessed abortionists. The jury and two alternates may be chosen today.

ELIMINATE QUESTIONS

"All the talesmen have heard these questions so often," said the court. Both sides then eliminated many of the lengthy questions by asking the following: "You have heard the discussion here on the law of testimony—do you agree with it?"

The prosecution had used up eight peremptory challenges and the defense four when Justice McCurn ordered the urors takn to the Hotel Bossert for luncheon. Each sidehas 20 for the 12 jurors and two additional for each of the two alternates.

Robert Roeck of 7710 Narrows Ave., display decorator, was challenged by Amen because he said he often sat with Judge Martin at at luncheon. Frank R. Gerstner of 653 E. 24th St. was excused because he is a political appointee. He is an accountant in the State Insurance Department and has been a Democratic poll watcher.

Robert W. Gunther, of 270 Hicks St., knew so many Democratic politicians and officeholders that Justice McCurn sustained a challenge for cause.

SAYS MARTIN WILL TESTIFY

Before court opened, Kleinman declared that Judge Martin definitely will take the stand in his own defense. Price had indicated this in yesterday's proceedings.

"Will the judge take the stand?" Kleinman was asked.

"Oh, yes," Kleinman said emphatically and smiled enigmatically. He did not furnish any details of what Martin will say when he faces Amen.

Justice McCurn excused four talesmen before the attorneys began their examination.

Judge Martin entered the courtroom, striding briskly to his seat, with two of his daughters accompanying him. Martin crossed his legs and clasped one knee. The dapper defendant wore a blue suit and had on a polka-dot tie. Since the trial opened, Martin has changed to a new suit every day.

WOULD BE EMBARRASSED

James J. Conaty, 51, of 119 Midwood St., was the first talesman to take the stand. Deacon Murphy, Amen assistant, began the day's probing.

Conaty said he would be "embarrassed" were he to serve. He was in the surety business and said he had done business with John B. Carroll and Price, Martin's attorneys. The talesman also knew District Attorney William F. X. Geoghan.

Conaty was extremely relieved when he was excused by consent of both sides. "I had another reason," he told Justice McCurn, "an illness."

Alfred E. Kegel, 46, real estate broker of 410 Prospect Park West, was the next talesman. His real estate office has been used as a polling place since 1928, he said.

At one point in Kegel's examination by Price, Murphy protested against Price's "summation." Justice McCurn agreed with Murphy, for he grinned broadly and sustained the objection. Kegel was finally challenged peremptorily by Murphy.

TOO OLD, EXCUSED

The next talesman, Clas J. Julstedt of 6701 Colonial Road, was excused, with a scattering round of applause in the rear of the court room, when he said he was 71. This was beyond the age limit for jurors.

Next to be questioned was Gunther, a district manager of the Maytag Company. He was challenged for cause by Murphy after he said Gunther would not be able to give an impartial verdict.

Talesman J. Shaw Kavanagh of 168 98th St. took the stand. Kavanagh said he was a "close personal friend" of Attorney General John J. Bennett Jr. and also knew District Attorney Geoghan and his indicted assistant, Francis A. Madden.

Kavanagh's answers, which crackled with dry wit, caused an outburst of laughter several times.

"There's been a great deal written about this case," Kleinman said.

LOT WRITTEN, NOTHING SAID

"There's been a lot written but nothing said," Kavanagh retorted. Kavanagh complained of "the stupidity of the investigator" who checked on his business, home address and family.

He said his neighbors were questioned by an Amen sleuth even before he got the jury notice. "They even asked how much money I made and how much meat my wife bought."

"Would it prejudice you?" asked Deacon Murphy, Amen aide.

"Not against the Attorney General," said Kavanagh. "Only against the stupid investigator."

Kavanagh was approved by both sides and sworn in as juror No. 8.

After a short recess Talesman Herman Brody of 84 74th St. was called to the stand. Under questioning by Amen he said he knew many of the defense figures, including Price. He was excused by consent of both sides.

Arthur A. Nelson, 52, of 8419 Fort Hamilton Parkway was the next talesman. Nelson said he was controller of the American Surety Company. Nelson was immediately challenged peremptorily by the defense after he said he knew William A. Lourie, whose name has been mentioned frequently in the case.

SPEEDS QUESTIONING

Amen next questioned John Schiffentecker, 55, a real estate man of 18 Herkimer St. Amen speeded his questioning, apparently determined to finish selection of a jury by the end of the day.

The defense did not bother to examine Schiffentecker, Kleinman announcing, "No challenge for cause," when Amen said he was satisfactory. Kleinman then challenged Schiffentecker peremptorily.

Robert E. Rowley, 48, of 7721 Ridge Boulevard, the next talesman, said he worked in the repair service of the New York Telephone Company. Rowley told Kleinman he had not assisted police in wire-tapping.

For the first time Amen referred to Martin's acting in his own defense, and asked Rowley if this would influence his verdict. Rowley said it wouldn't. Rowley was accepted by both sides and sworn in as Juror No. 9.

The seven jurors selected yesterday and Monday are:

WILLIAM A. REYCROFT, foreman, 41, of 2148 Troy Ave., bank examiner.
EDWIN MAURER, 41, of 101 Marine Ave., manager.
ROGER MULLIN, 52, of 451 E. 22d St., accountant.
JOHN H. PILKINGTON, 41, of 24 Colonial Gardens, engineer.
MARTIN W. LEWIS, 46, of 1011 E. 18th St., company president.
EDWARD A. HOLIHAN, 39, of 390 Pacific St., company vice president.
HENRY C. BAINBRIDGE, 60, of 429 Clinton Ave., company treasurer.

Danzig Nazis Send Warsaw New Protest

Firm Note to Poland Cites Six Alleged Violations of Rights

European Situation

DANZIG—Vigorous protest sent to Poland over alleged violation of sovereignty of Free City. German charges Polish soldiers shot at him.

LONDON—Prime Minister Chamberlain announces Britain is making new proposals to Russia, expresses confidence of "full agreement" shortly.

HONGKONG—British liner Ranpura halted at sea by Japanese after two shots are fired across her bow.

Danzig, May 24 (U.P.)—Danzig sent a vigorous new note to Poland today protesting alleged violation of the sovereignty of the Free City over which Germany and Poland have been in bitter controversy.

Following a German chauffeur's report that he had been fired on near the Polish frontier this morning, Arthur Greiser, Nazi vice president of the Danzig Senate, dispatched a protest to the Warsaw Government.

The note contained six points, understood to include:

1. Harmless passersby on the frontier at Dirschau, in Danzig territory, have been shot at by Polish soldiers.
2. That an official Danzig commission, of which the Polish diplomatic representatives had been informed, was hindered in its investigations by Polish soldiers, with bayonets fixed on their rifles.
3. Polish soldiers crossed into Danzig territory while on patrol duty.
4. Polish military airplanes flew over sovereign Danzig territory.
5. An unarmed and harmless Danziger who was on a holiday was murdered at Kalthof by the chauffeur of a Polish diplomatic representative.
6. The chauffeur was taken by Polish diplomats for security over the Polish frontier.

'SERIOUS,' SAYS BERLIN

The note demanded that the Polish Government take steps to reestablish peace and order on the frontier and find means of "quieting the almost hysterical attitude" of Polish fficials "before irreparable harm has been done."

[Meanwhile well informed Nazis close to the foreign office in Berlin said that they considered the situation "serious." The Nazis said that, in event the Danzig Senate protests to Warsaw are not answered satisfactorily, the German Foreign Office may make representations to the Polish Government.]

NEW BRITISH OFER

London, May 24 (AP)—Prime Minister Chamberlain announced today that the British Government was making new proposals to Soviet Russia for her adherence to the British-French front and he had every reason to hope it would be possible to "reach full agreement at an early date."

He said that as a result of conversations at Geneva between Foreign Secretary Viscount Halifax and Ivan Maisky, Soviet Ambassador to London, "all relevant points of view had now been made clear."

[Chamberlain also said that the Government was considering the question of de Facto recognition of the annexation of Czechoslovakia by Germany and Hungary, the United Press reported.

["It is not to be taken that the Government is considering such recognition," he said, but later added that the matter "is under consideration."]

Speaking in the House of Commons, the Prime Minister reported on the latest stage in the long-drawn negotiations between Britain and Russia for their projected mutual aid accord.

Earlier a two-hour Cabinet meeting had heard a detailed report of Lord Halifax' talks at Geneva with Maisky and French Foreign Minister Bonnet.

Informed quarters said that the Foreign Secretary urged immediate acceptance of Russia's terms for a three-power mutual assistance pact among Britain, France and Russia.

Chamberlain told the house he hoped to be able to announce the completion of an agreement with the Soviet Union by the time Parliament reconvened June 5, after the Whitsun recess.

Paid $55,000 To Manton, Lotsch Asserts

Says He Gave Him Money to Obtain Favorable Decisions

Continued from Page 1

told him "he would see that I got a favorable decision in the appeal." Thereafter, he paid $5,000 to Fallon, who assured him that the favorable decision was forthcoming "and to write the opinion and he would hand it to Judge Manton."

The opinion was written by Lotsch's law partner, Theodore Kenyon, "and I took it and gave it to Mr. Fallon."

"You mean," asked Judge Chestnut, obviously amazed, "that you gave him the draft of an opinion for the United States Circuit Court of Appeals."

"That's what he said."

OBJECTION HALTS ANSWER

"When the opinion came down did it follow the language of the draft opinion prepared by Mr. Kenyon?" inquired United States Attorney Cahill. But a defense objection halted the answer.

Lotsch, who was still under direct examination when the luncheon recess was called, also testified that, in pursuance of Judge Manton's promise to have Federal receivers use the Lotsch bank for their deposits, receivers for the Fox Theater Corporation and the Prudence Corporation made initial deposits of $50,000 and $25,000, respectively, in the Fort Greene Bank.

Both Lotsch and Fallon are codefendants who have pleaded guilty.

Lotsch testified that in addition to his banking activities he had been a patent lawyer and had represented prior to 1935 the P. and D. Manufacturing Company, being sued for patent infringements in Brooklyn Federal Court by the Electric Autolite Company.

At this point a request by defense Counsel Noonan that the court instruct "Government agents" to move away from the defense table resulted in a heated altercation.

Obviously annoyed, Mr. Cahill denounced the request as "prejudicial and unfair" and insisted that the nearest Government representative was not within hearing distance of the defense table.

MET FALLON IN '35

Lotsch went on to say that through a friend, who told him "I ought to meet William J. Fallon, he is a good friend of Judge Manton's" he was introduced to Fallon in the Spring of 1935.

Subsequently, he swore, he accompanied Fallon to Judge Manton's chambers in the old Federal Building on Park Row.

"Did you have a conversation with Judge Manton?" Cahill asked.

"Yes, Judge Manton wanted a $25,000 loan from the bank with which I was connected," Lotsch said.

The witness testified that he asked the other officers of the bank to grant Manton the $25,000 loan but the best he could do was to get a $10,000 loan with the promise that a further loan of $15,000 would be considered at some future date.

In urging his bank to grant the loan, Lotsch swore, he told his fellow officers that as a result we would "probably be able to get large deposits from the Fox and Prudence Companies."

HINTED FAVORABLE VERDICT

Sometime later, Lotsch testified, Fallon told him that if the loan went through there would be "a decision favorable to me."

"He meant the appeal pending in the Circuit Court?" asked Cahill.

"Yes," the witness answered.

He testified that on advice of Fallon he instructed his associate counsel in the appeal, a Mr. Kenyon, to prepare a draft opinion on the case. This was done, he added, and given to Fallon, who said he would turn it over to Judge Manton.

Fallon, the witness swore, told him that for an outright gift to him of $5,000 and the further loan of $15,000 to Manton that "I could be assured of a favorable decision in the case."

"When Judge Manton's opinion was handed down was it similar to the draft opinion handed over to Fallon?" Mr. Cahill asked. Objection to the question was sustained by the Court.

LOAN FOLLOWED DECISION

In July, 1935, Lotsch related, a favorable decision was handed down by the Circuit Court and ten days later an additional loan of $15,000 was made to Manton by the bank.

"Did the bank subsequently receive substantial deposits from the Fox Theater Corporation?"

"Yes," Lotsch said.

The Government alleges that Manton promised Lotsch that the bank would receive large deposits from receivers appointed in Federal Courts.

WENT TO SEE MANTON

He testified that he went down to see Manton in his chambers in October, 1935.

"Did you have a conversation with Judge Manton?"

"Yes, he asked me to arrange an additional loan of $25,000."

Lotsch said he told the jurist that this would be impossible and suggested that perhaps Manton could put up collateral and use the name of some other person in obtaining the loan.

The name of James J. Sullivan, president of the National Cellulose Corporation, in which Manton had a substantial interest, was suggested, it was brought out, and [illegible] was made in October, 19[illegible] livan upon Manton's

ATLANTIC CITY, N. J.

Loll on The Lido Beach on YOUR "CRUISE" ASHORE

AS YOU stretch out among the colorful cabanas, you realize the importance of the proper setting for the full enjoyment of a Traymore sojourn. Here is indulgence of an inimitable sort—at sea yet not at sea! For here you have all that the sea offers—plus the services of a great hotel and the diversions of a world famous resort. Come now—or for the summer. Rates are moderate.

THE **TRAYMORE** on the Boardwalk ATLANTIC CITY
Bennett E. Tousley, Gen. Mgr.

Mid-season Fun for an Early Vacation

Here midsummer sports and pleasures hit their stride early in June. Beach cabanas. Bathing from the hotels. Fishing and sailing parties. Superb meals. Restricted clientele.

Leeds and Lippincott Company
CHALFONTE-HADDON HALL
On the Boardwalk
ATLANTIC CITY
For Reservations Call LOngacre 5-4500

COOL your VACATION WITH a SEA BREEZE

TAKE your vacation where you can surely escape summer's heat—in the cool surf and soft sea air—made more enjoyable by the Seaside Hotel's delicious food, entertainment and sprightly Surf 'n Sand Room. But make reservations now—summer weekly rates are especially inviting. On the boardwalk, of course
N. Y. Office: 535 Fifth Ave. Tel. VAnderbilt 6-0069
The Seaside
Harrison Cook, Res. Mgr.
ATLANTIC CITY

CHECK THESE VALUES
VACATION where Values are Greatest
VACATION SPECIAL
ROOM BATH MEALS Friday to Sunday. $11 PER PERSON $12—$14
Big, delicious meals, delightful surrounding, seawater baths, beach bathing from hotel, shaded decks overlooking ocean. Special mid-week and weekly rates.
Write for reservations. F. Ernest Todd, Res. Mgr. N. Y. Office: 535 Fifth Ave., VAnderbilt 6-0133
The SENATOR ATLANTIC CITY

THE BREAKERS
On the Boardwalk
ATLANTIC CITY
Unexcelled Kosher Cuisine Under Supervision of Atlantic City Rabbi Mosheh Shapiro
SUMMER SEASON WEEKLY RATES AS LOW AS $32.50 PER PERSON TWO IN A ROOM, WITH BATH AND MEALS
EUROPEAN PLAN $15.00 PER PERSON TWO IN A ROOM, WITH BATH

Marlborough-Blenheim
ATLANTIC CITY
Directly on the Boardwalk, in the fashionable Park section
JOSIAH WHITE & SONS CO.

HOTEL STRAND
ATLANTIC CITY
PENNA AVE and BOARDWALK
DELIGHTFUL ROOM with BATH Including CONTINENTAL BREAKFAST SPECIAL WEEKLY RATES GARAGE on PREMISES
$3 PER DAY EACH — 2 IN A ROOM

BROOKLYN EAGLE RESORT & TRAVEL INFORMATION BUREAU
"Service to the Public for Almost 50 Years"
This is the largest and most complete bureau of its kind in America, with a record of almost 50 years of service. It influences the expenditure of more than $3,000,000 a year for vacation trips and hotel accommodations.

PRINCESS
South Carolina Ave. "Just off Boardwalk"
$3.50 DAILY With Meals WEEKLY $20
Special Family and Group Rates
ORCHESTRA Free Ocean Bathing From Hotel DANCING
WRITE FOR BOOKLET AND EUROPEAN PLAN RATES
Fireproof Garage H. Rae Scull OWNER

MILLER COTTAGE HOTEL 9 N. GEORGIA AVE. $2.50 up day; $17.50 up weekly, including excellent meals. Also European Plan. Bathing. Parking. Ph. 4-9294. Cap. 250. E. Crouthamel, Mgr.

ELBERON Tenn. and Pacific Av. Opp. Catholic Church Robert B. Ludy, Inc. ROOMS $1.00 UP Per Person DAILY

HOTEL EDISON Michigan Ave., near Beach. Central. Free parking. Daily $1. Special weekly. Running water all rooms. Private baths.

ATLANTIC CITY BOOKLET FREE Write Room 109, Convention Hall, Atlantic City

ASBURY PARK, N. J.

Hotel **MONTEREY**
ON THE BEACH ASBURY PARK N. J.
A FAMOUS North Jersey Coast RESORT HOTEL under KNOTT MANAGEMENT American or European Plan
Make Reservations NOW for a Summer of Surf Bathing, Sporty Off-Shore Fishing, Golf, Tennis and Riding along Beautiful Trails. Only 90 Min. from World's Fair.
BOOKLET ON REQUEST

THE ASBURY CARLTON
ASBURY PARK, N. J.
7th Ave., Facing Ocean
A refined, popular-priced, ocean-front hotel. Fireproof. Thoroughly modern. Every room with private lavatory or bath. Elevator.
American Plan $5 up
European Plan $3.50 up
OPEN ALL YEAR
Phone 4200 Asbury Park
H. S. Jackson, Manager

THE KESWICK 209 3d Ave. Block to beach. Attractive outside rooms. New innerspring mattresses. Amer. plan from $16 wkly. Europ. from $8 wkly. B. M. Kane A. P. 1715

THE ASBURY INN 305 Seventh Avenue, near Beach. American plan, $17, $18, $20 wkly. European, $8 up; $1.50 up daily. June rate $15 wkly. A. P. 9057

RENN TOWERS 217 SECOND AVE., ASBURY PARK, N. J. Block to ocean; nr. churches & amusements. Ocean view & ideal rms. Mod. rates. Ph. 454

CHATHAM 304 FOURTH AVE. All outside rooms. Running water. $1.50 up single. Spacious veranda. LEILA M. HAVENS

DANA HALL 209 Sunset Ave. Blk. to beach. Spacious verandas. Sensible rates. Am., Eur. plans. Bklt. A.P. 9178. M.E. Gracey

WINDSOR 3rd Ave. A. P. 1487. Amer.-Europ. Exceptionally fine food. Spacious porch. Sundeck. All year.

MERTEN 404 5th Ave. A. P. 3438 Amer. plan. Home cooking. Moderate. Rooms with baths and showers.

HOTEL LEONARD 602 5th Ave. Short walk to beach. Amer.-Europ. Christian clientele. A. P. 9170.

MAYVIEW 300 7th Av., Asbury Park Near Beach. Reasonable. American or European. Tel. 1711. Booklet.

THEDFORD 6th Ave. A. P. 197. Christian clientele. Near the ocean. Special weekly rates. Amer.-Europ. R. M. Currie.

WYANDANK 215 Third Ave, Asbury Park Moderate Rate. American Plan. G. A. Chesbrough.

BELMAR, N. J.

LLANYMOR HOTEL BELMAR, N. J. Tel. 561 3D AVE. BLOCK TO BEACH. CAP. 100 Bathe from your room. Modern throughout. Now open. June rates $3-$3.50 daily, $18-$21 weekly, including meals. Christian clientele. 23d season. JOHN HILLIG

CAPE MAY N. J.

CAPE MAY, N. J. 20 miles at sea; bathing, golf, all outdoor sports. Booklet, complete information, Room 136, City Hall.

OCEAN GROVE, N. J.

NORTHEND HOTEL
OCEAN GROVE, N. J.
Open June 23 Acommodates 400 Guests
Concert Orchestra Free Parking
Directly on the BOARDWALK
Dining Room and Solarium Built Over the Ocean
Swiming Pool and Game Room
Elevator Service from Boardwalk Level
From $6 Daily, $36 Weekly MEALS INCLUDED
All Outside Rooms . . . Booklet Available
PHONE ASBURY PARK 1492
RICHARD B. FREDEY, Mgr.

SHAWMONT 17 Ocean Avenue, Ocean Grove, N. J. A Better Class House. On the Beach. ANY 3 DAYS IN JUNE, $2.75 Up SINGLE Convenient to World's Fair Inquiry Invited. I. A. SHAW.

LILLAGAARD Overlooking Ocean 5 Abbott Avenue Airy rooms, running water. $16 up double weekly, with excellent meals. Ph. 4049. W. E. HYKA

MAJESTIC HOTEL On Ocean Front. Elevator. Private baths reas. Europ. Restaurant. Mrs. G. R. Haines.

ARDMORE-SUMMERFIELD Ocean Pathway at the Beach. Private porches. Baths. Ph. 2784. Booklet. E. E. Shaw.

GRAND ATLANTIC $1.50 up daily. Block to beach. Lower Weekly and Three-Day Rates.

AVON-BY-THE-SEA, N. J.

STRATFORD INN
AVON-BY-THE-SEA, N. J.
All improvements, good table, tennis courts; free parking space for cars. Bathing from the hotel. NO BAR. Tel. A.P. 2650.
SAMUEL W. TAYLOR, Owner Management.

LAKE HOPATCONG, N. J.

GREEN CROFT HOPATCONG, N. J., at Lake Ideal for young people; water sports, golf, riding; socially restricted; nr. churches. Bklt. $19-23 WKLY. Tel. 220. A. E. Fitzburgh

STYX VILLA, LAKE HOPATCONG, N. J. Motorboating, canoeing, bathing, dancing; hot, cold water all rooms. Rates $17.00 to $21.00. Hopatcong 223. Mrs. C. MATHIESEN

ITHANELL On lake. Modern. Water sports. Tennis. $17-$22 weekly. Booklet. O. S. BLAKESLEE

SPRING LAKE, N. J.

The Colonial HOTEL
SPRING LAKE BEACH N.J
CATERING TO SELECT CLIENTELE
ONE BLOCK FROM OCEAN & LAKE
No charge for ocean and pool bathing.

New ATLANTIC Hotel
SPRING LAKE BEACH, N. J.
Overlooking ocean. Free bathing, ocean and pool. Elevators. Sun deck. Dining terrace. Tennis, delicious meals.
Booklet—N. Y. Office: ELd. 5-0300

The SHOREHAM
A PREFERRED HOTEL AT SPRING LAKE BEACH, N.J.
American Plan Rates, Double with Bath from $6 day a person; $30 wkly. Ocean & Pool Bathing free to guests.
Phone 2400. F. N. VAN BRUNT, Owner.

THE WASHINGTON
Spring Lake Beach, N. J. Open until Oct. Rooms with bath or hot and cold water. Excellent food; attractive rates.
Mrs. RICHARD KEMPF, Spring Lake 3155

WILDWOOD, N. J.

WILDWOOD
BY-THE-SEA—N. J.
World's FINEST and SAFEST BATHING Beach
For Booklet Write Bureau of Publicity

NEW JERSEY

NEW LAKE END HOTEL
GREEN POND, NEW JERSEY
"Located on Water's Edge"
The Beauty Spot of New Jersey
A MODERN HOTEL, ALSO CABIN BUNGALOWS WITH OPEN FIREPLACE; EQUIPPED FOR CHILLY DAYS. BOATING, BATHING, TENNIS, GOLF, SADDLE HORSES. BOOKLET.
Mrs. J. L. SHAWGER

LAKELAND o' JERSEY
Free New Booklet, Scenic Retreats. More fun, less cost at 7 glorious mountain lakes; 1000-foot altitude. All sports. Hotels; cottages. Write Secy's Off., LAKELAND COUNCIL, Cranberry Lake, N. J.

NORTH SHORE HOUSE
Located on shore of Swartswood Lake. Tennis, boating, bathing, fishing and indoor games. Modern improvements. Rate $16 to $20 per week. Write for booklet.
NORTH SHORE HOTEL, Inc, Swartswood Lake, N. J.

LONE RANGE RANCH SWARTSWOOD, N. J. Box 16 Special week-end and Decoration Day rates.

CULVERMERE The REAL VACATION for YOUNG MEN and YOUNG WOMEN Box 650, Culver Lake, N.J.

THE PINES - SWARTZWOOD, N. J. Phone Newton 915-F-12 Table supplied with fresh vegetables. Free boating, swimming, tennis, dancing. Rates $16-$20. Booklet. EARLE E. HILL

PENNSYLVANIA

THE GLENWOOD
MILL RIFT, PA.
Special week-end party June 16-17-18, $3.50-$4.00 per day, A. P. All sports, bathing, dancing. Acc. 150 guests. Christian. 2½ hours from N. Y. C. via Erie R. R. Tel. Port Jervis 9943.
EDW. L. STODDARD.

Get FREE booklet, Hotels & Boarding Houses at Lackawanna R. R. ticket offices, or send 3c postage, R. F. Irwin, 140 Cedar St., N.Y.C.
THE POCONOS 3 HOURS AWAY

GREENWA HENRYVILLE, PA. All improvements. Bathing, boating, recreation hall, tennis, all sports; exceptional meals; Christians. Bklt.

The Gilchrist LAKE COMO, PA. Elev. 2000 Ft. Good Food Bathing. Modern. Putting, tennis, shuffleboard. Rates $18-$25. GEO. E. GILCHRIST.

POCONO LODGE Matamoras, Pa. Irvine De Remer. All outdoor sports. Saddle horses. Badminton. Christian clientele. Rates $18-$22. Write for information.

STARLIGHT INN Starlight, Pa. G. E. Fay On Lake Modern House. Good Table. Bathing, Fishing, Tennis, Dancing. $18-$21. Booklet.

Island Lake House Starrucca, Pa., on Lake, elev. 2,000 ft. Modern, all sports. Bklt. Charles Buhling.

DELAWARE VIEW FARM Shobola, Pa. Modern improvements. Boating, bathing, fishing, tennis, golf, swimming pool. Excellent meals. $14-$16. E. Wm. Burgess

HIGHLAND LAKE HOUSE Greeley, Pa. Mod. impts. Boating, bathing free. Tel 1R14 Lackawaxen. Christians. $14-$18. OTTO WINKLER

SWISS CHALET GREELEY, PA. Rudolph Perta. Modern. All sports on premises. $18-$20.

Beach Lake, Pa.

HOTEL DUNEDIN
Beach Lake, Wayne Co., Pa.
150 feet on water's edge; 1400 feet elevation. Modern. Running water, hot and cold, in every room; showers. Fresh vegetables served. Tennis, boating, bathing, golf nearby; bowling, other amusements. Near churches. Rate $16 June and Sept. $18 July and Aug. Booklet. 30th season.
FLOYD L. BAYLY, Prop.

LAKE VIEW HOUSE
Directly on Beach. BEACH LAKE, PA. Modern improvements. Hot and cold running water all rooms. All outdoor sports. Boating, bathing, fishing, bowling. Spacious grounds, large veranda. Good food. $18 weekly. Tel. Beach Lake 9007.
F. DROSSEL MEYER

LAZY-J DUDE RANCH Beach Lake, Pa. New management 110 miles from N. Y. Expert supervision. All sports. $18 up. Booklet.

Tuscarora Cottage Beach Lake, Wayne Co., Pa. On lake. Modern impts. Boating, bathing, fishing, amuse. $15-$18. R. Van Gorder.

EAST SHORE HOUSE BEACH LAKE, PA. Tel. 22R6. Home away from home. Ideal vacation spot. GILBERT OLIVER

Bushkill Falls, Pa.

BUSHKILL Falls HOTEL $18 wkly up M. Clark Mgr.
BUSHKILL, PA.
All Sports Orchestra Saddle Horses
Write for Special June Rate Booklet

PENNSYLVANIA

Canadensis, Pa.

PINE KNOB INN CANADENSIS, PA. Modern Swimming Pool. Sports. Tennis. Recreational Hall. Booklet. A. C. STEFFENS.

SPRUCE MT. HOUSE Accommodates 80. Private pool, tennis, horses, billiards, shuffleboard. Cresco 447R3.

GAY TIMES AT THE PINES Capacity 100. E. W. HELBIG, CANADENSIS, PA.

PINEHURST, Canadensis, Pa. Acc. 90. Excellent meals. Bathing, tennis, billiards, ping pong, box ball alley, etc. Bklt. A. E. & H. R. Gravel. Cresco 13

VILLA CAPRIOLI, Canadensis, Pa. In the heart of the Poconos. Italian-American cuisine. Modern improvements. All sports available. Tel. Cresco 9415

Cresco, Pa.

POCONO MOUNTAIN INN American-European. Open all year. Sky-Terrace Bar, Grill. All sports. N. Y. Office: 17 State St. BO. 9-8644.

Deleware Water Gap, Pa.

THE MOUNTAIN HOUSE Attractive. Modern. All Sports and Amusements. Mrs. E. Hauser & Sons

East Stroudsburg, Pa.

ECHO LAKE FARMS Star Route B in the Poconos. German-American kitchen. All water sports. Orchestra. Outdoor dancing. Saddle horses. $18-$20 wkly.; also special Spring rates. Gentile patronage. Apply booklet.

MAPLEHURST INN E. Stroudsburg, Pa. In the Poconos All sports. Swimming pool. Excellent meals. Dance barn. Swing orchestra. Reasonable. Acc. 200. Booklet. W. E. BURNETT.

RIP VAN WINKLE HOUSE—Own produce; swimming, sports, horses. Amer. plan. Reasonable rates. Stroudsburg 19R22.

Kirvin House R. D. 1. American plan. Fine food. Modern. $20 weekly. Riding, tennis, swimming. M. Strain

SHADY INN In Pocono Mts. Fresh vegetables, own farm; bathing, boating nearby; modern. $15 wkly. G. A. Shotwell

Greentown, Pa.

MAPLEWOOD FARM All products own farm. Homelike, restful. $14 up weekly. KATHERINE GRIMM.

Henryville, Pa.

HENRYVILLE HOUSE Recreation Hall, Dancing Nightly, Orchestra, Bath, Fish, Horses. $15 up wkly. Bklt. R. Henry.

Woodycrest Cottage, Henryville, Pa. Home cooking. Modern. Bathing, tennis, shuffleboard. Moderate rates. Booklet. M. MUNCH

BROOKSIDE FARM, Pocono Alps, Henryville, Pa. German cooking. Bathing. Modern. $14-$15 up weekly. A. HOMANN

Milford, Pa.

SAGAMORE Bungalow Camp. Twin Lakes, in Poconos. Restricted; young men and women, single or married. Orchestra, all sports. Now open. Booklet. Box 675, Milford, Pa.

Laurel Villa Milford, Pa. Hot & Cold water all rooms. All sports. $18 up. Bklt. H. N. DOSCHER

THE ARLINGTON MILFORD, PA. Modern impts.; Ideal for real vacation. $14 up. Booklet.

INDIAN POINT HOUSE, Milford, Pa., on Delaware River. Ideal location. Running water all rooms. $17 up. Booklet. P. C. McCARTY

Minisink Hills, Pa.

WILLOW DELL HOUSE On Silver Lake Minisink Hills, Pa. Excellent meals. Water sports, tennis, etc. $18-$19. horses; casino, swing orch.; Christian clientele; bklt. B.

HAVAREST HOUSE Amer. plan. Sports. Restful surroundings. Picnic grounds. Reasonable rates. C. Schmidt, Owner

Pocono Mountains, Pa.

WE **Pamper Mortals** ON VACATION AT **POCONO MANOR**
Excellent golf, riding, swimming . . . indoors and outdoors filled with entertainment for everybody—that's P.M. for your summer vacation. Delightfully cool, friendly and informal. Farm-fresh food. Bring the family to the top of the Poconos for the summer.
N. Y. Office: 535 Fifth Ave. Tel. VAnderbilt 6-3154
HERMAN V. YEAGER, General Manager
POCONO MANOR, PA.

Lenape Village
A POCONO CAMP
Adults and Families
• Rustic cabins with modern conveniences on lake. Central dining room. Riding, tennis, fishing, swimming, golf. Day or week. Selected clientele. Booklet. Mrs. J. E. Keiser, Drexel Court Apts., Drexel Hill, Pa.

COOL OFF Swim..ride..play tennis. Enjoy your favorite sport, a grand rest, pleasant social life at this beautiful 2,000-acre resort atop the Poconos. Three charming hotels. Christian clientele. Extremely moderate rates. Write Now.
LUTHERLAND
POCONO PINES, PENNA.
N. Y. OFFICE: 11 W. 42nd ST. • LOngacre 5-2136

THE ONTWOOD
MT. POCONO, PA.
CENTER OF SOCIAL ACTIVITY
Mt. Pocono's newest hotel, accommodating 150. Private baths or running water in all rooms. American plan. Delicious food. Golf, saddle horses, tennis, billiards. Orchestra. Hostess. Write for weekly schedule of sports and social events. Booklet. Tel. Mt. Pocono 160. CHARLES A. WEIR

DEVONSHIRE PINES Highest. Coolest. Mt. Pocono, Pa. Rooms with bath. Excel. view. From $22.50 wkly. Cap. 150. All sports, golf. Booklet. Gilbert D. Coan

Mountain Lake House Marshalls Creek, Pa. Orchestra evenings. Tennis, saddle horses. New swimming pool. Furnished cottages. Booklet. J. E. HUFFMAN.

VACATION PARADISE EAST STROUDSBURG, PA. OAK GROVE HOUSE — POCONO MTS. GLENWOOD HOTEL

FAMOUS FOR FOOD MT. AIRY HOUSE. Modern. Golf, tennis, riding. Own farm, dairy. $18-$25. Bklt. J. Martens

PARADISE INN Cresco, Pa. Modern. Specious lawns. Boating, bathing, dancing, tennis, riding. 21st season. E. M. STAPFF.

ECHO LAKE HOUSE Echo Lake, Pa. Amer. & Europ. Fine food. Reasonable. Sports. Bushkill 9176R3.

ONAWA LODGE MOUNTAINHOME PENNA. FAMOUS FOR "CRUISE-WAY" VACATIONS

THE BELMONT MT. POCONO, PA. All Sports. Rooms with bath and r. w. Booklet. J. E. Cornish

PLEASANT RIDGE HOUSE Mountainhome, Pa. Cresco 9422. Swimming pool. Orchestra. All sports.

POCONO LAKE HOTEL Pocono Pines, Pa. $18 to $25 weekly. Excellent table. Bathing, boating, saddle horses.

Marshalls Falls House Marshalls Creek, Pa. In the Poconos. Amer. Plan. Own farm. Dancing. Sports. Moderate.

HAWTHORNE INN & COTTAGES Best location in Poconos. Inspiring view. Family resort. L. E. Dengler, Mt. Pocono.

Shawnee-on-Delaware, Pa.

BENNE-KILL LODGE Modern. All sports. Excellent cuisine. Restricted clientele. Booklet, Phone Stroudsburg, Pa., 2083R1

RHODE ISLAND

IT'S TIME TO GO
Swimming in
Rhode Island
LESS THAN 4 HOURS FROM THE WORLD'S FAIR

For a summer sojourn or after your visit to the World of Tomorrow, rest and relax in the Smallest State. Give your family a real vacation.

- Bathing on famous beaches, sea and stream fishing, boating, yachting.
- Brilliant social events, moonlight dancing, summer theatres, seaside drives.
- Visits to scenes famous in American history and tradition; a mellow, peaceful countryside.
- Golf on fine courses, fast tennis, riding on miles of woodland trails.
- Snapshots of Colonial homes, lovely gardens, palatial estates, scenic views.
- Fresh seafood—lobster, clams, quahaugs—deliciously prepared.

To enjoy Rhode Island's traditional hospitality to the full, write for information on accommodations for a week-end or all summer . . . designed to suit your comfort and your budget.

Send this Coupon by the Next Mail!

SECRETARY OF STATE
219-4 State House, Providence, R. I.
Please send me information on Rhode Island.
Name..........
Address..........
City.......... State..........

VACATIONS GO FURTHER IN THE SMALLEST STATE

KENNETH RIDGE Watch Hill, R. I. On Ocean Beautiful estate. 11 baths. Booklet. Aileen Gray.

Block Island

Well, If I were looking up a place to stay through the hot summer, I would write the
VAILL HOTEL and Cottages
BLOCK ISLAND, R. I.
for their folder, which tells more than can be put in an advertisement like this.
The Owner supervises the management, guaranteeing good food, clean beds, and Nature supplies pleasant views and cool air.
Rooms with and without bath. *FREE use of private GOLF course as well as Tennis Courts and Bathing Beach.*
J. P. MALOOF, Prop.
ONLY GOLF COURSE ON ISLAND

BLOCK ISLAND, R. I.
"A Vacation to Remember"
The NARRAGANSETT
On waterfront. Free bathing, boating, tennis. Hot and cold running water in every room. Own farm products. Reasonable. Booklet. C. A. MOTT, Prop.

ATLANTIC INN Block Isle, Rhode Isle. Moderate. Excellent location. Booklet. Same owner-manager for 20 years. M. W. KEARNEY, 955 75th St., Brooklyn.

NEW HAMPSHIRE

"The House with the View" in the White Mountains
HOTEL LOOKOFF
Tennis—Golf—No Fee to Guests
Orchestra—Elevator—Excellent Table
Opens July 1 Restricted Clientele
Merrill & Sanborn, Ownership-Mgt.
SUGAR HILL, N. H.

BEN MERE INN
LAKE SUNAPEE, N. H. OPENS JUNE 30
An ideal resort for recreation in foothills of N. H. Golf nearby, bathing, boating, fishing, riding, tennis, shuffle board. Concerts and dancing. 100 Rooms, Amer. Plan. Booklet. Lewis R. Dudley. Ownership-Management. *Winter: Hotel Stratford, Tarpon Springs, Fla.*

Beaver Lake House
ON BEAVER LAKE
DERRY VILLAGE, N. H.
Beautiful spot; good beds; best of food; homelike, quiet and restful. Swimming. Recreation room. Rates $18 to $23 weekly, including meals. For booklet write JAMES DAVIS, Prop.

HANCOCK HOTEL
HANCOCK, N. H.
On Beautiful Lake Norway
A delightful vacation spot. Excellent accommodations, good food, all sports. $18 weekly, $3.50 daily. Write for booklet or phone Hancock 8067. R. STAHL, Mgr.

EMERSON INN
- at INTERVALE, N. H.
- in the White Mountains
- A snug mountain inn for the perfect vacation. Tennis, golf, swimming, fishing, riding, tramping. Own farm and dairy. All rooms with hot and cold running water. Refined Christian clientele. Weekly rates $23-28. Booklet. C. E. EMERSON, Host.

WINNIPESAUKEE Farm
AND ANNEX, LACONIA, N. H.
Golf, Boating, Bathing, Tennis—Garage. Baths and Electric Lights. Hot and Cold Water. Modern Non-Housekeeping Bungalows. New Innerspring Mattresses. Rates $17 to $24 weekly. Booklet.
G. ELMER SANBORN, Prop.

SPRUCE MT. LODGE and CHALETS
JACKSON, N.H.
WHITE MOUNTAINS
20 private bungalows, open fires, baths, all complete. Central dining room. Many young people. Selected clientele. ALL SPORTS. Best food. Homelike atmosphere. Booklet.
M. E. Slade, Proprietor

NEW HAMPSHIRE

CRAWFORD HOUSE
Discriminating people return each summer to the Crawford House at Crawford Notch. Up-to-date rooming space—the best of food—music by Boston Symphony players—Golf—Tennis—Swimming—Riding—Boating—Hiking—no hay fever. Season June 30-Oct. 4. Rates with meals $6 a day and up. Booklet and diagnosis of weekly rates—address: Barron Hotel Co., Crawford Notch, N. H.
Or ask Mr. Foster Travel Offices.
CRAWFORD NOTCH WHITE MTS. N. H.

Iron Mountain House and Meserve Hall
JACKSON, NEW HAMPSHIRE
The name Meserve has been connected with a hotel in Jackson since 1864. We are prepared to make your stay restful and enjoyable. Excellent food, good beds. Golf, tennis, fishing, bathing, dancing, horseback riding available. Rates $24.50 to $31.50 weekly. Booklet.
WILLARD A. MESERVE & SON, Props.

BEMIS CAMPS Overlooking Lake Kimball
The "back to nature" vacation in the White Mts.—with all the comforts of home. A spot entirely different from any other summer home colony. Fishing, mountain climbing, horseback riding, tennis, water sports, camping-out trips, night around the camp fire—all help to make Bemis Camps a popular resort. No hay fever. $15 to $25. Christian clientele.
H. E. BEMIS, South Chatham, N. H.

NEW ENGLAND INN and MODERN GUEST BARN
INTERVALE NEW HAMPSHIRE
REAL NEW ENGLAND
Atmosphere, background and food. 75 guests. Mountains, lakes, restful, quiet. Recreational facilities nearby. Only Christian clientele. Write for rates and folder to this beautiful old Inn.

WILSON and COTTAGES
WHITE MTS. JACKSON, N. H.
Wonderful view of Mt. Washington from 1,200 feet elevation. Large estate. Mountain climbing. Tennis, Golf, Dancing. Bathing in 90-foot pool, right on lawn. Rooms in hotel or private cabin. Bountiful table. Cool, clean, free from mosquitoes. Rates $18 to $25 weekly. Gentiles. Booklet. Write
Mrs. LOUISE S. PROCTOR.

FERNCROFT FARM INN, Near Lake Winnepesaukee, Alton, N. H.—Enjoy the beautiful view in pleasant surroundings. Homelike, modernized house with excellent table. Fresh farm products. Saddle horses, movies, dancing, bathing, etc., near. Illustrated booklet. Rates $16-$18 week, $3.00 day. Mrs. W. A. CROSBY.

POINT BREEZE On Lake Wentworth WOLFEBORO, N. H. 40-acre pine grove; home cooking; fresh vegetables; social hall; bathing, boating, bass fishing, tennis; modern sanitation; running water in all rooms; golf nearby. Christian clientele. $16.50-$19.00 weekly. Booklet. C. E. STEVENS, Prop.

Burkehaven Hotel Lake Sunapee, New Hampshire RATES $23 to $30 WEEKLY. BOOKLET.

THE BROCKLEBANK NEW LONDON, New Hampshire A friendly place. Rates $18 to $25 weekly

Red Gables and Cottages New London, New Hampshire On Lake Pleasant. Elev. 1200 ft. All sports. Gentiles. Rates $17 to $21 weekly. Booklet.

HUNTOON HOUSE ON KEZAR LAKE North Sutton, N. H. Homelike. Good food. Rates $18 to $25 weekly

HAMPTON BEACH, N. H., for health and happiness. Write for illustrated booklet and hotel guide. Secretary Chamber of Commerce, Box 105

PEMIGEWASSET Plymouth, N. H. Center of lake and mt. region. Bklt. W. B. Horrocks.

THE MONADNOCK White Mountains, Colebrook, N. H. On direct route to Montreal and Quebec. Booklet.

The BROOKLYN EAGLE Maintains the **Largest Resort & Travel Bureau** Conducted by a newspaper in the United States

MAINE

VACATION PROBLEMS ANSWERED IN THIS FREE BOOKLET
MAINE
The Land of Remembered Vacations

What's your idea of a *perfect* vacation? Here's the answer—all in one beautiful booklet. Because Maine offers you rest or sport . . . on wooded mountains or rock-bound seacoast. Hiking, camping, fishing, tennis, golf, everything your heart desires! You get more for your money in Maine.

You can swim and boat in salt water or fresh. Enjoy the incomparable Maine food. Live in the midst of Maine hospitality at famous hotels, modest inns or comfortable tourist houses. Write for the free illustrated booklet that tells where to go and what to do in Maine. Mail the coupon.

SEE THE MAINE EXHIBIT AT THE NEW YORK WORLD'S FAIR . . . THEN SEE **MAINE**

GET MORE FOR YOUR MONEY—IN MAINE
MAINE DEVELOPMENT COMMISSION
Tourist Service, Dept. 331
St. John Street, Portland, Maine
Please send me the new illustrated Maine Official Vacation Guide for 1939.
Name..........
Address..........
City.......... State..........

The Wonderland of Maine
KENNEBUNKPORT
Cape Porpoise
Goose Rocks Beach
Fine Sandy Beach—Sailing—Many excellent Golf Courses. 4 Municipal Tennis Courts and 2 Shuffleboards available to the public.
Every Summer Attraction
Modern Hotels. Summer Cottages for Rent.
For Free Booklet Write
KENNEBUNKPORT INFORMATION BUREAU
Box 1010, Kennebunkport, Maine

Old Orchard Beach
Playground of Two Nations
WORLD'S FINEST BEACH
18-hole Golf Course—Every Sport and Entertainment
Hotels—Cottages—Tourist Homes—Overnight Camps
Write Publicity Bureau
OLD ORCHARD BEACH MAINE

SQUAW MOUNTAIN INN
ON MOOSEHEAD LAKE MAINE
NOW OPEN—all outdoor sports; private golf course. NO HAY FEVER. Country Club atmosphere; delicious food; select clientele; American Plan from $5. Fine roads and train service. Come fishing—bring the family.
Write for booklet
Or ask any Mr. Foster Travel Office
PHILIP SHERIDAN Manager
Greenville Junction, Maine

MAPLE NOOK CAMPS On Belgrade Lakes
Individual cabins with bathrooms, hot and cold water, open fires, screened throughout. Sandy bathing beach. Free guest boats and tennis courts. All sports. Excellent meals. $32 weekly. Reduced June and September rates. Illustrated booklet. L. E. IMMELN, Oakland, Me.

The NONANTUM
KENNEBUNKPORT, MAINE
One of the most popular hotels at this exclusive resort.
Golf . . . and every recreational feature.
Elevator, steam heat, booklet
Complete Sprinkler System
FELIX BRIDGER, Manager

SPARHAWK HALL
Surf Bathing—Golf—Tennis—Riding
Music—Playhouse—Elevator—Booklet.
Rates Upon Request. Selected Clientele.
OGUNQUIT, MAINE

KAMP PEACOCK
On Lake Maranacook
Box E, Winthrop, Maine
A modern camp with modern conveniences, delightfully located at water's edge; nearly all diversions. Select clientele. I guarantee the kamp to be as represented in free 32-page booklet. Write
ELLSWORTH E. PEACOCK.

THOMPSON'S CAMPS On Sebago Lake, Naples, Maine Excellent salmon and bass fishing. Booklet.

LAKESIDE INN NORWAY, MAINE Restricted. Booklet On Lake Pennesseewasee

ALDEN FARM CAMPS on East Lake, Oakland, Maine All Sports. Box 2. MRS. FRED ALDEN

PINEWOOD CAMPS, Canton, Me. Maine's finest vacation spot. Every vacation pleasure. Grand food—a good time all the time. Moderate rates. Restricted clientele. Booklet. B. W. RICHARDSON.

OCEAN VIEW HOTEL, Biddeford Pool, Me. On Ocean Front. Fine Beach. Golf, Tennis, etc. Write for Illustrated Booklet.

BRUNSWICK HOTEL OLD ORCHARD BEACH, MAINE on the ocean. Christian clientele. Booklet.

GREEN ACRES INN AND CABINS, CANTON, ME. Golf, tennis, horses, bathing, boating, fishing, etc. $26.25 up. Restricted clientele. Bklt. E. E. Poland

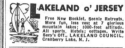

SPRUCEWOLD LODGE
and CABINS
BOOTHBAY HARBOR, ME.
Log cabin hotel and 1, 2 and 3 bedroom cabins with maid service. American plan. Balsam scented woods and ocean vistas; cocktail lounge, golf, tennis, sea bathing, also salt water swimming pool; fishing in fresh or salt water; riding; no mosquitoes or hay fever; also attractive housekeeping cabins completely furnished with 2, 3 or 4 bedrooms, living room, fireplace, kitchenette, bath and electricity. For week, month or season.
PARKER T. NICKERSON Manager
Write for BOOKLET

THE ASPINQUID
Ogunquit-by-the-Sea, Me.
Famed for home comforts and excellent table. Fresh vegetables and sea foods in attractive variety. Nearest hotel to bathing beach. Mr. & Mrs. L. E. Hall, Ownership Management. Moderate rates. Opens June 25th. Booklet.

BELVEDERE INN
Lake Maranacook, Maine
Including log cabins and bungalows for 2 to 6 persons with complete hotel service. Rooms, baths, running water. Dancing, bathing, fishing, canoeing, tennis courts. Weekly rates, including meals, $18-$25 (double), $22 and $24 (single). Restricted clientele. Booklet.
A. L. NELSON

MIGIS LODGE
On Sebago Lake
South Casco, Maine
An ideal vacation spot for particular people. Modern cabins on lake shore. Excellent food—Relaxation—Sports. Bass Fishing. Selected clientele.
Booklet. Mrs. G. Gulick Robinson.

MARANACOOK HOTEL
and 8 Annex Cottages along lake shore, in beautiful natural park. Large lobby, central dining room, good table, spring water. Bowling, Tennis, Dancing, Canoes and Boats, Indoor Activities. Rates, American
Cottage rooms $18-22, Hotel rooms $21-28
New management
Restricted. Write for Booklet E
MARANACOOK, MAINE

JAMAICA POINT CAMP
ON GREAT POND, LARGEST OF BELGRADE LAKES
Ideal vacation spot. Individual cabins. Hot and cold running water. Electric lights and baths. $31.50 and up. American plan. Also housekeeping cabins. Excellent bass, trout and salmon fishing. Boats, canoes and guides furnished. Accommodations for 70. Christian clientele. For folder write JAMAICA POINT CAMPS, Oakland, Maine

VERMONT

"On the Water's Edge"
Moosalamoo Park House Salisbury, Vt.
On Lake Dunmore Cottages $17.50 up
Main lodge and cottages, each cottage with private porch, modern improvements. Ideal country. Excellent fishing. Home cooking. Rates $17.50 double, $20 single. Christian clientele. Write for booklet.
Mrs. W. F. BENTLEY, Mgr.

ALL SPORTS AT YOUR DOOR—18-hole Golf, Tennis, Riding Trails, Boats, Fishing, Swimming, 100 modern rooms, 75 private baths. Restricted patronage. Literature.
LAKE MOREY INN
W. P. Lyle FAIRLEE, VERMONT

VERMONT FREE BOOK
"Unspoiled Vermont", vacation preview—a riot of pictures of Green Mountain resorts and tours.
Pub. Service 59 State House, Montpelier, Vt.

LAKEVIEW IN THE MOUNTAINS R.F.D. 1, Rutland, Vt. Fishing (boats free), tennis, saddle horses. Restricted. $16.50-$18. Bklt. A. J. Forguites

BONNIE OAKS INN FAIRLEE, VERMONT. Write for Booklet 8

LAKE VIEW HOUSE, POULTNEY, VT. On Lake St. Catherine. Modern. All sports. Cottage for rent. Low rates. Booklet.

THE FAY FARM IN THE PINES, Bennington, Vt. 300 acres. Rooms hot, cold water. Good meals. Swimming, shuffleboard, riding, golf. Free car meets Albany boat, round trip $4. Booklet.

OAKLEDGE MANOR Burlington, Vt. on Lake Champlain All activities, Select clientele, $25 up, Box H, R. C. Hill

Entered in the Brooklyn Postoffice as 2d Class Mail Matter W BROOKLYN, N. Y., SATURDAY, JUNE 24, 1939

NEWS behind the NEWS IN WASHINGTON

Paul McNutt Stays Right in the Spotlight

Often enough the candidate who first tosses his hat in the Presidential ring lives sorrowfully to see it trampled upon. Such a risk is being taken by Paul V. McNutt of Indiana, but a few of the wise ones here are advising against scratching off his name too early. The gentleman, it seems, is smart.

Political comets nearly always leave a train of scorched lesser luminaries. McNutt had some of those. When he left for the Philippines they said he was off for political Siberia. And after that affair with President Quezon over whom should be toasted first, the ridicule reached historic proportions.

Paul V. McNutt

Yet his current return to the United States, this time presumably to stay and run for the Democratic nomination, finds him as much in the spotlight as a man could be coming back to a country so busy with important affairs. His campaign organization paved the way for part of the show, including a statewide demonstration in Indiana and a wholesale distribution of publicity material.

Stood Up for U. S.

From the Philippines have come reports that by his hard-handed attitude in the cocktail affair he saved face for the United States in the Orient. In the Orient that is important. It seems that at a diplomatic party some one proposed a toast jointly to the President of the United States and the President of the Philippines. McNutt declined to let it be used as a precedent.

He notified each foreign consul that a toast for the President of the United States is to be separate and not jointly with the President of the Philippines. If more toasts are desired, then one may be given first to the U. S. High Commissioner (himself) and next to the President of the Philippines. The United States, said McNutt, comes first until the islands are independent. Filipinos boiled for a time with indignation.

Just where McNutt stands with President Roosevelt is anybody's guess. It is reported substantially here that before McNutt let his name be put up for 1940 he went to Roosevelt and asked if it would embarrass the President. Mr. Roosevelt reputedly said the more the merrier, but added that he was making no commitments.

Many Pros and Cons

As a candidate, he has advantages and disadvantages, as viewed by friends and foes. Many New Dealers distrust him. They call him the "man on horseback," a term that comes close to "dictator." Yet a recent meeting of Republicans in Indiana sought to damage him by crediting him with responsibility for many "New Deal" ideas as Governor of Indiana.

He revised the tax system in Indiana, substituting a gross profits tax as the major revenue source. It lowered the tax on farms and homes but made the Governor the principal dispenser of money, giving him a terrifically powerful weapon to be applied in reapportioning revenue among the lower branches of government.

From a strictly campaign proposition McNutt has advantages. McNutt has a good radio voice. And he will go well in the news reels. He is as handsome as a Roman general. Everytime his athletic figure is contrasted with the potty forms of some of his opponents he will swing 50 feminine votes.

And he is incredibly sure of himself. It is related, perhaps partly as an illustrative fable, that when American Legionnaires asked him several years ago if he would be a candidate for national commander, they reminded him that it would be useful politically. He was quoted as replying:

"I know it will. Some day I expect to be President."

—PRESTON GROVER.

Ears to the Ground

By Clifford Evans

This Is Our Town Brooklyn

Golfer Ralph Strafaci and Adelaide DeMartino are romancing. They plan to wed in October . . . Lawyers around town are pushing 22d A. D. Assemblyman Daniel Gutman for the Municipal Court Justice Democratic nomination to oppose Justice John Bladen in the election this Fall . . . Why was the Williamsburgh Community Council testimonial dinner to Louis Notkin suddenly called off? Could it be because ex-Magistrate David Malbin, an invited guest speaker, is an anti-organization candidate for City Court justice—and the scene of the affair was Knapp Mansion in Kings County Democratic Leader Frank V. Kelly's backyard?

Daniel Gutman

The Ned (Bay Ridge) Strauses are celebrating their 30th wedding anniversary . . . Word is around that Samuel Leibowitz will not personally defend Joseph Kress, one of the defendants in the Rubel holdup case. The trying will be done by some one in Leibowitz' office . . . The wedding bells will ring on Sunday for Charles Manzo, secretary to Municipal Court Justice George Joyce, and Angelina Mastrorillo . . . Flatlands Civic Association President Franklin B. Horbelt will campaign as the taxpayers' representative when he makes his run this Fall for the City Council . . . The Kings County Bar Association is holding a radio symposium today over Station WARD. Speakers will be William Pinckney Hamilton Jr., Denis M. Hurley and former Deputy Controller Milton Solomon . . . Charles Richman, who shifted his allegiance from Coney Island to Manhattan Beach, is being seen around town with Rose Rosenthal, granddaughter of Ralph Jonas . . . Long Island University athletic director Clair Bee airplanes to Texas tomorrow.

• • •

Take a Letter

Dear Cathy:

You know this district attorney muddle we have here, with no one knowing who the Democratic candidate will be? Well, Samuel Leibowitz, the lawyer, is beginning to worry the boys. They know that Leibowitz is tough, that he is against the political machine, that he has plenty of dynamite ready to use and that once he gets going he'll hit awfully hard, fast and furious. What is disturbing folks on the other side of the fence is that he is so quiet at the moment. They prefer hearing him. Otherwise he worries them.

By the way, one of the Mayor's closest advisors told me that there's something doing between LaGuardia and Manhattan D. A. Tom Dewey. He said that it comes from inefficiency in the Police Department and that Dewey has enough concrete evidence regarding vice, gambling and the policy racket to split the administration wide open. That won't happen, though, so everything's okay. The information, however, did come in handy in another direction. Seems that the Mayor is disappointed in Commissioner of Investigation Herlands, who was planted in Brooklyn as a district attorney build-up, and would like to drop him rather than get him the Republican-Fusion backing. But Herlands is out of Dewey's office and the Mayor isn't taking any chances.

• • •

Page 1 News

The special Department of Investigation, created under the new charter, is all set to go. Official announcement is expected shortly. Deputy Commissioner of Correction David Marcus, who turned down a judgeship in preference to police work, is set to head the bureau which is a combination of G-Man and law enforcement activities. Harvey Fosner of the Guggenheim Foundation is slated to serve as counsel for the department, to be assisted by William Richter. Fosner and Richter figured prominently in the early stages of the fur racket investigation. Although plans call for captains and other officers, the "brains" is Detective Grottano. Fifty secret police are expected to comprise the staff . . . The Kings County Democratic Organization is attempting to ditch a major officeholder who will be up for re-election this Fall . . . Municipal Court Justice Jacob Strahl will address the Glenmore Junior H. S. graduation class on Tuesday . . . Contrast: Rabbis and priests work side by side in concentration camps in totalitarian countries—while today the Zionist Organization of America and the Catholic Press Association will occupy the same floor at the Hotel Commodore . . . The story is told about the Rubel holdup men being awakened by a bell late one night while hiding in a Riverside Drive apartment. The apartment was on the first floor and from a window the vestibule could be seen. There wasn't any one ringing the bell—simply a policeman romancing a young lady who accidentally had leaned against several of the house bells. One of the bandits opened a window, leaned out and shouted at the cop, "How would you like it if I reported you to the Police Commissioner?" The policeman apologized and scampered off . . . A testimonial dinner given last year in honor of a prominent judge is now being investigated . . . Hal LeRoy taps today at Manhattan Beach, while George Jessel is there tomorrow.

Radio Phone Reports Freeport's First Tuna

Freeport, June 24—The Freeport waterfront habitues welcomed the first tuna of the season yesterday about noon when by way of radio telephone, Capt. Ben Eldred, 50 miles off shore on his Empress Ann, announced that he had just landed a 50-pound fish.

William B. Bradley of the South Shore Power Squadron was sitting in the office of the Freeport Boatman's Association when the call came and persons there talked back and forth with Captain Eldred for some time.

Captain Eldred's boat is one of the best known party boats that sail out of Freeport and he was one of the first to get equipped with a two-way radio telephone.

Brooklyn Scenes . . . The Boardwalk . . . No. 70

Looking at this photograph of the uncrowded Coney Island Boardwalk you can almost feel the cooling breezes blowing across it from the wide ocean. Summer is here and the Boardwalk attracts thousands of borough residents who seek escape at the seashore from the heat of city streets. This camera shot was taken on an average day from an upper floor of the towering Half Moon Hotel. (Photograph by Jules Geller.)

Chinese Aviatrix Sees People Unconquered

Miss Ya Chin Lee Returns From 10,000 Mile 'Charity' Flight With Hopes Still High

Despite the "appalling" Japanese bombings of civilian centers in her country and other war atrocities, her people will never be conquered by Japan, in the opinion of Miss Ya Ching Lee, beautiful and charming young Chinese aviatrix who on March 20 took off from Floyd Bennett Field on a solo flying tour in behalf of her war stricken people, and just three months later ended it without mishap in the same place.

Welcomed back yesterday by five women members of the New York branch of the Women's International Association of Aeronautics at an informal luncheon at the Hotel Bossert, Miss Lee had nothing but praise and graditude for the reception given her in this country throughout her 10,000-mile trip.

Though she made no speech, the flyer told reporters she raised about $10,000 in cash and received pledges for about $20,000 more in her campaign for civilian relief funds for the 36,000,000 refugees, mostly women and children, in her native country.

She told the people here, Miss Lee said, that the "spirit of the Chinese people is holding up wonderfully—it becomes stronger every day." The Japanese aggression had a disastrous effect at first, she added, but in the past year the Chinese have learned to organize a united defense.

HAS OPPOSITE EFFECT

"The bombings of cities were intended to break our morale," Miss Lee declared, "but they are having the opposite effect and are making us stronger in our determination. We will never be conquered by Japan."

Flying a Stinson, gull-wing monoplane lent to her by Walter Beech, aircraft manufacturer, Miss Lee stopped at 40 of the countries biggest cities, flying West along the Southern route and East along the Northern border.

"Americans have been marvelous," she reported. "So kind and generous to me. The sympathy has been overwhelming."

"Wherever I went, people opened their hearts. It gave me a great uplift to feel people are so sympathetic and it is a wonderful message for my people that the Americans are with us."

FLYING SIX YEARS

Dressed in a simple, clinging, white and pink flowered Chinese gown, Miss Lee said she had been flying since 1933. She smiled with universal femininity when a reporter asked her age but admitted it was "about that" when 23 was suggested.

She received her pilot's license in Geneva, Switzerland and then came to this country for advanced training at the Boeing School, in California. She spent several years touring China to promote civilian flying before coming here for her good-will tour.

During her training in California, she became a member of the Caterpillar Club.

"Did you have to bail out?" she was asked.

"I fell out," she related, "My safety belt became unbuckled while flying upside down over San Francisco Bay. I landed in the water, two miles out and couldn't swim so I just floated on my back until an amphibian rescued me 25 minutes later. That 25 minutes was a lifetime."

EXPECTS TO BE BUSY

Her plans for the immediate future are indifinite. What she wants most right now is rest, she said, but feared she won't have a chance to get much. Besides another mission or two she may undertake before returning home, she is writing a book on flying now, and intends to write another, on her American tour, when that is finished.

Ends Flying Tour

Miss Ya Ching Lee

Squalus Hero's Brother Wants to Be a Sailor

Greensboro, N. C., June 24 (AP)—Robert Duval Maness, 18-year-old brother of Lloyd B. Maness, hero of the Squalus submarine disaster, has applied for enlistment in the U. S. Navy. Young Maness was graduated from High School in May but waited until he was 18 to file application.

His brother was credited with slamming a door in the Squalus and saving 33 men from drowning.

Over Million Pupils Start Vacation Friday

Commencement Exercises for 71,500 Of All Schools to Begin on Monday

Some 1,210,000 public school students in the city will start on their eagerly-awaited ten-week Summer vacation next Friday afternoon. Commencement exercises for 71,500 graduates start Monday.

Schools throughout the city will graduate 25,000 elementary, 20,000 junior high and 25,000 senior high school pupils, in addition to 1,500 students of trade and vocational schools.

The high point of Brooklyn's Commencement week will be Wednesday when 14 high schools are scheduled to hold exercises.

A touch of human interest to the city's graduation exercises will be added when 60 children, unable to attend public schools because of physical incapacity, receive diplomas at individual exercises.

More than 40,000 teachers, supervisors and principals will also begin vacations. They leave the State education budget slash problem and the results of the special session of the State Legislature in regard to that question to members of the city's administrative staff, who have been requested to remain on duty. They have been asked to be on 24 hours call.

Regents examinations have been held during the past week and will continue next week. But the routine school work, as school officials well know, will not be intensive during the last few days of the school term, as concentration is not always possible with the lure of country and seashore lurking around the corner for the students.

The Board of Education will provide 388 playgrounds, 24 athletic fields and 42 swimming pools for the vast throng of school children who take to the streets when the Spring term ends. More than 1,600 teachers have received assignments to supervise these recreational facilities.

Some 200,000 children are expected to attend playgrounds, open from 10 a.m. to 5:30 p.m. Monday through Friday from July 5 to Aug. 31. Athletic fields will be open from 9 a.m. to 9 p.m., except Saturday and Sunday, when the hours will be 10 a.m. to 6 p.m.

The swimming pools, always a refuge from hot streets for thousands of youngsters, will be open from 9 a.m. to 5 p.m., except Saturday and Sunday.

Mark A. McCloskey, director of recreational and community activities for the Board of Education, will supervise the Summer program.

A new high school in Brooklyn will be among eight new buildings available in the Fall to relieve overcrowding and to make it possible to scrap inadequate structures.

Museum Displays Primitive Cotton Of Pre-Inca Days

On exhibition in the Central American galleries of the Brooklyn Museum is a mantle of cotton and vicuna wool, five feet long and 24 inches wide, said to be the most famous textile if its kind.

The cloth is Pre-Incan in origin, probably dating from a period earlier than 1000 A. D., and was purchased by the Museum from the John T. Underwood Memorial Fund, on the recommendation of Dr. Herbert J. Spinden, curator of American Indian art and primitive cultures.

The textile was brought to this city by Miss Anne Morgan for an exhibition of Peruvian Art and was formerly shown at the Paris International Exhibition.

It was found in a tomb at Paracas, Peru, a few years ago. Dr. Spinden believes it was part of the funeral dress of a chief or priest.

All Aboard for the World of Tomorrow

About 1,000 neighborhood children visited the World's Fair yesterday as guests of the Upper Broadway Civic Association. Photo shows the first contingent of happy youngsters leaving for the exposition from Hopkinson Ave. and Broadway. (Eagle Staff photo.)

Heffernan Says—

Old Barkentine At Canarsie Revives Memories

James Ford, to whom the Ireland in which he was born is an ever-verdant memory, and the America of his adoption, in which his children were born, a present and precious reality, took me for an automobile ride in his motorcar on Sunday.

We saw from the Shore Road, Manhattan's man-made mountain of fabricated peaks jutting out into the bay—so clear the atmosphere under the cloudy sky you could imagine it within rifle range.

Mr. Heffernan

We saw, as we rounded Fort Hamilton, every detail of the Staten Island shore, St. John's famous dock tower beyond the familiar Quarantine station, and Fort Wadsworth's granite bastion frowning under the rising hills. The old Quarantine Islands—Hoffman and Swinburne—on the west bar stood out, came clear against the silver gray background.

Canarsie Brings Memories

Then we arrived at Canarsie. Two memories came to me as I stood gazing at the hummocks of sand Mr. Moses has pumped in for this particular link in his circumferential parkway.

Somewhere in the late 90s the New York newspapermen covering Brooklyn decided one Summer evening as they sat in the reporters' room under the eaves of the old Municipal Building in Joralemon St., to get themselves a fish dinner. The "Main" office of the telephone company was then in Smith St., and occasional gifts of candy and pleasant chats with the operators in the lonely hours of the night had made us all pretty friendly with the night force. Those were leisurely, inefficient days, when there wasn't much telephone business in Brooklyn after 10 at night and regulations regarding telephone conversations were rather loose. So we called up the night supervisor and asked her to keep a record of all calls in which we might be interested for several hours, and by "L" and the old steam line from East New York we moved on Canarsie. There on the cool porch of an old hotel looking out over the rippling waters of Jamaica Bay we feasted on clam chowder, broiled lobster and a fresh-caught bluefish, stuffed and baked.

On Sunday I saw that old hotel, but from its porch the vista is one of heaped-up sand; the water is no longer in sight.

'Disaster at Sea'

The second memory is of a stormy Winter night. In the barroom of the same hotel in front of a great pot-bellied stove a group of baymen in shining oilskins and sou'westers stood. Two reporters were pleading with them to furnish transportation by boat to Ruffle Bar where it was reported a man and a woman were weather-bound and in peril. At last two of the sturdy chaps took their long oars from a corner of the barroom, after stuffing a ten-dollar bill each into his capacious pocket, and led us down to a heavy fishing dory. The sky was a scurry of racing clouds, the wind a-shrieking, bellowing blast, and the water as black as the Styx. For three hours, sitting in the stern sheets, we watched our Charons battle with the wind, the crashing ice cakes and the dirty, high-running sea.

We found those whom we sought finally, snug enough in a cabin warmed by blazing driftwood, and we cussed the lying tipster who has sent us on a fool's errand, all the way back to Canarsie Beach.

Days of Canvas

Down by the pier on Sunday I saw a relic of those days, a white barkentine moored to the stringpiece. Her red-leaded deck and white-leaded strakes were sadly in need of attention, and her catted anchor high above the bluff bow looked as if it would never drag mud again.

No canvas showed on her bare yardarms and fore-and-aft rigging. The name, Nordern, was painted on her stern. A "ship's husband," in blue sweater and blue cap, told us she was of Scandinavian built, and had made her last voyage to Denmark six years ago. She was launched in 1883. He said a Captain Ambrosia owned her now, but whether she was again to take the sea, or like so many an old windjammer, find a ship's grave far from the place of her birth, he didn't know.

I always feel a sense of regret when I see these old square riggers. I can recall the picture of South St. and Erie Basin long ago, when their bowsprits reached over the docks and streets.

Better Than Lights

Washington, June 24 (AP)—James A. Noe, Louisiana State Senator and now candidate for Governor, will have his full name in the call letters of his New Orleans radio station. Elmer Pratt, a Washington attorney, said today the Federal Communications Commission had agreed to allow Station WBNO to change its call letters to WNOE.

BIG BARGAINS AT LITTLE PRICES
Everyday at A&P SELF SERVICE FOOD STORES

Are you

Among the SMART THOUSANDS who serve these fine, fresh coffees and

SAVE UP TO 10c A POUND

Eight O'Clock Mild and Mellow 2 1 lb. bags 29c
Red Circle Rich and Full-Bodied 2 1 lb. bags 35c
Bokar Strong and Vigorous 2 1 lb. bags 39c

Guaranteed Meats at Really Low Prices

A&P meats are selected for quality, carefully protected by constant refrigeration, and cut by master butchers. A&P stands squarely behind every pound of meat it sells, and guarantees that you will be satisfied.

LEGS OF LAMB GENUINE SPRING LAMB—CHOICE GRADE lb. 23c
Genuine spring lamb, carefully selected to meet A&P's higher standards of quality.

HAMS SMOKED—10 to 12 lb. Average—Whole or Either Half. Armour's Star, Ferris, Wilson's Certified, Cudahy's Puritan and Sunnyfield lb. 23c
These fancy, sugar-cured hams are the very finest hams produced by leading packers.

FOWL MILK-FED SIZES UNDER 4½ lbs. lb. 21c SIZES 4½ lbs. and OVER lb. 23c
The extra fine quality of A&P milk-fed fowl insures better dishes for light summer menus.

PRIME RIBS OF BEEF A&P Quality Steer Beef Cut From 1st Six Ribs lb. 23c
A&P quality steer beef is your assurance of tender, delicious roast beef.

BROILERS & FRYERS FRESH-KILLED Sizes 2 to 3½ lbs. lb. 23c
Extra fancy young spring chickens fresh from nearby farms. Tender, juicy, delicious.

POT ROAST BONELESS CHUCK lb. 25c
One of the best-flavored pot roasts, and one of the most economical. A&P quality steer beef.

Loin Lamb Chops . lb. 39c
Shoulders of Lamb (CHUCKS) Whole lb. 17c
Veal Shoulders WHOLE lb. 15c
Pork Loins FRESH WHOLE or EITHER HALF lb. 19c
Pork Chops SHOULDER and HIP CUTS lb. 19c
Fresh Calas SHORT CUT PORK SHOULDERS—WHOLE lb. 17c
Spare Ribs FRESH . . lb. 13c
Frankfurters SKINLESS . lb. 23c
Chuck Roast BONE IN . lb. 17c
Cross-Rib Pot Roast lb. 27c
Chopped Beef . . lb. 19c
Plate & Navel Beef FRESH or CORNED lb. 10c
Brisket Beef BONELESS FRESH or CORNED lb. 27c
Ducks LONG ISLAND—EXTRA FANCY lb. 17c
Sliced Bacon SUNNYFIELD SUGAR-CURED 2 ½ lb. pkgs. 23c
Smoked Calas SHORT CUT PORK SHOULDERS lb. 19c
FRESH FILLET COD and HADDOCK . . lb. 15c

Ready-to-Eat Meats for Quick Summer Snacks

Sliced Boiled Ham lb 39c | Salami HARD lb 39c | Spiced Ham SLICED lb 29c
Thuringer . . lb 23c | Liverwurst or Bologna REG. lb 23c | Meat Loaf lb 25c

A&P FINE TEAS
Preferred by 5 out of 6 of our customers!

Of every 6 pounds of tea sold in A&P Stores, 5 pounds are A&P Teas. And the reason for this overwhelming choice is easy to explain: *Each A&P tea offers a quality far higher than what you would expect at the price for which it sells.* A&P can give you so much extra quality for your money because A&P imports, blends, packs and sells its brands—and thus eliminates many unnecessary expenses. These savings are shared with you!

NECTAR ½ lb. 27c
OUR OWN ½ lb. 20c
MAYFAIR ½ lb. 37c

Since 1859 A&P has imported, blended and packed fine teas

String Beans NEW 1939 PACK STANDARD QUALITY No. 2 can 5c
Crab Meat IMPORTED—AKO BRAND med. can 17c
Hormel's Spam . 12 oz. tin 25c
Dole's Pineapple Juice 18 oz. can 9c
Tomato Juice IONA BRAND 3 lge. 24 oz. cans 20c
Sliced Beets . . 16 oz. jar 10c
Encore Mayonnaise pt. jar 17c qt. jar 33c
Mayonnaise HELLMANN'S ½ pt jar 15c pt. jar 25c
Baby Foods STRAINED CLAPP'S, HEINZ or BEECH-NUT 3 for 22c
Minute Tapioca . . pkg. 10c
Ann Page Tapioca Quick Cooking 2 pkgs. 15c
Plain Gelatin ANN PAGE—PURE Four Envelopes to pkg. 3 pkgs. 25c
Knox Gelatin . . pkg. 18c
Wheaties . . . . pkg. 10c
Wheat Flakes SUNNYFIELD 2 8 oz. pkgs. 15c
Corned Beef Hash PRUDENCE 2 1 lb. cans 29c
Kellogg's Pep or RICE KRISPIES pkg. 10c
Puritan Baked Beans 2 28 oz. glass jars 29c
Flour SUNNYFIELD ALL-PURPOSE 3½ lb. bag 10c 7 lb. bag 19c 24½ lb. bag 55c
Flour Gold Medal, Hecker's or Pillsbury 3½ lb. bag 15c 7 lb. bag 29c 24½ lb. bag 79c
Social Teas or FIG NEWTONS N. B. C. 2 pkgs. 17c
Pineapple Gems DOLE'S 3 14 oz. cans 25c
Jack Frost Sugar Confectioner's or Powdered 1 lb. carton 6c
Sugar JACK FROST 5 pound paper bag 23c 10 pound paper bag 45c
Tomato Juice SUN-RAYED or CAMPBELL'S 4 cans 25c

Tomatoes STANDARD QUALITY No. 2 can 5c
Rinso . . . . 2 lge. pkgs. 35c
Armour's Corned Beef 2 12 oz. tins 29c
Waldorf Paper . . 4 rolls 15c
Sliced Beef ENCORE or A&P BRAND 5 oz. jar 21c
Kirkman's Borax Soap 7 cakes 25c
Green Giant Peas 2 17 oz. cans 27c
Presto Cake Flour . lge. pkg. 21c
Del Maiz Corn Niblets 12 oz. can 10c
Baking Powder ANN PAGE It's Dependable 12 oz. can 12c
Crisco or Spry 1 lb. can 18c 3 lb. can 48c
Pink Salmon COLD STREAM Firm, Tender Meat 2 1 lb. cans 21c
Sanka or Kaffee Hag 1 lb. tin 30c
Bisquick . . . lge. pkg. 25c

Nectar TEA BALLS ORANGE-PEKOE pkg. of 15 14c pkg. of 30 27c
Tomato Soup ANN PAGE Rich, Delicious 3 cans 16c
Campbell's Beans . 4 1 lb. cans 25c
Ivory Flakes . . lge. pkg. 20c
Gold Dust . . . lge. pkg. 15c
Fairy Soap . . 3 cakes 10c
Octagon Laundry Soap 3 cakes 10c
Babbitt's Cleanser . 3 cans 10c
Cleansing Tissues Fastidia 3 cartons of 200 sheets 25c
Chipso FLAKES or GRANULES lge. pkg. 19c
20 Mule Team Borax 2 pkgs. 27c
P&G Soap WHITE NAPTHA 8 cakes 25c
Lifebuoy Soap . . 3 cakes 16c
Ivory Snow . . lge. pkg. 20c
Palmolive Soap . . cake 5c
Kellogg's Corn Flakes 8 oz. pkg. 6c
Corn Flakes SUNNYFIELD 8 oz. pkg. 5c
Grape-Nut Flakes 3 pkgs. 25c
Salad Oil ITALIAN COOK pt. can 18c qt. can 29c gal. can 83c
Jell-O or Royal DESSERTS ALL VARIETIES 2 pkgs. 9c
My-T-Fine Desserts 3 pkgs. 14c

"SPEAKING AS A MOTHER"
by Pearl S. Buck
in the August issue
WOMAN'S DAY only 2c

CIGARETTES

POPULAR BRANDS carton of 10 pkgs. 1.15★ | Avalon, Paul Jones Twenty Grand, Wings carton of 10 pkgs. 89¢★

★ Plus Tax where in effect.

FRUITS and VEGETABLES

ELBERTA FREESTONE
PEACHES lb. 5c 6 pound basket 29c

Luscious Elberta Freestone Peaches laden with juice. And at a price that will enable everyone to enjoy them in their favorite manner. Fresh Peach Pie, Peach Cobbler, Peach Ice Cream or with cream.

ORANGES CALIFORNIA med. size 18 for 25c small size 25 for 25c
SEEDLESS GRAPES THOMPSON'S . 2 lbs. 15c
GOLDEN BANTAM CORN FROM NEARBY FARMS ear 2c

FROM NEARBY FARMS BEETS OR CARROTS 4 bchs. 10c
FROM NEARBY FARMS TOMATOES RED-RIPE lb. 5c
LONG ISLAND . . . . . U.S. No. 2 POTATOES Grade 10 lbs. 10c
CALIFORNIA ICEBERG LETTUCE medium size head 7c
CALIFORNIA RED PLUMS 2 lbs. 15c
MARYLAND CANTALOUPE medium size 5c

TODAY'S BIGGEST SALAD DRESSING "BUY"

IMAGINE getting a salad dressing you'll *prefer* for quality and flavor—one that actually contains *more of the fine ingredients* that make a dressing truly good—at this remarkably low price!

No wonder Ann Page outsells all other brands of salad dressing and mayonnaise *combined* in A&P Stores! This high quality at low cost is possible only because Ann Page is both made and sold by A&P, thus eliminating many in-between expenses.

SPECIAL OFFER

To introduce you to Ann Page, we offer you a beautiful Beetleware salad serving fork and spoon (10⅞ in. long) for only 25¢ and the coupon attached to each jar.

25¢ QUART JAR

ANN PAGE SALAD DRESSING

FANCY DAIRY PRODUCTS!

Sharp Cheese Whole Milk American Deliciously Sharp & Tangy lb. 21c
Swiss Cheese FANCY DOMESTIC lb. 25c
Bleu Cheese IMPORTED . lb. 29c
Swiss Cheese GENUINE IMPORTED SWITZERLAND lb. 45c
Muenster Cheese FANCY lb. 15c
Butter SILVERBROOK CREAMERY—Cut from Tub lb. 25c
Butter SUNNYFIELD — SWEET or SALT Our Very Best Tub Butter lb. 27c
Roquefort CHEESE GENUINE IMPORTED lb. 45c
Edam Cheese LOAF—40% Butter Fat IMPORTED lb. 25c
Selected Eggs LARGE MIXED COLORS GRADE B doz. 22c
Eggs MIXED COLORS Every Egg Guaranteed—GRADE C doz. 19c
Baby Goudas IMPORTED 40% Butter Fat lb. 25c | Cream Cheese BORDEN'S STAR lb. 23c
Mild Cheese YOUNG AMERICAN lb. 19c | Gold'N Rich Cheese lb. 33c

Above Prices Effective Thursday — Friday — Saturday

SHOP and BUY WITH CONFIDENCE

PRICES EFFECTIVE ONLY IN A&P SELF SERVICE STORES AND SUPER MARKETS IN BROOKLYN AND LONG ISLAND

NEWS behind the NEWS IN WASHINGTON

Our Big Guns Can't Go to South America

The last-minute legislative jam in the Senate stopped the War and Navy Departments from extending our hemispherical defense network down along the coasts of South America.

Legislation was proposed to let Latin American republics buy our most modern air and coast defense weapons direct from the Army and Navy. The law already permits them to buy munitions here from private concerns. But private U. S. concerns don't manufacture heavy-caliber coast defense weapons nor the speed-firing and sighting devices for anti-aircraft operation.

Sen. Vandenberg

The only place the Latin-American countries have been able to buy such equipment in Europe. They are buying it extensively Prices are much lower than for American stuff. Only recently Brazil placed an order for $60,000,000 worth of German artillery and other war material. Germany took cotton, coffee and other raw products in exchange.

Brazil is building three destroyers from American steel, but, now that they are about finished, she can't buy U. S. guns for them although the U. S. Navy has large stocks.

The State Department doesn't like the idea of European nations, notably Germany and Italy, supplying South American nations. The department thinks it is likely to win the Latin Americanes away from the U. S. orbit.

* * *

Ammunition Must Fit

The Army and Navy have an equal interest in the thing. In case of a world war, the U. S. and the other American republics likely would be shoulder to shoulder in defense of this hemisphere. If the republics to the south were equipped with European weapons they could buy no fresh supplies of ammunition during the war. And nothing made by the U. S. would fit.

The Army and Navy hoped—and expected—that orders for anti-aircraft and coast defense weapons would come from a number of South American nations.

Although the bill permitted them also to buy battleships or smaller craft, the Navy people don't expect they will. The Navy does not look for much hemispherical defense from the Latin-American navies. One modern battleship and a few heavy cruisers could put all the South American navies to rout.

But of special importance to the Navy are bases and safe harbors along the American coast. In a war these bases would be of tremendous importance. Rio de Janeiro, for instance, would need anti-aircraft weapons to shoot away raiding bombers. It would need coast defense weapons to protect the docks and war stores for the fighting forces.

Altogether six American republics have indicated they would like U. S. weapons. Sumner Welles, Under-Secretary of State, has told House and Senate Foreign Relations Committees that all the Latin-American nations approve the legislation.

The Other Side

The House passed the bill late in the session but opposition in the Senate Foreign Relations Committee held up the legislation until the final hours of the session. By the time it was released from the committee, it was too late. Four Republican members, Borah of Idaho, Johnson of California, White of Maine, and Vandenberg of Michigan, said the bill would do far more harm than good.

Instead of promoting hemispherical good feeling, they said, it would breed discord and rivalry in Latin America. If the U. S. agreed to build a ship or two for one South American country, they said, all others would get panicky. After all, the balance of power in South America is almost as delicate as in Europe.

Further, they argued, there is a genuine dislike in America for putting the U. S. in the munitions business.

"The U. S. shouldn't be huckstering military weapons and battle ships to our neighbors to the south," said Johnson.

The Army and Navy and State Departments answered that the countries can already buy whatever they wish abroad, so discord would not result just because they bought American.

The thing will come up again next session and probably will skid through like a wet duck.

PRESTON GROVER.

Ears to the Ground

By Clifford Evans

Confidentially Speaking

Manhattan District Attorney Tom Dewey—What is there to the story that those recent killings were not the work of Lepke at all, but were inspired by labor interests? . . . **Dixie Davis**—Your mother-in-law expects you and Hope Dare to spend your honeymoon in Las Vegas, N. M. . . . **Richard Whitney**—Although the bars of Sing Sing separate you and Wall St., you will be quizzed very shortly in connection with a lawsuit being launched by a brokerage house against the N. Y. Stock Exchange . . . **Larry MacPhail**—While all your ushers show a high degree of courtesy and efficiency in performing their tasks at Ebbets Field, the lad sporting badge No. 116 is just about tops . . . **Music-Maker Abe Lyman**—I thought you'd like to know that you have a namesake conducting a Jewish Hour on Monday over Radio Station WBNX . . . **Park Commissioner Robert Moses** — Somehow it seems a shame that parking on Shore Road is prohibited. It is undoubtedly the most beautiful spot in Greater New York and the cool breezes from the Narrows afford excellent escape from the heat. But your signs and the gendarmes move you on . . . **N. Y. Giants Manager Bill Terry**—As far as Dodgers fans are concerned, your first baseman's name should be pronounced BOOnura . . . **Ella Fitzgerald**—Although your recording of "Stairway to the Stars" has been released only three days, I thought you might like to know that more than 33,000 discs already have been purchased . . . **Mayor LaGuardia**—Do you remember that Board of Education meeting in connection with the budget-trimming when you appointed your secretary, Edmund Palmieri, to sit in for that one day as a board member so that there would be a quorum? Well, don't be surprised if you get word that Commissioner of Education Frank P. Graves rules that meeting illegal on the ground that you do not have the privilege of appointing anybody for only one day—because the tenure specifically is for seven years! . . . **Adrien Rollini**—That rendition of "Night Must Fall" which your trio offered the other night at the Piccadilly Circus Bar was about the trickiest ever . . . **A. David Benjamin**—The questions you tossed at County Judge William O'Dwyer, Democratic D. A. candidate, yesterday will not be answered because of all the doubt that you will be the Republican D. A. standard-bearer on Election Day . . . **Hi-De-Ho Cab Calloway**—Cora Green, who sang with you at the Cotton Club, is in Greenwich Village at the 7th Ave. Place.

His Honor

* * *

Chatter and Such

Brownsville boxing fans are afraid that their favorite lightweight's recent escapades may get him into heaps of trouble . . . Despite larger crowds than they've had in many years, Coney Island concessionaires are so in the habit of complaining that they can't get out of the old habit of singing the blues . . . Miss Juana (Coney Island Lovely) Fern celebrated her birthday the other day. She's of voting age, she says, and nothing else . . . Roger Brock, Democratic candidate for the Municipal Court bench to replace the ailing Justice John Victor Cain, has a brother, Edmund, on the faculty of Catholic University in Washington, D. C. . . . Latest thrill: Fishing from the Manhattan Beach rocks . . . Overheard on the Hotel Half Moon Ocean Terrace—"She's a changed girl now. At one time she was interested in the social register. But now it's strictly the cash register." . . . Julius Reinlieb, Republican candidate for the Municipal Court from the Third Judicial District, already has a decision over the Democrats—in court. He served as attorney in a case against Tammany Hall and was awarded a cash verdict . . . Barney Ain, Brooklyn's nationally-famous basketball authority, writes from Buenos Aires, where he recently addressed the Hakoah Club there on intricacies of the rim-tossing sport . . . The 52d St. Tony's is staging turtle races . . . Hotel St. George Comptroller Pat Douris was a soccer star in England almost 30 years ago. He played with the Celtics in Belfast and Shelbournes in Dublin and was selected on the All-British team. He now spends his spare time golfing—in the low 80's . . . Composer Johnny Mercer thinks that his pal Bing Crosby is the country's top singer when you list them in crooner-logical order . . . Ninety men and 20 officers will represent Mitchel Field in the Army air maneuvers scheduled for Malone, N. Y. . . . Singer Dee Williams of the Bermuda Terrace was laid low with an attack of laryngitis, but now is back at the microphone.

* * *

Fusion vs. G. O. P.

The Fusion party will not go along with A. David Benjamin, Republican candidate for District Attorney. Benjamin is considered not strong enough to be in the same ring with County Judge William O'Dwyer, the Democratic candidate.

Fusion is considering drafting either Commissioner of Investigation William Herlands or Brooklyn Magistrate Matthew J. Troy. The plan is to present a candidate sufficiently impressive to cause Benjamin to withdraw from the Republican field and Magistrate Charles Solomon to resign from the American Labor party slate so that all anti-Democratic forces can band together behind one candidate—Troy or Herlands. This is a move in desperation and is being engineered with crossed fingers.

FEATURES SPORTS

BROOKLYN EAGLE

CLASSIFIED COMICS

Entered in the Brooklyn Postoffice as 2d Class Mail Matter

BROOKLYN, N. Y., THURSDAY, AUGUST 10, 1939 W

The Army Goes to 'War'

The anti-aircraft guns of the 62d Coast Artillery, Fort Totten, swing into action.

Men on horseback must haul rubber-tired guns and get them there, too. Time was when horseback soldiers were elite of Army.

The infantry moves up during a mock war. Top: Zero hour, and a line of Army pursuit planes is ready to hop off and drive the "enemy" away.

Machine gun men spurn wisps of noxious smoke, set up their guns and fire.

3,000 Brooklyn And Long Island Men to Take Part In the Maneuvers

These are days when the world is shrunken in size. Giant transatlantic air liners commute across the Atlantic and the Pacific oceans almost daily. Steamships cut down the time between Europe and America, carrying on board thousands of passengers.

The wars of Europe, century-old struggles for the balance of power, are not so far away from us as we used to think. The Atlantic is no longer the broad gulf which permitted us to say that in a military sense America has nothing to fear from land-hungry aggressors grown ravenous on the leaner meat of small nationns.

A fleet of air liners might bring to remote camps in Canada thousands of invading troops prepared for a sudden sharp blitzkrieg in American territory. Latin American countries may become the victims of European penetration and provide similar bivouacs for enemy soldiers and aviators ready for a thrust at the vital Panama Canal.

Our 'War' Significant

So it is that in these days of war scares—as Paris builds air-raid trenches and London gets a stock of gas masks for its civilians—the forthcoming military maneuvers at Plattsburg, N. Y., take on more than the usual academic importance to us.

When a Black invading force is depicted during the games as having crossed the Atlantic and pushes across from a New England shore it will not represent the fantastic imaginations of army theorists. It will represent instead a vivid possibility in this shrunken world of ours.

And in another sense thousands of families in Brooklynn and Long Island will have that possibility brought home to them.

Beginning this morning when a small advance detachment began the trek to Plattsburg, between 2,500 and 3,000 borough and Long Island residents left for the up-State camps with their National Guard units.

Off to Plattsburg

Five officers and 55 men, under the command of Capt. Elmer S. Johnson, reported at the 14th Regiment Armory, 1402 8th Ave., at 5 a.m. today. Within an hour they were on their way to Plattsburg in station wagons and trucks. It will be their job to stake out the 14th Infantry base camp and make it ready for the arrival of the regimental equipment.

At midnight Sunday the remainder of the thousand men and 65 officers of the regiment will leave for Plattsburg prepared to take part in the largest peacetime war maneuvers ever held in the United States.

Earlier the same day members of the 1st Battalion of Brooklyn, who are part of the 105th Field Artillery, will set out in trucks. From Jamaica the 1st Battalion of the 104th Field Artillery is also to leave for up-State at 7 a.m. Sunday.

The 500 men and 30 officers in the 102d Quartermaster Regiment of Brooklyn depart at 5 o'clock Sunday morning under the command of Col. Foster G. Hetzel. Both they and Squadron C of the 101st Cavalry are to make the trip by truck.

Maj. Gen. Hugh A. Drum, commander of the 2d Corps Area, will be in charge of the first American field army headed by a single officer since the Civil War.

The climax of the war games is to be reached from Aug. 23 to 25. A Regular Army force, smaller than the field army, is to oppose the latter's preponderant manpower with modern high-speed military equipment.

Among the imaginary defenders of American territory will be the completely mechanized 7th Cavalry Brigade of the Regular Army.

The maneuvers will test the effectiveness of horseless cavalry under the conditions of present-day warfare. It will be the task of the horse-mounted 101st Regiment of Brooklyn to oppose the mechanized defending unit.

The 14th Infantry, commanded by Col. William R. Jackson, will serve in the field army as part of the 1st and 2d Corps of the National Guard.

Here Is What an Army Is Made Of

During the next few weeks you'll probably read much of battalions, platoons and brigades—and of corporals, captains and colonels. So here, briefly, is the lineup of army units* and their commanders.

Unit	Composition	Commander
Squad	8 men	Corporal
Section	3 squads	Sergeant
Platoon	2 sections	Lieutenant
Company	2 platoons	Captain
Battalion	4 companies, or 392 men	Major or Lt. Colonel
Regiment	3 battalions, or 2,000 men in wartime	Colonel
Brigade, Infantry	2 regiments	Brigadier General
Brigade, Field Artillery	3 artillery regiments plus ammunition train	Brigadier General
Division, Infantry	About 20,000 men (wartime); 2 Inf. brigades, 1 F. A. brigade, 1 engineering regiment	Major General
Division, Cavalry	2 cavalry brigades, 1 regiment of horse artillery, 1 armored car squadron	Major General
Corps	2 or more infantry divisions plus artillery, engineering service and aviation	Major General
Army	2 or more corps and 2 cavalry divisions plus artillery, signal service, engineer service and aviation	Major General

*In all units larger than regiments, organization is complicated by addition of either "overhead" or "specialist" services, or both. Divisions, for instance, need such added units as quartermaster and medical regiments, and signal, military police, ordnance and tank detachments.

Slight Mistakes Department

Marietta, Ohio, Aug. 10 (AP)—Firemen from a sub-station passed firemen from central station on the Muskingum River bridge.

Their trucks were headed in opposite directions—although they were going to the same fire.

A case of "mixed call box signals," the chief said.

Depew, N. Y., Aug. 10 (AP)—A group of judges waited to review a volunteer fire department parade.

The marchers, instead of passing the reviewing stand, traveled another route.

The judges commandeered a car, pulled ahead of the marchers, and reviewed from their new location.

Buenos Aires, Aug. 10 (AP)—Maria Luisa Tarantino, 23, heartbroken, wrote a farewell note, drank the contents of a dark bottle.

At the hospital doctors put her to bed. She had taken an enormous amount of cognac.

Cobourg, Ont., Aug. 10 (AP)—An American visitor here made two gross blunders.

He drank from a bottle of whisky in public.

He stood outside the window of a police station while doing it.

Condenser

Miami, Fla., Aug. 10 (AP)—Attorney Ernest E. Roberts won his case after making the shortest opening address ever heard in Dade County court of crimes.

"He didn't do it," was all Roberts said of his client, charged with operating a slot machine.

But the court said this commendable brevity had nothing to do with the legal victory.

Roberts won dismissal of the charge because officers didn't have a search warrant.

He never got around to proving that his client "didn't do it."

Boomps! Look What Those English Have Sent Us . . .

1. Hands . . .

Hands, knees and BOOMPS-A-DAISY!
I like a bustle that bends.
Hands, knees and BOOMPS-A-DAISY!
What is a BOOMP between friends?
Hands, knees, oh! don't be lazy,
Let's make the party a wow.
Now then hands, knees and BOOMPS-A-DAISY
Turn to your partner and bow, BOW-WOW!

That's the way you dance the Boomps-a-daisy, England's newest dance mania. It gets its name from the fact that at one important stage of the routine, partners bump posteriors—oh, ever so delicately, but still a boomp—as demonstrated here by Annette Mills, who originated words and boomps, and her partner.

These pictures give you the idea—and it may pay you to take a long look, for the darn thing's already spreading to the U. S.

2. Knees . . .

3. BOOMPS-A-DAISY!

Says U. S. Troops Lack Training

Washington, Aug. 10 (AP)—Gen. George C. Marshall, the Army's new chief of staff, reported today after inspecting preparations for another "Battle of Manassas" that the troops need more training for large scale operations.

He said the Army suffers by comparison with foreign forces, and with the Navy and Air Corps, because of lack of opportunity for war games such as will be waged in Virginia and New York State next week.

At the same time Marshall noted that the smooth mobilization of nearly 20,000 National Guardsmen at Manassas, Va., for the mass maneuvers of the First Field Army, disclosed "impressive advances" in fighting efficiency in the four years since similar maneuvers were staged in the East.

VALUABLE TRAINING

"These large scale operations," he said "are the most valuable training the Army can receive and there should be more of it by all means."

The approximately 8,000,000 men under arms in a tense Europe are represented largely by reservists, who Marshall noted are called into service for weeks and months at a time.

"Our National Guardsmen have but two weeks in the field," he said. "The Navy and Air Forces do not have to rent ground and can meneuver at any time.

"If at the close of their Summer training we could match the troops at Manassas with the larger force about to be mobilized in New York, we might really learn something valuable. But taht is impossible. The guardsmen can't remain away from their civil jobes that long.

JACKSON WOULD USE 'EM UP

"Then extra care has to be taken to harden te men gradually. In their present shape, a Stonewall Jackson would use them up in a week."

About 45,000 regulars and guardsmen will be mobolized beginning Saturday in the Plattsburg, N. Y., area.

Heffernan Says—

The 1940 Battle May Yet Begin Before Year Ends

Old Lyme, Conn., Aug. 10—Senator Barkley, Administration leader in the Senate, and Speaker Rayburn of the House, declared upon the adjournment of Congress, after the smashing blows administered to the New Deal, that when the recalcitrant Democrats got home they would learn that they had been in error and that the President would ultimately win his fight for the measures, including his foreign relations measures, which the Democratic-Republican coalition had defeated.

Mr. Heffernan

A keen Washington correspondent, Mr. Arthur Krock of the New York Times, notes that something less than a third of the Democratic legislators had joined the capably managed Republican bloc at any one time.

What the two experienced Congressional leaders and the Washington correspondent fail to realize is that the dissatisfaction among the rank and file Democrats is [illegible] adequately reflected in the Congressional roll calls of the last few months. I doubt that Representative Somers can now count on one-third of the regular Democratic votes in his district, where his puppeting at the command of the White House has not been satisfactory. And the veteran dean of the Brooklyn delegation, Tom Cullen, is beginning to learn that even in his district his constituents feel that their Representative is paying too much attention to the Cohen-Corcoran crowd and too little to the South Brooklyn stock without which his power would wither and fail.

Let People Decide

The New Deal leaders are declaring that President Roosevelt and his backers will carry the fight to the people, particularly the foreign policy fight. That is precisely where it belongs. And I have a notion that the old-line Democrats will be glad to meet the President in that field. They remember Wilson's appeal for a Democratic Congress to hold up his hands in 1918 and the election in that year of a Republican House. They remember the "great and solemn referendum" of 1920 and the defeat of Wilson's chosen candidate for the Presidency.

Remembering These Things

They remember the "purge" campaign of 1938 and the victory of all but one of the President's legislative opponents. They have marked the loss of New England and powerful Middle Western States to the New Deal as indicated by the 1938 gubernatorial and Congressional elections. So they will welcome any battle in the open—for several reasons.

For one, it will put an end to the secrecy which has beclouded the President's foreign policy. It will sharpen in the public mind the issue of "foreign entanglement" and on that issue the great majority of Americans are against the Administration. They are sick of propaganda; those who formerly used it with such skill have made the dosage too great.

Those who study the psychology of revolution know that too great a swing in the direction of radicalism always has its reaction in the opposite direction. In the classic French Revolution generous ideals such as undoubtedly actuated Mr. Roosevelt in 1932 led men to disregard the fundamentals of their national constitution, but the anarchy that follows invariably causes reversion, and the institutions that were derided and overthrown are once more established in the minds and hearts of the populace.

A Battle Ahead

Robert Moses, in a Harvard lecture which I have been reading, referred to Mr. Dooley's good-humoredly cynical observation that the Supreme Court follows the election. Mr. Roosevelt has provided us with the worst Supreme Court we have known since the old partisan days of Federalism at its worst. The confusing and confused thinking manifest in the recent Free Speech decision is indicative of the effect of court packing.

Mr. Roosevelt's relief policy has given us a huge debt and a vast army of public employes and beneficiaries who feel that they have a vested right in government support.

His foreign trade agreement policy has brought our labor, in large measure peonized by WPA, into competition with the enforced and poorly paid labor of the Old World. Our imports grow in leaps and bounds, our exports decline.

That is the story which will be brought into the open if President Roosevelt takes the stump in his grand tour for the powers Congress denied him.

It will mean the beginning of the battle of 1940 in the Autumn of 1939.

Son Born in Capital To Barrys of Queens

Washington, Aug. 10 (AP)—A son, their second child, was born yesterday to Representative and Mrs. William B. Barry of St. Albans, L. I.

Won Letters at 2 Colleges

Danny Taylor, N. Y. U. shotput star, won his varsity track letters at two colleges. Taylor attended Columbia University for two years before entering N. Y. U. At Columbia he won the I. C. A. A. A. A. shotput championship. He plays the saxaphone, clarinet and trombone in his own orchestra evenings and during vacations. His hobby is saving stamps.

BROOKLYN EAGLE SPORTS

★★ BROOKLYN, N. Y., SUNDAY, AUGUST 13, 1939 SECTION D

Rast Is Good in Air

Zipp Newman, Birmingham (Ala.) News: "Alabama can send Holt Rast, the end, into the air with supreme confidence this year . . . They will have footballs No. A aviator for a target . . . Rast has licenses to fly both land and sea planes with 50 hours of solo flying to his credit."

Bimelech Takes Saratoga Special, Winning by Three Lengths

Dodgers, Yankees Win—Giants Lose

Riggs Pressed to Beat Hecht, 7-5, 10-8, 6-4 in Eastern Net Final

Briar Sharp 2d, Andy K. 3d in Spa Race

Bradley Colt Makes It End-to-End in $9,500 Triumph

By W. C. VREELAND
Brooklyn Eagle Staff Correspondent

Sarasota Springs, Aug. 12—Bounding along like a startled antelope and never fully extended, Bimelech, bay colt, two, by Black Toney—La Troienne, carrying 122 pounds, and with F. A. Smith in the saddle, carried the popular colors of Col. E. R. Bradley home in front in a hollow victory by three lengths.

Briar Sharp was second, half a length in front of Andy K., who beat Now What a length for third money. The time, 1:10 4-5, was two-fifths of a second off of the track record, which El Chico tied when he won this stake last year.

STANDOUT OF SEASON

It was the easiest triumph for a juvenile with any pretense to class this season. And it was accomplished without the slightest apparent effort on the part of Bimelech.

It was a thousand pities that Colonel Bradley was unable to see it. Illness kept him confined to his bed in Garden City, L. I., but he anticipated the victory, for all along this season he has been telling his friends that Bimelech was the fastest young colt that he has had in several years.

And it was Bimelech's high flight of speed, maintained from start to finish, that caused him to win not only the $9,000 prize but the admiration of 17,000 racing fans who came out to the Spa track this afternoon. And by that open success Bimelech dashed to the front and held his place as the claimant for the title—Prince of the T. Y. C.

It was the second start and second triumph of Bimelech this year. Like his first race it was—no contest. It was just a fast spin that first exhausted and then tied up, fairly in knots, all competition. The fact that he was opposed to Andy K. who had won the Arlington Classic, and had finished first in the United States Hotel Stakes a wek ago, but had been disqualified when he interfered with Flight Command; Flight Command, Call to Colors, Now What, the best filly of the season; Briar Sharp, Stagefright and Ballast Reef shows the quality of his opponents.

Bimelech's victory at Empire City track, plus his fast trial since, had so impressed the racing fans and the layers of odds that at post time he paraded to the post a decided favorite at 7 to 2, black down from 8 to 5. Andy K. was second in favor with Call to Colors third, Flight Command fourth and Now What fifth. Long prices we eroffered against the others.

Bimelech and Now What went away winging at the start and soon were clear of their opponents. Now What tried to keep pace with Bimelech but the son of Black Toney, the smallest colt in the field of starters of the same size and substance as El Chico last year, raced away from her.

INCREASES ADVANTAGES

Bimelech kept increasing his advantage, tied Now What up for speed by the time she hit the homestretch, and with Smith holding hmi under easy restraint, the reins taut, and the bit pressing against his tongue, won with speed in reserve. Andy K. moved up fast around the turn for home and then began—bearing out—his old trouble.

This failure to keep a straight course enabled Briar Sharp to close a big gap from sixth place and nip second money. His odds were 15 to 1 for place. Flight Command was in a contending position for half a mile and then faded away. Call to Colors failed to show the least trace of his great speed when he won his initial start.

Mrs. B. F. Whittaker's Sickle T., backed down from even money to 4 to 5, raced head and head with Masked General all the way in the struggle for the Champlain Handi-

Continued on Page 2

Gains Final

Bobby Riggs

Leading Davis Cup candidate defeated Ladislav Hecht yesterday to enter final round of Rye tournament. Riggs meets Frankie Parker today for title.

Nat'l Midget Title to Bower

Philadelphia Racer Wins 150-Mile Grind Before 55,000

Westbury, Aug. 12—Gaining the lead on the 287th lap, Morris (Babe) Bower of Philadelphia, driving a red and white No. 9 Offenhauser, raced to an 11-second triumph over Joe Garson of Great Neck, L. I., in the 150-mile National Midget auto racing championship over the half-mile Roosevelt Raceway track here today before a record midget racing crowd of 55,000 fans.

Always among the leaders, despite pit stops on the 178th lap, Bower began to catch Garson after the 275th lap was passed when the brakes on Garson's No. 19 Offenhauser began to feel the wear and tear of the grind. Garson took over the lead on the fifth lap from Ernie Gesell of Inwood and held it through the 286th lap though he had two pit stops of 31 seconds each during the 148th and 263d laps.

Twenty-nine cars went to the starting line and during the grueling grind 1 1fell by the wayside as only seven were given the checkered flag. Such favorites as Bill Schindler of Freeport, Frank Bailey of New Brunswick, Bill Holmes of New York, Len Golen of Wilmington, Karl Hattel of Los Angeles, and Bill Morrissey of Newark, failed to survive.

Gesell beat Garson, who had the pole to the first turn and held the lead until the fifth, when the Great Neck ace moved into first place as Gesell went to the pit. Garson, driving steadily, built up a two-lap advantage before he went to the pits for the first time and was still one lap ahead of Mel Hansen of Los Angeles, when he returned to the track. This one-lap lead was held until Bower made his bid.

The triumph was worth $1,350 to Bower as Garson took down $1,000 for second. Perry Grimm of Los Angeles, in third, won $775, while Sam Hanks, another West Coast star, gained $550 for finishng fourth. Paulie Russo of Chicago, in sixth, won $330 while Hansen won $440. Paul Swedberg of oLs Angeles, won $220 for finishing 23 laps behind the winner. Brad Stilwagen of Rockville Centre was eighth as the field was flaged down after Swedberg took the checker.

The order of finish:

1. Morris Bower, Philadelphia— 3:02:41.1
2. Joe Garson, Great Neck— 3:02:53.1
3. Perry Grimm, Los Angeles— 3:04:02
4. Sam Hanks, Los Angeles— 3:05.47
5. Mel Hansen, Los Angeles— 3:07:50
6. Paul Russo, Chicago— 3:15:54
7. Paul Swedberg, Los Angeles— 3:18:10

Did not finish: Ernie Gesell, Brad Stillwagen, Bill Schindler, Frankie Bailey, Len Galen, Mike Josephs, Jim Forte, Honey Purck, Harold Hoffbauer, Henry Renard, Joseph Dorf, Jerry Walters, Bill Holmes, Karl Hattel, Cletus O'Rourke, Buster Walke, Len Duncan, John Lalli, Mickey Lowak, Bill Baker, Bill Morrissey, Tony Bonadoiss.

Czech Refugee Bows After Brilliant Duel

Marble-Fabyan Duo Retains Eastern Doubles Laurels

By HAROLD PARROTT
Brooklyn Eagle Staff Correspondent

Rye, N. Y., Aug. 12—Bobby Riggs, the unpredictable anchor man of our Davis Cup team, whipped out all his artillery today to blast Ladislav Hecht, the charging Czechoslovakian, off the Westchester Country Club's center grass court in a truly amazing exhibition.

Hecht, a fugitive Jewish Czech, was at no time fleeing from Riggs today as he fought every inch of the way to finally yield at 7—5, 10—8, 6—4.

As if to meet Hecht's bristling challenge, Riggs was on the ball every minute as he turned back the foreigner's heavily topped cross-court forehand shots, deft volleys and sliced backhands that bit the chalk lines, to move into the finals of the Eastern grass court championships.

Riggs meets Frankie Parker in the final tomorrow at 2 o'clock, and if he wins he will retire his second handsome silver bowl in as many weeks.

The women's Eastern singles final, between world champion Alice Marble and her understudy and doubles partner, Sarah Palfrey Fabyan, will follow the men's singles.

The men's doubles final will wind up the championships.

HECHT KEEPS TRYING

Hecht is a beautiful player, and he soon showed why he lasted into the round of eight at Wimbledon last year. The 25-year-old top-ranked Czech gave his first indication that he would not yield easily when he trailed at 2—5 in the first set but kept trying, broke Riggs back again and twice held his own service to deuce the set at 5—games all.

At this point Hecht's heavily-cut service was bothering Riggs. There were many protracted rallies, and only Bobby's uncanny ability to anticipate the next shot and keep the ball in play enabled him to finally break the Czech's delivery in the twelfth game.

The second set was a brilliant duel in which Riggs showed none of his characteristic tendencies to dawdle. Bobby went all out when he trailed at 3—5, put together three games of perfect tennis, won them all for a 6—5 lead, and then saw Hecht hold his own serve to deuce the match at 6—all.

STAVES OFF RIGGS

Hecht pulled many brilliant shots out of his racquet to stave Riggs off twice at set point in the 14th game, when Bobby made a great bid to break the Czech's service.

Riggs was fighting every inch of the way at this point, for Hecht led at 40—15 in that 14th game, and yet Riggs had two set points before he lost it, and the count went to 7—all.

The break came at 8—9 with Hecht serving. The Czech again led 4—15, but Riggs attacked, and his crisp volleys finally maneuvered the Czech out of position for the crusher.

What impressed critics most in the second set was the manner in which Riggs, after losing his serve in the fifth game and trailing at 2—3, 2—4, 3—4, 3—5, attacked Hecht just as the Czech was about to serve himself out for a 6—4 win. The foreigner's double fault at 15—all in this game was a vital break, and when Riggs won the game, four points to two, the set was deuced at 4—all. Riggs was volleying with a master's touch and covering court like an antelope coping with Hecht's raking drives.

Some of the spice was gone from Hecht's game in the final set, but still Riggs showed no tendency to loaf. Games went to 2—all, then to 3—2 for Riggs. Then Bobby broke Hecht for a 4—2 lead, but the Czech came right back to break Riggs and hold his own delivery for 4—all. Riggs then finished off the match in grand style, winning seven of the

Continued on Page 2

One Stride Too Slow and Tuck's Out

Tuck Stainback of Dodgers misses a hit by a stride on roller to Majeski and Buddy Hassett makes putout at first in ninth inning yesterday as Dodgers beat Bees at Ebbets Field, 10 to 3 (Eagle Photo)

Flock Downs Bees, 10-3, on 13-Hit Attack

Rout Posedel to Tie Giants for Fourth—Pressnell Prevails

By TOMMY HOLMES

The Dodgers industriously whacked the ball to every portion of the Flatbush landscape yesterday afternoon as they bowled over Casey tSengel's Boston Bees by the score of 10 to 3 to rise above the .500 mark once

Boston	ab	r	h	o	a	Dodgers	ab	r	h	o	a
Garms,rf	5	1	1	1	0	Hudson,2b	5	1	1	4	0
Simmons,lf	2	0	0	1	0	Lavagetto,3b	3	1	0	1	2
Outlaw,lf	2	0	1	0	0	Coscarart,3b	1	0	0	0	3
Hassett,1b	4	0	0	7	0	Walker,cf	4	1	2	3	0
Cuccin'llo,2b	3	0	0	6	4	Stainback,cf	1	1	0	0	0
Warstler,2b	0	1	0	0	0	Parks,rf	3	1	1	1	0
West,cf	4	1	2	3	0	Camilli,1b	3	2	2	9	0
Majeski,3b	4	0	1	3	3	Phelps,c	2	1	2	3	0
Lopez,c	1	0	0	2	1	Hayworth,c	1	0	0	1	0
Masi,c	3	0	1	1	0	Koy,lf	3	1	2	5	0
Sisti,ss	4	0	0	0	5	Durocher,ss	4	0	1	0	3
Posedel,p	1	0	0	0	0	Pressnell,p	4	1	2	0	1
Shoffner,p	1	0	0	0	0						
aSullivan	1	0	0	0	0						
Totals	35	3	6	24	13	Totals	34	10	13	27	9

a Batted for Shoffner in 9th.

Boston	1	0	0	0	0	0	0	2	0	—3
Dodgers	0	1	6	0	0	2	1	0	x	—10

Errors—Durocher, Lavagetto, Sisti. Runs batted in—Walker (2), Phelps (2), Koy (2), Parks, Camilli (2), Pressnell, West (2). Two-base hits — Garms, Hudson, Koy. Home runs—Camilli, Phelps, West. Stolen base—Camilli. Sacrifice—Phelps. Double plays—Majeski, Cuccinello and Hassett, 2. Left on bases—Boston, 7; Dodgers, 5. Bases on balls—Off Pressnell, 2; off Posedel, 2; off Shofner, 2. Struck out—By Pressnell, 3. Hits—Of Posedel, 7 in 2 2-3 innings off Shoffner, 6 in 5 1-3. Wild pitch—Pressnell. Losing pitcher—Posedel. Umpires — Sears, Campbell and Moron. Time—2:10. Attendance—5,987.

more. Victory lifted the Dodgers over Pittsburgh's Pirates and boosted them into a fourth-place tie with the Giants.

Thirteen Brooklyn hits off Barnacle Bill Posedel and Milburn Shoffner included Dolph Camilli's 18th home run of the season and Babe Phelps' fifth. Tot Pressnell's path to his sixth victory of the season was a complacent stroll along Easy St. after the third inning in which a sustained Brooklyn bombardment netted sx runs.

It was an easy victory for the knuckle ball specialist who, like the Dodgers, rose above the .500 mark, Pressnell having been charged with five defeats. He allowed only six hits with Max West's home run with one aboard in the eighth being responsible for two-thirds of the Boston runs.

The romp left the Dodgers highly optimistic about continuing to defy nature and swarm all over the Bees today. Said Bees are doing very badly. This was their fifth straight defeat and Stengel's nonplussed New Englanders have won only three of their last 17 games.

CAMILLI HITS 18TH

The Bees obtained a short-lived lead in the first inning which Debs Garms opened with a double down the left field line. Garms took third after Koy acught a Simmons fly in left, scored when Pressnell unloaded a wild pitch.

Camilli's home run which just cleared the right field screen tied the score in the second and in the third the Brooklyn bombardment really began.

Pressnell singled and Sudson drove him to third with a double. Lavagetto walked and the bases walked and the bases were filed. Dixie Walker smashed home two runs with a line single to right. Art Parks singled to center, scoring Lavagetto. Camilli walked and the bases were filled again. Max West leaped against the center field wall to catch a long fly from Babe Phelps, Walker scoring from third. Camilli stole second and then Ernie Koy doubled against the top of the left field wall, and Parks and Camilli scored to complete the six-run inning.

Koy's drive finished Posedel who was relieved by the left-handed Shoffner. That noble southpaw did all right until the sixth when Phelps hammered his long home run over

Continued on Page 3

Yankees Crush Athletics, 18-4

Dahlgren Clouts Two Home Runs to Lead 17-Hit Winning Drive

Special to the Brooklyn Eagle

Philadelphia, Aug. 12—The world champion Yankees served notice on the American League in general and the Boston Red Sox in particular

Yankees	ab	r	h	o	a	Philadelphia	ab	r	h	o	a
Crosetti,ss	1	1	1	0	1	Siebert,1b	5	1	2	12	0
Rolfe,3b	6	2	3	1	3	Moses,rf	4	1	0	2	0
Keller,rf	5	3	3	5	0	Johnson,cf	3	0	1	2	0
DiMaggio,cf	4	1	1	5	0	Hayes,c	4	0	1	4	2
Dickey,c	4	1	0	5	0	Brucker,c	1	0	1	1	0
Rosar,c	0	0	0	0	0	Tipton,lf	4	1	1	4	0
Selkirk,lf	6	2	2	3	0	G'tenb'g,2b	2	1	1	0	1
Gordon,2b	5	3	2	1	3	Ambler,2b	2	0	1	0	0
Dahlg'n,1b	6	4	4	7	0	Newsome,ss	3	0	1	0	2
Hil'brand,p	2	1	1	0	0	Lod'g'ni,3b	3	0	0	2	3
Sundra,p	3	0	0	0	0	Joyce,p	0	0	0	0	0
						Dean,p	1	0	0	0	0
						Potter,p	1	0	0	0	0
						xCollins	1	0	0	0	0
						Nelson,p	1	0	1	0	0
Totals	42	18	17	27	7	Totals	35	4	10	27	8

xBatted for Potter in sixth.

Yankees	0	6	1	2	3	1	5	0	0	—18
Philadelphia	0	2	2	0	0	0	0	0	0	— 4

Errors—Newsome, Tipton, Lodigiani, Ambler. Runs batted in—Dahlgren 6, Hildebrand, Rolfe, Keller 2, DiMaggio, Gordon 2, Selkirk 2, Crosetti, Gantenbeing 2, Lodigiani, Siebert. Two-base hits—Gordon, Tipton, Newsome, Rolfe 2. Three-base hit—Keller. Home runs—Gordon, Siebert, Dahlgren 2. Sacrifices—Crosetti 2, Lodigiani, Gantenbeing, Sundra. Double play—Siebert (unassisted). Left on bases—Yankees, 9; Philadelphia, 12. Bases on balls—Off Hildebrand 2, off Sundra 4, off Joyce 2, off Potter 3, off Nelson 2. Struck out—By Hildebrand 2, by Sundra 2, by Dean 1, by Potter 1, by Nelson 1. Hits—Off Hildebrand 5 in 2 2-3 innings; off Sundra, 5 in 6 1-3; off Joyce, 7 in 1 1-3; off Dean, 1 in 1 2-3; off Potter, 6 in 3; off Nelson, 3 in 3. Hit by pitcher—By Potter (Crosetti); by Nelson (DiMaggio). Passed ball—Hayes. Winning pitcher — Sundra. Losing pitcher—Joyce. Umpires—Quinn, McGowan and Grieve. Time—2:35. Attendance—4,000.

that all the talk about a Yankee crackup was merely an idle dream.

Smashing out 17 assorted hits that were good for 18 runs the Yankee Bombers crushed the Philadelphia Athletics for the second successive day by an 18—4 margin here today. Joe Gordon hit his 18th home run of the season and Babe Dahlgren connected for two, his 10th and 11th of the campaign.

SUNDRA GETS DECISION

Oral Hildebrand, who started for the Yanks, was batted from the hill in the third and Steve Sundra went the rest of the distance to become the winning hurler.

After a double play had stopped

Continued on Page 3

Lloyd Defeats Riddell In Nat'l Links Final

By RALPH TROST
Staff Correspondent of the Brooklyn Eagle

Southampton, Aug. 12—A good wind and a good golf course just about beat two good golfers into the ground here this afternoon when Larry Lloyd and John Riddell met in the final of the National Links invitation tournament. Riddell was hit hardest — and he, co-medalist and high prices favorite— lost, 4 and 3 in a final that was strictly tired-businessman golf.

Riddell, who missed very little in his semi-finals in which he smothered his clubmate, Celestin Durand, 4 and 3, just couldn't beat down. And, in the end, even the silky putting touch disappeared, Riddell three-putting the greens of the last five played. The blond-thatched Lloyd, who had played so many good shots in his semi-finals in which he always held the upper hand over young Gamble Wodward (the score was 2 and 1), wasn't much better. Larry really missed only one shot up to the ninth, but at that he was out in 44, seven over par.

The start of the finale was rather tough. Riddell hooked his drive on the first and had to play his second from the knobs. He took three to get to the green—and then he three-putted, giving Lloyd, who was well on in two, a win with a bogie five. The second hole saw Riddell hook another drive and then leave his second in the bunker.

The Garden City player, however, got a life when Lloyd, after plugging the "bell hole" and the match was squared when Lloyd, after plugging straight down the middle of the hog's-back path 4th, three-putted again. Riddell actually went out in front on the 8th where Larry was short with an iron second after deliberately hooking his drive into the 11th fairway to escape the right hand bunker. But then John kicked the situation back into a Mexican standoff at the 9th where he pushed an iron shot into a bunker and there was thoroughly beached.

On the 13th, John hit too strongly with his iron but the ball hung on the back edge. He took three to get down and lost that hole.

What seemed a certain win he turned into a loss on the cape 14th. Larry cut his drive into a trap. From there he overclubbed and went clear across the green. Riddell was neatly on in two, 20 feet from the hole. But then Lloyd played a grand explosion from the soft sand and holed a 12-footer. Riddell putted 30 inches short—and missed that. Instead of getting back to a two down status, John became four down—and one more hole, a half in 4s, put an end to the struggle.

Willie Turnesa, Holt Finalists

U. S. Amateur Titlist Beats Sheehan in Eastern Semi-Final

Syracuse, N. Y., Aug. 12 (AP)—Syracuse's own Bill Holt will meet Willie Turnesa of Elmsford, national amateur champion, in tomorrow's final at the Syrace Yacht and Country Club course to determine the Eastern amateur golf titleholder for 1939.

Turnesa uncovered some of the most brilliant shots ever seen in central New York today as he humbled burly Tommy Sheehan of Notre Dame, 9 and 5.

Eddie Sams of Fort Erie was eliminated, 5 and 4, in the other semi-final as Holt showed his local fans some of the golf which carried him into the semi-final of the recent British amateur.

Nearly 1,500 persons were on hand to watch the closing holes of the two matches this afternoon. Turnesa was 1 under par with 70 in the morning round, finish 3 up, but he really went to town after lunch as he went out in 31 for the course record for the nine holes and walked in from the 10th green, which he shared with a par 3.

The cards:

HOLT VS. SAMS—MORNING
Holt, out— 3 4 4 3 5 4 3 4 3—33
Sams, out— 5 3 3 3 4 4 4 3 4—35
Holt, in— 2 4 4 4 5 4 3 4 4—34—67
Sams, in— 2 5 4 5 6 4 4 4 3—36—71

HOLT VS. SAMS—AFTERNOON
Holt, out— 4 4 4 3 5 3 4 5 4—36
Sams, out— 4 5 4 4 5 3 3 5 5—39
Holt, in— 3 5 4 5 5
Sams, in— 3 6 3 4 x

TURNESA VS. SHEEHAN—MORNING
Sheehan, out— 4 4 4 4 4 4 4 5 4—37
Turnesa, out — 4 4 4 3 5 4 4 5 3—36
Sheehan, in— 3 6 3 5 5 3 3 4 4—36—73
Turnesa, in — 3 5 3 5 5 4 2 4 3—34—70

TURNESA VS. SHEEHAN—AFTERNOON
Sheehan, out— 4 5 4 4 6 4 4 4 4—39
Turnesa, out— 3 5 4 3 4 2 4 3 3—31
Sheehan, in— 3
Turnesa, in — 3

Phillies Top Terrymen, 4-3

Five Double Plays Aid Mulcahy—May, Suhr, Danning Hit Homers

The last-place Phillies made it two in a row over the Giants by turning back the Terrymen, 4—3, yesterday at the Polo Grounds. The Giants outhit the Phils, nine to six,

Philadelphia	ab	r	h	o	a	Giants	ab	r	h	o	a
Scharein,ss	3	1	0	4	5	Moore,lf	3	0	1	4	0
D. Hafey,rf	4	0	0	4	0	Jurges,ss	3	0	2	0	4
Marty,cf	3	0	0	2	0	Demaree,cf	4	0	0	3	0
Ar'vich,lf	4	0	2	1	0	Ripple,rf	4	0	0	4	0
Suhr,1b	3	2	2	11	2	Danning,c	4	2	3	3	1
May,3b	4	1	1	1	2	Bonura,1b	4	1	1	9	0
Hughes,2b	3	0	0	4	4	T. Hafey,3b	3	0	0	1	1
Millies,c	4	0	1	0	0	Kamp'is,2b	3	0	2	3	2
Mulcahy,p	4	0	0	0	0	Salvo,p	0	0	0	0	0
						xScalzi	1	0	0	0	0
						Lynn,p	0	0	0	0	0
						xxOtt	0	0	0	0	0
						Brown,p	0	0	0	0	0
						xxxMcC'hy	1	0	0	0	0
						Cofmman,p	0	0	0	0	1
Totals	32	4	6	27	13	Totals	30	3	9	27	9

xBatted for Salvo in third.
xxBatted for Lynn in fifth.
xxxBatted for Brown in eighth.

Philadelphia	0	2	1	1	0	0	0	0	0	—4
New York	0	0	0	0	2	0	0	0	1	—3

Errors—Scharein. Runs batted in—May 2, Arnovich, Suhr, Bonura, Ott, Danning. Two-base hits—Danning, Bonura. Home runs—May, Suhr, Danning. Stolen base—Scharein. Sacrifice—Ott. Double plays—Suhr, Scharein and Suhr; May and Suhr; May, Hughes and Suhr; Hughes, Scharein and Suhr; Suhr (unassisted). Left on bases—New York 3; Philadelphia 5. Bases on balls—Off Salvo 1; off Mulcahy 1; off Brown 2; off Coffman 1. Struck out—By Salvo 1; by Lynn 1; by Brown 1. Hits—Off Salvo, 4 in 3 innings; off Lynn, 1 in 2; off Brown, 1 in 3; off Coffman, 0 in 1. Hit by pitcher—By Mulcahy (Jurges). Losing pitcher—Salvo. Umpires—Ballanfant, Dunn and Klem. Time—1:45. Attendance—6,998.

but the cellar dwellers pulled five double plays, which enabled the staggering Hugh Mulcahy to go the route and win his seventh decision of the season as compared with 14 losses.

The Giants used four pitchers but it was Manuel Salvo, the starting hurler, who was touched for three of the four Philly runs and was the losing pitcher. Japhet Lynn came in to pitch in the fourth and was greeted by Gus Suhr's home run, the only run that he allowed. Walter Brown and Dick Coffman finished the game without being scored on.

Three of the four Philly runs were the result of home runs. Merrill May clouted his first of the season in the second inning with Gus Suhr

Continued on Page 3

36 Horses Go Under Hammer For $64,250 at Saratoga Sale

Saratoga Springs, N. Y., Aug. 12 (AP)—Thirty-six head of yearlings, broodmares and weanlings went under the hammer for $64,250, an average of $1,810, at the Saratoga auction sale of horses today.

Fiske Waring of New York paid top price when he purchased a bay colt by Blue Larkspur out of Batter Cake, consigned by Charles W. Williams, for $4,600. William Woodward, owner of the Belair Stud, went to $4,200 for a dark bay colt by Granville, one of his great horses, out of Knights Star, which was sent to the auction by Kenneth N. Gilpin's Kentmere Farm of Virginia.

Colonel Wall of Washington, D. C., and Drea Asbury of Cincinnati also went up to $4,200 to get horses they desired. Wall took the broodmare, Teddy Squaw, and Her Suckling by by the imported stallion, Teddy, out of the ring, and Asbury bid in Teddy Star, a broodmare. Both were consigned by the Kentmere Farm.

Six Augusta Players Injured in Crash

Savannah, Ga., Aug. 12 (AP)—Six players of the Augusta Baseball Club of the Sally League were slightly injured today 13 miles south of Savannah when their motorcar skidded on wet pavement and crashed into a tree.

Those in the car, driving to Jacksonville for a series opening Sunday, were First Baseman Kenny Ouzts, Third Baseman Johnny Russian, Outfielder Bill Johnson, Pitchers Bill Jeffcoat and Charlie Biggs and Right Fielder Rebel. All were treated at a Savannah hospital, then dismissed.

Major League Records

National League

YESTERDAY'S RESULTS

Brooklyn, 10; Boston, 3.
Philadelphia, 4; New York, 3.
Chicago, 6; Pittsburgh, 4.
Cincinnati, 8; St. Louis, 4.

STANDING OF THE CLUBS

	W.	L.	Pct.		W.	L.	Pct.
Cincin.	66	36	.647	New York	51	50	.505
St. Louis	56	43	.566	Pittsb'gh	49	49	.500
Chicago	57	49	.538	Boston	43	58	.426
Brooklyn	51	50	.505	Philaa.	30	69	.303

GAMES TODAY

Boston at Brooklyn (2).
Philadelphia at New York (2).
Pittsburgh at Chicago.
Cincinnati at St. Louis (2).

GAMES TOMORROW

Pittsburgh at Cincinnati.
Chicago at St. Louis.

American League

YESTERDAY'S RESULTS

New York, 18; Philadelphia, 4.
Boston, 9; Washington, 5.
St. Louis, 17; Detroit, 3.
Cleveland, 3; Chicago, 2.

STANDING OF THE CLUBS

	W.	L.	Pct.		W.	L.	Pct.
New York	72	32	.692	Detroit	55	50	.524
Boston	65	37	.637	Washing'n	47	59	.443
Clevel'd	54	47	.535	Phil'phia	36	69	.343
Chicago	56	49	.533	St. Louis	30	72	.294

GAMES TODAY

New York at Philadelphia (2).
Washington at Boston (2).
Chicago at Cleveland (2).
St. Louis at Detroit.

GAMES TOMORROW

St. Louis at Chicago.
Cleveland at Detroit (2).

International League

YESTERDAY'S RESULTS

Rochester, 5; Jersey City, 3.
Montreal, 7; Syracuse, 2.

STANDING OF THE CLUBS

	W.	L.	Pct.		W.	L.	Pct.
Jersey C.	67	50	.573	Newark	62	60	.508
Rochester	66	53	.555	Baltimore	53	64	.453
Syracuse	68	55	.553	Montreal	48	69	.410
Buffalo	65	54	.546	Toronto	47	71	.398

GAMES TODAY

Jersey City at Rochester (2).
Newark at Montreal.
Toronto at Syracuse.
Baltimore at Buffalo.

GAMES TOMORROW

Newark at Montreal.
Jersey City at Buffalo.
Baltimore at Toronto.
Syracuse at Rochester.

Sarazen's 210 Leads Shute By Stroke in Dapper Dan Open

Pittsburgh, Aug. 12 (AP)—Stocky little Gene Sarazen battered his way today into the final 18-hole round of the 10,000 72-hole Dapper Dan Open Golf tournament with a three-day total of 210, one stroke ahead of Denny Shute, Huntington, W. Va., former Ryder Cup star.

The 37-year-old East Brookfield, Coon., veteran labored around the Wildwood Country Club course under a broiling sun in a three over par 73, seven strokes above his course record-breaking 66 of yesterday.

Shute, the day's best bet to catch Sarazen, started out nicely and finished even par for the first nine, but ran into trouble and took a 72 for a 54-hole total of 211.

A high cross wind baffled a field of the nation's best golfers and scores skyrocketed from the sub-par rounds of yesterday. Ralph Guldahl, Madison, N. J., and Vic Ghezzi,

Continued on Page 2

Danzig Circled by Polish Troops, Berlin Claims

Weather Forecast
By U. S. Weather Bureau
Partly Cloudy and Warm Tonight and Tomorrow.

BROOKLYN EAGLE
DAILY AND SUNDAY

Wall Street Closing
Racing Extra
★ ★ ★ ★ ★ ★

98th YEAR—No. 234 | Entered in the Brooklyn Postoffice as 2d Class Mail Matter | BROOKLYN, N. Y., THURSDAY, AUGUST 24, 1939 | THREE CENTS

WAR IMMINENT

Chamberlain Vows United Fight After Nazi Defi

F. D. R. Appeals to Italy

President Asks King to Propose Pacific Solution

Message Asserts 'Absolute Right' Of Poland to Keep Its Independence, Says Hostilities Can Be Averted

Washington, Aug. 24 (AP)—President Roosevelt renewed today his efforts to avert a European war by appealing to King Victor Emmanuel of Italy "to formulate proposals for a pacific solution of the present crisis."

The president sent word to the king that if the Italian Government could do so. "You are assured of the earnest sympathy of the United States.

"Again a crisis in world affairs makes clear the responsibility of heads of nations for the fate of their own people and indeed of humanity itself. It is because of traditional accord between Italy and the United States and the ties of consanguinity between millions of our citizens that I feel that I can address Your Majesty in behalf of the maintenance of world peace."

ENVOY DELIVERS PLEA

Ambassador William Phillips on arrangements made by Mussolini and Foreign Minister Count Ciano, had an audience with King Victor Emmanuel and presented the president's message orally.

The text of the communication then was made public here by Secretary Hull as the President himself hurried back to Washington for conferences with his advisers on foreign affairs.

The president told the king:

"It is my belief and that of the American peopl^ that Your Majesty and Your Majesty's government can greatly influence the averting of an outbreak of war.

SECOND APPEAL TO ITALY

"Any general war would cause to suffer all nations whether belligerent or neutral, whether victors or vanquished, and would clearly bring de-

Continued on Page 2

Pope Stresses 'Grave Hour' in World Appeal

Justice Can't Be Had Through Violence, He Says in Broadcast

Castel Gandolfo, Italy, Aug. 24 (U.P.)—Pope Pius XII tonight broadcast an appeal for peace for the world "in its grave hour."

"It is a grave hour in the world," the Pope said. "We feel we must talk of peace.

"Jesus wants all men to be brothers."

The Pope said that "we make a new and warm appeal to the governments and the rulers and the people" for peace.

He deplored the use of force as an instrument for solving international problems. Justice cannot be obtained through violence, the Pontiff continued.

"Men must try to reason out their problems," he said.

"Wars of the future will only be causes for bloodshed and destruction of our fatherlands. We pray that the rulers may make their utmost efforts for peace."

The Pope declared that "the whole world wants peace."

"The hearts of mothers and fathers are beating with ours," he said. "The world wants bread and work, not steel and war."

He called upon all men to intensify their prayers for a better future," and concluded by imparting the Apostolic Benediction to the world in Latin.

His voice was strong and clear and he spoke rapidly. The benediction was not in the original text of the speech.

Narragansett Results

FIRST RACE—Three-year-olds and up; three-quarter mile.

Cania (Packer)	8.30	5.60	3.40
Gentle Knight (Taylor)	—	15.30	8.40
Peon (Krovitz)	—	—	3.50

Time, 1:12 1-5. Cavour, Little Mike, Miss Whim, Apprehend, War Grand, Pomplit, The Trout, Stavka, Martin Boy also ran. (Off time, 2:23½.)

Saratoga Results

FIRST RACE—Old River, first; Second Helping, second; Camomar, third.

Saratoga Scratches

First Race—Hide, Port Wales, La Scala, Burnt Bridges, Kens Pop.
Fifth Race—Southern Gal.
Sixth Race—Lieber, Stepahead, Suncrax, Uvalde, Taunton, Nipponese, Night Serge.
Weather, clear; track, fast.

In the Eagle Today

	Page		Page
Books	24	Jimmy Wood	16
Brain Teaser	24	Let's Go to Fair	14
Brooklyn Fact	12	Line on Liners	22
Cassel's Cartoon	12	Obituaries	13
Clifford Evans	15	Pollock	15
Comics	25	Radio	24
Crossword	24	Real Estate	23
Dr. Brady	25	Resorts	10
Edgar Guest	12	Robert Quillen	25
Editorial	12	Serial	24
Events Tonight	22	Shipping	22
Financial	19-20	Shops	8
Garden Corner	24	Sports	16-18
Grin and Bear It	12	Society	6
Heffernan	15	Theaters	11
Helen Worth	6	Washington	15
Hy Gardner	10	Women	6-9

Lavagetto in Lineup Despite Bite by Dog

Although his left hand was badly gashed by the teeth of an angry dog, Harry (Cookie) Lavagetto, Dodger third baseman, will be in the lineup tonight when his team plays the pace-setting Cincinnati Reds at Ebbets Field, it was announced today by Manager Leo Durocher.

The animal, a small fox terrier, was ordered tied up pending an examination by officials of the Department of Health to determine if it is infected with rabies.

To celebrate yesterday's victory a group of about 50 fans gave a dinner last night in honor of Cookie and four other Dodger players, including Manager Leo Durocher, at the Withers Restaurant, 32 Withers St. The dog wandered into the dining room and Lavagetto reached down to pet it but the animal snapped, digging its sharp teeth into his hand.

EXTRA

Danzig Encircled By Poles, Nazis Claim

Berlin, Aug. 24 (AP)—The official German news bureau DNB in a special dispatch from Danzig asserted tonight that the Free City had been encircled by a mixed Polish division in the south and west, and that the danger of an immediate coup d'etat was very great.

The DNB dispatch said:

"By this concentration of a war-equipped Polish division at the immediate frontier of Danzig territory the danger of an imminent coup d'etat has come exceedingly close."

Latest Bulletins

Berlin, Aug. 24 (AP)—The Foreign Office summoned foreign correspondents to a special press conference set for 6:30 p.m. No intimation was given of the reason.

Berlin, Aug. 24 (AP)—Reichsfuehrer Hitler unexpectedly arrived at Berlin's Tempelhof airdrome tonight from his mountain retreat near Berchtesgaden.

Warsaw, Aug. 24 (U.P.)—Poland, rapidly completing "very far-reaching" military preparations, tonight protested to Germany two alleged violations of the Polish frontier by armed bands of Germans.

Warsaw, Aug. 24 (AP)—Well-informed circles reported today that a German patrol crossed the Polish border this morning and occupied an estate about three-quarters of a mile within Polish territory near Ilawa.

Brussels, Aug. 24 (AP)—Long lines of German military trucks were reported today by border observers to be moving within sight of the Belgian town of Eupen, former German territory.

Koenigsberg, Germany, Aug. 24 (AP)—Foreign Minister Von Ribbentrop expressed the conviction that Adolf Hitler would master the present European crisis as he has all others, as he returned today from Moscow. Germany, he asserted, is unbeatable.

Danzig Senate Votes Forster, Nazi Radical, as New Ruler

Poland Shuts Border—Tense City Waits Decree Speeding Shift to Germany

Danzig, Aug. 24 (AP)—The Danzig Senate in solemn session voted today to make Albert Rorster, Nazi party gauleiter of Danzig, the Free City's chief of state.

This means that Arthur Greiser, who has hitherto been head of the little state as its Senate president, ceases to be chief executive.

Danzig's customs officers reported to Free State officials that Poland had closed the border between Poland and Danzig at 11 a.m. (6 a.m. Brooklyn time).

Danzig's officials earlier had shut off telephone connections with Gdynia. This was said to be a reprisal against Polish action in refusing to accept calls for Gdynia.

It was announced officially that the German Navy's 13,200-ton cadet training ship Schleswig Holstein would visit the Free City, anchoring tomorrow in Danzig Harbor.

A report by DNB, official German news agency, that the British Consul General had left Danzig proved untrue.

[In Berlin the Propaganda Minister announced that the cruiser Koenigsberg will "visit" Danzig within a few days, the United Press reported.]

The elevation of Forster gives

Continued on Page 2

Story on Page 5

U. S. Advises Tourists to Quit Europe

Envoys Warn Against Delay—F. D. Lands, Speeds to Capital

London, Aug. 24 (AP)—United States Ambassador Joseph P. Kennedy today issued a statement advising all American tourists in the British Isles to sail for home at once.

American officials estimated that there are now between 3,000 and 4,000 American tourists in England, Scotland and Wales.

Simultaneously the United States Embassies in Paris and Berlin officially and unequivocally advised Americans to leave immediately.

The Paris Embassy declared that "in view of the situation prevailing in Europe," American citizens are urged to make arrangements to leave France.

At the Berlin Embassy the following statement was issued:

"The American Embassy upon inquiry has been informing and is continuing to inform Americans that it is desirable to leave Germany."

Kennedy's statement said that "in a day or two" it might not be possible for them to get sailings for New York and warned them that if they stayed they might be subjected to "inconvenience, possibly danger."

SHIPS ARE AVAILABLE

Nice, France, Aug. 24 (AP)—American Consular authorities at Nice, working with United States Navy, have completed preliminary preparations for removing all United States citizens from the zone between the Italian frontier and Nice in case of emergency.

MORGENTHAU DEPARTS

Oslo, Norway, Aug. 24 (AP)—Henry Morgenthau Jr., United States Sec-

Continued on Page 2

Hope for Rain Fades; Heat to Stay a While

This morning, at least, the Weather Man promised refreshing showers throughout a day that could not exactly be called cool.

But by the afternoon forecast, even that damp bit of hope had disappeared, and the outlook now is "partly cloudy and warm tonight and tomorrow."

The temperature at 1 a.m. was 82, with humidity down to 48. Yesterday's humidity averaged 45 percent, and indications were that today's maximum temperature would remain at 85 degrees, as compared with yesterday's 88.

'Free Hand' Demanded By Hitler in Answer To Briton's Message

How Europe Is Swinging Toward War

LONDON—Prime Minister Chamberlain tells Commons Britain faces "imminent peril of war." Reiterates pledge to Poland; asks for dictatorial powers.

WASHINGTON—President Roosevelt addresses peace plea to King of Italy. U. S. Embassies in London, Paris and Berlin urge Americans to leave immediately.

BERLIN—German troops poised for march on Poland. Ultimatum to Warsaw today believed likely. Prompt reply to be demanded.

DANZIG—Albert Forster, Danzig Nazi leader, proclaimed dictator of Free State. Decree affecting status of Free City is drafted.

PARIS—Additional reserves called. Total at arms now 2,150,000.

MOSCOW—German Foreign Minister Von Ribbentrop leaves by plane for Berchtesgaden where Hitler awaits his report on signing of treaty with Russia.

ROME—Allied with Germany and ready to fight alongside Axis partner.

WARSAW—Poland ready to fight; protests invasion of German patrols.

Italy Will Support Reich Says Gayda

Rome, Aug. 24 (U.P.)—Italy will be on the side of Germany in any war over Danzig because Italy's interests are involved, Virginio Gayda, authoritative and quasi-official Fascist editor, said in the Giornale D'Italia today.

Placing responsibility for war or peace on Britain and France, Gayda, said that Italy's interests were involved in the dispute over Danzig because the Free City was part of the "greater European problem."

Rome, Aug. 24 (AP)—Premier Mussolini discussed military matters today with the chiefs of the Italian army, navy, air force and Fascist militia.

Stocks Stage Rally After Early Drop

The stock market staged a smart comeback this afternoon after prices had suffered declines extending to 3 points in morning trading. Trading volume was heavy at the start, 240,000 shares changing hands the first hour. At 2 o'clock transactions totaled 1,120,000 shares.

Precipitate declines in the Chicago and Winnipeg wheat markets induced the stock market to rally sharply shortly before noon, and the tape was a minute behind due to the heavy trade. Prices moved up and in some issues early losses were replaced by slight gains.

Says Any Nation That Blocks Path Will Be to Blame if War Results —Parliament Speeds Dictator Rule

London, Aug. 24 (AP)—Prime Minister Chamberlain declared in the House of Commons today that Adolf Hitler had demanded a free hand for Germany in eastern Europe and had told Britain that any country which interfered was to blame for an ensuing war.

"God knows I have done all that is possible in efforts for peace," said the Prime Minister after he had declared Britain's obligations to Poland "remain unaffected" by what he called an imminent peril of war.

Speaking against the background of a rapidly arming Europe, the Prime Minister asked Parliament to enact an emergency powers bill, giving the government virtually dictatorial authority to deal with any emergency.

Text of Chamberlain's Speech on Page 21.

The cheers that rose from all sides of the House at the close of his 33-minute speech indicated quick acceptance of his demand.

"As we think, so shall we act unitedly," Chamberlain said solemnly and the House rose and cheered.

The Prime Minister said Hitler's claim to a free hand i neastern Europe without interference came as a reply to a message delivered to the German Chancellor yesterday through the British Ambassador in Berlin, Sir Nevile Henderson. This message, Chamberlain said, restated Britain's own position.

ISSUE OF WAR RESTS WITH REICH

"The German Chancellor's reply includes what amounts to a restatement of the German thesis that eastern Europe is a sphere in which Germany ought to have a free hand," said the Prime Minister.

He went on to say that "we still hope reason and sanity will find a way out." But he said, "The issue of peace or war does not rest with us."

"If all efforts to find a peaceful solution—and God knows I have done my best—fail and we find ourselves forced to embark upon a struggle bound to be fraught with suffer-

Continued on Page 2

Believe German Ultimatum Will Give Poles Few Hours

Berlin, Aug. 24 (AP)—German troops stood ready today to back up Hitler's demands upon Poland and the British Government notified its consuls to advise British nationals in Germany to leave.

Simultaneously the United States Embassy for the first time began to tell inquiring citizens "unofficially" that it would be best for them also to depart.

With the Nazis seeking the establishment of Germany's pre-war esatern boundaries, one high Foreign Office official declared it was "very necessary" for Polish Foreign Minister Jozef Beck to go to Hitler quick- in his Bavarian mountain retreat.

Envisaging a possible reenactment by Beck of the trip to Hitler's chalet last March by President Emil Hacha of Czecho-Slovakia, the Foreign Office official said:

ZERO HOUR SEEN NEAR

"The Poles know exactly what we want of them."

The inference was that Poland had been appraised fully of Germany's demands, but that perhaps no zero hour yet had been set for her reply.

This zero hour was expected tonight after Foreign Minister Joachim von Ribbentrop, following the swift conclusion of th eRussian-German non-aggression pact, returned from Moscow and made his report.

There was a feeling that the best guess was that there would be a limited ultimatum to Poland of only a few hours.

Poland's only hope to avoid war then would be to send her Foreign Minister to Berchtesgaden to capitulate.

"Don't think for one moment that

Continued on Page 2

Appearing with this issue is the

Brooklyn Eagle's Annual Educational Directory

a 20-page tabloid supplement devoted to news of the educational world.

Weather Forecast
By U. S. Weather Bureau
Partly Cloudy, Moderate Temperatures Tonight and Tomorrow.

BROOKLYN EAGLE
DAILY AND SUNDAY

Wall Street Closing Racing Extra
★ ★ ★ ★ ★ ★

98th YEAR—No. 241 | Entered in the Brooklyn Postoffice as 2d Class Mail Matter | BROOKLYN, N. Y., THURSDAY, AUGUST 31, 1939 | THREE CENTS

BRITAIN MOBILIZES ALL ARMED FORCES

Orders Evacuation Of 3,000,000 From London, Key Cities

London, Aug. 31 (UP)—Great Britain announced tonight that she had decided on complete mobilization of her vast naval, regular army and air power against the threat of a new European war. The order calls up the remainder of the regular army reserve and the supplementary reserve.

The government's portentous decision—announced in an offici communique at Prime Minister Neville Chamberlain's residence at 10 Downing St.—increased the strain of Europe's war of nerves to an almost unbearable pitch.

Already 12,000,000 men were under arms and massed on the continental frontiers, the great British war fleet was strung out in battle array cross the North Sea and orders had been given to evacuate 3,000,000 helpless persons, children, women and invalids from England's cities to the countryside starting tomorrow.

The text of today's communique said:

"In continuation of measures already adopted, it has been decided on complete naval mobilization, and to call up the remainder of the regular armv reserve and supplementary reserve.

"A further number of the Royal Air Force volunteer reserve will also be called up. Officers and men should await further instructions which will be made public immediately by each of the three service departments."

The Dominion high commissioners met in the Dominions Office for a conference with Sir Thomas Inskip, Dominion Secretary.

Air raid precautions controllers throughout the country were instructed to take up their duties tonight.

Local authorities everywhere were ordered to set up air raid emergency committees. Twenty-four-hour shifts were detailed to construct public air raid shelters and covered trenches were ordered opened.

Zero Hour May Come Tomorrow

In Berlin, in Paris, in Rome and in Warsaw, similar and almost complete preparations for war had been made as the deadlock between Germany and Poland tightened until it seemed to some observers that it might soon surge beyond hope of further diplomatic maneuvers.

The possibility of further exchanges between Great Britain and Adolf Hitler continued open, but in the German capital high Nazi sources said that the positions of both sides seemed to have been made clear and that the Nazi Fuehrer might decide that another diplomatic message was unnecessary or futile.

Whether that meant that action would be Hitler's next

Continued on Page 2

London Stock Exchange to Close

London, Aug. 31 (AP)—The London Stock Exchange will be closed tomorrow, shortening the trading week by one day.

Transportation facilities will be so occupied with the evacuation of children from London tomorrow that normal Exchange dealings would be rendered extremely difficult.

Washington, Aug. 31 (U.P.)—A high official said today he believed the Federal Government should not do any financing during September because of the existing European crisis.

The Crisis in Brief

LONDON—Great Britain orders mobilization of land, sea and air forces; 3,000,000 children, women and invalids to be evacuated from cities tomorrow; Stock Exchange closed. Page 1.

BERLIN—Nazis report 'pause' in crisis negotiations but that negotiations are not broken off. It was uncertain if the latest British memorandum would be answered. Page 1.

VATICAN CITY—Pope Pius again appeals to big powers to maintain peace. Page 1.

PARIS—French Cabinet meets in urgent session with President Lebrun. Page 1.

WARSAW—Government spokesman says German secret police have occupied Danzig railway station and hoisted the Swastika flag over it. Page 3

BRATISLAVA—German troops, estimated at 400,000, mass against Polish frontier. Page 3.

BRESLAU—Correspondent finds eastern German roads choked with troops streaming toward Poland. Page 3.

MOSCOW—War Commissar announces new army laws which it was believed might add 500,000 men to the Soviet army as Soviet Parliament votes to consider ratification of Russian-German pact. Page 3.

City Signs Pact For 151-Million IRT Purchase

Board of Estimate Ratifies Agreement With 1 Dissenting Vote

With one dissenting vote, the Board of Estimate at a special meeting today ratified the agreement for acquiring the Interborough Rapid Transit system and Manhattan Railway properties for $151,248,187, and the Mayor and Controller executed the agreement for the city.

Borough President Harvey of Queens voted against ratification. Borough President Lyons of the Bronx, voting for the plan, took a crack at "those transit geniuses," Samuel Seabury and A. A. Berle Jr., who previously represented the Board of Estimate on transit matters, and called their plan for unification "one of the most infamous ever attempted to be put over on the city." The present plan saves the taxpayers $147,000,000, Lyons said.

SEEKS TO CONDEMN ELS

The Board of Estimate, at the same time, formally applied to the Transit Commission for permission to condemn the 2d and 9th Ave. elevated lines in Manhattan. Cost of condemnation of the elevated structures could be met by special assessment bonds amounting to $11,000,000. This would bring the total price to be paid for the B. M. T. and I. R. T. systems within the $315,000,000 in securities which the city is permitted to issue for acquisition of lines exempt from its debt limit.

In answer to a reply put by Herbert L. Carpenter, Brooklyn civic worker, Controller Joseph D. McGoldrick explained that the $11,000,000 in bonds would not apply to the condemnation of the Fulton St. elevated line.

MAYOR SOUNDS WARNING

Mayor LaGuardia signed the contract buying the I. R. T. in City Hall at 1 p.m. and at the same time issued a warning to junior security stockholders that if they attempted to fight the sale in court "the city would drive the hardest and cruelest bargain it possibly could."

"You'll just be wiped out if you fight this," the Mayor said.

The entire matter must go to the United States District Court for approval since the I. R. T. is in the hands of a receiver.

Representatives of various civic groups in the city attended the meeting and voiced approval of the acquisition. One dissenter was Sol G. Solomon of Woodmere, L. I., an

Continued on Page 21

Dodger-Cub Twin Bill Off Until Tomorrow

Rain again forced the postponement of both the Dodger-Cubs and the Giants-Cards double-headers scheduled at Ebbets Field and the Polo Grounds today.

Because of an open date on the calendar, the Dodgers and the Cubs will play the double-header tomorrow.

The Giants' and Cards' twin bill will be played off in St. Louis when the Giants stop off there on their final swing through the West.

Narragansett Desults

FIRST RACE—Three-year-olds and upward; three-quarters of a mile.

Yankee Skipper (Sniedr)	33.50	12.90	5.90
Cania (Packer	—	4.70	2.80
Bilboquet (Firedman)	—	—	2.70

Time, 1:16. Jessie O., Gentle Knight, The Lake, Flag Unfurled, Brilliant Rock, Fair Sonja, Dorothy Owsley, The Jurist, More Poise also ran. (Off time, 2:18½.

SECOND RACE—Cycle, first; Goster, second; Crestonian, third.

In the Eagle Today

	Page		Page
Books	24	Hy Gardner	26
Brain Teaser	24	Jimmy Wood	16
Brooklyn Fact	12	Let's Go to Fair	21
Cassel's Cartoon	12	Line on Liners	22
Clifford Evans	15	Obituaries	13
Comics	25	Radio	24
Crossword	24	Real Estate	23
Dr. Brady	25	Robert Quillen	25
Edgar Guest	12	Serial	24
Editorial	12	Shipping	22
Events Tonight	22	Shops	8
Financial	19-21	Sports	16-18
Garden Corner	24	Society	10
Grin and Bear It	12	Theaters	11
Heffernan	15	Washington	15
Helen Worth	10	Women	8-10

Ill, but Glad to Be Back

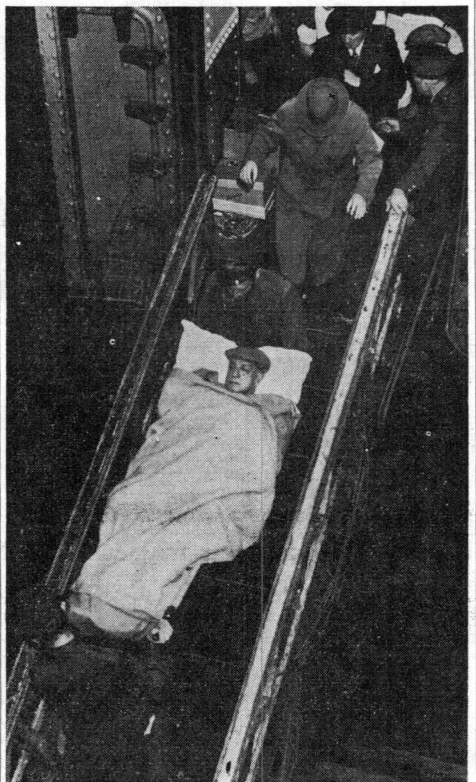

Charles M. Schwab, 77-year-old chairman of the Bethlehem Steel Corporation, arrived back in the United States today aboard the liner Washington. The elderly captain of American industry suffered a slight heart attack three weeks ago and was recuperating in a London hotel when the tense European situation forced him home ahead of time. (Wide World photo.)

F. D's Mother Arrives Home From Europe

John Roosevelt, Wife and C. M. Schwab Also Among 984 Aboard the Washington

The United States liner Washington returned today with 984 passengers, including Mrs. James Roosevelt, 83-year-old mother of the President, who cut short a week her vacation in war-threatened Europe.

Up bright and early at 7:30 a.m., when the ship docked, the elder Mrs. Roosevelt said she was having a good time in Paris visiting her sister, Mrs. Dora Delano Forbes, but decided to come home on the advice of American Ambassador William Bullitt in Paris. Her grandson, John Roosevelt, and his wife, the former Anne Lindsay Clarke, were returning on the Washington and Mrs. Roosevelt said she moved right in their suite.

HOPES SISTER 'HUSTLES'

"Now, I hope my sister hustles and gets over here," Mrs. Roosevelt stated.

Waiting at the pier were Mrs. Eleanor Roosevelt and her aunt, Mrs. David Gray. They rushed up

Continued on Page 3

Warmer Weather But Cloudy Skies On Tap Tomorrow

Rain continued to fall today from leaden skies, with accompanying chilly, below-normal temperatures. All this raw, damp weather, according to the Weather Bureau, is really the outer edge of the first northeaster of the season, a mild one, which has been blowing up the Atlantic seaboard from the Virginia Capes to the New England coast, and for which coastal storm warnings have been up for the past three days.

The storm, which delayed New England shipping yesterday, is moving out to sea, according to the Weather Bureau.

The rain here will continue until tonight, the Weather Bureau said, followed by cloudy skies tonight and tomorrow and somewhat warmer temperatures tomorrow.

Although the mercury was expected to go to 72 today, it was only 62 at 1 p.m., nine degrees below the normal average for the date. Yesterday's temperatures averaged 65, six below normal for the date.

Up-State farmers reported serious drought conditions still existing with wells and watercourses at very low levels, whereas New Jersey farmers reported that too much moisture was delaying the harvesting of late fruit crops and may affect the late peach crop.

Would Buy Danzig, Present It to Hitler

New Roads, La., Aug. 31 (U.P.)—Allen Ramsey Wurtele, retired naval officer, proposed a means of settling the Polish-German dispute without bloodshed today. He would purchase Danzig and the Polish Corridor by popular subscription from Poland and present them to Germany. He offered to contribute $5,000.

"In America, this Polish land—which is poor and capable of growing a little hay and some Irish potatoes—would be worth about $10 an acre," he said. "It is estimated that the total land could be bought for not much in excess of $70,000,000.

"This may sound screwball, but it isn't half as screwball as a general European war."

Pope Issues 11th-Hour Plea To Save Peace

Appeal to Powers Comes With Order For World Prayers

Vatican City, Aug. 31 (U.P.)—Pope Pius XII issued an urgent appeal to the Powers today to halt their war preparations and preserve peace.

Simultaneously the Pope issued from his Summer residence at Castel Gandolfo an order that Catholic churches throughout the world offer special prayers for peace.

The Pope transmitted his appeal to the envoys of all the Powers accredited to the Vatican, through Cardinal Maglione, Papal Secretary of State.

It was delivered by Cardinal Maglione when he summoned to his office the ambassadors and ministers attached to the Holy See.

FIVE ENVOYS RESPOND

Among those who responded were the German, French, Italian and Polish ambassadors and the British minister.

The new Belgian ambassador to the Holy See arrived today ahead of time and will present his credentials immediately because of the gravity of the situation.

A copy of the Pope's peace message was delivered to William Phillips, United States Ambassador, by Mons. Borgongini-Duca, papal nuncio to Italy, because the United States is not officially represented at the Holy See.

It was stated that the message was presented informatively, as a copy of the Pope's general appeal to governments throughout the world, and not as a special message to President Roosevelt.

Phillips immediately transmitted the message to President Roosevelt through the State Department.

An international pilgrimage of 20,000 persons representing the Catholic workers and youth organizations of 20 countries, which was scheduled to be held in Vatican City on Sept. 2, has been indefinitely postponed.

2 NEW PEACE MOVES

Paris, Aug. 31 (U.P.)—Official dispatches from Rome and Berlin today convinced France that both the Italian Government and the Vatican are making new moves for peace.

The Pope was reported to have cabled President Roosevelt asking

Continued on Page 21

Norma Shearer, Sailing Home, Lauds French

Paris, Aug. 31 (U.P.)—Norma Shearer, American motion picture star, sails for home on the liner Manhattan today, having cut short her third visit to Paris. She said Parisians were so full of cheerfulness and good humor that she found it hard to believe war was imminent.

"I'm leaving," she said, "convinced that everyone wants peace, and I'm hoping and praying that war will be avoided. It may seem cowardly for me to go, but if we Americans can't help we owe it to the French to relieve them of the responsibility of having us here.

"One by one the various classes have been called to the colors, and I've seen them going off joyously, the men full of confidence, the women smiling, devoted and brave. Never has a nation seemed so splendid or so inspiring."

Next Move Up to London, Berlin Says

Nazi Cards on Table—'Pause' in Crises Negotiations Seen

Berlin, Aug. 31 (AP)—Authorized Germans said tonight that a "pause" had come about in crisis negotiations with Great Britain but that negotiations "are not broken off."

Announcement of full mobilization of the British fleet, coming on top of Poland's extension of mobilization yesterday, these persons indicated, were at least partly responsible for the "pause."

'CARDS ON TABLE'

As a result, it was uncertain whether British questions, put to Adolf Hitler by the British Government in a memorandum handed to the Fuehrer last night, would be answered.

This morning it was said that the questions would be answered. Foreign Minister Joachim von Ribbentrop, however, it was then said, had given Sir Nevile Henderson, the British Ambassador, an oral indication of what the German reply would be.

Asked whether any new moves were to be expected as a result of the "pause," this afternoon's informants said:

"We have laid our cards on the table. Whether the British will come forward with any more suggestions we do not know."

These quarters said that British fleet mobilization had "increased the tension" in that the general situation late today was "very unclear."

The Italian Ambassador, Bernardo Attolico, called at the Foreign Office this afternoon after twice having seen Sir Nevile. It was said the Italian Government was "in constant contact with Berlin."

RUSSIAN 'TRUMP CARD'

Adolf Hitler was reported to be ready to play a Russian trump card in an effort to convince the Poles they should come to Berlin to negotiate.

The Russian Councillor of Embassy called at the Foreign Office while hints were spread that unless Poland bows to pressure being put upon her Hitler intends to announce some degree of military cooperation with the Soviets.

Should Hitler win Stalin over to actively assisting Germany militarily, Poland would find herself in a highly precarious position.

Further mobilization orders in Poland yesterday were interpreted by the Berlin Government as the

Continued on Page 21

Married Men Barred From Joining Army

Washington, Aug. 31 (U.P.) — The Army issued a blanket regulation today forbidding married men or those who have other dependents to enlist.

Officials said the order, issued by Maj. Gen. E. S. Adams, Adjutant General, tightened previous regulations. Previously, married men could enlist only if they had approval of post commanders or if they had sufficient income to support dependents.

Original enlistments are now barred if a man is married, has children, a mother or other dependents. An enlisted man now may not marry if he is below the rank of sergeant. Formerly he could marry if given special permission.

$17,000,000 Liner America Launched by Mrs. Roosevelt

Newport News, Aug. 31 (AP)—The passenger liner America, a major unit in the Maritime Commission's program to rehabilitate the American merchant marine, rode down the ways to the James River today, christened by Mrs. Franklin D. Roosevelt in what the President described as "one of the most important events to take place in the world this year."

The First Lady, before smashing a bottle of American champagne against the stately prow of the $17,000,000 vessel, read a letter from the President to Rear Admiral Emory S. Land, chairman of the Maritime Commission. Mr. Roosevelt said the launching "signifies an early return of the merchant fleet of the United States to a dominant position on the oceans of the world."

Referring to the Maritime Commission's building program, the President said:

"The tense state of the international situation makes it particularly desirable that we have a merchant fleet capable of carrying our commerce if and when foreign ships are withdrawn, and, should the unfortunate necessity arise, of serving as the necessary supply force for naval vessels. You and I know, from our work during the war, the disabilities of a navy which lacks an adequate merchant fleet. With all itis enormous potential combat power, such a navy is tied to its land bases."

Daladier Calls Cabinet Session

Emergency Meeting Follows Conference With British Envoy

Paris, Aug. 31 (AP)—The French cabinet met in urgent session tonight with President Lebrun, only three hours after Premier Daladier had conferred with British Ambassador Sir Eric Phipps.

As the Premier entered the meeting at the Presidential Palace he announced that the session "is not called to consider general mobilization." He gave no indication however, of the reason he did call it.

The French Government drove swiftly ahead with its preparations for war, if it must come, by decreeing that Paris henceforth must be blacked out.

Meanwhile the diplomatic lines for peace negotiations were kept open, awaiting the next move by Germany's Fuehrer.

Acros the Rhine border, however, French sources said, the German army was already on a wartime footing.

Through the Paris police an order was issued putting into execution

Continued on Page 21

London Cut Off From Continent

London, Aug. 31 (AP)—All telegraphic and telephonic communications between London and the European Continent were interrupted tonight.

At the same time many normal lines of communication between London and the United States were halted.

(This message came to the United States in duplicate by wireless and one cable company).

The London office of the Associated Press was informed at 7:09 p.m. (2:09 p.m., Brooklyn time), that the British censorship would begin within a few minutes, cutting in on the wires carrying its dispatches.

What was happening to communications between various European countries was not known immediately. (At least one channel between Paris and New York remained open.)

ONLY GOVERNMENT CALLS

Only government calls and calls for the Bank of England are being permitted to go through by telephone, the International Telegraph and Telephone Company stated in Manhattan today.

Calls to continental Europe were

Continued on Page 2

Bees Sell Simmons To Cincinnati Club

Boston, Aug. 31 (AP)—President Bob Quinn of the Boston National League Baseball Club announced today veteran Outfielder Al Simmons had been sold to the Cincinnati Reds for a "nominal sum."

Weather Forecast

[illegible]

BROOKLYN EAGLE

DAILY AND SUNDAY

Wall Street Closing
Racing Extra
★ ★ ★ ★ ★ ★

[illegible] FRIDAY, SEPTEMBER 1, [illegible] THREE CENTS

QUIT WAR ON POLAND OR FACE GT. BRITAIN, LONDON WARNS REICH

NAZI BOMBERS RAID MANY CITIES; F. D. VOWS TO KEEP AMERICA OUT

Throngs Flee English Cities

London, Sept. 1 (AP)—(Passed through British censorship)—Prime Minister Chamberlain declared tonight that unless Germany would suspend aggressive action and withdraw her forces from Poland, Britain would unhesitatingly fulfill her obligations to Poland.

Chamberlain made the statement at an extraordinary session of Parliament. If the reply to this last British warning is not favorable, he said, the British Ambassador to Berlin, Sir Nevile Henderson, will be instructed to ask for his passport.

Meanwhile the British Press Association said it understood Parliament would reconvene at 10 a.m. (5 a.m. Brooklyn time) tomorrow.

The Prime Minister said a bill would be introduced making the ages for military service between 18 and 41 years.

He began addressing the Commons at 6:04 p.m. (1:04 p.m. Brooklyn time) and finished at 6:30 p.m. (1:30 p.m.).

The Prime Minister said he did not suggest that the German reply "is likely to be otherwise" than unfavorable. News of the German air raid on Warsaw came as he spoke.

Chamberlain declared:

PLACES FULL BLAME ON HITLER

"We shall stand at the bar of history knowing that the responsibility for this terrible catastrophe rests on the shoulders of one man—the German Chancellor!"

The Prime Minister's statement came a few

Continued on Page 8

Spare Cities, President Begs Europe

Appeals Against Bombing Civilians Wilson Quits Post

Washington, Sept. 1 (U.P.)—President Roosevelt today pledged his Administration to make every effort to keep the United States out of war.

He also announced resignation of Hugh R. Wilson as Ambassador to Germany, and appealed to the four major European Powers to avoid the "inhuman barbarism" of bombing civilians and unfortified cities. He let it be known that summoning of a special session of Congress and invocation of the Neutrality Act are not an immediate prospect.

[Meanwhile Adolf Hitler sent President Roosevelt his reply to the President's appeal for peace last week, the Associated Press stated. The German Embassy forwarded it to the State Department this morning and the department was expected to make it public shortly.

[A well-informed person described the reply as being "very positive."]

Asked at a press conference whether he cared to say anything about the chance of this country staying out of war, Mr. Roosevelt replied:

"Only this: That I not only sin-

Continued on Page 8

Axis Broken, Hitler Hints To Reichstag

Pledges Friendship To Soviet and Vows He Will Win or Die

Berlin, Sept. 1 (AP)—Germany and Poland are waging an undeclared war. At noon today an official announcement said the Nazi air force had gone into action over Polish territory and that the German army was "counter-attacking" all along the German-Polish frontier.

German land forces, the announcement said, were determined to break all resistance.

The official statement that war was on came shortly after Fuehrer Hitler left the Reichstag amid cheers for his declaration that he would enforce a Polish settlement or die fighting in the army gray uniform he wore.

The commanders-in-chief of Germany's army, navy and air force—Col. Gen. Walther von Brauchitsch, Admiral Erich Raeder and Field Marshal Hermann Wilhelm Goering—issued "orders of the day" pledging loyalty to Hitler and the Reich.

The army and navy orders were

Continued on Page 8

Allied Envoys Ready to Leave Berlin, Chamberlain Warns

Nazi German troops invaded Poland today by land, sea and air, and brought on the immediate threat of war by Great Britain and France.

While German columns were moving into three Polish sectors, Prime Minister Chamberlain told a cheering Parliament in London this afternoon that the responsibility for bringing on a world catastrophe was "on one man"—Hitler—and that Britain would stand by her promise to Poland unless Nazi military aggression ceased and German forces were withdrawn at once.

A formal British declaration of war was thus withheld, but only temporarily. France, meanwhile, ordered a full mobilization and called its Parliament into session tomorrow, with every indication that that Power, too, would take war measures against the ancient Teutonic foe.

Chamberlain presently, the United Press reported, announced that both Great Britain and France had instructed their Ambassadors in Berlin to ask for their passports unless German armies withdrew from Polish soil.

REICHSFUEHRER STRIKES SWIFT BLOW

Adolf Hitler struck swiftly without an ultimatum or a declaration of war. His warplanes simply flew into Poland and bombed at least 17 cities and towns, some reports including Warsaw, Polish capital. His columns marched across the Polish border on three sectors, from East Prussia, Pomerania and Silesia. President Ignacy Moscicki proclaimed a state of war—technically different from a declaration of war but in its effects the same.

While Poland's allies thus gave every indi-

Continued on Page 9

Chamberlain Speech Puts Blame on Hitler

London, Sept. 1 (By Radio-A.P.)—The text of Prime Minister Chamberlain's speech:

I do not propose to say many words tonight. The time has come when action rather than speech is required. Eighteen months ago I prayed that the responsibility might not fall on me to ask this country to accept the awful arbitrament of war. I fear that I am not able to avoid that responsibility. The responsibility for this terrible catastrophe lies on the shoulders of one man.

At any rate, I could not wish for conditions on which such a burden would fall upon me clearer than they are today as to where I stand (cheering). The German Chancellor has not hesitated to plunge the world into misery in order to serve his own senseless ambitions. No man can say that the government could have done more to try and keep open the way for honorable and equitable settlement of the dispute

Continued on Page 9

Italy's Cabinet Bars Military Aid to Hitler

Rome, Sept. 1 (AP)—The Italian Cabinet announced today that Italy would refrain from starting any military operations. The Ministers had met with Premier Mussolini at 3:50 p.m. (10:50 a.m. Brooklyn time) to decide Italy's course of action as an ally of Germany.

They met knowing of French mobilization and that Hitler had declared Italy's aid would not be solicited in the German hostilities with Poland for the time being.

Before the Cabinet met at Viminale Palace, where Il Duce has an office as Minister of Interior, British Ambassador Sir Percy Loraine had sought an interview with Italian Foreign Minister Count Galeazzo Ciano to learn Italy's intentions.

MESSAGE FROM HITLER

[The United Press revealed that Adolf Hitler had telegraphed Mussolini that he does not at this time require Italian military aid.

[The text of Hitler's telegram follows:

["I thank you most cordially for the diplomatic and political help you recently gave Germany in behalf of her rights. I am persuaded

Continued on Page 8

11,000 Americans Wait For Passage Home

More than 7,000 American tourists in Europe sailed for home yesterday, and another 2,000 will sail today, Lynde Selden, executive vice president of the American Express Company, estimated today on the basis of cables received from abroad.

An estimated 11,000 are abroad, he said, and these are "being accorded every consideration by the various foreign governments and railway officials, and delays, where unavoidable, are being taken with patience and good nature."

Latest Bulletins

Paris, Sept. 1 (AP)—The French Government was reported tonight in circles close to the Foreign Ministry to be considering an ultimatum to Germany, demanding an immediate halt in hostilities with Poland and withdrawal of German troops from Polish territory.

Washington, Sept. 1 (AP)—Secretary Hull announced today Great Britain and France had agreed to refrain from bombing civilian populations in response to an appeal from President Roosevelt.

Berlin, Sept. 1 (U.P.)—Air raid sirens shrieked throughout Berlin at 7 o'clock tonight.

Washington, Sept. 1 (AP)—The United States received, as a neutral, today its first warning from the German Government not to violate neutrality in the air over Danzig and Poland.

Berlin, Sept. 1 (U.P.)—Polish artillery bombarded the Beuthen Railway Station, in the Polish Corridor, at 11:30 a.m. today, the DNB, official German news agency, announced.

London, Sept. 1 (U.P.)—An Admiralty spokesman said today that the Admiralty knew nothing of reports that a British warship had intercepted the German liner Bremen which left New York Wednesday. The spokesman said the reported seizure appeared unlikely inasmuch as Great Britain was not now at war.

On the War Front

LONDON—Chamberlain addressing Parliament issues last warning to Hitler. (Page 1.)

BERLIN—German troops cross Polish border; Nazi planes bomb Warsaw and other cities in Poland. (Page 1.)

PARIS—France orders general mobilization; decrees state of siege; House of Deputies and Senate to meet tomorrow. (Page 2.)

ROME—Italy decides against military action at this time. (Page 1.)

WASHINGTON—President Roosevelt pledges his utmost to keep U. S. out of war. Hitler replies to F. R.'s note. (Page 1.)

DANZIG—Chief of State Albert Forster turns Free City back to Germany for third time in history. (Page 7.)

BROOKLYN—Germans in Ridgewood take news of war calmly (Page 7); Greenpoint Polish colony ready to fight for motherland (Page 2); subway crowds discuss the crisis on way to work. (Page 5.)

LONDON—Children evacuated from London as precaution against air raids. (Page 4.)

ARMED STRENGTH—Figures on comparative military, naval and air forces of European powers. (Page 8.)

THE CRISIS—Chronological table of events leading to war. [illegible]

Full Text of Hitler's Speech to Reichstag

Berlin, Sept. 1 (U.P.)—The official text of Adolf Hitler's speech to the Reichstag today follows:

Delegates and men of the German Reichstag:

For months long we have been suffering under the torturing problem which the Versailles treaty, that is the dictate of Versailles, once left us, a problem which in development and distortion has become unbearable for us.

Danzig was and is a German city. The Corridor was and is German. All these territories owe their cultural development only to the German people. Without the German people, the lowest barbarism would reign in all these eastern districts.

Danzig was separated from us. The Corridor with her German districts in the east was annexed by Poland and above all the German minority living there was mistreated in the most fearful fashion.

About 1,000,000 people of German blood were forced to leave their homeland in 1919 and 1920. As al-

Continued on Page 8

In the Eagle Today

[illegible]

Narragansett Results

FIRST RACE—Three-year-olds and up; three-quarter mile.
[illegible]
SECOND RACE—[illegible]

BROOKLYN EAGLE
AUTOMOBILE Show NUMBER
BROOKLYN, N. Y., SUNDAY, OCTOBER 15, 1939
SECTION G

NATIONAL AUTO SHOW OPENS TODAY

New Cars Bigger 'n' Better And the Prices Are Down

If you really don't want to buy a 1940 model automobile it would be well to keep away from the automobile shows or the retail salesrooms—because the motor car industry this year has turned out some of the finest looking cars in its history.

Sleek isn't the word for them. They all look bigger and more massive than ever; even the lowest priced units look like the $2,000 car of a few years back.

Gone almost entirely is the "shark nosed" appearances of last year. The chrome-plated grilles are retained; many of them have been lowered, but the hood has been straightened up. Most of the new models have the alligator type of hood cover.

Carrying batteries under the hood cover, most of the new units have a locked-down cover which can be released only by operating a lever at the side of the instrument panel. Finger-tip gear shifting under the steering wheel is virtually universal.

There are few mechanical departures in the coming year's models, most of the designers' efforts having been to make the vehicles roomier and more attractive to the eye. The new "sealed beam" lights will be found on practically every 1940 model; more accessories have been made "standard."

The most drastic mechanical change in the coming models is Oldsmobile's automatic gear shift, eliminating both the standard type of clutch and the clutch pedal. This feature, however, is to be optional equipment, at a small additional cost.

All units are priced lower than comparable types of last year. Where prices have not actually been cut, additional equipment has been made standard. The price reductions have been made on the expectation of increased sales. Leading observers of the industry are looking for the production and distribution of approximately 4,000,000 units in the 1940 model season.

Models Abound in Beauty, Feature Improvements

Beauty of line and detail of appointments are revealed in practically every new model on display today at the National Automobile Show.

There are minor improvements — many of them—also some major ones that will mean greatly increased buyer satisfaction.

Several makes have curved rear windowglass to help carry out the rounded contours at the rear and avoid a flat area there.

A large proportion of doors are equipped with concealed hinges, thus eliminating projections around door. Some makes have door handles partly recessed into body moldings which also are in chrome, so that the handles are less prominent, although they project enough to provide a convenient grip. Most exterior handles are curved inward so as not to catch in clothing, this being one of the many features promoting safety. Doors on many new models are provided with rotary latches and close securely without slamming. Some makes have doors for rear compartments equipped with safety catches to prevent them from being opened by children when the car is in motion — another safety precaution.

SOME HAVE MORE POWER

Engines, having attained truly remarkable refinement and dependability in past years, include fewer changes than in almost any recent years. Some have slightly increased power and the latter are ample in all cases for rapid acceleration, good hill climbing and as high a top speed as driving safety warrants.

Nearly all new models are equipped with dual tail lamps and the latter are usually flush with fenders or nearly so. Some are at higher levels than formerly to reduce the chance of breakage. Rear lights on a number are fitted with transparent plastic lenses which are tougher than glass and developed to withstand exposure to the weather without appreciable deterioration. Quite a few of the 1940 crop have gravel guards or plates of steel in body color bridging the space between the rear bumper and the body

Continued on Page 3

Design by Robert H. Blend
Pratt Institute

40th Exhibit to Run Week At Grand Central Palace

Today at noon, the culmination of four decades of progress in automotive engineering—four decades of revolutionizing all industry and changing the habits of people—will be dramatized at the National Automobile Show.

This 40th anniversary of the big event will occupy four great floors of Grand Central Palace from today until next Sunday inclusive. Opening day hours are noon to 11 p.m. Beginning Monday, the hours are 10:30 a.m. to 11 p.m., and next Sunday, the closing day, doors will open at noon and close at 7 p.m.

The dates scheduled — three weeks earlier than in recent years—include two Sundays, the opening and closing days. This is an innovation. A major point in the selection of this period is the contribution that it will make to the stabilization of employment in the automobile industry and its network of supplying industries. Also, there are numerous conventions in New York this week. It is expected that many out-of-town visitors will take advantage of the opportunity to attend both the Automobile Show and the World's Fair.

Passenger cars shown are Bantam (American), Buick, Cadillac, Chevrolet, Chrysler, Crosley, De Soto, Dodge, Graham, Hudson, Hupmobile, Lagonda (English), La Salle, Nash, Oldsmobile, Packard, Plymouth, Pontiac, Standard (English), Studebaker and Willys.

Commercial vehicles include Chevrolet, Dodge, Federal, Hudson, Mack, Plymouth, Studebaker, White and Willys.

There is the usual display of accessories, parts, body work and shop equipment.

A flat 40c admission charge for the show will be in effect for the first time. This will apply throughout the day and evening. Its adoption in place of the usual 55c afternoon and 75c evening ticket recognizes the fact that in the four decades since the national show was established as an annual affair, the motor vehicle has come to be an essential part of the individual lives of people in all walks of life; also that ownership and interest in the car is universal in the United States. The

Continued on Page 3

Weather Forecast
By U. S. Weather Bureau
Partly Cloudy and Colder
Tonight and Tomorrow
Detailed Report on Page 20

BROOKLYN EAGLE
DAILY AND SUNDAY

Wall Street Closing
Racing Extra
★★★★★★

99th YEAR—No. 14 | Entered in the Brooklyn Postoffice as 2d Class Mail Matter | BROOKLYN, N. Y., MONDAY, JANUARY 15, 1940 | (Copyright 1940 The Brooklyn Daily Eagle) | THREE CENTS

BAIL OF $850,000 HOLDS 17 IN PLOT TO SEIZE U. S. RULE

Norway Hints Defiance in Reply to Reds

Note Reported Citing Transport of Arms As Not a Violation

Moscow, Jan. 15 (AP)—Soviet Russia warned today of "danger" in her relations with Norway and "especially Sweden," publishing both her protests to them charging violations of neutrality and their not "entirely satisfactory" answers.

In both cases the Russian protests dealt with anti-Soviet attacks in the press and in quarters close to the governments of the two countries and with men and material going from them to the aid of Finland.

Similarly-worded replies from Norway and Sweden disputed the Russian assertions and expressed hope for continued good relations with the Soviet Union.

Norwegian defiance of the Soviet was indicated in a United Press dispatch from Oslo, disclosing that Norway, in its reply to the Russian protest, had hinted it would permit the transport of arms across Norwegian territory to Finland.

The note, sent to Moscow on Jan. 6, denied that arms had been transported across Norway in the past, but said that it was not considered such would be in violation of international law.

The statement was taken to mean that in the future Norway might permit countries such as Britain and France to send arms through Norwegian territory.

SWEDEN SENDS NEW NOTE

[Foreign Minister Christian E. Guenther of Sweden sent a new note to Moscow today asserting that the Swedish Government has no political grievances against Russia and expressing hope for early elimination of all misunderstandings between the two countries, the United Press said.

[The note deplored attacks against Sweden appearing in the Russian press and broadcast by the Russian radio and said that there was no reason for the Soviet com-

Continued on Page 2

Young Reds Drafted

London, Jan. 15 (U.P.) — The Moscow radio announced today that Russian men aged 19 to 20 had been called to the colors. The Moscow radio broadcast was by Colonel Chernikh, who said that all men born in 1921 must immediately register for military service at special bureaus at Moscow.

He said the order also applied to all students in schools and universities who were born in 1922 and who are in their final year of studies.

Johnson St. Crowds Boo Alleged Conspirators

Booing crowds line Johnson St. as alleged conspirators against the United States were brought in for arraignment. Center panel Shows John F. Cassidy, one of the defendants (left), with G-man. (Eagle Staff photos.)

Suspect Ready 'To Talk'; More Arrests Are Due

Band Set to Start Bomb Terror In City When Seized by FBI—Scheme Believed Hatched Here

Bail of $50,000 each set in Brooklyn Federal Court today held 17 members of the Christian Front charged with a fantastic plot to overthrow the Government of the United States and set up a dictator.

The round-up of the little band and the seizure of a small arsenal in a Brooklyn home, including ammunition allegedly stolen from two National Guard regiments, was just the beginning of Government activity in that direction.

"We have only scratched the surface," United States Attorney Harold M. Kennedy declared in announcing that more arrests could be expected.

Watched by G-Men Since Summer

G-men under J. Edgar Hoover, director of the Federal Bureau of Investigation, have had the men under close observation since Summer, but closed in on them over the weekend because of information that they planned immediate action.

"Of course, we believe this entire conspiracy or scheme was fantastic but we could not wait until these people decided to hang a bomb," Mr. Kennedy said.

Literature Seized in Boston

Boston, Jan. 15 (AP)—Police seized membership cards and literature today from the New England headquarters of the Christian Front. Members of the police radical squad" turned over the data to Police Superintendent Edward W. Fallon, who announced earlier he had no evidence whatever of any revolutionary plans, but added there was evidence that the group was anti-Semitic."

A National Guard investigation was ordered by Maj. Gen. William N. Haskell, State National Guard commander, immediately after Government charges that the seized ammunition was military property.

Crowds thronged the Brooklyn Federal Building and lined the streets around it as the defendants were brought from Manhattan, one by one, in separate private automobiles. Three F. B. I. men guarded each prisoner. All the prisoners were handcuffed.

City Police Aid Marshal's Staff

For the first time in a decade, New York City police entered the corridon of the Federal Building, augmenting Marshal Jaeger's 12 assistants in their efforts to hold the

Continued on Page 6

Other pictures and stories on pages 3, 4 and 6.

Belgians, Dutch Mass Million

Lowland Nations Brace at Frontiers In Face of Threat

Amsterdam, Jan. 15 (AP)—Under virtually complete mobilization, the armies of Belgium and the Netherlands were massed today behind frontier defenses to meet any German threat to the lowlands' neutrality.

Close to 1,000,000 Belgian and Netherlands soldiers were reported already at or ordered to positions along the meandering border—a 300-mile wall through which Germany would have to smash to outflank the British-French Allies on the Western Front.

[The official German News Agency D. N. B. said that military measures had been taken by Belgium and Holland at the instigation of the French and British, the United Press reported. "In view of the impossibility of activity along the Maginot line they (France and Britain) now are seeking to provoke Germany in Holland and Belgium," D. N. B. said.]

In Belgium there were disturbing reports of new concentrations of Nazi attack troops, while in the Netherlands a government communique spoke of "certain less favorable symptoms in the international situation."

KING ASSUMES COMMAND

[A United Press dispatch pointed out, however, that King Leopold had assumed supreme command of all the armed forces today, as his father, King Albert, had done in the World War.]

The semi-official Belga News Agency issued a note in Brussels denying what it called "alarmist stories" being "spread in Belgium and abroad" and said additional mobilization was proof only of the vigilance of the government.

"No threat hase been hidden from the Belgian public," the note said, "and the independence of sources of information and the liberty of

Continued on Page 2

Red Fliers Raid Finland Again

Resume Bombings In South—Finns See Attack on Morale

Helsinki, Jan. 15 (AP)—The Russian air force, attacking again after unleashing yesterday the worst aerial offensive of the Russian-Finnish war, resumed bombing raids on south Finland today.

Two air alarms were sounded in Helsinki shortly after noon. No damage was reported downtown, but some bombs were reported to have fallen in the outskirts.

As a result of yesterday's widespread attack Finns feared that Russian strategy called for a powerful assault on behind-the-lines morale to break military resistance at the front.

The general staff in its communique today said that more than 300 Russian planes took part in yesterday's raids, and that three were shot down and three more reported shot down.

The Finns charged that some of the Russian bombers over the far northern front had come "by way of Norwegian territory."

RAIL CENTER BOMBED

It was indicated that Vasa, important coastal city on the Gulf of Bothnia and railroad center, suffered the severest damage among the larger cities. Business structures in the city of about 32,000 pop-

Continued on Page 2

Guard Probes Source Of Front's Firearms

State Unit to Investigate 'Every Angle' To Root Out Criminals, Haskell Asserts

Officials of the New York National Guard and F. B. I. agents are working in close co-operation in an effort to determine the source of the rifles and ammunition possessed by the 17 Christian Front members.

Maj. Gen. William N. Haskell, commander of the New York National Guard, placed Lt. Col. Edward Bowditch, Inspector General of the 27th Division, in charge of an investigation into "every angle" of the plot insofar as the guard is concerned.

At the direction of Governor Lehman, Brig. Gen. Walter G. Robinson, adjutant general of New York State, ordered an investigation at the Brooklyn Arsenal to determine if the plotters had obtained ammunition and supplies there, it was announced at Albany today.

Robinson emphasized that no arsenal workers were suspected of connection with the plot. The Governor acted in his capacity as commander-in-chief of the State's Naval and Military forces.

In a statement given out at National Guard headquarters General Haskell said it may develop that the rifles and ammunition seized in Brooklyn may not be Guard equipment.

Capt. John T. Prout Jr., one of the prisoners, has been relieved of his command at the 165 Infantry, Lexington Ave. and 25th St., Manhat-

Continued on Page 6

Italian Ocean Flier Lands Short of Goal

Buenos Aires, Jan. 15 (U.P.)—Col. Angelo Tondi, Italian aviator attempting a distance record flight from Rome to Patagonia, landed today on the Brazilian island of Fernando Do Noronha, 380 miles northeast of Pernambuco.

The Italian Embassy here announced that Tondi had landed at 10:50 a.m. after there had been widespread concern for his safety because of messages saying that one of the three motors on his Savonia Marchetti plane had failed.

Earlier Tondi had flown through a severe storm over the South Atlantic, just south of the equator.

Tondi took off from the Guidonia Airport, Rome, in hope of making a nonstop flight to Patagonia, at the extreme southern tip of South America.

U. S. Liner Quits Genoa

Genoa, Jan. 15 (U.P.)—The United States liner Manhattan left today for New York.

Vamps Accept Legion Offer

Make Arrangements For Annual Parade With Donated Bands

The "grand old men" of the Kings County Volunteer Firemen's Association today gratefully accepted the offer by the Kings County American Legion to make possible the vamps' traditional Washington's Birthday parade.

The Legion's offer was made following a regretful announcement Saturday by the volunteers that the city's economy wave had stricken from the budget the $1,500 appropriation for the parade.

When Michael V. Mirande, county commander of the Legion, read in the Brooklyn Eagle that lack of bands had forced cancellation of the colorful march for the first time in 48 years, he immediately offered the Legion's county band and drum corps and other musical units from the 70 posts in the county.

Today arrangements were completed with former Magistrate Alfred E. Steers, the new president of the old timers.

And to mark the comradeship between the younger men who fought for their country and the older men who offered their services on the home front, the Legionnaires will follow the thinning line of volunteers with delegations from their own posts.

Mr. Steers said that he was "not surprised" that the Legion should

Continued on Page 2

Crowds Boo Prisoners, But Some Cheer Cassidy

Crowds which lined the streets around the Federal Building had little sympathy for the Christian Front defendants today.

Many booed as motor cars bearing the prisoners drove up to the Johnson St. entrance.

Cries of "show your face" were heard above the tumult when one after another of the handcuffed prisoners attempted to "cover up" as cameramen, crowded together on the courthouse steps, used their flashlights.

Only from one section of the estimated 400 spectators came cheers and that was when John F. Cassidy, leader of the Christian Front in Brooklyn, arrived. Then there were a few greetings of "Hello Jack," from a group numbering about ten.

The crowd began gathering as early as 9:30 a.m., and by 10 a.m. numbered between 400 and 500 persons. The two policemen on duty had difficulty keeping traffic moving until extra police, requested by Capt. William Richter of the Poplar St. station, arrived.

Inspector Charles P. Dorschell in charge of the 11th Division said he had ordered 12 patrolmen and a sergeant to the scene. After their arrival the street was cleared for traffic.

It was reported earlier that the appearance of the large crowd had given rise to a rumor that efforts might be made to "spring" the prisoners, but this was denied by police.

Miss Ingersoll Lauds Mayor's Stand on Milk

Miss Asho Ingersoll, chairman of the Milk Consumers Protective Committee, today praised Mayor LaGuardia's appeal to the public to buy grade B milk instead of grade A on the ground that it is just as good and costs less.

Miss Ingersoll, daughter of the Borough President, declared: "There has been too much confusion in the minds of the public already between safety and quality. The Health Department's job is to guarantee a safe and pure milk supply. With the proposed single grade of milk, there is nothing to prevent the milk companies from selling a higher butterfar-content milk."

In the Eagle Today

	Page		Page
Books	22	Lindley	13
Brain Teaser	22	Line on Liners	20
Brooklyn Fact	10	Obituaries	11
Comics	23	Pattern	22
Crossword	22	Radio	22
Dr. Brady	23	Ray Tucker	10
Edgar Guest	10	Real Estate	21
Editorial	10	Robert Quillen	23
Events Tonight	20	Serial	22
Financial	17-19	Sermons	12
Garden Corner	22	Ships	20
Grin and Bear It	10	Society	7
Harold Parrott	14	Sports	14-16
Heffernan	13	Theaters	9
Helen Worth	7	Want Ads	20-21
Jimmy Wood	14	Woman's	7

Hialeah Park Results

FIRST RACE—Two-year-olds; three-eighth mile.

Miss Frances (P. Rob'ts)	12.40	4.30	3.30
Chance Cut (Arcaro)	—	2.60	2.20
Red Mantilla (A. Rob'son)	—	—	3.10

Time, 0:34. Subura, Whiskachance, Bawbee, Rubaiyat, Cook Book, Brown Flower, Nutmeg Lass also ran. (Off time, 2:02.)

Chart on Page 16.

SECOND RACE—Four-year-olds and upward; three-quarters of a mile.

Cerisse III (F. A. Smith)	6.50	4.10	2.90
Hezdrel (W. D. Wright)	—	9.80	5.50
Weepor (Wholey)	—	—	5.40

Time, 1:14 1-5. aClapair, aBerwyn, Jock's Betsy, Col. Scott, Penabud, Cave Hill, Joe D., Travel Agent also ran. (Off time, 2:32½.)

a H. Pleet entry.

Hialeah Park Daily Double on first and second races paid $68.60.

Alleged Plotters as They Waited to Face U. S. Court

Here are some of the alleged plotters as they waited to be arraigned in Federal Court today. (Eagle Staff photo.)

Congress Group to Give Data on Army Posts

Washington, Jan. 15 (AP)—Members of a Congressional delegation which made a 25,000-mile airplane tour of military establishments said today they were going to give Gen. George C. Marshall, Army Chief of Staff, some startling information about his organization.

Marshall has asked them to report their views and findings directly to him.

Members of the group, which toured Army posts in this country, Panama and Puerto Rico, already have recommended that production of the Army's new semi-automatic rifle be speeded up and that some of the military posts, dating back to Indian fighting days, be abolished.

Allies, Reich Agree It's Quiet at Front

Berlin, Jan. 15 (U.P.)—The German high command's communique said today that "there were no particular events" on the front.

Paris, Jan. 15 (U.P.)—The high command's communique reported today that the night had been quiet on the front.

Amsterdam, Jan. 15 (AP)—Two soldiers were killed and four injured today in an explosion during army exercises in Groningen Province, the government press service announced.

Brussels, Jan. 15 (AP) — Reports from Luxembourg said one shell landed on the Luxembourg side of the Moselle River near Perl today in an exchange of French and German artillery fire.

WARMING UP FOR THE RACES

This may sound like heresy, but it really is chilly these Winter nights in Florida. Testimony of that is revealed in the announcement that fans at the dog races in Miami are being warmed on cold nights by steam heat equipment under the seats.

Flaring Tempers Helping Rangers in Ice Race

SPORTOPICS

By JIMMY WOOD
Sports Editor

Those Armstrong-Montanez Odds

You can still get 3 to 1 that Henry Armstrong will outlast Pedro Montanez in their Garden duel for the welterweight title Wednesday night . . . That is, you can try to get it . . . Of course, you can't be ruled off for trying, as some wit once put it, but you might become somewhat weary if you try long enough to get 3 to 1 on Pedro to lift Hennery's one remaining championship headpiece.

However, if you're fortunate enough to encounter any citizen off base far enough to offer 3 to 1 on Hennery to hold his title it would be advisable to snatch this golden opportunity by the neckband. Hennery should be favored to win, but not at 3 to 1. The price is out of line.

Indeed, some of the smart persons in the boxing business believe that the 3 to 1 quotation is strictly sawdust spread by gamblers, who will get chumps to lay this price to them and then hedge off at a shorter price on the champion.

By this cute move these reckless gamblers stand to win no matter whether Hennery or Pedro comes galloping down with the decision.

The fact remains that betting on boxing still follows the flow of dough. If no Montanez money shows up Armstrong may well go into the ring at the out-of-line 3 to 1 odds. If, however, there's a flood of Montanez money in the Garden lobby on the night of battle the quotation probably will shrink to 9 to 5 or even shorter.

This is just one of the many peculiarities about our boxing business. The betting odds are seldom, if ever, based on the possibilities, established on the relative abilities of the gladiators, their records or their styles of battle. The odds, it seems, are always controlled by the amount of money that shows up for either fighter.

One certain winner, of course, will be Uncle Mike Jacobs. A combination of circumstances tends to make this certain every time Uncle Mike hoists Hennery into the ring for a main event.

At first Hennery himself was a standout as an attraction. He mowed down every one they put in front of him. In front of him, he mowed himself into three titles, the first man in boxing history to hold so many championships at the same time.

Then Hennery gave up the featherweight title. After this he tried another whirl with Lou Ambers for the lightweight title and Lou got back the crown. Some say that Referee Arthur Donovan was a great help to Luigi in this bout in that Arthur called every low one Hennery laid in but overlooked all of Luigi's offenses against the code of ring combat such as thumbing, goughing and elbowing.

Anyway, Hennery dropped the decision and forthwith all hands decided that he was on the decline, ready for some strong, young fellow to pop him over—and out.

Of course, ring customers, being what they are, can't afford to miss out on a "kill." Having followed Armstrong in all his victories, having watched him batter down all opposition, they wouldn't think of blowing the chance to see Hennery himself hammered to the canvas.

Well, this Pedro fellow is a strong boy. He probably is the best body puncher we have had around in quite a spell, and many ring sharps feel that a body-puncher is just the type to take Hennery.

They toss out the 15-round decision Pedro dropped to Ambers and also rule out the verdict he lost to Davey Day, the only decisions that have gone against him during his professional career. The Montanez followers hold that Pedro wasn't himself in these engagements. They lay these losses to a variety of ailments that Pedro was supposed to have suffered at the time.

Well, it may be that Pedro wasn't himself when he lost to Ambers and Day. It may be that he'll be just the strong, young boy to relieve Hennery of the welterweight championship. And it may be that you may be lucky enough to get 3 to 1 on him to top Hennery.

However, you must bear in mind that in taking 3 to 1 you are betting on Hennery's decline, not on Pedro's ability to beat him. If, as some say, Hennery has slipped far enough it should be a nice night at 3 to 1. If he hasn't we fear that Pedro will be in for a very disastrous evening, along with the gentlemen who reached out for the 3 to 1.

Bruins in Action in Front of Ranger Net

Bruins found Goalie Kerr a tough problem to solve last night at Madison Square Garden, and Rangers eventually won to gain first place in the league. Scrimmage scene shows action in front of Blueshirt net. Left to right are Pike of the Rangers, Cain of Boston, Kerr on the ice, Coulter of Rangers, A. Jackson of Bruins and L. Patrick of Rangers with both feet in the air. (Wide World photo.)

Ire Big Factor As Blueshirts Subdue Bruins

Boston Yields League Lead in Garden, Bowing by 4 to 2

By HAROLD PARROTT

A peevish penchant for getting the Rangers ripping mad had today cost the Boston Bruins the league lead, a bitter 4-2 spanking instead of their first Ranger scalp of the season, and a terrific diminution of caste in the ice loop.

Mac Colville, usually a mild-mannered impersonation of Mr. Milquetoast on skates, summed it all up last night after the smoke of battle had cleared.

"When Dit Clapper skated over to me in the first period and shook his finger under my nose, I really got mad,". he confessed. "Clapper said he'd shove his stick down my throat if I wasn't careful, but I told him to save his breath for skating."

Hockey Standings

Club	W.	L.	T.	Pts.	G.	O.G.
Rangers	17	4	7	41	87	42
Boston	18	7	3	39	90	59
Toronto	16	10	4	36	85	63
Chicago	11	14	1	23	51	77
Detroit	7	16	4	20	46	73
Americans	9	19	1	19	57	83
Montreal	8	17	1	18	58	77

Last Night's Results
Rangers 4, Boston 2.
Americans 2, Chicago 1.
Detroit 3, Toronta 2.

Games Tomorrow.
Rangers at Americans.
Toronto at Boston.

A hoarse-throated throng of 16,214 saw the blustering Clapper make that bullying move, and a few minutes later they also saw pussyfoot Mac slam home the goal that broke a 1-1 tie and put the Rangers out in front for the night.

TEMPER BEGETS VICTORY

The smaller Colville was hopping mad and so were the rest of the Rangers. "Big talkers, small skaters," they tabbed the Bruins.

It was the third time in five games with the Bruins that the Rangers' temperatures had risen enough to steam them up to come from behind to win. In 95 percent of their victories the Rangers score first. But when Milt Schmidt grabbed the first goal last night it was the third time this season that Boston had drawn first blood against the Blueshirts.

With the Rangers holding four wins and one tie in their five meetings with Boston this season, the Bruins have become the newest "cousins" in the sport world.

Inability of the Bruin "Sauerkraut Line" to function against the Ranger "Roughnecks"—Miller, Watson and Heil—and the Bostons' failure to dent the Rangers when the Blueshirts are a man short have definitely helped to establish the Hub clan as painfully close kin to the high-riding Rangers.

The facts are these: In five games against Rangers the Kraut line, famed for its nifty machinations, has scored only three times, although it has notched 32 goals this season. And all three goals have been solo efforts by that master mechanic, the speedy Schmidt. Boby Bauer and Porky Dumart admitted after last night's game that they just can't get an introduction to Kerr in the Ranger nets.

But it was Boss Frankie Boucher who pointed out the reason for Schmidt's first goal last night—the one that put Boston out in front, 1—0.

BABE PRATT SLIPS

It was a Ranger mistake that made only the more clear and evident the usual perfection of the Blueshirt machine.

"When we are a man short, we press the play, break up the opposition's efforts to move the puck up," said Boucher. "We have been so successful that only three goals have been scored on us all season when we have had players in the penalty box. But tonight Babe Pratt forgot himself and pressed in too far while the three forwards were harrying the Bruins; as a result, Schmidt got the break, and got away alone. Pratt shoul dhave been between Milt and the goal. He wasn't. But that doesn't happen often."

And that's another valid reason why the Bruins can't make any headway against the Blueshirts. When fists start to fly, both sides suffer casualties usually, as players are sent to the penalty box.

Against other teams in the league the Bruins can organize power plays, and take advantage of the short-handedness, to score. Against the Rangers they can't.

Cooney Weiland, who runs the Bostons now, admitted that last night after the game. "It's gambling hockey the Rangers play, forechecking like that," said Weiland, "and I am sure it will begin to backfire on them soon."

Cunningham Set To Call It a Day

Kansan Miler to Quit At End of Season—Anxious to Go to Work

The iron man of track, Glenn Cunningham, is going to quit running before his joints get rusty.

Just when people were beginning to wonder if the durable Kansan would lope along forever, he disclosed in a radio interview last night that this would be his last season of competition.

"For a long time now I've postponed my retirement from active competition, but it's one of those things that can't be put off forever," he said. "This will be my last year.

"I've continued in competition these past two years mainly with the hope of trying for my third successive Olympic team. Now conditions on the other side have made the holding of the Olympic games impossible. So why go on?"

Cunningham, who is married and has two daughters, one six weeks old, said he was "more and more anxious to enter my chosen professional field" and expressed a desire for "a teaching position in a department of health and physical education, preferably somewhere in the Midwest."

Since deceiving a doctorate from New York University in 1938 Cunningham has had a position as lecturer for the extension division of the University of Kansas.

Cunningham's career as a runner dates back to an accident when he was eight years old in his native Peabody, Kas. His legs were burned so badly it was thought he would never be able to walk. When he regained their use he began running to develop them.

He gained prominence in track at the University of Kansas and in 1932 earned a place on the U. S. Olympic team. However, his greatest fame came after his graduation. He competed in meets all over the United States and in many foreign countries.

In 1933 he was voted the James E. Sullivan award as the person who had done most for amateur athletics. In 1934 he set a world record for the mile of 4:06.7 which stood for three years until Sydney Wooderson of England did 4:06.4.

Boys in Quandary Over Title Odds

3-1 Odds Favoring Armstrong Puzzles Cauliflower Alley

By HAROLD CONRAD

The boys along Cauliflower Alley have been pondering over a complex problem in mathematics these past few days. They're trying to figure out why Henry Armstrong is a 3-to-1 favorite to turn back Pedro Montanez when they clash for Henry's welterweight title in Madison Square Garden Wednesday night.

Three-to-one odds are pretty good odds on a prize fight when two good fighters get together, and since they're touting Pedro as the toughest welterweight contender Armstrong has ever met, he must be a pretty fair battler. Still, they're betting even money that Henry will knock Mr. Montanez out somewhere along the 15-round route they are scheduled to step.

Why? One answer is that Pedro has tissue-paper eyebrows. That he cuts easily. Another is that he hasn't whipped a top-flight man in more than a year and that he hasn't even seen action since September.

The Puerto Rican was stopped by Davey Day in his last Garden appearance. Pedro was winning that fight from here to Panama, but he suffered a cut eye early in the scrap. The referee finally had to stop the fight and awarded it to Day on a technical knockout. The record books don't say anything about who was winning the battle. They merely say Davey Day stopped Pedro Montanez in eight rounds and that's what the boys pay off on.

Since Armstrong happens to be the type of puncher who cuts his opponents up, the experts are looking for the Puerto Rican to win by this same sanguinary method.

Cage Fisticuffs

Newark, N. J., Jan. 22 (AP)—A fist fight between two players broke up last night's basketball game between the professional Hebrew Club and the Cancos, New Jersey amateur champions, for the benefit of the President's Infantile Paralysis Fund.

The Hebrew Club was leading, 26—13, near the end of the first half, when Art Hillhouse, Cancos center and former L. I. U. star, and Murray Hellweil, Hebrew Center and ex-Union Temple star, engaged in a fist fight under one of the baskets.

Spectators swarmed over the floor and Walter Okrasinski, Cancos manager, ordered his team from the court. He said he wished to avoid "a riot." An A. A. U. officia lwas hit during the melee.

See Chance for Montanez to Win With Body Attack

The Montanez followers scoff at this forecast. The Puerto Rican is unquestionably a punishing hitter. His percentage for knockouts is almost as high as Armstrong's. He has flattened 49 foes in 95 contests and he has led up to many of these knockouts via a stiff body attack. As a matter of fact Pedro does rate as one of the best body punchers in the business and this is why the scoffers scoff.

In all his lengthy campaign Armstrong has never been subjected to a real body attack, and it is common talk that Henry doesn't like to take it around the midsection. They tell you that his headlong, semi-crouching style was developed primarily to protect his belly.

The bookmakers, those fellows who made the odds, have been pretty consistent this Winter. They've been wrong all season. If Henry's waspwaist is as sensitive as they say it is, they're liable to be wrong once more.

It looks as though it's merely a question of taking three to one on a pair of tissue-paper eyebrows or laying the same odds on a weak tummy. Take your pick.

Make Way There For Boucher Jr.!

Nephew of Famous Ice Star Blazing Trail of Own in Eastern Loop

By BEN GOLD

The king is dead. Long live the king!

Frankie Boucher, center on the most famous front line in Ranger history along with Bill and Bunny Cook, has long since packed his skates away and now coaches the team he once starred for, but his nephew, Frankie Boucher Jr., is now lifting the torch and seems destined to follow in his famous uncle's footsteps.

Frankie Jr., who came to the Rovers last season, is a clever stick handler and a smart strategist and appears headed for the senior team in the Four R farm system, the Rangers. Yesterday at the Garden Frankie climaxed his greatest season by establishing a new assist record for the Eastern Amateur League.

The Rovers turned back the Baltimore Orioles, 7—6, and Frankie had the amazing total of six assists on six of the seven Rover goals. The lone tally that Frankie had no part of was Al Collings' unassisted tally in the first period.

Boucher has been working on the second line with Mitchel Pechet and Len Loree, and the combination has been going so good that they bid fair to replace the front line of Rimstad, Collings and McKay if and when the veterans get the call to advance to the Philadelphia Ramblers, the next step in the Ranger farm system.

Pechet, who has been going at a terrific pace, added three more goals to his total and is steadily gaining ground on the league leaders. Boucher is also in the midst of the scoring battle and at last reports was battling for fourth place.

Immediately after the game, which was played as the first part of the twin bill, both teams hopped a special train for a return engagement with the Orioles in Baltimore in the evening. The Rovers won again, 4 to 1, scoring all of their goals in the first period. Boucher contributed an assist on the second tally.

In the other contest the Boston Olympic Juniors continued their mastery over the Metropolitan League teams by trouncing the Sands Point Tigers, 5—2. The Olympics had previously defeated the Exchange Brokers and the Manhattan Arrows.

The 13,327 fans, probably remembering the great free-for-all the Olympics staged at their last appearance at the Garden, waited impatiently for a repeat performance but it wasn't until the final period that they were party rewarded. Wally Aggett and Allen Foster started swinging fists and several of the others showed a readiness to join in the frolic but the referees quickly got the upper hand and trouble was avoided.

Hawks Conquest Boosts Amerks

Chicago, Jan. 22 (AP)—A two-goal rally in the third period gave the New York Americans a 2-to-1 victory over the Chicago Black Hawks last night before 14,903 spectators.

The Hawks, making their first appearance since snapping the winning streak of the New York Rangers a week ago, took an early lead but could not hold it against the stubborn Americans.

The victory boosted the New Yorkers from the league cellar to sixth place and left the Hawks in fourth place, three points ahead of Detroit.

Detroit, Jan. 22 (AP)—Flashing the finest attack they have shown at home this season, the Detroit Red Wings climbed into fifth place in the National Hockey League by beating the Toronto Maple Leafs, 3 to 2, here last night.

Connie Brown, stocky forward the Wings brought up from their Indianapolis farm club, provided two of the Detroit goals while Ken Kilrea, also a former Hoosier performer, got the other. The result left the Leafs in third place behind the Boston Bruins and Rangers.

Budge Nears End of Trail In Pro Tennis

Miami Beach, Fla., Jan. 22 (U.P.)—Tennis fans are fed up with watching Don Budge lick his professional cohorts and since there is no worth-while talent to lure from the amateur ranks, there probably will be no pro tennis troupes touring the country this year.

With about $85,000 in the bank and the dollars still rolling in, the titian-thatched Mr. Budge can look back on his first year in the pro ranks today and attest that there is more to the professional game than wielding a racquet for hardware and glory.

"I know I can't make that much every year," he said. "My income will take a sharp drop this year, and I expect it. Most of that money came from my tours with Fred Perry and Ellsworth Vines, and I don't think we will make any tours this year."

And why?

Let Jack Harris, the sponsor of pro tennis, tell you.

"Don defeated Perry 28 matches to 8 and Vines 22 to 17. They played in all the big cities and fans wouldn.'t go for the same gang. We need new blood, now—a player who can give Budge a fight. And, until we find one, Budge won't make any more tours."

When Bobby Riggs, No. 1 amateur, was suggested for the transfusion problem, Harris just smiled.

"As good a player as Bobby is, I don't think he would stand a chance with Budge. After all, Bobby is only 21 and still has lots to learn. Anyway, I understand he's not interested in turning professional."

Budge favors an open tournament, but he thinks all the amateurs would be on the sidelines by the semi-finals.

Jose de Capriles Victor in Epee Meet

Jose R. de Capriles of the Salle Santelli triumphed in the open individual electric epee fencing competition yesterday at the Salle Santelli. He won six of his seven matches in the final round, bowing only to Ralph Marson of the New York A. S. C., 3—0.

The runner-up was De Capriles' brother, Miguel, also representing the Salle Santelli, while Henrique Santos of the New York A. C. placed third.

Linney Wins Packer Trophy for Bobsleds

Lake Placid, N. Y., Jan. 22 (U.P.)—William Linney of Lyon Mountain, N. Y., set a four-man course record on the Mt. Van Hoevenberg Olympic bobsled run yesterday to win the Samuel H. Packer trophy.

Linney, following in the steps of his famous older brother, Bob, retired A. A. U. champion, piloted his team down the mile track in 1:08.59—nearly 60 miles per hour average—under perfect weather conditions. His time for the four heats was 4:35.11.

Lions' Sale Held Up

Dayton, Ohio, Jan. 22 (U.P.)—The fate of the Detroit Lions National Football League franchise remained undetermined following a meeting of the executive committee of the league last night.

A syndicate of New York and Chicago business men purchased the franchise from George A. Richards recently and the executive committee met to decide whether the transfer should be ratified or rejected.

Lott Regains Squash Title

Atlantic City, N. J., Jan. 22 (AP)—Hunter Lott of Philadelphia dethroned H. Sherman Howes Jr. of Boston in the finals of the Atlantic Coast squash rackets championships yesterday.

Lott's victory by a 15-10, 12-15, 15-13, 17-15 score earned him the title he relinquished in 1939 to the Bostonian in a similar four-set final. The year before Lott downed Howes in the final after a hard battle.

Boro Hockey Standard Upheld As Nicks Eclipse Garden Foe

The St. Nicks ice hockey club of Brooklyn is satisfied that it has finally convinced even the most doubting fan that it can hold its own with anything the Garden's Metropolitan League teams have to offer.

Last night the Nicks, leaders of the New York Amateur League, took on the Exchange Brokers, pacesetters in the Met loop, and handed them a 6—4 defeat in a hard-fought battle at the Brooklyn Ice Palace.

To cap off the night's entertainment, the Brokers and the locals tangled in one of the wildest free-for-alls ever witnessed at the Ice Palace. It started innocently enough, with just Tom Leahy and Blake Shepard trading blows and falling to the ice. The officials seemed to have the situation in hand when the unpredictable Pete Grace, St. Nick goalie, skated out to center ice to pile on Leahy. That was all that was needed to start the boys and for several minutes the battle raged furiously.

The Green and White skaters were nursing a 5—4 advantage at the time with only two minutes remaining in the final chapter. When the ice was finally cleared Jim Burke insured the triumph by taking a pass from Doug Cochrane and batting it into the cage.

The teams were deadlocked at 2—2 at the end of the opening period but in the second chapter the St. Nick speed boys, George Roberts and Cochrane, tore the Broker defense to shreds, the former scoring twice and the latter once to give the locals a 5—2 margin.

The lineup:

Pos.	St. Nicks	Exchange Brokers
Goal	Grace	Elias
R.D.	Burke	Piereth
L.D.	Shepard	Leahy
C.	Roberts	Tilley
R.W.	Merriam	McDonald
L.W.	B. Cooke	H. Sniffen

Spares—St. Nicks: Iglehart, Cochrane, Stockhausen, Breckenridge, Thomas; Brokers: Torgerson, Davis, Horn, Callahan, Heffernan, Zigmund, L. Sniffen, Redmond, Baolto.

Scoring—First period: 1. St. Nicks, B. Cooke (Merriam-Roberts), 2:33; 2. Exchange, L. Sniffen (Redmond), 4:44; 3. Exchange, Redmond (Lahey), 11:39; 4. St. Nicks, Cochrane (Merriam), 14:29. Second period: 5. St. Nicks, Roberts (Iglehart), 1:25; 6. St. Nicks, Cochrane (Burke), 4:19; 7. St. Nicks, Roberts, 14:05. Third period: 8. Exchange, McDonald (Redmond), 3:10; 9. Exchange, Redmond (Callahan), 9:27; 10. St. Nicks, Burke (Cochrane), 14:48.

Penalties—Merriam, Hefferman, H. Sniffen (2), Leahy, Shepard.

Referee—Fred Connor and Bill Clyde. Time of periods—Three of 15 minutes each.

BOTH SIDES

By HAROLD PARROTT

Enter Jack Harris, the Designing Villain

No wonder Jack Harris, smoothie promoter of professional tennis, pops up with an offer to put 10 of his net employees against the 10 best amateurs in the land, for "bare expenses!"

Mr. Harris, althruistic soul, suggests that the gate receipts from this extraordinary "team match" be applied to the furtherance of amateur tennis, the helping of poor little amateurs.

If the tennis fathers ever fall for this one, it will take a fund the size of the national debt to put amateur tennis back on a paying basis again.

Mr. Harris' hirelings would wallop the reputations right out of our not-so-starry first ten. Regardless of what Brash Bobby Briggs, apologizing for the amateurs, says about them beating the pros!

And after the disastrous denouement, Riggs, Parker and Cooke would have to tour the tank towns. Mr. Harris could just walk in and take over Forest Hills for his pros and fill the place.

No, Mr. Harris is not so dumb!

Fame Has Faded, Not Shots

A team match between the "best ten" in each camp would be disastrous for our amateurs. An open tournament would not be so bad, because the draw sheet would surely bring a few of the best pros into collision; if they knocked each other off, it might be possible for Riggs, say, to sneak into the semi-finals.

Here is the way the Harris notion might line up the team match:

Amateurs	Pros
Bobby Riggs	Don Budge
Don McNeill	Elly Vines
Elwood Cooke	Bill Tilden
Frank Parker	Lester Stoefen
Welby Van Horn	Bruce Barnes
Joe Hunt	Dick Skeen
Sidney Wood	Walter Senior
Bitsy Grant	Berkeley Bell
Gil Hunt	Keith Gledhill
Wayne Sabin	Ben Gorchakoff

Some of these pros have not been in the headlines recently. Stoefen, for instance, is not as glamorous now as in the days when his blistering service and classic profile made this tall, blond one of the striking figures of the amateur circuit.

But Stoefen now is a far better tennis player. He still hits as hard as ever, has added better ground strokes. He actually out-hit and beat Budge in one epic match in England last Summer.

Tilden is far from through, even at 48. In fact, smart men of tennis would not bet on any of the 10 amateurs named above in a three-set match against Tilden—except possibly Riggs, or a McNeill who was "hot." Tilden beat Vines at Wembley, England, last Summer. He owns every stroke in the game and what a "noodle."

Budge and Vines need no comment. No simon-pure player in this country could figure to take either.

Only in the lower half of the top ten competition would the amateurs have a chance. And Skeen, Senior, Bell, Gledhill and Gorchakoff, all of whom have toured with Harris companies, are good, although their reputations are not glossed-up by amateurism.

Tournament—on Paper

Several years ago the eminent Dr. Phil Hawk, in his book "Off the Racket," rigged up a highly imaginary open tournament. In the pages of the book, he played the tournament to its completion; he described strokes, breaks of the matches, and even the scores.

In Dr. Hawk's starry field were immortals who played a generation apart: England's Dohertys, our Maurice McLoughlin, France's Cochet and Borotra, Australia's Norman Brookes and Jack Crawford at his peak—and Bill Tilden.

How brilliant this field was might be deduced from the fact that Vinny Richards lost in the second round of play (to Borotra) and Bill Larned, a real immortal, bowed in the third round (to H. L. Doherty).

In the theoretical quarter-finals, Tilden beat Borotra, Brookes beat Cecil Parke, a great British player of 1914; H. L. Doherty of the flawless style beat McLoughlin, Fred Perry beat Crawford. Tilden won the final from Doherty—in an 18—16 fifth set!

There would be nothing so nebulous about Mr. Harris' proposed team match, however. There is not an amateur whom Budge wouldn't take easily. Van Horn, who reached our national finals last September, got but three games in three sets the year before from Budge, in the Nationals! Welby didn't improve that much; it was just that the field, without a dominating Budge, deteriorated.

The amateurs might call in help from other countries—in theory, anyway. Bromwich, Quist and Von Cramm would help. But Mr. Harris might then drag in Hans Nusslein, who is perhaps the second-best pro in the world. The German dominated Europe for years as Budge dominated the pros since he turned. Nusslein was just a whisper behind Budge when they played in the $5,000 Wembley tournament in England last year.

So you see, any way you look at it—it's Mr. Harris' party. If—and it's a big if—he can lure the shamateurs into it.

Shibicky Back Again on Hospital List

Alex Shibicky, who hurt his side in practice last week, doesn't think he'll be ready to whirl against Americans tomorrow night. . . . He went out for his first turn with the Colville line last night but the pulled muscle—it's under his heart—made him quit. . . . The Rangers' new medico, Dr. Diana, has him strapped up like a mummy. . . . Mac Colville should practice getting peeved. . . . That important goal he shot last night was only his sixth of the season, but he might do better if he were more irascible. . . .

The Bruins were really handing out the bruises last night, with Portland and Clapper busiest. . . . Art Coulter, Ranger captain, did the big walloping work for the Blueshirts. . . . The Bruins scored three goals that aren't in the records because two were after Referee Stewart's whistle had tootled, and the third went in off Art Jackson's arm, instead of his stick. . . . Clint Smith got the first Ranger goal as the climax to one of those "blueprint" plays. . . . Lynn Patrick slipped him the puck, although the Garden announcer said it was two other guys.

Alfie Pike is the hustling sort who gives as well as takes and he clinched in nifty fashion in Shibicky's berth. . . . Rangers have a fine chance to gain a four-point lead tomorrow night by beating A's, because Toronto Leafs will hit the Bruins in Boston with a do-or-die attitude. . . . Bryan Hextall, who scored the third Ranger goal, now has 15, tops in the league. . . . It was a hard-slamming play and Brimsek really skidded nto his own net, wth the disc under him.

Smitty added the fourth and final Ranger goal late in the third, getting a fast break and feinting Brimsek before tucking it away. . . . The "immortal" Brimsek has now been debunked. . . . Rangers have solved the young Minnesotan for 19 goals in five games, while Bruins have put only 10 pucks behind Kerr. . . . Begins to look as if Eddie Shore meant a lot to Brimsek—and the Bruins.

HAROLD PARROTT.

Hitler Rejects U. S. Hands-Off Warning

Wall Street Closing
RACING EXTRA
★★★★★★

BROOKLYN EAGLE

LOCAL WEATHER FORECAST: Clear and cool tonight; cloudy, warmer tomorrow

Wall Street Closing
RACING EXTRA
★★★★★★

99th YEAR • No. 185 • DAILY AND SUNDAY • BROOKLYN, N. Y., FRIDAY, JULY 5, 1940 • Entered at the Brooklyn Postoffice as 2d Class Mail Matter—(Copyright 1940 The Brooklyn Daily Eagle) (F. D. S. Corporation) • 3 CENTS

THEFT OF DYNAMITE IS PROBED FOR CLUE IN BOMBING AT FAIR

FRANCE BREAKS WITH BRITAIN ON FLEET GRAB

'Unjustifiable Aggression' Cited —Battleship Blown Up and 2 Set Afire in Clash, Admiralty Admits

Berlin, July 5 (AP)—The German Government was notified officially this morning by the French Government at Vichy of severance of diplomatic relations with Great Britain.

(Earlier it was reported in Geneva that the French Cabinet decided yesterday to break off diplomatic relations with England because of the British fleet's "unjustifiable aggression" against the French fleet at Mers El-Kebir.

(The French diplomatic representative at London adhering to the Petain Government will be recalled immediately, the Geneva dispatch said.

(London diplomatic circles said this morning that "up to the present" the British Government has received no intimation from the French Government that it intended to break off relations with Great Britain.

(The French charge d'affaires in London protested to the Foreign Office today over the British action against the French fleet in the Mediterranean. The French embassy called the protest "as drastic and as stern as it is possible to make.)

FEAR FOR DALADIER

London, July 5 (AP)—The German-controlled Brussels radio in a broadcast heard here reported today that the 15,363-ton French liner Massilia, which left Bordeaux June 16 with former French Premier Edouard Daladier aboard, was overdue and missing.

The broadcast said former French Education Minister Delbos and former Interior Minister Mandel also were aboard the ship.

Battleship Bretagne Blown Up

Geneva, July 5 (AP)—A French Admiralty communique, published in the press of territory not occupied by the Germans, stated today that the French battleship Bretagne was blown up and the battleships Dunkerque and Provence and the flotilla leader Mogador set on fire during the battle with the English fleet yesterday at Mers El-Kebir.

The communique, which agreed generally with the facts given the British House of Commons yesterday by Prime Minister Churchill, added that the six-hour ultimatum did not give the French fleet time to weigh anchor before the British opened fire.

"Vice Admiral Gensoul replied (to the British ultimatum) there could not be a question of the French fleet joining the British

Continued on Page 2

Anglo-French Caribbean Battle Seen Imminent

Island of Martinique Blockaded by British, Washington Informed

Washington, July 5 (U.P.)—French sources in Washington said today that the French island of Martinique, off the coast of Venezuela, had been blockaded by British cruisers and that fighting might be imminent.

The sources said the island authorities had sided with the Petain government and that the British sought to prevent a shipment of American airplanes, which had been delivered to the island from California, from falling into German control.

The island has some French submarines in its harbor and a number of smaller craft. There is a force of French marines on the island. Some French gold is stored there.

It was reported that some of the American airplanes had been uncrated and might be assembled and able to take part in the fight if it should materialize.

Well Within Safety Zone

The British Embassy said that it had no news regarding the reported blockade. Spokesmen were unable to give details as to British ship movements in that area, although it was recalled that there is a strong British naval base at Jamaica, another of the Caribbean islands.

The Martinique area is well within the safety zone proclaimed by the 21 American republics. Hostile acts by belligerents are forbidden in the zone, but it was not known immediately what action might be taken to prevent or halt any battle which threatens to develop there.

Several American warships in the

Continued on Page 2

Rumanians in Battle; Reds Rush New Army

Bucharest, July 5 (U.P.)—The Rumanian general staff said today that fighting broke out Wednesday between Rumanian and Soviet troops when the Russians advanced beyond the frontiers set for their occupation of Rumanian territory. Loss of life occurred in the fighting, the general staff reported.

Budapest, July 5 (AP)—Reports that new Soviet troops and mechanized equipment have arrived in Bessarabia, the province ceded to Russia by Rumania, sharpened tension in the Balkans today and led to the belief that Moscow is planning new demands on Rumania.

In Sofia, Bulgaria, circles close to the Soviet said Russia was taking an increasingly stern stand toward political developments and internal disorders in Rumania, where pro-Axis Premier Ion Gigurtu formed a new government yesterday.

Moscow was said to be particularly disturbed over reports that 300 workmen were killed in a recent military action against demonstrations at Galati in Rumania.

Doubt Success of Switch

Sofia political circles took the view the new Rumanian Government was confronted with an extremely difficult task in consolidating public opinion and restoring order. Doubts were raised in some quarters that the conflicting interests could be reconciled.

The Budapest press generally regarded the revision of the Buchar-

Continued on Page 2

Hitler Rejects U. S. Warning On Americas

Berlin, However, Says It Gave No Indication Of Desire to Interfere

BULLETIN

Washington, July 5 (U.P.)—The German Government, in a formal note made public by the State Department today, rejected this country's warning to keep hands off the Western Hemisphere.

Chancellor Adolf Hitler's government at the same time, however, said Germany had given no indication of any desire to interfere in the Western Hemisphere or to seek territory here.

Hyde Park, July 5 (AP)—At a time when Europe is fighting a bloody war and the United States is embarking on a vast defense program, President Roosevelt named disarmament today as one of five essentials to permanent world peace.

At a press conference he listed these objectives which he said must be realized before a permanent peace could be assured.

1. Freedom from fear, so that people will not be afraid of being bombed from the air or attacked by another nation. That, he said, means removal of the weapons which cause fear, or disarmament.
2. Freedom of information. That is important, Mr. Roosevelt asserted, because the whole country must be able to get news of what is going on in every part of the country and in every part of the world, without censorship. He said it meant not freedom of the press alone but freedom of every means of distributing information and that without it there could not be a stable world.

Cites Advantages Here

3. Freedom of religion. Under democracies, the President said, this freedom has been maintained fairly well but not in coun-

Continued on Page 2

Man Who Scarred Capone Sentenced To 60 Days in Jail

Frank Callucio, 42 of 264 6th Ave., who for the past 20 years has been described as the man who gave Al Capone his slashed face and the nickname Scarface, was sentenced today in Flatbush Court to serve 60 days in jail following his conviction on a vagrancy charge.

Callucio was arrested on March 27, last, in a bar and grill at 216 4th Ave., in a general police round-up and charged with vagrancy. He explained that he had the food concession in the bar but on June 21 was found guilty.

Magistrate Joseph C. H. Flynn sentenced Callucio to the jail term. The District Attorney's office had requested it. Hyman Barshay, former Assistant District Attorney, was counsel for Callucio and asked for a suspended sentence, which was refused, then asked for a stay of sentence until Monday which was also refused. Barshay had asked for the stay in order to take the matter to the Supreme Court.

Suffolk Downs Results

FIRST RACE—Three-year-olds and upward: three-quarters of a mile.

Athanasian (T. Bates)	6.40	4.20	3.00
Ghost Train (T. Atkinson)	—	5.00	3.00
Free Again (Allgaier)	—	—	2.60

Time, 1:16 2-5. Raceaway, Buddy's Sister, Cordate, Blue Covert, Myrna Lee, The Jurist, Modest Manners, Royal Chemist also ran. Off time, 2:23.

Empire City Results

FIRST RACE—Two-year-olds; 5½ furlongs.

Alcinous (Roberts	40.20	19.70	7.30
Possibility (Arcaro)	—	32.00	13.30
Rancho's Boy (Durando)	—	—	6.80

Time, 1:07 3-5. Janegri, Hup Nancy, Albiona, Illuminated, Dotwill, Sun Idele, Supper Show, Cherriko, Pessimist also ran. Off time, 2:17.

SECOND RACE—Star of Padula, first; Essiaytee, second; Jelwell, third.

Wide World photo

REMOVING BODIES OF BOMB VICTIMS—Mangled remains of two detectives killed in the explosion of a time bomb at the World's Fair yesterday are carried from the scene of the tragedy, concealed beneath sheets. The bomb exploded shortly after it had been taken from the British Pavilion and placed on the ground near the fence seen in the background.

HERO OF EXPLOSION—Detective Frederick C. Morlock Jr. of 190 28th Road, St. Albans, who carried the bomb from the British Pavilion to a secluded spot 300 yards away, where it exploded. Had the blast occurred in the pavilion hundreds might have been killed. Morlock was slightly injured.

Gibraltar Bombed By French Plane

Gibraltar, July 5 (AP)—Airplanes attacked Gibraltar three times without success today in the first air raids of the war on this British naval stronghold.

The raids started in the early hours. Searchlights went into action. Several bombs were dropped but all fell into the sea and there were no casualties and no damage.

In the third raid a plane was seen attempting to make a dive-bombing attack but was driven off by shore batteries.

Berlin, July 5 (U.P.)—The German wireless in a dispatch from Madrid today said that a French airplane had dropped bombs at the British fortress of Gibraltar.

The dispatch said:

"A French airplane dropped bombs over the British fortress of Gibraltar at 6 o'clock Friday morning, a report from Algeciras (Spain) states.

"British anti-aircraft opened fire on the airplane. Further details were not known in the Spanish capital, but it is assumed that the French airplane wanted revenge for the British assault on the French fleet lying at Oran."

Victim Answered Call To Fair on His Day Off

If Weather Had Been Nice, Cop's Family Says, He Would Not Have Received Fatal Summons

By MARY HOSIE

All the "whys" and "might-have-beens" crowded in today upon the Socha family as they waited for the body of Detective Ferdinand Socha, victim of the bomb blast at the World's Fair yesterday, to be brought home to them.

"It never should have happened," said Detective Socha's younger brother, Henry, in the grief-ridden Socha home at 545 Graham Ave.

Henry, who acted as spokesman for the family, sat at a kitchen table on the first floor of the Graham Ave. house and explained how it never should have happened. Upstairs his mother sat crying. All she was able to say was, "My boy. Oh, my boy." Detective Socha's wife, Jennie, over her first terrible shock, had gone out to buy some mourning clothes for the funeral. Another brother, Theodore; two sisters, Helen and Clementian, and the father of the family, Joseph, were receiving visitors.

Victims Were Partners

"It was his day off," said Henry. "If it had been a nice day, instead of a gloomy one, he probably would have been out on a trip with his wife and he never would have been home when his partner called."

Detective Joseph J. Lynch, also a victim of the blast was Socha's

Continued on Page 3

STATE CONTRACT LET OUTSIDE N. Y. DESPITE PROTEST

By JOSEPH H. SCHMALACKER

Cries of anguish over the annual headache-producing New York State income tax questionnaire, which John Q. Public gets from Albany before he is compelled to fork over $92,000,000 for the State Treasury, developed unexpectedly today, nearly one year ahead of schedule.

The occasion was the action of State officials in awarding a State contract for the printing of the blanks to an out-of-State printing firm in the face of protests aimed at getting the work for printers in New York City who must pay their own share of the Empire State's income taxes.

Indignant and insistent protests figuratively mingled with the roar of the presses in New York City's printing industry when it developed that the contract had gone to a Philadelphia low bidder.

The successful bidder was the William Mann Company, which, according to Vincent J. Ferris, secretary of the Allied Printing

Continued on Page 2

WILLIAM P. EARLE JR. IS CRITICALLY ILL

William Pitman Earle Jr., husband of Councilman Genevieve B. Earle and a prominent figure in the Brooklyn Big Brother Movement for the last 30 years, was reported today to be in a critical condition in Long Island College Hospital. Mr. Earle entered the institution a month ago suffering from an abdominal complaint.

One of the founders and former president of the Brooklyn Heights Association, Mr. Earle has lived at 11 Cranberry St. for many years. He is a partner in Earle Brothers, 38 Pearl St., Manhattan, dealers in crude gums, and married the former Genevieve Beavers on Oct. 27, 1913.

Eagle, News Guild Sign New Contract

The Brooklyn Eagle and the Eagle Unit of the New York Newspaper Guild today signed a contract for those employes of the Eagle in guild jurisdiction.

The contract has been in negotiation for several months and its consummation today marks a complete understanding between the paper and the guild.

The contract grants minimum wage scales, higher severance pay and three-week vacations to employes who have been with the paper for five years. The term of the agreement is for one year.

On behalf of the guild the contract was signed by Nat Einhorn, executive secretary of the New York Newspaper Guild, and I. Kaufman, chairman of the Eagle Unit. For the paper, Frank D. Schroth, publisher, and William F. Crowell, secretary, signed.

Bundist Is Arrested-- Front, Red Leaders Released After Quiz

BULLETIN

The first arrest in the investigation of the fatal bombing at the World's Fair yesterday was made this afternoon when police of the W. 68th St. station in Manhattan, acting on a secret tip, seized Ceasar Kroger, an alien and member of the German-American Bund, at the building where he is superintendent, 38 W. 181st St., Manhattan. In Kroger's quarters, police said, were found two automatic revolvers, one of them loaded, and several rolled maps of the city, with various locations delineated. Kroger was booked at the station on a Sullivan law charge and held for further questioning.

Police launched an investigation today into the unsolved theft of 39 sticks of dynamite from a Manhattan construction company on the possibility that this was the explosive used in the bomb which claimed the lives of two detectives yesterday at the World's Fair.

While John F. Cassidy, Brooklyn leader of the Christian Front; Paul Crosbie, Queens County chairman of the Communist party, and others were questioned and released, police acted on a tip given by the Brooklyn Eagle and summoned for questioning the watchman from whom the dynamite was stolen on May 29.

The explosive was seized from a building project of the Goodwin Construction Company at 26 W. 68th St., Manhattan, at 4 a.m. by an armed bandit who forced the watchman, Cesidis Antonelli of 185 West End Ave., Manhattan, to raise his hands.

After the gunman had fled, Antonelli notified the superintendent, William Weinstein, who, in turn, called police at 7:45 a.m. After a superficial inquiry, the Brooklyn Eagle learned, there were no more developments in the case.

$1,000 Reward Offered

Meanwhile, a reward of $1,000 for the apprehension of the criminal or criminals who planted the bomb in the British pavilion at the Fair was offered by the Detectives' Endowment Association, of which Detective Dennis J. Mahoney is president. Police Commissioner Valentine announced he had signed checks for $500 to each of the victim's widows.

Cassidy, who with eight others, was acquitted two weeks ago on charges of conspiracy to overthrow the Government, returned to his home at 3015 Farragut Road after waiting in line with some 100 others for brief questioning.

"The Christian Front definitely is against all violence," declared Cassidy. "We deplore the tragic occurrence at the Fair and sincerely hope that the culprits will be caught and punished."

Crosbie was picked up by police at his home, 39-22 49th St., Long Island City, shortly after midnight,

Continued on Page 3

U. S. Orders W.G.BishopHeld On Alien Charge

Accused Plot Leader Already in Jail—Bail Is Increased $2,000

By WENDELL HANMER

William Gerald Bishop, reputed leader of the seditious activities attributed to the defendants in the recent plot trial, today was ordered arrested by the Department of Justice as a possible alien, illegally in this country.

A warrant for his arrest on this charge was received from Washington by Federal Marshal Arthur G. Jaeger. He delivered it to Acting Warden Thompson of the Federal Detention Headquarters in Manhattan, where Bishop has been held in default of bail since his arrest last Jan. 13.

Originally $50,000, Bishop's bail subsequently was reduced to $10,000 and again was lowered to $5,000 by Judge Robert A. Inch in Brooklyn Federal Court on Wednesday. The warrant directs that in the event he succeeds in raising the $5,000, he shall be arraigned on Ellis Island and his bail there fixed at $2,000 pending a hearing on the alien charge.

Jury Disagreed in His Case

Bishop, never a member of the Christian Front, was one of five defendants who failed of acquittal at the trial, which ended June 24. The jury disagreed as to him on both counts of the trial indictment —conspiracy to overthrow the Government and conspiracy to steal Government property.

At the trial Bishop testified that he was born in Salem, Mass., about 39 years ago. He said fire had destroyed that community's vital statistics, which prevented his producing a birth record. In several exhibits introduced in evidence Bishop was shown at various times to have claimed other places of birth. Bishop himself testified that when he was one he was taken to Canada, five years later to Europe and that after spending the World War years in an Austrian internment camp, returned here.

Reminding that on Wednesday he had been instructed to ask a further reduction if unable to raise the $5,000 bail then set, Emanuele Trotta, Bishop's lawyer, today asked Judge Inch to reduce the $5,000 to $3,000. Judge Inch refused, saying that the new development had changed the situation. Bishop now must post a total of $7,000 bail to regain his liberty pending disposition of all charges against him.

Jehovah's Witnesses Sect Is Banned in Canada

Ottawa, Ont., July 5 (U.P.)—Jehovah's Witnesses, the sect whose members refuse to salute the flag on religious grounds, were banned in Canada today.

WHERE TO FIND IT IN TODAY'S EAGLE

Bridge	Page 22
Children's Section	Page 22
Comics	Page 9
Crossword	Page 20
Dr. Brady	Page 22
Ed Hughes	Page 14
EDITORIAL	Page 10
Events Tonight	Page 20
FINANCIAL	Pages 17-18-19
Garden Corner	Page 22
Going Places	Page 6
Grin and Bear It	Page 10
Jimmy Wood	Page 13
Lindley	Page 12
Line on Liners	Page 22
Lost and Found	Page 2
Movies	Page 7
Novel	Page 22
OBITUARIES	Page 11
Pattern	Page 22
RADIO	Page 9
Real Estate	Page 21
Society	Page 5
SPORTS	Pages 13-14-15
Theaters	Page 7
Tucker	Page 10
Wall Street	Page 17
Want Ads	Pages 20-21
Woman's	Page 4

Wide World photo

OCTOBER FORECAST?—Brooklyn's six members of National League All-Star team figure game Tuesday at St. Louis will give them preliminary peek at American League competition. They expect to have something to do with an American League team this Fall when the Dodgers play the best in the junior circuit in the World Series. And as far as Dodger fans are concerned there is no "if" about winning the pennant. Left to right, Brooklyn's contributions to All-Star game are Pete Coscarart, Whit Wyatt, Babe Phelps, Cookie Lavagetto, Leo Durocher and Joe Medwick.

FLOCK PLAYERS LIKELY TO SPICE ALL-STAR GAME

Durocher and His Five Mates To Provide Pepper in Tuesday's 'Dream Battle' at St. Louis

By TOMMY HOLMES
Staff Correspondent of the Brooklyn Eagle

Boston, July 6—Selected short subjects in the baseball field:

THAT 'DREAM GAME'—The All-Star game to be played at Sportsman's Park, St. Louis, Tuesday afternoon will be the eighth annual event of its kind and it may be the last. In theory the game presents a colorful conflict and another good reason for its existence—the benefit of a fund for indignant ball players—is certainly a worthy cause.

But ball clubs find the promotion of the game a nuisance and have discovered in recent years that interest in the game is purely local. St. Louis fans who can see the game are reasonably excited this year, but fans in other cities are not heated up a bit.

Wonder what the Dodger contingent led by Leo Durocher will accomplish Tuesday afternoon? Durocher has been Brooklyn's one and only All Star hero of the past. He played the full game at shortstop for the National League at Cincinnati two years ago and was outstanding in a 4-to-1 victory.

The last two N.L. runs of that game were Durocher's work. He came to bat against Lefty Grove after Frank McCormick had led off the seventh inning with a single and laid down a perfect bunt. Jimmy Foxx fielded the ball and fired it into right field when Charley Gehringer failed to cover first. McCormick scored, and when Joe DiMaggio's late throw to the plate was also wild Durocher also completed the circuit.

The business of getting four bases on a bunt, even though the journey was enhanced by two errors, is typical of Durocher's wideawake play. The entire Brooklyn club plays that kind of baseball now. Given an opportunity Tuesday, Pete Coscarart, Harry Lavagetto, Babe Phelps, Joe Medwick, Whit Wyatt and Leo himself ought to spark the proceedings with plenty of National League pepper.

Ross Tops West

WEST DOWN — ROSS UP—Next to the marvelous Mr. Medwick, the National League outfielder in greatest demand at last Winter's trading conferences was Max West of Boston. The rangy Westerner had hit .285 for the Bees in 1939, had 19 homers, was generally rated the most improved player in the league.

Bob Quinn didn't take any of the numerous offers he had for West and may never again have a chance to make a really good deal for him. Pitchers have changed their style of working on West. Instead of mixing them up, they aim to make him hit high fast balls that he can't pull and Max has been in a slump since the season started.

Next Winter Chester Ross probably will be the outfielder, if any, that other clubs will try to lure from Boston. A 22-year-old right-hander who played at Evansville, Ind., last year, Ross looked somewhat funny in left field on several occasions early in the season. But Casey Stengel stayed right with him. "The boy will make mistakes," explained Stengel. "But I think he will learn, and he is a really good hitter right now."

To the Dodgers Ross has looked like the best freshman hitter in the league this year. He bought himself a large share of Dodger admiration in one game last week when he reached out and hit a pitch over the outside corner of the plate 'way up behind the Ebbets Field score board in right field. There is no type of pitch more difficult for a right-handed hitter to meet with power and when you see a kid deliver that kind of a belt you need little other evidence to know he belongs.

Wire Chief the 'Culprit'

A GOOD, GAME GUY—Stewart Boggs, wire chief at the Philadelphia press boxes, was innocently responsible for perhaps the cruelest nickname ever tied to a ball player. It happened several years ago. The Phils piled up a big early lead against the Dodgers and some one remarked that the Quakers ought to win.

Stew shook his head. "Probably," he said, "when I handle the box score I'll find that line again, 'Losing pitcher—Mulcahy.'"

The game went on, the Dodgers staged a series of rallies, finally won by something like 12 to 11. And, sure enough, Hugh Mulcahy, in the game as a relief pitcher, put the man on base who scored the run that put Brooklyn ahead and took the rap for the defeat. To a large portion of the populace he has been Losing Pitcher Mulcahy ever since.

Mulcahy has done plenty of losing, at that. Up until this season he had a lifetime record of 29 victories and 60 defeats for a little more than three full campaigns. "He must be a good pitcher to lose so often," was one sage remark, and if you stop to think you realize that there is more truth than poetry in this paradox. Bad pitchers don't get in there that often.

The truth is, of course, that Losing Pitcher Mulcahy is a good pitcher with a bad ball club. For the first time he gets some official recognition of his talent this year. As a member of the 1940 National League squad, he is in line for his first opportunity to lose an All Star game.

Diz as Preacher Grandma's Idea

That Is if He Fails in Pitching Comeback in Texas League

Tulsa, Okla., July 6—Dizzy Dean, trying to rekindle the $185,000 bonfire in his right arm with Southwestern sunshine, is optimistic over the preliminary results.

"It's getting better," says the Dizzy One of his new "side-wheeler" delivery that he is attempting to develop as a means of relieving the muscle misery that has plagued him.

"The new delivery still throws me off balance a little, but we're working on that."

Dutch Reuther, the scout who was sent along with Dizzy from the Chicago Cubs to coach him while he tries to reconstruct his pitching form, says he, too, can see improvement.

The concrete evidence that Diz isn't doing so badly was displayed to the packed grandstands in the first two Sunday ball games that Dizzy pitched for the Tulsa Oilers in the Texas League. Diz won both games.

His persistence and his enthusiasm under trying conditions have convinced his Oiler teammates that Dean is determined his return to the Texas League will be a short one and that he soon will be back with the Cubs.

The whole thing, of course, was Dizzy's idea at the start. His brother, Paul, once returned to the Texas circuit and he now is doing all right with the New York Giants.

"Paul's 100 percent better for having returned to the Texas League," says Dizzy, who feels that if Paul did it he can too.

Dizzy doesn't even consider the possibility that he won't be able to make the grade again with the Cubs, and his Texas League fans seem to have the same philosophy—all except one of Dizzy's staunchest friends. She doesn't attend baseball games, but she has it all figured out what Dizzy can do if his arm fails him permanently.

The lady is 87 years old and she is Dizzy's grandmother, Mrs. C. M. Dean of Beggs, Okla.

Her idea: If Dizzy ever is washed out of baseball, she thinks he would make a fine preacher.

BALL USED IN No. 200 TO BE FITZ'S PRIZE

If and when he snares his 200th National League victory, Freddy Fitzsimmons is grabbing the last ball for his own trophy case. In that case are many horsehide trophies. Some from as far back as 1925, when Fred broke in under McGraw.

He has been giving away to close friends the balls he used to pitch the victories from 190 on. For instance, Ball No. 199 now is owned by Dr. Ernie Weymuller of Manhattan. But Fitz swears No. 200 isn't getting away.

PARROTT.

Schedule Favors Dodgers, Giants in Flag Race

Cincinnati, (AP)—The Cincinnati Reds may have the toughest road of any of the National League pennant contenders to travel in September. The Reds are home only eight days during that final month of the season. For this reason, some observers look for Brooklyn and New York to fight it out for the pennant, since they have a better closing schedule. That is, if they're in the fight then.

Kampouris on Way Back

A newly developed home run swing may send Alex Kampouris, Newark second baseman, back to the big show. The Greek infielder had 15 circuit blasts at the last counting.

BUSHWICKS AND SPRINGIES IN TWIN BILL TODAY

A real neighborhood baseball brawl involving the Springfield Greys and Bushwicks at Dexter Park and a star bill at Erasmus Field, which will pit the Bay Parkways against the Police and Fire Department nines, tops the semi-pro docket today.

The Bushwicks were walloped at Sherwood Oval last Monday night by the hated Springies, and mean to take a two-ply revenge this afternoon. Manager Joe Press has groomed his two aces, Jimmy Pattison and Bots Nekola. Nekola Thursday night blanked the Cedarhurst Club which has given the Bushwicks so much trouble this season.

The Springies are famed for their punch at the plate, but the Bushwicks have thumpers like Buddy Hall, who is still over .340; Solly Mishkin and Al Cuccinello, both well over .300.

The Springfields' mound staff will really be put to a test today and tomorrow. After today's double bill, the Sherwood Oval crew must gird for action tomorrow night against the formidable Homestead Grays, who walloped them a few weeks ago, 8—2.

Gray With Parkways

The Bay Parkways have taken a new lease on life with the addition of Pete Gray, whose appearance in the Erasmus Fielders' lineup was the signal for a spurt last season, too.

The Parkways beat the Bushwicks Thursday for the first time this season, and Gray's bat was busy. Working with Pete in Harry Hesse's outfield now are Larry Fischer (.409), Johnny Maruska (.381) and Eddie Boland (.337). This is probably the hardest-hitting garden corps in semi-pro ranks.

The firemen will oppose the Parkways in the first game, which will see the Hessemen facing Ken Auer, formerly of Fordham. Ken's brother, Roy, may pitch for the police nine, which also has Grosso, Parente, Lowe and Stuve on the hill staff.

Hot Off the Spikes

The Parkway pitching staff now includes Gene Bowe, Abe Spiro, Wally Holbrow and Eddie Speangler . . . The Springies' attack, which the Bushwicks must quell today, features George Cella, hitting .385 after recovering from a leg injury and Manager Tremper, socking .390.

Other Games Today

The House of David tackles the Queens Club at Queens Park today in two battles . . . The Cuban Stars go under the arc tonight at Cedarhurst Stadium . . . The House of David will play Barton's Nighthawks tonight at New Hyde Park.

A's Top Yanks, 8-7, in 10th

Continued from Page 1

run in the fifth and two more in the sixth to tie the score at 5—5.

Charlie Keller gave the Yanks a 7—5 margin in the eighth frame with his homer with Bill Knickerbocker on base.

Bump Hadley, who walked the first batter in the tenth and then was taken out, was charged with the defeat while Bill Beckman, who came on to toil for a seemingly hopeless cause in the first half of the tenth, was credited with the win, his first triumph of the season . . . When Hayes first hit his game-winning drive in the tenth, both base runners sprinted around the bases to score as did Hayes and at first Frankie was credited with a home run and the final score was recorded as 10—7.

However, the official scorer quickly rectified the mistake, crediting Hayes with an automatic double. McCoy was credited with scoring the winning tally . . . The teams will conclude their series with a doubleheader tomorrow . . . The Yanks will then return to the Stadium to open a stand against the West on Thursday.

NINE, TEN AND OUT!

Yankees	ab	r	h	o	a	Philadelphia	ab	r	h	o	a
Crosetti,ss	4	2	1	4	1	Lillard,ss	3	2	2	1	2
Kn'b'ker,3b	4	1	1	2	2	Gant'b'n,3b	1	0	0	0	0
Keller,rf	6	1	1	1	0	Moses,rf	5	0	1	0	0
DiMag'o,cf	5	0	2	4	0	McCoy,2b	4	1	2	2	3
Selkirk,lf	3	0	1	0	0	Johnson,lf	4	0	0	3	0
Dickey,c	5	0	0	5	2	Siebert,1b	5	0	1	11	1
Gordon,2b	5	0	1	5	3	Hayes,c	6	2	4	4	0
Dahlg'n,1b	4	2	2	7	1	Ch'pm'n,cf	5	0	2	5	0
Ruffing,p	2	0	0	0	1	Rubel'g,3b	2	1	0	1	4
Hadley,p	3	1	1	0	1	Dean†	1	0	1	0	0
Murphy,p	0	0	0	0	0	Brancato,ss	0	1	0	1	0
						Ross, p	4	1	1	1	1
						D.Miles‡	1	0	1	0	0
						Beckman,p	0	0	0	1	0
Totals	41	7	10	*28	11	Totals	41	8	15	30	11

*One out when winning run scored.
†Batted for Rubeling in ninth.
‡Batted for Ross in ninth.

Yanx	1	1	0	0	1	2	0	2	0	0	—7
Philadelphia	1	1	0	3	0	0	0	0	2	1	—8

Errors—McCoy, Ross. Runs batted in—Keller (4), McCoy, Dahlgren (2), Lillard (2), Moses, Johnson, Knickerbocker, Miles, Gantenbein, Hayes. Two-base hits—Moses, DiMaggio, Hayes. Home runs—Dahlgren (2), Keller. Sacrifices — Knickerbocker, Lillard. Double play—Dickey and Knickerbocker. Left on bases—Philadelphia, 15; Yanx, 11. Base on balls—Off Ross, 6; Ruffing, 5; Hadley, 3; Murphy, 1. Struck out—By Ross, 1; Ruffing, 2; Hadley, 3. Hits—Off Ruffing, 7 in 4 innings; Hadley, 7 in 5 innings (none out in 10th); Murphy, 1 in 1-3 inning; Ross, 10 in 9 innings; Beckman, 0 in 1 inning. Wild pitch—Ross. Winning pitcher—Beckman. Losing Pitcher—Hadley. Umpires—Grieve, Summers and Rue. Time—2:44. Attendance—5,486.

Hawley Triumphs In Montclair Final

Mountain Lakes, N. J., July 6—Donald Hawley of Orange, 11th ranking eastern player, won the Mountain Lakes Club Invitation Tennis tournament for the seventh consecutive time today as Louis Brownstein of San Diego, Calif., bowed in a stiff finals contest, 2—6, 6—0, 6—8, 6—4, 6—0.

Brownstein, seeded seventh in the tournament, pulled three upsets to reach the bracket against Hawley. Brownstein's net game was working to perfection in the early sets and his volleying was a tough nut for Hawley to crack.

It was nip-and-tuck to the final set, when the victor's superior court strategy proved the deciding margin.

Hawley gained a first leg on a $500 challenge trophy. He retired the two previous cups.

The women's title went to Miss Millicent Hirsh of New York, New Jersey feminine champion. She quickly disposed of Miss Eunice Dean, San Antonio, Tex., 6—1, 6—2.

Turner a Converter

Jim Turner, 210-pound guard drafted by the Brooklyn football Dodgers, beat Georgia and Brown for Holy Cross with points after touchdowns.

Major League Averages

NATIONAL LEAGUE

CLUB BATTING

Club	g.	ab.	r.	h.	hr.	rbi.	sb.	pc.
New York	**64**	**2237**	**313**	**617**	**39**	**290**	**18**	**.276**
Chicago	72	2532	336	675	35	311	26	.267
Pittsburgh	64	2200	312	588	36	284	28	.267
St. Louis	63	2236	287	592	55	268	25	.265
Boston	60	2090	267	547	25	233	24	.262
Cincinnati	67	2313	317	599	48	287	32	.259
Brooklyn	**65**	**2271**	**309**	**582**	**37**	**284**	**28**	**.256**
Philadelphia	65	2192	218	524	28	198	9	.239

CLUB FIELDING

Club	g.	po.	a.	e.	dp.	pc.
Cincinnati	67	1833	800	50	71	.981
New York	**64**	**1716**	**781**	**61**	**47**	**.976**
Philadelphia	65	1738	801	75	56	.972
Chicago	72	1955	885	92	66	.969
Brooklyn	**65**	**1812**	**670**	**81**	**43**	**.968**
Boston	60	1573	694	75	75	.968
St. Louis	63	1690	670	87	59	.964
Pittsburgh	64	1690	794	99	57	.962

BATTING RECORDS

Player, Club	g.	ab.	r.	h.	hr.	rbi.	sb.	pc.
Danning, N. Y.	**61**	**235**	**38**	**83**	**11**	**56**	**3**	**.353**
J. Martin, St. L.	41	105	11	37	2	20	1	.352
Davis, Pittsburgh	42	115	15	40	5	14	0	.348
Walker, Brooklyn	**56**	**216**	**33**	**73**	**3**	**28**	**1**	**.338**
May, Phil	57	200	26	67	0	25	2	.335
Gleeson, Chi	54	206	34	67	3	36	2	.325
Nicholson, Chi	60	213	34	69	9	46	1	.324
Hershberger, Cin	30	62	3	20	0	16	0	.323
Orengo, St. Louis	50	147	30	47	5	23	4	.320
Gustine, Pitts	53	204	23	65	1	23	6	.319
Herman, Chi	70	288	47	91	4	37	1	.316
Moore, New York	**61**	**246**	**44**	**77**	**4**	**24**	**4**	**.313**
Garms, Pitts	30	67	14	21	1	14	1	.313
Ross, Boston	61	231	42	72	8	37	3	.312
Phelps, Bklyn	**52**	**167**	**26**	**52**	**8**	**31**	**1**	**.311**
Moore, Bklyn-Bos	40	142	22	44	4	16	0	.310
Lombardi, Cin	58	214	30	66	8	42	0	.308
Demaree, N. Y.	**41**	**160**	**31**	**49**	**3**	**26**	**2**	**.306**
Marion, St. Louis	43	151	17	46	0	13	2	.305
Rowell, Boston	43	131	12	40	1	19	2	.305
Medwick, StL-Bkln	**56**	**231**	**35**	**70**	**6**	**31**	**0**	**.303**
Berger, Cin-Phil	22	43	3	13	1	5	1	.302
Cavarretta, Chi	49	153	32	46	2	20	3	.301
Miller, Boston	59	217	24	65	5	36	5	.300
Leiber, Chicago	50	185	23	55	5	34	0	.297
F.McCormick, Cin	67	270	45	80	8	43	1	.296
Whitehead, N. Y.	**64**	**285**	**36**	**84**	**2**	**18**	**4**	**.295**
Rizzo, Pitt-Cin-Phi	58	208	31	61	10	31	1	.293
Young, New York	**61**	**243**	**33**	**70**	**2**	**36**	**1**	**.288**
Ott, New York	**64**	**222**	**43**	**64**	**6**	**35**	**2**	**.288**
P. Waner, Pitts	42	118	18	34	1	17	1	.288
Hack, Chicago	67	266	51	76	1	17	5	.286
Gallagher, Bklyn	**18**	**42**	**4**	**12**	**0**	**3**	**1**	**.286**
West, Boston	59	219	38	62	3	30	1	.283
Van Robays, Pitts	54	206	22	58	1	30	0	.282
Witek, New York	**41**	**142**	**14**	**40**	**1**	**11**	**0**	**.282**
Mueller, Phil	51	135	14	38	1	14	1	.281
Hopp, St. Louis	39	57	10	16	0	3	0	.281
Mize, St. Louis	62	229	40	64	20	51	1	.279
Fletcher, Pitts	64	229	42	64	11	52	1	.279
Vosmik, Brooklyn	**50**	**198**	**25**	**55**	**1**	**19**	**0**	**.278**
Camilli, Brooklyn	**65**	**239**	**39**	**66**	**7**	**44**	**6**	**.276**
L. Waner, Pitts	40	58	11	16	0	1	1	.276
Collins, Chicago	24	58	7	16	1	12	4	.276
Owen, St. Louis	42	102	7	28	0	10	1	.275
Lopez, Bos-Pitts	50	164	24	45	2	21	2	.274
Lavagetto, Bklyn	**65**	**249**	**38**	**68**	**3**	**32**	**3**	**.273**
Koy, Bklyn-St. L.	42	125	18	34	3	20	3	.272
Bowman, Pitts	29	48	6	13	1	10	0	.271
Craft, Cincinnati	60	235	29	63	5	27	2	.268
Handley, Pitts	52	183	30	49	1	10	4	.268
Moore, St. Louis	52	191	27	51	6	22	7	.267
Mazzera, Phil	15	34	6	9	0	5	0	.265
Vaughan, Pitts	64	246	41	65	1	38	5	.264
Todd, Chicago	53	201	17	53	4	19	1	.264
Dallessandro, Chi	49	145	18	38	0	13	1	.262
Reese, Brooklyn	**40**	**134**	**26**	**35**	**2**	**12**	**9**	**.261**
Frey, Cincinnati	67	258	49	67	7	26	11	.260
Slaughter, St. L.	59	223	30	58	4	18	1	.260
Cuccinello, Bos-NY	**49**	**173**	**19**	**45**	**3**	**33**	**1**	**.260**
Brown, St. Louis	21	77	5	20	0	3	2	.260
Franks, Brooklyn	**23**	**54**	**4**	**14**	**1**	**7**	**0**	**.259**
Marty, Phil	47	168	19	43	3	12	0	.256
S. Martin, St. L.	60	253	30	64	4	20	1	.253
Durocher, Bklyn	**34**	**91**	**8**	**23**	**1**	**11**	**1**	**.253**
Hassett, Boston	60	235	37	59	0	15	3	.251
Goodman, Cin	55	212	34	53	5	25	1	.250
DiMaggio, Cin-Pitt	36	104	20	26	9	15	4	.250
Elliott, Pitts	58	234	31	58	3	24	4	.248
Werber, Cin	67	271	45	67	7	27	8	.247
Jurges, New York	**53**	**194**	**20**	**48**	**2**	**33**	**1**	**.247**
M.McCormick, Cin	40	129	12	34	1	10	2	.245
Coscarart, Bklyn	**54**	**205**	**23**	**50**	**6**	**32**	**3**	**.244**
Warren, Phil	39	99	10	24	4	15	0	.242
Gilbert, Brooklyn	**35**	**91**	**17**	**22**	**2**	**8**	**1**	**.242**
Russell, Chicago	41	134	9	32	2	19	0	.239
Cooney, Boston	31	67	7	16	0	3	2	.239
Klein, Phil	59	216	27	51	6	27	1	.236
Sisti, Boston	46	166	22	39	2	13	2	.235
Myers, Cincinnati	28	85	9	20	2	9	0	.235
Seeds, New York	**23**	**68**	**5**	**16**	**1**	**9**	**0**	**.235**
Bragan, Phil	57	210	16	49	4	21	1	.233
Arnovich, Phil-Cin	54	196	17	45	0	17	0	.230
Mahan, Phil	58	225	25	51	1	14	1	.227
Padgett, St. Louis	44	128	13	29	5	20	0	.227
Brubaker, Pitts	27	66	7	16	0	6	0	.227
Warstler, Bos	28	54	5	12	0	4	0	.222
Hudson, Brooklyn	**31**	**68**	**6**	**15**	**0**	**6**	**0**	**.221**
Schulte, Phil	48	182	21	40	0	6	1	.220
Atwood, Phil	42	105	2	23	0	13	0	.219
Mattick, Chicago	65	234	15	51	0	21	4	.218
Mattick, Chi	65	234	15	51	0	21	4	.218
Wasdell, Brooklyn	**18**	**55**	**10**	**12**	**0**	**6**	**1**	**.218**
Joost, Cincinnati	42	138	10	30	1	13	3	.217
Gutteridge, St. L.	33	56	8	12	1	8	1	.214
Rucker, New York	**26**	**75**	**8**	**16**	**0**	**3**	**0**	**.213**
Mulcahy, Phil	17	43	3	9	0	5	0	.209
Masi, Boston	26	58	4	12	0	4	0	.207
Galan, Chicago	46	130	22	26	2	10	4	.200
Young, Pitts	25	56	6	11	1	8	0	.196
Walters, Cin	18	56	7	11	0	8	2	.196
Derringer, Cin	17	51	2	10	0	5	0	.196
Gamble, Cin	22	31	8	6	0	0	1	.194
Berres, Pitts-Bos	33	63	3	12	0	2	0	.190
Glossop, N.Y.-Bos	34	114	18	21	4	9	1	.184
Mancuso, Bklyn	**24**	**55**	**7**	**10**	**0**	**4**	**0**	**.182**

PITCHING RECORDS (Four Decisions or More)

Pitcher, Club	g.	ip.	h.	bb.	so.	w.	l.	pc.
Mooty, Chicago	10	46	28	18	16	5	0	1.000
Fitzsim'ns, Bkln	**9**	**58**	**54**	**10**	**16**	**7**	**1**	**.875**
Tamulis, Bklyn	**16**	**68**	**57**	**11**	**22**	**5**	**1**	**.833**
Sewell, Pitts	13	49	61	20	14	4	1	.800
Carleton, Bklyn	**12**	**84**	**71**	**20**	**45**	**4**	**1**	**.800**
Melton, N. Y.	**16**	**75**	**72**	**28**	**53**	**7**	**2**	**.778**
Blanton, Phil	8	45	44	13	16	3	1	.750
Walters, Cin	17	125	107	46	47	11	4	.733
Errickson, Bos	15	89	87	43	17	5	2	.714
Thompson, Cin	17	122	94	56	54	10	5	.667
Pressnell, Bklyn	**15**	**45**	**36**	**13**	**18**	**4**	**2**	**.667**
Lohrman, N. Y.	**13**	**80**	**80**	**14**	**30**	**7**	**4**	**.636**
Turner, Cin	10	78	76	15	23	5	3	.625
R'ff'nsb'rg'r, Ch	19	54	55	16	26	3	2	.600
Russell, St. L.	22	45	48	21	13	3	2	.600
Beggs, Cin	12	33	28	6	12	3	2	.600
French, Chi	20	122	114	34	56	9	6	.600
Gumbert, N. Y.	**16**	**106**	**106**	**39**	**41**	**7**	**5**	**.583**
Shoun, St. L.	29	73	65	15	38	4	3	.571
Derringer, Cin	17	141	135	22	53	9	7	.563
Hubbell, N. Y.	**13**	**96**	**95**	**24**	**36**	**5**	**4**	**.556**
Casey, Brooklyn	**14**	**63**	**62**	**19**	**20**	**5**	**4**	**.556**
Hamlin, Bklyn	**14**	**79**	**78**	**16**	**39**	**5**	**4**	**.556**
McGee, St. L.	17	96	100	44	30	6	5	.545
Wyatt, Bklyn	**18**	**109**	**116**	**32**	**56**	**7**	**6**	**.538**
Passeau, Chi	21	136	115	39	50	8	8	.500
Cooper, St. L.	15	79	93	40	31	4	4	.500
Dean, N. Y.	**7**	**40**	**33**	**9**	**10**	**2**	**2**	**.500**
Moore, Cin	10	30	23	19	15	2	2	.500
Mulcahy, Phil	16	129	126	50	41	7	8	.467
Brown, Pitts	21	88	87	25	33	5	6	.455
Warneke, St. L.	14	85	85	20	34	5	6	.455
Schumacher, NY	**14**	**85**	**79**	**34**	**42**	**5**	**7**	**.417**
Sullivan, Bos	16	95	86	48	32	5	7	.417
Butcher, Pitts	16	66	73	27	18	4	6	.400
Bowman, Pitts	13	93	100	37	26	4	6	.400
Piechota, Bos	8	27	22	19	8	2	3	.400
Bowman, St. L.	13	41	45	19	20	2	3	.400
Posedel, Bos	17	99	115	32	47	5	8	.385
Lee, Chicago	20	111	128	45	36	6	10	.375
Olsen, Chicago	18	62	63	20	24	3	5	.375
Higbe, Phil	19	131	115	67	58	5	9	.357
Lanier, St. L.	15	39	46	20	17	2	4	.333

AMERICAN LEAGUE

CLUB BATTING

Club	g.	ab.	r.	h.	hr.	rbi.	sb.	pc.
Detroit	69	2414	393	690	58	358	22	.286
Washington	72	2558	342	721	27	304	48	.282
Boston	68	2412	362	673	63	343	17	.279
Chicago	67	2335	321	652	37	297	22	.279
Cleveland	72	2482	342	677	56	318	18	.273
Philadelphia	68	2337	333	637	50	306	20	.273
St. Louis	74	2602	376	685	66	353	25	.263
New York	**68**	**2277**	**323**	**570**	**67**	**296**	**28**	**.250**

CLUB FIELDING

Club	g.	po.	a.	e.	dp.	pc.
Cleveland	72	1907	720	61	69	.977
St. Louis	74	1975	917	77	91	.974
Chicago	67	1767	678	68	45	.973
Boston	68	1855	793	76	75	.972
Detroit	69	1873	755	80	62	.970
Washington	72	1878	821	89	70	.968
Philadelphia	68	1817	762	106	53	.960
New York	**68**	**1813**	**794**	**58**	**73**	**.978**

BATTING RECORDS

Player, Club	g.	ab.	r.	h.	hr.	rbi.	sb.	pc.
Mills, New York	**17**	**31**	**5**	**13**	**1**	**7**	**0**	**.419**
Gelbert, Wash	18	49	7	20	0	7	0	.408
Radcliff, St. L.	68	260	39	93	3	34	3	.358
Wright, Chicago	65	257	40	91	3	38	3	.354
Appling, Chicago	62	236	34	82	0	36	0	.348
Finney, Boston	63	283	45	98	4	35	0	.346
Greenberg, Det	64	253	50	87	15	69	0	.344
Williams, Boston	64	250	59	86	10	50	1	.344
McCosky, Detroit	62	257	58	88	3	20	1	.342
Simmons, Phil	21	41	7	15	1	9	0	.341
Solters, Chicago	41	134	20	45	3	26	2	.336
Travis, Wash	59	233	29	78	0	30	0	.335
Rosar, New York	**22**	**63**	**7**	**21**	**2**	**7**	**2**	**.333**
Peacock, Boston	31	57	[illegible]	19	[illegible]	9	0	.333
Mack, [illegible]	[illegible]	[illegible]	[illegible]	[illegible]	[illegible]	41	2	.327
Hayes, [illegible]	[illegible]	[illegible]	[illegible]	[illegible]	[illegible]	37	4	.327
Rosen[illegible]	[illegible]	[illegible]	[illegible]	[illegible]	[illegible]	15	2	.317
Cramer, [illegible]	[illegible]	[illegible]	[illegible]	[illegible]	[illegible]	26	1	.316
Moses, [illegible]	[illegible]	[illegible]	[illegible]	[illegible]	[illegible]	25	2	.315
Weath[illegible]	[illegible]	[illegible]	[illegible]	[illegible]	[illegible]	19	1	.315
Grace, [illegible]	[illegible]	[illegible]	[illegible]	[illegible]	[illegible]	8	0	.313
Sulliv[illegible]	[illegible]	[illegible]	[illegible]	[illegible]	[illegible]	21	0	.312
Walke[illegible]	[illegible]	[illegible]	[illegible]	[illegible]	[illegible]	53	13	.311
Higgin[illegible]	[illegible]	[illegible]	[illegible]	[illegible]	[illegible]	34	3	.311
Lewis, [illegible]	[illegible]	[illegible]	[illegible]	[illegible]	[illegible]	30	6	.309
Case, [illegible]	[illegible]	[illegible]	[illegible]	[illegible]	[illegible]	30	17	.308
Hoag, [illegible]	[illegible]	[illegible]	[illegible]	[illegible]	[illegible]	18	2	.308
DiMag[illegible]	[illegible]	[illegible]	[illegible]	[illegible]	[illegible]	2	1	.308
Selkirk, [illegible]	[illegible]	[illegible]	[illegible]	[illegible]	[illegible]	36	2	.307
Foxx, [illegible]	[illegible]	[illegible]	[illegible]	[illegible]	[illegible]	65	4	.305
DiMag[illegible]	[illegible]	[illegible]	[illegible]	[illegible]	[illegible]	46	0	.305
Tresh, [illegible]	[illegible]	[illegible]	[illegible]	[illegible]	[illegible]	32	0	.304
Keller, [illegible]	[illegible]	[illegible]	[illegible]	[illegible]	[illegible]	47	4	.303
Trosky, [illegible]	[illegible]	[illegible]	[illegible]	[illegible]	[illegible]	50	1	.301
Knick[illegible]	[illegible]	[illegible]	[illegible]	[illegible]	[illegible]	5	0	.301
Myer, [illegible]	[illegible]	[illegible]	[illegible]	[illegible]	[illegible]	5	0	.300
Hemsl[illegible]	[illegible]	[illegible]	[illegible]	[illegible]	[illegible]	32	1	.299
Sieber[illegible]	[illegible]	[illegible]	[illegible]	[illegible]	[illegible]	39	3	.298
Bonur[illegible]	[illegible]	[illegible]	[illegible]	[illegible]	[illegible]	43	1	.298
York, [illegible]	[illegible]	[illegible]	[illegible]	[illegible]	[illegible]	51	2	.298
Bell, [illegible]	[illegible]	[illegible]	[illegible]	[illegible]	[illegible]	30	1	.298
Johns[illegible]	[illegible]	[illegible]	[illegible]	[illegible]	[illegible]	46	4	.297
Early, [illegible]	[illegible]	[illegible]	[illegible]	[illegible]	[illegible]	5	0	.296
Wilson, [illegible]	[illegible]	[illegible]	[illegible]	[illegible]	[illegible]	4	0	.296
Tebbet[illegible]	[illegible]	[illegible]	[illegible]	[illegible]	[illegible]	19	4	.295
W. Mi[illegible]	[illegible]	[illegible]	[illegible]	[illegible]	[illegible]	10	0	.295
Boudr[illegible]	[illegible]	[illegible]	[illegible]	[illegible]	[illegible]	36	2	.294
Averil[illegible]	[illegible]	[illegible]	[illegible]	[illegible]	[illegible]	16	0	.289
McQui[illegible]	[illegible]	[illegible]	[illegible]	[illegible]	[illegible]	43	1	.286
Gehrin[illegible]	[illegible]	[illegible]	[illegible]	[illegible]	[illegible]	46	4	.284
Heffne[illegible]	[illegible]	[illegible]	[illegible]	[illegible]	[illegible]	25	3	.278
Berard[illegible]	[illegible]	[illegible]	[illegible]	[illegible]	[illegible]	50	3	.276
Kreev[illegible]	[illegible]	[illegible]	[illegible]	[illegible]	[illegible]	25	8	.272
Bloodw[illegible]	[illegible]	[illegible]	[illegible]	[illegible]	[illegible]	40	2	.271
Chapm[illegible]	[illegible]	[illegible]	[illegible]	[illegible]	[illegible]	24	6	.270
Doerr, [illegible]	[illegible]	[illegible]	[illegible]	[illegible]	[illegible]	43	3	.268
Dean, [illegible]	[illegible]	[illegible]	[illegible]	[illegible]	[illegible]	4	0	.267
Gante[illegible]	[illegible]	[illegible]	[illegible]	[illegible]	[illegible]	2	0	.267
Campb[illegible]	[illegible]	[illegible]	[illegible]	[illegible]	[illegible]	26	2	.266
Chapm[illegible]	[illegible]	[illegible]	[illegible]	[illegible]	[illegible]	32	1	.266
Clift, [illegible]	[illegible]	[illegible]	[illegible]	[illegible]	[illegible]	35	2	.264
Labbs[illegible]	[illegible]	[illegible]	[illegible]	[illegible]	[illegible]	21	2	.263
Turne[illegible]	[illegible]	[illegible]	[illegible]	[illegible]	[illegible]	4	0	.263
Tabor, [illegible]	[illegible]	[illegible]	[illegible]	[illegible]	[illegible]	37	5	.262
Bartel[illegible]	[illegible]	[illegible]	[illegible]	[illegible]	[illegible]	29	4	.260
Kuhel, [illegible]	[illegible]	[illegible]	[illegible]	[illegible]	[illegible]	39	6	.260
Welaj, [illegible]	[illegible]	[illegible]	[illegible]	[illegible]	[illegible]	16	7	.257
Swift, [illegible]	[illegible]	[illegible]	[illegible]	[illegible]	[illegible]	19	0	.254
Rubel[illegible]	[illegible]	[illegible]	[illegible]	[illegible]	[illegible]	17	3	.253
Cullen[illegible]	[illegible]	[illegible]	[illegible]	[illegible]	[illegible]	20	0	.252
Gordo[illegible]	[illegible]	[illegible]	[illegible]	[illegible]	[illegible]	41	10	.250
Dahlg[illegible]	[illegible]	[illegible]	[illegible]	[illegible]	[illegible]	25	0	.250
Henri[illegible]	[illegible]	[illegible]	[illegible]	[illegible]	[illegible]	14	1	.250
Heath, [illegible]	[illegible]	[illegible]	[illegible]	[illegible]	[illegible]	27	2	.249
McCoy, [illegible]	[illegible]	[illegible]	[illegible]	[illegible]	[illegible]	36	1	.247
Kenne[illegible]	[illegible]	[illegible]	[illegible]	[illegible]	[illegible]	17	1	.246
Rolfe, [illegible]	[illegible]	[illegible]	[illegible]	[illegible]	[illegible]	20	3	.246
Judnic[illegible]	[illegible]	[illegible]	[illegible]	[illegible]	[illegible]	40	5	.242
Cronin, [illegible]	[illegible]	[illegible]	[illegible]	[illegible]	[illegible]	46	3	.241
Lillard, [illegible]	[illegible]	[illegible]	[illegible]	[illegible]	[illegible]	14	0	.239
Pofahl, [illegible]	[illegible]	[illegible]	[illegible]	[illegible]	[illegible]	13	1	.235
Newso[illegible]	[illegible]	[illegible]	[illegible]	[illegible]	[illegible]	7	0	.234
Ferrel[illegible]	[illegible]	[illegible]	[illegible]	[illegible]	[illegible]	11	0	.232
West, [illegible]	[illegible]	[illegible]	[illegible]	[illegible]	[illegible]	5	0	.231
McNai[illegible]	[illegible]	[illegible]	[illegible]	[illegible]	[illegible]	31	1	.228
Keltne[illegible]	[illegible]	[illegible]	[illegible]	[illegible]	[illegible]	31	2	.227
Dickey, [illegible]	[illegible]	[illegible]	[illegible]	[illegible]	[illegible]	25	0	.226
Hudson, [illegible]	[illegible]	[illegible]	[illegible]	[illegible]	[illegible]	2	0	.220
Bruck[illegible]	[illegible]	[illegible]	[illegible]	[illegible]	[illegible]	1	0	.220
Susce, [illegible]	[illegible]	[illegible]	[illegible]	[illegible]	[illegible]	3	1	.208
Branc[illegible]	[illegible]	[illegible]	[illegible]	[illegible]	[illegible]	13	2	.205
Leona[illegible]	[illegible]	[illegible]	[illegible]	[illegible]	[illegible]	2	0	.204
Desau[illegible]	[illegible]	[illegible]	[illegible]	[illegible]	[illegible]	10	0	.201
Fox, [illegible]	[illegible]	[illegible]	[illegible]	[illegible]	[illegible]	3	1	.200
Croset[illegible]	[illegible]	[illegible]	[illegible]	[illegible]	[illegible]	17	5	.194
Strang[illegible]	[illegible]	[illegible]	[illegible]	[illegible]	[illegible]	4	2	.186
Milnar, [illegible]	[illegible]	[illegible]	[illegible]	[illegible]	[illegible]	2	0	.176
Feller, [illegible]	[illegible]	[illegible]	[illegible]	[illegible]	[illegible]	8	0	.167
Pytlak, [illegible]	[illegible]	[illegible]	[illegible]	[illegible]	[illegible]	7	0	.138

PITCHING RECORDS (Four Decisions or More)

Pitcher, Club	g.	ip.	h.	bb.	so.	w.	l.	pc.
Newso[illegible]	[illegible]	[illegible]	[illegible]	[illegible]	[illegible]	11	1	.917
Rowe, [illegible]	[illegible]	[illegible]	[illegible]	[illegible]	[illegible]	5	1	.833
Smith, [illegible]	[illegible]	[illegible]	[illegible]	[illegible]	[illegible]	9	2	.818
Wilson, [illegible]	[illegible]	[illegible]	[illegible]	[illegible]	[illegible]	4	1	.800
Heving, [illegible]	[illegible]	[illegible]	[illegible]	[illegible]	[illegible]	4	1	.800
Ross, [illegible]	[illegible]	[illegible]	[illegible]	[illegible]	[illegible]	4	1	.800
Dietric[illegible]	[illegible]	[illegible]	[illegible]	[illegible]	[illegible]	4	1	.800
Milna[illegible]	[illegible]	[illegible]	[illegible]	[illegible]	[illegible]	11	3	.786
Feller, [illegible]	[illegible]	[illegible]	[illegible]	[illegible]	[illegible]	13	4	.765
Breue[illegible]	[illegible]	[illegible]	[illegible]	[illegible]	[illegible]	6	3	.667
Grove, [illegible]	[illegible]	[illegible]	[illegible]	[illegible]	[illegible]	4	2	.667
Allen, [illegible]	[illegible]	[illegible]	[illegible]	[illegible]	[illegible]	5	3	.625
Russo[illegible]	[illegible]	[illegible]	[illegible]	[illegible]	[illegible]	5	3	.625
Bridge[illegible]	[illegible]	[illegible]	[illegible]	[illegible]	[illegible]	6	4	.600
Lawso[illegible]	[illegible]	[illegible]	[illegible]	[illegible]	[illegible]	3	2	.600
Hash, [illegible]	[illegible]	[illegible]	[illegible]	[illegible]	[illegible]	7	5	.583
Leona[illegible]	[illegible]	[illegible]	[illegible]	[illegible]	[illegible]	9	7	.563
Pears[illegible]	[illegible]	[illegible]	[illegible]	[illegible]	[illegible]	6	5	.545
Auker, [illegible]	[illegible]	[illegible]	[illegible]	[illegible]	[illegible]	7	6	.538
Ruffi[illegible]	[illegible]	[illegible]	[illegible]	[illegible]	[illegible]	7	6	.538
Smith, [illegible]	[illegible]	[illegible]	[illegible]	[illegible]	[illegible]	6	6	.500
Dean, [illegible]	[illegible]	[illegible]	[illegible]	[illegible]	[illegible]	6	6	.500
Babic[illegible]	[illegible]	[illegible]	[illegible]	[illegible]	[illegible]	6	6	.500
Newh[illegible]	[illegible]	[illegible]	[illegible]	[illegible]	[illegible]	5	5	.500
Harris[illegible]	[illegible]	[illegible]	[illegible]	[illegible]	[illegible]	5	5	.500
Bento[illegible]	[illegible]	[illegible]	[illegible]	[illegible]	[illegible]	4	4	.500
Dickm[illegible]	[illegible]	[illegible]	[illegible]	[illegible]	[illegible]	4	4	.500
Chan[illegible]	[illegible]	[illegible]	[illegible]	[illegible]	[illegible]	4	4	.500
Lyons[illegible]	[illegible]	[illegible]	[illegible]	[illegible]	[illegible]	4	4	.500
Galeh[illegible]	[illegible]	[illegible]	[illegible]	[illegible]	[illegible]	4	4	.500
Gorsic[illegible]	[illegible]	[illegible]	[illegible]	[illegible]	[illegible]	3	3	.500
Hudli[illegible]	[illegible]	[illegible]	[illegible]	[illegible]	[illegible]	3	3	.500
Donal[illegible]	[illegible]	[illegible]	[illegible]	[illegible]	[illegible]	2	2	.500
Coffm[illegible]	[illegible]	[illegible]	[illegible]	[illegible]	[illegible]	2	2	.500
Kenn[illegible]	[illegible]	[illegible]	[illegible]	[illegible]	[illegible]	6	7	.462
Bagby[illegible]	[illegible]	[illegible]	[illegible]	[illegible]	[illegible]	5	6	.455
Lee, [illegible]	[illegible]	[illegible]	[illegible]	[illegible]	[illegible]	5	6	.455
Potter[illegible]	[illegible]	[illegible]	[illegible]	[illegible]	[illegible]	5	6	.455
Rigne[illegible]	[illegible]	[illegible]	[illegible]	[illegible]	[illegible]	7	9	.438
Maste[illegible]	[illegible]	[illegible]	[illegible]	[illegible]	[illegible]	3	4	.429
Hudso[illegible]	[illegible]	[illegible]	[illegible]	[illegible]	[illegible]	6	9	.400
Heuss[illegible]	[illegible]	[illegible]	[illegible]	[illegible]	[illegible]	3	5	.375
Hard[illegible]	[illegible]	[illegible]	[illegible]	[illegible]	[illegible]	3	5	.375
Chase[illegible]	[illegible]	[illegible]	[illegible]	[illegible]	[illegible]	5	10	.333
Hayn[illegible]	[illegible]	[illegible]	[illegible]	[illegible]	[illegible]	3	6	.333
Kram[illegible]	[illegible]	[illegible]	[illegible]	[illegible]	[illegible]	3	6	.333
Knott[illegible]	[illegible]	[illegible]	[illegible]	[illegible]	[illegible]	3	6	.333
Nigge[illegible]	[illegible]	[illegible]	[illegible]	[illegible]	[illegible]	2	4	.333
Bildil[illegible]	[illegible]	[illegible]	[illegible]	[illegible]	[illegible]	2	4	.333
Murp[illegible]	[illegible]	[illegible]	[illegible]	[illegible]	[illegible]	2	4	.333

Higbe Halts Giants, 8-2

Continued from Page 1

then hit the road for the All-Star game in St. Louis on Tuesday and the consequent opening of the third Western trip. . . . Yesterday's paid attendance was 5,645, one of the smallest Saturday gatherings of the season for the P. G. . . . The Giants were anxious to leave the P. G. for they have fared poorly there this season while they have played brilliantly on the road. . . . Billy Jurges and Frank Demaree are expected to be back in the line-up by the time the Giants open their trip.

HIT BY PUNCHING BAG

Philadelphia	ab	r	h	o	a	Giants	ab	r	h	o	a
Mahan,1b	6	3	1	7	0	W'teh'd,3b	5	0	1	1	1
Klein,rf	5	1	3	4	0	Rucker,cf	5	0	0	4	0
Mueller,2b	2	1	1	3	4	Moore,lf	5	0	0	2	0
Rizzo,lf	4	1	1	2	0	Young,1b	3	0	1	6	0
May,3b	3	1	0	0	0	Danning,c	4	1	1	7	0
Marty,cf	4	1	2	3	0	Ott,rf	3	1	0	2	1
Bragan,ss	5	0	2	5	4	Cul'nello,2b	4	0	2	3	1
Atwood,c	5	0	0	3	0	Witek,ss	2	0	1	2	3
Higbe,p	5	0	2	0	2	Dean,p	2	0	0	0	1
						Lynn,p	0	0	0	0	0
						aMcCarthy	1	0	0	0	0
Totals	39	8	12	27	10	Totals	34	2	6	27	7

aBatted for Lynn in 9th.

Philadelphia	0	0	0	1	1	0	4	1	1	—8
Giants	0	0	0	2	0	0	0	0	0	—2

Errors—Marty, Rucker, Bragan. Runs batted in—Bragan 2, Cuccinello, Witez, May 2, Klein, Rizzo 2. Two-base hit—Cuccinello. Sacrifice — Dean. Left on bases—Giants 10, Philadelphia 11. Bases on balls—Off Dean 4, off Higbe 4, off Lynn 2. Struck out—By Dean 2, by Higbe 2, by Lynn 3. Hits—Off Dean—6 in 6 innings (none out in 7th), off Lynn 4 in 3. Wild pitch—Dean. Balk—Higbe. Losing pitcher—Dean. Umpires—oGetz, Pinelli and Reardon. Attendance—5,645.

Holt, Billows Advance on Links

Manchester, Vt., July 6 (U.P.)—Two New Yorkers, Bill Holt of Syracuse and Ray Billows of Poughkeepsie, came through quarter-finals of the 13th annual Robert Todd Lincoln Memorial Cup golf tournament late today and were favored to meetin the finals on rugged Ekwanok Country Club course tomorrow.

By virtue of easy victories Holt was to meet Kenneth Corcoran of Oyster Harbors, Mass., in tomorrow morning's 18-hole semi-final, while Billows was to play C. W. Price of Burlington. An afternoon final round of 18 holes will complete four days' play in which there were 191 entrants.

Semi-Pro Nines To Play Benefit

Five pitchers have been selected by the eight managers of teams in the Metropolitan Baseball Association to take part in the third annual Hospitalization Fund game between the M. B. A. All-Stars and the Black Yankees at Erasmus Field Thursday night.

The Bushwicks will have Emile (Mike) Meola, former Browns and Red Sox hurler, in the game while the Bay Parkways will be represented by their ace, Abe Spiro, and the Springfield Greys will send Hal Benne into the fray. Benne has won all nine starts this season. Bill Simmons, Cedarhurst veteran, and Ed Estwanick, Barton's Nighthawks southpaw, are the other moundsmen chosen.

Porter Beats Peterson In Broad Channel Tennis

Bill Porter defeated Arthur J. Peterson, 2—6, 6—4, 6—4, in the first round of the Class B tennis singles championship yesterday at Broad Channel Bathing Park. Adolph McCook lost to Hauflee, 7—5, 7—5, and Bill Whiteford conquered Chaumont, 6—2, 6—1.

Vince Paul beat Len Belter, 6—2, 4—6, 6—4, in a Class A tennis ladder challenge match. Ed George beat Phil Sands, 6—3, 6—4, and Joe Pecht gained the nod over Mike Abandond, 6—2, 6—1, in the

Querida Remains R Class Leader In Babylon Series

Special to The Brooklyn Eagle

Babylon, July 6—A record fleet of 96 boats crossed the starting line today and sailed the course in jig-time with a light sail breeze that blew steadily out of the southwest in the second race of Babylon's three-day invitation regatta.

Only four of Thursday's winners managed to stay on top. Duncan Arnold sailed his Querida home more than three minutes ahead of Gil Haight's Apache in the R class, and Carol King trimmed Julian Davies by nine seconds in the Timber Points. Wilbur Ketcham, in the Narrasketucks, and George Winters in the kephyrs both finished in the money, while the rest of the skippers were all shuffled up.

After rounding the mark in the second place, the first time around the course, Eddie Ketcham sailed his Draco II home over a minute ahead of Horace Havemeyer's Gull 2. Bill Picken, in Fo-Fo, finished third, 30 seconds astern of Havemeyer. Today's finish puts Havemeyer one point ahead of Ketcham in the series standing.

Doug Westin won handily in the Interclub class with Bill Sullivan in Phantom, finishing second. In the Cape Cod Knockabout class, Miss Nancy Underhill finished over a minute ahead of Sperry Lea's Horizon, while Prall Culviner sailed his Bucaneer home in third place. In the Snipe class, Jean Galbreath returned Tit for Tat, when she beat Florence Picken's Popeye. Robert Hornfeck sailing Dipsy Doodle was third. At this point, both Miss Picken and Miss Galbreath are tied for first in the series standing.

Gerry Wynkoop, sailing Bixie, won in the Comet class when his brother Dan fouled and dropped out of the race. Bob Gusravino was second in Kinkajou.

STARS—START 3:06—COURSE 8 MILES

Yacht and Owner	Finish
Draco II, Edward Ketcham Jr.	4:53:16
Gull II, Horace Havemeyer	5:54:38
Fo-fo, William Picken	5:55:14

4, Gull, William Hayward; 5, Finesse, Walter Podolak; 6, Vim II, Horace Havemeyer Jr.; 7, Wings, Everitt and Austin; 8, Typhoon, William Picken 3d; 8, Chief, Charles Lawrence; 10, April, William C. Foster; 11, Okla, H. Buys; 12, Vesta, Paul Maynard; 13, Interlude, Meville Smith; 14, Fatima, Hilda Lynn. Cottontail, Andrew Haire, and White Mist, Vincent Turecamo, did not finish.

INTERCLUB—START 3:09
COURSE 8 MILES

Yacht and Owner	Finish
Flying Cloud, Douglas Westin	4:48:53
Phantom, William Sullivan	4:50:45
Typhoon, William Bonyun	4:51:14

4, Gail, George C. Furman.

CLASS R—SRTART 3:09
COURSE, 8 MILES

Yacht and Owner	Finish
Querida, Duncan Arnold	4:49:40
Apache, Gilbert Haight	4:52:46
Allouette, Collins Brothers	4:54:19

ZEPHYRS—START 3:12
COURSE 8 MILES

Yacht and Owner	Finish
Duchess, George Winters	5:06:21
Circe, William Carpenter	5:06:40
Zym-Zym, James Swan	5:07:27

4, Debutante, W. B. Harwood Jr.

NARRASKETUCKS—START 3:18
COURSE 8 MILES

Yacht and Owner	Finish
Undine II, Bergen Chichester	5:10:24
Lucky Lady, Roy Van Nostrand Jr.	5:11:22
Coquette, John P. Robbins	5:11:53

4, Flying Arrow, E. Carlton Arink; 5, Taquam, Gorton Baldwin; 6, Tar, Dodd Brothers; 7, No. 16, Stephen Conger; 8, Vixen, Mrs. Betty Wanser; 9, Smoothie, Mrs. Jane Collins; 10, No. 21, Eugene Connett; 11, No. 15, R. S. Gibbs; 12, Papoose, W. R. Wiley; 13, Sweet Sioux, Betty and Bill King; 14, Scud II, Andrew Underhill Jr.; Rascal, Kenneth Smith; 16, ery Ladyship, Miss Paige. Shaver II and William Torrey withdrew.

TIMBER POINTS—START 3:21
COURSE 8 MILES

Yacht and Owner	Finish
Winsome II, Carol King	5:20:21
Bay Bee II, Julian Davies 3d	5:20:29
Three Star, Muriel Van Vranken	5:22:05

4, Oppie, Thomas D. Orr.

CAPE COD KNOCKABOUTS—START 3:24
COURSE 4 MILES

Yacht and Owner	Finish
Scud, Nancy Underhill	4:24:37
Horizon, Sperry Lea	4:26 12
Buccaneer, Prall Culliner	4:26:25

4, Malice, Terry McGuirk; 5, Audrey, Osborne Elliott; 6, Talisman, Mary D. Sayre; 7, Red Cloud, W. A. Rich; 8, Romona, J. W. Taussig; 9, Sandy, Healey Brothers; 10, Red Head, Peter Ross; 11, Puffin, Phyllis Van de Water; 12, Sam II, Mary Ann Shanks; 13, Good News, Paul Fishel; 14, Whitecap, Charles Ross; 15, Snapper, Cornelius Edert.

COMETS. START, 3:27. COURSE, 4 MILES

Bixi, Gerardus Wynkoop	4:28:16
Kindajou 3d, Rafael Gustavino	4:29:22
Snix, George W. Marshall	4:30:21

4, Fireball, Walbridge and Zimmerman; 5, Lucky, Alex Pearson; 6, Sunbeam, John Maynard; 7, No. 708, Robert Zimmerman; Duchess, Daniel Wynkoop, withdrew.

SNIPES. START, 3:30. COURSE, 4 MILES

Anne, Jean Galbreath	4:33:06
Popeye, Florence Picken	4:35:46
Dipsy Doodle, Robert Hornfeck	4:36:35

4, Sub Deb, Deborah Cassidy; 5, Tomcat, Marguerite Arink; 6, Merry Mac, Merritt McCully; 7, Torch, R. W. Morgan; 8, Mystery, William Abbott; 9, Skoal, John Rupee; 10, Dew Drop, Edwin Eyre; 11, No. 3052, Beth Blossom; 12, Classy, Marjorie Reynolds; 13, Tricky, J. G. Baxter; 14, Ozzie, F. Davies; 15, Nyen, Millicent George; 16, We'll See, R. Messon; 17, No. 287 (owner's name unknown); 18, Wild Cargo, Gloria Haight; 19, Teeteh, Charlotte Robbins; No. 1543, did not finish.

MALLARDS. START, 3:33
COURSE 4 MILES

Caprice, Edward Macy	4:38:22
Damzel, E. R. Kretz	4:38:30
Fol de Rol, H. A. Gartner	4:39:25

4, Four Winds, Jack Roundbeck; 5, Ibis, Leben Sailor.

FRENCH YIELD TRAPPED FLEET

Wall Street Closing
RACING EXTRA
★ ★ ★ ★ ★ ★

BROOKLYN EAGLE

LOCAL WEATHER FORECAST: Partly cloudy, warm tonight and tomorrow

Wall Street Closing
RACING EXTRA
★ ★ ★ ★ ★ ★

99th YEAR • No. 189 • DAILY AND SUNDAY • BROOKLYN, N. Y., TUESDAY, JULY 9, 1940 • Entered at the Brooklyn Postoffice as 2d Class Mail Matter—(Copyright 1940 The Brooklyn Daily Eagle) (F. D. S. Corporation) • 3 CENTS

JAPAN DEMANDS U. S. APOLOGY

Eagle Staff photos

AT RITES FOR BROOKLYN BOMB VICTIM—Marching behind casket of Detective Ferdinand Socha, killed in explosion of time bomb at World's Fair, are Mayor LaGuardia, Police Commissioner Valentine, Godfrey Haggard, British Consul General; Grover Whalen, Capt. Lawrence McNair of the Navy and Col. J. J. O'Hare of the Army.

City Posts $25,000 Reward For Tip on Fair Bombers

Appeals to Subversive Groups —1,000 at Sleuth's Funeral

A frank appeal to members of any subversive organization to divulge possible connections with the fatal bomb explosion at the World's Fair was seen today as the Board of Estimate, in its first meeting at City Hall, voted unanimously to appropriate $25,000 reward for information leading to the apprehension of the "person, persons or organization" which planted the bomb in the British Pavilion.

Full secrecy of identity was promised informants, lending support to the interpretation that the appeal for information was directed at members of alien organizations.

Mayor LaGuardia announced at the meeting that he had conferred with Police Commissioner Valentine and other police officials, and declared:

"If it is not essential that the informant appear as a material witness, arrangements will be made to conceal that person's identity."

The Mayor said any information could be given directly to the Police Department, either in person or by phoning CAnal 6-2000, Manhattan Hearquarters.

Declaring that if it had not been for the courageous action of members of the police force, two of whom were killed and six injured in removing the bomb before examination, the toll of life would have been much greater. He added

Continued on Page 19

Stratoliner Makes Record-Setting Flight

Lands Load of Celebrities at LaGuardia Field After 12-Hour Hop From West Coast

After a smooth and uneventful maiden trip from the West Coast, a Transcontinental and Western Air stratoliner landed at LaGuardia Field at 10:28 a.m. today with a planeload of celebrities and an unofficial record for commercial flights.

Twelve hours and 13 minutes earlier, the 23-ton, $450,000 Boeing transport had left Burbank, Cal., making only one stop, at Kansas City.

The first flight westward was made by a stratoliner which left LaGuardia Field last night at 9:30 o'clock, 45 minutes before the eastbound ship took off from California.

Although the original schedule had called for additional stops at Albuquerque, N. M., and Chicago, the Eastbound ship made only the single stop for fuel.

Former schedules of TWA called for an eastbound time of 15 hours 42 minutes and the new stratoliner schedule called for a time of 13 hours 40 minutes.

The 33-passenger plane, one of five being put into service by TWA, was piloted by Capt. Jack Zimmerman, chief pilot of the eastern division, and carried two other en-

Continued on Page 3

New Soviet Demands Feared by Turkey

Istanbul, Turkey, July 9 (U.P.)—Turkey expected new demands from Russia in the next few days and authoritative sources said there was little hope of an agreement.

It was believed that the demands would be stiffer than those Russia made last year for a mutual assistance pact, a change in control of the Dardanelles more favorable to Russia, and less friendly relations between Turkey and the Allies.

Britain Finding Poles Make Good Air Fighters

London, July 9 (AP)—The Air Ministry reported "very satisfactory progress" today in the training of thousands of Polish airmen as bombing crews in England.

Some of the best trained pilots, many of whom fought in France, probably will fly fighter planes.

ARMY TO ENLIST 'PARASHOTS' TO SPOT RAIDERS

By ED REID

Thousands of citizens living throughout New York State, and principally in the northern part, will be enlisted this Summer in an Air Raid Warning Corps, similar to the widespread organization existing in war-torn England, it was learned today.

The plan, evolved by Lt. Gen. Hugh A. Drum, commandant of the Second Corps Area, is based on the experiences of the "parashots" and other citizen groups functioning as guards against German air invasion in the British Isles.

The "brains" of the air raid corps will be centered at Plattsburg, where 100,000 members of the National Guard and Regular Army will engage in maneuvers during August.

A call for volunteers in the corps will be issued a couple of weeks before the concentration of soldiers in the Plattsburg area begins. Each civilian spotter will be given the number of the Army's air defense corps at the encampment and will in turn be given a place on a huge map of New York State, to be set up on a board at headquarters.

Without warning during the training period mass air raids will take place on the camp at Plattsburg and it will be up to the spotters to warn the Army men of the approach of the planes.

As each civilian calls in with his

Continued on Page 19

French Yield Trapped Fleet At Alexandria

Ile de France Reported Seized by British—Richelieu Is Crippled

BULLETIN

London, July 9 (AP)—Reuters, British news agency, quoted Japanese reports from Singapore today that the British had seized the 43,450-ton French liner Ile de France.

London, July 9 (AP)—The battleship Richelieu, 35,000-ton pride of the French Navy, has been crippled by British naval and air action, a cheering House of Commons was informed today as another section of France's fleet was taken by the British.

While A. V. Alexander, First Lord of the Admiralty, told the House of the British raids on the Richelieu at Dakar, French West Africa, yesterday, announcement was made in Alexandria, Egypt, that the French would turn their entire flotilla there over to Great Britain.

The Richelieu was struck first by depth bombs from a motorboat under her stern to wreck her propeller and steering gear, but the coup de grace on the new, mighty dreadnaught was delivered by aerial torpedoes dropped by British planes, Alexander disclosed.

He said she is dowr by the stern, listing heavily to port and lying in a heavy pool of oil.

The blow disposed of the seventh French battleship, the Admiralty First Lord said, leaving only the Jean Bart, a sister ship of the Richelieu still so far from completion that she cannot be ready for action for months.

France had eight capital ships when the armistice was signed, he

Continued on Page 19

Borough Aide Accused Of Taking $5,500 Bribe

BULLETIN

The first extraordinary Amen grand jury in a presentment handed up today to Supreme Court Justice MacCrate charged that George H. Green, an inspector in the Division of Highways and Sewers in the Brooklyn Borough President's office, has taken at least $5,500 in bribes and is unfit to remain in the city's employ.

Willkie Chooses Martin To Direct His Campaign

House Minority Leader Named G. O. P. National Chairman

Washington, July 9 (AP)—Representative Joseph W. Martin Jr. of Massachusetts, House minority leader, today was named chairman of the Republican National Committee and director of the Willkie Presidential campaign.

John D. M. Hamilton, present committee chairman, was selected as executive director. He will work under Martin at a salary of $25,000 a year.

Wendell L. Willkie, the Republican Presidential nominee, announced the appointments to a press conference after he had met with a subcommittee which the national committee authorized to make the selections.

Stassen Heads Advisers

Willkie also announced that Governor Harold E. Stassen of Minnesota, who was keynoter and Willkie's floor manager at the Republican Convention, would head a large campaign advisory committee.

Other appointments included formal selection of Russell Davenport of New York, former managing editor of Fortune magazine, to serve as Willkie's personal representative who will work with Martin, and the assignment of Oren Root Jr., young New York lawyer, to organization work among independent Willkie clubs.

May Pick N. Y. as Headquarters

Campaign headquarters, Willkie announced, will be established in either Chicago or New York. He added that an effort would be made to have the headquarters "convenient" to Martin, thus indicating that New York was the preferred city.

Walter S. Hallanan, of West Virginia, announced the sub-committee's action in approving the appointment of Martin was unanimous. Hallanan announced that Sinclair Weeks of Massachusetts had been chosen chairman of the executive committee of the National Committee. J. Russel Sprague of New York was named to the executive committee.

Reich, Italy Plot Threefold War On Great Britain

Gayda Sees Blockade, Empire Contacts Broken And Defeat at Sea

Rome, July 9 (AP)—An Italian-German agreement for a three-fold attack on Britain was reported today by Virginio Gayda, usually authoritative Fascist editor.

The axis partners, Gayda said, are determined:

1. To blockade the British Isles.
2. To break Britain's empire contacts.
3. To defeat her "at home, in imperial territories" and at sea.

Each axis power has definitely assigned tasks for these goals, Gayda, editor of Il Giornale D'Italia, said.

Italy's job, he declared, is to strike at the British at four places on land and harass British shipping in the Atlantic, Mediterranean, Red Sea and Indian Ocean and, above all, immobilize a large part of Britain's seapower in the Mediterranean.

Renew Raids on Britain

London, July 9 (AP)—At least two persons were reported killed and a number injured in widespread German aerial raids over England, Scotland and Wales last night and today.

A lone German dropped a load of bombs on a Welsh town this afternoon, killing at least two persons and injuring others.

(In Berlin, the high command said the air force bombs had hit shipyards at Devonport, oil tanks at Ipswich and elsewhere, explosive plants at Harwich, chemical plants in Billingham, and a cruiser, a destroyer and five merchantmen in the English Channel and North Sea.)

British and German planes fought an air battle over southeastern England this afternoon. Empty machine-gun cartridges fell like hail on the town over which the battle was fought.

Berlin, July 9 (AP)—All of 12 British bombing planes attacking the German-held airport of Stavanger-Sola on the Norwegian coast today were shot down, 11 by German planes and one by anti-aircraft fire, DNB, the official German news agency, reported.

Suffolk Downs Results

FIRST RACE—Three-year-olds; ¾ mile.

Kilta Verse (Taylor)	34.20	14.00	8.60
Brave Light (Krovitz)	—	6.00	4.20
Fortunate Boop (Bates)	—	—	5.40

Time, 1:12 2-5. Secret Service, Dance Step, Meadow Gold, Ariel Cape, Savin Pomp, Scotch Bonnie, Tell Me, Magnetism, Lou Bright also ran. (Off time, 2:20.)

SPECIAL MATCH RACE—Four-year-olds and up; mile and one-sixteenth.

Challedon (G. Woolf), first; Many Stings (Berger), second.

(No betting.) Time, 1:44 1-5.

Quiz Points to 2 In Slaying of Cop

After questioning five men for many hours, Deputy Chief Inspector William T. Reynolds announced this afternoon that the holdup murder of Patrolman Nicholas Marino on May 23, 1939, was "very near solution."

Inspector Reynolds made his announcement in the detective squad room of the Boro Park Precinct where the five were questioned. He said the examination had boiled down to a point where two of the men were under suspicion as the killers.

Apprehension of the group was credited to three detectives of the Boro Park station who picked up two men early today and later brought in the three others.

BRITISH PLANES BOMB ETHIOPIAN RAIL CITY

Cairo, July 9 (AP)—British bombing planes have raided the Ethiopian railway town of Diredawa and scored direct hits on railway workshops, the Royal Air Force announced today.

Diredawa is on the Jibuti-Addis Ababa railway, running from the African East Coast to the capital of Italian Ethiopia.

FRENCH VOTE BILL TO FORM FASCIST RULE

Senators and Deputies Quickly Adopt Move To Revise Constitution

BULLETIN

Vichy, France, July 9 (AP)—The French Senate adopted today the Government's resolution for revision of the French constitution by a vote of 225 to 1. It previously had been adopted by the Chamber of Deputies.

Zurich, Switzerland, July 8 (U.P.)—The French Parliament at Vichy hurried through the formalities of establishing a new totalitarian model state today after a warning by Vice Premier Pierre Laval that resistance would mean the sacrifice of "an honorable peace" and "our free institutions."

The action of the French Chamber of Deputies in approving transfer of full powers to the government of Marshal Henri Philippe Petain to establish the new constitution coincided with Berlin reports that "criminal" charges might be instituted against two former French Premiers and Gen. Maurice Gamelin.

Edouard Daladier and Paul Reynaud, two Premiers who were in power before the French military collapse, were named in Vichy dispatches broadcast by the German wireless. These dispatches concerned French proposals to punish persons responsible for "the inadequacy of French means of fighting the war."

Reports Not Confirmed

The German dispatches from Vichy referred only to confirmed reports that some members of the French Parliament were urging action against Gamelin, the former Premiers and a number of generals and civil administrators in northern France. These members blamed the ousted officials for the defeat of France and also for "the declaration and continuation" of the war, according to the Nazi reports.

The Petit Dauphinois, in a dispatch from Vichy, quoted Laval as saying:

"I bring you not the conviction

Continued on Page 19

BERLIN RENEWS DRIVE ON BRITISH SHIPPING

Berlin, July 9 (AP)—A new, intensive campaign to destroy British merchant shipping has been launched by German naval and air forces and may be expected to continue indefinitely, informed Nazi sources indicated today.

Opening of the drive was acclaimed by the authoritative commentary Dienst aus Deutschland, which said 330,000 registered tons of merchant shipping flying the British flag or bound for Britain were destroyed in the last eight days, exceeding all previous figures for any entire month since outbreak of the war.

Tokio Seizes British Ship Hauling Arms

Nipponese-American Relations Held Periled By Clash at Shanghai

Shanghai, July 9 (U.P.)—A British steamer carrying munitions from the French garrison at the French Tientsin concession to the French garrison in Shanghai was seized by the Japanese navy today.

The ship, the Shenking, operated by the Butterfield-Swire Company, a British firm, had been permitted by the Japanese to sail from Tientsin but was seized upon its arrival in Shanghai waters.

British naval authorities, investigating the seizure, denied rumors that the Idzumo, flagship of the Japanese fleet at Shanghai, had machine gunned the Shenking.

Shanghai, July 9 (AP)—Major General Saburo Miura, commander of Japanese gendarmes, demanded an apology today from the commander of United States Marines in the International Settlement for alleged maltreatment of 15 plainclothes gendarmes while in Marine custody.

He declared that "speedy settlement of the incident is necessary or the matter is likely to take a grave turn."

[The United Press quoted a Japanese embassy spokesman as intimating that rejection of the demand might affect the whole course of Japanese-American relations.]

Miura previously had apologized for presence of the gendarmes in the American defense area of the International Settlement in violation of an agreement not to enter without American military authorities' consent.

Col. Dewitt Peck, marine commander, replied yesterday, "It's a lie," in denying the Japanese had been maltreated. In a letter to Colonel Peck Miura said that despite his previous agreement to consider the incident closed, "discovery of new facts revealing that the Americans insulted the entire Japanese army" made necessary further consideration of the case.

Colonel Peck, who indicated informally that no apology would be forthcoming, said today he had asked the Japanese to explain additional violations of the agreement.

Threaten Hongkong

Tokio, July 9 (AP)—Informed quarters asserted today Japan is prepared to take military action against the British crown colony of Hongkong if Great Britain continues refusal to close the Burma route of aid to China.

Empire City Results

FIRST RACE—Two-year-olds; ⅝ mile.

Abbot's Maid (Wagner)	33.50	9.50	6.50
Halcyon Days (James)	—	3.10	2.60
Rodia (Shelhamer)	—	—	10.60

Time, 1:01 4-5. Periover, San Stefana, All Gray, Sting-Me-Not, Cheer Ersie, Alca-Gal, Jassion, Grand Court, Our Grace also ran. (Off time, 2:17½.)

SECOND RACE — Whip-away, first; Strength, second; Conscript, third.

WHERE TO FIND IT IN TODAY'S EAGLE

Bridge	Page 22
Children's Section	Page 22
Clifford Evans	Page 16
Comics	Page 23
Crossword	Page 20
Dr. Brady	Page 22
EDITORIAL	Page 10
Events Tonight	Page 20
FINANCIAL	Pages 17-18-19
Garden Corner	Page 22
Grin and Bear It	Page 10
Harrold Parrott	Page 13
Jimmy Wood	Page 15
Line on Liners	Page 22
Lost and Found	Page 20
Movies	Page 9
Novel	Page 22
OBITUARIES	Page 11
Pattern	Page 22
RADIO	Page 23
REAL ESTATE	Page 21
Resorts	Page 6
Shipping	Page 20
Society	Page 7
SPORTS	Pages 13-14-15
Theaters	Page 9
Tucker	Page 10
Wall Street	Page 17
Want Ads	Pages 20-21
Woman's	Page 8

Artist Denies Murals Were Red, Hits Destruction Edict as Vandalism

By DAVID ROBINSON GEORGE

Elderly August Henkel, American-born artist whose murals in the Administration Building at Floyd Bennett Field were ordered destroyed by the WPA as "Communist propaganda," is a firm supporter of the United States Government, the Bill of Rights and the principles of democracy.

His voice shaking with emotion over the loss of his job and the destruction of the paintings on which he spent three years of arduous work, he told the Brooklyn Eagle today that his only reason for refusing to sign an oath disavowing his faith in Communism or Fascism was because he considered it an invasion of his Constitutional rights.

Declaring the affadavit was ridiculous, Henkel said:

Denies 'Tampering'

"As an American, I feel that my politics are my own affair and I do not need to disclose them to any Government agency any more than I would need to tell how I vote in an election.

"When I refused to sign the oath, I asked to be allowed to make a statement over my name, but they would not let me."

As to the charge by Colonel Somervell that Henkel tampered with the murals after they were approved by a member of the Municipal Art Commission, the artist declared:

"That is a lie. The paintings were locked up in Art Project headquarters at 110 King St., Manhattan, from the time I finished them until they were hung."

Hits 'Official Vandalism'

"I cannot heelp but believe that I am dreaming," he said slowly in the living room of his modest home, at 103-04 217th Lane, Queens Village. "I wonder when I am going to awaken and discover that such official vandalism cannot be."

Then, turning bitter, the 59-year-

Continued on Page 19

Wall Street Closing
RACING EXTRA
★ ★ ★ ★ ★ ★

BROOKLYN EAGLE

LOCAL WEATHER FORECAST: Thunderstorms and cooler tonight and tomorrow

Wall Street Closin
RACING EXTRA
★ ★ ★ ★ ★ ★

99th YEAR • No. 206 • DAILY AND SUNDAY • BROOKLYN, N. Y., FRIDAY, JULY 26, 1940 • Entered at the Brooklyn Postoffice as 2d Class Mail Matter—(Copyright 1940 The Brooklyn Daily Eagle) (F. D. S. Corporation) • 3 CENTS

CONVOY RAIDED OFF IRELAND

U. S. Perils Relations, Tokio Warns

MAYOR BACKS DRAFT AS AID TO U. S. UNITY

But Urges Changing Bill to Emphasize Industrial Training

Washington, July 26 (U.P.)—Mayor LaGuardia of New York, who served as a World War aviator, indorsed the principles of compulsory military training today as a means of promoting national unity.

However, he recommended numerous changes in the pending Burke-Wadsworth compulsory selective service bill which would require the registration of 42,000,000 American men from 18 to 65 for selection for some form of national service.

He told the House Military Affairs Committee that emphasis should be placed on training youth, starting with boys just out of high schools, to take places in skilled industrial work, rather than merely placing them in military service categories.

Universal service to one's country, the New York Mayor said, would greatly unify the country and make citizens realize their national responsibility.

Vandenberg Urges Change

LaGuardia was the first of several witnesses at today's House committee session. This committee, as well as the Senate Military Affairs Committee, hope to have the measure ready for floor consideration next week

Drastic changes in the proposed legislation, however, will be sought on the Senate floor, where a move developed to try other methods of raising a big army.

Senator Arthur H. Vandenberg (R., Mich.) suggested that curtailment of the army's enlistment period from three years to one year would stimulate enlistment and might make conscription unnecessary.

LaGuardia said national unity was a great factor in the success of the German army.

"Their method," he said, "is abhorrent, repulsive to me. They did it on a philosophy of murder and

Continued on Page 2

Eagle Staff photo by Jules Geller

OH BOY!—This is young John Lyons' idea of how to keep cool during a heat wave and it appears to be a successful one. John is 3 and lives at 489 6th St. He's testing the temperature on the Long Meadow in Prospect Park.

Ride Victim Found In Stolen Car Left At L. I. Curb 2 Days

Special to the Brooklyn Eagle

Valley Stream, July 26 — The body of an unidentified man, believed by police to be a gangster who had been taken for a "ride," was found today in the back of an auto parked on the corner of Merrick Road and Montague St.

Otto Schneider, a bartender, noticed that the car was there yesterday and this morning, looked into the back seat and saw the man sprawled there, face down. He had been shot through the right side.

The license plates revealed that the car had been stolen. Police are searching nearby woods in an effort to find a gun.

Police said the plates had been stolen from Irving Radner of 1240 Sherman Ave., the Bronx.

Ex-Jurist Found Dead

Oklahoma City, July 26 (AP)—Eugene F. Lester, 68, former chief justice of the State Supreme Court, was found dead last night in a hotel room with a bullet wound in his head. Acting Coroner Ben LaFon returned a verdict of suicide. A note blamed ill health.

Empire City Results

FIRST RACE—Three-year-olds; about three-quarter mile.

Rancho's Girl (Meade)	3.60	2.80	2.50
Well Read (I. Anderson)	—	7.80	4.70
Argos (Driscoll)	—	—	4.90

Time, 1:09. Career Girl, Alseleda, Gwynne H, June Date, Sun Fox, Pamunkey, One Strike, Refreshing, Durable also ran. Off time, 2:19.

Suffolk Downs Results

FIRST RACE—Four-year-olds and p; three-quarter mile.

Cordate (A. Anderson)	16.80	7.00	4.80
Whisper (W. L. Taylor)	—	5.40	4.00
ttie (Yarberry)	—	—	11.40

Time, 1:13. Spanish Maid, Chardash, ospectus, Minstrel Wit, Sky Cloud, Blue rotto, Rollsbuzzy, Story Time, Ghost rain also ran. Off time, 2:22⅕.

Mercury Hits 93, New High For Year; Showers on Way

While the Weather Bureau was predicting thunder showers tonight and a break in the week-old heat wave tomorrow, the temperature climbed today to a new high for the year, reaching 93 at 2 p.m. The previous high for the year was 91, on June 4.

At the street level, a thermometer in the shade at Johnson and Washington Sts. registered 95 as against the more official Weather Bureau figure of 93 at 2 p.m.

As the mercury thus rose to sizzling heights, the humidity dropped off to 55 percent, without, however, making New Yorkers any more comfortable.

The thundershowers were predicted for late this afternoon, tonight and tomorrow, with cooler weather tomorrow night.

Winds were expected to shift from southwest to northwest, the change contributing a share to the less torrid times immediately ahead.

Temperatures were generally higher this morning than yesterday, the lowest being 73 at 5 and 6 a.m. as against 70 the day before, but the humidity was 82 at 9 a.m., a slight recession from the day before.

HEAT AND HUMIDITY

	TODAY		YESTERDAY	
	Temp.	Hum.	Temp.	Hum.
Midnight	77	—	72	—
1 a.m.	76	—	72	—
2 a.m.	76	—	72	—
3 a.m.	75	—	71	—
4 a.m.	74	—	71	—
5 a.m.	73	—	70	—
6 a.m.	73	—	70	—
7 a.m.	74	—	72	—
8 a.m.	73	85	72	95
9 a.m.	77	82	73	92
10 a.m.	80	76	74	89
11 a.m.	84	71	76	82
Noon	88	68	77	83
1 p.m.	90	61	81	75
2 p.m.	93	55	85	66

30° 4 MILES AWAY (UP)

A temperature of below freezing was reported four miles from LaGuardia Field at noon today by Joseph Browne, chief meteorologist of Transcontinental and Western Air, Inc. The report was of the air temperature at 20,000 feet above the field, where weather balloon and radio observations recorded a temperature of 30 degrees above zero.

Urges Navy Conduct Bearn From Martinique to U. S.

Washington, July 26 (AP)—Representative Melvin J. Maas (R., Minn.), minority member of the House Naval Committee, proposed today that the United States dispatch a naval force to Martinique to escort the French aircraft carrier Bearn with 100 airplanes aboard to an American port.

Conscription Is Called 'Totalitarian' By Boro Catholic Newspaper

In a Page 1 editorial, the Tablet, official organ of the Brooklyn Catholic Diocese, today declared against conscription as "totalitarian, dictatorial, regimentation and destructive of liberty."

"The Burke-Wadsworth bill was conceived with an autocratic mind," the Tablet editorial stated. "It is a departure from American traditions. It is being jammed down the throats of the people with great haste. It is based on fear. We oppose it. We believe conscription in peace times is not democratic, is not American."

The editorial pointed out that both the Democratic and Republican national conventions refused to indorse a draft or conscription plank in their platforms.

The Tablet urged its readers to write to their Senators and Representatives in Washington urging them to vote against the draft bill "as they told their delegates to the conventions that they want no war nor a part of any war."

The editorial pointed out that Canada, New Zealand and Australia, who are all at war, have not as yet enacted conscription.

AMERICAN TRADE CUT IN NORTH CHINA

Japan Hints Supply Of Pacific Rubber, Tin Will Be Blocked

BULLETIN

Washington, July 26 (U.P.)—The United States today approved charter of an American tanker to a Russian concern to take a load of gasoline to Siberia, although similar applications by Japanese and Spanish firms had been rejected.

Tokio, July 26 (U.P.) — Japan has asked the United States seriously to consider the possibility that any embargo on American supplies of scrap iron and oil to Japan may aggravate Japanese-American relations, it was reported today.

A veiled warning as to the strain any embargo would put on Japanese-American relations was reported to have been sent by the Foreign Office and there were indications that Japan may consider the possibility of retaliation against any American embargo on oil and scrap iron by seeking to cut off the United States supply of rubber and tin from the South Seas.

Halt U. S. Trading

Shanghai, July 26 (AP)—Coincident with United States action licensing all oil and scrap iron exports it was reported today that Japanese restrictions have halted

Continued on Page 2

SAY U. S. APOLOGIZED

Shanghai, July 26 (AP)—A Japanese Embassy spokesman declared today that two recent Japanese-American incidents at Tsingtao involving United States sailors had been settled with American expressions of regret.

E. M. TRAVIS DIES AT 78; FORMER STATE OFFICIAL

Prominent Republican, Ex-Senator, Controller, Was in Realty Business

Eugene M. Travis, formerly a powerful figure in Republican circles of Brooklyn, serving as State Senator from 1907 to 1912 and State Controller from 1915 to 1920, died last night in his home at 436 Grand Ave. after a brief illness. He was 78.

Before forging to the forefront as a politician, Mr. Travis was a prosperous importer of fruits and vegetables, and, since retiring from public activity in 1930, had been engaged in the real estate business as a member of the firm of Moebus & Travis.

In addition to his business and political affairs, he was an active layman of the Methodist Church, frequently attending local and national conferences, and for many years was a leader in activities of Masonic and other fraternal organizations.

A veteran of numerous hotly-contested campaigns for public of-

Continued on Page 11

TOO WARM FOR MARE

An old gray mare—a fish dealer's truck horse—found the weather so warm today that she took to the water. The mare, said bystanders, deliberately raced down the pier at the foot of Beekman St., Manhattan, early this afternoon, dived into the East River and swam and splashed happily about for an hour before she was fished out with a crane.

Raider Disguised as Swedish Craft Sank 2 Ships in Neutrality Zone

Rescuers of 25 Relate How Hidden Guns On German Boat Opened Fire in West Indies

By FRANK REIL

The German armed raider which sank two British ships recently near the West Indies, well inside the Neutrality Zone was disguised as a Swedish ship and did not reveal its true identity until it was close to its victims and ready to go into action with six-inch guns hidden below deck.

The Norwegian freighter Leif, which rescued 25 crew members of the Davisian who had been in a leaking lifeboat for seven days, docked at Pier 22, foot of Atlantic Ave. today, and brought back the first complete details of the raider and how it has been operating.

Nazi Flag Unfurled

The rescued British seamen who were landed at Samana, Dominican Republic, by the Leif, related to officers of the rescue ship that the raider was called the Narvik and had the national colors of Sweden painted on her sides, just like all other Swedish ships.

But when the Davisian, on her way to Trinidad, got close, a tarpaulin bearing a large Nazi swastika was dropped over the Swedish colors and several hidden guns on the raider went into action.

The Davisian, a vessel of 6,433 tons, had only one gun, a four-inch piece on her stern. The British ship, although completely surprised by the raider, returned fire but the ship's gunner, who had only two weeks training, was wounded along with four other seamen.

Taken Aboard Raider

Third Officer Nils Stromsvig, who was on watch when the men from the Davisian were picked up, was told that the ship had to surrender and all her men were put aboard the raider which was described as a new ship of about 10,000 tons and capable of a speed of almost 19 knots.

The Davisian was then sunk by

Continued on Page 2

HOUSE GROUP ASKS U. S. SHIPS FOR REFUGEES

Foreign Affairs Body Approves Measure To Remove Children

Washington, July 26 (AP)—Chairman Bloom (D., N. Y.) said today the House Foreign Affairs Committee had approved unanimously a bill to permit the use of United States vessels to remove refugee children from European war zones—an arrangement President Roosevelt described as possible.

Under the bill each vessel so used shall have painted plainly on both sides an American flag "and a statement that such vessel is a refugee-child rescue ship of the United States or under United States registry, so that night or day there can be no mistake as to the identity of such vessels."

Also any American vessel to be used for child rescue work must have its safe conduct granted by all nations at war.

Asserting that the United States had a deep desire to do everything possible to help remove children from England, President Roosevelt said today the Administration eventually might ask for reasonable assurances that refugee children could obtain safe passage to this country.

The first step, he told a press conference, involves providing perhaps 10,000 children in Britain with passports.

The next step, he said, would be to find out what the British

Continued on Page 3

Court Holds Truck Driver In Serious Injury of Boy

Carlo Calabrese, 34, a truck driver of 2628 Atlantic Ave., was held in $3,000 bail today in Felony Court for hearing Sept. 9 on charges of simple assault and driving without a license.

Detective Lawrence Shannon of the Miller Ave. station said that on July 24 Calabrese's truck struck and seriously injured Henry Fuchs, 9, of 2712 Atlantic Ave. On Jan. 18 last, Calabrese was arrested on a homicide charge after colliding with a police car, as a result of which Patrolman Michael Lonto died. The charge subsequently was dismissed.

$50,000 Food Goes to Paris

Washington, July 26 (U.P.)—The Red Cross announced today that $50,000 worth of food is en route to Paris from Switzerland to relieve a desperate food situation in the former French capital.

Woman, 63, Beaten And Critically Hurt; Son, 26, Is Sought

Mother in Hospital With Fractured Skull—Cops Told of Family Row

A 63-year-old mother was taken to Coney Island Hospital in a critical condition with a fractured skull today and detectives of the Sheepshead Bay station sought her 26-year-old son, who is charged with beating her.

Neighbors told the police there were indications that a family row was going on in the basement apartment at 1963 E. 15th St., occupied by Mrs. Marie Santanagaro and her two sons and a daughter. Such family battles have been frequent, the neighbors said.

The son, Frank, allegedly struck his mother and she fell to the floor, hitting her head on a sharp object. Frank fled when neighbors called the police.

Detective Harry Taylor was stationed at the mother's bedside in the hospital, to question her if she regains consciousness. The other members of the family refused to talk.

MADDEN DISBARMENT URGED IN REPORT OF REFEREE KAPPER

Disbarment of former Assistant District Attorney Francis A. Madden is recommended in a 30-page report filed with the Appellate Division by Official Referee Isaac M. Kapper, who heard charges preferred by the Amen grand jury and which replaced an indictment alleging Madden, while in office, took money from physicians in the abortion racket.

Details of the report will not be divulged until it is read in court Sept. 23. At that time Assistant Attorney General Charles J. Buchner of Amen's staff will present a motion asking the Appellate Division to confirm the report.

In addition to the charges concerning the doctors, Madden was accused of falsifying expense vouchers for his New Jersey investigations connected with the Paul Wendel kidnaping case and of presenting a spurious receipted bill for $36, allegedly spent at a New Jersey hotel. At the hearing before the referee, Madden denied all the charges. Notices that the Amen forces will move Madden's disbarment was served late yesterday on Robert McGowan Smith, who defended the accused attorney.

FRENCH MAN WARSHIPS TO HELP BRITAIN

Nazi Planes Keep Up Continual Battle for Control of Channel

London, July 26 (AP)—German bombers made a daring thrust at Britain's "back door" today by attacking a convoy off the North Irish coasts. Others kept up the continual battle for control of the English Channel by striking again at the southeast coastal towns.

Observers heard heavy gunfire the British replied to the attack and saw flashes of ships' guns as on the convoy off the north Irish coast—the first made in that area since the start of the war.

British planes streaked out to engage the Germans, and soon one bomber was seen to fall.

MAN FRENCH WARSHIPS

London, July 26 (AP)—The British Admiralty announced tonight that "steps are already well advanced for manning French warships which arrived in our ports before the signing of the armistice between France and Germany."

The announcement added: "A number of French ships of varying sizes are now being manned and prepared for sea entirely by officers and men of the free French naval forces headed by Admiral Meselier.

"One ship manned entirely by Frenchmen has already been at sea taking an active and successful part in operation."

Early reports indicated the southeast coast attacks were not as severe as yesterday when Britain fought off combined plane and torpedo boat raids.

The British reported shooting down 26 raiders and driving off a fleet of nine German mosquito boats which attacked a 21-boat convoy just off the mouth of the Thames.

Five Ships Sunk, Seven Damaged

Her own losses, Britain said, were five small merchant ships, totaling 5,104 tons. In addition five other small boats totaling 5,133 tons, and two destroyers, were damaged.

German claims of 53,000 tons of boats sunk by aircraft in this raid were called "grossly exaggerated."

The planes attacked the convoy in successive waves of 30 planes each, the Admiralty said, but were driven off with great losses.

The destroyers were damaged, the Admiralty added, when dive bombers attacked them twice as they returned from chasing mosquito boats.

The British also announced the loss of a trawler, the Fleming, when it and another trawler were attacked by four dive bombers.

Berlin, July 26 (AP)—The German high command announced in a special communique that German speedboats sank three merchant ships totaling 22,000 tons off the

Continued on Page 2

IN TODAY'S EAGLE WHERE TO FIND IT

Bridge	Page 20
Children's Section	Page 20
Comics	Page 9
Crossword	Page 18
Dr. Brady	Page 20
Ed Hughes	Page 14
EDITORIAL	Page 10
Events Tonight	Page 18
FINANCIAL	Pages 16-17
Garden Corner	Page 20
Going Places	Page 6
Grin and Bear It	Page 10
Harold Conrad	Page 6
Heffernan	Page 12
Helen Worth	Page 4
Jimmy Wood	Page 13
Lindley	Page 12
Line on Liners	Page 20
Lost and Found	Page 2
Movies	Page 7
Novel	Page 20
OBITUARIES	Page 11
Pattern	Page 20
RADIO	Page 9
Real Estate	Page 19
Society	Page 5
SPORTS	Pages 13-14-15
Theaters	Page 7
Tucker	Page 10
Wall Street	Page 16
Want Ads	Pages 15-16
Woman's	Page 4

Wide World photo

THEY DIDN'T COME BACK—In this picture, passed by the German censor, are shown, in Belgium, some of the English troops who never got to Dunkirk and who were not evacuated. English soldiers are shown lying dead beside their motor lorries. Note two (in helmets showing, in foreground) lying in almost identical positions, apparently dropped at the same instant by bullets from the same machine-gun spray.

JAPAN PROPOSES TO RULE INDIES AND INDO-CHINA

Government of Konoye Plans New State Based On Broad Totalitarianism

Tokio, Aug. 1 (AP)—The government of Premier Prince Fumimaro Konoye announced today a plan for a brand-new Japanese state, based on a sweeping totalitarianism at home and dedicated to an independent foreign policy which would extend Japan's domination southward over French Indo-China and the Dutch East Indies.

In a statement of policy the government outlined a strongly centralized and unified state designed for creation of "a new order for Greater East Asia," with the yen bloc—Japan and her continental satellites whose currencies are based on the yen—as the foundation.

Extensive Rearming Planned

The statement failed to take Japan any closer to the Rome-Berlin Axis, despite the totalitarianism at home. It pulled Japan away from the other Western Powers, however, and called for an extensive rearmament program.

Foreign Minister Yosuke Matsuoka said Japan had discarded the policy of trying to win the friendship of "recalcitrant nations." As for the European war, he said Japan for the present would maintain a policy of noninvolvement.

The government's statement coined the phrase "Greater East Asia" in naming the sphere Japan aims to dominate—previously it had been simply "East Asia," meaning Japan, Manchukuo and the occupied sections of China.

Of this Matsuoka said:

"Needless to say, the term 'Greater East Asia' includes the South Seas. The final aim is establishment of a stabilizing force for a self-sufficiency embracing not only Japan, Manchukuo and China but also Indo-China and the East Indies."

President Roosevelt's ban on the export of aviation gasoline to points outside the Western Hemisphere was interpreted by the Admiralty spokesman as a move against Japan, Germany and Italy which might lead to "repercussions."

The American aviation gasoline embargo, he said, was "an attempt to kill two birds with one stone," namely the Rome-Berlin Axis and Japan.

Defense Appeal Averts Strike in Boeing Factory

Seattle, Aug. 1 (U.P.)—A threatened strike of 6,700 employes of the Boeing Aircraft Company was averted temporarily today by a last-minute appeal from Secretary of Labor Frances Perkins in the interest of national defense.

The Aeronautical Mechanics (A. F. of L.) Union voted a 10-day extension just before a midnight strike deadline. Union spokesmen said they were confident an agreement would be reached before the new deadline.

Negotiators were deadlocked over the issue of a proposed wage reduction of 7½ cents an hour for beginner workmen, who now receive 62½ cents. The company had granted a 10-cent raise in higher brackets.

Miss Perkins' telegram appealed to both sides for an extension because of the B[illegible] plant's part in national pre[illegible]s.

The plan[illegible] unfilled order for 300 a[illegible] [illegible] he British [illegible]rchas[illegible] [illegible]sion and is pro[illegible]cing an un[illegible]sclosed number of [illegible]ing fortress bombers for the Unit[illegible]d States Army.

U. S. OIL MAN DEFENDS AID TO NAZI AGENT AS BUSINESS

Capt. Torkild Rieber, chairman of the board of the Texas Company, has been assisting Dr. Gerhardt Alois Westrick, German attorney and Adolf Hitler's special emissary to American businessmen, only because he considered it "simply very good business," Captain Rieber declared today.

Published reports disclosed Dr. Westrick, who came to the United States four months ago, has been living secretly on the estate of Harold A. Callan at 168 Mamaroneck Road, Scarsdale, where he has been seeing oil company officials and other business leaders.

At the Texas Company's Manhattan offices, it was said that Rieber's relationship with Dr. Westrick had "no political significance" and Rieber himself asserted:

"Westrick is a lawyer in Germany who represents some of the largest American firms. For us, he has handled several contracts and before the war used to come here two or three times a year. At the start of this visit of his, I was away. Later, he called me and said he wanted to move to the country so that his children could be put into a school."

Dr. Westrick moved into the Callan residence on May 6 and since then observers have noted a long parade of visitors by automobile, many of them being American oil company executives. To his guests, the visiting German has painted glowing pictures of profits to be expected from business to be done with a friendly Nazi Germany after Great Britain has been conquered.

'NO PLOT,' WIFE ASSERTS

"We don't plot anything here or anywhere else," Mrs. Westrick, wife of the German emissary, told reporters today in an interview at the Scarsdale estate.

She denied that there ever were any "large number" of callers at her home and said that the only visitors were personal friends.

"In his work my husband tries to be fair to both countries," she said.

'Curb Superintendents' Replace Blah-Blah Artists at Boro Hall

Sidewalk superintendents were in the majority in Borough Hall Park today as, for the first time in years, not one noonday speech was made in this happy hunting ground for the leather-tongued soap-box orators.

The orators wouldn't stand a chance, anyway. They would have had to make more noise than the steam shovels and cement mixers, which are busy tearing the place to pieces in the interest of a bigger and more beautiful park at the foot of Borough Hall steps. Even a soapbox orator would find this difficult, and there is the added consideration of the edict prohibiting public speaking in the park or on the steps until the WPA finishes its job.

In a few words those in charge of the transformation proclaimed today that, although aware that the WPA'ers have already made the well-worn steps virtually inaccessible, they are mindful of the persistence of the blah-blah artists.

In fact, a bit of questioning revealed, they are prepared to call on the police to enforce their banishment of the glib haranguers on such topics as the war, religion, the next election, proper diet and the unpredictable Dodgers.

But they expect no trouble from the bootblacks and elderly checker players who have been wont to frequent the park, deeming those folk amenable chaps who know when they aren't wanted and when their lives and limbs may be in danger.

At any rate, it won't be until the venerable park has become something more seemly to look upon, and the statue of Henry Ward Beecher has been pedestaled in a new location, that the soapboxers can retake their battleground.

Mrs. Roosevelt, Flying To Capital, Shuns Politics

Mrs. Eleanor Roosevelt, wife of the President, departed from La Guardia Field for Washington on an Eastern Airlines plane at 11 a.m. today. She would talk only briefly to reporters, and took her place in the plane 10 minutes before it was to start.

Replying with a shrug of the shoulders to a request for her opinion on the swing of some Democrats to the Willkie bandwagon, Mrs. Roosevelt said: "Well, what can one think?"

See War Issue In Local Vote

Continued from Page 1

who want peace are going to fall for his private platform of 'immediate aid' to the only remaining member of the Allies?"

Mr. Cassidy's letter was an answer to a previous one written to the Brooklyn Eagle by Mr. Serri.

"I have been bombarded by the newspapers, asking whether I intend to run for public office," Mr. Cassidy added. "Thus far I have made emphatic denials of any such intentions. BUT . . . I still believe in keeping America out of the war and in keeping the war out of America. Be careful, Mr. Serri, or the 6th Congressional District might yet vote for Peace."

His Privilege, Says Foe

Mr. Serri promptly replied that if Mr. Cassidy wished to enter the primary it was entirly his privilege.

"If he wants to enter the primary and make this a test of the question of isolation or aid to England, which I favor, I'd welcome it, in fact," Mr. Serri said.

"My platform is entirely plain. I'm for aid to England to stop Hitler before he has a chance to come to the United States. If he once becomes the overlord of all Europe we won't be big enough to stop him if he decides to come over here."

"I'm completely willing to let the voters decide this issue. By all means, let's have it tested."

The 6th Congressional District embraces virtually all of Flatbush, which is the 21st A. D., and also the 17th and 18th Assembly Districts. The number of enrolled Democrats who would be qualified to go to the polls in the district's primary is 101,637.

DROP SABOTAGE AS CAUSE OF FIRE ON SHIP HERE

British Freighter Blaze Believed Started by Spontaneous Combustion

Fire Marshal Thomas Brophy said today that the cause of the fire which broke out late yesterday afternoon in a hatch of the British freighter Port Fremantle, tied up at the foot of Congress St., was "definitely not sabotage." It appeared likely that spontaneous combustion was responsible.

Deputy Fire Marshals Martin Scott and William A. Finn, he said, were investigating and had been directed to make a detailed report.

Twelve firemen, including Battalion Chief Thomas Loughlin of the 25th Battalion, were overcome by smoke and burning rubber fumes while fighting the blaze.

The fire was confined to one hatch and Battalion Chief Anthony Jerick of the 32d Battalion said he believed the blaze was probably caused by spontaneous combustion. However, an immediate investigation was ordered.

Passengers Safe

The ship was scheduled to sail last evening for New Zealand with a cargo of potash and rubber. Ten passengers on board when the fire broke out a few minutes before sailing time were put safely ashore.

Ship line agents were unable to say when the ship would sail.

Four firemen were taken to hospitals. Those taken to Long Island College Hospital were Lawrence Mahn, 29, of 147-01 Hillside Ave., Jamaica, and William Batteau, 28, of 186-86 115th Ave., St. Albans, both attached to the fireboat Fire Fighter.

Taken to Holy Family Hospital were Battalion Chief Loughlin, 58, of 50-28 213th St., Bayside, and Fire Lt. Charles Heileman, 44, of 84-27 Doran Ave., Glendale, attached to Hook and Ladder Company 110.

Boro Phone Book Listings Up 1,000

Brooklyn's telephone listings have jumped by about 1,000 over last Winter's directory listings, to a total of 294,000 in the new August, 1940, directory which carriers for the New York Telephone Company started to distribute today. A total of 269,000 copies will be distributed by Aug. 9.

The Brooklyn business classified directory, known as the "Red Book," contains a civic page entitled "Brooklyn—New York City's Greatest Borough," with lists of places of interest and illustrations of the Brooklyn Museum, old Lefferts mansion, the Soldiers and Sailors Arch and a night baseball scene at Ebbets Field.

Lt. Col. Suavet Named Head Of State Arsenal in Boro

Albany, Aug. 1 (AP)—Lieutenant Col. Henry E. Suavet, 47, New York State National Guard ordnance officer of the 27th Division, was named today assistant adjutant general and officer in charge of the State arsenal at Brooklyn.

Suavet succeeds Col. William A. Taylor, 64, who was retired yesterday because of age regulations.

Chief of L. I. Peace Haven Held On Charge of Sanitary Violation

Special to the Brooklyn Eagle

Oakdale, Aug. 1—William Schmidt, superintendent of Peace Haven, headquarters of the Royal Fraternity of Master Metaphysicians, was arraigned here yesterday on a charge of violating the sanitary code after a trio of local officials discovered a soil pipe leading from the former Vanderbilt mansion directly to the adjacent Connetquott River.

Peace Haven has become famous as the scene of an experiment whereby the metaphysicians hope to raise "Baby Jean," a baby girl they adopted, to achieve immortality by isolating her from all possible impurities of thought, word or deed.

An unusually low tide led to the discovery of the soil pipe by Chief of Police Richard N. Tucker of Islip, who asserted that he had been conducting a quiet investigation for some time after complaints had been registered by local residents. He was assisted in his sleuthing by Dr. Charles E. Low, Deputy Health Commissioner of Suffolk County, and Rodney E. Cook, County Sanitary Engineer.

'Italo' Sends Boro Man Notice Of Marriage to 'Miss Germany'

A macabre "wedding announcement" for the marriage of the "Italian Empire and Miss Germany," naming Switzerland along with Europe's conquered nations as "witnesses" and declaring that "confetti" would be thrown by the armed forces of the axis powers reached Brooklyn today from Italy.

The announcement, apparently issued in May, set June for the event and was sent to an Italian-American who served with the United States forces in the World War and who asked that his name be withheld.

Italy entered the current war on June 10.

The notice named as witnesses to the marriage "Baroness Norway, Countess Holland, Viscount Belgium, Prince Luxemburg, Duchess Poland, with her adopted daughter, Danzig; the noble Lady Switzerland and numerous other admirers and guests."

The "wedding trip" according to the announcement, was to take the bridal couple "through the magnificent State of Gibraltar, the Suez Canal, with a stopover in Jibuti, Tunis, Corsica, Malta and Cyprus."

"The Italian and German aviation, marine and troops in mutual accord will distribute the confetti without being parsimonious," it continued.

The leaflet was signed "Grand Master of Ceremonies—Italo."

Schoolship 'Hazing' Charge Brings Action Against 18

Philadelphia, Aug. 1 (AP)—A 17-year-old cadet's charges of "severe hazing" brought today demands for the resignations of two shipmates aboard the Pennsylvania schoolship Annapolis, and disciplinary action against 16 others.

The State navigation Commission informed two first class cadets they must resign or be dismissed and reprimanded another for "attempting to suppress" an investigation into the charges. The rest were shorn of their ratings and deprived for 30 days of shore leave privileges.

Transit Employe Brings Test Suit

A test suit to determine whether membership in the Transit Workers Union is necessary for an employe to continue working for the transit lines under the ownership of the city, has been started in Manhattan Supreme Court by Edward Maguire, I. R. T. station agent and treasurer of the United Transitmen's Association. Maguire resigned from the T. W. U. several days ago to provide a basis for a decision.

The suit was started by service of the papers on the New York City Transit Commission. The complaint asks a declaratory judgment setting forth the status of Maguire, who with all other employes of the transit lines taken over by the city are now classified as civil service men.

Coney Island's boardwalk attractions as viewed from the sky.

A pretty highdiver in the waters of Coney Island.

Surf Avenue, Coney's main street, is the scene of many a celebration.

Shows to Migrate From Fair Midway To Coney in 1941

Parachute Jump Among Rides Moving to World's Greatest Playground

By JO RANSON

Coney Island, the world's most amazing outdoor recreation center, will become an even more powerful drawing card next season with the arrival of a flock of the more successful rides and shows now on display along the midway of the New York World's Fair.

Officials of the two major amusement parks in Coney Island, Steeplechase and Luna Park, yesterday revealed that they were dickering with outdoor showmen at the Fair to bring their attractions to Surf Ave. in 1941.

Several deals have already been arranged, particularly one for presenting the celebrated parachute jump on the boardwalk end of Steeplechase Park. It was reported that a five-year lease was signed for the parachute jump. Milton Sheen, outdoor showman now operating Luna Park, plans to install at least eight World's Fair attractions on the Luna midway next year.

Mayor's Aid Sought

Furthermore, the Coney Island Chamber of Commerce headed by C. J. Hilbert, has been in communication with Mayor LaGuardia in an attempt to have him interest Fair exhibitors in coming to Coney Island in 1941.

Mr. Hilbert, in writing to Mayor LaGuardia, stated that "an influx of new exhibits, shows, rides, etc., would naturally go a long way toward injecting a new spirit of progress in this community and we know that you have always shown an interest in Coney Island and feel that you will co-operate in any endeavor for its general welfare."

Business at Coney so far this year has been "fair" in the opinion of veteran concessionaires. The recent heat wave was of some value to the operators of soft drink and other refreshment stands, bathhouses and parking spaces. At one time during the torrid weather there was a complete sellout of soft drinks with little likelihood of getting more that day. "Ride" men didn't do so well during the heat wave, but there was a noticeable pickup in the last few days.

Boardwalk Improvement Hailed

Park Commissioner Moses' boardwalk and beach improvements have been hailed by all Coney Island merchants as a shot in the arm of business. His reconstructed boardwalk from Stillwell Ave. to Ocean Parkway and the presence of white sand on a portion of the beach evoked the highest praise from the strand's inhabitants.

The Coney Island Chamber of Commerce, however, has set as one of its major objectives for next year the continuation of the white sand to Sea Gate. This they hope Park Commissioner Moses will give them for 1941. The chamber is also desirous of improving the approach to Coney Island from Ocean Parkway, and of obtaining a local law which will bring the open front sidewalk photographers under the jurisdiction of the License Department.

Approximately eight such establishments would be affected, and according to the Chamber of Commerce "time will prove this regulatory action will benefit both the public and the concessionaires affected."

Fireworks an Attraction

The chamber reported that its Tuesday night fireworks displays bring as many as 350,000 persons to the beach. The fireworks last for 18 minutes and cost about $750 for each exhibition.

Commissioner of Licenses Paul Moss yesterday said that he was highly pleased with the manner in which the chamber and the concessionaires were co-operating with his department.

"They are helping me to make Coney Island a fine place for the millions who come there during the course of the Summer," he said. "Coney Island, I am sure, will have a fine future and I take great pride in the small part I had in building it up."

Mr. Hilbert was voluble in his praise of both commissioners, Mr. Moses and Mr. Moss.

"We can't find any fault with their work in this area. They have been most co-operative," he declared.

The president of the Chamber of Commerce also went on record as saying that Coney Island could stand more foot patrolmen during the Summer months.

"More police," he said, "would help us in preventing people from parading through the streets in their bathing suits. We want them to wear bathrobes or similar apparel on their way to the water."

Enterprises Tabulated

A recent tabulation of the number of business enterprises in Coney Island from the south side of Surf Ave. up to and including the boardwalk from W. 5th St. to W. 37th St., revealed that there were 448. They were as follows: Amusement devices, 39; auto parking, 12; bars and grills, 22; bathhouses, 30; candy and popcorn stores, 22; custard stands, 16; furnished rooms, 34; games, 50; hotels, two; lunch stands, 36; penny arcades, three; photo studios, eight; pony tracks, three; rathskellers, 30; refreshment stands, 65; restaurants, 11; shooting galleries, 14; shows, five; souvenir stores, 14, and miscellaneous, 32.

That is the backbone and muscle of the greatest playground in the world, a small area crowded with thrills and spills that played to more than a million people last Sunday.

It's Wise to Ask Doctor About Sun Tan Lotions

Many preparations are on the market which guarantee to give you a tan without a burn. Some of them are effective in screening out the heat rays. Others depend on a dye which discolors the skin to give a tanned effect. It is wise to ask your physician's advice before purchasing these cosmetics.

Follow Five Rules To Swim Safely

You'll enjoy swimming in the waters of Coney Island, but before you plunge into the briny deep make sure that you are familiar with the American Red Cross rules for safe swimming. There are plenty of life guards around but they have enough to do without coping with "showoff" swimmers. Remember, even expert swimmers face the danger of drowning. The rules for sensible swimming are as follows:

1 Don't swim alone; you may become exhausted and there may be no one near to help you.

2 Don't swim for at least two hours after eating a hearty meal; otherwise you are likely to be stricken with abdominal cramps which may render you helpless. If you are subject to cramps, stay close to shore.

3 Don't dive into water unless you are sure of its depth. Make sure that the water is at least six feet deep and free from under-water rocks, logs and the like.

4 Don't go on long swims, unless accompanied by a boat.

5 Don't forget that you get just as much exercise swimming in water 5 feet deep as in water 500 feet deep, and it is much safer. If you get tired in 5 feet of water, you can stand up and rest.

Sun-Worshipers Should Obey 'Tan' Commandments

Here's Medical Advice On How to Avoid Burn And Acquire Nice Color

Coney Island's mighty, powerful sun can be either a blessing or a nightmare, depending upon how you behave on the beach. As Dr. Charles F. Pabst, chief dermatologist and press reference chairman of the Medical Society of the County of Kings, has so often pointed out, over exposure to strong sunlight may cause serious consequences.

Not many persons realize it, but 200,000 working days are lost by illness attributed to sunburn. And the strange part of it is that most of this sunburn is "deliberately and intentionally acquired."

There is a sane way of absorbing the rays of the sun, and thanks to Dr. Pabst's "Tan" Commandments, the millions who plan to go to Coney Island and other beaches and who'll follow his advice, will undoubtedly go home much wiser and happier. Dr. Pabst's suggestions are so important that we suggest you cut them out and paste them on top of the picnic basket or thermos bottle. Here are the suggestions:

1—Acquire a coat of tan, provided you are not a heliophobe, by means of short exposure.

2—Don't sleep on the beach in the direct rays of the sun.

3—Don't drink highballs or strong liquor while exposed to the Summer sun.

4—Don't sit in the sun when the body is wet after bathing; the drops of water on the skin act as tiny magnifying lenses and increase the burn.

5—Don't go bareheaded in strong sunlight.

6—Don't read books or play cards in the direct rays of the sun.

7—Don't sprinkle perfume on the skin before exposure to the sun; a severe inflammation of the skin called perfume dermatitis may result.

8—Don't recline in strong sunlight after strenuous exercise.

9—Don't forget that blonds and brunettes react differently to the sun's rays; blondes and redheads burn more easily and seldom tan a deep hue.

If your skin will redden, blister and burn but never tan, you are a heliophobe, and should not expose yourself, as every new exposure means a new burn.

Well, there you are, ten excellent tips on what not to do when you reach the sandy shore of Coney Island.

Boy Scout Day Aug. 26 At Steeplechase Park

Arrangements have been made with the management of Steeplechase Park in Coney Island for Boy Scout Day on Monday, Aug. 26. Scouts from all parts of Greater New York will be admitted on the following basis: 50-cent tickets will be sold for 25 cents. Twenty-five-cent tickets will be sold for 15 cents.

Save Minnie-the-Bass, Is Plea to Fishermen

Traverse City, Mich. (U.P.)—Residents around Spider Lake hope the sportsmen will leave Minnie alone this season.

Minnie, a five-pound bass, is the pet of the resort, because she takes food from any one who offers it by hand. So far, though, she has shunned hooks.

Her old playmate, Popeye, was caught by a visiting fisherman two years ago, and her present companion, Billy, is still alive but wary after taking a hopper three years ago.

Villepigue's at Bay Steeped in Tradition

Steeped in tradition is Villepigue's at Sheepshead Bay. The present site was chosen by the doughty "Big Jim" in 1918 when the original restaurant, a stone's throw from the Sheepshead Bay track, proved too small to hold the crowd of sportsmen, socialites and other notables who flocked to partake of his fine cuisine.

Foresters to Hold Yule Fund Outing

The New York State Court of the Foresters of America will join in sponsoring an outing at Steeplechase Park, Coney Island, on Aug. 17. Proceeds will benefit the organization's Christmas basket fund. Last year's outing provided funds for 120 food baskets for needy families. Games and contests for children and adults are a feature of the program.

'Frozen Alive' at Luna After Run at the Fair

Among the popular attractions on the Midway in Luna Park is "Frozen Alive," a show in which a young lady spends a portion of her time resting in a cake of ice. This rather sensational presentation is guided by Renee Zouray.

"Frozen Alive" was first seen at the World's Fair last season and this marks the first time that the exhibition is on view at Coney.

Wall Street Closing
RACING EXTRA
★★★★★★

BROOKLYN EAGLE

LOCAL WEATHER FORECAST: Showers, moderate temperature tonight and tomorrow

Wall Street Closing
RACING EXTRA
★★★★★★

99th YEAR • No. 227 • DAILY AND SUNDAY • BROOKLYN, N. Y., FRIDAY, AUG. 16, 1940 • Entered at the Brooklyn Postoffice as 2d Class Mail Matter—(Copyright 1940 The Brooklyn Daily Eagle) (F. D. S. Corporation) • 3 CENTS

BOMBS ROCK LONDON; 2,500 PLANES ATTACK

BULLETIN

Berlin, Aug. 16 (AP)—DNB, official German news agency, said today German military planes over London's environs had started big fires on either side of the Thames and that "everywhere smoke was rising, everywhere hits and bomb craters were visible."

Berlin, Aug. 16 (AP)—British and German fighting planes were engaged in a fierce battle over London this afternoon, authorized German sources said.

These sources said huge explosions were observed in outlying sections of the British capital in the wake of a Nazi bombing raid.

The explosions were seen at Purfleet and Barking, both in the East End of London. Large gunpowder magazines are situated at Purfleet.

(The Barking-Purfleet section is just a short distance north of the Royal Woolwich arsenal. In the vicinity are clustered London's most important docks and nearby is the huge Imperial gas works.

(The whole section is also the site of important manufacturing plants.

An estimated 2,500 Nazi warplanes—twice as many as in yesterday's juggernaut smash at the island kingdom—were seen speeding at great height across the English coast.

[A German air armada, well-informed sources told the United Press, was sent to London for the express purpose of bombing military objectives.

[The reports from well-informed German sources said that British fighters had engaged the German planes and that a most violent engagement was being fought out high over the skies above the British capital.

[The reports said that the German bombers were raining bombs on Barking, on the Thames River, well within the London metropolitan area.

[Present indications are, it was said, that the air battle over London is one of the most severe fought thus far in the war.

[Fighting is spreading in the London area, a later report from the same quarters said.]

Earlier authorized German sources announced that the fleet of bombers was on its way to London.

These sources had said the huge air fleet was heading for military objectives on the outskirts of the city and was not expected to bomb the center of the city.

These sources said the Nazi air force "will undertake to prove that no power on earth can stop it from dropping bombs on English soil wherever it desires—even if it should be necessary on the city itself."

Authorized German sources said Nazi air raiders destroyed 11 airplanes and ten baloons during today's fighting over Britain. The Germans admitted the loss of three planes.

Bomb Industrial Area

D. N. B. official news agency, said that a large number of bombs had been dropped in early day and night raids on the Austin Company

Continued on Page 2

Eagle Staff photo

GOLD? SO WHAT?—Mrs. Violet Klimwich examines the gold-bearing rock in cellar of her home, 136-50 37th Ave., Flushing, but doesn't plan to do anything about it. She works as a charwoman and can't believe she can get rich quickly.

Real Gold Mine for Sale In Flushing--Don't Rush

Charwoman Asks $50,000 for House and All—Says Even John D. Can Bid for Property

For all Mrs. Violet Klimwich cares, John D. Rockefeller himself or anybody with $50,000 can have her property at 136-50 37th Ave., Flushing, as an apartment house or business site and she'll throw in the "gold mine" in her cellar.

The 43-year-old widow, who works as a charwoman in the RCA building in Rockefeller Center for $19 a week is totally disinterested in the gold which Government assayers say is waiting to be mined beneath her house to the amount of $19.50 per ton.

"I'm so used to hardship," she declared today, "that I can get along without money. I don't want to get rich in a hurry. I just want to be comfortable."

She recalled that last year she heard Mr. Rockefeller wanted to acquire some property in her neighborhood, but when she tried to see him he was always too busy.

"Maybe," she mused, "he'll have to come and see me now. Who can tell?"

Rocks that glittered were found on Mrs. Klimwich's property last April by workmen who were fixing the plumbing. She sent samples to the Assay Office and has now received a formal report telling her that the rocks really contained gold.

But she's "too smart" to try mining the stuff herself, she confided, because:

(1) It takes a lot of digging to dig up a ton of gold-bearing rock and it might cost $19.50 to get the $19.50 in each ton.

(2) It would make the house very uncomfortable to live in.

(3) She is no gold miner.

Mrs. Klimwich's husband died 12 years ago. She received the Flushing property from her mother, who now lives with her as well as two sons and two daughters. One of the boys has a mechanic's job. The plot is 62x122 and has three houses on it, two of which Mrs. Klimwich rents.

Saratoga Results

FIRST RACE—Four-year-olds and up; Steeplechase; about two miles.

aYork Miller (McKenna)	14.60	4.80	6.20
Bay Dean (C. Brooks)	—	3.40	2.80
aRockden (Clements)	—	—	6.20

Time, 4:18 4-5. Wambaw, He Goes, Drinthorn, Bold Fellow also ran. Off time, 2:30.

aG. Pc ry entry.

U. S. May Hang Man In Old Boro Tower

Noose Faces Cook Under Federal Law—Accused of Slaying in Row Over Woman

By FRED ANDERSEN

There may be an old-fashioned hanging in the cupola of the Brooklyn Federal Building.

The Federal Court today took jurisdiction of the first murder case it has had in many years and the potential candidate for the noose is Edward McGivney, 28, a cook in the Government's maritime academy on Hoffman Island.

McGivney is charged with the stabbing last Saturday of William Pasht, second-class seaman, and William Harkins, first-class seaman. Pasht died early today in Marine Hospital, Staten Island. The three, while on shore leave, argued over a woman and it is charged that when they returned to their quarters McGivney rushed to his kitchen, got a knife and attacked the seamen. Harkins is recovering. McGivney donned a life preserver and swam for five hours before he was captured.

Prosecution Up to U. S.

Assistant U. S. Attorney James G. Scileppi, in charge of the criminal division, after delving into the legal aspect of Hoffman Island as Government territory, decided that he and not the State authorities must handle the case and plunged into the detailed investigation to present to the Federal grand jury a charge of murder against McGivney.

As a result McGivney may be hanged in the old tower of Brooklyn's Federal Building, provided, of course, he is found guilty by a jury.

"What his fate may be I cannot say before the jury has passed on it," said Mr. Scileppi, "but so far as the law is concerned the Federal authorities still have the right, in their discretion, to hang a convicted murderer in the cupola of this building.

Law Was Amended

"If that is done, the hanging must be under the direction of the judge who pronounces the hanging sentence, the United States marshal and the United States District Attorney. Only a few years ago the law was amended permitting the Federal Court to send a condemned murderer to a State prison for electrocution, but it is not mandatory."

McGivney, who was arraigned Tuesday on an assault charge, is in the West St., Manhattan, Jail, under $25,000 bail fixed by U. S. Commissioner Edward E. Fay.

Alien Registry Office Opened Here by Quayle

300 Postal Employes Will Be Selected To Act as Interpreters

The 400,000 Brooklyn aliens will be registered at the station set up for that purpose on the fourth floor of the old Brooklyn Eagle Building, 305 Washington St., Postmaster Frank J. Quayle Jr. announced today. He is organizing a special staff of 300 employes of the Postoffice Department to handle the work and is finecombing the personnel to find men who can speak and translate the various foreign languages to help the aliens who cannot speak English.

A pamphlet of instructions has been issued to carriers and employes at all stations and substations so that they can answer any and all questions that may be asked of them by aliens.

Stiff Penalties Set

The registration station will be open an dready for work at 9 a.m. Monday, Aug. 26. It will remain open until 9 p.m. each weekday, except Saturdays, when it will close at 6 p.m. All registrations must be in by Dec. 26. Those who do not register may get six months in prison and be fined $1,000.

Those who make false answers are subject to a like fate and if any forget to tell the officials their new address within five days after they move, following registration, they may get 30 days in jail and a fine of $100.

Postmaster Quayle said that

Continued on Page 2

Woman's Body, Weight About Neck, Found in River

The body of an unidentified woman, about 59, was found today by the Marine Division of the Police Department, floating at the foot of Loew Ave. and North River, Manhattan. A rope and small lead weight were around her neck.

Mexican Peasants Revolt

Mexico City, Aug. 16 (AP)—Fourteen persons were reported killed and at least 40 wounded in the village of Felipe Santiago, Mexico State, when a band of 200 armed peasants staged a raid yesterday.

F. D. R. Bares Defense Talks With Britain

Parley on Acquisition Of Bases Centered On the Panama Canal

Washington, Aug. 16 (AP) — President Roosevelt announced today that the United States is "holding conversations" with Great Britain on acquisition of naval and air bases by the United States "with special reference to the Panama Canal."

The Chief Executive made the announcement at his press conference but cautioned reporters repeatedly not to tie it up with any speculation about the release of American destroyers to Great Britain.

Voluntarily, Mr. Roosevelt authorized the following direct quotation on the negotiations for bases:

"The United States Government is holding conversations with the government of the British Empire with regard to the acquisition of naval and air bases by the United States for American hemisphere defense with special reference to the Panama Canal."

The President then said that he had another item of news on which he also would make a direct, quotable statement, which was:

"The United States Government is carrying on conversations with the Canadian Government looking toward defense of the American hemisphere."

Mr. Roosevelt did not go into de-

Continued on Page 2

Powder Plant Blast Kills 5 Workers

Joplin, Mo., Aug. 16 (AP)—Five men were killed today in an explosion which wrecked a unit of the Atlas Powder Plant six miles east of Joplin in Southwestern Missouri.

The plant, which employs approximately 400 men and is one of three powder plants in this vicinity, has been producing nearly 2,000,000 pounds of T.N.T. monthly. Over half of the production is being purchased by British agents, officials said.

Because of the large British orders, a new T.N.T. unit was started last February and is ready to start operating next week.

The blast demolished the "No. 2 punch house" in which the five victims were working. Each unit of the plant is built in the center of a dirt retaining wall designed to direct the force of explosions away from other units.

The explosion did not touch the recently-completed T. N. T. unit.

Italians Bomb Greek Warships, Athens Reports

Gayda Charges Sinking Of Cruiser by Torpedo Was a 'British Plot'

Athens, Aug. 16 (AP)—A high authority said here tonight the commanders of two Greek destroyers bombed by warplanes today had reported by radio to the Navy Ministry that the attacking planes were Italian.

The Government carefully refrained from any comment, insisting that the planes were of "unknown" nationality.

Nevertheless, the high authority said the officers of the two destroyers, the Vasilevs Georgios I and Vasipissa Olga, crafts of 1,350 tonnage, had carefully watched the planes through field glasses and reported "an absolute identification."

Escape by Zig-Zagging

The destroyers, according to reports reaching Athens, escaped damage by zig-zagging at full speed. They did not open fire on the planes.

It also was reported that a Greek merchantship identified as the Frin was bombed by "unknown" warplanes while lying in an unidentified Greek harbor.

(Virginio Gayda, authoritative Fascist editor, wrote today in Il Giornale d'Italia that the torpedoing of the cruiser Helle yesterday was part of a British plot to precipitate a crisis between Italy and Greece. The editor disclaimed any Italian responsibility for the sinking of the ship by an unidentified submarine.)

Diplomatic observers expressed belief that the secret attacks left Greece virtually with an undeclared war on her hands. Officials, however, declared the government had not yet taken any defensive military measures.

Turkey Ready to Act

Istanbul, Aug. 16 (AP)—Premier Rafik Saydam conferred with the Greek Minister today and then held long conferences with army and navy leaders as Turkey took an increasingly serious view of the Italian-Greek situation.

The Turkish press hinted strongly that any open Italian move against Greece might see this country involved in fulfillment of the British-Turkish mutual assistance pact.

'Here I Come,' Shouts Man; Plunges to Crowded Street

New Haven, Aug. 16 (U.P.)—Shouting "Here I come" to a horrified crowd in the congested business center of the city, a man tentatively described as Joseph L. Owens, 50, of 1151 Bedford Ave., Brooklyn, dove to his death today from a seventh floor ledge of the First National Bank building.

An elevator operator in the building said the suicide had slugged him, pushed him from the cage and started the car The operator said he had thrown an emergency switch which halted the elevator at the seventh floor.

Owens then ran into a lawyer's office, climbed through a window and perched on the ledge.

He gazed down into the street for several minutes, crossed himself, and then leaped.

He plunged to his death as fire apparatus arrived and police entered the building to try to save him.

Police said Owens struck a lower ledge of the building in his descent and that he died instantly when he struck the pavement.

Identification was made from several letters found in Owens' pockets.

Several hundred persons witnessed the suicide. They shouted to Owens to go back into the office, but he paid no attention to them. He stood on the ledge for almost five minutes before he jumped.

Authorities were checking with New York police to verify the identification.

Hinted at Suicide

At 1151 Bedford Ave., which is a diner, Mrs. Marie Arms, the owner, said that Joseph L. Owen's received his mail there and had no home. His last address was 175 Gates Ave., where he had a small furnished room.

Last night, Mrs. Arms said, he looked "very tired" and announced:

"I am going on a long trip—and I'm not driving there."

He had just received a special delivery letter from his brother Eugene of Worcester, Mass., she said and with a disappointed look muttered, "No money."

For the last two weeks he had been driving a fruit truck between New York and Maine.

According to Miss Etta Dahm of 175 Gates Ave. he often appeared to be downhearted and once said: "I just can't get along here. I'm going to New London."

Berlin, Unworried, Reports Crop Prospects 'Good'

Berlin, Aug. 16 (AP)—Europe's 1940 crop prospects were described as "average good" today by German agricultural experts, who said the Reich's food situation was excellent with record root crops (potatoes, beets, etc.) in the offing.

These experts said the rationing system had greatly helped Germany to reduce cereal consumption, and declared there was absolutely no cause for worry since the Reich's grain supplies were still plentiful.

Figures were unavailable, it was said, because statistics on Germany's food supplies are regarded as a military secret.

Rockingham Park Results

FIRST RACE—Three-year-olds; three-quarters mile.

Dona's Pal (Caffarella)	22.60	8.80	9.00
Count Titz (Atkinson)	—	9.20	6.00
Canslip (Anderson)	—	—	8.80

Time, 1:14. Katie M., Bully Time, Erudite, Steeler, Johnny .. Texstar, Axelson, Pluto, Buzz Me also ran. Off, 2:35½.

6,000 Planes Locked In Battle Over England

London Clamps Down Censorship As Foe Strikes Again and Again

London, Aug. 16 (AP)—A great air battle for England and England's heart thundered tonight over these islands and invading Nazi planes rode the skies above London.

All day long the kingdom had been pounded by a vast fleet of some 2,500 German bombers and fighters.

And then, as Germany wirelessed to London and the world that more were yet to come, this capital of empire itself was drawn into the theater of action—the theater of the great showdown.

A censorship fell tight upon London.

(For more than two hours the Associated Press in New York received from London no news dealing with the raids.)

(The Germans announced in Berlin that in a thunderous engagement over London their bombers had observed big explosions in the eastern sections of the capital. These reports indicated that powder magazines had been hit in Purfleet and Barking in London's squalid East End.)

At 2 p.m. the Associated Press office in New York was still in contact with its London office, but it was apparent that censorship was preventing London from sending any news of today's fighting there.

The Dow-Jones ticker in New York said the London stock market closed during the air raid, but later trading resumed and the market closed steadier.

In some quarters, it was considered possible that the Nazi Fuehrer hoped to blast Britain into surrender without even sending troops across the channel for a land invasion.

Between 6,000 and 6,500 British and German planes were probably engaged in the terrific conflict. The British, with about 4,000 first-line defense planes, were believed certain to have thrown every available aircraft into action to stem the Nazi hurricane.

Aside from the metropolitan area, the raiding Nazis sprayed Britain with explosives from Scot-

Continued on Page 2

WHERE TO FIND IT IN TODAY'S EAGLE

Children's Corner	Page 20	Lost and Found	Page 2
Comics	Page 9	Movies	Page 7
Crossword	Page 18	Mr. Billopp	Page 20
Dr. Brady	Page 20	Novel	Page 20
Ed Hughes	Page 14	OBITUARIES	Page 11
EDITORIAL	Page 10	People in Politics	Page 12
Events Tonight	Page 18	RADIO	Page 9
FINANCIAL	Pages 16-17	Real Estate	Page 19
Fulton Lewis Jr.	Page 10	Society	Page 5
Harold Conrad	Page 6	SPORTS	Pages 13-14-15
Heffernan	Page 12	Theaters	Page 7
Helen Worth	Page 4	Wall St.	Page 16
Jimmy Wood	Page 13	Want Ads	Pages 18-19
Lindley	Page 22	Woman's	Page 4

Greeks Smash Italians at Key Points

WALL STREET
Closing Stock Prices
★ ★ ★ ★ ★

BROOKLYN EAGLE

WALL STREET
Closing Stock Prices
★ ★ ★ ★ ★

LOCAL WEATHER FORECAST: Cloudy, cooler tonight; fair, moderate temperature tomorrow

100th YEAR • No. 304 • DAILY AND SUNDAY • BROOKLYN, N. Y., SATURDAY, NOV. 2, 1940 • Entered at the Brooklyn Postoffice as 2d Class Mail Matter—(Copyright 1940 The Brooklyn Daily Eagle) (F. D. S. Corporation) • 3 CENTS

PRESIDENT PLEDGES NO WAR: STIRS HATRED, WILLKIE SAYS

GREEKS SEIZE KEY POINTS, SMASH ENEMY

Many Captives Taken In Overwhelming Push 7 Miles Into Albania

BULLETIN

Bitolj, Yugoslav Frontier, Nov. 2 (U.P.)—Greek troops which last night invaded Albania and took the Village of Bikliksta, threatening to cut off Italian troops in the Breznica area of Greece, advanced farther today and reached a point seven miles inside the border, according to reports from the Village of Stenja, on Lake Presba.

Athens, Nov. 2 (U.P.)—Greek mountain troops, thrusting more than three miles into Albanian territory after overwhelming Italian resistance, have captured a series of strong Italian positions and taken nine Italian officers, 153 men and a number of horses and mules, the high comma..d said in a communique today.

(Italian airplanes have bombed troops disembarking at the vitally important island of Crete, dominating the Aegean Sea, south of the Greek mainland, an Italian high command communique asserted. It was not specified whether the troops were Greek or British troops sent from Egypt.

(It was believed that results of the bombing were excellent, the communique said, adding that Italian bombs struck some steamships in the harbor and damaged port works in the island.

(A statement in the communique that Italian troops were carrying

Continued on Page 2

ROME GETS BAD NEWS

Rome, Nov. 2 (U.P.) — The war correspondent of the newspaper Messaggero, with Italian troops in Greece, admitted in a dispatch today that the Italians were having tough going.

He said the invaders faced the flower of the Greek Army, which was well supplied with British equipment ranging from uniforms to long-range artillery.

WHERE TO FIND IT IN TODAY'S EAGLE

Bridge	Page 7
Bruce Bliven	Page 7
Children's Corner	Page 7
Clifford Evans	Page 4
Comics	Page 6
Crossword	Page 7
Dr. Brady	Page 7
Ed Hughes	Page 12
EDITORIAL	Page 8
Events Tonight	Page 18
FINANCIAL	Page 14
Grin and Bear It	Page 8
Harold Parrott	Page 11
Heffernan	Page 4
Lost and Found	Page 2
Meet Your Leader	Page 7
Movies	Page 18
Novel	Page 7
OBITUARIES	Page 9
Patterns	Pages 6-7
People in Politics	Page 4
RADIO	Page 6
Real Estate	Page 17
Society	Page 5
PORTS	Pages 11-12-13
aters	Page 18
er	Page 8
Ads	Pages 16-17
's	Page 5

78,000 Will Witness Army-'Irish' Grid Tilt

Notre Dame Installed Topheavy Favorite; Rams Set to Bounce Back Against Tarheels

By JIMMY WOOD
Sports Editor

Hemmed in by solid walls of humanity estimated at 78,000, reported to have spent $350,000 for the privilege of sitting in at the colorful traditional football spectacle, undefeated Notre Dame battles Army today at the Yankee Stadium.

The setting is just as picturesque as ever. As usual, the Subway Alumni of the "Fighting Irish" appeared to be in the majority and bet freely at the odds of 4 to 1 on their idols from South Bend.

The customary parade of the Cadets will precede the game. The Army mule will be conspicuous, as will be Clashmore Mike, the Notre Dame canine mascot.

Some Predict Major Upset

Despite the fact that the West Pointers go into the fray with one of their worst records of recent years, one win, one tie and two successive losses, the combat will lose none of its glamour. Some were of the opinion that the underdog would rise on his hind legs and deliver one of the major upsets of the season. However, most believed that Elmer Layden's boys would rout Uncle Sam's warriors by an overwhelming score.

Fordham's game with North Carolina's Tarheels is the only local competition for the big subway classic, but the Rams, smarting from their upset defeat last week, are likely to spray a good game on the Polo Grounds lawn. North Carolina is a worthy foe, having come along fast after an early dunking by Wake Forest.

Epic battles are brewing at other focal points on the football map. Cornell's 16-straight defeatless streak, cherished so dearly in the Ithaca sanctum, is in real jeopardy this afternoon at the hands of a battling Columbia team which is far better than the eleven which

Continued on Page 9

AMERICA'S HONEY — The California Bee Keepers Association today chose Brenda Marshall (above), young film star, as "America's Honey." The film star was chosen because "she represents sweetness combined with modern beauty."

Court Sets Date for Trial Of 7 Electrical Unionists

County Judge Charles S. Colden in Long Island City yesterday tentatively fixed trial date for Harry Van Arsdale Jr., business agent of Local 3, International Brotherhood of Electrical Workers, A. F. of L., and six other union members on charges of rioting for Jan. 13.

The men were indicted as the result of disorders at the plant of the Triangle Conduit and Cable Company, Elmhurst, on Sept. 24. A strike has been in progress at the plant for several months. Argument on demurrers to the indictment, adjourned to yesterday from last week, again was deferred because expected superseding indictments had not yet been handed up.

Today's Scratches

Empire

2—Yawl, Arestino, Maezaca, Market Wise.
3—Mary Schulz, Sir Bevidere, Early Settler, Brown Queen, Cattistock, Wisbech.
5—Sickle T.
6—Early Delivery.
7—Newark.
Raining and sloppy.

Pimlico

1—Walter Light, Commentator, Zenana, Legenda, Blue Marvel, Joanny.
2—Hornblende, Hop Skip.
3—Fly Catcher, Greenwich Time, Suspect, Santi Quaranti, Dundrillin.
4—Barograph.
5—Alumino.
7—Pagliaci, Abrasion, Polymelior, Equistar.
8—Dnieper, Orius, Centerville, Strolling By, Quaroma, Channing.
Cloudy and muddy.

Rockingham

1—Gay Frank.
2—Count Eleven.
3—Mollie Gal, Suprema.
6—Night Editor.
Drizzling and slow.

RAF Turns Back Nazi Raiders From Ambush in Clouds

Spitfires Swoop Down, Scatter Enemy Planes On Way to Bomb London

London, Nov. 2 (AP)—A bomb struck a crowded bus and probably killed several persons in a night raid on London, it was reported today as Britain's fighters beat off three day attacks on the capital.

The raiders were pounced upon and scattered by patrols of British Spitfires which swooped from high cloud ambushes along the southeast coast.

Using the same surprise tactics, the fast British planes were credited with splitting up another large wave of German planes, this time Messerschmitt fighters, which tried to penetrated inland while the morning sun was at their backs.

The Air Ministry reported seven raiders shot down before noon, in addition to five downed by anti-aircraft gunners overnight.

Some raiders, however, streaked

Continued on Page 2

Von Papen Hunts Pheasants

Berlin, Nov. 2 (U.P.)—Baron Franz von Papen, German Ambassador to Turkey who arrived in Berlin from his post at Ankara late yesterday, has gone pheasant hunting, authorized German quarters said today. Papen was said to have spent only a short time in Berlin.

Berlin Theater Crowds Bombed In Heavy Assault

Raid Toll Uncounted —Thousands Caught In Movies and Cafes

Berlin, Nov. 2 (U.P.)—British planes, in a raid which caught tens of thousands of people in theaters, movies, restaurants and cafes, rained high explosive and incendiary bombs on the Berlin area last night, killing and wounding "a number" of persons, a government communique said today.

In a raid on Amsterdam, it was said, at least 26 persons were killed.

The air raid sirens shrieked in Berlin just when the fashionable west end was crowded with pleasure seekers, and the subways were crowded with those going home.

[British airplanes, in a smashing attack on German objectives during the night, bombed Berlin, the great Krupp armaments works, 15 airdromes at some of which German planes were just taking off to attack Britain, and various industrial objectives, the British Air Ministry asserted.

Hit War Plants, R. A. F. Says

[Several of Berlin's principal railroad stations and freight yards were attacked, a communique said.

[Among other targets were synthetic oil plants at Magdeburg and Gelsenkirchen, an industrial factory near Gelsenkirchen, the Krupp works at ssen, where a blast furnace was bombed, and the railroad junction at Osnabruck.

[Aircraft of the coastal command bombed German gun emplacements at Cape Gris Nez across the Channel.

[It was indicated strongly that British planes had made raids on Italy for the second straight night. There were two air alarms at Berne, Switzerland. Such alarms in the past have invariably meant a British raid on Italy.]

As soon as the sirens sounded managers of most theaters appeared on their stages, announced

Continued on Page 2

Seize Nazis in Raid On Greenland Post

A German-language broadcast by the British Broadcasting Corporation today said a German expedition of 50 men had been captured in an unsuccessful attempt to seize the meteorological observation station at Greenland. The Norwegian patrol boat Fritjof Nansen made them prisoners, it said. The broadcast was heard here by the Columbia Broadcasting System Company.

The broadcast, quoting a report from Stockholm, Sweden, said "for a long time the German air force has been experiencing the lack of exact weather forecasts, hindering successful air operations because Berlin did not get much support from the Danish and Norwegian personnel of the Weather Bureau at Greenland.

Weather Bureau officials in New Lork said Greenland had six to 10 observation posts and that before the war six were heard regularly in this country.

A German weather station in Greenland would enable the Nazis to forecast weather three to four days in advance, officials told the Associated Press.

Dr. James H. Kimball, chief meteorologist here, said that both Germany and the United States were severely handicapped in making weather forecasts after Britain cut off the Greenland reports.

G. O. P. Challenger in City To Wind Up His Campaign

Calls Boro Blast Tactics of Lenin, Trotsky, Hitler

Wendell L. Willkie returned to New York City today for the climactic address of his Presidential campaign.

Meanwhile, he lashed out at President Roosevelt for the Chief Executive's address in Brooklyn last night, which, said Willkie, was designed to 'stir up class hatred and divide our people," combining "the tactic of Lenin, the strategy of Hitler and the preaching of Trotsky."

The Republican Presidential nominee, resting before his final campaign appeartnce tonight at Madison Square Garden, issued a statement calling Mr. Roosevelt's address his "fourth defense speech —defense of his own administration."

Says G. O. P. Offers Unity

Saying his opponent "cuaims that the Republican ticket has the support of many different elements of our populations," Willkie continued:

"The answer to that is obvious. It is because our party is today the only one which offers unity to the country . . .

"In a desperate effort to block this movement of unity, the third term candidate stooped to the use of an alleged quotation which, if made, was discreditable. This quotation is supposed to have come from some one in Philadelphia having no connection with the National Republican ticket."

(Mr. Roosevelt in his Brooklyn speech, said "a prominent leader of the Philadelphia bar" had been quoted in the New York Times as saying the President's only supporters "are paupers, those who earn less than $1,200 a year and aren't worth that, and the Roosevelt family."

Cites 'Kicking' of Policeman

"This all to prevailing Republican sentiment" was described by the President as "a direct, vicious

Continued on Page 5

BRITISH PLANE CHEERED FLYING OVER ATHENS

Athens, Nov. 2 (U.P.)—Great throngs in the streets and on roofs today cheered a British Sunderland flying boat as it flew over the city just before an air raid alarm warning of the approach of Italian planes.

The British plane was forced down in Crete a month ago and interned by the Greeks. The Royal Air Force here already has opened offices for administrative work in connection with expected arrival of a British air force.

Ten to Start Flying Course Today on Scholarships

Ten young men will receive their first flying lessons today after receiving scholarships, enabling them to become full-fledged aviators on call for national defense duty, from City Council President Newbold Morris at exercises at Floyd Bennett Field.

The scholarships, the first awarded by the Volunteer Pilot Training Fund, go to Joseph Bongiorni, Jay Frank Pearson, John Joseph Martin, Meyer Wilen, John O'Shea, Gordon Robotham, Jerome Simpson, George Hester, William Boeppel and Clevis Yancey Tollett, all of whom applied for CAA civilian pilot training, but were rejected because the non-collegiate quota was filled.

Wide World photo

DELIVERS FIGHTING SPEECH—President Roosevelt denounces "unholy alliance" of radicals and reactionaries in his militant address at the Academy of Music.

Roosevelt Here Hits G.O.P. 'Unholy Alliance'

Reds, Nazis, Reactionaries Joined Against Him He Charges—24,000 Mass at Academy Rally

By JOSEPH H. SCHMALACKER

President Roosevelt pressed forward to save his third term from defeat in his own State today after a dramatic political shift of tactics against opponents at the climax of his campaign in Brooklyn's New Deal Democratic stronghold.

While the President invaded Western New York, before entering Pennsylvania and Ohio, rejuvenated Brooklyn allies took up the cue fashioned in last night's Academy of Music speech and launched a weekend drive for votes on the basis of his charge that a "new unholy alliance" had been formed to seek the New Deal's defeat.

The change of tactics unfolded itself before thousands of cheering, flag-waving and noise-making Democrats in a densely-packed rally as the President put aside his discussion of defense and charged, in effect, that disciples of Nazism's brown shirts and the Soviet's Reds had leagued themselves with reactionary forces to destroy the New Deal.

Charges Alliance of Foes

Striking at his foes in a burst of political warfare to the hilt, the President roused his followers with the declaration that bitterly discordant elements, which had been viciously attacking one another, were now enlisted in a common cause to win the campaign.

The President delivered his speech

Continued on Page 3

ROOSEVELT ODDS DROP

Betting odds have dropped off to 7 to 5 for President Roosevelt to carry the nation, and now are 6 to 5 in favor of Wendell L. Willkie carrying New York State, according to C. W. Ruff Valentine, broker, of Maiden Lane St., Manhattan.

N. Y. Clerk Arrested At Detroit in Theft

Detroit, Nov. 2 (AP)—Two New York detectives have completed a 38-State, 16-month pursuit with the arrest of a young trust company clerk, who, they said, is wanted in connection with the disappearance of $22,000 from his firm.

Detectives Joseph McKeown and Otto Drescher said they apprehended Joseph Flanagan, 27, former clerk in the Bronx County Trust Company, last night as he stepped off a bus from Windsor, Ont., after an attempt to enlist in the Royal Canadian Air Force.

The detectives said Flanagan had been sought since June, 1939, when he suddenly left his job and investigation revealed $22,000 was missing.

Roosevelt Cites Record in Talk At Rochester

Aboard Roosevelt Train En Route to Cleveland, Nov. 2 (AP) —"Your President says this country is not going to war."

Those words were addressed by Franklin D. Roosevelt to a rain-drenched crowd that gathered around his train at the Rochester station.

In an informal speech, Mr. Roosevelt reviewed what he termed a "fortunate record" established while he was Chief Executve of New York State and the nation.

He was the only Governor to serve four years without calling on the National Guard "to put down riots," he said, and in his seven and one-half years as President the army and navy "had never been called out except in a cause of humanity."

"And so it seems to me," he said, "that a fellow with that kind of a record over a good many years must have his head on the ground and I don't believe he has his finger on the trigger."

Flays G. O. P. for Fleet Tale

President Roosevelt told what he said was a story about the Republican National chairman in Washington who, he related, had said in a press conference—off the record but with word to reporters to spread it around—that the President had ordered a portion of the fleet westward and that the day after election he would order all of it to the Philippines—an action that would be regarded by Japan as hostile.

That type of thing, he said, was "more dangerous to our international relations" than anything ever done by his Administration.

He repeated that "your President says this country is not going to war."

In discussing his record at Washingtton the President said it never had been necessary to call out the Army or Navy to restore civil peace or to put down riots.

On the way to Cleveland to close out his last full day of campaigning with another major political address tonight, Mr. Roosevelt paused to speak from a platform adjoining his special train to an applauding throng of thousands at Rochester, home of plants making photographic equipment for the armed forces.

Senator James Mead, running for re-election, was waiting to greet the Chief Executive, while a band and the crowd whooped it up as the train pulled in from New York.

GO TO CHURCH TOMORROW

For Religious News, Sermon Topics, etc. All Denominations

TURN TO THE Church News Page IN TODAY'S Brooklyn

Grid Dodgers Favored To Top Giants Tomorrow

BROOKLYN EAGLE

SPORTS

SATURDAY, NOV. 2, 1940

W

Record Crowd to See Interboro Rivals Tangle at Ebbets Field

By LOU NISS

The Dodgers will play the strange role of favorites when they meet the Giants at Ebbets Field tomorrow before the largest football crowd in the history of Brooklyn. Ever since the Dodgers-Giants grid rivalry began in 1926 the Giants always have been rated tops in the betting and only once in 22 games have the Dodgers managed to completely upset the dope. That was in 1930 when the Dodgers won, 7 to 6, on Jack McBride's scoring run and Benny Friedman's point after touchdown.

This was Brooklyn's only victory against 18 defeats and three ties. Generally the Dodgers have made a good fight of it, and many of the games were close. The Dodgers expect to see that tomorrow's game also runs true to form, and the players are confident they will win despite the absence of Bruiser Kinard and Ralph Kercheval, shelved by injuries.

Crowd of 40,000 Possible

There is no doubt that a record crowd will be present. Almost enough tickets already have been sold to near the mark of 35,000 who jammed Ebbets Field in 1923 to see Notre Dame beat Army. Besides 10,000 general admission seats will be on sale when the gates open a few hours before game time.

With the 3,000 added sideline seats, the field will house 40,000 comfortably, and no one will be greatly surprised if there is a sell-out.

Brooklyn's improvement under Coach Jock Sutherland is the answer to the increased interest in the Dodgers. In other years the Dodgers had trouble winning from other weak sisters in the race and would take fearful beatings from the tough Western teams. This year they lost only to the Bears and Redskins, but looked like a real football team, even in defeat.

The Dodgers will not be at full strength for the Giants, but the absence of Ralph Kercheval and Bruiser Kinard has been nullified to a great extent by the Giants' loss of Tuffy Leemans, their ace ball carrier.

Other Dodgers who have been on the hospital list have shown enough improvement to assure their presence in the lineup. Ace Parker definitely will be in the starting backfield with Rhoten Shetley, Pug Manders and Banks McFadden; John Golemgeske will be back at tackle, though he may not start, and Mike Gussie also will be available at guard.

Coach Jock Sutherland has pointed the Dodgers for this game, just as he used to point Pittsburgh for some of its big ones. He feels that beating the Giants will put football over the top in Brooklyn, and that has been his aim all year. Sutherland has never held out much hope of winning the National League championship, but he has set his mind on beating the boys from the wrong side of the bridge. It might be unfortunate for President Roosevelt that the game is being played before Election Day, for if the Dodgers win some normally Democratic Brooklynites might write in Sutherland's name on the ballot.

CHEER UP, FANS!

It rain-rain-rained last night and this morning but the Weather Bureau, having the football crowds in mind, predicted that the rain would end early this afternoon. Tonight, according to forecasters, will be cloudy and tomorrow fair.

SCHOLASTIC FOOTBALL TWIN BILL POSTPONED

The schoolboy football double-header scheduled for Ebbets Field this afternoon has been postponed because of the heavy downpour. Thomas Jefferson High School was to have met Brooklyn Tech, while the undefeated James Madison eleven was slated to go against New Utrecht.

No new date has been set for the games, but plans are under way to reschedule them as a twin attraction at Ebbets Field in the near future.

INVITE F. D. TO TOSS FIRST BALL IN 1941

President Larry McPhail and Manager Leo Durocher of the Dodgers sent a telegram to President Roosevelt at the Academy of Music rally last night welcoming him to Brooklyn. He was informed that the Dodgers were for him and invited the national executive to throw out the first ball on opening day next Spring.

Italy's Tax Disbursements

Special to the Brooklyn Eagle

ROME—Tax disbursements for the ten provinces of Italy for the week ending Nov. 2, 1940, were as follows, with figures representing thouasnds:

Naples.....	32—16—81— 4—48
Bari.......	23—74—42—27—46
Florence...	19—56— 6—14—22
Milan......	71—14—82— 4—73
Palermo....	78—10—12—64—27
Rome......	69—49—18—24—84
Turin......	20—46—64—85— 8
Venice.....	76—30—56—81—79
Cagliari....	30—15—48— 6— 8
Genova....	57— 7—26—84—81

Quarterbacks Back Where They Started

Were Once Forbidden To Lug Ball; Now They Get No Chance

By RALPH TROST

Who does call the signals?

Once it was the captain. Now, some say, it's the coach. Anyway the business of calling signals has gone through a most interesting evolution—and, as far as the records go, we're celebrating the 60th anniversary of the little man who isn't there any more, the fellow dubbed "quarterback" who was once forbidden to run with the ball and now doesn't get any chance.

Back in 1880 when the orderly massing of players on either side of the line supplanted that disorderly hangover of rugby, the "scrum," the quarterback was created. He was the liason officer who operated between the line and the backs—a sort of public relations counsel. I never did know why he couldn't run with the ball.

Anyway, in 1880 football got a quarterback. And like the coxwain on a crew, he got smaller and louder with each passing year. And he had a long reign, too. He lived, and yelled, through the days of the flying wedge, through the era of long hair that blossomed in the 90s, through the great schism of 1895 when Princeton, Navy and Yale had one set of rules and Cornell, Harvard and Penn another.

The quarterback survived the first backfield shift, a machination of Alonzo Stagg, he held his own through Dr. Williams' famed Minnesota shift, the real forerunner of the Notre Dame style. But 20 years ago he started to skid.

Until that portrait-painting basketball player, Bob Zuppke started teaching football at Illinois, the quarterback was the field general. Hints, cues, tips, etc. were sneaked to him through substitutes and other manners. But to the public at large, the little fellow with the big voice was still the boss. But in 1921 came the huddle.

In the huddle any one could talk and, according to stories, most of them did. In a short time it was discovered that an end could give the signals as well as a quarterback. Then came the vogue for defensive signals.

Nowadays it's hard telling who does call the signals. Last year, at Columbia, the offense signals were called by the end, the defense by the center. There were all sorts of methods and it wouldn't surprise us a bit to learn that, somewhere, the attack signals were called by the center and the defense signals by a tackle.

In today's play there's only one style in which the quarterback, generally a little fellow of no more than 165 pounds, seems to have authority. It's in the Notre Dame arrangement of men. Wherever the N. D. system is employed, there you'll find the quarterback directly behind center, his left hand probably leaning lightly on the center's back, yelling loudly. Suddenly there's a shift and he disappears. And when he shifts off to another spot he takes with him the last reminder of the day when the quarterback was the real boss on the field.

BOTH SIDES

By Harold Parrott

AGELESS ROCK—When you come right down to it there was only one Rockne. We're not going to go maudlin or sobby on you, but——

Here it is almost the 10th anniversary of his death . . . this is the 10th Irish team since that plane crash on Kansas' thawing fields in the Spring of 1931 snuffed out his life . . . and the man is still a living legend.

He comes back, reincarnate in the person of Pat O'Brien, to startle you in a moving picture.

And every once in a while you get a jolt when somebody puts on the record of Rockne's famous dressing-room "fight talk."

Will Rockne never die? We think not. The stories through which he walks and talks bear him up, and they'll last as long as football.

Other coaches have had better records. Other coaches worked wonders with, with maybe, less material.

But Rockne had that electric something, that ability to pump a man or a team full of color. Rockne . . . Notre Dame . . . The Four Horsemen, are still magical names in football.

BATTLE OF BRILL RUN—But perhaps the Rockne stunt that appealed most to the public was the Pennsylvania slaughter, otherwise known as the Battle of Brill Run, in 1930. It was one of the Rock's last great splurges. It had his unmistakeable touch.

The whole setup was there, for Virtue to triumph. Rockne fixed it so Virtue would, and did. Knute played it up to the hilt. And how the public loved it!

Brill, you see, had been at Penn, had quit, and had gone to Notre Dame. Marty wasn't in the right U. of Penn. fraternities or something, and they never gave him a break there. And he let it be known that Lud Wray was his Hitler. A slave-driving, unappreciative coach who thought only of his own gain.

Brill at Notre Dame came to be a star. But he was a right halfback, a blocking back, and the year that N. D. moved in against Penn at packed Franklin Field Marty hadn't carried the ball much.

Rockne fixed it so that he DID carry it that day. Brill scored three touchdowns. Oh, yes, the score—60 to 20!

That delighted the football public from Coast to Coast. That was one Sunday morning Pop and little Willie both choked over their cereal, trying to tell Mom how Marty Brill had come back to get the best of the terrible man who'd persecuted him, and how Wray writhed under the walloping.

"Goodness gracious," said a million mothers that morning, "that Mr. Wray must be a terrible man . . ."

No we hate to spoil an old story, but we know Mr. Wray who is now an assistant at Manhattan, and how he ever got that reputation is beyond us. He's the nicest, mildest sort of gent you'd want to meet.

HIS LAST TEAM—Well, what we started to say was that Rockne certainly bowed out on a high note . . . his 1929 and 1930 teams were both unbeaten and untied national champions.

That 1930 team . . . whatever became of 'em all? . . . where are they, these boys who must be thinking of Rock's last game today?

Well . . . Brill is coaching at Loyola in Los Angeles . . . Bucky O'Connor, the converted fullback who scored two touchdowns in the victory over Southern California that was Rockne's valedictory game, is a doctor practicing in Detroit . . . Johnny (One-Play) O'Brien, the end, is dead, cracked up in an automobile smash.

Tommy Yarr, the All-American center, is with a Kansas City loan company . . . Nick Lukats, halfback, has had some success in the movies and is in the current one about Rockne . . . Marchy Schwartz, great All-American running back, helps Clark Shaughnessy at Stanford U. . . Mike Koken, Schwartz's mate, is with a trucking form in South Bend . . . Paul Host, who rose to captain by 1932 runs, a department store in Chicago.

Joe Sweewetski is the head coach at Holy Cross and Ed Kosky freshman coach at Fordham . . . Tom Kassis, left guard, is in the dry goods business in Wyoming . . . Tom Conley, end and captain, coaches John Carroll in Cleveland . . . Al Culver, tackle, is a Chicago lawyer . . . Joe Kurth, another tackle, is a Western radio announcer . . . Bert Metzger, famed watch-charm guard, is with a Chicago dairy farm.

They scattered to the four winds, that great 1930 team . . . But today, a decade later, they'll be together again . . . in thoughts, at least . . . thoughts of Rockne.

Jock Sutherland Approached on Ohio State Job?

By EDDIE BRIETZ

By Associated Press Correspondent

Nobody has denied the Dayton News' exclusive—that Jock Sutherland has been approached "unofficially" on his availability for the Ohio State job, just in case . . . Joe Louis has dropped six pounds since taking the stump . . . When she goes on the air tonight La Marble would do her fans a favor if she'd spike or confirm those reports she's all set to turn pro . . . Ted Williams still is sore at the papers. One of the Boston sheets wired the Beantown players for their draft numbers. Only guy who didn't reply was Theodore, the problem child.

Seven sets of brothers cavort on the Colby (Kans.) High squad . . . Some sort of record was hung up in the Lawrence College-Coe game when both teams scored a touchdown before 38 seconds of the last half had elapsed.

Wide World photo

'PPING OFF A DOWN—Bill Redmond of Poly Prep gets off to a ten-yard gain in first ›od of game with Brooklyn Prep at Boys High Field yesterday. Poly battled favored ›ent to 6—6 tie. (Story on following page.)

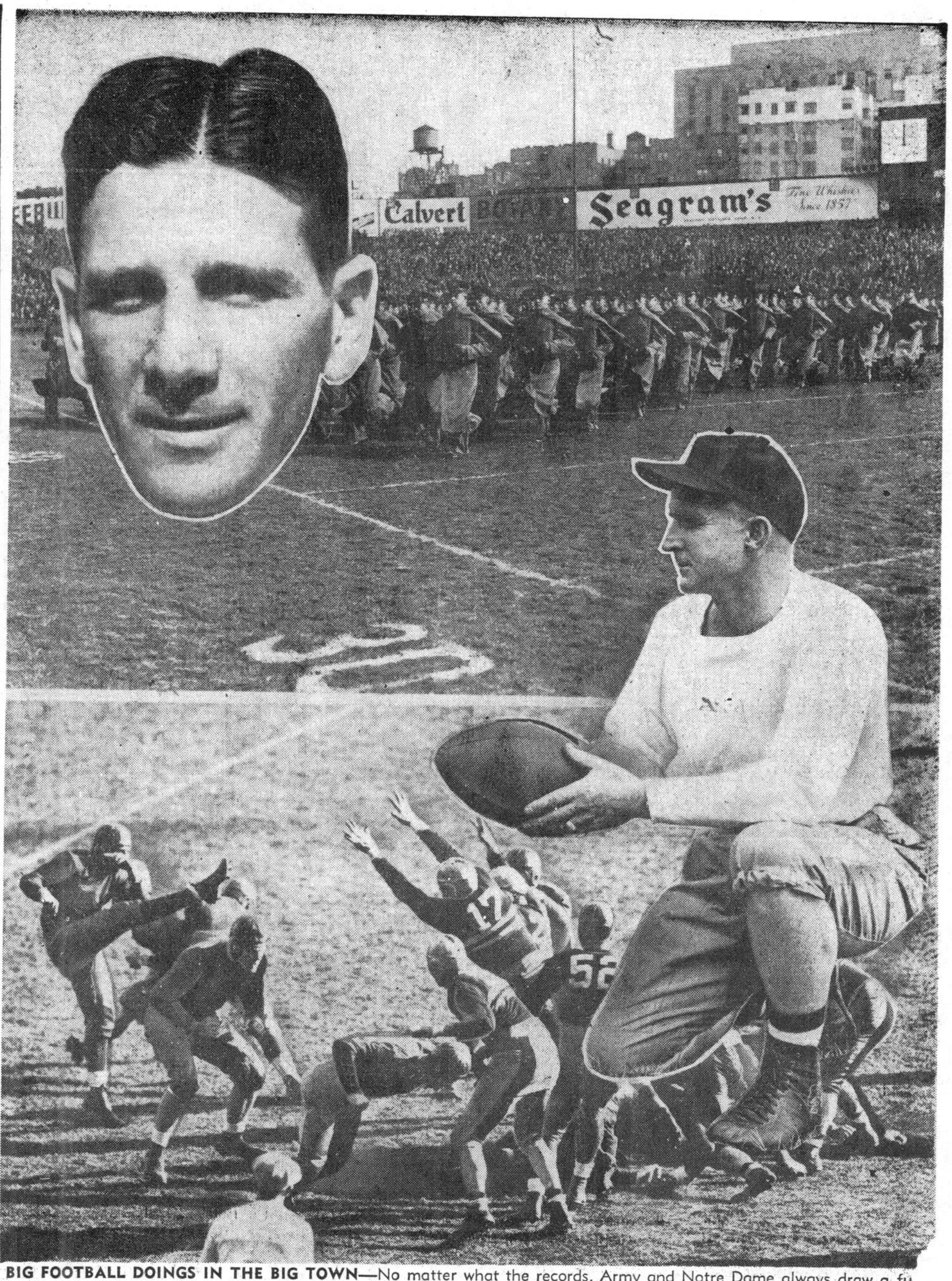

BIG FOOTBALL DOINGS IN THE BIG TOWN—No matter what the records, Army and Notre Dame always draw a fu house when they meet at the Yankee Stadium each season. Today's game drew 78,000, the majority Notre Dame famous subway alumni. Coach Elmer Layden (left) of Notre Dame and Captain Bill Wood (lower right), Army coach, ar not new rivals. They were opposing fullbacks when Army played Notre Dame at Ebbets Field in 1923.

Overlin's Pilot Hesitates On Return Go for Belloise

Steve Earns Draw With Champion In Sizzling Middleweight Match

By HAROLD CONRAD

Half the crowd of 13,000 customers booed the decision in Madison Square Garden last night which saved Ken Overlin's middleweight title. The other half cheered. If you ask us, both halves were right. If Steve Belloise, his ambitious challenger, didn't lose it, neither did Ken win it. Our score corresponded with Referee George Walsh's tally. We called it a draw, seven, seven and one.

But in deference to that unwritten law of the ring never to take a champion's title in an even match, there was nothing else to do but give Mr. Overlin the decision. The two judges didn't quite agree with one half of the crowd. George Kelly gave it to Overlin, nine and six, while George Lecron cast his vote for Ken, 11 and four. We're not quite sure Mr. Lecron was looking at the same fight.

But regardless of the pros and cons of the issue, New York saw a great fight and it ranks along with the Armstrong-Zivic battle as one of the outstanding matches of the past few years. A rematch would be a natural and, promoter Mike Jacobs with an eye to the gate receipts, knows this better than anyone. He would like to throw the pair back in there in a couple of months, but Chris Dundee, Overlin's manager, hasn't quite made up his mind. That should give you a pretty good idea of what kind of an opponent this Belloise kid is.

Steve had the title wrapped up and all ready to take home in the sixth round when he dropped Ken halfway through the round and peppered him unmercifully until the bell sounded, but he never put over that final crusher.

Steve really missed the bus, for he didn't hit Overlin another good punch again until the 11th. The swashbuckling sailor made an amazing comeback in the seventh round, and even the loyal Belloise rooters rose and cheered him to the man. But Ken didn't stop there. He extended the rally to the next round, and the next and next, and Belloise had to win four of the following rounds to make it close.

Belloise wasn't as bitter over the verdict as some of his supporters, and he summed the evening's action up most aptly. Said Steve: "You can't hit 'im when you can't see 'em." Not original, but too true.

THREE EX-CHAMPS STRING WITH CHAMP

It looks like the boys, meaning ex-heavyweight champions Jack Dempsey, Max Baer and Jimmy Braddock are ganging up on Joe Louis. Joe is in Wendell Willkie's corner, but Dempsey, Baer and Braddock, seated with District State Tax Appraiser David F. Soden, were prominent last night at the Roosevelt rally in the Academy of Music. The trio of ex-champs also attended the Kings County Democratic Organization dinner in the Hotel Granada, which preceded the rally. Max and Jimmy, with their arms around each other, kept chinning in a love-feast.

For a veteran of 13 years of campaigning, Overlin was roundly criticized for not taking a count after being knocked down. He claimed he was off balance and wasn't hurt by the punch that flattened him. Ken said the punch that caught him getting up was the one that hurt.

Right after the fight, when Belloise started to make for his dressing room, he couldn't walk down the main aisle. It was all cluttered up with people. Steve found out later that his brother, Mike, former featherweight champion, was jamming up the aisle. He had fainted when Harry Balogh announced the verdict.

Solly Kriger made a game but futile attempt against rugged Tommy Tucker in the eight-round semi-final. He fought back hard after being floored by Tommy in the sixth, but Tucker earned the decision. Featherweight champ Petey Scalzo outpointed Bernie Friedkin of Brownsville in an eight-round thriller to even up an old score. Bernie held him to a draw last Summer.

RANGERS OPEN RACE TONIGHT

Six of the seven National Hockey League clubs begin their 1940-41 season this weekend with a calm disregard for the fact that many of the players are subject to calls to military service in Canada and that, if the war situation becomes serious enough, they may never finish the campaign.

The club owners aren't particularly worried about that possibility. During the off season most of the athletes got in their required 30 days training with the Canadian militia and returned to the rinks in better condition than usual as a result.

The season opens tonight just where it left off last Spring with the world champion Rangers playing the Maple Leafs at Toronto. These finalists in last year's Stanley Cup playoffs are favored to fight it out with the Boston Bruins for the league championship this season.

Await Officials' O. K. on Snavely

Only reports from the officials who worked the recent Cornell-Ohio State football game were needed today to officially exonerate Cornell coach Carl Snavely of charges that he signalled from the bench during the game.

Asa Bushnell, executive director of the Central Office for Eastern Intercollegiate Athletics, announced in answer to a letter from L. W. St. John, Ohio State director of Athletics, who accused Snavely of "unsportsmanlike conduct," that he had written to the four officials asking specifically for their further views.

CORNELL LOSES BIG HAL, 17 OTHERS NEXT JUNE

By HAROLD PARROTT

Brooklyn Eagle Staff Correspondent

Ithaca, N. Y., Nov. 2—Hal McCullough, Brooklyn's 170-pound whizbang contribution to Cornell's all-conquering team, joked as he girded for his last game up here in the Willkie belt today, which the rest of the big Reds planned to make a big one—for him. They think Hal needs a "benefit," because he hadn't scored a single point for the big Red this year going into today's game.

Up here Willkie and the Cornells are both considered a cinch. Ninety percent of the big Red squad, it was found today, are for Wendell. And Cornell was 3 to 1 over Columbia today.

Look for Lean Days

Eighteen of the first 22 Cornells exit in June. Look for some lean days at Ithaca then, so that cry baby Harvard and whistle-blowing Yale will have little to howl about.

McCullough's leather-lugging days are nearing an end. After today's farewell in Ithaca, only road games with Yale, Dartmouth and Penn remain for Cornell. Mac says he won't play pro-football no matter how fat the offer.

The Cornells were planning a McCullough day today because, although Hal's kicking, running and the 24 completed passes he's fired in 36 throws this year have put the big Red on Sensation Street, the Boys High bombshell hasn't scored a single point this year.

The only losing varsity game this smiling 170-pound flash has been in during his varsity career at Cornell is the 19—17 defeat Syracuse pinned on the Big Red in 1938.

McCullough is not in good shape today. His legs are both taped, and the muscles therein are giving him no end of grief. He has not been able to kick all week. Army was the team that gave him the going-over, he says.

Carl Snavely joked about being worried because his "signal cylinders," for transmission of plays from the bench, were not on hand yet. Ohio State's charges of signaling are derided on every corner up here.

But nobody could laugh off Columbia's scrappy 30-man squad, which came over here this morning, after spending a quiet Friday plotting a tremendous upset. Lou Little didn't even work his men out in football suits yesterday. But he had a brain session in the afternoon and went over battle strategy to hobble McCullough and Cornell.

Boro, City, L. I. Vote Charts on National, Local Contests on Pages 20 and 21

Wall Street Closing RACING EXTRA ★★★★★★

BROOKLYN EAGLE

Wall Street Closing RACING EXTRA ★★★★★★

LOCAL WEATHER FORECAST: Partly cloudy, colder tonight; tomorrow cold

100th YEAR • No. 308 • DAILY AND SUNDAY • BROOKLYN, N. Y., WEDNESDAY, NOV. 6, 1940 • Entered at the Brooklyn Postoffice as 2d Class Mail Matter—(Copyright 1940 The Brooklyn Daily Eagle) (P. D. S. Corporation) • 3 CENTS

ROOSEVELT WINS 40 STATES: LABOR PEACE HIS FIRST GOAL

Cashmore, Leibowitz Beat Foes Two to One

G. O. P. Grabs 3 Assembly Seats —F.D.R. Wins 353,192 Edge Here

By JOSEPH H. SCHMALACKER

President Roosevelt's plurality over Wendell L. Willkie in the New Deal Democratic stronghold of Brooklyn stood at 353,192 votes today after a record demonstration of the borough's voting power in the tradition-shattering third term election.

The returns, giving the President a margin of less than two to one over his Republican opponent, spelled a loss of approximately 172,000 from his plurality of 525,000 votes in the election of 1936.

The tally gave Mr. Roosevelt 750,017 and Mr. Willkie 396,825.

The New Deal's sweep, though it bore with it the election of the Democratic slate of borough and country-wide candidates and each

Story of Long Island results on Page 2.

Congressional and State Senatorial nominee on the party's ticket, failed to accomplish the same result in the Assembly elections.

Cashmore, Leibowitz Elected

Borough President John Cashmore polled 645,146 votes in a three-cornered race and received a plurality of 339,105 votes over the runner-up, Emil N. Baar, the Republican candidate. Andrew Armstrong, the Labor party candidate, polled 129,965 votes.

Samuel S. Leibowitz, the Demo-

Continued on Page 12

How Boro Voted On Presidency

(By Assembly Districts)

A.D.	Willkie (Rep.)	Roosevelt (Dem., A.L.)
1.	11294	11807
2.	42878	122568
3.	7901	12995
4.	6013	19552
5.	12452	16812
6.	7602	22218
7.	12282	16167
8.	8385	10765
9.	53211	48891
10.	17597	15870
11.	17834	26807
12.	18948	22339
13.	7764	13076
14.	5131	18282
15.	6904	15372
16.	38262	99866
17.	10830	18370
18.	23367	92443
19.	8218	12764
20.	21005	18526
21.	35642	53651
22.	19800	39812
23.	5532	21064
Totals	396825	750017

The segregated vote for Roosevelt and the vote for the minor parties follow:

Roosevelt (Dem.), 615381, (A.L.), 131749; Thomas (Soc.), 3937; Babson (Pro.), 464.

(Queens, Nassau, Suffolk and other N. Y. State Counties on Page 20 and 21.)

Prepare Capitol Bleachers For Inauguration on Jan. 20

Washington, Nov. 6 (AP)—All the votes weren't counted yet but workmen hammered and sawed away today building wooden bleachers for the Jan. 20 inauguration on the east steps of the Capitol.

With 11,000 spectator seats to put up the contractor, declining to take a chance on the weather, got an early start.

P. R. WINS TEST IN ALL BOROUGHS BUT RICHMOND

Voters Overwhelmingly Reject Proposition To Discontinue System

Voters in all boroughs, with the exception of Richmond, overwhelmingly signified their desire to save proportional representation by voting against the proposition which would have resulted in the election of city legislators by State Senatorial districts.

The total vote was 782,768 against the proposition and 565,879 for it. Brooklyn voted 258,281 to save P. R., with 195,438 favoring the change. Queens voted 176,392 against the proposition, with 109,554 "yes" votes.

Other borough tallies were: Manhattan, 123,123 yes and 174,747 no; Bronx, 119,652 yes and 158,927 no, and Richmond, 18,112 yes and 14,421 no.

Supported by Democrats

The proposition also would have provided for the election of councilmen-at-large, due to unequal representation by Senatorial districts. It was strongly supported by the five Democratic county organizations and as strongly opposed by the Citizens' Budget Commission, Mayor LaGuardia and labor groups.

Opponents of P. R. contended that the system had been shown to be ineffective and that it failed to give local sections their proper representatives.

Supporters of P. R. warned that a "yes" vote on the proposition would return the structure which opened the old Board of Aldermen to criticism.

Nazi Headsman Sets Mark

Berlin, Nov. 6 (AP) — The heads of five convicted traitors rolled under the executioner's axe today in the biggest single day's death toll for espionage.

Points to Signs Pickets Carry At P. O. Service

'There's Your Story,' He Tells Reporters, Hinting Quick Action

Hyde Park, Nov. 6 (U.P.) — President Roosevelt indicated today that unification of organized labor may be the first objective in the third term to which he was elected in yesterday's Presidential election.

Mr. Roosevelt offered this clue to his trend of mind at his native Hyde Park village, while laying the cornerstone for a new postoffice.

Workmen, standing in the background of the ceremonies, bore placards reflecting the split in labor which developed between the Congress of Industrial Organization and the American Federation of Labor—a split which was broadened when John L. Lewis, president of the C. I. O., threw his full support behind Willkie.

"When Lewis Resigns Labor Will Prosper," one sign read. "Not Mr. Lewis But Labor Unity," another proclaimed.

Nodding toward the placards,

Continued on Page 12

HARVEY WILL STAY IN GOOD OLD U. S. A.

Despite the fact that he had previously been quoted as saying at a meeting in Hartford, Conn., that he would "go to Canada," if Wendell L. Willkie was defeated, Borough President Harvey of Queens declared last night that he would remain in New York.

"I have changed my mind," Harvey declared after learning that the election had been conceded to President Roosevelt. "I'm not going to Canada. If 130,000,000 Americans can take it, so can I. I think I'm needed more here."

When reports of his Hartford speech were first published, Harvey asserted that he had been misquoted. He declared that he actually told his audience that the "American people should move to Canada if Willkie is defeated."

The Vote for President

(By the Associated Press)

State	Voting Units	Units Reprtg.	Popular Vote Roosevelt	Popular Vote Willkie	Indicated Elect'l Vote Rvlt.	Indicated Elect'l Vote Wlke.
Alabama	2300	1376	175001	27334	11	—
Arizona	430	311	45362	24903	3	—
Arkansas	2169	857	63006	14027	9	—
California	13692	11168	1312992	929247	22	—
Colorado	1610	949	125898	144363	—	6
Connecticut	169	169	417858	361869	8	—
Delaware	249	217	57233	45404	3	—
Florida	1428	1120	295190	109639	7	—
Georgia	1720	1422	196956	29233	12	—
Idaho	792	502	68383	56830	4	—
Illinois	8378	8047	2069317	1945292	29	—
Indiana	3898	3556	807525	829418	—	14
Iowa	2453	2260	536677	579715	—	11
Kansas	2734	1997	228752	322956	—	9
Kentucky	4343	2435	321801	211456	11	—
Louisiana	1712	618	160720	26884	10	—
Maine	629	628	164769	163885	—	5
Maryland	1331	1246	364168	250362	8	—
Massachusetts	1810	1698	981571	869248	17	—
Michigan	3632	3033	861753	838731	19	—
Minnesota	3696	1919	395222	371736	11	—
Mississippi	1668	668	89845	4232	9	—
Missouri	4479	4129	867684	775343	15	—
Montana	1915	638	85143	55674	4	—
Nebraska	2043	1876	241739	323316	—	7
Nevada	260	217	22235	16344	3	—
New Hampshire	294	294	125625	109992	4	—
New Jersey	3631	3612	1012291	945750	16	—
New Mexico	919	508	75822	54189	3	—
New York	9319	9293	3256726	3021421	47	—
North Carolina	1916	1749	574924	182702	13	—
North Dakota	2261	962	63397	74011	—	4
Ohio	8675	8099	1565088	1443748	26	—
Oklahoma	3613	3227	433577	371554	11	—
Oregon	1693	922	111959	108959	5	—
Pennsylvania	8119	8106	2164138	1883714	36	—
Rhode Island	259	259	181881	138432	4	—
South Carolina	1277	696	82368	4131	8	—
South Dakota	1963	1445	87495	121644	—	4
Tennessee	2300	2125	323710	150531	11	—
Texas	254	224	504433	118198	23	—
Utah	831	457	84511	52100	4	—
Vermont	246	246	64244	78335	—	3
Virginia	1716	1705	236354	109597	11	—
Washington	3018	1717	228749	151957	8	—
West Virginia	2389	1426	313257	226780	8	—
Wisconsin	3038	2950	686546	666851	12	—
Wyoming	697	615	51156	46389	3	—
Totals	127245	103966	23175051	19388426	468	63

Willkie Urges Nation To Unite All Efforts

Concedes Defeat With Plea to Erase Clashes—Asks People Join in Drive for Defense

Conceding the election of President Roosevelt, Wendell L. Willkie expressed gratitude today to the thousands of his supporters, urging them to continue their campaign "for the unity of our people in the completion of our defense effort, in sending aid to Britain and in insistence upon removal of antagonisms in America."

Speaking over all major radio networks after he had dispatched a telegram of congratulations to the President, Mr. Willkie said that he accepted the result of the election with complete good will.

"The popular vote shows the vitality of our democratic principles

Continued on Page 12

Garvin Elevated To Supreme Court By Big Majority

Kings County Judge Edwin L. Garvin, Democrat, today had defeated William R. Bayes, Republican, who is chief justice of the Court of Special Sessions, and Louis P. Goldberg, American Labor party, for the vacancy in the Supreme Court, Second Judicial District.

Judge Garvin polled 1,026,068 to 844,023 for Justice Bayes and 177,897 for Mr. Goldberg. The Democratic candidate polled 608,099 in Brooklyn, while the Republican candidate polled 334,329, and the A. L. P. candidate, 139,623.

The Second Judicial District includes Brooklyn, Queens, Nassau, Suffolk and Richmond. Judge Garvin polled 281,492 in Queens, while Justice Bayes received 276,410 votes and Mr. Goldberg, 29,786.

The Supreme Court Justice-elect has served as a Special Sessions justice, as a Federal district judge and as a county judge. Judge Garvin also served as chairman of the board of trustees of the Brooklyn Public Library.

War News Squeezed Out

Ottawa, Nov. 6 (AP)—News of President Roosevelt's re-election squeezed war news out of the headlines of most Canadian newspapers.

Market Slumps At Election News

Wall Street's reaction to the results of the election was a pronounced decline in share values ranging to four points in some cases. There was a wave of emotional selling at the start of the market, blocks ranging to 10,000 shares appearing at substantially lower levels.

However, within a few minutes of the opening, the trend was reversed and a few gains over the previous close were set up and opening losses sharply pared.

The improvement was of short duration and after the first hour the market continued progressively lower, with losses extending to approximately three points in major issues by the final hour. Steels, motors, oils, utilities and airplane issues were all affected and no section of the market was immune to the trend.

Sales at 2 o'clock exceeded a million shares but final-hour trading was at a slower rate than previously. Utilities were among the weakest spots in the list.

President Piles Up 472 Electoral Ballots In 3d Term Sweep

By the United Press

President Roosevelt's big electoral college lead over Wendell L. Willkie mounted steadily today and latest returns forecast increased New Deal strength in both houses of Congress.

The popular vote was closer. Late this afternoon United Press tabulations showed the popular vote divided: Roosevelt, 22,039,853; Willkie, 18,408,829.

The returns conclusively gave Mr. Roosevelt 25 States with 348 electoral votes. He led in 15 other States with 124 electoral votes. That would make a total of 472 electoral votes.

Willkie had clinched five States with 28 electoral votes and was ahead in three States with 31 electoral votes. That would give him 59 electoral votes.

Democrats had made a net gain of 15 House seats from Republicans, but this may be whittled down some. The outlook was for Republicans to win one more Senate seat, but this will be offset by the retirement of two Anti-New Deal Democrats—Senators Rush Holt of West Virginia and William H. King of Utah—in favor of two party members more sympathetic to the New Deal.

Win 15 Governorships

Republicans had elected seven governors and paced Democrats in seven other gubernatorial contests. Fifteen Democratic gubernatorial candidates had won and four others were in the lead.

Willkie, who probably will pile up the largest popular vote ever cast for a losing candidate, conceded defeat shortly after 10:30 a.m.

The New Deal had broken through Republican defenses in New England and in the great industrial States of the Middle East. The solid South held solid and the Far West went to Roosevelt although Oregon was fighting ground. The Middle West proved a Willkie stronghold.

The President told his Hyde Park neighbors that they would find him "the same Franklin Roosevelt that you have known for a great many years."

G. O. P. Loses in House

It appears also that the G. O. P. again lost the House of Representatives. On the basis of incomplete returns the House seems to have

Continued on Page 12

NEW DEAL HOLDS CONGRESS RULE; MORE SEATS WON

Democrats Win 226 House Posts and at Least 15 Senate Contests

Washington, Nov. 6 (AP)—The Democrats, riding a tide of votes with President Roosevelt, kept control of both House and Senate in Tuesday's election.

An official tabulation showed they had won 226 House seats, for more than a majority, to 109 for the Republicans. In addition, one incumbent American Laborite was re-elected. A majority is 218.

Contrary to Republican predictions that they would gain from 50 to 80 seats, the returns indicated that the Democrats might win a few more than their present House strength of 258.

The Democratic majority in the new Senate, convening next Jan. 3, was hardly in danger but any vestige of doubt was eliminated when the tabulation showed they had

Continued on Page 12

Pimlico Results

FIRST RACE — Two-year-olds; three-quarters of a mile.

Hasty Notion (Garner) 33.10 11.10 7.80
Light of Morn (Lynch) — 4.60 3.00
Sailor King (Roberts) — — 9.30

Time, 1:13 4-5. Fantastical, aBrigadette, Low Road, Yawl, Tar Miss, aCeltic Knight, Socratic, Ophelia II, Hermar also ran. (Off time, 1:17.)
a E. G. Hackney entry.

SECOND RACE—Three-year-olds and up; six furlongs.

Ceiling Zero (Bierman) 9.30 4.50 3.10
Coquelicot (Anderson) — 3.30 2.80
Aristocracy (Dennis) — — 3.40

Time, 1:14 4-5. Storminess, Brookie Boy, L'Ondee, Queen Meadow, Harebell, Star Strewn, Adam's Needle, Arrow Girl, Lady Balko also ran. Off time, 1:45.

DAILY DOUBLE PAID $186.10

THIRD RACE—Three-year-olds and upward; about two miles (Steeplechase).

Dolly's Love (J. Penrod) 9.00 4.40 3.10
Good Chance (E. Roberts) —3.40 2.70
Oneechee (W. King) — — 3.00

Time, 3:53 2-5. Simoon, Bay Dean also ran. (Off time, 2:16.)

FOURTH RACE — Wayriel, first; Cherry's Child, second; Lerno, third.

Pimlico Mutuels

THREE RACES PAID ——— $120.90

Rockingham Park Results

FIRST RACE—Four-year-olds and upward; three-quarters of a mile.

Hittie (Taylor) 21.20 7.80 4.20
Perlette (May) — 3.40 2.60
Patapsco (Vercher) — — 2.80

Time, 1:14 1-5. Count Eleven, Day Is Done, Sky Cloud, Whisper, Epsom Prince, Fire Finch, Vital Lady, Weebag also ran. (Off time, 1:20.)

SECOND RACE—Three-year-olds and up; three-quarters of a mile.

Gala Star (Snyder) 24.60 8.20 7.00
Adolf (May) — 7.00 4.20
Lady Orchid (Briggs) — — 7.40

Time, 1:14 3-5. Maestrung, Key Man, Devil's Mate, Flag Post, Short Measure, Commencement also ran. Off time, 1:48.

DAILY DOUBLE PAID $200.

THIRD RACE — Two-year-olds; three-quarters of a mile.

Bright Arc (Bomar) 11.00 5.40 4.00
Thorino (W. L. Taylor) — 7.60 6.00
Silver Tower (Snyder) — — 7.00

Time, 1:15 1-5. Periover, Take Wing, Dainty Ford, Cavu, Alkyon, Beamy also ran. (Off time, 2:16.)

FOURTH RACE—Mill River, first; War Grand, second; Bereit, third.

WHERE TO FIND IT IN TODAY'S EAGLE

Bridge	Page 25	Line on Liners	Page 25
Children's Corner	Page 25	Lost and Found	Page 2
Comics	Page 24	Movies	Page 10
Crossword	Page 26	Novel	Page 25
Dr. Brady	Page 25	OBITUARIES	Page 15
Ed Hughes	Page 18	Patterns	Page 25
EDITORIAL	Page 14	RADIO	Page 24
Events Tonight	Page 28	Real Estate	Page 27
FINANCIAL	Page 22	Shopping with Susan	Page 6
Grin and Bear It	Page 14	Society	Page 9
Harold Conrad	Page 10	SPORTS	Pages 17-18-19
Heffernan	Page 11	Theaters	Page 1[illegible]
Helen Worth	Page 8	Tucker	Page 14
Jimmy Wood	Page 17	Wall Street	Page 22
Lindley	Page 27	Want Ads	Pages 26-27
		Woman's	Page [illegible]

Wide World photo

FAMILY FOR ANOTHER FOUR YEARS—President Roosevelt and his family receive the cheers of neighbors the porch of the Roosevelt home at Hyde Park as the nation returned the President to the White House for a erm. Left to right are the President, Franklin D. Roosevelt Jr., Mrs. Franklin D. Roosevelt Jr., Mrs. John Roose- hn Roosevelt, Mrs. Sara Delano Roosevelt, the President's mother, and Mrs. Eleanor Roosevelt, the First Lady.

good or bad though it may be. The most categoric instructions have been issued to the military command at the front and to civil authorities not to send to Rome for publication any news which has not been rigorously and personally—I say personally—controlled.

"On this subject I want to recall the cry of joy which arose in the House of Commons when (British Prime Minister Winston) Churchill gave the good news regarding the air attack on Port Taranto by British torpedo-carrying planes. Three ships were struck, but none was sunk, and only one of them has been, as announced by our war communique, seriously damaged so that repairs will require a long time. The other two will, according to unanimous opinion of experts, be rapidly restored to their full efficiency.

3. "It is like the Third Punic War, which concluded and will conclude with the destruction of the modern Carthage—Britain. A strong people like the Italians do not fear the truth; they demand it. That is why our war communiques are documents of truth. We list the blows which we give and which we receive."

The Fine-toothed Comb

Experts, neutral staff officers, commentators and students of rhetoric immediately began to take the speech apart. After all it was the first public utterance by Mussolini since his oration declaring a state of war with France and England. What did it all portend? Observed some:

1. Having spoken, Il Duce appeared on the balcony overlooking the big square and took ten bows in four minutes, while his populace cheered itself hoarse.

2. Familiar was the Axis alibi that captured documents in an occupied territory (this time France) made it imperative to invade Greece.

3. Apology for failure to achieve "lightning war" in Greece grew into a vaunting defiance that it didn't matter whether it took "two months or a year," Greece would be smashed. "I will never turn back," he shouted. Thought some: He was preparing his people for a longer adventure in Greece than they had anticipated. Thought others: He was assuring Adolf Hitler he could handle the adventure himself.

4. His likening his campaign (begun June 10 last) to the Third Punic War was thought by some to be an acknowledgment that he knew he had a life and death fight on his hands.

5. His loud protestations to truth were taken to be for home consumption. Recollected some: First Rome communique on the Battle of Taranto had admitted damage only to one warship. Mussolini's speech conceded damage to three. Recollected others: Il Duce himself said orders had been given that no news was to be reported that had not been "personally controlled." This was gayly submitted to literal interpretation in other than Axis capitals.

6. His assurance to his people that when peace came it would be "an Axis peace" was surprising, since nobody had suggested otherwise. Was he reminding Hitler that Rome was an Axis partner, too?

7. Could it be that a speech by Hitler a week ago and another by Mussolini so shortly after meant things weren't going nearly as well as expected on the Axis side and that both were really speaking over their peoples' heads to Moscow, which still maintained the silence of the Comrade Sphynx, after Foreign Commissar Molotov's brief visit to Berlin?

Mighty Sequel

Almost on the dot of Il Duce's bows to the thousands in the square before the Palazzo Venezia at the conclusion of his speech, Rome communique made joyous announcements. Thus:

1. An aerial torpedo had hit a British cruiser in the harbor of Alexandria. British Admiralty said: Pish and tosh.

2. An attempt to seize the Isle of Galdaro in the Dodecanese had been repulsed by "land, sea and air." In fact it reported: "Quick reaction of our land, sea and air forces chased off the enemy, who retreated rapidly." Some N. Y. C. papers interpreted it as a repulse to the British Navy. However . . .

The Greeks had another version. Reported the Ministry of Home Security from Athens:

"Citizens of the Dodecanese Islands living and working in Greece sailed on the night of Nov. 17-18 with a group of Dodecanesians and others on a motor launch from a Greek anchorage and landed on a small island of the Dodecanese Islands.

"The group attacked the police post and captured the police head and three carabinieri (policemen) with their equipment. The group further attacked a naval guard and in the fight which followed three naval guards, including the petty officer in charge, were killed.

"The raiders returned with four prisoners and equipment to the anchorage from which they sailed."

Only the Shadow Knows

Deep this Sabbath continued the mystery of why Marshal Maxime Weygand, the man who was called back from virtual exile in Syria to try to retrieve the lost Battle of France last Summer, was refusing to come home to Vichy on order and there bask in the smiles of Adolf Hitler's French Yes-man government.

Meanwhile, spirited was the controversy over who ordered the Armistice. First put forth partisans of Marshal Henri-Philippe Petain, hero of Verdun ("They Shall Not Pass") of Armageddon No. 1, that it was Marshal Weygand who had asked the Bordeaux government to apply for a surcease from strife. But hotly retorted partisans of Marshal Weygand: Petain compelled the plea for an armistice, on threat of resignation. Said France wouldn't ever be ruled from North Africa. Signs were that Vichy wasn't exactly one big happy family.

Meanwhile, men wondered just what Weygand might be up to. If he has been heard from, Vichy has been keeping mighty silent about what he had to say. Certainly he was still in North Africa. Speculated some: Might it not be that his presence and the confidence of France's colonial troops in him would be the cause for (a) Adolf Hitler's speech of eternal defiance to England and (b) Il Duce's ditto.

Follow Up on Big News

Of the convoy of 38 ships sunk, according to Berlin, beyond peradventure by the Nazi pocket battleship (assumed to be Admiral von Scheer) in the battle with suicidal British auxiliary cruiser Jervis Bay (See Trend, Nov. 17), London reported that the 33d had crept home to port. She was the battered tanker San Marina. Only 16 of her crew remained and her charts had burned.

Seems the raider set her afire. Crew abandoned ship. When Jervis Bay drew the attention of the German, crew rowed into the dusk, waited for 36 hours and then rowed back and managed to put the fire out. Four men were reported lost.

The roll of heroes continued to pile up, as detail after detail of the Jervis Bay's valiant self-sacrifice trickled by the censor.

Angel From Ohio

She's tiny and 66, this gray-haired, pink-cheeked, China-blue-eyed little old lady with the disarming appearance of utter helplessness. But she is Althea Patterson, daughter of former Governor John M. Patterson of Ohio, U. S.A., and, what's more, she is a branch prexy of E. O. N., Greek relief organization at Salonika.

She drives a battered 9-year-old motorcar and rides like a blessed fury through the bombed areas of Macedonia, bent upon succor to refugees. She came to Salonika for three days, back in 1924, but has stayed on, helping out. American consuls have striven to keep her safe at a farm school eight miles outside Salonika but she just says: Boo! Officials deny her permits to go into danger areas, so she just cranks up her motor and chugs off, anyhow. Bringing blankets and medical supplies and coffee and often just water.

In Salonika they call her "the Good Samaritan."

Why Eire Balks

Albeit England could use Lough Swilly and other Irish ports to choke off the U-boat menace and albeit nobody for a moment, even in Dublin, thinks that Adolf Hitler and Benito Mussolini have any kind thoughts for so little a state as Ireland, Eamon de Valera still holds stoutly to his neutrality, for all that blackouts have been practiced within his domain. His reason:

"To give us back the ports only on condition that they would be returned to Britain when she wanted them would in fact be not to restore them at all.

" . . . You in the United States are 3,000 miles away from immediate bombings. If we handed over the ports to Britain we would thereby involve ourselves directly in the war, with all its consequences.

"I can understand Britain's position and if I could do anything to relieve the suffering of the British people I would do so."

When asked how about the swap of U. S. A. destroyers for leases of air and naval bases in British possessions, de Valera said: "A great power like the United States is sufficiently strong if it became involved in war to influence the course of the war. But Ireland is a small nation and cannot hope to do that."

Also said that while U. S. A. was announcing it was staying out of the war, it could in fairness hardly ask Ireland to take a step which would pitch her right into battle.

Wide World photo

GOOD-BYE TO ALL THIS—S. S. Europa, once blue-ribbon mistress of the Seven Seas, was reported by the British to have been bombed at Bremen and practically ruined last week. Europa was sister-ship of S. S. Bremen, reported sunk in the Kattegat, loaded with German troops for Norway. British cities have been tumbling under blitzkrieg but even a German censor with lips buttoned up tight has been unable to hide the fact that German cities and ports have been getting theirs, too. And so civilization, like time, marches on.

BLITZKRIEG

How It Works, Cont'd

MONDAY, Nov. 18—Koritza, base of the fan of the Italian assault upon Greece, entered upon a grievous day. The Greeks were at the battlements. One Italian unit, with 132 tanks, was cut off and somehow the Greeks had a word for it—the situation, that is. Some said the tanks were trying to flee into Yugoslavia, but that was discounted. Along the Kalamas River the Greeks, believe it or not, were "mopping up." However . . .

Athens was also warning the world to beware of its early successes. Remember Finland. It was going all out and seemed to realize that Mussolini had hardly begun. But . . . Il Duce's prestige was sliding downhill as he brought his terrific might against the Grecian 7,000,000 population and got tossed right back. In brief, the Greeks were still doing pretty well by themselves.

London proudly announced that an "Army Co-operation Command" had been set up and immediately those who put two and two together to make sixteen plus a half were talking about an imminent British invasion of the Continent. Which amounted to so much hoopla in the minds of all who had any experience in war. Britain was still on the defensive and a man named Portal was still High Command of all King George VI's air forces.

Il Duce of Fascismo made a speech. (He pops off at the beginning of the week, even as Der Fuehrer of Greater Germany makes a practice of popping off at the end.) Said he: British were the biggest liars in the world. (See "Delenda Est Carthago.") Also: He would bust the Greeks in two, no matter now long it took. (See They Just Can't Stop Him.)

King Boris III of Bulgaria paid a secret visit to Adolf Hitler, in Germany. (See story on page 1.) What could it mean?

Could mean this: If Hitler struck for the Aegean through Bulgaria, it would signify that Mussolini couldn't carry his own weight against the Greeks. It would also mean that Hitler was aiming (a) for the Suez Canal (Mussolini's job) or (b) the Mespot oil fields (through Turkey.)

London, for a change, had a quiet Sabbath, thanks to cloudy weather. R. A. F., strange to say, spent a big Sunday bombing various German objectives.

British had the nerve to shell, from guns of light naval units, the port of Mogadiscio, in Italian Somaliland. Raised particular dickens, too, and gave the lie to Italian claims they had taken command in the Indian Ocean. Would this be just a coincidence in Mussolini's talking war?

TUESDAY, Nov. 19—Seems King Boris III came to Berchtesgaden (something his wily father, ex-King Ferdinand, would have required wild horses to drag him to) last Sunday. It must have been pretty imperative. And from what Trend understands, it must have been pretty much a bargain.

Meanwhile, British and Germans were bombing the daylights out of each other. Hysterical press, uninformed about bombing, said Neville Chamberlain's Birmingham was in flames. Fact was that Birmingham has a pretty good fire-fighting apparatus and the reports all came from Berlin. To be sure, Adolf Hitler would try to wipe out important British centers of industry. By the same token, British would try to bomb German centers of industry into a sort of do-nothing nervelessness. Remember that British have a way of announcing bad news first. Later reports this day had it that the Krupp works at Essen, a long bomber's flight, were unable to resume work upon the morrow. And the steel works at Stuttgart, said the grapevine, have been unworkable since last Oct. 29. Same goes for Dusseldorf. There is, in this war, quite a give and take.

Nasty British bombed North Italy again, and, with release of famed long-range, 3,000-mile American bombers, could skip Italy and lay a few eggs in (a) Italian-occupied Greece (of which at this writing there is none) and Toulon, base of the French fleet that decided to play Yes-man to Adolf Hitler via Vichy. Or North Africa. And where was the A. W. O. L. Marshal Maxime Weygand, who refused to come home to the bosoms of Marshal Petain and M. Pierre Laval, who proclaimed only week before last the totalitarian end of democracy? Berlin, Rome and Vichy would like to know. (See Foreign Affairs.) Meanwhile Japan was keeping mighty sociable.

WEDNESDAY, Nov. 20—Greeks were still doing very well by themselves. Much to Rome's annoyance. Meanwhile, the whole Balkan set-up was being mustered into the Axis, take it from Berlin. Reservations: Yugoslavia had yet to declare itself. Turkey was talking about a stout resistance "if attacked." Rumania, staggered by its earthquake, was giving up. Bulgaria, calling up its troops, was marking time.

Mighty above all else was the silence from Moscow, lair of Der Fuehrersky von Kremlin, Uncle Joe Stalin.

Italians still talked big, while the Greeks bore down upon Koritza. An appeal from Athens to Washington won the response that it would be "carefully considered." Greeks warned the world not to be deceived by their initial successes against Il Duce's not so mighty army. Were quite aware that if the papa of Fascismo really decided to bear down, their weak forces could hardly hope to triumph. However, in this case, Greece was in a position where England could help out. And was. Dodecanese Isles, proud naval Suez Canal-threatening bases of Mussolini, were now entirely surrounded. Note: British discovered Il Duce had no important naval units in the Dodecanese. Yet that was to be his contribution to the Axis for the reduction of the Suez Canal.

During the night, though, Italians had something to rejoice about. A Wellington bomber was forced down in Sicily. Some said on account of engine trouble (which would seem to be borne out because every man-jack aboard was saved without bailing out and the plane went up in flames). When you are downed in enemy territory, you fire your plane. Others said the plane was shot down by anti-aircraft. All the saying, thus contradictory, was from Rome. Big item was the capture of Britain's Air Marshal Owen Tudor Boyd, who was in the plane. He was second in command of the British Mediterranean forces.

King George VI convoked Parliament, bombs or no bombs, and had nice things to say about his gratitude to U. S. A. for help in the line of aid short of war. London had a respite, by the way. Its favorite fog came tumbling down. Nazis bombed coastal towns, however, and boasted that Birmingham, home of the late Rt. Hon. Neville Chamberlain, the Great Appeaser, was out of commission. British scoffed at the very idea.

THURSDAY, Nov. 21—Koritza was indeed in Greek hands and not only that, Italian bases on the Adriatic were under gunfire, too. Il Duce's Greek adventure was in a mighty bad way. Meanwhile, Hungary, always a playmate of Berlin, signed up with the Axis, but diplomatically this didn't mean very much. It was too much like the Dutch capturing Holland. The Turks, unofficially, squawked (a) by press and (b) by radio. Warned they would oppose the Axis if attacked. (Didn't say anything about helping out the Greeks, though.) Moscow continued to keep a buttoned-up lip, albeit it is sworn to protect Turkey, just as Turkey is sworn by the same treaty to come to the succor of the Soviets if they get into a jam requiring the shooting of guns.

A French battleship moved into Gibraltar and joined up with the "Free Frenchmen" movement. Spanish sources said it must be the Paris, a 22,000-ton dreadnought. But the Paris was already with the British fleet. Most figured the Spaniards were wrong and that the warship must be the Strassbourg, 26,000 tons, with nine 15-inch guns, mounted three to the turret, which at Oran escaped, damaged; went to Toulon, got repaired, sailed out and joined up its old ally. Incident was taken to mean that the French were by no means supine under the Yes-man government of Marshal Henri-Philippe Petain and M. Pierre Laval at Vichy, where the word of Adolf Hitler goes.

French were having trouble with their bonuses to papas and mamas of large families. Inference was that the Nazi occupiers of the most prosperous part of La Patrie were tying up the money.

London got a strafing again and so did the Midlands; but the Germans, snug in their homes, had to trundle out to air raid shelters, too, because the naughty British were bombing their cities all over the Ruhr, the Palatinate and even much farther east. All was not sweetness and light in the Third Reich, either.

FRIDAY, Nov. 22—While U. S. A. recovered from its annual festival of Thanksgiving and realized it really had something to be thankful for, word came through that King Boris III had been warned by Moscow to gang mighty warily in the company of Berlin.

Word also came that King Christian of Denmark spoke like a real king, thus: He noticed the swastika flag of Germany was flying over one of his buildings. This was in violation of his agreement with Adolf Hitler. Said the king to the sentry: "That flag must come down before 12 noon." Distressed sentry called up Nazi headquarters. Was instructed to shoot anybody sent to take the flag down. Five minutes before noon, King Christian appeared. Said he: "Take that flag down." Said the sentry: "I'll shoot any soldier who tries to." Added: "Who is the soldier to carry out your orders, Majesty?"

"I am the soldier," thundered King Christian.

The flag came down, plenty pronto, on the dot of noon.

Folks were again wondering about Marshal Maxime Weygand, the Frenchman in North Africa who wouldn't come home to Vichy under orders. Could it be that France was down but not out?

Meanwhile, Rome admitted that the Greeks had captured the Italian base of Koritza, ten miles deep in Albania, after 11 days of fighting. This was only 24 hours after it happened, pretty good truthfulness from any belligerent.

Balkans continued in a state of "unrest" while Birmingham (a) got bombed again and (b) proudly proclaimed it was still carrying on, industrially. Same time, Greeks were burying women, in a mass funeral. They had died in the retreat of the Italians (and Trend would not blame Il Duce's forces for deaths incident to a rear guard action, either):

Diplomats were still sipping their brandy in snifters and smoking $1 cigars and wondering what would come next. Feverish was the activity in European chancellories but so far, mouse-like was the result. Mountains were certain to labor but what they would bring forth over the weekend, man kneweth not.

One thing was sure: The Axis had to pull off something big, if only to reassure the Japanese boy-friends Tokio had not crawled out on a limb, to join up with Der Fuehrer and Il Duce.

Not even Ambassador Joseph Kennedy's pessimism about Britain's future could quite shake out of the heads of neutrals that England, like Greece, was doing pretty well by itself, right now. Of course, the morrow might bring another tale.

SATURDAY, Nov. 23—Rumania signed up with the Axis this A. M. and folks were somewhat amused, seeing that Bucharest has been under the Nazi thumb since last month. (See Foreign Affairs.) Turkey declared martial law. Birmingham was bombed again and Nazis insisted they could see the flames, 175 miles away, on the French coast, which was some seeing. Most believed, however, that Nazi aviators, up aloft, saw the fires, not Nazi soldiers on the ground.

Greeks continued to do mighty well by themselves. So well, in fact, that Rome announced: "Once Gen. Ubaldo Soddu's troops are organized, they will occupy all of Greece, literally flying through the entire country. It would be foolish to say the Greeks are not brave fighters, but even they will be helpless against what is to come." This Sabbath was the 26th day of Italy's war on Greece. Not one free Italian soldier at the moment is on Greek soil. Alas, Greeks are even on Albanian soil.

Uruguay, despite warnings from Generalissimo Francisco Franco's Spain, self-appointed guardian of Latin-American culture, continued to negotiate with U. S. A. in re: naval and air bases. Meanwhile, with many flourishes and ruffles of drums, Madrid announced it would resume air service to South America. The route: Seville-Buenos Aires.

Diplomats continued to sniff brandy and wonder what the morrow would bring forth. Dope was that Slovakia would sign up with the Axis next. Not that Slovakia wasn't signed, sealed and delivered the very day Germany moved in upon Czechoslovakia. Action of the Slovaks in that adventure was the first of many famous sell-outs since.

A Lonely Hearts Club in London, run by the Red Cross, was getting under way. The members: Husbands whose families had been evacuated. All meals (at least one hot one a day) and laundry cost 17s. 6d (about $3.50) per week.

Martinque was getting mighty mad because American businessmen wouldn't take orders for necessities, particularly those required for the harvest of the sugar crop next January. Called it a "financial blockade."

Thomas E. Naylor, Labor Member of Parliament, announced he would seek "a truce of God" (ancient Crusaders' cessation

Wide World photo

A STUKA AIMS FOR IT'S QUARRY—Picture above, unretouched in our Art Dep't, purports to be a Nazi dive-bomber swooping in upon its prey, apparently at dawn, judging from the clouds, presumably over English Channel. Picture was released by German censor (Dr. Paul Josef Goebbels' dep't of propaganda). Apparently the Nazi plane is after the Flying Dutchman, famed in song and story. For behold, the ship is up in the clouds, too. Could it be that it had been pasted on the beginnings of a swell photo of the Stuka in the morning zephyrs and rephotographed? If not, why isn't the tanker pictured firing hell-for-dear-life with its anti-aircraft? Trend wouldn't know.

Wall Street Closing
RACING EXTRA
★★★★★★

BROOKLYN EAGLE

Wall Street Closing
RACING EXTRA
★★★★★★

LOCAL WEATHER FORECAST: Cloudy, much colder tonight; snow, continued cold tomorrow

100th YEAR • No. 22 • DAILY AND SUNDAY • BROOKLYN, N. Y., THURSDAY, JAN. 23, 1941 • Entered at the Brooklyn Postoffice as 2d Class Mail Matter—(Copyright 1941 The Brooklyn Daily Eagle) (F. D. S. Corporation) • 3 CENTS

U. S. AND BRITAIN CAN'T BEAT HITLER, LINDBERGH ASSERTS

Best if Neither Side Wins, He Says, Urging Peace Now

Wide World wirephoto

OPPOSES LEASE-LEND BILL—Col. Charles A. Lindbergh is shown as he testified before the House Foreign Affairs Committee today, expressing opposition to the lease-lend bill.

Opposes Aid Bill—Sees America Safe From Any Invasion

Washington, Jan. 23 (U.P.)—Col. Charles A. Lindbergh told the House Foreign Affairs Committee today that he would prefer to see "neither side win" in the European war "and would like a negotiated peace."

Lindbergh also said he believed that even American entry into the war with Great Britain could not bring victory without an internal collapse in Germany.

"I would prefer to see neither side win," Lindbergh said. "I'd like to see a negotiated peace. I believe a complete victory for either side would result in the prostration of Europe such as we never before have seen."

Lindbergh, opposing the Administration's British-aid bill, made this statement when Representative Luther A. Johnson (D., Texas) noted that Lindbergh never had expressed sympathy for either side.

"It would be better for us if the war ends without a conclusive victory," Lindbergh said.

"It would not be best to see Germany defeated. A negotiated peace is the best for us. I have sympathy for the peoples of both sides, and not with their aims."

Doubt Bill Spells Victory

Lindbergh declared he did not believe the measure could enable Britain to win.

"I don't think anything short of war, or beyond war, will win this war on the present basis," Lindbergh said.

"Even with the active help of the United States, Britain could not invade the Continent and wi unless there is a German internal collapse," Lindbergh testified.

Lindbergh added that the fall of the British navy would "not seriously menace the United States."

Johnson repeated his question, asking which side's victory would be better. Lindbergh replied tersely:

"Neither."

Applause burst out in the committee room where 500 spectators had gathered.

Says We Can't Force Peace

"I think," Lindbergh testified, "that Europe would be in a more peaceful condition if we take no part in her wars, either the last or this one.

"I don't believe we can force peace on Europe," he said. "I think it would be constructive if the attitude of this country were for peace."

He told Representative James A. Shanley (D., Conn.) that the pending bill would be a step toward "projection of the United States into European quarrels."

Lindbergh said he saw no signs as yet of German collapse.

"In other words," Representative Joe L. Pfeiffer (D., N. Y.) asked, "the Germans are sure to win?"

"She already controls the Continent," Lindbergh replied. "I don't say she can invade England."

"What makes you think Germany will stop after conquering England?"

"The only thing that will stop aggression is sufficient strength to stop that aggression. I think we can build sufficient strength to stop it."

Would Halt Plane Exports

Lindbergh told the committee that he believed it a mistake to export American war planes at this time; that this nation has "but very few hundred at best" thoroughly modern warplanes while in Europe each side "has some thousands."

"I think our export at this time is injuring our defense," Lindbergh told Representative John M. Vorys (R., Ohio). Signs of prostration already are evident in Europe, Lindbergh said. Any attempt to invade before a collapse comes, he said, would result in a loss of life "incomparably greater than in the last war and Europe won't stand that."

He said he did not believe England could be invaded before she collapses internally, but "of that I am not sure."

America encouraged the British to declare war, Lindbergh contended.

"I think we encouraged them to get into the war when they were not prepared for it," he said, adding that attitude probably would be resented after the war.

"The main problem here," said Representative Charles A. Eaton (R., N. J.), "is the pending bill, os-

Continued on Page 2

BORO WARNED ON DANGER OF COURT 'BREAK'

Dark Basement Halls Provide Ideal Ambush, State Official Reports

Eagle Bureau, Capitol Building.

Albany, Jan. 23 — John L. Schoenfeld, State Correction Commissioner, sounded an official warning today of "dangerous procedure" in the handlnig of prisoners at the Brooklyn Felony Court by New York City's Department of Correction.

He issued a report that the city's Department of Public Works spent money to build an entrance on State St., in order to comply with a recommendation of the State Commission of Correction for devising a safe method to bring prisoners from vans and police wagons to the court pens. However, he said, it was the State Commission's understanding that the Police Department solely uses the entrance.

"The practice of releasing prisoners from the vans in the courtyard, then taking them via the dark basement upstairs," his report continued, "is a dangerous procedure. There seems to be no reason why the vans of the Department of Correction cannot use the State St. entrance which leads directly to the pens."

Commissioner Schoenfeld said that when an investigation was made, a double doorway, leading into a large room, was open, as well as a door leading to the building's boiler room. Expressing concern for what might occur, his report added:

"These places provide a hideaway for friends of prisoners, who might be armed and might make a surprise appearance while the correction officers were leading a group of prisoners along this dark corridor."

His report made sharp criticism of sanitary conditions in the detention pens and said "the place was anything but clean," He said the building custodian explained

Continued on Page 10

$13,000 Pay Forgeries Hold Boro Mother, 61, 28 Years With Firm

Gray-Haired Clerk Admits Falsifying Checks After Failing to Get Raise, Say Amazed Cops

One of the Big City's foremost theaters, the brightly lighted stage of the lineup room in Police Headquarters, featured an unusual act today in the person of 61-year-old, motherly, gray-haired Mrs. Catherine Carmody.

Behind silver-rimmed spectacles two tired blue eyes looked out over the glare, squinting at the gathering of officers and reporters and thieves, as detectives who saw the little figure in the dark seal coat remarked that if it was an act it was a good one, for Mrs. Carmody has admitted stealing $13,000 from her employers, they sa.id

Mrs. Carmody, who lives with her unemployed husband and two grown children at 1543 58th St., was charged with forgery on the complaint of Leon Thurlow, vice president of the Decorated Metal Manufacturing Company of 199 Sackett St. She was arrested last night by Detective Daniel Curtis of the Rapelyea St. station.

Juggling of Books Charged

For two and a half years, police said, Mrs. Carmody, who was a $1,600-a-year payroll cleck, had juggled the books of the company.

They said that the beginning of the forgeries was inspired by a raise given to the other employes and not to Mrs. Carmody who up to Sept. 15 had been in the employ of the company for 28 years.

For many years she handled the $3,500 weekly payroll of the firm and the method she used to steal the money was quite familiar to them, police said.

When an employe was laid off

Continued on Page 10

2 DIE, 12 INJURED AS TREES TEAR AIRLINER APART

Transport Crashes As It Circles to Land At Port in St. Louis

St. Louis, Jan. 23 (AP)—Only a mile from safety, a big Trancontinental & Western Airliner crashed before dawn today approaching Lambert-St. Louis Municipal Airport, killing the chief pilot and a passenger and injuring 12 other persons.

Flying on instruments, Capt. P. T. W. Scott, 36, of New York City, paassed over the field at 4:13 a.m. (Central time), and three minutes later he was dead in the wreckage wreckage of the ship, "The Sky Sleeper."

J. F. Mott, a TWA employe who boarded the plane as a passenger at Kansas City, also was killed.

Far behind schedule, the airliner, en route from Los Angeles to New York, flew low across the field and then banked to the left in making a swing for a landing from the southwest.

Residents of the neighborhood heard an angry roar of the twin motors, apparently when the pilot "gunned" his engines in an effort to climb. A "big flash" followed.

The possibility that radio trouble might have been a factor in the accident was suggested by Earl Bierman, radio operator in the con-

Continued on Page 10

Site for Huge Plane Plant Bought by Brewster

Philadelphia, Jan. 23 (U.P.)—The Brewster Aeronautical Corporation of New York today announced the purchase of five Bucks County farms on which it will build one of the nation's largest airplane assembly plants and industrial airports.

The first unit of the plant, costing $2,000,000, will be completed by July 1 and will employ 4,000 persons. When the entire plant is completed total employment will reach 10,000 company officials said.

COUNCIL OUSTS KERN AS HE SHOUTS 'LIAR'

Ordered to Remain Away Until Subpenaed —Charges 'Nazi Tactics'

Paul J. Kern, president of the Municipal Civil Service Commission, was ejected today from the turbulent City Council investigation into the workings of the Commission and its chief.

The Commissioner was formally ordered out and was politely accompanied by a sergeant-at-arms to the nearest exit, for asking questions and, finally, using a short and not-nice word.

The question he asked was: When would he get a chance to answer charges against him? And the short word he used, directed at Emil K. Ellis, committee counsel, was "liar."

Won't Try to Get Back

On the City Hall steps, the ejected Mr. Kern told reporters that he would probably not try to get back to the committee hearings.

"They are too dull," he said. "This is only tripe."

And then he revealed that he planned a rival investigation of his own, beginning next Monday, at which witnesses will be called to disprove charges as soon as they are made before the Council committee. Sidney Z. Searles, assistant counsel to the committee, has already been subpenaed to appear at the Kern hearing and others will follow.

"Some of the past activities of Mr. Ellis and Mr. Smith" (Alfred E. Smith Jr., committee chairman) will thus be exposed, Mr. Kern said.

Compares It With Nazis

Of his ejection, Commissioner Kern commented that it sharply resembled "the People's Courts of Nazi Germany, where the defendant is denied the right to be present." That right, he pointed out, has been in the English common law and so in American practice, for the past 400 years.

The day's dramatic ejection followed a series of committee maneuvers, which somehow cancelled themselves out, to keep Mr. Kern off the hearing-room floor. The hearing itself moved today from the New York County Court Building to the council chamber in City Hall. A detail of half a dozen policemen was set to guard the door, each with typewritten instructions

Continued on Page 10

Eagle Staff photo

"YOU ARE DIRECTED TO LEAVE AND STAY OUT"—Civil Service Commissioner Paul J. Kern (left) conducted out of the Council chamber in City Hall by Sergeant-at-Arms Hugh O'Neill after the Council committee investigating Civil Service had ordered him out.

British Tanks Drive 100 Miles to Derna

Guns, Planes Start Battering City—Admiral, Four Generals and 14,000 Captured at Tobruk

By the United Press

Great Britain threatened today to drive the Italians completely out of western Libya as advance tanks and Royal Air Force planes followed up the capture of Tobruk by starting to batter Derna.

The British brought their bag of Fascist prisoners in the desert blitzkrieg to about 100,000 with the capture of more than 14,000 men at Tobruk, including four Italian generals and an admiral.

While their comrades mopped up Tobruk, R. A. F. fliers and advance tank units began operations at Derna, 100 miles further west in a direct line and plunged across the desert plateau almost half-way to Benghazi, capital of Libya.

In East Africa the thrust into Italian Eritrea went deeper and the Italians were reported taking defensive positions 60 to 75 miles from the Sudan frontier.

Royal Air Force planes blasted at German dive-bomber bases in Sicily, Italian bases in the Dodecanese Islands and Italian positions in Albania.

Fires Visible 80 Miles Away

Cairo, Jan. 23 (AP)—British headquarters announced today that the capture of Tobruk, Italian Libyan base, was completed last night and that more than 14,000 prisoners were taken.

British casualties were said to be less than 500.

Royal Air Force headquarters, in reporting heavy raids on Derna, said bombs started fires which the R. A. F. said could be seen 80 miles away. Derna would be the immediate major objective of a British drive farther along the Libyan coast.

Barracks "and other military targets" were hit by tons of bombs, the communique said.

Military circles said that, with the fall of Tobruk, the British had "captured, destroyed and disintegrated" 11 Italian divisions in the desert campaign. It was made plain that the estimate of 100,000 prisoners "is merely an estimate and the number may run higher or lower." (Italian divisions ordinarily average about 12,000 men.)

Capture of two generals brought to 14 the total number of Italian generals so far reported captured in the North African offensive.

British Bomb Sicily

Rome, Jan. 23 (AP)—British planes have again raided Catania and another place in Sicily which was not identified, the Italian high command reported today, "without causing damage."

The British also attempted a raid

Continued on Page 2

Tunney Group Begins Drive on School Reds

Boro College Represented as New Student Organization Is Formed to Ferret Out Isms

Organization of a new student group to combat the influence of the allegedly Communistic American Student Union here and ferret out subversive groups was launched today at a meeting sponsored by the National Foundation for American Youth, of which Gene Tunney is national chairman.

Student representatives of six colleges and three high schools, including Brooklyn College and James Madison High School, attended the meeting, held in N. F. A. Y. headquarters in the R. C. A. Building, Radio City.

To Distribute Booklet

Proposals were made for the publication and distribution of a 40-page booklet, "How to Stop the Junior Fifth Column," which will describe methods of detecting and fighting subversive organizations

Continued on Page 10

11 in Jehovah Cult Are Jailed Here

Ten men and a woman, members of the religious sect known as Jehovah's Witnesses, today were convicted of disorderly conduct by Magistrate Eilperin in Flatbush Court. They were accused of carrying placards assailing organized religion and handing out anti-Catholic papers on Flatbush Ave. between Church Ave. and Albemarle Road on Jan. 8, disrupting traffic and disturbing the peace.

The magistrate offered to suspend sentence on promises not to repeat the offense, but defense counsel Hayden Covington refused and said the case would be appealed.

Magistrate Eilperin then sentenced each of the men to $50 fine or ten days imprisonment and the woman to a $5 fine or one day in jail. All elected to take the jail sentences.

The defendants were Mrs. Grace De Cacca, 51; her husband, John; George Messner, William Daily, Joseph Bogannon, David Lustrom, Peter Warco, Raymond Petry, Walter Crabb, Robert Morgan and Albert Cummings. All listed their addresses as 124 Columbia Heights, the headquarters of the sect.

Hialeah Park Results

FIRST RACE — Two-year-olds; three-eighths of a mile.

xSir War (R. Howell)	4.40	2.70	2.30
Chills (Gilbert)	—	16.80	7.30
Millo (Wright)	—	—	6.10

Time, 0:34 4-5. Notes, White Bait, Scotch Broth, Glastofield, Dan's Choice, At Liberty, Brenner Pass, Robert Mc. Alchanc, xRiposte, xIslam's Islam also ran. (Off time, 2:03.) xField.

SECOND RACE—4-year-olds and up; seven furlongs.

La Joya (Calvin)	69.60	36.40	11.30
Commencement (Emery)	—	10.30	5.00
Gold Mesh (Kingslay)	—	—	3.00

Time, 1:25. Pirata, Cantata, Marching Feet, Josie's Pal, Miss Frakes, Brilliant Stone, Day is Done, Amnesty, Dusky Girl also ran. (Offtime 2:33½.)

DAILY DOUBLE PAID $196.60

Bulletin

Hendley Loses Quiz Contempt Appeal

Albany, Jan. 23 (U.P.)—The Court of Appeals upheld today a contempt citation against Charles J. Hendley, president of the New York City Teachers Union, for failing to appear with documents before a legislative committee.

WHERE TO FIND IT IN TODAY'S EAGLE

Bridge	Page 21	Music	Page 11
Children's Corner	Page 21	Novel	Page 21
Comics	Page 20	OBITUARIES	Page 13
Crossword	Page 22	Patterns	Page 21
Dr. Brady	Page 21	People in Politics	Pake 14
Ed Hughes	Page 16	Real Estate	Page 23
EDITORIAL	Page 12	Shipping	Page 18
Events Tonight	Page 24	Shopping	Page 9
FINANCIAL	Page 18	Society	Page 8
Grin and Bear It	Page 12	SPORTS	Pages 15-16-17
Heffernan	Page 4	Theaters	Page 11
Helen Worth	Page 6	Tucker	Page 12
Jimmy Woods	Page 15	Wall Street	Page 18
Line on Liners	Page 21	Want Ads	Pages 22-23
Movies	Pages 10-11	Woman's	Pages 6 and 8

BROOKLYN EAGLE
REAL ESTATE
SUNDAY, JAN. 26, 1941 • SECTION D

TRANSFORMATION OF OLD BRIGHTON BEACH—Have you seen the old Brighton Beach section since its transformation from a Summer resort which contained the famous Brighton Beach Hotel, Brighton Music Hall, Great White Way, bathing pavilion and band stand, to a thriving residential section? Well, here's what the place looks like now with the exception of the home colony on Corbin Place, which Fred C. Trump, prominent home builder, has started and visualized by the artist. The other part of the sketch shows buildings now in the locality. The first unit of Mr. Trump's development will contain 200 moderate priced houses to be sold on convenient payments and long term mortgages. Mr. Trump predicts that, judging from the present interest shown in the development, "all of the Brighton houses will be disposed of by July 1 of this year." This is the eighth Trump borough development.

Extensive Home Projects Being Planned for 1941

Borough and Long Island to Be Scene of Activity, Revealed

Indications are that 1941 will witness extensive home building in this borough and on Long Island. Building firms have announced plans for many operations in which moderately priced houses will predominate. Several projects are being arranged for the eastern section of Flatbush and two are considered for the Fort Hamilton section of Bay Ridge.

F. H. A. Projects

Twelve operative building firms who during the past three years have created a new residential community of 12,000 people in 3,000 small homes in the New Hyde Park-Hillside Ave. of Nassau County, have filed plans with the Federal Housing Administration covering the erection of 1,200 new units capable of housing between 5,000 and 6,000 in this same area, according to a statement made yesterday by State Director Thomas G. Grace. These additional sub-divisions, all of which will carry Federal Housing Administration insured mortgages, will be entirely completed during the first six months of 1941 and because the price range is from $4,300 to $5,500, Mr. Grace said a ready sale of the new homes is anticipated. Another element in the sales situation, he added, is that the area involved is only between 30 and 40 minutes automobile or bus travel from Long Island City, Farmingdale and other industrial centers which are included in the defense program.

Old Farms Transformed

Four years ago, according to Mr. Grace, the 15,000 acres now included in the New Hyde Park-Hillside Ave. developments were occupied by the Wicks, Stoothoff, Schumaker, Rhodes and Wiggins farms and contained about 15 old-fashioned farm houses. The development of the section into a progressive and prosperous residential community has been accomplished almost entirely by operative builders working through the Jamaica insuring office of the Federal Housing Administration.

Mortgage insurance liability assumed by the Federal Housing Administration in this particular area amounts to about $10,000,000 at the present time. With the added construction planned for the current year, this liability will be increased to approximately $15,000,000.

The Hillside Heights development of Realty Associates of Brooklyn was the beginning of the large community which has now grown up in this part of Nassau County, and these builders are among those who have planned additional operations during 1941. Others are New Hyde Park Homes, Droesch Homes, Lakeville Estates, Hillside Park Oaks, Pilgrim Estates, Charles Rorech, Hyde Park Manor, Somerset Homes, Hillside Tuxedo, North Shore Park Homes and Blue Bird Homes.

Because of the rapid growth of the new community, Mr. Grace said, it has been necessary to make provisions for additional schools and churches and also to allot space for an area for tradespeople.

Future of Real Estate Market Problematical, McKenna Admits

Peter J. McKenna, real estate merchandising counsel, says the 1941 market for suburban homes is the most difficult to predict in the 20 years of his real estate experience. "We have been through booms and depressions during the last two decades, and we all know their effect," Mr. McKenna admits. "But today, with most of the world at war," he states, "the immediate future of real estate is highly problematical.

"It may reach volumes unknown in recent years, with a newly prosperous citizenry investing in homes the surplus of incomes fattened by the multi-billion dollar Defense Program. The curve of purchasing power already is strongly upward. And the probability of a paralleling upward curve in rents will stimulate this gathering trend toward home-buying.

"Conversely, a shortage of building materials brought about by the same Defense Program, may slow down the increasing momentum of home building to a virtual standstill, as it did during World War 1.

"Thus, the immediate outlook for real estate does not rest in the hands of home buyers or of home builders. The destiny of 1941's home building activity will be directed by the Government and by defense demands on private industry.

"Official bodies in Washington assure us that there will be an ample supply of building materials throughout the entire year, even in the face of 'all out' military requirements, and this claim is supported by the materials makers, who insist that production is sufficient to supply all private needs after defense requirements are satisfied.

"It is logical that the nation, with productive energies that make it the industrial Titan of all times, easily should take these intensified demands in its stride.

"A home, remember, whether it is built on Long Island or anywhere else in the United States, is a national product—with its materials drawn from virtually every corner of the country.

"Montana and Arizona mines provide its copper. Missouri furnishes the lead. The South Central and far Western States supply the lumber. Glass comes from Pennsylvania. And the slate, metal, paint, paper, wall boards and other materials also hail from various portions of the nation."

Show Model Houses In Nassau Colony

Two new model dwellings were opened last week in the Terracewood Homes community of Valley Stream, where Schlossman Brothers, builders, report having built and sold more than 90 homes.

The new model dwellings are fully detached, occupying plots from 40 to 50x100 at Valley Stream Boulevard and Cedarstream Ave., Valley Stream, L. I. The homes are of English, Early American and Dutch Colonial design, ranging from one-story to two and a half stories and including five to six rooms. Construction is brick, stone, stucco, frame and steel. Oil burners and Kohler plumbing fixtures are standard equipment.

MODEL DWELLING—This new house in the Hillside Park Oaks residential colony at Hillside Ave. and New Hyde Park Road, New Hyde Park, where a total of 35 houses is being built by Sam A. Harris, is exhibited as the model house in the community.

HAS NEW OWNER—Mrs. Jessie Griffiths of this borough has purchased this recently completed dwelling located at Lakeview Ave. and Knollwood Road, Rockville Centre, from the builder, Junard Construction Company. There is a growing Brooklyn colony in the community.

UPWARD TREND IN PRICE SEEN BY REALTY MAN

Turn of Market Due, Says Richard I. Hussey, Flatbush Broker

An upward trend in real estate prices is at hand, according to Richard I. Hussey of the firm of Hussey and Hoeh, prominent Flatbush real estate organization.

"It is so long since we have heard an optimistic note with a real true ring in real estate that we are not inclined to believe it when we do hear it," Mr. Hussey asserted yesterday in discussing the realty situation. "However, if the public does not want to follow the traditional habit of buying at top and selling at the bottom it is high time to look at the facts. We are at the bottom of the longest decline in prices and the severest depression in our history. What would lead us to the conclusion that the turn is at hand?

"The answer is that many different indices point upward. Foreclosure activity has been declining for some time and by the end of 1940 had almost reached the 1926 level. In other words fewer distressed properties are on the market and the foreclosed properties have passed from weak into strong hands. Rising prices of building materials and labor being diverted into defense industries will slow up new construction and increase the cost of new buildings. Coupled with this the demand for labor at good wages carried by defense preparations will be felt inevitably in general business and will favorably affect real estate.

"From every point of view it would appear that the buying point has been reached and should be taken advantage of. Never before have we had such a favorable market for the home buyer. Low prices, low interest rates, long term mortgages and small down payments present a combination of the most favorable factors that we have ever had.

"It is our firm conviction that the home buyer should buy now, before he misses these opportunities."

Bay Ridge Transaction

Bulkley & Horton Company sold through E. J. Hollahan of the Bay Ridge office the one-family dwelling 265 85th St., for John Nicholas, to a client for occupancy. Kraft Brothers was the co-operating broker.

Leningrad Rail Center Reported Seized

Wall Street Closing
RACING EXTRA
★★★★★★

BROOKLYN EAGLE

Wall Street Closing
RACING EXTRA
★★★★★★

LOCAL WEATHER FORECAST: Partly cloudy, cooler tonight; increasing cloudiness, occasional rains tomorrow

100th YEAR • No. 249 • DAILY AND SUNDAY • BROOKLYN, N. Y., MONDAY, SEPT. 8, 1941 • Entered at the Brooklyn Postoffice as 2d Class Mail Matter—(Copyright 1941 The Brooklyn Eagle, Inc.) • 3 CENTS

PRIZED U. S. BOMBSIGHT SECRET IN NAZI HANDS

OUST PETITIONS OF CASHMORE, SPENCE URGES

G. O. P. Attorney Cites 'Fraud Conspiracy' at Appellate Hearing

Contending that the petitions designating Borough President Cashmore, Democratic candidate, as a contender in the Republican primary election "are the result of a criminal conspiracy in which many serious crimes were committed, Kenneth M. Spence, counsel for the Brooklyn Republican organization today asked the Appellate Division to reverse Supreme Court Justice Garvin's ruling holding that 3,241 "good signatures" out of the 7,796 names on the petitions were sufficient to keep Mr. Cashmore's name on the ballot.

Mr. Spence argued before Presiding Justice Lazansky and Justices Hagarty, Carswell, Adel and Taylor that "the petition is so riddled with forgery, perjury and fraud that the whole must be rejected."

Counsel disclosed that at a Sunday morning conference, yesterday, Justice Garvin had declined to alter his Saturday night decision so as to make further deductions from the "valid" signatures.

'2,314 Valid at Most'

Mr. Spence gave the appeal justices a schedule showing his contention that there are at most 2,314 valid signatures, and that that number is subject to still further reductions as a result of Justice Garvin's rulings, although the latter, Mr. Spence declared, did not make the corresponding deductions from the total he arrived at.

Must Be Taken as Whole

Questions by the Appellate Justices as to whether one or two invalid signatures on a page would "disfranchise" the other 19 or 18 electors who had signed it brought

Continued on Page 2

Aqueduct Results

FIRST RACE—Three-year-olds and up; one and three-quarter miles (over hurdles).

Arms of War (Bostwick)	6.30	3.90	2.90
Scotch Tar (Bauman)	—	4.80	3.10
The Beak (Bellhouse)	—	—	3.30

Time—3:15 3-5. Jacket, Brown Prince III, Betty's Buddy, Shogun also ran. Off time 2:02.

SECOND RACE—Two-year-olds; three-quarters mile.

aAlibi Babe (Skelly)	8.60	3.70	4.10
Inscogert (Strickler)	—	3.90	3.20
aShemite (Schmidl)	—	—	4.10

Off time 2:31.
a-Green Pastures entry.

Narragansett Park Results

FIRST RACE—Two-year-olds; three-quarters of a mile.

Shrimpie (Atkinson)	17.00	8.00	6.00
Poppycock (Gonzalez)	—	8.10	6.30
Reckless Saxon (Dattilo)	—	—	9.60

Time, 1:13 1-5. Syam Saxon, Try Do It, Flag Spoon, Mine, Sunburst, Strutting Miss, Maequel, Little Romona, Amazia also ran. Off time, 2:16½.

SECOND RACE—Marjorie S., first; Tripit, second; Possibility, third.

DAILY DOUBLE PAID $90.20.

WHERE TO FIND IT IN TODAY'S EAGLE

Bridge	Page 19	Novel	Page 19
Comics	Page 16	OBITUARIES	Page 11
Crossword	Page 18	Only Yesterday	Page 4
Dr. Brady	Page 4	Patterns	Page 4
EDITORIAL	Page 10	RADIO	Page 16
FINANCIAL	Page 8	Real Estate	Page 19
Grin and Bear It	Page 10	Sermons	Page 20
Harold Conrad	Page 5	Society	Page 6
Harold Parrott	Page 15	SPORTS	Pages 13-14-15
Heffernan	Page 4	These Women	Page 4
Helen Worth	Page 7	Theaters	Page 5
Horoscope	Page 4	Tucker	Page 10
Jimmy Wood	Page 13	Uncle Ray's Corner	Page 4
Lindley	Page 4	Wall Street	Page 8
Movies	Page 5	Want Ads	Pages 17-18-19
Neighborhood News	Page 9	Weather Table	Page 11
		Women	Page 7

Eagle Staff photo

BACK IN CLASSES—Pupils in Class 4B at Public School 5, Tillary and Bridge Sts., salute the flag as a prelude to the start of a new term today and the end of Summer vacation.

MORAN TO QUIT WPA IF NECESSARY TO RUN

Labor Party Candidate for Sheriff Offers To Resign in Event Hatch Act Applies

BY JOSEPH H. SCHMALACKER

Leroy V. Moran, a WPA inspector assigned to the City Controller's office and a candidate for Sheriff in Brooklyn, told the Brooklyn Eagle today he will resign his post if he finds his candidacy is in conflict with the provision of the Federal Hatch Act.

His status presents a novel question which is regarded as one of the first of its kind to arise in a Brooklyn campaign.

Mr. Moran, a lifelong resident of Brooklyn, is an American Labor party candidate on the same ticket with Special Sessions Justice Matthew J. Troy. The latter, an independent Democrat, is the Labor party candidate for Borough President and is running also on the Republican ticket.

Will Decide by Oct. 1

Mr. Moran made his offer to resign in response to inquiries which were made to him at Controller McGoldrick's office, where he is employed as an inspector of WPA materials, although he is paid by the WPA.

He said he was drafted to run for Sheriff. His status, which he said he considered now to be problematical, is being studied by the party's law committee.

"My campaign won't start until Oct. 1," he said, "and if I find that my candidacy for Sheriff is in conflict with the provisions of the Hatch act, I shall, of course, resign my position. There was never any intent to disobey the provisions of the act."

For several days reports have persisted in political circles that a proceeding is contemplated to challenge Moran's status. His WPA position makes him an inspector of building and other materials.

Paris Nazis Arrest 100 Prominent Jews

Vichy, Sept. 8 (U.P.)—German authorities in Paris today arrested 100 prominent Jews and held them as hostages for maintenance of order in the city.

The drastic action by the Nazi occupation officials came as execution of another French citizen for alleged anti-Nazi acts was revealed.

The Germans already hold between 10,000 and 12,000 persons, many of whom are regarded as hostages for good behavior of the populace.

The official French news agency said those arrested "belonged to liberal professions, principally the bar." The arests were called "preventive."

The hostages, said the news agency, are "being held responsible for the maintenance of order."

Among those held were Pierre Masse, Senator for the Herault Department; Theodore Valensi, a famed lawyer, and Arthur Veil-Picard, a well-known race horse owner.

Million Glad (?) Students Romp Back to School

Welfare Department Distributed Clothing Valued at $838,032

With sharpened pencils and spotless copybooks clutched in their hands, more than 1,000,000 boys and girls trotted off to the city's public and parochial schools today to delve for another ten months into the intricacies of reading, writing and arithmetic.

The precise number of bright young faces that turned in the direction of elementary, vocational, junior and senior high schools was not available from official sources, but it was estimated that 1,010,680, or 40,000 less than last February, would be pretty nearly correct.

A steady decline in enrollment in recent years, resulting from fewer births and reduced immigration, has been hailed in many quarters

Continued on Page 11

Cooler Weather Today, May Rain Tomorrow

If you noticed a slight nip in the air as you hurried to work this morning, you were quite correct. The Weather Man said it would be cooler today, with moderate northwest winds doing their best to blow away the last days of Summer.

The Weather Man, thinking benignly about the children who reluctantly crawled off to school today, predicted cooler weather tonight. He ventured a forecast of occasional rain for tomorrow.

Flames Envelop Berlin in Biggest Raid of the War

U-Boat, Damaged By U. S.-Built Plane, Surrenders in Atlantic

London, Sept. 8 (U.P.)—A great force of giant British bombers lashed the "heart of Berlin" for two hours in the biggest raid of the war, causing many big fires and "extensive damage," the Air Ministry reported tonight.

A year and a day after the first mass raids on the London docks hundreds of British planes, including huge, new four-motored bombers, roared across Germany to strike in force at Berlin by the light of a full moon.

The Air Ministry admitted that 20 bombers were missing, indicating the intensity of the raid. The Ministry said the raid was carried out by a "very powerful force."

"Great fires sprang up in the city and extensive damage was done," the Air Ministry said.

Describing the attack on Berlin as "heavier than any yet made on the German capital," the Air Ministry reported that a "great many" high explosives were seen to burst around one of the main railway stations there.

U-Boat Gives Up to Plane

Meanwhile, a German submarine, severely damaged by bombs from an American-built Lockheed plane, surrendered in the Atlantic and has been brought into a British harbor, the Admiralty announced.

British warships, summoned to the scene, towed the damaged U-boat into port. Badly damaged in

Continued on Page 11

4 Hurt, 2 Critically, As Truck Capsizes

Four workmen were injured, two seriously, when an open-body truck in which they were riding turned on its side as it made a turn from Smith St. in to 3d St. at 1 p.m. today.

Two of the men were pinned beneath the truck body, which was torn loose from the chassis. The two others were thrown clear and landed in the street.

Pedestrians who witnessed the accident notified police that a school bus had collided with another vehicle. Police, however, reported that no school vehicle was involved in the accident.

All of the injured were rushed to the Long Island College Hospital.

PRESIDENT'S MOTHER—This is the most recent portrait of Mrs. Sara Delano Roosevelt, mother of the President, who died yesterday at her Hyde Park home at the age of 86.

World Mourns Mrs. Roosevelt

Rites Tomorrow—F.D.R. Postpones Radio Talk

Hyde Park, Sept. 8 (U.P.)—An American flag fluttering at half-mast from the Franklin D. Roosevelt Library symbolized today the grief of the President and his family over the death of his mother, Mrs. Sara Delano Roosevelt.

Mrs. Roosevelt, 86 years old, one of three women who have lived long enough to see their sons become President of the United States, died yesterday following a collapse of her circulatory system

Story of Mrs. Sara Delano Roosevelt's life on Page 3.

brought about by old age. Death came in a bedroom of the ancestral Roosevelt estate here with her son and her daughter-in-law, Mrs. Eleanor Roosevelt, at her bedside.

Funeral services, which will be private, will be held at 3 p.m. tomorrow from the home and she will be buried on the left side of her husband, James Roosevelt, who died in 1900, in the family plot in the yard of St. James Episcopal Church here. Only members of the family and intimates will attend and friends and the public were specifically requested not to send flowers.

Thousands of messages of condolences were arriving at the tem-

Continued on Page 11

Spy Theft Linked To Norden Worker In Queens Plant

The Nazis have America's most prized aviation secret, the famous Norden bomb sight, United States Attorney Harold M. Kennedy revealed in Brooklyn Federal Court today.

He made this sensational disclosure in the course of a 45-minute opening address to the jury before Judge Mortimer W. Byers that is trying 16 alleged German spies.

The Norden sight, successor to the earlier Sperry sight, reputedly is so accurate that it enables a flier at 10,000 feet altitude to drop a missile into a flour barrel.

The 16 on trial, together with 17 who have pleaded guilty and are awaiting sentence, were indicted July 25 as German agents who failed to register as such with the State Department and additionally as conspirators who collected and transmitted data about the American defense effort to Germany.

The first witness called was Raymond D. Muir, an attache of the State Department. He testified that none of the 16 defendants had registered.

One a Norden Employe

Kennedy's bomb sight revelation came in the outline of what he expects to prove against Herman Lang of 74-36 64th Place, only one of the 16 residents in the Brooklyn-Long Island area. A naturalized citizen born in Germany, Lang was a machinist and draughtsman for Carl I. Norden, Inc., Queens manufacturers of the famous sight.

"Lang," the prosecutor related, "went to Germany in 1938. While there, we'll prove, he furnished particulars of the bomb sight. When he returned and resumed his occupation with the company, he continued supplying information. We'll prove he received compensation for this—that 10,000 marks are on deposit for him now in Germany."

Ring Started in Germany

Organization of the alleged spy ring of the arrested 33, plus others who are now abroad and eluded the FBI roundup, was conceived and launched in Germany by Nazi officials, Kennedy said.

Agents sent here did the recruiting, paying the local hirelings with German funds. Cited as an exception to those recruited here was Edmund Carl Heine, who has been

Continued on Page 2

HERMAN LANG of 74-36 64th Place, Glendale, shown behind a deputy Federal marshal during today's luncheon recess in Brooklyn Federal Court, was accused by United States Attorney Kennedy of supplying details of the famous Norden bomb sight to Germany.

Leningrad Rail Center Is Reported Seized

Second Largest Soviet City Now Cut Off On All Sides, Says Nazi High Command

Berlin, Sept. 8 (U.P.)—The Nazi high command reported in a special communique late today that the encirclement of Leningrad has been completed.

The high command's statement was contained in a special communique from Adolf Hitler's field headquarters on the eastern front.

The high command reported that the River Neva which flows through Leningrad from the southeast had been reached "on a broad front."

Mobile units of the German Army, it reported, smashed through the strong line of Russian defenses to the Neva, capturing the town of Schlisselburg, railroad center through which pass the lines linking Leningrad with the rest of Russia.

Thus, said the high command, the ring around Leningrad has been closed and the city is cut off from all communication by land.

While the Nazi mobile units fought their way through to the Neva, Finnish troops were said to have advanced down the narrow peninsula between Lake Ladoga and Lake Onega, blocking off access to Leningrad from the east.

The high command said that Schlisselburg, less than 20 miles outside Leningrad proper, had been stormed by crack German units.

While the Luftwaffe pounded relentlessly at Russian defense lines, railroads and highways outside the former Czarist capital, the Finns pushed eastward and cut the Leningrad-Murmansk Railroad and blocked the entire isthmus between Lakes Ladoga and Onega.

Nazis Call Berlin Raid 'Detestable, Lout's Trick'; Vow Swift Revenge

Berlin, Sept. 8 (U.P.)—The German press today quoted civilian descriptions of the "fearful crash" of British bombs in a Royal Air Force raid on Berlin during the night and denounced the attack as a "lout's trick" and a "crime."

In angry outbursts German newspapers, for the first time since the heavy British air raids on Berlin of last Fall, promised vengeance as the official news agency reported that 27 civilians had been killed.

Describing the damage in the capital, the newspaper Nachtausgabe said that in a northern section of the city virtually the entire roof and iron balconies of a four-story apartment house were torn off by the concussion of a high explosive bomb.

Called 'Shameful Act'

One German was quoted as telling of a "fearful crash" as a bomb landed. "Our first thought," he said, "was: 'Quick, out of the cellar.'"

Berliners bombed out of their homes, the newspapers reported, were given temporary refuge in schools and other public buildings where coffee and sandwiches were distributed.

Propaganda Minister Paul Joseph Goebbels' newspaper, Der Angriff, reported that in one row of houses where a British bomb crashed all the casualties either were in the front halls or on the street outside.

The Nachtausgabe, concluding its account, said:

"These shameful acts will be re-

Continued on Page 2

DEFIES DOCTORS' ORDERS TO SEE DODGER GAMES

Hilda Chester, the Dodgers' most fervent rooter, revealed today that she watched her favorites play Saturday and Sunday, defying doctors' orders because the boys "needed me."

Now out of the hospital, Hilda hailed Leo Durocher as "one swell fellow." She plans to see the team off at Grand Central Station today.

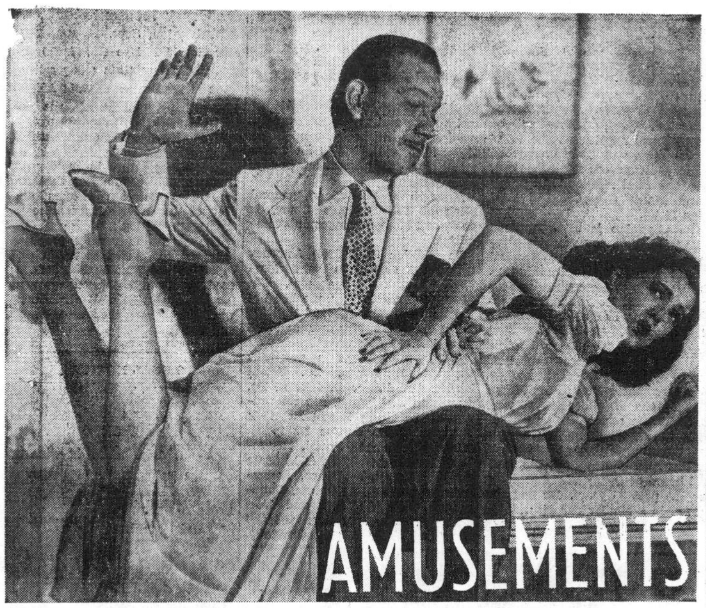

THE WAY TO TREAT 'EM—Melvyn Douglas illustrates the old-fashioned technique on Ellen Drew in "Our Wife," which comes to the N. Y. Paramount next Wednesday.

'The Wookey' Is Greeted With First-Night Cheers

New Play About English at War Has Laughter and Bombs in It

By ARTHUR POLLOCK

The sounds that came from the audience at the Plymouth Theater last night made it clear that "The Wookey," which opened there, is a hit. There were cheers at the end, cheers good and loud. It was pleasant to hear them, for this play by Frederick Hazlitt Brennan is an honest picture of what may very well be happening in England as a result of the German bombings. Mr. Brennan hasn't been there himself, but he reads the papers and has drawn conclusions.

"The Wookey" tells of the manner in which the English people are taking over the war. The author makes no stoical, tight-mouthed, traditionally heroic Englishmen of them, men and women mawkishly inhibiting their fears and refusing in the best school-tie manner to admit them. They are ordinary folk. And "The Wookey" is no horror play either. More often than not it is funny, though in its equipment are no pretentious jokes made while bombs fall. Most of these people are amusing people of Cockney speech. They complain freely—at least, the head of the family does—about the way the war is being run, about the way it was brought on.

Nobody, I think, is going to call it a play of the first class. Too much wood has gone into the making of it for that. The characters are stiff and machine-made. The author defines them but hardly succeeds in creating people to fit his definitions. Very little spontaneity is noticeable. The play moves from beginning to end not so much by its own inherent power as by virtue of the fact that the author made a plot for the action to follow. An unsteady, incomplete story it is, woven together with small skill. Its success will come from its oddities and its spectacle.

Mr. Wookey has a tugboat on the Thames and before the war starts makes trips to France. He fought in the last war and will have nothing to do with this one because he thinks those at the head of the government are bunglers. And besides, he told them exactly what to do, wrote them about it. And what did they do? They never answered. Let them run their own war. Hitler attacks Poland and then goes into France.

Even then the stubborn, tough-minded little Mr. Wookey isn't stirred. They started it. Let them finish it. But he has forced his sister-in-law, sent to the clink for doing a strip-tease in a theater, to marry a man and have children, and now he hears that his brother-in-law is in a tight spot in a place called Dunkirk. Since he is a relative and he believes in the family, he will go and try to get him back to England. The man is dead. But Wookey makes any number of trips back and forth, brings hundreds of soldiers safe home to England. And then what do "they" do? They take his boat away from him because he owes a bill for the gas and oil he used in saving his countrymen. He is mad. He writes to Churchill.

Then he is bombed out by the Germans. His wife is killed. He is mad again. There aren't enough bomb shelters along the docks and little protective anti-aircraft fire. Now, though, his small, lusty voice is beginning to be heard. A colonel is sent to him to discuss the question of protection. The dock workers have chosen him their representative. The colonel tells him the anti-aircraft guns are needed to protect the airdromes on which the Germans are centering the fire. And the district is to be evacuated. So he sends his frightened daughter and his heedless little son and his sister-in-law away to the country and remains alone to fight Hitler along the docks.

There is a good deal more to it than that. An Irish swain for his daughter, strained comedy about plumbing fixtures he brings home for the bathroom, any number of things thrown in without making a fluent whole. It is Edmund Gwenn who wins most of the acting honors as Stonewall Wookey himself. Norah Howard plays his wife nicely, Carol Goodner is her sister, Heather Angel his thin daughter, George Sturgeon his self-centered little son, Horace McNally the vigorous Irish suitor who begins to join the fight only at the end.

Fifteen thousand dollars, they say, have gone into the sound effects alone.

'THE WOOKEY'

A play by Frederick Hazlitt Brennan. Presented at the Plymouth Theater by Edgar Selwyn. Staged by Robert Sinclair. Settings by Jo Mielziner.

THE CAST

Ernie Wookey	George Sturgeon
Aunt Gen	Carol Goodner
Mrs. Wookey	Norah Howard
Primrose Wookey	Heather Angel
Constable Simpson	Henry Newbray
Walt Gibbs	Neil Fitzgerald
Mr. Wookey	Edmund Gwenn
Rory McSwiggin	Horace McNally
Cousin Hector	Byron Russell
Mr. Archibald	Byron Russell
A. R. P. Warden	Roland Bottomly
Dr. Lewishorn	Everett Ripley
First Boy	George Wilson
Second Boy	Gilbert Russell
Third Boy	John Moore
First Girl	Grace Collins
Second Girl	Cora Smith
Vack Lady	Olive Reeves-Smith
Curate	Sean Dillon
Colonel Glenn	Charles Francis

THE WOOKEY himself, Edmund Gwenn.

'West Point Widow' Comes to Criterion

Anne Shirley and Richard Carlson Try Vainly to Make Her Problem Real

By HERBERT COHN

The Army doesn't like the Criterion's "West Point Widow," according to reports, for it makes a West Point upper-classman seem an awful heel. The Army could dislike "West Point Widow" on other grounds as well, just as less official folks might. "West Point Widow" isn't a very good picture. It doesn't make much sense.

It tells about a nice, naive young girl who married and honeymooned with a West Point cadet. Cadets can't get married, though, and stay at West Point, so this marriage was annulled with the boy promising to wait faithfully for the girl, the girl making the same pledge to the boy. They part, and they stay apart, he at West Point, she nursing at a New York hospital.

But the girl has a baby. She names it Jenifer and keeps it hidden in her boarding-house room where a cheerful Negress who has tremendous faith in the vitamin value of pork chops plays nursemaid while the nice, naive mother is working at the hospital. The nurse doesn't let her one-time husband know he's a father because she thinks he'd give up his career to come and marry her all over again. And she doesn't tell his Park Ave. mother either because the same thing might happen. So she just struggles along on her own, taking courage from the gardenia that comes each week with a card from the cadet. No letter. Just a gardenia.

There's a nice young doctor, Richard Carlson, at the hospital, and after he discovers what the young nurse is doing he pitches in and makes life as pleasant as he can for her. He falls in love with her and it's pretty clear that she would fall in love with him, too, if it weren't for that weekly gardenia.

Always the inevitable outcome is clear. It's only a matter of waiting around for it to happen. It is interesting, while waiting, to contemplate how a cadet who made so fine and lasting an impression on so nice a girl could be such a rat, as this cadet obviously is, without the nice girl discovering it before the wedding. Or certainly before the annulment. But that's love in the movies. It pushes naivete to the breaking point and even further.

Anne Shirley and Richard Carlson, as the nurse and the helpful doctor, try hard to keep "West Point Widow" afloat. Maude Eburne helps some as a messy boarding-house keeper, and Frances Gifford helps some more as the maid. But "West Point Widow" is far beyond them and they won't get many to believe in it. So the Army can stop fretting.

Elsa Maxwell Coming To Cedarhurst Tuesday

Elsa Maxwell, playing in W. Somerset Maugham's comedy, "Our Betters," begins a week's engagement at the New Central Theater, Cedarhurst, on Tuesday. Estelle Winwood is featured in the cast, which includes Jayne Cotter, Kenn Randall, Carl Gose, William Swetland, Tom Rutherford, Margo Railton, Lowell Gilmore, Marshall Bradford, James Gelb and Ricardo Montalban.

N. Y. Paramount to Show 'Our Wife' Wednesday

"Our Wife," Columbia's new comedy of marital life, starring Melvyn Douglas, Ruth Hussey and Ellen Drew and produced and directed by John M. Stahl, will open a premiere engagement at the Paramount Theater Wednesday.

The supporting cast is headed by such prominent players as Charles Coburn, John Hubbard, Harvey Stephens and Theresa Harris.

Loew's Theater-Goers To Hear F.D.R. Tonight

Loew's theaters throughout the New York area and in some 50 other cities will so arrange their shows tonight as to include a broadcast of President Roosevelt's important radio address to the nation.

This effort to bring to the movie-going public an important radio speech is the second of its kind made so far. President Roosevelt's 4th of July address was broadcast from Loew stages at the suggestion of Defense Commissioner Mayor LaGuardia. The public reaction was so favorable that Loew's will repeat with the Thursday radio broadcast.

RKO Theaters to Pick Up President's Speech Tonight

President Roosevelt's radio address tonight will be heard in all RKO theaters. Programs will be arranged so there will be a break at 10 p.m.

Reds Smash Moscow Break-Through

Wall Street Closing
RACING EXTRA
★★★★★★

BROOKLYN EAGLE

Wall Street Closing
RACING EXTRA
★★★★★★

LOCAL WEATHER FORECAST: Clear, cooler tonight; partly cloudy, moderate temperature tomorrow

100th YEAR • No. 267 • DAILY AND SUNDAY • BROOKLYN, N. Y., FRIDAY, SEPT. 26, 1941 • Entered at the Brooklyn Postoffice as 2d Class Mail Matter—(Copyright 1941 The Brooklyn Eagle, Inc.) • 3 CENT.

60,000 WILL PARADE IN HUGE DODGER FETE

Eagle Staff photo

A COUPLE OF ROOTERS—Mrs. Dolph Camilli and 2-month-old Bruce, one of the five Camilli children, who provide behind-the-scenes inspiration for the great first baseman.

LITTLE WOMEN HAVE SERIES $$ ALL SPENT

Camilli Cash Earmarked for Ranch Repairs—Kimballs and Coscararts Coast-Bound

The Dodgers' wives are much like other wives. If the players themselves didn't know what they were going to do with the World Series money, the wives did.

Take Mrs. Dolph Camilli, whom we found home at 35 Sterling St. today, with big Dolph, little Dolph, 4; Doug, 5; Richard, 9; Diane, 2, and Bruce, 2 months.

While big Dolph was being punched in the nose by little Dolph with a pair of boxing gloves his dad had brought back from Boston, Mrs. Camilli said she'll live up to a very ancient baseball tradition—get a new fur coat.

Will Go to California

The Camilli household is almost all packed and after the series they wil go back to Latonville, in

Continued on Page 3

ODDS FAVOR YANKS

Jack Doyle, noted betting commissioner, today reported odds on the World Series varied from 2 to 5 in favor of the Yankees to 2 to 1 against the Dodgers.

Fred Schumm, Brooklyn betting commissioner, said the Yankees were 9 to 5 favorites.

Weather for Series Open 'Unpredictable'

The weather will be clear and cooler tonight and fair and cool tomorrow, the Weather Bureau predicted today, but what it will be next Wednesday afternoon, Oct. 1, at Yankee Stadium, the forecasters were loath to say.

"Unpredictable," they finally ventured.

Lepke's Attorney Cites 'Pampering' Of Reles by State

Star Witness Lodged In Hotel, Allowed Visits By Wife, Venireman Told

Lawyers' faces turned scarlet today as County Judge Taylor referred to "static" in ending an acrimonious verbal clash between Assistant District Attorney Burton B. Turkus and former Assistant District Attorney Hyman Barshay at the murder trial of Louis (Lepke) Buchalter and two henchmen.

The trial had been marked by drabness through inability to seat more than one of 165 prospective blue-ribbon jurors questioned thus far, and nerves were noticeably on edge when Max Oliver, an insurance supervisor of 362 Linden Boulevard, stepped forward to undergo examination.

Taking his position as counsel for Lepke, Barshay, without naming Abe (Kid Twist) Reles, the prosecution's star witness against murder-for-money gangsters, asked

Continued on Page 17

Zanuck, Vet, 'Hates War and Propaganda'

Washington, Sept. 26 (INS)—In an atmosphere supercharged with clashes between members, Darryl F. Zanuck told a Senate subcommittee today that he does not seek to inflame the people to go to war.

Himself a private in the World War, the dapper vice president of 20th Century-Fox issued a sweeping denial of all charges of war propaganda against the movies.

"I want to say first that no man who was in France during the last war can look upon war with anything but the deepest abhorrence," said Zanuck.

"I feel that it is the duty of every American to give his complete co-operation and support to our President and our Congress, to do everything to defeat Hilter and preserve America. If this course of necessity leads to war, I want to follow my President along that course."

Amen Reveals New Threats to Thwart Probe

Posts Extra Guards For Star Witnesses in Bebchick Slaying Quiz

Revealing "new threats" to thwart his investigation of police corruption in the numbers racket, Assistant Attorney General Amen today posted special guards for star witnesses in his inquiry into the slaying of Abe Bebchick, the Brownsville policy czar he had been seeking to question.

Without disclosing the nature of the threats or the names of the witnesses, the special prosecutor announced through his assistant, Harold N. Cohen, that the "ride" given Bebchick on Wednesday morning had prompted him to take more seriously all efforts to silence potential informers.

Promising an "important development" before nightfall, Mr. Amen denied reports that he had in custody a "payoff man" who had handed Bebchick bribes to 20 policemen, and that he had launched a thorough investigation of the failure of his detective staff to locate Bebchick a month ago.

"Of course," he said, referring to District Attorney O'Dwyer's revelation that Bebechick had remained in his familiar haunts in recent months, "I questioned our men. But I have no reason to suspect there was anything improper in their failure to bring Bebchick to my office."

To Quiz Henchmen

As six more police officers, including two captains, were brought before the two Amen grand juries to testify regarding policy racket protection, Capt. John J. McGowan, in charge of the Brooklyn homicide squad, sent a number of detectives to out-of-town centers to question Bebchick henchmen.

At the same time police of the Empire Boulevard station learned from a man identified only as "Zoo" that he had been hired as private chauffeur for Bebchick Tuesday night and saw him leave a restaurant at Utica Ave. and Eastern Parkway and drive away with two men shortly before 2 a.m. His body was found five hours later.

Meanwhile, funeral services for the slain gangster, who was 38 and lived at 9214 Avenue B, were conducted by Rabbi Abraham P. Block of Temple Petach Tikvah in the Jewish Memorial Chapel, 1406 Pitkin Ave. Only his mother, four brothers, three sisters and a handful of friends went from the chapel to burial services in Montefiore Cemetery, Springfield.

Six Policemen Questioned

A total of six plainclothesmen were questioned yesterday before Amen's two extraordinary grand juries, but the Assistant Attorney General pointed out that the actual slaying of Bebchick had not been discussed because that was solely within jurisdiction of District Attorney O'Dwyer.

The O'Dwyer office continued to incline to a belief that the policy king's success in a dice game had been directly responsible for his death, and Acting Deputy Chief Inspector William T. Reynolds reported that police were "leaning more strongly than ever" toward a robbery motive.

'Not a Big Shot'

Bebchick, whose sizable policy operations were confirmed in a raid on his "bank" at 626 Lincoln Place Wednesday that yielded thousands of slips, $1,300 in cash and the arrest of four henchmen, is said by Amen to have averaged $8,000 a day in illicit wagers on numbers.

WH-E-E-E-E!!! A Brooklyn Fan (the girls come pretty in Brooklyn) screams a welcome to her Dodger heroes at Grand Central.

REPUBLICAN DEAL WITH LABORITES REPORTED HERE

But Leaders Are Mum On Compromise Move To Strengthen Ranks

By JOSEPH H. SCHMALACKER

Republican-inspired reports that another campaign compromise is being attempted to strengthen the G.O.P., as well as American Labor party fences, filtered through political circles in Brooklyn today, despite the failure of efforts to promote a deal at an earlier stage of the campaign.

Leaders in both party ranks, while making no denials, insisted they were lacking information which would suggest that the two parties are on the verge of the agreement.

American Laborites themselves were concerned at the moment with a new flareup in the form of a Supreme Court mandamus proceeding between the A.L.P.'s embattled left and right wing factions.

An application signed by Supreme Court Justice Wilson on its submission by the Brooklyn left wing,

Continued on Page 17

DELAY CITY RAID DATA 'TO PREVENT ALARM'

When the situation "justifies it," the city's residents will receive pamphlets telling them exactly what to do in the event of an air raid.

Mayor LaGuardia yesterday revealed that instructions have been printed but distribution has been delayed "because we don't want to alarm the people."

The Mayor spoke at a luncheon meeting of the Fashion Group, Inc., at the Hotel Astor, Manhattan.

Reds Crush Panzers Hitting Moscow Line

Offensive Ordered By Hitler Costs Foe 20,000, Says Soviet

Moscow, Sept. 26 (U.P.)—Soviet dispatches claimed today that Russian troops have crushed an elite Nazi Panzer column which was attempting a direct break-through from Bryansk to Moscow as part of an offensive personally ordered by Adolf Hitler.

The Nazi attack was led by the Panzer forces of Col. Gen. Heinz Guderian, veteran of German break-through actions in Poland and at Sedan.

Guderian's forces were said to have made three separate attempts to crack the Russian lines and finally to have fallen back after suffering 20,000 killed, wounded and captured.

The offensive, a dispatch to the government newspaper Izvestia by

Continued on Page 17

574,000 Captured, Foe Doomed in Trap Near Kiev, Nazis Claim

Berlin, Sept. 26 (U.P.)—A special communique of the high command said tonight that a total of more than 574,000 Russian prisoners had been captured east of Kiev and that the "destruction" of trapped enemy forces was imminent.

War materials were captured in such great quantity that the total cannot yet be estimated, the communique said, and more prisoners are being taken as the trap is "mopped up."

Authorized sources admitted that the Russians had made strong counter-attacks in an unspecified area, but said they had been repulsed. They also reported that German bombers sank nine ships in a Soviet convoy on Lake Ladoga, three of them during attempted landing operations.

Official news agency dispatches said big Russian counter-attacks, in which hundreds of Don Cossack

Continued on Page 17

Narragansett Park Results

FIRST RACE — Two-year-olds; three-quarter mile.

Misfit (McCreary)	14.20	6.40	4.20
Reckless Saxon (Dattilo)	—	3.40	2.60
Sunburst (Briggs)	—	—	3.00

Time, 1:13 1-5. Pettine, Love Note, Bright Flyer, Accuse Me, Green Hickory, Benefice, Hidden Charm, Celia, Gallant Peggy also ran. Off time, 2:18.

SECOND RACE—Skipper's Mate, 1st; Tide's In, 2d; Ida Streng, 3d.

Belmont Park Results

FIRST RACE—Four-year-olds up; three-quarter mile.

Firozepore (B. James)	5.90	3.70	2.50
Sizzling Pan (Robertson)	—	3.40	2.40
Sherton Ann (Strickler)	—	—	2.60

Time, 1:11 1-5. Black Bun, Sir Gibson, Merry Knight, Carvale also ran. Off time, 2:06.

SECOND RACE—Michigan Sun, first; Whiscendent, second; Columbus Day, third.

500,000 to See Monday Turnout Headed by Team

Plans were laid in Borough Hall today for a mighty Victory Parade Monday afternoon to honor the flag-winning Brooklyn Dodgers.

The players themselves—Pete Reiser, Whitlow Wyatt, Dixie Walker, Kirby Higbe, Dolph Camilli, Peewee Reese and the rest—will be the center of attraction in the procession through Brooklyn streets.

With them and behind them will come bands playing, flags waving and Dodger fans marching by the thousands. And other Brooklyn fans, the planners predicted, will turn out to see and cheer to the number of 500,000 and more.

For details on the Dodgers' victory and how Brooklyn took it, see:

Wives' story and pictures, Page 1.

Fan story on Page 15.

Other pictures on Page 15.

How they won, how the Cards lost, and former Brooklyn winners in sports section.

The number of actual paraders, it was estimated, would be about 60,000.

Several tentative parade plans were merged when Borough President Cashmore today called a group of representative Brooklyn leaders. At the same time he issued a proclamation making Monday "Brooklyn Dodgers Day" and calling on all citizens to join in the demonstration "for Brooklyn's heroes."

The committee resolved to ask Mayor LaGuardia, who was in Washington, to declare Monday a half holiday for public school children and for all city employes who could be spared from their jobs.

Store Half-Holiday Sought

Major stores in the city also would be asked to declare a half holiday, permitting employes and patrons to give up the afternoon to the Dodger demonstration.

Announcement of parade plans was held up until after Larry MacPhail, Dodger president, and Leo Durocher, manager, after due consideration, gave the word that the players would be available.

The National League champions will spend Monday morning in the Yankee Stadium to familiarize themselves with the home grounds of their World Series foes. At 3 p.m. they will be in Ebbets Field, where they will be turned over to the parade committee members.

All veterans organizations in the borough were represented at the conference and an order was issued to "all county commanders of veterans organizations and to all veterans" to have all post colors and all musical units report at 2 p.m. Monday at Eastern Parkway and Prospect Park Plaza in preparation for the parade.

Will March to Boro Hall

The line of march was expected to be from that point to Borough Hall, where a reviewing stand, swiftly thrown up over the week-end, would hold reviewing officers and guests of honor.

It was probable that, for the first time, a big Brooklyn parade would go by way of Fulton St., now cleared of the old "Black Spider" elevated structure.

Invitations to attend as guests of honor were sent to President Roose-

Continued on Page 15

PROCLAMATION

TO THE PEOPLE OF THE BOROUGH OF BROOKLYN:

WHEREAS, the Brooklyn Dodgers, under the leadership of Leo Durocher, have brought to our Borough its first National League Pennant in twenty-one (21) years, and

WHEREAS, every one of Brooklyn's three million citizens are justifiably proud of their great baseball team, and

WHEREAS, it is fitting that the Dodgers be honored for their long and courageous pennant fight, now, therefore, be it

PROCLAIMED that Monday, September 29th, 1941, is hereby designated BROOKLYN DODGERS DAY, and the people of Brooklyn are hereby urged to do their part in making this day one to be remembered by hanging out flags and joining in the demonstration for Brooklyn's heroes of 1941.

John Cashmore
President of the Borough of Brooklyn

WHERE TO FIND IT IN TODAY'S EAGLE

Bridge	Page 27	Neighborhood News	Page 23
Comics	Page 24	Novel	Page 27
Crossword	Page 26	OBITUARIES	Page 17
Dr. Brady	Page 24	Only Yesterday	Page 13
EDITORIAL	Page 16	RADIO	Page 24
FINANCIAL	Page 22	Real Estate	Page 27
Going Places	Page 12	Society	Page 8
Grin and Bear It	Page 16	SPORTS	Pages 19-20-21-22
Heffernan	Page 13	Theaters	Page 11
Helen Worth	Page 10	These Women	Page 13
Horoscope	Page 27	Tucker	Page 16
Jimmy Wood	Page 19	Uncle Ray's Corner	Page 13
Lindley	Page 13	Wall Street	Page 22
Movies	Page 11	Want Ads	Pages 25-26-27
		Woman's	Page 1[illegible]

BROOKLYN EAGLE
FRIDAY, SEPT. 26, 1941
W

Dolph Camilli — Whit Wyatt — Pete Reiser — Kirby Higbe

Dodger Victory Richly Earned

SPORTOPICS By
JIMMY WOOD
Sports Editor

THAT CAMILLI MAN—The Dodger Victory Committee's poll of the fans reveals that Dixie Walker is the most popular Dodger and Dolph Camilli the most colorful one. Perhaps the committee will blushingly deny that it pulled a master stroke and decided not to limit the voting to the most valuable player, but we have a feeling that such was the case.

Had it been a most valuable player contest there could have been no logical winner but Camilli. Don't get us wrong, Greenpoint, we're not implying that Walker is not the most popular Dodger. It's true what they say about Dixie. He's a grand guy and a grand ball player. So is Camilli.

To paraphrase Ed Sullivan, it couldn't have happened to two nicer guys. The very fact, however, that Walker is voted most popular suggests also that he has more color than Camilli. Color is a strange commodity. Personally, we think Leo Durocher, Peewee Reese, Fred Fitzsimmons and Ducky Medwick rate over Walker in the rainbow league, but the fans have spoken and we guess we know when we're licked.

As to the relative playing merits of Camilli and Walker—well, it isn't even close. Camilli is not only the most valuable Dodger but the most valuable player in the league, which latter claim undoubtedly will be confirmed by the Baseball Writers of America in a few days.

To settle all arguments on the most valuable player score, let's put it this way:

Which one of the two do you think the Dodgers would have missed more had one of them been missing this season? We'll answer that one: Camilli.

Without Walker the Dodgers probably would have missed the Bronx Express. Without Camilli, however, they would have been stopped at the turnstiles. It was Dolph's power hitting combined with his fine art of playing first base that carried the Dodgers to the National League flag.

It's quite a personal triumph for Camilli, too, for he was 33 last April, when he started his 16th semester in organized baseball. Many baseball men thought he was past his playing peak, for at that age most athletes are and Dolph had a rather poor season last year.

Perhaps Dolph is past his peak. It may be that the campaign he is now winding up—his best ever in the big leagues—was an inspired performance. It came at the right time and next year Camilli probably will collect his fattest salary yet. As Burleigh Grimes used to say, a ball player gets paid for what he did the year before.

Of all the expensive player deals made for Brooklyn by Larry MacPhail, the earliest one, that which brought Camilli from the Phillies for Eddie Morgan and $45,000, probably has paid the biggest dividends.

Smart operators in ivory said Camilli wasn't a pennant-winning player. They pointed out that he had failed to stick with the Cubs when that club was a contender and had only looked like a lion thereafter because he was among the lambs in Philadelphia. The smart operators were wrong.

A glance at the highlights of his 1941 record as of today will reveal how wrong they were: League leader in home runs with 34 and league leader in runs-batted-in with 119.

He'll be a handy guy to have in there against those Yankees—but that's next week. More immediate items on the Dodger fans' social calendar are the presentations to Walker and Camilli at the Brooklyn Paramount and Fox tonight.

And now a bow to the Cardinals. They made it a rousing race and our Dodgers have the satisfaction of topping a great young team. Those Cards almost hustled their way to a flag and they might have made it but for a flock of injuries to key men. Then again it might not have been so close had the Dodgers not kept Walker on the bench while experimenting with Paul Waner early in the season.

Say, come to think of it, that Dixie Walker is going to have a nice contract case next year, too. Have you got a match, Mr. MacPhail?

Racers in Action

With no other circuit track in operation, Castle Hill Speedway will be the scene of a big meet tonight. Every top driver will be on hand, including Johnnie Swier, Greenpoint ace, who returned to action Tuesday night after a six-week layoff to win the main event

Series Dope in Sunday's Eagle

If you want to know every angle of the World Series coming up between the Dodgers and Yankees, be sure and get a copy of Sunday's Eagle. Our staff of experts, led by Tommy Holmes, who has traveled with the Dodgers for many lean years, and Harold Parrott, will cover every detail of the blue ribbon classics. In addition we will have features by staff writers of International News Service and United Press. The Eagle photographers will cover the series pictorially.

Wyatt-Fitz Parlay Is Southworth Tip

Card Manager Picks Whit to Win Two Series Games From Yanks

By HAROLD PARROTT

Pittsburgh, Sept. 25—Billy Southworth cashed in his chips in the N. L. pennant race like a good sport last evening and stuck in some World Series advice for the Dodgers.

"I'll be rooting for Brooklyn," he said. "So will all of us Cardinals. We're for the National League victory, of course. But I certainly wouldn't want to be going into this big series without a starting left-handed pitcher," as Durocher is."

Outside the wind-blown dusk was falling fast. The glum Cardinals, having tossed the sponge in at last—Max Butcher beat them, 3—1, not allowing a clean hit until the eighth—were in no hurry to get out of tomblike Forbes Field, where their pennant hopes had been buried as the Dodgers won in Boston.

"The Yankees are a great ball club," said Southworth. "But so much of their power is left-handed—Keller, whom I know from the International League; Dickey, Selkirk; Henrich, Rolfe—that I can't help thinking, as I've been thinking for a month, how well our southpaws—Pollet, White and Lanier—would do against a club like that.

"Don't get me wrong," the Cardinal boss added, hurriedly. "The Dodgers have fought and they beat us fair and square at every turn and they're entitled to that pennant. Why, take that Whit Wyatt. He's a pitcher for my money. And he'll worry those Yankees plenty, whether they go to the plate right or left-handed."

Southworth thought a minute, then added: "I would pick Wyatt to win both his starts. He has everything. But, then, where are you? You can't fastball those Yankees. Kirby Higbe can't afford to get into any holes with that ball club. He'll have to stay ahead of every batter, for if he doesn't they'll fall on him like a load of brick if he has to come in there with that ball."

How about Curt Davis?

Southworth cringed. "No curve ball," he said. "I know he's pitched good ball against us at times this season. If you can be sure his pitches are sinking the day you call on him, well, he'll give you a whale of a well-pitched game. But you've got to have a curve like Wyatt's to really stop those Yankees. I know, because we played them this Spring when Lanier and White pitched so well against McCarthy's team."

After Wyatt, Southworth's pick for a Dodger pitching hero in the big bucks series is Freddy Fitzsimmons. "Fred has just the sort of stuff to throw a club like the Yanks off stride," said the Redbird boss. "Well rested, Fitz is sure to give you a well-pitched game. He's broken our hearts at times this year, and you remember 1936, don't you?"

We did, of course—with the ball that glanced off Fitz' glove, winning a 2—1 World Series game for the Yanks at the Stadium.

Outside it was getting late. "It's late for Fitz, too," was Billy's shouted parting through the gloom. "But I'll bet on him to do it—this one last time. Fitz and Wyatt. Don't say I didn't tip you off."

HOME, SWEET HOME—Here Mickey Owen reaches the platter with a neat slide to bring in the Dodger run in the second inning.

WYATT CAN'T BELIEVE IT YET, CALLS IT DREAM

There were some strange reactions among the group of Brooklyn's pennant winning performers: For instance, a crack from Leo Durocher, the manager of the Flatbush heroes, who for three weeks has come close to a new record for lack of sustenance and lack of rest. Said the manager, "I felt sure they could win. In fact, I didn't see how they could miss with the spirit these boys possess."

And then there was Whit Wyatt, who shut out the Braves in the game, that clinched the pennant . . . While the boys were whooping it up in the clubhouse, Whit merely sat there in front of his locker . . . "I can't believe it," he said over and over again. "I bounced all over the major and minor league map for years and years and suddenly find myself pitching the game that clinches the pennant for the Dodgers." Wyatt halted, then added what sounds like something from Horatio Alger. "I think, I still think," he said, "that I'm dreaming."

And Fred Fitzsimmons, oldest of the Dodgers and one of the toughest. The big, round man had tears in his eyes. "Damn it!" he said again and again, "I'd live all right without the World Series check we're going to get. But what means so much to me is that we did come through for Brooklyn and the Brooklyn fans. If ever a town deserved a pennant and if ever fans

Continued on Page 18

MAJOR LEAGUE STANDINGS

FRIDAY, SEPT. 26, 1941

National League

STANDING OF THE CLUBS

	Brooklyn	St. Louis	Cincinnati	Pittsburgh	New York	Chicago	Boston	Phila'phia	Won	Lost	Percentage	Games Behind
Bkn.	—	11	14	12	14	13	18	17	99	53	.651	—
St.L.	11	—	12	16	15	11	14	17	96	55	.636	2½
Cin.	8	10	—	10	15	14	13	16	86	65	.570	12½
Pitt.	10	6	9	—	14	13	12	16	80	71	.530	18½
N.Y.	8	6	7	8	—	13	15	16	73	78	.483	25½
Chi.	9	9	8	9	9	—	11	14	69	83	.454	30
Bos.	4	8	9	10	5	11	—	14	61	91	.401	38
Phil.	3	5	6	6	6	8	8	—	42	110	.276	57
Lost	53	55	65	71	78	83	91	110	—	—		

YESTERDAY'S RESULTS

Brooklyn 6, Boston 0.
New York 3, Philadelphia 2.
Pittsburgh 3, St. Louis 1.
Cincinnati 6, Chicago 0.

GAMES TODAY

Cincinnati at Pittsburgh—Riddle (18-4) vs. Brandt (0-0).
Other clubs not scheduled.

GAMES TOMORROW

Philadelphia at Brooklyn.
New York at Boston.
St. Louis at Chicago.
Cincinnati at Pittsburgh.

American League

STANDING OF THE CLUBS

	New York	Boston	Chicago	Detroit	Cleveland	Wash'gton	St. Louis	Phila'phia	Won	Lost	Percentage	Games Behind
N.Y.	—	13	14	11	15	14	18	14	99	51	.660	—
Bos.	9	—	16	11	9	14	9	14	82	69	.543	17½
Chi.	8	6	—	10	17	13	11	10	75	76	.497	24½
Det.	11	11	9	—	12	7	11	13	74	77	.490	25½
Cle.	7	13	5	10	—	12	11	15	73	77	.487	26
Wsh.	4	8	9	15	10	—	11	11	68	82	.453	31
St.L.	4	13	11	11	7	11	—	11	68	82	.453	31
Phil.	8	5	12	9	7	11	11	—	63	88	.417	36½
Lost	51	69	76	77	77	82	82	88	—	—		

YESTERDAY'S RESULTS

No games scheduled.

GAMES TODAY

Washington at New York (2)—Chase (6-16) and Wynn (3-0) vs. Russo (13-10) and Chandler (9-4), 1:30 p.m.
Cleveland at St. Louis (2)—Feller, (24-13) and Milnar (12-15) or Smith (11-14) vs. Auker (14-15) and Galehouse (9-9).
Chicago at Detroit—Benton (13-6) vs. Rigney (12-13).
Other clubs not scheduled.

GAMES TOMORROW

Washington at New York, 2:30 p.m.
Boston at Philadelphia.
Cleveland at St. Louis.
Chicago at Detroit.

Better Club Really Did Win Most Gruelling Scramble in History of Senior Circuit

By TOMMY HOLMES

Champions of the National League, the Dodgers roared back into town today and I do mean roared. Training rules were suspended, champagne flowed in their special train from Boston as Leo Durocher's dead-game athletes celebrated their victory on the five and one-half-hour trip.

A long, hard duel with the St. Louis Cardinals that started way back in May ended shortly after 5 o'clock yesterday when Cookie Lavagetto fielded Max West's sharp grounder, juggled the ball an instant, then fired it over to Dolph Camilli at first base for the 27th putout that sealed a five-hit, 6-to-0 pitching triumph for Whitlow Wyatt.

The scoreboard already showed that the courageous Cardinals of old St. Louis had lost in Pittsburgh, so the boys knew that they were in, that the pennant was clinched. They dashed for the box, almost tore Wyatt apart, then carried their war whoops of triumph into the dressing room where the evening-long celebration started.

Most Gruelling of All Races

And here was a team that really deserved a party. Casey Stengel, the gnarled and wrinkled manager of the Braves, put it in a few words when he dropped in to congratulate Durocher.

"A great ball club," said Stengel, "and your boys won it by yourselves, which is the hard way."

Durocher invited Stengel to the Brooklyn clubhouse at the World Series games next week. Casey grinned and replied, "The way you fellows play ball, you don't need me."

Now that it's all over, you can see the better club won in the most gruelling, two-team race in the entire history of the National League. Since early May, the Cardinals and the Dodgers have been racing neck and neck, never more than four games apart in the standings. You owe a salute to the Cardinals, as courageous a ball team that ever stepped out upon a diamond. But it was their misfortune to run into a Brooklyn outfit just as game and with a little more ability.

Who won the flag for the Dodgers? "Everybody," said Durocher, calm for the first time in weeks. And then Leo seemed a bit afraid that one Dodger in particular might be overlooked. He added, "We couldn't have won without Hugh Casey's relief pitching."

Correct enough. But they also would not have won the pennant if they hadn't been tops in about every worthwhile department.

For example, Brooklyn has the athlete who'll, almost without a doubt, be named the most valuable player of the National League for 1941. He is Dolph Camilli, who'll lead the league in home runs, runs batted in and whose fielding finesse at first base is something terrific.

They also have the league's leading batter—a brash young left-handed slasher named Pete Reiser. And Reiser not only will wind up with the batting championship, but also may lead the league in runs scored, hits, two-base hits and three-base hits.

They have the two top pitchers of the league in the afore-mentioned Whit Wyatt and Kirby Higbe, both of them winners of 22 ball games.

And if Billy Herman isn't the best second baseman in this National League, I'll start from the beginning and try to learn this baseball racket all over again.

And, there is Dixie Walker, a great clutch ball player; Curt Davis, a grand spot pitcher; Peewee Reese, a kid shortstop who has been a bit over-awed by his surroundings but who is growing up rapidly; Harry Lavagetto, Mickey Owen and Herman Franks, both great competitors as catchers, and Freddy Fitzsimmons, than whom there is no whomer as a seasoned fighter who has been through the mill; Joe Medwick, who swings at the plate by ear but devastatingly; Lew Riggs, Wasdell, and all the rest.

Holmes Right Again!

Not forgetting Durocher, a dynamic leader who did enough worrying for the entire club during the final stretch drive. And you can say it and say it again that Durocher was the gent whose spirit and fight co-ordinated the talent of a scrambled ball club composed of oldsters, middle-aged big leaguers and kids hardly dry behind the ears.

Without attempting the double-jointed job of patting myself on the back, I'd like to point out that I did pick the Dodgers to win and did pick them because I thought they were the best ball club in the league. And they did finish up that way in spite of the numerous replacements that the Cardinals brought in on the scene—fellows like young Pollet and Musial who made it plenty close.

As Stengel said, the Dodgers won the flag the hard way. They were three games out when they started their final road trip which involved not only a swing of the Western towns but series in Philadelphia and Boston. They were three games in front when they left Ebbets Field and, after winning 11 and losing six on the road, returned two and a half games in front with only two games left to play.

It's a ball club that you can be proud of, boys and girls.

SLIDIN' MICKEY—Dodgers' catcher, Owen, covered a lot of ground at Braves Field yesterday. Here he is making a three-point landing to arrive at second base ahead of the throw. Note the ball striking him. Al Roberge is straining for the toss. A few minutes later Mickey slid home to score.

Everybody Goes Beautifully Wacky In Mad Pennant Spree for Our Boys

Professors Jig, Grandmas Howl, Kids Parade

A man smiled at a pretty girl on the subway coming in from Flatbush this morning. Instead of turning distastefully away, as she would have done yesterday, she smiled back. A woman in Bay Ridge couldn't believe her ears when her husband praised her cooking at breakfast.

An isolationist and an interventionist had a pleasant chat as they walked down Court St.—the first time they have been able to stand the sight of each other since 1939.

You get the idea. The lion and the lamb, you might say, were skipping around together, the best of friends.

You've guessed the explanation. It's that era of peace and good feeling that descended on Brooklyn around 5 o'clock yesterday when the Dodgers finally upped and ended the suspense by showing everybody who is the boss of the National League.

For 10 or 15 minutes before 5 o'clock Brooklyn hardly breathed. It was that quiet you'd think it was a courtroom with the jury filing in. Strong men gasped and swallowed as they cocked an ear to radios pouring Red Barber's voice from store doors and automobiles.

Terrific Suspense

Taxicab drivers didn't bother to look for prospective fares—nobody wanted to go anywhere.

A fat woman listening on Fulton St. sat heavily on the curb. She was unable to carry both the suspense and her weight. Bus drivers and trolley motormen found reasons to linger at stops where radios blared. A bemused bartender in Williamsburg held a glass under the beer tap till beer foamed over his hand and sloshed down into his shoes.

Then it came, that news Brooklyn had waited for through 21 years of hope deferred. Where a moment before there had been silence there now was a noise that burst and rolled and screeched and howled till it startled the gulls skimming over the harbor.

Dignified men slapped the backs of perfect strangers.

An aloof professor at Brooklyn College stepped off a neat buck-and-wing in his study—we have this on the solemn word of his amazed wife.

Drinks on House

A thrifty barkeeper out on Flatbush Ave. so far forgot himself—and the State law—as to set up a round on the house.

A grandmother in Canarsie, who has never in her life seen a ball game, jumped up with such violence that she knocked over and smashed to hell the new $29.95 radio that brought her the news.

From there on it was carnival night in Brooklyn.

Kids organized parades which were joined by their elders. Horns brayed enthusiastic if unmelodious tunes. The front page of the Eagle's extra editions announcing the result were pasted on windows and were carried as banners.

Hold Open House

Starry-eyed enthusiasts clustered under the windows of the Dodger office on Montague St. Larry MacPhail was holding open house, his seamy face wearing an expression so seraphic you couldn't believe it.

Hotels, restaurants, bars, lodge halls—any place where people could gather—filled up with Brooklynites who announced they were Dodger fans, were prepared to argue that the Yankees belong in the Three-Eye League, and who dared say different?

The air was a confusion of babbling. "Lavagetto . . . ah, he's the boy . . . Durocher is the sweetest damn manager . . . I told you the Pirates . . . the Cards . . . Waner . . . Fletcher . . . I got two complete sets coming for every game . . . my cousin's girl friend knows where you can pick up two or three sets . . . it'll only hold 35,000, packed in . . . the Stadium . . . Pete Reiser . . ."

And so on, and on, and on.

HAIL, THE CONQUERING HEROES COME—Part of the cheering crowd in Grand Central Terminal last night which met the champs (otherwise the Dodgers) on their return from Boston.

VICTORY SIDELIGHTS

Official recognition to Brooklyn's "Day of Days" came from Mayor LaGuardia in congratulatory telegrams to Larry MacPhail, president of the Dodgers, and to Leo Durocher, fiery manager of the ball club.

To Durocher, the Mayor said: "A long haul since 1920, but with a playing manager with your spirit and experience, Brooklyn is now placed in a position that it should hold in the National League. Congratulations to you and your splendid, fighting team. Greetings from one temperamentalist to another."

Mr. LaGuardia, facing a situation which will call for the greatest of diplomatic tact and care next Wednesday when he undoubtedly will be called on to toss out the first ball in the opening game of the World Series, sent the following wire to MacPhail:

"Congratulations. As Mayor of the City of New York, I am now really proud of Brooklyn.

"I am prouder still to be lucky enough to be Mayor at a time when the Dodgers return to their rightful place on the top of the heap in the National League. It is most unusual for a Mayor to be able to boast of two champion teams in one season.

"Best regards."

District Attorney O'Dwyer sent a brief but warm message to Durocher which stated: "Brooklyn is mighty proud of you and the boys and we will back you through a victorious World Series."

Yankees 'Burned'

Several hundred followers of the faithful Flatbush flock gathered on the site of old Washington Park, original Dodger ball park, 5th Ave. and 4th St., burned an effigy of the New York Yankees.

Another Dodger demonstration burned a Cardinal effigy from an electric light pole at 4th Ave. and 8th St., while motor traffic along the thoroughfare, a main artery, stood still with horns blowing full blast for nearly half an hour.

'We Win' Signs Rampant

In various sections, shop windows, doors and building walls sported the tremendous "WE WIN" headline from the front page of yesterday's late edition of the Brooklyn Eagle. The Eagle office was flooded with telephone calls throughout the evening and well into the morning with requests for additional copies of the paper which heralded loudly the recording of an historic event in the borough's glorious history.

As local taverns were reported to be doing a flood-tide business with all loyal fans working without effort to tie-on a world championship hangover, toast after toast was offered to the hometown heroes, to Max Butcher, a Dodger castoff who pitched Pittsburgh to a victory over the Cardinals and froze the St. Louis pennant hopes.

Leibowitz Closes Court

Judge Samuel Leibowitz and a jury were hearing testimony in a grand larceny case in County Court yesterday when the jurist's secretary tiptoed up to the bench and handed the Judge a slip of paper. As Assistant District Attorney John J. Rooney was in the process of examining a witness, Judge Leibowitz interrupted.

"Here is news of great moment to Brooklyn," the judge said. "Brooklyn has defeated Boston. Pittsburgh has defeated St. Louis. The pennant is ours. Trial adjourned."

'I Told You So'

On the heels of the glorious victory, the following comments were received by Eagle reporters:

BOROUGH PRESIDENT CASHMORE—I knew it the minute I threw out the first ball last Spring. They are a great ball team. But you ain't seen nothing yet. Watch out Yanks, the Brooks are coming!

GEORGE C. WILDERMUTH, president of Dodger Knot Hole Club—It's just as I predicted last April at the "welcome home dinner." How can the Yanks beat that team. Those darlings must win and will win. They can't lose!

SUPREME COURT JUSTICE FRANCIS D. McGAREY—They're the gamest team that ever had the privilege of denting the sod in Ebbets Field in years.

David F. Soden, State Tax Commissioner and one of the flock's perpetual boosters: "Felicitations to the team."

HE MANAGED ALL RIGHT—Leo Durocher, Dodger manager, walks calmly into Grand Central Terminal at head of his champions.

Dodger Fete Set for Monday

Continued from Page 1

velt, Senators Robert F. Wagner and James M. Mead, Governor Lehman, Mayor LaGuardia, District Attorney O'Dwyer, members of the Board of Estimate and others.

Meeting with the Borough President to make the plans were John J. Kenny, Kings County commander of the American Legion; Joseph H. O'Neill of the Brooklyn Real Estate Board; Deputy County Clerk James A. Kelly, William A. Halloran, president of the Allied War Veterans Association of Brooklyn; Ivan Boxell of the Brooklyn Chamber of Commerce; Hy Emanuel of the recently formed Brooklyn Dodgers Victory Committee; J. L. Kalischer, chairman of the committee; John J. Wims, past county commander of the Military Order of the Purple Heart; John Durant, past county commander of the Veterans of Foreign Wars; David Martin, managing director of the Hotel Bossert; Arthur H. Bernstein, State commander of the Jewish War Veterans; John J. Vical of the Disabled American War Veterans, and Henry J. Davenport, president of the Downtown Brooklyn Association.

Others on a larger, rapidly growing celebration committee were Joseph N. Aimee, county commander Veterans of Foreign Wars; Bernard E. Perelson, county commander Jewish War Veterans; Ray Austin, county commander Catholic War Veterans; John Starkey, Military Order of the Purple Heart; Col. William A. Dawkins, United Spanish War Veterans; Newton Avrutus, exalted ruler Brooklyn Lodge of Elks; Gerald Graham, regional director, and Fred Milligan, county president, Loyal Order of Moose.

Also Edward Whalen, master fourth degree Knights of Columbus; John J. Rooney, county president Ancient Order of Hibernians; John Cassidy, county chairman Fraternal Order of Elks; James J. White, Celtic Circle; Max Lustig and Sydney Harnett, Knights of Pythias; George Wildemuth, president Knothole Club; Frank J. Nolan, Clarendon Club; John Savarese, Charles Pace and Louis Camaradello, Italian-American Democratic Clubs; Frank J. Longo, president Dodger-Boosters-Frank Long Club; James J. Sullivan, Mansfield Club; Joseph Martin, Sheepshead Bay Sportsmen's Club; Nathan Dinkes, chairman Jeffersonian Club; Nick Drackalackas, president American Hellenic Club.

Also Martin Peterson, president Utican Club; Henry Karutz, president Kings County Grand Jurors Association; Adolph Gross, president Kingston Avenue Merchants Association; Frank Braxl, 86th Street Board of Trade.

Meanwhile, our dashing Dodgers—shoved, kissed and hugged as 10,000 delirious Brooklyn rooters gave vent to emotions stirred by 21 years of "waiting till next year"—could be forgiven if they looked forward to a clean-cut World Series triumph over the Yankees.

In a hectic outburst unmatched in history of Grand Central Terminal the precious Dodgers learned last night the heights to which the enthusiasm of the boys and girls from Flatbush, Greenpoint, Gowanus, etc., can ascend if given a bit of encouragement by their idols at Ebbets Field.

The festivities that completely disrupted the rail center resulted, of course, from the fact that the Durochermen had clinched the National League pennant by defeating the Braves, 6 to 0, yesterday, while the St. Louis Cardinals were losing to Pittsburgh, 3 to 1.

Veteran police observers scratched their heads and vainly tried to recall a comparable situation as rabid fans jammed the spacious structure and welcomed their beloved heroes home from Boston without thought of law and order.

It might even be said that the carefree crowd overflowed to the "rafters," for many found places on the taxicab ramp at the sidewalk level and peered through slits in the station's back wall to await patiently the appearance of Durocher & Co. and add their cheers.

The terminal's regular constabulary, accustomed to handling the arrivals of Presidents, movie stars and royalty, was obliged to adopt a "What's the use?" attitude, and the players themselves aided and abetted their admirers by quickly getting into the swing of things.

The closest descriptive term for this outpouring of devotion by hitherto pennant-frustrated fandom to "dem bums" is to liken it to a mob scene from a moving picture such as "Ben Hur."

But there was nothing staged about this jamboree. Crowds started to congregate spontaneously soon after the Dodgers had won the pennant. No one, least of all the police, whose original detail of 100 had to be increased before the "never-to-be-forgotten" night was over, knew what to expect next.

Jack Pierce, said by many to be "Dodger Fan No. 1," was there, blowing up his "Cookie" balloons and tossing them from a balcony to the crowd below, where they were batted about with abandon. Pierce also donned his "jinx" mask, just in case there were any curious Giant or Yankee fans around.

Giant-Yank Fans Quiet

If there were any, they kept quiet, for the crowd, a large percentage of whom sported hilarious banners, chanted at intervals, "Four straight over the Yanks," without a dissenting vote.

It was a typical Brooklyn crowd, curiously good-natured despite its high spirits. That is, until the players got off the train. Then its joy overcame its caution, as police lines were recklessly broken.

Long before that time, members of an impromptu band which has played at Ebbets Field during games, appeared with a banner which read, "Dodger Rooters Band—Loyal Greenpoint Rooters."

They started down the staircase to the pit of the lobby, proceeding through an area set off by police. The cops forced them back, only to be met by lusty boos.

"We want the band," went up in mighty roars.

They got it. Police Inspector George W. Heitzman explained to newspapermen that they had to let the band perform when and where it felt like or the crowd would have rushed the lines then and there.

Unprecedented Celebration

"Talk about being a diplomat," another sweating officer declared. "This Brooklyn crowd has them all beaten. There's never been a celebration like this here."

In the crowd, clergy rubbed elbows with newsboys. Wives left notes for their husbands to prepare their own suppers and skipped up to Grand Central.

The kleig lights and flashlight bulbs temporarily blinded them, but they kept waving their banners.

Camilli for President

"Camilli for President," one of these motley banners modestly proclaimed.

Mayor LaGuardia and District Attorney O'Dwyer, rivals for the Mayoralty post, would have gotten a kick out of another banner, which read: "Durocher for Mayor."

At that, he probably could have gotten himself elected last night.

"The Bums Done It," and "Our Bums Won" was painted on other makeshift standards.

Copies of the Brooklyn Eagle, with its large "We Win" headline, were prominently displayed.

Throughout all the bedlam and adding to it came the half-screech, half-wail of Mr. Pierce.

"Cookie," was its theme, taken up by the fans and re-echoed throughout the station where many famous personages have returned, but none to such a mass reception.

"When are our bums coming?" the clamoring crowd wanted to know.

Then the train pulled in and the players tumbled out. There was Kirby Higbe, Ducky Medwick, Freddy Fitzsimmons, Johnny Allen, Jimmy Wasdell, Lavagetto and the rest of the crew.

They were kissed on both cheeks by males and females. Their hands were shaken. Then they ducked out of the station.

Fitzsimmons was met by his wife and daughter. Some of the other married players were met by their wives.

No Rough Stuff

Despite the enthusiasm practically no rough stuff occurred. Only one woman was observed swinging her handbag at a man whom she claimed pushed her out of the way.

Wasdell, shunted aside in the melee by a working photographer, thought he had been pushed heedlessly and threatened to swing until he was apprised of his error.

'Red' Hero, Too

One person was carried off on the shoulders of the crowd. It was not a player, but "Red" Barber, popular announcer for the Dodger games, who broadcast the arrival ceremonies.

Not in the crowd per se, but waiting at the train-side for the arrival were two fans who could not possibly be 100 percent Dodger rooters, but who showed their esteem for the game Brooklyn club. They were Mrs. John McGraw, widow of the popular pilot of the Giants, and Mrs. Lou Gehrig, widow of the baseball immortal.

When the crowd started to push, considerate cops took Salvatore Merchese, 16, of 699 Sackett St., who is small for his age, out of the line and into a safe vantage point. Salvatore has a broken arm, received in—you guessed it—a sandlot baseball game.

Boro Hotels Mobbed

The players returned to their quarters in Brooklyn, only to be met at the various hotels and private residences by more enthusiastic crowds.

Lavagetto solved one problem by keeping everybody happy. Seemingly bitten by the "kissing bug," he embraced females willy-nilly.

"He kissed me. Cookie kissed me." These words, uttered by a multitude of females, were heard over and over again.

And far, far into the night the celebrations were continued.

AFTER THE BATTLE—The Dodgers themselves, in their dressing room in Boston after that final 6—0 victory yesterday, enthusiastically relaxing.

FULTON ST. TO BE READY

Th paving of Fulton St. from F[...] Ave. to Borough Hall w[...]pleted just in time for tha[...]ade on Monday, if it is decided to route the huge victory procession along Brooklyn's main business thoroughfare. Should this be the case, it will be the first time in many, many years that Fulton St. (remember when it used to be cluttered with elevated pillars and trolley tracks?) has been chosen as the main avenue for a parade of the proportions that this one is sure to assume.

CANDIDATE READS VICTORY NEWS—District Attorney O'Dwyer, Democratic candidate for Mayor, at his home in Bay Ridge looks over a late edition of yesterday's Brooklyn Eagle and reads that the campaign is over, the returns are in and we—the Dodgers, of course—have won.

THEY CHEERED WITH MUSIC—The Greenpoint Royal Rooters at the welcome home meeting at the Grand Central with their Brooklyn Dodgers Band.

$$$$ WORTH OF BALLPLAYERS—The champion Dodgers are shown en masse in this picture made today at Ebbets Field just before their game with Philadelphia. Perched on the sod is Batboy Jackie Bodner. Bottom row, left to right, are Trainer "Doc" Wilson, Harry Lavagetto, Peewee Reese, Pete Reiser, Red Corriden, coach; Leo Durocher, Charles Dressen, coach; Kirby Higbe, Mickey Owen and Lew Riggs. Second row, left to right, Joe Medwick, Curt Davis, Tom Drake, Larry French, Whitlow Wyatt, Ed Albosta, Luke Hamlin, Newell Kimball, Billy Herman and Johnny Allen. Top row, left to right, are Hugh Casey, Dolph Camilli, George Pfister, Jimmy Wasdell, Herman Franks, Roy Spencer, Pete Coscarart, Fred Fitzsimmons, Augie Galan and Dixie Walker. Team appears confident of beating the favored Yankees in World Series starting at the Stadium on Wednesday afternoon.

BROOKLYN EAGLE

SPORTS

CLASSIFIED ADVERTISEMENTS

REAL ESTATE

SUNDAY, SEPT. 28, 1941 • SECTIONS C-D

WHIRLY AGAIN 2D--SOME CHANCE WINS

Market Wise Beat Calumet Farm Ace by Nose As Stablemate Takes $57,900 Futurity

By JOE LEE

Whirlaway took another tumble from his lofty perch at Belmont Park yesterday when he was beaten by Market Wise, but an obscure stablemate, Some Chance, took the sting out of the defeat by carrying Calumet Farm's banner to a $57,900 victory in the Belmont Futurity.

Louis Tufano's Market Wise which was purchased for $1,000 from Mrs. Dodge Sloan as a two-year-old, clipped one full second off the North American track record in the 22d running of the Jockey Club Gold Cup, covering the two miles in 3:20 4-5 to beat Whirlaway a nose at the finish in a tremendous burst of speed through the stretch which had the crowd cheering wildly right to the wire.

Belair Stud's Fenelon was third, eight lengths behind the triple crown champion, while Abbe Pierre, the only other starter, trailed the field home.

Whirlaway did not look bad in defeat, but Market Wise was just too much horse for him in the closing strides. By his victory in the Gold Cup, the three-year-old colt boosted his earnings to $57,840. In his last 22 starts he has won eight, was second three times and third six times. It is quite likely that Market Wise's next appearance under silks will be in the $50,000 New York Handicap which will climax the Autumn meeting of the Westchester Racing Association next Saturday.

Basil James, aboard Market Wise, kept his charge in third position throughout most of the race with Fenelon leading Whirlaway by a length as they passed the mile and one-half mark. As they hit the stretch, Whirlaway was on top with Market Wise right at his head. James went after Robertson in the drive for the wire and just nipped him in the final 10 yards. Market Wise paid $10.90. Whirlaway was installed the favorite by the crowd at 1-3.

Some Chance won the 52d running of the Futurity, richest stake in the world for two-year-olds. The Jones-trained racer covered the six and one-half furlongs of the Widener course in 1:16 4-5, beating Greentree Stable's Devil Diver by a half a length with Caduceus, Mrs. W. M. Jeffords' colt, third.

The chestnut colt boosted his to-

Continued on Page 5

Yanks 11-5 Choice To Defeat Dodgers

Madcap Brooklyn shoved aside ice packs and bromides today and wearily arose from its Mardi Gras celebration of the Dodgers' National League pennant victory to find that New York's Yankees are 11—5 favorites over the Beloved Brooks in the 38th World Series that begins Wednesday.

This fact failed entirely to dampen the feverish interest in this intra-city feud. If the battle goes its seven-game, best-four-for-seven limit, a new World Series attendance record probably will be set.

Early ticket sales indicated that both Yankee Stadium and Ebbets Field will be jammed to the rafters for the first four games, and that crowded conditions will continue to prevail until a decision is reached. Baseball officials freely predicted that, in case seven games are played, more than 325,051 patrons will flock through the turnstiles, that figure being the high mark attendance set in 1926, when the Yankees-Cardinals post-season engagement went the full route.

Yankee Stadium, where the opening contest and second game will be played, can accommodate as many as 80,000 spectators. Ebbets Field, scene of the third, fourth and fifth games, offers sitting, standing and squatting space for as many as 38,000. Provided more than five games are necessary, they will be played at the Stadium. The

Continued on Page 4

Flock in Confab Over Series Swag

Boys Pass Up Hitting Practice For Powwow---Leo, Gernano Agree

By HAROLD PARROTT

The Dodgers gave their financial problems a two-hour rassle in the dressing room yesterday but at 2:15 they had to come up for air—and for the Phillies. They didn't have time for hitting practice.

Only members of the team who'd been on the roster all season were eligible to vote, so Johnny Allen, Larry French, Augie Galan and even Herman Franks sat outside in the dugout—wondering.

Jackie Bodner, the batboy, was wondering, too. Tim Sullivan, Yankee batboy, was voted $500 in the 1936 series, $750 the next year, $1,000 the third season and $1,500 as the Yanks won their fourth flag in 1939.

A visitor to the Dodger clubhouse was Frank Gernano, who won a September decision over Umpire George Magerkurth at Ebbets Field last year. Gernano congratulated Durocher, and vice versa. "You were right a year ago," said Durocher.

Red Barber circulated in the pressbox — unfamiliar territory for him. He said they'd given the air away to a football game. But the

Continued on Page 4

DODGER FANS SET RECORD AT GATE

Yesterday's crowd at Ebbets Field brought the total attendance for the season in the Flatbush baseball orchard to 1,202,383. That, of course, is a new record for Brooklyn. Seventy-eight games have been played here and there is one more to go, this afternoon's finale with the Phillies, which already is a virtual sell-out so far as reserved seats are concerned.

There should be plenty of room in the unreserved sections though, because cautious fans bought their tickets early to make sure of not being shut out of a final game that might have decided the National League pennant.

Nova's Mysterious Ring Drill Stumps Experts in Camp

By HAROLD CONRAD
Brooklyn Eagle Staff Correspondent

Greenwood Lake, N. Y., Sept. 27—The blinds were pulled tight and a pale, yellow light shone through the dust in Doc Bier's stuffy gymnasium at Pompton Lakes today. It was sort of a Dr. Jekyllish background for the scientific experiment which Ray Carlen thinks may cause a change in heavyweight titleholders when Joe Louis and Lou Nova clash in their 15-round extravaganza at the Polo Grounds tomorrow night.

Carlen saw a resemblance between Louis and Light Heavyweight Champion Gus Lesnevich. He refused to make clear exactly what this resemblance is, but he decided to hold this secret workout so Nova could familiarize himself with this move that both Louis and Lesnevich are supposed to make.

Around 2 p.m. Nova, his trainer, Ray Arcel, Carlen, Lesnevich and his manager, Lew Diamond, solemnly filed into the gym. No one was allowed near the place. The great experiment took about 20 minutes. When the five men came out Nova stepped into the outdoor ring and boxed two rounds with Jim Neville. If he was trying to practice what he had just learned in the secret session it wasn't obvious.

They just sparred around for the two rounds but when it was over Carlen and Nova departed to their quarters with an air of triumph.

Continued on Page 4

College Results

LOCAL

Brooklyn College J. V. 6—Poly Prep 0
Manhattan 20—St. Bonaventure 13
N. Y. U. 25—Penn M. C. 7

EAST

Albright 14—Muhlenberg 3
Amherst 31—Bates 7
Brown 20—Wesleyan 6
Bucknell 6—Lebanon Valley 0
Buffalo 19—Susquehanna 0
City College 20—Colby 16
Coast Guard 7—Connecticut 0
Colgate 6—St. Lawrence 0
Dartmouth 35—Norwich 0
Delaware 7—West Chester Trs. 7
Geo. Washington 25—Mt. St. Mary's 0
Lehigh 13— Hartwick 13
Maryland 18—Hampden Sydney 0
Navy 34—W. and M. 0

Continued on Page 4

Keller Returns To Lineup as Yanks Bow, 4-3

Lefty Gomez's chance of a starting assignment in the coming World Series took a decided drop today as the Washington Senators belted him for five hits and four runs in the first inning, all they needed to defeat the champion New York Yankees, 4 to 3, at the Yankee Stadium.

However, Yankee World Series prospects took a big upward trend when Charley Keller, slugging outfielder, out for two weeks with a bad leg, returned to the lineup. He failed to hit safely in four trips to the plate.

George Case started the fireworks in the first by beating out a hit, stole second and scored on Welaj's single. Layne flied out but Travis and Vernon kept the base-hit barrage to score Welaj. After Ortiz walked to fill the bases, Evans singled Travis and Vernon home with what proved to be the winning runs.

Bonham and Murphy followed Gomez and kept the Senators from scoring for the remainder of the game.

After holding the Yanks scoreless for five frames, Masterson was batted out in the sixth when the Yankees scored three times, Sturm starting it with a single. Rolfe forced him, Henrich then singled. Joe DiMaggio doubled, scoring Rolfe and Henrich. It was DiMaggio's

Continued on Page 4

Braves Subdue Giants by 5-4

Boston, Sept. 27 (INS)—A Giants' ninth-inning rally failed as the Braves beat them by a score of 5 to 4 today.

The Braves got their first counter in the second inning on Waner's single and Miller's double. In the third they hopped on Harry Feldman for four runs which was enough for the Braves to hold the lead until the finish.

Going into the ninth three runs behind, the Giants hopped on Al Javery, Boston's second pitcher, and before Errickson came to his rescue

Continued on Page 4

MAJOR LEAGUE STANDINGS

National League

YESTERDAY'S RESULTS

Philadelphia 7, **Brooklyn 3.**
Boston 5, **New York 4.**
Chicago 6, St. Louis 5.
Cincinnati 15, Pittsburgh 9.

STANDING OF THE CLUBS

	W.	L.	Pct.
Brooklyn	99	54	.647
St. Louis	96	56	.632
Cincinnati	88	65	.575
Pittsburgh	80	73	.523
New York	73	79	.480
Chicago	70	83	.458
Boston	62	91	.405
Philadelphia	43	110	.281

GAMES TODAY

Philadelphia at **Brooklyn.**
New York at Boston.
Cincinnati at Pittsburgh.
St. Louis at Chicago.

American League

YESTERDAY'S RESULTS

Washington, 4; **New York, 3.**
Boston, 5; Philadelphia, 1.
Chicago, 10; Detroit, 6.
Cleveland, 4; St. Louis, 3.

STANDING OF THE CLUBS

	W.	L.	Pct.
New York	101	52	.660
Boston	83	69	.546
Chicago	76	77	.497
Detroit	75	78	.490
Cleveland	75	78	.490
St. Louis	69	84	.451
Washington	69	84	.451
Philadelphia	63	89	.414

GAMES TODAY

Washington at **New York.**
Cleveland at St. Louis.
Chicago at Detroit.
Boston at Philadelphia.

Reiser Pulls Arm Ligament In Practice; Dodgers Bow

X-Rays Ordered as Precautionary Measure, Though Pete Says Wing Is O.K.–Rookies Play in 7-3 Defeat

By TOMMY HOLMES

Something happened at Ebbets Field yesterday afternoon that hadn't happened in Brooklyn for 21 years. The Dodgers lost—the tail-end Phillies beat them, 7 to 3—and nobody cared a bit. The fighting men of Flatbush merely grinned; they had clinched the pennant two days before. A crowd of 11,806 cash customers apparently paid no attention to the game, were satisfied merely to gaze upon their heroes in their working clothes. And an hour after the game was over, half the crowd was still in the park, waiting to cheer each Brooklyn player as he left the clubhouse.

Something else happened that frightened the boys for a while. Throwing in to the home plate at the tail-end of fielding practice, Pete Reiser pulled a ligament in his right elbow. His throwing arm hurt and Pete said so.

And so Reiser was the only regular Brooklyn player who did not appear in the first absolutely carefree ball game the Dodgers have had since their stop in Port Arthur, Tex., on the Spring training trip. Panicky at the thought that the National League's batting champion might not be able to open the World Series against the Yankees, Leo Durocher immediately called for Dr. Frank Glenn, specialist from New York Hospital.

By the time Dr. Glenn arrived, Reiser said that his arm felt okay. The doctor could find nothing wrong, but ordered X-rays as a precautionary measure.

The game itself was merely an opportunity for Durocher to show his regulars to the Brooklyn fans and then ring in all the reserves he could locate. Two men in the ball game were making their first appearance before the critical Flatbush clientele. Ed Albosta, a thin rookie righthander, was Leo's starting pitcher and allowed the Phillies no hits at all until he suddenly blew up with two out in the sixth inning and the Quakers staged their game-winning five-run rally. The other was George Pfister, a boy who looked like a whale of a young catcher. Pfister's throwing to bases had the fans talking—and plenty.

Continued on Page 5

GRID DODGERS TRIM EAGLES BY 24-13 COUNT

By HAROLD PARROTT
Eagle Staff Correspondent

Philadelphia, Pa., Sept. 27—The Philly Eagles were flattened here tonight, 2—13, by the Dodgers, before 16,341 fans, in a National League game.

So was Red Friesell, football's best-known official, flattened and sent to the hospital, but by whom wasn't quite clear.

The Eagles were suspected because Friesell's "accident," which knocked him so cold that ambulance had to call for him on the Dodger 40-yard line and drag him to Temple Hospital with a fractured left leg, followed closely on three 15-yard penalties which cost the Philly outfit a second Dodger touchdown and put them behind, 14—0. Merlyn Condit, new Dodger halfback, scored every one of those 14 points.

Even with Friesell out of the way, the Eagles never dug their way out of the hole. They scored in the last few seconds of the first half to make it 14—7, but in the fourth quarter Dean McAdams kicked a 24-yard

Continued on Page 4

HAVE YOU GOT YOURS?—Here's a closeup of the tickets that will get you into Ebbets Field Friday, Saturday and Sunday. If you haven't got them, the next best thing will be reading the Brooklyn Eagle which won't miss a trick on the series.

Bridges Ruled Red, Faces Deportation

Wall Street Closing
RACING EXTRA
★★★★★★

BROOKLYN EAGLE

LOCAL WEATHER FORECAST: Partly cloudy, cooler tonight; cloudy, occasional rains tomorrow

Wall Street Closing
RACING EXTRA
★★★★★★

100th YEAR • No. 270 • DAILY AND SUNDAY • BROOKLYN, N. Y., MONDAY, SEPT. 29, 1941 • • 3 CENTS

MILLION ROAR SALUTE TO PARADING DODGERS

Bridges Ruled Red; Court Calls For Deportation

Immigration Bureau Decision Now Goes To Appeals Board

Washington, Sept. 29 (INS)—The United States Immigration Service today found that Harry Bridges, West Coast C. I. O. leader, is a member of the Communist party and ruled that because the party "advocates and teaches the overthrow" of this Government by force and violence he should be deported to his native Australia.

The decision was handed down by Judge Charles B. Sears of New York, who, acting for the Immigration Service, recently concluded lengthy hearings on the Bridges case. His decision reverses a previous one made by Dean James Landis of the Harvard Law School who, in a similar role, found that there was no evidence that the labor leader was a party member.

Appeal Is Permitted

But the decision by no means concludes the case. It now automatically goes to the Board of Immigration Appeals. If the board concurs then it will be up to Attorney General Biddle to decide whether to issue a deportation order, and, should one be issued, Bridges may then appeal to the Federal Courts.

Judge Sears' report flatly indicted the American Communist party for having as its objective the "overthrow by force and violence of the Government of the United States."

Communist Since 1920

He found that Bridges, who is president of the International Longshoreman's Union (C. I. O.) had been a member of the party since entering the United States in 1920.

Cites Violent Aims

Judge Sears found further that the Communist party, of which Bridges has been a "member," and an "affiliate," "advocates and teaches the overthrow by force and violence of the Government of the United States."

The judge's decision also cited

Continued on Page 9

Harry Bridges

ECCLES URGES LONGER WEEK, WAGE CONTROL

Sees Inflation Certain Unless Strong Teeth Are Put Into Price Bill

Washington, Sept. 29 (U.P.)—Chairman Marriner S. Eccles of the Federal Reserve Board declared today that the United States cannot escape runaway inflation without heavier taxes than those now provided and some form of control on wages and farm prices.

Eccles said also that the threat of inflation may make "advisible" the extension of the 40-hour work week to 48 hours.

Testifying on the Administration's proposed price control bill before the House Banking Committee, Eccles implied that the suggested legislation—which does not attempt to curb wages—does not go far enough.

Eccles told the committee that all strikes are "intolerable in times of national peril," since the normal national economy as well as the

Continued on Page 8

GOP Nominates Freedman for Supreme Court

To Oppose Kleinfeld —Johnston Indorsed • For Re-election

By JOSEPH H. SCHMALACKER

Republican delegates from five counties voted unanimously at their judicial convention in Brooklyn this afternoon to nominate Jacob A. Freedman of 20 Plaza St., as the G. O. P. candidate to oppose Justice Philip M. Kleinfeld in the coming Supreme Court elections.

Mr. Freedman's nomination was voted after the convention, also by a unanimous vote, had indorsed Associate Justice John B. Johnston, Democratic member of the Appellate Division, for reelection under the principle of retaining justices who have served acceptably during their terms of office.

ALP Tieup Tabooed

The convention, which met in the Appellate Term of the Brooklyn Supreme Court, functioned harmoniously after Queens and Long Island Republican leaders had received assurances that no tie-up would be attempted with the American Labor party on the G. O. P. Supreme Court slate.

Warren B. Ashmead, the Republican leader of Queens, declared that borough was happy to join in Mr. Freedman's nomination. Mr. Ashmead said he had received the assurances of John R. Crews, the Brooklyn Republican leader, that Mr. Freedman would run for the judicial office as "a Republican, and only as a Republican."

Must Give Up County Race

Mr. Freedman's selection for the Supreme Court compels him to relinquish the nomination for the Kings County Court bench which he received in the Republican primary elections. This opens the door to a possible G. O. P.-American Labor party agreement whereby a Labor party candidate may be substituted on the G. O. P. ticket for the vacancy in the County Court nomination.

If this occurs, William Stanley Miller, a justice of the Court of Special Sessions, who is now the Republican candidate for Surrogate, is expected, in return, to receive the Labor party's indorsement for the Surrogate's Court race.

Former Supreme Court Justice

Continued on Page 9

Eagle Staff photo

SALUTE TO A GREAT TEAM—Cheering fans choked the Borough Hall section to pay thunderous tribute to our Dodgers today. These loyal rooters were part of more than 1,000,000 Brooklynites paying homage.

3 CONVOY CRUISERS SUNK, ROME CLAIMS

Battleship Nelson Reported Torpedoed In Big Sea Battle

Rome, Sept. 29 (U.P.)—Italian sources reported today that Fascist warplanes and warships attacked a British convoy carrying American war supplies in the Mediterranean, sinking three cruisers, damaging four other warships including a battleship believed to be the 33,950-ton Nelson, and sinking at least three freighters.

The damage to the huge Nelson, believed to be flagship of the British Mediterranean fleet, was claimed by the newspaper Lavoro Fascista in a dispatch datelined from a "Mediterranean air base."

The Nelson is one of the most powerful battleships in the British fleet and, since the sinking of the 42,100-ton Hood, one of the biggest.

An official communique claimed that the battleship was damaged by a hit on the prow by a torpedo fired by a Fascist torpedo plane.

The British Version

[A sharply conflicting version was given in London in which the Admiralty declared that an impor-

Continued on Page 9

Nine Italian Cities, Heart of War Output Area, Bombed by RAF

Rome, Sept. 29 (U.P.)—British planes bombed nine Italian cities during the night, while other British planes bombed the Island of Rhodes off the Turkish coast, the high command said in a communique today.

Casualties were put at 23 killed and 43 wounded in all.

Genoa, Turin, Spezia, Savona and Marina were bombed in the northern industrial area. It was said that British planes flew over Milan without dropping bombs.

Palermo, Trapani, Marsala and Castelvetrano were bombed in the Sicily raid, the communique said.

Nine persons were killed and 26 wounded at Palermo, two were killed in Genoa and seven wounded, and 12 were killed in the Rhodes attack, according to the communique.

The other casualties were indirect ones. Four persons were wounded at Spezia, a naval base on the Gulf of Genoa, by anti-aircraft shell fragments. At Milan, where it was said no bombs were dropped,

Continued on Page 9

SPY SURVEYED BORO SHIPPING, G-MAN TESTIFIES

Suspect Compiled Data On Machinery, Tools Being Loaded at Piers

FBI Agent Gordon R. Granthan testified in the Brooklyn Federal Court spy trial today to a survey of shipping at the Brooklyn waterfront, between Fulton and Amity Sts., made last Feb. 20 by Felix Jahnke.

Jahnke, one of 17 German spies who have pleaded guilty and are awaiting sentence, lived in a top-floor apartment at 563 Caldwell Ave., the Bronx, with Axel Wheeler-Hill. The latter is one of the 16 defendants on trial. In his apartment FBI agents seized a short wave transmitter that allegedly was used by the spy ring for communicating with the Nazis.

Wheeler-Hill himself made a shipping survey of the Brooklyn

Continued on Page 9

Marching Throngs Go Wild, Scream 'Murder the Yanks'

Dodgerville tossed aside its dignity today and in an enthusiastic outburst of triumphant bands, flying banners and deep-throated cheers, saluted our great baseball heroes in Brooklyn's largest parade since the Armistice.

A voluble, proud army of more than 60,000 men, women and children, bright in every color of the rainbow, marched from Grand Army Plaza, with the National League champions near the front in automobiles, while cheering crowds packed the sidewalks, hurled confetti and screamed: "Murder those Yankees!"

As the crowds jammed the streets earlier police estimates were quickly revised and police declared that easily more than 1,000,000 men, women and children greeted the champions. Police officials said the reception by far exceeded that given to Wrong-Way Corrigan, the ocean flier.

As the crowds along Flatbush Ave. and Fulton St., caught sight of Durocher, Reiser, Reese, of Medwick, Wyatt, Higbe, of Camilli, Fitzsimmons, Owen, they shouted their tribute, waved flags and tooted horns.

Nobody in that mass of men, women and children cared a whit about any notables. What notable could match a Dodger?

The kids howled their adoration and the Dodgers waved back, gulping at the grand reception. At that, it was difficult to place the adults and the youngsters in separate divisions—everybody was young and everybody was hailing the champs.

Marching, dancing, the scheduled line of 12 abreast sometimes erupted into 15 and 20 as emotional fans burst through the police lines to join the triumphant procession.

At the head of the cavalcade was a band of mounted policemen, their horses prancing to the sound of horns, trumpets and drums. The cops laughed and sometimes joined in the hurrahs, pointing to the many banners on the streets which exhorted, "Beat the Yankees!"

As the parade swung by Bergen St., patrolmen from Police Headquarters had a tough time restraining some of the police reporters who almost forgot they were assigned to cover that part of the line of march.

Banker and bartender slapped

Continued on Page 9

Moscow Won't Risk A Kopek on the Yanks

Even Lord Beaverbrook's a Dodger Fan On Gorki St. (Bedford Ave. to You)

Moscow, Sept. 29 (INS)—Even Moscow stands behind the incredible Brooklyn Dodgers . . . and you can take that from no less an authority than Quentin Reynolds, Flatbush resident and noted war correspondent, long a sports writer and now representative of Collier's Magazine.

Reynolds told International News Service in an interview today that he couldn't find a single kopek of Yankee money among the huge corps of delegates to the three-power arms conference under way here.

"The day the series opens," Reynolds said, "I'm going to take my stand outside a newspaper kiosk and wait for my copy of the Vechernaya Moskva.

"This stand will be on Gorki St.—the Bedford Ave. of Moscow. I won't care how long I have to wait because I will make believe I am standing in line outside Ebbets Field waiting to get in and see the Dodgers murder those Yanks.

"When the three-power conference got together here it had to cease all activity last Thursday night to celebrate the magnificent victory of my Dodgers. I have done my best but unfortunately everyone on the mission, including W. Averell Harriman and Lord Beaverbrook are Dodger fans and I haven't been able to get a single bet down.

"When the Dodgers finish off the Yankees, please ask Larry MacPhail to bring them over here. This is a place for real fighting men."

Louis Spots Challenger 1/4 Lb. in Bout Tonight

By HAROLD CONRAD

Dr. William Walker poked his stethoscope at the chests of Joe Louis and Lou Nova today and pronounced the champ and challenger in perfect shape for their 15-round title battle at the Polo Grounds tonight. Louis scaled 202¼, the heaviest he has ever weighed for a titular match. Nova weighed 202½.

The weighing-in ceremonies were held in Madison Square Garden instead of the Boxing Commission offices and a couple of thousand people clogged the streets outside of the Garden. Only newspapermen and photographers were admitted to the weigh-in, but there were 450 of them.

Louis and his seconds were the first to arrive, having motored in from Greenwood Lake training camp. Joe wore a snappy green sports coat, green hat and a light tan topcoat. Nova strolled in a few minutes later with his brain trust, wearing a blue sports coat and an open-necked shirt with no tie.

The fighters traded brief hellos. Nova seemed to be calm and extremely confident, but his blood pressure indicated he was under a nervous strain.

It was announced that Julian Black, the champ's manager; Jack Blackburn, his chief trainer, and Manny Seamon, his assistant trainer, would be in the Bomber's corner tonight. Nova will have in his corner his manager, Ray Carlen; his trainer, Ray Arcel, and Bobby Dawson and Jimmy August as assistants.

The betting hovered around 13 to 5, give or take a point, with Louis favorite. Promoter Mike Jacobs continued to do a land office business with his ticket sales and he was confident the gate would reach the $600,000 mark with a crowd of 65,000.

Cool and cloudy weather was forecast. In the event rain forces a postponement, the fight will be held Wednesday night.

Panto Case Enters Lepke Juror Quiz

The name of murdered Pete Panto, longshoreman labor leader whose body was found imbedded in quicklime several months ago in Lyndhurst, N. J., today crept into the questioning of a talesman in the first degree murder trial in County Court of Louis (Lepke) Buchalter, Emanuel (Mendy) Weiss and Louis Capone.

The prospective juror, Benjamin Protter, a writer of European affairs, who lives at 772 Linden Boulevard, is a brother of Marcy Protter, labor lawyer who headed the committee probe which resulted in the finding of Panto's body. The quizzing by one of the defense attorneys continued until the lunch recess.

District Attorney O'Dwyer some time ago declared that in his opinion Panto's murder was perpetrated by Weiss.

The prospective juror said he never discussed the case with his brother.

It Happened In Brooklyn

MAN HELD FOR TRIAL ON OPIUM CHARGE

William D'Ambrosia, 43, of 464 Nostrand Ave. was held for trial when arraigned today before Magistrate Solomon in Brooklyn Felony Court accused of possessing opium and a hypodermic needle. After D'Ambrosia was taken to Kings County Hospital Sept. 21 suffering from an overdose of narcotics, police said they found the drug and needle in his home.

5 FIREMEN OVERCOME IN SYNAGOGUE BLAZE

Five firemen were overcome in a one-alarm, smoky fire which broke out at 11 a.m. today in the basement of the Temple Auditorium, a Jewish synagogue at 251 Rochester Ave., in the East New York section.

DODGER TICKET 'SPEC' WINS COURT'S SYMPATHY

Thomas Dunne, 24, of 1949 E. 15th St., alleged to have offered for sale four tickets to the Dodger-Phillies baseball game in the street near Ebbets Field, yesterday, was charged with disorderly conduct in the Brooklyn-Queens Night Court. The complaint was made by Patrolman Andrew Langert of the 12th Division office.

Dunne told Magistrate Henry Soffer that he had purchased the tickets for three friends and himself and that when the friends failed to put in an appearance he decided to sell the tickets. The magistrate, indicating that he believed his story, fined him $5, with the alternative of spending a day in jail, then suspended application of the penalty.

Additional News Briefs on Page 9.

Rockingham Park Results

FIRST RACE—Four-year-olds and up; three-quarters mile.

Maetown (Jedlinski)	8.80	4.20	4.00
Whodunit (Krovitz)	—	9.40	6.80
Woof (Harrell)	—	—	7.60

Time, 1:14. Skeeter, Maefleet, Blossom Queen, Joy Bet, Wulfstan, Ugin, Claro also ran. Off time, 1:20½.

SECOND RACE—Four-year-olds and up; three-quarters mile.

Maeline (Taylor)	3.80	3.00	2.40
Judfry (Hettinger)	—	8.40	4.40
All Time High (Daniels)	—	—	3.00

Time, 1:13 3-5. Bully Time, Tetratown, Miss Co-Ed, Savant also ran. Off time, 1:50.

DAILY DOUBLE PAID $13.00

THIRD RACE—Four-year-olds and up; three-quarters mile.

Black Look (Atkinson)	3.40	2.80	2.40
Baba (Connolly)	—	5.40	3.40
Minstrel Wit (Woolfe)	—	—	2.60

Time, 1:14. Blackbirder, Flosilda, Dovie Lou, Liberty Torch also ran. Off time, 2:19.

Belmont Park Results

FIRST RACE—Four-year-olds and up; seven-eighths mile.

Sun Galomar (Young)	13.40	7.60	5.50
xMaydig (James)	—	7.90	5.60
Noroton (Hildebrant)	—	—	10.70

Time, 1:25 3-5. Hi-Kid, Galvale, Fortification, Peter Porter, Rissa, Gallant Stroke, Ara-Ornis, Abmeres, Ken's Pop, xArmagnac, xAttracting also ran. Off time, 2:06½.

xField.

SECOND RACE—Two-year-olds; three-quarters mile.

Silver Grail (James)	6.80	4.10	3.30
Burgaway (Skelly)	—	26.40	12.10
Sound Effect (May)	—	—	5.00

Time, 1:12 2-5. Magician, Brave Friar, Topless Tower, York River, Little Pitcher, Plantagenet, Star Quest, Philharmonic also ran. Off time, 2:38.

DAILY DOUBLE PAID $38.10

Hawthorne Results

FIRST RACE—3-year-olds and up ¾ mile.

Wonana (Wielander)	7.20	3.80	2.60
Hour Al (Martin)	—	9.00	4.20
Myrica (Brooks)	—	—	2.20

Time, 1:13 3-5. Brave Up, Mr. Mais, Black John, Fairab, Stray Chord, Turkey Hash, Sally I, Fair Jule, Tea Gossip, also ran. Off time, 2:21½.

WHERE TO FIND IT IN TODAY'S EAGLE

Bridge	Page 21	Neighborhood News	Page 9
Comics	Page 18	Novel	Page 21
Crossword	Page 20	OBITUARIES	Page 11
Dr. Brady	Page 18	Only Yesterday	Page 17
EDITORIAL	Page 10	Pattern	Page 17
Events Tonight	Page 22	RADIO	Page 18
Financial	Page 8	Real Estate	Page 21
Grin and Bear It	Page 10	Sermons	Page 22
Harold Conrad	Page 4	Society	Page 6
Harold Parrott	Page 15	SPORTS	Pages 13-14-15-16
Heffernan	Page 17	Theaters	Page 4
Helen Worth	Page 17	These Women	Page 4
Horoscope	Page 17	Tucker	Page 10
Jimmy Wood	Page 13	Uncle Ray's Corner	Page 17
Movies	Page 4	Want Ads	Pages 19-20-21
		Woman's	Page 7

Bleacher Scene at Yankee Stadium as Umpire Called, "Play Ball!"

Eagle Staff photo

Ebinger Delivers Own Pastries as Drivers Strike

Head of Baking Firm Chauffeurs Truck—3,000 Out in City

Walter D. Ebinger, president of the Ebinger Baking Company, today drove a truck out of the firm's main building at Bedford Ave. and Albemarle Road as his 14 drivers walked out in a city-wide strike called by Local 802 of the Teamsters Union A. F. L.

Driving truck No. 13, the company head delivered pastries to stores at Tilden and Flatbush Aves., Flatbush Ave. near Dorchester Road and Flatbush Ave. near Newkirk Ave.

Mr. Ebinger, after making the deliveries, returned perspiring, to the main building. He announced that the 52 company stores would have no pastries tomorrow and that his bakers had been sent home pending settlement of the dispute.

Claims 3,000 on Strike

Paul J. Sullivan, president of the local, declared that 194 baking concerns throughout the city were affected by the strike, with 3,000 union members responding to the strike call.

He said the men had been getting $42 minimum a week, plus $6 commission for receipts over $300, and that they sought a minimum of $45 a week, plus $8 commission.

70,000 Jam Park in Opener

Continued from Page 1

prised at all the mystery and reporting that Rolfe and Keller were fit and, yes, that Ruffing would pitch.

There was no sign of the Dodgers and it was rumored they weren't in their dressing room at all but had failed to show up.

The Brooklyn cavalcade was definitely on the scene, however. It roared up with a motorcycle escort shortly before 11. The big busload had been delayed for 20 minutes before leaving the Hotel New Yorker because Secretary John McDonald overslept.

See Davis On Mound

The driver who piloted Brooklyn's precious busload up to the Bronx stated authoritatively that Curt Davis would pitch. Davis just looked wise and said nothing. He never says anything, anyway. His fellow Dodgers call the big hunter from Utah "Daniel Boone."

At 11 o'clock the bleachers and $2.30 unreserved seats upstairs were packed, with hot-dog hawkers doing a land-office business as lunch time neared.

Although the noise and shouts and clatter from upstairs set up a continual din, there was hardly a soul in the mezzanine or grandstand. It was like sitting in an empty house with a haunted attic.

Diamond in Top Shape

Workmen rolled the canvas off the infield shortly after 11 o'clock. The diamond seemed in tip-top shape. A band parked in left center struck up a tune as the first Yankee heads bobbed out of their dugout at 11:22.

Charley Keller, the King Kong Yankee, came up with an armful of baseballs and tossed them out on the mound. Dodger supporters booed lustily, but Yankee cheers matched them, decibel for decibel, this time.

Johnny Schulte, the coach, started to pitch as Stan Bordagaray, ye olde Dodger, was the first to take his practice swings. He was the nearest thing to a bona fide Dodger the fans had seen all morning, and they cheered him lustily.

Yanks Bombard Stands

As the Dodgers appeared at four minutes before noon the Yankees began to pump homers into the bleachers, as if to instill terror into Dodger hearts. Twink Selkirk hit the first. Then almost every Yankee hit one. The third-string catcher, George Pfister, was the first Dodger to show his head, and Herman Franks and Kirby Higbe were right behind him.

The boos that greeted the Flatbush flock proved beyond a doubt that Dodger fans didn't outnumber Yank adherents.

On his way to the dugout Wyatt stopped to chat with Bill Dickey, who sent him some fishing plugs after the All-Star game in Detroit.

"That Dickey's the finest fisherman I've ever seen," Wyatt told us. He might have added he hoped Bill would go fishing for that curve of his at the plate when he pitches tomorrow.

Instead, the Dodger ace only grinned and said, "He's one of the finest fellows in baseball and a great hitter."

Yankee redhots booed lustily when the Durocher men ran on the field. Then the Dodger rooters came to life with an answering roar.

Two hours before game time the bleachers and upper tier seats were completely sold. One somewhat disconsolate gentleman remarked he had shelled out $6 for "a standing room" ticket.

In the upper grandstand three rabid Dodgers fans from Somerville, N. J., encamped at Section 10 with a huge banner in tribute to "Dem Bums." They were Gerald Neesen, Frank Paternoster and Tolin Bisso, all garage workers.

Baseball, like love, is something you don't have to understand to enjoy. Two lithe things in their early teens wandered about the upper tiers looking for seats and asking every usher where home plate was. They confessed they knew nothing of baseball but came for the fun of it.

Arriving between 12 and 12:30 were Mrs. Durocher, Nellie Durocher, Jean Wanamaker, Larry MacPhail's secretary; Mrs. Fred Fitzsimmons, Helen Fitzsimmons and Mrs. Joe Medwick.

Today is Mrs. Fitzsimmons' birthday and she hopes it's a good luck sign. To be sure she wore the 255-win pin awarded Fred at Ebbets Field last year, her good luck pin.

Mrs. Durocher sat in a box behind Larry MacPhail, next to the Dodgers' dugout. Mrs. Durocher looked stunning in a violet turban, with a high crown of mink, a black dress and gorgeous orchid. She carried a mink coat and wore her good luck pin, a jeweled bird. "Keep 'em flying and bring home the pennant," she said.

Larry MacPhail was a page out of Esquire—a symphony in brown—as he took his box seat beside the Dodgers' dugout.

His guest was Branch Rickey of the Cards.

"I'm rooting for Brooklyn today. I think it's a hot team; it's ready," said Rickey.

SURE, HE WAS THERE!—Just one of those lads from the Bronx who think the Yanks have a chance.

Our Fans Take Over Stadium

Continued from Page 1

and planted his fedora on the dugout roof.

Fusilleers Blare Forth

The initial burst of music of the day came shortly after 9 when the Flushing Fusilleers, a honky tonk band, blared forth.

The five members, Louis Mannellino and John Tinney, drummers; Joe Darberi and James Mannellino, trombonists, and Angelso Alvarella, cymbals, had waited on the bleacher line since 5 this morning.

California Rooters

Something akin to the long-distance record for Dodger rooting went to young George Robert Roxburgh of San Diego, Cal. He came all the way across the continent with most of the members of the American Legion's junior baseball championship team.

Roxburgh, who helped pitch his team to the Legion's championship, occupied a seat in the lower grandstand with young James S. Kennerly, a teammate and also from San Diego.

Sentiment among the out-of-towners was heavily for Brooklyn. "Brooklyn? I certainly am rooting for the Dodgers," Sherwood Shumaker of Winston-Salem said emphatically. "I've come 600 miles to see this."

Mr. Shumaker identified himself as a main office associate of the R. J. Reynolds Tobacco Company.

Fans for 25 Years

From Richmond, Va., came Mr. and Mrs. Charles B. Lake.

"Mrs. Lake and I have been going to World Series games for 25 or 30 years," said Mr. Lake, who is assistant to the president of the Chesapeake & Ohio Railroad.

Mr. Lake voiced a fine degree of impartiality when the Brooklyn Eagle's agent asked him to pick the likely series winner.

"The Yankees have the class, as I see it, and Brooklyn has the spirit, the momentum."

Mr. and Mrs. Lake will be at Ebbets Field when the series moves to Brooklyn.

Four out of the first five fans waiting in line at the bleacher gate of the Stadium were Dodger fans. One of them, Pat Alvarello, 20-year-old machinist of 2361 Atlantic Ave., said: "I been to Philadelphia and I been to Boston with the Dodgers. I say we're in."

RROADWAY ROSE GETS 30 DAYS FOR 'PUTTING BITE' ON ENTERTAINERS

Ann (Broadway Rose) Dym, who lives at Grafton St., in the Brownsville section, today was sentenced to 30 days in jail—with no alternative of a fine—in West Side Court, Manhattan, after her conviction on a disorderly conduct charge.

The notorious panhandler was arrested last night in front of a restaurant at 1624 Broadway, Manhattan, where Patrolman Louis Unger of the W. 54th St. station, charged that Broadway Rose was grabbing prominent entertainers by the arm and "annoying them until they gave her some dough."

The Game in Detail

FIRST INNING—Walker came up amid a great ovation. Dixie looked at two balls that were low. A third ball was waist high and outside. The next was also a ball and Walker walked on four straight pitches. Herman hit the first pitch to Rolfe, who tossed him out, Walker moving into second. Reiser went after the first pitch and skied to DiMaggio, Walker remaining glued to second. Camilli swung murderously and missed for a strike. The next was a ball, high and wide. Ball two was low. Camilli took another vicious swing and missed for a second strike. Dolph made another swish in vain and sat down on strikes.

No runs, no hits, no errors, one left.

Sturm gazed at a strike through the middle. Sturm tagged the second pitch over Lavagetto's head for a single. Rolf took a wide ball. Davis made a vain attempt to pick Sturm off first. Another ball was waist high and wide. Rolfe hit to Camilli and Dolph whipped the ball to Reese for the putout on a close play. Henrich ignored a curve around his knees for a strike. Henrich forced Rolfe, Herman to Reese, the relay to Camilli not being in time for a double play. DiMaggio received a big hand as he strolled up to the plate. He took a high one outside for a ball. Joe cut at the next and fouled down the first-base line. DiMaggio flied to Medwick near the foul line.

No runs, one hit, no errors, one left.

Second Inning—Medwick swung and missed the first pitch and fouled off the next for a second strike. Ruffing wasted one outside for a ball. Joe cut at a curve ball and missed for strike three. Lavagetto belted a long foul into the right field stands. Cookie made a vain lunge at the next for a second strike. Lavagetto made Ruzzuto go to his left to get his bounder and hurl him out. Reese jumped away from an inside pitch for Ball 1. Peewee looked at one through the middle for a strike. A second strike resulted from a foul into the stands. A second ball was in close. Reese skied to Keller.

Nno runs, no hits, no errors, none left.

Keller gazed at a ball knee high and wide. A second ball was well outside. Charley sent a towering fly to Reiser Dickey bashed the first pitch to Herman, who retired him at first. Gordon let a strike clip the outside corner. The count leveled with a ball low and outside. Joe fouled off a second strike. Ball two was close and knee high. Gordon fouled down the third base line. And another into the stands. A third foul went into the stands and there was a wild scramble for the souvenir. Gordon got off a prodigious home run into the left field stands for a home run, the first of the series. It was a 370-foot drive. Rizzuto made Medwick circle a couple of times to gather in his fly.

One run, one hit, no errors, none left.

THIRD INNING—Owen elected to look at the first and it was a called strike. The count went to two strikes via a foul into the stands. Ruffing's half speeder was a ball low and outside. Mickey lofted to Keller. Davis was loudly cheered as he stepped to the plate and had a strke called. Keller also collared Davis' lift. Walker made it the third putout by taking Dixie's hoist after a ten-yard run near the foul line.

No runs, no hits, no errors, none left.

Ruffing also got a big hand as he came to the plate. Davis shot a curve across for a strike and Red swung and missed a sinker for a second. The next serve was a wide ball. Ruffing was turned back, Reese to Camilli. Sturm looked at a strike and a ball from which he had to jump away. Ball two just missed the inside corner. Sturm went out, Camilli to Davis, who covered first. Rolfe cut at the first and he fouled for a strike. A second strike was the outcome of another foul. Rolfe shot a long foul into the right field stands. Ball one was high and wide. Rolfe checked his swing at an outside pitch and it was a second ball. Rolfe went down swinging on strikes.

No runs, no hits, no errors, none left.

FOURTH INNING—Herman let a strike sail by and Billy fouled off the next attempting to bunt for a second strike. The ensuing pitch was a ball that was high. Herman hit three fouls in succession and smashed to Rizzuto, who pegged him out. Reiser took a called strike and fouled down the left-field line for a second strike. A high inside ball drove Pete back. A change of pace missed the target for ball two. Reiser took a mean cut and tipped it for a foul and Dickey held onto the ball for a strikeout. Camilli went after the first pitch and fouled it off. Dolph let a second strike curve in there. Camilli went for a fast ball up around his shoulders, missed and struck out for his second time.

No runs, no hits, no errors, none left.

Henrich gazed at a strike and Tommy then popped to Reese. DiMaggio got off a 370-foot drive to left field and Medwick leaped up against the fence and made a spectacular spear of the drive. Joe fell turfward with the ball in his gloved hand and the crowd went wild with excitement. Keller took a strike and ball. Charley went all the way around trying to connect with a sinker and a second strike was the decision. Keller two missed the outside corner. Ball three made Keller fall back. Ball four was outside and Keller walked. It was the first pass issued by Davis. Davis tried to pick Keller off first but it was no soap. Dckey doubled off the fence in center, 407 feet away. Keller, who was on his way with the pitch, scored standing up. Gordon was intentionally passed. Rizzuto looked at a ball and bounced out, Herman to Camilli.

One run, one hit, no errors, two left.

FIFTH INNING—Medwick got another generous clapping when he came up and immediately looked at a ball. Joe poked a fly to left center and DiMaggio hauled it in. Lavagetto also hoisted to DiMaggio off the first pitch. Reese let a ball down the middle go by for a strike. Peewee lined over Gordon's head for the Brooks first hit. Owen had a strike and fouled for a second. Ball one missed the outside corner. Owen tripled between Keller and DiMaggio, Reese scoring. Owen made it at third with a headlong slide. Davis went gunning for the first and fouled it off. Curt looked at a ball and then grounded to Rizzuto, who whipped him out.

One run, two hits, no errors, one left.

Ruffing looked at an inside strike and a ball outside. Red lifted to Reiser. Sturm took a pitch inside near the hands for a ball and a fast ball above the knees for a strike. Sturm broke his bat bounding out to Herman. Rolfe let a fast ball sail by for a strike. Rolfe pasted an overhand curve ball into center for a single. Henrich flied deep to Walker.

No runs, one hit, no errors, one left.

U. S. AND CANADIAN FLIERS LIKE DODGERS

London, Oct. 1 (U.P.)—Eight radios today broadcast a play-by-play account of the first game of the World Series.

Interest in the series is widespread in Britain, but particularly heavy in the air forces, because of the American Eagle Squadron and the Royal Canadian Air Force.

The Eagle Squadron has so much money down on Brooklyn that the Yankees are only 4 to 3 favorites. The Canadian also backed the Dodgers with pounds, shilings and even pence.

Manilla, Oct. 1 (U.P.)—Soldiers and sailors were forgetting about raid raid drills today until the Yankees and the Dodgers settle their World Series.

Tokio reported that Japanese sports writers had polled their reders and found they liked the Yankees, 2 to 1.

Reds Ridicule Reports Of Peace Overtures

Moscow, Oct. 1 (U.P.)—Soviet spokesman S. A. Lozovsky today ridiculed Italian and German reports that Russia had made peace overtures to the Axis as committees of the tri-Power conference began a new day of planning fast and effective materiel aid to the Russian army and navy.

British and American circles regarded the reports of Russian peace feelers as efforts to sabotage the conference by arousing their suspicions that material sent to Russia might be wasted if the Soviet made peace with Hitler.

Three Students Injured In School Race Battle

Detroit, Oct. 1 (U.P.)—Three students of Lincoln High School in suburban Ferndale were injured today in fighting between white and Negro youths.

Ferndale police reported that one wihte boy was cut so seriously that hospitalization was required. Two others, they said, were painfully mauled. The trouble started yesterday, police sad, when two white and two Negro boys scuffled after school. The Negro boys returned today supported by a larger group of their friends and the fight started.

Davis Knocked Out in the 6th

Continued from Page 1

to left field for a clean single. Rolfe rapped a grounder down to Camilli and the able first baseman's snap throw to second just did reach Peewee Reese in time for a force play.

Rolfe in turn was forced at second on Henrich's grounder to Herman. And then Davis induced the great DiMaggio to lift a high, easy fly to Medwick in left.

Medwick opened the Dodger second by waving vaguely at a high third strike. Rizzuto, the stocky Yank shorstop from Richmond Hill, made a neat stop behind second and threw out Lavagetto. Reese flied to Keller and that was that.

Davis, working smoothly, got the first two Yankees out in the second, then the first explosion of the Bronx Bombers came without warning.

Homer in Left Field Stands

Gordon's homer sailed high and hard into the lower left field stands, just inside the foul line and about ten rows high.

Rizzuto followed with a hard hit ball in the same direction but Medwick went back and made the catch near the fence.

Three successive flies to Keller in left field finished the Dodgers in the third. That made it four straight putouts for the Yankee left fielder. In the Yankee third the Bombers expired painlessly, Rolfe becoming the first Series strikeout victim of Davis.

Dodgers Hitless in Fourth

Again the Dodgers went hitless in the fourth, Ruffing striking out Reiser and Camilli in most discouraging fashion.

The most spectacular play of the day occurred with one out in the Yankee fourth. DiMaggio hit one solidly and the ball sailed out toward the left field stands. At the base of the fence, Medwick waited for what seemed an interminable period.

Just as the ball sailed within reach of the customers, Medwick leaped, speared it with his glove, rebounded off the wall, fell to the turf, rolled over once, then stuck up his glove to show that he still had the ball. It was a terrific catch and brought down the house.

But that was merely a prelude to more misery for the Dodgers. Keller walked and Bill Dickey whacked a long double off the wall in right center, Keller scoring the second New York run before the ball could be returned to the infield.

Gordon was purposely passed, then Rizzuto grounded to Herman to end the inning.

Finally with two out in the fifth came the first Dodger hit—a neat line single Peewee Reese plunked in right center. And that was swiftly followed by the first Dodger run.

Fiery Mickey Owen delivered the wallop, a hard low liner to left center. DiMaggio raced over and stopped the ball with a backhand thrust of his gloved hand, but then overran it. Reese was over the plate and Owen slid safely into third for a triple by the time the Yanks had the situation in hand. But Mickey died on third as Rizzuto threw out Davis.

At noon the field was cluttered with newspapermen, photographers and assorted celebrities. The Yankees were taking batting practice and the sun was breaking through the overcast skies before the Dodgers ended their clubhouse meeting and ambled out on the field.

Well in the van was lean, spare Curt Davis, veteran right hander, who had just been told to go to work.

Roar Greets Dodgers

Brooklyn supporters greeted the Dodgers with a resounding roar and there were just enough New York boos mixed in to make the scrappy National League champions feel at home.

Just before 12:30 Babe Ruth, the magnificent old slugger whose bat virtually built the Yankee Stadium, entered a third base box, was immediately recognized, received a cheer and then the Dodgers went to work.

Luke Hamlin started pitching and the first batter to face him was Durocher himself. The most encouraging signs of the early drill were two successive smashes Camilli parked in the rightfield stands.

After Hamlin flipped for 15 minutes, Ed Albosta, rookie righthander, stepped in to feed them to the Brooklyn maulers.

Durocher, who persistently declined to pose with other managers in the course of the regular season, willingly permitted photographers to lead him over to shake hands with McCarthy.

"You're one man I am glad to see," said the Lip, and McCarthy merely grinned his Irish grin.

Mayor LaGuardia walked across the field to great Baseball Commissioner Landis. Ruffing came out to warm up for the Yanks and only then did Durocher reveal that Davis would start.

Boy's 40-Foot Climb Maroons Him for Hour

Uncle Clambers Up Rocks to the Rescue And Firemen's Aerial Ladder Saves Both

Eight-year-old Richard A. Brown of 427 Linden Boulevard went on a climbing spree today and was marooned for one hour and ten minutes before a fire company's aerial ladder rescued him.

Richard and his mother, Mrs. Celia Brown were visiting his grandmother, Mrs. Esther Horowitz, of 1793 Riverside Drive, Manhattan.

At 10:30 a.m. the boy and his aunt, Mrs. Sarah Sands, of 3395 Sedgwick Ave., Manhattan, went for a walk on the drive. While Mrs. Sands sat on a bench, Richard began to climb the rocks at the rear of the Cloisters at Fort Tryon Park.

Having ascended 40 feet, Richard suddenly discovered that he could not descend. He began to yell.

Mrs. Sands ran to get help and brought back her brother Sidney Horowitz, 28. Horowitz managed to reach Richard but he, too, could not descend.

Hook & Ladder Co. No. 36, commanded by Lt. William McNulty, solved their dilemma. The firemen erected their aerial ladder and brought the two safely to the ground.

Casey Fails Fitz, Blowing Two Plays

Freddie's Patient Coaching Forgotten by Relief Man

HAROLD PARROTT

Inside angle on the two-run eighth inning the Yankees put together on Hugh Casey yesterday was the two plays the 200-pound pitcher "blew" completely.

One was Henrich's pulled ball between first and second which Camilli stabbed at but Coscarart came over and got. When Pete came up with the ball he found Casey hadn't started for the mound in time, wasn't covering the bag.

It was ironic that old Fred Fitzsimmons, master-fielder and tutor of the Dodger pitchers, should see the younger Casey, whom he is always exhorting to hustle and work, start to blow his ball game that way.

But that wasn't all.

With Rolfe (who had also singled) on second and Henrich on first, Casey went to 3 and 2 with DiMaggio. As Hugh stood on the nound, Pete Coscarart, who had een playing almost directly beind second, cut in toward the bag. t was a play. Casey was supposed o step back, wheel and pick Rolfe ff. Rolfe seemed to be moving oward third, and might have been rapped.

Ierry-Go-Round Is On

But Casey didn't step back. He itched, DiMaggio rapped the ball to center (the third of the four traight hits off Casey that inning) nd the merry-go-round was on. olfe, under way, scored easily on at one.

Why didn't Casey turn and throw second? Did he miss the signal? idn't he hear the Dodger shouts om the bench?

Casey knew the answers, but we idn't have the heart to ask the eorgian, who sat in front of his cker in abject misery after the ame. It was ironic that Casey resses with his back to Fitzsimons.

"We would have won, 1 to 0, if itz could have stayed in there,"

Continued on Page 4

OFFICIAL FIGURES, STANDING, SCHEDULE

STANDING

	W.	L.	Pct.
New York Yankees (A. L.)	2	1	.667
Brooklyn Dodgers (N. L.)	1	2	.333

RESULTS

First game (at Yankee Stadium, Oct. 1):

		R.	H.	E.
Dodgers	0 0 0 0 1 0 1 0 0	2	6	0
Yankees	0 1 0 1 0 1 0 0 x	3	6	1

Batteries—Davis, Casey, Allen and Owen, Franks; Ruffing and Dickey.

Second game (at Yankee Stadium, Oct. 2):

		R.	H.	E.
Dodgers	0 0 0 0 2 1 0 0 0	3	6	2
Yankees	0 1 1 0 0 0 0 0 0	2	9	1

Batteries—Wyatt and Owen; Chandler, Murphy and Dickey, Rosar.

Third game (at Ebbets Field, Oct. 4):

		R.	H.	E.
Yankees	0 0 0 0 0 0 0 2 0	2	8	0
Dodgers	0 0 0 0 0 0 0 1 0	1	4	0

Batteries—Russo and Dickey; Fitzsimmons, Casey, French, Allen and Owen.

SCHEDULE

Fourth and fifth games at Ebbets Field, Sunday and Monday, Oct. 5 and 6.

Sixth and seventh games (if necessary) at Yankee Stadium, Tuesday, Oct. 7 and Thursday, Oct. 9.

THIRD GAMES TOTALS

	1941	1940
Attendance (pd)	33,100	52,877
Receipts	$158,844.00	$219,151.00
Players' share	81,010.44	111,767.01
Clubs' share	27,003.48	37,255.67
Leagues' share	27,003.48	37,255.67
Commission share	23,826.60	32,872.65

TOTAL FOR THREE GAMES

	1941	1940
Attendance (pd)	167,888	115,310
Receipts	$684,444.00	$511,693.10
Players' share	349,066.44	260,963.48
Clubs' share	143,358.96	86,987.83
Leagues' share	143,358.96	86,987.83
Commission share	102,666.60	76,752.96

Higbe to Face Donald in 4th Contest Today

Kirby Called Turn Last Winter but Thought He'd Oppose Feller

By HAROLD PARROTT

Higbe vs. Donald!

That's the pitching setup for the fourth game of this World Series at Ebbets Field today.

It will give the chin-up, swaggering, devil-may-care little Carolinian, Higbe, his first chance to pitch in a World Series—a chance he has been looking forward to since last Winter when Larry MacPhail snagged him from the Phils for $100,000 cash. He said then he'd pitch against—and beat—Bob Feller in the World Series.

If Kirby can beat Atley Donald today, he'll be more than satisfied.

Experts have been saying for a month that Higbe will be courting decapitation if he lays that fast one within reaching distance of the Yankee bats. It's reasoned that the Yanks love fast-ballers (Higbe has no change of pace) and that he wouldn't have won 15 games in the other league, although he won 22, lost 9 in the National League.

Dodger players to whom we talked last night don't agree with this. "If Higbe's curve ball is working, he will pitch as well as Wyatt and Fitz against the Yanks," said one. "If he gets into a hole with that fast one, he can make them hit into double plays with that hook, for it really explodes. But to do this he has to have control. He isn't worth a nickel out there without his control."

Durocher himself echoed this. "I don't know where the idea came from that Higbe hasn't a curve," said Leo. "He has, and it's a dandy. It bothered the Yanks last Spring and it will bother them tomorrow."

Higbe was just two innings short of being a 300-inning pitcher for the Dodgers this year. He fanned 123 men (Wyatt whiffed 177) but walked

Continued on Page 5

Now for Our Sunday Punch!

Continued from Page 1-A

She regained her composure after a fit of weeping.

Meanwhile, the injured pitcher was removed to the clubhouse and big Casey started warming up in the right field bullpen.

"Get some runs for Fitz," was a cry that started up in the stands as the Dodgers came to bat in the seventh. Pete Reiser made a brave start. His first World Series hit was a terrific double against the screen above the wall in right center.

But no one behind him could do anything about this scoring opportunity. Medwick struck out, Harry Lavagetto grounded out to Red Rolfe at thrd and Dolph Camilli merely looked at a called third strike.

Observers thought that Casey didn't show much as he warmed up in right field and it is a cinch that he didn't have much when he started pitching to the Yankees.

The burly Southerner got by Johnny Sturm, first man up in the eighth, but only because Reiser caught a line drive in left center.

Then Rolfe lined a single to right.

Tommy Henrich didn't hit the ball any too well but his grounder was accidentally well placed between first and second. Camilli rushed to grab it and throw to second base for a force play, but the ball got past him. Pete Coscarart, tearing over from second behind Camilli, fielded the ball but had no play, since Casey didn't get to first base ahead of the hitter. And so Yankees were safe on first and second.

DiMaggio Scores Rolfe

The great Joe DiMaggio, handcuffed by Brooklyn pitching in the first two games of the series, lined a single to center, scoring Rolfe and sending Henrich to third.

Charley Keller hit a long line single to center, scoring Henrich and sending DiMaggio to third.

Casey was pulled right there and left-hander Larry French moved in to relieve. French couldn't have done a better job. He induced Bill Dickey to ground sharply just to the left of second base. Reese grabbed the ball, spiked the bag for a force play and then fired a bullet to Camilli to complete a double play at first.

Walker Starts Rally

The violently partisan Dodger crowd yelled for a rally in the Brooklyn half and got it. But said rally wasn't quite enough.

Dixie Walker, who hadn't yet made his first hit of the series, lashed one to right center. Keller tore over and threw himself at the ball but could do no more than block it, and Walker went to second for a double.

But Mickey Owen's best was a big hopper back to the box. Russo fielded the ball and threw him out while Walker held second. Augie

Continued on Page 4

SPORTS
CLASSIFIED ADVERTISEMENTS
REAL ESTATE
SUNDAY, OCT. 5, 1941 • SECTIONS C-D

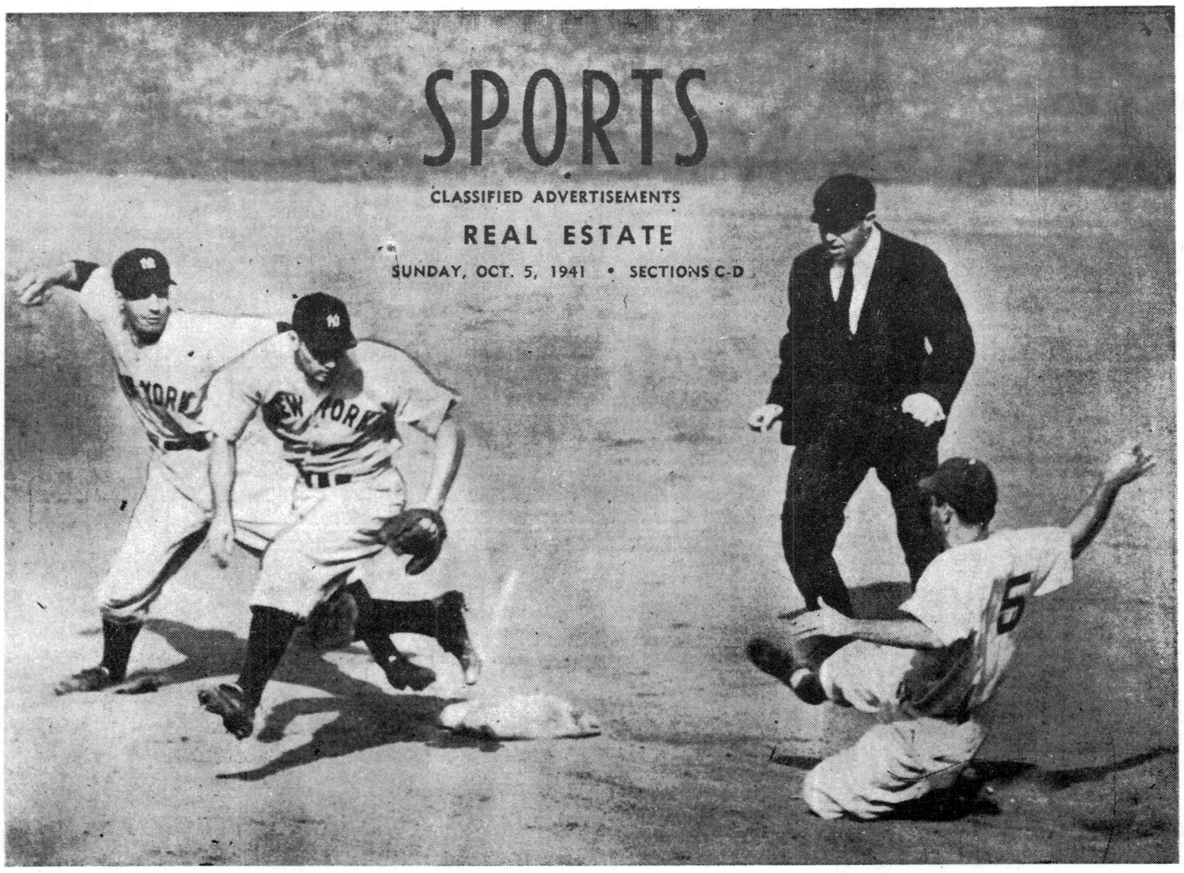

END OF DODGERS' SECOND-INNING THREAT—Phil Rizzuto throwing to Johnny Sturm to complete double play that squashed Brooklyn hopes in second inning. Harry Lavagetto opened inning with walk and then Rizzuto made sparkling pickup of Dolph Camilli's grounder, stepped on second to force Lavagetto and tossed to Sturm for the double killing. That's Joe Gordon stepping out of the way of Phil's throw.

MacPHAIL EXPLODES, BLASTS HUGH CASEY

Hurler's Indifference in Warming Up Draws Red-Head's Fire—DiMag' Gets Surprise

By HAROLD CONRAD

Larry MacPhail emitted a lot of blasts after the game, but one of his loudest was against Hugh Casey because the two-ton tosser didn't warm up properly in the bull pen. When it was obvious that he would have to come to the rescue of the stricken Fitzsimmons, Casey was just lobbing 'em in as though he had all day to warm up.

Talk about winning your own game, that's exactly what young Marius Russo did yesterday. In addition to pitching four-hit ball, he knocked Freddie Fitzsimmons out of the box—and we mean knocked him out. The liner Russo bounced off Fitz's knee-cap was one of the hardest hit balls of the game.

DiMaggio hit a towering fly in the fourth and ran all the way to second while Camilli was making the catch. Joe had his back to the play and when turned around he saw the ball on the ground. He thought he was safe and Umpire

Continued on Page 5

Governali Passes Columbia to 13-6 Win Over Brown

Columbia's injury-ridden Lions, striking swiftly through the air in the second and third periods, defeated determined Browns, 13—6, at Baker Field yesterday.

A crowd of 12,000 watched Paul Governali throw strikes to Steve McIlvenan on two identical touchdown plays to give Columbia its fourth victory over Brown in their 11-game series.

The injury jinx which has pursued the Lion since the first day of practice was still going strong, however, as Don Snavely, its great center, was laid out in the first five minutes with a recurrence of the twisted knee he suffered three weeks ago.

Governali, in leading the Lion to victory, threw 22 passes, eight of which were completed for a total of 127 yards. The former Evander Childs star also did the Columbia

Continued on Page 4

Princeton Drubs Williams, 20-7

Princeton, N. J., Oct. 4 (INS)—Princeton University's varsity gridders opened their campaign with a 20—7 victory over the Williams College eleven in Palmer Stadium here today. Capt. Bob Peters tallied once and passed to Right End Dick Schmon for another Tiger touchdown.

After pounding the Williams line during the first period, the Orange and Black took to the air in the second quarter and Right Halfback Bob Perina drew first blood when he dropped a 20-yard pass to Bill Sheridan in the end zone. Peters plunged over from the two in the third quarter and connected on his toss to Schmon a few plays later. Bob Hayes threw a 50-yard pass to End Al Hearne for the Purple's only touchdown in the fourth quarter.

CREDIT DUE DICKEY, SAYS MODEST RUSSO

"Give credit to Big Willie Dickey," Marius Russo said yesterday in the Yankee dressing room after limiting the Dodgers to four hits and setting them down, 2—1.

"Willie came out to me and had me in check when I felt a little wobbly. He steadied me. It's great when you have a catcher like him."—COHEN.

Fordham Wins, 16-10, on Pass In Last Minute

In the gathering twilight at the Polo Grounds yesterday, the old reliable, Steve (Flip) Filipowicz, came through once again for Fordham.

Goaded on by a Southern Methodist eleven that seemingly had the football game tucked away, erratic Fordham pulled itself together under Flip's powerful right wing twice to surge back in the waning seconds of its contest with the Texans yesterday, winning by a narrow 16—10 margin.

Only five and one-half minutes remained to play. Big Joe Pasqua, the boy with the "million-dollar toe," had just booted an "impossible" 44-yard field goal to put the Mustangs out in front by a 10—7 count. Fordham held the ball but on its own 35. Part of the crowd of 28,500 moved slowly toward the exit gates.

Try for a Tie

It was Flip's job now. Fading to his right, he criss-crossed a pass to Claude Pieculewicz who was stopped on the Mustang 31. Again Flip threw, this time to Jimmy Noble, to the 12. Three bucks at the Texan line yielded no gain.

Fordham decided to play safe and try for a tie. This time another Steve—Hudacek—dropped back and from a difficult angle, tied the count with a placement.

Three minutes remained. Those Ram Rose Bowl dreams were fading. Then the break came. Little Dick Miller, after slipping through the Ram line for 10 yards, fumbled and stocky Joie Kovach wrestled

Continued on Page 4

SANTILLI BREAKS ARM, OUT FOR SEASON

Alex Santilli, Fordham right tackle, who was carried from the field in the final quarter of yesterday's game with Southern Methodist University, suffered a broken left arm, it was revealed after the contest. Santilli was treated in the Polo Grounds clubhouse by Dr. Gerald Carroll and later sent to Union Hospital in the Bronx. It is expected that he will be out for the season.

College Football

EAST

Army	19	Citadel	6
Bates	7	New Hampshire	6
Bucknell	12	Muhlenberg	0
Clarkson	20	Ithaca	0
Coast Guard	48	Worcester	0
Colgate	7	Penn State	0
Cornell	6	Syracuse	0
Dartmouth	47	Amherst	7
Hamilton	21	R. P. I.	0
Hobart	13	Union	0
Holy Cross	13	Providence	0
Maine	14	Northeastern	12
Mass. State	8	Connnecticut	6
Navy	40	West Virginia	0
Norwich	21	Colby	7
N. Y. U.	6	Lafayette	0
Pennsylvania	19	Harvard	0
Princeton	20	Williams	7
Purdue	6	Pittsburgh	0
Rochester	13	Oberlin	6
St. Lawrence	13	Ohio Northern	0
Susquehanna	6	American U.	0
Trinity	9	Vermont	7

Continued on Page 4

Alsab, Fenelon Break Records

World's Two-Year-Old Mark Falls—New Belmont Time in $50,000 'Cap

Belair stud's Fenelon returned to his top form when he swept to a handy triumph over Louis Tufano's Market Wise in the $50,000 added money, long distance New York Handicap before a crowd of 27,000 fans at the windup of the Belmont Park Fall meeting yesterday.

Corydon, from the Greentree Stable, took third in advance of eight others who contested the issue over the two-and-one-quarter-mile course.

Mrs. Albert Sabath's sensational Alsab smashed to an eight-length triumph over the best Eastern two-year-olds to win the 71st running of the $10,000 added Champagne Stakes and virtually clinched juvenile honors for the year.

13th in 20 for Alsab

In registering his 13th win in 20 starts, Alsab ran the eight furlongs in the fastest time in history for a two-year-old. He was clocked in 1:35 2-5—three-fifths of a second faster than the 1:36 hung out by Twenty Grand at Churchill Downs 11 years ago.

Fenelon's victory came as a complete reversal of his showing in last Saturday's Jockey Club Gold Cup when he was beaten eight lengths by Market Wise and Whirlaway.

Fenelon, with Jimmy Stout aboard, took the verdict in the new track record time of 3:37 flat, which clipped one and four-fifth seconds off the old mark established by Mrs. Marie Evans' Shot Put.

Market Wise, because of his smashing victory over Whirlaway

Continued on Page 4

WORLD SERIES

THIRD GAME BOX SCORE

New York Yankees

	AB.	R.	H.	O.	A.	E.
Sturm,1b	4	0	1	12	0	0
Rolfe,3b	4	1	2	1	2	0
Henrich,rf	3	1	1	2	0	0
DiMaggio,cf	4	0	2	2	0	0
Keller,lf	4	0	1	2	0	0
Dickey,c	4	0	0	4	1	0
Gordon,2b	3	0	1	2	4	0
Rizzuto,ss	3	0	0	2	3	0
Russo,p	4	0	0	0	4	0
Totals	33	2	8	27	14	0

Brooklyn Dodgers

	AB.	R.	H.	O.	A.	E.
Reese,ss	4	0	1	3	1	0
Herman,2b	1	0	0	0	1	0
Coscarart,2b	2	0	0	0	3	0
Reiser,cf	4	0	1	5	0	0
Medwick,lf	4	0	1	3	0	0
Lavagetto,3b	3	0	0	1	0	0
Camilli,1b	3	0	0	11	0	0
Walker,rf	3	1	1	2	0	0
Owen,c	3	0	0	2	1	0
Fitzsimmons,p	2	0	0	0	2	0
Casey,p	0	0	0	0	0	0
French,p	0	0	0	0	0	0
Allen,p	0	0	0	0	0	0
Galan	1	0	0	0	0	0
Totals	30	1	4	27	8	0

Runs batted in—DiMaggio, Keller, Reese. Two-base hits—Reiser, Walker. Three-base hit—Gordon. Stolen bases—Rizzuto, Sturm. Left on bases—New York, 8; Brooklyn, 4. Bases on balls—Off Fitzsimmons, 3; Russo, 2. Struck out—By Fitzsimmons, 1; Russo, 5. Hits—Off Fitzsimmons, 4 in 7 innings; Casey, 4 in 1-3; French, 0 in 2-3; Allen, 0 in 1. Double plays—Rizzuto and Sturm; Reese and Camilli. Losing pitcher—Casey. Umpires—Grieve (A.), plate; Goetz (N.), first; McGowan (A.), second; Pinelli (N.), third. Time—2:22. Attendance—33,100.

THERE GOES YOUR BALL GAME—Joltin' Joe DiMaggio pounding out the hit that brought home Red Rolfe with the first run of the game in the eighth inning yesterday. Immediately after Charley Keller singled to score Tommy Henrich with what proved to be the winning run as the Yankees beat the Dodgers, 2 to 1, to win the third game of the World Series and take a 2 to 1 lead in games.

THE PAYOFF—Bill Dickey slides in with second and winning run of second inning as Yankees won world championship by beating Dodgers, 3 to 1, in fifth game of series at Ebbets Field yesterday. Previously Charley Keller had scored and Dickey had gone to second on wild pitch. Joe Gordon's single brought Dickey home.

Dodgers Lucky to Win One Game, Says McCarthy

Flock Has Great Club, Admits Joe, Pointing to Sweeps in Other Series

By LOU E. COHEN

The game was over, the celebration in the Yankee dressing room was quieting down, the photographers and newsreel men were gone and Manager Joe McCarthy was finished accepting handshakes, back-slaps and words of praise. He was sitting in front of his locker, drying himself after a shower. Tired from the excitement, he wasn't doing any talking—until some one said it was too bad that two of the games had to be won on "breaks" such as Freddie Fitzsimmons' injury and Mickey Owen's error.

"Whatthehell!" McCarthy spoke up. "The Dodgers were lucky to win a game. We usually win the series four in a row. Those Dodgers are a great team. You can't take that away from them, but don't expect me to sit here for hours praising them. I have a great bunch of ball players of my own."

INJURED — Bill Dickey hit dirt when struck in groin by Lew Riggs' foul in first inning.

Joe DiMaggio was asked about his near-battle with Whitlow Wyatt in the fifth inning, broken up only after players from both teams and umpires had swarmed onto the field.

Yanks Wanted to Beat Wyatt

"Oh, it was nothing," Joe smiled. "I flied out to center field and as I passed by Wyatt I said to him, 'This ball game isn't over yet!' And in return he cursed at me so I went at him."

DiMaggio's remark to Wyatt came after he had fanned twice and then lofted to Reiser.

Tiny Bonham, who pitched well, was elated as the players kissed and hugged him.

"Gosh! I've always hoped to pitch a World Series game and win it," he enthused. "I feel good."

"That Wyatt is one fellow we wanted to beat," Frankie Crosetti said.

"Well, it's all over now," came from Charlie (Red) Ruffing.

Ed Barrow, Yankee president, came into the dressing room and wrapped his arms around DiMaggio.

Tommy Henrich was elated over his home run which cleared the right field fence. "That's a thrill, to hit one off Wyatt. He's a great pitcher."

An usher came over to DiMaggio and whispered in his ear. DiMag got up off the locker-room stool and walked over to a big, strapping fellow. It was Lefty O'Doul, one-time Dodger.

It's Southward, Ho! for Dickey

Everybody was happy—as it always is with the victors. Art Fletcher was on top of a trunk leading the singing of "Sidewalks of New York," and Earle Combs, another Yankee coach, went around shouting that he was going to get high—until some one reminded him that he was strictly a cola drinker.

Frenchy Bordagaray said he was leaving town immediately to take care of business interests which will keep him engaged through the Winter. Bill Dickey is heading for Florida and will stay there "until I get fed up with it."

Marius Russo, who twirled a four-hitter Saturday, is using his series share to buy a house for himself, his wife and his baby—due in December. Phil Rizzuto will settle some family debts, take a trip and bank any money left over.

Red Rolfe had a tough series. He was weak after fighting off a siege of colitis and then suffered several painful bruises. Rolfe will rest a while in New England and doesn't know whether he'll return to his annual Winter post of coaching basketball at a small New Hampshire college.

Joe Gordon and Charlie Keller will spend the Winter hunting.

And as each Yankee dressed and left the locker room, he walked by the Dodger quarters and smiled to himself. Somehow, there's nothing so pleasant as being on a winning team.

NOW WHAT?—Umpire McGowan listens to beef by Durocher and Wyatt on called ball for Joe Gordon.

BOX SCORE OF FIFTH WORLD SERIES GAME

YANKEES

	ab	r	h	po	a
Sturm, 1b	4	0	1	9	0
Rolfe, 3b	3	0	0	3	0
Henrich, rf	3	1	1	1	0
DiMaggio, cf	4	0	1	6	0
Keller, lf	3	1	0	4	0
Dickey, c	4	1	1	2	0
Gordon, 2b	3	0	1	0	3
Rizzuto, ss	3	0	1	2	2
Bonham, p	4	0	0	0	1
Totals	31	3	6	27	6

DODGERS

	ab	r	h	po	a
Walker, rf	3	0	1	0	0
Riggs, 3b	4	0	1	1	3
Reiser, cf	4	0	1	2	0
Camilli, 1b	4	0	0	9	1
Medwick, lf	3	0	0	0	0
Reese, ss	3	0	0	2	3
aWasdell	1	0	0	0	0
Owen, c	3	0	0	9	1
Coscarart, 2b	2	0	0	3	3
bGalan	1	0	0	0	0
Herman, 2b	0	0	0	0	2
Wyatt, p	3	1	1	1	1
Totals	31	1	4	27	14

aBatted for Reese in ninth inning.
bBatted for Coscarart in seventh inning.

Yankees	0	2	0	0	1	0	0	0	0	—3
Dodgers	0	0	1	0	0	0	0	0	0	—1

Error—Reese. Runs batted in—Gordon, Reiser, Henrich. Two-base hit—Wyatt. Three-base hit—Reiser. Home run—Henrich. Double plays—Owen and Riggs; Reese, Coscarart and Camilli; Herman, Reese and Camilli. Earned runs—Yankees, 3; Dodgers, 1. Left on bases—Yankees, 6; Dodgers, 5. Bases on balls—Off Wyatt, 5 (Henrich, Keller, Rolfe, Gordon, Rizzuto); off Bonham, 2 (Medwick, Walker). Struck out—By Wyatt, 9 (DiMaggio (2), Bonham (4), Henrich, Keller, Rizzuto); by Bonham (2), (Camilli, Reiser). Wild pitch—Wyatt. Umpires—McGowan (A. L.), plate; Pinelli (N. L.), 1b; Grieve (A. L.), 2b; Goetz (N. L.), 3b. Time—2:13. Attendance—34,072.

Farley, Ever the Politician, Sits Behind Dodgers, Roots for Yanks

By BILLY GOODRICH

Former Postmaster General Jim Farley was seated behind the Dodger dugout yesterday and this caused a wit to ask if he had turned against his favorites, the Yankees. "Heavens, no!" bellowed the genial Irishman. "Don't even think of such a thing! I like it over here, and besides they treat me right. However, I prefer those Yankee-doodle dandies."

Pat O'Doherty, pug-nosed, smiling "brawn of a lad," will succeed Timmy Sullivan as the Bronx Bombers' batboy next season. Pat's 15 years of age, a Stuyvesant High School student and already a favorite with the Yanks, who like his winning smile.

FORCED — Johnny Sturm of Yanks forced at second in first inning but Coscarart's throw wasn't fast enough to get Red Rolfe for double play at first.

Sullivan will be called into the Army within a few months, and so he spent the last few weeks breaking O'Doherty in. "Why, he works like a veteran already," said Sullivan. "Just look at him put those bats into the right ring! I know the champs will like him."

Marse Joe McCarthy and Eddie Collins of the Boston Red Sox were in a huddle before the final World Series game. The Yankee boss and Collins discussed the series in general and the most important thing—a trade.

Ernie Bonham, strapping right-hander who handcuffed the Dodgers, was the coolest guy on the Yank bench before game time. You'd never think it was his first World Series attempt.

The fans booed Joltin' Joe DiMaggio after Wyatt fanned him in the first inning, and Bill Brandt, National League publicity director, quipped, "That's just for being too good." DiMag will stay around Manhattan for a month, then head home to the Coast for some fishing.

Phil Rizzuto, better known as The Flea, who seemed as big as an elephant to the Dodgers on the defense, rode Wyatt from the start to the finish.

RED LIGHT — Pete Reiser checks self going into third after triple with two out in first. That's Red Rolfe with hand upraised, but he's waiting for ball, not directing traffic.

Wyatt didn't care to talk much about his verbal row on the field with Joe DiMaggio.

"It's just one of those things that happen in the heat of battle," Wyatt explained. "He said something to me and I said something to him. It's over now. Let's forget it. Joe is a great player and I like him."

Coach Earle Combs of the Yankees hugged Joe Gordon on the way back to the dressing room after the game and kept shouting. "Here's my idea of a real second baseman—and a ball player's player!"

COMING EVENTS CAST THEIR SHADOWS

Believe in coincidences? Well, here are a couple:

Everyone knows that the Yankees won the last three games against the Dodgers at Ebbets Field. How many recall that the Yankees also won the first three games against the Dodgers at Ebbets Field early in the season?

The games were the last three of the exhibition series between the two clubs and were played April 11, 12, and 13. The Yanks won by 7-6, 3-2 and 3-0. Bonham, who won yesterday, was the winning pitcher in the final game April 13, while Russo contributed to the first exhibition victory.

GORDON GOOD, BUT HE'S NO FRISCH--LEO

Durocher Says Flock Made Hurlers Look Great by Weak Hitting

By HAROLD PARROTT

We lost in five games, and no questions asked, except by Little Rollo, who will want to know 20 years from now how and why those Yankees beat our brains out. And what will you say?

Rollo's Aunt Matilda may roll her eyes and say it was because those Dodgers were such a brawly team, and that Mr. Durocher's language was so terrible.

On the other hand the Brooklyn Rooters' Second Guess Squad may decry the fact that Leo the Lip erred in playing Mickey Owen behind the plate in that Fateful Fourth Game, or, that it was because "Casey-Is-Ready" was NOT ready in the Terrific Third game of the series.

However, taking all arguments with a ton of salt, the one and only fact does remain that the Yankees ARE the 1941 World Champions, and played just that kind of ball.

It's a fact that there isn't one position in the field at which you could say the Dodgers had the edge over the Yankees in this five-game series.

Which, of course, narrows it down to pitching. The flipping of Curt Davis, Whit Wyatt, Fred Fitzsimmons and—in the fourth game—Hugh Casey, kept us close.

Last evening in the dressing-room Durocher admitted the Yanks were a great club. "But," said Leo, "we made their pitching look great because we weren't hitting. No pitcher like that Tiny Bonham today, who was throwing fast balls all afternoon because he does not own a curve, should make us look so bad."

Gordon Star—Leo

Durocher admitted the Yanks were good, and he admitted Joe Gordon was their No. 1 star in this series, too. But he put a brake on enthusiasts who talked about Gordon as an "All time great."

"Gordon, good as he was," said Lip, "couldn't carry Frankie Frisch's glove when Frank was in his prime. Don't forget Frisch was great defensively, too, besides which he was hitting .340 and stealing all those bases!"

Those words may help you keep a better perspective.

And now, how about these conclusions:

BIGGEST STAR—Gordon, with his seven hits, six walks and amazing defensive play. His one error became the Dodgers' winning run in the second game.

BIGGEST RIVALRY—Reese vs. Rizzuto, with the Yank getting the nod on greater sureness afield. Had a bad series at the bat (two hits) although he was a .300 hitter all season.

BIGGEST SURPRISE—Johnny Sturm's outpointing of Dolf Camilli for first-base honors. Sturm got six hits, had only one lapse on a thrown ball; Camilli fielded well, but fanned six times, looked puny at bat to be the No. 1 Dodger flop.

BEST STRATEGY—By Joe McCarthy, who said little, but juggled his pitchers to get the most out of them, while Durocher found himself thwarted by his own well-laid plans and sunk by his own super-strategy. McCarthy figured Ruffing to lead off as the bell-cow, for steadiness and psychology; he admitted later he thought Russo was his best bet, and he saved Marius to beat Fitz, whom he figured would be tough for his free-swingers!

FACTS AND FIGURES OF 5TH SERIES GAME

The official attendance and receipts of the fifth game of the World Series and the totals for all five games, as compared with the same figures last year, follow:

Fifth Game Totals

Attendance (pd.)	34,072	55,189
Receipts	$161,921.00	$224,597.00
Clubs' share	68,816.42	80,453.72
Leagues' share	68,816.42	80,453.72
Comm. share	24,288.15	33,689.95

Totals for Five Games

Attendance (pd.)	235.773	224,592
Receipts	$1,007,762.00	$957,598.10
*Players' share	431,378.91	373,830.56
Clubs' share	212,611.88	220,063.91
Leagues' share	212,611.88	220,063.91
Comm. share	151,165.60	143,640.11

*Does not include share of radio rights. Of the players' pool, the winners' share will be $181,179.14 and the losers' $120,786.10. The amount to be divided among second, third and fourth place teams in each league is $129,413.67.

RESULTS AND STANDING OF WORLD SERIES

Final Standing

	W.	L.	Pct.
Yankees (A. L.)	4	1	.800
Dodgers (N. L.)	1	4	.200

Results

First game (at Yankee Stadium, Oct. 1).

										R	H	E
Dodgers	0	0	0	0	1	0	1	0	0	—2	6	0
Yankees	0	1	0	1	0	1	0	0	x	—3	6	1

Batteries—Davis, Casey, Allen and Owen, Franks; Ruffing and Dickey.

Second game (at Yankee Stadium, Oct. 2).

										R	H	E
Dodgers	0	0	0	0	2	1	0	0	0	—3	6	2
Yankees	0	1	1	0	0	0	0	0	0	—2	9	1

Batteries—Wyatt and Owen; Chandler, Murphy and Dickey, Rosar.

Third game (at Ebbets Field, Oct. 4).

										R	H	E
Yankees	0	0	0	0	0	0	0	2	0	—2	8	0
Dodgers	0	0	0	0	0	0	0	1	0	—1	4	0

Batteries—Russo and Dickey; Fitzsimmons, Casey, French, Allen and Owen.

Fourth game (at Ebbets Field, Oct. 5).

										R	H	E
Yankees	1	0	0	2	0	0	0	0	4	—7	12	0
Dodgers	0	0	0	2	2	0	0	0	0	—4	9	1

Batteres—Donald, Breuer, Murphy and Dickey; Higbe, French, Allen, Casey and Owen.

Fifth game (at Ebbets Field, Oct. 6).

										R	H	E
Yankees	0	2	0	0	1	0	0	0	0	—3	6	0
Dodgers	0	0	1	0	0	0	0	0	0	—1	4	1

Batteries—Bonham and Dickey; Wyatt and Owen.

Great Year for Flock Despite Series Defeat

Dodgers' Showing in Exciting Classic Nothing to Be Ashamed of, Says Holmes —Yanks Were Worried Down to End

By TOMMY HOLMES

"I'm not superstitious," said the late Ring Lardner, "but I do think that it's bad luck to bet against the Yankees."

That's the same quotation I used the afternoon I picked the Dodgers to win the Series in six or seven games. And I was wrong, and Lardner's classic phrase still stands.

The Yankees have that winning habit in World Series competition and there's no doubt about that. Since 1926, the Yanks have competed in eight of these struggles for the baseball championship of the green footstool and they have won eight straight. That's par for the course.

They have beaten no less than six different National League clubs—everybody but the Phillies and the Braves, who in that period haven't been unfortunate enough to have met Joe McCarthy's mauling mob.

AFTER THE BATTLE—Manager Leo Durocher (left) of Dodgers and Manager Joe McCarthy of Yankees congratulate each other on the fine play of both teams during the exciting series.

Our Dodgers have to be ashamed of nothing. The Yankees came into the Series much the favorites—in fact, varied pre-Series dope gave Leo Durocher's men nothing more than an outside chance. And yet, the Yankees, with all of their devastating power and finesse, were a worried lot right down to the minute when Jimmy Wasdell lined to DiMaggio to end the classic. It was not the picnic that the Yanks expected. It was a hollow victory.

Yanks Got Break

That the Yankees were on the receiving end of every good break that bobbed up in the five-game drama, will not be denied, not even by the Yanks and McCarthy. And as Durocher put it when the smoke of battle had cleared, "The Yankees are too good a ball club to be beaten without an even break in luck."

Two of the four Yankee victories were guided by the hand of Lady Luck. It takes a pretty fair memory to recall when a team ever suffered such cruel breaks as Durocher's scrappy outfit did in this Series.

Go back to Saturday afternoon when gallant Fred Fitzsimmons for all his 40 years, set down the Yankee power for six innings and seemed well on his way to his first Series triumph. Then the fast turn of events—a line drive off the bat of Marius Russo that almost took off Freddy's leg—sent the vetern knuckle-baller out of the game. And with him went the Dodgers' chance to take a 2—1 lead in the Series. Sure, Russo pitched a whale of a game, but Fat Freddy was with him to the tragic moment.

As heart-rending as that was, the worst had yet to come. Sunday afternoon, in the fourth game, with the Dodgers fighting to get back on even terms, saw the strangest finish to a ball game that has ever been recorded in Series history. And again, Lady Luck was in the Yankee lineup. Mickey Owen's disastrous error, after Hugh Casey had seemingly clinched a heroic relief effort by fanning Henrich for the third and final "out" in the game, which turned a sure Yankee defeat into triumph in short order. You probably wouldn't believe it could happen if you didn't see it.

Fourth Game the Crusher

That was really the crusher, and the McCarthymen really won the championship then and there. Had Owen held that ball, there is no telling what would have happened in the remaining games. Durocher would have been in the driver's seat, ready to fire Curt Davis and Whit Wyatt in games five and six and with that kind of pitcher working normally, you're always in the ball game.

Still a Great Year

Yesterday's clincher was the first game of the Series in which Joe McCarthy's young men showed any kind of marked superiority over the Dodgers. They didn't outgame Wyatt by winning on a score of 3—1. Not even the best of pitchers can win many a game with a one-run margin, and the silent Georgian had to get that himself. His double on which he eventually scored was the only offensive which the Dodgers could organize against the shoots of Ernie Bonham.

They're taken up the old battle-cry in Flatbush again, but the faithful won't see their Dodgers in a more gallant or heroic stand than they did this season. It was a great year.

THRONG'S OVATIONS STIR MICKEY OWEN

Catcher Gets Tumultous Reception At Bat—Dodgers' Series Shares Set Mark

Mickey Owen, the Dodgers' hard-working catcher, probably will never forget the famous fourth-game error of his. But the chances are that in future years whenever the picture of that curve slipping away from his glove returns to his mind's eye to haunt and torment him, another picture, comforting and encouraging, will be right behind it.

That will be the recollection of three tumultous, tear-bringing ovations rendered as from one voice from the huge throng on each of his appearances to the plate as a batter.

They say the fans are bitter and cruel in defeat. Maybe they are, but more than one spectator at Ebbets Field yesterday gulped hard to swallow that big lump when Mike came up to bat. And gulping the hardest of all was the fiery little catcher of the Dodgers.

The Dodgers gained a distinction in defeat. They will draw the largest individual shares of any losing club in history. Each Brooklyn player will get a check of $4,808, while the Yanks collected $5,917.31, sixth largest purse for the winners. Babe Phelps, Angelo Giuliani, Paul Waner, Mace Brown and Alec Kampouris were ignored entirely.

This division did not include the return from the radio rights.

Larry MacPhail has nothing but bright optimism for the future. He pointed out that the Dodger farm teams play against eight of the Yankee farms, six of the Reds' farms, ten of the Cards' and four or five of the Tigers' teams and this year the Dodger farmhands beat all their other rivals on the season's plays.

HOLMES

WANTS DODGER FANS TO JACK UP 'CUTS'

What will our loyal Dodger rooters think up next?

From W. O. Ritchie of Flatbush comes this suggestion:

In order to increase each Dodger's cut of the World Series melon, which amounts to $4,808, so that it will equal the Yankees' slices of $5,917, Mr. Ritchie asks whether there are 60,000 Flatbush fans who would consider the fun they had listening to the broadcast of the games worth a buck a head. Mr. Ritchie calculates that if there are 60,000 such fans they would raise enough to equal the Yankees' share of the World Series swag.

THAT MAN'S HERE AGAIN—Charley Keller, who ruined Dodgers all through series, slides into third base on Bill Dickey's single in second. Yankee trouble-maker scored first run against Dodgers on wild pitch a moment later.

U. S.-Jap Clash Inevitable, Says Knox

Wall Street Closing
RACING EXTRA
★★★★★★

BROOKLYN EAGLE

LOCAL WEATHER FORECAST: Partly cloudy and warmer tonight and tomorrow

Wall Street Closing
RACING EXTRA
★★★★★★

100th YEAR • No. 295 • DAILY AND SUNDAY • BROOKLYN, N. Y., FRIDAY, OCT. 24, 1941 • Entered at the Brooklyn Postoffice as 2d Class Mail Matter—(Copyright 1941 The Brooklyn Eagle, Inc.) • 3 CENTS

ROOSEVELT INDORSES MAYOR

New Moscow Drive Is Repelled

Fire Captain Killed Fighting Smoky Blaze in Edgemere

Fire Capt. Walter Sandberg, 50, attached to Hook and Ladder Company 121, Rockaway Beach, was killed today while fighting a smoky fire in the three-story frame dwelling at 315 Beach 54th St., Edgmere. Captain Sandberg was overcome by smoke and was carried from the third floor to the street by other firemen.

Captain Sandberg, who lived at 88-27 137th St., Jamaica, was the second member of his fire company to be killed within the year. Last February Lt. Benjamin Parcell died when he fell from the roof of a building in Broad Channel while fighting a blaze.

TEACHER HURT AS NEW BLAST ROCKS COLUMBIA LAB

An explosion at 11 a.m. today in the physics laboratory of Columbit University shook the top five floors of the building and resulted in severe burns to a research worker.

The blast was caused by dust igniting when a substance known as pyroforic flamed up while being packaged in the laboratory. The work was being done by Dr. Walter Zinn, 34, of 14 Linden Terrace, Leonia, N. J., who was taken to St. Luke's Hospital with second degree burns of the hands.

BOOK AGENT FORCED TO DISCONTINUE 'RED DECADE'

By threat of legal action, Corliss Lamont, chairman of the new defunct Friends of the Soviet Union, has persuaded Baker & Taylor, book distributors, to discontinue "The Red Decade or the Stalinist Penetration of America," by Eugene Lyons, it was learned today. Mr. Lamont, it was stated, objects to the fact that the book implies he approves of mass homicide. Also, he denies that he is "a stinker." The American News Company, it is understood, has refused to cease handling the book. Mr. Lamont, son of Thomas A. Lamont of J. P. Morgan & Co., once predicted that the United States will have a Communist form of government by 1959.

UNION HEAD'S PLEA AVERTS ROBINS DRYDOCK STRIKE

A strike today at the Robins Drydock and Repair Company yards, foot of Dwight St., Erie Basin, was averted by the appeal of John Green, International president of the Industrial Union of Marine and Shipbuilding Workers of America, for further time to negotiate with the company.

About 4,000 of the 6,000 Robins employes met last night in Prospect Hall, Prospect and 5th Aves., in closed session to vote whether Local 39 should strike this morning.

After the meeting Joseph Burge, New York regional director of the union and chairman at the session, disclosed that sentiment at the meeting was overwhelmingly in favor of an immediate walkout, but that a telegram from Green to delay action was heeded.

ULTRA VIOLET-RAY CONVICTS EX-JOCKEY

John H. Fallehy, 59, ex-jockey, trainer and horse-owner, today owes his forgery conviction to an ultra-violet ray machine at the pay-off windows of Aqueduct Race Track. At his trial before County Judge Thomas Downs and a jury in Long Island City, Ira Plinnock, track cashier, testified that the machine showed that numbers on three $10 mutuel tickets, which Fallehy presented for payment June 11, had been altered to carry the numbers of a winning horse rather than a losing horse. Fallehy protested that he was merely cashing the tickets for an acquaintance.

HIGH COURT UPHOLDS DAILY WORKER CONVICTION

The Appellate Division of the State Supreme Court unanimously confirmed today the jury conviction of the Daily oWrker and its managing editor, Clarence Hathaway, for criminal libel. Each had been fined $500 and Hathaway also was sentenced to 30 days in the Workhouse.

In 1936 the paper published an attack on the murdered editor of a Minneapolis paper for his policy on labor-political matters. The action against the Communist paper yas initiated by Mrs. Edith Liggett, widow of the murdered man.

U. S.-Japanese Clash Certain, Knox Asserts

President Is Drafting Huge New Arms Plan To Help Defeat Axis

Washington, Oct. 24 (U.P.)—President Roosevelt disclosed today that he is drafting a huge new armament program to help defeat the Axis, and Secretary of Navy Knox declared that an American-Japanese "collision" is inevitable if Japan continues her expansion program.

The President revealed the broad aspects of the new arms production plan at a press conference. He described the program in his own words as comprehensive but not all-out. The first part of the program will be a doubling of tank production, he said.

Knox, addressing a group of ordnance manufacturers and officers of naval establishments, declared:

"The situation out in the Far East is extremely strained.

Knox Fears 'Collision'

"We are satisfied in our minds that the Japanese have no intentions of giving up their plans for this expansion. If they pursue that course a collision is inevitable."

In disclosing plans for the new armament program, Mr. Roosevelt said the tank expansion item was the most important on the list at this time and that he probably would ask Congress to authorize its start in the near future. He said the expansion would go beyond OPM Director William S. Knudsen's original estimate of a boost in medium tank production from 1,000 to 2,000 a month.

Mr. Roosevelt would give no figures, however.

He said that he was uncertain

Continued on Page 4

Eagle Staff photo

STILL HOPEFUL—Mr. and Mrs. Joseph Igneri of 1362 E. 5th St. look at a picture of their son, Orlando, 22, whom they are still trying to have released from the Army so that their home may be saved from foreclosure.

Parents to Fight Ban On Trainee's Release

If Son Could Enlist in Navy, Difference In Pay Would Tide Them Over, They Claim

If their son could only enlist in the navy instead of remaining a trainee, everything would be much simpler, and their fear of poverty would be relieved to some extent, Mr. and Mrs. Joseph Igneri said today.

But he has tried to enlist and has been turned down and a United States judge has said his induction into the army cannot be changed. At their home, 1362 E. 5th St., mother and father looked bleakly at the future and found it unpromising.

Orlando Igneri, their 22-year-old son, is now at Camp Upton. Yesterday he applied unsuccessfully before Federal Judge Robert A. Inch to be released from the army so that he could help support his parents and his brother, John, 26, might wed.

He argued that with the mother and father to be supported, his brother would find it difficult to take on the added expense of a

Continued on Page 21

Fresh Shakeup Hits Two More Red Marshals

Voroshilov, Budenny Now Army Organizers —Soviet Sure of Victory

Kuibyshev, Oct. 24 (U.P.) — Front line reports said today that the Germans launched new attacks with fresh troops on the Moscow defense lines at Mozhaisk and Maloyaroslavets but Red Army forces beat back the assaults at all critical points.

Soviet war correspondents reported that at a number of positions Russian troops launched local counter-attacks.

The front reports followed the statement of S. A. Lozovsky, Soviet press spokesman, that the Germans already have suffered losses of several hundred thousand men and that Russia, shaking up the Soviet high command, is organizing large new armies, prepared to fight on for years, if necessary, to achieve victory.

Lozovsky announced that Marshals Klementi Voroshilov and Semyon Budenny, commanding the Leningrad fronts, had been relieved of their commands and that Marshal Semyon Timoshenko, formerly on the central front, had taken over Budenny's command. Lozovsky said Timoshenko was shifted "for internal military reasons."

He disclosed that Voroshilov and Budenny, two heroes of the early days of the Soviet, were organizing new armies.

Insist Nazis Checked

In one of the firmest Russian statements of the entire war he said Adolf Hitler had failed of his main objectives, that he would never get them, that Russia was supremely confident of victory and that if this was not the last great German offensive it was one of the last.

Lozovsky asserted that the Germans had been thrown back in several sectors of the Leningrad front, that they had now concentrated their main strength on the Moscow front.

He asserted that the greatest German drive on Moscow, from the west and southwest in the Mozhaisk-Maloyaroslavets areas, had been definitely checked; that to the north the Russians held half of Kalinin, 100 miles from Moscow, and that at no point were the Ger-

Continued on Page 2

Praises LaGuardia Administration as 'The Most Honest'

Washington, Oct. 24 (U.P.)—President Roosevelt today indorsed Fiorello H. LaGuardia for re-election as Mayor of New York and praised his administration of the city as the most honest and efficient in his recollection.

Despite his stride across party lines to back the candidacy of the Republican candidate, Mr. Roosevelt deprecated reports that it might result in the resignation of Edward J. Flynn as chairman of the Democratic national committee.

When told that newspapers had speculated on such a possibility, the President replied that he did not think there was any story in that situation. Flynn and other New Yorg City and State Democratic leaders are backing the candidacy of William O'Dwyer, the Democratic challenger.

Text of Statement

The President indorsed LaGuardia in a formal statement, which permitted direct quotation to heighten its effectiveness. The text of the statement:

"Although my voting residence has always been up-State, I have lived and worked in the City of New York off and on since 1904. I have known and observed New York's mayors since that time.

"I am not taking part in the New York City election, but because the City of New York contains about half the population of my State, I do not hesitate to express the opinion that Mayor LaGuardia and his administration have given to the city the most honest and, I believe, the most efficient municipal government of any within my recollection.

"The fact that the city's election has no relationship to national policies, but is confined to civic policies, is attested by the fact that the constitution of the State provides for the municipal election in off-years when neither a Governor nor a President nor members of the House of Representatives or Senate of the United States are to be chosen."

In the last sentence of his statement Mr. Roosevelt appeared to say, in effect, that he was divorcing his indorsement of LaGuardia from any State or national Republican organization.

Although the move jolted New York City and State Democratic organizations, it had been expected. Flynn was reported to have attempted to prevent or minimize Mr. Roosevelt's indorsement of LaGuardia.

50 MORE FRENCH HOSTAGES SLAIN IN NAZI REPRISAL

Vichy Reports Plea By Petain Wins Stay For 100 Also Doomed

Vichy, France, Oct. 24 (U.P.)—Fifty French hostages were executed by German firing squads today for the slaying of a Nazi major at Bordeaux, but a communique said that Marshal Henri Philippe Petain had secured postponement of the deadline for execution of 100 others.

The original communique said that "German authorities" ordered postponement of the execution deadline but later a correction was issued saying that the postponement was agreed to by "the Reichs Chancellor and supreme commander of the Reichs' forces"—Adolf Hitler.

The executions brought to 100 the number of hostages put to death in retaliation for the slaying of German officers at Bordeaux and Nantes.

A German announcement said that Pierre Lerein, a resident of Floriac Gironde, near Bordeaux, was executed yesterday on a charge of illegal detention of arms and explosives.

His execution brought the total

Continued on Page 21

Masquerading Nazi Sought on Steamship

Buenos Aires, Oct. 24 (U.P.)—Police were expected to search the Spanish steamer Cabo de Hornos when it arrives today for a German masquerading as a Jewish refugee.

He was said to have documents and instructions for Leo Hirsch, who reportedly is being sent here to replace Gottfried Sanstede, former German press attache and alleged Gestapo chief in Argentina.

O'Dwyer Levels Attack Against Markets Head

The campaign fire of District Attorney O'Dwyer, Democratic mayoralty candidate, was directed today against the Markets Department with charges that Commissioner William Fellowes Morgan Jr. has utilized municipal radio station WNYC for discriminatory advice on foods.

"If I ever have a commissioner who makes use of the city radio station—if there is one—to advertise one product to put two out of business, he will be fired," O'Dwyer said.

O'Dwyer unleashed his attack on Commissioner Morgan yesterday by denouncing to 500 food merchants and their employes the action of the Markets Department in permitting its consumers' bureau to conduct programs on WNYC in which fresh fish was extolled over dried fish.

"There is a place to discuss the merits of fresh fish versus dried fish," he told his listeners, assembled at a rally held by the O'Dwyer-for-Mayor division of the fruit and vegetable industry in Washington Market, Manhattan, "but that place is not the city radio station."

Rabbi Assails Valentine

Rabbi Samuel Peiper of the Community Reform Temple, noting Police Commissioner Valentine's

Continued on Page 21

WHERE TO EIND IT IN TODAY'S EAGLE

Bridge	Page 25	Novel	Page 25
Comics	Page 22	OBITUARIES	Page 15
Crossword	Page 24	Only Yesterday	Page 11
Dr. Brady	Page 11	Patterns	Page 11
EDITORIAL	Page 14	RADIO	Page 22
FINANCIAL	Page 20	Real Estate	Page 25
Going Places	Page 13	Society	Page 6
Grin and Bear It	Page 14	SPORTS	Pages 17-18-19
Harold Conrad	Page 7	Theaters	Page 12
Heffernan	Page 11	These Women	Page 11
Helen Worth	Page 8	Tucker	Page 14
Horoscope	Page 11	Uncle Ray's Corner	Page 11
Movies	Page 12	Wall Street	Page 20
Music	Page 12	Want Ads	Pages 23-24-25
Neighborhood News	Page 21	Weather Table	Page 15
		Woman's	Page 8

Attorney Accused Of 'Baiting' Court

A controversy over whether or not Attorney Jesse Climenko was a "lone sheep" today brought an unscheduled recess in the murder trial of Louis (Lepke) Buchalter, Emanuel (Mendy) Weiss and Louis Capone.

Climenko, soft-voiced, Harvard-trained Lepke counsel, had spent less than ten minutes in cross-examining the day's first witness, Mrs. Sylvia R. Greenspan, 28, of 401 Schenectady Ave., daughter of Joseph Rosen, the murder victim, when the controversy developed.

Judge Taylor made a remark which the attorney said he had not heard. He asked that it be repeated. The judge replied that Climenko "did not listen" and "I consider your conduct impertinent." Counsel asked mor an exception, whereupon the judge ordered a 15-minute recess so that Climenko might "compose himself."

When court was resumed, with the jury absent, the judge said from the bench that a practice of "baiting of the court" had grown up, with the purpose of "getting a ruling on which to base a reversal on appeal" and he would not have it. When Climenko said he reserved the right to take exceptions, the court promised to "deal with you at the proper time," adding:

"I think you are the lone sheep in the ranks of defense counsel in this attitude."

Former General Sessions Judge Alfred J. Tally, counsel for Weiss, then said that he, too, took exception to the court's remarks and that Climenko was not a lone sheep.

At this point Judge Taylor rose and announced a recess.

Mexican Cactus Narcotic Rising as Menace in U. S.

Reno, Nev., Oct. 24 (U.P.)—Dr. Charles Tranter said today that a little brown button from Mexican cactus—a button which the Indians call "the sacred mushroom of the Aztecs" that brings "beautiful dreams and beautiful music"—is gaining wide favor as a narcotic by Easterners.

Tranter, a Reno physician, said that use of peyote, the button, is becoming so prevalent it is as dangerous as the marijuana wave of five or ten years ago.

"It is a menace to America if unchecked," he said. "I have proof it is widely used in the East where socialites hold peyote parties. There are more peyote addicts than those suffering from diphtheria and smallpox combined."

REFUGE

A thrilling new serial by Vida Hurst begins in the Brooklyn Eagle Monday.

It's a timely dramatic story about a beautiful refugee girl who comes to America to find happiness and security.

Army Honors Boro Man For Gallantry in 1918

The Silver Star was awarded to Joseph Klein of 852 Crown St. for gallantry in action when he was a first-class private in the A. E. F., the War Department announced today.

Mr. Klein rescued two wounded soldiers with another soldier's aid while under machine-gun fire at Haudiomont, France, on Nov. 9, 1918. The citation said that with the assistance of the soldier he attacked the enemy machine-gun nest which was holding up the advance of his company, killed the crew and disabled the gun.

Illiteracy No Grounds For Divorce, Court Rules

Los Angeles, Oct. 24 (U.P.)—Illiteracy is not grounds for a divorce, the Superior Court ruled today, because Andrew Johnson, 17th President of the United States, could neither read nor write until taught by his wife.

Superior Judge Peirson M. Hall denied Mrs. Lucile Forbes, 18, an annulment from Robert Forbes, also 18. She had charged he concealed his inability to read or write and declared she had to read the funny papers to him.

Eagle to Mark Century Of Progress Over WOR

Arthur T. Robb, editor of Editor and Publisher; James H. Furay, vice president and a director of the United Press, and Frank D. Schroth, publisher of the Brooklyn Eagle, will be the speakers on a broadcast over Station WOR Sunday evening commemorating the Eagle's 100 years of existence in the field of American journalism.

The program, designated as "A Century of Newspaper Making," will be heard from 10:15 to 10:30 p.m.

Messages from President Roosevelt and Governor Lehman will also be read during the broadcast.

To commemorate the 100th anniversary of its founding on Oct. 26, 1841, by Isaac Van Anden, the Brooklyn Eagle will publish on Sunday a special 76-page Centennial Edition in addition to the regular issue. This fully illustrated supplement will be divided into three sections, historical, residential and industrial.

As a second added feature, an exact facsimile of the first issue of the Brooklyn Eagle will be distributed with every copy of the Centennial Edition.

A ten-point program for the future progress of Brooklyn, drafted as a composite of ideas advanced by leading citizens, will be presented for the first time Sunday on the front page of the main news section of the Brooklyn Eagle.

Empire City Results

FIRST RACE — Two-year-olds; three-fourths of a mile.

Cherrydale (Westrope)	33.70	10.70	6.60
Feathery (Meade)	—	3.40	2.70
Tower Maid (Stout)	—	—	4.10

Time, 1:09. Field Lark, Vain, Lover's Lass, Ninety Days, Furenuf, Quatrebelle, Violante also ran. Off time, 1:52.

SECOND RACE — Four-year-olds up; mile and one-eighth.

Commendador II (M'C'y)	10.70	5.40	4.10
Gangplank (Schmidl)	—	5.90	4.30
Ken's Pop (Sisto)	—	—	14.80

Time, 1:54. Cortez, Aladdin's Dream, Llavin, Stable, Rheanus, Miquelon, Franco Saxon, Dark Watch also ran. Off time, 2:22.

Laurel Results

FIRST RACE—Three-year-olds and up; three-fourths of a mile.

Docket (Berg)	8.00	5.50	4.10
High Bud (Hacker)	—	21.20	10.90
Bill K (Bocson)	—	—	22.30

Time, 1:14 1-5. Lady Jaffa, aJoanny, Dusty Dunlin, Shall We Dance, Balkanese, Rough Egg, Dividend, Baby Mowlee, Aler-lin also ran. Off time, 1:37.
aShouse-Babylon entry.

SECOND RACE — Three-year-olds and up; two miles (Steeplechase).

Greenwich Time (Cruze)	5.30	3.00	2.70
Fatty (Brooks)	—	3.00	3.00
Heliograph (Clements)	—	—	3.80

Time, 4:01 2-5. Harem Honey, Stockwood, Worthful also ran. Off time, 2:02½.

Rockingham Park Results

FIRST RACE—Three-year-olds and up; three-fourths of a mile.

Eleventh Hour (Dattilo)	5.60	3.40	2.60
Foggy Day (Scocca)	—	5.00	3.20
In Dutch (T. Bates)	—	—	3.60

Time, 1:14 2-5. Libra, High Caste, Lina's Son, Eviva, Lady Ariel, Athanasian, Staid Lady, Curlique, Viajero also ran. Off time, 1:20½.

SECOND RACE — Three-year-olds and up; three-quarters of a mile.

Good Actor (Taylor)	11.00	4.80	3.00
Sun Girl (Bates)	—	3.20	2.40
Jackinthebox (McMullen)	—	—	2.60

Time, 1:14. Butterman, North Sea, Apropos, Sir Quest, Buck's Image, Aristocracy, Hittie, Miss Co-Ed, Updo also ran. Off time, 1:52½.

DAILY DOUBLE PAID $30.60

THIRD RACE—Two-year-olds; three-quarters mile.

Reckless Saxon (Dattilo)	4.60	3.20	2.40
Scarcity (Taylor)	—	6.40	3.60
Kempy (Mehrtens)	—	—	2.40

Time, 1:14. Affianced, Mindful, Zite, Decade, Tiara also ran. Off time, 2:20.

Sportsman's Park Results

FIRST RACE—Three-year-olds; one and one-sixteenth miles.

High Name (Trombley)	6.00	4.00	2.60
Florizan Black (Jemas)	—	17.80	8.00
Texas Way (Brooks)	—	—	3.80

Time, 1:55. Himulus, Ambo, Bud B., My Hobby also ran. Off time, 2:01.

Lehman Denounces Mayor for Abuse

Wall Street Closing
RACING EXTRA
★★★★★★

BROOKLYN EAGLE

Wall Street Closing
RACING EXTRA
★★★★★★

LOCAL WEATHER FORECAST: Cloudy, cooler tonight; tomorrow partly cloudy, cool

101st YEAR • No. 299 • DAILY AND SUNDAY • BROOKLYN, N. Y., TUESDAY, OCT. 28, 1941 • Entered at the Brooklyn Postoffice as 2d Class Mail Matter—(Copyright 1941 The Brooklyn Eagle, Inc.) • 3 CENTS

DEFENSE STRIKES BRANDED AS SABOTAGE IN SENATE BILL

Lehman Denounces LaGuardia, Says He Hit New Low in Abuse

Charges Mayor Hurls Epithets For Intimidation

Governor Lehman came squarely into the Mayoralty campaign today when he denounced Mayor LaGuardia in one of the severest rebukes he has ever administered to a public official.

The statement, which charged that the Mayor has reached a "new low" in abuse, followed on the heels of a speech the Governor made in the Bronx last night in which he said LaGuardia could not serve both the city as Mayor and the nation as civilian defense director at the same time.

Lehman said the people of New York City are "sick and tired of Mr. LaGuardia's unbridled tongue." As for himself, the Governor said, he could not be intimidated. He made the statement at his home, 820 Park Ave., apparently in answer to a speech by the Mayor yesterday.

Lehman accused the Mayor of making statements contrary to fact on the decision of the Court of Appeals, which ruled out an election for State Controller on Nov. 4.

Scores Mayor's Epithets

"Last night, in discussing the decision of the Court of Appeals in regard to the election of State Controller," the Governor said, "Mayor LaGuardia was not only grossly abusive but his statements were completely contrary to the facts."

"The Mayor, not only in this campaign but for a long time since, in his capacity as chief executive of the city, has abused and vilified every one who opposed him or criticized him.

"'Thief,' 'double-crosser,' 'crook,' 'bum' are among the milder of the Mayor's epithets. The people of the

Continued on Page 3

WINTRY WINDS DUE TO CHILL BORO TONIGHT

Winter will step into Brooklyn and the suburbs tonight when a northwest wind is scheduled to bring temperatures ranging from 32 to 38 degrees and a frost. It will be partly cloudy and moderately cold tomorrow, the Weather Bureau declared.

WHERE TO FIND IT IN TODAY'S EAGLE

Bridge	Page 19
Clifford Evans	Page 4
Clubwomen	Page 7
Comics	Page 16
Crossword	Page 18
Dr. Brady	Page 4
EDITORIAL	Page 8
Events Tonight	Page 10
FINANCIAL	Page 14
Grin and Bear It	Page 8
Harold Parrott	Page 11
Heffernan	Page 4
Helen Worth	Page 6
Horoscope	Page 4
Movies	Page 5
Music	Page 5
Neighborhood News	Page 15
Novel	Page 19
OBITUARIES	Page 9
Only Yesterday	Page 4
Patterns	Page 7
RADIO	Page 16
Real Estate	Page 19
Society	Page 7
SPORTS	Pages 11-12-13
Theaters	Page 5
These Women	Page 4
Tucker	Page 8
Uncle Ray's Corner	Page 4
Wall Street	Page 14
Want Ads	Pages 17-18-19
Weather Table	Page 9
Woman's	Page 6

Beauticians Strike in 500 Boro Shops, Smear Paint on Placards

One thousand beauticians in about 500 shops in sections of eastern Brooklyn went on strike today for wage increases and other benefits.

Mud packs hardened into clay and operators smeared their paint on picket signs as P. Charles Di Neri, secretary-treasurer of Local 7, Beauty Culturists Union of America, C. I. O., said the strike would be extended during the week.

The shops affected are in East New York, Brownsville, Crown Heights and Flatbush.

A three-year contract between the Empire State Master Hairdressers Association, the employers organization and the union expired Oct. 15. The union seeks a $17.50 minimum wage for manicurists and a 10 percent general wage increase for others.

Demands include one week vacation with pay; elimination of staggered hours, an 8:30 p.m. closing time and one full day a week off; four legal holidays annually and a 50 percent commission over a certain amount taken in by each beautician.

WATCHMAN SAVES MAN ENVELOPED BY FLAMES

Quick action by James Pennington, watchman at the Long Island Lumber Company, 42-14 11th St., Long Island City, today saved Richard Washington, 39, Negro, of 55 W. 128th St., Manhattan, from being burned to death. Gasoline became ignited as Washington was pouring it into the tank of a crane in the yard and the Negro's clothing caught fire.

Pennington pulled him away and quickly tore off Washington's coat, shirt and underwear.

HONOR NAVY YARD DRIVERS FOR SAFETY RECORD

Rear Admiral Edward J. Marquart, commandant of the Brooklyn Navy Yard, will present a certificate of honorable mention today to the enlisted drivers of navy passenger automobiles assigned to the Navy Yard, in recognition of a flawless safety record.

The certificate was issued by the National Safety Council, in connection with the council's national fleet safety contest for passenger cars in the Eastern area, group four, for the period from July 1, 1940, through June 30, 1941. The certificate was received at the Navy Yard yesterday from Secretary of the Navy Frank Knox.

'ANGELS'' REVELRY DISTURBS BORO 'HEAVEN'

You can't make unnecessary noise even in 'heaven' and get away without at least an investigation into your hilarity, it was disclosed yesterday in Pennsylvania Avenue Court.

Holy Love, appearing before Magistrate Jacob Eilperin on a summons to investigate, admitted that she and friends had been less quiet than usual in her "heaven" at 69 Osborn St., at 2 a.m. on the morning of Oct. 19, but she explained that she was a disciple of Father Divine "and it was all in the interest of religion, Judge."

Abraham Kaperskin, a neighbor at 57 Osborn St., whose slumber was disturbed, insisted that the "unearthly sounds" which he heard coming from the heaven were at least partly due to vocalization and the strains of an orchestra, but the court dismissed the summons after warning Holy Love to be less noisesome in the future.

Widow Claims Double Indemnity For Buggsy's Death in Chair

Declares Execution Falls in 'Accidental' Category—Insurance Firm Seeks Ruling

Life insurance law is in the making today in Brooklyn Federal Court as an aftermath of the electrocution last June 12 of Martin (Buggsy) Goldstein, a member of the Murder-for-Money gang.

With Harry (Pittsburg Phil) Strauss, he was executed for the murder of Irving (Puggy) Feinstein, another underworld character.

On Feb. 3, 1936, Buggsy obtained from the Prudential Insurance Company of America a $6,000 policy embodying a double imdemnity accidental death clause. His widow, Beatrice, named beneficiary in the policy, has filed a claim with the company for the $12,000 payment.

The insurance company has now filed suit for cancellation of the policy, posing the following questions for a judicial determination:

In withholding from an insurance company that he is a murderer and therefore liable to conviction and execution does an insured practice a fraud which fails to disclose his true status as an insurable risk?

In the absence of a specific clause in a policy covering payment for death at the hands of the State, must such death be deemed within the purview of the policy?

If payment must be made, is execution to be deemed accidental death and the payment to be double the face amount of the policy?

The basis of the insurance company's complaint is that the policy was fraudulently obtained. Buggsy's widow has 21 days in which to file an answer.

Quiz on Mayor's Election Fund Suddenly Ends

The Crane-Gerard investigation into Mayor LaGuardia's election campaign expenditures ended suddenly today with an explosion of charges and counter-charges, and cries of "slush-fund" and "quitter!"

Before the end came, testimony had been given before Frederick E. Crane, former Chief Judge of the Court of Appeals, and James W. Gerard, former Ambassador to Germany, that the Mayor's campaign cost was $287,135.68—as against charges of a "million-dollar slush fund" which had brought the probe into being. The Mayor had named Crane and Gerard to hold non-partisan hearings.

At today's hearing, in Judge Crane's offices at 61 Broadway, Manhattan, the fatal quarrel developed over submission of certain of the LaGuardia campaign expense books for audit by accountants to be named by the Democrats.

Fights 'Fishing Expedition'

Corporation Counsel William C. Chanler, representing the Mayor, said he would not permit it, that the Democrats wanted only a chance to go into "a long fishing expedition." He would not object, however, to an audit by a certified public accountant picked by any three reputable newspapers in the city.

Robert Daru, chief counsel for Mr. O'Dwyer in the hearing, insisted he had been promised an audit of the books and had a right to assume that that was made in good faith.

"This inquiry now reaches the

Continued on Page 3

Empire City Results

FIRST RACE — Two-year-olds; three-quarter mile.

Brother Dear (Strickler)	4.20	2.90	2.60
Crab Apple (Meade)	—	6.60	5.00
Gay Chic (Hildebrand)	—	—	6.90

Time—1:12 1-5. Catineau, Blue Nose, Philharmonic, Michigan Brown, The General, Pinochle, Coppit also ran. Off time, 1:49½.

SECOND RACE — Three-year-olds and up; three-quarters mile.

Schuylerville (Rodriguez)	14.10	6.40	3.00
Misting (Oliver)	—	4.40	2.60
Celaeno (Meade)	—	—	2.40

Time, 1:11 2-5. Khaymazon, Valjohn, Seenie, Ocean Line also ran. Off time, 2:25½.

DAILY DOUBLE PAID $43.60

Laurel Results

FIRST RACE — Two-year-olds; three-quarter mile.

Anonymous (S. Young)	13.40	6.40	5.70
Smart (McCombs)	—	5.90	4.70
bClifton's Dawn (Howell)	—	—	4.60

Time—1:16 2-5. aMad Witch, Lucky Number, bOlympian, Mintwitch, aEpistle, Glynland, Tovarich, Newfoundland, Prison Ship also ran. Off time, 1:36½.

aMidkiff-McDowell entry; bFeltner-Allen entry.

SECOND RACE—Four-year-olds and up; two miles; steeplechase.

Bell Man (Leonard)	15.90	5.70	2.90
Flemar (Bosley)	—	4.20	2.30
Buck Langhorne (Cruz)	—	—	2.30

Time, 4:05 2-5. Round Bend, Garrynamona, Nursery Pranks also ran. Off time, 2:02.

Rockingham Park Results

FIRST RACE—Three-year-olds and upward; mile and one-sixteenth.

Lou Bright (Gysin)	7.60	3.80	3.20
Six Shooter (T. Atkinson)	—	4.40	3.20
Premier Avril (T. Bates)	—	—	3.80

Time—1:51 3-5. Detroit II, Charlie's Lady, Eleventh Hour, Right As Rain also ran. Off time 1:22.

SECOND RACE — Four-year-olds and up; three-fourths of a mile.

Peter Argo (McMullen)	8.00	4.60	3.40
Claro (Daniels)	—	6.00	3.80
Bully Time (Dattilo)	—	—	4.80

Time, 1:14 4-5. Sadie F, Mowseen, Clean Swept, Rural Mail, Whisper, Set, Grandioso, Hittie, Sir Quest also ran. Off time, 1:52.

DAILY DOUBLE PAID $33.00

THIRD RACE—Two-year-olds; one and one-sixteenth miles.

Mellow (Dattilo)	5.60	3.00	2.40
Grandiloquent (Lindy)	—	6.80	4.00
Header (Ryan)	—	—	2.60

Time—1:53 1-5. Four-in-Hand, Arieante, Marymick, Infinite Maid, Fay Jay, Strutting Miss also ran. Off time, 2:20.

River Downs Results

FIRST RACE—Two-year-olds; one mile and forty yards.

Barney's Gal (Delucia)	25.00	11.60	6.40
Jack K (Meloche)	—	10.00	5.80
Darby Dee Dee (W'daman)	—	—	5.40

Time, 1:42 2-5. Texalite, xAgrawan, xIvy Roll, Brillmiss, Total Loss, xMiss Pert, Two Roses, Griffin Hills, xEasy Hal also ran. Off time, 2:20.

HUNTED THUG KILLS HIMSELF IN GUN CHASE

Two Others Seized In Bebchick Murder —Onlooker Wounded

A running gun duel through the corridors and over the fire escapes of the Abbey Hotel, 51st St. and 7th Ave., Manhattan, today ended with the suicide of a murder suspect, the capture of two other suspects and the wounding of an onlooker.

Fatally wounded by a bullet from his own revolver was Abe (Joe Miller) Bitler of 2301 E. 23d St., Brooklyn, who had boasted not long before that "no one will ever get me alive." Shot through the right temple at 2:30 a.m., he died in Roosevelt Hospital at 6:30.

Before he turned his weapon on himself, Bitler fired twice at William Ortmann of Detroit, 52, composer and theatrical manager, whom he mistook for a detective. In the Roosevelt Hospital, Ortmann, shot through the left side of the heart and the abdomen, was said to be in a critical condition.

Sought by Boro Cops

Those arrested were Samuel Kovner, 28, of 5811 18th Ave., Brooklyn, and Samuel Kablonsky, 23, who

Continued on Page 2

'ALARMING' PERIL SEEN BY SOVIET AS BATTLES RAGE

Reds Counter Attack On Moscow, Donets Fronts, Train Reserves

Kuibyshev, Oct. 28 (U.P.)—Soviet counter-attacks on both the Moscow and Rostov-Donets Basin front were reported in Russian dispatches today but the situation on the southern front was said still to be "most alarming."

The fighting for Rostov and the Donets industries was described as raging with unabated ferocity.

Far back of the fighting lines, the Moscow newspaper Pravda reported, new Russian reserve troops are being trained. These reserves, it was said, are being assembled as far east as the Trans-Baikal region of Siberia.

In a four-column leading article, Pravda proclaimed anew Russia's intention of fighting the war to the end.

Industries Moved East

Russian heavy industries, in substantial part, it said, have been

Continued on Page 2

Nazis Rage at F. D. R. Charge Address Is 'Final Step to War'

Roosevelt Branded 'Greatest Liar, Faker In World History'

Berlin, Oct. 28 (U.P.)—Nazi spokesmen strongly denounced President Roosevelt's Navy Day speech today and the authoritative Hamburger Fremdenblatt charged that the Chief Executive's address last night was "in more than one sense a final step toward an undeclared shooting war by the United States against Germany and her allies."

Nazi spokesmen and the controlled German press attacked Mr. Roosevelt with almost unprecedented rage, directing their fire particularly at his charges that Germany contemplates creation of a Nazi-dominated hegemony in South America and world wide abolition of organized religion.

Call President 'Liar, Faker'

The authorized spokesman said that "Roosevelt evidently has the ambition to go down as the greatest liar and faker in world history."

[Meanwhile, in Rome Premier Mussolini told a cheering throng of 50,000 Fascists that the United States and other anti-axis forces will be crushed by the axis.]

The Berlin afternoon press published front-page articles denouncing Mr. Roosevelt as a "liar, faker, warmonger, lunatic and hireling of hte Jews."

It was regarding as noteworthy that for the first time in recent years the Nazi press and spokesmen reacted almost immediately to President Roosevelt's address. Ordinarily no reaction is produced for at least 24 or 36 hours after a Presidential statement.

The first printed quotations from the Roosevelt speech dealt with his charges regarding Nazi intentions toward South America and religion.

The Lokalanzeiger headlined "Roosevelt's Silly Forgery" and said, editorially: "Roosevelt has not hesitated to libel Germany with regular forgeries in order, by these unbelievable methods, to create something like a moral alibi for his criminal plans. Roosevelt wants conflict. That is to say Judah wants to drive Americans into war."

See President Running Amok

The Deutsche Allgemeine Zeitungs said:

"The warmonger in the White House spoke, foaming at the mouth. His chasing after war has become a veritable running amok."

"Such an example of shamelessness, rottenness, beastliness and idiocy never has been offered to a modern nation," an authorized informant said. "Never has such a specimen of mental breakdown been

Continued on Page 2

Nation Moving Past Short of Hostilities Status, Talk Reveals

Washington, Oct. 28 (U.P.)—President Roosevelt's emphatic statement that "the shooting has started" was spectacular notification today that the nation is moving beyond short-of-war boundaries into the field of limited naval hostilities.

America has been attacked and Germany fired the first shot, Mr. Roosevelt last night told his worldwide broadcast audience and the total defense and Navy Day diners in the Hotel Mayflower here.

His address, charging Nazi plans to abolish religion and to take over South America and parts of Central America, including the Panama Canal, seemed to combine significantly with a dramatic reminder that the dead and injured aboard the destroyer Kearny were the sons of many States.

The whole appeared to be a summons to the hesitant at home, in Latin America and, perhaps, even in the Vatican, to join the crusade against Hitler. Mr. Roosevelt's own estimate of his speech was that the religious phase was the most newsworthy.

Calls for Speedy Arming

He called again for the speedy arming of American merchant ships, insisted they must be free to carry munitions directly to British ports and promised that the navy would protect American shipping. The Neutrality Act had been "outmoded by force of violent circumstances."

Mr. Roosevelt was interrupted 12 times by applause but the big outburst of whoops and cheering came when he directly denied the right of John L. Lewis, president of the United Mine Workers of America, to shut down production in captive coal mines.

In 101 razor-sharp words Mr. Roosevelt dealt with business and labor obstruction to national defense.

Must Multiply Output

"Our national will must speak from every assembly line—yes, from every coal mine,' 'the President began, but was interrupted by a burst of cheering at the interpolated reference to coal mines, "in the all-in-

Continued on Page 2

Service on Bronx I. R. T. Resumes After Flood

After a nine-hour tieup, caused by a burst water main, subway service on the I. R. T. division in the Bronx resumed today. Over 500,000 commuters were affected by the break in service. The water was from nine to 15 feet deep in several places.

PRISON TERMS PROPOSED TO HALT TIEUPS

Lewis an 'Arrogant Labor Leader' in Coal Walkout, Says Byrd

Washington, Oct. 28 (U.P.)—Senator Josiah W. Bailey (D., N. C.) introduced legislation today to define as sabotage against the Government situations like the captive coal mine strike called on John L. Lewis.

Bailey introduced the measure as an amendment to the neutrality act revision measure now being debated in the Senate. It would impose a maximum fine of $10,000 and ten years' imprisonment for violations.

Under the terms of Bailey's proposal, which followed President Roosevelt's third appeal to Lewis to call off the captive coal mine strike, sabotage would be broadened to include stoppages in the production of "materials or articles ordered by any department or bureau of Cabinet official for the national defense."

(The United States Steel Corporation curtailed operations today because of the work stoppage in its captive mines. Benjamin F. Fairless, president of U. S. Steel, announced that the corporation's subsidiaries in the Chicago, Pittsburgh and Youngstown districts would have to curtail their production 10 to 20 percent because of the mine closings.)

Mr. Roosevelt last night denounced a "dangerous" minority of labor leaders as a menace to national security. His statement was considered in some Congressional quarter as tacit agreement to some form of legislation to curb strikes.

Chairman Elbert D. Thomas (D., Utah) of the Senate Labor Committee suggested that it might be "beneficial" to extend to all labor disputes the compulsory mediation features of the railway labor act. But he cautioned against hasty legaction at this time.

Condemns Lewis

Bailey introduced his amendment shortly after Senator Harry F. Byrd (D., Va.), made a floor

Continued on Page 2

MAYOR DISPLAYS PUNCH IN MAKING HIS POINT

Political speeches [illegible] sometimes physically dangero[illegible] illustrated by Mayor [illegible]a last night at Seth Low [illegible]nior High School.

Describing the Governor's dilemma in the Controllership development, and saying "Herbie gave himself a punch in his own jaw," the Mayor socked his own chin, nearly knocking himself out.

GUARDING BRITAIN'S LIFELINE—Somewhere in the Atlantic, as President Roosevelt rallied America to "battle stations" in the war to destroy Hitlerism, this American submarine is heading to sea with flags flying and deck guns at "ready" for any emergency.

Street Closing
CING EXTRA
★★★★★

BROOKLYN EAGLE

Wall Street, Closing
RACING EXTRA
★★★★★★

LOCAL WEATHER FORECAST: Rain tonight; cloudy, followed by clear, colder tomorrow

R • No. 340 • DAILY AND SUNDAY • BROOKLYN, N. Y., MONDAY, DEC. 8, 1941 • Entered at the Brooklyn Postoffice as 2d Class Mail Matter—(Copyright 1941 The Brooklyn Eagle, Inc.) • 3 CENTS

.. S. DECLARES WAR; ,500 AMERICANS DIE

ashington, Dec. 8 (UP)—Casualties on the Hawaiian l of Oahu in yesterday's Japanese air attack will nt to about 3,000, including about 1,500 fatalities, hite House announced today.

he White House confirmed the loss in Pearl Harbor of old battleship" and a destroyer, which was blown

everal other American ships were damaged and a number of Army and Navy airplanes on Hawaiian were put out of commission, the White House dis- d.

t reported at the same time that American operations st Japan were being carried out on a large scale, re- g already in the destruction of "a number of Japa- planes and submarines."

Manila, Dec. 8 (UP)—Press dispatches reported that 100 0 troops, 60 of them Americans, were killed or injured y when Japanese warplanes raided Iba, on the west t of the Island of Luzon, north of the Olangapo naval

BATTLE OFF HAWAII

TED PRESS

he United States and Britain smashed back pan today on a 6,000-mile Pacific war front flamed from Hawaii's coral beaches to the shores of Malay and Thailand.

he American battle fleet was reported chal- g the Japanese striking force which raided ii with heavy loss of life and naval damage. at naval engagement was rumored in the s west of America's Pacific Gibraltar.

Here is the picture:

ondon: Prime Minister Churchill carries Britain into against Japan with a formal declaration before ment.

okio: Japanese naval command claims sinking of battleships Oklahoma and West Virginia; damage other battleships; damage to four heavy cruisers; destruction of U. S. planes; probable sinking of aircraft carrier (rumored to be the Langley), cap- f "many" enemy ships; sinking of U. S. mine- er Penguin at Guam.

hailand: Apparently caving in to the Japanese little or no fight; Tokio claims Japanese troops into country under "agreement" reached with k Government; Japanese reported swarming outhern Thailand in preparation for drive on ore.

ingapore: British battling Japanese landing forces have established series of beachheads along n coast; Royal Air Force heavily engaged.

anila: Waves of Japanese bombers attack key in Philippines, including U. S. Army base at Fort burg, Davao and the vicinity of Baguio. Japanese s rumored but not confirmed.

hina: Japanese attack Hongkong twice by air; over Shanghai International Settlement; occupy n British Concession and intern 200 American ma-

acific Isles: Japanese attack American islands of

Continued on Page 2

118 Japs Seized Here; City Put On War Footing

Boro and L. I. Speed Defenses—Mines, Nets To Be Placed in Bay

At least 118 Japanese aliens throughout the city and Long Island were seized and interned at Ellis Island between midnight and 9 a.m. in a roundup which is continuing.

Meanwhile, as Mayor LaGuardia placed New York City on a war footing, Brooklyn and Long Island prepared defenses at vital port facilities, army and navy stations, utility and defense production plants and airports.

Coast Guard officials announced that mines or a submarine net will block off all but a 2,000-foot channel through the lower bay. Protective devices will be installed in the bay between Norton's Point, Coney Island, and Hoffman Island. The army followed with an announcement that several mine tenders have been turned over for duty with bases at Fort Hancock, Sandy Hook.

Guard LaGuardia Field

Extra police were on duty today at LaGuardia Field, patrolling the three entrances and the Pan American seaplane base. From the Astoria precinct patrolmen were assigned at the 85th St. entrance where the road leads directly to

Continued on Page 10

Communists Pledge Full Loyalty to U. S.

The National Committee of the Communist party of the United States today was on record with the declaration that it "pledges its loyalty, its devoted labor and the last drop of its blood in support of our country in this greatest struggle that ever threatened its existence."

The statement, signed by William Z. Foster, national chairman of the national committee of the party, pledged "everything for victory over world-wide Fascist slavery."

WAR BULLETINS

JAPS BOMB MANILA FORT

NBC reported from Manila this afternoon that the Philippine capital "is now being bombed." The Japanese are bombing with "fiendish accuracy," it was reported. The Japanese attacked Fort William McKinley, just outside Manila, and Nichols Airfield on the outskirts of the city.

NAZIS DROP MOSCOW DRIVE

Berlin, Dec. 8 (UP)—A Nazi military spokesman said tonight that Germany has abandoned attempts to capture Moscow for this Winter. He said the severe Russian weather caused the Germans to end large-scale operations on the Eastern Front for the Winter. (Earlier details on Page 2.)

FIRST CASUALTIES LISTED

The first United States casualties in the Japanese attacks were revealed today in word sent to the parents by the Navy Department. (An official list of casualties is expected to be issued at Washington later.)

The dead: 1st Lieut. Hans Christiansen, 21, Woodland, Cal.; 2nd Lieut. George A. Whiteman, 21, Sedalia, Mo., and Private George G. Leslie, 20, Arnold, Pa.

4 LATIN REPUBLICS JOIN U. S.

By mid-afternoon today four Latin Republics, Cuba, Costa Rica, Nicaragua and Haiti, declared war on Japan as Pan-American solidarity began expressing itself, the International News Service reported. Mexico, Uruguay, Salvador and Colombia were preparing similar action while the latter nation was reported ready to cede Pacific and Caribbean bases to the United States.

HONGKONG REPELS 2 RAIDS

Hongkong, Dec. 8 (UP)—Two air raids by Japanese planes on Hongkong were beaten off by anti-aircraft fire today and damage was not important, a British command communique said.

(The Japanese report claimed that in a surprise attack on a British airdrome north of Hongkong 12 planes were set afire.)

3 JAP TROOPSHIPS HIT

San Francisco, Dec. 8 (UP)—The Singapore Radio, heard by a United Press listening post here today, reported two American-built Hudson bombers operating off the northern Malayan coast had scored direct hits on two Japanese troopships and another Hudson bomber had scored a direct hit on a barge loaded with Japanese soldiers.

U. S. INTERNS 736 JAPS

Washington, Dec. 8 (UP)—Attorney General Francis Biddle announced today that Federal Bureau of Investigation agents had seized 736 Japanese nationals in the United States and in the Hawaiian Islands last night.

Continued on Page 10

WHERE TO FIND IT

Bay Ridge	Page 9	Music	Page 4
Bridge	Page 23	Neighborhood News	Page 8
Clubwomen	Page 18	Novel	Page 23
Comics	Page 20	OBITUARIES	Page 13
Crossword	Page 22	Only Yesterday	Page 6
Dr. Brady	Page 6	RADIO	Page 20
EDITORIAL	Page 12	Real Estate	Page 23
FINANCIAL	Page 10	Sermons	Page 7
Grin and Bear It	Page 12	Society	Page 18
Harold Conrad	Page 4	SPORTS	Pages 15-16-17
Harold Parrott	Page 15	Theaters	Page 4
Heffernan	Page 6	These Women	Page 6
Helen Worth	Page 19	Tucker	Page 12
Horoscope	Page 6	Uncle Ray's Corner	Page 6
Jury	Page 8	Wall Street	Page 10
Lindley	Page 6	Want Ads	Pages 21-22-23
Movies	Page 4	Weather Table	Page 13
		Woman's	Page 19

Washington, Dec. 8 (UP)—Congress today proclaimed existence of a state of war between the United States and the Japanese Empire 33 minutes after the dramatic moment when President Roosevelt stood before a joint session to pledge that we will triumph—"so help us, God."

The Senate acted first, adopting the resolution by a unanimous roll call vote of 82 to 0, within 21 minutes after the President had concluded his speech.

The House voted immediately afterward and by 1:13 p.m. a majority of the House had voted "Aye.' The final House vote was announced as 388 to 1. The lone negative vote was cast by Representative Jeannette Rankin, (R., Mont.), who also voted against enter into World War 1.

The resolution now has to be signed by Speaker Sam Rayburn and Vice President Wallace before it is sent to the President at the White House. His signature will place the United States formally at war against the Japanese Empire, already an accomplished fact.

The resolutions were before both Houses within 15 minutes of the time Mr. Roosevelt ended his seven-minute, 500-word extraordinary message.

There was a half second of uncertainty in the House when Representative Rankin objected to unanimous consent for immediate consideration of the war resolution.

Miss Rankin Hissed

Speaker Sam Rayburn brushed the objection aside. It was she who, in the small hours of April 6, 1917, faltered, wept and finally voted "No" against a similar resolution aimed at Germany.

When the clerk came to her name on the roll call today she voted "No" again. A chorus of hisses and boos greeted her vote.

Representative Harold Knutson (R., Minn.), who also voted against American entry into the World War in 1917, said today this nation "has no choice but to declare war on Japan."

"I do not see that we have any other choice," Knutson told reporters. "They declared war on us."

Miss Rankin and Knutson are the only present members of the House who voted against war in 1917.

Only Two Remain Seated

Only Miss Rankin and Representative Clare Hoffman (R., Mich.) had remained seated when the House gave a standing ovation in response to Roosevelt's solemn statement:

"I ask that the Congress declare that since the unprovoked and dastardly attack by Japan on Sunday, Dec. 7, a state of war has existed between the United States and the Japanese Empire."

In a staccato of short sentences the President told where the Japanese had hit yesterday throughout

Continued on Page 2

TEXT OF ROOSEVELT CALL ON CONGRESS

To the Congress of the United States:

Yesterday, Dec. 7, 1941—A date which will live in infamy—the United States of America was suddenly and deliberately attacked by naval and air forces of the Empire of Japan.

The United States was at peace with that nation and, at the solicitation of Japan, was still in conversation with its Government and its Emperor looking toward the maintenance of peace in the Pacific. Indeed, one hour after Japanese air squadrons had commenced bombing in Oahu, the Japanese Ambassador to the United States and his colleague delivered to the Secretary of State a formal reply to a recent American message. While this reply stated that it seemed useless to continue the existing diplomatic negotiations, it contained no threat or hint of war or armed attack.

"Deliberately Sought to Deceive U .S."

It will be recorded that the distance of Hawaii from Japan makes it obvious that the attack was deliberately planned and many days or even weeks ago. During the intervening time the Japanese Government has deliberately sought to deceive the United States by false statements and expressions of hope for continued peace.

The attack yesterday on the Hawaiian Islands has caused severe damage to American naval and military forces. Very many American lives have been lost. In addition, American ships have been reported torpedoed on the high seas between San Francisco and Honolulu.

Yesterday the Japanese Government also launched an attack against Malaya.

Last night Japanese forces attacked Hongkong.

Last night Japanese forces attacked Guam.

Last night Japanese forces attacked the Philippine Islands.

Last night the Japanese attacked Wake Island.

This morning the Japanese attacked Midway Island.

Japan has, therefore, undertaken a surprise offensive extending throughout the Pacific area. The facts of yesterday speak for themselves. The people of the United States have already formed their opinions and well understand the implications to the very life and safety of our nation.

As commander-in-chief of the Army and Navy I have directed that all measures be taken for our defense.

Always will we remember the character of the onslaught against us.

Calls for War on Jap Treachery

No matter how long it may take us to overcome this premeditated invasion, the American people in their righteous might will win through to absolute victory.

I believe I interpret the will of the Congress and of the people when I assert that we will not only defend ourselves to the uttermost but will make very certain that this form of treachery shall never endanger us again.

Hostilities exist. There is no blinking at the fact that our people, our territory and our interests are in grave danger.

With confidence in our armed forces—with the unbounding determination of our people—we will gain the inevitable triumph—so help us God.

I ask that the Congress declare that since the unprovoked and dastardly attack by Japan on Sunday, December seventh, a state of war has existed between the United States and the Japanese Empire. FRANKLIN D. ROOSEVELT.

The White House, Dec. 8, 1941.

Mercury Drops to 25°, Coldest Weather of Season

The city experienced its coldest temperature of the season when the mercury dropped to 25 degrees at 4 a.m. today, but rising temperature and cloudiness was forecast for the rest of the day. The highest temperature expected today is 40 degrees. Tomorrow will be clear, according to the Weather Man.

Charles Town Results

FIRST RACE — Two-year-olds; about ½ mile.

Olympian (Loturco)	3.20	2.80	2.20
Rolls Rough (Shaffer)	—	9.20	4.80
Chief Teddy (Grant)	—	—	3.60

Time, 1.27 2-5. Prison Ship, Duca..., Susan's Sally, Loch Raven, Tuleyrie's Bay also ran. Off time, 1.33.

SECOND RACE — Three-year-olds and up; six and a half furlongs.

Glitter Girl (W. Kelly)	8.00	4.20	3.60
Two Ply (Carrillo)	—	4.20	3.60
High Rose (W. Kirk)	—	—	8.00

Time, 1.21 2-5. Paloomia, Joanna, Great Bear, Meadow Gold, Compound also ran. Off time, 2.02½.

33 Nazi Spies Get Stiff Prison Terms Here

Wall Street Closing
RACING EXTRA
★★★★★★

BROOKLYN EAGLE

Wall Street Closing
RACING EXTRA
★★★★★★

LOCAL WEATHER FORECAST: Cloudy and colder tonight

101st YEAR • No. 1 • DAILY AND SUNDAY — BROOKLYN, N. Y., FRIDAY, JAN. 2, 1942 — Entered at the Brooklyn Postoffice as 2d Class Mail Matter— • 3 CENTS

JAPS OCCUPY MANILA

25 Nations Sign Fight-to-Finish Pact

33 Nazi Spies Get Stiff Prison Terms Here

Courtroom Jammed As Byers Metes Out Heavy Sentences

Stiff sentences, some close to the maximum, were imposed in Brooklyn Federal Court today by Judge Mortimer W. Byers on the 33 persons who were part of the Nazi espionage system in this country.

Three women who took part in the work of supplying the German war lords with vital American information felt the heavy hand of the law. All of them stalked out of the courtroom without showing tears or trace of emotion.

Lilly Barbara Carola Stein, 27, of 232 E. 79th St., Manhattan, Vienna-born model, got the heaviest of the women's sentences. She must serve ten years, the maximum on the second count of transmitting information to Germany. Included in that is another sentence of two years for conspiracy, for the court ruled that all double sentences imposed be served concurrently. Prisoners must serve out unpaid fines at the rate of one day for each dollar.

Lightest Term Is Year

The lightest sentence of all, a year and a day, was given to Evelyn Clayton Lewis, 31, of 24 W. 76th St., Manhattan, Arkansas-born artist, who told Judge Byers she was deeply humiliated by her disgrace. She fell in love with a Nazi spy and followed him blindly in obeying orders, and Judge Byers told her that an infatuation was no excuse for disloyalty to one's country.

Else Weustenfield, 41, of 312 W.

Continued on Page 2

Cashmore Names Joseph Reich as Boro Secretary

Democratic Leader Of 6th A. D. Succeeds Schanzer in Post

Appointment of Joseph Reich as Borough Secretary was announced today by Borough President Cashmore.

Mr. Reich, who is Democratic leader of the 6th A. D., fills the vacancy caused by the resignation of Borough Secretary Albert D. Schanzer. Mr. Schanzer recently was appointed by Governor Lehman to the Appeals Board of the State Unemployment Insurance Department.

Mr. Reich served in the Assembly with the Borough President in the early 1920s, and subsequently they also served together for ten years as members of the old Board of Aldermen.

Mr. Reich is a World War veteran, past commander of Brooklyn Post, 500, American Legion, of which Mr. Cashmore is a member; past commander of Williamsburg Post 224, Veterans of Foreign Wars; past national advocate general, Jewish War Veterans, and also is actively identified with other fraternal, charitable, civic and religious organizations in this borough.

Until abolition of the office under the country reform proposition voted at the last election, Mr. Reich had been Deputy Kings Register.

He resides with his wife at 85 Pulaski St.

Eagle Staff photo

WOMEN SPIES JAILBOUND—Lilly B. C. Stein (left), Viennese model, sentenced to ten years in prison, and Evelyn C. Lewis, Arkansas-born artist, sentenced to a year and a day. They are two of the 33 convicts given prison terms by Judge Byers in Brooklyn Federal Court today as Nazi spies.

BALS TO COMMAND O'DWYER'S SQUAD

Creation of Confidential Investigating Group Agreed On at Conference With Mayor

District Attorney O'Dwyer today awaited certificates of appointment promised by Mayor LaGuardia to create a new confidential investigating squad responsible only to the prosecutor.

Agreement on creation of the secret squad was reached yesterday by the Mayor and Mr. O'Dwyer after a half-hour conference at City Hall. Both officials emerged from the parley in amicable moods.

It was the first time they had met face to face since their nomination last September as opponents in the recent Mayoralty election, and it was apparent that their bitter political feud which flared publicly three weeks ago had been smoothed over.

Backs Mayor's Statement

The Mayor issued a statement declaring that Mr. O'Dwyer had submitted a "very constructive plan" for realignment of police working on his broad criminal inquiry. The prosecutor, on returning to his office, smilingly expressed satisfaction with the results and said his comment for the moment

Continued on Page 21

LaGuardia Ouster As OCD Head Asked

Washington, Jan. 2 (INS)—Charging that New York City's defense organizations are confused and without a head, Rep. Martin J. Kennedy (D., N. Y.), today demanded the removal of Mayor LaGuardia from his job of Director of Civilian Defense in Washington.

"In behalf of the seven and one-half million people in my city, I plead with the President to replace Mr. LaGuardia," Kennedy said in a speech on the floor.

"Some time ago we had an air raid warning. It resulted in terrible confusion. No one knew what to do and our Mayor was nowhere to be found—he was thousands of miles away, and his only comment was to insult the people of his city."

2 Belgian Hostages Shot by Germans

Two Belgian hostages have been shot down by German occupational authorities and a large number arrested following widespread acts of sabotage, the British radio reported today in a broadcast heard by C.B.S.

Tropical Park Results

1—Queen Echo, 11.20-5.40-3.20; Bold Turk, 3.70-2.60; War Declared, 4.50. Off time, 2:04.

2—Sassy Mate, 8.20-4.10-3.70; Silent Host, 6.10-4.70; Alley, 7.30. Off time, 2:32½.

DAIL DOUBLE PAID $60.80

U. S. WARSHIP HIT IN DUTCH WATERS

Naval, Air Aid to East Indies Revealed In Jap Raids on Vessel and Two Planes

Batavia, N. E. I., Jan. 2 (U.P.)—United States naval and air co-operation with the Dutch defenders of the East Indies was disclosed today in a war communique which said an American warship and two airplanes had been attacked by the Japanese.

The warship escaped serious damage during enemy aerial bombardment in a northern sector of the East Indies (possibly off Borneo or Celebes Islands), and the American aircraft were not damaged, according to the communique.

The communique, distributed by the official news agency, said:

"In the northern part of the archipelago, Japanese aircraft attacked one of the warships of the American fighting forces which are co-operating with the Netherlands naval forces in defense. No serious damage was done.

"In the same area, two American planes were attacked by a number of Japanese aircraft but did not suffer damage."

The Dutch officially reported that Japanese aircraft, attempting to "terrorize the population" had bombed and machine gunned the settlement of Laboean Bilik, on the Sumatra east coast.

Jap Islands Bombed

Sydney, Australia, Jan. 2 (INS)—Unleashing their first major offensive action out of Australia, British planes were revealed today to have attacked enemy targets in the Japanese-mandated Caroline Islands.

A communique issued at Melbourne said R. A. F. planes bombed ground installations and seaplanes at Kapingamarang Island in the Caroline group, 1,200 miles from Australia.

Another official communique said four Japanese transports had been sunk off the coast of Thailand.

The attack on the Caroline Islands marks the first punishment inflicted on Japanese territory.

If the assault was launched from Australian soil it means that the British flyers made an extended flight across the Coral Sea and the Netherlands East Indies far up into the Pacific.

CHINESE TROOPS ENTER BURMA TO BOLSTER BRITISH

Malaya Command Declares 'Considerable Help' Is on the Way

Singapore, Jan. 2 (U.P.)—A communique issued by the Malaya command at the Kuala Lampur base in the west coast defense area said today that "considerable help is en route for the armies defending Malaya."

It was believed here that the communique was meant to indicate that Sir Henry Pownall, new commander in chief in the Far East, intended to fight for every inch of ground and to allay any feeling in the provinces that everything was being sacrificed to the defense of Singapore.

[An announcement in Chungking disclosed that fully equipped Chinese troops have entered Burma at the request of the British and are now under command of Gen. Sir Archibald Wavell, British commander in chief in India.

[The Chinese high command, a spokesman said, was preparing to send more Chinese tropps abroad whenever requested to do so by the British or other Allies.]

Japs Raid Singapore

It was admitted that there was little word from the east coast, where the Japanese had claimed the capture of Kuantan, 200 miles from Singapore, but it was said that British patrols and artillery were active.

A Japanese air attack on Singapore Island during the night did little damage and caused no casulaties, it was said.

British planes, attacking a Japanese airdrome in Kedah Province, up the west coast from Penang

Continued on Page 21

3 Baby Girls Greet 1942 At Boro Hospital

Although the first 1942 baby was born at the Bronx Maternity Hospital at 12:01 a.m. yesterday, three baby girls followed soon afterward at St. Catherine's Hospital in the Williamsburg section. Their parents are named Peropat, Di Carri and Miezwa.

The new Archbishop Spellman Pavilion at St. Vincent's Hospital, Manhattan, just opened, started its career with the birth at 3:35 a.m. of a daughter to Dr. and Mrs. John H. Kilgus of 475 Clinton Ave.

50c. Biscuit Theft Costs Peggy O'Neil $120

London, Jan. 2 (INS)—The original "Peg o' My Heart"—Actress Peggy O'Neil—was $120 out of pocket today because, according to the police, she stole 50 cents' worth of biscuits and chocolate from a London store.

Miss O'Neil protested her innocence, but the magistrate thought otherwise and fined her $80 plus $40 costs. "The seriousness of the crime should not be measured by the value of the goods stolen," he said.

Bardia Captured; Free 1,000 Captives

Cairo, Jan. 2 (U.P.)—British Imperials have captured Bardia, Axis stronghold between Tobruk and the Egypt-Libya border, general headquarters for the Middle East said today.

In taking Bardia the Imperials released more than 1,000 British prisoners of war who had been held there by the Axis. The total number of enemy prisoners taken at Bardia was not known immediately.

Bardia, German-Italian stronghold which the British passed by in their drive against the main Axis forces, was taken by South African troops this morning.

A special communique by Royal Air Force Middle East headquarters in Cairo said that during 1941 the R. A. F. shot down or destroyed on the ground 2,095 enemy aircraft on all Middle East fronts ranging from Greece to Italian Somaliland.

Boy Slayer of Family Breaks Minnesota Jail

St. Paul, Minn., Jan. 2 (U.P.)—State police blocked northern Minnesota roads today, hunting Richard Dehler, 16-year-old farm youth who escaped from a Little Falls jail where he was held awaiting trial for slaying his father, mother, brother and sister.

U. S., Britain, Russia, China Act on Pledge

Won't Accept Separate Peace—F. D. R. to Give Details of Declaration

Washington, Jan. 2 (U.P.) — The United States, Great Britain, China and Russia have signed a declaration that they will fight the Axis to a finish and that none of them will accept a separate peace, it was learned today.

Mr. Roosevelt was expected to announce the pact late this afternoon.

It was understood that several other nations also have agreed, or soon will agree, to the anti-Axis pact. Several envoys visited the State Department during the day, including Panamanian Ambassador Ernesto Jaen Guardia, who told reporters he had signed a declaration of anti-Axis solidarity.

[The INS said that the grand pact is being signed by 25 nations in the office of Assistant Secretary of State Adolf Berle Jr.

[By 12:45 p.m. the diplomatic representatives of some 15 nations had called at the State Department to affix their signatures to the agreement, according to the INS.]

The declaration was said to be brief and to contain only two points—a pledge to enter into no separate peace and a pledge to co-operate toward victorious conclusion of the war.

The agreement apparently is the first concrete result of the talks Mr. Roosevelt and British Prime Minister Winston Churchill have been holding here with spokesmen for nations opposing the Axis. The conferences also have covered supply and command problems.

Signed by Churchill?

No details were available immediately, but it was pointed out the chief executives of the two great English-speaking nations are currently in the White House and presumably signed the agreement for the United States and Great Britain. Also in Washington are T. V. Soong, new Foreign Minister of the Chinese Nationalist Government, and Russian Ambassador Maxim Litvinov, who also is the Soviet Vice-Commissar for Foreign Affairs.

Envoys from these countries visited the State Department today and were believed to have signed the pact: Australia, Belgium, The Netherlands, Costa Rica, Honduras, El Salvador, Cuba, Haiti, Guate-

Continued on Page 21

Hitler Hanged in Effigy By Chicago Celebrants

Chicago, Jan. 2 (INS) — Adolf Hitler was hanged in effigy as part of Chicago's New Year's celebration, apparently by someone with aesthetic as well as political sensibilities.

The effigy, left hanging in a tree, consisted chiefly of a leather jacket, trousers and shoes, with the head representing the mustached physiognomy of the German dictator.

Queens Man Among 9 Lost On Army Bomber Flight

March Field, Cal., Jan. 2 (U.P.)—A twin-motored bomber missing in the San Bernardino Mountain area with nine men aboard was "presumed" lost today. The ship, a Martin B-26, flew into bad weather with seven other planes on Tuesday night and had been unreported since, March Field Headquarters revealed.

Second Lt. Frank A. Kobal, Queens Village, N. Y., was a crew member.

BASE AT CAVITE ALSO IS SEIZED

Defenders Take Strong Positions North of Capital, on Fortified Isles

Washington, Jan. 2 (UP)—The city of Manila and the United States naval base at nearby Cavite fell into Japanese hands today.

Valiant American and Filipino defenders under Gen. Douglas MacArthur had to abandon the capital and the base, but they still held strong positions north of Manila and on fortified islands that command Manila Bay.

The fall of undefended Manila was announced in a War Department communique which said:

"Advanced elements of Japanese troops entered Manila at 3 p.m., Jan. 2, 1942 (Manila time) (1 a.m. E. S. T.).

Evacuation of Cavite was reported by the Navy in another communique, stating:

"All ships and naval personnel were removed from the Manila-Cavite area prior to enemy occupation."

Meanwhile President Roosevelt told newspapermen to expect an important announcement from the White House late today. Mr. Roosevelt's announcement of impending big news came as he and British Prime Minister Winston Churchill quickened the pace of their efforts to perfect British-American war plans.

The loss of Manila, which had been in United States

Continued on Page 21

MacArthur Wounded, Tokio Report Says

Tokio, Jan. 2 (Official Japanese Broadcast Recorded by by the United Press in New York)—Gen. Douglas MacArthur, United States commander in the Philippines, was reported by official Domei News Agency today to have been wounded in the right shoulder and removed to the island fortress of Corregidor in Manila Bay.

[In Washington the War Department said that it had no report that General MacArthur has been wounded.]

According to the Domei report, MacArthur was wounded by shrapnel and was being treated either at Corregidor or in Australia. The agency said he may have been removed to Australia on a hospital ship that recently left for Port Darwin and that the Philippine Government had been reported moved to Port Darwin.

Assert Americans Encircled

It was asserted that part of the American forces in Batangas prov-

Continued on Page 21

WHERE TO FIND IT

Bay Ridge News	Page 8	Lindley	Page 23
Bridge	Page 25	Movies	Page 10
Comics	Page 22	Music	Page 23
Crossword	Page 24	Neighborhood News	Page 9
Dr. Brady	Page 23	Novel	Page 25
EDITORIAL	Page 12	OBITUARIES	Page 13
FINANCIAL	Page 20	RADIO	Page 22
Going Places	Page 11	Real Estate	Page 25
Grin and Bear It	Page 12	Society	Page 18
Harold Conrad	Page 23	SPORTS	Pages 15-16-17
Harold Parrott	Page 15	Theaters	Page 10
Heffernan	Page 23	These Women	Page 23
Helen Worth	Page 19	Tucker	Page 12
Horoscope	Page 23	Uncle Ray's Corner	Page 23
Jo Ranson	Page 22	Wall Street	Page 20
Jury	Page 9	Want Ads	Pages 24-25
		Woman's	Page 19

WALL STREET
RACING EXTRA
★★★★★★

BROOKLYN EAGLE

WALL STREET
RACING EXTRA
★★★★★★

LOCAL WEATHER FORECAST: Partly cloudy and continued cold tonight.

101st YEAR • No. 5 • DAILY AND SUNDAY • BROOKLYN, N. Y., TUESDAY, JAN. 6, 1942 • • 3 CENTS

F. D. R. VOWS U. S. WAR ON ALL AXIS FRONTS

Outlines A. E. F. for Britain, Huge Plane, Tank Output

185,000 Aircraft, 120,000 Land Dreadnoughts Ordered for '42-'43

Washington, Jan. 6 (UP)—President Roosevelt, in a promise of victory to come, told Congress today that he would order United States armed forces to world-wide war fronts to find the enemy and "hit him and hit him again whenever and wherever we can reach him."

He warned of a "heavy price for freedom" in money, work and blood and fixed the war budget for the next fiscal year at $56,000,000,000.

Most of these billions will go into a tremendous production effort far exceeding anything the world has seen—185,000 planes, 120,000 tanks and 55,000 anti-aircraft guns to be produced during 1942 and 1943, the President said.

Far from trying to clothe the projected production in military secrecy, Mr. Roosevelt departed from his prepared text to tell Congress that "I hope all these figures I have given become common knowledge in Germany and Japan."

U. S. Forces—land, sea or air—will take up defensive or offensive positions as circumstances warrant in the British Isles, many points in the Far East, on all the oceans and on bases within and without the New World to protect the Western Hemisphere.

Mr. Roosevelt's personally delivered annual message to Congress on the state of the union at war outlined a staggering production program of airplanes, tanks, guns and shipping—a program calculated to stagger the Axis.

"Let no man say it cannot be done," he said. "It must be done—and we have undertaken to do it."

Continued on Page 2

SPEECH HIGHLIGHTS

Washington, Jan. 6 (UP)—Highlights of President Roosevelt's address to Congress today on the state of the Union:

OFFENSIVE WAR—"We cannot wage this war in a defensive spirit . . . We shall carry the attack against the enemy—we shall hit him and hit him again wherever and whenever we can reach him."

UNITY OF NATIONS—"We must guard against divisions among ourselves and among all the other united nations . . . American armed forces must be used at any place in all the world where it seems advisable . . . at many points in the Far East . . . on all the oceans . . . in the British Isles . . ."

WHEN WILL THE WAR END?—"There is only one answer to that. It will end just as soon as we make it end, by our combined efforts, our combined strength, our combined determination to fight through and work through until the end—the end of militarism in Germany and Italy and Japan."

U. S. WAR OBJECTIVES—" . . . are clear; the objective of smashing the militarism imposed by war lords upon their enslaved peoples— . . . of liberating the subjugated nations— . . . of establishing and securing freedom of speech, freedom of religion, freedom from want and freedom from fear everywhere in the world."

PRODUCTION—"In this year, 1942, we shall produce 60,000 planes . . . 45,000 tanks . . . 20,000 anti-aircrat guns . . . 8,000,000 deadweight tons (of shipping) . . . next year, 125,000 airplanes . . . 75,000 tanks . . . 35,000 anti-aircraft guns . . . 10,000,000 tons."

JAPS SUFFER HEAVY LOSSES IN LUZON RAIDS

7 of 50 Bombers Hit by Corregidor And Batan Defenders

Washington, Jan. 6 (U.P.)—Japan sent 50 bombers in a heavy air attack against Gen. Douglas MacArthur's last-ditch fighters in the Philippines, the War Department reported today, but suffered severe losses in the new bombardments of fortress Corregidor and American strongholds in Batan Province.

American and Philippine ground defenses damaged at least seven of the Japanese bombers—a 14 per cent casualty toll for the enemy—and it seemed likely that most of these seven planes had been put permanently or temporarily out of the war.

That brought the score of Corregidor's powerful anti-aircraft defenses to 15 Japanese planes known downed and at least seven damaged in recent air bombardments.

The Army reported that the latest Japanese attack extended over four hours yesterday but that casualties to American forces and damage to their positions were light.

U. S. Shows Aerial Punch

The Japanese attack did not appear to compare in effectiveness with the assault by long-range heavy American bombers upon enemy naval concentrations off Da-

Continued on Page 11

PREDOMINANT COLOR WILL BE KHAKI!

Philadelphia, Jan. 6 (U.P.)—The International Association of Clothing Designers today considered recommendations for changes in men's clothing styles to conserve materials.

Recommendations, to be acted upon, include:

1. Abandonment of vests and two-pants suits.
2. Cuffless trousers.
3. Shorter topcoats and overcoats.
4. An end to the pocket flap.
5. Fewer buttons.
6 Brighter colors.

Raid Warden, Fined for Parking, Urged to Use Bike or Skates

Judge, an Air Guard Himself, Gives Advice to Clear Streets of Autos

Air raid wardens can help keep the streets clear of parked cars by leaving their automobiles home and going about their business on bicycles or even roller skates, Magistrate Peter M. Horn urged today in Queens Traffic Court.

He made the suggestion when passing sentence on Leo A. Levy, senior post warden in the Astoria precinct, who was charged with parking his car for four hours in front of 37-27 82d St., Jackson Heights, last Friday. Levy explained he was on business ordered by Sector Warden Harry Hollander, but the magistrate, a sector warden himself, imposed a $4 fine.

Bicycles, he pointed out, are now used by wardens in London and even roller skates may have to be used.

New Boards Formed Here

Formation of two new tire-rationing boards in Brooklyn and a change of address for another borough board were announced today by Harold W. McGraw, city administrator of the Federal project. Both new boards will meet at the East New York Savings Bank, 2650 Atlantic Ave. The new bodies are:

Board K-5—Chairman, Leslie L. Finkelday, realtor; Arthur S. Gatehouse, banker, and Henry F. Ohlau, businessman.

Board K-6—Chairman, Harold R.

Continued on Page 11

14 Women Volunteers On Duty at Boro Field

Fourteen members of the Brooklyn division of the American Women's Voluntary Services were busy today as guides, receptionists and drivers at Floyd Bennett Field.

Members of the corps will serve as chauffeurs tomorrow night when 54 Powers models attended a servicemen's dance at Fort Hamilton.

Gets Canada Jail Term On 13th Illegal Entry Try

Toronto, Jan. 6 (U.P.)—Walter Griffiths, a Negro citizen of the United States, likes Canada. In 14 years, he illegally entered 12 times, was always caught and deported.

He was brought before a judge yesterday for his 13th illegal entry. The judge told him he could stay this time, a year at the least, two years at most, but in jail.

Legion Forming Own Unarmed 'Regiment' Here

Home Defense Unit To Get Basic Training Prescribed by Army

An unarmed "regiment" was in the process of formation today by the Kings County American Legion, in a move which Legionnaires believed would be widely copied throughout the nation.

Existing laws forbid formation of any armed home defense units outside of the present State Guard, according to Col. John D. Humphries, commander of the 13th New York Guard and a member of the 13th American Legion Post which is sponsoring the plan for the new regiment.

Membership in the regiment is open to all veterans of the county, with instruction to begin within a week or two in the basic training prescribed by the U. S. Army. Training sessions will be held once a week for 13 weeks.

Colonel Humphries, who is tentatively slated to head the instruction, said that the regiment might "branch out into anything, after completing the fundamental training."

A resolution calling for the regiment's formation was enthusiastically approved at a meeting last night of the 13th Post at the 13th Regiment Armory, Sumner and Jefferson Aves. The resolution was introduced by Stephen V. Hrewniak, post commander, and has the indorsement of County Commander John Kenny.

All to Undrego Basic Training

Colonel Humphries, who addressed the meeting, stressed the fact that all Legionnaires and other veterans would have to undergo basic training on joining the regiment, even if they had

Continued on Page 11

BRITISH SMASH JAP LANDINGS ON MALAYA

Guns Rout Bombers—Put 'Scorched Earth' Policy in Effect

Singapore, Jan. 7 (U.P.)—British coastal defenses smashed new Japanese landing attempts on the west coast of Malaya, anti-aircraft guns drove off enemy bombers again tonight and dispatches from the north said that a vigorous "scorched earth" policy had been carried out in areas yielded to the invaders.

British forces generally have destroyed everything that might be of use to the enemy before they fell back before increasingly powerful Japanese forces, according to front line dispatches.

(Whetner the big rubber, tin and other resources of the rich Malaya Peninsula sector now in Japanese hands had been destroyed—representing vast wealth—was not specifically stated in this dispatch.)

Japs Find No Food

The dispatches said that the British opened food stores and warehouses and invited the public to remove goods before the Japanese arrived in some towns. In one instance, 100,000 sacks of rice were removed and Japanese forces found no food when they arrived.

British guns threw up a heavy barrage and British fighter planes took to the air at dusk when Japanese bombers attempted to renew attacks on Singapore, driving them off after a few bombs had done slight damage.

A new landing attempt on the west coast resulted in practically annihilating enemy parties, it was reported, but other landing attacks were believed being attempted by the enemy.

(Dispatches did not say but it appeared that the new Japanese landing attempts were north of the Kuala Lumpur area. They may have been feeler blows, intended to prepare the way for a more ex-

Continued on Page 2

Tropical Park Results

1—Queen Echo, 10.50-6.90-4.70. Miss High Hat, 20.10-8.60; Catomar, 6.40. Off time, 2:02½.

2—Leib Light 3.60, 2.40, 2.30; Dan's Choice, 3.80, 3.40; Here Now, 5.70. Off time, 2:32½.

DAILY DOUBLE PAID $19.20

Icy Brakes, Doors Delay Thousands In Subway Tieups

Winter's Coldest Day Halts B.M.T., I.R.T. and Independent Trains

Thousands of persons were delayed on city subway trains today, the coldest day of the Winter, by six instances of mechanical difficulty caused by the weather.

A Manhattan-bound Brighton local developed mechanical trouble at 7:30 a.m. at Whitehall St. that delayed the train eight minutes.

Frozen brakes halted an I. R. T. train at 6:12 a.m. at 135th St., Manhattan. Although the train

Continued on Page 11

Merger of Courts May Solve Space Problem in Boro

Proposed Legislation Would Ease Congestion In Supreme Tribunal

By JOSEPH SCHMALACKER

Albany, Jan. 6—A New York City Court consolidation proposal, which is awaiting introduction in the Legislature, contemplates at least a partial solution of the Brooklyn Supreme Court's acute space shortage problem, it was indicated here today.

The proposal, if ratified, would mean consolidation of the County Courts of Kings, Queens, the Bronx and Richmond and the New York County Court of General Sessions with the Supreme Court. The County Courts in Kings and the other counties, as well as the Court of General Sessions, are limited to criminal jurisdiction.

The Brooklyn Supreme Court

Continued on Page 11

Quick-Witted Cabbie Traps 2 in $117 Holdup

A quick-witted taxicab driver, known only as Nick, caused the arrest today of two Newark youths who were fleeing from the $117 holdup of a night clerk at the Chelsea Hotel, 23d St. and 7th Ave., Manhattan.

The two men, Gennaro Bifalco, 24, and Anthony Juliano, 19, leaped into the cab after holding up Harry Beale, the clerk, at 5 a.m. Nick, noticing they carried guns, shouted to two policemen at the corner who seized them. Two unloaded revolvers were found in the possession of Bifalco and Juliano.

ROCKEFELLERS GIVE $200,000 TO RED CROSS

Washington, Jan. 6 (U.P.)—The American Red Cross announced today that Mr. and Mrs. John D. Rockefeller Jr. and their six children have contributed $200,000 to the American Red Cross war fund.

MERCURY DROPS TO 11 FOR WINTER LOW MARK

No need to say it was cold. The mercury, according to the weather man, officially dropped to 11 degrees at 7:45 a. m. for the coldest day so far this Winter. It is not expected to rise above 28 today.

Happiest Mother Hears From Son Who Survived Pearl Harbor Blow

Sea Cliff, Jan. 6—One of the happiest women in this village today was Mrs. Henry P. Graham of 29 Main Ave., who received a telephone call from Seattle. At the other end of the wire was her son, Ensign Henry Graham, 24, of the battleship West Virginia. He was in Pearl Harbor during the Japanese raid on Dec. 7.

Mrs. Graham, who had not heard her son's voice for a year and a half, said he told her he had just reached the West Coast and that "I haven't a scratch but I have to start from scratch." He explained he needed a full supply of clothing, having lost everything except his class ring and a watch. Graham was graduated from Annapolis in 1940 and in July of that year was assigned to the West Virginia.

10 WOMEN GUARDS START DUTIES AT AIRPORT

In th presence of Mayor LaGuardia, who was leaving the airport for Washington, ten women who will act as guards and guides at LaGuardia Field began their duties in the Administration Building today.

The women, under command of Lt. Lillian Hoelderlin of Jackson Heights, are a part of a volunteer group which has been training under police supervision for guard and guide duty at various public places. They will be assigned to the airport in groups of ten, each group working a four-hour shift.

Continued on Page 5

Pacific Clipper Safe Here; Skirted War in World Trip

With a 31,500-mile globe-girdling flight behind it, the Pan-American Airways Pacific Clipper today dropped down at the LaGuardia Field seaplane base after having skirted the war in the Pacific safely under a pre-arranged emergency route plan.

The clipper arrived at Auckland, N. Z., on Dec. 7, the day Japan struck in the Pacific on a routine flight and from then on, without passengers, freight or mail, it followed the emergency flight plan which carried it around the globe and safely into New York.

Capt. Robert Ford, 35-year-old pilot who has been with Pan-American since 1933, was in command. Its other officers were: John H. Mack, first officer; Roderick N. Brown, second officer; James G. Henriksen, third officer; Homans K. Rothe, and John B. Parish, engineering officers; John S. Steers, fourth officer; John D. Poindexter and Olav Hendrickson, radio officers, and Barney Sawicki and V. C. Edwards, flight stewards.

Girdles Globe in 409½ Hours

The time consumed from San Francisco around the world to New York was 409½ hours. The clipper was not officially heard from after it left Auckland Dec. 15 until last night when it was within a few hours of New York.

Although not permitted under current military emergency regulations to discuss the flight in detail, Ford revealed that he flew 6,026 miles over land, most of it jungle or desert; made 18 stops under 12 different flags, crossed and sometimes recrossed the South Pacific, Indian and Atlantic Oceans; Australia, the Timor Sea, Netherlands East Indies, Bay of Bengal, Arabian Sea, Persian Gulf, Red Sea, the Nile, Congo and Amazon Rivers, South America and the West Indies.

A standard Boeing clipper ship, the plane had to be serviced in flight and an extra engine was practically picked to the bone of parts by the time it docked at New York.

THE BROOKLYN EAGLE'S ANNUAL

Business and Financial Review

Containing the opinions of business leaders, important facts, analyses of current conditions and future prospects.

In Today's Eagle

WHERE TO FIND IT

Bay Ridge	Page 5	Movies	Page 7
Bridge	Page 29	Music	Page 7
Clifford Evans	Page 7	Neighborhood News	Page 4
Clubwomen	Page 8	Novel	Page 29
Comics	Page 10	OBITUARIES	Page 13
Crossword	Page 28	Only Yesterday	Page 6
Dr. Brady	Page 6	RADIO	Page 10
EDITORIAL	Page 12	Real Estate	Page 29
Events Tonight	Page 4	Society	Page 8
FINANCIAL	Page 11	SPORTS	Pages 25-26-27
Grin and Bear It	Page 12	Theaters	Page 7
Harold Parrott	Page 25	These Women	Page 6
Heffernan	Page 6	Tucker	Page 12
Helen Worth	Page 9	Uncle Ray's Corner	Page 6
Horoscope	Page 6	Wall Street	Page 11
Income Tax	Page 6	Want Ads	Pages 28-29
Jury	Page 4	Weather Table	Page 13
		Woman's	Page 9

New York City's Greatest Need—A Full-Time Mayor

6 SECTIONS

BROOKLYN EAGLE

EVERYWHERE 5c

LOCAL WEATHER FORECAST: Warmer, no rain or snow today.

101st YEAR • No. 17 • DAILY AND SUNDAY — BROOKLYN, N. Y., SUNDAY, JAN. 18, 1942 ●●●

3 SHIPS SUNK IN TOKIO BAY

Carole Lombard, 21 Killed in Plane

RAID NETS 4 HERE IN HUGE POLICY RACKET

Ramshackle Building Yields Slips Showing 4 Million Weekly Take

Police in Brooklyn last night cracked down on what they called a big-time policy racket gang operating on a scale bigger than anything since the lush, lurid days of the late Dutch Schultz.

Detectives under Inspector Michael J. Murphy, chief of Police Commissioner Valentine's confidential squad, did it with a raid on a ramshackle structure at 66 Adams St., temporary headquarters of the game.

Seized were four men said by police to be the topnotch policy czars and a vast number of policy slips indicating a play of just under $4,000,000 a week.

Moved Headquarters

Chief of the four policy kings, according to the police, was Frank Weber, 46, of 223 24th St., brother of Louis Weber, now on parole after serving in the penitentiary for his own policy doings. Taken with him were Paolo Rodriguez, 49, of 1021 DeKalb Ave.; Carmelo Mora, 40, of 349 6th St., and Gustavo Monelt, 30, of 158 Hicks St.

After several hours of questioning the four were booked at the Poplar St. station on the charge of operating a policy game. After be-

Continued on Page 2

RAID LADDER — Police entered this window at 66 Adams St. in seizing suspected leaders of what they called the biggest policy ring in the city.

Mrs. Wallace Christens First of Flying Boats

Stratford, Conn., Jan. 17 (U.P.)—The first of three flying boats of the American Exports Lines, Inc., was christened today by Mrs. Henry A. Wallace in ceremonies at the Vought-Sikorsky plant.

Designed for non-stop trans-oceanic air service, it was the first of three built for the corporation at an aggregate cost of more than $3,000,000.

The wife of the Vice President of the United States succeeded in christening the airship with the traditional bottle of champagne on a special steel shaft which was constructed along side the plane after she was unable to break it against the bow.

WHERE TO FIND IT

SECTION A

Edgar Guest	Page 8
Editorial	Page 8
Heffernan	Page 8
Letters to the Editor	Page 8
Lindley	Page 7
Obituaries	Page 11
Resort	Page 10
Schools	Page 9
Travel	Page 10
Tucker	Page 8

SECTION B

Bridge	Page 6
Club News	Page 5
Helen Worth	Page 4
Society	Pages 1, 3 and 6
Woman	Page 4

SECTION C-D

Crossword Puzzle	Page 6D
Dr. Brady	Page 6D
Financial	Page 7D
Horoscope	Page 7D
Real Estate	Page 7D
Sports	Pages 1-4C
Want Ads	Pages 7-10D

TREND SECTION E

A Review of the Arts	
Movies	Page 8
Music	Page 5
Old Timers	Page 4
Radio	Page 7
Theaters	Pages 6-7

SECTION F

Eight Pages of Comics.

Lewis Proposes CIO, AFL Resume Labor Peace Talks

Green Promptly Accepts Offer by Miners' Chief For Unified Leadership

Washington, Jan. 17 (U.P.)—President John L. Lewis of the United Mine Workers Union tonight proposed that the C. I. O. and A. F. L. resume peace talks to bring labor under a "unified and competent leadership," and his offer was accepted promptly by A. F. L. President William Green.

President Philip Murray of the C. I. O. left Washington 10 days ago for a rest and was not available immediately for comment on Lewis' proposal. Other C. I. O. leaders declined comment pending action by Murray.

Lewis wrote identical letters to Green and Murray, stating that the "sequence of events since the last (peace) meeting some two and one-

Continued on Page 2

MAYOR GIVES JOB DECISION IN TALK TODAY

Broadcast Expected To Announce Quitting of Either of His Posts

Mayor LaGuardia may announce his decision to resign either from the Mayoralty or the directorship of Office of Civilian Defense in a radio address at noon today.

He will speak then over WNYC, the city station, the unrevealing title of his address being "A Message to the People."

The Mayor yesterday continued in his new policy of refusing to see reporters, and written questions sent in to him remained, with one exception, unanswered. Aides in the Mayor's office explained that all questions that any reporter might possibly ask will be covered in the Mayor's broadcast.

Denies His Resignation

One written question which the Mayor did not answer referred to the rumor, which flew rapidly around the city yesterday, that he had already resigned as Mayor. The question was almost instantly returned, with the words sprawled across the bottom: "Absolutely Not!"

The Mayor has clung to his policy of journalistic non-intercourse since his return from Washington last Thursday. Among unanswered questions were some on the Mayor's six-day week for municipal employes. City workers were on their second eight-hour Saturday yesterday, and in many city departments the general discontent was sharpened by the circumstance that there was little or nothing to do.

Complain and Watch Clock

The Brooklyn Marriage License Bureau issued 210 licenses yesterday—only 25 of them between noon and 5 p.m. Most of the time the bureau's staff of 10 sat, complained and watched the clock. Criticism of the six-day week order came yesterday from the Federation of Municipal Employes, A. F. of L. affiliate.

The federation's president, Henry Feinstein, in a letter to the Mayor, asked for an opportunity to present facts as to the sixth working day for city employes and to recommend remedies.

Other employe organizations which have protested are the State, County and Municipal Workers of America, C. I. O., and the Civil Service Forum, unaffiliated.

Continued on Page 2

Exploding Airliner Hurls Bodies Hundreds of Yards on Mountain

Star's Mother and 15 Army Men Victims—Clark Gable Tries in Vain to Reach Scene

Las Vegas, Nev., Jan. 17 (U.P.)—Mountain climbers today found the burned bodies of beautiful Carole Lombard and 21 other persons who perished in the head-on crash of a TWA sky liner into the sheer face of Table Rock Mountain.

Six hundred feet below the rugged summit the ruins of the big silver transport ship lay crumpled in a gully.

Above on the rock face of the cliff was a telltale smudge which showed where the plane had struck, probably at almost 200 miles

GABLE FILM HALTED

Hollywood, Jan. 17 (INS)—Work on Clark Gable's new picture at MGM "Somewhere I'll Find You" was suspended temporarily today.

an hour, and burst into flaming explosion which hurled the bodies of the occupants hundreds of yards away.

All Died Instantly

Death for all—the movie star, her mother and press agent, a woman passenger and 15 United States Army airmen—must have been instantaneous.

A member of the searching party—Indians, miners and soldiers—who clambered down the mountainside to break the news to Miss Lombard's grief-stricken husband, Clark Gable, said gasoline and surrounding pine trees had flared in a monstrous funeral pyre after the crash.

He said the bodies were charred so badly they were unrecognizable.

Tossed Coin With Press Agent

The blond movie star was flying home from a speech at Indianapolis at which she boosted sales of defense bonds and stamps. She was born at Fort Wayne, Ind., as Jane Peters 33 years ago.

She had tossed a coin with her press agent, Otto Winkler, to determine whether they and her mother, Mrs. Elizabeth K. Peters, should fly or take a train. Tails won. They flew, Miss Lombard eager to return to Gable, the movie idol she called "Pappy."

Gable was waiting at the Los Angeles airport when they told him there was a delay. Then they broke the news that the plane had crashed. He flew at once in a chartered Western Air Express plane to Las Vegas and started into the snowclad slopes wearing a polo coat and oxfords.

Gable Almost Frantic

Hardy mountain men, whose shoes had been ripped to shreds in the night's search, shook their heads. There were no horses be-

Continued on Page 3

MOURNED—Film star Carole Lombard lost her life in her country's service, the Treasury Department said last night. She made the ill-fated flight in connection with her efforts to help the Government raise defense funds.

9 Army Men Die In Two Crashes

Spokane, Jan. 17 (INS.)—All eight members of the crew of an Army bomber were killed outright today in a crash two and one-half miles north of the Pendleton (Ore.) Air Base, the Second Air Force announced tonight.

Dies in California Crash

Riverside, Cal., Jan. 17 (U.P.)—An Army pursuit place from March Field crashed and burned today in the Santa Ana River bottom five miles west of Riverside, killing the pilot. Army authorities withheld the name of the pilot of the single-seated craft pending further investigation.

2 Die in Atlantic Crash

Washington, Jan. 17 (INS)—The Army Air Corps today gave up hope for Pilot Lt. James Allison Fannin, 33, of Memphis, after discovery of the body of his fellow flier, Lt. Rush Williard of Bay City, Mich. in the Atlantic Ocean 45 miles off Cape Charles, Md.

The two fliers had been missing since Wednesday night when they left Knoxville, Tenn., on a routine flight to Washington.

U. S. Gets 'Conscience Pay'

Washington, Jan. 17 (U.P.)—The Treasury today received $36 from an anonymous person "for over pay in the World War." The money was mailed at Wichita, Kan., and has been deposited in the Treasury's "conscience fund."

CRASH OFF N. J. SINKS SHIP; SECOND AFIRE

2 Merchantmen, Blacked Out, Collide Within Sight of Atlantic City

Washington, Jan. 17 (INS)—One merchant ship sank and another was afire as a result of a collision off the New Jersey coast tonight, the Navy Department announced.

The merchant ship San Jose sank following a collision with the steamship Santa Elisa within sight of Atlantic City, a Navy Department spokesman said.

The Santa Elisa, apparently badly damaged, was burning.

The glow of the flames could be seen along the Atlantic City beach front.

The steamship Wellhart picked up 18 survivors and the steamer Charles L. O'Connor saved 11, including a master, first mate and third mate.

The Navy spokesman did not reveal the size of the ships nor their destinations.

Further details were referred to the Fourth Naval District at Philadelphia.

Apparently the ships were traveling under wartime blackout. Coast Guard and merchant ships in the area, it was believed, were rushing to the scene.

U-Boats Still Lurk Off Coast, Navy Warns

Washington, Jan. 17 (U.P.)—The Navy said tonight that enemy submarine action off the Atlantic Coast continues but revealed no further details of U-boat operations.

It reported in a communique that "enemy submarine activities off the Northeast coast of the United States continue."

Navy destroyers and patrol planes, it was assumed, are sweeping coastal waters ready to attack any German submarines at the slightest sign of their presence.

2 Eagle Carriers Lose $21.90 in Defense Stamps

Two newspaper carrier boys last night reported that between 5 and 6 p.m. Friday they had lost two envelopes containing $21.90 worth of Defense Stamps they had received for sale to subscribers to whom they delivered the Brooklyn Eagle.

If found, the stamps should be returned to the boys—J. Bacigalupo, 1330 Rogers Ave., who lost $12.40 in stamps on Flatbush Ave., between Farragut and Glenwood Roads, and J. Hartigan, 162 E. 28th St., who lost $9.50 worth on E. 25th St., between Clarendon Road and Tilden Ave.—or to the Circulation Manager, Brookly Eagle.

U. S. Sub Knifes Into Jap Waters For Daring Attack

Washington, Jan. 17 (UP)—An American submarine has invaded the most closely-guarded waters of the Japanese Empire—those off Tokio Bay—and has sank three Japanese vessels, the Navy announced tonight.

The Navy announcement came as Gen. Douglas MacArthur and his American and Filipino troops fought valiantly against a storming Japanese attack upon their Batan Peninsula positions in the Philippines.

The Navy communique revealed the most daring American naval operation of the war—a feat rivaling that of Army Capt. Colin Kelly in sinking the Japanese battleship Haruna.

Slipped Into Jap Harbor

The submarine, presumably one of those attached to Admiral Thomas C. Hart's Asiatic fleet, slipped into the closely-protected waters off Japan's greatest naval base, Yokusuka, within a few miles of Yokohama, heart of the vast Japanese sea empire.

The American underseas craft attacked and sank three Japanese merchant ships and managed to flash a report of its success to American naval headquarters. Whether it is still operating in the dangerous Japanese waters was not revealed.

It was the first time in nearly 100 years that an American naval craft had entered Japanese waters on a mission of war or warlike nature.

The successful attack was carried out in the same waters where Commodore Matthew Perry sailed nearly 100 years ago, his guns ready for action, in the historic voyage which opened up Japan to contact with the western world.

Battle Nears Crisis

In the Philippines, the battle was approaching a crisis and still there was no indication whether American and Philippine reserves would be able to roll back the onrushing Japanese hordes.

Japanese propaganda reports—unconfirmed by the United States War Department—claimed that MacArthur was now fighting a stubborn withdrawal action, slowly falling back toward Mariveles and Fortress Corregidor, whose heavily armed rock chambers guard the entrance to Manila Bay.

Admit 'Tenacious' Resistance

[A Berlin report from Tokio claimed that Japanese forces have landed south of Olangapo and are striking toward the rear of MacArthur's lines southeast of Subic Bay. The report said United States resistance "continues tenacious," because the fate of the whole Batan position depends upon the outcome of these operations.]

The American communique admitted that MacArthur's men are "greatly" outnumbered but said, nonetheless, that "our soldiers are stubbornly contesting the attempted advance."

For three days the Japanese have hurled their forces against MacArthur's stone wall. Failing in initial direct assaults they adopted their Malayan tactics of infiltration in small, picked parties. Some of these forces, it was presumed, have

Continued on Page 2

British Launch All-out Malayan Counter-Drive

Aussies Pace Attack Aiming to Turn Tide In Singapore Battle

With Empire Forces in West Malaya, Jan. 17 (U.P.)—Imperial armies grappled hand to hand today with powerful, tank-led Japanese invaders of Johore State in a supreme bid to turn the tide of battle for Singapore.

Abadoning the delaying tactics of a dismal retreat hundreds of miles down the peninsula, the powerfully reinforced British Imperials, paced by Australians, were turning on the enemy with everything they had under orders to "hold and destroy him."

The Australians' biggest task was to wipe out a Japanese bridgehead on the south bank of the Muar River 90 to 100 miles northwest of Singapore. It bore the potential menace of a flanking maneuver around the west end of the reorganized battle line.

(Axis broadcasts claimed the Japanese had broken through the Muar and were within 50 to 70 miles of Singapore.)

'Good Fight Coming'

"A good fight is coming," Maj. Gen. Henry Gordon Bennett, commander of the Australian Imperial force told me Friday night. "Thus far things are going our way, but we must expect heavier assaults with tanks, planes and artillery backing up the Jap infantry."

Bennett said that, by conservative estimate, 800 Japanese were killed Thursday in the main action so far by the Australian troops, whose own casualties were slight. The main Japanese forces have not shown up since then, he said.

He said also that Imperial bombers and fighters "played havoc" with a Japanese column in which more than 1,000 trucks were creeping along 22 miles of roadway leading up to the fighting zone.

[Tokio reports said Japanese troops pushing down the west coast were in the Batu Pahot sector on the Simpang River, 70 miles from Singapore and "will probably knock at the doors of Singapore Island Sunday."

[On the central front the Japanese claimed they had captured Batu Anam, ten miles southeast of

Continued on Page 2

Vast Expansion Looms For New York Guard

May Have to Be Increased Many Times, Says Gen. Ottman

By DAVID ROBINSON GEORGE

New York's new State Guard may have to be increased many times over its present roster of 15,292 men "to cope with the situation" before World War II is ended.

This is the considered opinion of Maj. Gen. William Ottman, commanding general of the Guard, who in civilian life is chairman of the board of the United States Printing & Lithographing Company, 85 N. 3d St., a major Brooklyn industry and one of the largest of its kind in the world.

"I can see," he declared in the library of his home at 103 E. 73d St., Manhattan, "somewhere between a possibility and a probability, that unless this war comes to an unexpected end, sooner than experts predict, the New York Guard will have to be augmented many times over."

Gen. Ottman said, at the Guard's various regimental headquarters.

Guardsmen will get actual field training this Spring and Summer if a recommendation made by General Ottman is carried out.

Urges Training in Field

Regulation Army equipment, including overcoats and two-piece uniforms, are arriving daily, Gen-

"At a recent meeting of all brigade commanders with Governor

Continued on Page 2

GENERAL'S SON ENLISTS

William Ottman Jr., son of the General, has just enlisted as a private in the 12th Regiment, the same outfit his father joined as a private in 1916. The regiment has headquarters in the old armory at 62d St. and Columbus Ave. The son is president of the George Ehret Brewery.

Nazi Field Marshal Dies of Apoplexy

Berlin, Jan. 17—(Official German Broadcast Recorded by the United Press in New York)—Field Marshal Walther von Reichenau, 56, one of the first German military commanders to throw in his lot with the Nazi movement, died of apoplexy today while being transferred to his home for medical treatment.

[Von Reichenau was one of three prominent militarists giving early support to Hitler. The others were Gen. Werner von Fritsch, who died mysteriously in Poland, and Gen. Werner von Blomberg, who was ousted.]

Until recently an army group commander on the Southern front in Russia, Reichenau won his marshal's baton as a commander in Poland and for operations as chief of the Sixth Army in action against France. The Axis forces recently had suffered heavy defeats on the South Russian front.

Hitler Orders State Funeral

Adolf Hitler ordered a state funeral for Reichenau, son of a prominent artillery general, and instructed Reichsmarshal Hermann Wilhelm Goering and Field Marshal Gerd von Rundstedt to represent him at the services.

During the World War Reichenau

Continued on Page 2

Forced Landing Fails To Keep Student Down On His First Solo Flight

George H. Schwender, 20, of 73-21 70th St., Glendale, made a forced landing in a Porter-Field monoplane yesterday at the foot of Florence Ave., 1,500 feet east of Gerritsen Ave., Marine Park. Forced down because of a clogged gasoline feed line, Schwender made a perfect landing, cleaned out the line and then took off for Roosevelt Field.

Schwender was en route to Roosevelt Field from Poughkeepsie on his first solo flight. A student at Pratt Institute, Schwender was flying a plane owned by Urbant Aviation School, Roosevelt Field.

New York City's Greatest Need—A Full-Time Mayor

AMUSEMENTS

'Invaders' at the Capitol

By HERBERT COHN

"The Invaders," which began its engagement at the Capitol Theater yesterday and was shown to an audience dominated by military leaders last night, is an adventure story with a purpose. It is exciting as a melodrama, but it is no less exciting as an anti-Nazi political document. It looks at a half dozen German seamen, landed from a submarine in the Hudson's Bay country, sees how they have been steeped in the narrow philosophy of Nazism and watches them as they try to infect non-Nazis with their undemocratic thoughts.

It listens while the leader of the German landing party bursts in on Johnny, the trapper who hadn't heard that Germany had invaded Poland, and tries to convince him that the Nazis want to "liberate" the French. Johnny, who was satisfied with the kind of freedom his people already had, quickly decided he didn't care for the Nazi brand of "liberation." The Nazis got rid of him before they headed south for the border of neutral United States.

The invaders came next upon a camp of Hutterites, a religious sect that lived and worked communally, each member doing the kind of work he could do best for the benefit of the others in his cult. The Hutterites were of German descent, and the invaders talked to them about the superiority of Aryans, the "super race" that Bismarck envisioned. But the Hutterite leader, Peter, knew about Nazism, about its oppressions, about its lack of freedom, its paganism, its hate for non-Aryan humans. Peter's fervid answer to the Nazi leader, a defense of freedom, tolerance and brotherly love, won one of the Nazi seamen to his side and sent the others packing.

And so the invaders went on, meeting next an expatriate American lazying on a Canadian lake while writing a book about the Nazi-like Blackfoot Indians, a tribe that, fortunately, had petered out. The writer was an easy-going fellow, complacent enough until the invaders destroyed his manuscript, burned his copy of Thomas Mann's "Magic Mountain" and slashed his Picassos. That made him fighting mad. When the invaders left his lake there was one less in the party.

And by the time the border was in sight there was only one left to meet the surly Canadian soldier who was dodging military police because he was A. W. O. L., but who soon remembered how to handle a Nazi when he was face to face with one.

There is a magnificent political drive to this story by Emeric Pressburger, one fraught with significance and bald warnings. It is heroic, dynamic, meaningful and hugely impressive, and it stands solidly as the most effective expose of Nazi thought to reach the screen in this war. It is intelligently written, yet a great part of its effectiveness stems from the sensitive direction by Michael Powell, director of "U-Boat 29," and from the sterling performances by Eric Portman as the Nazi leader; Laurence Olivier, Leslie Howard and Raymond Massey, as the trapper, writer and soldier, respectively; Anton Walbrook as the Hutterite leader, and Glynis Johns, a fresh young actress, as a Hutterite girl.

"The Invaders" is a credit to them all—a stirring and enlightening film and an engrossing entertainment.

FOR GOO'NESS SAKES—Lou Costello in "Ride 'Em, Cowboy," current feature at Loew's Criterion.

Doug Fairbanks At Loew's Met.

Old Papa Dumas is telling one of his swashbuckling fables at Loew's Metropolitan Theater this week, and it winces up with a traditional sabre scene, with the grunting of fighting men and the clanking of their steel. It's a good, exciting scene, with Douglas Fairbanks Jr., an old hand at fencing, and Akim Tamiroff sparing no effort. It's part of "The Corsican Brothers," the Edward Small adventure with Ruth Warrick, and, incidentally, it's the best part.

"The Corsican Brothers" is dated. It seems silly today for one severed Siamese twin to wince with pain when the second, in a Corsican castle a dozen miles away, is being horsewhipped. But sympathetic reactions are an important part of the Met's film. They are always happening, and Fairbanks and Director Gregory Ratoff always take them seriously.

Akim Tamiroff plays the part of the villain in the Dumas story, which Howard Estabrook and George Bruce have liberally transcribed for the screen. He's different from Fairbanks; he doesn't take himself seriously at all. He makes his Corsican sound like a visitor from the Steppes and he struts and mugs outrageously in scenes that Dumas must have treasured for their emotion.

But whether he reveres old Dumas or not, Tamiroff is right about "The Corsican Brothers." It's best when it's joshed and when its story about the twins—Doug Fairbanks as both of them—brought up separately in completely opposite surroundings but falling in love with the same girl and disliking the same persecutions, is played down in favor of the sword play.

"Miss Polly," a comedy featurette with ZaSu Pitts and Slim Summerville paired is co-featured at the Met.

H. C.

MOVIE TIME TABLE

ALBEE—"Son of Fury," 10, 1:20, 4:40, 8, 11:20; "Playmates," 11:40, 3, 6:20, 9:40.
FOX—"Captains of the Clouds," 12:14, 3:31, 6:48, 10:04; "Blondie Goes to College," 11, 2:17, 5:34, 8:51.
METROPOLITAN—"The Corsican Brothers," 11:01, 1:49, 4:37, 7:25, 10:13; "Miss Polly," 1, 3:48, 6:36, 9:24.
PARAMOUNT — "Bahama Passage," 11, 1:51, 4:42, 7:33, 10:24; "Steel Against the Sky," 12:33, 3:24, 6:15, 9:06.
STRAND—"Close Call for Ellery Queen," 11:20, 2, 4:40, 7:40, 10:25; Stage Show, 1:05, 3:50, 6:50, 9:30.

MANHATTAN

CAPITOL—"The Invaders," 10:14, 12:34, 2:54, 5:14, 7:34, 9:54, 12:14.
CRITERION — "Ride 'Em Cowboy," 9:57, 11:56, 1:43, 3:36, 5:29, 7:22; 9:15, 11:08, 1:01.
MUSIC HALL — "Woman of the Year," 10:43, 1:34, 4:33, 7:32, 10:23; Stage Show, 12:37, 3:36, 6:35, 9:30.
PARAMOUNT — "The Lady Has Plans," 10:01, 12:53, 3:55, 7:07, 10:14, 12:13; Stage Show, 11:48, 2:50, 6:04, 9:14.
ROXY—"Roxie Hart," 11:30, 2:20, 5:05, 7:50, 10:40; Stage Show, 1:20, 4:10, 7, 9:45.
RIVOLI—"To Be or Not to Be," 10:20, 12:40, 3, 5:20, 7:40, 10, 12:20.

AMUSEMENTS—MANHATTAN BEACH

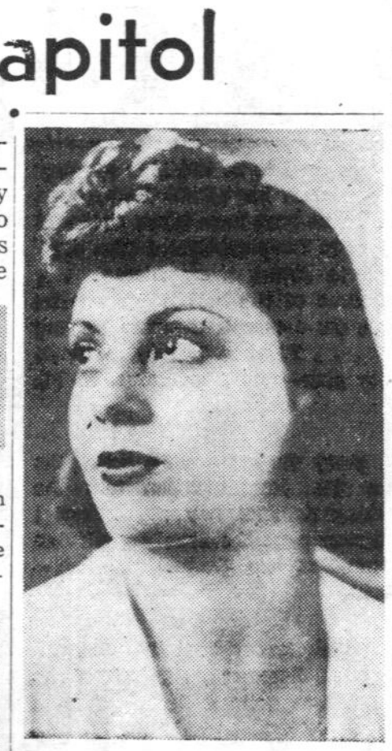

FLORA FREIMAN plays a leading feminine role in "The Blacksmith's Daughters," a Jewish folk play which the Peretz Hirshbein Yiddish troupe is presenting this weekend at the Parkway Theater.

Flatbush Offers Earl Carroll Revue

By ROBERT FRANCIS

That streamlined version of Earl Carroll "Vanities" which has been making its way eastward via the top vaudeville houses since last July took over the stage for a week at the Flatbush Theater yesterday. The management has adopted a policy this year of interpolating these unit revues at odd times between their usual "name band" programs. Most of them have been a pleasant change and the current one is quite up to standard.

This reviewer can't entirely subscribe to the program billing of the two dozen cuties as "the most beautiful girls in the world." That covers a lot of territory. But the ladies are very pretty, indeed, in all degrees of dress and undress. And there is much of the latter, as befits a "Vanities" revue. They all dance and sing nicely, and while most of the sets consist of simple backdrops which are a necessity with a touring unit, there are a couple of production numbers in the opulent Carroll manner. The patriotic finale with red, white and blue lamps is particularly effective.

On the comedy side, the Slate Brothers, who have been absent from these parts for a couple of years, return to provide more than a quota of belly laughs. The Wiere Brothers add a lot more.

Jon Zerby and Inge Wiere contribute a novelty dance routine; Fay Carroll handles the solo vocal assignments commendably and, lest anything be left out, there is toe dancing by Jeanne Devereaux. It's a good all-'round show with something for everybody.

'Remarkable Andrew' A Captivating Satire

"The Remarkable Andrew" checked into Loew's State Theater yesterday and acted out a screenplay that Dalton Trumbo wrote from his own popular novel. Andrew is a captivating fellow, full of charm and good habits. He's diligent, clean-living, neat and healthy. He's not ordinary, but he's real enough. He might be one of thousands of young men you can find around town.

He also has a rigid belief in what is right, and the courage to back up his conviction. But what really makes him remarkable is that Gen. Andrew Jackson, for whom he's named, comes to him when he needs help. And when the going is genuinely tough, Old Hickory summons General Washington, Ben Franklin, Chief Justice Marshall, Tom Jefferson, and even Jesse James and a skinny ordinary private from the Revolution to help straighten him out.

Andrew gets into trouble without wasting much time. He discovers a shortage of $1,240 in the Shell City treasury books when the time comes to close them for the fiscal year. His boss will take responsibility, but that doesn't suit Andrew. They're his figures and he wants them right. He insists, even when he's suspended and threatened with firing. Andrew suspects crooked work and he'll have none of it. That's when General Jackson comes. The General, quite innocently, causes Andrew more trouble for, like Mr. Jordan, he is visible only to Andrew and when Andrew walks along the street talking to him, folks think he's talking to himself. The same applies to the rye Andrew buys for the parched General. Folks think Andrew's gone daft and taken to drink. Even some of his friends turn against him.

There is crooked work, of course. Most of the top local politicans are in on it and they're planning to make Andrew their goat. They're going to try him for grand larceny before a fixed judge, and it looks bad for him. That's when Washington, Franklin, Jefferson and Marshall come. In their day, each had helped establish American principles to protect a good, honest fellow like Andrew who was only trying to bring criminals to the bar. Andrew remembered some of the things they had said about freedom of speech and honesty and democracy and he told them to the jury. But he needed facts, as well, and his reincarnated friends helped him there, too.

"The Remarkable Andrew" is a warm and captivating whimsy, beautifully played by Bill Holden as Andrew, Brian Donlevy as General Jackson and Ellen Drew as Andrew's girl. It has wit and drama and charm. But more than that, it is a cunning commentary on political chicanery and a forceful and inspiring statement of the truths for which we believe we're fighting today. "The Remarkable Andrew" is one of those few pictures that should be seen by everybody, even though it might be tucked away in a second-run theater or as the second feature of a double bill in Squeedunk.

With 7,764 bookings reported, the Walt Disney-Treasury Department short, "The New Spirit," has set a record for domestic showings, the War Activities Committee announced today.

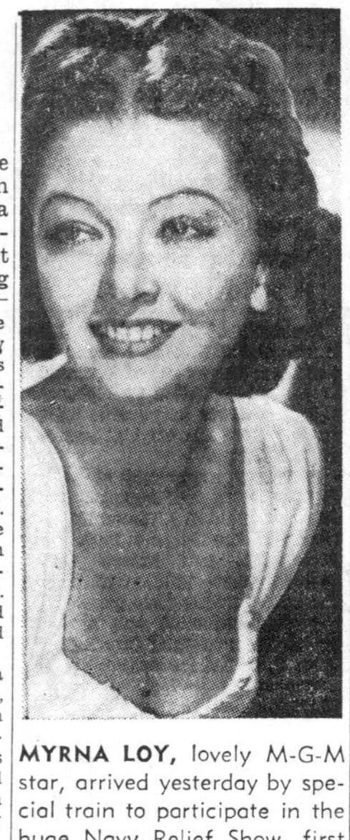

MYRNA LOY, lovely M-G-M star, arrived yesterday by special train to participate in the huge Navy Relief Show, first big service benefit, to be held next Thursday night at Madison Square Garden. Proceeds will go to the Navy Relief Society.

Greco at Met.

Anthony Greco, who coaches college fencing, will direct the fencing contest between Long Island University and Brooklyn College, to be held on the stage of Loew's Metropolitan Theater Monday evening.

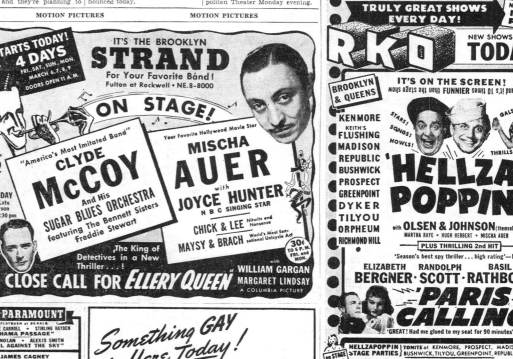

Goossens Conducts; Menuhin Is Soloist

Philharmonic-Symphony Introduces Works by Goossens and Mohaupt

By MILES KASTENDIECK

Eugene Goossens officiated at the Philharmonic-Symphony concert in Carnegie Hall last night and Yehudi Menuhin saved the evening with a spirited performance of Dvorak's Concerto for Violin and Orchestra in A Minor, thus commemorating the centenary of the composer, according to the program. Two works were given a first hearing: Goossens' Phantasy for Strings in One Movement and Richard Mohaupt's Symphony No. 1. The cause of contemporary music maintained its status quo.

This was something of a routine concert in spite of the nature of the program. The reason might be found in a similarity of performance no matter what the music. Only toward the end when it was doing its best for the new symphony did the orchestra sound at all in good form. Except for the Haydn, the music was of little consequence while the performance of the Haydn was hardly more than acceptable.

The ease and assurance with which Mr. Menuhin tossed off the Dvorak were indicative of the facility of his playing as well as of the playable character of the music. There were no demands on his inner interpretative sense nor was his performance marked by exceptional distinction. It was noticeable that his tone was not big and full, but that technically he was playing true to form and reputation.

Recent progress in contemporary music had led to the opinion that we had grown out of the kind of music that the works of Goossens and Mohaupt presented. The former was innocuous, well enough made and agreeable to the ear; the latter was irritating, experimental and much fuss about little matter. Mr. Mohaupt calls his work a symphony, but once again the term is loosely used. It amounts to a dissertation on rhythm in four movements based on classical forms. Something of a hybrid piece, it stems directly from Moussorgsky and makes its bows to Ravel, at no time establishing enough individuality to command concentrated attention.

'Junior Miss' on Sunday For the Stage Relief Fund

An extra performance of Max Gordon's comedy hit, "Junior Miss," by Jerome Chodorov and Joseph Fields, will be presented Sunday evening at the Lyceum Theater to aid the Stage Relief Fund.

MOTION PICTURES

STAGE PLAYS—BROOKLYN

STAGE PLAYS—MANHATTAN

FEATURE FILMS SHOWING TODAY

BAY RIDGE
Electra, 75th St. and Third Ave.......... Kit Carson; also Scattergood Pulls the Strings
Stanley, Fifth Ave. and 75th St. ...... Chocolate Soldier; also Nine Lives Are Not Enough

BEDFORD
Crown, 527 Empire Blvd. PR. 2-0070..... Down in San Diego; Ellery Queen and Murder Ring
National, 720 Washington Ave.......... Look Who's Laughing; also Borrowed Hero
Rogers, 333 Rogers Ave. PR. 4-2230.... Down in San Diego; Ellery Queen and Murder Ring
Savoy, Bedford Ave. and Lincoln Pl..... Hellzapoppin; also Paris Calling

BENSONHURST
Colony, 18th Ave. and 65th St.......... The Wagons Roll at Night; Gentleman From Dixie

BOROUGH HALL AND DOWNTOWN
Duffield, Duffield and Fulton Sts....... The Feminine Touch; also Unholy Partners
Momart, Fulton St. and Rockwell Pl.... Charlie Chan in Rio; Man Who Talked Too Much
St. George Playhouse, 100 Pineapple St. Unholy Partners; also The Feminine Touch
Terminal, Fourth Ave. and Dean St..... Chocolate Soldier; Confessions of Boston Blackie

BRIGHTON BEACH
Oceana, Brighton Beach Ave.-Hoff St... Smilin' Through; also Mr. and Mrs. North

BUSHWICK
Empire, Ralph Ave. and Broadway .... One Foot in Heaven; also You're in the Army Now

FLATBUSH
Astor, Flatbush Ave. near Church....... Skylark; also New York Town
Flatbush, Church and Flatbush Aves.... Earl Carroll Vanities; also Slate Bros., Buster Shaver with Olive and George
Granada, Church and Nostrand Aves.... One Foot in Heaven; also You're in the Army Now

EAST FLATBUSH
Avenue D, Avenue D and E. 43d St..... One Foot in Heaven; also You're in the Army Now
Rugby, Utica and Church Aves.......... One Foot in Heaven; also You're in the Army Now

GERRITSEN BEACH
Graham, 311 Whitney Ave............. They Died With Their Boots On; Blues in the Night

PARK SLOPE
Carlton, Flatbush and Seventh Aves..... I Wake Up Screaming; also Skylark
Plaza, Flatbush Ave. and Park Place ... Kitty Foyle; also Raiders of the Desert
Sanders, Prospect Park West-14th St.... One Foot in Heaven; also You're in the Army Now
Venus, 1224 Prospect Ave............... How Green Was My Valley; Moon Over Her Shoulder

KINGS HIGHWAY
Jewel, Kings Highway at Ocean P'kway.. Hold Back the Dawn; Henry Aldrich for President

AVENUE U SECTION
Avenue U, Ave. U and E. 16th St..... Chocolate Soldier; Confessions of Boston Blackie
Traymore, Avenue N and E. 46th St.... My Lucky Star; also Drums Along the Mohawk

RIDGEWOOD
Colonial, Broadway and Chauncey....... H. M. Pulham, Esq.; also Tarzan's Secret Treasure
Ridgewood, 1673 Myrtle Ave.......... H. M. Pulham, Esq.; also Tarzan's Secret Treasure
Rivoli, Myrtle and Wilson Aves.......... Nothing But the Truth; also Buy Me That Town

SHEEPSHEAD BAY
Sheepshead Th., Sheepshead Rd.-Voorhies I Wake Up Screaming; also Swamp Water

SOUTH BROOKLYN
Sander's Globe, 228 15th St.......... International Lady; also Moonlight in Hawaii
Minerva, Seventh Ave. and 14th St...... Kitty Foyle; also Lady Scarface

Today's LOEW'S Movie Guide

LOEW'S KINGS, Flatbush and Tilden Avenues; LOEW'S PITKIN, Pitkin and Saratoga Avenues ... "SUNDOWN" Gene TIERNEY, Bruce CABOT and "KATHLEEN" Miss Shirley TEMPLE

LOEW'S ALPINE, 69th Street and Fifth Avenue; LOEW'S BEDFORD, Bedford Avenue and Bergen Street; LOEW'S BROADWAY, Broadway and Myrtle Avenue; LOEW'S CONEY ISLAND, Surf and Stillwell Avenues; LOEW'S GATES, Gates Avenue and Broadway; LOEW'S KAMEO, Eastern Parkway and Nostrand Avenue; LOEW'S 46TH STREET, 46th Street and New Utrecht Avenue; LOEW'S PREMIER, Sutter Avenue, Hinsdale Street; LOEW'S ORIENTAL, 86th Street and 18th Avenue ... Bob HOPE • Vera ZORINA • Victor MOORE "LOUISIANA PURCHASE" In Technicolor — PLUS — JACKIE COOPER "Glamour Boy" with Susanna Foster

LOEW'S PALACE, East N. Y. Ave. and Douglass St. ... H. M. Pulham, Esq., Hedy Lamarr, Robt. Young, Ruth Hussey; Tarzan's Secret Treasure, Weissmuller
LOEW'S BAY RIDGE, 72d Street and Third Avenue ... Claudette Colbert, Remember the Day, John Payne; Don Ameche, Joan Bennett, Confirm or Deny
LOEW'S BORO PARK, 51st Street and New Utrecht Avenue ... Man Who Came to Dinner, Bette Davis, Ann Sheridan; Blue White and Perfect, Lloyd Nolan
Extra—VAUDEVILLE at BORO PARK Tonite!

LOEW'S BREVOORT, Brevoort Place and Bedford Avenue; LOEW'S WARWICK, Jerome and Fulton Streets ... In Technicolor Jeanette MacDONALD • Brian AHERNE "SMILIN' THROUGH" and Gracie ALLEN, "MR. AND MRS. NORTH"

LOEW'S CENTURY, Parkside and Nostrand Avenues ... Birth of the Blues, Bing Crosby, Mary Martin; The Night of January 16th, Robert Preston
LOEW'S MELBA, Livingston Street and Hanover Place ... Dr. Kildare's Victory, Lew Ayres; Yank on the Burma Road, Laraine Day

Century SHOWS TODAY

KINGSWAY Kings Highway, Coney Island Ave. ... Olsen and Johnson, "HELLZAPOPPIN"; and "PARIS CALLING"
AVALON, Kings H'way and E. 18th St.. "H. M. Pulham, Esq." & "Tarzan's Secret Treasure"
PATIO, Flatbush Ave. and Midwood St.. "SMILIN' THROUGH" & "MR. & MRS. NORTH"
MIDWOOD, Avenue J and E. 13th St...; MARINE, Flatbush Ave.-Kings H'way...; MAYFAIR, Avenue U-Coney Island Ave..; ALBEMARLE, Flatbush Av.-Albemarle Rd.; FARRAGUT, Flatbush Av.-Farragut Rd.. ... Betty Grable, Victor Mature, Carole Landis "I WAKE UP SCREAMING"; and "SWAMP WATER"
ELM, Avenue M at East 17th St........ "Remember the Day" and "Confirm or Deny"
RIALTO, Flatbush Ave.-Cortelyou Rd...; VOGUE, Coney Isl. Ave. and Avenue K.. ... Rosalind Russell, Don Ameche, "THE FEMININE TOUCH"; and "UNHOLY PARTNERS"
NOSTRAND, Kings H'way-Nostrand Av.; PARKSIDE, Flatbush and Parkside Avs.. ... Martha Scott, Fredric March, "ONE FOOT IN HEAVEN"; and "YOU'RE IN THE ARMY NOW"
COLLEGE, Flatbush Ave.-Avenue H..... "You Belong to Me" and "International Lady"
TRIANGLE, Kings H'way-E. 12th St... "The Chocolate Soldier" & "Confessions of Boston Blackie"
QUENTIN, Quentin Rd. at E. 35th St... "I Cover the Waterfront" & "Let 'Em Have It"

7TH ★★★★★★
Sports Extra
Wall Street Financial News

BROOKLYN EAGLE

LOCAL WEATHER FORECAST: Showers, rising temperatures tonight.

101st YEAR • No. 75 • DAILY AND SUNDAY • BROOKLYN, N. Y., TUESDAY, MARCH 17, 1942 • Entered at the Brooklyn Postoffice as 2d Class Mail Matter—(Copyright 1942 The Brooklyn Eagle, Inc.) • 3 CENTS

M'ARTHUR TAKES OVER AUSTRALIA COMMAND

Eagle Staff photo

AND THE CYMBALS CLANGED!—William Keating, center, of Division 35, Ancient Order of Hibernians, struts along carrying an ancient Irish shillalah in the borough's annual St. Patrick's Day parade, flanked by two other wearers of the green.

'TWAS GREAT DAY FOR OUR IRISH DESPITE MIST

Brooklyn's Sons of Erin March With Gusto In Boro Hall Review

"Sure, 'tis a foine day for the Irish and 'tis one good St. Patrick's Day parade."

A kindly mother, bubbling with irrepressible Irish enthusiasm, so exclaimed as she stood on the corner of Livingston and Court Sts., flanked by her young son and daughter, and watched 1,200 loyal Brooklyn sons who stem from the Emerald Isle march past in honor of Ireland's patron saint.

As the line of march swung into Court St., Mrs. Mary Brosnan of 400 Butler St., wearing a Kelly green coat, hat and gloves, lifted aloft 2-year-old freckle-faced Eileen and patted Timothy Jr., 4½, on the head, exclaiming:

"There's your father, and a mighty proud man he is today."

Little Eileen, holding the Irish flag, and Timothy, waving the Stars and Stripes, shouted greet-

Continued on Page 2

CHINESE PREDICT ATTACK ON SIBERIA

Chungking, March 17 (U.P.)—A Chinese Government spokesman said today that China regards it as "very probable" that Japan will launch an attack upon Siberia.

This belief, he said, was supported by a meeting of high Japanese military officials in Manchukuo.

Tropical Park Results

1—a-Through Train, 13.90, 5.70, 3.20; Hoosier, 4.20, 3.00; Piccadilly, 3.40. Off-time, 2:04. a-Coupled with Cockaigne.

2—Fly Gent, 21.90, 7.60, 4.30; War Declared, 5.30, 3.30; Royal Blue, 3.00. Off time, 2:32½.

DAILY DOUBLE PAID $108.00

3—Son O Hal, first; Mersa Matruh, second; Bay Ridge, third.

2 German Spies Face Death on Guilty Pleas

Ship Designer and Army Private Nabbed Under Wartime Statute, Linked to Nazi Ring

An ex-German navy man who once helped design American destroyers and a German-born private in the United States Army, both of whom have pleaded guilty of wartime espionage, today faced possible death penalties.

First to be arrested since the United States entry into the war, both men were linked with the now defunct Brooklyn spy ring and are accused of acting as Nazi spies and sending airplane and shipping information to Germany by invisible ink messages written between the lines of letters to mail drops in Mexico, South America and Europe.

The two men are Richard Friedrich Fruendt, 56, of 11 E. 75th St., Manhattan, and Pvt. Peter Franz Erich Donay, 33, assigned to Governors Island, who has been in the army jail at Fort Jay since Dec. 10.

Working with them, according to the FBI, was Richard Ernst Weber, a radio mechanic, who resigned last

Continued on Page 2

20 Lost as U. S. Collier Is Sunk By Enemy Sub Off Atlantic City

Six survivors of an American collier torpedoed and sunk off Atlantic City early Saturday floated in the sea for six hours, clinging to an overturned lifeboat from which 20 of their shipmates had been thrown into the water, the navy revealed today.

The vessel, whose name and tonnage were unannounced, carried a crew of 34. In addition to the six rescued from the capsized lifeboat, eight others—including the captain and chief officer—were picked up from life rafts by rescue craft and brought to New York.

Nineteen of the 20 men first reported lost after the lifeboat was overturned by force of a second torpedo blast are missing and presumed lost.

FACING ARSON TRIAL, L. I. VAMP DISAPPEARS

Mineola, March 17—John Seifert Jr., 19, one of the nine North Bellmore volunteer firemen charged with starting more than 30 fires, has been missing for 12 days, it was disclosed today in District Court here when the case was called to trial. Judge Cyril W. Brown said he would issue a warrant for the seizure of Siefert and adjourned the case to March 31.

Continued on Page 18

NAVY BACKS BUILDING OF EXPRESS ROAD

Withdraws Objection To Razing of Factory On Park Ave. Route

The Navy Department has withdrawn its original objection, it was learned today, and work will begin immediately on construction of the express highway through Brooklyn's Park Ave.

Rear Admiral H. L. Brinser, inspector of naval material, has informed Controller McGoldrick by telephone that he is no longer opposed to demolition of the seven-story concrete building at 35 Steuben St., which is in the path of the proposed speedway.

Previously the Admiral had contended that the structure was needed by the Kollmorgen Optical Company of 2 Franklin Ave., which has important naval contracts and could find no other housing facilities needed for the plant's expansion except the building on Steuben St.

Demolition of the concrete building and other structures was ordered Feb. 5 last by the Board of Estimate without a dissenting vote

Continued on Page 2

DRAFT LOTTERY FOR 9 MILLION TO START AT 6 P.M.

Stimson to Pick First Number—Drawing Due To Last All Night

Washington, March 17 (U.P.)—Approximately 9,000,000 men who registered for selective service last month will learn within the next 24 hours the order in which they will be examined for induction into the armed forces.

The first wartime draft lottery since Oct. 1, 1918—but the third in the last 17 months—will begin at 6 p.m. in the departmental auditorium here.

Secretary of War Stimson, reaching into the historic "goldfish bowl" which has been used for every draft lottery since July 20, 1917, will draw the first number.

Brig. Gen. Lewis B. Hershey,

Continued on Page 2

FIND YOUR NUMBER

The Brooklyn Eagle tomorrow will publish the new draft order numbers drawn in today's Selective Service lottery. Men from 20 to 44, affected by the new Selective Service drawing, will find their new numbers conveniently listed in the order of their present registration numbers.

REDS SMASH BIG GAP IN DONETS LINE

Germans Suffering Heavy Losses, Hurl Reserves Into Battle

Moscow, March 17 (U.P.)—The Red Army has opened a large breach in German positions in the Donets Basin, front dispatches said today. The enemy was reported counter-attacking despite heavy losses, however, with furious fighting in progress on a wide southern front.

The pounding effect of the Soviet attacks was illustrated by dispatches reporting that only 100 Germans out of a battalion and two companies (about 1,300 men) escaped in one sector after a Russian artillery and infantry assault.

But the Nazis were throwing reserves into the battle and launching strong tank counter-attacks. Dispatches said the action continued with the outcome not yet clear.

Break Temporary, Nazis Say

(London and Berlin reports recently have told of big-scale fighting in the Ukraine, including a Russian drive that carried into the suburban streets of Kharkov and at some points broke through the Axis defense line in the Kharkov-Orel sector. One temporary break in the southern front was acknowledged by Berlin, which asserted the hole in the defense line later was closed during fighting in a snowstorm.)

'Pulverize' Positions

Soviet artillery aided in the fighting by "pulverizing" prepared positions of the Germans.

Later, however, the German command launched a counter-attack in which two full regiments and 30 tanks attempted to close the breach.

Soviet tanks counter-attacked, damaging 15 enemy tanks in the first day of fighting. Further news of the engagement was awaited.

'Black Clouds' Terrorize Nazis

London, March 17 (U.P.)—Reports from Russia today told how "Black Clouds"—Soviet counterpart of British Commandos—were striking terror into the hearts of German garrisons.

FIRST ASSEMBLY LINE MINESWEEPER LAUNCHED

A minesweeper built for the United States Navy on the assembly line plan of production was launched today at the yard of the Wheeler Shipbuilding Corporation, 154th St. and East River, Whitestone.

The minesweeper, one of 16 under construction at the Wheeler plant, was christened YMS-42 by Mrs. Allene Gokey, wife of Com'r N. W. Gokey, Navy Bureau of Ships, Washington.

As the minesweeper was carried on a marine railway into the water, more than 800 workmen cheered and several hundred other persons in a grandstand applauded.

Stomach Righted, Bouncing Joey Stands the Family on Its Head

Everything is right today in the Lucchese household at 515 Linwood St. since Baby Joe's upside-down stomach has been righted.

Mama, Mrs. Margaret Lucchese, said joyfully: "He can eat anything now. He's got a healthy appetite."

Papa, Benjamin Lucchese, said: "We can't get him to go to bed now. He's full of life. He wants to play all the time."

The other children, all five of them, simply grin their pleasure. They are Vincenza, 12; Anthony, 11; Philipe, 9; Jerome, 7, and Salvatore, 6.

Little Joe has returned home after a month at the Flower Hospital, Manhattan, where a delicate operation was performed to correct his stomach, which has been in the wrong position since birth. Hospital officials declined to name the surgeon who operated.

Because of the inverted stomach, the boy previously had been unable to eat the foods customary for children his age or to play as he pleased.

The father, a building laborer, said over and over: "The operation was a success. Thank God!"

Gen. Douglas MacArthur

QUITS BATAAN BY PLANE ON F. D. R. ORDER

He'll Lead Big A. E. F. And Allied Forces in Battle for Continent

Washington, March 17 (UP)—Gen. Douglas MacArthur, foremost commander of the United Nations, arrived in Australia from the beleaguered Philippines today and has assumed supreme command of Allied forces there in Australia's hour of peril.

The famous defender of the Philippines reached Australia after a secret airplane flight, only a few hours after official disclosure that American troops—air and ground forces "in considerable numbers"—had landed in Australia and were preparing to counter Japan's blows against the southwest Pacific bastion.

MacArthur, the War Department announced, was ordered by President Roosevelt to leave the Philippines 23 days ago and go to Australia "as soon as the necessary arrangements could be made."

Wife Accompanies Him

It had been conceded by top military authorities for weeks—while demands for MacArthur's "rescue" from the Philippines were made in Congress and in Australia—that a Presidential order would be necessary to make him leave his valiant little army that has held the Japanese at a standstill on the Bataan Peninsula battlefront.

MacArthur was accompanied to Australia—nearly 2,000 miles south

Continued on Page 3

M'Arthur Move Thrills Boro Man-in-the-Street

Irish Waiting for Parade Are Jubilant, Hail 'His Real Chance' on St. Patrick's Day

Brooklyn's man-in-the-street and woman, too, are in favor of General Douglas MacArthur's transfer from the Bataan Peninsula to the "wider arena of Australia, where he can really throw his weight around." But the verdict is not unanimous.

The dissenters, several of whom declined to give their names, said "We ought to call all our generals back to this country. We've got to think of America first."

The happiest keynote was struck by two motherly looking housewives, Mrs. Joseph Moriarty of 1421 E. 57th St. and Mrs. Thomas Conway of 311 Hicks St., who thought it an omen that a "MacArthur should be given his real chance on St. Patrick's Day."

"He's a good man wherever he'll

Continued on Page 3

WHERE TO FIND IT

Bay Ridge	Page 18
Clifford Evans	Page 4
Clubwomen	Page 6
Comics	Page 14
Crossword	Page 16
Dr. Brady	Page 15
EDITORIAL	Page 8
Events Tonight	Page 5
FINANCIAL	Page 13
Grin and Bear It	Page 8
Harold Parrott	Page 11
Heffernan	Page 8
Helen Worth	Page 6
Horoscope	Page 14
Jury	Page 15
Movies	Page 4
Music	Page 4
Neighborhood News	Page 5
Novel	Page 17
OBITUARIES	Page 9
Only Yesterday	Page 15
RADIO	Page 14
Society	Page 6
SPORTS	Pages 11-12-13
Take My Word	Page 15
Theaters	Page 4
These Women	Page 15
Tucker	Page 8
Uncle Ray's Corner	Page 15
Want Ads	Pages 16-17
Weather Table	Page 3
Women's	Page 7

40,000 'FAMINE ORPHANS' ROAM STREETS OF ATHENS

Ankara, Turkey, March 17 (U.P.)—A Winter of starvation has left between 30,000 and 40,000 "famine orphans" in Athens. They have been collected from the streets and placed in asylums. Their parents, according to the refugees, either abandoned the children or died of starvation.

Dozens of pale, haggard civilians collapse daily on the streets of Athens and Piraeus from hunger.

In a first-class restaurant a small portion of vegetables, a slice of bread and a piece of meat the size of a match box costs the equivalent of $15 or $20.

Mavro Mihailis, former Greek Foreign Minister, has estimated at least 1,000 starvation deaths occur daily in Athens and Piraeus.

40-MILE SPEED LIMIT IS ASKED BY LEHMAN

Albany, March 17 (U.P.)—A 40-mile-an-hour speed limit was asked of the Legislature today by Governor Lehman in accordance with a request from President Roosevelt.

In a speical message, Lehman asked the Legislature to enact the required legislation promptly in order to conserve motor vehicles, gasoline and tires.

Legislative leaders said they intended to amend the Rapp Bill to set a 40-mile limit. The measure, originally specifying a 50-mile-an-hour limit, is scheduled for passage tomorrow in the Assembly.

128 Dead, Toll Rising In Wake of Tornadoes

By United Press

The death toll mounted today as more bodies were found in the broken path of ruin left yesterday by tornadoes spreading from north central Illinois southward through five Mississippi Valley States.

The known dead stook at 128 this afternoon, but wreckage in Kentucky, Tennessee and Mississippi was expected to yield more bodies, and many of the 200 known to be injured in these States as well as Illinois and Indiana were in critical condition.

Property damage approximated $3,000,000, but this estimate undoubtedly will be revised upward as details are reported from isolated sections where communications were broken.

A State-by-State picture:

Mississippi—75 know fatalities property damage still estimated only in "millions" from a twisting funnel of wind that struck at north central Greenwood and ripped southward through a score of towns and communities, leaving many thickly settled centers without electric power or communication.

Tennessee—16 dead; damage as yet unestimated, but greatest in western central section; damage at Bolivar's Western State Hospital alone was believed to be $100,000.

Kentucky—16 dead in western Muhlenberg, Grayson and Hardin Counties, 10 of these at the mining community of Browder; delayed reports due to disrupted communications led to the fear that Ken-

Continued on Page 2

Dodgers Get 3 Hits, Bow to Red Sox, 8-1

Higbe, Chipman and Head Fail on Mound As Hub Rookies Hold Flock Scoreless for Seven Innings—Casey Proves Effective

By TOMMY HOLMES
Staff Correspondent of the Brooklyn Eagle

Sarasota, Fla., March 21—The Dodger batting attack, which flourished to the extent of 19 hits against the Yankees yesterday was a scandal to the Jaybirds here this windy March afternoon. Held to three singles by a couple of over-ripe rookie pitchers, our N. L. champions were beaten, 8 to 1, by Boston's Red Sox before a polite crowd of 750 clients.

The boys blamed it on the wind—a stiff, steady breeze that came in over the center-field fence and directly into the batter's face at home plate. Just why the same wind did not check the 10-hit Red Sox attack goes unexplained, unless you want to call the fact that the Red Sox play in drafty Boston an explanation.

Leo Durocher used four pitchers—Kirby Higbe, Hugh Casey, Bob Chipman and Ed Head. All of them suffered, except Casey.

Dodger Run Forced In

Yank Terry and Oscar Judd were the veteran rookies who humbled the proud Dodgers. Terry is a 29-year-old righthander who learned a trick turntable delivery out at San Diego last season which effectively masks a sneaky, fast ball. He'll probably be a starting pitcher for Joe Cronin this season. Judd, a 32-year-old lefthander, is back from Louisville for another trial.

Alex Kampouris got one of the Dodger singles and Lew Riggs got the other two. The final Riggs hit was the only one that figured in the scoring. Reese walked with two out in the Brooklyn eighth and Riggs followed with the hit. Then successive bases on balls to Reiser and Galan forced over the Brooklyn run.

The Red Sox opened up on Higbe in round one by scoring two runs without the aid of a hit. That was largely Higbe's own fault. He gave Dom DiMaggio a base on balls and then threw wild into center field after grabbing the double-play ball Johnny Pesky slapped right back to the box. DiMaggio continued to third on the error, scored while Reese threw out Ulysses Lupien, once baseball captain at fair Harvard. Pesky scored from second when Reese booted Jim Taber's grounder.

Chipman Greeted With Singles

Higbe was untouchable for the rest of his turn and Casey completed three innings without serious trouble. In fact, it was the seventh before the Red Sox broke loose again. Chipman by this time was on the mound.

Johnny Welaj, John Peacock and Judd greeted the Northport, L. I., southpaw with successive singles for one run. Rizzo threw out Peacock trying to reach third on Judd's hit, but then a pass to DiMaggio and Pesky's short single filled the bases. Lupien singled through Galan for another run and Heber Newsome walked, forcing over a third. The fourth run of the inning was Pesky's after Medwick caught Bobby Doerr's fly but the

Continued on Page 2

BROOKLYN EAGLE
SPORTS
CLASSIFIED ADVERTISEMENTS
REAL ESTATE
SUNDAY, MARCH 22, 1942 • SECTIONS C-D

Rangers Drop Cup Clash to Leafs, 3-1

Toronto Takes Playoff Opener As Drillon, Metz and Apps Score

Toronto, March 21 (U.P.)—Toronto's surprising Maple Leafs beat the league-leading New York Rangers, 3 to 1, in the Stanley Cup playoff opener tonight on Toronto ice before 13,313 fans.

Brilliant play by the big Leaf line of Syl Apps, Gordon Drillon and Nick Metz gave Toronto the first victory in the best four-of-seven series. It was a rough clash and the players' blood boiled over. The finish took on the aspect of a brawl and only timely action prevented a general fracas.

Tomorrow night the foes come to grips again in Madison Square Garden.

The Rangers got off to a fast start, but their lead was short-lived. Big Babe Pratt took a pass from Phil Watson at the blue line and broke through the center of the Leafs' defense to light the bulb in 2:26. It was a 20-foot shot and Goalie Broada never had a chance.

Drillon evened the score at 4:15 on a pass from Syl Apps with a low one in close. A little more than a minute later Metz put Toronto in front when he picked up a loose puck and scored on a screened backhand shot from the edge of the crease.

Both teams battled furiously throughout the rest of the period with the Leafs pressing continually. The action was fast and rough, but Bill Henry made a gallant stand in the Rangers' net. Referee King Clancy meted out three penalties, two to the home team.

Leafs Increase Lead

Toronto increased its lead in the second period on Syl Apps' goal at 14:14. The pace slowed somewhat in the middle stanza and the Leafs carried the play to the New Yorkers

Continued on Page 2

JUST AN OFF DAY, PALS!

Dodgers	ab	r	h	o	a	Red Sox	ab	r	h	o	a
Reese.ss	3	1	0	3	4	D.DiM'o.cf	3	2	1	0	0
Riggs.3b	4	0	2	2	3	Pesky.ss	5	2	1	2	4
Reiser.cf	3	0	0	3	0	Lupien.1b	4	0	1	10	0
Galan.1b	1	0	0	7	1	Tabor.3b	2	0	1	1	2
Medwick.lf	4	0	0	3	1	L.N's'me.3b	1	0	0	0	3
Rizzo.rf	4	0	0	0	1	Doerr.2b	4	0	0	2	3
Dapper.c	4	0	0	2	0	Finney.rf	4	1	1	1	0
K'pouris.2b	3	0	1	3	3	Welaj.lf	3	2	1	7	0
Higbe.p	1	0	0	0	0	Conroy.c	2	0	1	1	0
Casey.p	0	0	0	1	0	Peacock.c	2	0	2	2	0
Chipman.p	0	0	0	0	0	Terry.p	2	0	0	1	1
Head.p	0	0	0	0	0	Judd.p	2	1	1	0	0
aHerman	1	0	0	0	0						
bPadgett	1	0	0	0	0	Totals	34	8	10	27	13
Totals	29	1	3	24	13						

aBatted for Chipman in eighth inning.
bBatted for Head in ninth inning.

Dodgers ——— 0 0 0 0 0 0 0 1 0—1
Red Sox——— 2 0 0 0 0 0 4 2 x—8

Errors—By Higbe, Reese, Riggs. Stolen bases—Lupien. Double plays—Reese, Kampouris and Galan; Pesky, Duerr and Lupien. Bases on balls—Off Higbe 1, Chapman 1, Head 1 Casey 1, Terry 2, Judd 5. Struck out—By Higbe 1, Head 1, Terry 1, Judd 2. Hits—Off Higbe, 1 in 3; Terry, 2 in 6; Casey, 2 in 3; Chipman, 5 in 1.

HERE'S LOOKING AT YOU—The handsome soldier admiring his new outfit is none other than Billy Conn, former light heavyweight champion who is in training for his greatest bout—against the Axis.

NATS RALLY TO NOSE OUT GIANTS, 4-3

Ott Reads Riot Act but Team Suffers Tenth Defeat in 12 Starts

Special to the Brooklyn Eagle

Miami, March 21—Mel Ott read the riot act to his stumbling Giants before today's game with Washington and while the little manager did infuse more life and hustle into the New York play, the result was unchanged. The Giants sustained another defeat, 4 to 3, as the Nats rallied to win. It was their 10th loss in a dozen games.

The Giant regulars played throughout the game. Ott did not substitute a second team as he had hitherto, and the team held Washington even until the ninth when it again ran afoul of the 18-year-old sensation of the Washington camp, Eddie Lyons. This cocky high school rookie from Winston-Salem, N. C., opened the ninth with a stinging double past Billy Weber and rode home on another two-bagger by Stan Spence.

Three days ago, in Orlando, Lyons whipped the Giants with a pinch single for the decisive tally. Senator camp-followers are hailing Lyons as another Pete Reiser.

Adams Finishes Poorly

This time the Giants fielded well enough, despite one unimportant error by the kid second baseman, Connie Ryan, and they hit opportunely. The defeat must be charged to mediocre twirling by Ace Adams, who finished the game after Hal Schumacher had worked the first four innings.

That so-often-fatal faux pas of the Giant staff, walking the first man up, was indulged in by Adams in the seventh when he had a 3—1 lead. Three hits followed and the score was tied. Harry Danning doubled and Bill Jurges drove him in with a single in the fifth off Winn. Werber walked to open the sixth and after two were out, Mize singled. Leiber walked and Danning singled off Bill Zuber, a tall Mennonite from Iowa, for two tallies.

Schumacher had his usual early season trouble with control, filling the bases with free tickets in the second, but he escaped damage. Three singles in the fourth chipped a run off his delivery.

Bob Repass, Senator shortstop, made the fielding gem with a leaping catch of a liner by Ott. Leiber pulled a beauty in center, where he had been shifted to make room for Rookie Willard Marshall in left.

Mize admits his ailing right shoulder is not yet in good condition, but he made two hard throws to second for force plays . . . Ryan's error proved a break for the Giants. He dropped the ball on a force play at second and George Case broke from third for home. Ryan threw him out . . . The last time the Giants won a game Hubbell pitched. And the only two games the club won were on Sunday. Ott is using the lucky combination today, Hubbell on Sunday, against the Senators. Bob Carpenter will share the job with Hub.

The box score:

Senators	ab	r	h	o	a	Giants	ab	r	h	o	a
Case.lf	4	0	2	3	0	Werber.3b	2	1	0	1	3
Spence.cf	5	0	1	1	0	Marshall.lf	4	0	0	4	0
Campb'l.rf	3	0	0	1	0	Ott.rf	4	0	0	1	0
Ortiz.rf	2	0	1	0	0	Mize.1b	4	1	1	6	4
Vernon.1b	5	0	1	14	0	Leiber.cf	3	0	1	3	0
Early.c	4	0	0	4	2	Danning.c	4	1	2	3	1
Galle.3b	3	1	0	0	0	Jurges.ss	4	0	2	4	3
Repass.ss	2	0	1	2	6	Ryan.2b	4	0	1	3	3
Pofahl.2b	2	1	1	2	4	Schum'r.p	1	0	0	2	2
Wynn.p	2	0	0	0	1	Adams.p	1	0	0	0	1
Zuber.p	1	1	1	0	0						
Cathey.p	0	0	0	0	0						
aLyons	1	1	1	0	0						
Totals	34	4	9	27	13	Totals	31	3	7	27	17

aBatted for Zuber in ninth inning.

Senators ——— 0 0 0 1 0 0 2 0 1—4
Giants ——— 0 0 0 0 1 2 0 0 0—3

Errors—Ryan, Pofahl. Runs batted in—Pofahl, Jurges, Mize, Danning, Case, Vernon, Spence. Two-base hits—Danning, Lyons, Spence. Double plays—Repass and Pofahl; Vernon, Early and Repass; Schumacher, Jurges and Mize. Left on bases—Senators, 9; Giants, 5. Bases on balls—Off Wynn, 1; off Schumacher, 3; off Adams, 3; off Zuber, 2. Struck out—By Schumacher, 1; by Wynn, 1; by Zuber, 2; by Adams, 1; by Cathey, 1. Hits—Off Schumacher, 4 in 4 innings; off Adams, 5 in 5; off Wynn, 4 in 5; off Zuber, 3 in 3. Winning pitcher—Zuber. Losing pitcher—Adams. Umpires—Goetz (N. L.) and Summers (A. L.). Time of game—1:58.

Gordon Drillon

N. Y. U. Fencers Bag College Title

New York University won the 49th Intercollegiate Fencing Association tournament at the Salle Santelli last night, copping the three-weapon championship for the eighth time in 10 years.

The Violet duelists retained the epee crown, lost the foils title to Columbia and regained sabre honors for a total of 76½ points.

Army finished second with 72½ points. Columbia was third with 64½, while Penn and Penn State tied for fourth with 56 each. Princeton and Yale deadlocked for sixth with 53½. Navy finished 12th.

Columbia captured foils honors for the first time in two decades. The Lions captured the event with 28 points, Army was second with 25 and N. Y. U., defending champions, took third place honors with 22 tallies.

N. Y. U. won the sabre title by scoring 28 points. Army also took second place in this event with 26 tallies. Princeton was third with 23, Penn fourth with 22, Yale fifth with 20, and Columbia sixth with 19 points.

The Violets won the epee competition with 26½ points.

HAWKS TO DONATE PROFITS TO WAR FUND

Chicago, March 21 (U.P.)—The Chicago Blackhawks of the National Hockey League will donate their complete profits from the 1942-43 season to a wartime relief agency, Maj. Frederic McLaughlin, president of the club, announced today. The contribution is expected to amount to between $40,000 and $50,000.

HEADLINERS—Joe DiMaggio, famed Yankee slugger (left), and Hugh Casey, Dodger hurler, turned in neat performances in yesterday's exhibition games. DiMaggio poled out his first home run against Cards, while Casey allowed the Red Sox only two hits in pitching three scoreless innings. Yanks won, but our Dodgers met defeat.

COSCARART'S GRAND SLAM HELPS BUCS ROUT A'S, 7-2

Hollywood, Cal., March 21 (U.P.)—Pete Coscarart's fourth inning homer with the bases loaded sparked the Pittsburgh Pirates to a 7—2 triumph over the Philadelphia Athletics today. The score was deadlocked when Coscarart connected, and Vince DiMaggio added another run with a circuit swat in the fifth.

Both teams connected for nine safeties, the A's contributing an error. Ken Heintzelman, Al Butcher and Joe Sullivan hurled for the Pirates, with Newman Shirley and Luman Harris working for the A's.

The score by innings:

	Innings	R.	H.	E.
Pittsburgh (N)	0 1 0 4 1 0 0 0 1	7	9	0
Philadelphia (A)	0 1 0 0 0 0 0 0 1	2	9	1

Batteries—Heintzleman, Butcher (4), Sullivan (8) and Baker; Shirley, Harris (5) and Castiglia.

Brown's Rally Wins

Deland, Fla., March 21 (U.P.)—A five-run rally in the sixth inning gave the St. Louis Browns a 5-to-4 triumph over the Braves today. The Braves previously had taken the lead with two in the second and a pair in the fifth.

Three Boston errors aided the Browns as they rapped Manuel Salvo and Dick Errickson for seven hits. The Braves got ten hits off Al Hollingsworth and John Niggeling.

Veteran Outfielder Johnny Cooney, delayed by his wife's illness, made a belated appearance in the Braves' Spring training camp today. Shortstop Eddie Miller makes his playing debut with Boston tomorrow. Outfielder Tommy Holmes of Brooklyn continues to be the best-looking recruit in camp.

The score by innings:

	Innings	R.	H.	E.
Boston (N)	0 2 0 0 2 0 0 0 0	4	10	3
St Louis (A)	0 0 0 0 0 5 0 0 x	5	7	1

Batteries—Salvo, Errickson (5) and Lombardi, Montgomery (6); Hollingsworth, Niggeling (6) and Swift, Ferrell (6).

White Sox Defeat Cubs

Los Angeles, Cal., March 21—Behind the five-hit, shutout hurling of veteran Ted Lyons and John Humphries, the White Sox trounced the Cubs, 6—2, today. Bill Lee started for the Cubs and was charged with the defeat.

	Innings	R.	H.	E.
Chicago (N)	0 0 0 0 0 0 0 2 0	2	6	2
Chicago (A)	0 0 2 1 1 1 0 1 x	6	9	1

Batteries—Lee, Schmitz (6) and McCullough; Lyons, Humphries (4) and Turner.

Tigers Bow, 3—1

Lakeland, Fla., March 21 (U.P.)—In an exhibition tilt marred by seven errors, the Cleveland Indians topped the Detroit Tigers, 3 to 1, today.

Continued on Page 2

Mioland Sets Track Mark in Tropical Romp

Miami, March 21 (U.P.)—Charles S. Howard's Mioland regained with interest whatever lustre he lost in the Widener Cup as he galloped home a four-length winner in the $7,500 Coral Gables Handicap at Tropical Park today.

The big horse from the West Coast carried high weight in the field of ten starters and was under triple wraps at the wire. Signator, who set the pace, was a surprise second, a length and a half before Llanero. Our Boots duplicated his Widener performance by finishing a fast closing fourth. The time for a mile and one-eighth was 1:49 2-5, two-fifths off the track record set a year ago by Bonzar.

Stable Jockey Buddy Haas made up most of Mioland's 125 pounds and he waited with his horse while Signator and Sir Marlboro went head and head for six furlongs.

At the far turn Haas let the big fellow go and from there on in the others could never get close. Signator gamely held on for the place award while Llanero closed a little ground for third.

Mioland was a slight favorite and returned $6.50, $4.50 and $3.60. His victory was worth $6,165. Signator paid $10.80 and $6.30, Llanero, $14.40.

Night Tide just managed to get up in time to win the first race, scoring by a nose over Bad Cold. The latter had the lead to the stretch but chucked it in the run for the wire. Arched was third.

Form players were rewarded in the second race when Putitthere stepped down in front at even money. Implicit was second with Mersa Matrush getting in for the short end.

Newcomer Smashes College Swim Record

New Haven, Conn., March 21—A new sprint sensation asserted himself in the Eastern Intercollegiate Swimming championships in the Yale pool today when Ed Hall, sophomore from Massachusetts State, hit a dazzling 51.1 seconds for the 100-yard freestyle. His time not only broke the intercollegiate record, but came within a tenth of a second of Johnny Weissmuller's world mark.

REV. ELLIOTT OF GRID DODGERS NOW IN ARMY

The Rev. Wilson Elliott has notified the Brooklyn football Dodgers he would be unable to play in the National League next Fall, it became known yesterday. Elliott, a six-foot-two, 230-pound tackle from the University of Chattanooga, has enlisted in the army as chaplain. He was Brooklyn's 17th choice in the player draft last December.

WAR'S INROADS TO CHANGE 1942 GRID PICTURE

By JACK GUENTHER

The college football heroes won't report for practice for at least six months more, but you can dust off the little black book and jot down the first new record right now—never before in all the game's history have so many head coaching changes been effected at the major gridiron schools.

Attribute the unprecedented turnover to the war, poor 1941 performances, or even to the natural inclination to seek greener pastures. A United Press survey disclosed today that 15 nationally famed coaches have left their old jobs. Some have joined the army, others the navy and the rest have moved on to bigger fields of operation.

Many Colleges Affected

The roll call is a long one and includes the names of schools from every major conference save one—the Southwest.

Here is the list of switches as it stands toady: In the East four schools have been affected. At Fordham—Jim Crowley has joined the navy as a physical instructor and Backfield Coach Earl Walsh will succeed him. At Navy—Major Swede Larson, recalled to active duty, has turned over the Middies to the backfield coach, Commander John Wheichel. At Yale—Spike Nelson joined the army and has not been replaced. At Holy Cross—Joe

A similar number of changes have been made on the coast. At Stanford—Clark Shaughnessy resigned today to go to Maryland and Assistant Jim Lawson was elevated to the top job. At Washington—James Phelan's contract was not renewed and Frosh Coach Pest Welch moved up. At Southern California—Sam Barry has joined the navy and Jeff Cravath was recalled from San Francisco to succeed him.

In the Middle West there are four new coaches. At Minnesota—Bernie Bierman joined the marines and Dr. George Hauser, his assistant will carry on. At Nebraska—Major Biff Jones has returned to West Point as graduate manager and Assistant Glenn Presnell was elevated. At Illinois—Bob Zuppke resigned and Line Coach Ray Eliot was placed in command. At Purdue—Mal Edwards resigned to join the navy and Frosh Coach Elmer Burnham moved up.

The other three switches took place in the South. At Duke—Wallace Wade accepted an army commission and Backfield Coach Eddie Cameron will work in his place for the duration. At Tulane—Red Dawson resigned to become backfield coach at Minnesota and Claude Simon, an assistant, won the job. At Maryland—Shaughnessy will move in and Al Heagy, Al Woods and J. Faber move out.

Gloria Callen Shears Backstroke Record

Miss Gloria Callen broke the world 100-meter indoor backstroke swimming record when she covered the route in 1:14.8 last night in an A. A. U. meet at the New York A. C. The old mark of 1:16.3 was set by Mrs. Eleanor Holm Rose.

Yankee Homers Top Cards, 4-3

DiMag, Gordon Belt Four-Baggers—Donald Retires 15 Men in Order

Special to the Brooklyn Eagle

St. Petersburg, Fla., March 21—On the spectacular rebound from a trouncing by the Dodgers, the Yankees today clustered a few superlatives. Joe DiMaggio accomplished his first home run of the year, Joe Gordon belted his second in two games with a man on base in the eighth, Charley Keller made an amazing catch in the eleventh, and Swampy Donald turned in five brilliant innings of runless and hitless pitching.

The sum total of all this was a 4—3 victory over the Cardinals, who had won three straight from the world champions. Their series of nine meetings now is tied, 3 to 3.

The 18-hit blitz by the Superbas did not agree with Joe McCarthy's tender stomach, so he called a meeting this morning and urged the Bombers to start bombing. In fact, he did more than urge. Tommy Henrich, who has been slow in training and had hit only .220 in a dozen contests, was frowned upon by the management. He was benched in favor of Mike Chartak.

Borowy Yanked in Ninth

With all their achievements and spirit, the Yankees came very near suffering their seventh setback in the Grapefruit League instead of scoring their seventh victory. Hank Borowy, who had not hurled since March 6 because of a finger blister, proved stable-worn and almost spilled the beans. He had to be yanked in favor of Red Branch with two on and nobody out in the ninth.

Branch promptly walked pinch-hitter Crabtree to load the bags, and it took a double play, started by Phil Rizzuto, to keep the damage to one run. With the tie on third, Jimmy Brown ended the game with a foul to Gerry Priddy.

In the eighth inning, with one out and Cardinals on second and third, Keller dashed to the left-field screen, leaped high and clutched Terry Moore's bid for a homer—and the game.

With the best demonstration of pitching seen in Florida this year, Donald was the real hero. Not only did he not allow a hit or a run, but his control never broke. He retired 15 Red Birds in order and only three of them were able to drive a ball out of the infield.

When Borowy got rid of the Cards just as expertly in the sixth, the press box began to wonder about Grapefruit League no-hitters. But with one gone in the seventh, Moore eased a single into left and broke the spell. The Cards got only three more hits.

DiMaggio's homer came off Al Jurisich's first pitch in the second inning.

The losing hurler was the rele-

Continued on Page 2

Joe Gordon

Snead-Wehrle, Nary-Haas Pairs Gain Golf Final

St. Augustine, Fla., March 21 (U.P.)—Defending champions Sammy Snead and Wilford Wehrle defeated Chandler Harper and Sam Bates today in the semi-finals of the national amateur-professional best-ball golf tournament, one up in 36 holes.

In the other semi-final match Bill Nary, California professional, and Fred Haas, New Orleans, pulled out to win, one up after 37 holes, from medalists Al Brosch, Farmingdale, L. I., and Harry Offutt, St. Petersburg, Fla.

In the morning round Snead birdied the second, sixth and eighth holes, putting the Snead-Wehrle team three up. Harper came back with a birdie four on No. 15 to cut the lead to two up at the end of the round.

In the afternoon Harper came back with three birdies, but Snead birdied two more to win, one up.

Nary and Haas finished even with the Brosch-Offutt team in the morning round. The identical scores

Continued on Page 2

Ruffin Earns Decision Over Parker at Grove

Bobby Ruffin, 136, flashy Astoria lightweight, evened up matters trouncing Morris Parker, 131½, Newark Negro, in the feature eight-round bout at Ridgewood Grove last night before a capacity crowd of 3,000 fans. They had met three previous times. Parker won twice and Ruffin now holds two wins, too.

It was a fast, exciting, hard-fought contest. In the second round Ruffin dropped Parker with a right to the jaw for no count. Despite his defeat, Parker gave a good account of himself against the dancing master.

In two sixes Harold Gibson, 120½, Harlem, defeated Mario Morales, 122, Havana, and Johnny Greco, 135, Montreal, defeated Joe Torres, 139, Puerto Rico.

In fours, Julie Bort, 132, Brooklyn, defeated Bobby Henderson, 129, Brooklyn; Tommy Marino, 125, Brooklyn, overcame Johnny Price, 130, Montreal; Teddy Delson, 158½, New York, scored over Johnny Landy, 153, New York; Angelo Gonzales, 130½, New York, won from Gregory Costello, 131, Fordham.

7TH ★★★★★★ Sports Extra
Wall Street Financial News

BROOKLYN EAGLE

LOCAL WEATHER FORECAST: Cool tonight.

101st YEAR • No. 83 • DAILY AND SUNDAY • BROOKLYN, N. Y., WEDNESDAY, MARCH 25, 1942 • Entered at the Brooklyn Postoffice as 2d Class Mail Matter—(Copyright 1942 The Brooklyn Eagle, Inc.) • 3 CENTS

U. S. NAVY SMASHES TWO JAPANESE BASES

Find Your Objective, Let 'Em Have It

EAGLE'S EYRIE—From the broad deck of a U. S. aircraft carrier like this one our filers roared into Far Eastern skies to carry the war to the Japs on Marcus and Wake Islands.

TERSE ORDER SENDS PLANES TO ATTACK

By JOE JAMES CUSTER

Aboard a U. S. Aircraft Carrier in the Pacific, March 4 (Delayed) (U.P.)—Today we attack Marcus Island and the entire ship is astir in the wee hours of the morning.

I'm up at 3, but I find the bombing squadron pilots have already had breakfast and are relaxing, some of them sprawled languidly in deep-cushioned chairs and dozing.

They've already obtained their instructions, and noted the special, last-minute details marked on the huge blackboard in the "ready room."

Their soft-spoken, affable Irish squadron leader walks in briskly for a last-minute conference with the air group commander. In a low-pitched, conversational tone he informs his men:

(a) They're not to fly over our surface ships.

(b) They're to attack immediately any enemy ships they sight.

"Be sure you're dressed warmly," he counsels, stuffing cotton in his ears, "for it'll be cold up there. Get into your formations as quickly as possible. When you reach the island pick out your objective and let 'em have it. Then scram the hell out of there."

His remarks mark the zero hour, and the aviators rise to their feet and file out to the flight deck.

They're a young-looking bunch—"probably average about

Continued on Page 2

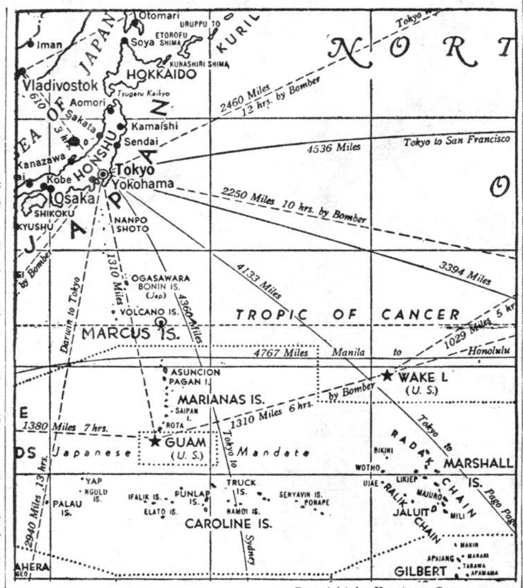

Copyright by Hagstrom Company.

DIMMING THE RISING SUN—The United States Navy announced today its forces had blasted Japanese-controlled Marcus Island, a base only 990 miles from Japan's congested Yokohama.

MARCUS, WAKE ISLES BLASTED

Wreck Airport, Guns, Barracks 990 Miles From Yokohama

Washington, March 25 (UP)— U. S. Pacific fleet task force carried out surprise attacks on Japanese-owned Marcus Island, only 990 miles southeast of Tokio, and on Japanese-occupied Wake Island, smashing shore installations, sinking two patrol boats and demolishing three large seaplanes, the navy announced today.

The communique reported U. S. losses as only two aircraft, one in each of the attacks.

The task force was commanded by Vice Admiral William F. Halsey, who headed the naval forces which raided the Japanese-controlled Marshall and Gilbert Islands last Jan. 31.

TOKIO GETS BLACKOUT JITTERS

Copyright, 1942, by United Press

Aboard a U. S. Aircraft Carrier in the Pacific, March 4 (Delayed)—The United States Navy knocked at Japan's front door today when planes from this aircraft carrier dumped 12 tons of high explosives on installations on Marcus Island, 990 miles southeast of Tokio.

Eight days previously, it now can be revealed, a U. S. naval force delivered a crushing blow at installations on Wake Island, which the Japanese had captured from heroic American marine defenders.

Naval authorities believed the two raids shattered, for some time at least, links in Japan's chain of fortified bases extending southeasterly from Tokio to the Marshall Islands, Japan's Eastern outposts.

The attack on Marcus Island—only a stone's throw from Tokio as distances are measured in the vast area of the Pacific—carried the war into Japan's home waters.

It gave Tokio and Yokohama their first taste of blackout jitters and was expected to divert a portion of Japanese material and manpower from other vital areas in the southwest Pacific.

Marcus' proximity to Tokio served as a special stimulant, the pilots expressing a desire to head an adequate force on a concentrated attack upon that city and Yokohama.

Only American losses were one plane in each attack.

A hard hitting combination of cruisers, destroyers and

Continued on Page 2

10 Bulls on Loose in Williamsburg Tossed for Loss by Cops' Lassos

Ten bulls got loose in Williamsburg today and, as if they were in ten china shops, broke down walls, caused people to run helter-skelter and generallp disturbed the peace. Twenty policemen with lassoes captured them.

The animals were being transported in a truck of Max Bell & Sons, 287 McKibbin St., to the slaughter-house of the C. Lehman Packing Company, 321 Johnson Ave. On S. 9th St., between Roebling and Havemeyer Sts., something broke, the tailboard of the truck fell and the bulls jumped. Scattering, they galloped off in several directions but chiefly toward Pete McGuinness' "Garden Spot of the Universe," Greenpoint. But they didn't get near enough to find out whether the garden spot had good grazing. It took police a little over an hour to clear the streets.

NITZBERG APPEALS FROM 2D DEATH SENTENCE

Ossining, March 25—Irving (Knadles) Nitzberg, 32, convicted for the second time of the slaying of Albert Shuman in Brooklyn, has filed notice of appeal with Sing Sing Prison Warden Robert Kirby, thus automatically postponing his execution, originally set for early in June.

HEATER FUMES FELL FAMILY OF FOUR

Lawrence Arena, 29, a longshoreman, his wife, Madeline, 28, and their sons, James, 4, and Alfonso, 2, were overcome last night by fumes from a gas-burning water heater in their home at 118 Wyckoff St.

The mother and children quickly lost consciousness, but Arena managed to crawl to a front room window and summon aid before collapsing. They were revived by an ambulance doctor from Holy Family Hospital and members of Police Emergency Squad 13.

Continued on Page 12

Firm Ends 'Bonuses,' Cuts Pay, War Profits

Cleveland, March 25 (U.P.)—Jack & Heintz, Inc., whose generous wage and bonus system was brought to light by the House Naval Committee in Washington, voluntarily limited profits to 6 percent today and announced that officers' salaries would be cut $85,000 each.

The company is working on orders from the army and navy for aircraft parts totaling $58,000,000.

William S. Jack, president, said "any profits above 6 percent will be refunded to the army and navy," and the 6 percent profit will be kept by the company as a reserve.

"We will reduce officers' salaries from $100,000 to $15,000," he said. "No further bonuses will be paid to officers and no further dividends will be paid for the duration of the war.

"We have been so busy, with our minds concentrated on production that we didn't realize the effect on the public of paying our officers $100,000 and bonuses."

Testimony before the House Committee revealed that Jack and two other officers were paid $100,000 a year and large bonuses and that Jack's secretary was paid a salary of $25,000 and a bonus, totaling almost $40,000, last year, and that she had received $18,295 the first 10 weeks of this year.

Employes were given monthly banquets, gold watches and insurance policies.

EXECUTIVES IN 15 WAR PLANTS GOT 22-1,331% RAISES

House Committee Told Of Big Pay Boosts When Defense Program Began

Washington, March 25 (U.P.)—Executives of 15 naval ordnance construction concerns received salaries during the first year of the defense program that were as much as 1,331 percent higher then earnings in 1934, the House Naval Affairs Committee was told today.

Chief Counsel Edmund H. Toland advised the committee today that his staff had completed a survey of salary increases among ordnance contractors who had supplied information in response to questionnaires.

Toland made his report at the committee's hearings on the Smith-Vinson bill to limit war profits to 6 percent and suspend overtime payments for work in excess of 40 hours a week in war industries.

Using salaries paid to corporation executives from 1934 to 1940 as the basis of comparison, Toland said that 26 out of 41 executives received more than 100 percent increases during the period. Fourteen of the 26 received more than 200 percent, 10 received more than 300 percent, seven received more than 400 percent and five received more than 500 percent.

"The tremendous increases," Toland said, "in compensation paid officials, of course, cannot be attributed solely to defense work as 1934 was considered one of the depression years, yet there were a number of large increases in 1940 over 1938, the first year of business. Salaries during this period showed increases as high as 181 percent.

"While the salaries of officials increased tremendously during the first year of the defense program, incomplete figures for 1941 indicate that there will be a much greater increase as the program progresses.

"An example of the individual companies comprising the 15 selected as a sample showed a wide variation in the percentage increases during the period 1934-1941 (using the first and last year for which complete information was furnished (range from approximately 22 percent to 1,331 percent (J. B. Armitage, chief engineer of the Kearney & Tucker Corp.)

Higher Wages Urged At Catholic Conference

Opening Session of Regional Meeting Hears Appeals for Distribution of Wealth

A halt to attacks on organized labor and fairer distribution of wealth among the working people were urged by speakers today at the opening session of the three-day Brooklyn Regional meeting of the Catholic Conference on Industrial Problems at the Columbus Club, 1 Prospect Park West.

More than 200 at the morning meeting were addressed by the Rev. Benjamin L. Masse, S. J., associate editor of America, national magazine of the Jesuits; Dr. Walter Willigan, professor of economics at St. John's University; Russell L. Greenman, manager of the industrial department of the Brooklyn Chamber of Commerce, and William Collins, regional director of the A. F. L. in Greater New York.

Declaring that a wartime prosperity tends to obscure the grow-

Continued on Page 8

Lindbergh Takes Ford Plane Post

Detroit, March 25 (U.P.)—Charles A. Lindbergh has been employed by the Ford Motor Company in the engineering department of its giant Willow Run bomber plant, Ford Personnel Director Harry H. Bennett announced today.

Bennett said the position was offered to Lindbergh by Henry Ford yesterday during a detailed inspection of the bomber plant. Lindbergh was in Washington today, presumably to confer with the War Department regarding his new post.

"Mr. Ford merely offered Lindbergh the job," Bennett said, "and Mr. Lindbergh agreed to take it."

Last January Lindbergh offered his services to Henry L. Stimson, Secretary of War, and it was announced that he would be entrusted with a civilian mission involving technical research for the War Department.

NURSES AIDE WEEK PROCLAIMED BY MAYOR

Mayor LaGuardia has issued a proclamation designating the week of April 6-12 as Victory Nurses' Aide Week, it was announced today by Mrs. Winthrop W. Aldrich, vice chairman of the Greater New York Civilian Defense Volunteer Office.

The proclamation emphasizes the drive to train 10,000 women in the city to perform the nurses' aide duties in the city hospitals, which have lost many nurses because of the needs of the armed forces.

Tropical Park Results

1—Mar Le. 5.30. 3.70, 3.00; Handy Justice, 6.70, 4.20; Range Dust, 4.50. Off time, 2:04.

2—Commencement 11.30, 6.00, 3.80; Chigre 36.80, 9.90; Kleig Light 2.80. Off time, 2:32½.

DAILY DOUBLE PAID $34.50.

3—Bayridge, first; Louisville II, second; No Count, third.

Red Demands Allies Drive Against Nazi

London, March 25 (U.P.)—Soviet Ambassador Ivan Maisky demanded today that the United Nations seize the initiative from Germany and make a supreme effort to open a Spring and Summer offensive which will turn 1942 into the victory year of the war.

Maisky made his statement in awarding the Order of Lenin to four British pilots who fought on the Russian front.

TENTATIVE GAS RATION 5-10 GALLONS A WEEK

Washington, March 25 (U.P.)—Motorists in the newly-restricted areas embracing 15 Eastern States, Washington and Oregon and the District of Columbia will receive at least five gallons of gasoline weekly under tentative rationing plans.

No definite figures have been set, officials said today, but no amount under five gallons has been mentioned. Some have suggested as much as ten.

Officials said there is a possibility that motorists will be allowed to accumulate their weekly gasoline coupons for Summer vacations.

JAPAN OCCUPIES ISLAND GROUP IN BENGAL BAY

Approaches to India Menaced by Seizure Of Penal Settlement

New Delhi, India, March 25 (U.P.)—Japanese armed forces have occupied the Andaman Islands in the Bay of Bengal and pushed northward in fierce battles with Chinese and British forces in the Toungoo sector of central Burma, communiques said today.

Occupation of the Andaman Islands on the approaches to India had been expected since the fall of Malaya and British forces recently were withdrawn from the islands, which are 2,600 square miles in area and lie 180 miles south of Burma.

"A considerable portion of the population, including women and children and a number of convicts, also was evacuated," the communique said.

Flank Allies in Burma

On the Burma land front a Japanese flank attack snapped the northward communications of the Allied forces at Toungoo and a big battle was in progress both north and south of the town, where the situation was officially reported to be serious.

The Burma command reported that a force of 1,000 Japanese cavalry and "plain clothes men" had slipped around the main defense lines south of Toungoo and cut the Toungoo-Mandalay road about 20 miles north of the Burma defense positions.

Chinese forces immediately were thrown into an attack on the Japanese flanks in an effort to recapture an airdrome north of Toungoo.

Lt. Gen. Joseph Stilwell, U. S. A., commands the Chinese forces in Burma.

"The situation on the Toungoo front is serious," the communique said.

Order Tax Returned

Employers in the State have been ordered to return 25 percent of the money they have withheld from out-of-State employes to pay their 1941 State income tax. The 25 percent represents the reduction recently enacted by the Legislature,

Draft Bribe Conviction Of Three Is Upheld

The conviction of a former draft board chairman, a Bronx contractor and the latter's son, found guilty of conspiring to have the son evade the draft by payment of a $1,000 bribe, today had been upheld by the United States Court of Appeals.

Daniel J. Houlihan, the former draft board chairman, was sentenced to a two-year prison term; the father, James O'Connell, 62, faces a year's term, and his son, Francis, 27, was sentenced to two years. All are Bronx residents.

Pneumonia Cases Rise, But Deaths Drop

Last week saw 175 new cases of pneumonia in Brooklyn and 18 deaths, Health Commissioner Rice reported today. This represents an increase of five cases but a drop of 10 deaths, as compared with the previous week.

Deaths from all causes were 499, a drop of 81 from the preceding week. In the corresponding week of 1941 there were 547. There were 897 births, a decrease of 81 from the previous week. In the similar week last year there were 793.

WHERE TO FIND IT

Bay Ridge	Page 9	Lindley	Page 14
Bridge	Page 23	Movies	Page 13
Civil Service	Page 6	Music	Page 13
Clubwomen	Page 11	Neighborhood News	Page 9
Comics	Page 20	Novel	Page 23
Crossword	Page 22	OBITUARIES	Page 15
Dr. Brady	Page 21	RADIO	Page 20
EDITORIAL	Page 14	Real Estate	Page 20
Events Tonight	Page 4	Society	Page 11
FINANCIAL	Page 12	SPORTS	Pages 17-18-19
Grin and Bear It	Page 13	Take My Word	Page 21
Harold Conrad	Page 13	Theaters	Page 13
Harold Parrott	Page 17	These Women	Page 21
Heffernan	Page 14	Tucker	Page 14
Helen Worth	Page 10	Uncle Ray's Corner	Page 21
Horoscope	Page 20	Want Ads	Pages 21-22-23
Income Tax	Page 16	Weather Table	Page 15
Jury	Page 21	Women's	Page 10

Give Boys a Sendoff? Boro Answers 'Yes'!

7TH ★★★★★★ Sports Extra
Racing • • All Sports

BROOKLYN EAGLE

LOCAL WEATHER FORECAST: Occasional rain, colder tonight.

101st YEAR • No. 92 • DAILY AND SUNDAY • BROOKLYN, N. Y., FRIDAY, APRIL 3, 1942 • Entered at the Brooklyn Postoffice as 2d Class Mail Matter—(Copyright 1942 The Brooklyn Eagle, Inc.) • 3 CENTS

BORO HERO SAVES 34 MATES, SENDS SOS ON SINKING SHIP

HEROIC DOCTOR RETURNS HOME—Dr. Leonard H. Conly, who, suffering from two broken ribs, attended at a birth in an overcrowded lifeboat after his ship was torpedoed, is shown at his home, 912 Herkimer St., with his wife and their 2-year-old son, Leonard H. Jr.

Weary Doctor Home After Lifeboat Birth

'Great Little Stowaway,' He Chuckles—Orders Boro Office Dusted for Business

After an absence of many months Dr. Leonard Conly, 42, arrived today at his home, 912 Herkimer St. He slowly lifted himself from the front seat of his brother's automobile, climbed slowly up the stoop and eased himself upon the comfortable sofa in the parlor.

Two of his ribs are broken, mementos of his heroic feat in a raging sea when he delivered a baby boy in an overcrowded, partially swamped lifeboat and brought the infant's mother safely through her ordeal without instruments or sanitary devices.

"What's there to talk about?" he demanded, making a brave effort to conceal a sudden twinge of pain. His own baby boy, Leonard Jr., 2, gurgled happily and seized his coat lapel.

Orders Office Dusted

Dr. Conly seemed exhausted from the 40 sleepless hours in the tossing lifeboat. Mrs. Desanka Mohorovicic,

Continued on Page 4

Give Boys a Sendoff? Boro Answers 'Yes'!

Perelson of Jewish War Veterans Joins Drive With Plan for Neighborhood Celebrations

War veterans in their forties know well how it feels to be a boy of 20—or older—going away to war.

Looking back over the years they can recall each a different youth making the big change-over from school or home or a beginning job to the unpredictable life of a soldier in uniform. Maybe more than any actual war experience to come that change scares a boy, no matter how brave in the face of real danger, gives him a feeling of being suddenly left alone.

Veterans of that older war have been therefore quick to support a move for a borough-wide method of giving a send-off to Brooklyn's young men of the war of 1942 just before they are inducted into the service of Uncle Sam.

Continued on Page 4

Standard Sales To Axis Airlines In Brazil Bared

Berle Says Company Refused to End Pacts Until U. S. Blacklisting

Washington, April 3 (U.P.)—Assistant Secretary of State A. A. Berle Jr. testified at a Senate hearing today that last October representatives of Standard Oil Company (N. J.) refused to breach a contract to supply gasoline to Axis air lines in Brazil.

Berle said that two days after the initial refusal Standard agreed to co-operate with the State Department. During those days the Government began action to blacklist Standard's Brazilian subsidiary and "news of it traveled fast," Berle commented.

The refusal was based, Berle said, on the ground that Standard's Brazilian subsidiary had a contract with Condor, German-controlled Brazilian air line, to supply aviation gasoline and oil. The Standard officials said, he added, that failure to make deliveries might bring a suit and loss to the company.

Supplied Italian Airline

The information, Berle said, was conveyed to him at a conference on Oct. 21, 1941, with a "Mr. Palmer," whom he identified as attorney for Standard, and another unnamed company representative.

Berle testified after William Lavarre, Commerce Department Latin-American expert, told the committee that Standard sold gasoline to the Italian Lati Airline in Brazil until the flying firm was blacklisted by this Government.

Lavarre said that the Commerce Department had held conversations with Standard Oil officials, who "were threatened twice" before the blacklist "put Lati out of business."

"Do you mean," Senator Harold H. Burton (R., Ohio) asked Berle, "that Standard took the position that it could make any contract it wanted, against the vital interests of the United States, and keep it because to breach it would lose the company money?"

"The position they took was that they were going to keep the con-

Continued on Page 2

CHINESE RETAKE BURMA AIRPORT NEAR TOUNGOO

Much War Material Captured as Troops Advance Southward

Chungking, April 3 (U.P.)—A Chinese communique issued at Lashio tonight said that Chinese forces in Burma were advancing against the Japanese and had re-captured Keyungkang Air Field.

(The Kyungon Air Field is about ten miles north of Toungoo and presumably is the same as Keyungkang Air Field mentioned in the Lashio communique. The field was first seized by the Japanese in their flanking operations north of Toungoo but Chinese troops fought their way out of the trap with the aid of reinforcements coming down from the north.)

The communique said that the Chinese advance was resumed on Wednesday (presumably pushing southward toward Toungoo) and that much war material was captured.

Chinese troops in the Toungoo

Continued on Page 2

5 Army Fliers Die In Bomber Crash

West Greenwich, R. I., April 3 (U.P.)—Five army fliers including two officers were killed when a medium bomber on a routine flight crashed, exploded and burned in woods on Hopkins Hill.

A spokesman for the First Corps area at Boston said the charred bodies had not been identified.

He said that the bomber, reported overdue at Westover Field, Mass., carried two officers and three enlisted men when it crashed.

Several hours after the accident was reported by farmers living in the isolated area a charred body was extricated from the wreckage.

Two truckloads of soldiers and four State troopers reached the scene and recovered the charred body. They reported that all that remained of the plane was a single engine, wing tips and a small section of the fuselage buried in a fire-blackened crater.

New Drug Sobers Dogs, May Work on Humans

Boston, April 3 (U.P.)—Black coffee and other amateur remedies for inebriates may go by the boards if a new drug—sodium pyruvate—works as well on human beings as it has on "drunken" dogs.

Chemical chasers sobered up the dogs three times faster than normal after they became intoxicated by consuming alcohol equivalent to a half-pint of whisky gulped by a 130-pound man.

Experiments on dogs with the drug were reported by its discoverers—Drs. W. W. Westerfield, Robert Berg and Elmer Stotz of Harvard University.

Tropical Park Results

1—Bottle Imp, 3.70, 2.80, 2.40; Poalty 4.60, 3.10; Stepping Out, 3.80. Off time, 2:36.

2—Zite, first; Gala Orte, second; Retion, third.

Bowie Results

1—Four Stars, first; Ariel Boom, second; [illegible], third.

Eagle Staff photo

HE SENT THE MESSAGE THROUGH—Ignace Choinacki, 24, of 218 Barbey St., radio operator on a freighter torpedoed at sea, who stayed on board after first torpedo smashed radio mast. He set up emergency sending apparatus and again and again sent out urgent call for help. He is shown on his arrival here greeted by sister, Lillian.

Priorities Force City to Send Rookie Cops on Duty Unarmed

The Police Department, it was learned today, has been unable to obtain revolvers for 57 rookie patrolmen appointed in January. The new cops, who attend police school in the daytime but have two-hour patrols at night, are being sent out on duty unarmed.

The department, is was learned, has been trying for months to obtain 300 revolvers but so far has been able to get only 50 guns after prolonged negotiations with priorities officials in Washington. These, with 90 obtained from other sources, equipped only 140 of the 197 men appointed in January.

WOMAN SLEUTH NABS 2 IN NARCOTICS RING HUNT

The residents of a lower East Side neighborhood in Manhattan will be startled to learn that the friendly woman who was so interested in their affairs is Detective Margaret Leonard. She put on old clothes, rented a flat near Monroe and Catherine Sts. and hunted for a narcotic peddling ring.

As a result, Thomas Russo, 22, of 27 Prince St., and Edward Angelico, 25, of 86 Catherine St., today are under arrest on narcotic selling charges. Police allege that Ralph Prisco, shot to death Monday in an attempted holdup of the Associated Auto School at 317 Flatbush Ave. was an accomplice of the two under arrest. Police said Detective Leonard's investigation showed Angelico's flat was used as a hiding place for narcotics.

80 DEALERS FARE LIGHTLY ON PINBALL CHARGES

Eighty Queens storekeepers today had received suspended sentences on their pleas of guilty to possessing pinball machines when arraigned in Felony Court, Ridgewood, before Magistrate Hockert. They were given summonses during police raids last January.

Continued on Page 4

Gas Firm Cancels Plea For $1,000,000 Boost

The Brooklyn Union Gas Company has agreed to withdraw its application for an increase in rates, the Public Service Commission announced today. Had the proposed increase been granted, Brooklyn and Queens consumers would have had to pay $1,000,000 more annually.

The company first announced its intention of seeking higher rates in 1938, with the result that the commission immediately began rate proceedings which have continued until the present. The proceedings were ended today with the company's withdrawal of its application.

Another important Brooklyn Union Gas proceeding also was ended by agreement between the firm and the commission.

This proceeding involved the commission's proposal that the company's books and accounts be so adjusted that nearly $6,500,000, which, according to the commission, represented excess of book cost over the original cost, be eliminated from the company's capital structure.

The commission proposed that the adjustment be made by reducing the stated value of the company's capital stock from $60 to $40 a share, a reduction from the present stated value of $37,268,300 to $29,814,500. The company's depreciation reserve also was to be increased from $15,736,000 to $32,144,000.

All of these adjustments, according to the commission, have been ratified by the company's stockholders, and only a few minor details remain to be settled.

U-Boat Shells Tug Off Coast--3 Vessels Lost in Caribbean

The heroic story of a Brooklyn youth, Ignace Choinacki, 24, of 218 Barbey St., and the shelling of a tugboat off the Atlantic coast after a five-mile chase were described today by 85 survivors of four sinkings, 74 of whom were landed in New York Harbor.

Three freighters and the tugboat and several barges towed by the tugboat were sunk by enemy submarines, the navy revealed. The freighters were torpedoed in the Caribbean. Choinacki was a radio operator aboard one of them.

The tug was sunk Tuesday morning. When the submarine first began shelling the tug and barges, the tug captain cut the lines and swung his craft away in an effort to escape.

Chases Tug for 5 Miles

The raiding sub pursued the tug for five miles and succeeded in sinking the vessel. It then returned to pour more shells into the barges, sank two of them, and fled. The tug's master and chief engineer, and nine crew members from the barges were rescued.

Choinacki's ship, like the other two, medium-sized freighters, was the first to go down, on Feb. 22 last. Fifteen or 16 members of the tugboat are missing, while a total of 20 crew members from the freighters sunk are also missing.

While Choinacki's ship was 190 miles off Trinidad a torpedo struck her, smashing the radio mast. The crew of 35 tumbled into lifeboats—all but Choinacki. He remained behind, working furiously to set up an emergency sending set. It was 9 at night, but the men in the lifeboats could see him moving about on the doomed deck.

Finally he got his set working. Six times he sent out the call for help—SOS . . . SOS. Only then he thought of himself—and not himself alone. There was a tiny pet monkey on board, the only living thing besides himself. He held it

Continued on Page 4

SEE ROOSEVELT MOVE TO SETTLE INDIA'S DEMANDS

Chungking Speculates On Intervention—Cripps, Wavell Study Problems

New Delhi, April 3 (U.P.)—Success of Great Britain's effort to win India's aid in the war depends upon settlement of three demands of the All-India Congress, it was understood today.

(Dispatches from Chungking reported speculation on the possibility that President Roosevelt might intervene in the negotiations in an effort to bring about a settlement of India's demands. An Axis broadcast also reported efforts by China's Chiang Kai-shek to aid a settlement.)

Sir Stafford Cripps, Britain's emissary to India, and Gen. Sir Archibald Wavell, commander-in-chief in India and Burma, today consider three Congress demands, which were:

1. A strong voice in control of India's defense.

2. Provision for election instead of appointment of representatives of Indian States to the Constitutional Assembly.

3. Elimination of the right of provincial States to decline to adhere to the dominion plan.

Hope for Accord Rises

(The All-India radio reported a "more optimistic atmosphere" among All-India Congress leaders today, indicating hope for an agreement when Wavell and Cripps meet Saturday evening with Congress President Maulana A. K. Azad and Jawaharlal Nehru.)

The position of the Working Committee of the Congress on the three issues was set forth in a communication to Cripps yesterday, and it is expected that he will communicate his government's reaction to Maulana Abul Kalam Azad, president of the Congress, and Jawaharlal Nehru, powerful left wing Congress leader, later today.

If a satisfactory answer can be given to these demands there is every hope, observers said, that a majority of the Congress Working Committee would accept the modified offer of Great Britain. Rejection of the demands, however, probably would mean rejection of the modified offer.

Concerning the first demand it was understood that the Working Committee insisted that India have a Defense Minister with powers similar to those held by the Minister in Canada and Australia, or that they be allowed to work out their own strategy and operations plans.

U. S. Intervention Seen

Chungking, China, April 3 (U.P.)—Chinese quarters believed today that President Roosevelt may be asked to mediate in an effort to prevent collapse of negotiations in New Delhi on Great Britain's offer of post-war dominion status for India.

Official sources declined comment but unofficially there was increasing speculation on suggestions that Mr. Roosevelt be urged to act.

Store Clerks Collect Funds To Care for Foundling

Clerks of the linen department at R. H. Macy & Co. today started a collection to care for a 3-week-old girl abandoned by its mother yesterday on a supervisor's desk on the sixth floor of the Manhattan department store.

The girl, who has red hair and blue eyes, was the center of attraction for a time after its discovery during the noon rush hour yesterday. She was taken to the New York Foundling Hospital.

WHERE TO FIND IT

Bay Ridge News	Page 4
Bridge	Page 19
Comics	Page 18
Crossword	Page 18
Dr. Brady	Page 5
EDITORIAL	Page 10
Going Places	Page 8
Grin and Bear It	Page 10
Harold Conrad	Page 17
Heffernan	Page 10
Helen Worth	Page 7
Horoscope	Page 16
Jury	Page 5
Lindley	Page 10
Movies	Page 9
Music	Page 9
Neighborhood News	Page 4
Novel	Page 19
OBITUARIES	Page 11
RADIO	Page 16
Real Estate	Page 19
Society	Page 6
Sports	Pages 12-14-15
Take My Word	Page 5
Theaters	Page 9
These Women	Page 17
Tucker	Page 10
Uncle Ray's Corner	Page 17
Want Ads	Pages 18-19
Woman's	Page 2

★★★★★★ Sports Extra

Wall Street Financial News

BROOKLYN EAGLE

LOCAL WEATHER FORECAST: Rain and cool tonight

101st YEAR • No. 98 • DAILY AND SUNDAY • BROOKLYN, N. Y., THURSDAY, APRIL 9, 1942 • [illegible] • 3 CENTS

BATAAN OVERTHROWN; 36,800 BATTLE TO END

Fate of Exhausted Troops In Doubt; Bay Forts Hold Out

Washington, April 9 (UP)—Thirty-six thousand American and Filipino troops, exhausted by short rations, disease and lack of relief, were overwhelmed on Bataan Peninsula today by a fresh and numerically superior enemy.

Secretary of War Stimson, who disclosed for the first time the number and plight of the Bataan defenders, was unable to say how many of the 36,853 Yanks and Filipinos were killed, captured or wounded.

He said that every effort was being made to get as many of them as possible to Corregidor and other American fortresses that still hold out in Manila Bay. But it appeared doubtful that any substantial number could be evacuated.

Stimson also revealed for the first time that some aid had been run through the Japanese sea blockade to the men fighting in the Philippines, but at heavy cost.

"Several ships" of supplies pierced the blockade, Stimson said, and part of the supplies arrived at Corregidor and Bataan. "But for every ship that arrived we lost nearly two ships," Stimson said in counting the cost of the relief attempts which failed.

First news that American defense of the peninsula had collapsed came in a 5:15 a.m. communique from the War Department which said that the American right flank had been turned and that a counter-attack failed because the men were exhausted. The communique added that the Bataan defenses "probably have been overcome."

Stimson, who had just conferred with President Roosevelt, said at a press conference that in addition to the United States-Filipino troops on bloody Bataan there were some 20,000 civilian refugees there.

They had fled to Bataan at the time of the Japanese occupation of Manila. Their presence made the food situation more critical and handicapped the defenders.

Continued on Page 9

Bugle Blows At Jamaica Track Today

Lid-Lifter of Long Racing Season Here May Draw 20,000

By HAROLD PARROTT

They're off a-galloping today at the Jamaica Track, the horses and the iron men.

It's the lid-lifter for the long Metropolitan racing season, and more than 20,000 may turn out to see a program, headed by the $7,500 [illegible] Handicap, which may make one of the best Jamaica meetings ever. The seven-race program got under way at 2 p.m.

Because Santa Anita didn't operate, a number of horses and horsemen are inordinately hungry at this time of year, and the Jamaica fields promise to be sparkling. Never before, veteran horsemen say, have so many top [illegible] been on hand at this time of year. Jamaica, rebuilt two years ago at a [illegible] cost, is [illegible] to welcome today's throngs, but it hasn't the frills of [illegible] Hialeah or its Queens neighbor, Belmont Park. The racing bug is not too prissy about flamingoes or [illegible] when he wants to get his bet down, however.

Plenty of Betting Cash

Officials expect a large handle in the mutuels this afternoon. They know there is a lot of loose money around; Florida's racing season proved that, with the Hialeah handle, for instance, just a bit below last year's, when there was no war.

Mention of the war brings to mind that the racing folk haven't recognized it yet. They've taken no cognizance of the "war efforts" of other sports like baseball, and apparently haven't given much thought to admitting armed service men for anything but the regular fee.

Only 89 percent of the money that's bet today will roll back to the winners, for there is an 11 percent take in the works of the mutuel machines. The customers don't seem to notice this, however, and will climb all over one another today to place their bets. The students of form like to bet at Jamaica, for it is a kite-shaped track that brings out the real sprinting ability of a horse and races are truly run here, as we say in our set, Throckmorton.

Today's turnout may be in the nature of a picnic crowd, with plenty of food hampers likely to be seen unless the picket line thrown around the track by Local 249, Pari-Mutuel Sellers and Cashiers Union, A. F. L., is withdrawn. Truckloads of food were rerouted to Belmont Park yesterday when their drivers refused to go through the picket lines.

Synthetic Tires 2 Years Off

It will be at least two years before the average citizen, if he still has the price, can buy synthetic rubber tires, the Academy of Political Science, meeting in the Hotel Astor, was told yesterday by Robert P. Russel, executive vice president of the Standard Oil Company of New Jersey.

Mayor, Valentine Seek Jurist to Try 32 Cops On Charges of Graft

Mahoney Considered—Dewey and Al Smith Mentioned if Ex-Justice Is Not Available

Mayor LaGuardia and Police Commissioner Valentine today joined in the search for a jurist to preside at the departmental trials of the Brooklyn policemen accused of taking $1,000,000 graft a year for protection of a $100,000,000 gambling ring.

Of the 40 patrolmen and higher police officials accused in grand jury presentments handed up yesterday, only 32 are to be tried, the others having resigned from the department.

The Mayor and commissioner want to find some one with the "character and qualifications" of Jeremiah T. Mahoney, who would give the men a fair trial and the charges against them a fair and full hearing.

Presided at Bail Trials

Mr. Mahoney, former Supreme Court Justice and former candidate for Mayor, presided at the police trials of a lieutenant and ten sergeants between December, 1939 and May, 1940, on charges of bail bond irregularities brought, as were the present graft charges, as the result of an investigation by Assistant Attorney General Amen.

Four of the ten were found guilty and dismissed from the force, one was fined, five were permitted to retire and one man died.

Judge Mahoney was named a special deputy police commissioner for the duration of the trials, and at the close turned his salary over to the Police Pension Fund.

Whether he would be able to take over the trial job this time was not known, but his name was first on the list of those under consideration. Should he be unavailable, other names were tentatively considered, including those of former Gov. Alfred E. Smith and former District Attorney Thomas E. Dewey.

Meanwhile the 32 policemen were under suspension without pay.

14 Have Retired

The suspensions were announced a few hours after six grand jury presentments were handed up to Supreme Court Justice MacCrate accusing 40 plainclothesmen and nine higher police officials—49 in all—of collecting the graft tribute.

Fourteen of the 49 had already retired from the department while under investigation, and apparently no further action would be taken against them. The status of three

Continued on Page 2

Airport Funds Approved Amid Fraud Charges

$591,000 Fee to Private Consultant on Idlewild Job Flayed as 'Grab'

Funds for construction of the new Idlewild airport in Queens were made available today by Mayor LaGuardia at a public hearing during which a feature of the project was denounced as "larceny," "an outrageous grab" and "a swindle."

The provocative feature was the $591,000 fee which Jay Downer, State Parkway Commission engineer, is to receive in private capacity as consultant on the draining, filling, lighting and paving of the airport. The total cost of this work, including the consultant's fee, is $9,000,000.

The money was obtained from the navy in payment for Floyd Bennett Field. Its assignment to Idlewild was effected by a local law. When the Mayor signed the measure, Joseph E. Kinsley of the Bronx, chairman of the City Council finance committee, asserted, "You have not heard the finish of this!"

Charges 'Steal'

Previously, protesting the impending signing, Kinsley, referring to the Downer fee, demanded:

"Is it just because the parkway funds are being curtailed that he is to be moved to more lucrative fields?"

Joseph Goldsmith, president of the Taxpayers Union, said it was rumored that "there was a steal" connected with the measure.

Leopold B. Rossi, secretary of the Civil Service Forum, said it represented the "kind of larceny that cannot be prosecuted in the courts" yet is unfair to city employes "who are about to be fired to pay this sum to a private engineer when city engineers in the past have performed this kind of work."

Harold Campbell of the Civil Service Technical Guild said the unit cost of the project would be 50 percent less if civil service engineers did the work.

Answering his critics, the Mayor said he "had never heard anything based on more misapprehension and misstatement of facts."

He said the Idlewild job presents an engineering feat of the first magnitude, that it had been carefully examined and will cost less with a consultant on the job than without.

He stated that the army and navy were vitally interested in speeding it to completion and that the project had been given priority rating.

Hughes to Celebrate 80th Birthday Tomorrow

Washington, April 9 (UP)—Charles Evans Hughes, retired chief justice, went by automobile today to New York, where he will spend his 80th birthday tomorrow with his three children and nine grandchildren. He was accompanied by Mrs. Hughes.

Hughes retired from the court last July 1, finding the strain of judicial work too heavy for his years, but he now is said to be in good health. Mrs. Hughes, who is 77, has been ill much of the last year.

British Lose 2 Big Cruisers In Bengal Bay

Sunk by Jap Fliers—Naval Battle Looms—Ceylon Coast Bombed

London, April 9 (UP)—An Admiralty communique revealed today that the eight-inch-gun heavy cruisers Cornwall and Dorsetshire had been sunk by Japanese airplanes operating in the Bay of Bengal and which, in their latest attack, bombed the Trincomalee Naval Base on the Ceylon coast today.

It was believed here that the losses may be merely the prelude to the greatest naval battle of the war, exceeding both in ferocity and strategic potentialities the naval battle off Java.

Such a battle, if it took place, naval quarters said, might decide the fate of Ceylon if not of India.

Radio Rome reported last week that a strong British naval formation, including the 31,100-ton battleship Malaya, had left Gibraltar for the Indian Ocean.

Admit Merchant Ships Sunk

The All-India Radio said it was announced officially at New Delhi that Japanese naval and air forces had sunk "several" merchant ships in the Bay of Bengal.

Between 400 and 500 survivors of the merchant ships already have been landed at Indian ports, the radio said.

Sought Jap Fleet

Dispatches from India and Ceylon reported British naval as well as air force units ranging the Bay of Bengal in search of the Japanese fleet, including aircraft carriers, which had attacked ships and towns of Ceylon and the Indian coast.

The Admiralty gave no details of the sinking of Cornwall and Dorsetshire.

Continued on Page 10

WPB Cuts Supply Of Gas to Stations

Washington, April 9 (UP)—Direct rationing of gasoline to motorists may be averted in East and West Coast curtailment areas under a War Production Board order today for further reduction in filling station deliveries.

The order, effective April 16, will restrict gasoline deliveries to filling stations in 17 eastern States, the District of Columbia, and Washington and Oregon to 66 2-3 percent of the average received in December, January and February. These filling stations and other bulk consumers now are receiving 80 percent of their former average.

Oil Coordinator Harold L. Ickes said the order may make it unnecessary to institute rationing.

"If the reduction works satisfactorily," he told a press conference, "we may go to Price Administrator Leon Henderson and tell him that we see no occasion for card rationing."

The order will continue to leave it up to filling stations to distribute their quotas of gasoline among their customers as they see fit.

Other details on Page 9

Jamaica Results

1—Very Snooty, 6.70, 4.40, 3.20; Tindell, 68.20, 15.80; Brooming Home, 3.90. Off time, 2:06½.

2—[illegible], 6.20, 4.30, 3.80; Jamerica, 8.20, 5.30; [illegible] Trap, 4.60. Off time 2:33.

DAILY DOUBLE PAID — [illegible]

3—[illegible] Whistler, 1st; Photo for place.

Tropical Park Results

1—[illegible], 13.20, 5.80, 4.20; [illegible], 4.20, 4.60; [illegible], 3.80. Off time, 2:07.

2—[illegible], 6.20, 4.60, 3.30; Barney's [illegible], [illegible]; [illegible], 3.10. Off time, [illegible].

Wingate Didn't Get Sendoff in '17 But Insists Boys of '42 Should

Soldier, lawyer, judge and veteran of World War I, George Albert Wingate had this to say today of the proposal for a community send-off plan to Brooklyn boys inducted into America's fast-growing army:

"I didn't get a sendoff myself. We were hustled overseas in a hurry. But I think it would be a very fine thing, a very gracious gesture. I should think it would definitely heighten and improve the morale of the families of those going away, their relatives and their friends, and of the men, too."

A Brigadier General and Kings County Surrogate for nearly a quarter of a century ending last Dec. 31, Mr. Wingate joined the National Guard as a private in the old 23d Regiment when a boy of 18.

He has been an active figure in that organization, in the army itself in war time, in the American Legion and in the civilian activities of lawyer, judge and distinguished citizen.

"Our boys today," he said, "go away fairly quietly and for unknown destinations. For military reasons, to keep their number and the time and direction of their de-

Continued on Page 10

10-Day Tank Drive Crushed by Reds

32 Machines Wrecked in the Crimea—Entire Russian Line Under Plane Assault

Kuibyshev, Russia, April 9 (UP)—Fleets of newly built Nazi tanks and dive bombers are assaulting Russian positions all along a 1,200-mile front from Leningrad to the Crimea where reinforced Red armies are awaiting Germany's Spring offensive, dispatches from the front reported today.

In the Crimea, near besieged Sevastopol, Russian forces were said officially to have crushed the Germans' biggest tank assault since the battle of Moscow, in a battle that raged for ten days.

The Germans hurled a fleet of 100 tanks at the Russian positions in the assault that cost them 32 of the tanks, eight of which were seized by the Russians in workable condition.

Drove Breach in Red Lines

At one time during the battle the Germans drove a breach in the Russian lines, but Soviet tanks and infantry regained the position.

Increasing numbers of enemy tanks and planes—many of the latter Junkers-88 bombers said to have left German factories less than a month ago—struck "feeler" blows all along the front in an apparent effort to find spots for the first pushes of Adolf Hitler's Spring drive.

Official dispatches said, however, that every attack had been thrown back with heavy German losses inflicted by Russian tanks, anti-tank guns and anti-tank riflemen whose numbers have been increased during the last two months.

61 Enemy Planes Destroyed

Reinforced squadrons of Nazi dive bombers, attacking in groups of 20 or more planes, were said to be in widespread action against the Russian positions.

In two days, the Red air force was credited with destroying 61 enemy planes, including 19 bombers.

The official Communist party newspaper Pravda said the Red armies, reinforced by millions of specialist reserves as well as new tanks and planes, were ready for the Spring campaign everywhere along the front.

Hitler-Heiler Hails America But Too Late

American-born William Grohs, 30, couldn't remember in court today how he ran into trouble with Hiram Donnelly, Brooklyn shipyard worker, but Donnelly's testimony that Grohs was heiling Hitler and saying unprintable things about America in a waterfront bar and grill convinced Magistrate Joseph Glebocki in Bay Ridge Court.

Despite protestations by Grohs that "America is more or less of a heaven to me," Magistrate Glebocki declared Grohs guilty of disorderly conduct and ordered him held without bail for sentencing next Tuesday.

Donnelly, a World War veteran who lives at 1671 8th Ave., said that he ran into Grohs in a bar near the Bethlehem Steel Company Shipyard at the foot of 27th St., Brooklyn.

Made Unprintable Remarks

Grohs was heiling Hitler and shouting that "America will be ruled by Germany!" Donnelly said.

Continued on Page 10

Marshall Saddened By News From Bataan

London, April 9 (UP)—Gen. George Marshall was advised of the apparent fall of the American defenses of Bataan today as he began work, and well-informed quarters said that, while he did not comment, he appeared depressed.

It was added that he was watching all developments closely.

To Swap Diplomats

Radio Berlin, quoting a dispatch from Tokio, said today that 63 Allied diplomats in Hongkong would be exchanged for Japanese diplomats in Great Britain and the United States.

Of these, 49 are Americans, two Dutchmen, five Belgians, three Norwegians and four Canadians, the dispatch said.

Bowie Results

1—Joquita, 6.60, 3.70, 2.80; Colleen M, 8.90, 5.60; Spanish Sun, 3.60. Off time 2:32.

2—Gentle Savage, 1st; No Bodies, 2d; Southern Jane, 3d.

Boro Woman Is Cleared In Theft of $1,000 Watch

Anne Sador, 26, of 25 Marlborough Road, was exonerated today of complicity in the theft of a $1,000 wristwatch which she sought to sell last November to a Manhattan dealer for Sigmund Bostrup, 42, engineer of a Manhattan hotel.

Bostrup, who received five to ten years' imprisonment from General Sessions Judge Sullivan on his guilty plea, said he had stolen the watch from a guest's room but Miss Sador believed it to be his legitimate property.

Simplified State Form For Tax Goes to Assembly

Albany, April 9 (UP)—Adoption of a simplified State income tax return chart, similar to the new Federal form, approached realization today with Senate approval of the Desmond bill. The measure would eliminate complicated calculations for taxpayers by providing an average deduction for all classes of incomes up to $5,000. The bill now goes to the Assembly, where little opposition is anticipated.

M'Arthur Kin Heading For War on Luftwaffe

Montreal, April 9 (UP)—A 20-year-old second cousin of Gen. Douglas MacArthur, with the wings of the Royal Canadian Air Force pilot newly pinned on his chest, is heading for the war against the Nazi Luftwaffe over Europe.

He is leading aircraftsman Thomas T. Wells of Montreal, whose grandmother was a sister of General MacArthur's mother. Wells enlisted in the R. C. A. F. last July, and yesterday graduated as a pilot.

WHERE TO FIND IT

Bridge	Page 17	Music	Page 7
Clifford Evans	Page 7	Novel	Page 17
Comics	Page 14	OBITUARIES	Page 9
Community News	Page 16	RADIO	Page 14
Crossword	Page 15	Real Estate	Page 19
Dr. Brady	Page 16	Society	Page 6
EDITORIAL	Page 8	SPORTS	Pages 11-12-13
FINANCIAL	Page 18	Take My Word	Page 15
Grin and Bear It	Page 8	Theaters	Page 7
Harold Parrott	Page 11	These Women	Page 14
Heffernan	Page 8	Tucker	Page 8
Helen Worth	Page 5	Uncle Ray's Corner	Page 15
Horoscope	Page 14	Want Ads	Pages 16-17
Jury	Page 15	Weather Table	Page 9
Movies	Page 7	Women's	Pages 6-8

See $40,000 Gate at Flock Navy Fund Game

7TH ★★★★★★ Sports Extra

Wall Street Financial News

BROOKLYN EAGLE

LOCAL WEATHER FORECAST: Cooler tonight

101st YEAR • No. 127 • DAILY AND SUNDAY • BROOKLYN, N. Y., FRIDAY, MAY 8, 1942 • Entered at the Brooklyn Postoffice as 2d Class Mail Matter—(Copyright 1942 The Brooklyn Eagle, Inc.) • 3 CENTS

JAPS LOSE 17 SHIPS, EPIC BATTLE RAGES ON

HERO'S HOMECOMING—At the Bulkeley home, 45-42 45th St., Long Island City. Lt. John D. Bulkeley, hero of the fighting in the Philippines, today sees for the first time his young son, Baby John D. Jr. Left to right: Mrs. Hilda Bulkeley, wife of the lieutenant; Mrs. Elizabeth Bulkeley, his mother; young daughter, Joan, and the lieutenant and his son.

Plane Carrier, 2 Cruisers, 8 Other Enemy Craft Sunk

Gen. MacArthur's Headquarters, Australia, May 8 (UP)—United States and Allied warships tonight were believed to be pressing a fight to the finish against a strong Japanese fleet after sinking or damaging 17 enemy ships in the greatest naval battle of the war.

The battle of the coral sea, which may decide the whole strategy of the southwest Pacific war, is being fought out "mercilessly" by an Allied air and naval force of "considerable strength" striking at a Japanese attempt to advance "in force," according to Allied sources.

The belief was expressed that the Allied warships would make every effort to prevent breaking off the action which United Nations forces apparently have been seeking for weeks.

In two phases of the battle so far announced in Allied communiques, a total of 13 enemy warships and four transports or supply ships have been knocked out. Of these 11 ships, including nine warships, were listed as sunk, among them two cruisers, two destroyers and one aircraft carrier. Eight enemy planes have been shot down.

(A Tokio broadcast quoted the Japanese high command as saying that the Allied losses included an American battleship of the 32,600-ton California type, a Brit-

Continued on Page 2

GATE OF $40,000 SEEN AT FLOCK'S NAVY FUND GAME

Even Peanut Vendors And Cops Put Cash on Line at Ebbets Field

The fans flocked to Ebbets Field today for the first Navy Relief Fund game.

The twilight contest between our Devastating Dodgers and their natural baseball enemies, the Giants, had drawn several hundreds by noon and, as the hours passed, thousands more lined up before the ticket windows.

Cops were there, but paying admission like everyone else—the hot dog vendors, batboys, newspapermen and the players themselves.

Expect $40,000 Gate

Gate receipts of $40,000 at least were expected, all to go to the Navy Relief Society, which, since Jan. 1, has distributed $13,897 in loans and $2,575 in outright grants to 309 and 122 families of navy men in Brooklyn alone.

The Brooklyn Eagle will donate

Continued on Page 13

JAPANESE LOSSES

By United Press

The greatest sea battle of the war, which started Monday and still was in progress today northeast of Australia, had resulted so far in these reports and claims of naval losses:

Japanese Ships Sunk (11)

One aircraft carrier.
One heavy cruiser, probably of 10,000 tons.
One light cruiser, probably 6,000 tons.
Two destroyers.
Four gunboats.
One supply vessel.
One transport sunk during air attack on Louisiade Islands.

Japanese Ships Damaged (Six)

One aircraft carrier, probably a total loss.
One heavy cruiser.
One light cruiser.
One seaplane tender of 9,000 tons.
One supply ship.
One transport.

Non-Essential Drivers Face 3-Gal. Gas Limit

Washington, May 8 (U.P.)—Price Administrator Leon Henderson declared today that the basic gasoline ration for non-essential motorists in the East would be two or three gallons a week.

He confirmed that the western parts of New York and Pennsylvania had been withdrawn from the rationing area, along with West Virginia.

Henderson told a House Interstate Commerce Subcommittee that the East coast gasoline supply, which will be rationed after May 15, would permit distribution to non-essential users at a rate "between two and three gallons a week, probably nearer two, with no prospect of getting it above three."

He estimated, however, that non-essential motorists accounted for only about one-third of all car owners in the rationed areas. The term non-essential, he said, is applied to "automobiles not used for vocational or necessary purposes."

The other two-thirds will get varying additional amounts.

"We will furnish enough gasoline to get the worker to and from his job," Henderson told the committee.

Henderson said he expected to receive from Oil Co-ordinator Ickes' office within a few days the actual figures on the amount of gasoline which will be available for passenger cars.

Henderson told the House Committee he was "very proud" of the way people had responded to the sugar rationing program and said he felt that their response to a "meal-ticket" gasoline rationing plan would be as good.

He said that OPA and the War Production Board hoped it would not be necessary to ask local rationing boards to police the gasoline regulations. But if such a step becomes necessary, he added, it will be done.

Hero Bulkeley Home, Sees Baby First Time

Wife Greets Him at LaGuardia Airport—He'll Rest, Then Return to 'Finish Job'

By GERTRUDE McALLISTER

Lt. John D. Bulkeley, American naval hero who carried General MacArthur away from the battered shores of Bataan, came home to his family today—home to his wife, his parents, his daughter and a new son, sleeping peacefully in his basinette unaware of the importance of the occasion.

The alert eyes of the tired, khaki-clad father sparkled and after a momentary appraisal, he said:

"He's grand."

And then the lieutenant asked to be left alone—alone for a while to enjoy "peace and quiet for the rest of the day."

Lieutenant Bulkeley's arrival in the United States came as a surprise, his wife, Hilda, being informed late yesterday. But she was at LaGuardia Airport when his plane arrived at 10:22 a.m. after a flight from San Francisco.

Before leaving for his home at 45-42 41st St., Long Island City, the lieutenant, his arm about his wife, stepped before the newsreel cameras and said modestly:

"I am most happy to be back in the United States. We served the navy to the best of our ability but we did only what was expected of us; no more, no less. We were helped by a bit of luck. We intend to go ahead with more motorboats and finish the job we started."

Then he was off for his home. Neighbors were on the sidewalk as he stepped from the automo-

Continued on Page 13

WARM WELCOME—Lt. John D. Bulkeley is greeted at LaGuardia Field by his wife, Hilda.

TRADES PINT OF BLOOD FOR SUGAR RATION CARD

Tonawanda, N. Y., May 8 (U.P.)—A Tonawanda woman thought it was fair enough to exchange a pint of blood for a sugar rationing card.

She went to the wrong school for her card and stood in line. Without question she permitted a Red Cross blood bank attendant to take a pint of her blood, as he explained it was "for the soldiers and sailors in the United States armed forces."

When i' was over she asked for her sugar rationing card. They sent her to the right school.

Dominican Steamer Sunk

Trujillo, Dominican Republic, May 8 (U.P.)—It was announced officially today that a German submarine had sunk the Dominican steamer San Rafael, 1,973 tons, and that 30 crew members are missing.

Jamaica Results

1—Regal Boy, 3.90, 2.90, 2.40; Flying Son, 5.70, 3.80; Is I Is, 4.00. Offtime 2:06½.
2—Miranda Z., 105.70, 48.90, 21.60; xRosy Dollar, 15.00, 7.80; Bonnie Golos, 8.00. Offtime 2:37½.
x Field.

Daily Double Paid $294.20.

Pimlico Results

1—Tweendeck, 51.20, 20.50, 8.60; Piccadilly 5.30, 4.20; Magdala, 7.60. Offtime, 2:35½

Narragansett Park Results

1—Misty Lady, 3.80, 2.90, 3.00; Montbars, 5.20, 4.50; Seaman, 7.20. Offtime, 2:49.

U. S. Agrees to Purchase Brazil's Spare Rubber

Rio De Janeiro, May 8 (U.P.)—The United States has agreed to purchase all Brazilian rubber for the next five years not required for domestic uses, Finance Minister Arthur De Souza Costa said today.

All rubber manufactured products not needed for internal consumption also will be sold to the United States and a working agreement for the sale of automobile tires has been reached, he said.

Brooklyn Man Killed By Train in Valley Stream

Valley Stream, May 8—A man identified as George E. Love, 60, of 479 Ridgewood Ave., Brooklyn, was killed by a train today at the Long Island Railroad station.

Witnesses said they saw Love run along the platform before he was struck by a westbound express. He was identified through papers found in his clothes. The accident caused a 13-minute delay. J. A. Everett of 187-10 105th Ave., Hollis, was the motorman of the train.

Individual Tax Rise Is Proposed

Washington, May 8 (U.P.)—The House Ways and Means Committee's staff of experts today proposed an individual income tax increase that would yield less than half the $4,300,000,000 sought from this source by the Treasury.

The staff plan was presented to the committee by Colin E. Stam, who said it would raise $1,900,000,000.

Stam proposed, committee members said, retention of the present individual income tax exemptions of $1,500 for a married couple, $750 for a single person and $400 for each dependent.

Axis Loses 101 Planes In Assault on Malta

London, May 8 (U.P.)—The defenders of Malta, using fighter planes and anti-aircraft guns, destroyed 101 Axis warplanes during April, but despite this high toll the enemy dropped 7,000 tons of bombs, a military commentator announced today.

AND THEN FIRING SQUAD—WHAT SHOULD HE DO?

Pompton Lakes, N. J., May 8 (U.P.)—Councilman Harry Davenport received this invitation from the Pompton Lakes Post of the American Legion to make a memorial address:

"You are invited to be one of the speakers at our Memorial Day meeting. The program will include a talk by the Mayor, recitation of the Lincoln Gettysburg speech by a high school pupil, your talk and then the firing squad."

He hasn't decided whether to accept.

WHERE TO FIND IT

	Page		Page
Bridge	21	Lindley	12
Comics	18	Movies	11
Community	7	Novel	21
Crossword	20	Obituaries	13
Dr. Brady	6	Parrott	15
Editorial	12	Radio	18
Events Tonight	6	Real Estate	21
Fighting Men	6	Society	9
Financial	19	Sports	15-16-17
Going Places	10	Take My Word	6
Grin and Bear It	12	Theaters	11
Heffernan	12	These Women	6
Hitler Helpers	6	Tucker	12
Home Front	6	Uncle Ray	6
Horoscope	6	Want Ads	19-20-21
Jury	6	Weather	13
		Women	8

'Should Brooklyn Get a Divorce?' -- *See Sunday's Eagle*

Dodgers Call on Davis Against Lee

7TH ★★★★★★★ Sports Final

Wall Street Financial News

BROOKLYN EAGLE

LOCAL WEATHER FORECAST: Warm tonight

101st YEAR • No. 156 • DAILY AND SUNDAY • BROOKLYN, N. Y., SATURDAY, JUNE 6, 1942 • Entered at the Brooklyn Postoffice as 2d Class Mail Matter—(Copyright 1942 The Brooklyn Eagle, Inc.) • 3 CENTS

AT LEAST 8 JAP SHIPS HIT IN SEA-AIR BATTLE

Dodgers Send Davis Against Lee of Cubs

DODGERS	CUBS
Reese,ss	Hack,3b
Vaughan,3b	Merullo,ss
Reiser,rf	Cavarretta,cf
Medwick,lf	Nicholson,rf
Walker,rf	Russel,1b
Camilli,1b	Novikoff,lf
Owen,c	Stringer,2b
Herman,2b	McCullough,c
Davis,p	Lee,p

Umpires—Conlan, Reardon and Goetz.

Chicago, June 6—The Dodgers called on Veteran Curt Davis to give them the edge over the Cubs here today after the teams had split a twin bill yesterday. Davis, who has a record of seven victories and one defeat, was opposed by Big Bill Lee.

U. S. Persists in Effort To Aid War Prisoners

Washington, June 6 (U.P.)—The Red Cross and the State Department are continuing efforts to send a shipload of food and medical supplies to American prisoners of war in Japan, Senator Dennis Chavez (D., N. M.) said today.

Chavez said major obstacles to the plan were failure so far to get permission from Japan to land at Manila and difficulty in obtaining a neutral ship.

Suffolk Downs Results

1—Valdina Flare, 8.60, 4.60, 3.20; Liberty Patsy, 6.40, 4.00; Shemite, 3.40. Off time, 2:33½.

2—Hyead, first; Very Graceful, second; Scorcity, third.

Detroit Results

1—xTide's Dream, 33.20, 12.60, 8.20; Royal Shawl, 7.80, 4.80; Last Bubble, 4.40 Off time, 2:25.

xField.

2—Arial Toy, 1st; Lochlea, second; Sugarage, third.

THIRD RACE—$1,200; claiming; three-year-olds and up; six furlongs.

P.P.		Wt.	P.P.		Wt.
1	Sumatra III	110	7	Countmein	102
2	xSt Dismas	110	8	Goodanwarm	108
3	Remote Control	115	9	xMiss Mahoot	93
4	xMiss Westie	101	10	xLady Sponsor	95
5	Red Horizon	103	11	Handy Justice	113
6	Drawby	105	12	Wise Fire	108

FIRST	SECOND	THIRD

Thistle Down Results

1—Lucky Pompi, 12.20, 5.20, 3.40; Try Flight, 3.20, 2.40; Wise Margaret, 4.20. Off time, 2:32½.

2—Little King Pin, first; Dinner Horn, second; Ted Greenock, third.

Charles Town Results

1—Navigation, 7.60, 3.60, 3.00; Zyloxxie, 5.40, 3.80; Don Dash, 4.40. Off time, 2:36½.

Delaware Park Results

FIRST RACE—$1,100; maidens; two-year-olds; five furlongs.

P.P.		Wt.	P.P.		Wt.
1	Wise Advice	118	9	xDr. R. Young	113
2	Hadawin	118	10	Wessex	118
3	Wadedale	118	11	Bayford	118
4	xGothic	113	12	xMad Venture	110
5	Identic	118	13	Lordwin	118
6	xBuzz Buzz	113	14	Bright Quest	118
7	Omada	115	15	Thesus	118
8	Calvert	118	16	Oyster C'ker	115

FIRST	SECOND	THIRD
2	1	10

Lincoln Fields Results

FIRST RACE—Purse, $1,000; maiden two-year-olds; five furlongs.

P.P.		Wgt.	P.P.		Wgt.
1.	Hi Murt	114	10.	Cideam	117
2.	Blue Shot	117	11.	Town Victory	117
3.	Wee Ann	114	12.	Air Sickle	117
4.	xContemplat'n	112	13.	Saboteur	117
5	River Captain	117	14.	Chance Grey	117
6.	Prognostic	114	15.	Ever Flying	117
7.	Brilliant Jr.	117	16.	Dr. Rush	117
8.	Chain Break	117	17.	Lucky Trip	117
9.	Wise Paisano	117	18.	Indian Watch	117

FIRST	SECOND	THIRD
1	5	2

BASEBALL RESULTS

NATIONAL LEAGUE

Dodgers	0							—
Cubs								—

Batteries—Davis and Owen; Lee and McCullough.

Giants								—
Cards								—

Braves	0	0						—
Reds	0							—

Batteries—Tobin and Lombardi; Walters and Lamanno.

AMERICAN LEAGUE

Indians	0	0						—
Yankees	3	0						—

Batteries—Dean adn Hegan; Ruffing and Rosar.

W. Sox	0	0	2	0				—
Red Sox	1	0	0					—

Batteries—Grove and Tresh; Hughson and Conroy.

Tigers	1	0	3	0	1	1	1	—
Senators	0	0	0	1	0	0		—

First Game—Batteries: Bridges and Tebbetts; Zuber and Early.

INTERNATIONAL LEAGUE

Buffalo	5	0	0	0				—
Newark	0	0	0	0				—

First Game—Batteries: Gentry, Garbark; Washburn, Robinson.

Montreal	1							—
Baltimore	2							—

Batteries—Macon and Dopper; Roche and Becker.

Toronto at Syracuse, night game.

BELMONT RESULTS

1—Rurales 18.40-6.80-4.30, Tweedy 9.30-5.70, Famous Victory 10.50. (1:53)

2—Miss Q. 16.30-7.60-4.90, Lotopoise 4.60-3.60, Fresh Start 4.50. (2:28)

DAILY DOUBLE PAID $146.00

3—Mad Policy, first; Chuckatuck, second; Cupid, third.

FOURTH RACE—$5,000 added; the National Stallion Stakes; two-year-olds; five furlongs, Widener Course.

1—aCorona Corona
2—Bull Penn
3—Portido
4—bSun Cap
5—Hickory Head
6—Ocean Wave
7—Tip Toe
8—Dove Shoot
9—bSupermont
10—Rosewell
11—Four Freedoms
12—Quillon
13—aSlide Rule

aW. E. Boeing entry; bFoxcatcher Farms entry.

FIRST	SECOND	THIRD
4	1	

Charts, Entries and Selections on Page 10

Tokio Claims Four Subs Sunk in Japan Waters

Tokio, June 6 (U.P.)—(Japanese broadcast recorded by United Press in New York)—Japanese Imperial Headquarters said today that in the first days of June four enemy submarines had been sunk in Japanese waters, including Tokio Bay.

DIMOUT TIME

Saturday, June 6

Sun rises, 5:29; sun sets, 8:28.

Sunday, June 7

Sun rises, 5:28; sun sets, 8:29.

Believe Hitler Warned Mannerheim of Disaster

Stockholm, June 6 (U.P.)—Finnish observers believed today that Adolf Hitler flew to Finland to remind Field Marshal Karl Gustav Mannerheim that Germany and Finland faced catastrophe together if the Axis were defeated, rather than to congratulate him on his 75th birthday.

Well-informed quarters said Hitler was dismayed by Mannerheim's decision to have no part in Germany's "Summer offensive" and to let the Nazis try to cut the Leningrad railway and storm Leningrad by themselves.

RAF BATTERS RUHR AGAIN IN 24-HOUR DRIVE

Waves of Planes Bomb Naples—Raiders 22 Miles From Rome

London, June 6 (U.P.)—Britain's great four-engined bomber planes, to a total of 300 or more, attacked the German Ruhr war industry center during the night for the third time in five days of their new devastation raids, the air ministry announced today.

Throughout the night, as they struck again at the heart of Germany's war production, light bombers and night fighters hurled bombs and poured machine gun bullets into targets over a wide area of German occupied territory.

Planes based on the Mediter-

Continued on Page 2

LATE NEWS BULLETINS

BENNETT FIELD DISPUTE CERTIFIED TO W L B

Washington, June 6 (U.P.)—Secretary of Labor Frances Perkins today certified to the War Labor Board a jurisdictional dispute involving 250 workers at Floyd Bennett Field, New York, Earlier Details on Page 2

46 SURVIVORS FROM 3 U. S. SHIPS LAND AT GULF PORT

A Gulf Coast Port, June 6 (U.P.)—Survivors from three United Nations merchant ships sunk by Axis submarines have been landed at gulf ports, the navy announced today.

The entire crews, totaling 46 men, were saved from two of the vessels, a medium-sized Norwegian freighter and a small unarmed British cargo ship. Ten of a crew of 35 on a medium-sized American merchantman lost their lives when a single torpedo sent the ship to the bottom in two minutes.

CHUHSIEN DEFENDERS BEAT OFF JAP ATTACKS

Chungking, June 6 (U.P.)—Chinese defenders of Chuhsien, railroad center and important Allied air base in Chekiang Province, have beaten off more thrusts by encircling Japanese forces and still hold the besieged city, it was announced today.

Baby Born in Blackout As Nurse Holds Torch

100,000 Throng Coney Walk in Citywide Test —Mayor Pronounces It Complete Success

The apparent success of New York's first citywide practice blackout, embracing an area of 321 square miles, was attributed today to the co-ordinated action of the Civilian Defense personnel and the close co-operation of its 7,500,000 residents.

Called on only eight hours notice by Mayor LaGuardia, the city's 19,000 policemen, 6,500 firemen and 170,000 air raid wardens mobilized their forces with dispatch and at 9:30 last night a blanket of darkness covered the five boroughs as each community quickly snuffed out its lights for the 20-minute test.

As the lights at Beth-El Hospital, Rockaway Parkway and Avenue A, went out, a six-pound, six-ounce baby girl was born as a nurse held a flashlight. Dr. B. Greenberg completed the delivery 5 minutes after the blackout started. The mother is Mrs. Lillian Stiss, 23, of 238 Legion St.

No Disorder Noted

Brooklyn and Queens were the first to douse their lights and then in quick succession the street light patterns of the other boroughs vanished. Bridges, tunnels and highways went dark and the throbbing life of the city continued behind closely screened windows.

From vantage points on Brooklyn Heights and the Williamsburgh Savings Bank Building, a few lights seemed to pierce the darkness in midtown Manhattan, but soon they were quickly extinguished under the careful scrutiny of the air raid wardens.

There was no disorder. Not a wheel turned except those of police

Continued on Page 7

Probe of Amen Flops as Seven Refuse to Testify

Proceedings brought to determine whether Assistant Attorney General Amen should be examined on charges of willful neglect and omission of duty floundered today after a lengthy closed session on Bay Ridge Magistrate's Court, during which seven principal witnesses refused to testify.

Later, Magistrate Charles G. Keutgen declined to discuss the hearing, which arose from an information suggesting willful neglect and omission of duty on Mr. Amen's part in not obtaining indictments against policemen recently named in grand jury presentments charging police protection of a $1,000,000 gambling ring.

The information was filed by former Police Inspector John Reddan, named in the presentment as having retired while under investigation in the gambling inquiry.

Wants Name Cleared

He had demanded that Mr. Amen permit him to appear again before the grand jury "to clear my name."

The hearing yesterday featured long legal arguments by Robert H. Elder, Reddan's attorney, and William J. Butler, legal expert of the Amen staff.

Mr. Butler, making it plain that he did not concede the magistrate's jurisdiction to hear such a proceeding, made a "special" motion to quash the subpenas that were issued by Magistrate Charles Solomon. Magistrate Keutgen did not announce any decision and declared the proceeding would be "in camera." Forthwith the newspa[illegible]

Continued on Page 7

WHERE TO FIND IT

	Page		Page
Bridge	13	Novel	13
Churches	8	Obituaries	7
Clifford Evans	14	Radio	4
[illegible]	4	Sermon Topics	8
Crossword	12	Society	5
Dr. Brady	5	Sports	9-10
Editorial	6	Take My Word	4
Financial News	3	Theaters	14
Grin and Bear It	6	These Women	5
Heffernan	6	Tucker	6
Horoscope	5	Uncle Ray	5
Jury	5	Want Ads	11-12-13
Movies	14		

CITY'S SIRENS TESTED

A second test of air raid sirens installed by police was made in Brooklyn today, and on a signal from the Telegraph Bureau at Police Headquarters, Manhattan, the sirens sounded a warbling note for two minutes. There followed a silent period and three minutes later a steady note was sounded for two minutes.

The signals started at noon and ended at 12:05 p.m.

Observers reported that the sirens could be heard for a considerable distance, though not quite so loudly as last Saturday.

Nazis Near End Of 'Suicide Trail,' Biddle Declares

Chattanooga, Tenn., June 6 (U.P.)—Germany entered the "home stretch of a suicide trail" April 27 when the Reichstag voted Adolf Hitler the power to punish every German without regard to their "duly acquired rights," Attorney General Francis Biddle said today.

He hold the Tennessee Bar Association the German people, by surrendering those rights, had plunged themselves into the "last ugly phase of their cycle of self-enslavement—the phase of complete, undisguised despotism."

"From now on Adolf Hitler's will —and what is more tragic for the German people, his intuitions—will supersede all law," Biddle added.

He said the "duly acquired rights" were not comparable to the rights of a citizen of a democracy, but that they did provide trial for the accused, special privileges as a reward for special merit, and superior rank to those entitled to it by German standards, and protected officials against removal without cause.

In denying these rights to his people, Biddle said, Hitler crossed the line which "the Kaiser would not have dared to cross in the name of outright monarchy."

Biddle said he did not mean to predict revolt in Germany, but he asserted that "there is such a thing as the sabotaging of a nation's soul."

"The comment of the Russians, immediately after that session of the Reichstag last April, sums it up rather neatly," he said. "'Hitler's Spring offensive has begun.' Moscow announced; 'it is against the German people.'"

U. S. Relentlessly Pursues Enemy

Major Setback Near Midway Hinted —Damage to Our Forces Not Revealed

Pearl Harbor, Hawaii, June 6 (UP)—At least eight and probably more warships and transports of a powerful Japanese invasion fleet have been damaged in the Pacific where the enemy is withdrawing under relentless attack of American naval and air forces.

A spokesman for Admiral Chester W. Nimitz' Pacific Fleet headquarters here revealed the total of at least eight enemy ships damaged — and perhaps any number up to 16 or 20 — as the battered Japanese fleet fled from its humiliating and possibly disastrous defeat near Midway Island.

Admiral Nimitz, in an earlier communique, had said:

"As more reports come in it appears that the enemy's damage was very heavy indeed, involving several ships in each of the carrier, battleship, cruiser and transport classes."

At Least 2 of Each Class

To clear up the use of the word "several," whether it meant several in each individual class or several among the four categories, the spokesman said:

"The communique may be interpreted to mean that more than one ship was damaged in each class mentioned."

Thus, with the U. S. naval-air forces "continuing the battle," at least two Japanese battleships, two cruisers, two aircraft carriers and two transports have been damaged.

The disclosure that the major enemy fleet included transports made it evident that United States Navy, Air Force, Army and Marine defense forces had repulsed a definite Japanese invasion attempt—on Midway or even a more vital objective.

Carrier Torpedoed 3 Times

One enemy aircraft carrier, first damaged by aerial bombs, was later struck by three submarine torpedoes, the fighting commander in chief of the Pacific Fleet announced in one of the most dramatic communiques of the war.

Reciting the damage to the enemy fleet, Admiral Nimitz said:

"This damage is far out of proportion to that which we received.

"While it is too early to claim a major Japanese disaster it may be conservatively stated that United States control remains firm in the Midway area.

"The enemy appears to be with-

Continued on Page 7

8th Jap Sub Destroyed After Sinking 2d Ship

Melbourne, June 6 (U.P.)—A Japanese submarine which sank a second merchantman off the southeast coast, was sent to the bottom by RAF bombers, bringing the total of enemy undersea craft destroyed in six days to eight, it was announced today.

The Japanese submersible, lurking off the coast of New South Wales State in the new offensive against the vital Pacific supply line from the United States, torpedoed an Australian merchantman.

The stricken ship broke in halves and sank within 30 seconds, but as it sank, with probably 38 of its 43 men trapped inside, a Royal Australian air force plane roared over and its avenging bombs sunk the submarine.

Racing to the rescue, the plane swept to within 20 feet of the

Continued on Page 2

U. S. Annexes All Ships Under Dutch Control

London, June 6 (U.P.)—All ships controlled by the refugee Netherlands Government were requisitioned today for the use of the United States Government.

Peter A. Kerstens, minister of commerce and industry for the Netherlands Government in exile, announced that the ships will be held under charter to the British War Transport Ministry until six months after the war.

The charter was negotiated through the transport ministry in behalf of the United States, the agreement being signed by Averell Harriman, U. S. lend-lease representative in London; Lord Leathers of the British transport ministry and Kerstens.

Announcement of the decree, made through Aneta, Netherlands news agency, said the ships would be placed at the "disposition of the American authorities."

Netherlands officials emphasized that the action did not mean that the Government had taken ownership of the fleet but merely would control its use until after the war when the ships would be returned to their owners.

Before the fall of Java, the Netherlands merchant fleet totaled about 2,750,000 tons and it was believed that most of the fleet still is afloat.

The ships will be operated under the Dutch flag and with their Dutch crews, the announcement said.

WHIRLY IN TOP RACING SHAPE

Picked to Win Brooklyn Handicap—$100,000 War Aid Aqueduct Outlook

By JOE LEE

The Queens County Jockey Club will ring down the curtain on one of the most successful meetings ever held at Aqueduct tomorrow and all of the receipts will go to Army-Navy Relief and the USO. The $30,000 added Brooklyn Handicap and the $5.000 added Great American are the fixtures-features of a program which should net $100.000 for war aid.

The eyes of the turf world are centered on the Brooklyn Handicap, for Whirlaway, the bushy-tailed glamour boy of the turf, will be strutting his stuff in an effort to pass the $400,000 mark and at the same time move a step closer to Seabiscuit's all-time record for money winning.

Served Notice Monday

Whirlaway served notice on his rivals last Monday in winning the Celt Purse by a nose over Attention, setting a new standard of 1:49 2-5 for the mile and one-eighth. Ben Jones, trainer for the Calumet Farms, is in excellent spirits these days, for his charge will go into the Brooklyn in the best shape of his career.

With Market Wise out of the Brooklyn because of a cough which he developed just before the Carter Handicap, Attention looms the most dangerous rival for Whirlaway. Max Hirsch, trainer for Mrs. Parker Corning, reported that Attention came out of Monday's race in excellent condition and will be sent right back for another crack at Whirlaway tomorrow. Incidentally, Attention beat Whirly in the Arlington Classic last year.

The Comet will shoulder 128 pounds, Attention getting a six-pound concession, one more pound than he carried in the Celt last Monday. I look for Whirlaway to win. Others expected to start in the Brooklyn are Our Boots, Waller, Olympus, Swing and Sway, Salford II, Third Degree, Corydon and Tola Rose.

BRIDLE BITS—Yesterday's mutuel handle, which totaled $1.038,708 for the eight races, was the largest weekday figure of the meeting . . . Miss Discovery was claimed by J. Freedman, Present Arms went to C. C. Ortlieb and Kentown was haltered by F. J. Hastings . . . Ira Hanford's suspension ends today, not July 26 as was reported yesterday . . . The daily double pool of Samhar and Refulgent paid off at $38.20 with 1,117 persons holding winning tickets . . . The betting in the double pool totaled $47,474 . . . Jockey Nick Coule is awaiting a call from the U. S. Army . . . The apprentice allowance rule has been modified . . . The stewards of the Jockey Club have decided that apprentice jockeys in the future will be allowed seven pounds until they have ridden 20 winners and five pounds thereafter . . . This will go into effect after the ruling has been published in the Racnnk Calendar three times.

Hickey Shuts Out Edison for Pfizer

Effective pitching by Hickey, who allowed four scattered hits, enabled Pfizer to whitewish Edison in a twilight game in the Brooklyn Industrial League at the Parade Grounds last evening, 6—0. Hickey walked but one batter. Kucklinca got half of Edison's hits. The Pfizer hitsmiths pounded the service of Sanders for 11 safeties.

Box score:

Pfizer	ab	r	h	o	a	Edison	ab	r	h	o	a
Chewins,lf	4	1	2	0	0	Keegan,2b	3	0	0	5	3
Correll,cf	3	0	2	1	0	Moore,cf	3	0	0	1	0
G'sman,2b	2	0	0	2	5	C'ntino,ss	2	0	0	0	0
Tim'ney,1b	4	0	0	14	1	C'brasi,1r	3	0	0	8	0
Mayer,ss	4	1	1	2	4	Graham,lf	3	0	1	2	0
Roche,rf	3	1	1	1	0	Berry,rf	2	0	0	0	0
Sturm,3b	3	2	1	0	3	K'linca,3b	3	0	2	2	4
McCune,c	3	1	2	0	0	Britt,c	3	0	0	3	1
Hickey,p	3	0	1	1	1	Sanders,p	2	0	1	0	2
aRivoire	1	0	1	0	0	bPender,p	0	0	0	0	0
						cPecarrico	0	0	0	0	0
Totals	30	6	11	21	14	Totals	24	0	4	21	10

aRan for Cassentino in 7th inning.
bPitched for Sanders in 7th inning.
cBatted for Correll in 6th inning.

Pfizer ——————0 0 1 2 0 3 0—6
Brooklyn Edison——————0 0 0 0 0 0 0—0

Errors—By Cassentino, Calibrasi, Graham, Timoney. Two-base hit—Graham. Home run—Sturn. Sacrifice hit—Roche. Double plays—Edison, Sanders, Britt, Calibrisi; Calibrini (unassisted); Kugan, Calibrasi. Bases on balls—Off Hickey, 1; Sanders, 1; Pender, 0. Struck out—By Hickey, 0; Sanders, 1; Pender, 0. Hit by pitcher—By Sanders (Gassman). Hits—Off Hickey, 4; Sanders, 11; Pender, 0. Umpires—Hildebrand and Madden.

Ruth Wins From Lauri

Ruth McGinnis, female pocket billiard champion of the world, defeated Onofrio Lauri, ex-State titlist, 100-21, at the Brooklyn Billiard Academy last night. Tonight Miss McGinnis will oppose Arthur Rubin, one of the outstanding stars of the city.

Sports Today

BASEBALL

Dodgeds vs. Cincinnati Reds at Ebbets Field, Bedford Ave. and Sullivan Place, 3 p.m.
Giants vs. Pittsburgh Pirates at Polo Grounds, 8th Ave. and 157th St., 3 p.m.
Newark Bears vs. Syracuse Chiefs at Ruppert Stadium, 262 Wilson Ave., Newark, 7 p.m.

GOLF

Women's Long Island championship at North Hempstead C. C., Port Washington, 9:30 a.m.
Women's Westchester-Fairfield championship at Scarsdale G. C., Hartsdale, N. Y., 9:30 a.m.
Long Island junior championship at Cherry Valley Club, Garden City, 9 a.m.
New Jersey junior championship at Plainfield C. C., 9 a.m.

HORSE RACING

Queens County Jockey Club meeting at Aqueduct, L. I., 1:45 p.m.

TENNIS

National pro championships at West Side T. C., Forest Hills, L. I., 1:30 p.m.

WRESTLING

MacArthur Stadium 15th Ave. and 86th St., Brooklyn, 8:30 p.m.

112 ATHLETES GIVEN AWARDS AT LAFAYETTE

Pincus Reveals School Hopes to Expand Its Program Next Term

Max Pincus, chairman of the Health Education Department of Lafayette High School, presented 142 awards to 112 members of the school's six athletic teams and in his address revealed that he has hopes of expanding the inter-scholastic athletic campaign when the institution goes into its fourth year next term.

Pincus lauded Coach Seymour Yudell and the soccer team for bringing Lafayette its first city title in the school's short history. It was Lafayette that shared the city P. S. A. L. soccer title with James Monroe after both had played to a scoreless tie in the finals. Yudell presented each player a gold soccer ball, a gold medal and a major L.

Hy Tummenelli was the recipient of the George Wingate medal, given for outstanding improvement in health education, on his high ratings in the rigid P. S. A. L. tests.

Awards:

Football

Major L—Co-captain Seymour Jetter and Irwin Stein, Larry Aaronoff, Sal Badalomenti, Larry Braverman, Bill Christgau, Joe Curasi, Frank Faviario, Harold Feldman, Norman Goldstein, Sam Klein, Mark Lomolino, Charles Matarese, Pete Pappas, William Melnick, Tony Palato, Mel Solomon, Murray Swelka and Ed Kassman, manager.
Minor L—Bernard Fleischman and George Digman.

Soccer

Gold Soccer Balls—Sid Arms, Murray Schneider, Manny Schweisberg, John Rebba, Tom Raleigh, John Scott, Julius Adelsberg, John Quontanoui, Harvey Lasky, Sid Lubin, Frank Milek, Jerry Shapiro, John Bonanno, Vic Fugollo and Frank D'Angelo.
Gold Soccer Medals—Sid Arms, Murray Schneider, Manny Schweisberg, John Rebba, Tom Raleigh, John Scott, Julius Adelsberg, John Quontanoui, Harvey Lasky, Sid Lubin, Frank Milek, Jerry Shapiro, John Bonanno, Vic Fugollo and Frank D'Angelo.
Major L—Murray Schneider, Maurice Schweisberg, John Rebba, Tom Raleigh, John Scott, Julius Adelsberg, John Quontanoui, Harvey Lasky, Sid Lubin, Frank Milek, Sid Arms, Saul Shanes, Lenny Quartaro, Jerry Shapiro, Vic Fugallo, William Rothberg, Curtis Peterson, John Bonanno, Frank D'Angelo, Sid Bush, Elmer Meninchetti.
Minor L—Anthony Curreri, Mario Gullo and John Macrie.

Handball

Major L—Burt Grenberg and Leonard Michaelman.
Minor L—Harold Kitt, Seymour Shekter, Herbert Feder, Zwlich Kaplan, Arnold Buckberg, Vincent Galbo and Manager Irwin Lasky.

Basketball

Major L—Co-captain Murray Robinson and Al D'Amato, Norman Mager, Arthur Darrow, Murray Weiss, Stanley Edelman and Sol Kritzer.
Minor L—Norman Goldstein, Harry Murphy, Michael Kwitnicki and Sam Klein.
Insignia L—Harry Rubin, Tony San Fillipo, Herbert Sterenfeld, Walter Palsey, Seymour Olshin and Ed Davis.

Fencing

Major L—Marvin Gottlieb, Seymour Wollman, Bernard McCloskey, Martin Sadock, Sol Feder, Seymour Meyersen and Al Polesek.

Baseball

Major L—Howard Hillman, John Malafronte, Stanley Rusinski,, Frank Panarello, Angelo Pellegrino, Jack Kanner, Nino Ruggiero, Bob Cianchetti, John Gambino, Joe Martello, Harold Paulucci, Seymour Mont, John Raffa and Ernest Steck.
Minor L—Mike Remer, Joohn Cataldo, Arnold Harris, Peter Plaia, Irwin Walowitz, Jack Sheer, Sheldon Baum and Jack Cohen.
Insignia L—Jack Durante, Joe Klecker, John DiGregorro, Gene Blasanstein, Seymour Doveck, Albert Halikas, Anthony Guarino, John McHugh, Seymour Polatsek, Jack Corso, Ralph DePrima and Albert Halikas.

Coach Joseph Laub of Lafayette is introducing something new to high school football. On Aug. 29 he will take his squad of 30 gridders up to camp in Parksville, N. Y., and on Sept. 1 he will begin conditioning his lads for the opening of their grid campaign against Brooklyn Tech at Brooklyn College Field, Sept. 26.

Dodger Diary

June 26, 1941—Dodgers won home night game, 11—2, Wyatt giving Boston five hits and fanning eight. Dixie Walker hit triple and three singles. Boston scored in the eighth for first run off Dodger pitching in 43 innings.

1931—Robins sewed up game, with eight-run outburst in first inning, off Burleigh Grimes and Jim Lindsey of Cardinals. Johnny Frederick collected a homer, two doubles and a single in five times at bat as Dodgers won, 16—5.

1916—Brooklyn scored eight runs in fifth inning against Giants in opener of twin bill in Flatbush, but Giants came back with four in seventh, and won, 11—8. In the second game, Rube Marquard gave the Dodgers a 2—1 win in 12 innings, allowed the Giants a run in the first frame, then pitched 11 scoreless rounds.

1915—Zach Wheat singled in eighth to rob Grover Cleveland Alexander of no-hitter in 4—0 win for Phils. It was second of four one-hitters for Alex during the season, which set modern record.

BILL GOTTLIEB.

Joe Lee's Aqueduct Form

FOR SATURDAY

FIRST RACE—$1.500: the Air Corps Hurdles: three-year-olds and up; mile and one-half over hurdles.

P.P.	Horse	Jockey	Wt.
4	**Blanket**	**Maier**	157
6	**Top Milk**	**McMillan**	130
3	**War Magic**	**Neilands**	134
1	Gunbearer	Alimony	130
2	Wyoming 2d	No boy	134
5	Rice Cake	Walker	137

SECOND RACE—$1.500: the Marine Corps; maiden two-year-olds; five furlongs.

P.P.	Horse	Jockey	Wt.
6	**Bollinger**	**Basile**	116
3	**Gouache**	**May**	116
11	**Play Ground**	**No boy**	116
1	Ariel Play	Robertson	116
2	Bold Glance	No boy	113
4	Le Havre	Stout	116
5	Gallant Witch	No boy	113
7	Old Westbury	Meade	116
8	Gloriana	Schmidl	113
9	Pentland Firth	Meade	116
10	xPartido	Garza	111

THIRD RACE—$1.500: claiming: the U. S. Coast Guard; three-year-olds and up; six furlongs.

P.P.	Horse	Jockey	Wt.
2	**Halcyon Boy**	**Longden**	115
1	**Grail Bird**	**James**	119
3	**xHubbub**	**Wahler**	103
4	Cassis	Mehrtens	103
5	Porter's Girl	McCreary	103
6	Hard Jester	Robertson	119

FOURTH RACE — $.000 added; the Great American; two-year-olds; six furlongs.

P.P.	Horse	Jockey	Wt.
4	**Supermont**	**Gilbert**	119
1	**Best Irish**	**Longden**	115
5	**aFour Freedoms**	**Wright**	115
2	aFamous Victory	James	110
3	Breezing Home	Nodarse	110
6	Swimmin Hole	Peters	115

aMare's Nest Stud Farm entry.

FIFTH RACE—$5,000 added: the Army and Navy Handicap; three-year-olds and up; six furlongs.

P.P.	Horse	Jockey	Wt.
1	**Doublrab**	**Thompson**	125
5	**Sheriff Culkin**	**No boy**	119
4	**Overdrawn**	**Meade**	117
2	Augery	Stout	113
3	Parasang	James	112
6	Imperatrice	May	115
7	Col. Teddy	McCreary	112
8	Bayview	Longden	113

SIXTH RACE — $30.000 added: the Brooklyn Handicap; three-year-olds and up; mile and one-quarter.

P.P.	Horse	Jockey	Wt.
4	**Whirlaway**	**No boy**	128
6	**bAttention**	**Meade**	122
9	**aSwing and Sway**	**Longden**	110
1	aThe Rhymer	Arcaro	112
2	Waller	Thompson	111
3	bTola Rose	Mehrtens	106
5	Olympus	James	110
7	Paper Boy	Wahler	105
8	aCorydon	No boy	108

aGreentree Stable entry. bA. J. Sackett and Mrs. P. Corning entry.

SEVENTH RACE—$2.000: allowances; Merchant Marine; three-year-olds and up. Mile and one-sixteenth.

P.P.	Horse	Jockey	Wt.
10	**Dandy Fox**	**No boy**	113
3	**Bar Fly**	**Thompson**	118
8	**Lord Kitchener**	**James**	113
1	Blue Gino	No boy	101
2	Yankee Chance	Woolg	115
4	xDark Discovery	Garza	105
5	xBelplay	No boy	109
6	Meissen	Schmidl	114
7	Chaldon Heath	Woolf	113
9	xCheesestraw	Wahler	110
11	Obash	Gilbert	117
12	Barrancosa	Basile	109

EIGHTH RACE—$1.500: claiming: U. S. O.; three-year-olds and up. Mile and one-eighth.

P.P.	Horse	Jockey	Wt.
14	**xCharlene**	**No boy**	111
9	**Ring Star**	**Meade**	120
4	**Sir Lancelot**	**Laidley**	121
1	Prince A. O.	Greco	113
2	Miquelon	Longden	121
3	a-Castigada	Zufelt	113
5	xHaut Mond	Loveridge	112
7	xEnoch Borland	No boy	116
6	Smart	No boy	105
8	xNightland	Wahler	109
10	Day Off	Thompson	114
11	xSinging Torch	Loveridge	115
12	Hoptown Lass	Wright	109
13	Bootless	Wright	114
15	Sergeant Bob	Rollins	113
16	a-Happy Home	No boy	108

a-C. A. O'Neil Jr. entry.
x-Apprentice allowance claimed.
Track fast.
BEST—WHIRLAWAY.

Mermaids in Title Meet For Army Fund July 5

Eight events, two of them closed to daughters and sons of members, form the complete program for the women's A. A. J. championship swimming and diving meet which will be held for the benefit of Army Emergency Relief at the Sleepy Hollow Country Club, Scarborough-on-Hudson, N. Y., on Sunday afternoon, July 5.

Gloria Callen has already entered to defend her Metropolitan 110-yard backstroke title, while Marilyn Sahner will compete in the 100-yard invitation scratch race. Another crown-holder, Miss Margaret Russell, South Atlantic champion, will appear in the 100-yard invitation breaststroke handicap.

Schroeder Leads Field Into College Net Semis

New Orleans, June 26 (U.P.)—Two singles and a doubles match will be played today to complete makeup of the semi-final round in the 58th national intercollegiate tennis tournament.

Top-seeded Ted Schroeder of Stanford, the nation's ranking player, eliminated Jack Rodgers of Rice, 6—2, 6—3, to win his semi-final berth along with Emery Neale, unseeded player from Stanford, who routed seventh seeded Earl Bartlett of Tulane, 6—2, 6—4, yesterday.

No other matches were played.

Greenberg, Mulcahy Out of July 7 Game

Washington, June 26 (U.P.)—Sergt. Hank Greenberg will be missing from the service team lineup for the July 7 game with the major league All-Stars at Cleveland because the former Detroit slugger will be too busy trying to win his "wings".

Greenberg is attending the Army Air Corps candidate training school at Miami Beach, Fla., and can't take time out for baseball, the War Department said today.

Pitcher Hugh Mulcahy and Outfielder Joe Marty, formerly of the Philadelphia Phils, and Infielder Johnny Berardino, once with the St. Louis Browns, also will be unable to play.

Pros Hold Tennis Clinic At Forest Hills Sunday

The free tennis clinic for boys and girls, under the sponsorship of the Professional Lawn Tennis Association, which was scheduled for last Sunday and postponed because of rain, will be held at Forest Hills this Sunday in conjunction with the final day of the national professional tennis championships.

Boys and girls, as well as adults, are invited to attend the clinic and receive instruction from the outstanding professionals on the various strokes of tennis, footwork and court strategy. Don Budge, Bobby Riggs, Charlie Wood, Bruce Barnes, Wayne Sabin, Karel Kozeluh and others will lecture and demonstrate.

Navy Ring Go Pairs Overlin With Apostoli

Middleweights Settle Grudge Tonight in Norfolk Encounter

Norfolk, Va., June 26 (U.P.)—Sailors Fred Apostoli and Ken Overlin, former middleweight champions, settle their five-year grudge tonight at Foreman Field in the Navy's first bix boxing bout of the war.

Betting is even and heavy on this 10-round bout in which Boatswain's Mate Apostoli of the Norfolk Naval Training Station seeks revenge from Machinist's Mate Overlin of the Norfolk Naval Air Station.

Apostoli has been gunning for Overlin ever since "Conga Ken" ruined Apostoli's New York debut with an upset decision at the old Hippodrome back in 1937, before either was champion.

Because of this grudge and because of the intense rivalry between the two stations, the demand for tickets is so great that officials expect a sellout crowd of more than 10,000—largest fight attendance in the South since the Jack Sharkey-Young Stribling bout at Miami Beach, Fla., in 1929. A crowd of 40,000 saw that one.

Proceeds go to the Navy Relief. They are expected to exceed $13,000.

Boxing will return to Madison Square Garden late in July with two matches—one involving Lightweight Champion Sammy Angott and the other Heavyweight Tami Mauriello.

Angott will tangle in a return non-title 10-round bout with young Ray Robinson, Harlem's unbeaten welterweight, on July 30. Robinson outpointed Angott in a close fight in Philadelphia last July.

Mauriello of New York, who recently held Bob Pastor to a draw, will battle Red Burman of Baltimore in a 10-rounder on July 23. The winner is promised an August match with Lee Savold of Des Moines.

World featherweight champion Chalky Wright's brother, Lee, will make his local ring debut Tuesday night when he meets Danny Kapilow of Coney Island in an eight-rounder at MacArthur Stadium.

A six-rounder will send Jimmy Carollo, national Golden Gloves heavyweight champion who turned pro several weeks ago, against George Stovall of Harlem. They fought a sizzler in the amateurs, and State Athletic Commissioner Bill Brown, who saw the battle, suggested a rematch when he learned both had turned pro.

Frank Ciaffone May Oppose Smith

Frank Ciaffone, Abraham Lincoln High School pitching ace who may win a contract with a Brooklyn farm team, will be on the mound in one of the games when the Dodger Rookies oppose the Floyd Bennett Naval Air Station nine Sunday in a doubleheader at Celtic Oval, Avenue Z and E. 13th St., Sheepshead Bay. Proceeds will go to the Navy Relief Fund.

It is probable that Frank Ciaffone and his cousin, Larry Ciaffone, will form the battery against the Sea Birds' Roland Smith and Bill Schwietter. Smith is a former Yankee farm hand, while Schwitter starred in baseball and basketball at Manhattan College.

Bill Rinker, six-foot-four southpaw from Seton Hall College, may pitch the other game for the Rookies. Other possible starters for Bennett Field are Porter Lens, who was with Twin Falls in the Pioneer League and Bunny Drafts, former Oklahoma City, Texas League, pitcher.

P. S. 194 Wins Finale

The Public School 194 baseball team ended a successful season by winning from Public School 152 by a score of 7—1.

RUNS OF THE WEEK

NATIONAL LEAGUE

Teams	F.	S.	S.	M.	T.	W.	T.	Tls.
Chicago	12	1	7	x	8	3	7	38
New York	10	8	7	x	7	3	x	35
St. Louis	3	4	13	x	x	3	4	27
Brooklyn	4	10	5	x	6	x	4	29
Boston	6	4	3	x	x	9	0	22
Cincinnati	6	7	4	x	0	4	0	21
Pittsburgh	7	0	7	x	2	x	x	16
Philadelphia	4	0	4	x	4	1	1	14
Totals	52	34	50	0	27	23	16	202

AMERICAN LEAGUE

Teams	F.	S.	S.	M.	T.	W.	T.	Tls.
Cleveland	5	1	3	x	7	9	4	29
Detroit	5	7	6	x	2	0	7	27
Boston	1	x	12	x	6	1	3	23
St. Louis	4	5	5	x	5	4	x	23
New York	4	0	6	x	6	6	x	22
Philadelphia	0	3	8	x	5	0	1	17
Chicago	0	x	6	x	x	6	2	14
Washington	6	6	4	x	x	0	0	11
Totals	20	22	50	3	31	26	17	163

INTERNATIONAL LEAGUE

Teams	F	S.	S.	M.	T.	W.	T.	Tls.
Newark	18	18	5	x	0	x	4	45
Syracuse	4	15	12	x	3	3	3	40
Buffalo	16	4	13	x	x	6	x	39
Montreal	3	16	7	3	x	9	x	38
Jersey City	5	11	11	x	5	x	1	33
Toronto	3	9	4	2	x	4	5	27
Baltimore	5	2	5	x	6	2	2	22
Rochester	3	3	9	x	x	2	4	21
Totals	57	78	66	5	14	26	19	265

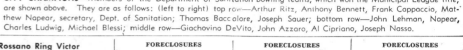

CITY CHAMPIONS—Members of the Department of Sanitation bowling teams, which won the Municipal League title, are shown above. They are as follows: (left to right) top row—Arthur Ritz, Anthony Bennett, Frank Cappaccio, Matthew Napear, secretary, Dept. of Sanitation; Thomas Baccalore, Joseph Sauer; bottom row—John Lehman, Napear, Charles Ludwig, Michael Blessi; middle row—Giachovino DeVito, John Azzaro, Al Cipriano, Joseph Nasso.

Rossano Ring Victor Over Kessler in Eight

Vinny Rossano scored an eight-round victory over Milton Kessler in the feature boxing bout at the Fort Hamilton Army Reservation last night.

In the eight-round semi-final Corp. Marty Clark drew with Buddy Moore.

Johnny Greco knocked out Jimmy Pierce in 2:22 of the second.

The scheduled four-rounders resulted as follows: Cocco Rossano technically knocked out Willie Bush in 2:15 of the first and Joe Governale, Red Hook, technically knocked out Ray Ford Murray in 2:19 of the third when the referee intervened.

OUT-OF-TOWN BOUTS

Appleton, Wis.—Phil Zwick, 128, Kaukauna, Wis., knocked out Sam Scully, 130, Omaha, Neb., in the third.
Elizabeth, N. J.—Wallace Cross, 209, East Orange, N. J., outpointed Danny Cox, 180, New York, in eight.
Philadelphia—Henry Allen, 182, Philadelphia, outpointed Mike Alfano, 202, New York in eight.
Fall River, Mass.—Young Byron, 140½, Boston, outpointed Billy Tordiglione, 145, Boston, in 10.

BANKRUPTCY NOTICES

PHILIP GROSS, Bankrupt.
Notice is hereby given that July 29, 1942, has been fixed as the last day for the filing of objections to the bankrupt's discharge at the office of EUGENE F. O'CONNOR JR., Referee in Bankruptcy, 44 Court Street, Brooklyn, New York.

JOSEPH ZUCKERMAN, Bankrupt.
Notice is hereby given that July 29, 1942, has been fixed as the last day for the filing of objections to the bankrupt's discharge at the office of EUGENE F. O'CONNOR JR., Referee in Bankruptcy, 44 Court Street, Brooklyn, New York.

FORECLOSURES

SUPREME COURT, KINGS COUNTY—THE KINGS COUNTY SAVINGS BANK, plaintiff, against WARREN JONES, individually and as Administrator of the Estate of FRANK JONES, deceased, et al., defendants.
Pursuant to judgment of foreclosure and sale entered in the above action, dated June 13th, 1942, I, the Referee therein named, will sell at public auction to the highest bidder, by MORRIS REICH, auctioneer, in the Brooklyn Real Estate Exchange Salesroom, No. 189 Montague Street, Brooklyn, New York, on the 10th day of July, 1942, at 12 o'clock noon, the premises directed by said judgment to be sold, situate in the Borough of Brooklyn, County of Kings, City and State of New York, described as follows:
Southerly side of Putnam Avenue, 60 feet west of Classon Avenue; being a plot 20 feet wide front and rear by 80 feet deep on each side, and known as No. 62 Putnam Avenue.
Dated, June 17th, 1942.
BRYAN BRADY, Referee.
TAYLOR & ROBERTS, Attorneys for Plaintiff, 7 Hanover Street, New York City. je19-6t F&Tu

SUPREME COURT, KINGS COUNTY—SOUTH BROOKLYN SAVINGS AND LOAN ASSOCIATION, plaintiff, against JOHN A. MACCARINO, et al., defendants.
Pursuant to judgment entered herein, dated June 5, 1942, I will sell at public auction, by MICHAEL J. REILLY, auctioneer, at the Brooklyn Real Estate Exchange, 189 Montague Street, Brooklyn, New York, on June 30, 1942, at 12 o'clock noon, the mortgaged premises in the Borough of Brooklyn, Kings County, directed by said judgment to be sold, being a plot of land situate on northerly side of 38th Street, distant 214 feet east of 3rd Avenue, having uniform width of 36 feet and uniform depth of 100 feet 2 inches.
Dated, Brooklyn, N. Y., June 9th, 1942.
HENRY BONOWITZ, Referee.
DANIEL McNAMARA, Plaintiff's Attorney, 322 9th Street, Brooklyn, N.Y. je9-6t Tu&F

SUPREME COURT, KINGS COUNTY—JAMES H. BRICE, as Trustee, etc., plaintiff, against TONY ZANELLI, also known as ANTHONY ZANELLI, et al., defendants.
Pursuant to judgment of foreclosure and sale, dated June 2, 1942, I will sell at public auction, at the Brooklyn Real Estate Exchange, No. 189 Montague Street, Brooklyn Boro, New York City, at 12:00 o'clock noon on July 2, 1942, premises directed by said judgment to be sold, being a plot of land, with improvements thereon, in said Brooklyn Boro, known as the westerly part of Section 29 on "Map of 233 lots of Flatlands on the north side of Vernon Avenue, belonging to HENRY V. VANDERVEER, Map No. 708," and described as follows:
BEGINNING at a point on the northerly side of Butler Street, distant one hundred twenty-five feet three inches westerly from the corner formed by the intersection of the northerly side of Butler Street with the westerly side of Lawrence Street, as laid out on said map, which point of beginning is where the northerly side of Butler Street is intersected by the centre line of Section 29, as laid down on said map; running thence northerly at right angles to Butler Street and along the centre line of Section 29 one hundred thirteen feet to the southerly side of Section 24, as laid down on said map; thence westerly along the southerly side of Section 24 twenty-five feet to the easterly side of Section 30, as laid down on said map; thence southerly along the easterly side of Section 30 one hundred thirteen feet to the northerly side of Butler Street, and thence easterly along the northerly side of Butler Street twenty-five feet to the point or place of beginning.
EXCEPTING, however, from the premises above described so much thereof as has been taken for the opening of Albemarle Road.
ALSO all the right, title and interest of the said mortgagor of, in and to Albemarle Road lying in front of and adjoining said premises to the centre line thereof.
TOGETHER with all fixtures and articles of personal property now attached to or used in connection with the premises.
Dated, June 8, 1942.
JACOB ZANE HOFFMAN, Referee.
CHARLES E. CHALMERS, Plaintiff's Attorney, 60 East 42nd Street, New York City. je9-6t Tu&F

SUPREME COURT, KINGS COUNTY—LUDWIG HEPP and ANNA HEPP, plaintiffs, against MARY W. RICHARTZ, defendant.
Pursuant to judgment entered June 10th, 1942, I will sell at public auction, by WALTER A. HALLOWELL, auctioneer, at Brooklyn Real Estate Exchange, 189 Montague Street, Brooklyn, N. Y., on July 7th, 1942, at 12 noon, the mortgaged premises in Kings County. Beginning at the corner formed by the intersection of the northerly side of Ridge Boulevard (formerly 2nd Avenue) with the westerly side of Marine Avenue; running thence westerly along the northerly side of Ridge Boulevard 100 feet; thence northerly parallel with Marine Avenue 100 feet to the centre line of the block between 94th Street and Ridge Boulevard; thence easterly along the centre line of the block and parallel with Ridge Boulevard 100 feet to the westerly side of Marine Avenue, and thence southerly along the westerly side of Marine Avenue 100 feet to the corner, the point or place of beginning. Subject to covenants and restrictions of record. Reference being made to said judgment for more complete description of said premises.
FRANCIS M. VERRILLI, Referee.
GEORGE A. ALIANO, Attorney for Plaintiffs, 185 Montague Street, Brooklyn, N. Y. je16-6t Tu&F

SUPREME COURT, KINGS COUNTY—THE PRUDENTIAL SAVINGS BANK, plaintiff, against DAISY A. ELLIOTT, et al., defendants.
Pursuant to judgment entered June 6, 1942, I will sell at public auction, by McGUINNESS & REILLY, auctioneers, at Brooklyn Real Estate Exchange, 189 Montague Street, Brooklyn, N. Y., on June 30, 1942, at 12 noon, the mortgaged premises in Kings County, more particularly described in said judgment, beginning on the south side of Hart Street, 300 feet east of Evergreen Avenue, then south parallel with Evergreen Avenue 195 feet to north side of Cedar Street, then east along Cedar Street 50 feet, then north parallel with Evergreen Avenue 169 feet 5 inches to southwest side of Myrtle Avenue, then northwest along Myrtle Avenue 50 feet 2½ inches to south side of Hart Street, then west along Hart Street 6 feet 9¼ inches to beginning. Together with street rights.
JAMES F. DULLIGAN, Referee.
DELATOUR, KENNEDY & MILLER, Attorneys for Plaintiff, 185 Montague Street, Brooklyn, N. Y. je9-6t Tu&F

SUPREME COURT, KINGS COUNTY—HOME OWNERS' LOAN CORPORATION, plaintiff, vs. GIOVANNI ORLANDO, also known as JOHN ORLANDO, et al., defendants.
Pursuant to judgment dated June 5th, 1942, duly entered, I will sell at public auction to the highest bidder, by MAX W. FEDERMAN, auctioneer, at the Brooklyn Real Estate Exchange, 189 Montague Street, Brooklyn, N. Y., on the 7th day of July, 1942, at 12:00 o'clock noon, premises in said judgment directed to be sold, with the improvements thereon, situate in the County of Kings, State of New York, on the east side of West Street, distant 180 feet north from the corner formed by the intersection of the east side of West Street with the north side of Avenue W; premises being 20 feet in width front and rear by 100 feet in depth on both sides, part of distances through party walls; known by street number 2273 West Street; more particularly described in said judgment herein referred to.
Dated, June 15th, 1942.
MARY E. BROPHY, Referee.
LEO SLUTZKY, Plaintiff's Attorney, 66 Court Street, Brooklyn, N. Y. je15-6t M&F

SUPREME COURT, KINGS COUNTY—ANNA MORALES RODGERS, plaintiff, against AMELIA CORONADO STRATTON, et al., defendants. NOTICE OF SALE.
In pursuance of a judgment of foreclosure and sale, duly made and entered in the above-entitled action and bearing date the 10th day of June, 1942, I, the undersigned, the Referee in said judgment named, will sell at public auction, at the Brooklyn Real Estate Exchange, 189 Montague Street, in the Borough of Brooklyn, City of New York, on the 15th day of July, 1942, at twelve o'clock noon of that day, by MICHAEL J. REILLY, auctioneer, the premises directed by said judgment to be sold, and therein described as follows:
ALL that certain lot, plot or parcel of land, with the buildings and improvements thereon erected, situate, lying and being in the Borough of Brooklyn, County of Kings, City and State of New York, bounded and described as follows:
BEGINNING at the corner formed by the intersection of the easterly side of Eighth Avenue with the northerly side of Third Street; running thence easterly along the northerly side of Third Street 97 feet 10½ inches; thence northerly parallel with Third Street 97 feet 10½ inches to the easterly side of Eighth Avenue, and thence southerly along the easterly side of Eighth Avenue 95 feet to the corner, the point or place of beginning.
TOGETHER with all right, title and interest of the mortgagor in and to Third Street and Eighth Avenue, lying in front of and adjoining said premises to the centre line thereof; be the said several distances and dimensions more or less; together with the building and appurtenances thereof.
Said premises will be sold in one parcel subject to any state of facts which an accurate survey would show, and subject to a certain mortgage made by Park and Third Street Construction Co., Inc., to Prospect Park West Apartments, Inc., dated June 27, 1921, and recorded in the Kings County Register's office in Liber 4967 of Mortgages at page 263, on July 8, 1921, and a certain bond and mortgage made by Park and Third Street Construction Co., Inc., to Metropolitan Life Insurance Company, dated June 28, 1921, and recorded in the Kings County Register's office in Liber 4967 of Mortgages at page 229, on July 8, 1921, as consolidated by agreement in writing dated June 29, 1928, and recorded in the Kings County Register's office in Liber 7088 at page 158, on June 30, 1928, and subject to the rights of tenants and occupants of the premises other than those named as defendants in this action.
Dated, New York, June 15th, 1942.
MILTON W. BERGER, Referee.
JOSEPH V. McKEE, Attorney for Plaintiff, Office and Post Office Address, No. 14 Wall Street, Borough of Manhattan, New York City. je19-6t F&Tu

SUPREME COURT, KINGS COUNTY—EDWARD HAAS, plaintiff, against FRANK SCHNEIDER and ANNA SCHNEIDER, his wife, defendants.
In pursuance of a judgment of foreclosure and sale duly made and entered in the above entitled action and bearing date the 29th day of May, 1942, I, the undersigned, the Referee in said judgment named, will sell at public auction to the highest bidder, by McGUINNESS & REILLY, auctioneers, at the Brooklyn Real Estate Exchange, No. 189 Montague Street, in the Borough of Brooklyn, County of Kings, on the 29th day of June, 1942, at twelve o'clock noon, the premises directed by said judgment to be sold and therein described as follows:
ALL that certain lot, piece or parcel of land, with the buildings and improvements thereon erected, situate, lying and being in the Borough of Brooklyn, County of Kings, City and State of New York, bounded and described as follows:
BEGINNING at a point on the southerly side of Beadel Street, distant two hundred and twenty (220) feet easterly from the corner formed by the intersection of the southerly side of Beadel Street with the easterly side of Morgan Avenue; running thence southerly parallel with Morgan Avenue and part of the distance through a party wall one hundred (100) feet; thence easterly parallel with Beadel Street thirty (30) feet; thence northerly again parallel with Morgan Avenue one hundred (100) feet to the southerly side of Beadel Street; thence westerly along the said southerly side of Beadel Street thirty (30) feet to the point or place of beginning.
TOGETHER with all the right, title and interest of the party of the first part in and to the land lying in the bed of the street up to the center iine thereof immediately adjoining and adjacent to said premises.
Dated, June 4, 1942.
JOSEPH H. DAVIS, Referee.
DAVIS, WAGNER, HEATER & HALLETT, Attorneys for Plaintiff, 120 Broadway, New York City, N. Y. je8 12 15 19 22 26

SUPREME COURT, KINGS COUNTY—THE CONRAD POPPENHUSEN ASSOCIATION, plaintiff, against DORA SCHWARTZBERG and SADIE QUICKSILVER, individually and as Executrices, etc., et al., defendants. NOTICE OF SALE.
Pursuant to a judgment of foreclosure and sale, dated June 8th, 1942, and duly entered herein, I will sell at public auction, at the Brooklyn Real Estate Exchange, 189 Montague Street, Brooklyn, Kings County, New York, at 12:00 o'clock noon on July 14th, 1942, by NATHANIEL SHUTER, auctioneer, the premises in said judgment directed to be sold, with the improvements thereon, situate in Brooklyn, Kings County, City and State of New York, on the southerly side of Livonia Avenue, distant 20 feet easterly of Hinsdale Street, having a width of 20 feet front and rear and a depth of 60 feet on both sides; being known as 508 Livonia Avenue, Brooklyn, New York, and as more particularly described in said judgment.
Dated, June 19th, 1942.
WILLIAM V. KEENAN, Referee.
FREDERICK S. RAUBER, Plaintiff's Attorney, 39-15 Main Street, Flushing, New York. je22-6t M&F

SUPREME COURT, KINGS COUNTY—HOME OWNERS' LOAN CORPORATION, plaintiff, against LILLIE BROWN, et al., defendants.
JOSEPH L. PLAN, Attorney for Plaintiff, 2 Lafayette St., N. Y. City.
Pursuant to judgment of foreclosure and sale, dated June 17, 1942, entered herein, I will sell at public auction to the highest bidder, by MAX FEDERMAN, auctioneer, at the Brooklyn Real Estate Exchange, 189 Montague Street, Brooklyn, N. Y., on July 14, 1942, at 12 o'clock noon, the mortgaged premises in Kings County, State of New York, directed by said judgment to be sold, known as 3024 Brighton 4th Street, Brooklyn, N. Y., being a parcel 20 feet wide front and rear by 100 feet deep on both sides, situated on the westerly side of East 4th Street, now Brighton 4th Street, distant 180 feet southerly from the southerly side of Ocean View Avenue; together with and subject to driveway easements; reference being made to said judgment for a more complete description thereof.
Dated, June 22, 1942.
HENRY I. PERLIN, Referee.
je22-6t M&F

SUPREME COURT, KINGS COUNTY—THE KINGS COUNTY SAVINGS BANK, plaintiff, against WILLIAM WILLENBACKER, et al., defendants.
Pursuant to judgment of foreclosure and sale entered in the above action, dated May 29th, 1942, I, the Referee therein named, will sell at public auction to the highest bidder, by JOHN A. HARTIGAN, auctioneer, in the Brooklyn Real Estate Exchange Salesroom, No. 189 Montague Street, Brooklyn, New York, on the 30th day of June, 1942, at 12 o'clock noon, the premises directed by said judgment to be sold, situate in the Borough of Brooklyn, County of Kings, City and State of New York, described as follows:
Property on southwest side of Evergreen Avenue, 68 feet 8¼ inches northwest of Grove Street, 20 feet 4¼ inches wide in front, 20 feet ¼ inch wide in rear, 80 feet 7¼ inches in depth on southeasterly side and 77 feet 9 inches in depth on the northwesterly side, and known as No. 426 Evergreen Avenue.
Dated, June 8th, 1942.
EDWARD A. VOSSELER, Referee.
TAYLOR & ROBERTS, Attorneys for Plaintiff, 7 Hanover Street, New York City. je9-6t Tu&F

SUPREME COURT, COUNTY OF KINGS—ROLAND C. DIEHL and JENNIE C. SULLIVAN, plaintiffs, against DEW HOLDING CORP., et al., defendants.
MACKELLAR & GERBRACHT, Plaintiff's Attorneys, No. 43 Cedar Street, Borough of Manhattan, New York City.
Pursuant to judgment entered June 8, 1942, the undersigned will sell at public auction, at the Brooklyn Real Estate Exchange Salesroom, No. 189 Montague Street, Borough of Brooklyn, County of Kings, City and State of New York, at 12 o'clock noon on the 8th day of July, 1942, by FRED G. SCHAEFER, auctioneer, the mortgaged premises directed by said judgment to be sold, described as follows:
ALL that certain lot, piece or parcel of land, with the buildings thereon erected, situate, lying and being in the Borough of Brooklyn, County of Kings, City and State of New York, bounded and described as follows:
BEGINNING at the corner formed by the intersection of the easterly side of East 10th Street as laid down on the Map of the Town Survey Commission of Kings County and the northerly side of Church Avenue as widened: running thence northerly along the easterly side of East 10th Street forty-three feet six and one-half inches to a point distant five hundred eighty feet southerly from the southerly side of Caton Avenue; thence easterly at right angles to East 10th Street and part of the distance through a party wall one hundred feet; thence southerly parallel with East 10th Street eight feet eleven and three-eighths inches to the northerly side of Church Avenue, and thence westerly along the northerly side of Church Avenue one hundred five feet nine and five-eighths inches to the corner, the point or place of beginning.
TOGETHER with all the right, title and interest of the mortgagors of, in and to the land lying in front of and adjoining said premises to the centre line thereof.
Said premises will be sold subject to covenants and restrictions contained in deed recorded in the office of the Register of the County of Kings, in Liber 804 of Conveyances, at page 317; to party wall agreements recorded in said Register's office, in Liber 3139 of Conveyances, at pages 545 and 546, and in Liber 3250 of Conveyances, at page 263, so far as such covenants and restrictions and party wall agreements are now in force and effect, and to the state of facts as is shown on a survey of said premises made by HOMER L. BARTLETT, INC., dated July 26, 1928, and to any state of facts which an accurate survey of said premises would show since said date.
Dated, June 16, 1942.
JOHN J. M. O'SHEA, Referee.
je17-6t W&F

SUPREME COURT, KINGS COUNTY—MANUFACTURERS TRUST COMPANY, plaintiff, v. ANNA ROSENZWEIG, et al., defendants.
NEWMAN & BISCO, Plaintiff's Attorneys, 29 Broadway, N. Y. C.
Pursuant to judgment entered June 18th, 1942, I will sell at public auction at the Brooklyn Real Estate Exchange, 189 Montague Street, Brooklyn, N. Y., by ALLEN M. TEPLITZ, auctioneer, on July 20, 1942, at 12 o'clock noon, the mortgaged premises and personal property directed by the judgment to be sold, situated on the westerly side of Ocean Parkway, distant 200 feet northerly from the northwest corner of Avenue V and Ocean Parkway, fronting 30 feet on Ocean Parkway and the same distance in the rear, with a depth of 140 feet on each side and known as 2160 Ocean Parkway.
Dated, June 23, 1942.
WILLIAM ZIEGLER JR., Referee.
je26-6t F&W

SUPREME COURT, KINGS COUNTY—AURORA GRATA LODGE NO. 756, F. & A. M., plaintiff, against GILDA SHEVLIN, et al., defendants.
Pursuant to judgment herein dated April 24, 1942, I will sell at public auction at the Brooklyn Real Estate Exchange, 189 Montague Street, Brooklyn, New York, on July 15, 1942, at 12 o'clock noon, by G. V. McMAHON, auctioneer, mortgaged premises directed by said judgment to be sold, on the northerly side of Fillmore Avenue, 59 feet west of East 34th Street; fronting 19 feet on Fillmore Avenue with a uniform depth of 90 feet, more fully described in mortgage recorded in Kings County Register's office in Liber 8163 of Mortgages at Page 1.
JAMES A. DAYTON, Referee.
WATSON, KRISTELLER & SWIFT, Plaintiff's Attorneys, 68 William Street, New York, N. Y. je24-6t W F

SUPREME COURT, KINGS COUNTY—THE PRUDENTIAL SAVINGS BANK, plaintiff, against ANNA ALPEROWITZ, et al., defendants.
Pursuant to judgment entered June 22, 1942, I will sell at public auction, by McGUINNESS & REILLY, auctioneers, at Brooklyn Real Estate Exchange, 189 Montague St., Brooklyn, N. Y., on July 15, 1942, at 12 noon, the mortgaged premises in Kings County more particularly described in said judgment, beginning on the east side of Chester St., 166 feet 2 inches south of Broadway, being 16 feet 8 inches in width front and rear, by 100 feet in depth on both sides, together with Street rights.
NEIL M. LIEBLICH, Referee.
DELATOUR, KENNEDY & MILLER, Attorneys for Plaintiff, 185 Montague St., Brooklyn, N. Y. je24-6t W F

BOTH SIDES

By Harold Parrott

JUST BUDDY AND RUFF—Well, doesn't that stop you cold? . . . Two old gaffers who didn't figure they belonged with The Great Yankees . . . up and won that World Series opener yesterday for the champions . . .

Sure, Red Ruffing and Buddy Hassett did something for the Yankees yesterday . . . But another way to figure it is that the Yankees—just BEING Yankees—did something for them . . . And I'll try to tell you why, as Red and Buddy told it to me just a while ago . . .

HASSETT HEARTBREAKS—"Tell you the truth," said Hassett, "I took a job as a plumber's apprentice last Winter up-State. When the Braves shipped me to Ed Barrow in February in 'part payment' for Tommy Holmes I didn't foresee 'Yankees.' I saw Newark or Kansas City ahead . . . then Binghamton, perhaps. Well, I'd had enough disappointments . . . For a kid who'd been bought by the Yankees in college, dreamed of taking Gehrig's job, asleep and awake, for years . . . Then was sidetracked to Brooklyn, where I hit around .300 three straight years and still was a 'failure' . . . Well, I'd had enough, that was all . . ."

There was a misfortune in Buddy's family that prevented him from marrying . . . he was able to save precious few dollars from his baseball earnings for the future . . . Then a year ago last Spring the Braves got Babe Dahlgren . . . and Casey Stengel, Buddy's old pal, announced to one and all that Boston had "the best infield in the National League" . . . With Dahlgren playing first and Hassett on the bench . . . That hurt! . . . Of course, Dahlgren was exploded before very long . . . And although Hassett won his job back with Casey and hit .296 there are some wounds that those things can't heal . . . He was still a "failure" . . .

THEN THE WORM TURNED—Well, some of the newsmen weren't very kind to Buddy this Spring as he left his plumber's tools in the North and decided to give baseball one more whirl . . . Ed Levy, they said, was a cinch to take that first base job . . . Hassett, at 30, was trying so hard he looked terrible . . . getting in his own way . . .

Today, where's Dahlgren? Where's Levy? Where are those experts who counted Buddy out in St. Pete, in Spring training?

But I'll tell you where Buddy Hassett, who made the clean basehits that drove in the first and third Yankee runs yesterday, is today . . . He's sitting up on top of the world—and it's a new experience for that never-say-die Irishman!

"WHAT WOULD THE YANKS WANT WITH ME?"—And Ruffing . . . Big Red didn't think he was ever major league stuff in 1930, when . . . But let him tell it himself . . .

"I'd lost 22 ball games the year before for the Red Sox," big Red told me, "an' 25 the year before that. I was a big kid, an' strong, but I just couldn't get that ball over the plate. Why, I walked over 100 batters each year.

"One day we were in Philadelphia and I saw Charley Wagner, our manager, talking on the long-distance phone," he said. "I'd been waiting for that, felt sure I was going back to the minors. I expected it.

"In the dugout that afternoon Wagner called me over," Red laughed. "He said, 'I made a deal for you, Red, so go an' get your stuff packed.' I was moving into the clubhouse when I thought to ask, 'What league, Charley?' 'What league? you big goof,' he says. 'Why, this league, of course. The Yankees have been after you for weeks.'"

Ruff laughed as he lived that happy day over again. "I said to him, 'You're kiddin'. What would the Yanks want with a wildman like me?' He said, 'You're goin' to be a great pitcher some day, Ruff; just keep at it.'"

Well, Ruff belonged, all right, even though he found it hard to believe . . . He's won something like 215 ball games for the Yanks since then . . . He's the greatest money pitcher the Yankees ever had, and the Yankees are fast company, as if you hadn't noticed . . .

Southworth Signs 1943 Contract

St. Louis, Oct. 1 (U.P.)—President Sam Breadon of the St. Louis Cardinals announced last night that Billy Southworth, who piloted the club to its first National League pennant in eight years, has signed a contract to manage the Cards in 1943. The announcement was made within a few hours after the Cards lost the first game of the Series.

Terms of the contract were not disclosed.

Southworth returned to the Cards as manager late in the 1940 season when the Red Birds were slipping fast. He took control of the jittery youngsters, gave them self-confidence and the Cards finished that year in third place. They were two and one-half games behind the pennant-winning Brooklyn Dodgers at the close of last year's race. Southworth previously had served a brief term as pilot of the club in 1929.

QUICK CORRECTION—Joe DiMaggio made a slight mistake going into third on Bill Dickey's single in eighth inning of World Series opener yesterday. He overslid, but promptly took care of it by hooking the bag with his hand. Joe got three hits as Yankees beat Cards, 7—4, in series opener at St. Louis. Whitey Kurowski is the third baseman, Cal Hubbard the ump.

With His Wood He Did It—Did Hassett!

John Aloysius' Bat Was the Difference In Opener—Ex-Dodger Stood Out Over Ruffing as Yankees Got Jump on Cards

By TOMMY HOLMES

Staff Correspondent of the Brooklyn Eagle

St. Louis, Oct. 1—Joe McCarthy of the Yankees hasn't the air of a man who'd be highly sympathetic toward the audible arts. Once a year or so he might go for a rousing Irish come-all-ye but, as a general rule, I do not think he cares much about singing ball players.

But if John Aloysius Hassett, the left-handed lyric tenor of the Bronx, cares to throw his voice around a bit before the second game of the World Series here today I do not think the manager of the world champions will mind a bit.

Yes, sir, the light-hearted young man who first-based for the Dodgers before Dolph Camilli came to Brooklyn and then was lost in the semi-obscurity of a Boston Brave uniform before he bobbed up with the Yankees this Spring was the hero of the 7—4 Yankee victory in the opening game.

That is to say that Buddy was the difference. He was the guy who got Mort Cooper on the run, the Irishman with the piece of wood whose execution brought on a sad state of St. Louis Cardinal jitters, leading to a large enough edge to withstand a desperate Redbird drive in the ninth inning.

And while I'd like to see the Cardinals as National League representatives in a World Series look a good deal better than they did yesterday I might say that the laurel of World Series hero would not descend upon the brow of a better fellow than Hassett.

Planned Adjectives for Ruffing

It was only after this dizzy-mad ball game was over that one realized that Hassett was the star of the afternoon. Right up to the finish the boys in the press box were polishing a few thousand well-chosen adjectives to apply to Charley Ruffing, the veteran right-hander. McCarthy started Ruffing against Cooper over the objections of experts who are helping Joe manage his ball club.

The early mystery of the day was why the Cardinals carried bats to the plate. They did not get a hit until two men were out in the eighth inning when Terry Moore singled.

But in the ninth the Cardinals exhibited that abysmal ignorance of which they were guilty throughout the entire National League season. They did not know they were beaten. And as they surged, Ruffing suddenly started to feel his 37 years. Before they were retired the Yankee pitcher was peering dejectedly from the bench and the New York club looked actually scared.

Ruffing got one man out in the ninth. Walker Cooper scratched a hit past Rolfe, then Ruffing got a second man out. Then Sanders walked, Marion tripled, O'Dean and Brown singled. Three runs were already in when Spud Chandler came to Ruffing's rescue. Another scored when Moore greeted Chandler with a single. Slaughter singled, too, and there the bases were loaded with the three tying runs and Rookie Stan Musial at the plate.

Chandler got Musial on a well-hit ball. Hassett went over to his right and speared a not-too-simple grounder. He just did get it to Chandler, covering first, in time to end the game.

But that of course is not why Hassett was the difference. The competent Morton Cooper was not the pitcher he was on at least five occasions against the Dodgers this season, but yet he might have won had it not been for John Aloysius. It was a Hassett double just inside left field line that smaked over the first Yankee run in the fourth. The Yanks scored another in the fifth mainly because Roy Cullenbine—another ex-Dodger, by the way—doubled.

Then in the eighth with two out Hassett singled over the third Yankee run and that blow seemed to send the Cardinals into an advanced case of the shakes. Slaughter let in two more runs by muffing a fly in right field. In the eighth the Yankees scored two more unearned runs because Cooper's relief, Max Lanier, was too nervous to know whether he was pitching or peeling potatoes. He threw one ball into the Yankee bullpen on a bunt and then made a ridiculous muff of a ball Johnny Hopp tossed back to him from first while another run scored.

Afterward Billy Southworth though that the equanimity of his Cardinals had been restored by that last-inning bid. That could be. But to this observer the Yanks seem to be sitting pretty with one vicory bagged and the St. Louis pitching ace out of the way for a few days.

BROOKLYN EAGLE
SPORTS
THURSDAY, OCTOBER 1, 1942

Cards Sidetrack Gordon, Keller

Our Mr. Holmes Admits He Didn't Know the Flash Could Look So Bad

St. Louis, Oct. 1—The Cardinals didn't look too hot in the first World Series game. But one thing you can say for them is that they took charge of Charles Keller and Joseph Gordon.

After the 1941 World Series, Gordon was acclaimed as the out-standing hero of the championship series and Keller got the second highest vote. Yesterday the Cardinals got them out about as often as the '41 Dodgers got them out in the entire series.

Keller Flattered by Pass

Each Yankee slugger came to the plate five times. Keller walked to get on base once and Gordon did not get on base at all. Keller struck out twice. Gordon struck out three times.

I didn't know that Gordon could look so bad. Cooper whiffed him twice on sweeping curves that must have been six inches outside and not more than a couple of inches off the ground.

SLATS MARION of Cards checks in at third on triple that drove in two runs for Cards in ninth inning yesterday. Red Rolfe covers the bag.

The Yankees beefed plenty about the way Umpire George Magerkurth called balls and strikes. This was due less to the quality of the Magerkurth judgment than to the difference of opinion as to what constitutes a low strike in the two major leagues.

A knees high pitch is a ball in the A. L., a strike in the N. L. and Mort Cooper's fork ball and curve were down around the knees all the time he was in there.

Charley Keller did a lot of looking askance and another Yankee who seemed puzzled was Phil Rizzuto, the shortstop, who is as low slung as a scotty.

Friend Magerkurth appeared a bit bewildered by Rizzuto's squawk, probably wondering how any pitcher could throw a ball too low for such a little guy to hit.

Ruffing scored his seventh World Series victory. The red-headed Yankee has lost only once in these things. His victory score is a World Series record. A teammate, Lefty Gomez, has won six. So has Waite Hoyt, an old Yankee, and Chief Bender, an old, old star of the Athletics.

The Yankee pitcher kept the Cardinals under control mainly with fast balls until he wearied in the ninth. His relief, Spud Chandler, did no outstanding job judged solely by results. But he was breaking off a pip of a curve and each of the three Cardinals who faced him had two strikes on them before they hit the ball.

The Cardinal jitters were not hard to understand. Of the 15 players Southworth used only Harry Gumbert and Ken O'Dea, who made brief appearances, appeared in a World Series game before. Only Hassett and Cullenbine of the Yanks were novitiates.

The crowd of 34,385 was the most silent World Series throng I've ever seen. Violently pro-Cardinal, they did indeed have little to yell about until the ninth.

And it's a darned good thing for this series that the ninth inning did happen. Until they suddenly got to Ruffing, the Cards looked completely demoralized.—HOLMES.

Yankees 5—3 Favorites In Second Series Game

St. Louis, Oct. 1 (U.P.)—James J. Carroll, St. Louis betting commissioner, offered odd of 3 to 5 on the New York Yankees to win today's World's Series game with Ernie Bonham pitching. He held the St. Louis Cardinals at 7 to 5 with Johnny Beazley on the mound.

Carroll said there were no more prices quoted on the outcome of the Series because the Yankees had been odds-on favorites before their victory yesterday. Previously he had held the Yanks at 9 to 20 and the Cardinals at 9 to 5.

SCORES BY PHONE

The New York Telephone Company has arranged to provide Eagle readers with an accurate and up-to-the-minute record of the World Series. Please call MEridian 7-1212 and, at the conclusion of the time announcement, the score at the end of each inning will be given.

OFFICIAL FIGURES ON CONTEST NO. 1

Official figures on the first game of the World Series, as compared with the same figures last year, follow:

	1942	1941
Attendance	34,385	68,540
Receipts	$151,797	$265,396.00
Players' share	*	$135,351.96
Club's share	*	$45,117.32
Leagues' share	*	$45,117.32
Commission share	*	$39,809.40

*Division of the receipts to the players' pool, Commissioner Landis' share and the United Service Organization were not immediately made public.

FRIENDLY ENEMIES—Joe McCarthy, manager of the world champion Yankees, left, and Billy Southworth, Cards' skipper, pose amicably enough. The photographer didn't catch the conversation, but we suspect Southworth was telling Joe that things were going to be different out there today. Yankees beat Cards, 7—4, in series opener yesterday.

Colgate's Hopes Are High For Victory Over Cornell

Red Raider Grid Squad Fortified By Its Best Soph Talent in Years

By RALPH TROST

Ithaca, Hamilton and Hanover may be a long way from this neck of the woods, but for the next two weeks happenings at Cornell, Colgate and Dartmouth will hold the spotlight. These three colleges have always attracted a tremendous number of students from this sector. This week it's Colgate—Cornell. Next week, Colgate—Dartmouth.

Bill Wright

Top billing this week is, of course, the Colgate—Cornell game at Ithaca, where the Red Raiders from the Chenango, fortified by the best sophomore talent Colgate has had in years, will try to make up for several years of defeats.

The Red Raiders looked forward to 1942. Like Cornell, the boys from the Chenango gave many men to the service. Both teams have been hit where it hurts—Cornell in the fullback spot, Colgate on the wings. But even that hasn't changed the situation much.

Had Fortmann for 'T'

Colgate, this year, can win. And no matter what they may say, there'll be tremendous disappointment around Hamilton (and numerous Long Island hamlets) if they don't. And there's also going to be a strong feeling of disappointment in these same areas if the Red Raiders don't, without warning, go completely away from Andy Kerr's long-used double-wingback stuff into the ultra modern Chicago Bears' version of the "T". Danny Fortmann, one of the Bears' stoutest linesmen, the team captain and all that, spent a great deal of time this year back in the Chenango Valley. And not, the alumni hope, for no good reason.

Strangely, back of the alumni hopes is a lad from Ithaca—of all places. His name is Hart. He's the quarterback. In the opinion of some of the most critical, he has just the zip in both handling the ball and timing the team that Colgate has needed.

Cornell, more than any other, has the Long Island talent. The husky W. B. Wright, a Freeport youngster, was called on to handle the fullback burden and did well against Lafayette. His pass defense, and interception, was of tremendous help. Another Long Islander is Wally Kretz, from Amityville. He also figured importantly.

Andy Kerr

OUT OF THE BOOK—Dartmouth's team includes a goodly number of lads who are skilled at other sports besides football. Sayers, Captain Douglas' relief, is so good a baseball player that Jeff Tesreau would have been pleased if he ducked football (and possible injury) altogether. Jeff thinks he has another major leaguer like Red Rolfe in the big first baseman. Sayers, by the way, is the only Indian who won a baseball letter as a freshman. Burroughs, the No. 1 blocking back, is an all-around athlete—whose leg fracture, suffered when skiing, healed amazingly fast. His relief, Carey, is the same sort of all-around athlete, as is Moe Monahan out at end. Moe is the best lacrosse player in school, among other things.

BOX SCORE OF FIRST WORLD SERIES GAME

New York (A. L.)	AB.	R.	H.	O.	A.
Rizzuto, ss.	3	0	0	2	2
Rolfe, 3b.	5	2	2	0	1
Cullenbine, lf.	3	1	1	1	0
DiMaggio, cf.	5	2	3	3	0
Keller, lf.	4	0	0	4	0
Gordon, 2b.	5	0	0	2	1
Dickey, c.	4	1	2	9	0
Hassett, 1b.	4	1	2	5	1
Ruffing, p.	4	0	1	0	0
Chandler, p.	0	0	0	1	0
Totals	38	7	11	27	5

Dickey and Hassett scored in eighth on Slaughter's error.

Rolfe scored in ninth on Lanier's error.

Cullenbine scored in ninth on Lanier's error.

St. Louis (N. L.)	AB.	R.	H.	O.	A.
Brown, 2b.	4	0	1	1	2
Moore, cf.	4	0	2	1	0
Slaughter, rf.	4	0	1	1	0
Musial, lf.	4	0	0	1	0
W. Cooper, c.	4	1	1	8	1
Hopp, 1b.	4	0	0	11	1
Kurowski, 3b.	3	0	0	1	0
Marion, ss.	4	1	1	3	2
M. Cooper, p.	2	0	0	0	1
Gumbert, p.	0	0	0	0	1
a-Walker	1	0	0	0	0
Lanier, p.	0	0	0	0	1
b-Sanders	0	1	0	0	0
c-O'Dea	1	0	1	0	0
z-Crespi	0	1	0	0	0
Totals	35	4	7	27	9

a—Batted for Gumbert in eighth.
b—Batted for Kurowski in ninth.
c—Batted for O'Dea in ninth.

New York	0	0	0	1	1	0	0	3	2	—7
St. Louis	0	0	0	0	0	0	0	0	4	—4

Errors—Lanier, 2; Brown, Slaughter. Runs batted in—DiMaggio, Hassett (2), Marion (2), O'Dea, Moore. Two-base hits — Hassett, Cullenbine. Three-base hit — Marion. Sacrifice — Cullenbine. Left on bases—New York, 9; St. Louis, 9. Bases on balls—Off M. Cooper, 3; off Lanier, 1; off Ruffing, 6. Struck out—By M. Cooper, 7; by Lanier, 1; by Ruffing, 8. Hits—Off M. Cooper, 10 in 7 2-3; off Gumbert, none in 1-3; off Ruffing, 5 in 8 2-3; off Lanier, 1 in 1; off Chandler, 2 in 1-3. Winning pitcher—Ruffing. Losing pitcher — M. Cooper. Umpires — Magerkurth (N.), plate; Summers (A.), first base; Barr (N.), second, and Hubbard (A.), third. Time—2:35. Attendance—34,385.

Nashville Vols Win, Deadlock Dixie Series

Shreveport, La., Oct. 1 (U.P.)—The Nashville Vols knocked Floyd Speer off the mound in an explosive seventh inning last night and tied the Dixie Series at two games each by beating Shreveport '5—1.

The Volunteers hit Speer and relieft hurler Al Bronkhurst for 10 hits and showed their heaviest batting power of the series. Vito Tamulis, meanwhile, allowed only four hits. Shreveport got its lone run in the second inning.

The teams play their fifth game here tonight.

Grid Dodgers Race Against Time—Getto

By PAUL GOULD

This year's Dodgers the best in the team's history?

That 35—14 shellacking handed the Philadelphia Eagles Sunday in the league opener an indication the club will have its highest scoring outfit yet?

The Eastern Division championship a strong possibility?

Coach Mike Getto dug his cleats into the pliant Ebbets Field turf and conceded nothing of the sort.

"It's a race," he said slowly, "a race against time."

Depends on Veterans

The Dodgers' chances, it develops, largely hinges on how long the veterans can go without injuries. During this time the coach works like all fury to transform his collegiate All-Americas, the "surefire" prospects, into first-class professional material.

"Professional football," Professor Getto expounded, "is like a postgraduate course in the game, with the college part the undergraduate study. When a college star gets into the pro league he's got to learn a lot of new things—particularly how to co-operate with skilled men who are mechanically perfect."

A few years ago, Getto pointed out, a great All-America star from the South broke into the Dodger camp. There was so much written about him he seemed hotter than a three-alarm fire—yet he barely made the team!

The way the Dodgers shape up, they have 14 or 15 veterans who have to shoulder the burden for five more weeks. Mike estimates that it takes two-thirds of a season to acclimate the college newcomers into the pro stratosphere and if the regulars can go without injuries for another month then he'll concede the team will go places.

"Take that game Sunday," Mike pointed out. "The Eagles scored two touchdowns on our newcomers. They threw two passes, our defenses slipped and there were two scores. Now, there's the difference between college and pro ball. In college if the defense falls down, a first down, a 25-yard gain results. But not against Isbell and Hutson or any polished pros. One pass, one slip—one touchdown."

The "youngsters" who Getto has weighed in the scale and found not wanting include Robertson, the U. S. C. back; Courtney, Syracuse ball-toter; Tofil, the Indiana end; Jeffreys, Missouri guard, and Eliason, another end. Eliason hails from Minnesota Teachers (never heard of them) and was a sleeper, the Dodger scouts pulled out of a hat. He's a comer, Getto says.

FIRST BLOOD FOR THE RED BIRDS—Whitey Kurowski of the Cards crosses home plate in the third inning of the game with the Yanks yesterday at Yankee Stadium. It was the first run of the day, the second one coming in the last frame. Cards, behind White's great pitching, beat Yanks, 2—0.

Woolf Rides Occupation, Whirly to Belmont Triumphs

Tables Turned on Alsab in Gold Cup —Futurity Nets Marsch Colt $56,690

Whirlaway won the $25,000 Jockey Club Gold Cup and Occupation romped home in the $70,000 Futurity at Belmont Park yesterday with Iceman Georgie Woolf up on both winners, completing an astounding stake double.

Riding with his accustomed icy-veined assuredness, Woolf had Whirly under triple wraps in the early stages of the Cup as The Rhymer galloped in front with Alsab close behind. At the far turn Carroll Bierman on Alsab tried the stunt of stealing away which worked in their recent match race but it was a different Whirlaway today and he doggedly charged at the 'Sab in the last furlong to win by three-quarters of a length.

Alsab easily took the place by eight lengths over Bolingbroke while The Rhymer was a weary and distant fourth. The time was 3:21 3-5 for two miles. The score was worth $18,350 and brought the Calumet champ's total earnings to $511,486. It wiped out the sting of the nose defeat suffered by Whirly behind Market Wise in this same race last year and also avenged his recent licking by Alsab in their match race. Whirly paid $3.10 and $2.10. Alsab was $2.30. Because of the four-horse field there was no show betting.

31,805 See Race

Occupation's victory was surprisingly easy. Made a second choice to the stretch-running Count Fleet by the crowd of 31,805, the John Marsch colt outbroke his field to go to the front in the opening quarter and—with Woolf snugging him all the way—bounced past the judges five on top and just breezing.

The long shot, Askmenow, was second and Count Fleet third. The winning son of Bull Dog ran six and one-half furlongs down the straightaway of the Widener course in 1:15 1-5 and earned $56,690 to zoom his earnings for this year to $177,515. The Marsch colt clinched the two-year-old crown by his victory and is easily the top colt among the juveniles in earnings.

Occupation returned his backers $7.10, $4.50 and $2.70. Askmenow paid $16.40 and $5.80 for outlasting Count Fleet for the place. The Count, favorite at three to two, was unable to gain in the drive and was $2.60 for show.

COLGATE WHIPS CORNELL FOR 1ST TIME SINCE 1919

Ithaca, N. Y, Oct. 3 (U.P.)—For the first time since 1919, Colgate's football team defeated the Big Red of Cornell today.

Andy Kerr's seasoned Red Raiders of the Chenango punched out an 18-to-6 victory before 12,000 spectators in the 29th meeting of the teams.

After the opening kickoff, the visiting Maroon Marauders drove to the Cornell 20, were frustrated by a pass interception but soon started toward the goal again.

Jules Yakopovich returned a punt to the Cornell 35. Al Hanover drove off tackle and tossed a pass to fullback Mike Micka to bring the ball to the four. Three plunges afterward Micka scored.

Yakopovich's 45-yard dash with a Cornell pass interception to the Cornell 30 set up the second touchdown in the first period. A holding penalty failed to daunt the raiders as Freshman Walt McQuade rifled a pass from the 44 to end Batorski on the 20 and Batorski romped across.

Colgate drove 85 yards, with Micka's battering smashes counting heavily, for their touchdown in the second period. Except for Yakopovich's one gallop of ten yards, Micka himself moved the leather to the Cornell 35. There Ed Phinney hurled a pass which end Walt White gathered on the one before he fell. Micka punched across the score.

Cornell moved from its 29 to its

Continued on Page 4

BOX SCORE OF THIRD WORLD SERIES GAME

ST. LOUIS (N. L.)

	AB	R	H	O	A	E
Brown, 2b	4	1	1	1	2	0
Moore, cf	4	0	0	3	0	0
Slaughter, rf	4	0	1	3	0	0
Musial, lf	3	0	1	2	0	0
Cooper, c	4	0	0	8	0	1
Hopp, 1b	4	0	0	8	0	0
Kurowski, 3b	2	1	1	2	2	0
Marion, ss	3	0	1	0	1	0
White, p	2	0	0	0	0	0
Totals	30	2	5	27	5	1

NEW YORK (A. L.)

	AB	R	H	O	A	E
Rizzuto, ss	4	0	2	2	6	0
Hassett, 1b	1	0	0	1	0	0
Crosetti, 3b	3	0	0	1	1	0
Cullenbine, rf	4	0	1	0	0	0
DiMaggio, cf	4	0	2	2	0	0
Gordon, 2b	4	0	0	3	3	0
Keller, lf	4	0	0	2	1	0
Dickey, c	3	0	1	5	1	0
Priddy, 3b, 1b	3	0	0	10	1	0
Chandler, p	2	0	0	1	2	0
aRuffing	1	0	0	0	0	0
Breuer, p	0	0	0	0	0	1
Turner, p	0	0	0	0	0	0
Totals	33	0	6	27	15	1

a-Batted for Chandler in 8th.

St. Louis	0	0	1	0	0	0	0	0	1	—2
New York	0	0	0	0	0	0	0	0	0	—0

Runs batted in—Brown, Slaughter. Stolen base—Rizzuto. Sacrifice—White. Left on bases—St. Louis 5, New York 6. Bases on balls—Off Chandler 1, Turner 1. Struck out—By Chandler 3, White 6. Hits—Off Chandler 3 in 8, Breuer 2 in 0 (pitched to three batters in 9th), Turner none in 1. Double play—Keller, Dickey. Struck out—Moore 2, Slaughter, Cullenbine, DiMaggio, Gordon, Chandler, Crosetti, Ruffing. Walks — Kurowski, Musial. Winning pitcher—White. Losing pitcher—Chandler.

Umpires—Barr (N.), plate; Hubbard (A.), first base; Magerkurth (N.), second; Summers (A.), third. Time—2:30.

Williams Finally Licks Tiger After 40 Years

By RALPH TROST
Brooklyn Eagle Staff Correspondent

Princeton, N. J., Oct. 3—After 40 years of vain pursuit, little Williams College finally caught up with Princeton. And the Purple gave it to the Tiger—but good, coming out ahead, 19—7, after apparently, in real Williams-Princeton tradition, having handed the Tiger victory on hand embroidered doily.

The little band—there were only 28 in the Williams squad—veritably gave Princeton a touchdown by playing sucker to a series of third-down passes from kick formation. Then they started coming and, except for lapses, kept the game well under control. When it was all over, Princeton had as pretty a collection of statistics as you ever gazed at with 14 first downs to Williams' five and a total yardage of 334 to Williams' 189. But the Purple had the ball game — and that's what it wanted.

When Williams finally buckled down to business, they splashed deep purple over Princeton's hopes with a heavy mop. They splashed it on with a three-play 64-yard touchdown march, a 55-yard run back of a low Perina kick—and then a 45-yard pass play with an 18-year-old former Exeter captain, Pat Higgins of Elmhurst, lugging the leather.

Princeton's lone tally was little Davy Marshall's. It was the first score of the game and the one that had made the Williams cause look

Continued on Page 2

OUT OF ACTION—Buddy Hassett heads toward dugout after breaking thumb.

TENNESSEE'S PASSES UPSET FORDHAM 40-14

Filipowicz Handcuffed By Vols' Defense in Rough-and-Tumble Go

Knoxville, Tenn., Oct. 3 (U.P.)—University of Tennessee's underrated eleven—tied last week by South Carolina—put on a surprising show of power today to overwhelm Fordham, 40 to 14, before a crowd of 24,000.

Steve Filipowicz, Fordham's passing ace, was almost completely throttled by Tennessee's screening 6—2—2—1 defense. But he scored one touchdown early in the first quarter, intercepting a Tennessee pass on the Southerners' 48 and racing untouched for the score.

Tennessee's previously considered weak line succeeded in outpowering the Ram forward wall, furnishing protection for a long series of Tennessee backs who completed passes almost at will.

Came Rough, Tackling Fierce

The game was rough and at one time during the second quarter nine policemen held the entire Fordham squad back from the playing field when a Tennesee man tackled a Fordham ball-carrier practically in Fordham Coach Earl Walsh's lap.

Walter Slater scored the Vols' first touchdown early in the second period, going over after a Tennessee drive brought the ball from the Tennessee 33 to the Fordham one.

From then on the game was a nightmare for Fordham. Slater

Continued on Page 4

Penn Capitalizes On Harvard Miscues To Score by 19-7

Cambridge, Mass., Oct. 3 (U.P.)—Pennsylvania's powerful veterans rolled up a 19—7 victory today over a game Harvard team of football novices who fought back to score in the final minutes before 12,000 fans in Harvard Stadium.

Battering Bert Stiff, a pre-season All-America nominee, hammered and kicked Pennsylvania into an early 19—0 lead. Harvard's looping defense, used with effect in last week's opening game, failed to shackle Pennsylvania's first-half running attack.

Pennsylvania forced Harvard back when a long and accurate kick by Stiff rolled out on the Crimson four. A disastrous fumble by halfback Don Richards was recovered by quarterback Dick Martin to give Pennsylvania a scoring opportunity in the first five minutes of play.

In four plays, Stiff slammed his way through the center of the

Continued on Page 4

Bierman Team Ends Minnesota Streak

Minneapolis, Oct. 3 (U.P.)—The old coach came back to Minneapolis today with a team of sailors who shattered the 18-game Minnesota winning streak he had established. A crowd of 37,500 spectators watched the Iowa Pre-Flight Naval Training School, coached by Lt. Col. Bernie Bierman, win the game, 7 to 6.

Minnesota's last previous defeat was at the hands of Nile Kinnick and the "Cinderella Boys" of the 1939 University of Iowa by a 13—9 score.

The touchdowns came in the first quarter and were scored in electrifying fashion.

Minnesota hopped into the lead eight minutes after the opening kick-off when Bill Daley, the Gophers' left halfback, sprinted 55 yards on a perfectly executel play.

Shortly before the opening period ended Fisher punted to Herman Frickey, who caught the ball on the fly on the Gopher two-yard line instead of letting it roll across the goal line. Punting from behind his own goal line, Frickey kicked back to Fisher and the former Ohio State star took it on the Minnesota 38-yard line and ran for the touchdown. Fred Gage of Illinois made the conversion to put the Cadets in front to stay.

HAIL THE HERO—White, winning hurler, walks off field amid congrats from mates.

'Shuttle Relay' Ga. Tech Backs Rip N. D., 13-6

Leahy Leaves Sick Bed To See 11-Game Streak Of Irish Come to End

South Bend, Ind., Oct. 3 (U.P.)—A smart, fast squad of Georgia Tech Yellow Jackets scored a brilliant 13-to-6 upset over Notre Dame today to hand the Irish coach, Frank Leahy, his first defeat in 22 games.

Leahy left a sick bed to direct Notre Dame strategy. With nearly 30,000 fans, he watched a Tech hold off the Irish througnout the first half and then strike swiftly for the first score late in the third quarter.

The Irish had to come from behind in the final quarter to keep from being shut out.

N. D. Streak Broken

Three sets of fast, tricky backs, who came on and off the field at appropriate moments, like a shuttle relay, deployed behind a line that was both quick on the draw and tenacious.

For Notre Dame the loss ended a streak of 11 games without defeat, although Army tied the Irish last year and Wisconsin gave a possible tip-off on the Irish future with a 7-all tie last Saturday at Madison.

It was the first defeat for Leahy, first as head coach at Boston College in 1939. He won 11 games at B. C. in 1940, won eight and tied one here last year and tied last week with Wisconsin.

Both teams threatened in the first half, Tech storming to the very shadows of the Irish goal in the waning minutes. But even so the Engineers' touchdown with three minutes of the third quarter left came with shocking suddenness.

Eddie Prokop, sophomore brother of Joe, who once played for Notre Dame, set up the score with a 14-yard pass which Herb Coleman, Irish soph center, tipped into the air only to see it fall into the hands of Pat McHugh on the one-yard line. Ralph Plaster, who scored here as a sophomore two years ago,

Continued on Page 4

Manhattan Subdues Muhlenberg, 27-7

Manhattan's football team swamped a fighting Muhlenberg eleven, 27 to 7, at the Polo Grounds yesterday. The Jaspers scored a pair of touchdowns in the opening period, one in the third and fourth, respectively.

The Mules' sole tally came in the closing minutes of the fourth quarter.

The victors tallied in the initial quarter via the aerial route. Frank Kiresecker set up the first touchdown, breaking loose for two end runs. Bill Burns took over from the 12-yard stripe to Earl Lambert, who went two yards for a touchdown. Jim Worst's kick was good for the extra point.

Three minutes later the Jaspers scored again. Harry Ulrich scampered 25 yards to put the leather on

Continued on Page 4

FOOTBALL RESULTS

LOCAL

34	Columbia	Maine	2
27	Fort Totten	B'klyn Coll.	7
27	Manhattan	Muhlenberg	7

EAST

27	Amherst	Springfield	19
14	Army	Lafayette	0
21	Bates	Trinity	12
33	Boston Coll.	W. Va.	0
18	Bowdoin	Wesleyan	0
28	Brown	Rhode Island	0
26	Carnegie Tech.	Westminster	0
40	Coast Guard	Worcester	0
18	Colgate	Cornell	6
26	Connecticut	Mass. State	0
58	Dartmouth	Miami	7
40	Delaware	Drexel	0
25	Duquesne	Holy Cross	0
59	Franklin & Marshall	Ft. Hamilton	0
20	Gettysburg	W. Maryland	10
14	Maryland	Lakehurst	0
14	Montclair Teachers	Panzer	7
35	Navy	Virginia	0
19	Pennsylvania	Harvard	7
14	Penn State	Bucknell	7
40	P. M. C.	Hartwick	7
20	Pittsburgh	S. M. U.	7
30	Rochester	W. and J.	0
27	Rutgers	Vermont	20
19	Williams	Princeton	7
33	Yale	Lehigh	6

SOUTH

18	North Carolina	South Carolina	6
14	Florida Naval Station	Miami	0
21	Alabama	Mississippi	6
27	Alabama Poly	Tulane	13
26	Florida	Tampa	6
40	Georgia	Furman	7
7	North Carolina State	Clemson	6
40	Tennessee	Fordham	14
26	Vanderbilt	Purdue	0
20	Wake Forest	Duke	7
21	W. and M.	V. P. I.	7
13	West. Kentucky	Marshall	13

WEST

27	Colo. State	Colo. Mines	0
21	Fort Riley	Kansas State	7
13	Georgia Tech	Notre Dame	6
25	Great Lakes	Iowa	0
67	Illinois	Butler	0
7	Iowa Cadets	Minnesota	6
20	Michigan	Michigan State	0
26	Missouri	Colorado	13
26	Nebraska	Iowa State	0
3	Northwestern	Texas	0
32	Ohio State	Indiana	21
39	Ohio U.	Akron	0
35	Wisconsin	Marquette	7

SOUTHWEST

27	Rice	L. S. U.	14
19	Texas A. and M.	Texas Tech.	0
13	Texas Christ.	Arkansas	6
23	Tulsa	Oklahoma	0

FAR WEST

0	Washintgon U.	So. California	0
13	Oregon State	California	8
14	Santa Clara	Stanford	6
18	Cal. Cadets	U. C. L. A.	7
7	Washington State	Oregon	0
27	College of Pacific	Chico State	6

SCHOLASTIC RESULTS

14	Erasmus Hall	B'klyn Tech	6
24	Madison	Tilden	6
13	B'klyn Prep	All Hallows	6
0	Boys	Jefferson	0
12	Adams	Mt. St. Michael's	2
32	Peddie	St. John's	13
31	Lincoln	Manual	0
26	Flushing	Lafayette	0
40	St. Benedict's	La Salle M. A.	13

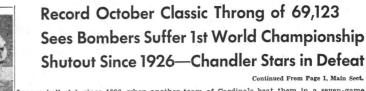

White Blanks Yankees, 2-0; Cards Take Series Lead, 2-1

Record October Classic Throng of 69,123 Sees Bombers Suffer 1st World Championship Shutout Since 1926—Chandler Stars in Defeat

Continued From Page 1, Main Sect.

League ball club since 1926, when another team of Cardinals beat them in a seven-game series. Incidentally, White shut them out and it was the first time the Yanks had been held scoreless in a World Series since Jess Haines turned the trick that very same year.

However, it was not White's pitching that caused the Yanks to wake up today beefing about life in general and the particular situation in general. They passed up their ordinary appetite for ham and eggs because they cannot understand the type of ball club they are playing.

The Cardinals are whizzing along in this World Series just as they whizzed through the closing stages of the National League pennant race. They are marvelous on defense and rely on the percentage that the opposite club will beat itself.

Here is how the Yanks beat themselves on this bright and shining afternoon. First, here is a real believe-it-or-not. The Yanks argued the Cardinals into a run over the protests of Southworth's St. Louis speedsters. The other Cardinal run scored on an error and was unearned.

Yanks Outhit Victors

Meanwhile, Mr. McCarthy's maulers over the nine-inning stretch hit White's baseballs harder and farther than any Cardinal teed off against Spud Chandler, Marvin Breuer and Jim Turner, who operated on the mound for the Yanks.

Cards Superb in Defense

But always when the Yankees were lucky to swing from the hips and connect with the ball, a Cardinals outfielder had the presence of mind to catch it. One of these defensive maneuvers was as great a play as you'll ever see. That was Terry Moore's catch of Joe DiMaggio's rifle shot in the sixth inning.

But that wasn't all. Stan Musial's shoulder blades were pressed against the low letf field rail in the Bronx when he caught Joe Gordon's line drive in the seventh. Then Country Slaughter faded back to the rightfield wall and

Continued on Page 3

BROOKLYN EAGLE
SPORTS
CLASSIFIED ADVERTISEMENTS
REAL ESTATE
SUNDAY, OCT. 4, 1942 • SECTIONS C-D

REPORT FLOCK SEEKS RICKEY AS PREXY

A hot report making the rounds last night had it that the Brooklyn Baseball Club's board of directors had asked Sam Breadon, president of the Cardinals, for permission to dicker for Branch Rickey Sr., vice president and general manager of the St. Louis club. Rickey may succeed Larry MacPhail as chief of the Dodgers.

Rickey is known to have made up his mind to quit the Cards when his current contract expires in the near future.

PARROTT.

'Breaks' Decided, Says McCarthy

Yankee Manager Declares Chandler Pitched Better in Defeat Than White

By HAROLD PARROTT

Joe McCarthy, whose job of running these world champion Yankees has been pretty much plush and profit, still is far from convinced that the Cardinals are something new and deadly, even though he does find himself down in a World Series two games to one for the first time in his Yankee career.

"We hit the ball harder than they did all day," said Joe in his little cubicle under Yankee Stadium after the crowds had died away, "but they got a few breaks—that's all."

Somebody said Hank Borowy would stop the Cards Sunday.

"Stop 'em," snorted McCarthy. "They've been stopped all the while. We got to hit a few balls in the right places—that's all."

Somebody asked if the Cardinal pitcher, Ernie White, had seemed fast out there to the Yankees.

'Spud Pitched Better'

"I dunno and don't care," said McCarthy. "We hit more balls hard off White than they did on Chandler, so I would say Spud pitched better, even if he did lose. Only ball they hit hard was Musial's base hit in the fourth."

What made it harder for McCarthy to bear, of course, was that his protest on Marion's bunt in the third inning with Kurowski on first and none out broke the ball game open for the Cards. Marion was thrown out on his first bunt, but McCarthy squawked that the ball had hit the plate and then hit the Card shortstop's bat for the second time.

Marion then produced another topped ball to Chandler's right and beat it out. Another bunt and an infield out brought Kurowski with a tissue paper run—the only one of the game until the ninth.

Thus McCarthy won the argument but lost the run. Kurowski

Continued on Page 3

Governali, Germann Pace Columbia to 34-2 Maine Rout

Columbia's touchdown twins, Paul Governali and Ken Germann, went to work again at Baker Field yesterday and the result was an easy 34—2 triumph for the Lions, their second victory in as many weeks, over Maine.

Germann, who turned in a fine defensive game and did most of the Columbia kicking, scored three times. Twice he took touchdown passes from Governali, one of them on a play that covered 70 yards, and in the third period he went over on a reverse offtackle smash from the Maine 19-yard line.

Governali, too, was brilliant. Passing Paul completed nine of 11 aerials for a total gain of 261 yards and scored the first Lion touchdown himself on a plunge from the two-yard line. In addition Governali made the longest scrimmage gain of the day—a 28-yard run from a fake pass formation in the first quarter.

The Lion second team scored another one with but a minute left to the game. A 23-yard pass from Don Kasprzak and a 25-yard run by Otto Apel, who plucked the ball out of the air, was good for the fifth Columbia touchdown. Leno

Continued on Page 3

HASSETT OUT OF SERIES WITH BROKEN THUMB

Buddy Hassett, Yankee Cinderella man in the first World Series game, is out of play for the duration, Joe McCarthy says. A White pitch mashed Buddy's left thumb against his bat in the first inning yesterday and he had to retire.

The thumb is fractured, according to Dr. Emmett Walsh, Yank physician, who inspected the X-ray plates that Hassett had taken at the hospital immediately after the game.

This means that Jerry Priddy will play first, with Red Rolfe and Frankie Crosetti alternating at third.

IN ON THE KILL—Two familiar faces at Yankee Stadium yesterday were those o[illegible] Col. Larry MacPhail, ex-president of the Dodgers, and Leo Durocher, Dodger pilot. They watched Cards blank Yanks and chortled to see National League color-bearer triumph, 2—0.

U. S. to Demand Axis War Criminals

7TH ★★★★★★ Sports Extra

Wall Street Financial News

BROOKLYN EAGLE

LOCAL WEATHER FORECAST: Cool tonight

101st YEAR • No. 278 • DAILY AND SUNDAY • BROOKLYN, N. Y., WEDNESDAY, OCT. 7, 1942 • Entered at the Brooklyn Postoffice as 2d Class Mail Matter—(Copyright 1942 The Brooklyn Eagle, Inc.) • 3 CEN

LET'S GO, BROOKLYN, PILE UP YOUR SCRAP!

Eagle Staff photos

TODAY IS THE DAY—And all over Brooklyn workers, housewives and business men are piling up the scrap where city trucks can pick it up tomorrow. At left, workers burn down an old fire escape at the Navy Canteen, Navy and Concord Sts. In center, Mrs. David Diamondstone hands up an old boiler to Mrs. David Jaffe, right, seated on pile of scrap in front of their home at 125 Ocean Parkway. At right, employe of S. Klein, Inc., coal and building materials concern, heaps up heavy contributions at 1237 38th St.

SIDEWALK'S YOUR BATTLE LINE TODAY

And It's Up to You To Throw at Least 70 Million Lbs. at Axis

Today is the day Brooklyn's millions deliver their own private kick in the pants to Hitler and Hirohito.

Today at 3 p.m. Brooklyn begins putting out its scrap. Tomorrow morning at 6:45 the Department of Sanitation's trucks start rumbling through the graying light to pick up the stuff with which your Uncle Samuel's sinews of war will be strengthened.

All day long 250,000 volunteers, shock troops in Brooklyn's battle for material, were going from door to door, flat

Continued on Page 15

WELL DONE, RICHMOND!

Scrap to the amount of 15,897,845 pounds—7,949 tons — or twice the goal set, was collected in Staten Island yesterday, which was its Scrap Collection Day, according to figures announced early today. Even then more scrap was still coming in, and the final total was not expected to be determined until all collections were hauled to receiving centers in another day or two.

The collection averaged 89 pounds per capita, as compared to 28 pounds per capita collected last week in the Queens drive.

"Up to expectations," said Mayor LaGuardia. "A darn good show."

Reds Hurl Bombers At Hard-Pressed Foe

Soviets Cut Off Fleeing Nazis, Kill 1,200 —Force of Drive in Stalingrad Increases

Moscow, Oct. 7 (U.P.)—Marshal Semyon Timoshenko threw strong forces of Stormovik bombers into his counter-offensive above Stalingrad today, and his columns, advancing over a wide area, drove into a town, cut off fleeing Axis forces and klled 1,200.

The desperate Germans, trying to take Stalingrad before Timoshenko's relief offensive and approaching Winter trapped them, steadily increased the force of their thrusts within the city.

Dispatches said several German divisions (probably 45,000 men), tanks and 1,000-plane sorties were hammering incessantly at a small industrial district in the northwestern section of Stalingrad. But at no point, the Soviet high command said, did the Germans advance.

Order Troops to Hold

General Rodimtsev, one of the great heroes of the battle of Stalingrad, ordered the city held at any cost.

"I am confident that, in spite of

Continued on Page 12

YOU MUST REGISTER IN ORDER TO VOTE

Registration hours today are from 5 p.m. to 10:30 p.m. They're the same tomorrow and Friday; Saturday's will be from 7 a.m. to 10:30 p.m.

Remember — America's fighting men in foreign war zones probably won't have the opportunity of voting at Nov. 3d's elections. Stay-at-homes do have this opportunity and more—the privilege and the duty to vote.

But remember, too—you must register to vote.

Do it today.

SENATE REJECTS MOVE TO BOOST CORPORATE TAX

Approves 40% Rate For Combined Normal And Surtax Levy

Washington, Oct. 7 (U.P.)—The Senate, by a 75-to-9 vote, today rejected a proposal by Senator Robert La Follette (Prog., Wis.) to boost the combined normal and surtax rates on corporate incomes to 50 percent, and approved a Finance Committee recommendation to set the rate at 40 percent.

The 40 percent rate is 5 percent lower than the 45 percent rate which the House wrote into its version of the pending revenue bill. The existing combined rate is 31 percent.

Casts Lone Negative Vote

The 40 percent rate was then approved by voice vote, with La Follette's voice the only one heard to shout "No."

The action on the corporation rates came after La Follette had filed a minority report on the tax bill in which he charged that the measure in effect taxes "bread out of people's

Continued on Page 12

U. S. TO DEMAND SURRENDER OF WAR CRIMINALS

F. D. R. Plans Allied Commission to Probe Barbarism After Conflict

Washington, Oct. 7 (U.P.)—President Roosevelt, deploring the continuance of barbaric enemy crimes against civilian populations in occupied countries, declared today that this Government at the end of the war will demand the "surrender to the United Nations of war criminals."

"With a view to establishing responsibility of the guilty individuals through the collection and assessment of all available evidence, this Government is prepared to cooperate with the British and other Governments in establishing a United Nations commission for the investigation of war crimes," the President declared in a statement.

Mr. Roosevelt promised that "just

Continued on Page 12

Mother of 7 Prefers Jail To 'Selling' 2 Babies

Destitute Boro Woman Trailed Husband, A Soldier, Across Country Till Luck Ran Out

Los Angeles, Oct. 7 (U.P.)—Social agencies offered help today to Mrs. Grace Elizabeth Grotheer, a soldier's destitute wife, who testified in court that she had gone to jail to avoid "selling" two of her children to a wealthy benefactress.

She told Superior Judge Robert Scott that bad luck had dogged her and her seven children and that her army allotment checks had been delayed.

Mrs. Grotheer and the children —Margaret, 12; Aloysius Jr., 11; Charles, 9; Theresa, 7; Grace, 4; Johnny, 16 months, and Mary three months, left her home in Brooklyn at 351 Central Ave., to follow Sgt. Aloysius Grotheer from camp to camp.

They kept pace with him as far as Los Angeles, but the allotment checks didn't. Money ran out. Neighbors reported their condition to authorities, who arrested Mrs.

Continued on Page 15

Civic Leaders Rally Behind New Jail Fight

Pledge to Support Goldstein Action for Showdown in Court

Brooklyn civic leaders today rallied behind the latest and at the moment the most hopeful attack upon the antiquated Raymond Street Jail building. Attorney Joseph Goldstein has obtained a Supreme Court order requiring the State Correction Commission to show cause on Friday why its refusal to demolish the civic disgrace should not be reversed.

Robert Alfred Shaw, president of the Brooklyn Hill Association, placed every resource of the association at former Judge Goldstein's disposal today.

Ready to Appear in Court

Mr. Shaw said he was ready to appear in court and produce documentary evidence to show that many residents of Brooklyn want the ancient jail torn down. He agreed that the 448 cells in the prison and the many steel bars would be of vast help to the scrap

Continued on Page 15

Babs Taylor Swallows Glass in Hospital

Special to the Brooklyn Eagle

East Hempstead, Oct. 7—Barbara Lucy Taylor, 28, member of a prominent Long Island family whose repeated wrecking of police booths landed her in jail, was in Meadowbrook Hospital today after, according to the police, she swallowed pieces of glass yesterday.

Miss Taylor, serving a 90-day term, to expire Oct. 30, in Nassau County jail on a charge of maliciolus mischief, was taken from her cell to the hospital last Sunday for a nervous condition and was to have been returned to the jail yesterday.

While eating her lunch, it was reported, she placed a glass container in her mouth and bit on it. She was reported to have said she would rather die than return to jail.

George E. Mulry, Miss Taylor's attorney, said a conference to discuss her case will be held this afternoon by a representative of the district attorney, her mother, Mrs. Cyril F. Taylor and a psychiatrist appointed to examine Miss Taylor.

Warden Seized for Selling Scrap; OCD Would Get Funds, He Claims

Mrs. Anna De George of 315 Avenue P was so shocked to see the heap of scrap she and neighboring women had collected being sold to a junk dealer that she called the police.

As a result, Rubin Moskowitz, 44, of 6402 24th Ave., an air raid warden, and Benjamin Meadows, 48, of 1900 Rockaway Parkway, the junk dealer, were haled into Brooklyn-Queens Night Court on a charge of petty larceny. Moskowitz said the money was to be used to pay the expenses of the OCD headquarters and the air raid wardens' quarters.

Adolph Rose, salvage zone commander of the Bath Beach Precinct, maintained that the procedure was perfectly legitimate, adding that air raid wardens in his zone had collected and sold $2,200 worth of scrap. Magistrate Francis X. Giaccone directed all persons concerned to appear before him in Coney Island Court Oct. 15.

Continued on Page 4

BELMONT PARK RESULTS

1—Miss Sugar 5.20-3.40-2.70, Cananea 7.50-4.80, Chipamink 4.20. (1:33)
Prince Quillo won but was disqualified.
2—Royal Nap 11.80-8.60-5.70, R'p'g Glory 13.90-6.90, S. Bound 5.30. (2:06½)
DAILY DOUBLE PAID $220.40

SHOW GIRL, 20, JOINS THE TOMMY MANVILLE REVUE AS NO. 6

New Rochelle, Oct. 7—Tomm Manville is going to do it again!

The much-married heir to th Manville millions will take his sixtl wife Sunday afternoon in civil cere monies at his estate, Bon Repose here, it was learned today.

Clad in a conservative dark business suit, Manville appeared for a license today before City Clerk Charles U. Combes, with blond and pretty 20-year-old Wilhelmina Connelly Boze, South Carolina show girl, who is to become the sixth Mrs. Manville.

Rockingham Park Results

1—Ballast Reef, 12.00, 4.20, 2.80; Becomly, 2.80, 2.20; Kleig Light, 3.60. Off time, 2:20.

Laurel Results

1—Picture Flag, 5.40, 3.80, 2.90; Super Foot, 13.10, 6.50; Calvert, 3.70. Off time, 2:05.

WHERE TO FIND IT

	Page		Page
Bridge	27	Movies	21
Civil Service	23	Novel	27
Comics	24	Obituaries	15
Crossword	26	Parrott	17
Dr. Brady	23	Radio	24
Editorial	14	Real Estate	27
Events Tonight	8	Society	22-23
Fighting Men	23	Sports	17-18-19
Financial	19	Take My Word	24
Grin and Bear It	14	Theaters	21
Heffernan	14	These Women	23
Helen Worth	23	Tucker	14
Home Front	23	Uncle Ray	23
Horoscope	24	Want Ads	25-26-27
Jury	23	Women	23

GOING PLACES

Continued from Opposite Page

man. What more could one ask? Zimmerman's **Hungaria** will celebrate its fourth anniversary on Columbus Day. This restaurant has a reputation of long standing—if you haven't paid a visit you should.

Repetition is a good reminder—so here goes. Don't forget that Ross MacLean, baritone star of George White's Scandals, will open at Jack Dempsey's **Broadway Restaurant** on Tuesday; that the Show Bar of the **Enduro Restaurant,** opposite the Brooklyn Paramount Theater, is so popular and the entertainment so successful that the owner, Harry Rose, has renewed the entertainers' contracts for 60 days; that the Dixie Colonels, playing at the **Hotel Dixie** Lounge celebrate the fifth anniversary this evening; that Gloria Parker, who had a party in her honor at the **Hurricane** last week, introduced a new song called "Scrap Iron Jive"; the new show that opened at **Havana Madrid** elicited raves with the particular favorites the Trio Mixteco.

An ideal way to celebrate Columbus Day would be to enjoy the weekend program planned by Harry Rogers and his orchestra playing in the Ocean Terrace Dining and Cocktail Room of the **Half Moon Hotel,** Coney Island. The **Aloha Club** on Church Ave. is introducing Iris Ray, Louise Palmer, dancers. Bill Robbins, managing director of the **Park Central's** Cocoanut Grove, announces a new edition of "Hitting a New High," current musical revue which will open in about two weeks. Likewise there will be a complete new show at **Mother Kelly's.** Rosalie Grant, recently of the St. Moritz, is singing at the **Brevoort,** smart supper place.

What do you know, the **Restaurant Mayan** is helping the paper shortage by printing one day's menu on the back of the previous day's. Morton Downey, now starred at the **Hotel Savoy Plaza** Cafe Lounge, doesn't have to worry about his Celtic following since a representative throng of sons of Eire arrived to pay respects. Senor Wences, ventriloquist at the **Rainbow Room,** has been signed by the United States Department of Labor to make a technicolor short based on child entertainment. Because of the demand for dancing in the Bowman Room on Sunday nights the management of the **Biltmore** had Jeska deBabury and his Hungarian gypsy orchestra switch from concert music to Viennese waltzes.

The McGowan and Mack Ice Revue, currently at the **Boulevard** in Elmhurst, celebrates its first anniversary this week by introducing a new Gay Nineties routine.

SINGER-COMEDIENNE Gracie Fields begins an engagement tonight in the Wedgwood Room of the Waldorf-Astoria.

THE LOMBARDO BROTHERS, who have returned to the Roosevelt Grill.

THE LAWRENCE SISTERS, featured in the new Winter revue at the Embassy.

DOT MURRAY, songstress in the cocktail lounge at the Park Terrace.

FORD CRANE, master of ceremonies at the Rainbow Inn.

COLLETTE BAXTER, vocalist at Louise's Monte Carlo.

ZIGGY TALENT, saxophonist with Vaughn Monroe's band in the Commodore's Century Room.

BENNY GOODMAN and his band swings into the Terrace Room of the Hotel New Yorker.

BENNY FIELDS stars in the Greenwich Village Inn's revue, opening Oct. 12.

VOCALIST—Betty Engels, at Jack Dempsey's Broadway Restaurant.

ALYCE KING shares the billing with Alvino Rey and his orchestra at the Astor Roof, starting on Monday.

THEY DO RUSSIAN DANCE AT OETJEN'S

Connie Morano and Adele Paone have new singing parts in Will Morrissey's "Newcomers of 1942," musical revue in its seventh week at Oetjen's Restaurant. A Russian dance number, with Ann Drake, Selma and Miriam Stone, Loretta Hoyler, Johnny Federico, Jo Patti, James Amato, Don Rinaldi and Sid Bailey, is featured.

The show bar attraction at the Flatbush cafe now is a "2 to 4 a.m. Serenade."

Ballet Theater Pays Tribute to Fokine

By MILES KASTENDIECK

Paying tribute to the late Michel Fokine, the Ballet Theater gave a memorial performance at the Metropolitan Opera House last night. John Martin, dance critic of the New York Times, spoke briefly, and the audience stood for a moment of silence in the spirit of affirmation and recognition of the great choreographer's contribution to the dance.

Mr. Martin called attention to the fact that through his ballets Fokine will always be among the living. "He found an art dead and gave it life," and in doing so doubly achieved his own immortality. What modern ballet owes to him is inestimable.

The program was an excellent cross-section of Fokine's work, ranging as it did from "Les Sylphides," conceived in the classic tradition and undoubtedly the most enduring ballet of the romantic period, pivoting on the satiric "Petrouchka," and ending with the exhuberant "Bluebeard." Thus within the scope of a single evening one could appreciate the versatility, the inventive genius, and mastery of the man.

As for the performances, each indicated that the dancers rose to the spirit of the occasion. It has become more and more obvious that they have so increased in skill as to have developed a troupe of stars that make up their own little firmament. That Alicia Markova shone the brightest was even a greater tribute to the classic perfection of her dancing in "Les Sylphides."

"Petrouchka," in a restaged version on which Fokine was working at the time of his death, now has one of the most exciting, colorful and touching finales of any ballet. Though it started slowly, it ended triumphantly. Irina Baronova was the dancer; Richard Reed, the Blackamoor, and Yura Lazovsky, the puppet. And this time it was the puppet who stole the show. "Bluebeard," with a familiar cast, except for Karen Conrad and Nora Kaye, made a hit all over again. Conrad's spirited performance contributed its share.

BUY U. S. WAR BONDS AND SAVINGS STAMPS

HARRY JAMES, pet of the town's jive artists, leads his orchestra in the Blue Room at the Hotel Lincoln.

Personals

Former Municipal Court Justice Nathan Sweedler will address members of the Hancock Street Neighborhood Association on Tuesday night at 80 Hancock St.

Local girls who are members of musical organizations at Wilson College, Chambersburg, Pa., are Barbara Lake of Woodmere, Marjorie Jane McCormack of 629 68th St. and Betsy Morrow of 55 Remsen St.

Harold H. Boxer of 652 Lafayette Ave. has been elected president of Congregation Beth Jehuda for his ninth successive term.

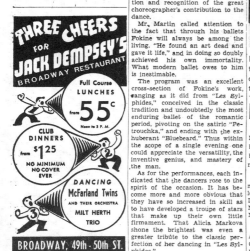

Lila Barbour

H. H. Boxer

Lila Barbour, singer, of 1615 Avenue W, was wed to Samuel Edelstein, Brooklyn attorney, yesterday in the St. George Hotel.

Morris Kavalsky of Flatbush celebrated his 25th birthday and his departure to the army at a party in the New Pelham Heath Inn.

Carol Ann and Mary Ann Gibson, twin daughters of Mr. and Mrs. John F. Gibson of 873 E. 7th St., have observed their third birthday at their home.

A dinner was given to William Yates of the New York Telephone Company in the Boulevard, Elmhurst, on the occasion of his 30th year with the company.

Patricia Trainor of 3301 Farragut Road was honored at a shower at Oetjen's Restaurant, Flatbush and Church Aves., on the occasion of her marriage.

BUY U. S. WAR BONDS AND SAVINGS STAMPS

3 SECTIONS

BROOKLYN EAGLE

EVERYWHERE 5c

LOCAL WEATHER FORECAST: Cool today.

101st YEAR • No. 289 • DAILY AND SUNDAY — BROOKLYN, N. Y., SUNDAY, OCT. 18, 1942 • •

U. S. NAVY GOES INTO ACTION IN BATTLE FOR GUADALCANAL

BATTLING BIG BLAZE—Firemen fight to control the five-alarm fire at 12th Ave. and 37th St. that spread a dense smoke screen over half of the borough and caused nearby residents to be routed from their homes.

5-Alarm Fire Roars Through Boro Plant

Flames Shoot High in Air, Endanger Nearby Homes—One of 7 Hurt Is Near Death

A spectacular five-alarm fire late yesterday roared through a four-story building at 12th Ave. and 37th St. and cast a heavy, black smoke pall over half of Brooklyn.

Feeding on cork insulation, the fire spread rapidly through the 60-foot high structure formerly used as an ice plant, leaving a workman near death from severe burns and injuring six firemen, including a volunteer auxiliary.

The fire in the building, which until two weeks ago housed a Knickerbocker Ice Company plant, shot tongues of flame skyward. Sparks fell on nearby frame dwellings, causing police to evacuate the residents.

Patsy Tarlo, 40, of 139 Duffield St., who was working in a one-story annex of the building when a spark from an acetylene torch ignited the cork insulation, was taken to Israel Zion Hospital, where his condition

Continued on Page 10

WHERE TO FIND IT

SECTION A		SECTION B	
Clubs	17	Art	8
Edgar Guest	20	Bridge	12
Editorial	20	Career Quiz	13
Fashions	16	Crossword Puzzle	12
Heffernan	20	Dr. Brady	12
Helen and Warren	18	Financial	10
Helen Worth	16	Movies	8-9
Letters to Editor	20	Music	8
Lindley	20	Novel	12
Obituaries	20	Radio	10
Old Timers	18	Real Estate	11
Resorts	10	Sports	1-4
Schools	19	Theaters	7
Society	13-15	Trend	5-6
Tucker	20	Want Ads	13-17

SECTION C
Eight Pages of Comics.

Turn to the Classified Pages and look under Instruction—Schools—for vital information about a future career.

Biddle Asks U. S. Tighten Spy Laws

Washington, Oct. 17 (U.P.)—Attorney General Francis Biddle tonight asked Congress to enact legislation providing penalties of death or life imprisonment for any one committing acts of sabotage or espionage, or otherwise aiding the enemy.

He sent to House Speaker Sam Rayburn (D., Texas) and Chairman Frederick Van Nuys (D., Ind.) of the Senate Judiciary Committee a proposed law, entitled the war security act, which would plug loopholes in existing laws and strengthen internal security in time of war.

The inadequacy of present law was revealed by legal technicalities which arose after the recent capture of the eight Nazi saboteurs and the arrest of their 14 confederates.

Men of Sunken Vessel Aided the Red Cross

Washington, Oct. 17 (U.P.)—The navy revealed today that the officers and men of the naval tanker Naches, which was sunk during the battle for Java, contributed $128 to the American Red Cross. Part of the sum was contributed before the ship was sunk by men now listed as missing.

HOUSE VOTES 18-19 DRAFT BY 345 TO 16

Restrictions on Use Of Youths Rejected In Four-Hour Debate

Washington, Oct. 17 (U.P.)—The House passed today and sent to the Senate legislation for the draft of 18 and 19-year-old youths to enable the army to build up a strong striking force of 7,500,000 men by 1943. The vote was 345 to 16.

When the measure is approved by the Senate and signed into law by President Roosevelt, most likely by next weekend, it will make available for induction some 1,050,000 of the 'teen age boys who registered last June. Their induction will begin in December, under present plans.

500,000 Volunteers Expected

Another 500,000 of the 18-19 class are expected to volunteer in the army, navy, marines or coast guard. while the others are being inducted.

The measure, debated for only four hours, was passed in near-record time. It was requested by the War Department on Tuesday as a means of giving the army greater resiliency and endurance. Officials complained that the average age of new troops was too high to weld together a fast-moving, hard-hitting army.

The way for passage was cleared when the house rejected, by a vote of 155 to 55, a last-minute attempt to lower the draft age in the bill to 19 instead of the 18 figure sought by the War Department with Mr. Roosevelt's approval.

Fish Amendment Defeated

That amendment, sponsored by Representative Ed Gossett (D., Texas) came after rejection of a series of others designed to impose restrictions on the use of the 18-19 service class. One amendment, by Representative Hamilton Fish (R., N. Y.), would have exempted men more than 40 years old from liability for military service.

At one point in the debate, when consideration was being given to proposals to require at least a year's training before 18- and 19-year-olds could be sent abroad, Representative James W. Wadsworth (R., N. Y.), read a letter of opposition from Gen. George C. Marshall, army chief of staff. Marshall said it would be "almost impossible for the army to operate" under such a restriction.

Maj. Gen. Lewis B. Hershey, national Selective Service director, told Congressional committees during the week that 450,000 in the 18-19 class would be called up for induction in December.

The draft of 18- and 19-year-olds would serve to delay the induction of many married men with wives but no children and single men with secondary dependents such as mothers, brothers and sisters.

400,000 Face Induction

Hershey said that about 400,000 in those dependency classifications would be inducted in November.

Hershey said that the proposed draft, together with the army goal of 7,500,000 men, would mean that married men with children will not have to be drafted in 1943. There are, as yet, no estimates on what 1944 requirements will be.

The House bill provides that

Continued on Page 2

SOVIET AIR FLEET RIPS NAZI PLANES AT STALINGRAD

But Communique Adds Defensive Fighting Still Prevails in City

Moscow, Sunday, Oct. 18 (U.P.)—Red Army defenders of Stalingrad fought hordes of German tanks and infantry at the northern rim of the city's defenses today and turned them back in at least one sector.

Northwest of the city, between the Volga and Don rivers, Marshal Semyon Timoshenko's relief offensive driving against the German left flank improved and consolidated its positions, the Russian midnight communique said.

Red Air Force Helps

The Soviet defenders of the steel city were receiving much-needed help from the Red air fleet, which battered German air formations

Continued on Page 2

Old L. I. Homestead Damaged by Fire

East Patchogue, Oct. 17—Fire this afternoon caused about $1,000 damage to the old Darrow homestead on Old Robinson Boulevard. Emily Darrow, 65, an invalid, who lived in a three-story section of the rambling structure, which was built about 100 years ago, was carried out by policemen and firemen. She was taken to a convalescent home. Her 87-year-old sister, Sarah, and a family living in the two-story section got out without assistance.

The fire is said to have started from a portable oil stove which was placed too near the wall.

PRINCETON SCORES UPSET IN TYING PENN

Football took over the sports scene yesterday and oddly enough, the biggest upset was the 6-6 tie which Princeton won from what was considered the powerhouse of the Ivy League, Pennsylvania. Other outstanding scores:

34	Army	Columia	6
23	Fordham	W. Virginia	14
25	Montclair Tchrs.	C. C. N. Y.	0
8	Alabama	Tennessee	0
7	Boston College	N. C. Pre-Flight	6
7	Brown	Lafayette	0
0	Cornell	Penn State	0
14	Dartmouth	Harvard	2
34	Duke	Colgate	0
13	Navy	Yale	6
19	Syracuse	Holy Cross	6

Our Losses Called Minor —Planes Still Use Airfield

JAPS SHELLACKED IN SOLOMONS—Air view of East Tanambago in the Solomons, where Japs again were trying to expel our forces, after U. S. planes had peppered it with bombs, leaving wrecked piers (foreground) and buildings damaged.

Washington, Oct. 17 (UP) — American naval forces are now in action in the battle for Guadalcanal, the navy reported late today in a communique which disclosed that thus far no full-scale land fighting has developed.

American losses in the battle thus far have been minor, but the navy described the enemy assault as "serious" and said that "in a battle of this nature losses must be expected."

Details of the part being played by the navy in resisting the savage Japanese attack were not given, but it was regarded as significant that the navy declared that "our land, sea and air forces of the army, navy and marine corps are engaged."

A reference to American planes still operating from Guadalcanal also quieted fears that the shelling and bombing of the American air field on Guadalcanal might have crippled United States air power.

After the announcement that the outcome of the Guadalcanal fighting still was undecided, the navy's communique—the first of the day on the situation in the southwest Pacific—related additional details of the recent action.

Three enemy bombers and five fighters were shot down during the air attack on Guadalcanal shortly after noon on Oct. 15.

During the night of Oct. 15-16 enemy surface vessels bombarded American positions on Guadalcanal for about an hour. A group of enemy vessels to the eastward of the

Continued on Page 6

Hyde Park Rally Ends Bennett Up-State Tour

Roosevelt's Friends Hail Candidate, Who Reaffirms Loyalty to President

By JOSEPH H. SCHMALACKER
Special to the Brooklyn Eagle

Poughkeepsie, Oct. 17—The first long journey of his up-State campaign tour was concluded under dramatic circumstances here tonight by Attorney General John J. Bennett Jr., the Democratic gubernatorial nominee.

Acclaimed by President Roosevelt's Dutchess County friends, who made him their guest of honor at a dinner in the Nelson House, the Democratic candidate not only reiterated his complete loyalty to the President in his role as Commander-in-Chief of the nation's armed and economic forces, but, in effect, came to grips with his political opposition's charges.

Without mentioning Thomas E. Dewey, his Republican opponent, by name, or referring specifically to accusations Mr. Dewey has made on the stump, Mr. Bennett apparently moved to spike the charges in a speech making it clear that all who supported him were aware, individually and collectively, that such support did not carry with it any return promise of obligations or "special favors."

Under No Obligations

Mr. Dewey's charges have included the assertions that the Brooklyn convention of the Democrats was a "surrender to the forces of reaction" and that the same forces were disinterested in the problems of the State and were merely waiting to "ambush" the Democratic national convention of 1944.

"I want to go on record now," declared Mr. Bennett, "that I made

Continued on Page 10

Big U. S. Convoy Reaches Britain

London, Oct. 18 (Sunday) (U.P.)—A large convoy has arrived safely in the British Isles under protection of British and American planes after being trailed four days by enemy submarines.

Although there was ample evidence that a pack of submarines had the convoy under surveillance and was prepared more than once to attack, presence of planes of the United States Navy and the R. A. F. coastal command prevented a torpedo attack.

Navy Catalina flying boats from Iceland bases and American-built bombers—Flying Fortresses, Liberators and Hudsons—joined in the attacks. After three attacks pilots reported sighting oil patches and wreckage, indicating possible victories over three of the underwater raiders.

Blind to Aid War In Army Darkrooms

Rome Air Depot, N. Y., Oct. 17 (U.P.)—Blind persons will have a chance to participate in the war effort here, Col. Richard J. O'Keefe, depot engineering officer, said today.

O'Keefe has hired several blind persons, explaining:

"We will have thousands of film magazines, used on aircraft cameras, that have to be loaded. I feel there is no reason why a blind person cannot do this work as well as one who has perfect vision." Film loading depends solely on touch, he said.

2,482 Auxiliary Firemen Enrolled in the City

A total of 2,482 new auxiliary firemen were enrolled during a city-wide recruiting campaign which featured Fire Prevention Week, Oct. 4-10, John J. McCarthy, assistant chief of the Fire Department, announced yesterday.

RAF RIPS FRENCH ARMS WORKS IN GREAT DAY RAID

Lancaster Bombers Hammer Famous Le Creusot Plant

London, Oct. 18 (U.P.)—Strong forces of Lancaster bombers, most powerful in the world, have carried out the greatest daylight attack of the war against the famous French Le Creusot armament works, an air ministry communique said today.

Target of the mass attack were the plants of the International Schneider Cartel at the industrial town 170 miles southeast of Paris, just 12 miles north of the unoccupied zone.

Schneider is among Europe's greatest manufacturers of heavy guns and other equipment for Axis armies.

"The attack was carried out with great determination," the commu-

Continued on Page 2

Night Flying Pigeons Train for War Fronts

London, Oct. 17 (U.P.)—United States Army headquarters announced today that several hundred pigeons were being trained for use as messengers for the American forces on the various war fronts.

The pigeons, being taught night flying, are put in battle condition with the aid of firecrackers and diving planes. They are given such soldier privileges as furloughs and medical care.

DIMOUT TIME

Sunday, Oct. 18:
Sun rises, 7:14; sun sets, 6:16.
Monday, Oct. 19:
Sun rises, 7:15; sun sets, 6:15.

U. S. Troops Reported Landed in Liberia

The British Broadcasting Corporation tonight broadcast a British Reuters News Agency dispatch from Monrovia, announcing that American troops have arrived in Liberia. The dispatch gave no details.

C. B. S. here later heard a B. B. C. broadcast that R. A. F. units had accompanied the United States troops to Liberia and already were conducting off-shore patrols against enemy U-boats said to be operating in West African waters.

Liberia, it was said, shortly may announce officially its adherence to the cause of the United Nations.

The Columbia Broadcasting System quoted the British radio as saying that "it is probable" that the German consul general and his staff "will shortly be asked to leave Liberia."

It said that other Germans were evacuated from the country some weeks ago and that President Roosevelt's representative, name ungiven, had just concluded extensive discussions with the president of Liberia.

Washington Silent

Washington, Oct. 17 (U.P.)—No official statement could be obtained tonight on the London advices that American rtoops had been sent to Liberia, but unofficial quarters viewed it as a logical move since it was announced last Spring that Liberia ultimately would be an important terminal for the American air services.

Monrovia, capital of the Negro republic, is a little more than 1,600 miles across the Atlantic from Reciffe, Brazil. It is about 900 miles south of Dakar, the Vichy stronghold on which the Nazis long have been reported to have designs.

7TH ★★★★★★ Sports Extra

Wall Street Financial News

BROOKLYN EAGLE

Weather—Cool tonight. Sunset, 5:50; Dimout, 6:20.

102d YEAR • No. 306 • DAILY AND SUNDAY • BROOKLYN, N. Y., WEDNESDAY, NOV. 4, 1942 • Entered at the Brooklyn Postoffice as 2d Class Mail Matter—(Copyright 1942 The Brooklyn Eagle, Inc.) • 3 CENTS

POLETTI IS EDGED OUT AS GOP SWEEPS STATE

ROMMEL RETREATS AS ALLIES LAUNCH ALL-OUT AIR DRIVE

Axis Quits Alamein Positions After Heavy Losses in Tank Battle

Cairo, Nov. 4 (U.P.)—Front reports late today said Marshal Erwin Rommel is abandoning his Alamein positions and retreating westward along the coastal road under an all-out Allied air attack in which the entire British and American bomber and fighter strength was employed.

Dispatches from the fighting scene said that Rommel started his withdrawal several hours ago.

The reports indicated the Axis forces have given up their fight in the forward desert area, presumably as a result of heavy losses suffered in the crushing British armored attack of the past three days.

London Sees Climax Near

(Twenty-four hours more of desert fighting, it was believed in London, may determine whether the Allies can bring the Axis to bay in North Africa in a sweeping campaign designed to regain control of the Mediterranean.

(Another day's fighting, it was felt, will determine whether the hammering blows of the 8th Army's tanks and planes can force Marshal Erwin Rommel into an all-out retreat.

It was believed here that Rommel is now more thoroughly on the defensive than he ever has been in the 18th months or so that he has been in charge of Axis operations in Africa.)

U. S. Planes Blast Foe

Huge formations of British and American bombers were roaring continuously over the coastal road west of Sidi Abd El Rahmen, dropping tons of bombs on the jammed columns of Axis trucks and troop transports streaming to the west.

United States and British fighter squadrons were thrown into the battle, smashing at the Daba-Fuka road and attacking every Nazi effort to provide an aerial cover for the withdrawal.

Nazis Abandon Tanks

The Germans, front reports said, abandoned scores of broken and damaged tanks on the battlefield at Tel El Aqqaquir where the

Continued on Page 11

Hold General Wainwright In China Camp, Japs Say

Tokio radio today made assertions which, if true, would constitute the first indication of the whereabouts of Lt. Gen. Jonathan M. Wainwright, commander in chief of American forces captured at Bataan, and Lt. Gen. A. E. Percival, British commander in the Malay Peninsula.

A Tokio broadcast said Wainwright and Percival were in a Japanese prison camp in Taiyuan in Shansi Province of Japanese-occupied China, about 300 miles southwest of Tientsin.

Safety Razor Manufacture Barred for Civilian Use

Washington, Nov. 4 (U.P.)—The War Production Board today prohibited all manufacture of safety razors for civilian use and cut output of blades to 80 percent of last year's production.

The order, which is expected to save approximately 800 tons of steel, authorizes safety razor production only for the armed forces, lend-lease and for export.

Report U. S. Troops Arrive in Palestine

London, Nov. 4 (U.P.)—The Exchange Telegraph Agency reported today in a dispatch from Istanbul that American troops had arrived in Palestine and Syria to reinforce British garrisons.

It said the Americans were welcomed by the populace in both countries.

SMOKE FELLS 30, 250 RESCUED IN LONG BEACH FIRE

New Law Affecting Volunteers Handicaps Department in Fight

Long Beach, Nov. 4—Repercussions of an ordinance passed only last Thursday were felt today when 18 paid firemen, lacking the assistance of some 70 volunteer firefighters of Long Beach, fought a stubborn blaze in a six-story, 90-family apartment house.

About 250 scantily clad persons were driven to the street shortly after 4 a.m. when flames swept through one tier of apartments from the ground to the top floors. Fifty were affected by smoke and 30 had to be treated at Long Beach Hospital.

Only three of the city's patrolmen were on hand to aid the firemen and volunteer fire companies finally had to be called from Rockville Centre.

Assails Ordinance

Former City Judge M. A. Vogel, retained to represent the volunteer firemen in an effort to invalidate the ordinance, which places the volunteer firefighters under command of the paid department, said the new law does not make it necessary for volunteer firemen to respond to alarms unless notified to do so by the paid fire commissioner. This, Vogel charged, was not done and hence none of the volunteers responded.

Declaring the ordinance inconsistent, Vogel said that under its provisions it would have been necessary for the Fire Commissioner to telephone the 70 volunters at their homes.

According to police, the fire started in a refrigerator on the ground floor of the Parkway Court at 225 W. Park Ave.

The tenants shivered in the cold wind while hasty arrangements were made to house them in neighboring homes and apartments. A large group was taken to the Central School, which was hurriedly manned by a Red Cross Canteen Corps. About 20 others were taken to the police station.

Tenants praised Sgt. James Cusack and Patrolmen Horton and Kaberstein, who dashed through the building rousing families and leading them to the street.

50 Affected by Smoke

Because of the lack of help, evacuation of the tenants was slow and the last 50 taken out were affected by the choking smoke. Thirty of these were taken to Long Beach Hospital but none was in serious condition and all were discharged as soon as temporary shelter was found for them.

Up until last Thursday, the city's paid fire force had jurisdiction only in getting apparatus to a fire, where the volunteer members would fight the blaze.

Arrives in Moscow

London, Nov. 4 (U.P.)—Radio Moscow announced today that Brig. Gen. Patrick Hurley, United States Ambassador to New Zealand, had arrived in Moscow aboard an American bomber. Radio Moscow said Hurley had arrived from Africa.

Late Election Figures

FOR GOVERNOR

	Dewey (R)	Bennett (D)	Alfange (ALP)	Pluralities
Brooklyn	222352	287695	149078	Bennett 65343
N. Y. City	733114	817675	348500	Bennett 84561
N. Y. State	2127607	1488901	400000	Dewey 638706

FOR LIEUTENANT GOVERNOR

	Wallace (R)	Poletti (D)	Poletti (ALP)	Pluralities
Brooklyn	189779	309716	155068	Poletti 275005
N. Y. City	719968	1217991*	——	Poletti 498023
N. Y. State	1962697	1937467*	——	Walace 25230

FOR CONTROLLER

	Moore (R)	O'Leary (D)	O'Leary (ALP)	Pluralities
Brooklyn	193307	440993*	——	O'Leary 247686
N. Y. City	648741	853390	340840	O'Leary 545489

FOR ATTORNEY GENERAL

	Goldstein (R)	Epstein (D)	Kahn (ALP)	Pluralities
Brooklyn	191064	314095	116487	Epstein 123031
N. Y. City	617882	883045	282343	Epstein 265163
N. Y. State	1791042	1488176	328863	Wallace 302866

FOR COUNTY JUDGE

Turkus (R)	Sobol (D)	Neuberger (ALP)	Pluralities
210548	284872	122374	Sobol 74324

FOR CITY COURT JUSTICE

Bartels (R)	Schwartzwald (D)	Rabino'tz (ALP)	Pluralities
193503	286950	133973	Schw'ld 93447

*Combined with ALP vote

Indict Astoria Couple as Traitors In Harboring of 2 Nazi Saboteurs

Herman Heinrich Christian Jacob Faje, 36, and his wife, Hildegarde C. Faje, 33, of 32-40 46th St., Astoria, were charged with treason in an indictment handed up today to Federal Judge Matthew T. Abruzzo for the alleged harboring of two of the four Nazi saboteurs who landed at Amagansett Beach last June.

It is alleged the defendants, both naturalized citizens, concealed and assisted Heinrich Harm Heinck and Richard Quirin, two of the quartet of Hitler agents who came ashore on Long Island from a submarine.

The couple are charged with receiving $3,600 from Heinck to safeguard for him. They face penalties of death or imprisonment of from five years to life, if convicted.

CREW OF GROUNDED SHIP RESCUES SOLDIER

Glen Cove, Nov. 4—It was disclosed today that three youths clinging to their overturned rowboat were saved Sunday afternoon by sailors of a freighter which had gone aground that morning on Matinecock Point.

The seamen lowered one lifeboat but it capsized and a second was smashed against the ship's side. The third and last boat, however, remained afloat and the crew rescued Pvt. Stanley Zamoickin, on leave from Fort Wadsworth; Edward Weincorkowski and Vincent Rufolo. Their boat capsized in a squall.

BOY, 11, ELECTROCUTED IN RAILROAD YARD

The neighborhood pals of Donald Clark, 11, of 214 Eldert St. will probably keep out of railroad yards for a long time, for Donald is dead today. He was killed while playing atop a freight car in the Long Island Railroad yard on Metropolitan Ave., Maspeth, yesterday afternoon. He came in contact with a live wire.

SCHOOL'S OUT AND GAS RATIONING TO BLAME

Mount Holly, N. J., Nov. 4—There is no school today for 140 youngsters and maybe none for the duration here unless officials relax the gasoline ration regulations to enable the four teachers of Tabernacle Public School to get there from their distant homes.

Mrs. Mary Devinney lives in Westville, 30 miles away. Mrs. Mae Stuckey lives at Roebling, 20 miles away, and brings with her Mrs. Claire Thompson and Mrs. Ruth Beddow of E. Riverton, who come 12 miles by bus to meet her. The Board of Education was told by rationing officials no gas allowance would be made unless Mrs. Devinney carried three passengers and Mrs. Stuckey one more, which was described as "obviously impossible because the school is in an isolated community."

SEAMAN TO FACE COURT IN DEATH OF BARTENDER

Hans Gabrielsen, merchant seaman of 44 Clinton St., will be arraigned in Brooklyn Felony Court tomorrow on a charge of homicide following the death of Dominick Nispoli, 28, of 228 Carroll St., in the Brooklyn Eye and Ear Hospital.

Nispoli, a bartender at a saloon at the Carroll St. address, was assisting two of his customers to the street about 2 a.m. last Sunday. Suddenly one of the men lunged at him and butted him in the throat with his head. Nispoli went to the hospital yesterday and died today.

Continued on Page 11

EMPIRE RESULTS

1—Chipamink 5.50-3.80-2.90, Regimental 6.40-4.00, Blue Shot 3.80. (2:05)

Republicans Gain in U. S., But Fail to Rule Congress

Take 5 Seats In Senate, 4 Governorships

Republicans today were clinching Senatorial, Congressional and gubernatorial gains won in Tuesday's election, but incomplete midday returns indicated continued Democratic control of the House of Representatives. The Democrats also will retain control of the U. S. Senate.

The election box score on the basis of incomplete reports was:

Republicans had won five new Senate seats and might stretch this triumph to ten seats.

A net gain of 39 House seats by Republicans indicated.

Republicans have won four Governorships, are leading in the race for a fifth and lost one to a Progressive in Wisconsin.

Fourteen Democratic and eight Republican Senate incumbents appear to have been re-elected.

For the House Democrats elected 192 members, Republicans 167, Progressives 2, American Labor party 1. Seventy-three contests remained undecided.

Here is what happened to some of the political figures who have been in the public eye in recent months:

Sen. George Norris (Ind., Neb.) defeated.

Sen. C. Wayland Brooks (Rep., Ill.), pre-war Isolationist, elected.

Sen. Josh Lee (D., Okla.), sponsor of prohibition proposed in draft bill, defeated.

Rep. Hamilton Fish (R., N. Y.), elected.

Sen. Prentiss M. Brown (D., Mich.), sponsor of price control laws; defeated.

Gov. Harold Stassen (R., Minn.), re-elected for third time.

Gov. Culburt Olson (D., Cal.), defeated.

Sen. William H. Smathers (D., N. J.), defeat indicated.

Gov. J. W. Bricker (R., O.), re-elected for third time.

Defeat of the veteran independent Senator George W. Norris of Nebraska was symptomatic of a

Continued on Page 2

THE WINNAH!—Thomas E. Dewey as he became the first Republican Governor of New York in 20 years. He is pictured with Mrs. Dewey, left, after election was conceded.

G. O. P. Seers Cost Party 4 Judgeships

Deal With Democrats Gave Republicans Only One Where All Five Would Have Won

Republicans of five counties in the Second Judicial District ran the gamut of joy and gloom over post-election results today.

While hailing Governor-elect Thomas E. Dewey's Statewide victory, the G. O. P. had time to bemoan some of its own political guesswork which in all probability robbed the Republican party of its chances of electing five Supreme Court justices, instead of one, for terms of 14 years at salaries of $25,000 a year each.

Brooklyn Republicans who are included in the judicial district with Queens, Nassau, Suffolk and Richmond Counties were virtually the only ones in a position to boast: "I told you so."

Agreed to Bi-Partisan Slate

The Republican and Democratic party units, over the protests of the Brooklyn Republicans, quietly agreed during the Summer to nominate a

Continued on Page 17

Spy's Girl Friend Admits Aiding Him

Hedwig Engemann, 34, described by the Government as the girl friend of Edward John Kerling, one of six executed Nazi saboteurs, pleaded guilty in Manhattan Federal Court today to charges of misprision of treason.

Judge Simon Rifkind set Nov. 18 for sen... Miss Engemann, indicted a week ago for having knowledge that Helmuth Leiner, awaiting trial for treason, had aided and abetted Kerling's efforts as a saboteur. Kerling was one of the eight saboteurs who were landed on United States soil from German submarines but were apprehended before they could institute their ambitious sabotage plans.

Miss Engemann faces a maximum sentence of seven years imprisonment, a $1,000 fine, or both.

Cambridge Students Greet Mrs. Roosevelt

Cambridge, Nov. 4 (U.P.)—Students and residents of this university town gave Mrs. Eleanor Roosevelt an enthusiastic welcome today when she arrived with Lady Reading to visit Queens College.

The streets were lined with cheering people, many of whom waved American flags. Mrs. Roosevelt later visited a service club operated by the Women's Volunteer Service and met and chatted with American, Canadian and British troops.

Massachusetts Rejects Birth Control Measure

Boston, Nov. 4 (U.P.)—Massachusetts voters rejected a "birth control amendment" which would have permitted doctors to give contraceptive advice to married persons as a health measure. Mounting returns showed a "no" majority of 91,585.

Bitterly opposed by the Catholic Church, and personally assailed by 81-year-old William Cardinal O'Connell, the margin of defeat was expected to be increased by returns from several unreported cities with large Catholic populations. Early returns from rural regions had put the "yes" vote in the lead.

U. S. Fliers Down 3 MES, Damage Many More

Cairo, Nov. 4 (U.P.)—United States pursuit planes yesterday shot down three Messerschmitt-109 fighters and probably destroyed or damaged many more, a communique from United States Army Air Force headquarters in the Middle East announced today.

American fighter-bombers started several fires, while medium bombers scored at least 17 direct hits on motor vehicles and started more than 20 fires, the communique added.

Rockingham Park Results

1—Mattie Sue, 8.40, 3.40, 2.60; Our Victory, 3.00, 2.40; Silt, 4.40. Off time, 2:03½.

2—Bill's Sister, first; Maemante, second; Two Kick, third.

SUGAR FIRM INDICTED ON ANTI-SLAVERY LAW

Washington, Nov. 4 (U.P.)—Attorney General Francis Biddle announced the United States Sugar Corporation and four of its employes were indicted today by a Federal grand jury at Tampa, Fla., on charges of violating the Federal civil rights and anti-slavery statutes.

The indictment, charging a conspiracy to hold Negro sugar cane workers in a condition of peonage, named as individual defendants:

M. E. Von Mach, personnel manager, Cwleistown, Fla.; Evan Ward McLeod, superintendent, Bare Beach plantation; Oliver H. Sheppard, superintendent, South Shore plantation, and a Mr. Neao, superintendent, Miami Lochs plantation.

Pimlico Results

1—Gala Light, 40.90, 15.40, 8.10; Mistrella, 9.70, 6.20; Susan Constant, 3.90 (1:20).

2—Pabrupt, 7.10, 4.90, 3.40; Avesta, 6.40, 4.60; Sentinel, 5.00. Off time, 1:51½.

DAILY DOUBLE PAID $221.90.

3—Nellie L, first; Toy-Quay, second; Winning Smile, third.

Bennett Beaten By Dewey in All But 4 Counties

By JOS. H. SCHMALACKER

Democratic hopes of salvaging at least one State office out of the Republican sweep in New York dwindled today as Thomas W. Wallace, Republican candidate for Lieutenant Governor, forged ahead of Charles Poletti, Democratic incumbent.

The Republican triumph, headed by Thomas E. Dewey's landslide plurality of about 650,000 votes over Democratic Attorney General John J. Bennett, never was threatened except for the contest over the Lieutenant Governorship. And that office seemed definitely Republican when returns came in from 75 percent of the up-State districts on which Poletti had pinned his hopes. With all but 137 districts reported Wallace held a lead of 25,200 votes.

Bennett, defeated in all but four of the State's 62 counties, received a plurality of 65,343 in Brooklyn, where his party extended its grip on legislative and Congressional seats and also elected County Judge-elect Nathan R. Sobel and Justice Jacob J. Schwartzwald of the City Court.

Poletti Held Slight Edge

Poletti this morning, when 431 districts were missing and he held a slight edge over Wallace, said he would demand a recount if the missing returns gave a plurality to his opponent. However, he tempered his remarks this afternoon when the later returns were made known. He then stated: "The re-

Tables of Results in Brooklyn, Queens, Nassau and Suffolk—Pages 16-17.

turns indicate a very close election. Pending the receipt of official returns and the soldiers' vote I am naturally withholding any comment."

At the Board of Elections it was

Continued on Page 17

2 Boro Companies To Make Army Shirts

The army yesterday awarded contracts for 100,000 khaki shirts to two Brooklyn firms. The Friendly Shirt Company of 304 Morgan Ave. was awarded a contract for 75,000 shirts, while the Shutley Shirt Company of 86 Meserole St. will furnish 25,000 garments.

Nazi Claims Denied

London, Nov. 4 (U.P.)—Authoritative sources said today that German claims of sinking 16 ships totaling 94,000 tons from a convoy off the Canadian coast "conform to their previous exaggerations."

WHERE TO FIND IT

	Page		Page
Bridge	23	Movies	19
Civil Service	18	Novel	23
Comics	20	Obituaries	11
Crossword	22	Parrott	13
Dr. Brady	20	Radio	20
Editorial	10	Real Estate	23
Election News	16-17	Society	9
Fighting Men	18	Sports	13-14-15
Financial	15	Take My Word	20
Grin and Bear It	10	Theaters	19
Heffernan	10	These Women	18
Helen Worth	9	Tucker	10
Home Front	18	Uncle Ray	18
Horoscope	20	Want Ads	21-22-23
Jury	23	Women	8

Cohan Sidetracked the Serious With 'I'm a Song and Dance Man'

GEORGE M. COHAN THE ACTOR—As he appeared in, left, "Ah, Wilderness" (1933) and "Return of the Vagabond" (1940).

Beloved by All, His Traits Were Modesty and Speed

A few years ago someone was praising George M. Cohan for having "re-energized the American theater."

The speaker said Cohan was "the Dean of the American Stage."

He added something about the "subconscious poetry" of Cohan's dramatic prose and the occasional "profundity" of his plays.

Cohan flashed a look at the speaker from under lowered lids,

Story of Mr. Cohan's death on Page 1.

opened the right corner of his mouth a notch and cracked:

"I'm a song and dance man."

That was George M. Cohan's summation of his career, composed on the instant and delivered without delay. It was characteristic of the man who did and was all the things the tribute payers said about him.

Appraisal Never Expanded

It illustrated two of his outstanding traits, modesty and speed. So far as the records show he never revised his own flash estimate of himself and never gave it another thought.

It was the Fourth of July, 1878, in a cheap Providence, R. I., theatrical hotel when George Michael Cohan was born, the son of Jeremiah Cohan, actor, and Helen Costigan Cohan, actress; brother of Josie Cohan, actress.

The frenzy, tempo and noise of Cohan's natal day never quite departed from him.

In his 50 years on the stage his rule was: speed, enthusiasm, energy; his motto: never make an audience wait for laughs.

Seasoned Trouper at 8

At 8 Cohan was a seasoned trouper—second fiddle in the orchestra for "Daniel Boone on the Trail."

At 11 he was a buck and wing dancer.

At 13 he was star of "Peck's Bad Boy."

At 15 he made his Broadway debut at Keith's as a "song and dance artist."

Of his Broadway debut he said:

"What a flop I was."

Cohan acted in more than 5,000 performances. He wrote or produced or collaborated on 100 plays. He composed 300 songs.

His "Seven Keys to Baldpate" in 1913, "Song and Dance Man," a tribute to his father, in 1923, and such other plays as "Get-Rich-Quick Wallingford" and "Forty-Five Minutes From Broadway" won him acclaim but did not affect his own estimation of himself.

In the early days the family performed as "The Four Cohans." Old-timers remember his curtain line:

"My mother thanks you, my father thanks you, my sister thanks you and I thank you."

'Retired' Many Times

Cohan's tempo sometimes became temper. He was always announcing: "I'm through with the stage." He never was for more than six months at a time.

He fought a running battle with theater managers. When he'd get a bad billing he'd confront the manager with threats to become famous, buy the theater and "throw you out."

The records show he carried out one piece of projected revenge.

In his youth he sent a song to a publisher and it came back with his cherished lyrics rewritten.

Twenty-five years later the same publisher asked him to revise an operetta. He did, with a vengeance. He practically rewrote it. And "The Royal Vagabond" was a smash hit.

Known as a Soft Touch

But Cohan was never mean. He was known throughout the profession as a soft touch. His "Okay, kid" meant, "Sure, here's $5. More if you need it."

His intimates—actors, producers,

THE ETERNAL SONG-AND-DANCE MAN—George M. Cohan in characteristic song-and-dance pose (1912) and, right, in "I'd Rather Be Right," good-natured joshing of President Roosevelt and the Supreme Court, in 1938.

servants—loved him. (His chauffeur once said, "When they made that guy they broke the mold.")

And so did audiences. When he pranced to the footlights, cocked a derby or straw hat over his right eye, and started his famous side-mouth delivery of song or wisecrack no audience ever held out on him.

At 26 he joined Sam H. Harris, another youngster, in an assault on Broadway. They started with "Little Johnny Jones," which the critics panned and the public paid in droves to see. They were together 15 years, parted company for 18, and got together again in 1937 to produce "Fulton of Oak Falls."

His friends always wondered at the dapper, chipper Cohan's vitality. While starring on the road in one play he carried along a second cast for whom he was writing and directing another play.

As F. D. R. in 'I'd Rather Be Right'

Cohan's most remarkable performance may have been in "The Song and Dance Man." Or perhaps as star of Eugene O'Neill's "Ah, Wilderness." Or, in 1937-38, as "Franklin D. Roosevelt" in "I'd Rather Be Right."

In "I'd Rather Be Right," Cohan impudently satirized the President while others of the cast performed a similar operation on the Supreme Court. The Supreme Court declared a third term unconstitutional and, just to prove it could be wrong, did the same thing for the Constitution itself.

After failing for years to please the critics, who invariably disagreed with the public, Cohan appeared nonplussed when he finally succeeded.

Critics' Praise 'Debunked'

After hearing praises of a play in which the professional examiners found all sorts of subtleties he hadn't consciously put in it, Cohan said: "It's just a show."

Cohan loved baseball, purple pajamas, shoes and Broadway. He hoped once that his namesake son would become a ball player. He was a little proud of his small feet and liked to buy shoes. Once after he had turned 60 he looked out of an automobile window at Broadway and remarked: "Gee, it's a grand old street."

Cohan was married twice. His first marriage, to Ethel Levy, New York and London vaudeville headliner, was dissolved. They had a daughter, Georgiana. He married Agnes Nolan of Boston in June, 1907. They had three children, Helen, Mary and George M. Jr.

Cohan was white-haired, although still slender, ruddy-faced and agile, when he first locked horns with the movies. Neither side liked the experience.

Of the film capital he said: "If I had my choice between Hollywood and Atlanta I'd take Leavenworth." Of the movies: "They didn't like me and I didn't like them."

Earnings Ran High

Cohan made a lot of money. In 1907 his income from royalties and acting and producing was estimated at $500,000. In 1929 when Harris lost $2,000,000 in the market crash Cohan offered to make it good. His friends believed he could have done it easily.

Everybody knows about "Over There," the war song he wrote in 1917. Congress awarded him a medal years later and President Roosevelt presented it to him on May 1, 1940.

He was modest about it. If he "hadn't written it on Thursday, somebody else would have written it on Friday. It just had to come."

Once in Washington an admirer called him the country's "Poet Laureate." He disclaimed the title but admitted he was "pretty handy" at song-writing.

But when the President handed him the medal for "Over There" he said:

"I hope America will never need another war song. But if we do need one, it will have to be written by some young fellow."

Dutch Official Says Food Of Europe Goes to Nazis

"The situation in the Occupied Countries of Europe is very grim and is getting worse," said the Jonkheer Henri Van Vredenburch, who with his wife, Irene, was among the 24 passengers to arrive on a Pan American Airways Clipper at the Marine Terminal, LaGuardia Field, late yesterday.

Jonkheer Van Vredenburch said: "The food situation is very bad. While you can't say it is as desperate as it is in Greece, it is still very bad and steadily getting worse. All of the food, apparently, is going to Germany, where I understand they have plenty of supplies taken from the Occupied Countries."

Mayor-Epstein Tiff Needs Final Act

Not Even Mr. E. Knows Whys and Wherefores Of the Missus' Latest Run-in With His Honor

Friends of Mrs. Ethel Epstein were chuckling today over her account of a bawling-out she gave Mayor LaGuardia for dismissing her as his labor secretary.

She said she raked her erstwhile chief over the coals for such things as bad relations with the press, avoidance of criticism and unfairness to herself and other employes.

Less partial observers meanwhile were pondering the choice of one of three conflicting versions of how the encounter in City Hall yesterday afternoon had come about.

Differs With Husband

According to Mrs. Epstein, she had come to say good by to associates and was talking to a group of girl secretaries when His Honor came along. Her husband, Solicitor General Henry Epstein, said last night that she had gone to City Hall to tell the Mayor what she thought of him. And the Mayor:

"That's her story of the conversation. She came here to ask me to give her job back. I am not interested in complaints from dismissed, disgruntled city employes who want their jobs back."

Mrs. Epstein's Account

The dialogue, as recorded in Mrs. Epstein's stenographic memory, was as follows:

Mayor—Hello, Eddie, dear.

Mrs. Epstein—Hello, I don't know what to call you.

Mayor—Wait a minute, Eddie. I want to see you. Stay around.

Mrs. Epstein—I'm sorry, I can't wait. If you want to see me, you see me right here. I'd like to know—why did you fire me?

Mayor—I had a bigger job in mind for you, but you spoiled it by giving out my letter to the newspapers.

Mrs. Epstein—Just give me one reason why you fired me. Why didn't you call me down here, instead of sending a letter? You didn't have the guts to tell me.

Mayor—You should not have criticized my administration in the radio speech you made Monday night. You said my first term was my best. No, Eddie, it wasn't. This is my best administration.

Mrs. Epstein—You are causing an open scandal by your failure to provide an agency where city employes can present their grievances.

Mayor—Oh, Eddie—how can you be so unfair?

Mrs. Epstein: You have lost all your friends.

Mayor: I am more popular than ever! I have a lot of friends!

Mrs. Epstein: Name one!

Mayor: You know the newspaper men hate me.

Mrs. Epstein: Whose fault is that? Why in the world do you handle newspaper men like that? Give me one instance in which you were misquoted.

Mayor: You know the newspapers are all prejudiced against me. Besides, I haven't any funds to set up the kind of an agency you're talking about.

Mrs. Epstein: Well, somebody in the Controllers' office told me that there is a cushion of funds over there that can be used.

Mayor: They don't know what they're talking about.

Attacks "Yes-Men"

Mrs. Epstein: That's the trouble—no one knows anything around here but you. You have too many yes-men around you and too many rubber stamps. You appointed a rubber stamp in place of Paul J. Kern as Civil Service Commissioner.

Mayor: I'll be seeing you around, Eddie.

Mrs. Epstein: Oh, no you won't.

At that point Mrs. Epstein said she walked out.

Son Home on Leave Hid Tale of Heroism

When young Leonard S. Edelstein, aviation radioman first class, U. S. Navy, who lives at 653 Blake Ave., was home on a furlough recently he didn't have much to say about the war to his parents, Mr. and Mrs. Jacob Edelstein.

After he had returned to duty, they learned he had been cited by his commanding officer for his part in freeing the life rafts of a rapidly sinking patrol bomber, thereby saving the crew. With him were J. D. Pyle of Norfolk, Va., and Carol E. Millikin of Beresford, S. D. The news came to his parents in a letter.

The rescue was effected in pitch darkness. The three men were ordered to remain aboard the sinking bomber, while the rest of the crew leaped into the sea.

The trio slashed at the moorings of one life raft, got it free and then tossed it to the men in the water. A second raft was sent to them but they could not find it in the darkness. After the rafts had been freed the three men jumped in the water.

Thirteen men clung to the single raft for a day and a half and were in danger of having high seas break their holds. Stinging jelly fish added to the discomfort.

Two squadrons of navy planes flew over without seeing the men but a lone flier later spotted them and summoned help.

The citation awarded the trio lauded their "meritorious action, which is in keeping with the highest ideals in the naval service."

3 SECTIONS **BROOKLYN EAGLE** EVERYWHERE 5c

Weather: Cold Today. Sunset, 5:45; Dimout, 6:15.

102d YEAR • No. 310 • DAILY AND SUNDAY   BROOKLYN, N. Y., SUNDAY, NOV. 8, 1942 • • •

U. S. INVADES FRENCH AFRICA: VAST FORCE OPENS 2D FRONT

Allied Forces Headquarters in North Africa, Nov. 8 (Sunday) (UP)—American troops by the scores of thousands opened their African offensive today with the world's greatest naval armada in the vanguard.

LEADS INVASION—Lt. Gen. Dwight D. Eisenhower, commander of the United States forces in the European theater, who heads vast American force which invaded French African colonies.

The Americans and British have landed in great force on the coast of North Africa.

It is the opening of offensive action in the European theater by Yankee doughboys, who are slogging into action on this side of the Atlantic for the first time since 1917-18.

The operation, launched under the cover of huge fleets of naval warships and airplanes, was described as the largest single American offensive action in history.

Washington, Nov. 7 (UP) — American army, navy, and air forces, equipped with the most modern armored weapons, are landing tonight on the Mediterranean and Atlantic coasts of French African colonies in the opening of the long-heralded second front, against the Axis, the White House announced.

The White House and the War Department announced the landing operations simultaneously shortly after 9 p.m. The invasion of Africa apparently is on a tremendous scale. It is commanded by Lt. Gen. Dwight David Eisenhower, commander of United States forces in the European theater.

The White House also issued the text of a broadcast message by Mr. Roosevelt to the French people informing them in their own language of the purpose of the expedition and assuring them that the Allies seek no territory and have no intention of interfering with friendly French authorities in Africa.

The announcements did not precisely locate the American landings. But it appeared possible that the maneuver could develop into the western end of a pincers strategy designed to crush German Field Marshal Erwin Rommel's Axis legions once and for all in North Africa.

[In London it was reported American troops descended on the coasts of North and West Africa in a nutcracker operation designed to drive the Axis from Africa, regain control of the Mediterranean and open the way for an attack northward to the European coast.

[The operation was of vast scope, involving U. S. land, air and naval forces, British naval and air forces and a small group of British infantry.

[Vichy reported that a huge Allied battle squadron had been observed steaming east of Oran, on the central Algerian coast, indicated that Algeria, Tunisia—immediately at the rear of the Axis positions in Libya—Morocco and Sengal may be involved.

[An American Army spokesman asserted that "this is the

Continued on Page 2

ROMMEL ARMY BELIEVED CUT TO 25,000

British Race to Close Trap on Germans Near Libya Border

Cairo, Nov. 7 (U.P.)—The Imperial 8th Army hurled armored forces, motorized infantry and swarms of planes tonight at the remnants of Marshal Erwin Rommel's once proud Afrika Korps—possibly only 25,000 out of an original 140,000 now trying to brace for a stand at Halfaya (Hellfire) Pass on the Libyan frontier, 240 miles west of the Alamein battleground.

The main body of the Imperial forces was reported to be well west of Mersa Matruh, 110 miles west of Alamein, and advance striking forces were believed to be as far as 00 miles west of Alamein or close to the Egyptian-Libyan frontier, 40 miles west of Alamein.

Meanwhile, Lt. Gen. Bernard L. Montgomery ordered his Eighth Army to finish the job of "removing the Germans from North Africa."

"There is much to be done yet, and it will call for a supreme effort and great hardship on the part of every officer and man," the British General messaged his troops.

"Forward, then, to our task of removing the Germans from North Africa! The Germans began this trouble, and they must now take the consequences."

British Capture 20,000

How many men Rommel had left in the Halfaya area could not be established. Already 20,000 prisoners have been counted in British hands. Rommel's desert casualties were estimated at something like another 20,000 and 75,000 Italian troops had been left far behind the swirling battleground, ready to surrender when the British can find time and men to round them up.

Rommel entered the desert battle with a maximum of 140,000 troops in the forward area. Unless he has been able to rush up reinforcements from the rear in large numbers, it was doubted that he had more than a division or two left to attempt another stand at Halfaya.

May Not Make Stand

It appeared possible tonight that the bruised and beaten Axis forces might not even attempt to stand at Halfaya but would instead continue their headlong flight as deeply as possible into Libya in an effort to open up a gap between themselves and the pursuing 8th Army. Such a maneuver, however, may already be doomed to failure.

Lieutenant General Montgomery has ordered that every attempt be

Continued on Page 2

'We Count on Your Friendship And Ask Your Aid,' French Told

Eisenhower Calls on People To Fly Tricolor and U. S. Flag

Washington, Nov. 7 (U.P.)—Lt. Gen. Dwight D. Eisenhower, commander of the United States forces invading French North Africa, tonight broadcast a proclamation in French to the inhabitants of that area saying the United Nations intended to save them from Italo-German invasion.

The text of his proclamation:

"Here is a communication from the American general, Eisenhower, commander-in-chief of the forces now disembarking in French North Africa. This is one of the General Staff officers who speaks to you, this communication, of the highest importance, is addressed to the French armies on land, sea, and air in North Africa:

"Frenchmen of North Africa, the forces which I have the honor of commanding come to you as friends to make war against your enemies.

"This is a military operation directed against the Italian-German military forces in North Africa. Our only objective is to defeat the enemy and to free France. I need not tell you that we have no designs either on

Continued on Page 2

HISTORIC BORO CHURCHES ACT FOR MERGER

Central Congregational, Clinton Ave. Community Parishioners to Meet

Historic Central Congregational Church and the Clinton Avenue Community Church will merge to become the Cadman Memorial Church if both congregations approve.

The fact that the official boards of the two institutions have agreed upon terms of consolidation was to be revealed from the pulpit of each at today's morning services. The announcement followed a considerable period of secret negotiations.

Both congregations will meet in their respective buildings—Central at 64 Jefferson Ave., and Clinton Avenue at Clinton and Lafayette Aves.—on Friday, Nov. 20, to vote for or against the proposed merger. If both vote affirmatively, necessary court action will be taken promptly to make the consolidation effective by Jan. 1.

As the agreement now stands, it is generally understood that the services will be held in the Clinton Ave. building, the historic structure on Jefferson Ave., headed for 35 years by the Rev. Dr. S. Parkes Cadman, being used only occasionally for special services because it has a larger auditorium.

The Rev. Dr. Moses Richardson Lovell, pastor of Central, will be the minister of the new church, and his assistant, the Rev. John J. Foster, will continue in that capacity.

Dr. Stamm Resigned

The Rev. Dr. Frederick K. Stamm, pastor of the Community Church, tendered his resignation some weeks ago. It will be effective at the end of the year, after which he will devote his time to his radio preaching and literary work.

The late Dr. Cadman, internationally known, had a distinguished list of predecessors, including the Rev. J. Clement French, the Rev. Henry Martyn Scudder and the Rev. A. J. F. Behrends. Dr. Lovell succeeded him after serving pulpits in Holyoke, Mass.; Waterbury, Conn., and Washington, D. C.

The Clinton Ave. institution, founded in 1848, included the Rev. Dr. Nehemiah Boynton among its famous preachers. Dr. Stamm, during his 14 years of service with the church, gained nation-wide recognition not only from his books but from his 12 years of Sunday broadcasts on a coast-to-coast National Broadcasting Company hookup.

Battery Tube Work Permitted to Continue

WPB Approves Tunnel Authority's Plea Pending Appeal From Previous Ruling

The War Production Board has granted permission to continue tunneling operations at the Manrattan end of the Brooklyn-Battery tunnel pending a final review of an appeal of last week's stop-work order, Commissioner William H. Friedman of the New York City Tunnel Authority announced last night.

Commissioner Friedman said that permisison was granted at a conference in Washington on Friday which was attended by Tunnel Authority Engineer Ole Singstad and representatives of the WPB who sougth to continue employment for 1,200 sandhogs.

Exception Filed

Following last week's order by the WPB to stop all work at the Manhattan end of the tunnel project at once, Alfred B. Jones, tunnel authority chairman, and other officials filed an exception on the grounds that compliance would work an "exceptional and unreasonable" hardship on the project.

The exception also was based on the fact that no steel, critical materials or equipment adaptable to any other purpose was being used and that the 1,200 sandhogs employed would be thrown out of work, aggravating the serious unemployment situation in New York City.

Since the Manhattan end of the tunnel is now being driven through solid rock, no cast-iron lining, such as that needed on the Brooklyn end and where work was shut down last month, is needed, it was pointed out.

"It is the contention of the Tunnel Authority that the completion of the $80,000,000 Brooklyn-Battery tunnel is a matter of prime importance to the defense of New York City and the entire eastern seaboard," Commissioner Friedman declared.

"If the East River bridges should be so damaged as to be rendered unserviceable, the completed tunnel would provide the only direct vehicular link between Brooklyn and Manhattan."

Commissioner Friedman also pointed out that on Oct. 29, 1940, President Roosevelt, at the groundbreaking exercises at the Brooklyn end of the tunnel, said that if there should be an attack on America, it would be safer for America and for all its cities to have tunnels instead of bridges.

The tunnel is now more than one-third bored through. It will be approximately two miles long, reaching from the Battery to the foot of Hamilton Ave., with an elbow under Governors Island.

Most of the arterial highways which it was designed to hook up have already been constructed. It will connect directly with the Belt Parkway on the Long Island side and with the West Side Highway and the East Side Drive in Manhattan.

ACTION AT POLLS HELD NECESSARY TO DOOM JAIL

Trumpler Doubtful It Can Be Achieved Through the Court

Tearing down of ye ancient firetrap, the 104-year-old Raymond Street Jail, may not be achieved until the people of Brooklyn compel action by making their will known in a political campaign, George H. Trumpler, former president of the Kings County Grand Jurors Association, declared yesterday.

Mr. Trumpler, chairman of the association's Raymond Street Jail Committee, indicated in a statement last night that he was not too hopeful of getting the necessary redress through court action. The basic trouble, he found, was that the State Commission of Correction, which has jurisdiction over the jail, consists 100 percent of non-Brooklynites and their attitude is, said Mr. Trumpler, "Let Brooklyn grumble!"

The whole matter will come up before Supreme Court Justice Wenzel on Nov. 30, following another hearing—two have already been held—before the commission. But Mr. Trumpler, like former Magistrate Joseph Goldstein, who is pressing the court action, sees no great prospects of favorable action. Mr. Trumpler stated:

Political Issue Urged

"Watching the court proceedings instituted by Ex-Magistrate Joseph Goldstein to compel the State Commission of Correction to close the Raymond Street Jail, it is very apparent that every loophole that the law provides will be taken advantage of to embarrass this legal action, which even if unsuccessful will at least be an interesting experiment to ascertain if redress in this matter is obtainable in our courts for the long suffering people of Brooklyn. If not, it will be necessary to make it a definite political issue which, of course, should be avoided if possible.

"Very unfortunate indeed is the fact that none of the members of the State commission are residents of Brooklyn for the Raymond Street situation is indigenous to Kings County. To the State Commission of Correction, however, with four members from Manhattan and the rest from up-State, the Brooklyn bastile is just another prison and is regarded from a purely academic viewpoint.

"What difference doth it make if millions are squandered on new and palatial city prisons throughout the city in smaller boroughs with Kings County left holding the bag with an antiquated and obsolete structure on its hands. Let Brooklyn grumble. That seems to be the attitude of the State Commission of Correction following the example set in the matter of all public buildings in Brooklyn by the present city administration."

5,188 Japanese Troops Slain In Solomons

Our Losses 1,000 —U. S. Forces Advance East of Airport

Washington, Nov. 7 (U.P.)—At least 5,188 Japanese troops have been killed in land fighting in the Solomons since United States forces invaded them on Aug. 7, the navy announced late today, indicating that American troop losses are around 1,000.

The navy set Japanese losses at this figure in a communique issued a few hours after disclosure that American Army forces on Guadalcanal advanced several miles against enemy forces east of Henderson Field on Friday. The earlier communique also disclosed that marines had repulsed light enemy attacks from west of the field.

The first communique said army troops crossed the Malimbiu River, encountering only light resistance. The Malimbiu stretches inland about four miles southward of Koli Point, near the scene of enemy landings Tuesday and Wednesday nights.

The second communique made no reference to American losses in the Solomons, but it was recalled that Secretary of Navy Frank Knox told a press conference Friday that Japanese losses there were running better than five to our one. That would set the U. S. losses at about 1,000 or less.

The navy said its figure for enemy losses was based "on an actual count of enemy killed in actions ashore and does not include estimates of those killed in enemy-controlled areas where no count could be made." The losses, it specified, all were inflicted by U. S. forces in

Continued on Page 2

F. D. Appeals to French Not To Obstruct A.E.F.

Washington, Nov. 7 (U.P.)—In connection with current military operations in French North Africa, the President has broadcast by radio to the French people the following message in French:

"My Friends, who suffer day and night, under the crushing yoke of the Nazis, I speak to you as one who was with your army and navy in France in 1918. I have held all my life the deepest friendship for the French people—for the entire French people. I retain and cherish the friendship of hundreds of French people in France and outside of France. I know your farms, your villages, and your cities. I know your soldiers, professors and workmen. I know what a precious heritage of the French people are your homes, your culture and the principles of democracy in France. I salute again and reiterate my faith in liberty, equality and fraternity. No two nations exist which are more united by historic and mutually friendly ties than the people of France and the United States.

Would Restore Liberty

"Americans, with the assistance of the United Nations, are striving for their own safe future as well as the restoration of the ideals, the liberties an dthe democracies of all those who have lived under the tricolor.

"We come among you to repulse the cruel invaders who would remove forever your rights of self-government, your rights to religious freedom, and your rights to live your own lives in peace and security.

"We come among you solely to defeat and rout your enemies. Have faith in our words. We do not want to cause you any harm.

"We assure you that once the menace of Germany and Italy is removed from you, we shall quit your territory at once.

"I am appealing to your realism, to your self-interest and national ideals.

"Do not obstruct, I beg of you, this great purpose.

"Help us where you are able, my friends, and we shall see again the glorious day when liberty and peace shall reign again on earth.

"Vive la France Eternelle!"

THREE SUBWAY CARS PASS OVER FAINTING GIRL, BUT SHE'S SAVED

Mrs. Louise Poepfer, 21, of 676 St. Mark's Ave., fell from the platform of the Hoyt-Schermerhorn subway station yesterday and was rescued after three cars of a Manhattan-bound train had passed over her.

Mrs. Poepfer, who recovered consciousness after she was lifted from a well between the tracks, told police she became dizzy before she fell.

Ambulance Surgeon Scozelli, from the Holy Family Hospital, to which she was removed, said she was suffering from a possible fracture of the skull, shock and lacerations.

Einstein Kin to Be Citizen

Camp Clairborne, La., Nov. 7 (U.P.)—Pvt. Henry H. Niedermeier, 21-year-old Berlin born grandnephew of Albert Einstein, was scheduled to become a U. S. citizen today in Federal District Court at nearby Alexandria.

WHERE TO FIND IT

	Page		Page
SECTION A		Schools	8
Bridge	10	Society	13-15
Dr. Brady	18	Tucker	20
Clubs	17	Women	16
Crossword Puzzle	10	SECTION B	
Editorial	20	Art	8
Fashions	16	Career Quiz	13
Financial	19	Movies	8-9
Heffernan	20	Music	8
Helen Worth	16	Real Estate	10
Horoscope	10	Resorts	16
Letters to Editor	20	Sports	1-4
Lindley	20	Theaters	7
Novel	10	Trend	5-6
Obituaries	21	Want Ads	11-15
Old Timers	18	SECTION C	
Radio	19	Eight Pages of Comics	

Turn to the Classified Pages and look under Instructions—Schools—for vital information about a future career.

2 Sons in Armed Forces, Astoria Vet Also Joins Up

Richard Thomas Johnston, 42, marched away yesterday as a volunteer with a quota of selectees from Local Draft Board 244, 21-77 31st Ave., Astoria, to follow his two sons as members of the armed services of the United Nations.

Johnston, a World War veteran of 22-11 Steinway St., received the cheers and good wishes of his wife, two daughters and his Astoria neighbors.

"I feel fine," Johnston said as he expressed confidence that he would pass the physical examination. His eldest son, Richard Jr., 20, entered the army a month ago, and his youngest son, Thomas Edward, 17, joined the Royal Canadian Air Force three months ago.

Doctor Killed in Trying To Save Wounded Soldier

Cairo, Nov. 7 (U.P.)—Capt. Edward T. Stone of Washington, D. C., an American volunteer medical officer with the Dunham Light Infantry, was killed attempting to reach a wounded man lying in the open under terrific artillery and machine gun fire, it was announced today.

Stone was talking with an army chaplain, Capt. F. N. Carpenter, during a moment's respite, when a corporal reported a wounded man 200 yards away.

Despite the intense curtain of fire Captain Stone set out accompanied by a sergeant and a corporal. The party had covered only a few yards when a shell burst killed all three.

440 City Stores Warned On Price Violations

Warnings of criminal prosecution for failure to comply with maximum price regulations have been sent to 440 retailers in this city by Sylvan L. Joseph, regional administrator of the Office of Price Administration.

He also disclosed that 600 other cases were being studied for evidence of deliberate and willful violation of regulations.

Of 1,575 stores checked in a recent investigation, Mr. Joseph said, only 535 were found to be complying fully with the regulations.

IRISH BEAT ARMY, 13—0; L. S. U. BEATS FORDHAM

Notre Dame blanked Army, 13—0, at Yankee Stadium yesterday before a near capacity crowd, largest of the wartime football season. Louisiana State U. tucked away Fordham at the Polo Grounds, 26—13. Moravian romped through C. C. N. Y., 32—0. And there was good grief elsewhere, too, such as Navy's seven to Penn's zero and Colgate's 35 to Columbia's 26. Other notable scorings:

20	Brown	Holy Cross	14
13	Cornell	Yale	7
19	Dartmouth	Princeton	7
7	Duquesne	St. Mary's	7
75	Georgia	Florida	0
7	Indiana	Minnesota	0
6	Iowa	Wisconsin	0
19	Lafayette	Rutgers	13
35	Michigan	Harvard	7
18	Penn State	Syracuse	13

L. I. Soldier Dies in Crash

Neosho, Mo., Nov. 7 (U.P.)—Sgt. Rayond F. Burns, stationed at Camp Crowder, was killed today when a jeep in which he was riding crashed into a ditch. Burns' home was at Far Rockaway, L. I.

Rangoon Docks and Ships Hit by U. S. Bombers

New Delhi, Nov. 7 (U.P.)—A large force of United States Army bombers successfully attacked the harbor area of Rangoon yesterday, scoring hits on warehouses and a small ship at the Japanese occupied capital of Burma, it was announced today.

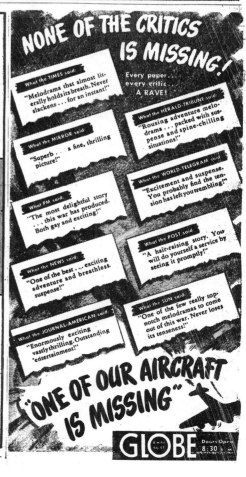

Motion Picture Theaters Play Important Part in War Effort

Take Tip From Britain And Relax in Movies

England Learned Usefulness of Screen To Boost the Spirits Early in Conflict

By JANE CORBY

In wartime more than ever, let's go to the movies! Why? Because entertainment and amusement in wartime are the vitamins of morale—they do for the war-weary spirit what A and D and B[1] complex do for the body. They bring relaxation, which is something with which a nation at war can do, and of all the means of amusement readily available to the public, soldier and civilian alike, there's nothing to top the movies.

In Britain, at the outbreak of the war, all the movie houses were shut. Then the ban was lifted, because the Government had found out that the British people could stand the bombings and the rationing better if they could laugh away an hour or two with Abbott and Costello, or worry about nothing more serious than whether or not Veronica Lake can really see out of the eclipsed eye.

Yes, the British know that the movies are an antidote even to incendiaries and crater holes and all-night alerts, and if Americans haven't, for the most part, had to find that out for themselves, they have at least discovered that for war-weariness, as a means of relaxation after a hard day's work, as an escape from the natural anxiety over the boys who are "somewhere" there is nothing in the world like the movies. The way that movie business has been upped all over Greater New York, according to the figures made public by various houses, shows that.

So, let's go to the movies. We can all do with a bit of strengthening of the morale. A quick look at the screens around town will help us make up our minds about what to see:

Springtime in the Rockies, having its premiere today at the Roxy, is a musical in Technicolor, all girls and dancing and laughter. Carmen Miranda and Betty Grable are both in it, and so are John Payne and Cesar Romero.

Road to Morocco, having its premiere today at the N. Y. Paramount, is triple-starred, with Bing Crosby, Bob Hope and Dorothy Lamour, gags and laughs and four new hit tunes.

The Navy Comes Through, new at the Criterion today, is a saga of the navy and the merchant marine, with thrilling sea fights.

Orchestra Wives has a top band—Glenn Miller's—in a top musical hit that has a gay plot. Ann Rutherford is one of six glamour girls who contribute a plentitude of charms.

Eyes in the Night is a murder mystery, with Edward Arnold starring as the blind sleuth who solves the crime, and "Friday," a new canine star, in the role of a seeing-eye dog.

The Major and the Minor gives Ginger Rogers a chance to show how cute a 12-year-old girl can be, for she plays a kid role that leads to frantically funny complications.

Wake Island is the rousing reenactment of the 14 days siege that will live forever. It's dynamite.

The Glass Key is a thriller and it really thrills. Veronica Lake, Alan Ladd and Brian Donlevy have the top roles and the story moves fast.

A Yank in Libya combines romance and laughs against the war drama in North Africa. There's a sinister sheik, an American war correspondent and a pretty girl, and Parkyakarkas, who looks after the comedy angle.

The Pride of the Yankees is the colorful life of Lou Gehrig, with Gary Cooper in the title role and all the thrill and excitement of baseball, with the re-enactment of events that are still alive in the memories of the majority.

Pardon My Sarong has Abbott and Costello having fun on a South Sea island, which is a funny idea in itself. The boys are zanies, all right.

Here We Go Again brings to the screen four radio characters that have been there before—Fibber McGee and Molly, Edgar Bergen and Charley McCarthy. There's a plot that serves to hold a lot of laughs together.

Desperate Journey is the breathtaking story of the adventures of five RAF members forced down in Germany. It has Errol Flynn, Ronald Reagan, Raymond Massey and other stars.

Talk of the Town is a romantic comedy, with Cary Grant and Jean Arthur—Cary's a fugitive, wanted for murder!

One of Our Aircraft Is Missing is the British-filmed tale of RAF fliers, forced to bail out over occupied Holland, and making their escape by means of the Dutch underground.

George Washington Slept Here is the lively screen dramatization of the play of the same name, with Jack Benny and Ann Sheridan piling laughs on laughs.

Now, Voyager presents a new Bette Davis, in this story of a young woman whose life has been all but spoiled by a selfish mother. Paul Henreid has the important male role.

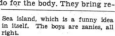

SONG AND DANCE TEAM Betty Grable and John Payne keep "Springtime in the Rockies," which opened today at the Roxy, in high gear despite certain romantic hurdles. Carmen Miranda is another member of the gorgeous cast.

DOROTHY LAMOUR, Bob Hope and Bing Crosby are on a "road" again, this time "The Road to Morocco," which opened at the N. Y. Paramount today. It's the setup you've asked for—and laughed at before—Lamour as the luscious native girl, Hope and Crosby as a pair of roistering vagabonds.

GOOGIE WITHERS will keep you on the edge of your seat in "One of Our Aircraft Is Missing," at the Globe Theater. She leads a bailed-out British bomber crew to safety through occupied Holland.

Jack Benny Picture A Continuous Laugh

By JANE CORBY

You'll laugh when Jack Benny goes upstairs and returns suddenly through the ceiling; you'll laugh when he falls into the old, disused but deep well; you'll laugh every time he just misses falling into the new well and laugh even harder when he finally does fall into it. If this gives you the idea that in "George Washington Slept Here" Jack Benny takes a lot of falls, that is correct. He falls and falls but he never flops! "G.W.S.H.," the Warner Brothers version of the Moss Hart and George S. Kaufman stage play, is a laugh hit from start to finish. It opened today at the Brooklyn Paramount.

With Jack Benny is Ann Sheridan, playing his wife, a nice and naive girl who longed for a home in the country furnished with antiques. The picture is all about how without waiting for Jack's approval she bought a convincingly dilapidated house because of its history: "George Washington slept here," and then broke the news gently to Jack, a fellow who liked living in the city. As the reluctant country gentleman Jack gives a perfect performance, and the wifely Ann, lovelier even than usual, shows a decided talent for comedy.

The story deals with the attempts of the pair to restore the shambles of a house to livability and to get a well that will provide water. But the nearby brook furnishes the only water for this cozy home for the duration of the film. In their efforts the pair are assisted by a lethargic caretaker played by Percy Kilbride who manages to surround Jack and Ann with piles of gravel and other restorative essentials at great expense—so great that bankruptcy finally faces the homemakers.

There's a disappointment for Ann when she learns that Washington never slept in the house, but Benedict Arnold did. There are comical complications when rich uncle Charles Coburn comes to visit and turns out to be penniless. There's an imp of a young nephew who adds to Benny's general misery and a meanie of a neighbor who makes an already difficult situation worse for Jack. There's a personable antique dealer who rouses Jack's jealousy when Ann appears to be taking him seriously, and altogether it's a completely hilarious picture.

VICTORY DRIVE UNDER WAY ON PLAZA ALLEYS

War Bonds, Stamps Given as Prizes In Unique Contest—Flatbush C Play Marks Reunion of Two Old Friends

By LOU E. COHEN

Victory bowling drives have been opened at the Plaza Bowling Center, as a means of selling war bonds and stamps. The top prize each month is to be a $25 war bond, paid for by the Plaza.

The contest operates as follows: Each bowler can roll on lanes 7, 8 and 9—which are the Victory Drives—all day Saturday, Sunday and holidays. The entry fee is 75 cents, as follows: 25 cents for three frames of big pins and the remainder into the prize fund.

If a bowler gets 70 or more in the three frames, he receives a 10-cent war stamp; for scores of 80 or better, there is a 25-cent war stamp, and for the high score of the month, or more 90-scores than anybody, there is a $25 war bond.

Whatever surplus funds there are will be awarded to the Red Cross, USO or any other war charitable organization as a contribution from the patrons of the Plaza Bowling Center.

Jack Meyer and Phil Eisenberg have been friends for 25 years. In recent years, however, the nature of their work took them in different routes. Last week, the Elite team in Flatbush C of the Brooklyn Eagle League came to the Keystone Recreation Center for its regular match—and for the first time in several years, Meyer and Eisenberg ran into each other. Meyer, it seems, is taking the place of his son, who bowled with Elite until drafted in the army; while Eisenberg is proprietor of the Keystone Recreation Center.

Syracuse women bowlers have pledged $4,000 to the National Bowlers Victory Legion . . . Joe Wilman and Adolph Carlson, two of Chicago's best pinmen, recently met in a formal match, Wilman winning by 1086—1043. They were going along even until the fifth game when Wilman shot 259, while Carlson "slipped" to 229 . . . The Curtiss-Wright Aviation plant at Buffalo has 208 sanctioned teams, while Bell Aircraft, also in Buffalo, has 231 units . . . George Markley, 70-year-old pin-setter in Milwaukee, recently set 112 games in one day.

LET 'ER ROLL!

Panthers Win in Sweep

The Panthers won three games from the Bedford Fishers in Borough Hall D at the Eagle Recreation, while M.A.R.S.A. blanked Hevey's Sparks, Kopper's Coke turned the same trick against the Central Paintmakers and the Carroll Juniors took two from the Pratt Postmen.

Scores:

Panthers				Bedford Fishers			
K'leman	143	139	89	Op'sano	124	—	—
Claps	110	—	113	J'menro	123	126	152
Anthony	173	142	125	P.Fi'etti	152	178	179
Stev'son	157	126	—	A.Fi'etti	179	165	133
Seeley	137	173	163	Balduc	174	134	138
L'Bruyere	—	134	133	Rella	—	176	131
Totals	720	714	623	Totals	752	779	733
M.A.R.S.A.				Hevey's Sparks			
Ge'mano	128	168	167	Por'nova	145	133	146
Favino	153	—	149	Freese	110	102	73
Franco	143	122	155	Monello	101	67	96
O'Brien	145	146	195	Ma'ma'n	114	141	167
Gulan	179	173	175	Carleo	157	164	156
Carbo	—	73	—				
Totals	748	682	841	Totals	635	607	638
Paintmakers				Kopper's Coke			
M'Mic'ele	87	—	103	Wallace	143	108	136
M'Aloney	106	191	112	Ritchie	166	146	135
Lib'tino	119	146	154	Pulcino	166	190	186
Di'stein	142	86	122	Sheerin	121	209	138
Gr'berg	137	172	192	Bahman	141	183	136
Didato	—	52	—				
Totals	591	647	683	Totals	737	836	731
Pratt Postmen				Carroll Juniors			
Keane	173	167	141	Monelli	155	164	168
Grau	124	—	115	Fusco	168	148	156
G'balvo	115	126	145	Cos'tino	167	123	147
Musto	113	185	151	DeVito	159	127	147
Meyers	130	178	171	Arcuri	191	153	138
Gehnrich	—	115	—				
Totals	654	771	723	Totals	840	715	746

Heim's Captures Lead

Heim's Tavern moved into first place in Bushwick D by downing Lawler Red in two out of three contests. Roberts Red and Blue also took two each, topping United Grocers and Lawler Blue.

Lawler Red				Heim's Tavern			
Johns'on	135	165	166	Cronin	172	209	118
Saccardi	142	154	170	Bell'ann	143	139	127
Wills	135	111	116	Miller	179	146	183
Busch	141	140	150	Illg	154	133	157
Wagner	190	157	156	Fie	160	143	161
Totals	743	727	758	Totals	808	770	746
United Grocers				Roberts Red			
W'r'man	121	148	142	Sc'nable	146	108	135
Maenno	126	147	108	Reilly	148	221	180
Scott	123	128	109	Walken	94	76	88
Minden	116	127	168	Gunther	117	157	112
H'cliffe	131	93	168	Johnson	135	218	134
Totals	617	643	795	Totals	640	780	649
Lawler Blue				Roberts Blue			
P'liague	156	128	154	Lutz	108	—	149
Cupesp	122	128	145	Hess	110	88	133
Br'mann	133	121	129	Cussics	178	155	175
Jacruso	133	161	136	Bresler	149	152	145
Staib	142	202	155	Walder	176	154	160
				Adams	—	97	—
Totals	687	741	719	Totals	727	642	762

DOES IT AGAIN—Andy Varipapa, Brooklyn resident and the greatest exhibition bowler in the U. S., rolled his 50th 300-game yesterday while bowling against George Huffman at Muncie, Ind.

United Hunts Entries

FOR FRIDAY

FIRST RACE—$1,500; claiming; two-year-olds; six furlongs.

P.P.	Horse	Jockey	Wt.
1	xxCherry T	Rienzi	104
2	xxLight Dress	Clingman	104
3	November	No boy	109
4	xxSusan Constant	No boy	104
5	Isolation	Rogers	112
6	xxBayborough	No boy	104
7	Bottle Imp	No boy	112
8	Light Chaser	Schmidl	112
9	xxLovely Delores	Crowther	104

SECOND RACE—$1,500; claiming; two-year-olds; six furlongs.

P.P.	Horse	Jockey	Wt.
1	xxTropics	Campbell	107
2	Chief of Statff	No boy	112
3	xxFly Whisk	Rienzi	107
4	Calvert	No boy	112
5	xxHalf Grand	Cost	107
6	Orpheum	Rogers	112
7	Gaykis	Wall	109
8	xxKievres	No boy	104

THIRD RACE—$1,500; the Belmont and up; two miles.

P.P.	Horse	Jockey	Wt.
1	xAfrican Boy	O'Neill	142
2	aKellsboro	Penrod	147
3	bSimilar	No boy	147
4	Mesa	Cruz	147
5	bSt. Patricks Day	No boy	147
6	bFelt Slipper	No boy	147
7	xxMad Policy	Owen	143
8	xxEmmas Pet	Malan	135
9	cBaskeroll	Brown	139
10	xaTioga	No boy	137
11	xcRed Rufus	Gallagher	130
12	aUntermyer and R. V. N. Gambill entry.		
13	bR. K. Mellon and W. Post entry.		
14	CC. M. Cline and Mrs. E. R. Owen entry.		

FOURTH RACE—$1,500; claiming; three-year-olds and up; maidens; seven furlongs.

P.P.	Horse	Jockey	Wt.
1	Night Bird II	Robertson	115
2	aPennyroyal	No boy	109
3	bSnooks Winters	No boy	118
4	Recap	Atkinson	115
5	Neutral	Rienzi	107
6	bByrd Boy	No boy	151
7	aGrand Venture	Schmidl	112
8	xxHegemon	Crowther	107
9	aMrs. D. A. Buckley entry.		
10	bK. N. Gilipin entry.		

FIFTH RACE—$1,500; the Cherry Malotte Steeplechase; three-year-olds and up; about two miles.

P.P.	Horse	Jockey	Wt.
1	Frederic II	No boy	145
2	Compass Rose	Penrod	131
3	xAlcadale	Gallagher	134
4	xxAhmisk	Owen	130
5	Burma Road	No boy	131
6	Knights Quest	Passmore	148
7	xMad Policy	No boy	140
8	xSimoon	Smiley	137

SIXTH RACE—$2,500; the Turf and Field; three-year-olds and up; one mile.

P.P.	Horse	Jockey	Wt.
1	Scotch Trap	Nodarse	111
2	Sundial	Atkinson	105
3	Bisby	No boy	105
4	Enterprise	Robertson	111
5	xxLlanero	Clingman	106
6	Bulldinger	No boy	115

SEVENTH RACE—$1,500; claiming; three-year-olds and up; seven furlongs.

P.P.	Horse	Jockey	Wt.
1	Port Harmony	Atkinson	105
2	xxMaechance	Rienzi	115
3	Hubbub	Smith	113
4	Cousin Man	Rogers	113
5	Grand Party	Schmidl	111
6	xxRoman Flag	No boy	111
7	Dress Boot	Robertson	117
8	xxBlue Warrior	No boy	111
9	Cheesestraw	No boy	111

EIGHTH RACE—$1,500; claiming; three-year-olds and up; one mile.

P.P.	Horse	Jockey	Wt.
1	Who Calls	Atkinson	108
2	xxHillblond	Rienzi	109
3	xxHere Goes	No boy	106
4	xxShipmate	Rienzi	106
5	xxxKey Man	Cost	107
6	At Play	No boy	114
7	Castigada	No boy	111

xThree pounds, xxfive pounds, xxxseven pounds.
Track fast.
Horses listed in order of post position.

Rockingham Park Entries

FOR FRIDAY

FIRST RACE—$800; claiming; maidens; two-year-olds; six furlongs

P.P.	Wt.	P.P.	Wt.
1 Still Pond	118	7 xMaster Pete	113
2 xLove Venture	110	8 Miami Sun	116
3 Miss Cold	115	9 Risanda	115
4 Esther Mac	115	10 Timothy C.	118
5 xFly Escort	113	11 Caroline F.	115
6 Jockstone	113		

SECOND RACE—$800; claiming; three-year-olds and up; six furlongs.

P.P.	Wt.	P.P.	Wt.
1 All Crystal	112	9 Centuple	116
2 xClassic Beauty	99	10 Rolls Buzzy	107
3 xCrown Gem	102	11 Tripit	113
4 xTwo Tops	102	12 Prince A. O.	107
5 Hunting Home	108	13 xMalinda B.	99
6 Maydig	107	14 Hardship	106
7 Don Pecos	113	15 Flying Silver	113
8 Count Cotton	110	16 Cleo Louise	104

THIRD RACE—$800; claiming; three-year-olds and up; six furlongs.

P.P.	Wt.	P.P.	Wt.
1 Reversal	113	6 xNot Yet	103
2 Bell Bottom	109	7 Old Wick	107
3 xMintson	111	8 Trimmed	111
4 xWithin	103	9 Canterup	108
5 xFair Hero	106	10 Lina's Son	116

FOURTH RACE—$800; claiming; two-year-olds; one and one-sixteenth miles.

P.P.	Wt.	P.P.	Wt.
1 Justa Woofing	112	6 xBurgoo Prince	107
2 Bit of Sugar	115	7 Private Earl	112
3 Is I Aint	118	8 Mokananne	118
4 xFlying Ned	113	9 xGhost Hunt	113
5 Southern Yam	115		

FIFTH RACE—$800; claiming; three-year-olds and up: mile and one-sixteenth.

P.P.	Wt.	P.P.	Wt.
1 xGentle Savage	108	6 Dark Level	113
2 Guardsman	113	7 Whiscendent	107
3 xBoats Crew	106	8 Apropos	110
4 Ask Me	110	9 Soberano	113
5 xDon Moss	106	10 xOvando	106

SIXTH RACE—$900; claiming; the Shore Road; three-year-olds and up; mile and one-sixteenth.

P.P.	Wt.	P.P.	Wt.
1 Rambunctious	115	4 Grand Day	115
2 Anzac	109	5 Gold Bill	118
3 Display Style	106	6 xPanthere C'k	110
		7 Texalite	106

SEVENTH RACE—$800; claiming; three-year-olds and up; mile and one-sixteenth.

P.P.	Wt.	P.P.	Wt.
1 xArmy Grey	105	5 Light Banset	101
2 xYannie Sid	105	6 Labeled Win	110
3 Hazel Lee	113	7 Catomar	110
4 xSmart Banset	101		

EIGHTH RACE—$900; claiming; four-year-olds and up: mile and one-sixteenth.

P.P.	Wt.	P.P.	Wt.
1 Off Shore	113	8 Noble Boy	113
2 Cosse	118	9 Mitza	110
3 Flaming High	113	10 Clapair	113
4 Hasty Wire	113	11 xSaxonian	111
5 Temulac	113	12 Gaspar deSalo	116
6 xDizzy B	108	13 xPilatesun	111
7 Ranchos Boy	116		

xApprentice allowance claimed.

xApprentice allowance claimed.

FINANCIAL

Stock Market Firm in Tone

Price Shifts Narrow In Moderate Trading

The stock market opened on a firm note today and continued so throughout the session. Prices changes were usually small and trading was not large, but early gains were held well for the most part and some issues moved forward again in afternoon dealings. Some of the so-called war group were down as much as a point in morning dealings, but large parts of the declines had been recouped late in the day. Some of the rail issues were fractionally off, but New York Central proved an exception with nearly a point gain due to the dividend declaration. International Telephone continued active and Canadian Pacific was also largely traded in.

Motors were usually steady and utility commons were holding around the previous close. Oils and mercantiles were not much changed.

Several issues made new highs for the year, including Dow Chemical, Commercial Credit, Commercial Investment Trust, and Allied Stores. American Can and Columbia Gas equaled their highs.

Bond Trading Dull

Trading in listed corporate bonds today was along dull lines. Prices moved within narrow limits and there were few changes to indicate any particular trend. Some of the rails displayed a firm tone at the opening, but many were unchanged to fractionally lower and movements after initial dealings were out of the way were irregular. New York Central refundings were among the firmer spots. Childs Co. 5s were weak in the industrials, dropping around three points.

In the foreign lists, bonds of occupied countries were firm to higher, but trading was light. Norwegians showed gains of around a point.

U. S. Treasury bonds were quiet and little changed.

Green Point Bank Honors Employes

The board of trustees of the Green Point Savings Bank, Brooklyn, has just honored with a special luncheon two of the bank's officers who have just completed 25 years of service. They are Nelson H. Vogel and William H. Noeth.

George W. Felter, president of the bank, on behalf of the board presented each guest of honor with a suitably engraved watch.

Mr. Vogel and Mr. Noeth came to the bank during the busy days of the first World War; both have progressed side by side through various clerical positions in the bank, and both were made assistant secretaries in 1932.

Companies Issue Earnings Reports

U. S. Gypsum Company reported today for nine months ended Sept. 30, 1942, net profit $3,878,148 after Federal income and excess profits taxes, etc., equal to $2.90 a share on common. This compares with a revised net profit of $5,045658, or $3.88 a common share, in the like 1941 period.

CERTAIN-TEED PRODUCTS CORPORATION—Nine months ended Sept. 30 net profit $800,797, equal to $10.96 a preferred share, against $1,145,665, or $15.68 a share, year ago.

TWIN COACH COMPANY—Nine months ended Sept. 30 net profit $522,235, or $1.10 a share, against $511,326, or $1.08 year ago.

Freight Traffic Drops

Washington, Nov. 12—Loadings of revenue freight during week ended Nov. 7 totaled 829,490 cars, a decrease of 60,969 cars from previous week and also a decrease of 44,092 cars from like week a year ago, according to reports to Association of American Railroads.

Cotton Seat Sold

Arrangements were completed today for sale of a New York Cotton Exchange membership at $3,000, up $225 from the previous transaction.

War Financing Drive Widened

Treasury Will Solicit Vast Sum From Public

Washington, Nov. 12 (U.P.)—Secretary of Treasury Henry Morgenthau Jr., announced today a new policy of Treasury war borrowing under which a determined effort will be made to obtain the major part of Government funds from the public rather than from banks beginning Nov. 30.

Government borrowing during December will be on an unprecedented scale, he told a press conference.

Morgenthau said he has set up a super-organization to promote Government borrowing from the public through an active selling and advertising campaign in which he has enlisted sales and advertising executives of private industry.

Involve Large Sums

He indicated future financial operations would be in very large sums, and that offerings of securities probably would be made not oftener than bi-monthly. The program includes a number of "tap" issues that will be available at all times for large investors, corporations and small investors.

He listed among the organizations enlisted to promote the gigantic borrowing program the New York Stock Exchange, Investment Bankers Association, National Association of Securities Dealers, Government Securities Dealers Association, Association of Stock Exchange Firms and the American Bankers Association.

OWI to Co-operate

He said he also was enlisting Elmer Davis, head of the Office of War Information, to make widespread announcements of Government security offerings.

Leaders in private industry allied with the new Treasury program include R. H. Grant, vice president in charge of sales of the General Motors Corp., who will organize a selling group to handle the securities and will advise Morgenthau on selling methods, as securities are offered. Miller McClintock, executive director, and Harold Thomas, vice chairman, of the Advertising Council, will advise Morgenthau in advertising new issues through the widest channels.

Morgenthau said first announcements of the amounts and kinds of securities to be offered Nov. 30 would be made next week.

Papsdorf Urges Club Funds Used For Bonds Gifts

Herman L. Papsdorf, president of the Hamburg Savings Bank has just announced that the bank will again distribute one of the largest Christmas Clubs in Brooklyn and Queens. The bank has already begun the preparation of over 21,000 vouchers for mailing to members who will receive over $740,000.

"Last year," said Mr. Papsdorf, "our Christmas funds were distributed just prior to Pearl Harbor and there was a tremendous increase in the purchase of defense bonds out of Christmas Club money. If we can judge by the great increase in the sales of war bonds during the year 1942, I believe that many more Christmas Club members will purchase bonds this year. In addition a bond makes a splendid Christmas gift."

"Many people are today earning a far better wage than ever before and there is a strong human tendency to indulge in certain luxuries and spending not heretofore possible. I feel it my duty to emphasize the need for continued and greater saving in these times. Disregarding for the moment the heavier tax payments we shall all be obliged to meet in the coming year, it is wise to look ahead a bit further to the day of victory and peace, when we shall return to our normal pursuits and once more be in the market for the purchase of a home, of a new car, refrigerators, radios and all of the things which have gone to make our great nation the best place to live on the face of the earth."

Mr. Papsdorf announced that the bank's two offices at Myrtle and Knickerbocker Aves. and Fulton and Crescent Sts. will be open on the evenings of Nov. 23, 24, 25 and 27 for the convenience of Christmas Club members who desire their Christmas funds before the regular date of cashing, which is Dec. 1.

Four Pipe Line Companies Propose Unification Plan

Plan for unification of Buckeye Pipe Line Company, Indiana Pipe Line Company, Northern Pipe Line Company and New York Transit Company will be presented to stockholders of the various companies for action in near future and if approved it is intended to make it effective by Jan. 1, 1943.

Under plan, Buckeye Pipe Line Company will be recapitalized with 1,352,000 new shares of capital stock and stockholders of constituent companies will receive new shares of Buckeye.

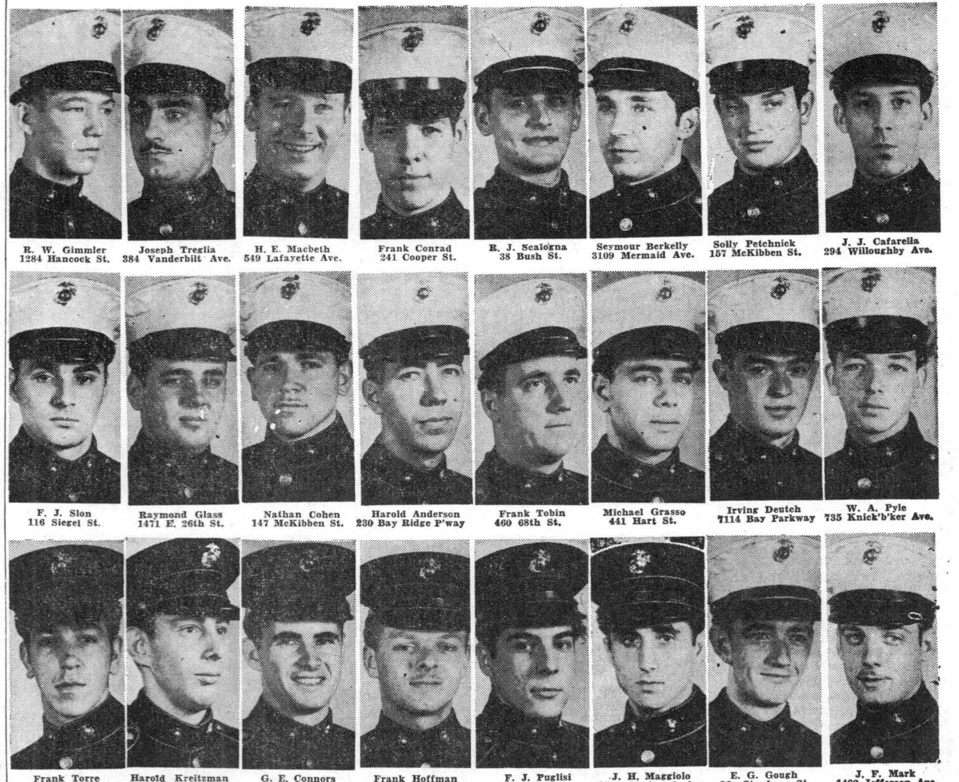

R. W. Gimmler, 1284 Hancock St. — Joseph Treglia, 384 Vanderbilt Ave. — H. E. Macbeth, 549 Lafayette Ave. — Frank Conrad, 241 Cooper St. — R. J. Scalogna, 38 Bush St. — Seymour Berkelly, 3109 Mermaid Ave. — Solly Petchnick, 157 McKibben St. — J. J. Cafarella, 294 Willoughby Ave.

F. J. Slon, 116 Siegel St. — Raymond Glass, 1471 E. 26th St. — Nathan Cohen, 147 McKibben St. — Harold Anderson, 230 Bay Ridge P'way — Frank Tobin, 460 68th St. — Michael Grasso, 441 Hart St. — Irving Deutch, 7114 Bay Parkway — W. A. Pyle, 735 Knick'b'ker Ave.

Frank Torre, 3712 Flatlands Ave. — Harold Kreitzman, 170 Quentin Road — G. E. Connors, 817 68th St. — Frank Hoffman, 945 DeKalb Ave. — F. J. Puglisi, 1580 76th St. — J. H. Maggiolo, 3501 Nostrand Ave. — E. G. Gough, 261 Stanhope St. — J. F. Mark, 1482 Jefferson Ave.

James Cavanaugh, 390 12th St. — V. J. Clarke, 48 Nortern St. — Augustus Slafani, 1778 W. 9th St. — H. L. Pearlstone, 1647 Sterling Place

THESE 28 Brooklynites have joined the marines during the past month and are now stationed at Parris Island, S. C., for recruit training. The pictures are published as a salute to the Marine Corps, which observed its 167 anniversary Tuesday.

Corp. Robert F. Fitzgerald, stationed at Fort Bliss, Texas, has been assigned to attend Officer Candidate School at Fort Monmouth, N. J.

Raymond C. Glass Jr. of 1471 E. 26th St. has been sent to Parris Island, S. C., to receive basic training with the marines. His brother, Edward, is an apprentice seaman training at Great Lakes, Ill.

Jack Axelowitz of 152 S. 8th St. has arrived at the air base at Sioux Falls, N. D.

Pvt. Arthur M. Sheehan of 519 5th St. has been assigned to the air depot at Oklahoma City, Okla.

W. B. Anderson

William Neilson

Awarded silver wings of army airmen at Randolph Field, Texas, were Walter B. Anderson of 683 51st St., William Neilson of 240 8th St., William R. Skeath of 335 95th St. and Harry E. Stengele, also of Brooklyn.

W. R. Skeath

H. E. Stengele

Willard John Dawley of 1000 E. 19th St. was recently graduated from the marine aviation radio school at Jacksonville, Fla., as the honor man in his class.

Solomon J. Zoller of 365 Lincoln Place has been promoted to lieutenant colonel at Fort Dix, N. J.

John Flood of 1158 Sterling Place has been assigned to drill instructors school with the Army Air Corps at Miami Beach, Fla. He attended St. John's Prep.

Edwin N. Buthorne of 32-74 33d St., Astoria, has been graduated as a second lieutenant from the Officer Candidate School at Fort Sill, Okla., and has been assigned to Fort Meade, Md.

E. N. Buthorne

H. F. Skelly

Pvt. Henry F. Skelly of 1131 New York Ave. has been graduated from the air corps school at Kessler Field, Miss., and has been assigned to Greenville, S. C.

Pvt. William Winkelseth of 244 Steuben St. has reported to Camp Blanding, Fla., for training. His brother George is stationed at Camp Davis, N. C.

John Cafarella of 294 Willoughby Ave. and his brother Howard have enlisted in the Marine Corps and are receiving basic training at Parris Island, S. C.

L. J. Barnard

E. F. Barnard

When it was announced that Sgt. Leonard J. Barnard of 246 50th St. was killed in action overseas, his brother, Corp. Edward B. Barnard, stationed at Fort Sam Houston, Texas, returned to comfort the bereaved mother.

Second Lt. William P. Goodwin of 1666 W. 2d St., recently commissioned at Victorville, Cal., is now instructing bombardier students at that base. He was a football star at St. John's Prep.

Pvt. Nathan Silverstein of 588 Belmont Ave. has arrived at Fort Benjamin Harrison, Ind., for basic training in finance.

Charles De Muria of 7418 14th Ave. has been transferred from Camp Stewart, Ga., to Camp Jackson, S. C. He was recently made private first class.

Pvt. Francis J. Rogers of 395 Fenimore St., in the Marine Corps, has been sent to New River, N. C., for special training.

Gerard Fremgen of 816 Herkimer St., a graduate of Alexander Hamilton High School, has enlisted in the marines and is stationed at Parris Island, S. C.

Giacomo F. Bertuccio of 1975 W. 7th St. has completed a course of signal instructions at Fort Monmouth, N. J.

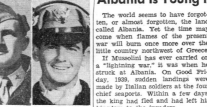

Reporting for special courses at Fort Knox, Ky., were John A. Cardin of 2064 W. 5th St., P. Laurence Masterson of 398 Prospect Ave., Arthur Rosen of 3809 Atlantic Ave. and Alvin W. Witcher of 483 Quincy St.

Pvt. William Obermayer of Brooklyn is now stationed with the intelligence department at the army flying school at Pecos, Texas.

Corp. Gilbert Amgott of 205 Bridge St. and Corp. Sherman A. Harmin of 1782 Coney Island Ave. have been enrolled in a signal course at Camp Murphy, Fla.

Two Queens fathers, veterans of the first World War, have joined their sons in the present army. John Treloar of 225-18 Merrick Boulevard, Laurelton, followed his son George, and Richard T. Johnston of 22-11 Steinway St., Astoria, has joined two sons.

Lt. John J. Killian of 271 New York Ave., son of Post Office Inspector S. J. Killian, has been promoted to captain with the 18th Field Artillery, Fort Sill, Okla. Captain Killian attended Boys High and the University of Illinois. He was member of the R. O. T. C.

Capt. John J. Killian

News for publication in this department should be addressed to the "Fighting Men" Editor, Brooklyn Eagle, Johnson and Adams Sts., Brooklyn, N. Y.

BUY U. S. WAR BONDS AND SAVINGS STAMPS

An inventor has added a catcher for trimmings to a motor-operated hedge trimmer.

Idle for almost 15 years a mercury ore deposit in Peru will be reopened.

Uncle Ray's Corner For Boys and Girls

Albania Is Young Nation but People Are of Ancient Race

The world seems to have forgotten, or almost forgotten, the land called Albania. Yet the time may come when flames of the present war will burn once more over the little country northwest of Greece.

If Mussolini has ever carried on a "lightning war," it was when he struck at Albania. On Good Friday, 1939, sudden landings were made by Italian soldiers at the four chief seaports. Within a few days, the king had fled and had left his kingdom to the invaders.

If you look at a map of southern Europe, you will notice that boot-shaped Italy has its "heel" close to Albania. Albania's population is only about 1,000,000. The area is a bit more than 10,000 square miles.

In one sense, Albania is a young nation. It became a free country in 1913—only 29 years ago.

From another point of view, it is one of the oldest nations in Europe. People of Albanian stock have lived there from the dawn of written history. During thousands of years, they have been under the power of Romans, Bulgars, Turks and other conquerors.

Portrait and statue of the Albanian hero, George Kastriota.

There is another name for the Albanians. They are classed as "Shkypetars," and are described as "a blond race, whiter than the Serbs or Bulgars." The meaning of "Shkypetars" is believed to be "Sons of the Mountain Eagle."

Albanians are mountain dwellers, and live chiefly by farming and raising livestock. They are the only people in Europe who are, at present, divided into tribes and clans.

The tribes and clans have kept a sense of freedom through all the time their land has been held by other nations. No matter who might claim the right to rule, they have lived in their mountains and have carried on their simple life very much as they chose.

When the Turks were spreading over southeastern Europe, the Albanians grew worried. The chiefs of their tribes joined together and made war, with George Kastriota as their leader. The Turks gained power in the end, but Kastriota held them off for many years, and became a hero to his people. His fame has lasted during the 500 years which have passed since he did his work.

(For HISTORY or TRAVEL section of your scrapbook.)

Tomorrow:

Uncle Ray

If you want a free copy of the illustrated leaflet, "Your Body at Work," send a stamped self-addressed envelope to Uncle Ray in care of this newspaper.

3 SECTIONS

BROOKLYN EAGLE

EVERYWHERE 5c

Weather—Continued cold today. Sunset, 5:38; Dimout, 6:08.

102d YEAR • No. 317 • DAILY AND SUNDAY

BROOKLYN, N. Y., SUNDAY, NOV. 15, 1942

NAZIS SABOTAGE BASE AT BIZERTE

U.S., Jap Warships Fight Running Battle

Rickenbacker Cheats Death Again; Is in Good Condition

Saved With Six Others After 24 Days on Raft

Washington, Nov. 14 (U.P.)—Capt. Eddie Rickenbacker, who cheated death many times on the ground and in the air, has done it again, the Navy Department announced today.

Twenty-four days after he disappeared in the South Pacific on a secret flying mission for the War Department, the navy said today, he had been found—alive and in good condition—on a rubber life raft 600 miles north of Samoa.

The man who drove the tires off racing automobiles as a youth, who fought German planes in the First World War when the odds were seven to one against him and who only a year and nine months ago, survived an air crash which killed eight others, had come through again.

Sharing the indestructible Rickenbacker's luck in his latest adventure were six others of the eight-man crew whose United States Army bomber was forced down in the Pacific wastes by lack of fuel last Oct. 21.

One Member of Crew Dies

An eighth member of the crew—Sgt. Alexander Kaczmarcyk of Torrington, Conn.—died in Capt. Rickenbacker's little yellow life raft several days ago and was buried at sea.

With Rickenbacker when a Navy PBY flying boat found him were Col. Hans C. Adamson, the pilot, and Pvt. John F. Bartek. Adamson's condition was also described as good, but the Navy said Bartek was in a serious condition, presumably from exposure. He is expected to recover, however.

Meanwhile, another PBY had located three other members of the crew, Lt. James C. Whitaker, Lt. John J. De Angelus and Staff Sgt. James Reynolds—on a small island in the same general area. Their condition was not immediately as-

Continued on Page 11

PICTURE OF A HAPPY WOMAN—Mrs. Eddie Rickenbacker receives the glad news.

Capt. Eddie Rickenbacker

NAVY REPORTS BOTH SIDES SUFFER LOSSES

Clash Seen as Start Of New Attempt to Retake Guadalcanal

Washington Nov. 14 (U.P.)—American warships are engaged in a running battle in the Solomons area with a Japanese fleet, which apparently is starting a new attempt to dislodge United Sates forces defending the vital airfield on Guadalcanal Island, the navy disclosed today.

Except to note that "both sides have suffered losses," the navy gave no details of the new action. Observers believed, however, that it comprised a number of hit-and-run fights rather than a toe-to-toe slugging match between the two fleets.

This belief was based largely on the fact that the communique referred to "a series of naval engagements," as well as to "the battle." The series commenced on the night of Nov. 12-13 and is still in progress, the communique said.

Followed Bombardment

The battle began only a few hours after U. S. warships had shelled Japanese positions on Guadacanal for 10 hours Thursday. That bombardment, reported by the navy yesterday, was interrupted only when a fleet of 31 enemy torpedo and fighter planes attacked the warships. Thirty of the enemy planes were shot down.

"No details will be reported while the battle is in progress," today's communique said. "To announce details of these actions while the battle is in progress would furnish the enemy with information of definite value to him."

It had been known for some time that the Japanese were concentrating their forces in the Northern Solomons, undoubtedly in prepara-

Continued on Page 7

AAA THREAT TO AXIS—Algerian and American Allies converse after United Nations force lands near Oran without opposition. Note American flag insignia on officer's sleeve. These burnoused and turbanned natives can be tough and vicious fighters against the Axis, if they choose. Photo was radioed from London.

AXIS LANDING MORE TROOPS BY LAND, SEA

Allies Mass at Border For Headlong Push—Planes Pace Attack

London, Nov. 14 (U.P.)—The battle of Tunisia, a sharp knife pointed at the soft underside of the European Axis, went forward tonight with air power leading the way for occupation by the British First Army.

Royal Air Force fliers with the British Eight Army pursuing the Afrika Korps ranged far westward and reported that the Germans in Tunisia had begun sabotaging installations at Bizerte, strategic Tunisian port.

[A dispatch dated Allied Headquarters, North Africa, said Allied troops moving toward a headlong push across Tunisia are still on the Algerian side of the frontier, consolidating the landing of new troops and equipment.

[Lt. Gen. Dwight Eisenhower, commander of the Allied forces in North Africa, went to Algiers and then returned to direct personally this new phase of operations.

[Additional landings of Axis forces in Tunisia—mostly Italians—were reported continuing by land and sea. It was assumed that the Royal Navy would cope with the seaward landings.]

(With regard to Axis landings in Tunisia, latest estimates here were that no more than 3,000 troops had arrived—most of them paratroopers and ground forces.)

French troops garrisoned in Tunisia were said to be engaged in bitter battles with the Germans while awaiting assistance from Britain's strong first army, last reported officially at Bone, 50 miles from the Tunisian frontier.

(In Washington, the War Department announced that Allied forces advancing from Algiers toward

Continued on Page 7

F. D. R. HAILS A. E. F. CHIEF

Washington, Nov. 14 (U.P.)—President Roosevetl today messaged Lt. Gen. Dwight D. Eisenhower, commander in chief of the North African operations, that the "highly sucessful accomplishments" of his forces were reassuring to the nation because they demonstrated perfect co-operation between the British and Americans.

Boro Gunner Tells How Lone Tank Bowled Over 50 Vehicles in Oran

By PHIL AULT

Oran, Algiers, Nov. 12—(Delayed)—(U.P.)—A single American medium tank went on a rampage in the center of Oran for half an hour Tuesday morning, rammed and destroyed three 75 mm. guns and 50 motor vehicles and emerged from the city with its armor plate pockmarked but with the French guns hanging from its front.

The crew of the tank, a General Grant, was exhausted when I talked with them four miles outside the city. Led by a sergeant, they had become separated from their unit and penetrated the city all alone, hours before other units entered.

The tank was ordered to smash a road-block set up near the Lasenia Airport south of Oran at 8 a.m.

It rumbled through the road-block at 20 miles an hour and ran point-blank into a mobile 75 standing in the middle of the road.

Boro Man Is Gunner

Corp. Bernard J. Kessel of 1640 Ocean Ave., Brooklyn, who mans the tank's own 75, explained that he had no time to load it.

"So we rammed him full speed,"

Continued on Page 7

RISING CURBS ON BUSES MAY REVIVE TROLLEYS

Fewer Vehicles, More Passengers, ODT Crackdown Cited

Brooklyn's bus travelers, a growing army of nearly half a million passengers a day, may have to go back to the old-fashioned trolley car, officials of the Board of Transportation indicated yesterday.

Increasing needs and restrictions of the war effort are responsible. Spencer S. Hamilton, assistant general superintendent in charge of surface transportation for the board in Brooklyn, with offices at 385 Flatbush Ave. Extension, pointed out that the Office of Defense Transportation already had ordered private bus lines in Manhattan and elsewhere to reduce bus operation by 15 percent, as a means of reducing the use of gasoline, tires and other materials. A similar

Continued on Page 8

Deny Guiana Invason

Rio de Janeiro, Nov. 14 (U.P.)—Official quarters today denied a report circulated by the German-controlled Paris radio that Brazilian forces had invaded French Guiana.

YALE BEATS TIGER, 13-6; B. C. RIPS FORDHAM, 56-6

Football continued upon its own war endeavor yesterday, with Yale beating Princeton, 13-6, at Columbia's Baker Field. Brooklyn College was happy with a 7-7 tie against C. C. N. Y. Michigan's great line mowed down Notre Dame's slants at Notre Dame, 32-20. Navy torpedoed Columbia at Annapolis to the tune of 13-9. Boston College went on a rampage through the "Blocks of Granite" of Fordham, 56-6. Manhattan finished up on the short end of the score against Jimmy Crowley's N. C. Pre-Flight team, 17-0.

Other scores were:

19	Army	V. P. I.	7
21	Cornell	Dartmouth	19
7	Harvard	Brown	0
44	Ohio State	Illinois	20
20	Wisconsin	Norththwestern	19
14	Colgate	Syracuse	0

Boro Career Man Gets City Tax Post

Peter Leckler of 120 E. 89th St., Brooklyn's career man in the City Tax Department, yesterday was appointed a member of the City Tax Commission at $9,000 a year by Mayor LaGuardia.

Leckler has been a tax assessor since 1923, and before that was a school teacher. Mayor LaGuardia, swearing him into office, complimented him as "a career man who has proven his worth, and his promotion from the ranks is in line with the policy I plan to continue as long as I remain in the job."

William Wirt Mills was appointed president of the commission at $12,000 a year. He had been acting president since president Joseph Lilly entered the armed service.

During the swearing in ceremonies the Mayor remarked that New York City's financial situation is not as bad as that in many other cities.

'Twon't Be a Fit Day For Man Nor Beast

Keep your overcoat buttoned today, but not around the hanger in the clothes closet. If you have not yet put anti-freeze solution in your car's radiator, this may be sad news by the time you read it, for the Weather Bureau predicted continued cold weather for today, and the strong winds that made the thermometer drop last night will keep on blowing.

Lehman Names Bleakley To Probe Compensation

Governor Lehman yesterday named William F. Bleakley, who opposed him for the Governorship on the Republican ticket in 1936, as a Moreland Act commissioner to investigate alleged abuses of the Workmen's Compensation Act.

Previously three urgent requests for an investigation, sent by Mayor LaGuardia, had been rejected by the Governor.

Cop Pleads for Toy Gun Bandit Driven to Holdup by Kin's Poverty

Police Detective William F. Fruin of the Butler St. precinct has a heart. So Francis Reilly, 25, a peddler, of 324 Prospect Ave., may get off lightly on a charge of assault and robbery. The answer comes on Monday, when Reilly faces a hearing in Brooklyn Felony Court.

Fruin's police mind was prompted to quick action by the screams of a woman rushing out of Henry Benter's butcher store at 76 Nevins St. Friday afternoon. With Detective Francis Connelly, he rushed in and found Benter holding a man in a hammerlock on the floor. The detectives saw the butcher's prisoner was the same man they had noticed pacing up and down in front of the store for half an hour or more.

A search of the prisoner yielded a toy gun and a note. The prisoner was Reilly, whose police record consisted of one conviction and a suspended sentence for peddling without a license in Nassau County.

The note read: "Dear Wife Anna—Please don't hold this act against me. I am fed up with living the way we are. If you were wise, you would have left me a long time ago. I love you and the kiddies. —Frank."

Fruin learned there are two little Reillys and a third is soon to be added. When Reilly was arraigned before Magistrate Hirsimaki in Felony Court yesterday. Fruin told the court the whole story—a lot more than required by strict adherence to police duty.

He pointed out that the Reilly family was in desperate straits when Reilly decided on his rash act. Benter said Reilly had staged an attempted holdup, with the woman present. Benter felled the would-be bandit with a blow, hammerlocked him and told the woman to scream for the police.

Magistrate Hirsimaki set the hearing for Monday and fixed bail at $1,000, after Reilly had pleaded not guilty.

2 DIE IN CRASH OF POLICE CAR CHASING SPEEDER

Cop, Store Manager Killed at Long Beach Taking Money to Bank

Special to the Brooklyn Eagle

Long Beach, Nov. 14—A policeman and a store manager were instantly killed and another policeman was injured seriously this afternoon when a polise car, on the way to a bank with the store's money, detoured to pursue a speeder and hit a telegraph pole on Lido Road, near the new naval station.

The dead were Patrolman Henry Horton, 50, of 525 E. Hudson St., Long Beach, and Harry Triebeg, 38, of 25 Long Beach Blvd., Long Beach.

The injured man is Patrolman Arthur Dacey, 50, of 518 W. Hudson St., Long Beach. He is in Long Beach Hospital with three broken ribs and other injuries.

Horton, who was president of the Long Beach Patrolmen's Benevolent Association, was driving the car when it started from the A. & P. store for the National City Bank branch on Park Ave., with Dacey in front beside him and Triebeg, assistant store manager, in the back, holding a bag with the store's money.

On Park Ave. at Edwards St. another car sped past the police car, going, one witness said, "at least 65 miles an hour." Horton turned his car in pursuit for the speeder and followed him beyond the city limit and along Lido Road. While negotiating an S curve about a mile from Lido Beach, the police skidded sidewise into a telegrapth pole.

Dacey managed to summon help and Nassau County police responded. The bag with the money, amount not disclosed, was kept in police custody.

San Salvador, Vichy Break

San Salvador, Nov. 14 (U.P.)—The Foreign Office announced today that San Salvador has severed relations with Vichy France.

Catholic Hierarchy Issues Post-War Plan

Prelates Assert Profit Element in Industry Must Be 'Subservient to the Common Good'

Washington, Nov. 14 (U.P.)—The Catholic hierarchy of the United States asserted tonight that "in the post-war world, the profit element in industry and commerce must be made subservient to the common good of communities and nations if we are to have a lasting peace with justice and a sense of true brotherhood for all our neighbors."

In a "statement on victory and peace" issued in the name of all archbishops and bishops in the country, the Catholic prelates declared that neither secularism nor exploitation nor totalitarianism but only "the spirit of Christianity can write a real and lasting peace in justice and charity to all nations—even to those not Christian."

"In the Epochal revolution through which the world is passing," the statement continuped, "it is very necessary for us to realize that every man is our brother in Christ.

Signed by Ten Bishops

"All should be convinced that every man is endowed with the dignity of human personality, and that he is entitled by the laws of nature to the things necessary to sustain life in a way conformable to human dignity."

The statement was approved by 102 members of the American hierarchy at the annual meeting of

Continued on Page 8

6 Convicted of Treason For Aiding Saboteur

Chicago, Nov. 14 (U.P.)—A Federal court jury tonight convicted six naturalized German-Americans of treason, the highest crime against the United States.

The verdict, returned by a jury of eight housewives and four men against the parents, aunt and uncle and two friends of Herbert Haupt electrocuted Nazi saboteur was the biggest treason conviction in the history of the nation.

The only crime mentioned in the constitution, treason carries a maximum penalty of death and a minimum of five years imprisonment and a $19,000 fine.

The jury was charged only with determining guilt or innocence. Sentence is left to the discretion of Trial Judge William J. Campbell, at 46 the youngest Federal judge in the Chicago district.

Those convicted were three middle-aged couples, all natives of Germany, who settled in Chicago and became naturalized citizens. They were:

Young Haupt's parents, Hans and Erna; his aunt and uncle, Lucille and Walter Froehling, the latter Mrs. Haupt's brother; and Otto and Kate Wergin, neighbors and friends of the other two couples.

Mrs. Haupt, Herbert's mother, and Mrs. Froehling broke into sobs when they heard the jury's decision. Mrs. Froehling was carried from the tiny courtroom by two baliffs.

Froehling and Wergin bowed their heads when they heard the verdicts. A separate one being read for each defendant, but the elder Haupt remained stoic.

Improve or Perish, Winant Warns World

Birmingham, Nov. 14 (U.P.)—U. S. Ambassador John G. Winant warned today that the world has before it a choice between the greatest future of all time or self-destruction.

"The greatest future of all time is before us, and also the gravest responsibility. We have the faith and capacity which if organized still will let old men dream dreams and young men realize visions," he declared.

WHERE TO FIND IT

	Page		Page
SECTION A		Women	20
Bridge	18	SECTION B	
Dr. Brady	18	Art	8
Clubs	21	Career Quiz	15
Crossword Puzzle	18	Financial	12
Editorial	22	Helen and Warren	11
Fashions	20	Movies	8-9
Fighting Men	18	Music	8
Heffernan	22	Old Timers	11
Helen Worth	20	Radio	12
Horoscope	18	Real Estate	10
Letters to Editor	22	Resorts	18
Lindley	22	Sports	1-4
Novel	18	Theaters	7-8
Obituaries	23	Trend	5-6
Schools	12	Want-Ads	13-17
Society	15-17	SECTION C	
Tucker	22	Eight Pages of Comics	

Turn to the Classified Pages and look under Instructions—Schools—for vital information about a future career.

Lip Is on Probation As Dodger Manager

Durocher's $25,000 Player Contract Includes 10-Day Clause—Little Skipper, Rickey Are in Full Accord on Discipline

By TOMMY HOLMES

In spite of the long delay in coming to terms, it appears today that the relations between Leo Durocher and Branch Rickey are cordial enough.

Rickey put it this way: "I have known Leo from away back and have had much to do with him and his affairs. I know his ability and his capacity, and our procedure in our conferences has been designed to have his ability and his capacity meet."

Nevertheless, it was impossible to escape the notion that Leo is more or less on probation, too. The $25,000 Dodger contract he signed was a player contract and contains the customary ten-day clause which leaves the club free to call everything off on ten days notice or ten days' pay.

Of course, such a contract might also have been designed to protect the club in the event that Durocher is drafted for the armed service.

Gambling Over-Emphasized

The Pullman poker games of the Dodgers last season probably were over-emphasized in the comment that accompanied the various conferences that led up to Durocher's re-engagement as manager, but there is no doubt that they figured in the discussions.

Branch Rickey clammed up on the subject. "I'd rather not go into the questions of discipline we discussed," said the new boss of Ebbets Field.

But Durocher went into the matter to some extent.

"There isn't any doubt," the Lip admitted, "that our card games were bad. As a matter of fact, I had arrived at that thought independently. Before I started talking to Mr. Rickey about next year's contract, I resolved that there'd be no more gambling for any real money on any other club I ever managed.

"Just how much effect our card games had on the play of the club on the ball field is something I don't know. If it had any effect at all. It was something I could have stopped and something I probably should have stopped.

"But just off-hand I can think of six players on our club who represented a very important part of our ball club. And not one of the six to the best of my knowledge and belief turned a card all season. You certainly couldn't blame card playing for the failure of Vaughan, Camilli, Medwick, Reiser, Walker and Wyatt to do as well as they did the year before.

"For Reiser, I'll take all the responsibility. I put Pete back into the lineup too soon after he ran head-on into that centerfield wall in St. Louis.

Played Poker in Flag Year

"I think we played cards just as much in 1941, the year we won the pennant, although not for perhaps stakes as high. But it doesn't make any difference. I don't suppose I gave it enough serious thought before but I realize now that it's bad practice. From now on, there'll be nothing tougher than a 15-cent limit on any card as long as I manage the Dodgers."

Personally, I don't know just what Durocher meant. Maybe he meant five-and-ten-cent poker. A 15-cent limit would make change-making pretty complicated.

Some one asked what other disciplinary rules had been decided upon for the 1943 Dodgers and Rickey interrupted to say, "I don't think I'd answer the question if I were you." So the question wasn't answered. Then some one asked if Brooklyn players would be prohibited from visiting the race track on off-days.

Durocher said, "I don't care to answer that," and Rickey said, "Well, I will."

B. R. continued, "There will be no restrictions whatever on what a ball player does in his spare time, and if we have men who do not know how to spend their spare time intelligently, perhaps we have the wrong sort of men."

Rickey added that there was a vast difference between playing cards and even going to the race track for amusement and recreation and getting involved in situations in which the man might be seriously hurt in a financial way.

BOTH SIDES

By Harold Parrott

A GOOD START—Had a ringside seat at a great show yesterday: Mr. Rickey vs. the press. It was his first joust with the 30, typewriter-thumpers who on occasion have raked and blasted MacPhail and Durocher.

Few will deny that Rickey is a top lawyer and executive, equipped to debate or fence with the best. What did HE think of his inquisitors?

Afterward he told me, "They hit hard, but they hit clean. I never thought I'd be asked questions like that. I felt I was up to my ears all the time, had to keep swimming. If one missed you, the next one would get you with a killing question if you left an opening. Tough, yes, but fair. And, above all, if you declined to answer—they were polite. It was my impression New York newsmen are the sharpest—the BEST at their trade."

Rickey was interested in how they felt toward him, too . . . and I'd wager he read today's stories as avidly as a playwright devours those first-night reviews.

DRESSEN NO. 1 TOPIC—Reporters' consensus seemed to be that Rickey's bow was a success, that a lot of questions had been answered. Thing that bothered them most was the firing of Charley Dressen, the little coach. No explanation on that one.

"Rickey did not give Dressen much praise," somebody cracked, "He did not cushion the dire deed."

"Well, the more you praise a guy," came the answer, "the bigger reason you got to give for letting him go—"

And that might be a bull's-eye answer.

"NEW DEAL," SAYS LIPPY—Durocher's reaction to the whole show was illuminating. Leo was a bit penitent about the poker games, the gambling on the club, admitted they might have hurt the Dodgers, said there'd be a 15-cent limit.

A few of the writers who'd scrapped with Lippy Leo at various times last season wasted no time coming to grips with him. What was his attitude toward the press going to be? Would they be welcome in the clubhouse?

"A new deal, fellows," said Leo, with a sincere ring. "With this man in charge things are going to be different, I don't have to tell you that. I will never say anything against MacPhail, who I still think is a great guy. But as you know Larry picked up every little thing and wanted it explained and sometimes flew off the handle and as you know I was always the guy who landed in the middle. At times I felt like a football. But this is a new deal."

PUTTING HIM ON THE SPOT—Did I hear a question from the back of the class as to the nature of some of the embarrassing questions which were fired at Mr. Rickey? Uh-huh. Well——

They asked him why Dressen was fired, and they asked what the new discipline rules were going to be, and they asked him (right in front of Durocher) whether there was a 10-day release clause in the player's contract that Leo had signed. And then somebody said "Was Durocher's salary slashed? We know that MacPhail was pretty free with the cash, and we hear you are here to cut salaries, Mr. Rickey."

From behind a barrage of cigar smoke, B. R. countered: "Let us not beg the question. That query springs from the fact that my players' salaries were lower in St. Louis than they are here. That is natural. Income is lower there. I am like the new coach who does not like to be told by his halfback how the old coach directed him to play. I am the new coach, and I do not care a hoot about the old coach. I will cut salaries if I think they can be cut and should be cut—but I will also raise salaries."

FITZ LIKE THE BABE?—Most emphatic was Mr. Rickey about the successor to Durocher, if and when. He did not think that successor would come from the ranks of the coaches on the club, he said. The exact way he put it: "I would rather see Durocher surrounded by men who are professional coaches (and coaching is a dead-level job) than by men who have a yen to manage the team."

He could not emphasize enough, he said, how desirous he was to have Fitz accept the Montreal managerial post. "I think he has all the qualifications," Mr. Rickey boomed, "both as to background, and character and ability, and definitely should expose himself to managerial work at this time."

Rickey further said he had made it a practice, although not a rule, to draw his managers from the ranks of his farm teams. "But some men feel that is a retrogression," he said, "They so abhor the minors. I have made the Montreal post so attractive for Fitz because I do not want him to feel that way, I want him to serve what you might call an 'apprentice-ship' in our system."

I could not help thinking of Colonel Ruppert and how he wanted Babe Ruth to serve his apprenticeship at Newark, and how the Babe never would . . .

Well, Mr. Rickey has ousted one Cardinal farm (Rochester from West Palm Beach, and moved the Dodgers in . . . and he has ousted another Card farm (Columbus) from Lake Worth and moved the young Dodger Montreals in there . . . now all he has to do is pry those Cardinals out of first place in the N. L. Could be!

Ruth Increases Lead

Ruth McGinnis, champion woman pocket billiard player of the world, increased her lead over E. W. Neves by taking the second block of their match last night at the Brooklyn Billiard Academy, Flatbush Ave. and Fulton St., 100 to 85. Ruth is setting the pace by 200 to 145. Their last block will be played tonight.

Schumacher Seeks Commission in Navy

Righthander Hal Schumacher, veteran pitcher of the Giants, has applied for a commission in the navy, it was reported today. The Giants first learned of Schumacher's action when navy officials queried the club for references.

TITLE HOPES, BOWL BIDS GO ON THE BLOCK

Ohio State's Meeting With Michigan Tops Tomorrow's Football

By PAUL SCHEFFELS

Every section of the nation comes up with a strong program for tomorrow's semi-final week of full play in the college football season with circuit titles and bowl bids holding most of the interest.

Only the Ivy League and Western Conference give no thought to post-season bowl bids as the Pacific Coast, Missouri Valley, Big Ten, Southeast and Southwest Conferences and Ivy League all reach the critical titular stage.

Headed by the Ohio State-Michigan game in the mid-West every part of the country lists a banner brawl including UCLA-Washington on the Pacific Coast, Georgia-Auburn in the South, Rice-TCU in the Southwest and traditional Yale-Harvard in the East.

Wolverines Favored

The Buckeyes have a chance to clinch Big Ten honors by beating Michigan but are slight underdogs against the Wolverines. Wisconsin, pointing for a tie, tackles Minnesota while Indiana goes to bat against Purdue. In non-conference contests, Great Lakes draws the favorite's role against Illinois, Iowa Pre-Flight over Nebraska, Notre Dame over Northwestern, Detroit over Arkansas and West Virginia over Michigan State. Iowa State takes the field against Kansas State in the only Big Six game. Tulsa rates the nod to clinch the Missouri Valley crown as its undefeated eleven meets Creighton.

The twin paragons of the Southeastern Conference—undefeated and untied Georgia and Georgia Tech—rule heavy choices to take Auburn and Florida in warm-up games for their classic battle next week. Other circuit games favor Alabama over Vanderbilt, Mississippi State over Mississippi and Tennessee over Kentucky.

William and Mary, unbeaten pacesetter in the Southern Conference, moves outside to play North Carolina Pre-Flight. In conference contests Davidson is given the edge over The Citadel, Furman over Clemson, Duke over North Carolina State and Maryland over Washington and Lee. TCU and Baylor, picked to whip Rice and SMU, need triumphs to go into a three-way tie with Texas for the Southwest Conference lead.

Stanford Choice on Coast

UCLA will try to pick up ground on idle Washington State in the Pacific Coast Rose Bowl race as it met Washington. Two other conference games pit Oregon State against Oregon with Stanford favored to down California. Wyoming is picked over Utah State in the only Big Seven game.

A grip on the Big Three crown is the stake between Harvard and Yale with the Elis given an edge. Army gets the nod to trip Princeton for command of the Ivy League while Dartmouth is favored over Columbia.

A pair of Big Six invaders are the choices to score intersectional triumphs, Missouri figuring to win over Fordham and Oklahoma over Temple. Boston College ranks as a prohibitive choice to trample Boston University, with Penn State-Pitt a tossup and Holy Cross chosen over Manhattan and Georgetown over George Washington.

Brooklyn College Team In A. A. U. Harrier Meet

The New York A. C., Manhattan College, Millrose A. A. and Brooklyn College have teams entered in the Metropolitan Association A. A. U. senior individual and team cross country championship to be held at Van Cortlandt Park Sunday, starting promptly at 2:30 p.m.

The outstanding entries are Frank Dixon, IC4A champion; J. Gregory Rice, New York A. C., defending champion; James Rafferty and George DeGeorge, New York A. C.; Edward J. Walsh and Robert E. Farley, Manhattan College.

Rangers Waste Scoring Punch

Mistakes Nullify Power of Attack—Leafs Latest to Profit by Boners

By RALPH TROST

Les Patrick and Lou Little should get together. The Rangers' manager and the Columbia coach have one thing in common. Their teams score often enough—but the opposition scores more.

The Rangers, in case you'd like to know, are averaging 3.63 goals per game, which isn't bad at all and usually yields a good percentage of victories. They are, at this stage, out-scoring the Boston Bruins, who are a rung higher on the ladder. They are caging that puck at a little better clip than another of the higher-ups, Les Canadiens.

But they are still losing. The Blueshirts dropped another game in Madison Square Garden last night when they came out on the short end of a 7—3 joust with the Toronto Maple Leafs, the Stanley Cup holders—in person.

Buzinski Stars in Net

It was an interesting game to watch. There was plenty of fast skating and some plain and fancy stops made by M. Buzinski, the Rangers' goalie. But there were also plenty of errors. If they had an error column in hockey the Rangers would own it lock, stock and barrel.

It's amazing how swiftly an error becomes a goal for the opposition. They were leading, 1—0, when Alfie Pike meant to tuck a puck past Syl Apps. But he got his stroke mixed somehow, didn't get clear—and in faster time than it can be written Syl chopped it at Buzinski, who stopped it, but Mel Hill was right there to tuck in the rebound. Where was the rest of the defense?

Only a few seconds later Nobbe Warwick was moving in mid-ice. He made a feint to pass Sweeney Schriner, forgot to take the puck with him and lo—Sweeney wafted the puck 35 feet and into the high right corner. To make matters worse, Gaye Stewart was off the ice for holding Snuffy Smith when the Rangers decided to outfox Mr. Apps. They even went into a huddle about it. They managed to weary Mr. Apps and he left the ice. Schriner thereupon entered, got the puck on a faceoff right in the middle of the ice and slammed the disc cleanly home.

That's what's been happening to the Rangers. They make a mistake and it costs a goal.

Maybe the worm will turn one of these days.

Cracked Ice

Lin Bend, one of the youngsters brought in to replace the lost Colville-Shibicky line, got his notice to scoot back to Canada and into the army. Technically he's returning for home defense service and can so insist. But nobody insists. It isn't popular. Rhys Thompson, who played for the Leafs, was up with the late, lamented Americans but sent back to New Haven for more experience . . . It didn't take Phil Watson long to ring up the first goal—which made it 115 straight without being shut out. It was strictly a solo, Phil's second in successive games. Phil stole the puck from Apps and got by two Leaf men before he suckered Hill out of position . . . Bucko McDonald continues as a thorn in the Rangers' side. Bucko was once farmed out because he couldn't get down to playing size. He loves to eat. The Rangers should work on this failing

HOCKEY STANDING

	W.	L.	T.	Goals F.	Goals A.	P.
Detroit	4	2	1	30	22	9
Chicago	4	2	1	28	23	9
Montreal	3	4	0	25	24	6
Boston	3	4	0	17	21	6
Toronto	4	2	0	29	17	8
N. Y. Rangers	2	6	0	29	51	4

Last Night's Results

Toronto, 7; Rangers, 3.
Chicago, 6; Detroit, 2.

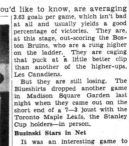

Arkie Vaughan

Rickey to Shop For Infielders At Chicago Mart

With the selection of a manager out of the way—and Branch Rickey admitted that no one except Leo Durocher had been seriously considered—the makeup of the Brooklyn infield is the next big consideration.

"I hope I can find a selling market for infielders at the Chicago meetings," said Rickey wistfully. "As matters stand, there are only three infielders we can count upon for next season—Billy Herman, Alex Kampouris and Durocher."

Vaughan Pulls a Camilli

It's now reported that Arkie Vaughan like Dolph Camilli is making sounds like retiring. Rickey fears Peewee Reese will be in the army.

He seems dead serious about Durocher coming back as a player. Talking about the club's training plans at West Palm Beach, B. R. said he thought they'd get started on March 1 or a little before. As a matter of fact I can think of a couple of fellows who ought to start getting in shape now. I mean Newsom and Durocher," he said.

Leo, who stopped practicing after Spring training this year and didn't get into a National League game, merely grinned.

The release of Chuck Dressen as Dodger coach was not a surprise, yet the reasons behind it are not clear. Rickey said he liked the bustling little guy personally and believed him to be an able coach. That seems to put the Dressen discharge at Durocher's door and Leo wasn't talking.

Dressen was around later. He received the verdict with his usual smile, said he'd go to Chicago for the Winter meetings and hunt up another baseball job.

Ted McGrew was to see Camilli today and there was a rumor from California that Camilli would like to intercept the Dodger scout. The story said Dolph wanted to save McGrew from wasted time, that Dolph's mind was made up to retire.

Rickey took the report that Vaughan would follow Camilli into retirement with his chin up. "I'm not unduly impressed by baseball retirements in November," he said. "And I repeat that I congratulate any man who feels that he has reached the stage of life when he is under pressure to do nothing he doesn't want to do. I've been trying to do that for 60 years."

And that incidentally recalls what Rickey calls his most important announcement of the day. He opened the meeting by saying, "I will not be 61 years old until Dec. 20. I am not 62 years old as has been stated in the metropolitan press." HOLMES.

HOCKEY OVERTIME PLAY ABOLISHED

Montreal, Nov. 20 (U.P.)—Frank Calder, president of the National Hockey League, announced today that overtime play will be abolished and that games resulting in tie scores at the end of the regulation three periods will be considered draws.

The action was taken, Calder said, "because of existing travel conditions."

A previously-rejected proposal to curtail the number of players on each squad will be reconsidered at a special meeting of the league governors in Boston, Nov. 23, Calder disclosed.

SPORTS

FRIDAY, NOVEMBER 20, 1942

WOULD PROVE WRIGHT WRONG—Willie Pep, above, hopes to win featherweight title from Chalky Wright in 15-round bout at Garden tonight. Pep is an 8 to 5 favorite, but Wright says those odds are out of line.

PEP 8-5 TO COP CHALKY'S CROWN

Connecticut hopes to have one of its sons crowned as a world's champion tonight after Willie Pep, Nutmeg State challenger, meets Boss Chalky Wright in the 15-round feature at Madison Square Garden. Connecticut has become so enthused over the idea that fans from up that way have bought out two-thirds of the house and at that rate Promoter Mike Jacobs is hoping they dig up a few more challengers.

Pep, having accomplished the amazing feat of winning 53 consecutive contests, rules an 8 to 5 favorite. The price was 2 to 1, but it dropped a few points when some of the boys r'used to be amazed by this record. They pointed out that many of Pep's victims were fourth-raters who couldn't lick anybody else anyway.

Case Rests With Wright

But streak or no streak, Pep has already demonstrated that he is a most capable performer. The case seems to rest with Chalky Wright, who seems to have lapses every now and then. His redeeming feature, though, is that he always manages to come through when the blue chips are up.

Wright held a one-quarter pound advantage over Pep when they weighed in today. Wright scaled 125¾, Pep 125½.

Twice before worthy featherweight contenders have sought to wrest the title from Chalky, but he discouraged them. Two months ago Lulu Constantino brought his youth and speed into the ring in an effort to upset Wright. But the way it wound up Chalky had all the speed and stamina, while Lulu was completely done-in at the end of the battle.

Pep seems to be the most popular fighter ever to come out of Connecticut, the State which has boasted such worthies as Bat Battalino and Louis (Kid) Kaplan. Several thousand rooters will make the trip down, not only from his native Hartford, but from New Haven, Bridgeport, Waterbury and other parts of the State.

Paired in the supporting six-rounders are Pete Kennedy, White Plains welter, and Harold Green of Brooklyn; Mario Morales, Cuban featherweight, and Ham Wiloby of Jamaica; Johnny Dell, Brooklyn featherweight, and Ray Velarde, of Mexico. Ossie Rodriguez, Puerto Rican featherweight, meets Jackie Lynch of New Orleans in the opener.

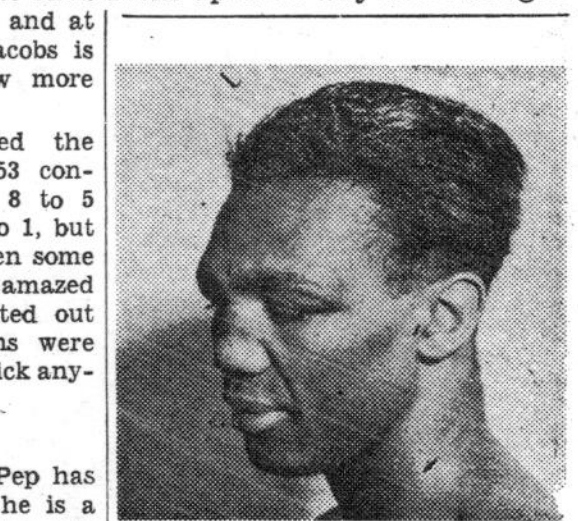

Chalky Wright

Harold Green has been matched to meet Georgie Harper in the eight-round semi-final to the 10-round feature at the Broadway Arena Tuesday night, which brings together Wicky Harkins and Indian Gomez.

Bobby Lakin, Jamaica welterweight, meets Frankie Cardinal, crowd-pleasing West Side battler, in the top six of an all-star card tomorrow night at the Ridgewood Grove.

Joe Aponte Torres, colorful Puerto Rican featherweight, faces Mexican Joey Silva of Philadelphia in the semi-final.

Bobby Ruffin of Astoria will meet Roman Alvarez, East Side lightweight contender, in the feature bout at the St. Nick's Arena Monday night.

THWARTED BY TURK—Goalie Turk Broda of the Toronto Maple Leafs goes down on one knee in first period to make a save on Lynn Patrick's thrust at the goal while Bucko McDonald (3) of the Leafs tries to help the goalie. Bryan Hextall (12) of the Rangers came in fast on this play to help Patrick, shown facing the camera. Leafs won, 7—3.

EAGLE GRID SELECTIONS

	LEO (U.P.) PETERSEN 55—35 .611	PAUL GOULD 54—36 .600	HAROLD PARROTT 53—37 .589	JIMMY MURPHY 52—38 .578	TOMMY HOLMES 51—39 .567	OFFSIDE McGLUGG 51—39 .567	RALPH TROST 40—35 .533	BEN GOULD* 43—47 .478	LES PATRICK† Guest Picker
PENN STATE PITTSBURGH	Penn State 14—7	Penn State 7—0	Penn State 20—6	Penn State 7—6	Penn State 21—7	Penn State 20—7	Penn State 13—7	Penn State 21—10	Penn State 7—0
AUBURN GEORGIA	Georgia 21—6	Georgia 20—0	Georgia 20—7	Georgia 12—6	Georgia 21—0	Georgia 35—0	Georgia 21—6	Georgia 42—7	Georgia 34—0
FORDHAM MISSOURI	Missouri 28—0	Missouri 13—6	Missouri 21—7	Fordham 7—6	Missouri 14—13	Missouri 14—13	Missouri 10—7	Missouri 14—13	Missouri 14—7
YALE HARVARD	Yale 7—6	Yale 10—7	Harvard 13—7	Harvard 7—6	Yale 14—7	Yale 12—0	Tie 7—7	Yale 7—6	Yale 6—0
ARMY PRINCETON	Army 13—7	Army 14—9	Army 20—7	Army 12—6	Army 21—14	Army 14—0	Army 21—6	Tie 13—13	Army 20—0
COLUMBIA DARTMOUTH	Dartm'th 13—6	Dartm'th 14—13	Columbia 30—20	Dartm'th 14—9	Columbia 28—21	Columbia 21—14	Columbia 28—26	Dartm'th 20—12	Columbia 27—21
MANHATTAN HOLY CROSS	Holy Cross 14—0	Holy Cross 20—0	Holy Cross 30—14	Holy Cross 14—7	Holy Cross 14—7	Holy Cross 12—0	Holy Cross 14—0	Holy Cross 21—7	Holy Cross 13—7
N'WESTERN NOTRE DAME	Notre Dame 21—6	Notre Dame 13—0	Notre Dame 21—7	Notre Dame 21—7	Notre Dame 21—7	Notre Dame 21—6	Notre Dame 6—0	Notre Dame 18—14	Notre Dame 21—6
MICHIGAN OHIO STATE	Michigan 21—19	Michigan 20—13	Ohio State 21—7	Michigan 12—6	Ohio State 21—14	Michigan 21—14	Michigan 42—41	Michigan 21—20	Michigan 14—13
WISCONSIN MINNESOTA	Minnesota 13—6	Minnesota 10—7	Minnesota 21—7	Minnesota 19—12	Wisconsin 14—7	Minnesota 14—0	Minnesota 7—6	Tie 7—7	Minnesota 7—6
LAFAYETTE LEHIGH	Lafayette 14—6	Lafayette 13—0	Lafayette 20—7	Lafayette 12—6	Lafayette 14—13	Lafayette 7—0	Lehigh 2—0	Lafayette 14—3	Lafayette 13—0
KENTUCKY TENNESSEE	Tennessee 21—7	Tennessee 14—0	Tennessee 32—14	Tennessee 9—6	Tennessee 20—7	Tennessee 33—0	Tennessee 13—6	Tennessee 7—0	Tennessee 14—7
CALIFORNIA STANFORD	Stanford 13—7	Stanford 19—7	California 20—7	Stanford 21—14	Stanford 21—7	Stanford 28—0	Stanford 6—0	Stanford 21—14	Tie 7—7
GA. TECH FLORIDA	Ga. Tech. 32—6	Ga. Tech. 40—0	Ga. Tech. 40—7	Ga. Tech. 28—0	Ga. Tech. 28—0	Ga. Tech. 21—0	Ga. Tech. 76—0	Ga. Tech. 50—6	Ga. Tech. 35—0
INDIANA PURDUE	Indiana 13—10	Indiana 14—0	Indiana 10—7	Indiana 19—6	Indiana 20—7	Indiana 13—0	Indiana 13—12	Indiana 18—9	Indiana 14—7

*Batting for Lou Niss, who is warming bench this week. †Hockey Rangers' manager.

War Restrictions Laying Groundwork For Vast Home Market, O'Hara Says

War conditions have tended to disrupt the business of private builders and realty brokers but the very restrictions which have brought many problems to them are serving to lay the groundwork for a vast market for homes in future years, in the opinion of Frank S. O'Hara of Jackson Heights, former president of the New York State Association of Real Estate Boards and retiring head of the New York State Society of Real Estate Appraisers.

In a survey of the New York State market prospects at the close of his term of office in the appraisal group, Mr. O'Hara yesterday predicted broad activity particularly in the residential field after the war, largely as a result of the great backlog of demand now being built up through emergency curbs on construction work and enforced delay in home ownership on the part of many thousands of families of men now in military service.

"Not only will builders be kept busy filling this demand but real estate men will find a wide field for their services in negotiating sales of new and used homes and home sites and in valuing properties in the light of the new economic conditions which will face the nation," he said.

"The momentum of the demand developed during the lean years of the depression, when building activity virtually came to a standstill, was just beginning to be felt when the national emergency brought delays and uncertainties which limited buying. Then the successive Federal orders restricting and finally ending all private building terminated the healthy boom in residential expansion which had been developing partioularly in Long Island communities.

"Five factors seem to presage one of the greatest revivals in home construction in the nation's history after the war, with New York sharing actively in this upswing. One will be the return of millions of reunited families to normal civilian life, with a consequent demand for modern living quarters on their part; another will be the normal need for new housing to replace the homes which become outmoded and to accommodate newly-married couples; still another will be the great backlog of potential demand now being built up by cessation of private construction work.

"Many families who will not wait for the completion of new construction when peace returns probably will turn to existing houses to fill their need, bringing an active market for used residences in New York City, its suburbs and in other parts of the State. Workers who have gone into defense plants elsewhere are due to return to their original places of residence in the State, some with sufficient savings to become home owners for the first time."

Mr. O'Hara, who has been active in disposing of HOLC holdings on Long Island, reported that inquiries in this classification were continuing to be heavy and that sales were being made at a satisfactory rate. One of the problems in keeping up with the demand, he explained, has been that of maintaining trained sales staffs in the face of the constant drain on personnel being made by war needs.

Mr. O'Hara will relinquish leadership of the New York State Society of Real Estate Appraisers, a branch of the State Realty Association, at a meeting to be held in Albany on Friday, Dec. 11. He will be succeeded by Ralph W. Arend of Utica.

SALE IN PRESIDENT ST.—This one-family dwelling, 1349 President St., has been sold by William J. Fleming of the Nostrand Ave. office of M. C. O'Brien, Inc., as broker, for the Kings County Savings Bank, to a client for occupancy.

IN FLATBUSH PROJECT—Two of the new two-family houses in the Dahill Homes, Inc., development, at Dahill Road and Fort Hamilton Parkway, built by James Dorment and Wesley Roche, were recently sold, according to Henry Goetz, sales director at the property.

FLATBUSH TRANSACTION—This one-family dwelling, 1083 E. 40th St., has been sold by Hussey & Hoeh, as brokers, for the Roosevelt Savings Bank, to Dr. Samuel A. Bark, for occupancy. The plot is 40x100 and the house contains six rooms and bath.

HAS NEW OWNER—This dwelling, built by the Gibson Corporation at Gibson, Valley Stream, has been sold to a worker in a nearby defense plant, according to Fred Simons, sales director at the property.

ADDITION TO LOFT ESTATES—Recently completed house in the Loft Estates development, facing Sunrise Highway, between Rockville Centre and Baldwin, built by Gust Svensen, Inc., and used as a model house, it was announced by Frank Kondla, sales director.

SURVIVES APARTMENT INVASION—Although the spread of apartment house developments in the Flatbush section during the past decade has swept away hundreds of handsome private dwellings not protected by zoning regulations, there remain many good-looking one-family houses, such as the one shown here, located in blocks zoned against apartments. Their owners have long fought any attempts to modify the regulations and will continue to oppose any invasion of the privacy of the neighborhood by unwelcome structures.

REAL ESTATE

Realty Problems To Be Discussed At Conference

Former Supreme Court Justice Joseph M. Proskauer will discuss the "Wage and Hour Law" at the luncheon of the Metropolitan Realty Conference to be held at the Hotel Commodore on Wednesday, Dec. 16, it was announced yesterday by the New York Metropolitan Association of Real Estate Boards.

Speakers at the all-day conference, which will open at 10 o'clock in the morning, include Bernard F. Hogan, president, the Greater New York Savings Bank, who will speak on "Co-operation in Realty Investments"; John B. McTigue, chief, Project Analysis Board, Construction Bureau WPB, on "Limitation on Building Construction Under War Production Board Order L-41"; Edward A. MacDougal, president, the Queensboro Corporation, on "The Mortgage Moratorium"; Herbert E. Bode of Hosinger & Bode, Inc., on "Reasons for Liquidation of Certificated Mortgage Issues Now"; William J. Demorest, vice president, William A. White & Sons, and chairman of Manhattan Volunteer Rent Control Committee, on "Rent Control," and Harold J. Treanor, counsel, Real Estate Board of New York, on "Assessment Review."

Lively Bidding For Property at Night Auction Sale

That there is widespread interest among investors and homeseekers in well-located property was demonstrated Wednesday night in the Real Estate Exchange, 189 Montague St., when the Jere Johnson Jr. Company, with Fred B. Snow as auctioneer, sold many parcels of real estate for the Kings County Trust Company.

Long before the auction started, the salesroom was filled to capacity and when the first building was offered there were many standing. By actual count 550 persons attended, according to Mr. Snow. The bidding throughout the sale was spirited, and choice parcels brought satisfactory prices, a representative of the trust firm stated. Two-family houses were of particular interest. In the group were representatives of banks and mortgage firms and realty organizations.

The properties bid in and the prices paid follow:

42 Smith St., two-story store and meeting rooms, $10,200; 295 Garfield Place, four-story and basement dwelling, $6,900; 588 7th St., three-story and basement dwelling, $5,800; 301 5th Ave., four-story store and apartment, $2,500; 2550 E. 23d St., two-family house, $6,250; 2314 Avenue I, two-family dwelling, $11,100; 8214 21st Ave., two-family house, $7,300; 1133 53d St., two-family house, $6,750; 1766 58th St., two-family house, $7,000; 2030 74th St., two-family house, $6,100; 1817 E. 12th St., two-family house, $5,000; 136 E. 40th St., two-family house, $5,200; 3122 and 3124 Mermaid Ave., one-story store, $1,750; 364 Chester St., three-story store and apartment, $3,750; 94 Powell St., one-family dwelling, $950; Greymore Hotel, Bay Shore, plot on Clinton Ave., $1,500; plot 100x450, on Ocean Ave., Bay Shore, $1,500; six lots on Parkswood Lakes, Babylon, $300; plot 165x195, on Hulse St. and Bellport, $150.

State Realty Men To Meet in Albany

Real estate men from all sections of the state will gather in Albany on Dec. 11 to launch officially the 1943 program of the New York State Association of Real Estate Boards.

High spot of the day will be the Inaugural Luncheon when A. N. Groves of Syracuse will be installed as president, succeeding George L. Long of Brooklyn. At the same time, Ralph W. Arend of Utica will officially take over the chairmanship of the New York State Society of Real Estate Appraisers, a division of the state realty group. He succeeds Frank S. O'Hara of Jackson Heights.

John Henry Improving

John E. Henry, downtown realty broker and long active in the affairs of the Brooklyn Real Estate Board, who underwent an operation on Nov. 25, is steadily improving, it was learned at his home yesterday.

Large Dwellings Now in Demand, Banker Reveals

When Reconditioned Find Realty Buyers, Stratton Declares

The gradual emergence of the larger house from the depths to which real estate buyers have confined it for a decade, is an interesting development of the Queens real estate market, according to Le Roy T. Stratton, vice president of the Queens County Savings Bank of Flushing and Corona.

"There have always been people who would like their homes situated on large landscaped plots, with ample room for lawns and gardens, but high assessed values with resultant high taxes and heavy carrying charges have kept many from purchasing these fine old dwellings.

"This type of home," continued Mr. Stratton, "has generally been reconditioned and has had most of the new modern 'gadgets' incorporated in it, without altering its 'homey' style. The banks have tried to sell such houses for several years—at higher prices, perhaps—but the small house further out has had the preference. Now the banks have greatly reduced prices, along with interest rates, from the 6 percent rate, which was once standard, and the tax commissioners have helped—in some cases substantially—by adjusting assessed values, so that carrying charges are no longer the bugaboo they once were.

"Whether a land market will develop after the war," continued Mr. Stratton, "nobody knows. It has after previous wars, and if it does, some of these large centrally located plots will become valuable.

"At present the impossibility of securing materials for private building renders these prime sites suitable only for the one and two-family dwellings that are currently erected thereon. It is not impossible, however, that in a few years some of them will house hundreds of families in the greatly improved apartments that will spring from the drawing boards of the architects when peace returns.

Slight Increase In Building Cost Of Small Houses

Construction costs of a standard six-room house increased only 5 percent from October, 1941, to October, 1942, as compared with an increase of 13 percent in the preceding 12-month period, the Federal Home Loan Bank Administration yesterday reported. During October, 1942, labor costs showed no change, while materials costs rose less than 1-10th of 1 percent.

Trends in the total cost figures for individual cities varied considerably during the three-month period from August to October. Seven of the cities reporting indicated increases in costs, six indicated no change and four showed decreases.

The Federal Home Loan Bank Administration, a unit of the National Housing Agency, reported that its index of material prices for October showed a figure of 121.6, as compared with the 1935-1939 base of 100. The labor cost index was 130.2, while the combined material and labor figure was 124.5.

Wholesale building material prices, as reported by the U.S. Department of Labor, showed no change during the month of October. Slight increases were indicated in the wholesale prices of lumber and paint and paint materials, but those were offset by a decline in the "miscellaneous items" group.

New Sales Rates To Be Effective First of the Year

The new sales commission rates, recently adopted by the Brooklyn Real Estate Board and which become effective on Jan. 1, 1943, are as follows:

"On the price obtained up to and including $8,000—5 percent.

On the excess over $8,000, up to and including $12,000—4 percent.

On the excess over $12,000, up to and including $100,000—2 percent.

On the excess over $50,000, up to and including $10,000—2 percent.

On the excess over $100,000—1½ percent."

The minimum commission of $100 on vacant land and $200 on improved property is continued, the Board explained. The present rate of 5 percent on industrial and waterfront property, and on hotels, theaters, concessions and amusement enterprises is not affected by the new rates.

The reason for the change, the Board announced, was to make the sales commission rates conform to those used in other parts of the Metropolitan area.

At a meeting held by the Realty Brokers of Bay Ridge, Inc., last Wednesday night, Allan Cuttle, chairman of the ethics and commission committee, reported on the new commission rates adopted by the Brooklyn Real Estate Board, and the board membership passed a resolution to endorse these new increased rates. Thomas J. Clark, president, presided.

Hotel Modernized

The Hotel Lexington, Lexington Ave. and 48th St., Manhattan, has undergone extensive modernization under the direction of its vice president and general manager, Charles E. Rochester. The changes include new decorations, new furniture and conversion of some of the larger suites into smaller units.

Demolition of Old Dwelling Recalls Its Varied History

Watching the demolition of the fine old dwelling at the northeast corner of Cortelyou Road and E. 18th St. Thursday, Arthur H. Bull, president of the Bull Realty Company, old-time Flatbush realty man, recalled the history of the house, including its sale 33 years ago by his father, Edward Bull, when he had a real estate office at 1090 Flatbush Ave. The house is being razed to clear the land and to save the taxes.

"This old house, like many another in the older part of Flatbush, had a remarkable history," said Mr. Bull. "In November, 1909, the house stood at the southwest corner of Flatbush Ave. and Dorchester Road. It was one of the old Flatbush mansions, possibly 100 years old, occupied for years by H. J. Roberts.

"The corner property was acquired by Emanuel Leiberman to use for store purposes, and the house was sold to Berthold B. Kramer for $700, who owned at that time the plot on which the house now stands.

"It was such a large structure that it became necessary to saw it in half before it would go through the streets. The first half was moved through Dorchester Road, Ocean Ave. and Cortelyou Road. The moving caused so much commotion on account of the Cortelyou Road trolley being put partially out of commission and the Fire Department objected so strenuously to cutting the overhead wires that the second half was taken all the way up to Beverly Road and down E. 18th St.

"William S. Rustin, the contractor who sawed the house in two, was highly complimented as a crowd gathered to watch the two sections come together and the siding line up to its original level. The property has changed hands a number of times and last April was sold by F. M. Ahern, as referee, to Pauline Gluck.

"Now, as it is being pulled apart, we see the way such houses were put together many years ago. Most of the newer homes are not brick filled, neither have they the well-preserved materials used in those days, with workmanship the builders had reason to be proud of.

"This house has stood idle for some time, all boarded up after its windows had been smashed by boys. A recent fire in the attic did not add to its appearance, thus it became an eyesore to the neighborhood.

"At the time of its purchase Mr. Kramer was a well-known Flatbush delicatessen store owner, who had a store on Flatbush Ave., opposite Linden Boulevard.

Buys Home on E. 31st St.

M. C. O'Brien, Inc., has sold for the A. Barton Hepburn Hospital of Ogdensburg, N. Y., the one-family semi-detached dwelling at 1564 East 31st St. to Wililam A. Lane of 244 E. 31st St.

Made Sales Agent For Foreclosed Queens Property

The Builders' Outlet Department of Butterly & Green, Jamaica realty firm, has been appointed exclusive sales agents for eight dwellings recently foreclosed and purchased by the Premium Realty Company.

The houses which are located on Francis Lewis Boulevard, half a block north of Merrick Road, Laurelton, are solid brick English type and contain six rooms.

Bay Ridge Transaction

Michael P. Curnin Inc., as broker sold the one-family house, 99 87th St., for the Brooklyn Trust Company to a client for occuppancy.

'Once On Honeymoon' Has Comedy, Thrills

Ginger Rogers, Cary Grant Co-Star In Romance With Blitz Background

By JANE CORBY

"Once Upon a Honeymoon," which opened at the Albee today, is the story of romance under difficulties between Cary Grant and Ginger Rogers, a delightful comedy-drama, with the two stars at their brilliant best. Leo McCarey, who produced and directed the film and collaborated with Sheridan Gibney on the original screen play, has upheld a reputation for doing the unusual in this picture by providing a romantic comedy against a background of Nazi terrorism in the early days of this World War. The result is a powerful film, a gripping picture that will entrance the whole family.

AMUSEMENTS

The story opens in Vienna just before the Anschluss, where Ginger, as Katie O'Hara, ex-strip teaser from Brooklyn, posing as a society girl, marries the suave Baron von Luber, Hitler's chief advance agent. Katie also meets Pat O'Toole, American broadcasting reporter, in Europe to check up on the baron's activities, who not only warns Katie against the baron before her marriage—in vain, of course—but finds various excuses to keep in their vicinity as they honeymoon through a Europe that is everywhere blitzed in their wake, a coincidence that even Katie finally admits must have some connection with the baron.

The three principals are in Warsaw when the dancer learns the truth about her husband, and she and the commentator make use of the Nazi assault on the city to make their escape. Followed by invading armies and Gestapo spies, the two Americans flee into Holland and France, where they meet the baron again for a surprise finish to the exciting story.

Walter Slezak, a newcomer to the American screen, gives a strong performance as the baron, and the excellent supporting cast, headed by Albert Dekker and Ferike Boros, contribute heavily to the picture's success.

Co-feature at the Albee is "Time to Kill," the latest Mike Shayne adventure, with Lloyd Nolan and Heather Angel.

BUY U. S. WAR BONDS AND SAVINGS STAMPS

IN YIDDISH MUSICAL — Seventy-three-year-old Sam Kasten dances with Molly Picon in "Oy Is Dus a Leben," at the Molly Picon Theater.

GAY OPERETTA — Paul Best, Dorothy Sarnoff and Everett West in a scene from the Americanized version of Johann Strauss' "Fledermaus," which is attracting large audiences to the 44th St. Theater.

'Life Begins at 8:30' In 2d Week at Roxy

"Life Begins at 8:30," new 20th Century-Fox comedy romance starring Monty Woolley and Ida Lupino, started its second and final week yesterday at the Roxy Theater.

In addition to the stars, the featured cast is headed by Cornel Wilde, Sara Allgood, Melville Cooper, J. Edward Bromberg and William Demarest.

Irving Pichel directed "Life Begins at 8:30," from the screenplay by Producer Nunnally Johnson and the play by Emlyn Williams.

Universal Employes Get Christmas Bonus

Christmas bonuses amounting to one week's salary will be given to Universal Pictures employes who have been in the company's service three months or more and whose weekly salaries are $40 or under.

This announcement follows resolution adopted recently by company's board of directors.

MOVIE TIME TABLE

BROOKLYN

ALBEE—"Once Upon a Honeymoon," 10, 1:05, 4:15, 7:20, 10:30; "Time to Kill," 12:05, 3:15, 6:20, 9:30.

MAJESTIC—"Living Ghost," 12:30, 3, 5:25, 7:50, 10:30; "Sheriff of Sage Valley," 11:30, 1:50, 4:25, 6:50, 9:25.

METROPOLITAN—"White Cargo," 12:40, 3:58, 7:16, 10:34; "Apache Trail," 11:15, 2:33, 5:51, 9:09.

PARAMOUNT—"Now Voyager," 11, 2:38, 6:16, 9:54; "Daring Young Man," 1:17, 4:55, 8:33.

STRAND—"Flying Tigers," 12:40, 3:50, 7, 10:15; "Street of Chance," 11:20, 2:35, 5:45, 9.

MANHATTAN

ASTOR—"For Me and My Gal," 10:05, 12:17, 2:29, 4:41, 6:53, 9:05, 11:17.

CAPITOL—"Journey for Margaret," 10, 12:05, 2:10, 4:15, 6:20, 8:25, 10:30, 12:25.

CRITERION—"Who Done It," 10:06, 11:59, 1:52, 3:45, 5:38, 7:31, 9:24, 11:17, 1:10.

MUSIC HALL—"Random Harvest," 10:30, 1:26, 4:25, 7:22, 10:21; Stage show, 12:30, 3:30, 6:30, 9:30.

PARAMOUNT—"Road to Morocco," 10:21, 1:12, 4:14, 7:20, 10:17, 11:39; Stage show, 12:09, 3:11, 6:22, 9:19.

ROXY—"Life Begins at 8:30," 1:05, 1:50, 4:45, 7:40, 10:25; Stage show, 1, 3:40, 6:45, 9:45.

Jerry Wald's Orchestra At N. Y. Strand Friday

Jerry Wald and his orchestra will headline the "in person" show at the N. Y. Strand Theater starting next Friday with the new Warner Bros.' film, "Flying Fortress". "Flying Fortress" stars Richard Greene and Carla Lehmann and was produced at the Teddington Studios in England. Songstress Anita Boyer will be featured with the orchestra. Jack Gilford, the Lime Trio and Betty-Jane Smith also will be seen in the "in person" show.

BUY U. S. WAR BONDS AND SAVINGS STAMPS

MOTION PICTURES

Didn't Know His Pockets Were Loaded, With Slugs

Jules Biderman, 63, of 2834 W. 19th St., was arraigned in Weekend Court yesterday on a charge of dropping slugs into a subway turnstile. He was arraigned on the complaint of Randolf Marrett, who said he saw Biderman drop the slug into the turnstile coin box.

There were six slugs in Biderman's pocket when he was arrested, but he told the court he formerly worked for a company that used the slugs for its vending machines, and that he did not even realize the slugs were in his pockets.

Magistrate Frances W. Lehrich paroled him for a hearing in Bay Ridge Court Thursday.

City Patrol Corps To Enlist Women For Varied Duties

Women volunteers for police service, clerical and transportation jobs are being sought by the City Patrol Corps, it has been announced at the headquarters of the Civilian Defense Volunteer Office at City Hall, Manhattan.

Volunteers for clerical work are not required to wear uniforms, drill or take a physical examination, but may do any of these if they desire. Fingerprinting is required of all volunteers. These women do office work for the patrol corps.

Volunteers for transportation service are urgently needed in all boroughs of the city except Richmond. They must use their own automobiles to transport members of the corps to their assigned posts of duty.

Volunteers for police duty are needed in all boroughs, according to Maj. Gen. Robert M. Danford, commandant of the City Patrol Corps. They assist policewomen assigned to duty in public places and are expected to serve a minimum of four hours per week. They may serve from 7 to 11 p.m. on week days and from 1 to 5 p.m. on Sundays and holidays. They also serve on various needed details.

Volunteers for clerical service work mainly during the afternoon and evening, and transportation service workers serve any four hours between 4 p.m. and midnight.

Crews to Be Sworn on Vote Board Wednesday

Presiding Justice Edward Lazansky, of the Appellate Division, will administer the oath Wednesday at 10:30 a.m., to John R. Crews, the Republican county chairman, who takes office Jan. 1 as a new member of the Board of Elections.

Commissioner Crews, named last week by the City Council for a two year term, succeeds Commissioner J. A. Livingston, who retires because of the age limit.

You'll want to read

On Tour . . . with your Personal Shopper

Shopping the town is a big job . . . but your personal shopper has done it for you. She brings you news of interesting stores, unusual merchandise, exceptional values, worthwhile places to buy. And all her findings are briefly but clearly reported. Save yourself valuable time and the perplexity of knowing where and what to buy.

TURN TO THE Society Pages IN TODAY'S BROOKLYN EAGLE

Eagle Staff photos

SANTA CLAUS IS COMING—Eagle cameramen scouted around through Brooklyn store toy departments for evidences of the coming miraculous visit of Santa Claus Friday. Here is a young lady full of anticipatory glee.

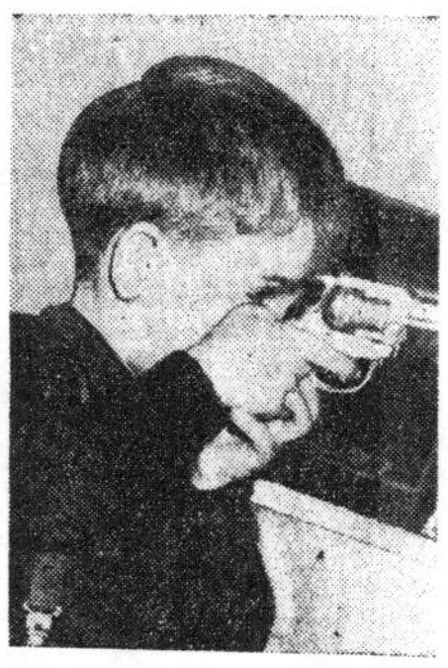

BANG, BING! — Appeal of firearms is distinct this year. Here a Brooklyn youngster emulates many of his elders now banging away with live ammunition.

THE NAVY—This youngster's predilection for the sea is clearly demonstrated by his uniform. But what is he doing with a toy field piece?

For Service Men

The New York City Defense Recreation Committee, 99 Park Ave. (at 40th St.), through the generosity of the entertainment world offers a partial list of free amusement and recreational activities available today. Afternoon tickets from 11 a.m., evening tickets from 4 p.m. Apply 99 Park Ave. for tickets.

The Brooklyn Defense Recreation committee, Concord and Navy Sts., and the T. V. S. O. Information Center and Lounge, 191 Joralemon St., also distribute free tickets to leading Brooklyn moving picture theaters and various other amusements on special occasions.

STAGE PLAYS

Tickets available for matinee and evening performances of many legitimate Broadway plays through the courtesy of the League of New York Theaters.

MOTION PICTURES

Tales of Manhattan—St. George Playhouse (Brooklyn).
White Cargo — Metropolitan (Brooklyn).
How Green Was My Valley—Tivoli (Brooklyn).
My Sister Eileen—Fox (Brooklyn).
Now, Voyager — Brooklyn Paramount.
Once Upon a Honeymoon—Albee (Brooklyn).

MUSIC

Philharmonic-Symphony Society—Carnegie Hall, 3 p.m.
Trapp Family Singers — Town Hall.
Dimitry Markevitch, cellist—Brooklyn Academy of Music.
Jewish Choral Society—Y. M. H. A.
"La Traviata"—Hunts Point Palace, Bronx, 3:15 p.m. (Uniform is pass).

SPORTS—OTHER EVENTS

Observatories Tour—Empire State Building (Uniform is pass).
N. B. C. Tours—Rockefeller Center.
Hayden Planetarium.
Soccer—Starlight Park Stadium (Uniform is pass).
Hockey—Madison Square Garden, 1:30 p.m. and 8:40 p.m.

PARTIES-HOSPITALITY.

Vassar Club—Apply 99 Park Ave. for passes.
Engineering Women's Club—Apply 99 Park Ave. for passes.
Nat'l Catholic Community Service—17 51st St., 3 p.m.
Jewish Welfare Board Club—1 E 65th St., 5 p.m.

THE TINKER—This lad, you can plainly see, is going to spend Christmas day busily absorbed in whatever Santa Claus leaves for him. Clearly the studious type.

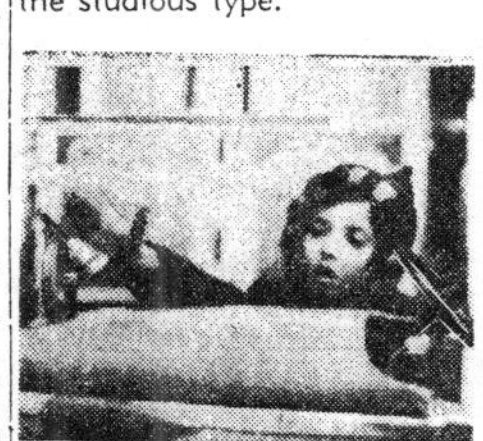

NOISE—Plenty of sound is one of the keenest of childhood pleasures. Here a little girl demonstrates her delight in ringing bell of toy auto.

3 L. I. Girls Study Child Recreation

Special to the Brooklyn Eagle:

Chambersburg, Pa., Dec. 19—Three Long Island girls are among the Wilson College students who are carrying on an experiment designed to show how any community can provide wholesome recreation for its children at small cost.

They are Virginia Coburn, daughter of Mr. and Mrs. Richard A. Coburn of 224-35 93d Road, Queens Village; Alice Hering, daughter of the Rev. and Mrs. Ambrose Hering of 65 Vincent Place, Lynbrook, and Ann Marquesee, daughter of Mrs. Jack Marquesee of 980 Benton Ave., Woodmere.

The experiment is under way at the neighborhood play center just established by the Wilson Social Service Association at an expenditure of little money and much ingenuity on the campus in one-time storage rooms. The willing subjects of the experiment are Chambersburg youngsters, who participate in handicrafts, dramatics, sports and games.

BUY U. S. WAR BONDS AND SAVINGS STAMPS

EMERALD BALL APPROVED—Bishop Thomas E. Molloy of the Catholic Diocese of Brooklyn is shown reading the first public announcement of this year's Emerald Ball during the annual visit by the officers and directors of the Association. The affair is given annually for the benefit of the Roman Catholic Orphan Asylum Society. In the photo are, left to right, seated, Paul H. Keller, financial secretary; Secretary of State Walsh, Bishop Molloy and William J. Grace, president. Standing, left to right, are Congressman Eugene J. Keogh, first vice president; Henry Mannix, James J. Brown Jr., Federal Housing Administrator Grace, Edward C. Dowden, the latter four of the board of directors; Collector of Internal Revenue Nunan, second vice president, and John J. Lynch, recording secretary.

APPROVAL DUE ON STABILIZATION PLAN FOR TAXES

Would Set Up Tax Reserves to Prevent Revenue Fluctuations

Although Governor-elect Dewey, his fiscal advisers and the legislative leaders have had comparatively little time to discuss administration policies, the belief expressed in usually well-posted sources last night was that one proposal due for approval would be the GOP tax stabilization reserve plan.

The plan, in effect, provides for setting up a system of tax reserves against future rainy days in the financial affairs of the State in order to prevent revenue fluctuations which result from business depressions.

The plan's sponsors argue the time is ripe for its approval because of the State's excellent financial position at present when a possible $80,000,000 so-called surplus or balance has been predicted for the end of the current fiscal year and Governor Charles Poletti has asserted another 25 percent reduction of State income taxes may be possible.

Other Plans Studied.

Aside from the quarterly payment plan on income taxes Governor-elect Dewey is known to be studying various proposals for State tax relief, including deductions for unusual medical and hospital expenses and for insurance payments in computing income tax returns.

The Republican tax reserve plan has been under consideration for a period of years. It was advocated in the report of the Joint Legislative Committee on State Fiscal Affairs in 1937. This group, headed by Chairman Abbot Low Moffat of the Assembly Ways and Means Committee, proposed a series of far-reaching budget and tax reforms, only a few of which have been accomplished.

The Republican-controlled Legislature of 1941 gave preliminary approval to a constitutional amendment authorizing the establishment of tax revenue stabilization funds to be used only if revenue for any year falls below a norm to be determined on the basis of past revenues.

In order to be acted upon by the voters at the election in November, 1943, the proposed amendment comes before the incoming Legislature for the second approval, which is required before any constitutional change may be passed on to the people.

Cites the Times

The joint legislative committee's report pointed out that in times of increasing prosperity the tax revenues of the State Government increase beyond immediate needs, but that in such times it has been considered "politically wise" to reduce taxes. In bad times, on the other hand, the report stated, it has always been necessary to impose new or additional taxes and resort to borrowing.

The report advocated creation of a system of tax reserves to effectuate a partial stabilization of revenue from the more widely fluctuating taxes in the State tax structure. The committee found that the levies mostly subject to wide fluctuation were the personal income, corporation and stock transfer taxes.

High School Fills Order

Portland, Ore. (U.P.)—Members of Benson High School's woodworking class were surprised but undaunted the other day at a hurryup order by the Red Cross for 1,100 cribbage boards to be included in packages to American soldiers overseas. In just 3½ days 18 boys of the department finished the boards, 130,000 drilled holes and all.

No Charge for 20th

Lock Haven, Pa. (U.P.)—If the stork makes its 20th visit to the home of Mr. and Mrs. James Roy Hill medical services will be free of charge. Dr. T. E. Teah, attending physician at the birth of the Hills' 19th child, a boy, told the proud father that "the next one is on me."

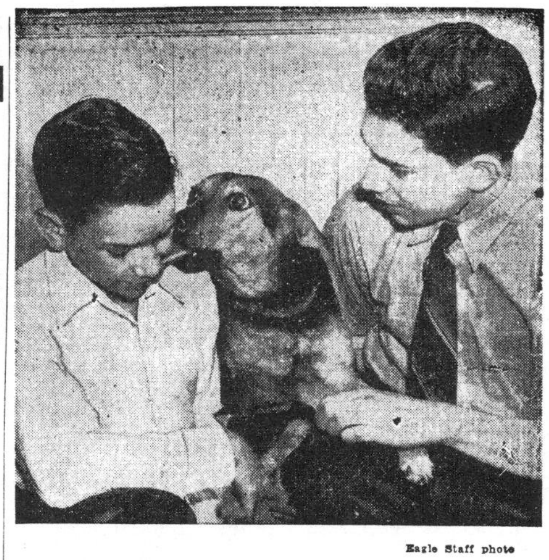

Eagle Staff photo

K-9 CORPS ROOKIE—Zuker, pet of Brooklyn boys, was accepted for the army by War Dogs for Defense. But gas shortage kept her from induction base. Left to right, Manuel Muniz, 12, and Primivito Muniz, 15, of 46 Henry Street.

Federation to Launch Campaign at Dinner

The Eastern Parkway Division of the New York and Brooklyn Federations of Jewish Charities will launch its annual campaign at a dinner on Tuesday, at 6:30 o'clock, at the Brooklyn Jewish Center, 667 Eastern Parkway, it was announced yesterday by Maurice Bernhardt, division chairman.

The affair will benefit the 116 health and welfare institutions affiliated with the two federations and will pay tribute to Samuel Rottenberg, on the occasion of his 70th birthday, for his lifetime of service to civic and philanthropic causes. Mr. Rottenberg was founder and for ten years president of the Brooklyn Jewish Center. Isidor Fine is chairman of the dinner committee.

'Flare Path' Looks Dim at the Miller

Girl Must Choose Between R. A. F. Pilot and Film Star in New Play

By ARTHUR POLLOCK

Terence Rattigan, who wrote "French Without Tears" some seasons ago, is in the R. A. F. now and has succeeded in doing a play about his fellow fliers without making the R. A. F. seem very exciting. He remembers too well. He remembers the old theatrical dodges. So there is corn in "Flare Path," which Gilbert Miller presented last night at Henry Miller's Theater.

A girl, actress, married to a flier, lived with a Hollywood actor for a year and ran away from him, though she loved him. The actor comes to the little hotel near the airdrome to take her away from her husband. But just as she is about to tell Teddy, the bomber pilot, that she's leaving him, he has to take off on a bombing flight to Germany. She sees him go and waits for his return. And that brings about a change in her. Noting the change, the actor tells her he can't live without her. Then the flier tells her that flying frightens him terribly and he needs her. That puts her in Candida's spot. Both need her. Which will she choose?

A movie actor! He hardly seems to be aware that there is a war. It makes for pretty trivial stuff. If it were trivial and spirited no one need complain too much. But "Flare Path" moves slowly, has no resilience in its talk, remains always tame. Once the actor translates for a wife a letter written in French by the Polish flier who is her husband and seems to be lost. A count, he married an English barmaid because he was lonely and she helped him find the address he wanted. The letter of goodbye gives a better picture of the man who wrote it than Mr. Rattigan can give us of any of his other characters who spend the evening talking.

The Poles, says Terry, the pilot who has to fight terror every time he goes up, fight fiercely, are eager to kill Germans. "But we are rather bored." he adds. The day before in confessing his fear to his wife in order to make a scene that the author wanted to be effective, a bore was not the term for bombing. Mr. Rattigan is said to have written his play in a hurry and no doubt did not mind if it turned out elementary.

A few moments of mild excitement it has. Most of the time, however, it moves along slowly, merely making believe. Margaret Webster's direction helps very little. The acting, like the writing, is done largely by cliche.

Perhaps Alec Guinness as Terry is the most successful of the players.

BEVERLY BAYNE, playing Mrs. Brown in "Claudia," which celebrated its 700th performance last night at the Forrest Theater.

At least the limpness of the play does not prevent his appearing to be a good actor. Nancy Kelly is pretty and earnest as the girl, Doris Patston does a good job as the barmaid who married the Polish count, Alexander Ivo is amusing as that bewildered nobleman, Arthur Margetson, as the Hollywood star, hasn't much chance; Gerald Savory is a bombardier who used to be a bus conductor, Helena Pickard his wife, Reynolds Denniston a squadron leader, and Bob White is the boy who works at the hotel run by a severe lady played nicely by Cynthia Latham.

Samuel Goldwyn has taken an option on the services of Lucille and Eddie Roberts, magical mentalists, touring army camps for the USO, and plans using them in the next Bob Hope picture.

BUY U. S. WAR BONDS AND SAVINGS STAMPS

HOLIDAY ATTRACTION at RKO neighborhood theaters starting today, is "You Can't Escape Forever." George Meeker, Joe Downing and Brenda Marshall are shown in a scene from this Warner Bros. production. Added feature is "The Navy Comes Through."

'Flying Fortress' Held 2d Week at B'klyn Strand

"Flying Fortress," a Warner Bros. picture starring Richard Greene who obtained a special leave from his duties in the tank corps of the British Army to appear in this picture, will be held over for a second week beginning tomorrow, at the Brooklyn Strand Theater. "Wildcat," co-featuring Richard Arlen and Arline Judge will be the second feature.

"Flying Fortress" deals with modern warfare in the skies—American eagles piloting two-ton "blockbusters" on German objectives. Richard Greene is seen as a reckless American flyer who joins the Atlantic Ferry Command.

Orchestra Leader Writes a Play

Leo Crane, orchestra leader and musical director, has completed the score and book of a musical comedy, "Nickel in the Slot," and has submitted it to several producers. It deals with a family who run a candy store in Brooklyn and suddenly finds its main source of income cut off when the Mayor decrees that all pin-ball machines are illegal.

MOVIE TIME TABLE

BROOKLYN

ALBEE—"Once Upon a Honeymoon." 12:30, 3:50, 7:10, 10:30; "The Great Gildersleeve," 11:25, 2:45, 6:05, 9:30.
FOX—"My Sister Eileen," 12:35, 3:48; "Counter Espionage," 11:15, 2:28; "Gentlemen Jim," 5:52, 8:51, 11:50; "Secret Enemies," 7:46, 10:45.
MAJESTIC—"City of Silent Men," 11, 2, 4:30, 7, 9:30; "The Rear of the Enemy," 12:30, 3:20, 6, 8, 10:30.
METROPOLITAN—"Who Done It?" 12:08, 2:52, 5:25, 7:58, 10:42, 1:26; "Behind the Eight Ball," 11:01, 1:15, 4:18, 6:51, 9:35, 12:19.
PARAMOUNT—"Road to Morocco," 11:05, 2:11, 5:17, 8:01, 10:45, 1:29; "Henry Aldrich, Editor," 12:48, 3:54, 6:49, 9:33, 12:17.
STRAND—"Flying Fortress," 12:45, 3:35, 6:20, 9:05, 11:50; "You Can't Escape Forever," 11:15, 2:10, 4:55, 7:40, 10:25.

MANHATTAN

ASTOR—"For Me and My Gal," 10:05, 12:17, 2:29, 4:41, 6:53, 9:05, 11:17.
CAPITOL—"In Which We Serve," 10, 12:27, 2:54, 5:21, 7:48, 10:15, 12:32.
PARAMOUNT—"Road to Morocco," 10:41, 1:32, 4:41, 7:50, 10:56, 12:37; stage show, 12:29, 3:40, 6:49, 9:58.
ROXY—"Black Swan," 11, 1:50, 4:50, 7:50, 11; stage show, 12:55, 3:50, 7, 10.

Gentleman Jim; Other Reviews

By JANE CORBY

Continued from Page 4

course of his career. The San Francisco waterfront provides the scenes of one of the most spectacular of Corbett's earliest fights, when society folks and waterfront hangers-on gather on a barge and along the shore to witness what was then an illegal boxing bout, and which is broken up by the police just as Corbett kayoed his man.

Highlight of the tale is Corbett's vanquishing of John L. Sullivan—"himself"—portrayed by Ward Bond. Sullivan's relinquishing of the golden belt is a touching scene, sympathetically played by Bond, a now pathetically deflated champion, and made poignant by Flynn's sudden transformation from a boastful, confident young man, to a quiet, understanding fellow who can appreciate the older man's feelings.

"Gentleman Jim" is a fine record of the early history of pugilism in this country, as well as robust entertainment.

The second feature at the Fox is "Secret Enemies," with Craig Stevens and Faye Emerson.

AT LOEW'S MET: 'WHO DONE IT?'

All is goofy on the holiday screen at Loew's Met, where beginning today Abbott and Costello start the hilarity rolling with "Who Done It?", and the Ritz Brothers, assisted by Carol Bruce, carrying on from there in "Behind the Eight Ball," which is having its first New York showing at the Metropolitan. It's a dual all-laff show which will be enjoyed by youngsters between the ages of six and 60 and which will cause more mature folk to gorget their 70 or 80 years.

"Who Done It?" is the eighth starring Abbott and Costello production. In this story they are supposed to be amateur sleuths; but there's a funny story about that—half way through the script when the picture was being made they weren't sure themselves. They went to Associate Producer Alex Gottlieb and told him they couldn't stand the suspense any longer. "Are we the criminals or not?" they demanded. "Right now it looks as if we're guilty." Bud and Lou, it seems, never read a script, as a usual thing; but this time the producer had insisted. Result: Two comics so tangled in their own plot that they didn't know whether they were going to end up as detectives or chasing themselves as criminals.

And the audience gets just as much involved, too, for the new fun film is a howling travesty on murder-mystery dramas and the kind of scientific crime detection in which they engage is nothing to get serious about. Action takes place for the most part in a vast studio broadcasting station, where the boys get into sound effects jams and Costello even tries to do a turn as a tightrope walker on the studio aerial dizzy stories above the sidewalk

The zany duo's supporting cast includes Patric Knowles, Louise Albritton, William Gargan and William Bendix, who give topnotch performances.

BUY U. S. WAR BONDS AND SAVINGS STAMPS

Buck Jones' Last Film At the Majestic Friday

"Dawn on the Great Divide," a Monogram Picture, starring Buck Jones, popular movie hero of many westerns, arrives at the Majestic Theater tomorrow. This is Buck Jones' last picture; he died in the Boston holocaust which cost hundreds of lives a few weeks ago.

"Dawn on the Great Divide" is a stirring story of pioneer days in the great West, with Mona Barrie, Raymond Hatton and Robert Lowery in featured roles. Also on the Majestic holiday program is "The Pride of the Army," with "Ace" the wonder dog. It is a suspense packed story of the spy war, with the dogs that take part in the war effort playing a leading role. Human stars include Billy Lee, Addison Richards, Bradley Page and Kay Linaker.

Special films included in the holiday attractions for the youngsters are "Pardon My Pups," with Shirley Temple, and "The Sweet Pie and Pie," with the Three Stooges.

Brooklyn Paramount, Fox Late Shows Tonight

The Brooklyn Paramount and Fox Brooklyn Theaters, in addition to their respective scheduled runnings of their feature screen attraction tonight, will present an extra late showing of the film programs in order that those of our patrons who find it impossible to attend the earlier shows, may see a later performance of the entire screen offering at both theaters.

The Brooklyn Paramount theater is currently showing the new Bing Crosby, Bob Hope, Dorothy Lamour film, "The Road to Morocco" together with the light and entertaining, "Henry Aldrich, Editor." The film program at the Fox is Errol Flynn's latest starring vehicle, "Gentleman Jim," the screen story of the life of James J. Corbett, in which he appears opposite Alexis Smith. The associate feature is "Secret Enemies," with Craig Stevens and Faye Emerson in the leading roles.

JOHN CARROLL—One of the Flying Tigers in the picture of the same name playing at the Loew's neighborhood theaters starting today.

'Arabian Nights' Due At Rivoli Christmas

On Christmas morning the management of the Rivoli Theater will present, following the currently showing "Palm Beach Story," co-starring Claudette Colbert and Joel McCrea, Universal's fiery adventure story "Arabian Nights."

MOTION PICTURES

She gave everything to the men she loved...
... What Must They Do To Win It?
That's Shera—Queen of the Harem. A thousand men dream of her beauty ... a thousand men fight for her love. Wild adventure ... exotic love await you behind guarded harem gates in the mysterious East!
WALTER WANGER'S MIGHTY PRODUCTION
Arabian Nights
IN TECHNICOLOR
starring JON HALL · MARIA MONTEZ · SABU
with LEIF ERIKSON · BILLY GILBERT · EDGAR BARRIER
SHEMP HOWARD · THOMAS GOMEZ · TURHAN BEY
A UNIVERSAL PICTURE
Maria Montez as Sherazade, the Desert Queen
GALA PREMIERE
Xmas Day 9:30 A.M.
RIVOLI
Broadway at 49th

MOTION PICTURES

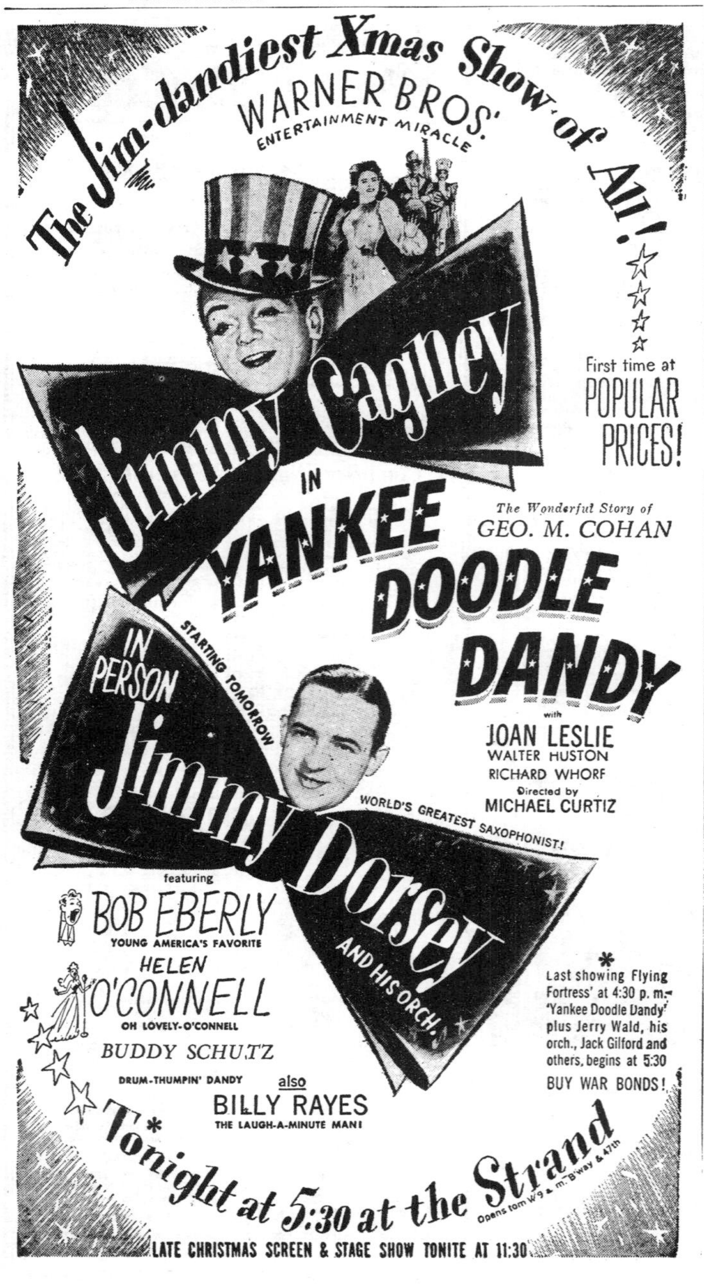

The Jim-dandiest Xmas Show of All!
WARNER BROS.' ENTERTAINMENT MIRACLE
First time at POPULAR PRICES!
Jimmy Cagney
IN
YANKEE DOODLE DANDY
The Wonderful Story of GEO. M. COHAN
with
JOAN LESLIE
WALTER HUSTON
RICHARD WHORF
Directed by MICHAEL CURTIZ
STARTING TOMORROW
IN PERSON
Jimmy Dorsey AND HIS ORCH.
WORLD'S GREATEST SAXOPHONIST!
featuring
BOB EBERLY
YOUNG AMERICA'S FAVORITE
HELEN O'CONNELL
OH LOVELY-O'CONNELL
BUDDY SCHUTZ
DRUM-THUMPIN' DANDY
also
BILLY RAYES
THE LAUGH-A-MINUTE MAN!
Last showing Flying Fortress' at 4:30 p. m.-'Yankee Doodle Dandy' plus Jerry Wald, his orch., Jack Gilford and others, begins at 5:30
BUY WAR BONDS!
Tonight at 5:30 at the Strand
LATE CHRISTMAS SCREEN & STAGE SHOW TONITE AT 11:30

HUMPHREY Bogart · INGRID Bergman · PAUL Henreid
HOLLYWOOD B'WAY, 51ST
WARNER BROS.'
CASABLANCA
A HAL B. WALLIS PRODUCTION
CONTINUOUS OPENS 11:30 A.M.

GIVE BONDS FOR XMAS!

What You Buy With WAR BONDS

Stop Spending, and **Save for the future.** That has been good advice since biblical days. You cannot buy tires today, but you can **start saving** to buy that new set of tires when they go on the market again.

Your regular investment of ten percent or more of your earnings in **War Bonds** through your **Payroll Savings Plan** will provide the necessary funds to buy those tires later and help win the war now. Let's **"Top that Ten Percent by New Year's."**

U. S. Treasury Department

NEW YORK'S GREATEST STAGE AND SCREEN SHOW!
Tyrone POWER · Maureen O'HARA
in THE BLACK SWAN
in Technicolor
A 20th Century-Fox Picture
ON STAGE
In Person CARMEN MIRANDA
and her BANDA DA LUA
NICHOLAS BROTHERS
Plus Other Big Acts!
Doors Open 10:30 A.M.
Roxy
7th Ave. at 50th St.
BUY WAR BONDS

SHOWPLACE OF THE NATION
RADIO CITY MUSIC HALL
ROCKEFELLER CENTER
HELD OVER—SECOND WEEK!
Ronald COLMAN · Greer GARSON
IN JAMES HILTON'S
"RANDOM HARVEST"
The Hall of Fame Picture · Directed by MERVYN LEROY
Produced by SIDNEY FRANKLIN · An M-G-M Picture
Great Christmas Stage Show: "THE NATIVITY," famed annual pageant, and "HATS OFF!" gay holiday spectacle, produced by Leonidoff, with Rockettes, Corps de Ballet, Glee Club, Symphony Orchestra, direction of Erno Rapee.
Doors Open 10:15 A.M. · Picture at: 10:20, 1:19, 4:18, 7:17, 10:19
Stage Show at: 12:26, 3:27, 6:26, 9:29 · Doors Open Friday 9:30 A.M.
FIRST MEZZANINE SEATS RESERVED IN ADVANCE · Phone Circle 6-4600
Buy U. S. War Bonds and Stamps For Christmas—Available in Foyer

Americans everywhere can help their country defeat the enemy aggressors by investing often and regularly in War Bonds and Stamps.

FOR THE GREATEST REVIEWS EVER ACCORDED A MOTION PICTURE —READ TODAY'S NEWSPAPERS!
The Greatest Human Drama of Our Time!
NOEL COWARD'S
"IN WHICH WE SERVE"
Starring NOEL COWARD
Released thru United Artists
CAPITOL B'WAY and 51st ST.
Continuous Performances · Popular Prices
BUY WAR BONDS AND STAMPS

Fighting Men Everywhere Join in Christmas Greetings

Thousands of Brooklyn's men in Uncle Sam's fighting forces, stationed in all parts of the country, streamed back to their home town during the past week for Christmas furloughs.

Many additional thousands, unable to obtain leave, will have their holiday dinners in army and navy posts in all sections of the nation, as well as on far-flung fighting fronts, with thoughts of home uppermost in their minds.

Many of the men are visiting their homes for the first time in many months, and the borough will extend a warm welcome to them as well as to recent inductees and enlisted men.

The following are some of those who are spending the holiday in Brooklyn and Long Island:

Petty Officer Arthur L. Guideli, U. S. Coast Guard, 7901 15th Avv., will celebrate his Christmas furlough by becoming engaged to Frances Ingeao, 8631 15th Ave.

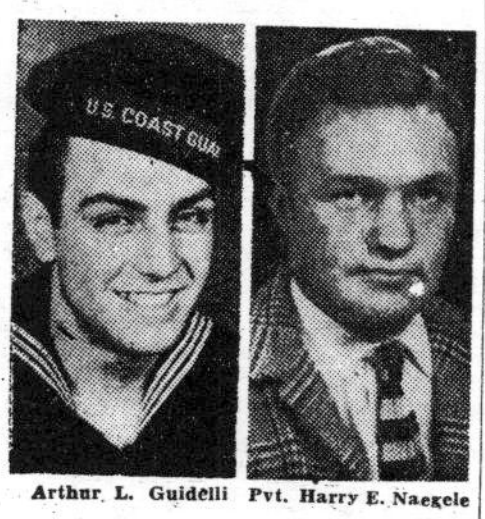

Arthur L. Guidelli Pvt. Harry E. Naegele

Pvt. Harry E. Naegele, 1880 Willoughby Ave., will be home from Langley Field, Va., to spend the holidays with his family. A brother, Jack, also home for Christmas, will go into active service with the Naval Reserve on his return to Notre Dame College. A third brother, Edwin, attending Bishop Loughlin High School, is planning to join the Canadian Navy. Anita Rita, a sister, is awaiting notification of appointment to the officers candidate school of the Waacs.

Pfc. Donald Sutherland of 20 Plaza St., who has won three medals for bayonet, rifle and hand grenade, expects to attend Officers Candidate School upon his return.

Donald Sutherland 20 Plaza St. Pvt. William F. Sweeney

Pvt. William F. Sweeney of Ft. Sill, Okla., will spend Christmas with his bride, Gertrude, at 901 80th Street.

Lt. Albert N. Blanchard, U. S. N. R., son of Mrs. William A. Blanchard, will spend Christmas at home, 1044 84th St. He is an instructor at Dartmouth College, Hanover, N. H.

Lt. Albert N. Blanchard

Roland J. Callahan, seaman, 308 E. 39th St., now assigned to Fort Trumbull, New London, Conn., where he is training for his third mate's rating.

Sgt. Arthur Bunin, stationed at Myrtle Beach, South Carolina.

Staff Sgt. Martin O'Brien from McDill Field, Fla, and his brother, Sgt. Patrick, stationed at Camp Chadbourne, La. Both live at 6621 Avenue T.

Corp. Harold F. Moles, 165 Gates Ave., from Cherry Point, N. C.

Pvt. George J. Evans Jr., 1042 75th St., who is attached to special training unit, Miami Beach, Fla.

Sgt. William Jasmagy of 50 Pulaski St.

Lt. Charles J. McCarthy of 257 E. 32d St., stationed at Camp Pickett, Va.

Lt. Michael Del Casino and Sgt. Anthony Del Casino of 235 Steuben St.

Joseph P. McGuire, enlisted reserve corps, 594 Rogers Ave., from Camp Paul Smith, N. Y.

Pvt. Richard Plum, 271 76th St., from Camp Pickett, Va.

Francis J. Rogers, 395 Fenimore St., with the marines from New River, N. C.

Second Lt. Frank E. Leonard Jr., 585 E. 7th St., stationed at Washington, D. C.

Sgt. Frank Monteleone, 351 Avenue W, from Gunter Field, Ala., where he is a sergaent crew chief.

Pfc. Anthony J. Curro, stationed at Ft. John Custis, Cape Charles, Va.

Pfc. David Gittner, 803 E. 35th St., home from Camp Gruber, Okla.

Pfc. Eugene Doerr, 5921 4th Ave., of the parachute troops.

Richard P. Scanlon, seaman, 175 Rogers Ave., from Great Lakes Naval Training Station.

Pvt. Walter Kearns, 559 Nostrand Ave., stationed at Ft. Eustis, Va.

Albert W. Spehr, 169 Rugby Rd. with the marines at New River, N. C.

Michael O'Donnell, seaman second class, of Brooklyn, from Ship Bottom, N. J.

Sgt. Robert Patrick Dunne, 37 Madison St., from Ft. Jackson, S. C.

Pfc. Raymond A. McMahon, 549 E. 26th St., from Camp Cooke, Cal.

Lt. L. A. Swenson, 762 E. 18th St., from Ft. Benning, Ga.

Second Lt. Alfred A. Gentilcore, 378 E. 46th St. with his bride, the former Raye Katz, from Camp Barkley, Texas.

Pvt. John M. Renehan, 234 Baltic St., from Camp Pickett, Va.

Pvt. Irving Abrams, 27 Hart St., at air corps radio school in Chicago. He will be gradutted from school early in January.

Marie A. Balandis, who is scheduled to report to the Waac camp in Daytona Beach, Fla. She formerly was employed by the Farm Credit Administration and the Veterans, Administration. She attended Girls Commercial High School.

2d Lt. Archie A. Ignatow, 365 Lincoln Place, recently commissioned from Carlisle Barracks, Pa., leaves for his new post at Fort Bragg, N. C., Jan. 3.

Pvt. Herbert Klein, 210 Roebling St., is at the Chicago School of Aircraft Instruments, Chicago, Ill.

Sgt. Thomas J. Hynes, 74 Lawrence Ave., stationed at Fort Jackson, S. C. His brother, Pfc. James F. Hynes, formerly at Fort Bragg, is overseas.

Charles Tagliani, 288 Lincoln Ave., a graduate of Boys High School, has just returned from Africa. He was formerly on the Hugh L. Scott.

Pfc. John J. Taylor, 2100 Flatbush Ave., now at Ordnance Training School, Aberdeen, Md. His brother, Pfc. William C. Taylor Jr., entered training in optic instruments at Mississippi Ordnance Plant, Flora, Miss.

Thomas Flery, 723 E. 9th St., is with the Army Paratroops at Fort Bragg, N. C.

Raymond Williams, 153 Garfield Place, at the Portland Naval Base, expects to be home for New Yar's.

Sgt. Daniel J. Grosso, 87 Hicks St., a graduate of St. John's Episcopal Preparatory School and St. John's University, now with the hospital medical detachment in St. John, British Columbia, and his brother, Edward, former Deputy Internal Revenue Collector, stationed in the air corps headquarters at Atlantic City, are both at home f.or the first time in a year.

William R. Nummy, pharmacists mate, 3d class, 108 Forbell St., home ffom active service during the African invasion, is on a 30-day leave.

Herman Martin Steinman, 2225 E. 26th St., with the amy air cborps is now stationed at Atantic City, N. J.

Staff Sgt. Eliot Levin, 276 Dover St., with the army air corps at Walterboro, S. C.

Lt. Robert B. Haber, 1195 E. 12th St., former football star and graduate of Erasmus Hall High School and Rutgers College, now stationed at Los Angeles, Cal. His brother, Lt. Seymour R. Haber, is with the Physical Training Department at Shaw Field, S. C.

Pvt. John Baldo, at Fort Benning, Ga., and his brother, Vincent, stationed with the Coast Guard at Fort McHenry, Md., of 169 Lake St., home for the holidays. A third brother, Pvt. Joseph Baldo, is somewhere in Ireland.

Henry J. Blackwell of Brooklyn was recently promoted to staff sergeant at the parachute school, Fort Benning, Ga.

Corp. Robert E. Topping, 1423 Mill Ave., who attended Erasmus Hall High School, now stationed in the medical corps at Lemoore, Cal.

Sgt. Cyrus Esposito, 354 42d St., at Fort Hancock, N. J.

Pvt. Fred R. Gregson, former Sperry worker and graduate of St. Augustine's High School, now at Miami Beach, Fla.

Staff Sgt. Bernard Zuckman, 1842 E. 29th St., Coney Island, is at Sebring, Fla.

Pfc. John Slattery, 777 Franklin Ave., is stationed at Cochran Field, Georgia.

Corp. Walter F. Balletto, 279 Warren St., formerly a teacher of English at the Brooklyn High School of Specialty Trades, is now at Camp Polk, La.

Sgt. David Johnsen, 62 Eaton Court, stationed at Gunter Field, Ala.

Seaman Fred Kroog, 115 St. Mark's Place, radio student at Boston, is on furlough with his two brothers, Ernest and Teddy, who will join the service immediately after the holidays.

Capt. V. T. Montemorano, army medical corps, will spend Christmas with his parents, Mr. and Mrs. A. Montemarano, 451 Carroll St. His two brothers, Corp. Joseph and Pvt. Angelo Montemarano, will also be home.

Pfc. R. W. Jensen, 338 92d St., Drew Field, Fla. — Pfc. G. W. Allen, 811 Beverley Road, Fort Jackson, S. C. — Richard Foley, 681 Vanderbilt Ave., Nashville, Tenn. — R. A. Schmitt, 451 Bainbridge St., Breezy Point, Va.

Lt. H. S. Wilms 301 E. 23d St. Camp Lee, Va. — Pvt. J. F. McGuinness 296 Sterling Place Stinson Field, Texas — Francis G. Alverzo 1460 E. 53d St. Little Creek, Va. — Pvt. Frank Dunn 8868 17th Ave. Los Angeles, Cal.

J. P. Jackson Jr. 1212 Glenwood Road Annapolis, Md. — Corp. Joseph Vignola 1253 65th St., Camp Chaffee, Ark. — Pvt. A. J. Christiano 458 Carroll St. — Pvt. Albert Parente 1373 56th St. Camp Jackson, S. C.

Pfc. Peter Senia 160 Ryerson St. Ft. Barrancas, Fla. — Frank Balestrine 942 67th St. Nashville, Tenn. — Kenneth Gibson 165 Columbia H'ghts — Pvt. G. W. Ansorge 2100 Westbury Court Fort Revere, Mass.

Second Lt. Daniel T. Drubin of 625 Rugby Road, was just commissioned upon graduation from the army air force bombardier school at San Angelo.

John T. Colgan 3415 Avenue K — Daniel T. Drubin 625 Rugby Road

John T. Colgan of 3415 Avenue K, having received his commission from Officers Candidate School at Fort Benning, Georgia, expects to spend the holidays in Brooklyn.

Corp. Don Boursheid, 348 56th St., stationed at Camp Gruber, Ala.

Pvt. Anthony Verde, 22 Morgan Ave., stationed at Atlantic Beach, Florida.

Second Lt. Arthur Carpinto, U. S. Coast Guard Medical Corps, and his brother, 2d Lt. Joseph Carpinto, U. S. Army Medical Corps, of 1833 71st St. Their nephew, 2d Cl. Seaman Joseph W. Detolla, 1535 72d St., stationed at Groton, Conn., will spend the holiday with them.

Staff Sgt. Thomas A. Dorney, 139 78th St., stationed at Fort Knox, Kentucky.

Pvt. Leonard Unger of 1013 Avenue J., a graduate of New Utrecht High School and St. John's Law School, is attached to the administrative staff at Pendleton Field, Ore.

Leonard Unger 1013 Avenue J — James J. Sullivan 310 12th St.

Machinist Mate James J. Sullivan of 310 12th St., has recently returned from Africa and is spending his Christmas leave with his family.

Vincent J. Denaro of 510 McDonald Ave., who is attending officer candidate school at Camp Davis, N. C., is spending his holiday furlough with his wife.

John H. Walters, U. S. Navy, will be with his wife and son over the holidays.

Aviation Cadet Norman B. Cabel, 739 E. 46th St., at Nashville, Tenn.

Sgt. John Edward Calacino of 109 Sterling Place, from Camp Hood, Tex.

Michael Sullivan of 372 13th St., stationed at Northport with the coast guard.

Pvt. Nils W. Person of 1645 Utica Ave., from Camp Edwards, Mass.

Aviation Cadet Milton Feinman of 6310 23d Ave., stationed at Nashville, Tenn.

Pfc. Walter J. Wolters of 8118 3d Ave., posted at Drew Field, Fla.

Pvt. Robert M. Heiberg of 750 54th St., from Atlantic City.

Corp. James E. Marsh of 4301 Foster Ave., now home on furlough from Camp Gruber, Okla., has recently become engaged to Florence M. Sullivan of 1350 Albany Ave.

Corp. James E. Marsh — Corp. Kenneth Forger

Corp. Kenneth Forger of 1434 E. 56th St. is stationed with the Signal Corps at Fort Monmouth, N. J. A brother, Pvt. Andrew H., is in the Army Air Force at Miami Beach, Fla.

Pvt. Walter J. Sabatowiz, 716 President St., is home on a 30-day furlough after spending a year in the Walter Reed Hospital, Washington, D. C.

Chief Petty Officer Jerome A. Yates, 1300 Schenectady Ave., is on leave after seeing service in Egypt.

Staff Sgt. Arthur Bunin, a graduate of Erasmus High School, is attached to the medical department, Myrtle Beach, S. C.

Pvt. George Vanderbilt, 73 Schaeffer St., of Camp Gruber, Okla., and his brother, who is in the navy, expect to spend their Christmas furloughs at home.

Sgt. John E. Crockett of Brooklyn, recently promoted to the rank of sergeant at Moody Field, Ga., will be home for Christmas.

Corp. H. J. Teitelbaum, 1844 Haring St., from Camp Claiborne, La., expects to enter officer candidate school at Duke University, N. C.

Seaman Eugene Jacob of 543 61st St., stationed at Newport, R. I.

Howard S. Johnson of 1616 E. 37th St., in the navy, from Great Lakes, Ill.

Staff Sgt. Vincent J. Sullivan of 5818 5th Ave., from Attica, N. Y.

Pvt. Thomas F. Ward, 42 Lincoln Ave., recently graduated from the air corps technical school at Chanute Field, Ill., is at home over Christmas.

Lt. James A. Parker of 7904 5th Ave., a recent graduate from Officers Candidate School, Miami Beach, Fla., will return to his new station at Bolling Field, Washington, D. C.

John Romano 1455 81st St. — James A. Parker 7904 5th Ave.

John Romano of 1455 81st St., who was graduated from basic training at the U. S. Naval Training School, Great Lakes, Illinois, will return to his duties as a hospital apprentice first class.

Corp. Michael D'Angelo of 1437 71st St. is stationed at Miami Beach, Fla.

Pfc. Ralph Proscia of 273 Bay 13th St. is on leave from Camp McCoy, Wis., to marry Miss Kitty McPhee of 197 17th St.

Seaman First Class Jack Tolson, 676 E. 43d St., stationed at Memphis, Tenn., celebrates a Christmas birthday with a ten-day furlough.

Charles Schneeman — Jack Tolson

Corp. Charles Schneeman, 1461 E. 63d St., is at Lowry Field, Colo. A graduate of Pratt Institute, he was formerly a magazine artist.

Second Lt. Frederick Shea of 356 Weirfield St., a graduate of Regis High School and Holy Cross College, was recently commissioned at Camp Davis, N. C. Shea spent seven months in Hawaii before entering officers candidate school.

Pvt. Gerard R. Cottam of 104-42 119th St., Richmond Hill, is stationed at Camp Gordon, Ga.

Pfc. John Jeans Jr., of 392 3d St. is now at Craig Field, Ala.

Second Lt. Leonard Gardner, 1324 St. John's Place, was recently commissioned at Fort Benning, Ga. A graduate of Boys High School. Lieutenant Gardner is one of the youngest men to hold that rank. He is 20 years old and enlisted in the army on July 4, 1940.

BUY U. S. WAR BONDS AND SAVINGS STAMPS

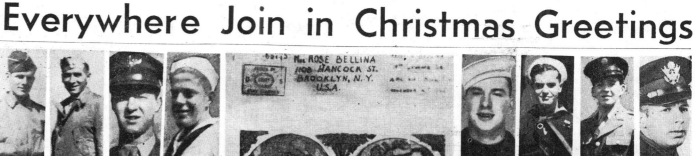

FROM MIDDLE EAST—One Brooklyn lad cannot be home for a Christmas furlough. Stationed in the Middle East is Sgt. Frank A. Bellina of 1108 Hancock St. He sent holiday greetings with the above card to his parents, Mr. and Mrs. Anthony Bellina.

Pfc. C. Lombardo Camp Gordon, Ga. — J. T. Burgess, Y.S.C. 3518 Avenue L Cape May, N. J. — Pvt. (f.c.) L. Lacosta 2281 E. 47th St. Syracuse, N. Y. — Edward McElhone 2017 Caton Ave. Pine Camp, N. Y.

CHRISTMAS AWAY—While many Brooklyn men are spending the holidays at home, these two local soldiers depend on the United Service Organizations for Yule cheer. Shown in the U. S. O. Club in Hempstead are, left to right, Sgt. Francis J. Romano of 1238 Holsey St. and Aviation Cadet John Jarembinsky of 130 17th St.

Gerard J. Bridges 249 12th St. — Edward F. Hall, 709 Decatur St. — Joseph N. Russo, 247 Woodbine St., Fort Mason, Cal. — Lt. John Richard Schippers 241A Brooklyn Ave.

Corp. M. A. Green 305 Jamaica Ave. Camp Pickett, Va. — Pvt. Michael DeMartino 78 Skillman St., Los Angeles, Cal. — Corp. Ed. Gorman 405 20th St. Ft. Ethan Allen, Va. — Clifford Foley 681 Vanderbilt Ave. Norfolk, Va.

C. H. Fairechio 985 Nostrand Ave. Camp Gruber, Okla. — John Beveridge Brooklyn, N. Y. Camp Gruber, Okla. — Lt. W. F. Heuer Jr. 1192 Brooklyn Ave., At Fort Belvoir, Va. — Sgt. A. Woods 150 Shepherd Ave. Camp Gruber, Okla.

Harry C. Buschman 1140 E. 43d St. Portsmouth, N. H. — Sgt. E. A. Caccavale 806 Hart St. Camp Myles Standish — Pvt. M. H. Schuhmann 19-21 Avenue K Camp Crowder, Mo. — Malcolm Cohen 16 Hawthorne St. M. M. 3d Class

With Our Fighting Men

1st Lt. Pierson E. Clair Jr. of 349 Linden Boulevard has received a new assignment which will take him to various posts in California and Arizona.

Sgt. T. W. Driscoll of 1170 Sheepshead Bay Road asks that Fighting Men convey his Christmas greetings to his Brooklyn friends from Fresno, Cal.

Staff Sgt. Roland L. Jones of 275 Albany Ave. was married to Dorothy Pate of Waco, Texas, and has returned to his brooklyn home. His brother, Thomas, was recently made a sergeant in Salt Lake City, Utah.

Robert J. Davidson of Brooklyn, fighting in North Africa, has been made a corporal. He is a graduate of Franklin K. Lane High School.

Frank Dolan of 2543 Church Ave. is stationed with a coast artillery unit in Colorado.

Seymour H. Rosenblum of 1680 Ocean Ave. has been graduated as a bombardier at Victoryville, Cal.

Benny Palma — S. H. Rosenblum

Pvt. Benny Palma of 1428 77th St. is now in Ireland. A neighbor, Thomas Polistena of 1670 81st St., is posted in the Panama Canal Zone.

Pvt. Bruno Sengstock of 409 Etna St. is at Fort Jackson, S. C.

Pvt. Apostolos Maravelias of 1665 E. 10th St. has been transferred from Fort Monroe, Va., to Fort Benning, Ga.

Thomas Skelly of 287 Classon Ave. has joined the navy, and a neighbor, Harry Burke of 283 Classon Ave., is with the army at Red Bank, New Jersey.

Roy Nielsen of 9016 3d Ave. is with the army air force at Miami Beach, Fla.

Ivan Stock of 601 E. 21st St. has arrived for basic training at Fort Benjamin Harrison, Ind.

Ivan Stock — Seymour Sklar

Seymour Sklar of 3145 Brighton 4th St. has completed primary flight training and has been transferred to Corpus Christi, Texas.

Pvt. Solomon Gitlin of 584 Bradford St. has arrived at the air force base at Atlantic City, N. J.

Aviation Cadet Frank D. Littel of 99 Lafayette Ave. is training to become a bombardier at Ellington Field, Texas.

Pvt. John F. English of 112 Adelphi St., now stationed at Camp Crowder, Mo., was recently home on a furlough.

News about the men and women of this community who are in service is welcomed to this department. Such news should be addressed to Fighting Men Editor, Brooklyn Eagle, Johnson and Adams Sts., Brooklyn.

Edward McElhone 2017 Caton Ave. Pine Camp, N. Y. — 900 Lafayette Ave. A. R. Israelsky Fort Dix, N. J.

WELL-EARNED REST—American and Australian anti-aircraft gunmen enjoy a bit of relaxation in New Guinea quarters after participating in a land battle in which 300 Japs were killed. The machine gun in foreground was captured during the battle. Though these men are primarily experts with "ack-acks," they can operate tommy-guns and keep them handy in case of trouble.

Peril to Judaism Seen in Zionism

The "permanent solution of the Jewish problem lies not in the establishment of Palestine as a sovereign State for the Jews but in the global efforts to rectify the wrongs afflicting all peoples and in the democratic principles of freedom, justice and humanity."

The statement, uttered by the Rev. Dr. Samuel E. Goldenson, rabbi of Manhattan's Temple Emanu-El, 5th Ave. and 66th St., last night, was echoed in considerable discussion today.

"I have found unacceptable the theory that the Jewish problem would be solved by the creation of Palestine as a Jewish sovereign State," he said. "The danger to Judaism in the Zionist doctrine is in its emphasis on the earlier and narrower features of our heritage. Realizing our unfavored position in many parts of the world, it should not be too difficult to understand that the very establishment of a Jewish State would make hostile countries feel freer to make their Jewish citizens feel uncomfortable and unwanted, if they have the excuse that the Jews have a place to go to and a place to which they belong, anyway."

Draft Official Joins the Navy

Port nd, Ore. (U.P.)—A draft board officia preferred fighting himself rather t sending others to do it.

After having signed up hundreds of draftees for military service, Carl Hering, Jefferson County draft board chairman, drafted himself recently into the navy—not the army.

"I've always wanted to enlist in the navy and, besides, one gets tired of seeing others always leaving for the big show," said Hering in his resignation letter.

Reduce Marine Insurance

Rio de Janiero (U.P.)—The Brazilian Insurance Institute announced a six percent maritime insurance reduction late in November, reflecting the success of Brazilian-United States naval anti-submarine activity on the sealanes around the eastward bulge of Brazil. The new rates are effective for shipping plying the entire length of Brazil's coastline.

BRITON ON ROAD TO ROME—In Bengazi, on North African coast, as British army moved in after Axis troops had been chased out, British tank fighter picks up an Italian propaganda book printed in English. Whatever the contents, title of the book may be pointing the way.

Investors Purchase Flushing Block Front

The one-story taxpayer, consisting of thirteen stores and a bowling alley, covering the block front on the west side of Main St., between 71st Road and 72d Ave., Flushing, L. I., has been sold to the 71-24 Main Realty Co., Inc., by Flushing Heights Realty Corp. for all cash over mortgages aggregating $77,082. The Flushing Heights Realty Corp. was represented by Sidney Hoffman, attorney, and the 71-24 Main Realty Co., Inc., by Jaffa & Silverman. Title insurance to the purchaser has been issued by Title Guarantee and Trust Company.

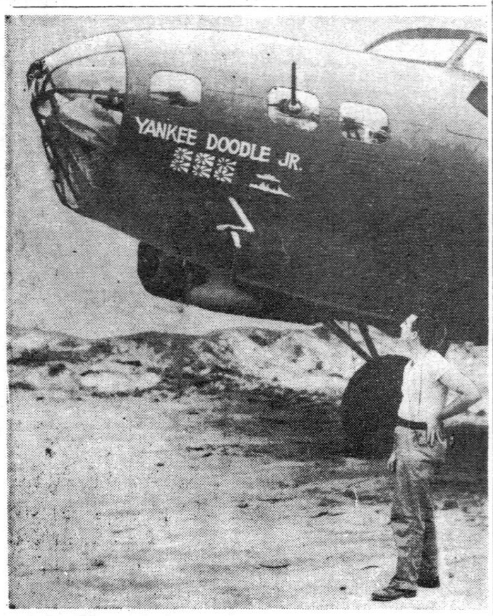

AXIS BEWARE—This United States Flying Fortress reveals its part in destroying the enemy in the South Pacific area. The silhouettes on the nose of the ship stand for a Japanese cruiser and transport sunk by the plane while each flag stands for a downed Zero.

Small War Plants Corporation Heads Facing Shakeup

Nelson Plans Move To Double the Output Of Arms This Year

Washington, Jan. 2 (U.P.)—Production Director Donald M. Nelson soon will shake up the high command of the Small War Plants Corporation as part of a program to double the output of arms in 1943, responsible officials said today.

Present plans, it was understood, call for the retention of Lou Holland, Kansas City, Mo., as head of the corporation. It was considered likely that Samuel Abbott Smith, Boston, a member of the board of directors, also would remain. But the tenure of three other directors was in doubt. They are: Albert M. Carter, Murphreesboro, Ill., banker; William S. Shiply, York, Pa., refrigerating executive, and James T. Howington, Louisville, Ky., industrialist.

WPB spokesmen said the shakeup probably would take place within two weeks. The corporation probably will continue to operate as a separate entity of the WPB but maintain closer contact with Vice Chairman Charles E. Wilson.

The Small War Plants Corporation, created to spread more of war business among little operators, was months in completing an organization and on Nov. 19, Holland reported that it had been able to negotiate only about $16,000,000 of war contracts for small firms.

Assails War Songs

Los Angeles, Cal. (U.P.)—The failure of the present war to inspire any "good" war songs is attributed by Dr. Walter H. Rubsamen, professor of music at the University of California, to the fact that the American musical ear has become so educated to jazz and syncopated rhythms that straight martial songs no longer appeal to it. "Praise the Lord and Pass the Ammunition" and "The Fuehrer's Face" mark the high-water mark of war song production to date, he said, "and a very sorry one at that."

Borough, L. I. Count 6 Dead After Safer but Wetter New Year's

Fewer Arrests but Hangovers Were Plentiful—Local Church Services Well Attended

After having welcomed 1943 with mixed emotions, flavored with reflections of past celebrations and tempered with thoughts of men fighting to the death in far corners of the globe, Brooklyn, Queens and Long Island counted up the score today—at least six dead, five seriously hurt and 13 recovering from various injuries of less consequences.

But the four counties, from Greenpoint to Greenport, were right in step with the rest of the nation in its trend toward a safer—and apparently saner—New Year's celebration, for the casualty figures were considerably lower than those last year.

Hotels, restaurants, night clubs and local bars and grills did a capacity business; liquor flowed like the proverbial water—with far more devastating effects, greenbacks were much in evidence and crowds, ditto.

Report Few Arrests

On the credit side were the police reports that drunks on the streets were comparatively rare, at least for a New Year's observance; the court records showing few arrests and the church announcements that holiday services were well attended.

Among the more serious observances of the new year's debut were the prayer and musical ceremonies held in the Council Chamber of City Hall at noon yesterday. Mayor LaGuardia, the speaker, told about 800 members of his official family that "It is going to be a hard year; stop to consider that we've been engaged only in preliminary skirmishes."

The people must "pray and hope for a speedy end that will eliminate not peoples but individuals and their regimes and their philosophy. We must remove them and then, without hatred in our hearts, approach the unfortunate people who have been misled by these cruel dictators," he said.

Following are some of the debits:

Pvt. Charles Jones, 25, attached to Company G, 113th Infantry, who was on his way home to visit his mother, Mrs. Jennie Jones of 1126 Pacific St., was killed instantly early yesterday morning by a hit-and-run driver at Coney Island Ave. and the Belt Parkway.

Drowns in Fall From Pier

Hugh J. Williamson, 60, a laborer of 1672 Davidson Ave., the Bronx, was drowned when he fell into the bay from Pier 1 at the foot of 58th St. just before dawn. Police said he apparently had tripped on the dimmed-out pier and lost his balance.

Allen G. Munn, 29, of 606 Islip Boulevard, Islip Terrace, and Harold Carrillion, 27, of 15 Willoughby Ave., West Islip, were fatally injured when the car in which they were riding got out of control and overturned on Farmingdale Road near Straight Path, Copiague. Robert Kesseler, 24, of Carleton Ave., East Islip, received a fractured skull.

John Patania, 40, of 2053 Second Ave., Manhattan, was killed instantly when a car police said was operated by Edgar Walton of Parkersburg, Va., struck him at Prospect and Third Aves., Brooklyn. Walton was not held.

Dies in Trolley Crash

Thomas O'Brien, 33, of 13 Sagamore St., Freeport, was killed when the car in which he was riding with his brother, Francis, 34, of the same address, crashed into the rear of a trolley car discharging passengers on Myrtle Ave. at 83d St., Glendale. Francis O'Brien received fractured ribs.

When a westbound electric Long Island Railroad train struck the car he was driving at the Bellmore Ave. crossing, Bellmore, Pvt. Chester Deyette of the Ordnance Department, Rome Airport, Rome, N. Y., and his companion, Jane Nash, 19, of Helen St., Seaford, were injured. Both were taken to the Mitchel Field post hospital, where it was said the soldier's condition is serious. Miss Nash suffered shock.

In two accidents occurring 15 minutes apart at the same intersection, Anna Stroud, 37, of 889 70th St., and John Jackson, 34, of 750 Park Ave., received leg injuries. Both were struck by hit-run drivers at 4th Ave. and Union St.

Frederick Beeman, 50, of 137-19 96th Place, Glendale, was taken to Unity Hospital with a possible skull fracture and broken leg after he was struck by a car at Liberty and Vai Siclen Aves. Francis McGuire of 131-54 135th St., Richmond Hill, was said to have been the driver.

Injured by Hit-Run Car

Harvey Brennan, 42, of 264 E. 28th St., was taken to Kings County Hospital with serious head and internal injuries when a hit-run driver struck him at Hawthorne St. and Nostrand Ave.

Francis Lee, 2d class seaman stationed at Floyd Bennett Field Naval Air Station, sustained a fractured skull when he was struck while crossing Flatbush Ave. by a car operated, according to police, by Anatole Pica of 6928 Louise Ave., Arverne.

Christina Edwards, 55, of 122 Bond St., was struck by a car said by police to have been driven by Vincent Guido of 183 Butler St., while she was crossing Bond St., near Dean St. She suffered a head and leg injury. Guido was released after questioning.

When his car, out of control, crashed into a light pole on the Belt Parkway near West Rockaway Parkway, Charles Pirozzo, 43, of 26-09 21st St., Astoria, sustained a fractured skull.

Mary Lukach, 24, of 360 Dean St. suffered fractured ribs and Thomas Palmeri, 26, of 167 Navy St., received a broken leg when the car in which they were riding with Francisco Cutrone of 73 Eldert St., struck a tree as Cutrone swerved to avoid hitting a pedestrian.

Cop Shot by Accident

Patrolman James McDonald of the Glendale Precinct was shot in the right leg when his service revolver fell out of a defective holster and discharged as he removed his coat in his home, 82-53 62d Ave., Elmhurst.

Irene Sadowsky, 15, of 225 19th St.; Helen Budnick, 18, of 301 23d St.; Grace Schiadone, 16, of 666 4th Ave., and Angie Derrazzi, 16, of 553 Brooklyn Ave., were stricken when the oven gas flame was extinguished while a chicken was roasting in the kitchen of the Sadowsky home. They were treated for gas poisoning.

Orderliness was apparent through the borough during the holiday, police reporting only about a dozen false fire alarme, compared to a usual average of 40. Only about 15 disorderly conduct cases came before Magistrate Frances W. Lehrich in Brooklyn Weekend Court. She granted suspended sentences after lecturing each person. The magistrate also observed her 20th wedding anniversary New Year's Eve.

Blame Dimout for 'Accidents

Police attributed most of the traffic accidents to the dimmed-out streets.

The first baby of 1943 was born in Brooklyn a few seconds after midnight yesterday to Mr. and Mrs. Jack Brand of 474 Quincy St., in Beth Moses Hospital. Young Miss 1943 is a six-pound girl. Mr. and Mrs. Robert Lee of 140-20 Sanford Ave., Flushing, took the Queens prize with a boy 30 seconds after midnight in Flushing Hospital.

Eagle Staff photo

PEARL HARBOR TO GUADALCANAL—Master Sergt. John Lillback is on a leave at his home, 1128 E. 34th St., Brooklyn. He was sergeant of the guard at Hickam Field, Hawaii, when the Japs attacked Pearl Harbor and has since seen action in the Philippines, New Guinea and the Solomons. He was awarded the Distinguished Flying Cross and Silver Star. Between battles he was married Oct. 24 in Australia. His bride is still there and he will return. Sergeant Lillback is an aerial photographer, radio operator and gunner.

F. D. R., GEORGE VI VOW CRUSHING BLOWS ON AXIS

Lashing Peace Is Aim, Says President—Hitler Sees Victory for Reich

By United Press

The following world leaders gave the following messages on the occasion of the start of a New Year:

President Roosevelt: (At a press conference)—"The United Nations have a three-fold task ahead at the start of 1943. First, to press on with the massed forces of free humanity till the present bandit assault upon civilization is completely crushed; second, so to organize the relations among nations that forces of barbarism can never again break loose; third, to co-operate to the end that mankind may enjoy in peace and in freedom the unprecedented blessings which Divine Providence, through the progress of civilization, has put within our reach."

Message From King

King George VI of Britain: (To President Roosevelt)—"I and all my peoples deeply appreciate all that the United States have achieved in the common cause under your inspiring leadership. We feel confident that the recent victories of the United Nations are but forerunners of heavy blows which in the coming year they will together strike at the enemies of civilization."

Adolf Hitler: (To the German people)—"The war was started by international Jewry, Roosevelt's Jewish brain trust, the Jewish press of America, Jewish broadcasting systems which are nothing else but an equally Jewish framework of the leadership of the Soviet Union . . . The day will come when one of the contending parties in this struggle will collapse. That it will not be Germany, we know."

Giraud Addresses Troops

Gen. Henri Honore Giraud, leader of the French in North Africa: (To French troops)—"In this fight, all France has eyes turned on us. Let us never forget that millions of prisoners in Germany and France are awaiting salvation from us. As I already have said to you, we are inspired by only one aim—France and her empire. We have only one watchword—victory."

Gen. Serge Ingr, Czech Minister of Defense: (In broadcast to Czech people)—"Germany's military defeat is sealed. It now is only a matter of time. Germany has lost her offensive war and is now on the defense."

Kane Claims 'Airtight' Case in S. I. Murder

While sorrowing relatives and friends attended requiem mass in St. Mary's R. C. Church in Port Richmond, Staten Island, today for 19-year-old Mary Ricoitch, found slain in a deserted spot last Monday, District Attorney Farrell Kane prepared to submit to the grand jury next week the circumstantial evidence he has gathered against her suspected slayer.

The prisoner is Dominic Taddio, 38, a war worker of 62 Tompkins St., Stapleton, father of three young children. His wife left them last July because, she told police, he was cruel and brutal.

Taddio is in Bellevue Hospital prison ward, to which he was removed when he collapsed after a 10-hour grilling. The suspect stuck to his denial of any knowledge of the crime.

Taddio was pointed out to police by Julia Larsen, 19, of 3561 Richmond Terrace, Mariner's Harbor, a friend and neighbor of the slain girl, as the man who had frequently driven both of them to work in his automobile. The prisoner denied that he had ever seen the Larsen girl before.

Examination of Taddio's car revealed bloodstains on the rear seat and floor. His jacket also was stained and was sent to the city chemist for analysis. District Attorney Kane declared that he had an "airtight" case against Taddio and did not need a confession.

ROUGH WEATHER HATS—Ensign Barbara Easley, left, of Hollywood, adjusts a borrowed sou'wester for Ensign Mary L. Kennedy of White Plains, on deck of patrol boat at United States Coast Guard Academy, New London. Both officers are former Waves and are now undergoing indoctrination course at academy to prepare them to handle future Spar enlistments.

MAYOR ASKS END OF TEACHERS' SABBATICALS

Suggests This Method To Add 1,000 Full Time Instructors to System

Mayor LaGuardia today called on the Board of Education to add more than 1,000 permanent full-time teachers to the city school system by recalling all those on sabbatical leaves, retiring physically unfit teachers over 60 now on leave and appointing substitutes to replace those retired.

In a letter addressed to Ellsworth B. Buck, president of the board, the Mayor revealed that "there are no less than 2,250 teachers drawing full pay on sabbatical leave." He expressed surprise that "out of this number, 740 are between the ages of 60 and 70."

Pointing out that sabbatical leaves are granted as "a peace-time provision to permit teachers a year's vacation for study, travel or health restoration," the Mayor tartly suggested that "there is not much benefit that can be obtained within the intent of the sabbatical year policy either to the system or to the individual" in the 60-70 year age group.

"In fact," he said, "it is a reasonable assumption that having reached the age of 60 they have acquired all the knowledge and experience that each particular individual could obtain up to that time and with previous sabbatical leaves."

The leaves, he said, mean the school system loses the service of experienced teachers while "underpaid and inexperienced" substitutes replace them. The situation is made worse, however, he added, because a shortage of substitutes recently has made it necessary to place full-time teachers in the replacement positions, thus involving payment of two full salaries for one post. Substitutes earn about one-half of the salary of the teacher on leave, the amount being deducted from the absent teacher's pay.

FIREMEN BALK AT STAGE, HAND 'NEAREST EXIT' SCRIPT TO MANAGERS

Theater audiences from now on will listen to the official warning issued by Fire Commissioner Walsh, telling just what to do—in case something happens. The warning, which long ago had been printed in theater programs, and tells the patrons to note the nearest exit and walk to it if an alarm is sounded, was recited at all stage theaters yesterday by individual firemen.

This extra "bit" on the program was vociferously applauded where firemen braved stage fright and did their own reciting. Many of the firemen, however, who would think nothing of rushing into cauldrons to save lives, quaked at a stage appearance and prevailed on actors or theater managers to read their lines while they stood by to give authority. In movie theaters sound trailers are being prepared and the message will be printed and spoken before each performance.

WAAC—Suzanne Tirlet, former secretary to author Eve Curie and an artist herself, has completed basic Waac training at Fort Des Moines and is taking a specialist course in hopes of being assigned overseas. Paris-born, she is now an American citizen.

Riverhead Town Board Gets G. O. P. Majority

Riverhead, Jan. 2—The Riverhead Town Board, formerly composed of three Democrats and two Republicans, became four-to-one when two new Republican members were seated yesterday.

One of the new members—Milton L. Burns—was appointed town supervisor by the board to take the place of Joseph V. Kelly, Democrat, who was inducted into the army on Dec. 18 last. The other—William J. Leonard—was elected justice of the peace on Nov. 3 last, to fill the vacancy resulting from the induction into the army last August of Henry M. Zaleski, Democrat. The town board is made up of four justices of the peace and a supervisor.

The town board, at yesterday's meeting, appointed Republicans to fill various positions recently held by Democrats, and, in most instances, increased the salaries attaching to the positions.

The largest increase, $600, was in the salary of the superintendent of the Riverhead Sewer District boosted from $1,800 a year to $2,400 a year. Alden Young, Republican, was appointed superintendent, to succeed Ernest Jeffries, Democrat.

Of every pound of meat being produced in the U. S. about 12 ounces will go to the civilian population, the remaining four ounces will be distributed among our fighting men and the armed forces and civilians of our Lend-Lease Allies.

SET FOR CITY—Ed Golub of St. John's University has shown such marked improvement in recent games that he figures to get a starting chance when the Redmen meet City College in the 22d renewal of their series at Madison Square Garden Wednesday night.

PLAY MAKER—Although small in stature, Hy Gotkin has proved himself valuable addition to St. John's University basketball team by his passing and play-making ability. When close-up baskets are scored by the Redmen, its frequently Gotkin who makes them possible.

Montgomery, Rico In 15-Round Go

Lightweights in Tournament Battle in Garden Ring Friday

A lightweight title match closed the boxing year 1942 at Madison Square Garden and now a lightweight tournament will open the year 1943 in the same ring.

On Friday night, Jan. 8, Promoter Mike Jacobs inaugurates the new boxing year with a program headlined by a 15-round contest involving two of the 135-pounders who seek a crack at the title.

Montgomery Faces Rico

Bob Montgomery, Philadelphia lightweight, opposes Chester Rico of the Bronx, in one of the 15-rounders. Montgomery was last seen at the Garden in August when he trounced Bobby Ruffin. His last ring appearance took place in the Quaker City several weeks ago when he evened his score with Maxie Shapiro who had outpointed him by a narrow margin a few weeks before.

Rico has developed during the past year into one of the country's leading lightweight contenders. His form has improved steadily, he has added a punch to his boxing ability, and he has made many stirring fights in recent months.

Johnny Greco, crack young Montreal lightweight, makes another Garden start in an eight-rounder. He is paired with Billy Speary, of Nanticoke, Pa. Greco scored an impressive kayo victory over Harold Green at the Garden last month.

In another eight Sonny Horne, Niles, Ohio, middleweight boxes Joe Agosta of New York.

Beau Jack, new lightweight champion who knocked out Tippy Larkin in the last Garden show, has a $1,500 forfeit on deposit with the State Athletic Commission, guaranteeing that he will defend his title against the winner of the lightweight tournament now in progress at the Garden and in other arenas.

St. Teresa, OLPH, Lourdes Leaders In CYO Jr. Loop

Beating back the opposition in its five games staged to date, St. Teresa's is leading the parade in Section 1 of the junior competition of the C. Y. O. basketball tourneys of Kings County. St. John the Baptist is in the runner-up slot, with four victories and one defeat.

The Section 2 action has Our Lady of Perpetual Help as the leader, with four successes and one reversal, while St. Rose of Lima has captured three, while dropping one. In Section 3 Our Lady of Lourdes is out in front, with four triumphs and no setbacks. Second is Queen of All Saints, with two wins and one defeat.

STANDINGS OF TEAMS
JUNIOR DIVISION

Section 1

	W.	L.
St. Teresa	5	0
St. John the Baptist	4	1
St. John's Home	4	2
St. Augustine	3	2
St. Matthew	1	4
St. Saviour	0	4
St. Thomas, 4th Ave.	0	4

Section 2

	W.	L.
Our Lady of Pepetual Help	4	1
St. Rose of Lima	3	1
St. Catherine of Alexandria	3	2
St. Brendan	2	2
St. Finbar	1	4
St. Charles Borromeo	1	4
St. Athanasius	0	3

Section 3

	W.	L.
Our Lady of Lourdes	4	0
Queen of All Saints	2	1
Sacred Heart	2	1
St. Vincent de Paul	1	1
St. Mary, Immaculate Conception	0	2
Annunciation	0	3

Shuffled Hawks To Face Rangers On Garden Ice

A strong Chicago sextet will take the ice against the Rangers in a National Hockey League game tonight in Madison Square Garden.

The revitalized Blue Shirts have been receiving a little more of the player accidents, which, oddly enough, got them galloping at the pace of former seasons.

Since last the Patrick-Boucher forces visited Detroit to break a long desultory streak with a 3—1 verdict, their close-by neighbors, the Hawks, have been making revisions calculated to stop the Rangers' newly-found strength.

Paul Thompson has shuffled about his speedy forward trios and has added two new stalwarts up there, giving lead to the possibility that h[illegible] have a plethora of talent on hand.

His defense quartet, smooth on attack as they are in rear-line positions, and with Earl Seibert, Aud Tuten, Red Mitchell and Weibe handing out body checks, the Hawks boast one of, if not, the hardest-hitting bruisers in the league.

Although Art Wiebe did not report until a week ago, he is always in condition and reports from Chicago state that after a couple of days on the ice he was in top condition to jump into the lineup.

The lineup:

Pos.	Rangers	Hawks
G.	1 Franks	Gardiner 1
D.	3 Heller	Seibert 17
D.	15 Garrett	Tuten 2
C.	6 B. Kirkpatrick	C. Dahlstrom 15
R. W.	12 Hextall	March 5
L. W.	9 Patrick	Hamill 3

Alternates—Rangers: Pike (2), Davidson (4), Warwick (8) Smith (10), Goldup (11), Cameron (14), Myles (18). Black Hawks: Purpur (4), Allen (6), D. Bentley (7), Mitchell (8), Johnstn (9), Thoms (12), Carse (16), M. Bentley (18), R. Bentley (19), Art Wiebe (??).

Leagues Set To Act Tuesday

Continued from Page 1

formation which will necessitate a change in our views."

Under a scheduled opening April 27 and closing Sept. 26, there are 153 possible playing dates. When days for travel and weather postponements are subtracted, doubleheaders would have to be played virtually every Saturday and Sunday during the 22 weeks the schedule runs to permit crowding in 154 contests. The practice employed by many teams of leaving the date following each night game open also would have to be abandoned.

The majors have played a 154-game schedule annually since 1920. In 1919 the playing card included only 140 contests.

Setting the opening day back to April 27 would permit clubs to train in the North without seriously handicapping their conditioning programs. Virtually all clubs have abandoned California and Florida training bases, but few of them have yet selected new "close-to-home" camps.

Other points that may be discussed by the magnates include series of five to seven games instead of the two-three-four-game series now in vogue, open dates for distant "jumps" so as to make the use of Pullmans unnecessary and the reducing of traveling squads from 25 to 20 players.

Bowling Booming All Over Country

Thousands of Newcomers Becoming Pin-Minded, Reports Varipapa

By PAUL GOULD

It's getting so that whenever Andy Varipapa comes to Brooklyn it's almost as auspicious an event as when he makes one of his much-heralded visits to a mid-Western city. Andy's becoming a stranger to his own heath, we're sorry to report, so great have become the demands for him elsewhere. Right now he's spending a little time with his family in Flatbush after a three-month junket, but in a day or so he'll be pushing off again.

Nine months of the year, from September through May, the borough's best-known bowler sallies forth on expeditions. Personal appearances featuring the trick shots for which he is famous, engagements against leading pinmen, instruction lessons for hundreds of embryo Varipapas, these in part constitute his program. His report about the growth of kegelspiel elsewhere is an eye-opener.

"What impressed me most in my trips to cities in Ohio, West Virginia, Indiana and Illinois," he said, "was the way thousands of newcomers are flocking to the sport. This is particularly so with regard to women. In defense cities especially the game booms almost 24 hours a day and the soldiers are taking it up, too."

Andy Varipapa

Conducts Schools in West

Andy put in long stands at Toledo and Chicago, where he conducted schools. En route to the Windy City, he made his 50th 300 game in Muncie, Ind., after having failed by a narrow margin several times. Then in Chicago he competed in the second annual national match-game championship. One hundred selected rollers had survived elimination tests all over the country and Andy was among the seeded stars. Where he finished 11th last year, this time he wound up third, close behind Frank Benkovic of Milwaukee. Connie Schwoegler of Madison, Wis., led the field. Huge crowds saw the tournament, 2,700 fans jamming the stands for each of the 10-day sessions.

Varipapa's next destination is Detroit, where he will again lecture and give personal instruction. Andy's method is to address his pupils for about 15 minutes and then have them take positions in the alleys. Here he puts them through their paces.

'Technique's the Thing'

"Bowling's not a game that can be mastered overnight," he says. "There's a certain rhythm to it which requires synchronization of different muscles. Bowling's a game of accuracy, and you've got to do everything right to click. Technique's the thing."

One of the most heartening signs Andy's encountered outside of New York is the number of youngsters taking to the sport. He had a chance to observe two newcomers in the Chi tourney, and based on their exploits he believes that soon the teen-age lads will be edging the veterans out of the headlines.

Among those he thought of highly were Buddy Bomer of Texas, a 27-year-old player, and Rudy Pugel of Milwaukee, barely 21.

'Keep your eye on them,' he advised. "They're budding champs."

Dell and Terranova Headline Fistic Show

For fistic entertainment with proper balance, the Broadway Arena on Tuesday night will offer three eight-round fights where the odds on each contest will be no more than 6 to 5 and take your pick, so evenly matched are the gladiators.

In the fight which takes top billing, East New York's Johnny Dell will come to blows with Phil Terranova, newly crowned Bronx featherweight champion, while the other eights will offer Billy Pinti with Joe Aponte Torres and Gus Levine with Wilce Rivera.

Terranova, former Golden Gloves champion under the aegis of Bobby Gleason, will be making his first start in the Halsey St. sock center, and his aggressive style of fisticuffing is a certainty to go over in a big way with the local fans. Dell, long a popular youngster in this borough, recently made a great fight with Lulu Constantino in a bout which sold out the arena.

Matchmaker Billy Brown has promised the winner a crack at Costantino either the last week in January or early in February. Dell would like a return bout with Lulu because the youngster insists that with the experience he has gained from their first battle, he feels confident he can now turn back Costantino. Terranova and the East Side Italian have never met.

Pinti, another youngster who tried to whip Costantino, will be facing a fighter of his own caliber and the fur is really expected to fly. Torres is a noted knockout artist, half of his fights having terminated by the kayo route, and with Pinti matching right hands with the Puerto Rican, the fight is not expected to go the limit.

As for the Levine-Rivers embroglio, this is a real grudge battle as there is little love lost between the pair. Hostilities sprung from a gymnasium workout in which both claimed that the other was shooting for a knockout and they are both eager for the chance to start belting one another's brains out. Ray Robinson, for whom Levine acts as a mascot, is expected to watch the fight from a ringside seat.

Two four-round fights will complete the program with Jimmy Cartelli, promising Red Hook battler, facing Lew Perez, Harlem spoiler, and Joey Verna, Williamsburg pride, meeting Bobby Morgan, West Sider.

CAGE LEADERS FACE TOUGH FOES TONIGHT

Jewish Center Meets 8th Avenue Temple In E. J. C. Contest

The two borough teams tied for the lead in Division 1 of the Eastern Jewish Center League are under strong threat of being dumped out of the top rung tonight by a pair of tough basketball rivals. Brooklyn Jewish Center, one leader, takes on a strong Eighth Temple team on the Center floor, while the other pacesetter, Jewish Community House of Bensonhurst, invades an always dangerous lair at the 92d Street Y. M. H. A.

B. J. C. and Bensonhurst each have scored two victories in three times out in league competition, while their opponents, who have split two decisions, can go into first place by winning.

The week's action on the cage front finds Brooklyn Battalion, Coast Guard, playing four successive nights. Wednesday they face Manhattan Beach Coast Guard, Thursday the Naval Recruiting Station, Friday Camp Upton and Saturday the Bedford Y. M. C. A.

Flatbush Boys Club returns to its court Wednesday night to meet Eastern District Y. M. C. A., then plays at 23d St. Y. M. C. A. the following evening. At the same time Ellis Island Coast Guard invades Fort Hamilton.

Bedford Y. M. C. A. renews rivalry with the Boys Welcome Hall outfit on the Bedford floor Saturday night while Metropolitan A. A. invades the Caseys in an Eastern District loop tussle.

STANDING OF EASTERN JEWISH CENTER LEAGUE:

DIVISION I

	Won	Lost	Pct.
Brooklyn Jewish Center	2	1	.667
Jewish Community House of Bensonhurst	2	1	.667
Eighth Avenue Temple	1	1	.500
92d Street Y. M. H. A.	1	1	.500
Hebrew Educational Society	1	3	.250

DIVISION II

	Won	Lost	Pct.
Williamsburg Y. M. H. A.	4	2	.667
Washington H'ts Y.M.H.A.	4	2	.667
Federation Settlement	5	3	.625
Harlem Hebrew Institute	3	2	.600
Jacob H. Schiff Center	0	7	.000

Whirly Heads Widener Field

Continued from Page 1

slipped through in the final yards to drop his nose in front in a finish that saw four horses heads apart on the wire. The Rhymer had been so little thought of that he was placed in the mutuel field with four others.

Bolingbroke Dark Horse

The early dark horse of the race, now on the grounds and showing plenty of speed in his workouts, is Townsend B. Martin's Bolingbroke, which already has one decision over "Mr. Longtail," gained in the Manhattan Handicap at Belmont Park last Fall. Watches were shattered on that Fall day as the rangy son of Equipoise outran Whirlaway in the straightaway to find the long mile and one-half route in 2:27 3-5 for a new American record.

It also will be Whirly's rubber meeting with Riverland, which capped a spectacular rise from the plater ranks last November by defeating Alsab and Whirlaway within the space of four days. Whirly, however, evened that score at the Fair Grounds a month later when he drove home the winner of the $15,000 Louisiana Handicap with Riverland two lengths back in third place.

Among others nominated are Best Seller, who was second in last year's race; Thomas Heard's consistent Boysy and Isidore Bieber's sturdy Bright Gallant.

Two Reds Have 4 Children

Outfielders Max Marshall and Gerald Walker of the Reds each is the father of four children.

St. John's and City Renew Cage Feud

Meet in 22d Game of Series—Redmen Hold 11–10 Edge

The renewal of two of basketball's oldest rivalries, City College vs. St. John's and N. Y. U. vs. Manhattan is the double-barrelled feature of the new week's court schedule in New York. Their playing form sharpened by the strenuous intersectional competition of the Garden's holiday week carnival, the home town teams are ready now to train their guns upon each other, and will, with these games, initiate the annual metropolitan championship round robin.

In other years these two games made up one Garden show, but this week they are spotted on different programs. The City-Redmen battle is listed for Wednesday, and the N. Y. U.-Kelly Green tussle for Saturday.

However, the Violets are to appear in the Garden on both nights. They renew another old rivalry, against Penn State, in the other half of the Wednesday program. The second of the Saturday games teams L. I. U. with the North Carolina Pre-Flight squad from Chapel Hill.

Redmen Hold Edge

The City-St. John's engagement is the 22nd of a series that has been keenly and evenly waged through the years. Eleven to ten is the series count, with the Redmen enjoying the one game advantage. However, City have won the last two, and no member of the present St. John's team includes a victory over the Beavers among the souvenirs of their playing careers.

But the Redmen are this year's early season favorites to win the metropolitan crown, and that estimate is supported by their two skillfully contrived Garden victories over Oklahoma and Tennessee. The mastodonic Harry Boykoff will give the Redmen a definite height advantage over the Beavers, and such skillful operatives as Levane, Baxter and Golub concede nothing to their rivals in the way of play making skill or shot making accuracy. The set-up casts the Beavers in an under-dog role, but that is nothing new. They were similarly underestimate before they beat St. John's last year and the year before.

In 23d Meeting

The Manhattan-N. Y. U. series is actually the longer of the two. Their game on Saturday will be the 23d since 1908. The Violets have dominated the action in recent years, but the Jaspers' new coach, Joe Daher, has revived basketball enthusiasm at Riverdale, and his team is pointing toward the game in the conviction that it can win.

The new Kelly Green outfit, featuring a couple of flashy freshmen in Tommy Tolan and Bill O'Brien and sophomore Warren Fenley (a tall center), has already accomplished what was thought to be impossible. Their four-game winning streak includes victories over Syracuse and Niagara, two of the Eastern seaboard's strongest. Niagara, in fact, is the team that wrecked St. John's all winning season. Fenley has proved himself to be an exceptional backboard retriever and the other two youngsters are scorers. Meanwhile the veterans, Dick Murphy and Dan Christie are playing the best basketball of their Manhattan careers.

Broberg in Cadets' Lineup

The North Carolina Cadets are coached by Dyke Raese, coach last year of West Virginia's New York Invitation Tournament champions. Dartmouth's Gus Broberg, one of the country's great shot-makers and scorers, is the team's leading player, but his supporting cast includes several stars from the South and mid-West.

C. G. Prepares New Permits For Power Boats

By JACK RAMSAY

Yachtsmen who left last week's monthly meeting of the United States Power Squadrons with the impression that pleasure boating would be ruled out of the realm of possibilities for the coming year and that only craft permitted afloat would be those serving the Coast Guard, had their fears for nothing.

It was learned that the Coast Guard has prepared a new form of permit for owners of pleasure craft. It includes a reference to fuel consumption and to the hours during which boats may be operated in 1943. It will not prohibit yachtsmen from utilizing their ships even if they are not enrolled in the Coast Guard Auxiliary or Coast Guard Reserves.

Told to Carry On

On the sailing side of the yachting picture it was the consensus of opinion among members at the International class annual dinner at the New York Yacht Club that races would be held as usual next year.

Capt. Kenneth Whiting, U. S. N., and Com. Sherman Hoyt, U. S. N., addressed the unusually well-attended gathering and pointed out that this present generation of yachtsmen are at sea in service of the navy and doing a swell job and it was up to the oldtimers to carry on and educate the coming generation of youngsters so that they would be marine-minded and fit and ready to take their places when called.

Despite dimout regulations which hide most yacht clubs these days behind shutters and make them appear dismal, the clubs were gay and merry places as the New Year was ushered in last Thursday night.

Men of the armed services were royally entertained at Sheepshead Bay Yacht Club in one of the best attended affairs at that popular club in years. Other clubs, scenes of get-togethers of families and members home on leave, included the Larchmont Y. C., Manhasset Bay Y. C., the City Island Y. C. and the Harlem Y. C. on City Island.

Harold A. Baker's School for Navigation at the Hotel Astor has added a course in meteorology to aid those who desire service in the many branches of Uncle Sam's growing forces. The instructor is Peter E. Kragt, prominent weather caster.

Paul A. Sperry is the new commodore of the Off-Soundings Club. G. W. Blunt White is vice commodore; Edgar S. de Meyer, rear commodore; Edward Southworth, secretary; Eliot L. Wight, treasurer, and Edward F. Sutherland, measurer. The race committee includes Dr. Eugene Walker, chairman; Robert Tippin and Sanford Lawton.

Hit Production Upped

The first ten hitters in the American League in 1942 made more hits than the first ten batsmen in the league in 1939. This past season the total for the top ten was 1,765. For the 1939 season the total was 1,687.

Melillo Returns to Politics

Oscar Melillo, who has retired as coach of the Cleveland Indians, is returning to a political job in the Pullman district on the south side of Chicago, probably writing finis to his baseball career.

CANDIDATE FOR CROWN—Bob Montgomery, Philadelphia lightweight, does a bit of bag punching in preparation for his 15-round meeting with Chester Rico in first bout of elimination tournament. Survivor of elimination series will get crack at Beau Jack's title.

Moschetti Key Man In St. John's Win

Braces Team's Defense Against Fordham To Share Honors With Trio of Scorers— West Virginia Five Worn Down By N. Y. U.

By GEORGE E. COLEMAN

Larry Baxter, Fuzzy Levane and Hank Boykoff rate plenty of credit for St. John's U. 63—47 triumph over Fordham U. at the Garden last night, which followed a win for New York U. over West Virginia, 52—51 in an extra-period tilt. Baxter netted 22 points, Levane 17 and Boykoff 11 to make the Redmen look better on the offense than they have at any time this season.

But there's another player who deserves just as much credit. The almost forgotten cager is Al Moschetti, No. 6, whom the fans haven't seen often since last season's City-St. John's contest, in which he missed six foul shots.

BOTH SIDES

By Harold Parrott

DODGER DEMOSTHENES — Mr. Branch Rickey was in full cry yesterday. Brooklyn's newest orator really turned it on, shifting conversational gears like some combination Kaltenborn-William Jennings Bryan-Raymond Gram Swing, with a patriotic dash of F. D. R. and just a touch of Billy Sunday.

This is not the public speaking department I know, and Mr. Rickey's local oratorical launching was notable for other reasons than his great gift of gab.

What I mean to say is that although B. R. seemed to be talking to the Brooklyn Rotarians out front, he was in reality talking AT a man on the end of the dais—Dixie Walker, spectacled and serious.

It was the first meeting between the popular Dodger outfielder, or perhaps ex-outfielder, and his new boss, or is he?

This time Rickey got in the last word, and indeed all the words, but you need not suppose Mr. Walker will always be speechless.

Dixie got a good idea of Rickey's conversational caliber yesterday, however, and he backed away cautiously. It was hard even to coax him into a picture (which you will see on this page) with the Mahatma. You can bet Dixie will go into those contract talks with his ears stuffed and his tongue wagging. He will have to go at some chatting clip to hold B. R. to a tie, however, if that gentleman really gets set to put the conversational convincer on Dixie and Dolf Camilli, another bashful, or "retiring" Dodger.

HEY, DIXIE, DIDYA BELIEVE IT? — Rickey remarked that, ah, yes, he realized the factors that might make Mr. Walker "hesitate" about returning to the Dodgers; undeniably fine factors, he said, like "continuity of employment," "the year-round paycheck," and so on.

Going off then on a tack that dealt with the debt baseball idols have to their public, B. R. framed a plea that would have touched the heart of a stone buddha.

The idol—could it have been Mr. Walker he meant?—must never break faith with his public, Mr. Rickey pleaded, sketching at some length the depth of influence such an idol has on "the 20 million youngsters who devour this nation's sports pages."

"The man of muscular skills," orated B. R., "holds more influence with our youth than the man of philosophic attainments." Did he look directly at Dixie?

Walker didn't bat an eye as Rickey dipped lightly into Henry James, the Bible, justified baseball which he said must have an "awareness" of what is going on in the world today, and at one time exploded in a good loud "Hell"—after which he halted dramatically, looked around the room, and said, with a twinkle in his eye "I withdraw that."

LOOKS LIKE QUITE A BOUT! — Mr. Walker also showed no emotion as Rickey went into a short exposition of how the team that "wants most to win" is usually the team that does win.

"Say the Dodgers win 75 games," hypothesized B. R., "and the Phillies win 75——"

He stopped as if he was shot. "No," he said, "That could never happen!"

Dixie didn't even chuckle at this mild slander on the Phils. Perhaps he was thinking of that jui-jitsu class he had to get back to, as athletic director at Sperry's.

Dixie hasn't won his "S" at Sperry's—at least, he wasn't wearing it. And definitely, Mr. Rickey hasn't yet won his Walker AWAY from Sperry's. First round a draw, I'd say!

"MR. RICKEY, I WANT YOU TO MEET——"—Well, who is it Mr. Rickey's meeting behind those studious-looking cheaters but his own right fielder! It was first time Dixie Walker had met his new boss, and it happened yesterday at Brooklyn Rotary Club luncheon in the Hotel Bossert, where B. R. wowed 'em with his oratory.

Holds Mullens in Check

Coach Joe Lapchick, however, knows that Moschetti did his job just as well as Baxter, Levane and Boykoff did theirs. Bob Mullens, the Rams' big scoring threat, started off with a three-point play, added a double and a free throw for Fordham's first six markers and then handed George Babich a pass for another basket. Hy Gotkin was rushed into the scramble to stop Mullens. He didn't do too well and with nine minutes to play in the first half the teams were deadlocked at 14-all. Out came Gotkin and in went Moschetti.

From then on the high-scoring Fordham Rams couldn't cope with the Indians' power, not only because the Redskins' sharpshooters went into high but because Moschetti was doing a swell job on the defense, Mullens netted exactly one lone foul in the remaining nine minutes and, in addition to spiking Fordham's big gun, Moschetti covered up and directed the defensive play of the Redmen, which is quite a job when one considers how weak the Redskins are defensively.

The second half started with St. John's on the right side of a 38—23 count and Moschetti began by taking over Tony Karpowicz, the town's leading scorer who had accounted for eight points in the early half. But if Mullens was first down the floor the St. Johns senior would pick up the tall, blond Ram. Karpowicz was soon forced to the bench, Moschetti had him tied into a knot and Mullens scored one basket, but not on Moschetti, Ed Golub had the Fordhamite on that one.

When Levane or Gotkin goes into Uncle Sam's armed forces Moschetti will be remembered for last night's work. Then Lapchick's lads may develop into a team that not only has plenty of scoring power but also a tight defense. As such they would be tough even for New York U.

Pressure Told on Mountaineers

Most fans feel that the Violets were quite lucky last night. If Floyd Stark, the Virginian center, hadn't thrown that back pass into the court Jerry Fleishman wouldn't have had the sucker shot to deadlock the count that forced the teams into an extra period. But it was the city slickers' constant battling that had the strong Mountaineers out on their feet. Stark was weary and his lapse was due to the constant pressure.

The Violets and Mountaineers played 39 minutes instead of 40 in regulation time. New York U. called a time out and the timekeeper forgot to switch off the clock. It seemed much longer to the West Virginians.

St. John's U.	G.	F.	P.	Fordham	G.	F.	P.
Levane	8	1	17	Karpowich	3	6	12
Rossini	0	0	0	Haggerty	1	3	5
Plantamura	1	0	2	Lucas	0	1	1
Baxter	9	4	22	Bach	1	0	2
Henry	0	0	0	Gebhardt	0	0	0
Boykoff	3	5	11	Babich	6	1	13
Moschetti	1	3	5	Cheverko	1	0	2
Golub	2	0	4	Mullens	3	4	10
Gotkin	0	2	2	Mulvihill	1	0	2
Spea	0	0	0	Graham	1	0	2
Pastushok	0	0	0				
Keller	0	0	0				
Totals	24	15	63	Totals	16	15	47

Referees—Kennedy and Quigley.

N. Y. U.	G.	F.	P.	W. Virginia	G.	F.	P.
Grenert	1	1	3	Walthall	7	4	18
Fleishman	5	4	14	Hamilton	6	0	12
Regan	2	0	4	Stark	5	2	12
Simmons	3	2	8	Nicksick	2	1	5
Legatt	0	0	0	Reaves	1	0	2
Lumpp	6	2	14	Davis	1	0	2
Mele	4	1	9				
Totals	21	10	52	Totals	22	7	51

Officials—Matty Begovitch and John Nucatola.

Phils' Rookie Inducted

Allentown, Pa., Jan. 13 (U.P.)—Eddie Freed, 23, who was slated for a regular outfield berth this year with the Philadelphia Phils, today was inducted into the army at the Allentown induction center.

RANGER SIX COULD REALLY USE BOUCHER!

At 40, However, Frank Doesn't Relish Idea Of Return as Player

By RALPH TROST

Yes, Frank Boucher is 40 years old. He has been out of active hockey more than four seasons. And, on his own word, a good, stiff body-check isn't absorbed by fellows in the 40s as readily as by the kids. Nor can the fellows in their 40s go as fast or as long.

But for all the arguments against it, there's still the idea in the Rangers' camp that if Boucher, as smooth a guy as ever wielded a stick, would try a comeback the Rangers would definitely gain. That knowledge of when to do it and how to do it—that's the stuff that Boucher still has. Aand doubtless can use.

Could Make Big Difference

One solid, smart hockey player can make a great deal of difference to the Rangers. Such a fellow could lift them out of the ruck and, maybe, carry them into the Stanley Cup playoffs again.

As the setup now stands, the Blueshirts (as you'll see tonight when they tackle the Detroit Redwings in the big Red Cross benefit game) have a really good first line

HOCKEY STANDING

Club.	W.	L.	T.	F.	A.	Pts.
Boston	14	9	6	103	99	34
Toronto	13	10	4	126	84	30
Detroit	11	8	7	85	67	29
Chicago	10	8	6	80	83	26
Montreal	8	13	5	85	107	81
Rangers	7	15	4	83	122	18

Tonight's Games

Detroit at Rangers.
Chicago at Montreal.

in Watson, Hextall and Patrick. With Bob Kirkpatrick's remarkable improvement this past month, that second line of Kirkpatrick, Warwick and Goldup should be almost equally strong. Boucher's return would make up a third line of Snuffy Smith, Scotty Cameron and —Boucher. Yeah, all three are centers and have been centers. But Boucher is smart enough to shift and so is Smith.

The trick, of course, is selling the idea to Boucher, who is a pretty shrewd gent and knows all the angles—including the fact that he dropped out of hockey when he was just about at his peak. He left in good health, with all bones intact, his own teeth, pretty good legs and a happy frame of mind.

It could be pointed out to Frank that Lester Patrick, the Rangers' manager, ceased active play at 37 but came back when he was 43 and played 26 games. Bun Cook, one of the fellows Frank played with for years, dropped out for just as long as Boucher, but, under pressure came back to play with his Providence team.

Bill Cook, whose major league career didn't start until he was 26, played until he was 40. So did Ching Johnson.

The part about Boucher that appeals so much is that Frank never got out of condition. When the preseason work started, he was in there with the boys and moved around faster than most. He gets out and works when they practice—and often shows the boys that he's considerably smarter than they.

What with one thing or another, this consideration of Boucher as player and coach (like Detroit's Ebbie Goodfellow) is solid thinking. If, since Christmas Eve, the Blueshirts hadn't been battling along at better than an even .500 clip—which is good enough to get into the playoffs, this whole idea might never have come up. But with the Rangers needing just a little lift—well, there it is—if some one can only put the convincer on Frank.

Cracked Ice—One of the sight of sights is seeing a goalie dress. By the time he gets those leg pads on, the only way he can finish up buckling himself in is on his knees . . . No team in the league has as much experienced, steady power up front as the Red Wings. Together, Sid Abel and Syd Howe, make up the best center pair in the league. That's one of the reasons Les Patrick picked them, not the Leafs or Bruins, to finish the season on top. One of the reasons they don't lead the league is—the Rangers.

BASKETBALL RESULTS LAST NIGHT

52	New York University	W. Va. (Overtime)	51
42	Penn State	Syracuse	28
39	Loyola	Western Michigan	38
49	Providence	Yale	37
36	Kansas	Oklahoma A. & M.	29
51	Penn	Maryland	49
46	Dartmouth	Seton Hall	40
63	St. John's	Fordham	47
66	Baylor	Texas A. & M.	58
37	Rockhurst	Kansas State	24
60	Norfolk Naval Station	Duke	53
41	Texas	S. M. U.	37
39	Middlebury	Albany S. College	36
38	Moorhead Teachers	Concordia	29
53	Scranton U.	N. Cumberland R. C.	48
48	Illinois Wesleyan	Illinois College	43
104	Defiance	Bluffton	39
59	Brown	Massachusetts Tech	38
33	Navy Pier	Chihcago Teachers	25
46	Minnesota	Michigan State	32
46	Dartmouth	Seton Hall	40
63	Amherst	American Interna'l	34
66	Cotawba	Guilford	29
43	Virginia Military	Virginia State	33
43	Williams	Mass. State	41
39	Gettysburg	Navy	37
47	George Washington,	N. Carolina Pre-Flight	45
39	Columbia	Army	23
42	Fort George Meade,	Kutztown (Pa.) Teachers	37
54	Aberdeen Proving Grounds,	La Salle	40
38	Swarthmore	Johns Hopkins	12
66	Newark	Wagner	53
	Waynesburg-St. Vincent, postponed.		
61	Cathedral	New York Aggies	39
37	Western Maryland	Loyola	4
531	University of Connecticut,	New Hampshire	40
40	Norfolk Naval Air Station,	Appalachian (N. C.) Teachers	36
50	Franklin (Ind.)	Hanover	43
60	Great Lakes	St. Joseph's (Ind)	32
50	Manchester	Concordia	29
41	Carbondale Teachers,	Illinois Normal	30
49	Iowa State Naval	Mason City	39
50	Fort Sheridan (Ill.),	Naval Training Sch ol (Chicagot)	49
32	Wartburg	Western Union	29
59	Indiana State Teachers,	Eastern Illinois Teachers	48
42	Kent State	Hiriam	37
38	Baldwin Wallace	John Carroll	33
53	North Texas Teachers,	Howard Payne	50
56	Southwest Texas,	Stephen F. Austin	41
39	College of Idaho,	Lewiston State Normal	36
34	Oregon	Idaho	31
49	Washington,	Harlem Globe Trotters	30

MAROON MAGIC—Al Moschetti of St. John's is hot on the heels of Fordham's Dan Graham as the latter moves the ball up court in game at Madison Square Garden last night. Bob Mullens, formerly of Brooklyn Prep, also follows play with startled gaze of man who is watching a feat of magic. Referee Quigley is blocked out of the play. St. John's beat Fordham, 63—47, after New York U. nipped West Virginia, 52—51, in overtime game.

WRIGHT SEEKING FISTIC REVENGE

By HAROLD PARROTT

There are plenty of personal angles to the two 10-round battles which highlight the Garden boxing show tomorrow night.

In different bouts will be Chalky Wright, the ringwise veteran who helped Jackie Wilson so much during the middleweight prodigy's early bouts—and Wilson himself, now a sergeant at Mitchel Field.

Take Wright's case. Edged out of the featherweight picture when Willie Pep took his title in a close battle in the Garden in November, Chalky is trying to make the lightweights move over and give him room as a contender.

Also Sidetracked by Joey

And to get his foot inside the lightweight door, Chalky must beat a boy who sidetracked him much as Pep did. That is Joey Peralta, Mexican buzz-saw. Wright had won 16 straight fights until Peralta unexpectedly put the skids under him in a Wilkes-Barre, Pa., bout in 1941.

That Wright-Peralta rematch sounds like a good affair, but Wilson's bout with Jake LaMotta, a rugged character from the Bronx, is quite a shindig too, c paper.

Wilson, according to assorted experts, is really the top welterweight in the biff business right now. He has had quite a job proving it because Red Cochrane, who is in the navy now and hence out of danger at least as far as Wilson goes, would never fight him. Fritzie Zivic gave Jackie a bit of a run-around, too, and Ray Robinson was not anxious to tangle with him. But tomorrow night the comparison boys will be busy because Robinson was not able to do too much with LaMotta last October. LaMotta is still tough, for two weeks ago he beat Jimmy Edgar. So the experts are anxious to rate Wilson, the new phenom, on how he does tonight against Jake.

Rated in other ways, Wilson is quite a handy citizen. When he went to the Coast from Cleveland, he did not rush his fistic career, for he wanted to complete his high school course first. He did, and besides his diploma he also has some skill as a cartoonist. His drawings have made some of the sports pages in Coast papers.

Building for the Future

At 25, Wilson is married, and he is smart enough to build for the future instead of just ramming ahead in this biff business and getting punchy. He is in the army because he eloped little more than a month before Pearl Harbor; Oct. 24, 1941, to be exact, the night he kayoed Kid Azteca.

Wilson was a Golden Glove and National A. A. U. champ, and he fought in the 1936 Olympics. He has handed out 32 kayoes in his 53 pro bouts. He has something, and the Garden bugs, seeing him for the first time, had better look quickly if they want to see what it is.

BASKETBALL 'PENALTY BOX' IS PROPOSED

Milwaukee, Jan. 14 — Bill Chandler, Marquette basketball coach, proposes that basketball adopt a "penalty box" plan similar to that in hockey in place of the four-foul rule. He proposes that on the fourth foul a player be removed from the game for a specified time, perhaps three minutes. During that period a mate could be substituted for him, and at its end he could go back into the game. Subsequent fouls would bring similar penalties.

LEO DUROCHER, Dodger manager, who is at the Mayo Clinic in Rochester, Minn., today for a physical checkup.

DiMaggio, Joining Army, Breaks Up Yankees–but Good!

Baseball men today were of the opinion that the Yankees had been definitely brought back to the field in the American League by Joe DiMaggio's announced intentions of joining the army.

Reconciliation Effected

In a statement from Reno yesterday DiMaggio said he had effected a reconciliation with his wife, the former Dorothy Arnold, and would enlist as soon as he could arrange his personal affairs. Mrs. DiMaggio would have completed six weeks of residence in Nevada today, thereby becoming eligible to file a divorce application.

Since last October Shortstop Phil Rizzuto, First Basement Buddy Hassett, Pitcher Charley Ruffing and Outfielder Tommy Henrich of the Yankees have gone into the service. All, including the veteran Ruffing, were key men. DiMaggio's decision leaves the team with only two outfielders, Charley Keller and Roy Weatherly.

President Ed Barrow of the Yanks said last night that he had not been officially informed of DiMaggio's plans, but was not surprised by Joe's decision. "I wish him Godspeed and good luck," said Barrow. "We are perfectly in accord with anybody who wishes to serve his country. Joe should make a fine soldier."

In State Squash Racquets

Donald Frame of the Harvard Club, defending New York State amateur squash racquets champion and Metropolitan titleholder, entered the final round of the New York State title tournament last night, winning from Lt. Edward C. Oelsner of the University Club, 15—8, 15—11 and 15—11 at the Downtown A. C. Frame will meet H. Williamson Pell of the Princeton Club today. Pell turned back Richard P. Cooley of Yale University by scores of 7—15, 15—5, 15—11 and 15—12.

Only Four Dodger Outfielders May Respond to Training Bell

By TOMMY HOLMES

While Harold Patrick Reiser, the regular Dodger center fielder, was getting himself inducted into the army at Jefferson Barracks, Mo., yesterday, Branch Rickey and Dixie Walker, the regular Dodger right fielder, were passing the time of day at the weekly luncheon of the Brooklyn Rotary Club.

And as the sun went down it looked very much as though the Dodgers had lost two regular outfielders for the duration. For Walker, looking very dapper and businesslike—he is wearing glasses this Winter—told the new Brooklyn chief just what he told the present writer a month ago, namely, that he feels his duty to himself and his family may lie in his present job with Sperry Gyroscope, and that he seriously considers retirement from baseball.

With Dolph Camilli talking retirement and Peewee Reese likely to get into the army, the 1943 Brooklyn infield was the most serious matter of concern to Rickey and Leo Durocher a few weeks ago. But now the shortage of baseball manpower has affected the outfield situation to an even greater extent.

Ten outfielders are on the Brooklyn reserve list, but it is extremely probable that only four will be available when and if the boys go away for Spring training a couple of months hence.

Jack Graham, a gangling rookie from Montreal, preceded Reiser into the army. Don Padgett and Johnny Rizzo are wearing navy blue. On the doubtful list along with Walker is Augie Galan. The little California Frenchman has been reported about to enter the armed forces, but Ebbets Field has heard nothing definite from him for weeks. Galan is 30 years old and unmarried.

Joe Medwick may be the only veteran regular left. The remaining outfielders include two rookies and a utility man. The utility man is our old friend, Frenchy Bordagaray. The newcomers are Luis Olmo, a husky Puerto Rican, who slugged for Richmond last Summer and grabbed just about all the batting honors in the Piedmont League, and Harold Peck, a star speedster at Milwaukee. Peck's speed may be impaired by last Fall's gun accident, which resulted in the loss of a couple of small toes. The Dodgers have a conditional arrangement with Milwaukee for his services and need not pay for him unless they keep him after opening day

PETE REISER, who was inducted into the army yesterday.

Medwick, of course, is strictly a left fielder. That was also Olmo's position at Richmond, although the Puerto Rican shifted around a bit and put in some time at third base. Peck was right fielder at Milwaukee. That would seem to make Bordagaray the Dodger center fielder for 1943.

I don't think, though, that Rickey will be happy to stand pat with his present outfield situation. At his press conference today he may reveal his plans to make a trade if such a thing is possible under the current sad market condition. He'll also talk some more about Spring training, although it seems unlikely that a definite decision by the Dodgers is close at hand.

Meanwhile the Winter banquet league is starting up. One of the guests at the dinner to George V. McLoughlin at the Cathedral Club tonight is our old friend, Bill Terry, headed here from Memphis. McLoughlin and Terry are old friends and Bill's visit here is natural enough. But at that the boys who are guessing that Terry might be seeking financial backing to buy the Phils may not be too wide of the mark.

Japs' Last Papuan Strongholds Seized

7TH ★★★★★★ Sports Extra

Wall Street Financial News

BROOKLYN EAGLE

Weather—Light rains today. Sunset, 5:57; Dimout, 6:27.

102d Year. No. 18. DAILY & SUNDAY • (Copyright 1943 The Brooklyn Eagle, Inc.) • BROOKLYN, N. Y., TUESDAY, JAN. 19, 1943 • Entered at the Brooklyn Post-office as 2d Class Mail Matter • 3 CENTS IN NEW YORK CITY ELSEWHERE 4 CENTS

PRESIDENT ORDERS STRIKERS BACK TO MINES IN 48 HOURS

Sees Nation Injured —Threatens to Take Action if Defied

Washington, Jan. 19 (U.P.)—President Roosevelt today directed striking anthracite coal miners to go back to work within 48 hours or face the consequences of "necessary steps" by the Government to protect the nation.

The President said the walkout was doing the country "serious injury."

Mr. Roosevelts directive was contained in telegrams sent to 33 national and local officials of the United Mine Workers.

Approximately 12,000 miners are still out in a strike which began 21 days ago because of a dispute arising from wage demands and an increase in dues levied by the union.

The President, acting as commander in chief of the armed forces, directed "all miners in the anthracite coal fields who are now out on strike to return at once to their jobs of producing vitally needed coal for their country."

WLB Order Ignored

He acted after the War Labor Board yesterday had advised him of its inability to end the strike.

One of the telegrams went to John L. Lewis, international president of the United Mine Workers, who had told the strikers to resume work.

George W. Taylor, acting chairman of the WLB, in a letter to the President, described the walkout as a violation of the labor-industry no-strike agreement and the WLB directive of Jan. 15 in which the Labor Board ordered the strikers to resume operations immediately and settle their grievances without halting production.

The board decided unanimously yesterday to ask the President to act, pointing out that when the strike began early in January the strikers gave as their reason an increase in dues levied by the union last Fall.

Asked Boost Despite Contract

Then, the board said, as the strike continued demands were made for an increase of $2 per day in wages despite the fact that the strikers were covered by a contract which does not expire until April 30.

The board estimated that there were approximately 13,500 miners still on strike yesterday. Some went back to work today.

The strike had inspired demands in Congress ranging from proposals to prosecute the union leaders to passage of legislation making it a crime to strike in time of war.

One member of the House who represents an anthracite mining region, Representative John W. Murphy (D. Pa.) planned "a personal plea to the miners in my district to go back to work."

3,000 Return to Work

Wilkes-Barre, Pa., Jan. 19 (U.P.)—Approximately 3,000 of 15,000 striking miners in Pennsylvania's northern anthracite field returned to work today pending settlement of their grievances.

The South Wilkes-Barre colliery of the Glen Alden Coal Company, first to close in the 21-day-old strike, reopened with a "weak force" after returning miners walked through heavy picket lines.

Officials of the company, world's largest anthracite producer, declined to estimate the number of men working, but said "coal is already being produced." . . . . . .

The Hudson Coal Company reported approximately 2,700 miners in the Olyphant local returned at three of their collieries and production was "almost normal."

There was, however, no indication of a general back-to-work movement.

At least 3,800 miners last night voted to continue the strike. They are employed at Glen Alden's Woodward and Huber mines and the Westmoreland shaft of the Lehigh Valley Coal Company. Lehigh reported its Prospect and Henry collieries remained idle. Eight hundred workers at the Inkerman shaft of the Volpe Coal Company joined the strike yesterday, but last night reversed their vote and resumed work today.

In the southern anthracite field the Lehigh Valley Company reported 1,600 miners at the Hazleton shaft who struck Saturday had returned to work. Union officials said that 1,000 other workers at its Nesquehoning shaft of the Edison Anthracite Company voted to return.

8th Army Battles Axis 50 Miles From Tripoli

4 Cities Seized—Report Rommel Flees to Tunisia

Cairo, Jan. 19 (U.P.)—Gen. Sir Bernard Montgomry's Eighth British Army has reached Zliten, on the Libyan coastal road 82 miles from Tripoli, a middle eastern command communique reported today.

On the southern inland flank the Eighth Army, having driven the Axis Afrika Korps out of Beni Oulid, 90 miles southeast of Tripoli, flicting tank losses, was in contact with the enemy toward Tarhuna, road junction 50 miles northnorthwest of Beni Oulid and only 50 miles from Tripoli, the communique said.

To reach Zliten, the Eighth Army passed through Misurata, the big German base for the Wadi Zemzem defense line.

British Sweep On

London, Jan. 19 (U.P.)—The British 8th Army stormed on toward Tripoli, less than 50 miles away today, and dispatches from Algeria said Marshal Erwin Rommel, deciding to abandon all of Tripolitania, had fled to Medenine, 68 miles inside Tunisia.

The 8th Army's northern column swept through Misurata, the big German base for the Wadi Zem Zem defense line, and yesterday was at Zliten, on the coast 82 miles from Tripoli, a Middle Eastern command communique said.

In their advance the British captured Misurata and Zliten.

But the greatest advance was made by the southernmost of the 8th Army's three advancing columns. It was in contact yesterday, the communique said, with enemy forces toward Tarhuna, a road junction only 50 miles from Tripoli. At the rate the 8th Army was advancing, it apparently was much closer than 50 miles to Tripoli today.

Nazis Attack in Tunisia

Two companies of German infantry, apparently attempting a diversion that would give the Afrika Korps a better chance to escape, attacked Allied positions northwest of Bou Arada in Tunisia. Two other companies came to their support and they made some gains, according to an announcement from Allied North African headquarters.

Far to the south of Tripoli another threat to the base developed when French forces from Tunisia were reported to be nearing a junction with another French column from Equatorial Africa. The latest report on the French force from Tunisia placed it at Tin-Abunda, 425 miles south of Tripoli.

Bombers Pound Foe

American and British bombers of the Middle East Command pounded the retreating Axis forces unceasingly, and struck blows intended to paralyze defenses in Tripoli.

WHERE TO FIND IT

	Page		Page
Bridge	15	Music	5
Comics	12	Novel	15
Crossword	14	Obituaries	7
Dr. Brady	12	Parrott	9
Editorial	6	Patterns	14
Fighting Men	11	Radio	12
Financial	13	Real Estate	15
Grin and Bear It	6	Society	4
Heffernan	6	Sports	9-10-11
Helen Worth	11	Take My Word	12
Home Front	11	Theaters	5
Horoscope	12	These Women	11
Income Tax	13	Tucker	6
Jury	11	Uncle Ray	11
Lindley	6	Want Ads	13-14-15
Movies	5	Women	4

Marcel B. Peyrouton

ALGERIA HELM PUT IN HANDS OF PEYROUTON

Ex-Envoy to Argentina Is Strong Laval Foe—Was in French Cabinet

Algiers, Jan. 19 (U.P.)—Marcel Peyrouton, former French Minister of Interior, was appointed Governor General of Algeria today.

Peyrouton succeeds Yves Chatel as Governor General. He recently was French Ambassador to Argentina and came her from South America by plane last week.

He left Buenos Aires on Dec. 29, saying he was going to North Africa to serve under Gen. Henri Honore Giraud, new high commissioner of the French North African possessions.

Peyrouton had resigned his diplomatic post when Pierre Laval, collaborator with Germany, rose to power in the French Government.

It was Peyrouton who signed the order for Laval's arrest when the latter was expelled from the French Cabinet in December, 1940.

Peyrouton served as resident general in Tunisia in 1939 and 1940 before becoming Minister of Interior in the Petain Cabinet. He was appointed Ambassador to Argentina in 1941.

Says Nazi Generals Plot To Overthrow Hitler

London, Jan. 19 (U.P.)—Prime Minister Johan Nyggaardsvold of the exiled Norwegian Government said today latest underground reports from Norway told of a plot among German generals to overthrow Adolf Hitler once the military situation becomes desperate.

In an interview Nyaardsvold quoted these sources that some of the German commanders were jealous of the power wielded by Hitler's SS Elite Guard troops and Heinrich Himmler's Gestapo.

"Until the situation becomes desperate, there is little chance of a major plot against Hitler developing," he asserted.

Urges Washington Exile Banner of Sliced Bread

Madera, Cal., Jan. 19 (U.P.)—The city council today sent to Washington a resolution demanding that "the man responsible" for no-slice bread "be run out of Washington as too dumb to help the government."

Last Japanese Strongholds in Papua Captured

Remnants of 15,000 Army Fighting in Rags And Near Starvation

Gen. MacArthur's Headquarters, Australia, Jan. 19 (U.P.)—United States and Australian troops have taken Sanananda Point and Sanananda village, the last Japanese strongholds in Papuan, New Guinea, Gen. Douglas MacArthur announced today in a special communique.

Japanese remnants, all who were left of the enemy's Papuan army of 15,000 shock troops, including naval landing parties and marines, were sliced into four isolated pockets, two on the north New Guinea shore and two inland, and their position was hopeless.

A Sydney Herald special correspondent at the front reported the Japanese were groggy, in appealing physical condition, wearing tattered uniforms and ribbons of boots which had rotted from their feet.

Japs on Small Beach Front

Opening their drive Sunday, the Allied troops cut the main road, leading inland, in the Japanese rear.

Following up this success, the Allies drove on to take Cape Killerton, at the northwestern side of the enemy beachhead, and Wye Point, 700 yards to the southeast.

The Japanese were left with a beach front less than 2,500 yards long and about the same depth inland.

The United States and Australian troops were thus very close to the biggest Allied victory of the southwest Pacific, the complete elimination of the Japanese army which landed at Buna, just down the coast, months ago, and started a confident drive for Port Moresby, the Allied base on the south coast, which was to be the springboard for an invasion of Australia.

DOG TO FACE TRIAL FOR SCALING FENCE AND KILLING TERRIER

Detroit, Jan. 19 (U.P.)—Timmie, 4-yera-old retriever, must stand trial, Jan. 27, for the death of Tippy, a wire-haired terrier that yapped at him once too often from behind his master's fence.

Timmie finally scaled the fence and when he did the 10-year-old terrier was killed. Prosecution will be under a Nineteenth Century statute decreeing death for vicious dogs.

Thomas P. Thompson, attorney retained by the defendant's owners, Mr. and Mrs. F. N. Pattison, said he would base his case on the contention that the statute applied only to dogs that killed sheep, cattle and chickens.

Hogan Calls Off Probe Of Mary Barton's Death

District Attorney Frank S. Hogan today declared that the case of Mary Barton, who died Sept. 8, 1941, was closed as far as he was concerned.

William L. Grundhofer, fosterfather of the night club dancer, who has continually charged that she was murdered, failed to appear at the prosecutor's office yesterday to substantiate his charges.

TRAP PERILS NAZIS NORTH OF LENINGRAD

General Retreat Looms As Reds Pound Salient After Freeing City

Moscow, Jan. 19 (U.P.) — Soviet troops pounded a vulnerable German salient outside Leningrad today and threatened to isolate the Axis armies on the northern front or force them into a general retreat, front dispatches indicated.

The northern Axis salient already has lost its northern anchor at the fortress of Schluesselburg, 25 miles east of Leningrad, which was taken when the Red army lifted the 16-month siege on the former Czarist capital.

Successful operations along this salient could become a springboard for a Russian thrust into the Baltics and perhaps a drive into East Prussia and Poland, observers said.

Smash On 1,250-Mile Front

The Russians were on the march along their 1,250-mile front in a smashing offensive rivaled only by the German advance in 1941. The Axis was confronted with danger spots along the entire front.

Simultaneously with its announcement that Leningrad had been freed, the Red Army reported yesterday its forces had driven across the Donets River and recaptured Kamensk, 90 miles north of Rostov.

Once the Soviets mop up the Kamensk area they will be in position to extend their bridgehead on the west bank of the Donets and push on toward Likhaya, the vital rail junction 16 miles to the south, which now is carrying the major role in supplying Rostov from the west. Such a drive would menace the entire Donets line of the Axis.

Reports from the Stalingrad area, where the remnants of 22 Axis divisions had been reduced from 220,000 men to less than 70,000, said the encirclement was tightened yesterday and 3,000 more Germans killed.

In the Velikie Luki area 250 miles south of Leningrad and 275 miles

Continued on Page 7

EXTENSION OF HERLANDS SCHOOL INQUIRY URGED

Councilman Louis P. Goldberg, Brooklyn American Laborite, was to introduce a resolution today urging Commissioner of Investigation Herlands to widen his investigation into the city school system to include the Board of Construction and the Bureau of Plant Operation and Maintenance.

These groups constitute a major part of the $18,474,587 budget submitted by the Board of Education for operation in 1943-44. Goldberg's resolution calls for Herland's to submit a report on them by March 1.

Joseph M. Conroy

DEWEY APPOINTS CONROY, COLLINS TO L. I. BENCH

Both Prominent in G.O.P. —To Occupy County Court Posts Until End of Year

By JOSEPH H. SCHMALACKER

Albany, Jan. 19—Governor Dewey's first judicial appointments in the Long Island area were made here today.

Joseph M. Conroy, 48, of 114-01 95th Ave., Richmond Hill, was named Queens County judge at $25,000 a year, to succeed Charles S. Colden, who was elected to the Supreme Court bench.

Henry J. A. Collins, 47, of Seaford was appointed Nassau County judge at $15,000 a year, to succeed Cortland A. Johnson, also elevated to the Supreme Court.

Both men, Republicans, have outstanding records in the legal profession. They will sit by appointment till the end of the year, when elections will decide their future careers. Senate affirmation of both appointments was considered certain.

Difference in Salaries

The difference in the two salaries is due to New York City's contribution of $10,000 to the State salary of $15,000 for county judges. Mr. Collins, however, will most likely get an additional $2,500 as judge of the Children's Court. Judge Johnson held both jobs and the local authorities may give Mr. Collins the additional post.

Mr. Conroy has been prominent in Queens Republican politics for many years. Born in Brooklyn Oct. 17, 1894, he attended Our Lady of Mercy Parochial School, Manual Training High School and Brooklyn Law School, being admitted to the bar in 1919.

He is a former president of the Queens Bar Association and was

Continued on Page 7

PRICE SLASH DUE IN WAR ON BLACK MARKET

Prosecution of 14 Meat Wholesalers Called 'Only the Beginning'

A general reduction in retail meat prices was looked for today as a result of the vigorous action taken by the Office of Price Administration to break up the black market.

As the opening gun in its campaign the regional office of the OPA launched prosecutions against 14 wholesalers and small packers and 29 of their officers and employes in Brooklyn, the Bronx, Newark, Paterson and Philadelphia.

Warrants charging ceiling price violations were served upon the individuals, five in the Bronx being immediately placed under arrest and held in bail for the grand jury by U. S. Commissioner Cotter in Manhattan.

The prediction of early benefit to consumers was made by Sylvan L. Joseph, regional OPA administrator, who emphasized that the drive was just beginning.

Only the Start of Drive

"It should not be assumed," said he, "that the arrests made are the culmination of this investigation. Rather they represent only the initial results. On the basis of facts already gathered cases are being prepared against several other wholesalers.

"Reports indicate that our widespread investigations have already

Continued on Page 7

U. S. Subs Sink 5 More Ships In Pacific Zone

Washington, Jan. 19 (U.P.)—United States submarines, striking at enemy shipping in the Pacific and Far East areas, have sunk five more enemy ships and damaged two others, the navy announced today.

Ships sunk included were a destroyer, a large cargo ship, a medium-sized cargo ship and a small patrol vessel.

Damaged were one large tanker and one small cargo ship.

Today's announcement brought to 112 the total of enemy ships sunk as a result of U. S. submarine operations in the Pacific since Pearl Harbor. Twenty-two others have been probably sunk and 29 damaged.

2 FAKE BERLINS FAIL TO CONFUSE PILOT

Royal Air Force Bomber Station Somewhere in England, Jan 19 (U.P.)—Two dummy cities, not one as previously believed, rigged up outside Berlin to mislead Allied fliers had no effect on the shooting eye of flight Sgt. H. Goodwin, 22, of Wyncote, Pa., who piloted a British Lancaster heavy bomber in Saturday night's smash at the capital. Goodwin said he dropped his two-ton "block-buster" right in the center of the real Berlin.

It has been known the Germans have made reports to confuse attackers by creating a fake Berlin beyond the outskirts of the real city but Goodwin and his mates saw two mock cities, both easily distinguishable from the real thing.

Chinese Foil 15th Attempt To Cross River to Yunnan

Chungking, Jan. 19 (U.P.)—Fighting continued on the Yunnan border today with Jaanese troops based at Kengtung, near the French Indo-China line, making their 15th unsuccessful attempt to cross the Nanlei River, according to a Chinese Army headquarters communique.

1,219 Casualties Listed By Navy; 36 in Boro, L. I.

14 Local Men Reported Dead, 9 Missing And 13 Wounded Between Dec. 16 and 31

Washington, Jan. 19 (U.P.)—The Navy Department today released casualty list No. 20, which included 1,219 men who were reported dead, wounded or missing in advices to their next of kin between Dec. 16 and 31, 1942.

The total included 418 dead, 403 wounded and 398 missing. The list named 84 men from New York, 32 from New Jersey and 19 from Connecticut in these categories.

The new list brought to a total of 21,497 the number of navy, marine corps and coast guard casualties reported between Dec. 7, 1941, and Dec. 31, 1942.

The figures showed that of 21,497 casualties 6,344 were listed as dead, 3,837 as wounded and 11,316 as missing.

List No. 20 included men from all

Continued on Page 3

Halifax Dined at Jewish Hospital; To Give Room to Honor Hero Son

Lord Halifax, British Ambassador to the United States, was a guest today at a luncheon and reception at the Jewish Hospital, 555 Prospect Place, and afterwards was conducted on a tour of inspection of the hospital.

The affair had been planned for Lord and Lady Halifax. Both accepted the invitation but only Lord Halifax arrived. His wife sent a note explaining illness of a son prevented her appearance.

The Ambassador was accompanied by the British Consul General and his wife, Sir Godfrey and Lady Haggard.

Louis M. Rabinowitz, vice president of the hospital, later announced that Lord Halifax was donating a room in the pediatric ward as a memorial to his son, Francis Hugh Peter Courtenay Ward, killed in action in the present war.

OPEN WINDOW IS DEATH'S DOOR TO SLEEPWALKER

The body of Max Cohen, 74, retired manufacturer, of 805 St. Mark's Ave., was found today on the sidewalk below a window open in his fourth floor apartment, where he lived with two daughters.

His daughters, who did not know of the occurrence until after the body had been found, said their father might possibly have been walking in his sleep, according to police. He had not been feeling well recently, they said. The police listed the occurrence as "fell or jumped."

Continued on Page 7

Eagle Staff photo

PACKIN'S GOOD—Snowball season opened officially today as the Winter's first real storm spread its carpet and the gale added a bite to the mixture. These lads are from St. Francis Prep, and the scene of their lively fun is Borough Hall. The civic center is a pretty sight while the snow stays clean.

6,850 Battle Heaviest Snow

Continued from Page 1

from third rails by dropping alcohol on it.

In keeping the streets cleared for traffic the Department of Sanitation kept 6,850 men and 392 pieces of equipmen, aside from dump trucks, busy, according to an announcement by Commissioner William F. Carey. As the storm continued more and more of the department's dump trucks were diverted from their normal task of gathering garbage to snow removal.

Will Call Reserves

Should these forces prove inadequate, the commissioner said, he would have recourse to the emergency roster of laborers and privatel-owned trucks registered for employment in case of need.

With the Weather Bureau forecasting that the snow would turn to rain before night—specifically, "sleet or freezing rain with strong winds and continued cold"—it was not regarded as likely that the emergency forces would be needed.

In Trenton, State Highway Commissioner Spencer Miller Jr. reported all highways open, with traffic considerably slowed by the storm.

Five children were shaken up in the Bronx in an accident caused by the storm. They were in a station wagon bound for All Hallows Institute, a Manhattan parochial school, when the vehicle was hit by a truck owned by the M. N. Beer Corporation on Homestead Ave. According to the police, the truck had skidded out of control. The children were taken to Fordham Hospital for a precautionary checkup.

In Garden City early today Edwin H. Pinkus, 22-year-old electrical engineer employed at the Sperry Gyroscope Company plant, was fatally injured when struck by an automobile while walking on Clinton Road, near the old Westbury Gold Golf Club. He died several hours later in Nassau Hospital, Mineola.

Borough Flier Wins Second Valor Award

Among the seven air corps officers awarded the Distinguished Flying Cross today by Lt. Gen. George C. Kenney, Allied air chief in the southwest Pacific, for making more than 50 operational flight missions, was 1st Lt. George F. Callahan of 128-16 148th St., South Ozone Park.

Earlier this month Lieutenant Callahan received the Cilver Star for gallantry in action. He shot down one out of a flight of eight Zeros and 15 Japanese dive bombers, which attacked his formation of planes.

Lieutenant Callahan is 27 and has been in service for about two years. He received his training and was commissioned in Alabama in October, 1941. He was stationed at Mitchel Field and was shipped to Australia shortly after Pearl Harbor.

He attended Jamaica High School and before going into service was employed by the Equitable Life Assurance Society in New York.

He is the son of Anna R. Callahan, who is an air raid warden and Red Cross worker. His mother is proud of letters from him, many of which go like this:

"We shot down (censored) Jap planes today. How about that, mom?"

Teachers to Meet

A meeting of the Catholic Teachers Association will be held Sunday at 3 p.m. at the Columbus Club for delegates and alternates.

New Stoppages Feared in Transit Pay Rise Protests

IND Maintenance Men Expected to Emulate Action of IRT Workers

Subway maintenance men on the IRT division of the city transit system who struck briefly yesterday in protest against "inadequate" pay increases are back at work, but officials of the Transport Workers Union, C. I. O., at whose urging they returned to their jobs, expressed fear of new stoppages among shop men of the IND division today.

Union leaders said the IND workers are paid today and outbreaks would probably develop as they did among the IRT workers yesterday, when the men learned for the first time that they had received "inadequate" pay increases or none.

Mayor LaGuardia on Jan. 6 announced he had arranged for increases totaling $1,093,000 a year to 13,0000 of the city's 32,000 subway employes. Union officials said 6,000 men have been given 2-cent-an-hour increases; 3,600, 4 cents, and 3,000, 5 cents.

Quill Assails Delaney

Yesterday's stoppages involved 2,500 men in eight I. R. T. shops, who stayed away from their jobs following their lunch hour for periods ranging from one to two hours. They returned after officials of the union had urged them to in line with labor's wartime no-strike pledge.

Michael J. Quill, T. W. U. president, and other union heads, expressed confidence that "our members will heed our plea to refrain from any further action and will follow faithfully the policy of the T. W. U. to settle this dispute by impartial arbitration."

Quill and Douglas L. MacMahon, president of the New York City local of the union, charged that yesterday's "brief interruptions" were the result of the "provocative policies" of John J. Delaney, chairman of the Board of Transportation, in refusing to deal with the union on behalf of the men or to submit the issues to arbitration.

The union had asked the War Labor Board to settle the issue but that agency, after a hearing, ruled that it did not have jurisdiction where the employer, as in this case, is a municipality.

The Mayor indicated that a showdown was nearing between Quill and the city government.

"The city has to decide whether or not a person not an officer of our city government can run our transit system," he declared.

William Jerome Daly, secretary of the Board of Transportation, called the stoppages "nuisance disturbances," which, he said, the union staged as a "publicity build-up" for Quill. He added that the men affected would be docked in pay for the time they had stayed out.

The largest of the stoppages occurred in uptown Manhattan, where 1,100 men took an "extended" lunch period. At the Corona shops 130 men took part in the stoppage.

In one of the shops in Manhattan the men hanged the Mayor and Delaney in effigy.

Flynn Resigns Post On Bronx Committee

Edward J. Flynn, nominated as Minister to Australia, today resigned as chairman of the executive committee of the Bronx Democratic County Committee. The resignation was in a letter to Harry E. Chambers, county chairman, who said that Flynn's successor would be chosen at a meeting next week.

Fire Wrecks 4 Buildings

Continued from Page 1

tions of the feet and face, treated on the scene.

Police Emergency Squads of the Miller Ave. and Grand Ave. precincts were at the scene, also the St. John's Hospital Emergency Unit and an ambulance from Bushwick Hospital. An emergency first aid station also was set up at a neighborhood drug store.

Trains Move Through Smoke

After the flames flared up shortly before 10:30 a.m., a column of dark smoke was blown across the structure of the Broadway elevated line. The elevated trains, with passengers looking out of the windows, moved slowly through the smoke as though passing through a tunnel.

Westbound local service on the Broadway-Brooklyn elevated line was routed over to the express track between the Gates Ave. and Broadway-Myrtle Ave. stations. This was done to enable firemen to use the outer track while directing the hose on the fire.

Eastbound trains on the Lexington Ave. elevated line went as far as the Nostrand Ave. station, then turned back. Meanwhile shuttle service was installed between the Nostrand Ave. and Gates Ave. stations.

Crowds Gather Despite Storm

Trolley traffic was still tied up shortly before noon. They were the Broadway and Putnam Ave. lines.

Despite the cold wind and the snow, crowds gathered on nearby streets. Police maintained fire-lines well back of the area in which the firemen were working. Ice coated the firemen's helmets and rubber coats. Water froze on parts of the ruined buildings and made the footing slippery.

The second alarm was sent at 9:35 a.m., the third at 9:57 a.m. and the fourth at 10:25 a.m.

According to police, the fire is elieved to have started in the Patkow Linoleum Co., located at 1589 Martiny's Sign Shop, S. S. Nicholas 5-10-25-$1 Store and Brownie's Cleaning Store. All the buildings are owned by the Fresh Pond Realty Co., 648 Lexington Ave.

BORO STUDENT WINS SECOND MUSIC AWARD

Kenneth Vincent Casey, 17, of 447 62d St., today has the distinction of getting the top excellence award twice in his school career. As a graduate of St. Michael's Diocesan High School, 43d St., he was given a $25 check by Bishop Molloy personally at the graduation exercises in the Bishop Loughlin High School Auditorium on Greene Ave. on Monday night.

In January, 1939, he got the general excellence award as a graduate of Our Lady of Perpetual Help Parochial School, 59th St. and 6th Ave. His name has been on the honor rolls of both schools continuously. In high school he was pianist of the orchestra. Kenneth is the son of Mr. and Mrs. Michael Vincent Casey and has a sister, Alice, a student in St. Joseph's College.

Amen Reforms Drafted in Bills

Continued from Page 1

racket, the net balance for the public at the conclusion of the investigation was $929,000.

Among his recommendations were changes in the law dealing with testimony in bribery cases and disclosure of grand jury testimony.

Consults Amen Aides

The understanding is that most of these recommendations will be embraced in the bills Senator Desmond is preparing to introduce. He said he had been in conference with some of the chief aides who served with Amen.

Meanwhile, both Senate and Assembly held brief sessions, with the Assembly adopting a resolution introduced by Minority Leader Irwin Steingut of Brooklyn congratulating President Roosevelt on his 61st birthday on Saturday.

Steingut's resolution hailed Mr. Roosevelt as the commander-in-chief who is leading the "battle against the forces of world oppression."

A bill calling for $300-a-year salary increase for memberse of the supervising, teaching, administrative and custodial staffs of the New York City Board of Education was introduced by Assemblyman Robert J. Crews, Brooklyn Republican.

BUY U. S. WAR BONDS AND SAVINGS STAMPS

Moses Receives Rotary Award

Park Commissioner Moses today was awarded the Service Medal of the Rotary Club of New York at a luncheon in the Hotel Commodore, Manhattan.

The award, "in recognition of outstanding service to the people of New York," was presented by Ray O. Wyland, president of the club and director of education for the Boy Scouts of America.

The diners included Newbold Morris, president of the City Council; Secretary of State Thomas J. Curran, Herbert Bayard Swope, chairman of the State Racing Commission; Maj. Gen. Sanderford Jarman of the Eastern Defense Command and Grover A. Whalen.

Commissioner Moses is the first person to be so honored by Rotary since the presentation to Gen. Evangeline Booth in 1940. Other recipients of the award include Dr. Alexis Carrel, Paul P. Harris, Robert Weeks DeForest and Thomas A. Edison.

Wise to Speak Here

Rabbi Jonah B. Wise of the Central Synagogue in Manhattan, will speak at the fourth institute lecture at the Bay Ridge Jewish Center, 4th Ave. and 81st St. Solon B. Hanft will preside.

Eastern District Presents Ambulance to Army

High spot of yesterday's graduation exercises of the Eastern District High School, Marcy and Keap Sts., was the presentation of an ambulance from the student body to the army.

The presentation was made by Florence Guzik, who was in charge of fund raising. It was accepted by Lt. Phelps Phelps for the army.

Funds were raised through an "odd penny drive," a faculty show, a picture exhibition, school dance and several community affairs.

Meyer Waks was the faculty member in charge of the drive. Dr. Samuel D. Moskowitz, principal of the school awarded the diplomas.

THE SCREEN

By Jane Corby

'The Crystal Ball,' 'Gone With the Wind,' 'They Got Me Covered,' on Borough Screens

"The Crystal Ball," which opened at Loew's Met today, has Paulette Goddard starring in that new type of role for which she is becoming famous, a get-your-man role which includes out-maneuvering strong opposition, this time from Virginia Field. Together the girls vie for the personable Ray Milland, and before Paulette is conceded the winner considerable light-hearted comedy has obliterated the wearisome events outside the moviehouse door for the duration of the film. It's the kind of picture everybody in the family can enjoy, too.

Besides the three headliners, "The Crystal Ball" has a happily chosen cast that makes the most of every rib-tickling situation. Gladys George, as Madame Zenobia, honky-tonk teller of fortunes; Cecil Kellaway, as Pop Tibbets, who runs a shooting gallery, and William Bendix, as Biff Carter, Ray Milland's chauffeur-valet, keep the story rolling merrily.

Trouble starts when red-headed Toni Gerard, played by Paulette Goddard, finds herself down to her last 38 cents in New York. Having come here from deep in the heart of Texas, to compete in a beauty contest, she is left stranded when the judges suffer from myopia and give the decision to a blonde. Sighting Madame Zenobia's outfit, she asks for 38 cents worth of fortune telling and Zenobia befriends her to the extent of getting her a job as a sharpshooting "shill" for Pop Tibbets.

Ray Milland steps into her life when he accompanies Virginia Field, playing an attractive young widow who considers him her property, to Zenobia's establishment, because the widow has lost an emerald ring and wants occult help in finding it. To see Ray Milland is to love him, as far as Paulette is concerned, and she sets herself to outdo the widow, making use of all the crystal-gazing at her command in order to win out. Before everything is settled to Paulette's satisfaction Ray Milland, an attorney, is all but disbarred over a land transaction to which Paulette has unwittingly committed him. But it all turns out to be hilarious good fun as the final reels are unwound.

CONRAD VEIDT as Major Strasser, who makes things tough for Ingrid Bergman, Paul Henreid and Humphrey Bogart in "Casablanca," which started its fourth week at the Paramount yesterday. "Stand By All Networks" is added attraction.

'Gone With the Wind' Now on Strand Screen

"Mammoth" is the word for that picture which made movie history, "Gone With the Wind," which is now back in Brooklyn, opening today at the Strand, for the benefit of the many who want to brush up on their memories of the lengthy, fascinating spectacle first screened at the end of 1939, and the few who happened to be in Timbuctoo or other distant points when it made the rounds the first time. One fact about "Gone With the Wind" stands out clear above all the rest: it's a picture that can't be ignored, and the temptation to see it again, and find out if it's as good as you thought it the first time, is almost certain to be irresistible.

The Strand is offering the full-length version—it takes three hours and three-quarters—in Technicolor. It is a magnificent production, with an overwhelming assortment of touching drama, by turns heartlessly grim, sweet and tender and sparkling with wit. It is boldly realistic in its language and finely acted by a huge cast.

The characters which Margaret Mitchell created between the covers of the book for which "best-seller" is a weak description, have been transposed, in all their vivid strength, on the screen. Again they live in an authentic Southern atmosphere, to walk the red clay of Georgia plantations, to be frenzied by Sherman's march on a gutted Atlanta, to mourn the collapse of an unique civilization and to make the best of the new life forced upon them at the end of the Civil War.

Briefly, the story of "Gone With the Wind"—in case there is still extant somebody who is not yet acquainted with the plot—is the story of a headstrong, tenacious woman, to whom the Civil War brought misery that she refused to endure, who swore that, through her own efforts, she would never be hungry again, and who twisted her life and sacrificed her friends to win her ends. It is a study of personalities, contrasting Scarlett O'Hara, the indomitable, played by Vivien Leigh, with Melanie Wilkes, the sincere and understanding wife of Ashley Wilkes, played by Olivia DeHavilland. Leslie Howard has the role of Ashley, wooed by the love pirate Scarlett. Clark Gable reached the apex of his career as Rhett Butler, the man who knew Scarlett O'Hara as well as she knew herself, and who was a match for her in practicality and greediness.

Other characters which have become immortalized for moviegoers are Laura Hope Crews as Aunt Pittypat, Thomas Mitchell as Scarlett's father and Hattie McDaniel as the delightful Southern Mammy. Talented supporting players have done their share of making "Gone With the Wind" a sensitive and intelligent photoplay, beautiful to see and compelling in its high drama.

'They Got Me Covered' Headliner at the Albee

"They Got Me Covered," the new Bob Hope-Dorothy Lamour laugh riot, opened today at the Albee with Bob Hope carrying off his role of world's zaniest newspaper reporter with smash hilarity. Why Bob proves his right to the title in the very first sequence, when he gets fired by the news agency he represents while acting as foreign correspondent in Russia, having overlooked the German invasion of that country.

Besides Bob and Dottie, the film has the services of Lenore Aubert as a slinky woman of mystery and John Abbott as the quarry of Axis agents, along with Otto Preminger as the head of the Axis ring. Edward Ciannelli, Donald Meek, Marion Martin—in the exotic role of "The Glow Girl"—and Philip Ahn and together they provide some of the best comedy situations in many a film month.

It's Bob Hope's efforts to retrieve himself after being fired and scoop everybody by getting an exclusive story on Axis agents in this country that lead to a lot of screwy complications. Bob starts off by going to see his girl friend, Miss Lamour, employed by the Washington office of his syndicate. There he stumbles on the activities of Axis spies, but trouble ensues as soon as he starts looking for it.

His informant dictates the story to a stenographer, but Gestapo men get the shorthand notebook, then kidnap the girl herself. Hope, trying to release her, is trapped by the Axis agents, the informant is killed and the gang, afraid to kill Hope for fear of exposing themselves, plan to discredit him before he tries to write his story. They frame up a marriage for him with "The Glow Girl," a strip-teaser!

How the plan works and the hero's desperate attempts to straighten everything out make for the side-splitting conclusion to the film, which gives Hope his funniest role to date and Dorothy Lamour a dramatic part in which she does not have to wear a sarong.

YETTA ZWERLING, Jewish comedienne, is featured in "The Rich Uncle," Yiddish musical comedy starring Menasha Skulnik this week-end at the Parkway Theater.

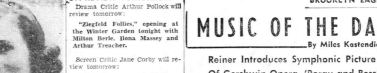

ON REVIEW TOMORROW

Drama Critic Arthur Pollock will review tomorrow:

"Ziegfeld Follies," opening at the Winter Garden tonight with Milton Berle, Ilona Massey and Arthur Treacher.

Screen Critic Jane Corby will review tomorrow:

"Slightly Dangerous," with Lana Turner and Robert Young, opening at the Capitol.

"The Hard Way," with Ida Lupino, Dennis Morgan and Joan Leslie, opening at the Fox. Also "Truck Busters."

Ethel Waters to Sing At the N. Y. Strand

Ethel Waters, international singing star, who recently completed the motion picture "Cabin in the Sky," has been engaged as the special featured attraction in the N. Y. Strand stage show headed by Jan Savitt and his orchestra, beginning Friday, April 9.

MUSIC OF THE DAY

By Miles Kastendieck

Reiner Introduces Symphonic Picture Of Gershwin Opera, 'Porgy and Bess'

That Gershwin's immortality will rest chiefly on the fact that he was a song writer was made the more apparent by the first New York performance of "Porgy and Bess": a Symphonic Picture, arranged for orchestra by Robert Russell Bennett and presented by Fritz Reiner at the Philharmonic-Symphony concert in Carnegie Hall last night. The potpourri of the material from the Gershwin opera had its moments, but they were for the most part those sections which incorporated the best-known melodies of the work. And what tunes they are!

Like the symphonic synchronization of Jerome Kern's "Showboat," this one of "Porgy and Bess" serves its purpose well and is a better job. Fritz Reiner was responsible for the arrangement, picked the sections and set the sequence of the numbers. Mr. Bennett complied to this plan, adding his part as he knew Gershwin would have liked it in such a symphonic version. The orchestration is full, sometimes flashy and sometimes noisy. There are saxophones and a banjo (appropriately used for "I Got Plenty o' Nuttin'") to give the right color.

While there is no story or program, the numbers follow in this order: Scene in Catfish Row, Opening Act III, Opening Act I, "Summertime," "I Got Plenty o' Nuttin," Storm Music, "Bess, You Is My Woman Now," The Picnic Party, "There's a Steamboat That's Leavin' Soon for New York," "It Ain't Necessarily So" and "Oh, Lawd, I'm On My Way." Whether anything was gained thereby is questionable.

All the theatrical element in the score came out in the Reiner interpretation, including considerable sentimentalization of the song hits. The performance would have gained by more even tempos, paced a bit faster.

In commemoration of Rachmaninoff, the orchestra played the finale from Tchaikowsky's Sixth Symphony, "Andante Lamentoso," before the beginning of the printed program. It happens that Rachmaninoff's last appearances in New York were with the Philharmonic-Symphony in Carnegie Hall on Dec. 17 and 18, 1942.

This concert was conducted more along the lines of the "old" Reiner in contrast to the "new" observed last week and the first week of his previous visit. His conception of Debussy's "Iberia" was not particularly enhancing and his interpretation of the Tchaikowsky Fifth Symphony was decidedly mannered. The program was poorly made, every selection on it began slowly and almost drearily.

FEATURE FILMS SHOWING TODAY

BAY RIDGE	
Electra, 75th St. and Third Ave.........	Yankee Doodle Dandy
Harbor, 92d St. and Fourth Ave........	Journey for Margaret; Red Skelton in Whistling in Dixie
Stanley, Fifth Ave. and 75th St........	Gone With the Wind
BEDFORD	
Crown, 527 Empire Blvd. PR. 3-8536...	You Were Never Lovelier; also A Night to Remember
Lincoln, Bedford and Eastern Parkway..	His Girl Friday; also If I Had My Way
National, 720 Washington Ave..........	For Me and My Gal; also The Omaha Trail
Rogers, 333 Rogers Ave. PR. 4-2230 ...	Now, Voyager; also Youth on Parade
Savoy, Bedford Ave. and Lincoln Pl......	Amazing Mrs. Holliday; The Falcon Strikes Back
BENSONHURST	
Colony, 18th Ave.-65th St. BE. 6-2231.	20 Mule Team; also 40 Little Mothers
BOROUGH HALL AND DOWNTOWN	
Century's Tivoli, Fulton St., Boro Hall.	In Which We Serve; also McGuerins From Brooklyn
Duffield, Duffield and Fulton Sts.......	In Which We Serve; also McGuerins From Brooklyn
Momart, Fulton St. and Rockwell Pl....	The Star Maker; also Western Union
St. George Playhouse, 100 Pineapple St.	In Which We Serve
Terminal, Fourth Ave. and Dean St.....	Journey for Margaret; also Whistling in Dixie
BRIGHTON BEACH	
Oceana, Brighton Beach Ave.-Hoff St...	Immortal Sergeant; also It Comes Up Love
BUSHWICK	
Empire, Ralph Ave.-B'way. FO. 9-7940..	China Girl; also Margin for Error
FLATBUSH	
Astor, Flatbush Ave. near Church.......	I Am the Law; also Four Mothers
Granada, Church and Nostrand Aves	Journey for Margaret; also Whistling in Dixie
Leader, Coney Island and Newkirk Aves.	Immortal Sergeant; also It Comes Up Love
EAST FLATBUSH	
Avenue D, Avenue D and E. 43d St.....	Life Begins at 8:30; also Tarzan Triumphs
Rugby, Utica and Church Aves..........	China Girl; also Margin for Error
GERRITSEN BEACH	
Graham, 311 Whitney Ave.............	Yankee Doodle Dandy
PARK SLOPE	
Carlton, Flatbush and Seventh Aves	In Which We Serve; also McGuerins From Brooklyn
Plaza, Flatbush Ave. and Park Place	Army Surgeon; also The Falcon's Brother
Sanders, Prospect Park West-14th St...	Dr. Gillespie's New Assistant; Underground Agent
Venus, 1224 Prospect Ave..............	For Me and My Gal; also Omaha Trail
KINGS HIGHWAY	
Jewel, Kings Highway at Ocean P'kway..	I Want a Divorce; also Gateway
AVENUE U SECTION	
Avenue U, Ave. U and E. 16th St.	Journey for Margaret; also Whistling in Dixie
Traymore, Avenue N and E. 46th St....	Journey for Margaret; also Whistling in Dixie
RIDGEWOOD	
Colonial, Broadway and Chauncey	Immortal Sergeant; also It Comes Up Love
Ridgewood, 1673 Myrtle Ave............	Star Spangled Rhythm; also At the Front
Rivoli, Myrtle-Wilson Aves. GL. 5-0744.	White Cargo; also About Face
SHEEPSHEAD BAY	
Sheepshead Th., Sheepshead Rd.-Voorhies.	Margin for Error; also China Girl
SOUTH BROOKLYN	
Sander's Globe, 228 15th St...........	Sutters Gold; also Come On, Leathernecks
Minerva, Seventh Ave. and 14th St.....	Yankee Doodle Dandy

Wyandanch Club Land Bought by Shirley

700 Acres of Famous Smithtown Property To Be Sold by Corporation in Plots

Walter T. Shirley, widely known land developer whose office is in 500 5th Ave., Manhattan, has purchased 700 acres of the famous Wyandanch Hunting and Fishing Club, in Smithtown, Suffolk County, L. I., from the Leeson Corporation of Manhattan, through Long Island Acres, Inc., of which Mr. Shirley is president.

The Leeson Corporation acquired the property about a year ago from the Central Hanover Bank which secured it in December 1940 from the Wyandanch Club through an order from the Supreme Court. In the recent transfer Charles L. Kahn was attorney for the seller, the Leeson Corporation epresented at the sale by its president, Frederick M. Leeston Smith of Manhattan.

The Wyandanch Club, organized about fifty years ago by leading New York business men and sportsmen, still retains nearly a thousand acres adjoining Shirley, where its present members fish in the big lake and well-stocked trout streams and shoot duck and other small game in the rolling, wooded hills. Among the organizers and early members of the Wyandanch Club were Eversley Childs of Bon Ami fame, General Wingate, Thomas Mills, Frank Bailey, Newbold Herrick, Arthur Whitney, Claud Pollister and Sam Brown.

The Club acquired its extensive fishing and hunting preserve from various "Smith" heirs and the Club's 2,000 acres represented by far the largest land holdings of any individual or corporation in Smithtown, since the death in 1691 of the famous Long Island Land King, Richard "Bull Rider" Smith, founder of Smithtown when his vast holdings, all of the present Smithtown and more, were divided by his will among his six sons and two daughters. According to Shirley's title searchers, Smith, in order to establish a clear title to the town named after him, was forced to buy deeds not only from Lion Gardiner, the first white owner, but also from six different Indian Chiefs, from a land pirate, from the towns of Huntington and Bookhaven, in addition to securing land grants from two English and from one Dutch Governor.

Shirley's Corporation now owns the 700 acres free and clear. The property will be wholesaled as acreage in plots of one-half acre to ten acres, priced according to the corporation at $300 an acre and upwards. The subdivision map, almost completed, calls for two parkways, 100 feet wide and a mile and a half long, running through the property from Jericho Turnpike to Hauppague Road with intersecting roads 50 feet wide. Contracts amounting to approximately $50,000 have already been awarded for improvements, clearing and road construction.

The property will be sold for Summer and year round homes, for Victory Gardens, also for investment to meet the insistent demand among New Yorkers for Long Island acreage. The extent of this demand is evidenced by the fact that only about 150 acres remain unsold of the former 1,000 acre Vanderbilt Estate at Lake Ronkonkoma where Shirley introduced his wholesale acreage plan last December after it had taken him two and a half years to sell 200 acres in lots. The Shirley organization has sold in acreage parcels, more than 600 acres in five months' time.

"I anticipate greater and great-

Continued on Page 35

REAL ESTATE

Names Committee To Study Plans for Post-War Housing

A. N. Groves, Syracuse, president of the New York State Association of Real Estate Boards, today announced the appointment of a post-war planning and housing committee "to develop a sane and sensible program for the future financing, construction and ownership of real property."

Robert H. Armstrong of Manhattan will head the committee.

The Brooklyn member is Victor J. Matthews. The members from Queens are Edward J. MacDougall of Jackson Heights, Thomas F. Malone of Jamaica and Edward F. Hossinger of Long Island City.

"There are no greater problems than those confronting real estate today," said Mr. Armstrong, commenting on the work of his committee. "Housing, finance, decentralization of both industry and business and the migration of huge segments of our population are but a few.

"Unless the real estate problems of this State are solved," he emphasized, "there is no doubt but that the bankruptcy of many communities must ensue."

Pointing to the problems that have been created within our economy during recent decades by the great social and industrial changes that have taken place, Mr. Armstrong said: "No longer does any business or industry dare to drift and merely ride on the wave of the future.

"Our entire national economy today is so complex," he said, "and the forces which control its direction are so at variance with one another that planning in its broadest sense has become necessary.

"The war has accentuated and accelerated recent changes in technology and construction, shifts in population and the increased participation of Government in business. No longer can an individual, any group, any business or group of business be responsible and answer only to themselves. There is a social responsibility which is demanded as well.

"Plans galore have been promulgated by various Governmental agencies and in State capitals, as well as from the desks of learned economists, but those interested in real estate have never offered one of their own."

LAKE RONKONKOMA BATHING BEACH—Here is a section of the private bathing beach on Lake Ronkonkoma, in one of the most beautiful spots on the lake to which purchasers of the former Vanderbilt estate plots have free beach rights. The property is being "wholesaled" by Long Island Acres, Inc., of 500 5th Ave., Manhattan, at the rate of about $99 per quarter acre.

IN LOFT ESTATES—One of the new homes in the Loft Estates residential colony, facing Sunrise Highway, between Rockville Centre and Baldwin, built by Gust Svensen, Inc. Frank Kondla, sales director, states that two of the recently completed houses were sold over the past weekend.

IN NEW HOME GROUP—Fifteen of these low cost houses of bungalow type have been completed by the Gibson Corporation at Gibson, Valley Stream. Fred Simons, sales director at the development, states that there has been active buying there during the past three weeks.

Flatbush Apartment Sold

Joseph Lampiase, as broker, sold for S. Klein to an investor, the four-story apartment house, having 20 apartments, at 1722 Caton Ave., corner E. 18th St., valued at $60,000, having an annual rental of $11,628. Julius Jay Flamm represented the seller and Abraham Yesnowitz represented the purchaser.

Brooklyn Apartments For Rent

Brooklyn Real Estate For Sale

Long Island Real Estate For Sale

Long Island Real Estate For Sale

Long Island Real Estate For Sale **Long Island Real Estate For Sale**

DONT THROW A BOMB FOR THE JAPS
HELP UNCLE SAM SAVE RUBBER
DONT BREAK GLASS OR THROW SCRAP METAL OR NAILS IN THE STREET

Offices—To Let

★★★★★★★ SPORTS
Wall Street Financial News

BROOKLYN EAGLE

Weather—Rain and wind today and tonight. Sunset, 7:50; Dimout, 8:20.

102d Year. No. 119. DAILY & SUNDAY • (Copyright 1943 The Brooklyn Eagle, Inc.) • BROOKLYN, N. Y., FRIDAY, APRIL 30, 1943 • Entered at the Brooklyn Post-office as 2d Class Mail Matter • 3 CENTS IN NEW YORK C ELSEWHERE 4 CE

LEWIS FIRM IN REPLY TO F. D. R.; 90,000 IDLE

Mother Hurls Two to Death, Ends Life in Six-Story Leap

Stabs Her Aunt In Astoria Spat Before Tragedy

A woman, about 28, shortly before noon today hurled two girls, apparently between 3 and 5 years of age, from the roof of a six-story apartment house at the northwest corner of 41st Ave. and 21st St., Long Island City, and then herself jumped to the ground.

The woman died in an ambulance on the way to St. John's Hospital, Long Island City.

The children died in the same hospital a short time after they were taken into the emergency ward and before police could question them.

Long Island City police announced at 1:30 p.m. that the woman, before she threw herself and her two children, stabbed an aunt during a quarrel in Astoria, according to police.

The dead woman was Mrs. Rose Tanelian, 28, of 31-21 97th St., Corona, police announced.

The dead children were her daughters, Marion, 5, and Florence, 4.

A group of men at Paretti's gasoline station at the southeast corner of 41st Ave. and 21st St. saw the woman on the roof of the apartment house, diagonally across the street. The house is a unit of the Queensbridge Houses, the low-rent housing project directly north of the Queensboro Bridge.

The men in front of the gas station saw the woman lean over the parapet and drop the two children into space.

Then, as horrified men started to weave their way through traffic on busy 21st St., the body of the woman thudded on the ground.

The woman and the two children

Continued on Page 18

BORO FLIER CITED IN RAID OFF SICILY

Sweeping in to bomb the Sicilian Straits with a group from Maj.-Gen. James H. Doolittle's strategic force, Second Lt. Robert C. Congdon of 135 Martense St. was forced to dive into the middle of defending enemy planes, it was announced today. In the ensuing dog fight the Brooklynite lieutenant scored lightning victories over his opponents and went to help in the bombing that resulted in the sinking of two Axis vessels and the damaging of at least nine others.

Dodgers, Giants Game Off; Play Two Tomorrow

Today's scheduled game between the Dodgers and the Giants at the Polo Grounds was postponed and the teams will play the first major league doubleheader of the season there tomorrow.

Plane Downed Off Cyprus

Cairo, April 30 (U.P.)—An enemy fighter was shot into the sea off Cyprus yesterday, a Royal Air Force communique announced today.

PIMLICO RESULTS

1—Valpuiseaux, 27.00, 11.40, 6.00; Meeting House, 7.60, 4.40; Bay Dean, 2.70. Off time, 11:59½.
2—Chain Miss, 10.40, 5.30, 4.70; Sparker, 6.00, 4.40; Mare Nostrum, 7.60. Off time, 12:31.

DAILY DOUBLE PAID $249.60

3—Magis Heels, 4.90, 4.00, 2.90; Banyan, 9.20, 5.90; Donavatra, 4.80. Off time, 1:01.
4—Ecomint, 7.80, 5.90, 4.20; Lost and Found, 8.00, $5.40; Charge, 3.50. Off time, 1:31⅕.
5—Farsight, 5.00, 2.70, 2.30; Saboteur, 2.70, 2.30; Precious Years, 2.70. Off time, 2:01.

He Crawled Into Jaws of Death--

Boro Sergeant Wins Silver Star For Extreme Heroism in Africa

Heroic action displayed while repairing communication lines under severe machine gun and artillery fire won Technical Sgt. Hugh Sparks, 39, of 9732 Fort Hamilton Parkway, the Silver Star citation.

The scene of action was North Africa during a heavy artillery duel between the Americans and Germans. Vital communication lines contacting two battalions were wrecked by enemy fire. Sgt. Sparks and a handful of men volunteered to repair the damage. Foot by foot they crawled through a veritable screen of machine gun and cannon fire. They managed to reach the lines, repair them and return safely. The success of the sergeant and his men permitted the battalions to accomplish their mission.

"I am not very surprised about Hugh," said Mrs. Sparks when she learned of her husband's courageous feat.

The sergeant had been an army man for almost all his mature years, enlisting long before the start of World War II. During his first few years in the service he was stationed at Fort Hamilton. At the advent of our entrance into the war, he was transferred to Fort Devens, Mass. He left for over-seas duty in July of 1942. He was with first divisions to land on North

Continued on Page 11

Sgt. Hugh Sparks

Lovelorn Girl Due for 2d Standup As Youth Is Held in New Robbery

A lovelorn girl from Cleveland is due for another Brooklyn standup tonight. Her boy friend, Salvatore Farranto, 16, of 466 Columbia St., is in custody of police again, this time on a charge of stealing $240 from Salvatore Carobene, a neighbor.

When Detective Clarence Gilroy collared him today, Farranto shrieked: "I guess I'm unlucky in love."

"How so?" asked Gilroy.

"Last time I got pinched I had a date with my girl, who came all the way from Cleveland, but I was in the coop. I had a date with her for tonight, and here I am again."

Farranto was at liberty in $1,000 bail, awaiting a hearing in burglary of a jewelry store at 252 Smith St. on April 13.

SHOT KILLS MAN FACING DRAFT BOARD RECALL

With a rifle beside him, Seymour Greenberg, 32, was found dead yesterday of a gunshot wound in his mouth in his room at 2230 E. 12th St. Police said the wound was self-inflicted. Neighbors, police reported, said he was scheduled to reappear before his draft board for reexamination.

THE LITTLE BLACKOUT WASN'T THERE

For more than three hours last night Brooklyn was all prepared for a rumored surprise blackout which never came.

Air raid wardens in white helmets and arm bands walked the streets, apprehensive civilians remained in expectantly and in Manhattan Commissioner Valenine remained at his desk until midnight. But the whistles never blew and many a mystified warden walked slowly home to sleep with one ear cocked for action.

KEAN AGAIN HEADS CONEY ISLAND C. OF C.

Charles J. Kean was elected for a third consecutive term as president of the Coney Island Chamber of Commerce, at its annual dinner meeting last night at the Half Moon Hotel, Coney Island. Three hundred men and women, representing the resort's largest interests, attended.

License Commissioner Paul Moss, City Councilman Edward Vogel and Municipal Court Justice Roger Brock spoke. President Kean said that despite war conditions, Coney Island anticipates one of its biggest seasons because of the curtailment of automobile driving.

Continued on Page 11

JAMAICA RESULTS

1—Docd'ough 29.30-9.30-3.80, Jack Dove 4.60-2.90, Dandy Jim 2.40. (2:05½)

OPA BOOSTS PRIME MEATS' POINT VALUES

But Lowers Those For Variety Types And Canned Fish

Washington, April 30 (U.P.)—Housewives must pay an additional point for 15 prime cuts of beef, veal and pork and a point less for 25 variety meats, canned fish and other special products purchased after 12:01

New Point Chart on Page 2

a.m. Sunday, May 2, the Office of Price Administration announced today.

The upward revision in the point values of prime cuts—steaks and roasts—resulted from a heavy consumer demand for lean meats and those which can be sliced into smaller portions, officials said. They said the changes did not reflect any worsening of the meat shortage.

OPA rejected industry demands that it reduced point values of sausage. Officials said they could not be lowered without diverting excess amounts of fresh cuts to sausages.

The value of sausage now is determined by the point value of meats that go into it. OPA said that it could not with justification manipulate point values so as to influence consumers to buy processed meats rather than the fresh cuts of meats from which sausage is made.

Five cuts of steak—round, top round, bottom round, round tip and flank—were advanced one point each. They now will cost 9 points per pound. Round top roast was advanced from 7 to 8 points a pound.

In veal, leg roasts were raised from 6 to 7 points; round steak cutlets from 8 to 9 points and sirloin steak or chops from 7 to 8.

Pork point values were raised a

Continued on Page 2

HEARINGS END IN RACE TRACK UNION DISPUTE

Evidence Presented To Show Political Favor Governed Jobs

Hearings before the State Labor Relations Board started two weeks ago into a union dispute at the Jamaica Race Track, ended at noon today after presentation of evidence on how to get a race track job by knowing the right politicians.

The proceedings, which were before Examiner Sidney L. Cahn in th SLDRB rooms at 250 W. 57th St., Manhattan, were technically on the petition of the ari-Mutuel Employes Guild, an unaffiliated organization, for recogntion as sole bargaining agent for ticket-takers and cashiers at the track.

The Muteul Ticket Agents Union, A. F. L., whose members have been

Continued on Page 18

Gen. Kenney Decorates Fliers Who Braved Odds

General MacArthur's Headquarters, Australia, April 30 (U.P.)—Lt. Gen. G. C. Kenney, air force commander in the southwest Pacific, today decorated the crew of a Flying Fortress which fought off 15 to 20 Japanese Zeros and braved anti-aircraft fire in a reconnaissance flight over Rabaul last November.

Red Cross $13 Million Over War Fund Goal

The National Red Cross War Fund has topped its goal of $125,000,000 by $13,000,000, Walter S. Gifford, national chairman of the fund, said today.

The final amount will be somewhat greater, Gifford added, since some localities which have not yet reached their goals will continue their campaigns.

Reds Decorate Budenny

By United Press

Marshal Semyon M. Budenny of the Red Army received the order of Lenin today, his 60th birthday anniversary, for "outstanding military service to the Soviet Government," the Russian radio announced. The broadcast was recorded by FCC monitors.

Is Silent on Strike; Insists on New Parley

Wildcat Strikes Spread—Pepper Sees 'Rebellion'

Washington, April 30 (U.P.)—Wildcat strikes in the nation's richest soft coal fields were spreading today despite President Roosevelt's ultimatum that they cease by 10 a.m. tomorrow.

A survey disclosed that the number of strikers in five Mid-Western, Eastern and Southern bituminous fields had climbed past the 90,000 mark.

White House Secretary Stephen T. Early said President John L. Lewis of the United Mine Workers had not replied to Mr. Roosevelt's demand that the strikes end and soft coal production continue.

In addition to the possibility that all 450,000 soft coal miners would quit work at the expiration of a 30-day contract extension truce tonight, there was the threat that 80,000 Pennsylvania anthracite miners also would stop production. The hard coal miners' contract expires at midnight tonight and negotiations for a new contract are deadlocked.

Both the soft and hard coal miners have been demanding a $2-a-day wage increase.

Two Contracts Expire

Within the next 24 hours the miners face two deadlines:

1. Midnight tonight—One month's extension of the soft coal contract between the U. M. W. and the Appalachian coal operators expires. Lewis has said that his miners will not "trespass" on mine property without a contract, action tantamount of a strike. In addition, the wage contract for 80,000 anthra-

Continued on Page 18

UMW Chief Charges Operators 'Wilfully Blocked' an Agreement —Miners Want to Work, He Declar

John L. Lewis, replying to President Roosevelt's u matum against interruption of war-vital coal producti today remained silent on his strike threat, but renewed mands for continued negotiations through collective b gaining in the wage controversy affecting 450,000 bitumin miners.

The bushy-haired president of the United Mine Work did not directly threaten a general coal strike, nor did give any assurance that the miners would obey Presid Roosevelt's back-to-work order.

Lewis' demand for continued negotiations came only a few hours before the expiration at midnight of the extension agreement during which bituminous mines in 26 States have kept open under the existing contract for the anthracite region in Pennsylvania.

Mr. Roosevelt yesterday ordered Lewis to send about 85,900 striking miners back to their jobs by 10 a.m. tomorrow under penalty of invoking his power "as President and Commander-in-Chief of the Army and Navy to protect the national interests and to prevent interference with prosecution of the war."

Want Agreement, Says Lewis

In his inconclusive message dispatched to the President, which followed a meeting of the U. M. W.'s international policy committee Manhattan, Lewis said:

"We want an agreement. want to work. The bituminous operators have willfully blocked making of an agreement. We spectfully advise that in our ju ment the making of an agreem through a renewal of collective b gaining is the logical means of p viding justice and equity to parties."

Lewis, in a letter to the Preside repeated his contention that War Labor Board has "prejudg the coal miners' case. He asser that the WLB, bound by the "li steel" wage ceiling formula, cc not make a decision "based u the equities of the miners' case."

Renews Stand

The letter took approximately same stand as that voiced by Le several days ago to Secretary of

Continued on Pag

Hirohito's Birthday Celebrated in Japan

Tokio radio today reported celebrations throughout Japan yesterday on the 42d birthday of Emperor Hirohito, including a two-hour military parade in the capital watched by the ruler.

British, Yank, Red Army Heads Meet in Teheran

London, April 30 (U.P.)—The Nazi Paris radio said today that the commanders of British, American and Russian troops in the Middle East are conferring at Teheran, Iran.

Mountain Siege Rage Within Sight of Tunis

Core of German Resistance Is Reached With Allies Suffering Heavy Casualties

Allied Headquarters, North Africa, April 30 (U.P.)—' battle for Tunisia became a grim mountain siege aln within sight of Tunis today after Allied armies yester fought off fierce Axis counter-attacks along the entire fr and edged forward again on the northern and southwestern flanks.

American infantry of the Second Corps, attacking entranched hill positions guarding Mateur junction, and French troops south of Pont Du Fahs junction, gained ground, but the Allied offensive now has fought forward to the core of German resistance and a high price must be paid for the next few miles leading to the Tunis plain.

The blackened wreckage of German tanks lay against the pale green hills around Djebel Bou Aoukaz, 11 miles east of Medjez-El-Bab, and there are many enemy dead on the rocky slopes along the front. But the Germans showed tremendous power of resistance and ragged Allied troops have suffered heavy casualties.

Nazi Resistance Stiffens

Until capture of certain remaining heights the way cannot be opened across the plains to Tunis, some 21 miles distant. The only way these heights can be taken is by storming.

In the last two days the Germans have definitely been trying to wrest the initiative from our troops in a general counter-offensive. So far they have failed but the struggle still was in progress as a part of the

Continued on Page 18

Nazis Report Alli Armada Off Afric

London, April 30 (U.P.)—A flee 150 landing barges, escorted by stroyers and and an aircraft rier, passed eastwards through Straits of Gibraltar yesterday, German Transocean News Age reported from La Linea today.

An escorted convoy of 23 tra ports and tankers also left Gibra yesterday, the German agency s

Later, Transocean added, British battleships Rodney, Mal and Renown, the aircraft carri Furious, Illustrious and Argus, f cruisers and eight destroyers a left Gibraltar.

Boro Woman Who Danced at 108 Succumbs on Her 110th Birthday

Instead of a family celebration yesterday to mark the 110th birthday of Mrs. Martha Davidian, plans for her funeral were being made at her home, 2 Avenue C, where she died at 3 p.m. of pneumonia. At her bedside were her two sons, several grandchildren and other relatives.

Two years ago at the wedding of her grandson, Leon Davidian in Washington, Mrs. Davidian insisted on making the trip to the capital, and there amazed the guests by dancing with the bridegroom and others. Up to that time she took great delight in cooking, sewing and doing other light household tasks. Her health began to fail soon after.

Born in Armenia on April 29, 1833, Mrs. Davidian came to this country 33 years ago and lived for more than 30 years at the Avenue C address. Her husband, David Davidian, died 45 years ago.

She is survived by two sons, Karekin Davidian of Brooklyn and Harry Davidian of Queens, a married daughter, Bahar, who lives in South America, and who is nearly 90 years old, and four grandchildren, Grace Davidian Parsekian, Ira Davidian, who is in the army, Leon Davidian and Veronica Kanboorian. There also are four great-grandchildren in this country and others in Europe and Asia.

The funeral will be held at 2 p.m. Sunday in the Armenian Apostolic Church, 207 E. 30th St., Manhattan. Burial will be in Cedar Grove Cemetery.

WHERE TO FIND

	Page		
Bridge	21	Music	
Comics	15	Novel	
Crossword	20	Obituaries	
Day by Day	6	Parrott	
Dr. Brady	15	Patterns	
Editorial	10	Radio	
Fighting Men	6	Real Estat	
Financial	22	Societ	
Grin and Bear It	10	Sports	1
Heffernan	10	Take My Word	
Helen Worth	9	Theater	
Home Front	6	Those Women	
Horoscope	15	Unc Day	
Letter Out	6	W ds	19
Movies	17	W	

Fun for All the Family--New Puzzles and Pastimes Page in Sunday Eagle

★★★★★★★ SPORTS 7 Wall Street Financial News

BROOKLYN EAGLE

Weather—Moderate temperature with light winds. Sunset, 8:27; Dimout, 9:27.

102d Year. No. 161. DAILY & SUNDAY • (Copyright 1943 The Brooklyn Eagle, Inc.) • BROOKLYN, N. Y., FRIDAY, JUNE 11, 1943 • Entered at the Brooklyn Post-office as 2d Class Mail Matter • 3 CENTS IN NEW YORK CITY ELSEWHERE 4 CENTS

PANTELLERIA FALLS; F. D. R. BIDS ITALY QUIT

MINERS' HOPE FOR ACCORD IS INDICATED

Tentative Pact in Pa. Seen as Basis—Fine Evokes Threat to Quit

Washington, June 11 (U.P.)—The United Mine Workers, threatening a new strike in protest against $1-a-day fines for last week's stoppage, still hope to negotiate a settlement of their dispute with mine operators on the basis of the tentative agreement with central Pennsylvania operators, a union spokesman indicated today.

He said certain other operators—in addition to the central Pennsylvania group—had indicated willingness to accept provisions of the tentative settlement with that group, which included payment of $1.30 a day as portal-to-portal pay.

Miners Serve Notice

The spokesman added, however, that union officials "don't know what these Government agencies will do." Apparently he referred to the possibility that the War Labor Board may refuse to approve terms of the agreement with the central Pennsylvania operators.

Members of John L. Lewis' U. M. W. already had started to serve notice that they were prepared to stop work again if the Government insists on collecting the $1-a-day fine for last week's five-day stoppage.

The Beaverdale Local No. 2233, in Cambria County, Pa., telegraphed solid fuels Administrator Harold L. Ickes that its members would quit work before they would pay the fine. While there are but 400 members of the Beaverdale Local, they expressed what appeared to be the

Continued on Page 15

Thomas A. Swift

T. A. Swift Dies As He Enlists Defense Aides

Leader in Boro Improvement Drives Collapses on Platform

Thomas A. Swift, executive secretary of the Downtown Brooklyn Association, who has been identified with innumerable campaigns for borough improvement, died last night while enlisting volunteers in the civilian defense drive on the stage of the St. George Playhouse, 100 Pineapple St. Mr. Swift, who was seized with a heart attack, was 50 years old.

Oscar Lager, manager of the theater, stated that Mr. Swift arrived at 8:30, and upon learning that his speech was scheduled for 9, took a seat in the rear of the

Continued on Page 11

UNION CLAIMS NORDEN CO. SLOWED WORK

Asks Investigation Of Charges—Firm Head Makes Denial

A demand for an official investigation of its charges that the Carl L. Norden Co., makers of the Norden bombsight, brought about a slowdown of production, was launched today by the organizing committee of Local 475, United Electrical, Radio and Machine Workers of America, C. I. O.

Theodore H. Barth, president of Carl L. Norden, Inc., made a vigorous denial of the charges of slowdown.

William B. Elconin, international field organizer of the union, at a meeting of his committee at 80 Willoughby St., told reporters that the committee was to meet today with officials of the War Labor Board, the NLRB and officers of the army and navy, in an effort to restore capacity production at the Norden plants, 80 Lafayette St. and 50 Varick St., both Manhattan. The Norden concern has received awards of an E pennant and two stars, the last one in March.

These awards, said Elconin, showed that the workers were doing their part and that the slowdown was part of the company's plan to defeat the efforts of the union to become the bargaining agency for the employes, 40 percent of whom are women.

Employes Resentful

Elconin, in the presence of the organizing committee and other officers of the local, declared that

Continued on Page 15

Overthrow Duce, Roosevelt Urges; 15 Million Lbs. of Bombs Hit Isle

Washington, June 11 (U.P.)—Citing the fate of Pantelleria, President Roosevelt today called again on the Italian people to overthrow their Fascist dictators and get out of the war.

Talking to his press conference shortly after being advised by Gen. Dwight D. Eisenhower of Pantelleria's surrender, Mr. Roosevelt said the people of Italy could feel assured that once their Fascist overlords are out of the way, the people will be given a free choice of a new government.

His remarks were an open renewal of the invitations voiced frequently by himself and British Prime Minister Winston Churchill for the Italian people to overthrow the Mussolini regime and throw themselves on the mercies of the Allies.

Scores Mussolini

Mr. Roosevelt reminded the people of Italy that the effect of the Allied campaign against Italy was the perfectly logical and inevitable result of the ruthless, traitorous course followed by Benito Mussolini.

Mussolini, the President said, has betrayed his own country in a struggle for personal power and aggrandizement.

Harking back to his "stab in the back" speech when Italy made an unprovoked declaration of war against France, Mr. Roosevelt said the United Nations had no choice but to prosecute the war against Italy until complete victory is won.

Offers Self Rule

When the German domination of Italy has ended, he said, the United Nations could well assure the Italian people of their opportunity to pick a non-Fascist government of their own choosing.

He expressed a hope in behalf of the United Nations that Italy

Continued on Page 15

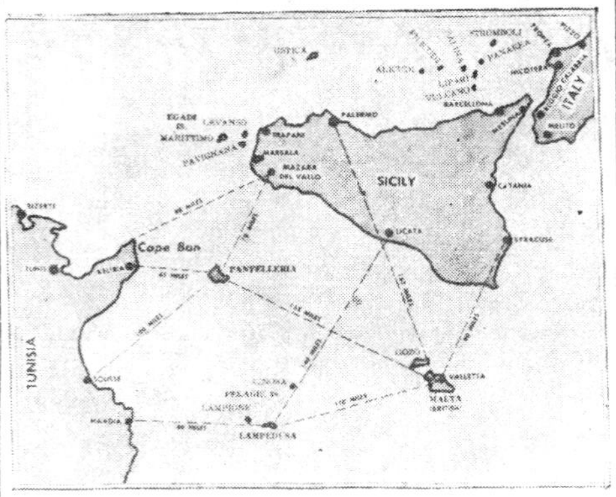

THE ROAD TO ROME—The reason why we wanted strategic Pantelleria is graphically shown on this map. The erroneously named Italian Gibraltar is just a short hop from Sicily and the Italian mainland itself.

By REYNOLDS PACKARD

Allied Headquarters, North Africa, June 11 (UP)—The vaunted Axis island fortress of Pantelleria ran up the white flag of surrender today after almost three weeks of unprecedented bombardment in which air power almost single-handedly for the first time reduced an enemy bastion and cleared the invasion path to Sicily.

The island, 62 miles from Sicily, surrendered by raising a white flag and putting a large white cross on the airfield at 11:40 a.m. and Allied troops began occupying it on the 20th consecutive day of attack from the air, supplemented by six British naval bombardments.

A total of 15,000,000 to 17,000,000 pounds of bombs was dropped on the 32-mile-square island of Pantelleria in the last 13 days of intensive attack. On Thursday a total of 39 Axis planes was shot down and the Allied ratio of planes lost was about one to 18 in the last phase of the offensive.

[Pantelleria covers 32 square miles. In contrast, Brooklyn covers 80.95 square miles.]

In the final phase of attack starting at dawn Thursday the greatest load of bombs ever dropped on such an area was loosed by many hundreds of Allied planes of all types which were over the target in such numbers that they had to "stooge around" in circles awaiting their turn to dump high explosives.

Storm Delayed Blows

Only once during the period from dawn Thursday until darkness was there a lull, and that was when a heavy thunderstorm momentarily halted operations, which ended with a smashing triumph for the theories of Lt. Gen. Carl A. Spaatz, American deputy commander of Allied air forces in Northwest Africa, and his superior, Air Chief Marshal Sir Arthur W. Tedder of the R. A. F.

The capitulation of the first stepping stone on the invasion route to Southern Europe came after a period of 20 days in which the island had been attacked each day and after a period of 13 days of major offensive in which it had been plastered in an all-out drive by the Allied air force—largely American planes — and shelled by the British Navy. Twice the garrison refused demands for unconditional surrender, the second rejection coming Thursday night.

Forty-nine Axis airplanes were shot down in the last two days of the offensive against Pantelleria, compared to a total loss of seven for the Allies in the whole Mediterranean theater.

A special communique from the headquarters of Gen. Dwight D. Eisenhower announced the surrender of the Pan-

Continued on Page 15

Victory First in History Forced by Air Power

Surrender of Pantelleria Is Smashing Triumph For Gen. Spaatz' Theories on Use of Planes

By VIRGIL PINKLEY

Advanced U. S. Air Base, North Africa, June 11 (U.P.)—The Axis garrison on bomb-torn Pantelleria Island ran up a white cross of surrender on the airfield today in an unprecedented capitulation brought about almost solely by aerial power.

Experts said it was the first time in history that a surrender had been forced so conclusively by aerial fleets which had pounded the island by the thousands for 20 days.

The British Navy shelled the Italian fortress island six times, but the vast part of the attack was carried on by American and R. A. F. planes of all types from Flying Fortresses to Spitfires. They never gave the enemy an hour's rest in the last phase of the onslaught.

The white flag was displayed over the harbor of Pantelleria, near St. Elmo Hill, and occupation of the fortress by Allied troops was ordered at once. It was a victory of special importance for Lt. Gen. Carl Andrew Spaatz, American deputy commander of Allied air forces in

Continued on Page 15

De Gaulle Snubs Meeting After Resigning Post

London, June 11 (U.P.)—A usually reliable American source said today that Gen. Charles De Gaulle had offered his resignation from the French Committee of National Liberation, but the committee had not yet accepted it.

Gen. Georges Catroux was understood to be trying to persuade De Gaulle to withdraw his resignation.

Algiers, June 11 (U.P.)—General De Gaulle remained away from a meeting of the French Committee of National Liberation today, presumably protesting that the committee had not heeded his demands for French Army reforms.

Charles Town Results

1—Sir Winks, 4.60, 3.00, 2.80; Meadow Clover, 4.20, 3.60; Blue Proof, 3.80. Off 1:20½.

2—Remolee, 5.40, 3.20, 2.80; Sonny H. 3.80, 4.20; Castine, 9.40. Off 1:47.

DAILY DOUBLE PAID 25.80

Union Gains in Fight to Organize Brooklyn and Queens Y. M. C. A.

The Social Service Employes Union, left wing C. I. O. affiliate which attempted to organize local chapters of the American Red Cross, has won a War Labor Board decision taking jurisdiction in its fight to organize the Brooklyn and Queens Y. M. C. A.

Local 19 of the S. S. E. U., according to Bernard Segal, president, will be given an informal hearing next Friday at the regional offices of the board in Manhattan.

Charitable and benevolent organizations are exempted from provisions of the Wagner act governing collective bargaining. Segal said today the union "had called off a strike scheduled for December, 1941, because of a desire to promote national unity and avoid interference with the important morale work of the Y. M. C. A."

The Y. M. C. A., of which Roy M. Hart is president, had no comment to make on the development.

4,510,000 APPLICATIONS FOR WAR RATION BOOK 3

A total of 4,510,000 applications for War Ration Book 3 from New York State families was received today at the Office of Price Administration. Consumers who failed to apply by mail were instructed to wait until Aug. 1 before applying at local rationing boards. School teachers and students will begin mailing books to mail applicants next week.

ARMY PLANE BLAZES IN AIR, PILOT ESCAPES

Mitchel Field, June 11—An army pursuit plane that caught fire in flight made a forced landing two miles south of Camp Upton, it was announced here last night.

The pilot, who escaped unhurt, brought the plane down, then put out the flames with a fire extinguisher. The plane was badly burned.

Continued on Page 11

AQUEDUCT RESULTS

1—Buzalong 10.00-5.00-3.40, Free Air 4.20-3.00, aBushel Basket 3.40. (1:38⅗)

aCoupled with Dog Show.

C. W. Ferry Appointed To State Taxation Post

Albany, June 11 (U.P.)—Charles W. Ferry, 56, New York City, today was appointed an estate tax appraising accountant by Commissioner Rollin Browne of the Department of Taxation and Finance. Ferry will be connected with the New York office of the department's estate tax bureau at an annual salary of $5,000.

Planning Further Cut In Liquor Allocations

A reduction of whisky allocations to retailers to 60 percent of their normal allotments is being planned by distillers, beginning July 1, to keep the rationing program in line with seasonal decline in volume. Present allocation is about 75 percent. of past sales.

U. S. Recognizes New Argentina Administration

Washington, June 11 (U.P.)—Secretary of State Hull announced today that the United States has recognized the new government of Argentina.

Hull said that the U. S. Ambassador at Buenos Aires, Norman Armour, had delivered the official notification at noon to the government headed by President Gen. Pedro Ramirez.

In response to questions at his press conference, Hull said he expected all of the Latin American countries which had not recognized the Ramirez regime yesterday would do so during the day.

Hull said he had no particular comment to make on the recognition by this Government, saying it was an ordinary step taken somewhat as a matter of routine when

Continued on Page 15

BASEBALL

(Morning Game)

Reds—— 0 0 1 0 0 0 4 2

Cubs—— 0 0 0 0 0 0 0

Batteries—Starr, Mueller; Warneke and Hernandez (7), McCullough.

WAR IN MEDITERRANEAN

Other stories about the fall of Pantelleria and its significance in the growing Allied offensive will be found on page 15 of this edition.

LEST YOU FORGET! TUESDAY'S TAX DAY

Through all the excitement of Congressional battling over new tax legislation, June 15 continues its inexorable advance and will definitely be here Tuesday.

The date is important because the second quarterly installment on the 1942 income—remember?—must be paid no later than midnight of that day, whether a withholding tax is adopted or not.

Reminder to this effect came from Joseph D. Nunan Jr., Collector of Internal Revenue for the 1st New York District.

Perjury Defendant Awaiting Sentence

Wilhelm A. G. Meyer, 54-year-old German army veteran and naturalized United States citizen, today was being held by Federal authorities for sentencing June 18, following conviction of having given false testimony before an Army board of officers. The false statements laid to Meyer involved his association and correspondence with Fritz Duquesne, a convicted Nazi spy.

Vying Riveters Play Tunes On Rafters of Borough Hall

Red-hot rivets few thick and fast and ack-ack-ack vibrations of riveting guns filled Borough Hall at noon today as two champ teams from the Sullivan Shipyards competed for the riveting championship of Brooklyn.

After ten minutes of high-speed operations, which demonstrated vividly to more than 3,000 cheering spectators the skill that goes into the building of ships for war, the four-man Green Team, headed by 44-year-old Luke Anderson, topnotch riveter, was declared the winner. They had driven home 73 rivets into steel plates which were propped up on a truck to simulate the hull of a ship.

The contest provided a dramatic windup to the ten-day citywide CDVO recruiting campaign to enlist 500,000 additional volunteers in defense services. Grover A. Whalen, director of the city CDVO, came across the bridge to congratulate the champ riveters and awarded service bars to five persons who have accumulated a grand total of 16,000 hours of civilian defense volunteer service.

Recipients of the service bars were Mrs. Tracy S. Voorhees, borough CDVO chairman; Mrs. Maurice B. Rich, CDVO vice chairman, and Howard E. Jones, director of Block Service Organization, 4,000 hours each.

The members of the winning riveting team were Luke Anderson, riveter; Joseph Ketcham, holder; Thomas McGovern, heater, and John Breslin, passer. Each will be awarded a $25 war bond.

350-Pound Tuna Is First Catch of Season

The first catch of the tuna fish season, a 350-pounder, has been consigned to Chesebro, Robbins and Grahame Company, 123 Fulton St. The monster tuna, caught off Newport, R. I., by Capt. Cliff Tallman of Newport, is now at Fulton Fish Market.

WHERE TO FIND IT

	Page		Page
Bridge	19	Novel	19
Comics	15	Obituaries	11
Crossword	20	Parrott	13
Dr. Brady	24	Patterns	20
Editorial	10	Radio	16
Events Tonight	20	Ration Calendar	5
Fighting Men	17	Real Estate	21
Financial	18	Society	6
Grin and Bear It	10	Sports	13-14
Helen Worth	7	Take My Word	17
Home Front	17	Theaters	9
Horoscope	24	These Women	17
Letter Out	16	Tucker	10
Lindley	10	Uncle Ray	17
Movies	9	Want Ads	19-21
Music	9	Women	[illegible]

Goldman Dedicates 'Hail Brooklyn' to Boro Music Lovers

Dedicated to the people of Brooklyn

Hail Brooklyn

MARCH

EDWIN FRANKO GOLDMAN

HAIL BROOKLYN MARCH, by Permission of the Copyright Proprietor, MILLS MUSIC INC.

HOPES MARCH WILL PROVE ANOTHER HIT

Trumpets tooted, piccolos piped and bassoons moaned in the good ol' Goldman Band fashion this past week at Carnegie Hall in rehearsal for the band's first public performance of Dr. Edwin Franko Goldman's new march, "Hail Brooklyn," the words and music of which are published herewith.

The first playing of the opus, which is dedicated to the people of Brooklyn, will take place Thursday night at the opening concert in Prospect Park. A first hearing of the work leaves the listener impressed with its sharp, swingy rhythm, leading into a "catchy" chorus.

As Dr. Goldman has often said, "If you can't sing, just la-la."

And there lies the story. For years Prospect Park listeners have cheered, whistled and shouted for "On the Mall," dedicated to another park in far-off Manhattan, and have joined in the famous chorus. Now Flatbushites will be able to call for a composition dedicated to their own borough, and they will gleefully join in the "la-la" procedure recommended by Dr. Goldman. for those who don't know the words.

Hopes It Will Be a Hit

"I sincerely hope that it will be a hit just as 'On the Mall' is," said the composer. "I have dedicated it to the people of Brooklyn for their interest in the Goldman concerts, their enthusiastic support and their immense enthusiasm."

Borough President Cashmore and other notables will be present when the march will bow in on Thursday night. Of course, the finale of the march will have all of the Goldman trimmings—at first the tune will be played softly so that all can join, and for the last chorus the trumpeters will stand up and blast away; the trombones will blare, and the drummers will be quite busy—especially on that final thump.

Wide Popularity Of 'Hail Brooklyn' Is Publishers' Joy

Among those who are happy about the new march "Hail Brooklyn," by Edwin Franko Goldman, are the publishers, Jack and Irving Mills, president and vice president, respectively, of Mills Music, Inc.

Irving, a former Brooklynite, is in far-off Hollywood, presiding over the West Coast destinies of the firm. Nevertheless, his former associations come back to him with emphasis as the words and music of the new composition reached him in California.

The Mills house has published such hits as Hoagy Carmichael's "Star Dust" and the more recent Hit Parader "Idaho." Jack Mills is hopeful that in "Hail Brooklyn" he has another "On the Mall." Some of the enthusiasm of the publishers for the success of the piece is shown in the cover of the sheet music, which is a montage of Brooklyn scenes.

Asks Added Day For Displaying Flag

Special to the Brooklyn Eagle

Washington, June 12—While the nation prepares for Monday's official observance of Flag Day, Representative Eugene J. Keogh of Brooklyn is sponsoring a proposed joint congressional resolution which would add another day to the code for displaying the national colors. His resolution, if approved, would sanction Gold Star Mother's Day, the last Sunday in September, as one of the days when the flag should be flown.

According to Representative Keogh this day was apparently omitted inadvertently from the codification of existing flag rules and customs. His resolution is a proposed amendment to the recognized code.

Eagle Staff photos

BROOKLYN ON HIS MIND—Concentrating on thoughts about our fair Borough of Churches, Dr. Edwin Franko Goldman leads his trusted men in a rehearsal of his new march, "Hail Brooklyn." Come to Prospect Park on Thursday night and hear it yourself.

THE OPENING PROGRAM

Part I

Jubilee March	Shostakovitch
Overture, "Hilaritas"	Shepherd
Prelude and Fugue	Riegger
American Plantation Dances	Arnold
Czech Rhapsody	Weinberger

Part II

Tone Poem, "Jupiter"	Holst
Fantasie, "The Land of the Free"	Rogers
James Burke, Cornetist	
"Suwannee River"	Foster-Dvorak
March, "Hail Brooklyn" (new)	Goldman
Finale, "Pines of Rome"	Respighi

Will Introduce Air Warden's Tune

Enric Madriguera, presenting his music at the Roxy Theater beginning June 16, will introduce a new song written by Congressman Louis Rabaut of Michigan, titled "I'll Be Okay in a Blackout," dedicated to the air raid wardens of America. Patricia Gilmore and the Madriguera Glee Ensemble will handle the vocal assignment of the number.

ARISE, BOYS—This is the row of trumpeters which will stand and blare forth the last chorus of Dr. Goldman's new march at its premiere in Prospect Park Thursday night. Blow good, fellers, we're depending on you.

Allies Rip Through Sicily Air Defenses

★★★★★★★ SPORTS 7 Wall Street Financial News

BROOKLYN EAGLE

Weather—Cooler with showers tonight. Sunset, 8:29; Dimout, 9:29.

102d Year. No. 166. DAILY & SUNDAY • (Copyright 1943 The Brooklyn Eagle, Inc.) • BROOKLYN, N. Y., WEDNESDAY, JUNE 16, 1943 • Entered at the Brooklyn Post-office as 2d Class Mail Matter • 3 CENTS IN NEW YORK CITY ELSEWHERE 4 CENTS

MAYOR OPENS CITY RECORDS TO FULL INQUIRY BY COUNCIL

Oona O'Neill

Charles Chaplin

Chaplin Gets License To Marry Oona O'Neill

Comedian Lists Age as 54, Bride-to-Be as 18 —Joan Barry Collapses on Hearing News

Santa Barbara, Cal., June 16 (U.P.) — Charlie Chaplin, white-haired film comedian, today obtained a license to marry Oona O'Neill, his drama protege and daughter of Playwright Eugene O'Neill.

The comedian and his bride-to-be were waiting at the courthouse entrance when Deputy Clerk Ira D. Altschul opened his office this morning.

Chaplin listed his age as 54 and said he was born in England. Miss O'Neill listed her birthplace as Bermuda and her age as 18.

The party left immediately by automobile shortly before newspapermen descending en masse on the courthouse.

Miss O'Neill and Chaplin, who disappeared from Hollywood last night, had been sought by newsmen since the first word of their elopement.

Even those close to the comedian knew nothing of his plans.

Accompanying the bridal couple were Harry Crocker, Hollywood columnist and friend of Chaplin, and Catherine Hunter, the star's press agent.

Chaplin and Miss O'Neill have known each other for eight months, becoming acquainted after she came to Hollywood to take part in a picture "The Girl From Leningrad." Chaplin reportedly coached her in her drama career after she was chosen debutante No. 1 in New York last year.

Chaplin had been married three times previously, to Mildred Harris, Lita Grey and Paulette Goddard.

In Hollywood, Joan Barry, who claims the movie comic is the father of her unborn child, collapsed when she heard of the elopement. Physicians were called to attend her.

King's Africa Tour Spurs War of Nerves

Axis Jitters Reported Rising at Reports Of Massed Invasion Barges Off Sicily

London, June 16 (U.P.) — A secret, flying visit by King George VI to inspect Allied forces in the Mediterranean theater today topped a war of nerves that left the Axis floundering amid wild speculation on the imminence of an invasion thrust somewhere on the rim of Europe.

When, how and where the blow "in its most intense and violent form" will hit the enemy as promised by Prime Minister Winston Churchill was as much a mystery as ever and there was no official suggestion that the King's inspection tour was linked to any impending operations.

But—

1. The censorship permitted disclosure from London that the Allies had massed invasion barges, landing craft and transports of all types on the south coast of England.

Axis Has Jitters

2. Axis broadcasts continued to report Allied invasion barges and convoys in the Sicilian Straits area.

3. The British press again referred to Axis reports of Allied troops massed in the eastern Mediterranean.

4. A dispatch from United Press correspondent Richard D. McMillan in Cairo said that the enemy was bewildered and unable to decide where to concentrate the bulk of his forces in the Mediterranean sector.

5. It was reported the Germans were engaged in anti-invasion maneuvers on the Norwegian coast.

Industries Hard Hit

6. A broadcast by the BBC reported that German industry, under Allied bombardment, was unable to maintain reserves of war weapons in view of the huge losses in Russia and North Africa and that equipment was not being shipped directly from factories to the front.

The King left Windsor Castle by automobile in great secrecy Friday night and went to the air field, where he boarded a service plane.

A few minutes after the King's plane took off, another plane carrying Cabinet members followed.

The King landed at the Algiers Air Field at 8 a.m. Saturday.

King George, accompanied by

Continued on Page 6

Dewey to Attend Parley

Albany, June 16 (U.P.)—Governor Dewey will leave Saturday to attend the 35th annual Governors' Conference at Columbus, Ohio, beginning Sunday.

ALLIES SMASH STIFF SICILY AIR DEFENSES

Open Concentrated Big-Scale Offensive Against Five Dromes

Allied Headquarters, North Africa, June 16 (U.P.) — Allied aerial fleets smashed through stiff Axis opposition to turn the shattering power of day and night bombardment against the big invasion stepping stone island of Sicily, a communique disclosed today.

A surprise visit of King George VI and other officials to British and American troop centers after a secret journey from London was disclosed at the same time officials revealed the inauguration of concentrated big-scale onslaughts against five airdromes in western Sicily.

The King was loudly cheered by American and British troops with whom he mingled on the beach and elsewhere, watching United States commando units go through their paces and talking to men in hospitals, on warships and in the field.

Everything from flying Fortresses to Spitfires took part in the renewed pasting of Sicilian airdromes. Bocca Di Falco, Castelvetrano, Trapani-Milo, Borizzo and Sciacca were hammered and Marsala radio station was heavily bombed.

Eleven Axis planes were shot down as the Allied forces encountered stiffer oppostion. Allied losses were seven planes.

It was the fourth day of intermittent air attack on Sicily by planes from the Northwest African or the Middle East forces. Many fires were started and enemy installations were wrecked, following up the attacks on Monday night by RAF Wellingtons which hit four Sicilian airdromes. Two radio stations at Marsala were set afire.

RAF Beaufighters also shot down four Axis bombers as they attacked North African coastal towns.

(Axis broadcasts described these attacks by the luftwaffe as directed against Allied concentrations of landing barges, transports and warships massed in the Sicilian straits for invasion of Sicily.)

Flying Fortresses dropped bombs among Axis aircraft on the ground at Bocca di Falco, but the extent of damage was uncertain.

(Reports reaching Madrid from France said that the Italians, apparently reeling under the initial air attacks and feeling that an Allied invasion thrust might overrun their island outposts, have moved important war supplies, port installations and vital records, as well as virtually all bomber squadrons, from Sicily, Sardinia and southern Italy to bases north of Naples.)

British Labor Party Keeps Door Closed Against Reds

London, June 16 (U.P.)—The Labor party conference voted today to maintain its ban against accepting the Communist party to membership. The ballot was taken after a heated debate. The vote was 1,951,000 to 721,000.

Swedish King Is 85

Sweden's tall, tennis-playing king, Gustav V, is 85 years old today.

Charles Town Results

1—Euchre, 10.80, 4.40, 2.80; Bugler, 3.40, 2.40; Corley's Pet, 3.00. Off time, 1:18.

2—War Smoke, 6.40, 3.60, 2.80; Lena Girl, 5.20, 3.40; Ginger Man, 4.40. Off-time, 1:43½.

DAILY DOUBLE PAID $53.80

3—Sunny Del, 11.60, 4.60, 2.20; Sally Lunn, 4.80, 2.20; Jack's Star, 2.20. Off time, 2:10.

Suffolk Downs Results

1—Miss Gosling, 3.80, 2.80, 2.40; Risanda, 10.40, 5.80; Baying, 2.40. Off time, 2:33.

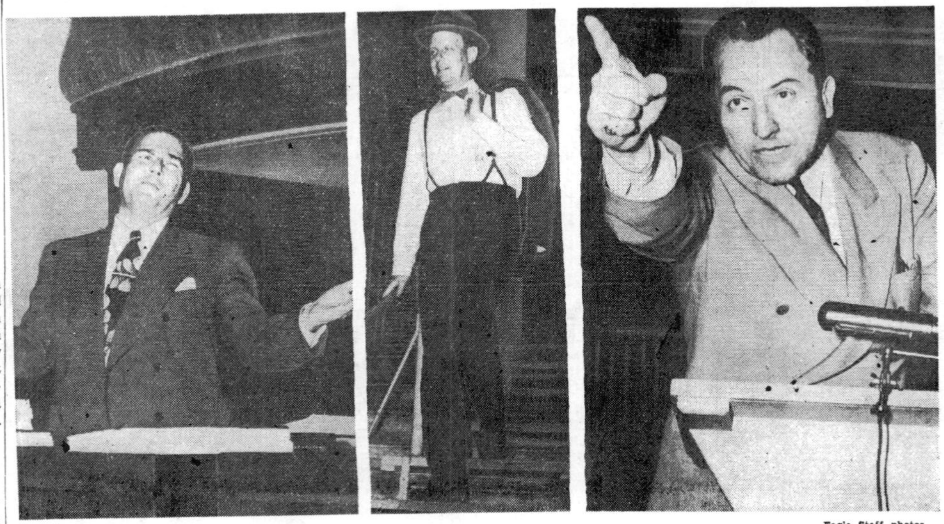

Eagle Staff photos

PRINCIPALS IN NEWEST CITY DRAMA—Brooklyn Councilman Walter R. Hart, left, as he brought to the City Council floor early this morning his resolution for an investigation of the city administration. Center is Council President Newbold Morris wearily leaving City Hall at 2:45 a.m. The belligerent councilman at the right is Majority Leader Joseph T. Sharkey of Brooklyn, who will lead the inquiry.

RANGERS SEIZE 75 MEN IN TEXAS RACE RIOTING

Mob Besieges Sheriff In Search of Negro Accused of Attack

Beaumont, Texas, June 16 (U.P.)—Texas State Guardsmen surrounded the police station today with fixed bayonets and sub-machine guns after Texas Rangers had arrested approximately 75 white men who had been attacking Negroes and destroying property in the Negro residential sections.

Approximately 100 men, most of them shipyard workers, were on the first floor of the 14-story courthouse building, demanding that the Sheriff hand over to them a Negro alleged to have assaulted a white woman. The Sheriff had permitted a six-man committee to go through his jail and see that the Negro was not in custody, but the men were not convinced.

All-Night Rioting

There has been night-long rioting, fighting and arson by mobs of white men in the Negro districts. Police sent to nearby Port Arthur and Orange for ammunition repelnishments called on the Texas Rangers, Texas Highway Police, Office of Civilian Defense Auxiliary Police and Texas State Guardsmen for help.

Chief of Police Ross Dickey described the situation as tense. No

Continued on Page 6

THUNDERSTORMS DUE, WEATHER MAN SAYS

The Weather Man warns that today's rising temperatures will be broken by scattered thundershowers this afternon and evening. It won't be uncomfortable, though, as the humidity is not keeping pace with the heat, even falling off a bit since this morning.

The W. M. hastily adds not to forget to take out the blanket for tonight. Those showers will be followed by fresh winds and colder tonight, slackening to moderately cool by morning.

Temperature at noon was 86 with humidity at 47 percent, a very good combination, according to the W. M.

Court Flays Hero Cop's Killers; Sentences Them to Die in Chair

Detective Joseph Miccio, thrice decorated for heroic action in seven battles during World War I, "was destined to sacrifice his life upon the altar of duty," County Judge Brancato declared today in sentencing the detective's two slayers to death in the electric chair during the week of July 25.

Detective Miccio was shot dead on Dec. 7, 1942, on Nevins St. near Dean St., by Joseph Palmer, 28, of 1723 Lexington Ave., Manhattan, and Vincent Sollami, 26, who never gave a home address.

"It was when questioning the two defendants in line with his duties as a detective that he met death at their hands," Judge Brancato added, excoriating the two slayers for their repeated crimes "with viciousness and utter disregard for human life."

SING SING CONVICT TESTIFIES IN MURDER TRIAL

Abe Yelin, 28, a convicted robber from Sing Sing Prison, was the first witness called today by Assistant District Attorney James McGough in the trial of three men on a charge of slaying Patrolmen Leon Fox on the night of Feb. 15, 1941.

Yelin testified that Joseph Indovino, 26, one of the men on trial, told him about planning the holdup during which the patrolman was shot, a few days before the shooting occurred. Yelin also testified that Sidney Rudish, 29, also on trial, told him about taking part in the alleged holdup later in the evening on which it occurred.

The third defendant on trial before County Judge Leibowitz is Morris Malinski, 26, of 714 Hinsdale St.

RECOVER BABY KIDNAPED IN MANHATTAN

Children playing in front of 316 W. 26th St., Manhattan, today saw a strange woman walk off with the baby carriage in which 8-month-old Carol Macinko had been left by her mother while she went into her apartment. When the mother returned to find baby and carriage gone she telephoned police and a radio alarm was broadcast.

Shortly afterward Patrolmen Kravik and Bannick, cruising in a radio car on W. 23d St., came upon the carriage, which was being pushed by a woman who said she was Rosalind Rogg, 23, of 1544 Minford Place, the Bronx.

Taken to the W. 20th St. station, she was questioned in connection with a series of similar baby kidnapings recently.

Continued on Page 15

AQUEDUCT RESULTS

1—At Play 5.30-3.70-2.90, Psychiatrist 13.50-8.10, Sun Triad 10.50. (1:34½)

2—Grant Rice 3.10-2.50-2.20, Red Blossom 3.70-2.90, Flary 2.60. (2:05

DAILY DOUBLE PAID $8.40

3—Guinea Club, first; Tasmania, second; Winged Hoofs, third.

225,000 TAX RETURNS LACK IDENTIFICATION

Many Mail Payments Did Not Include Bills, Says Nunan

Income tax payments mailed in by more than 225,000 residents of Brooklyn and the rest of the 1st New York District have found their way into the "unidentified returns" account, Internal Revenue Collector Joseph D. Nunan Jr. disclosed today.

Handled as unidentified, he explained, are all returns not accompanied by bills and therefore lacking the identifying account number.

Eventually about 100,000 of the returns will be traced to their proper accounts numbers through information in letters accompanying the payments.

The other unidentified tax payers, Mr. Nunan said, will not be credited with having made their June payments until, responding to notification of deliquency, they appear at the Internal Revenue office, 210 Livingston St., and prove the contrary.

Some Bills Mailed Late

At least 85,000 taxpayers in the 1st District, officials said, will have

Continued on Page 6

ODT ORDER HALTS S. I. BUS STRIKE THREAT

Staten Island was free today from the threat of a bus strike as a result of the decision of the ODT to restore half the mileage it had ordered cut from the lines operated by the Staten Island Coach Company. The company's bus drivers, members of Local 726 of the Amalgamated Association of Street and Electric Railway, had threatened to strike in protest against layoffs that would have resulted from the 20 percent mileage reduction.

Pep Reports for Induction

Hartford, Conn., June 16 (U.P.)—Featherweight Champion Willie Pep reported today at the army induction center for his final physical examination.

If the doctors stamp Pep okay he will leave for Fort Devens, Mass., June 30 to begin his basic training.

DIRECTS ALL DEPARTMENTS TO AID PROBE

But Bars City Funds From Sweeping Quiz Into Administration

By JOSEPH H. SCHMALACKER AND JACK RAMSAY

Mayor LaGuardia, bowing to the Democratic-controlled City Council's move in ordering an investigation of the city government, this afternoon threw wide the doors of his administration for a full inquiry.

The Mayor, in effect, directed all his commissioners and subordinate appointees to extend full co-operation to the Council's special investigating committee, headed by Democratic Councilman Walter R. Hart of Brooklyn, but served notice that he did not expect city funds to be spent for the inquiry.

Inquiry Voted by 18 to 5

Meanwhile, other developments piled up with almost unprecedented swiftness following a turbulent post-midnight meeting of the City Council at which the city's Democratic-controlled legislative body rushed through a resolution for the biggest investigation which the LaGuardia Administration has faced since taking office. The vote was 18 to 5.

District Attorney Frank S. Hogan of Manhattan was served with a subpena calling for the immediate production of all records and material in the stirrup pump case in which Milton Solomon of Brooklyn, a former deputy city controller, was acquitted by a jury in General Sessions of an attempted shakedown charge.

Herlands Faces Bar Probe

Meanwhile, it was learned that Commissioner William B. Herlands of the LaGuardia administration's Department of Investigation, who is believed to be one of the main targets in the Council's inquiry, was also facing a resumption of a tem-

Continued on Page 6

ARGENTINA SEEN BREAKING AXIS TIES

Buenos Aires, June 16 (U.P.)—Optimistic observers today interpreted President Gen. Pedro S. Ramirez' pledge that the new military government will "do what it ought to do" as confirmation that Argentina contemplates breaking off relations with the Axis.

These sources coupled Ramirez' remarks with the statement of Foreign Minister Vice Admiral Segundo R. Storni Friday that Argentina intends, "step by step, to achieve the position she could be in."

Ramirez expounded his government's foreign and domestic policies at his first press conference at the presidential palace.

Report New India Viceroy

London, June 16 (U.P.)—Reliable sources said today that a new Viceroy of India has been chosen and will be announced soon.

WHERE TO FIND IT

	Page		Page
Bridge	23	Obituaries	15
Comics	20	Parrott	17
Crossword	22	Patterns	22
Dr. Brady	20	Prevost	14
Editorial	14	Radio	20
Fighting Men	10	Real Estate	23
Grin and Bear It	14	Society	9
Financial	19	Sports	17-18-19
Helen Worth	9	Take My Word	24
Home Front	10	Theaters	12-13
Horoscope	20	These Women	24
Letter Out	10	Tucker	14
Lindley	14	Uncle Ray	24
Movies	12-13	Want Ads	21-22-23
Novel	23	Women	[illegible]

BASE NEAR JAPAN BLASTED

★ ★ ★ ★ ★ ★ ★ SPORTS 7
Wall Street Financial News

BROOKLYN EAGLE

Weather—Warmer tonight. Sunset, 8:23; Dimout, 9:23

102d Year. No. 199. DAILY & SUNDAY • (Copyright 1943 The Brooklyn Eagle, Inc.) • BROOKLYN, N. Y., TUESDAY, JULY 20, 1943 • Entered at the Brooklyn Post-office as 2d Class Mail Matter • 3 CENTS IN NEW YORK CITY ELSEWHERE 4 CENTS

AXIS TROOPS MUTINY AS ALLIES SPEED ON

Eagle Staff photo

CRUSHING CHISELERS—Housewives of the Kings Highway section march to court to see justice done in a black market case. Third from left is Mrs. Sonia Margulis, who got "gypped," and on the extreme right is John H. Harmon of the OPA who presented the case in court.

Black Marketeer Fined As Women Jam Court

Banana Dealer Pays $10 Levy as Indignant Housewives Quit Homes to Press Fight

More than a hundred residents of the Kings Highway section, members of the local consumer group, marched into Magistrate Charles E. Ramsgate's court on Schermerhorn St. today to demonstrate to the shopkeepers in their neighborhood that they can't charge higher-than-ceiling prices and get away with it.

The shopkeeper against whom they complained was Charles Richman, who conducts a fruit and vegetable market at 551 Kings Highway. Several days ago Mrs. Sonia Margulis of 1812 E. 4th St. bought a lot of groceries and asked for bananas. Richman, she told the court, disappeared into a back room

Continued on Page 2

Greenpoint Jeep Tells Africa About 'Garden Spot of the World'

The beauties of Greenpoint—"garden spot of the world," according to Pete McGuinness, Greenpoint's No. 1 citizen—are being advertised as far as the field of operations in North Africa.

Word to that effect was received today by Councilmanic President Newbold Morris in a letter from his former assistant, Capt. Thomas E. Stevens. The captain reported that he came upon Pvt. Frank Ganzone of 507 Graham Ave., Greenpoint, sitting in an army jeep, which bore upon its side the legend:

"The Greenpoint Jitterbug."

Ganzone said he was a long-time friend of Pete McGuinness.

NEGRO TROOPS TAKE OVER AQUEDUCT TRACK

The Aqueduct racetrack in Ozone Park is today the temporary Summer home of the Negro troops of the 372d Regiment. The soldiers, assigned to guard duty in New York, took over the track yesterday and will stay until Aug. 22, eight days before the Fall racing meet begins there.

Continued on Page 9

JAMAICA CHARTS

(Empire City Meeting)

1—W'tw'd Belle 185.90-61.40-21.00, P. R'ider 7.00-4.40, B. B'que, 4.90. (1:50½)

GOLDSTEIN ACTS TO ERASE CITY FROM JAIL FIGHT

Would Restrict Suit To Close Raymond St. Prison to State Board

The Supreme Court suit to discontinue the use of the ancient Raymond Street jail for the incarceration or detention of prisoners got off to a new start today when former Magistrate Joseph Goldstein, petitioner in the suit, launched a move to eliminate all the city officials from the case.

If it succeeds, only the State Correction Commission will be left, and the only point to decide then would be whether it was right or wrong in refusing to order discontinuance of the jail.

The city officials, including all members of the Board of Estimate, the mayor, controller and the New York City Department of Correction, were to be served today with an order signed by Justice Ughetta. This requires them to show cause on Thursday why Petitioner Goldstein should not be allowed to discontinue his suit as to them.

Not In Case At Start

They were not in the case originally, but were brought in after the State body asked the court to include them as defendants on the

Continued on Page 2

R, S, T Blue Food Stamps Become Valid Aug. 1

Washington, July 20 (U.P.)—The Office of Price Administration announced today that blue food stamps lettered R, S and T in War Ration Book II will become valid Aug. 1 and remain good for canned and processed foods until Sept. 7.

Stamps N, P and Q now in use will continue to be good until Aug. 7. The OPA urged families using fresh fruits and vegetables through the Summer months to destroy their excess or invalid stamps promptly. The agency pointed out it is illegal for a consumer to give his dealer stamps without receiving the equivalent point value in food.

Yanks Blast Base Close to Japan

Bombers Attack Paramushiru In Daring Thrust Into Kuriles

Washington, July 20 (U.P.)—Army airmen in four-motored Liberator bombers Monday morning blasted the important Japanese naval base at Paramushiru, on Japan's side of the North Pacific, and started "a number of fires."

They also scored "near hits" on an unknown number of enemy vessels around the base. "Near hits" frequently are as damaging to ships as direct hits.

This daring thrust by army fliers—made while their comrades half way around the world were bombing Rome—was announced today by the navy, which controls operations in the Pacific.

Is Strong Naval Base

The big enemy base, only about 1,200 miles from Tokio itself, is one of the strongest of Japan's naval bases. It is one of the northernmost of the 32 Kurile islands which extend northeastward for 700 miles from Japan proper.

Bombing of Paramushiru brought home to the enemy the likelihood of new air attacks on their homeland. Long-range planes, if able to operate from recently recaptured Attu, have to go only 765 miles to reach Paramushiru and a little more than 2,000 miles to reach Tokio.

The Consolidated Liberators which attacked Paramushiru might also have come from Amchitka, United States Aleutian base 965 miles from Japan's "Pearl Harbor of the North Pacific."

This was the first raid on Paramushiru to be announced by the navy. Observers generally had expected for some time that with American forces in control of Attu, Paramushiru—and probably other enemy installations in the Kuriles—would feel American bombs.

Kiska Blasted Again

The communique revealing the Paramushiru foray disclosed that on Sunday a force of medium and heavy army bombers attacked the main camp area and Gertrude Cove installations on Japanese-held Kiska, sole remaining enemy foothold in the Aleutians. Overcast prevented observation of results.

The communique also announced that on Sunday (Island Time) Japanese planes bombed the Allied base at Canton Island in the Phoenix group in the South Pacific. No casualties or damage was sustained, the navy said.

Race Track Taxes Help State Recoup Other Losses

State income tax revenues this year are about $20,000,000 below the budget estimate, despite the increase in personal incomes, the State Tax Commission has announced.

Fiscal experts said revenues from other taxes, notably pari-mutuel race track and stock transfer taxes, are running far enough above estimates to offset the loss.

WHERE TO FIND IT

	Page		Page
Bridge	17	Obituaries	9
Comics	13	Parrott	11
Crossword	16	Patterns	15-16
Dr. Brady	13	Prevost	8
Editorial	8	Radio	13
Events Tonight	10	Ration Calendar	18
Fighting Men	14	Real Estate	17
Financial	18	Society	4
Grin and Bear It	8	Sports	11-12
Home Front	14	Theaters	6
Horoscope	13	These Women	18
Letter Out	14	Tucker	8
Lindley	8	Uncle Ray	14
Movies	6	Want Ads	14-17
Music	7	Wartime Problems	14
Novel	17	Women	4

2d Lt. Julius Horowitz

Boro Flier Reports Dearth of Fighters In Rome's Defense

"Wear them proudly," wrote 2d Lt. Julius Horowitz when he sent his mother his pilot's Silver Wings. Today she is wearing them more proudly than ever, for she has just learned that her 21-year-old son was co-pilot of the Flying Fortress Queenie which dropped bombs on Rome's industrial objectives.

It was only six weeks ago that Julius said goodbye to his neighbers at a farewell party in his home at 213 Avenue N, before flying for Africa. This was his first mission and, said he to a foreign correspondent aboard the bomber, according to dispatches received here, "If they are all like that, it will be O. K. with me."

There was hardly any opposition from Axis air fighters, he informed reporters. In fact, the few they saw never came near enough to be seen clearly and apparently fought shy of approaching the Flying Fortresses.

Letter Received

Julius' father, Reuben, manager of a grocery warehouse, was not surprised when he learned of his son's part in the Rome bombing, for Julius had written in a letter dated June 20 that he expected to go into action "very soon." His mother could not be reached for comment, for she is on a vacation in the mountains.

Neighbors were overjoyed to hear the news of "our boy Julius." They always thought he had the makings of a hero in him.

"One of the nicest boys on the block," said one of the neighbors who thought a couple of his friends might have been with him on the mission.

A graduate of Eastern District High School, Julius enlisted in the air corps shortly after the attack on Pearl Harbor. He had always wanted to fly and couldn't wait to see some real action.

STEEL, RAIL CENTERS HIT IN ROME RAID

Only 5 of 500 Allied Planes Lost —166 Italians Killed

Allied Headquarters, North Africa, July 20 (U.P.)—American precision bombers smacked every ton of exploives squarely into the target area in the attack on Rome yesterday, severely damaging vital Axis rail hubs and hitting a steel works and chemical plant.

Pictures of the first raid on Mussolini's capital showed today the accuracy of the aerial attack.

Suffering only the lightest losses against weak Italian defenses, the bombers scored so heavily on the San Lorenzo Railroad yards that traffic was blocked through that vital rail transshipment point. Fifty hits in the Littorio yards caused a partial tieup there.

(The Italian high command, in a communique broadcast by the Rome radio, said that Naples, Italy's second port, was bombed last night. The Allied raid on Rome caused "very great" damage, the communique said. Casualties in the Rome raid, "so far as ascertained," were 166 persons killed and 1,659 injured, the communique added.)

The pictures, taken only an hour after the last of the 500 bombers and their escort of twin-engined Lightnings had flown over Rome, testified to the care used in the raid to avoid hitting religious or other cultural objects.

Say Bombs Still Go Off

(Axis announcements, admitting heavy damage in Rome, said that time bombs were still going off. Rome radio's estimate that 166 persons were killed in the heavy assault compared with 1,200 killed

Continued on Page 2

WARM SPELL TO STAY, WITH RISE TOMORROW

The present warm spell, which has not been uncomfortable, thanks to normal humidity, is due to continue, according to the Weather Man. Tomorrow may bring a slight rise in temperature but, barring unforeseen circumstances, the mercury is due to stay in the low 80s.

Fires on Trestles Delay Two L. I. R. R. Schedule

Long Island Railroad trains on two tracks, the main line and the Long Beach branch, were delayed yesterday by trestle fires of undetermined origin. The first delay, on the main line, was of 45 minutes' duration, and the second was for 25 minutes. The main break was at a bridge between Southold and Greenport.

Crash Kills Flying Cadet

Aviation Cadet Ray F. Ellis, 20, son of Mrs. Irene Ellis of 847 Herkimer St., was killed yesterday in the crash of his basic training plane at Waco, Texas, it was announced today at the Waco army air field relations office.

Gen. Giraud in London

London, July 20 (U.P.)—Gen. Henri Giraud, co-leader of the French Committee of National Liberation, arrived today from Canada.

Yanks Drive to Cut Sicily in Two Parts

Aim K. O. Blow in Central Area —Battle Still Rages for Catania

Allied Headquarters, North Africa, July 20 (UP)—The U. S. Seventh Army advanced northward across the waist of Sicily against little more than token resistance today and an Allied communique reported signs of mutiny as Axis troops surrendered by the hundreds.

The American drive, gathering momentum by the hour, threatened to split the defenders of Sicily. Under immediate threat, if not already captured, was the big enemy base of Enna, controlling the main east-west artery across Sicily and only 28 miles from the north coast.

(British military observers in London said the speed of the American advance threatened to deal a knockout blow to the whole Italian resistance in central Sicily. Radio Algiers said both American and Canadian troops have reached Enna.)

The see-saw battle for Catania raged more bitterly than ever today, with the British 8th Army tightening a strangle-hold on the east coast port.

Attack and counter-attack followed in rapid succession, and the Germans threw paratroops into action as infantry in their desperate efforts to hold off the forces of Gen. Sir Bernard L. Mortgomery at Catania and westward around the Gebini airdromes.

Another General Captured

Gen. Guilo Cesare Gotti Porcinari, commanding the 54th Naples Division, was captured, the fourth Italian divisional commander to be taken prisoner.

The 8th Army had established a number of bridgeheads north of the Simeto River, which runs just south of Catania, and have held them against many fierce thrusts by Nazi tanks.

The line held by Montgomery's men starts on the sea and runs inland about 22 miles to Rammacca, passing south of the Gerbini Airdrome area which had been reported gravely threatened by the Allied troops.

The Americans who took Caltanissetta were pushing on northward in mid-Sicily toward the important road junction of Enna and had reached the Caterina area, which lies west of Enna.

Thus the Canadians were hacking forward directly toward Enna while the American attack had swung slightly to the west in the Caterina sector, where roads lead to the north coast without passing through Enna. This suggested that the Americans might push on some 30 miles toward Termini-Imerese on the north coast without waiting for the fall of Enna.

Canadians Hurl Back Foe

The Canadians smashed back several enemy counter blows. Casualties

Continued on Page 2

6 Yanks Crash in Portugal

Lisbon, July 20 (U.P.)—Six crew members of an American bomber were interned last night by authorities when their plane was forced down by an oil leak on the Lisbon Airdrome. None was injured.

THREE-PRONGED SICILIAN DRIVE—Spectacular progress of American troops was reported in the Enna area, where one spearhead, driving northeastward, has virtually split the island, while another American column was believed thrusting tentatively northwest in direction of Sciacca and a third moving up the road and railroad due north to Lercara, all marked by arrows.

Walker's Bat Snaps Flock Losing Skein

Dixie Hits Two Home Runs in 4-for-4 Day As Fitz Gets Nod in 7-5 Win Over Phillies

By TOMMY HOLMES

Rising in what might have been wrath, our Brooklyn Dodgers yesterday afternoon bowled over the aggressive, hustling Phillies by a score of 7 to 5, thereby ending a heart-rending losing streak that had reached five straight games.

There were several heroes as the somewhat punchy players of Leo Durocher came to life.

One was Freddy Fitzsimmons. This stout old party, who'll be 42 years old next month, started the ball game and pitched long enough to get credit for the victory. He was blasted out in the eighth when the Phils scored three runs in about a minute and a half but thin-lipped Les Webber came in and checked the hostilities with the aid of some first rate fielding support.

But that wouldn't have been enough or nearly enough if it hadn't been for Dixie Walker, who led an 11-hit attack against three characters named Charley Fuchs, George Eyrich and Walter (Boom Boom) Beck with two home runs, a double and a single. That meant four hits in four times at bat for the gentleman from Dixie and he scored four runs, while batting across three.

In all justice, Mr. Walker was the hero of a crowd of 8,610 which included 7,625 cash customers.

Dahlgren Delivers

The Phils were the first to score, getting a run off Brooklyn's stout pitching antique in round one. Murtaugh and Northey scratched infield singles and Murtaugh reached third while Adams grounded to Herman, who started a double play. Wasdell walked and then Dahlgren reached out and poked a single to right, scoring Murtaugh.

Vaughan walked to open the three-run Dodger counter-attack and took second on a peculiar balk by young Mr. Fuchs. The ball slipped from the Phillie pitcher's hand as he was preparing to pitch. Paul Waner promptly pumped a single to center, scoring Vaughan. Camilli flied to center and then came Walker's home run, a long, graceful fly over the right field screen.

Fuchs was nudged for two more in the third. Camilli beat out a hit to Wasdell, rode to third on Walker's single to right. Herman smashed a hit through Dahlgren into left, scoring Camilli. Galan filled the bases with an odd-looking hit. It was a line drive, hit with such vehemence that it knocked Wasdell's mitt off his right hand and ten feet away. The ball bounced five feet into the air and Wasdell almost caught it with his bare hands as the thing came down. Then Camilli scored as Owen grounded to Murtaugh, who started a double play.

Fitz survived a bit of difficulty in the fourth. Dahlgren opened for the Phils with a single and was forced at second when Triplett slapped a knuckler right back at Fitz. Brewster's single to center advanced Triplett to second and Livingston's single to center scored him. Here Glenn Stewart batted for Fuchs and kindly grounded to Glossop for a double play. Eyrich, just turned 18 and a recent graduate of Reading High School, was the second Quaker pitcher. He provided the customers with the intriguing sight of the youngest hurler in the majors competing against the oldest.. He yielded one run in his three innings. Walker doubled in the fifth, went to third on Her-

Continued on Following Page

★ ★
BROOKLYN EAGLE
SUNDAY, JUNE 20, 1943

Sports Real Estate
Trend Radio
Theaters Classified Ads

Dodds Retains A.A.U. 1,500 Title

Runs Metric Event in 3:50, Best Time of Career—Burnham Far Back

By HAROLD PARROTT

Mayor LaGuardia's own private track meet overshadowed the first half of the National A. A. U. championships at Randalls Island yesterday.

Gil Dodds, the bespectacled divinity student, ran off with the 1500-meter feature by 30 yards yesterday, but there was far more interest in today's special event, the LaGuardia one-mile walk. Dodds won in 3:50, the fastest time of his career.

Today, when Gunder Hagg and Greg Rice stage their spiked shoe spectacle of the decade, everybody who sees the classic will have to qualify first in the LaGuardia walk, staged over a super sunbaked course from the subway to isolated Triboro Stadium, on cast-away Randalls Isle.

All Bus Service Stopped

Two thousand hoofers who attended the meet yesterday were forced to use their No. 17 leather by the Mayor as he unexpectedly stopped all bus and taxi service to the meet, which is for the benefit of the Army Air Forces.

And as LaGuardia's "every fan a competitor" campaign reaches its peak today, the language should be enough to make any divinity student plug his ears.

The new LaGuardia "track meet" for the paying fan was totally unexpected, for the Mayor is honorary chairman of the committee staging the two-day events involving competitors from coast to coast.

Buses whizzed by the portals of the Stadium yesterday, but they were not allowed to stop and pick up the 2,000 unfortunates who hit the road in the heat and hoofed it home.

Mr. LaGuardia's act, putting the

Continued on Following Page

Yankees Top Red Sox, 2-1, In 12 Innings

By HAROLD C. BURR

It would have been a heartbreaker for Spud Chandler to lose, but Ken Sears and Rollie Hemsley collaborated handsomely at bat to save Spud from defeat and give the Yankes a 2-to-1 victory over the Red Sox in 12 innings at the Stadium yesterday. These batterymen have to stick together.

Pinch-Hitter Sears' 470-foot long fly with the bases loaded in the ninth inning sent the game into overtime, and Hemsley's single, again with the cushions crowded in the 12th, broke up the old ball game. Chandler wasn't pitching then, going out for a pinch hitter in the ninth and Johnny Murphy received credit for the win, his sixth in eight decisions.

Until the ninth Chandler was hooked up with Oscar Judd, seeking his first American League triumph over the Yanks, in a scoreless tie. Not a visitor had got past

Continued on Following Page

DOUBLE SNUFFING OUT—Augie Galan, Dodgers, being forced on Mickey 'Owens' bounder in the third by Charley Brewster to Danny Murtaugh, who in turn whipped the ball to Jimmy Wasdell at first to complete a double play for the Phils yesterday at Ebbets Field. Murtaugh is seen throwing the ball, which is indicated by an arrow.

CARDS RALLY IN 8TH, TRIM CUBS BY 4-2

M. Cooper Scores 6th Straight Victory for Record of 9 and 3

St. Louis, June 19 (U.P.)—A three-run Cardinal rally in the eighth inning today subdued the Chicago Cubs 4 to 2 and put Mort Cooper, the big righ-hander who has now won six in a row, ahead of the major league pitchers with nine wins and three losses.

Chicago got to Cooper for two runs in the fourth, but the Redbird ace kept control of the remainder of the game while his mates tallied once in the sixth and three more times in the eighth for the victory.

Today's win ended a three-game losing streak for St. Louis—their longest this season—and kept the club in front of the National League by three games.

Chicago	ab	r	h	o	a	St. Louis	ab	r	h	o	a
Hack,3b	4	0	1	3	0	Klein,2b	4	0	1	1	4
Stanky,2b	4	0	0	1	2	Walker,cf	3	0	0	3	0
Cavar'ta,1b	3	0	1	8	2	Musial,rf	4	2	3	1	1
Nich'son,rf	4	0	1	2	0	Litwh'r,lf	4	1	2	2	0
Novikov,lf	4	1	1	2	0	W.Cooper,c	4	1	1	3	0
Goodm'n,cf	1	0	0	0	0	Kur'kski,3b	4	0	1	1	1
Merullo,ss	3	1	2	0	3	Sanders,1b	3	0	1	13	0
L'w'y,ss-cf	4	0	2	1	1	Marion,ss	4	0	1	3	4
McCul'gh,c	4	0	0	5	1	M.Cooper,p	3	0	0	0	0
Lee,p	3	0	1	2	1						
Wyse,p	0	0	0	0	0	Totals	33	4	10	27	10
Totals	34	2	9	24	10						

Chicago	0	0	0	2	0	0	0	0	0	—2
St. Louis	0	0	0	0	0	1	0	3	x	—4

Errors—None. Runs batted in—Lowrey (2), Litwhiler (2), Kurowski (2). Two-base hits—Lowrey, Novikov, Merullo, Musial (2), Kurowski. Three-base hit—Lowrey. Double play—Marion, Klein and Sanders. Bases on balls—Off M. Cooper 1, Lee, 1, Wyse 1. Struck out—By M. Cooper 3, Lee 2, Wyse 1. Hits—Off Lee, 8 in 7 2-3; Wyse, 2 in 1-3. Left on bases—Chicago 6, St. Louis 7. Losing pitcher—Lee. Umpires—Magerkurth, Dunn, Stewart. Time of game—2:04. Attendance—2,178.

Pirates Nip Reds, 4—3

Pittsburgh, June 19 (U.P.)—Bob Elliott singled in the 11th inning with two men on base to give the Pirates a 4-3 victory over the Cincinnati Reds here today. It was the second extra inning game between the two teams in two days.

Johnny Lanning, Pirate pitcher now under contract to the army as a private, won his fourth victory of the year in a relief role.

In the 11th Tommy O'Brien batted for Lanning and walked. Cincinnati. Manager Bill .McKechnie took out Bucky Walters and sent in Lefty Clude Shoun. Gustine tried to sacrifice but hit into a double play. Johnny Wyrostek singled to left and Barrett worked Shoun for a pass to set the stage for Elliott's winning smash.

Cincinnati	ab	r	h	o	a	Pittsburgh	ab	r	h	o	a
Frey,2b	6	0	3	3	4	Gustine,2b	5	0	0	3	1
Crabtree,rf	4	1	2	1	0	Wyrost'k,rf	6	1	1	0	0
Walker,cf	5	1	1	1	0	Barrett,lf	5	0	1	3	1
McC'm'k,1b	5	0	3	10	2	Elliott,3b	6	0	3	1	5
Mesner,3b	4	0	0	3	2	Flecther,1b	4	2	2	10	0
Tipton,lf	5	0	1	4	0	Lopez,c	4	0	1	7	2
Miller,ss	4	0	0	4	5	DiM'gio,cf	5	1	1	4	0
Mueller,c	2	0	0	2	0	Geary,ss	4	0	1	4	4
aVanderm'r	0	0	0	0	0	Klinger,p	3	0	2	0	0
Dephil'ps,c	0	0	0	1	0	Rescigno,p	0	0	0	1	1
bMarshall	1	1	1	0	0	dColman	0	0	0	0	0
Lakeman,c	0	0	0	1	0	eRussell	0	0	0	0	0
Walters,p	5	0	1	2	2	Lanning,p	0	0	0	0	0
Shoun,p	0	0	0	0	1	fO'Brien	0	0	0	0	0
Totals	41	3	12	c21	16	Totals	42	4	13	33	14

aRan for Mueller in seventh.
bBatted for Dephillips in ninth.
cTwo out when winning run was scored.
dBatted for Rescigno in ninth.
eRan for Colman in ninth.
fBatted for Lanning in eleventh.

Cincinnati	0	0	0	0	0	2	0	0	1	0	0	—3
Pittsburgh	0	1	0	1	0	1	0	0	0	0	1	—4

Error—Tipton. Runs batted in—Lopez, Klinger (2), McCormick (2), Marshall, Elliott. Two-base hits—Barrett, McCormick, Fletcher, Frey. Three-base hits—Fletcher, Elliott. Home run—Marshall. Stolen base—Miller. Sacrifices—Crabtree, Mesner, Lakeman. Double plays—Mesner to Miller ot McCormick; Shoun to Miller to Frey. Left on bases—Cincinnati 10, Pittsburgh 13. Bases on balls—Off Walters 6, off Klinger 1, off Lanning 1, off Shoun 1. Struck out—By Walters 2, by Klinger 4, by Lanning 3. Hits—Off Klinger, 9 in 6 1-3 innings; Rescigno, 3 in 2 2-3; Lanning, 0 in 2; Walters, 10 in 10; Shoun, 2 in 2-3. Winning pitcher—Lanning. Losing pitcher—Shoun. Umpires—Sears, Pinelli and Barlick. Time of game 2:41. Attendance—4,235.

Senators Top A's, 6—3

Philadelphia, June 19 (U.P.)—Backing Alex Carrasquel and Rae Scarborough with a 13-hit attack, the Washington Senators defeated the Philadelphia Athletics today, 6—3.

Although he was relieved in the seventh inning, Carrasquel was credited with his seventh victory of the season.

The Senators scored twice against Orie Arntzen in the first inning and picked up the rest of their runs off Bert Kuczynski, 1942 Penn football captain. Bob Johnson and Stan Spence each had a double and two singles.

Carrasquel had a shutout until Bobby Estalella led off the sixth in-

Continued on Following Page

TAKING FEATURE RACE—Vincentive, with Jockey Johnny Gilbert in the saddle, is shown winning the $25,000 added Dwyer Stakes at Aqueduct yesterday after fighting off a stretch bid by Famous Victory, No. 9, who finished second. Timed at 2:05 for the 1¼-mile distance, Vincentive paid the pretty price of $10.30 for each $2 ducat. Princequillo, No. 7, took the show honors.

JOCKEY ROBERTSON BADLY HURT IN SPILL

Alfred Robertson, veteran contract jockey for Mrs. Dodge Sloan's Brookmeade Stable, suffered a severse fall during the running of the first race at Aquedust yesterday and was removed to Physicians Hospital in Jackson Heights.

Robertson suffered possible concussion and back injuries when he was spilled off the plater Roman Glory in a jam on the stretch turn.

Simonson, Braun Reach Invitation Golf Semi-Finals

Special to the Brooklyn Eagle

Garden City, June 19—Golf every bit as hot as the weather was uncorked at the Cherry Valley Club in the annual member-guest invitation tournament here today. Best-ball scores three or four under par were nothing at all and the Frank Simonson-Burt Braun, Warren Smith-L. H. Harrison, Millard Webb-Celestin Durand and Dr. Ray Bowles-Frank Cravens teams battled their way into a semi-finals.

Hottest of all the golf was that which the Frank Giles-Dr. Joseph Kendrick team poured at the comedalists Harry Leyser and Neal Fulkerson. The victors had a putt for a 67 when the match ended, and when Kendrick, one of the victorious teams at Hempstead last week, has a putter in his hands there's a good chance of that putt going in.

Giles and Kendrick, however, couldn't keep up the pace all day. They had a nine-hole letup—and

Continued on Following Page

Pauline Betz Wins Clay Court Title

Detroit, June 19 (U.P.) — Pauline Betz of Los Angeles added a third national title to her tennis conquests today when she defeated Nancy Corbett of Chicago, 6—0, 6—1, to win the women's singles final in the national clay courts tennis championships at the Detroit Tennis Club.

Miss Betz, rated the nation's No. 1 feminine player, completely outclassed Miss Corbett, who is only a year out of the junior ranks. Although Miss Corbett forced several games to deuce, she was able to win only the second game of the second set.

Today's victory adds the national clay courts title to Miss Betz' indoor championship, won last Winter at Boston, and her outdoor championship, which she took at Forest Hills, L. I., last year.

The tournament closes tomorrow with Seymour Greenberg, Chicago, facing William Talbert, Cincinnati, in the men's singles final.

Giants Defeat Braves, 5 to 3, For Hub's 252d

Special to the Brooklyn Eagle

Boston, Mass., June 19—Carl Hubbell, who will be 40 on Tuesday, won his third straight victory of the season against nary a defeat, and the 252d of his career, with a 5—3 decision over the Braves today before 3,111 paid. The old master was not quite so sharp as he had been in his previous complete-game efforts, and needed help from reliable Ace Adams in the eighth when he tired. But King Carl still was the effective pitcher of years gone by when the Braves threatened and a man had to be put out to save the contest.

Aided by Two Double Plays

His four strikeouts were strategically spotted to cool off Boston rallies, and his support assisted him with two double plays. Although Hubbell allowed six walks as well as six hits, extraordinary extravagance for the old gent, his screwball and slider had the authentic touch in the pinches.

After the Braves landed on his slants for two in the first, Carl did not surrender another run until the seventh, when he had been given a 5—2 lead. His make-or-break ordeal occurred in the fifth. With two on and one out, Hub fanned Johnny McCarthy, and after walking Connie Ryan to fill the bases, he retired Eddie Joost on an infield roller on the 3—2 count.

Mickey Witek, who has hit Boston pitching at a .340 clip for ten games this campaign, knocked in three Giant runs, with a double and a single. Billy Jurges smashed three of the ten New York hits.

The Giants, hitting in timely fashion, as they had in Hub's other two triumphs, chased loser Red Barrett in the three-run third and shook their other two runs out of Dave Odom.

Successive doubles by Chet Ross and McCarthy after Charley Workman had walked, put Hubbell two runs in the hole in the first.

The Giants rallied for a 3—2 lead in the third, on singles by Jurges, Sid Gordon, Witek and Dick Bartell, with Mel Ott's walk and Ross' error on Gordon's hit thrown in. All runs were earned and Barrett turned over the mound to Odom, a 235-pounder who had been released by the Athletics in the Spring.

Odom wasn't damaged until the

Continued on Following Page

Smart Lookin Scores 3d Straight Turf Win

Boston, June 19 (U.P.)—Allen T. Simmons' Smart Lookin, a brisk running daughter of Reaping Reward, raced to a neck victory in the $7,500 Betsy Ross Stakes at Suffolk Downs today for her third victory in three starts as Sea Reigh was second and Vietta third.

Jockey Tommy Luther rode the Simmons filly over a five-furlong course in :59 4-5 for a net purse of $5,450. Smart Lookin paid $8.40, $3.20 and $2.50. Sea Reigh returned $2.80 and $2.20, Vietta was $2.40 to show.

RIVERLAND DESTROYED BY VET AT BELMONT

Louisiana Farm's Riverland, helpless in his stall with a shattered hip since he broke down in last Saturday's Carter Handicap, was destroyed yesterday by the track veterinarian at Belmont Park.

The big gelding broke down as the field left the gate. The word to destroy had to come from Lloyds of London, insurer of the horse.

Riverland was purchased for $6,000 last Fall by Clark from Howard Wells. He quickly rose in class and within five days last October defeated Alsab and Whirlaway. He earned about $94,000 for Clark in less than a year and reportedly was insured for $40,000.

VINCENTIVE WINS THE 55TH DWYER

Famous Victory Is 2d, Princequillo 3d—28,370 Wager $2,206,097 at Aqueduct

By RALPH TROST

Out in front all the way, that's the story of the 55th Dwyer Stakes at Aqueduct yesterday and, as 28,370 others will attest, W. L. Braun's three-year-old bay colt, Vincentive, never ran a better race as he picked up for his often disappointed owner $19,600 of the $25,000 added stake.

Seven times a starter this season, the bay managed to get too far behind, be blocked or accomplish any number of undesirable things as he piled up a record of being a great also—ran.

But yesterday, under the skillful handling of Johnny Gilbert, this son of Challenger 2d—Phenomenon by Scotch Broom, got in no tangles. He hit right for the lead in the historic mile-and-an-eighth grind and was never headed. And when the long Aqueduct stretch was hit, he had all that it took to fight off the challenge first of the fast-improving Irish horse Princequillo and then of the terrific stretch drive of famous Victory which finished second, a half-length behind.

No Race for the Books

As anticipated this running of the Dwyer was no race for the books. The running was in 2:05 more than three seconds back of Valdina Orphan's record and the slowest recorded since 1940 when the race was stretched to a mile and a quarter. But it was a great betting race, for the crowd couldn't make up its mind, though it finally went for the Fitzsimmons-trained Tip Toe, who broke down in the running and finished seventh with Famous Victory a second choice and Vincentive no better than third.

But once the race started it was all Vincentive, right up to within 100 yards of the finish when it seemed that Famous Victory might have the foot to draw up even.

Fairy Manhurst broke first from the barrier. But Gilbert drove hard for the lead and at the first turn had it. From there on there were

Continued on Following Page

Segura Annexes Intercollegiate Tennis Honors

Montclair, N. J., June 19 (U.P.)—Francisco (Pancho) Segura, University of Miami tennis ace, won the 14th annual Eastern Intercollegiate championship today with an easy 6—0, 6—1, 6—2 triumph over Robert Wasserman of Ohio State.

Segura also teamed with Manfred Berliner Jr. of Miami, to win the doubles title with a 6—3, 7—5, 6—1 victory over Richard Bender and Edgar Buttenheim of Princeton.

The little South American swept through the tournament without the loss of a single set, indicating that he probably will be a strong favorite to win the national championship at Forest Hills next Fall.

Segura's accurate smashes to the far corners and his astounding speed carried him into his victory over Wasserman, who was passed repeatedly as he rushed the net in an effort to carry the attack.

Pittsburgh-Philly Grid Merger Ok'd

Chicago, June 19—After reconsidering a vote taken during an earlier session the National Professional Football League voted tonight to permit the merger of the Pittsburgh Steeler and Philadelphia Eagle franchises.

The two Chicago teams, Bears and Cardinals, also had applied for a merger but withdrew the application after being rejected in the early vote on combination franchises.

Two bids for "after the war" franchises also were received. They were from Frank E. Mandel, Chicago investment broker representing a Boston syndicate, and Henry M. White, Baltimore oil man.

There were reports current that Ehlers and White might join their groups to guarantee Baltimore a club next Fall.

Paterson Wins World's Flyweight Championship

Glasgow, June 19—Jackie Paterson, former Glasgow ship worker, won British recognition as world flyweight boxing champion tonight when he scored a first-round knockout over Peter Kane, former champion from Lancashire, in their scheduled 15-round bout.

The fight was recognized as a title affair by both the British Boxing Board of Control and the New York State Athletic Commission. Little Dado of the Phillipines is recognized as champion by the National Boxing Association in the United States.

Experts Favor Rice To Outspeed Hagg

The most widely publicized international foot race in 18 years will be staged today at Triborough Stadium, Randalls Island, when feather-footed Gunder Hagg of Sweden, holder of seven world records, meets little Greg Rice, America's greatest runner, in a 5,000-meter test of stamina and speed.

Not since Paavo Nurmi of Finland invaded the United States in 1925 and matched strides with "Chesty Joie" Ray at old Madison Square Garden has there been such interest in a race.

Crowd Expected to Top 20,000

More than 20,000 fans are expected to witness this feature of the two-day National A. A. U. track and field championships. In addition to Hagg and Rice, eight other runners are entered in the 5,000 meters (three miles, 188 yards). However, they are expected merely to provide background.

Despite Hagg's record-shattering achievements abroad, betting was even at Toots Shor's yesterday. Rice, the former Notre Dame star who now is a chief specialist in the U. S. Maritime Service, was well supported in the wagering because of his 65 consecutive victories and because of his great personal popularity.

The majority of New York sports writers also favored Rice, for two reasons: (1) They wouldn't believe anyone can beat him until they saw it done, and (2) they figured the percentage is against any foreign track star making a successful American debut—particularly one who had made a month's voyage on a rolling tanker.

Rice received this backing despite clockings and running form that

Continued on Following Page

MAJOR LEAGUE RECORDS

National League

YESTERDAY'S RESULTS

Brooklyn 7, Philadelphia 5.
New York 5, Boston 3.
Pittsburgh 4, Cincinnati 3 (11 innings).
St. Louis 4, Chicago 2.

STANDING OF THE CLUBS

	W.	L.	Pct.	G.B.
St. Louis	32	18	.640	....
Brooklyn	32	24	.571	3
Cincinnati	26	23	.531	5½
Pittsburgh	26	23	.531	5½
Philadelphia	26	25	.510	6½
Boston	22	26	.458	9
New York	21	31	.404	12
Chicago	18	33	.353	14

TODAY'S GAMES

New York at **Brooklyn.**
Cincinnati at Pittsburgh (2).
Chicago at St. Louis (2).
Philadelphia at Boston (2).

GAMES TOMORROW

New York at **Brooklyn** (twilight).
Pittsburgh at Chicago.
St. Louis at Cincinnati (night).
Other teams not scheduled.

American League

YESTERDAY'S RESULTS

New York 2, Boston 1 (12 innings).
Washington 6, Philadelphia 3.
Cleveland 5, Chicago 4 (1st game).
Cleveland 10, Chicago 8 (2d game, 10 innings).
Detroit 4, St. Louis 3 (13 innings).

STANDING OF THE CLUBS

	W.	L.	Pct.	G.B.
New York	30	19	.612	....
Washington	29	24	.547	3
Detroit	24	24	.500	5½
Cleveland	26	26	.500	5½
Philadelphia	27	28	.491	6
Boston	26	29	.473	7
Chicago	21	26	.447	8
St. Louis	20	27	.426	9

TODAY'S GAMES

Washington at **New York** (2).
Boston at Philadelphia (2).
Cleveland at Chicago (2).
St. Louis at Detroit (2).

GAMES TOMORROW

No games scheduled.

Madriguera to Be Guest at La Conga

Enric Madriguera, currently headlining the Roxy stage show together with his pretty vocalist, Patricia Gilmore, will be guest stars at Jack Harris' La Conga on Monday night. Madriguera, one of the foremost exponents of Latin American music, will present a "Citation of Welcome" to ChuChu Martinez of La Conga's new show.

GOING PLACES

By RUTH G. DAVIS

What more can be said than has been said about the excellent food at **Tappen's** for nearly 100 years? Well, 98 years, anyway. If you can't believe what people have been saying for that length of time, you'll not be convinced now. The dinners at Tappen's are just as fine as ever they were, for rationing has had little effect on them. Primarily, one goes to this restaurant for a shore dinner, although there is always a filet mignon awaiting the guest who doesn't want fish. All right, you say, perhaps rationing is no problem—what about the curb on pleasure driving? Surely, it is a pleasure to visit Tappen's. Blessed be Jeremiah Tappen, who opened the restaurant in 1845. He picked an excellent location for, although once reached by buggie or boat, it is now accessible to subway, trolley or bus lines. Shore dinner enthusiasts are willing to travel long distances to get to Tappen's.

Newcomers to Brooklyn will want to know that Tappen's, located in Sheepshead Bay, is a landmark on Emmons Ave., between E. 26th and E. 27th Sts. The building, of course, is an old one with up-to-date equipment, done in a new coat of white paint each season. The dining room is large and airy, with a color scheme of red and white, and the massive HorseShoe bar has a reputation all its own.

If you can find time between the courses you might dance to Freddie Mitchell and his orchestra, which has arrived at Tappen's from Kelly's Stable. Marion Johnson is the featured singer. Tappan's is run by **Patrick O'Donnell**, president, and Eddie Goldsand, manager. Oldtimers will be glad to see Harry Wilson, the headwaiter, still on hand, ready to see that your slightest wish is fulfilled.

A new member—Billy Peterson, who is featured in the "Manhattan Holiday" revue in the Ice Terrace of the **Hotel New Yorker**, is an official member of the Society for the Prevention of Disparaging Remarks About Brooklyn. President Sid Ascher has welcomed the new member, who makes his home at 8054 5th Ave., and presented to the skater a scroll of honor. Brooklynite Sunny Skylar, who is doing the vocalizing with Vincent Lopez and his orchestra at the **Hotel Taft**, has collaborated with humorist Chic Gaylord on a musical comedy scheduled for Fall production. Continuous nightly entertainment is offered at the **Alp** every Friday and Saturday night. And the **Warfield Restaurant** is noted for its home cooking. Another borough spot for entertainment is the **Talk of the Town**, which features Scandinavian-American music. Don Paul plays for the dancing at **Hartman's**, where vaudeville is featured over the weekends. **McGough's** can brag of two shows nightly with George Chatterton as the m. c.

Benny Goodman, Swingdom's King of Clarinetists, following in the footsteps of his erstwhile protege Harry James, will arrive with his orchestra at the **Hotel Astor**. Bill Farrell, minstrel man, has begun his 450th consecutive week at the **Place Elegante**. The Ernest Franz Continentals continue as the orchestral attraction.

There'll be a new show at the **Hurricane** beginning Wednesday. It will be called "Rockin' in Rhythm." Duke Ellington, pianist, composer and orchestra leader, will again fill his triple role. The supporting cast includes Radio Aces, the tap-dancing Callahan Sisters and Coleman Clark, the table tennis champion.

July will bring with it some new Summer shows. Lou Walters will bring on July 6 to his **Latin Quarter** "Folies Romantique." The show is produced on the grand scale for which Walters is famed and is designed strictly as cool fare for the hot Summer trade. The scene of the revue will be the beaches of Coney Island. The inimitable Georgie Price, famed comedian and singer, will hold the spotlight as the star of the new show. Stanley Melba, the **Hotel Pierre's** entertainment director and maestro, announces that Myrus, the amazing Thought Detective, will return to the Cotillion Room on July 7 for an extended engagement. Incidentally, do you know that Stanley is a samba specialist. Tito Guizar, currently the star at the Starlight Roof of the **Waldorf-Astoria**, will leave on July 8 to make a personal appearance tour of the Mexican army camps.

A pleasing and patriotic idea—Managing Director Spencer L. Sawyer is playing host to a party that he calls "This Is America" at the Skyline Roof of the **Hotel Sheraton**. These midnight parties are a regular Thursday feature, with a different group of people from a cross-section of American life, each week as guests. The first party last night honored Americans named Smith, Jones, Brown, Johnson, Henderson, Moore and Wilson. Two entertainers will be right at home—King Johnson, the leader of the band and his vocalist, Rosemary Smith.

VOCALIST — Roberta Welch sings with Larry Keyes orchestra on the St. Regis Roof.

PATRICIA KING entertains with her dancing at Leon and Eddie's.

GRETCHEN HOUSER, singing with Joe Ricardel and his orchestra at the Clermont Inn.

ELLA FITZGERALD, featured singer at the new Cafe Zanzibar opening Wednesday.

Two of the owners of the Hotel Sheraton will also be present, as they answer to the names of Henderson and Moore. Invitations to these typically American Thursday night supper parties are obtained by the purchase of a $100 war bond. If you're an American, you're invited.

The Queen Mary Club will change its name—it will now be **Cafe Mocambo.** The club originally intended to take the name "The Zanzibar," but another new club had prior rights. The new show made its debut at the club on Tuesday with Madeline Holmes and Frances Williams the stars. Speaking of the new **Cafe Zanzibar,** atop the Winter Garden Theater, all indications point to it being a wow . . . With pink wall mirrors, and stuff. In addition to Don Redman's orchestra and singing star Ella Fitzgerald, already announced as set for the show by Joe Howard, the master mind of Zanzibar, are Avis Andrews, Maurice Rocco, the Rockin' Rhythm pianist, the Berry Brothers and Moke and Poke. Watch for the opening to be on Wednesday night.

On our highly recommended list is the **St. Regis Roof**, which is air-cooled and has delightful music, including Larry Keyes orchestra and Theodora Brooks and her Hammond organ play for continuous dancing. The Monday Servicemen's Nights at the Cocoanut Grove of the **Park Central** is quite popular. Each Monday the Grove offers service men and their friends a full course dinner, floor show and dancing all for the price of $1 per person. Sally Goodwin, blues singer, will make her New York night club debut at **Bill Bertolotti's** in the Village on Monday night. **Hickory House** has a new feature in food . . . the Victory lunch. The owners, taking a cue from a nearby war plant, now offers food high in the scale of nourishment, attractively prepared.

What next. The **Village Barn** is inaugurating a "Be Kind to Waiters'" night, the idea is being ushered in next Tuesday. The executive personnel will serve the waiters after the cash customers leave. Doodle contests will be revived at the **Restaurant Mayan** beginning next week. They were inaugurated last year and high competition ran among such champion doodlers as Myrna Loy, Robert E. Sherwood and Ethel Merman.

The comedy acrobatic team of Jules and Clifton is seen nightly in the fast-moving floor show at the **Boulevard** in Elmhurst. The slogan at **Felzmann's** in Bay Ridge is "Go Where the Crowds Go"—enough said. A couple of extra musts on your "night club" list include **La Martinique**, where Dick Haymes, handsome young crooner, is so popular; **Havana Madrid**, which boasts of Luisillo, brilliant young flamenco dancer of the team of Rosa and Luisillo, who is directing a new set of dances for the chorus; and **Versaillies**, where the revue is so good it is being held over indefinitely.

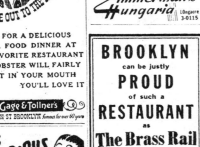

KING OF SWING — Benny Goodman brings his orchestra to the Hotel Astor Roof next Monday.

Where to DINE and DANCE

In Brooklyn

AMERICAN INN — 1506 KINGS HIGHWAY. NO COVER CHARGE. Take Brighton Line Subway to Kings Highway Station. AIR CONDITIONED. FINEST NIGHT SPOT IN FLATBUSH. Continuous Dancing and Entertainment Nitely. ALL-STAR FLOOR SHOW. Music by "Bangy" Edwards and his Rhythm Band. FINE LIQUORS AND GOOD FOOD

BEDFORD PLAZA — ESTABLISHED 1916. 1268-70 FLATBUSH AVE. SPECIAL SUNDAY DINNER 95c NOON TO 9 P.M. WEEKDAYS 85c, 5 TO 9 P.M. LUNCHEON FROM 40c. Choice Wines & Liquors. Air-Conditioned

CHESTERFIELD — AIR CONDITIONED. "BORO HALL'S SHOW PLACE" Dancing Nightly. Private Rooms for Parties. 25 WILLOUGHBY ST. (nr. Jay) MAin 5-9312

FELZMANN'S — 4TH AVENUE at 39TH STREET. Go Where the Crowds Go!—Dining—Famous for the BEST of Foods and Drinks. DANCING and FLOOR SHOWS NIGHTLY. Enjoy the Spicy Music of FELZMANN'S B'WAY BAND

HALF MOON HOTEL — BOARDWALK AND WEST 29TH STREET. Ocean Terrace. Private Banquet Rooms Available. Daily and Sunday Dinners - No Cover. - Free Parking

HOTEL GRANADA — Ashland Place and Lafayette Avenue, 1 BLOCK FROM ALL SUBWAYS. LUNCHEON - DINNER Served in the New Gay Crystal Room. 8 Private banquet rooms available for small or large parties. STerling 3-2060

HOTEL PIERREPONT — Pierrepont and Hicks Sts. Visit our newly decorated Mirror Room. A delightful place to dine and wine amid cheerful surroundings. Luncheon 60c. Dinner 85c, $1.00. Sunday Dinner 85c, $1.00. A la carte. Banquet facilities. Air-Conditioned. MA. 4-5500

Joe's — Borough Hall, 330 Fulton St. Air-Conditioned. Famous for Good Food and High Quality . . . at Popular Prices. Breakfast, Luncheon, Dinner and After Theater Cocktail Lounge. Est. 1909. CU. 6-9672

LA SALA'S — ITALIAN AMERICAN CUISINE. Eastern P'kwy at Bedford Ave. MAin 2-9280. Full Course Dinner, $1.50. J. C. Johnny & Syd Kaye's All-Girl Sing Orch. Nitely. Catering from 2 to 200. Jimmy La Sala, 'Squire of Kenmare St.'

MAMMY'S PANTRY — Dine in the BROOKLYN HEIGHTS or OLD DOMINION ROOM. Air-Conditioned. Montague and Henry Sts.

BANQUET ORMOND — (1274 FULTON ST., NR. NOSTRAND). STerling 3-8341. Acc. 25 to 400. Dining Room for Weddings, Receptions. Newly Decorated. Air Conditioned. Reasonable Rates.

RIVOLI — 1095-97 FLATBUSH AVE. AIR CONDITIONED. WEDDINGS, BANQUETS, CARD PARTIES, COMMUNION BREAKFASTS, Etc., 10 to 500. BU. 4-1334

NIGHT CLUBS

ALP — CABARET SHOW Friday, Saturday and Sunday. Continuous Entertainment Nightly—Singing Waiters. Also featuring Mary Griffin in Popular Melodies. 563 Fifth Ave., near 15th St.

ATLANTIS — ON THE BOARDWALK, STILLWELL AVENUE. NUMBER ONE SPOT IN CONEY ISLAND. ENTERTAINMENT, DANCING. EDDIE SMALL Orch.

NIGHT CLUBS

BALI — 2660 OCEAN PARKWAY At Belt P'kway, ES. 2-9838. MARION HARVEY, Mistress of Ceremonies. THE RENEES—PHYLLIS MERLE. OTHER STAR ACTS. TOMMY VARRELL'S ORCH. Added Attraction, Toni Vale, Dynamic Songstress

BARKLEY'S — 1620 AVENUE U. DEwey 6-9661. AL NESOR, M. C. ★ MARILYN MACK ★ SLIM DALE ★ PAT LU RAINES—ELINORE EDEN. JOE CROSBY GORGEOUS GIRLS. Hosts: Harry Siegel and Milton Rosenbaum • Tommy Dale and Orch.

Blue Mirror — 1251 FLATBUSH AVE., AT NEWKIRK. FOUR HAWAIIAN SERENADERS. MOKIHANA • CHARLES BOURNE. CONVENIENT. Never a Cover or Min.

Mae Flynn's — The Show Place of Flatbush. AIR-CONDITIONED. Dancing and Entertainment Nightly. All-Star Floor Show. Fine Liquors and Good Food. 1055 WASHINGTON AVE., EMPIRE BLVD., OPP. EBBETTS FIELD. ING. 2-9719

JOE GROS MGR. — CLUB WARREN — RALPH SHAW, M. C. RUTH RAND. MURIEL TERRY. BETTY BLAINE. Warren Cor. Bond Sts.

LEWIS — AIR CONDITIONED. FRED BURTON, The Human Pianola. 2301 EMMONS AVE. SHEEPSHEAD BAY. DON ALLEN, DON DIFLAVIO PLAY AND SING. 1369 FLATBUSH AVE.

NEW PARK VIEW — ENTIRE NEW SHOW SAT., JUNE 26TH. SALLY TESTA, BROADWAY BLUES SINGER. 143 CLASSON AVE. MA. 2-9250. Cont. Entertainment and Dancing. No Cover

PATIO — 630 FLATBUSH AVE. BU. 4-9021. BETTY ROYCE, Singer and Entertainer. Dancing Nitely to Charles Sameth's Orchestra. Continuous Entertainment -:- No Cover -:- Moderate Prices

TALK of the TOWN — Broadway Floor Shows Nightly. Scand.-American music. Moderate prices. 3rd Ave. at 47th St. Carmine Russo, Prop.

In Bay Ridge

Warfield Restaurant — 5701 THIRD AVE. (Cor. 57th St.) 43 Years at Same Address. Specialize in Home Cooking. Lunch Room Open 6 A.M. Dining Room from 9 A.M. Steak and Chop Dinners from 5 P.M. Special Dinners Served All Day Sunday. Reasonable Prices.

NIGHT CLUBS

HARTMAN'S — 4th Ave. at 100th St. Dance to the MUSIC of DON PAUL and his orchestra playing nightly. VAUDEVILLE WEEKENDS

McGOUGH'S — George Chatterton, M. C. 4th AVE. at 91st ST. TRUDY CHANDLER • SHEILA DAWN. EDITH DELANEY • HAVEN JOHNSON. LESLIE BRIGHTON • MILT MANN ORCH. 2 SHOWS NITELY • SH. 5-3210

SHORE ROAD CASINO — MARY LOU KING. DUDE KIMBALL, M. C.—JUNE IMHOFF. THE ALBERTAS—BILL HENRY'S ORCH. 4th AVE. & 101st ST. at BELT PARKWAY

Sheepshead Bay

TAPPEN'S — EMMONS AVE. & E. 27th ST.—SHORE DINNERS AND A LA CARTE. FREDDY MITCHELL & ORCHESTRA, FEATURING MARIAN ROBINSON. PAT O'DONNELL, Pres.

In Manhattan

MARINE GRILL, Hotel McAlpin, B'WAY AT 34TH ST. — JOHNNY MESSNER and his orchestra now more popular than ever. Nightly except Monday. No cover charge. Dinner from $1.75. Special Supper $1.25. Friday nights after 9:30 p.m. minimum $1.75 per person. Saturday nights and Holiday eves. $2.25. PE. 6-5700.

CHINESE RESTAURANTS

Lichee Wan 11 Mott St. — Chinatown's Restaurant of distinction. Lunch from 45c. Dinner from 65c; also a-la-carte. Open Sundays. Air conditioned.

FRENCH RESTAURANTS

MAISON GABY — 71 W. 68th St. SUS. 7-8218. Lunch 50c up. Dinner 95c up. Specialties: Guinea Hen, White Wine Sauce; Lobster, Filet Mignon, Frog Legs, BAR

RUSSIAN RESTAURANTS

KAVKAZ — 332 E. 14th ST. GR. 7-9132. "Russian atmosphere at its best"—excellent "Shashliks." A la "war" days. Roast duck and Vareniki.

SWEDISH RESTAURANTS

KUNGSHOLM — 142 EAST 55TH ST. DINE IN OUR SUMMER GARDEN. LUNCHEON • COCKTAILS • DINNER SERVED WITH SMORGASBORD. EL. 5-8183. MUSIC BY MUZAK. OPEN SUNDAYS

NIGHT CLUBS

BAL TABARIN — 225 W. 46th St. CI. 6-0949. "GAY PAREE IN N. Y." De luxe French Dinner $1.25. 3 revues nitely. 2 orchestras. Dancing. No cover.

BARN — (Village Barn) 52 West 8th Street. ST. 9-8840. WILLIE SOLAR. VIRGINIA CARROL & OTHERS. HOME of the HOBBY HORSE RACES. Join in the fun with Square Dances and Musical Chairs. 6 Star Acts 3 Shows Nightly Dinner from $1.50. AIR CONDITIONED

HOWDY REVUE — New Summer Revue; Gay—Colorful—Cast of 30. Continuous Entertainment; No Cover; 3 Shows. 17 WEST 3rd STREET. STuyvesant 9-8821

JIMMY KELLY'S — DINNER $1.50. REVUE 9-12-2:15 A.M. 181 Sullivan St. Air-Conditioned. AL. 4-1414. Open Sun.

SMALLS' PARADISE — 100% FIREPROOF Clover Leaf Bar & Room. 7th Ave. Sub. 1 block; 8th Ave. Sub. 2 blocks; 5th & 7th Ave. Bus at our door; 8th Ave. Bus 1 block. NEW REVUE—135th St.-7th Ave. AU. 3-9327. No Cover "Ballyhoo of 1943". 3 shows. Min. Sat. & Hol. Eve. only $1.50

UBANGI — THE HOTTEST COLORED SHOW on B'WAY. DINNER from $1.25. 3 SHOWS NIGHTLY. BROADWAY, Bet. 52d & 53d STS. CIRCLE 6-4959

In Queens and Long Island

CIRO'S — in the HOMESTEAD HOTEL, Kew Gardens, L. I.—BILL LESTER and his Orchestra. Dinner from $1.20. Cocktail Lounge—Dining Room.

Weismantel's Show Boat — 810 JAMAICA AVENUE. AP. 7-9853. FRANKIE BOOTH Presents—Twice Nitely CHERRIE DENNIS—STONE & VICTOR. LILLIAN LANE'S GIRLS ABOUT TOWN. DINING—DANCING—DIVERSION

Byrnes Summons Wallace and Jones

★ ★ ★ ★ ★ ★ ★

SPORTS 7

Wall Street Financial News

BROOKLYN EAGLE

Weather—Cooler with diminishing winds. Sunset, 8:31; Dimout, 9:31.

102d Year. No. 180. DAILY & SUNDAY • • BROOKLYN, N. Y., WEDNESDAY, JUNE 30, 1943 • Entered at the Brooklyn Post-office as 2d Class Mail Matter • 3 CENTS IN NEW YORK CITY ELSEWHERE 4 CENTS

Today's Good News:

U-BOAT PERIL BEATEN; WE INVADE JAP ISLAND

YANKS SEIZE BASE 5 MILES FROM MUNDA

Washington, June 30 (UP)—American forces, cutting through the Japanese defense perimeter, have landed on Rendova Island, only five miles from the enemy's Munda base in the central part of the Solomons Islands group.

A 22-word navy communique revealed the landing was accomplished yesterday morning—American time—by "combined U. S. forces." It gave no details and did not mention what enemy opposition, if any, was encountered.

Capture of the island would represent a 110-mile advance from the Russell Islands, heretofore the most northwestward part of the Solomons held by American forces. Rendova is 170 miles from the main Allied base in the Solomons or Guadalcanal.

Military experts believed that with U. S. forces firmly established on Rendova, it might not be necessary to capture Munda itself. That base is on New Georgia Island, which is separated from Rendova by the Blanche Channel, only a few miles across. The Rendova force, it was believed, might

Continued on Page 9

1st Barrage Balloons Soar on L. I.

BALLOONS ALOFT—First flight of barrage balloons in New York metropolitan area is watched by officers and civilians (left) yesterday on a golf course "somewhere on Long Island." Rising swiftly to 2,000 feet in two minutes, English-type sausage (right) prepares to ascend as helmeted soldiers take positions.

HEAVY FIGHTING IN FALL VOWED BY CHURCHILL

London, June 30 (UP)—Prime Minister Churchill today revealed the "total defeat" of enemy U-Boat attacks in the last 60 days—including the sinking of more than 30 enemy submarines in May alone—and warned invasion-jittery Axis Europe that "very probably there will be heavy fighting . . . before the leaves of Autumn fall."

Speaking at a triumphal ancient ceremony in which he received the freedom of the City of London at the blitz-wrecked Guild Hall, Churchill defied and jibed sarcastically at Germany and Italy but warned the Allied Nations that "we must not think the difficult times are over."

"Survival and victory are well within our grasp but hard and painful may be the process," he warned in renewing strongly Britain's promise to wipe out the Axis and then fight with all available means to force the Japs to submit "or bite the dust."

In addition to the "massacre of U-Boats" in the battle of the Atlantic during May and June, when Allied shipping was almost unmolested, Churchill covered the whole range of the war in his speech.

The Prime Minister said that:

1--The Allies will accept no compromise for ending the war which must be waged on the basis of unconditional Axis surrender.

2--There will "probably be heavy fighting in

Continued on Page 9

ARMY RAISES 30 BAGS OVER GOLF COURSE

Somewhere on Long Island, June 29 (Delayed) (U.P.)—The first balloon barrage in the New York metropolitan area was unveiled by the army today as the band on the clubhouse terrace of a well-known golf course played "The Stars and Stripes Forever" and army and navy officers and civilians watched more than 30 of the silver gasbags soar above the treetops into a cloudy sky.

Maj. Gen. Sanderford Jarman, whose anti-aircraft units extend from Maine to Florida, gave the command which sent the barrage on its baptismal flight, " raise all balloons to R. O. H. (ruling operational height).

This unit, with operating headquarters in a clubhouse just off the first tee, protects an important objective.

There are some 50 balloons in the unit, scattered several miles over the area and each manned by 13 men. The balloons rise only during raid alerts. They are of the Eng-

Continued on Page 11

Seek to Link Nazi Spy Suspect With Fatal Blast at World's Fair

Investigation is under way today to determine whether Erwin Henry de Spretter, Staten Island consulting engineer under arrest as a Nazi spy, had anything to do with the Fourth of July bomb explosion at the World's Fair in 1940, in which two detectives were instantly killed and six other persons were injured.

Police Commissioner Valentine and Inspector Arthur Wallander, director of the city's defense forces, today announced the start of a probe into de Spretter's movements at the time of the blast disaster. De Spretter had worked at the Fair making some of the models for the General Motors Futurama.

900,000 PUPILS BEGIN SUMMER VACATIONS

Brooklyn children today dashed madly out of classrooms for the last time until Fall—ten joyous weeks away.

For many of the city's 900,000 school children, however, the war will dominate their vacation work and play. Victory gardening, volunteer farm work and other war work will take up most of their time. And this Summer the usual trips to the country and seashore will be curtailed or cut out altogether, due to gasoline and travel difficulties.

Teachers will also contribute time to the war emergency with each required to serve one week without pay on emergency duty during the vacation. In addition, the Board of Education requires that they remain within one day's traveling time of the city to enable them to return to supervise the children in the event of a bombing.

BANDITS GET $450 IN TRUCK HOLDUP

Morton Schnaps of 434 Hinsdale St., driving a truck belonging to the Universal Cigarette Service, 175-15 Jamaica Ave., stopped early today for a red light on 101st Ave at 98th St., Ozone Park. Two men hopped suddenly into his cab, told him to be "sensible,' tucked him under the seat and drove off.

When they stopped they told him to remain as he was for 20 minutes. When Schnaps took stock he found he was minus collections of $450 and 12 cartons of cigarettes. He and his truck were near the rear entrance of the Aqueduct Race Track. Schnaps was not injured.

Continued on Page 11

BYRNES CALLS WALLACE, JONES FOR SHOWDOWN

Asks Face-to-Face Meeting in Effort To Settle Dispute

Washington, June 30 (U.P.)—War Mobilization Director James F. Byrnes today summoned Vice President Wallace and Secretary of Commerce Jesse H. Jones to his White House office for a face-to-face effort to settle their bitter dispute.

House Republicans, meanwhile, sought a full-dress Congressional investigation of the uproar caused by Wallace's charges that Jones was hamstringing the Board of Economic Warfare. Representative Richard B. Wigglesmorth (R., Mass.), noting that Jones had asked for an investigation, introduced a resolution calling for the inquiry.

Byrnes told a press conference that as long as "there are men of strong convictions in the departments there will be differences of opinion and when I hear abopt them I try to resolve them."

Cites F. D. R. Mandate

Announcing that he had asked Wallace and Jones to come to his office today, Byrnes said the purpose of the conference would be discussion of "the controversy which has been reported in the press."

Byrnes said he acted in accordanec with the assignment given him by the President when he was made War Mobilization Director, to see

Continued on Page 2

LaGuardia Defies OPA To Get Meat for City

Accepts Offer of Packers to Sell Direct To Retailers at Wholesale Ceiling Prices

In direct defiance of OPA, Mayor LaGuardia has accepted the proposal of independent packers to sell meat to retailers at wholesalers' ceiling prices. After a conference with Daniel P. Woolley, his Commissioner of Markets, he told reporteds today:

"I am doing this on my own responsibility."

This development followed hard on the heels of a disclosure that packers in New York City were prepared to go over the head of OPA and appeal to another Government agency — the Department of Justice—for a grand jury investigation of the price office's attitude.

When asked how much meat would be available under the new plan the Mayor answered: "One to 5,000,000 pounds."

The plan was originally submitted to OPA and the city by Nathan Sweedler, former Municipal Court justice and counsel for the Eastern States Independent Meat Packers and Slaughterers and last Friday Commissioner Woolley announced that the city had leased a meat stall in Washington Market to the Stamford, Conn., slaughtering firm of Sosnowitz & Lotstein. Sweedler said the firm was prepared to sell 10,000 pounds of meat weekly and that, with further outlets, up to 1,000,000 pounds a week could be routed to consumers.

Plans were upset the next day as OPA said thumbs down. Both

Continued on Page 11

Waac Director Hits At Rumors About Corps

Swampscott, Mass., June 30 (U.P.)—Rumors aimed at women in the armed forces and war industries suspiciously follow the Hitler doctrine of divide and conquer, Col. Oveta Culp Hobby, director of the Waacs, told the board of directors of the General Federation of Women's Clubs last night.

Referring to published reports of a secret agreement between the army and the Waacs to provide contraceptive and prophylactic equipment to members of the auxiliary, Colonel Hobby said the rumors were "malicious and untrue."

WEATHER MAN SEES COOL WAVE CONTINUING

While Brooklynites are reveling in the delightful breezes of the current cool wave, the Weather Man predicts more of the same with falling humidity, but cryptically adds "slowly rising temperatures."

There is no need for alarm—yet —because the mercury has a long way to go from today's readings in the low sixties to the torrid heights of the last week. The outlook seems pleasant for the time being, with moderate to fresh winds continuing to fan the city. And tonight will be cool again.

Midnight Is Deadline To Buy Auto Stamps

Tonight at midnight is the deadline for the purchase of $5 Federal auto use tax stamps required for the operation of any motor vehicle during the year ending July 1, 1944.

Stamps are on sale at Internal Revenue offices and postoffices. They must be placed in a prominent spot on all cars in use after midnight.

JAMAICA RESULTS

(Empire City Meeting)

1—Saucy Song, first; Dauntless Gal, second; Rosa Bonheur, third.

Heating, Cooking Stoves To Be Rationed Aug. 15

Washington, June 30 (U.P.) — The Office of Price Administration announced today that nation-wide rationing of heating and cooking stoves will begin by mid-August, instead of at the end of this month, as previously scheduled.

Charles Town Results

1—Idle Night, 31.20, 11.00, 7.60; Miss Pilgrim, 6.00, 4.00; Bob Junior, 4.20. Off time, 1:20.

SECOND RACE—Sug, first; Brush Off, second; Inmate, third.

Flying Fortresses Raid Motor Plant in France

London, June 30 (U.P.) — United States Flying Fortresses took over the Allied air offensive against Axis Europe in daylight yesterday with a precision bombing attack on Le Mans, France, it was announced today as a British spokesman revealed that the R. A. F. has tripled the weight of its attacks on Germany.

At the same time Foreign Secretary Anthony Eden told Commons that Britain has no intention of approaching the Italian Government with suggestions as to how it may save Rome from aerial bombbardment.

"I repeat that we would not hesitate to bomb Rome to the best of our ability and as heavily as possible if the course of the war should render such action convenient and helpful," Eden said.

Capt. Harold Balfour, Parliamentary Undersecretary of the Air, informed Commons that the Royal

Continued on Page 2

Brother of De Gaulle Escapes From Germans

Algiers, June 30 (U.P.) — Gen. Charles De Gaulle's brother, arrested and interned by the Germans, has escaped from a Nazi concentration camp, according to underground reports from France, the newspaper Echo D'Alger said today.

WHERE TO FIND IT

	Page		Page
Bridge	19	Obituaries	11
Comics	16	Parrott	13
Crossword	18	Patterns	17-18
Dr. Brady	16	Radio	16
Editorial	10	Society	6
Fighting Men	8	Sports	13-14-15
Financial	11	Take My Word	16
Grin and Bear It	10	Theaters	4
Home Front	8	These Women	8
Horoscope	16	Tucker	10
Letter Out	8	Uncle Ray	8
Lindley	10	Want Ads	17-18-19
Movies	4	Women	6
Novel	19		

Stories of Brooklyn Men and Women in U. S. War Service

Your Wartime Problems

By RICHARD HART

Many Overseas Men Find Company Deposit Excellent Method of Saving Money

It is good news that many of the members of our armed forces, particularly those overseas, are taking advantage of the plan to deposit their surplus funds with their finance officers.

Soldiers' deposits, which are repayable with 4 percent interest on discharge from the army, now total $21,000,000. This represents about 134,000 individual accounts. Approximately 80 percent of these are held by soldiers overseas, the remainder by troops in continental United States.

This arrangement is especially practical for overseas men. It is not wise for them to carry too much surplus money around. They get more money for overseas service and some of them are depositing this extra pay with Uncle Sam. This privilege is extended only to enlisted men. The soldier deposits his money with his company commander or the personnel adjutant and is given a deposit book.

The depositor may open his account with not less than $5 and may make subsequent deposits of that much or more. To insure against loss of records, duplicates are kept in the office of the Chief of Finance. In peacetime the soldier was not allowed to withdraw these funds until his discharge. Today withdrawals may be made in cases where hardship exists. However, this plan was never intended to be an easy checking account for our servicemen. It is primarily a demobilization fund.

To a point of being tedious this columnist will continue to harp on the necessity of the "nestegg" for the rainy day when the man or woman is demobilized or discharged. Any veteran of the last war waxes eloquent on this subject at the slightest provocation—and with reason! It is a bleak period in a man's life and fund of this sort can be a godsend.

CHECKS WASTE

Actually, a man serving overseas has little chance to spend money except on these useless trinkets which clutter up barracks bags. It is much better to put this money away because most of this souvenir junk must be ditched as the outfit moves up to the front. There is something pretty permanent about a bank deposit with Uncle Sam.

Ready cash in the army is always a hazard. Every outfit has its chronic borrowers. Nearly every barracks has its perpetual card or crape game. This is an easy way of whiling away the hours, but it can be very costly to those boys who do not know all the answers. Uncle Sam is a pretty straight fellow to lend money to in these days.

If you have a problem, write to Richard Hart, care of this newspaper. A stamped, addressed envelope will bring a personal reply.

On the Home Front

Precinct, zone and sector directors of the block service organization of the Brooklyn Civil Defense Volunteer Office are requested to attend a special meeting tonight in the Hotel Bossert.

The subject of training block service leaders will be discussed, according to Bernard A. Savage, Brooklyn director. He also announced the appointment of Mrs. Ely E. Kleinfeld as supervisor of precinct committee work. She will visit local branches and committee chairmen.

Home nursing classes for Central Queens have been started at the Corona Health Center and at Rockaway Beach Boulevard and 69th St., Averne.

A similar course will be launched next Tuesday morning at 93-32 Union Hall St., Jamaica, for a group of high school students.

The Kings County Jewish War Veterans will be host to several hundred service men on Sunday night in the Coney Island Service Men's Center, 529 Surf Ave., according to Leo Price, county commander. Joseph Lenowsky is in charge of arrangements.

Red Cross classes in canning will be held in the rooms of two Queens public utility firms, according to Mrs. Wilbur F. Howell of the Central Queens Chapter.

Sessions will be held in the New York and Queens Electric Light & Power Company office at 145-22 Jamaica Ave. and at the Brooklyn Union Gas Company auditorium in Jamaica. Registration may be made at chapter headquarters, 93-32 Union Hall St., Jamaica.

Irene Rosenberg, pianist, will be heard in a recital Sunday afternoon in the Brooklyn Museum. She will play selections by Bach, Beethoven, Chopin and Liszt.

Co-operating groups were the Civilian Defense Volunteer Office of the Bushwick-Stuyvesant area, the Charles W. Heisser Post, American Legion, and the Lexington Ave. branch of the Bendix Marine Division.

Residents of Miami Court recently dedicated a service flag for nine members of families in the street who are in the armed forces. They include Lt. Charles Botts, Pvt. James Kelly, Pvt. Sonny Carvel, Pvt. Thomas Duffy, Pvt. Victor Bovino, Pvt. Edward Cahill, Pvt. James Peerless, Pvt. J. Pensabini and Adelaide Dowling, who recently joined the Waves.

Ten Local Men On Prisoner List

Washington, June 30 (U.P.)—The War Department today made public the names of 789 United States soldiers held as prisoners of war by Japan. Nine of this number are from Brooklyn and one from Queens as follows:

BEIERSTEDT, Staff Sgt. Harold G.: Mrs. Kwai F. Pang, aunt, 1331 E. 29th St.

BLISS, 2d Lt. Raymond W., Jr.: Col. Raymond W. Bliss, M.C., father, headquarters 1st army, Governors Island.

GIARDINA, Tech. Sgt. Joseph A.: Joseph Giardina, father, 3815 12th St.

JANIEC, Pfc. William R.: Frank Madein, friend, 1469 President St.

KERNER, Staff Sgt. Benjamin: Mrs. Sarah Kerner, mother, 445 Watkins St.

McCANN, 2d Lt. Eugene Joseph: Mrs. Mary A. McCann, mother, 510 Ocean Ave.

McDONNELL, Chaplain, Capt. John J.: Mrs. Hannah McDonnell, mother, 1017 Dahill Road.

MATUOZZI, Staff Sgt. Robert E.: Robert E. Matuozzi, father, 16 Court St.

MILLER, Pfc. Thomas E.: Mrs. Anne Miller, mother, 139-18 97th Ave., Jamaica.

TANTURRI, Staff Sgt. Arthur J.: Ceasare Tanturri, father, 640 Lafayette Ave.

WEISSBUCH, Pvt. Elliott: Mrs. Netti Weissbuch, mother, 236 Vernon Ave.

LETTER OUT

1. Displace	Letter Out for something out of the ordinary.
2. Parsing	Letter Out and it's good for a drink.
3. Snuffler	Letter Out for plaited strips.
4. Aspired	Letter Out for compliments.
5. Yielder	Letter Out and he depended upon it.

Remove one letter from each word and rearrange to spell the word called for in the last column. Print the letter in center column opposite the word from which you have removed it. If you have "Lettered Out" correctly he is very fastidious.

Answer on Page 18

With Our Fighters

Corp. A. D. Carcaroma of 372 Avenue W has been graduated as a mechanic at Keesler Field, Miss.

Another new army sergeant is Harold I. Koltun of 2224 Benson Ave., promoted at Fort Benning, Ga.

A new sergeant at Greensboro, N. C., is Peter J. Felice of 4315 Clarendon Road.

John E. Licari of 123 Avenue S has been made a corporal at New Orleans, La.

Gertrude E. Kuehnmein of 217 Quincy St. has been sworn into the Waves.

Thomas J. McDonald of 434 44th St. has been made a technician fifth grade at Fort Knox, Ky.

Pfc. Gamliel Weisbach of 1659 47th St. has been graduated from the weather school at Grand Rapids, Mich.

Promotions announced in the Panama Canal Zone inclue those of A. A. Marciano of 2714 Avenue D, to sergeant, and James W. Finnegan of 902 Avenue C to corporal.

In the same area, Staff Sgt. Seymour Bender of 1769 51st St. has received the Air Medal for meritorious achievement.

Tech. Corp. Edward J. Salisbury of 270 60th St. has returned to Camp Rucker, Ala., after a furlough.

John S. Conway of 17 Horace Court, at Camp McCain, Miss., was wed to the former Alice Carbey of 7th St.

READY FOR BOMBER DUTY—Lt. Harold J. Rocketto of 2265 65th St. is shown with his wife after receiving the silver wings of a navigator.

R. D. Horne Jr. R. J. Smith

Receiving second lieutenants' commissions as fliers at Roswell, N. M., were Ralph D. Horne Jr. of 2714 Quentin Road and Russell J. Smith of 54 Lincoln Ave.

Louis Korotkin N. J. Stevason

New second lieutenants in the army air force, commissioned at Williams Field, Ariz. are Louis Korotkin of Ozone Park and N. J. Stevason of 1022 Dahill Road.

Joseph B. Milgram Jr. of 952 E. 19th St., who received basic training at Camp Claiborne, La., has been commissioned a second lieutenant at Fort Belvoir, Va., and after two weeks of special training at Richmond, Va., he will report to Spokane, Wash.

Robert Veech of 1933 E. 34th St., having completed preliminary naval training at Sampson, N. Y., was home on furlough. Joseph E. Kulaga of 310 Bedford Ave. has been transferred to Salt Lake City, Utah, after being graduated as a sergeant gunner at Fort Myers, Fla.

Charles Strong of 1487 E. 14th St., recently home on furlough after basic training at Camp Barkeley, Texas, is now taking a special course at Nashville, Tenn.

Corp. Harold M. Feuerstein of 897 Empire Boulevard has been made a sergeant at Savannah, Ga.

F. C. Keeney V. J. Musgrove

Francis P. Keeney, a New Utrecht High School Alumnus, and Vernon J. Musgrove, alumnus of Alexander Hamilton, have just been commissioned second lieutenants in the army air corps at Luke Field, Ariz.

Irene Richman of Jackson Heights was given a party in the Boulevard, Elmhurst, before leaving for the Waves.

Now attending advanced flight school, Monroe, La., Aviation Cadet George S. Loughlin of Brooklyn recently received his pre-flight diploma.

Lt. Frank J. Perrotta of 459 13th St. is now stationed in Seattle, Wash.

Abraham Schwartz of 1680 E. 17th St. has entered the signal corps. He is a member of the enlisted reserves.

Two Brooklynites have just completed special courses at the signal corps school, Camp Murphy, Fla. They are 2d Lt. Charles Lees of 4695 Bedford Ave. and 2d Lt. Andrew A. Ruda of 1953 71st St.

Corp. John J. Davis of 262 Winthrop St., now with the army air force at Boca Raton, Fla., expects to spend July 4 with his wife and son.

A. E. Mockler A. J. Platt

Pfc. Albert E. Mockler of 7691 Colonial Road is now home on furlough from Wake Forest, N. C. Augustus J. Platt of 150 St. James Place has been promoted to private first class at Camp Edwards, Mass.

M. L. Heller C. T. Moser

Marion L. Heller of 320 Sterling Place has returned to Camp Davis, N. C., after a furlough. Charles T. Moser, seaman second class, is home at 826 Rogers Ave. after seeing action in the Pacific.

Scheduled to get his silver wings, Aviation Cadet Joseph C. Gillen of 1299 E. 34th St., now stationed at Tucson, Ariz., will soon complete his last course of training as a pilot in the army air corps.

Pfc. Lewis M. Bellinger of 445 E. 5th St. is in training as an airplane mechanic at Lincoln, Neb.

As a result of "delay en route" during his transfer from Camp Lee, Va., to San Antonio, Texas., Lt. Kenneth W. Frey of 924 Lincoln Place, has the opportunity to spend a few days at home.

At Lawson Field, Ga., Pfc. James Cuglietto of 1957 61st St. was recently promoted to the grade of corporal.

The Red Cross mobile blood bank visited the Masonic Temple at Bushwick and Gates Aves., this week in a successful trip.

REPLACING MEN—Commissioned third officers in the Waacs at Fort Des Moines, Iowa, were, left to right, Lillian Griffin of 1920 E. 36th St., Winifred Goodman of 2717 Avenue W and Beatrice Warnoff of 789 McDonough St.

ATTENTION, PLEASE!

Sorry, but no photos used in the Home Front or Fighting Men columns can be returned. However, news of local men and women in service or active in Civilian Defense on the home front will be welcomed by the Brooklyn Eagle. Such news should be addressed to either Fighting Men Editor or Home Front Editor, Brooklyn Eagle, Johnson and Adams Sts., Brooklyn.

DRAFTIE

By Paul Fogarty

Take My Word For It

: : Frank Colby

A HANDBOOK FOR OFFICE WORKERS

Q. Should "are" or "is" be used with "company" and "corporation"?

A. "The company are; the corporation are" is a usage prevalent in England, but it is not good usage in America. Here, the preferred form is: The company is; the corporation is; the Government is; the Congress is, etc.

Q. Which is correct, "Someone's else book," or "Someone else's book"?

A. The modern and customary form is "someone else's book."

Q. Please tell us whether the second quotation mark is correctly placed in these sentences: He said, "Where are you going"? She answered, "It's none of your business"!

A. Punctuation marks (except commas and periods) belong within the quotation if they apply only to the matter quoted. Correct: He said, "Where are you going?" She answered, "It's none of your business!"

But note: Did she say, "It's none of your business"? In this sentence, the quotation mark does not belong with the matter quoted, but with the question, Did she say . . .?

Q. We can't decide whether to use one or two commas in this sentence: "The colors are red, white, and blue."

A. The punctuation is correct. In a series of three or more, place a comma before the conjunction "and," as: Our stocks include shoes, suits, hats, gloves, and underwear. She is efficient, attentive, and ambitious.

Q. How should a married woman sign a business letter?

A. She should not sign "Mrs. John H. Jones." Either of these forms is correct:

(Mrs.) Ethel M. Jones.
Ethel M. Jones.
(Mrs. John H. Jones).

Offered today only, my pamphlet of SYNONYMS. Get rid of your overworked words. Send a stamped (3-cent), self-addressed envelope to Frank Colby, 3221 Huntingdon Place, Houston, Texas.

THESE WOMEN!

By d'Alessio

"Now mind you, I don't want any that lay millions of eggs. I haven't room!"

Boro Prisoner of Japs Flew With Colin Kelly

"He was born during the last war and always said that was why he liked military life so much."

Joseph Giardina of 3815 12th Ave. is proud of his fighting son, Tech. Sgt. Joseph A. Giardina, who is at present a prisoner of war in Japan.

"He went to West Point for three years and he got in by examination, not pull," explained Mr. Giardina. "Then he left and went into the air corps. He is a radio mechanic and operator and has flown with Capt. Colin Kelly."

On March 27 Sergeant Giardina received the Distinguished Flying Cross. This his parents proudly display along with the last letter he wrote before he was reported missing last June.

Giardina was first stationed in Hawaii and then later at Clark Field. From there, his parents don't know everywhere he went, but he was on Bataan when it fell, they believe. At first he was held prisoner in the Philippines and then recently transferred to Japan.

"He always wanted to see the world, and now he's seeing it," said his sister.

Two weeks before he was taken prisoner, he had made the flight which earned him the DFC.

The last letter he wrote to his folks was on April 29, 1942, and in it he was full of encouragement for them. He said that he was "fine and dandy" and warned them to keep well, for "Health is wealth, you know." "If only I could get a letter from him—in his writing," said his mother. "We have received telegrams saying he was all right and a prisoner, but until I see his handwriting I'll wonder, worry."

At Christmas he had sent every one cards and also $100 for his mother. His letters always were interesting and newsy.

"We've all written to him, but he has not answered us yet. I suppose it takes time. We'll have to be patient."

Giardina is 28, was born in Europe and came to this country when he was four years old. He is a graduate of Lincoln High School, where he "was a very smart boy." He received a medal for Spanish at graduation.

Pa Gave Pep Talk To Soldier Son

Bolstering each other's courage with the old adage, "While there's life, there's hope," Mr. and Mrs. Robert E. Matuozzi of 742 Union St. have been rewarded after 18 months of waiting with the news that their son, Staff Sgt. Robert Matuozzi, is alive and a prisoner of war of the Japanese Government.

Shortly after the fall of Corregidor he was reported missing in action. The last communication they had from him was in February, 1942, when he telegraphed that he "was all right."

Twenty-four-year-old Sergeant Matuozzi had enlisted four years ago in the medical corps while working in a pharmacy. A graduate of Boys High School, he planned to study medicine at college. His brother, Norman, aged 18, now studying in the Pre-Medical School at Manhattan College, is in the reserve of the air corps. Another brother, Wilton, 22, now working at the Sperry Gyroscope Company, expects to enter service shortly. Mr. Matuozzi, a lawyer, when sending his son off to war, admonished him heartily, to "knock the hell out of the enemy."

Was a Painter Before He Enlisted

Pfc. William R. Janiec enlisted two years ago and on May 10, shortly after he enlisted, was in the Philippines. He also was at Pearl Harbor for some time.

Frank Madein of 1469 President St., a friend, has written several letters to Janiec but has received no answer. Two months ago a telegram from Washington informed them that he was a prisoner in Japan.

Private Janiec, 27, was born in New Jersey and worked as a painter before he enlisted.

Puzzled Over Status Of Prisoner-Nephew

Mrs. Kwai F. Pang of 1331 E. 29th St. is puzzled about her nephew, Staff Sgt. Harold G. Beierstedt. She has been informed that he is a Japanese prisoner. The War Department has said she can write and if necessary send a cable.

"But the Red Cross says we shouldn't send a cable—I don't know what it means," said Mrs. Pang. She hopes it doesn't mean that he is sick.

Beierstedt was on Corregidor and was taken prisoner there. Later, word was received saying that he had been transferred to Japan.

The last communication the Pangs had from their nephew was a Christmas card postmarked Nov. 21, 1941. All he said on it was, "I'm well." Then, on April 30 a telegram from the Government came.

Beierstedt enlisted four years ago. Previously he had been in the National Guard.

Chaplain Always Asked About the Dodgers

Capt. John J. McDonnell, a chaplain, was on Corregidor when it fell. Today his name appears on the list of prisoners in Japan.

Captain McDonnell enlisted three years ago and was stationed at Fort Devens, Mass., during the time he was in this country. When he went overseas he was stationed on "The Rock" for two years until it fell.

He was missing for a year before his parents received word that he was held prisoner. A month ago a telegram from the Red Cross reached their home at 1017 Dahill Road.

"When he wrote he always wanted to know about the Dodgers. He said he was well and getting along all right," said Mrs. McDonnell.

Captain McDonnell, 39, was born in Brooklyn, attended Cathedral High School and St. John's University. He was a curate at St. Mary Star of the Sea before he enlisted.

Foreboding Grips Mother of Soldier

Pvt. Elliott Weissbuch is listed on today's release as a prisoner of war in Japan.

Mrs. Netti Weissbuch of 236 Vernon Ave. is tearful about this news, because it only increases her sorrow. On June 24 her son's name appeared on a list sent by the International Red Cross to the War Department. The list was of the names of those who have died of disease in the Japanese prison camps.

Now, ironically, his name is on today's list. All Mrs. Weissbuch can say is, "I can't believe it."

Uncle Ray's Corner

For Boys and Girls

Huge Statue Honors Hero of Tarascan Indians

In west central Mexico there is a State which contains most of the members of a certain tribe of Indians. They are known as Tarascans and we hear of them as far back in the history of white men in the New World.

About 250,000 of the people of Mexico are classed as Tarascans. There are not nearly so many of them living today as there are Aztecs and Mayas.

In the time of Montezuma II much of Mexico was under the power of the Aztecs. The Tarascans, however, kept their freedom.

Cortez and his Spanish soldiers conquered the Aztecs, but the Tarascans fought off the invaders. In later years their lands were taken over as part of the Spanish colony of Mexico, but they were not willing to be "good subjects." The spirit of revolt was in them.

Among the heroes of these Indians is a man known as a "warrior priest." His full name was Don Jose Maria Morelos y Pavon, but he commonly is spoken of as Morelos.

In 1810 Morelos joined in an effort to win freedom from Spain. In the fighting which followed during the next five years he proved himself an able leader. He was captured, however, by Spanish troops and died before a firing squad.

In memory of Morelos a statue has been built on an island in a lake where Tarascans fish to this day. The statue is made up of concrete blocks and it rises as high as a six-story building. The hero failed to live to see Mexico win freedom, but he is honored for the work he tried to do.

Several weeks ago I spoke of the "dance of the old men" which Tarascans perform during a service in honor of the dead. They also have other dances, and it is their custom to wear masks while they dance.

In the market place of a Tarascan town, "food for the dead" is sold. Cakes and colored candy are on display and a person may buy one or more objects to take to a grave.

The candy or cake is placed on the grave at or near midnight. These simple folk no doubt expect the spirits to come back to the cemetery to enjoy something to eat. Flowers also are placed on the graves and at times a piece of meat.

(For TRAVEL or GENERAL INTEREST section of your scrapbook.)

Uncle Ray

Tomorrow—Bananas.

Ten illustrations by Frank C. Pape appear in the picture leaflet, AFRICA'S PEOPLE AND CUSTOMS. If you want a copy send a self-addressed envelope bearing a three-cent stamp to Uncle Ray in care of this newspaper.

Stories of Brooklyn Men and Women in U. S. War Service

Your Wartime Problems

By RICHARD HART

Better Not Urge Medical Discharges Against Physician's Advice

"Is there any way that we can hasten our son's discharge from the army because of a nervous condition?" asks Mr. Tom P. "He is one of those borderline cases and his doctors are willing to discharge him if we will sign a paper accepting his custody; otherwise, they are willing to keep him in service. Just why do we have to sign this paper and what can the army do for the boy that we cannot do better at home?"

It would be a mighty good thing for Mr. Tom P. to visit the boy in the hospital and have a heart-to-heart talk with the chief psychiatrist there. Plan to spend a full day with the boy, if regulations permit, and let him do most of the talking.

Home folks often make the mistake of accepting the custody of such cases in their sheer eagerness to get the boy back home. But this means that the responsibility for getting him completely well again is shifted from the army to the home, and usually these waivers make it impossible for the boy to get a pension.

THEY NEED REST

A good many of these nervous cases need only the rest and good food that the army can provide. There is no magic formula in psychiatry and often the turmoil of coming home, getting back on the job again proves too much of a strain. And families are so liable to spoil them in the meantime! We are still at that point where the man who has seen action is somewhat a novelty to citizens and the returning soldier is apt to get the viewpoint that the world is going to make a big fuss over him for the rest of his life. Alas, the veterans of the last war can testify how easy it is for people to forget!

This is the great argument for the rather heavy discipline most hospitals exercise toward their patients. In the convalescent stages it is not good practice to "baby" the patients; especially if they are upset by their experiences at the front. It hastens their recovery to keep them amid placid surroundings, with plenty of sleep and good food.

With the very best of intentions, families are likely to interrupt the convalescent process. It is hard to keep neighbors from plying the boys with questions about the one period of their lives they want most to forget. It is difficult to prevent the local service club from asking them to make speeches about their experiences with all the strain on the nerves that this entails. And as for seeing the girl friends again—wow, what fellow wouldn't get excited about this after North Africa or Iceland!

ASIDES TO READERS

To ADELAIDE: Why not write to him and say that you are planning to give him a birthday present but want him to specify what he wants? Then you can use his letter to send the package through the mail by showing his A. P. O. overseas postmark.

If you have a problem, write to Richard Hart, care of this newspaper. A stamped, addressed envelope will bring a personal reply.

1851-B

COOL AND TRIM

Just as smart a shirtwaist as you could ask for—well cut and beautifully detailed. Can go anywhere.

Barbara Bell Pattern No. 1851-B designed for sizes 12, 14, 16, 18, 20; 40 and 42. Corresponding bust measurements 30, 32, 34, 36, 38, 40 and 42. Size 14 (32) requires, with short sleeves, 3¼ yards 39-inch material.

Ready now, for your mid-season and fall sewing—a new Pattern Book for fall! Contains 85 new patterns for practical wartime fashions. 15 cents per copy. You may order it with a 15 cents pattern for 15 cents plus 1 cent postage.

For this attractive pattern send 15 cents, plus 1 cent for postage, in coins with your name, address, pattern number and size wanted to Barbara Bell (Brooklyn Eagle), Post Office Box 75, Station O. Manhattan. Allow 10 days for delivery.

ATTENTION, SERVICE MEN, RELATIVES AND FRIENDS! SEND FOR WAR BALLOT

Every male and female member of the military and naval forces of the United States, who is a resident of New York State and a duly qualified voter, has the right to vote at the general election to be held on Nov. 2, 1943, as fully as if he or she were personally present at home.

An application for a war ballot will be promptly sent by the State War Ballot Commission upon the written request therefor of any service men or of any relative or friend in his or her behalf. The application must be filed by midnight, Sept. 20, 1943.

Act promptly and mail a post card or letter to the commission at Albany, N. Y., or 80 Centre St., New York City, and state:

Rank and full name of member of armed forces; regiment, company, troop, or other command; name of camp, vessel or base; post-office address of camp, vessel or base; service man's home residence.

Sendoff for R. G. Bassman

A sendoff party will be given to Rudolph G. Bassman by his fellow co-workers this evening at the Pierrepont Hotel. Ruddy is to be inducted into the army. For a number of years he has been employed by the City Bank Farmers Trust Company, Montague St. Mr. Bassman was formerly a resident of the Heights. Herb Wheeler will be in charge of the arrangements.

LETTER OUT

1. Granges		Letter Out and she gets on your nerves.
2. Dampen		Letter Out and it's done to every child.
3. Ingots		Letter Out and any wasp can do it.
4. Divorcee		Letter Out and it's protected.
5. Psalter		Letter Out and let's eat.

Remove one letter from each word and rearrange to spell the word called for in the last column. Print the letter in center column opposite the word from which you have removed it. If you have "Lettered Out" correctly it will decay.

"Letter Out" correctly it will decay.

Answers on Page 12

With Our Fighters

Three brothers, Pvts. Dan and Pat and Pfc. Vincent Allocco of Brooklyn are serving with the medical corps in the armed forces. Vincent is in North Africa. Dan and Pat are at training stations in the United States.

Ruth Edna Thomson of 221-34 Hartland Ave., Queens, has reported to New River, N. C., for her basic training in the marine corps, women's reserve.

PENSACOLA APPOINTEES—Aviation cadets recently transferred to the naval air training center at Pensacola, Fla., include, left to right, Oscar J. Stone of 1610 E. 22d St., Thomas Carlisle of 287 Van Sicklen St., Thomas R. Collins of 95 Cambridge Place and Edwin J. McCue of 8408 3d Ave.

M. K. Coen — Robert Magdalin

Pfc. Michael Kenin Coen of 561 4th St. is expecting a furlough next month from his post with an armored division. Robert Magdalin of 437 Quentin Road has been transferred from Camp Lee, Va., to Centenary College, Shreveport, La.

WIN WINGS AND COMMISSION—Appointed second lieutenants upon graduating from schools at Midland and San Angelo in the West Texas Bombardier Quadrangle are, left to right, Philip Barnett of 1430 E. 8th St., Harold Cohen of 964 Eastern Parkway, Edward J. Garone of 1551 57th St., Midland, and Julian S. Collender of 2020 Kings Highway, San Angelo.

Stanley Czys — L. R. McDonough

Pvt. Stanley Czys of 146 18th St., who has been in Africa for six months, has received the Order of the Purple Heart. Pvt. Laurence R. McDonough of 1447 Flatbush Ave. is now in Hawaii.

From his station at Los Angeles, Cal., Pvt. Floriggi Raimondo of 714 61st St. is home on furlough.

Joseph E. McDonough of 1447 Flatbush Ave., who is in North Africa, has been promoted to corporal. His brother, Vincent R. McDonough, is at Parris Island, S. C., for marine corps basic training.

"AIR CONDITIONING" COMPLETED—Now qualified to navigate bombers against the enemy after completing training at the navigation school at Hondo, Texas, are, left to right, Lts. Dominick G. Farinacci of 342 61st St., Alfred M. Gertler of 1343 E. 13th St., Joseph W. Herbst of 257 Sherman St. and Abraham Inkeles of 5304 Tilden Ave.

BASIC TRAINING COMPLETED—Having finished training at Fort Knox, Ky., these soldiers are prepared for combat duty with an armored force unit. They are, left to right, Pvts. Charles T. Bell of 19 Hubbard Place, Frank V. Dibitetto of 1968 W. 10th St., Harry Myrand of 146 Lenox Road and Joseph V. Lentino of 276 Columbia St.

THE BEST REWARD OF ALL—Proudly Mr. and Mrs. Thomas A. LaMar of 425 101st St. congratulate their son, Thomas, following graduation exercises of engineer candidate school at Fort Belvoir, Va.

Erasmus Hall High School graduate, Richard Ferrer of 189 E. 34th St. is enrolled for a one-year course at the navy's new officer training station at the University of Rochester, N. Y.

With basic training at Camp Robinson, Ark., completed, Pvt. Stanley S. Berg of 540 Ocean Ave. has entered Louisiana State University, where he will study psychology.

Florence Eisen — H. C. Kocherian

Wave Florence Eisen of 255 Pennsylvania Ave. will leave soon for Washington, D. C., after a short visit, to work in the naval personnel department. Aviation Cadet Howard Charles Kochera of 228 E. 38th St. is studying meteorology at Grand Rapids, Mich.

A. J. Minnella — W. J. O'Brien

Antonio J. Minnella of 1775 50th St. has earned his wings from the parachute training school at Fort Benning, Ga. William J. O'Brien of 1263 E. 29th St. was commissioned an ensign in the naval reserve upon graduating from the naval air training center at Corpus Christi, Texas.

ATTENTION, PLEASE!

Sorry, but no photos used in the Home Front or Fighting Men columns can be returned. However, news and pictures of local men and women in service or active in Civilian Defense on the home front will be welcomed by the Brooklyn Eagle. Such news should be addressed to either Fighting Men Editor or Home Front Editor, Brooklyn Eagle, Johnson and Adams Sts., Brooklyn.

Dr. Brady says:

One of my contentions is that the morbid fear of "autointoxication," which happens only in the imagination, keeps many victims enslaved to physic.

Another contention of mine is that if no physic and no enema or other "aid" of any kind were available the victim of the constipation habit would be cured of the habit in five days. The trick is to hold the poor fish from his desire to resume taking physic for the necessary length of time to permit abused nature to re-establish automatic regulation—by the same mechanism as that which automatically regulates breathing and heartbeat.

The constipation or physic habit is a psychological problem. The trouble is in the mind, not in the bowel.

As long as people are in that state of mind one might as well holler down the rain barrel as try to tell 'em they're fools to go on like that. I know, because I've been doing my dangdest to bring 'em to their senses for a long time with the booklet "The Constipation Habit and Colon Hygiene" (for which I exact a three-cent-stamped self-addressed envelope and ten cents) and only a precious few of the people get the desired results, because they are so deeply imbued by the nostrum and quack teachings that they just can't believe the simple truth.

It is now well established that the B-complex vitamins, notably thiamin (B-1 and riboflavin (B-2 or G) and perhaps others are essential for good "tone" in the involuntary muscle of the stomach and intestine and that of the arterial wall and the heart itself. It is my belief that habitual deficiency in the intake of B-complex, due mainly to the general use of refined white flour in place of the whole wheat unbolted flour of a century ago, is a common predisposing factor of constipation habit and of colon derangement. So I suggest that every dose of cascara, for instance, should be combined with vitamin B-complex, every dose of digitalis should be combined with vitamin B-complex, for the real "tonic" action of B-complex on the involuntary muscle of alimentary tract or heart and arteries, as the case may be.

QUESTIONS AND ANSWERS

I Like It

I have had more different ailments, or believed I had, until I began reading your column. Then every little while I learned there is no such ailment as I thought I had, and although at first I dismissed your statements as the notions of a crank, in time I found your teachings unanswerable. Net result—now I'm very well, thank you, sir, except that I am some twenty pounds overweight. Mrs. D. B.

Answer—Thank you, Ma'am. A letter like yours relieves me of a lot of symptoms, too. Makes me feel I'm not just hollering down the rain barrel. Now that you've got your bearings, it is comparatively simple to take care of the twenty-pound handicap you carry. Send twenty-five cents and three-cent-stamped envelope bearing your address for booklet "Rules for Reducing"—tells how to do it and improve your health at the same time.

Girls, Don't Let 'em Get You Down

Mother is 75 years old. She runs and manages successfully a ten-room house, has four roomers, does all her own laundry, baking, cooking, general work for three of us. After a recent check-up her doctor wanted to give her some vitamin shots, but she pooh-poohs. M. W.

Answer—The picture you show of mother calls for a couple of poohs. A girl as much on her toes as she is should be able to swallow in the ordinary way whatever vitamins she may need. Some doctors are too fond of administering "shots" when the patient can as well take the medicine in the ordinary way.

THESE WOMEN!

By d'Alessio

"My husband is awfully fussy. He refuses to eat leftovers made from leftovers of the day before."

On the Home Front

Bay Ridge citizens crowded around the baseball diamond on Shore Road and 79th St. and watched the Bay Ridge Canteen Block Busters blast the Jewish Welfare Board, USO club's baseball team, 40 to 9. The victory made the Block Busters the champion team of canteens located in the Bay Ridge-Fort Hamilton area.

Buddy Thompson, Jameson, Terra, Carroll and Doemer of Bay Ridge scored home runs.

After the game all hands were guests at the Bay Ridge Canteen, 6216 4th Ave., where they took part in formal opening ceremonies of the new outdoor garden and dance floor.

An interesting program of entertainment has been arranged for Saturday night at the canteen.

Two medical field units, the funds for which were raised at a benefit concert at the Lincoln Hotel last Saturday, will be sent to the Russian Army. More than $4,500 was raised at the function, sponsored by the Long Beach Committee of the United Jewish War Effort.

One unit will be inscribed in the name of "Patrons and Frances K. Powell of the Hotel Lincoln, Long Beach." The other is in the name of the "Yeshiva of Flatbush," of which Nathan Flax is president.

With contributions still rolling in, Max D. Thorner, chairman of the committee, said that there should be sufficient funds for a third unit when total receipts are in. Each completely equipped unit costs $2,000.

The Rev. Dr. Theodore S. Ross of the Congregation Shaari Zedek will speak on the "Message of Israel" radio program tomorrow and the following Saturday, July 31, over the Blue Network station WJZ. "The Religion of a Sensible Person" is the title of this first talk.

More than 200 soldiers made blood donations and twice that number volunteered contributions to the Long Shore Red Cross at Fort Totten last Saturday. About 65 members of the North Shore Blood Donors Service, consisting of nurse aides, staff assistants, motor corps, grey ladies and canteen workers assisted. Mrs. Richard Ninet was chairman of the unit.

YOUR BIRTHDAY

By Stella

FRIDAY, JULY 23—Born today, you are under the sign of Leo and have a strong, self-reliant and determined mind which says and odes what it thinks. You like a lot of excitement and you are apt to see that things don't slow down too much wherever you are. You are original and some of your ideas seem a little startling at first. But if you stick to them they will be accepted eventually. When that time comes, you're off on a new road! You have a sharp mind and should develop the cultural side of your nature. You have excellent taste and know good from bad. You accept only the good, too, and will refuse anything but first rate. Your imagination is keen and your inventive mind may bring about something very interesting during your lifetime.

To find what the stars have in store for tomorrow, select your birthday star and read the corresponding paragraph. Let your birthday star be your daily guide.

Saturday, July 24

LEO (July 24-Aug. 23)—If you think before you act and don't let impulse lead you astray, you will get through the day successfully.

VIRGO (Aug. 24-Sept. 22)—Conservative action will help you make a wise decision to avoid future trouble.

LIBRA (Sept. 23-Oct. 23)—You can make progress today if, when evening comes, you avoid a dispute which might upset you.

SCORPIO (Oct. 24-Nov. 22)—If you can control your temper you can save yourself a useless argument.

SAGITTARIUS (Nov. 23-Dec. 22)—This is apt to be an irritating day for you.

CAPRICORN (Dec. 23-Jan. 20)—Think before you act and be conservative in all matters.

AQUARIUS (Jan. 21-Feb. 19)—Caution should be your watchword all day and throughout the evening.

PISCES (Feb. 20-March 21)—Nothing seems to go right today so just be patient.

ARIES (Mar. 22-Apr. 20)—If you are conservative with things you can weather today's troubles.

TAURUS (Apr. 21-May 21)—Let reason rule impulse and don't speak hastily in anger to anyone.

GEMINI (May 22-June 22)—Just one of those jittery days for you.

CANCER (June 23-July 23)—Definitely a poor day for all your activities.

WAR ENCYCLOPEDIA

THE DEMOLITION BOMB

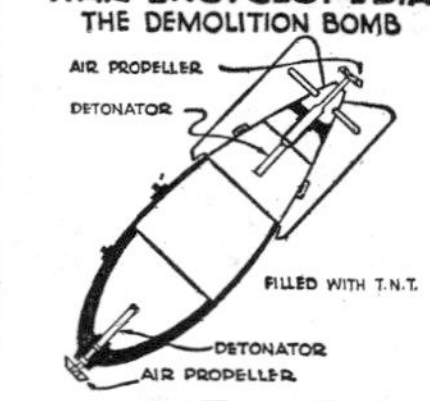

GLOSSARY OF ARMY SLANG

DOLL — A JAP

TAKE THEIR PULSES — TO KNOCK THEM OUT.

Uncle Ray's Corner

For Boys and Girls

Slight Breeze Makes Aspens Tremble and Rustle

Trembling poplar!

That is one of the names of the aspen tree, which belongs to the poplar family. The tree does tremble in a sense of the word. Even a very small breeze will set it a-flutter, indeed a breeze so small that a person might not notice it.

The aspen is not one of the most common trees, but it is found in many places. It grows from the northern part of Siberia to the British Isles, in Labrador and across Canada to Alaska. In the United States it is a native of both Maine and California, and that statement can be made about only a very few native trees. One of the others is the black willow.

The leaves of the aspen provide the rustling sound. They rub against one another when they are touched by a gentle breeze.

There is a legend that the cross on which Jesus was crucified was made from aspen wood. The legend says that the tree trembles for that reason!

The white wood of the aspen is soft, smooth and of light weight. If the bark is peeled off a month or two before the tree is cut, the wood will become harder and will make better timber. In parts of the earth where few other trees grow, the aspen has proved of special importance.

Aspen wood was used in making many of the old-fashioned wooden water pails, also for casks to hold herring. Some wooden trays and bowls are made from it today.

During the Middle Ages in Europe, aspen wood was valued for the making of arrows. While King Henry V was on the English throne, a law was passed that no man should use such wood for any other purpose. For any one who did so, there was a fine equal to about $25 in our money.

Aspens often reach a height of from 60 to 80 feet. Now and then they grow as high as 100 feet. The trunks may be as much as three feet thick.

These trees grow at points near sea level, also on the sides of mountains. In the United States and Mexico, dwarf aspens are found on mountains more than a mile and a half above sea level.

(For NATURE section of your scrapbook.)

Uncle Ray

Tomorrow: Notes on the F. B. I.

Ten illustrations by Frank C. Pape appear in the picture leaflet, AFRICA'S PEOPLE AND CUSTOMS. If you want a copy, send a self-addressed envelop bearing a 3-cent stamp to Uncle Ray in care of this newspaper.

DRAFTIE — By Paul Fogarty

Duce's Fall Held First Big Stroke in Freeing of Europe

EX-AGITATOR ITALY'S BOSS FOR 21 YEARS

By United Press

Benito Mussolini, who started political life as a small-time Socialist agitator and turned to Fascism to create the first dictatorship of its kind in modern history, ruled Italy for 21 years before war exploded the shell of his empire.

Less than 38 months after he stuck out his lower jaw and promised that his never-produced millions of bayonets would help kill off democracy, Mussolini's regime died with guns of the Allies firing within hearing distance of the Italian mainland.

It was an easier end than had ever been anticipated for Mussolini —and unexpected. As Mussolini's rise exemplified the waning of freedom in Europe, his fall was the first big stroke looking toward the freeing of Europe.

It came only four days before his 60th birthday.

Son of a Blacksmith

Mussolini, son of a radical-minded blacksmith, led his black shirt legions on Rome on Oct. 28, 1922, and became premier in a bloodless revolution, forcing King Emmanuel to yield. Mussolini himself went before the King, wearing his black shirt and keeping a pistol swinging from his hip.

Taking the title Il Duce, the leader, Mussolini promised that the Fascist black shirts, advocates of force, either would get the government quickly or would seize it at the expense of the "miserable dominant class."

He was then only 38, a strong, vigorous man. Behind him was a long record as a socialist editor and agitator. He was the forerunner from whom Hitler and various other imitators borrowed the ideas for Fascist forms of the corporative state.

Mussolini was born July 29, 1883, at Dovia Di Predappio, a village in northern Italia, where his mother was a school teacher and his father, Alessandro, a blacksmith. His father named him Benito Juarez after the Mexican revolutionary.

Brawling and various escapades interrupted his schooling. However, he was educated enough to become a teacher before he started bumming his way through Europe. He was arrested as a Socialist agitator when he came back to his home town and fomented a farm strike.

His wife, Donna Rachele, of Forli, lived in obscurity. She bore her husband five children.

Teamed With Hitler

Street brawling characterized the rise of Fascism. Unrest was rampant in Italy. At its height, the march on Rome occurred. With an amazing vigor that infected all the country, Mussolini set out to remake Italy.

Climax of this period came when he started to work with Hitler, set out to expand the Italian Empire and eventually conquered Ethiopia in 1936 in defiance of the League of Nations and Great Britain.

After Hitler forced the second World War on the world in 1939, Mussolini hung back until France was dying before Hitler's Nazi legions. Mussolini ordered Italian troops into the French Riviera on June 10, 1940.

Mussolini's present health was not known but he was believed to be failing. Recent pictures showed him losing weight although for years he has been the most active of the Fascists and forced his followers into feats of strength to prove themselves. He reportedly shunned liquor.

Many times assassins have tried to kill him. Once a bullet grazed his nose. Another time a bomb exploded outside his automobile. He boasted of his allegedly charmed life.

THE BIG "I AM"—President Roosevelt's April, 1939, proposal for a ten-year peace pledge prompted sneers and ridicule from the Premier of Italy. Here he is answering President's appeal.

IN MAY, 1938—It was temporarily correct to say: "The Mighty Mussolini visits the Mighty Hitler in Germany." Only five short years ago. Axis partners shown on Mussolini's visit to Germany.

TAKEN INTO CAMP—By 1942, Mussolini was merely a sounding board for Hitler. "I am confident of the outcome in Russia," he echoed. And at the same time he promised stronger air raid shelters for Italy. Candid camera caught Duce's sound and fury.

LATE IN 1938—The Chanticleer of Italy posed as a great, big human Peace Dove, yearning to have its own way in the world. In full regalia, with many medals on breast, he shouts his plans for peace—his peace.

DUCE'S OUSTER FORECASTS AXIS DOOM—HOOVER

Handwriting on Wall Looms for Hitler, Says Aussie Chief

By United Press

Persons in all walks of life today hailed the ouster of Mussolini as the beginning of the end for Italy and a definite sign that the Axis structure is crumbling.

Comment included:

Former President Hoover: The downfall of one of the world's greatest persecutors will give heart to every persecuted man and woman in the Axis-occupied world and it is the handwriting on the wall for his colleagues.

Vice President Wallace: Surely it won't be long now as far as Italy is concerned.

Mayor LaGuardia: I anticipate the complete capitulation of Italy within the next few days. He (Mussolini) will go down in history as the betrayer of Italy.

Prime Minister John Curtin of Australia: The repercussions on occupied countries cannot be overstated. Hitler sees in the fate of his ally the handwriting on the wall for himself.

Foreign Minister Ezequiel Padilla of Mexico: The machinery of the Axis is breaking up.

Count Carlo Sforza, Foreign Minister of Italy before the rise of Fascism: Mussolini's end is a happy event for the political, moral and international future of Europe.

Attorney General Francis Biddle: It looks like the first evidence of the internal breaking up of Italy.

War Manpower Commissioner Paul V. McNutt: The action would indicate the end of the fascist regime.

Italians Here Elated At Mussolini's Ouster

They Greet News Quietly as Manhattan's Mulberry St. Area Stages Demonstration

Italian-Americans in Brooklyn are taking the ousting of Mussolini quietly, although they were very happy about it and satisfied that Italy's part in the war would soon be over.

Police reported no demonstrations of any kind such as the impromptu block parties and parades which took place along Mulberry St. in Manhattan.

Mayor Warns Italians

With the knowledge that the present government under Marshal Badoglio has stated it would continue the war, Mayor LaGuardia warned the Italian people abroad in a special broadcast beamed to them last night that until the Fascist party is tossed out, the United States and Great Britain will not stop fighting Italy.

In an earlier statement the Mayor had said that Italy would capitulate in a few days and that the Badoglio proclamation that his government would keep up the fight should not be taken seriously.

The Mulberry St. celebrations included rounds of free drinks and triumphant cries of "Italia e salvado"—"Italy is saved." Elsewhere, from Harlem to the crowded tenements of the lower East Side, there was also general elation.

Photographers Tour Areas

Much of the feeling about the war was given impetus by the touring of news photographers in the Italian districts. It became quiet later on as the residents, many of whom have sons in the American fighting forces, learned that the Italians were keeping up the struggle.

Count Carlo Sforza, who was Foreign Minister of Italy before Mussolini came to power, echoed the theme of Mayor LaGuardia's propaganda broadcast.

"From the national Italian point of view," he said, "the Italian nation will judge the Badoglio cabinet according to what it is going to do at once."

He was pleased with the Italian dictator's downfall, calling it a "happy event for the political, moral and international future of Italy." The count claimed that Mussolini's end came as a direct result of the bombing of Rome.

Toscanini Ovation

A thunderous ovation was given Arturo Toscanini as the world-famous conductor mounted the podium last night to conduct a special war bond concert of the NBC Summer Symphony Orchestra. Toscanini, an avowed enemy of Mussolini, left his homeland because of his hatred for Fascism, which he didn't hide.

From the Italian press came comments of satisfaction. Generoso Pope, publisher of Il Progresso, in an editorial published today, called Il Duce's resignation the "logical and inevitable consequence of his betrayal of the Italian people."

One of the wildest demonstrations occurred at an anti-Fascist rally at Cooper Union, Astor Place and Cooper Square, when Representative Vito Marcantonio announced the news. Instantly the place became a bedlam with the audience putting up their fingers in the V salute.

8 U. S. CITIZENS INDICTED AS AXIS PROPAGANDISTS

Constance Drexel, Jane Anderson Named On Treason Charges

Washington, July 26 (U.P.)—Eight United States citizens who have been broadcasting Nazi and Fascist propaganda from Germany and Italy were indicted by a Federal grand jury today on a charge of treason.

Named in the indictment under the treason statute which carries a maximum penalty of death, were:

Frederick Wilhelm Kaltenbach, 48, formerly of Dubuque, Ia.; Robert Henry Best, 47, formerly of Sumter, S. C.; Ezra Pound, 57, formerly of New York; Douglas Chandler, 54, formerly of Baltimore; Edward Leo Delaney, 57, formerly of Olney, Ill.; Constance Drexel, 48, formerly of Philadelphia; Jane Anderson, 50, formerly of Atlanta, Ga., and Max Oscar Otto Koischwitz, 41, formerly of New York.

Attorney General Biddle, in announcing the indictments, said the grand jury's action "reaffirms the fact that the United States will not tolerate traitors either at home or abroad."

Betrayed Fellow Citizens

He said that it is the intention of the Justice Department to bring these people, when they are apprehended, to trial "before a jury of their fellow citizens, whom they are charged with betraying."

Miss Anderson is the ex-wife of Deems Taylor, music critic. After years of obscurity she rose to sudden prominence when Spanish Loyalists sentence her to death in 1938 for espionage.

Chandler formerly served as a columnist for the Baltimore Sunday American.

Miss Drexel traveled widely as a news correspondent and in 1937 worked on a WPA writers' project.

Delaney was formerly a bit-part actor.

Koischwitz served on the faculties of Columbia University and Hunter College, N. Y.

Kaltenbach was known as the American counterpart in Berlin of the British "Lord Haw-Haw."

Best was educated at Wofford College and Columbia University where he won a Pulitzer scholarship for study in Europe. He was a correspondent for the United Press until shortly before the United States entered the war.

Pound for a few years after the first World War enjoyed limited popularity as a poet.

Dinner Arranged To Honor Tilyou

Tribute will be paid to George C. Tilyou, retiring Kings County administrator of the War Price and Rationing Board at a dinner on the Marine Roof of the Hotel Bossert next Monday night.

Mr. Tilyou, whose resignation became effective Saturday, was the first borough administrator, and has seen the organization grow until it now has seven branches with rationing powers over 2,750,000 Brooklynites. He is succeeded by William Jagger, who was his assistant.

The dinner committee is under the chairmanship of William J. Grace.

Arkwright Resigns As Bar President

George A. Arkwright, who has been made Public Service Commissioner by Governor Dewey, has resigned as president of the Brooklyn Bar Association.

At a special meeting of the board of trustees of the association Hunter L. Delatour was advanced from first vice president to president. Mr. Delatour, a resident of Great Neck, is also the president of the Nassau County Bar Association. He had been a vice president of the Brooklyn Bar Association for four years and was chairman of its grievance committee. He will hold his new post as president until next June.

At the same meeting Sydney Strongin became first vice president, Walter Bruchhausen moved up to second vice president and Julius Applebaum was elected third vice president. Martin H. Weyrauch was elected to fill a vacancy as trustee for a year.

Free Show for Children

Century's Tivoli Theater will present a special Shangri-La show on Thursday. All children under 16 purchasing one dollar's worth of war stamps will be admitted free from noon until 3:30 p.m.

Probe Delays Trial of 6 Aides In Revenue Office

Employes Are Charged With Taking Fees for Helping Taxpayers

The cases of the six employes of the Brooklyn office of the Collector of Internal Revenue, 210 Livingston St., who were arrested at various times on charges of unlawfully accepting "fees" to help income tax payers with their returns, are awaiting final reports from the intelligence unit of the Treasury Department, Federal officials stated today in answer to questions about the delay in bringing the men to trial.

"As soon as the investigation is finished and the reports are filed here, we will be able to proceed," said United States Attorney Harold M. Kennedy.

Two of the men, Joseph Bogats of 3401 Avenue T, principal auditor of the collector's office, and Archie N. Maslow of 295-A Pulaski St., a senior auditor, were arrested at the Livingston St. office on March 13, while thousands of persons stood in line to pay their income taxes.

Andrew J. Hurley, a special agent of the Intelligence Unit, charged that the two had accepted a $200 gratuity the day before.

Richard Macaluso of 475 Suydam St., Max J. Marder of 1586 E. 22d St., Joseph P. Loftus of 134 Stuart Ave., Valley Stream; Richard Macaluso of 475 Suydam St., deputy collectors, and John Doherty, assistant chief of the auditing division, 2404 Ditmars St., Long Island City, were arrested and arraigned in April. All entered not guilty pleas.

Lana's Day-Old Daughter Rallies After Transfusion

Hollywood, July 26 (U.P.)—The day-old daughter of Lana Turner has reacted favorably to a blood transfusion for an anemic condition, the film star's physician reported today.

The 7 pound 14 ounce baby girl was born yesterday at Presbyterian Hospital and then was transferred to Children's Hospital. Anemia is rare in new-born infants. Miss Turner's condition was good.

Anything to Be Helpful

Napa, Cal. (U.P.)—The local police like to be courteous and helpful to the armed forces, so they are whistling for a cat. The wife of an army officer in a small town in Washington advised them that while shopping in Napa her pet cat, Perry, had gone AWOL. Fortunately, she explained, they only had to whistle the same as to a dog and the cat would jump into their automobile. They are still whistling.

Attorney Brands Hospital Union's Fight Audacious

Recalls Court Action Enjoining Strikers —Says Same Law Rules

"It seems to me to be a new piece of audacity," commented Benjamin C. Ribman, attorney, today, referring to the latest attempts to unionize hospitals. Mr. Ribman fought the 1937 strike activities of a union on behalf of the Jewish Hospital of Brooklyn and won an injunction signed by Supreme Court Justice Albert Conway, now on the bench of the Court of Appeals.

"The law is the same now as it was then," said Mr. Ribman. "Justice Conway's injunction was based on the plain provision that hospitals, charitable and religious institutions not conducted for profit are exempt from the little Wagner act, which governs litigation in labor disputes.

"I am at a loss to understand how the disputes were certified to the War Labor Board by the United States Conciliation Service. The union in the Jewish Hospital case lost again in the Appellate Division and then went out of business, and it is my belief that the latest attempt in Brooklyn should fail."

The hospitals that have been requested to appear before the War Labor Board or file briefs are Israel Zion, Beth El and Beth Moses of Brooklyn and Beth Israel of Manhattan. Local 444 of the State, County and Municipal Workers of America, C. I. O., filed complaints "on behalf of the employes."

Serves 720,000,000 Cups Of Coffee a Year in Capital

The catering organization in Washington, D. C., which serves meals in Government building cafeterias dispenses 720,000,000 paper cupfuls of coffee a year. The organization, defined as Government-controlled and called the Welfare and Recreational Association of Public Buildings and Grounds, is the world's largest food caterer and the largest user of paper cups and plates.

'Farm Front' Heroines

Erie, Pa. (U.P.)—For distinguished service on the "farm front," Eleanor and Cynthia Lane of Waterford were admitted to the Erie Times Legion of Honor. To relieve their father of a "hired man" shortage they aided in the harvest of 90 tons of hay, picked half a ton of cherries and a quantity of strawberries last Summer. Between "field hours" they gardened, drove horses and milked cows.

Isn't Seeking State Post, Says Steingut

Assembly Minority Leader Irwin Steingut, who holds the Democratic leadership of Brooklyn's 18th A. D., put the damper today on reports suggesting that he was seeking the Democratic nomination for Lieutenant Governor.

"I don't know a thing about it and I haven't spoken to a soul about it," he declared.

The reports were news also to Frank V. Kelly, Democratic county leader. He said there had been no meeting of the Democratic leaders to consider candidates.

The consensus among the Democrats is that a special election must be held in the Fall to fill the vacancy caused by the death of Lieutenant Governor Thomas W. Wallace, Republican.

Farley on West Coast; Confines Talk to War

Los Angeles, July 26 (U.P.)—Former Postmaster General James A. Farley, here on a three-day visit, refused to talk politics today but waxed enthusiastic over the future of the war.

"Voters aren't interested in politics now; they're interested in the war," said the former chairman of the Democratic National Committee. Farley foresaw the weakening of Germany through lowered civilian morale and said he was confident the Allies have plans to prevent the Japanese from keeping their acquired Pacific bases.

DORIS TO SHED MATE, ALSO JERSEY TAXES BY RENO RESIDENCE

Reno, July 26 (U.P.)—Doris Duke Cromwell, the wealthiest woman in the world, will establish permanent residence here so she can divorce James H. R. Cromwell, the former United States Minister to Canada.

The contemplated divorce, however, is only incidental, she said. Because of New Jersey's high State income tax, she can no longer make her home there, the tobacco heiress complained. And because of the war she is unable to make use of her $500,000 "little grass shack" in Hawaii.

Mrs. Cromwell arrived yesterday with a baggage car of effects, which included three horses, a shepherd dog and an automobile.

CHAMP FAT SAVER—Mrs. Mae Hambel of 2363 E. 75th St., who gained nation-wide fame last Winter when she appeared at the Brooklyn Salvage Committee's headquarters with 55 pounds of waste fat saved entirely in her own kitchen, is now headed for a new record.

Stories of Brooklyn Men and Women in U. S. War Service

Your Wartime Problems

By RICHARD HART

Company Clerk and Mess Sergeant Best Friends of a Soldier

Take it from an old army sergeant, the two best friends an enlisted man can have are (1) the company clerk and (2) the mess sergeant.

What a mistake the new recruit makes when he highhats the "lowly" company clerk as he fills in his service record. Often he is a non-military looking person with a shallow chest and a pale countenance, but his power in the outfit should never be underestimated. A friendly acquaintance with him is likely to be profitable—particularly for a soldier who wants to succeed. He sees all the recent army regulations, knows what opportunities for special training are popping and he often wields no small power in the granting of furloughs, leaves and passes.

Somebody ought to write a saga about this unsung hero of every war—the company clerk. He often works far into the night to get the allotment or insurance report out. If Uncle Sam operated on the Wages and Hours Act, he would earn a fortune in overtime. It is no fun to type out thousands of other fellows furlough papers, when you are often regarded as "too necessary" to get one for yourself. And a company clerk rarely can call his off time his own, particularly if the C. O. has a habit of coming back to the company office after dinner.

THE LAST MAN

The company clerk, being last in line, gets most of the blame for any inefficiency that crops up. The outfit thinks he is responsible when the allotment checks or insurance notifications are tardy. The officers blame him for the non-arrival of their travel orders or promotions.

YE MESS SERGEANT

Second unto the company clerk as a valuable friend is the mess sergeant. He can be of great value to any hungry man and his value increases precipitously when the outfit moves overseas. If he likes you he will want you to drop in late in the evening to sample the pies he is baking for tomorrow's dinner. If he dislikes you, you are liable to find yourself peeling onions, if ever you are assigned to K. P.

ASIDES TO READERS

To Mrs. A. S. Don't worry your pretty head about inequalities of rank or opportunity in the service. This is one of the hardships every one endures in the service.

If you have a problem write to Richard Hart, care of this newspaper. A stamped, addressed envelope will bring a personal reply.

On the Home Front

CD U.S.A. Bonds Knitting AIR WARDENS YMCA FIRST AID Flag War Stamps CORPS Blood Donors USO

Queens Village Legion Seeks Records for Men in Service

Queens Village Post of the American Legion is again conducting a drive to collect records for men in the armed forces. Various home front groups in the vicinity are aiding the campaign.

Legionnaires will embark on a house-to-house canvas Sunday, starting from headquarters at 214-59 Jamaica Ave. William C. Beinbrick of St. Albans is chairman.

A new home nursing class which will start Aug. 5 at 7 Hanson Place has been announced by Mrs. William L. Wolfson, chairman of home nursing of the Brooklyn Red Cross. There will be 15 two-hour sessions on Monday and Thursday nights.

The course will be conducted by Mrs. Edna M. Nilssen, a registered nurse.

Admiral Charles P. Plunkett Post, American Legion, will unveil an honor roll of members and sons and daughters of members in the armed forces Aug. 6 at 230 Adelphi St.

A gold star mother will dedicate the scroll in the presence of several Legion officials. William A. Reimann is chairman of the committee in charge.

The first anniversary of the Greenpoint Patriotic Organization will be observed at a dance Saturday night at Leviton's Ballroom, Diamond and Calyer Sts.

Veteran, civic, patriotic and political groups in the area have received invitations to be represented. Proceeds will be used for induction parties to draftees.

The Civilian Defense Volunteer Office of the 64th Precinct is pressing a salvage drive for brass, copper, bronze, tin cans and rags.

Pickups can be arranged by contacting the office at 551 86th St., according to Patrick M. Coyne, salvage chairman. Churches and social organizations in the area have been asked to co-operate.

A parade and street rally to send a medical field unit to the Red Army in the name of the late Master Sgt. Meyer Levin will be held Sunday at Mermaid Ave. and W. 31st St., Coney Island.

Air raid wardens of the area will march through the Coney Island streets. The women's division of the local chapter of the American Jewish Congress is sponsoring the event.

Believes in Doing

Burbank, Cal. (U.P.)—Mrs. William Bisset, chairman of the Burbank Red Cross Mothers Corps, believes in setting the shining example. She has one son in the navy and beginning immediately after Pearl Harbor she has given a blood donation every three months until she now has a gallon to her credit.

WAR ENCYCLOPEDIA
WEAPONS

HAND GRENADE
EFFECTIVE BURSTING RADIUS IS ABOUT 30 YARDS. BEST USED AGAINST ENEMY 30 TO 45 YDS. FROM THROWER. SHOULD BE THROWN FROM PROTECTIVE COVER

LETTER OUT

1. Bygone		Letter Out for hard black wood.
2. Chapelry		Letter Out and it's moralizing.
3. Caseous		Letter Out for reasons.
4. Brigades		Letter Out and you shorten it.
5. Comanches		Letter Out and they used to drive.

Remove one letter from each word and rearrange to spell the word called for in the last column. Print the letter in center column opposite the word from which you have removed it. If you have "Lettered-Out" correctly **"it will shine."**

Answer on Page 15

DRAFTIE — By Paul Fogarty

Mr. and Mrs. Joseph Schacher of 322 7th Ave. have four sons in the service: Philip and Samuel, who are stationed in this country, and two others serving overseas.

Recent winner of wings and commission at the army air force navigation school, Selman Field, Fla., La., is Herbert Brill of 289 Empire Boulevard.

Recently wounded in the Aleutian area, Pvt. William J. Moin of 1496 E. 45th St. has two little daughters and a son at home. They are Patricia Ann, 9; Florence Rita, 5, and William Robert, 7.

Interviewed Sunday on the BBC weekly shortwave program to America was the son of Mr. and Mrs. Weisner of 145 Penn St.

Cadet Benedict Intanato of 8671 24th St. is now a student at Butler University, Indianapolis.

R. H. Thomas — W. R. Grandely

Richard H. Thomas of 472 41st St. was commissioned an ensign in the Naval Reserve upon completion of the flight training course at Pensacola, Fla. William R. Gandely of 1568 Bergen St. was commissioned a second lieutenant in the marine corps following completion of training at Pensacola.

Pvt. Kenneth Hurwitz of Brooklyn, a graduate of Erasmus Hall High School, is completing his basic training at Camp Eustis, Va.

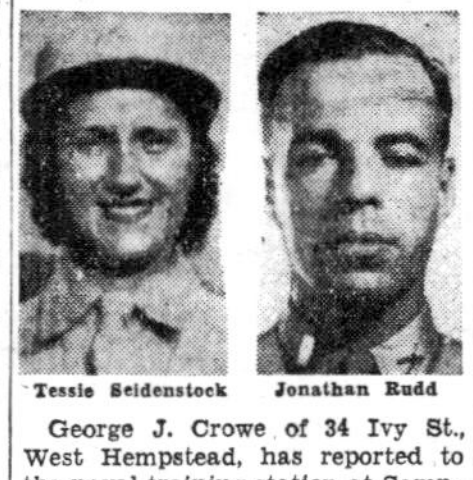

Tessie Seidenstock — Jonathan Rudd

George J. Crowe of 34 Ivy St., West Hempstead, has reported to the naval training station at Sampson, N.Y.

Recent winner of a Purple Heart, Peter F. Provenzale of 5019 Avenue I, has been promoted to first lieutenant. He is one of five brothers in the service.

Tessie Seidenstock, a Wac, was given a welcome home party on her first furlough from Daytona Beach, Fla. Jonathan Rudd of 806 Foster Ave. has been commissioned a second lieutenant at Fort Monroe, Va.

Nathan Goldstein — J. J. Zienkowicz

Nathan Goldstein, seaman first class, who resides at 1606 51st St., is in the South Pacific. Joseph J. Zienkowicz of 61 Sutton St. has been commissioned an ensign in the Naval Reserve at Corpus Christi, Texas.

Another group of brothers serving en masse are the four sons of Mrs. Rose DeLema of 34 Tompkins Place. Pvt. Mario, 23, is in the infantry at Camp Phillips; Pvt. Joseph, 23, is a marine at Parris Island, S. C.; Pvt. Nick, 25, is stationed at Fort Dix, N. J., and Pfc. Pasquale, 26, is overseas.

Stationed at Camp Edwards, Mass., is Pvt. Anthony A. Corroa of 1884 W. 6th St. He is one of four cousins serving in the armed forces.

MORE COMBAT NAVIGATORS—At graduation exercises at Hondo and San Marcos, Texas, aerial navigation training bases, these young men received their wings. They are, left to right, front row, Irving H. Fox of 551 Bushwick Ave., Anthony J. Laura of 1948 W. 10th St., Michael A. Birbiglia of 446 Monroe St. and David Barer of 1140 Blake Ave. In the second row, Nathan F. Abramowitz of 220 Highland Boulevard, Samuel Korbelak of 136 North 8th St., John J. Klokis of 393 South 2d St. and Sidney Ritterman of 428 E. 46th St.

R. J. Emerson — William Kalaher

Corp. Raymond J. Emerson of 3219 Clarendon Road has returned to Camp Hood, Texas, after a furlough. His brother Edward is a staff sergeant in the Panama Canal Zone. William Kalaher of 121 Rogers Ave. has been made a lance corporal at Fort Knox, Ky.

Another Erasmus alumnus now serving with the armed forces is Pvt. Michael Grande, who has just returned to Camp McQuade, Cal., after spending a ten-day furlough with his family.

Sidney Levine — R. W. Lau

Sgt. Sidney Levine of 7311 17th Ave. has completed training as an aerial gunner at Wendover air base, Utah. Robert W. Lau of 368 E. 32d St., now serving in the army's finance department at Duke University, N. C., has been advanced to the rank of second lieutenant.

Bernard Sobersohn of 2016 74th St. is now a member of the military police at Fort Niagara, N. Y.

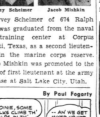

Harvey Scheimer — Jacob Mishkin

Harvey Scheimer of 674 Ralph Ave. was graduated from the naval air training center at Corpus Christi, Texas, as a second lieutenant in the marine corps reserve. Jacob Mishkin was promoted to the rank of first lieutenant at the army air base at Salt Lake City, Utah.

ATTENTION, PLEASE!

Sorry, but no photos used in the Home Front or Fighting Men columns can be returned. However, news and pictures of local men and women in service or active in Civilian Defense on the home front will be welcomed by the Brooklyn Eagle. Such news should be addressed to either Fighting Men Editor or Home Front Editor, Brooklyn Eagle, Johnson and Adams Sts., Brooklyn.

David Pinnelas — Harold Spilko

David Pinnelas of 4232 Bedford Ave. and Harold Spilko of 1061 Glenmore Ave. have been promoted to the rank of second lieutenant, bombardier, at the Victorville, Col., army air field.

Rosalie Benedetto of 313 72d St., recently sworn into the marines, has left home to begin training at Camp Lejeune, N. C.

P. R. Spennato — A. W. Stillwell

P. R. Spennato of 1621 W. 4th St. and Alfred W. Stillwell of 354 Bay Ridge Parkway received navigator wings at San Marcos, Texas.

Pvt. Edward Francis Brennan of 63 Dean St., who was inducted into the army in March, has completed training at Camp Wheeler, Ga. His brother, Harold Francis, is in Hawaii and another brother, Joseph, is stationed at Camp Campbell, Ky.

D. A. Rosmarin — L. L. Suttenberg

Daniel A. Rosmarin of 2111 Albemarle Road and Lawrence L. Suttenberg of 2150 75th St. have been appointed second lieutenants in the army finance department at Duke University, N. C.

Donald J. Hallameyer of 2604 Newkirk Ave. has been home on furlough from Pensacola, Fla., where he received his wings and was commissioned second lieutenant in the marine air corps.

Lt. William F. Helfert of 676 Halsey St. is home on a 13-day leave from his Florida training base.

THESE WOMEN!

By d'Alessio

"Our garden is doing quite well by us—we have chicken from it every day."

LIKE FATHER . . . is Aviation Cadet Clinton D. Burdick of 19 Montgomery Place, who expects to top his dad's first World War record of downing nine planes. The 19-year-old son of Howard Burdick, holder of the Distinguished Service Cross and the British Flying Cross, is training for combat pilot duty at the San Antonio Aviation Cadet center.

PETRILLO TO SEND ORCHESTRAS ON TOURS AT ROOSEVELT REQUEST

James C. Petrillo, president of the American Federation of Musicians, will send well-known symphony orchestras on road tours "because President Roosevelt is very much concerned" about the dearth of first class music for small towns.

Petrillo said today he conferred at the White House on the matter last December and the Federation appropriated $250,000 for full expenses. He said another $250,000 had been authorized if needed.

No orchestras have been notified of the plan, Petrillo said. Details of their one-night stands will be worked out by local unions, he said. The plan is to be put in operation next week.

Asked if the President said anything about the recording ban at the December conference, Petrillo answered:

"He didn't say a word, not one word about it—but I sure thought beforehand I was going to hear about it."

Petrillo said the concerts would be free.

Japs List Rubber Runway

By United Press

Tokio radio, quoting a dispatch from Kuching, North Borneo, said Wednesday that a rubber runway for a Borneo airfield had been completed. The broadcast, recorded by United Press at San Francisco, said that the rubber takeoff surface was "very successful," as it is unaffected by the heavy Borneo rains.

1852-B

SIMPLE, SMART

A two-piece that is as close to perfection as any style ever was. Trim, wonderfully fitting and wearable everywhere.

Barbara Bell Pattern No. 1852-B designed for sizes 34, 36, 38, 40, 42, 44, 46 and 48. Size 36 short sleeves requires 4⅛ yards 39-inch material.

For this attractive pattern send 15 cents, plus 1 cent for postage, in coins with your name, address, pattern number and size wanted to Barbara Bell, Brooklyn Eagle, Post Office Box 75, Station O, Manhattan 11, N. Y. Allow 10 days for delivery.

BUY U. S. WAR BONDS AND SAVINGS STAMPS

Uncle Ray's Corner

For Boys and Girls

Russians Used Pictures to Change Ways of Uzbeks

Yesterday we were speaking about the voyage of the Chelyuskin across the Arctic Ocean. After sailing from European Russia, it had almost reached Bering Strait when it was caught in heavy pack ice. Later it sank, and the 128 persons aboard were left on the ice in the East Siberian Sea.

Help came in the form of airplanes. A landing space was cleared in the pack ice, and the explorers were taken back to Russia by air.

The leader of the exploring party later made a statement about the northern parts of what is commonly known as "Siberia." Here is a shortened account of what he said before the present war started:

"We Russians are building towns and ports in the Arctic. We are planting vegetables and setting up schools and hospitals in what the world used to look upon as a frozen waste.

"The cold need not keep people from living in this region. It seldom is colder than 40 below zero in the Arctic Winter, and it gets that cold even in the Ukraine.

"The Summer is cool and short, but there is sunshine which lasts 'day and night' and this helps the growth of plants. Beautiful flowers, such as violets and forget-me-nots, grow in the Arctic.

Young Russian woman painting comic picture of a smoker in Uzbek town.

"Gold, silver, oil and coal exist under the frozen surface, and we are going to get those valuable minerals. People in our Arctic towns raise tomatoes, cucumbers, radishes and other vegetables in hothouses, and we are testing crops of wheat and oats.

"Our new Arctic towns grow fast. One of them, named Igarka, has 12,000 people in Winter and a Summer population of 20,000. They have theaters, dance halls, kindergartens and clubs. Airplanes provide them with fast transport."

Besides using land inside the Arctic Circle, the Russians have done a great deal to educate people elsewhere in Russia-in-Asia. These people are of many types and speak many languages. Some of them are "nomads." They live first in one place, then in another. They move about so their livestock can have new grazing lands.

From time to time, "campaigns" have been carried out to change certain customs. One tribe, for example, used more tobacco than was usual elsewhere. A picture campaign was started to show these people, known as Uzbeks, the harm which could come from smoking.

For TRAVEL section of your scrapbook.)

Uncle Ray

Tomorrow: Mexico's Smoking Mountain.

SUBMARINE WARFARE is the title of an illustrated leaflet. It contains 10 pictures by Frank C Pape and several hundred words of text by Uncle Ray. To obtain a copy send a self-addressed envelope bearing a three-cent stamp to Uncle Ray in care of this newspaper.

THE SCREEN

By Jane Corby

'This Is the Army,' Made Into Great Film, Has First Showing at Hollywood Theater

Wait till YOU see "This Is the Army" in Technicolor at the Hollywood Theater. You'll say it's a great show. You can say that again, too. It's a double-great show. first, because it's magnificent entertainment; second, because it's a fine democratic enterprise, the joint ... of American soldiers, Amer... best-loved songwriter, and ... of America's most important film companies, with the group of talented civilians working under its direction, all without salary or recompense of any kind, all working, mind you, simply for the good of the common cause. Is that a leaf right out of American democracy's book or is it?

The picture company to which the country is indebted for the film version of the soldier show, "This Is the Army," is Warner Bros. The soldiers who take part are the 350 who appeared in the original stage production. The cause for which picture producers, soldiers and civilians worked together in making the film, "This Is the Army," and to which the public may contribute simply by seeing the show, is Army Emergency Relief. All the profits of the film will go to this fund, and nobody, from Jack L. Warner, executive producer of the studio, and Hal B. Wallis, associated with him in the production, from Michael Curtiz, who directed the film with verve, and Casey Robinson and Capt. Claude Binyon, who wrote the script for the film version, and Kate Smith, who sings "God Bless America," to Joe Louis, who has a part in one of the production numbers and the other 349 soldiers who sing and dance and do acrobatics, to Irving Berlin, who wrote the music and lyrics and has given the last two years almost entirely to this show, nobody gets paid.

No empty gesture is this waiving of profits, either. Warner Bros. obtained the rights to the soldier show on the afternoon of the premiere of the stage version on July 4, a year ago, when Major Albert Warner turned over to Army Emergency Relief a check for $250,000 as an advance payment on a contract by which the company would receive 50 percent of the profits of the film. Three weeks later the Warner Brothers tore up their contract and drew up a new one, giving all profits from the film to Army Emergency Relief, thereby cutting themselves out of what they estimate as a probable profit of several million dollars.

The film version of "This Is the Army" presents the numbers performed in the stage version during its New York and coast-to-coast tour, with additional numbers, plus a story in which civilian players as well as army personnel take part. The 350 soldiers who appeared in the stage production fill their original parts in the picture, with bounce and vigor and entirely captivating enthusiasm.

Sgt. John Prince Mendes is there with the magic, in the number called "A Military Vaudeville Show," just as in the original, and so is the Allon Trio, the acrobatic act that went into the army so all three members could be together. The "ladies" of the chorus are the howl of the performance. Sgt. Alan Manson impersonates Jane Cowl and brings down the house. In general content, the film version is the same as the stage show, but there have been additions, a few substitutions, new songs have been added and a story has been superimposed on the original series of production numbers.

This story doesn't amount to so very much. As "This Is the Army," the stage show, is Irving Berlin's sequel to his World War I soldier show, "Yip, Yip, Yaphank," the film version of the soldier show of World War II is told in terms of a father-son story. Three buddies of World War I, played by George Murphy, Charles Butterworth and George Tobias, help put over "Yip, Yip, Yaphank," sail overseas, return from France after the war, and live to see the sons of two of them in the World War II army, and taking part in the new soldier show. Lt. Ronald Reagan, playing the son of George Murphy, is in love with Joan Leslie, in the role of the daughter of Charles Butterworth, but wants to wait till the war is over before marrying her. The love story, which ends in a marriage ceremony in the alley back of the theater where these new soldiers are giving their final performance before leaving for overseas, is the thread which holds the film story together.

Any way you look at it, "This Is the Army" is a big production. Applause came loud and frequently at the premiere and nobody got a bigger hand than Irving Berlin singing his own "Oh, How I Hate to Get Up in the Morning." As for "This Is the Army, Mr. Jones," the way that soldier chorus sings it makes it a song that keeps humming round in your head. "This Is the Army" is a great show—but we said that. Well, we're saying it again.

'THIS IS THE ARMY'

Warner Bros. picture, in Technicolor, produced by Jack L. Warner and Hal B. Wallis for Army Emergency Relief. Directed by Michael Curtiz, from a screen play by Casey Robinson and Capt. Claude Binyon, based on the stage show, Irving Berlin's "This Is the Army." Presented at the Hollywood Theater.

The Cast

Jerry Jones	George Murphy
Eileen Dibble	Joan Leslie
Maxie Twardofsky	George Tobias
Sgt. McGhee	Alan Hale
Eddie Dibble	Charles Butterworth
Mrs. Davidson	Dolores Costello
Rose Dibble	Una Merkel
Major Davidson	Stanley Ridges
Ethel	Rosemary De Camp
Mrs. O'Brien	Ruth Donnelly
Mrs. Nelson	Dorothy Paterson
Cafe Singer	Frances Langford
Singer	Gertrude Nieson
Kate Smith	Kate Smith
Mrs. Twardofsky	Ilka Gruning
Johnny Jones	Lt. Ronald Reagan
Joe Louis	Sgt. Joe Louis
Tommy	T. Sgt. Tom D'Andrea
Ollie Twardofsky	Sgt. Julie Oshins
Ted Nelson	Sgt. Robt. Shanley
Danny Davidson	Corp. Herbert Anderson

As Soldiers

1st Sgt. Allan Anderson, M. Sgt. Ezra Stone, S. Sgt. James Burrell, Sgt. Rose Elliott, Sgt. Alan Manson, Sgt. John P. Mendes, Sgt. Earl Oxford, Sgt. Philip Truex, Cpl. James MacColl, Cpl. Ralph Magelssen, Cpl. Tileston Perry, Pfc. Joe Cook Jr., Pfc. Larry Weeks, The Allon Trio

LUCILLE BALL takes her press agent, William Gaxton, to task in "Best Foot Forward," film version of the stage musical now at the Astor Theater.

'Wooden Soldiers' on The Music Hall Stage

Radio City Music Hall's 36 Rockettes march down a stairway 36 feet long with exactly 36 steps as the curtain rises on "Parade of the Wooden Soldiers" in the current stage spectacle, "Gala Russe," produced by Leon Leonidoff, and featuring the Don Cossack Chorus directed by Serge Jaroff.

The top step is 20 feet from the stage, and the Rockettes, smartly uniformed and marching with the stiff precision of the wooden soldiers they represent, maintain their world-wide reputation for holding a straight line as they descend.

BUY U. S. WAR BONDS AND SAVINGS STAMPS

MOTION PICTURES

FEATURE FILMS SHOWING TODAY

BAY RIDGE
Electra, 75th St and Third Ave........The Edge of Darkness; also Good Morning, Judge
Harbor, 92d St. and Fourth Ave........China; also My Heart Belongs to Daddy
Stanley, Fifth Ave. and 75th St........Keeper of the Flame; also Two Yanks in Trinidad

BEDFORD
Lincoln, Bedford Ave.-Eastern P'kway....Joy of Living; also Hunted Men
National, 720 Washington Ave..........Edge of Darkness; also Sarong Girl
Rogers, 333 Rogers Ave. PR. 4-2230 ....Air-Cond. Too Many Husbands; also American Empire

BENSONHURST
Colony, 18th Ave.-65th St. BE. 6-2231. Air-Cond. Bucket of Blood; Revolt of the Zombies

BORO PARK
Elton, 43d St. and New Utrecht Ave.....Flight for Freedom; also I Walked With a Zombie

BOROUGH HALL AND DOWNTOWN
Century's Tivoli, Fulton St., Boro Hall..The Desperadoes; also Johnny Doughboy
Duffield, Duffield and Fulton Sts.......This Land Is Mine; also Jitterbugs
Momart, Fulton St. and Rockwell Pl.... Remember the Day; also French Without Tears
St. George Playhouse, 100 Pineapple St. Air-Cond. The Desperadoes; also Three Hearts for Julia
Terminal, Fourth Ave. and Dean St.....Lady From Kentucky; also Newsboys' Home

BRIGHTON BEACH
Oceana, Brighton Beach Ave.-Hoff St...The Moon Is Down; Red Head From Manhattan

BUSHWICK
Empire, Ralph Ave.-B'way, FO. 9-7940. Presenting Lily Mars; Sherlock Holmes in Washington

FLATBUSH
Granada, Church and Nostrand Aves.... China; also My Heart Belongs to Daddy
Leader, Coney Island and Newkirk Aves..This Land Is Mine; also Jitterbugs

EAST FLATBUSH
Avenue D, Avenue D and E. 43d St..... Crash Dive; also Gildersleeve's Bad Day
Rugby, Utica and Church Aves..........Edge of Darkness; also Johnny Doughboy

GERRITSEN BEACH
Graham, 311 Whitney Ave..............Forever and a Day; also Tahiti Honey

PARK SLOPE
Carlton, Flatbush and Seventh Aves.....This Land is Mine; also Jitterbugs
Plaza, Flatbush Ave. and Park Place... Air-Cooled. This Woman Is Mine; also Tight Shoes
Sanders, Prospect Park West-14th St....White Savage; also Wings Over the Pacific
Venus, 1224 Prospect Ave...............Edge of Darkness; also Dixie Dugan

KINGS HIGHWAY
Jewel, Kings Highway at Ocean P'kway ..I Love You Again; The Hound of the Baskervilles

AVENUE U SECTION
Avenue U, Avenue U and E. 16th St....Edge of Darkness; also Swing Your Partner
Traymore, Avenue N and E. 46th St....Edge of Darkness; also Follow the Band

RIDGEWOOD
Colonial, Broadway and Chauncey...... Five Graves to Cairo; Henry Aldrich Gets Glamour
Ridgewood, 1675 Myrtle Ave.......... Five Graves to Cairo; Henry Aldrich Gets Glamour
Rivoli, Myrtle Wilson Aves. GL. 5-0744 Edge of Darkness; also Sarong Girl

SHEEPSHEAD BAY
Sheepshead Th. Sheepshead Rd.-Voorhies Crash Dive; also Gildersleeve's Bad Day

SOUTH BROOKLYN
Sander's Globe, 228 13th St. .... Sun Valley Serenade; also Go West
Minerva, Seventh Ave. and 14th St.....Lucky Jordan; also Lady Bodyguard

Boro Rallies to $3,331,000 Red Cross Drive

★★★★★★★★ SPORTS 7 Wall Street Financial News

BROOKLYN EAGLE

Weather—Strong winds tonight; clear, cold winds tomorrow.

103d Year. No. 58. DAILY & SUNDAY • (Copyright 1944 The Brooklyn Eagle, Inc.) • BROOKLYN, N. Y., WEDNESDAY, MARCH 1, 1944 • Entered at the Brooklyn Post-office as 2d Class Mail Matter • 3 CENTS IN NEW YORK CITY ELSEWHERE 4 CENTS

DRIVE ISOLATES 72,000 JAPS

OUT OF THE BATTLE—In a little while this casualty from the Cassino front will be getting Red Cross care in a hospital back of the lines. But that care cannot continue unless YOU support the Red Cross.

BULGARIA SAID TO ASK FOR TRUCE TERMS

Report Query to U. S., Britain—See Finns Out Of War Within Month

London, March 1 (U.P.)—Potential crackups at both ends of the Nazi satellite front in Europe were indicated today by reports that Finland might be out of the war within a month and that Bulgaria was asking the United States and Britain for armistice terms.

Moscow's confirmation of preliminary moves toward a settlement with Finland, together with a summary of what would be expected of the Finns, led diplomatic quarters to the conclusion that a Soviet-Finnish armistice might be arranged soon.

Usually reliable sources said they had received advices from neutral capitals indicating that Bulgaria was in the process of soliciting America and Britain for armistice terms.

Crisis Is Reported

"Startling developments" in Bulgaria were expected at any time. Reports of Cabinet crises and conferences in Sofia were reaching neutral capitals in a steady stream, informants said.

Bulgarians credited with important political connections were reported in or on the way to Turkey.

The Finnish Parliament in secret session last night tacitly voted full confidence in the government, perhaps even authorized it to accept Moscow's invitation to send a mission to Moscow to negotiate a separate peace.

The favorable action followed a lengthy debate, presumably relating to possible peace terms, a Finnish radio broadcast said.

Moscow Confident of Peace

Moscow, March 1 (U.P.)—Optimism prevailed in Moscow today that Finland would accept Russia's terms for an armistice.

The Soviet offer, much more moderate than had been anticipated, caused considerable surprise and satisfaction in certain quarters in Moscow. They believed that Russia had taken exceptional steps to make it easy for Finland to withdraw from the war and doubted the Finns could find any excuse to reject the terms.

Anzio Allies Shatter Dual German Attack

Infantry, Guns Halt Drive That Threatened To Develop Into Full-Scale Offensive

BULLETIN

Allied Headquarters, Naples, March 1 (U.P.)—Allied infantrymen and the flaming guns of the 5th Army shattered a double-barreled German armored attack on the Anzio front today, halting a drive that had threatened to develop into a full-scale Nazi offensive to wipe out the embattled beachhead.

Allied Headquarters, Naples, March 1 (U.P.)—German armored forces, equipped with radio-directed robot tanks loaded to the turrets with high explosives, struck with gathering force at the Anzio beachhead today in what appeared to be their third major attempt to hurl the 5th Army invaders back into the sea.

Grimly-fighting Allied forces were reported holding firm under every onslaught, but headquarters spokesmen indicated the full weight of the Nazi offensive was just beginning to enter the battle and that the decisive test lay ahead.

(A German high command communique said a "fairly large" Allied battle unit had been encircled southwest of Cisterna during the initial Nazi attack.

British Escape Trap

(Front reports received at Allied headquarters, possibly referring to the same incident, said a British patrol of company strength had effected a deep penetration of the enemy lines in the northern sector of the beachhead and remained there for so long that it was feared lost. The patrol later fought its way back to the Allied lines with a number of prisoners.)

The ten-day lull in the battle for the beachhead ended explosively when waves of German tanks and shock troops swarmed out of the ravines and caves southwest of Aprilia, on the Allied left flank, and broke against a stubborn wall of British infantry and artillery.

The attack followed a day and night of heavy artillery preparation during which the big guns of the Nazi 14th Army raked every corner of the 100-square-mile beachhead and German fighter bombers swooped low over the battle lines to bomb and strafe the Allied trenches.

The Allied infantrymen rose from their trenches to meet the oncoming German assault troops while massed anti-tank guns and field artillery ripped up the Nazi armor, halting the attack in its tracks.

Dies in Capital

Representative T. H. Cullen (Story on Page 15)

YANKS MOP UP ADMIRALTY ISLAND FOE

Captured Los Negros Airfield Aimed Directly At Group's Chief City

Allied Headquarters, Southwest Pacific, March 1 (U.P.)—United States invasion forces, thrusting across the Bismarck Sea to within 610 miles of Truk, have landed in the Admiralty Islands, captured an airdrome and rapidly are extending their beachheads against dwindling resistance, it was announced today.

The landing on tiny Los Negros Island, backed by powerful air and naval bombardment, advanced the American forces nearly 250 miles westward from New Britain and completed the southern prong of a pincers movement on the enemy's big aerial and naval base at Truk.

The penetration also gave the Allies a foothold for further operations against New Guinea, 250 miles to the south and brought the Americans only 1,300 miles from the Philippines.

Swarming ashore in landing boats from U. S. destroyers, dismounted elements from the 1st Cavalry Division took the Japanese defenders by "complete surprise" and quickly captured Momote airfield for a base of operations aimed directly at Lorengau, principal city on the main island of Manus.

Complete Conquest Near

"The enemy's resistance is being rapidly overcome," a communique from Gen. Douglas MacArthur said, indicating that the U. S. troops, which effected the landing Tuesday, were nearing, if they have not already completed, the occupation of Los Negros.

(Tokio radio, admitting the Admiralty landing in a broadcast, claimed "fierce fighting" was under way between Japanese garrisons and American forces which landed from "more than 15 transports.")

Penetration of the Admiraltys, a chain of 160 volcanic coral islands and atolls, virtually completed a strangle hold on the enemy's Southwest Pacific holdings, cutting practically all supply routes for the beleaguered Japanese.

Spokesmen estimated that the new landing, together with the seiz-

Continued on Page 15

Lepke Counsel Asks Writ of Habeas Corpus

If Plea Is Denied, Appeal to Washington May Save Murder Boss

Federal Judge Clarence Galston in Manhattan this afternoon will hear arguments on a writ of habeas corpus sought by J. Bertram Wegman, counsel to Louis (Lepke) Buchalter, scheduled to die tomorrow night in the electric chair at Sing Sing for murder with two henchmen.

If the court grants the writ, intended to give Lepke back to the jurisdiction of the Federal Court, under whose sentence he was serving time for a narcotics violation, the triple execution will be postponed. If the writ is dismissed after argument, Lepke's lawyer will appeal to Washington, which also might result in postponement of the execution.

Wegman's fight is a delaying action. Five times Lepke and the two gunmen have been reprieved. Wegman seeks the habeas writ on the ground that the Federal authorities had no right to surrender Lepke without first pardoning him as he has not finished a 14-year term for narcotics selling.

Wife, Son Visit Him

Lepke's wife, Betty, and his stepson, Harold, 20, visited him today in the death cell at Sing Sing. It was reported from the prison that he was optimistic that another reprieve would be obtained.

Rabbi Joseph Katz, prison chaplain, visited Lepke and remained with him for a half-hour. Lepke's appetite was good, he read the morning newspapers and exercised.

Several visitors also were received by Capone and Weiss. The former had a long talk with the Rev. Bernard Martin, Roman Catholic chaplain.

Joseph Palmer and Vincent Sallami, convicted of killing Detective

Continued on Page 15

Withdraws Complaint After Lawyer Apologizes

Susan Page, a portrait painter, of 115 Minna St., withdrew her complaint against a lawyer after he publicly apologized to her yesterday in Jefferson Market Court, Manhattan. The lawyer, Rudolph R. Loening, was haled into court for having had Miss Sage and her woman companion ejected from a box at a concert in Carnegie Hall. An usher had shown the two into Loening's box by mistake.

SAVE WASTE PAPER—USE THE PHONE

If you are unable to dispose of your waste paper through your regular channel, telephone your borough CDVO-WPB salvage office.

Brooklyn—MAin 5-0061.
Manhattan—MUrray Hill 3-9669.
Bronx—FOrdham 5-1500.
Queens—CLeveland 3-0175.
Richmond—GIbraltar 7-1000.

$3,331,000 Red Cross Drive Launched Here

Banners and Displays Rally Boro's Millions in Campaign

What is it worth to you that your boy overseas shall have blood plasma available when wounded?

Thus asks a Brooklyn leader, Branch Rickey, in the Red Cross drive to raise a $200,000,000 war fund in the nation, $3,331,000 in the borough.

As the drive was officially launched today, there was every indication that to the mothers, fathers, friends and neighbors of

Picture on 1st Page, 2d Section

Brooklyn's 260,000 young men in uniform, the Red Cross service to our men at war was worth far more than any money in the bank—and that the money goal would be raised.

From 1,000 of Brooklyn's tallest buildings, Red Cross banners fluttered; and on streets and rooftops, in subways and in doorways appeared the red cross on white, indicating that Brooklyn's millions were rallying to the Red Cross.

The Red Cross drive started, perhaps significantly, the day after the official conclusion of the Fourth War Loan drive, in which this borough turned in better than 100 percent of every war bond quota set—the overall quota, the corporation sales and sales to individuals.

Three giant Red Cross banners, fluttering against the sky in front of Borough Hall, at Flatbush Ave. Extension and Willoughby St. and at Pitkin and Saratoga Aves., seemed to give the public promise that the Red Cross quota also would be met and bettered.

Displays Aid Drive

Red Cross displays in store windows along Fulton St. and on Flat-

Continued on Page 15

MARKER JUMPS GUN

A workman with more strength than science put Brooklyn two-thirds over the top in the Red Cross drive only a few hours after the campaign started. The indicator in Borough Hall showed that the $2,000,000 mark had been reached. Red Cross officials, hastily adjusting the overoptimistic thermometer, explained the gadget was struck accidentally by a workman.

JURY CHOSEN TO TRY HANCOCK PERJURY CASE

Lie Detector Banned—Defendant's Husband In Front Row Seat

A jury of 11 men and a woman was quickly chosen in Kings County Court today for the trial of Mrs. Edna Hancock, 30, on charges of perjury growing out of the conviction—now reversed—of Murray Goldman of 145 Sumner Ave. for attempted rape.

If convicted, she would face a maximum sentence of five years in jail, $5,000 fine or both.

The Goldman conviction was thrown out after an announcement by County Judge Samuel S. Leibowitz that results of a lie detector test and other evidence had convinced him of the man's innocence, and, obviously referring to that, County Judge Peter J. Brancato, presiding at today's trial, told the assembled panel of jurors and prospective jurors:

"You may have heard or read something about lie detectors. Well, there will be none of that in this case. Lie detector testimony is without any value as evidence. The Court of Appeals has so ruled."

Second Rap at Lie Detector

It was the second judicial pronouncement against the lie detector to be made in the case, County Judge Franklin Taylor having made a similar statement in earlier court proceedings.

During the questioning of jury talesmen, Assistant District Attor-

Continued on Page 15

RANKIN TO FIGHT COMPROMISE VOTE PLAN

Washington, March 1 (U.P.)—Representative John E. Rankin (D., Miss.), leading exponent of State ballots for the soldier vote, declared today he would fight vigorously on the House floor to defeat the compromise Federal-State ballot plan approved by Senate-House conferees.

Rankin was the only one of the ten conferees who opposed the compromise reached after three weeks of discussions. He said it was a threat to the constitutional rights of the States.

Other conferees said the measure was as satisfactory a solution as could be worked out.

QUADS' MOTHER UNWED, SHE INFORMS PRESS

Heanor, Derbyshire, England, March 1 (U.P.)—Nora Carpenter, 23, who gave birth to quadruplets Monday night, told newspapermen today that, contrary to her earlier statement, she is not married.

Miss Carpenter's mother agreed with the correction of her statement. "There is nothing to be gained by hiding the facts and we would rather be honest about it," the mother said.

The maternal grandfather of the two boys and two girls is a miner.

RUSSIANS ENTER PSKOV SUBURBS, NEAR RAILWAY

Drive on Line to South Routs Foe, Puts Ostrov Under Direct Threat

Moscow, March 1 (U.P.) — Soviet armored forces broke into the outskirts of Pskov, invasion key to the Baltic States, today, and in a companion drive turned an enemy retreat into a rout only six miles from the last German-held north-south railway in northern Russia.

The Red Army's double threat to the main defenses guarding Latvia and southern Estonia gave promise of an early battle for the Baltic States themselves.

Front reports said Gen. Markian M. Popov's operations on the approaches to the Pskov-Idritsa-Polotsk railway northwest and west of Novosokolniki rapidly were assuming the character of a rout.

Racing 16 miles down the Porkhov-Ostrov highway, the Russians captured Khrmova, only six mies from the railway and 16 miles from Ostrov itself on the Pskov-Dvinsk trunk line. The advance practically paralyzed the enemy's movements along the Pskov-Polotsk raiway and brought Ostrov under direct threat.

Nazis Abandon Supplies

The Russian advance was so rapid that the Germans were unable to evacute their equipment, instead blowing it up or dumping it into lakes and marshes.

(A London broadcast said the Russians now control all railroads out of Pskov, where the Germans have rushed up reinforcements from the Ruhr.)

Front reports said the Germans were laying down a terrific artillery barrage, blowing up bridges, mining roads and frequently counterattacking in a final effort to save Pskov, but Red armies continued to close in relentlessly on the strategic junction from four sides.

More than 250 additional towns and villages fell to the armies of Gens. Leonid A. Govorov and Markian M. Popov north, northeast, east and southeast of Pskov yesterday.

Abuse Charged In Dewey Probe

Albany, March 1 (U.P.)—Assemblyman Hulan E. Jack and Daniel L. Burrows, New York City Democrats, charged on the floor of the Assembly today that special police conducting Governor Dewey's investigation of Albany County had been hounding, intimidating and abusing" the city's Negro citizenry.

Jack and Burrows said they had conducted an investigation after charges had been made by Sonny Jones, a Negro witness in the investigation, that representatives of Special Prosecutor George F. Monaghan's office "beat him and hung him out of the window o nthe 29th floor of the State Office Building."

"We are ab...utely amazer to learn of such brutal tactics as alleged to have been used, in using duress against innocent individuals who in no way were accused of wrongdoing," they said.

Betty Hutton Finds She Has 3 Cracked Ribs

Hollywood, March 1 (U.P.)—Blond Betty Hutton discovered today she has been walking around a month with three cracked ribs. The Paramount jitterbug was not aware of her injury until X-rays for a pain in the side showed the injury.

Doctors believe the star suffered the injury a month ago when she fell during an acrobatic dance routine for "Incendiary Blonde."

Moffett Hits Oil Waste; Demands Ickes' Ouster

James A. Moffett, former Federal Housing Administrator, today announced that he intends to demand the "resignation or impeachment" of Harold L. Ickes as Petroleum Administrator for wasteful and scandalous handling of the oil situation.

Moffett blasted Ickes on the charge that the Cabinet member was supporting the unnecessary expenditure of vast sums on a pipe line in Arabia, looking ultimately toward the use of oil in the post-war policing of Europe.

"A Senate committee should be appointed," Moffett said, "to determine whether the American taxpayer and public should be called upon to finance what appears to be an unjustified venture in bureaucracy."

Moffett asserted that the Arabian oil in question could be shipped much more cheaply per barrel by tanker and that tankers could do the job now, whereas it would take between 18 months and two years to complete the pipeline.

GRUMET HINTS LAWYER WROTE LONERGAN NOTE

Says Letter Contains Same Words Used in Court by Broderick

Prosecutor Jacob Grumet today inferentially charged that Edward V. Broderick, counsel for Wayne Lonergan, 26-year-old RCAF aircraftsman accused of murdering his pretty heiress wife, had written the controversial letter in which Lonergan is alleged to have renounced his claims to his wife's fortune.

Most of the morning session of the trial was taken up with a discussion of the letter, which Broderick had brought into court Monday and had shown to each talesman as he was questioned.

Court Reverses Decision

Even before questioning of jurors began today, General Sessions Judge John J. Freschi reversed his decision that the letter could be shown to jurors but was not to be made public nor read aloud in the courtroom. He declared that during yesterday's recess contents of the letter had been published in newspapers and that "counsel may as well have read it in open court."

The court, in a new ruling, refused to permit any prospective juror to see or read the letter. Only general questions concerning whether the talesman had heard of it would be allowed, he said.

Grumet dropped the bombshell near the end of the morning session when he expressed doubt that the date of the letter is "the true date" and said he had "serious doubt as to the authorship."

"If Lonergan wrote it, he refers to the Bernheimer-Burton fortune in exactly the same words used by Mr. Broderick in this courtroom Monday," Grumet asserted. "It is a striking similarity that gives us

Continued on Page 15

Sees Merchant Tonnage Of U. S. 3 Times Britain's

London, March 1 (U.P.)—Lord Winster said today that after the war the United States will have 30,000,000 gross tons of merchant shipping, three times that of Britain, and will have the initiative at sea if there is any desire to use it.

Strike Closes Schools

Pittsburgh, March 1 (U.P.)—A strike of 1,000 custodial, shop, storeroom and cafeteria workers in public schools gave a holiday to 82,000 school children today as unheated classrooms forced the closing of all 130 school buildings.

M'Arthur Visits Troops On Los Negros Island

'You Have Performed Magnificently,' He Tells Invaders of Admiralties During Inspection

By WILLIAM B. DICKINSON
(Copyright by United Press)

Aboard General MacArthur's Flying Fortress Over New Guinea, March 1—The American invasion of the Admiralty Islands, another stepping stone on the road to the Philippines and Tokio, was accomplished so quicky and easily that it left a smile of satisfaction on the face of Gen. Douglas MacArthur today as he returned to his base in New Guinea.

The general obviously enjoyed his experience yesterday, when he visited his troops and inspected their positions on Los Negros Island less than eight hours after they landed under Japanese fire and seized Momote airstrip.

The firing from enemy guns started when the first wave of landing boats, in one of which I was riding, reached a point about a mile from the entrance to Hyane harbor.

Capture Airstrip

After the first wave reached the edge of the airstrip, the second wave came in and took the left flank, the third rolling in five minutes later on the right flank, all advancing clear to the strip.

A Higgins boat brought in General MacArthur. After an hour detailed inspection of almost the entire beach, I asked MacArthur how he found the positions.

"Splendid," he replied. "Just fine."

Congratulates Gen. Chase

At the dock MacArthur congratulated Brig. Gen. William C. Chase, commander of the landing forces.

"My heartiest felicitations to you and your men," the General said. "You have performed magnificently. Hold what you have taken no matter against what odds. You have your teeth in him now. Don't let go."

MacArthur transferred this morning from the warship which returned him from the invasion to a PT-boat and reached the advanced base in New Guinea, where he conferred with Lt. Gen. Walter Krueger, commander of the U. S. 6th Army. Then he boarded his own Fortress for the flight over the mountains to his advanced headquarters in New Guinea.

By a special dispensation from the General, because we were the first newsmen to land on Los Negros, Tom Shafer, Acme News photographer, and I were permitted to accompany the General to the base in his plane.

Admiral Thomas C. Kinkaid, who was aboard, commented:

"From a naval point of view, Los Negros was a superb operation, excellently planned and well executed. I am perfectly satisfied."

MacArthur Spurns Danger

During his inspection of the landing beach MacArthur disregarded the possibility of danger. He scorned the green fatigue uniform which is standard for invading units of the 1st Cavalry Division and came in on a Higgins barge clad in a khaki gabardine trenchcoat and his gold-braided cap instead of a steel helmet.

WHERE TO FIND IT

	Page		
Bridge	20	Patterns	19
Comics	23	Prevost	14
Crossword	20	Radio	23
Dr. Brady	14	Ration Calendar	6
Editorial	14	Real Estate	20
Financial	4	Society	6
Helen Worth	6	Sports	18, 19
Horoscope	23	Take My Word	14
Movies	12, 13	Theaters	12, 13
Music	13	These Women	10
Novel	19	Tommy Holmes	18
Obituaries	15	Uncle Ray	10
Our Fighters	10	Want Ads	20-23
		Women	6

Buy War Bonds

BROOKLYN EAGLE

5c IN CITY AND LONG ISLAND

Weather—Snow, continued cold today.

103d YEAR • No. 62 • DAILY AND SUNDAY — BROOKLYN, N. Y., SUNDAY, MARCH 5, 1944 • • • • •

Forts Batter Berlin For 1st Time in War; 40 U. S. Planes Lost

Find Luftwaffe Almost Helpless To Meet Test

By United Press

The Berlin Radio went off the air suddenly early this morning after flashing a warning that "enemy planes" were approaching the capital. U. S. Government monitors reported the Nazi's station's abrupt blackout.

London, March 4 (U.P.)—American bombers blasted the outlying sections of Berlin for the first time in the war today and found the Luftwaffe virtually powerless to meet the historic challenge which opened the daylight offensive against Adolf Hitler's doomed capital.

Through a snow and cloud-packed sky where the temperature was 60 degrees below zero, B-17 Flying Fortresses delivered the blow that had been the dream of every American airman based in Britain. They were powerfully suported by American fighters, including waves of the new P-51 Mustangs.

Luftwaffe Caught Off Guard

The Luftwaffe's touted squadrons appeared to have been caught off guard. The few enemy planes that got through the thick cloud banks were reported none too eager to meet this crowning demonstration of our ability to blast the Nazi war effort to its central root—Berlin.

Fourteen heavy bombers and 26 escorting fighters failed to return from the widespread attacks, representing only a small percentage of what was described officially as a very strong force.

The American and Allied fighters shot down nine enemy fighters, in addition to a still-unannounced number of Nazi planes downed by the bomber gunners.

The terse announcement from U. S. European theater headquarters, signifying that bomb-weary Berliners now can know no respite from the aerial terror by night or day, said only that in the course of attacks on targets in Eastern Germany one American formation "reported attacking a target in the Berlin district."

"The flight was made through difficult flying conditions with clouds often as high as 30,000 feet," the communique said.

Flak Heavy Over Ruhr

But Fortress crews climbing out of their bombers back in Britain told of blasting the outer areas of Berlin after a terrible battle with the weather and heavy flak over the Ruhr although the resistance over Berlin itself was so weak as to prove anti-climactic.

The targets were attacked with the cloud-penetration technique but through breaks in the ceiling the crews saw parks and lakes in Berlin's outskirts and the great super highways leading into the heart of the city.

Some crews reported that the clouds opened as they dropped their bombs and they were able to watch them plummet down for direct hits on the target.

The return trip was virtually without incident except for the onslaught of the weather and many of the fliers came back suffering severe frostbite.

Brooklyn Letters to Cost 3 Cents After March 25

It will cost 3 cents instead of 2 after March 25 to mail a letter from one part of Brooklyn to another, Postmaster Frank J. Quayle pointed out in a statement last night.

The increased postage was ordered by the tax law which President Roosevelt vetoed and which was then passed over his veto. It abolished the 2-cent rate for local first-class mail and increased postage on parcels weighing more than eight ounces by 3 percent and not less than 1 cent a parcel. Money order rates are also increased.

Borough Flier Tells Vivid Story Of All-Yank Show at Nazi Capital

'Expected to Catch Hell's Jackpot, but Didn't,' Says Lt. Whalen—Pilot Ran Out of Oxygen

(The following eyewitness story on the Berlin raid was written for the United Press by Lt Edmund Whalen, 1349 Pacific St, Brooklyn, who joined the R. A. F. in 1941 and transferred to an American Spitfire fighter squadron last October. He flew a Mustang in today's U. S. raid on Berlin.)

LT. EDMUND WHALEN

An American Air Base Somewhere in England, March 4 (U.P.)—We expected to really catch hell's jackpot when we reached Berlin today, but we didn't.

We've gotten worse flak over Holland plenty of times, and the fighter opposition was both small and timid. The whole business seemed poor according to the Hun's usual standards.

We were already over Germany when we met our bombers, and although we saw a few enemy vapor trails, it was a long time before we actually saw any of their planes.

We just crisscrossed back and forth across the tops of our big bomb - carrying "trucks," and thrilled as we realized that at last it was to be the all-Yankee show we'd waited over three years to take part in.

Focke-Wulfs Appears

Finally, as we emerged from a layer of clouds at least 22,000 feet up, four vapor trails to the southeast turned out to be Focke-Wulfs. They were about 2,000 feet above

Continued on Page 6

Nazis Halted at Anzio 'Dead Woman's Corner'

American Troops, Backed by Strong Artillery Blows, Smash Tank-Led Assault

Allied Headquarters, Naples, March 4 (U.P.)—American troops, backed by strong artillery blows, have smashed a tank-led German assault at "Dead Woman's Corner" near Cisterna on the Anzio beachhead and the British have blunted two other light jabs possibly presaging a fourth all-out Nazi attack, it was disclosed today.

Reconnaissance photographs revealed at the same time that American Flying Fortresses struck a crippling blow against German communications in their attack Friday on the sprawling Littorio rail yards in Rome, where bombs ripped through more than 2,000 pieces of rolling stock.

The new German attacks were of local character as the battered enemy divisions—now revealed to total 12 against the beachhead alone—regrouped and recovered from the shock of their costly failure to crack the beachhead lines this week.

American guns knocked out three out of an attack group of eight German tanks at "Dead Woman's Corner," a mile and a half southwest of Cisterna, so named because the Italian village there is named Femina Morta—dead woman. German infantry groups behind the tanks did not attempt to press the attack.

It was disclosed that the Allies have taken 3,500 German prisoners since they stepped ashore at Nettuno and Anzio last Jan. 22 while the enemy's total loss in killed, wounded and prisoners was approaching the 20,000 mark.

Despite their losses, the Germans were massing more and more men against the beachhead. On the stalemated Cassino Front, meanwhile, warmer and clearer weather was reported but streams still were flooded and the mud hampered the 5th Army's effort to dislodge the Germans from their remaining strongholds in Cassino Town.

Business Organizations Took 80 P.C. of War Loan

Commercial, industrial and financial organizations led the way in the 4th War Loan as in previous drives, directly accounting for more than 80 percent of the total dollar volume of sales in New York State. This was announced yesterday by Nevil Ford, executive manager of the War Finance Committee for New York, in revealing an analysis of final figures.

Americans Blast 2 Japanese Bases In the Carolines

Yank Airmen Also Attack Enemy Positions In Marshall Islands

Pearl Harbor, March 4 (U.P.)—B-24 Liberators of the U. S. Army 7th Air Force, striking westward into the Carolines, attacked the Japanese bases of Ponape and Kusaie Thursday, Admiral Chester W. Nimitz announced today, while American medium bombers attacked isolated enemy positions in the Marshalls.

Big four-engined Liberators, apparently in small formations, dropped approximately eight tons of bombs on aircraft runways and buildings on Ponape and also attacked shipping at the dock area of Kusaie. The presence of Japanese shipping at Kusaie indicated the enemy may be reinforcing that stronghold, the easternmost of the Carolines and only 340 miles from Kwajalein.

Ponape and Kusaie are 385 and 678 miles, respectively, east of Truk.

While Thursday's attack was not very strong, its effect—along with other assaults—is to keep the Japanese from air attacks on American-held Marshall Islands.

As the heavies struck westward, army Mitchell medium bombers and navy Venturas of Fleet Air Wing 2 attacked two enemy bases in the eastern Marshalls with 17 tons of bombs, hitting airdromes and starting fires.

Some anti-aircraft fire was encountered by the American planes but all returned safely to bases.

These attacks were made on the same day as the latest navy air attack on Paramushiru in the Kuriles, announced yesterday, when Fleet Air Wing 4 sent a small force of Venturas against this Japanese stronghold in the North Pacific. These planes attacked from Attu, 765 miles to the east.

Jamaica Soldier Killed, 4 Hurt in Ohio Crash

Martins Ferry, Ohio, March 4 (U.P.)—Staff Sgt. Owen Gary, 22, of Jamaica, N. Y., was killed and four other persons were injured today when the automobile in which they were riding crashed into a street car on U. S. Route 40 near Bridgeport, Ohio.

Staff Sgt. Hugh Masterson of 6109 Hutchins Boulevard, North Bergen, N. J., and Corp. Frank Cerniglia, 33, of 147-34 108th Avenue, Jamaica, N. Y., driver and owner of the car, were injured critically and taken to Martins Ferry Hospital. Cerniglia's wife, Marie, and daughter, Florette, 11, also were injured.

The three soldiers were stationed at Camp Tyson, Tenn., and were en route to Jamaica on furlough. Masterson and Cerniglia were to be removed to Fletcher General Hospital at Cambridge, Ohio, when their conditions permit.

Swiss Spy Faces Death

Berne, March 4 (U.P.)—Maj. Ernst Pfister of the Swiss Army has been sentenced to death as the leader of a spy ring "operating for foreign powers," it was announced officially today.

Yanks Repel Attacks On Los Negros Airfield

Allied Headquarters, Australia, Sunday, March 5 (U.P.)—Fierce Japanese counter attacks against American defenses around Momote airfield on Los Negros Island in the Admiralties were repulsed Friday in actions lasting throughout the night, Gen. Douglas MacArthur's communique announced today.

"Wave after wave was destroyed before the Japanese finally recoiled in complete defeat after one of the fiercest encounters of the war," the communique declared in describing the successful American defense of positions won in the surprise landing last Tuesday.

The American troops had battled off Japanese attacks Tuesday nd Wednesday nights, and after inforcements landed Thursday pulsed enemy efforts to break the efense lines that night.

,000 Japanese Casualties

Japanese casualties since Tuesday on Los Negros Island, strategic point only 610 miles southwest of Truk, were estimated at 3,000.

American losses have amounted to only 61 killed and 244 wounded in the heavy fighting, the communique reported.

"Our troops are preparing to resume their advance," MacArthur's war bulletin said after reporting the new enemy attacks.

American destroyers joined in the campaign for complete occupation of the Admiralties when they steamed across the Bismarck Sea to shell Lorengau on Manus Island and Seadler Harbor.

It was the farthest north any U. S. destroyers operating under Admiral William F. Halsey's command have ever penetrated in the Southwest Pacific war.

NAZIS SUFFER HEAVY LOSS IN PSKOV BATTLE

Reds 19 Mi. from Latvia—Smash Open Road Toward Nikolayev

London, Sunday, March 5 (U.P.)—The Red Army advanced to within 19 miles of the Latvian border in a westward sweep below Pskov yesterday, while in Southern Russia the 3d Ukrainian Army, resuming its offensive south of Krivoi Rog, pushed across the Ingulets River on a 15-mile front and opened a road toward the German Black Sea stronghold of Nikolayev.

Moscow's broadcast communiques gave no report on the progress of the battle for Pskov, which front reports from the Soviet capital said was one of the fiercest of the Winter campaign. A supplementary Moscow radio account said the Germans were suffering heavy losses in futile attempts to take lost positions on the 22-mile crescent-shaped front spread halfway around the Baltic gateway city.

Berlin broadcasts said the German command had pulled its advanced posts back toward the main Nazi lines around Pskov.

Reds Widen Narva Bridgehead

Moscow anounced that on the Narva front in Northern Estonia the Russians hurled the Germans from several heavily fortified points and widened their bridgehead on the west bank of the Narva River, southwest of the isolated city of the same name. Berlin said a major battle was raging in the area and claimed one part of the Soviet bridgehead was wiped out.

Berlin also said the Russians were attacking along a 90-mile front in the Western Ukraine between Shepetovka and Lutsk, one enemy broadcast claiming that an advanced group of Russians was isolated near Shepetovka. Lutsk is 85 miles inside Poland while Shepetovka is on the Russian side of the pre-war frontier.

The Soviet bulletins offered no confirmation to the German reports, telling only of fighting on the northern and southern fronts.

Reds Take 6 Towns in North

In the North, the Russians captured six towns along a 22-mile front starting at the town of Panevo, 17 miles south of Pskov. Those forces were battering westward toward the Pskov-Warsaw railroad, one of two lines still available to the German garrison in Pskov, and the Latvian border beyond.

Moscow identified that front as being in the direction of Ostrov, a large town on the railroad and a prize highway junction which is 33 miles south of Pskov. By taking the town of Nemoevo the Russians moved to within seven miles east of Ostrov and 19 miles from Latvia.

Thirteen miles northeast of Ostrov they won Gusakovo while to the southeast they captured Shubina Gora and Sigorino, respectively 11 and 12 miles from Ostrov.

The southward thrust also threatened Kherson, 35 miles southeast of Nikolayev, with encirclement.

The Moscow radio meanwhile revealed that capital ships of the Soviet Baltic Fleet pulverized German defenses before the Red Army started its northern drive in mid-January in the Leningrad area.

Faces Grand Jury Action For Illegal Transmitter

Frederick A. Turner, 37, of 606 Kosciusko St., was released in $500 bail yesterday for Grand Jury action on a charge of operating a radio transmitter in his home without a license.

Louis de la Fleur, Federal Communications Commission intelligence officer, was the complainant against him before Federal Commissioner Martin C. Epstein.

LEPKE DIES IN CHAIR WITH 2 HENCHMEN

Louis Capone

Emanuel (Mendy) Weiss

Louis (Lepke) Buchalter

F. D. R. Orders Daniels Give Data to Senators

Aide Says He's Now Willing to Answer Queries—Writes Chairman About Talk With President

Washington, March 4 (U.P.)—President Roosevelt retreated tonight in the face of a Senate subcommittee's determination to force a test of strength between the executive and legislative branches and instructed his administrative assistant, Jonathan Daniels, to give information sought by the subcommittee.

Daniels said he now is willing to answer the questions which he refused to answer before a Senate subcommittee last Monday and which prompted the subcommittee to vote to recommend contempt proceedings against him.

In a letter to Subcommittee Chairman Ellison D. Smith (D., S. C.), Daniels said he had conferred with the President and Mr. Roosevelt "does not think that in this particular matter my testimony would adversely affect the public interest."

President Willing to See Group

"In fact," Daniels' letter added, "the President stated to me that if the committee wishes to discuss the matter with him personally, he will be happy to see the committe at any time."

Smith said Daniels' letter was "an admission that we have the power" to require executive officials to testify. He said he expects the contempt proceedings to be dropped if Daniels appears before the subcommittee and answers questions satisfactorily. But he added that he would have to take it up with the committee.

"It is very satisfactory to me," Smith said. "The whole thing was a question of whether Congress had power to investigate activities of an agency created by Congress, and whether executive department officials could be required to testify. This is an admission that we have the power."

Daniels Quizzed About Slattery

Smith's group, an agricultural subcommttee investigating the Rural Electrification Administration, had asked Daniels whether he had requested the resignation of REA Administrator Harry Slattery. Slattery testified Daniels had on three separate occasions.

Daniels, advised by Ugo Carusi, executive assistant to Attorney General Francis Biddle, refused to discuss the case on the grounds that it involved confidences between him and the President and that to answer the subcommittee's questions would "not be in the public interest."

There appeared little doubt that had Daniels not undergone a change of heart, the full committee would have approved the subcommittee's recommendation and presented it to the Senate.

Insists Argentina Cut All Axis Ties

Washington, March 4 (U.P.)—This country will have nothing officially to do with the present Argentine regime until it kicks out Axis spies, interns Axis officials, stamps out illicit traffic with the Axis and unequivocally enters "the realm of hemispheric solidarity," Acting Secretary of State Edward R. Stettinius Jr. said today.

In a surprise formal statement, Stettinius reviewed the circumstances under which Acting President Edelmiro T. Farrell assumed power from President Gen. Pedro Ramirez on Feb. 25 and added:

"This Government has reason to believe that groups not in sympathy with the declared Argentine policy of joining the defense of the hemisphere were active in this turn of affairs."

Authoritative sources indicated today that Great Britain will follow the policy announced by the United States in withholding recognition.

Stettinius' statement presumably was prompted by a declaration by the Chilean Government that the new Argentine regime was a legal continuation of the Ramirez regime and that the question of recognition therefore does not arise.

Tito's Forces Take Lastva In Southern Bosnia

London, March 4 (U.P.)—Fighting flared throughout all the Hercegovina region of southern Bosnia yesterday as Marshal Josip (Tito) Broz' Partisan forces captured Lastva, 20 miles east of Budrovnik, and smashed a German attempt to penetrate to Kalinovik, 30 miles south of Sarajevo, a communique from the Yugoslav People's Party of Liberation said today.

After capturing Lastva in vicious hand-to-hand fighting, the Partisans slashed through the Trebenice area for steady gains near the Adriadic, it was said.

Labor Draft Rejected By Truman Committee

Senators Praise Home Front Production Mark, Urge Limited Civilian Manufacture

Washington, March 4 (U.P.)—The Senate Truman Committee tonight rejected the proposed labor draft as merely "sacrifice for sacrifice's sake," proclaimed that the home front has answered its critics with a confounding production record, and recommended return of some industry to limited civilian manufacture.

Criticizing charges of military leaders that civilians are not equaling the sacrifices of the fighters, the war investigating committee in its third annual report declared that the "people will do any job" needed for them. It warned that frenzied additional conversion of civilians to war work will not help servicemen.

In 1941, 1942 and 1943, it said, civilians turned out 105,061 airplanes, 746 fighting ships, 23,867 landing craft, 1,899 Liberty Ships—20,450,800 deadweight tons—702 other commercial ships, 28,286 subsidiary navy vessels, and 1,567,940 military trucks. Additionally, Americans built $20,000,000,000 of the "best and most modern plant facilities in the world."

Give Figures on Output

Agriculture and industrial workers put in 45 percent more man-days of effort in 1943 than in 1939, and industrial labor increased its output by 89.6 percent in 1943 over 1939.

The report added: informed the committee that the bulk of the initial equipment and supplies for the War Department will have been manufactured within 60 to 90 days, and thereafter the job will be to supply items of special need, to replace material and to improve quality."

The committee rejected arguments that National Service legislation would end strikes, and warned that its administration would be so complicated that results would not be obtained until after the need has passed.

"On the whole, the performance of labor has been very good," it said. "The manpower problem is too complex and difficult to be solved by any such easy means as passing a draft statute."

The Government must enunciate a clear and understandable labor-relations policy, "written into law and administrated through one single agency instead of the dozen or so now operating in this field," it added.

It recommended a cautious return of some plants to manufacture of simple civilian goods of the

African Troops Threaten Jap Burma Defense Line

New Delhi, March 4 (U.P.)—West African troops have broken into the Kaladan River town of Apaukwa in Western Burma in a drive that threatens both Akyab, 38 miles to the south, and the main Japanese defense line in Arakan, it was announced today.

By Thursday evening, a Southeast Asia command communique said, the West Africans had captured moth of the enemy positions at Apaukwa. Their successful advance marked the deepest Allied penetration in Western Burma since British Imperial units were forced to withdraw from the Donbaik area, 22 miles northwest of Akyab last Spring.

Agent-General Pledges India to Security Plans

Sir Girja Shankar Bajpai, Agent-General for India in the United States, said yesterday that "whatever league or association for international security the United States, Russia, China and the British Commonwealth may form, India will readily join on a basis of obligations equal to their means and a status of complete and honorable equality."

Bajpai told the Metropolitan Opera 13th victory rally that India "has the same ideals as yourself, wherever right, liberty and honor lead, towards that noble goal she will march, head erect and heart

LAST VISIT—With their son, Harold, 22, Mrs. Louis Buchalter is seen leaving Sing Sing prison after a final visit with Lepke yesterday.

31 Seized in Miami Rail Black Market

Washington, March 4 (U.P.)—The Department of Justice announced today the arrest of 31 persons in Miami, Fla., including 16 railroad employes, for "black market" trafficking in railroad reservations.

The arrests climaxed a Federal Bureau of Investigation inquiry into complaints that Miami tourists have been forced to pay "tips" above lawfully prescribed rates to obtain their accommodations out of the Winter resort center.

The Justice Department said 15 of the persons were employes of hotels in the Miami area. They were charged with violating the general conspiracy statute, the department said.

The railroad employes were charged with violating a Federal statute which forbids the sale of any service to a passenger at a rate in excess of that charged other persons for the same accommodations.

Both violations carry a maximum sentence of a $5,000 fine and two years' imprisonment.

President Begins 12th Year in Office

Washington, March 4 (U.P.)—President Roosevelt, in the home stretch of his third term and possibly preparing to seek a fourth term, began his 12th year in the White House today by asking God for guidance in attacking the war, and political problems which lie ahead.

As he has done each year since he was swept into office by a nation wallowing in this slough of the worst economic depression in its history, the President sat with bowed head as his former headmaster at Groton School, the Rev. Endicott Peabody, sought divine aid for his former pupil.

Gathered about the Chief Executive in the East Room of the White House were Mrs. Eleanor Roosevelt and other members of the family; Crown Prince Olav of Norway, the Crown Princess and their three children; Supreme Court Justices, Congressional leaders, Cabinet officers, the high command of the armed services and civilians directing the battle of the home front.

As he started on his 12th year in office, the President remained a political enigma so far as a fourth term is concerned. Most Democrats, convinced that he is their only hope of victory in November, are confident that he will be drafted and that he will accept the nomination.

Country Club Burns

Lawrenceville, N. J., March 4 (U.P.)—Fire of unknown origin destroyed the Greenacres Country Club here today. Damage of $100,000 included $8,000 worth of liquor.

Racket Leader Tight-Lipped in Death Chamber

Louis (Lepke) Buchalter was executed in the Sing Sing death chair at 11.16 last night.

His two underworld henchmen, Louis Capone and Emanuel (Mendy) Weiss, convicted with him of the murder of Joseph Rosen, small time Brooklyn racketeer, went to their deaths a few minutes earlier.

Lepke died tight-lipped to the end. He made no farewell remarks.

He entered the execution chamber at 11:13 p.m., last of the three, and was pronounced dead three minutes later.

Capone, first to be executed, walked into the chamber at 11:02 and was pronounced dead at 11:05.

Weiss entered at 11:07 and was dead at 11:10.

When Lepke entered the death chamber, he looked around nervously, then steadied himself and glanced at the spectators. He sat in the chair unassisted, glancing from side to side as the guards strapped him in, watching every move they made until they put the mask over his face. He uttered no sound.

'Framed,' Says Weiss

Weiss came in escorted by Rabbi Jacob Katz and shouted, "I was framed up" as he was led to the death chair.

He was innocent, Weiss said, and Governor Dewey knew it.

He said, "the only reason I am going is because I am a Jew. Have been framed because I am a Jew."

He continued, "Give my love to my family and everybody else. I am innocent."

Weiss entered the death chamber apparently chewing gum.

Capone Composed

Capone, first to enter, walked in calmly, gave the guards no trouble, and sat down without a sound.

Weiss, in his speech to the audience, was very deliberate about it.

Father Bernard Martin preceded Capone into the death chamber, uttering prayers.

There were about 34 persons present, including 24 reporters.

As the men entered the death room, each halted, and the principal keeper said, almost inaudibly, as he stood in front of the prisoner, "Is there anything you have to say?" Only Weiss took advantage of the offer.

Each man received four electric shocks. After the fourth jolt was applied the prison physician, Dr. Charles C. Sweet, stepped up to the body in the chair, opened the man's shirt, applied a stethescope, and turning to the witnesses said, "This man is dead."

Then the attendants walked up, unbuckled the body, placed it upon a wheeled table, and pushed it into an anteroom, where autopsies were immediately performed.

Officials said that the bodies may be claimed any time after 9 a.m. tomorrow, by relatives. At 10:30 p.m. the family, which operate the Depot Square Hotel, closed the place, and asked patrons to leave, because they had to attend a wedding reception for a relative in New York City. Those who were ushered out included members of the bereaved families, who departed in automobiles, before the execution.

Last Plea Fails

The last door to a court stay of execution was closed shortly after midday yesterday, when the United States Supreme Court refused to intervene. And all afternoon and through the evening hours there was tense waiting for a last minute reprieve by Governor Dewey which never came.

As if himself convinced that his end was near, Lepke, who once ruled a vast underworld empire, issued a "last statement," declaring that "I am not guilty of the Rosen murder," and that "I did not receive a fair trial."

'Made No Deal'

He had made no "deal," he said, in his statement, to buy his life by "talking"—revealing the links between crime and politics in the

Continued on Page 6

WHERE TO FIND IT

	Page		Page
Art	24	Our Fighters	16
Bridge	5	Prevost	18
Camera Club	15	Radio	24
Clubs	15	Real Estate	17
Crossword	Comics	Resorts	17
Dr. Brady	16	Schools	17
Editorial	18	Society	12-14
Financial	10	Sports	21-22
Helen Worth	15	Theaters	25
Horoscope	5	Tommy Holmes	21
Movies	25-26	Trend	23-26
Music	25	Want Ads	27-31
Novel	10	Week Outdoors	24
Obituaries	19	Women	[illegible]
Old Timers	16		

LAST "ALL ABOARD"—Both young and old jam the rear platform of the last "L" train over Brooklyn Bridge.

200 Ride Last 'L' Train Across Brooklyn Bridge

Service Is Discontinued After 46 Years —To Modernize Span, Widen Auto Roadway

"L" trains across Brooklyn Bridge, inaugurated 46 years ago and once the major form of transportation between this borough and Manhattan, are no more today.

The last train to make the trip left Park Row yesterday, carrying with it a group of 200 passengers, many of whom remembered when one train followed another in rapid succession over the span, sometimes at the rate of several each minute.

One of the veterans making the trip was Fred Decker, 61, of 249 Conklin Ave., who made the first trip on the line at the age of 15 and later got a job as a motorman and piloted trains across the bridge for 32 consecutive years. For him there is "no sound like the clicking of an 'L' train over the Brooklyn Bridge."

Another oldtimer was the motorman, Harry Page of 36 Logan St., who has been running trains over the span for 16 years, and who estimates that this final trip was his 12,776th trip, "or something like that."

The gathering was well sprinkled with the younger element, mostly autograph and souvenir seekers. They got signatures and they also obtained the destination signs on the last train, which was "Eastern Parkway."

Autographs solicited included those of Henry B. Brainerd, former president of the National Railway Historical Society, and Mrs. John Connors of 66-53 60th Place, Ridgewood, who has traveled for 40 years on the line.

Discontinuance of service was the first step in a $1,580,000 plan to modernize the bridge. Trolley tracks will be transferred to the former "L" route and the roadway will be widened for automobiles.

Passengers going to Manhattan today received free transfers at the Bridge-Jay St. station for any trolley going over the bridge. For those traveling to Brooklyn, transfers will be given on trolleys at Park Row for the DeKalb, 7th Ave. and Smith St trolley lines in addition to the Myrtle and Lexington Ave. "L's."

Today's Profile

The Rev. Dr. Moses Richardson Lovell, pastor of the Cadman Memorial Church, would be an actor if he had another life to live.

Although he never regretted being a minister, he feels that one lifetime isn't enough in which to do all the interesting things the world offers. He made his stage debut in Boston University. The high point of his career was his role in "A Midsummer Night's Dream."

Rev. Moses R. Lovell

Interested in social work, he started the Brooklyn Life Adjustment Center in 1939, in which Catholic, Jewish and Protestant psychiatrists hold the only clinic of its kind in the country. Every Monday night persons troubled with mental disturbances are seen at the church and helped to solve their problems.

The idea came to him in New Hampshire, where within a short period of time, a man he knew attempted to commit suicide, a member of his congregation kept rousing him at 3 o'clock in the morning, and some one tried to shoot him. He decided then that the human race needed a little help.

With his son, Moses Richardson Jr., in the navy and his daughter, Mary Elizabeth, married, he and his wife live at 125 Brooklyn Ave. When people ask his age, he says he's 40 plus. Born in Massachusetts, "under the sign of the codfish," he came to Brooklyn in 1938. He decided he was cut out for the ministry at the age of five. A clergyman, to him, must be a combination of dramatist, poet, thinker and prophet. As a prophet he says that the war in Europe will be over in October of this year.

The theater and travel are his favorite hobbies. He has been in Europe four times and thinks that Norway is the most beautiful country in the world.

His travels have brought him to a strange conclusion—"The more I see," he says, "the more I believe that every one in the world has lived in Brooklyn at some time or another."

WINDELS SEES 10c FARE HOPE IN MAYOR'S TALK

While radio listeners were wondering today whether Mayor LaGuardia's broadcast address yesterday meant that he was for or against a ten-cent subway fare, one Brooklynite, who did not hear the speech, was apparently satisfied that it gave encouragement to his side of the question.

This was Paul Windels of 10 Pineapple St., chairman of the Committee of Fifteen, whom the Mayor referred to as "the sage of Crabapple Street."

"As the Mayor's statement has been reported to me," said Mr. Windels, "he has indicated that he will go along with the self-sustaining subway fare if the other political groups of the city also will go along. I should say then that the Citizens Transit Committee is making a lot of progress."

Reference was to the practical advice, standing out of the welter of pros and cons in the Mayor's address, that the way to go about getting a higher fare is to first sell the idea to the city's county political leaders. Said the Mayor yesterday over WNYC:

Need Politician's Nod

"Who is sponsoring an increased fare? One having the best of intentions, good will and sincerity can shout from the top of the tallest skyscraper until he is blue in the face and he will not bring about a change until the politicians are willing to give the nod.

"Let me suggest to the Committee of Fifteen to get an expression, a public expression, from Ed Flynn of the Bronx and Frank Kelly of Brooklyn. Find out how Johnnie Crews of Brooklyn and Tommy Curran of Manhattan feel on the subject. Let these four men speak out. When these men state that they are for the increased fare the Legislature will pass the law, the City Council will approve and the increased fare will go into effect."

Asked to comment, Kings County Republican leader John R. Crews said:

"In 1921, as members of the Legislature, the Mayor and I agreed to oppose the Miller traction bill (for a higher fare). When I ran for re-election the Mayor indorsed me and praised me as a progressive.

"In 1921, as a member of the Legislature, the Mayor, who then was president of the Board of Aldermen, and I agreed to oppose the Miller traction bill (for a higher fare). When I ran for re-election the Mayor indorsed me and and praised me as a progressive. I've been consistent in my policies."

Opponents Find Comfort

Opponents of a higher fare could find comfort in portions of the Mayor's speech, in which he declared that any proposal to increase the fare would be defeated three to one in a referendum; denied that a higher fare was necessary because of the physical condition of the transit lines, and pointed out that even owners of homes valued up to $10,000 stood to lose more through the year by a boost of the fare to 10 cents than through the increase in property taxes to make up the deficit in the operation of the transit lines.

Within a few days, the Mayor told his hearers, he expects to announce the appointment of a justice to preside in a School Part of the Children's Court to handle cases of truancy. Under the plan, which he said has the approval of John E. Wade, Superintendent of Schools, the new justice will sit not in a court but in a school building, spending one day a week in each borough.

On the subject of food, the Mayor urged a boycott against fish dealers who take advantage of the lenten season to charge exorbitant prices for fish not under price control—specifically bass, sea bass, striped bass, fluke, mackerel, porgies, carp, whitefish, clams and lobsters.

Scout Troop 167 Leads Paper Drive

Boy Scout Troop 167 of the Bedford-Stuyvesant district today leads the borough Scout drive for waste paper with 62,000 pounds contributed toward a Brooklyn total of 116,048 pounds for the Scouts, according to the Greater New York Council.

Other large collections are those of Troop 365 of the Bushwick-Arlington district, 36,484 pounds; Troop 147 of the Flatbush district, 32,000 pounds, and Troop 425 of Sheepshead Bay, 10,200 pounds. Most troops report that proceeds go to Summer camp funds.

Meanwhile, plans were being completed for the second weekly collection of scrap paper Wednesday, when officials hope to exceed the 706 tons gathered last week.

Department Store Wage Scales Tentatively Set

Approvable wage rates ranging from $20 to $72 a week for 75,000 employes in 53 department stores in the metropolitan area, but which are not automatically applicable, were announced yesterday as tentatively established by the Regional War Labor Board.

The new rates are set as standards for 40 selling and nonselling jobs. Their establishment does not constitute an order requiring all employers to pay them as minimum wages.

"Permission to raise wages to the approval level must still be received from the WLB by an employer," Thomas L. Norton, regional board chairman, said.

Navy Lifts Age Limit For Medical Specialists

To make more physiclians available for service in the U. S. Navy Medical Corps, the maxmum age for specialists has been raised from 50 to 55, it has been announced by Capt. Kenneth G. Castleman, director of the naval officer procurement for the 3d Naval District. He added that the navy will now accept for "limited shore duty only" certain physicians who cannot meet the regular physical requirements.

Borough Neurologist Wins Army Promotion

Dr. Zachary R. Cottler of 465 Ocean Ave., chief of neurology and attending surgeon at Station Hospital, Morris Field, Charlotte, N. C., has been promoted from captain to major in the Medical Corps. He is the second Brooklyn army doctor to figure in the news over the weekend. Lt. Col. Noah Barysh was previously mentioned for his contributions to army medicine in England.

Major Cottler had been on the staffs of Kings County, Trinity and Jewish hospitals.

WORKING TOGETHER—The Red Cross drive got off to a good start in Flatbush, thanks to the efforts of these three left to right): Mrs. Ceil M. Walsh, captain of Division 5; Magistrate Nicholas H. Pinto and Mrs. Joseph Tannenberg, district supervisor of Divisions 4, 7 and 10.

College to Hold Red Cross Rally

Leo Durocher will be the principal speaker at the Red Cross War Fund rally to be held on Brooklyn College campus March 8. Harry Gideonse, president of the college, will preside.

In announcing the event, David L. Tilly, chairman of the fund's commerce and industry division, extolled Brooklyn's contributions to the war effort both in manpower and in money donated to the Red Cross.

The rally at Brooklyn College is but one of several events scheduled for the coming week. In four days of last week city-wide collections amounted to $3,872,000. John P. Stevens, general chairman of the appeal, announced.

The borough's share of New York's $22,386,000 quota is $3,331,000. The nation-wide goal is $200,000,000. To raise this fund Stevens said average daily collections of $722,000 will be required.

Ambrose B. Acker, chairman of the Queens Red Cross drive, announced the need for more canvassers to raise the borough's $1,083,000 quota.

Report Turks to Resume Talks on Arms Shipments

London, March 6 (U.P.)—A Turkish commission is expected to leave for London soon to discuss possible resumption of military shipments to Turkey, the Exchange Telegraph Agency repoted from Istanbul today.

Both the United States and Britain suspended shipments of military supplies to Turkey after a breakdown in military talks that might have led to Turkey's entry into the war.

4 BORO CLERICS SIGN PROTEST OVER BOMBING

Four prominent Protestant clergymen of Brooklyn are among the 28 signers of a protest issued yesterday against the "obliteration" bombings of German cities—labeled as a participation on the part of Christian people, even though thousands of miles away, in "a carnival of death." The protest is published as a foreword to an article on "Massacre by Bombing" written by Vera Brittain, British author, for the March issue of Fellowship, monthly organ of the Fellowship of Reconciliation, a pacifist organization.

The Brooklyn signers are the Rev. Dr. J. Henry Carpenter, executive secretary of the Brooklyn Church and Mission Federation; the Rev. Dr. Phillips Packer Elliott, pastor of the First Presbyterian Church; the Rev. Dr. John Paul Jones, pastor of the Union Church of Bay Ridge, and the Rev. Dr. John H. Lathrop, pastor of the Unitarian Church of the Saviour. Also among those who signed the protest are Dr. John Haynes Holmes, a resident of Brooklyn and pastor of the Community Church, Manhattan, and the Rev. Dr. E. Stanley Jones, former Methodist missionary to India, who is well-known to Brooklyn audiences.

The clergymen note that in World War I "some shreds of the rules of war were observed to the end." But today even the "fragments" of a Christian conscience are "disappearing" among combatants, they say.

This Time It's Poker To Quiet Her Nerves

Mrs. Sarah Ronner, 45, of 602 Sutter Ave., who still has to explain in East New York Court a charge that a stud poker game suddenly turned into a birthday party as raiding police entered her apartment, now has another explanation to make to a court.

Patrolman William Warden of the 12th Inspection District told Magistrate Francis X. Giaccone in Weekend Court yesterday that when he entered the kitchen of Mrs. Ronner's apartment he found six women playing stud.

Mrs. Ronner pleaded she was "a sick and nervous woman" and that she invited the women to play because the game quieted her nerves. The last time police entered the apartment, they claimed, the stud game had stopped and women were singing "Happy Birthday to You."

Samuel Brill, 55, of 80 E. 31st St., was charged with operating 11 tables of stud poker and four tables of rummy in the Rockaway Mansion, 691 Rockaway Ave., for "benefit of the Saratoga Spring Cure and Convalescent Home." His case will be heard March 8 in East New York Court.

Lorenzo Stanzello, 60, of 1582 W. 4th St., charged with bookmaking, told Magistrate Giaccone the five slip found in his pocket represented "daily doubles" he was playing by telephone himself. The arresting officer, however, said five different men had been seen giving Stanzello the slips and that each time Stanzello made a phone call. His case comes up in Coney Island Court March 16.

★★★★★★★ SPORTS 7 Wall Street Financial News

BROOKLYN EAGLE

Weather—Partly cloudy, colder tonight; clear tomorrow

103d Year. No. 70. DAILY & SUNDAY • (Copyright 1944 The Brooklyn Eagle, Inc.) • BROOKLYN, N. Y., MONDAY, MARCH 13, 1944 • Entered at the Brooklyn Postoffice as 2d Class Mail Matter • 3 CENTS IN NEW YORK CITY ELSEWHERE 4 CENTS

EIRE FACES ALLIED SANCTIONS

Doolittle Is Nominated For Lieutenant General

President Recommends Promotion Of Much-Decorated Tokio Raid Leader

Washington, March 13 (U.P.)—Maj. Gen. James H. Doolittle, leader of the 1942 raid on Tokio and now commander of the 8th Air Force in Britain, was nominated by President Roosevelt today for promotion to lieutenant general.

Maj. Gen. J. H. Doolittle

Doolittle, 47, was famous as a speed flier and test pilot during the 1920s and early 30s. Called to active army duty July 1, 1940, as a major, he was assigned to the 8th Air Force in July, 1942, while he was a brigadier General. The following September he was named to command the 12th Air Force in North Africa. Promoted to major general, Doolittle then was made commanding general, north African strategic air force, in March, 1943. He became commander of the 15th Air Force on Nov. 1, 1943, and on Jan. 1, 1944, he took his present post.

One of the most decorated air generals in the army, Doolittle was awarded the Congressional Medal of Honor for leading an air raid on Tokio. He also holds the Distinguished Flying Cross, given him in 1922 for a none-stop flight from Florida to California; the Oak Leaf Cluster for the DFC for test flying in 1924; the Distinguished Service Medal for his service of commander of the Northwest African Strategic Air Force! the Silver Star and the Air Medal With Three Oak Leaf Clusters.

Red Cross Booths Put Up at Key Spots

5,000 Volunteers Will Aid in Drive For Funds—Report Lunch to Honor Banker

From today until the end of the 1944 Red Cross War Fund campaign, Brooklyn residents will find it easy to make their contributions toward the borough's $3,331,000 goal.

Red Cross booths were set up this morning at 400 key locations in the borough, including all banks, department stores, postoffices, restaurants and skating rinks, for the solicitation of funds and to stimulate further interest in the appeal. The booths, which will be maintained until April 5, will be staffed by volunteer uniformed Red Cross workers who will operate under the supervision of Mrs. Ruth Nathan, chairman of the booths and theaters section.

Contributions solicited by the approximately 5,000 volunteers, who will serve in this undertaking, will be credited toward the community appeals goal of $500,000.

Mrs. Nathan of 290 Empire Boulevard, a veteran Red Cross worker, having served in a volunteer capacity for seven years, said the booths would be manned during all hours the location was open. She predicted complete success in this undertaking and said "my workers will go after those dollars the house-to-house canvassers do not get and the extra dollars that will go to make the current campaign a complete success. We want to impress upon the people that they must make greater sacrifices, just as our fighting men are 'making greater sacrifices."

Meanwhile, it was announced today by David L. Tilly, chairman of the Commerce and Industry Division, that George Whitney, vice chairman of the Greater New York 1944 Red Cross War Fund and president of J. P. Morgan & Co., will be the guest of honor at Brooklyn's first report luncheon tomorrow. Reports on the contributions secured by 60 C. & I. sections and divisions will be submitted by sectional heads, while County Clerk Francis J. Sinnott, head of the Community Appeals Division, will report on the progress of his group.

Sydney Moseley, news commentator and analyst for Station WOR, will be the principal speaker at the affair, which will be held at 12:30 p.m. at the Hotel St. George roof. Red Barber, general chairman of the campaign, and Dr. L. Wendell Fifield, pastor of the Plymouth Church of the Pilgrims, will also speak.

THE RED CROSS AT WORK —IT NEEDS YOUR AID

The American Red Cross is charged with the duty of providing recreation for convalescent men in army and navy hospitals. It furnishes them with games, radios, books, pianos and magazines and arranges motion picture shows both in ward and recreation halls and other enterment.

This is only one of the many services of the American Red Cross.

SIWASH, BESOTTED DUCK, ROUTS JAP ROOSTER; GETS MARINE CITATION

Auckland, N. Z., March 13 (U.P.)—Siwash, a beer-drinking duck, won belated recognition today for mowing down one Japanese rooster during the marine invasion of Tarawa.

Lt. Col. Presley M. Rixey, commander of the marine battalion in which Siwash served as official mascot, entered the fowl in the battalion's record with this citation:

"For courageous action and wounds received at Tarawa; with utter disregard for his personal safety, Siwash, on reaching the beach, without hesitation engaged the enemy in fierce combat, namely one rooster of Japanese ancestry. Although wounded on the head by repeated pecks he routed the opposition. He refused medical and until all wounded members of his gun crew had been cared for."

State Traffic Deaths Score Record Drop

Albany, March 13 (U.P.)—The State's 1943 motor vehicle death toll of 1,765 was the lowest on record and marked a drop of 19 percent from the previous year's rate of 2,184 deaths, Motor Vehicle Commissioner Clifford J. Fletcher reported today.

He attributed the reduction to less travel rather than to better driving practices.

Mrs. Roosevelt Visits Defenses in Trinidad

Port of Spain, Trinidad, March 13 (U.P.)—Mrs. Eleanor Roosevelt visited army and navy installations in Trinidad over the weekend.

She said she found morale of troops in Trinidad "normal and just about what one would expect."

Fresh Air Fiend Has Firemen Biting Nails, Slinging Nets, All for Naught

The eternal office argument on whether the windows should be opened or closed was no nearer settlement today after firemen and passers-by attempted to "rescue" Marion Simms, 66, of 22-23 42d St., Astoria, from a roof of 601 W. 50th St., Manhattan, where she had gone to get "some fresh air."

This morning Miss Simms, an artist in a toy factory at the 50th St. address, quarreled violently with a coworker. Miss Simms wanted a window up. The coworker wanted it closed.

The plant foreman intervened and suggested that Miss Simms take the day off and get some fresh air. Instead of going home she went to the roof and walked around the edge.

Passers-by who saw her on the edge of the roof summoned fire apparatus which responded with life nets. Several persons attempted to "rescue" her by climbing to the roof. When approached by would-be rescuers Miss Simms blithely reported, "I'm simply after some fresh air." She was taken to Roosevelt Hospital and then sent home.

Reds Drive Toward Odessa

Gigantic Battle Driving Nazis Out of Ukraine

Moscow, March 13 (U.P.)—Russian troops, waging a titanic battle for the liberation of the entire western Ukraine, have slashed into the Odessa provincial district and today were reported pushing on toward the big Black Sea port.

The 2d Army of the Ukraine, smashing up against the Bug River in the Gaivoron sector, penetrated the extreme northwest corner of the Odessa provincial district 130 miles above Odessa.

The swiftest advances were credited to the army of Marshal Ivan S. Konev. Striking down through the Ukraine at a pace of almost a mile an hour, his troops had turned the German retreat into a panicky flight, in which even small arms and gas masks were abandoned.

Pravda said a gigantic battle to drive the last Nazi soldier out of the Ukraine was in full swing, with Soviet troops spreading out along the lower Bug and slashing southward west of the river.

Nazi Lines Tottering

The entire German position in the Ukraine was tottering under the hammer blows of four Red armies which threatened Vinnitsa, Tarnopol, Proskurov and Nikolaev.

"The ghost of Stalingrad is with the German army," Pravda said. "The Germans are thinking only of avoiding a repetition of Stalingrad. They are more sensitive to our cutting roads behind their lines. Our armies now are advancing toward the western frontiers."

Smashing through to the Middle Bug on a steadily widening front, Konev's 2d Ukrainian Forces drove enemy remnants into the river and hundreds drowned.

A lightning 20-mile advance yesterday brought Konev's forces to the middle Bug along a five-mile front after engulfing more than 60 towns and villages.

Cut Rail Link

The capture of the railway junction of Gaivoron, on the north bank of the Bug, cut a line linking Pervomaisk with the Odessa-Warsaw trunk line and brought the Russians to within 41 miles of the Odessa-Warsaw line itself, 50 miles northeast of Bessarabia and 130 miles north of Odessa. Dzulinka, five miles northwest of Gaivoron, also was seized.

The 4th Ukrainian Army intensified pressure against the Germans' southeastern flank with an advance from its new bridgehead on the northwest bank of the lower Dneiper to Tyaginka, 22 miles northeast of Kherson.

At the opposite end of the 500-mile battle line, the 1st Ukrainian Army tightened its siege arc around the railroad junction of Proskurov on the Odessa-Warsaw line with the capture of Matskovtsy, four miles to the west, and Nizhnie Volkovtsy, six miles to the southwest.

The battle for Tarnopol, 60 miles west of Proskurov, was reported in its fourth day of street fighting.

See Mass Action By Million Czechs

London, March 13 (U.P.)—A million Czechs were believed responding today to a call from their exile government to begin active resistance against the Germans on a scale that may develop into an armed uprising.

With the Red army less than 120 miles from the old borders of Czcho-Slovakia, the exile government in a broadcast ordered its followers to "go over from individual exploits to organized mass action.

"Form fighting detachments," the broadcast said almost on the eve of the fifth anniversary of the Germans' entry into Prague. "Don't resist as individuals. Set up national committees. Form armed groups from guerrilla bands with the most resolute men and women capable of bearing arms."

The broadcast marked the first formal appeal by an exile government to its native underground to go over to the offensive and affected about one-sixth of oppressed Europe's potential underground army of 6,000,000.

R. A. F. Bomb Strikes Where Goebbels Was

By United Press

Nazi Propaganda Minister Dr. Paul Joseph Goebbels left a hotel room where he was entertaining guests the night of Feb. 15 only a few minutes before an R. A. F. bomb struck, killing all his guests, according to a broadcast from Madrid by CBS correspondent Glenn Stadler.

Stadler said the incident was revealed by a neutral traveler from Berlin.

Heads Motor Corps

Huntington, March 13—Mrs. Reed Chambers, chairman of the American Red Cross Volunteer Services, has appointed Mrs. A. Earl Heacock as captain of the motor corps. Mrs. Heacock will succeed Georgia Dolan, who recently resigned.

Allied Artillery Rips Germans at Anzio Beachhead

Bombard Highways To Prevent Thrust As Mud Bogs Armies

Allied Headquarters, Naples, March 13 (U.P.)—Allied long-range guns raked German positions around the Anzio beachhead with good effect yesterday, but bad weather grounded most of the opposing aerial forces and limited ground fighting throughout Italy to isolated patrol clashes, a communique announced today.

The bombardment ripped through enemy front line positions and the network of roads leading down to the beachhead from Rome in an apparent effort to prevent the Nazis from massing in strength for another thrust at the Allied lines.

Supporting the 5th Army gunners, small formations of Allied fighters and fighter-bombers ranged over the beachhead throughout the day, bombing and strafing enemy concentrations and transport at Campo Leone, Gezano, Cisterna and Velletri. Not a single enemy plane attempted to interfere.

Allied and German skirmishers stabbed repeatedly at the opposing lines, but the rains and mud prevented any large-scale infantry or armored operations.

Similar conditions bogged down the main 5th Army front around Cassino and in the lower Garigliano River valley. On the British 8th Army's eastern front, the Germans threw three small patrols of about 40 men each against the Indian positions near Orsogna, but all were repulsed after fairly heavy Nazi casualties.

American and British warplanes struck north of the battle lines at German communications in the Rome-Orvieto-Terni area, starting large fires in enemy supply centers

Continued on Page 2

FOSS, MARINE AIR ACE, RETURNS TO PACIFIC BUT WON'T SEEK RECORD

A South Pacific Air Base, March 13 (U.P.)—Maj. Joe Foss, marine flying ace, has returned to the South Pacific with a new squadron, which he trained as a unit in the United States.

But Foss, who tied Capt. Eddie Rickenbacker's World I record by downing 26 Japanese planes during the Guadalcanal campaign, is aiming for team work rather than personal accomplishments.

"We're not out for records," Foss said. "I just want to do our job well and bring all these kids home safely. If we get Zeros, it will be a result of team play."

Marine Public Relations Officer Ist Lt. Penn T. Kimball disclosed that the squadron, numbering a half-dozen fliers under 21 years of age, was cchedulеd to go into action soon. The men will be flying speedy Corsairs.

Goering--Going--Gone

HAMBURG "HAMBURGERED"—This photo, which came from neutral sources, shows the havoc wrought by American and British bombers on Hamburg during July and August, 1943. The big German port has been hit many times since then.

2 AMERICAN OFFICERS AIDING YUGO PARTISANS

Lead Successful Operations on Dalmatian Islands

London, March 13 (U.P.)—Two unidentified American officers are leading Partisan detachments in successful operations on the Dalmation islands of Brac and Hvar, where Marshal Josip (Tito) Broz's forces are attemptin gto clear the Adriatic stepping stones in event of any Allied operations against the mainland of Yugoslavia, a Partisan communique said today.

The announcement was the first official disclosure that American officers were taking active participation with the Partisans in their fight against the German occupation army.

The detachment on Hvar was said to have engaged superior Nazi forces but reportedly took a heavy toll of enemy troops.

On Brac, the other group of Partisans under a U. S. officer made a successful attack near the township of Pucin, capturing considerable booty.

Upholds Eire's Action

London, March 13 (U.P.)—George Bernard Shaw told the Daily Sketch today that Eire was justified in refusing to abandon her neutrality and that "the suggestion of sanctions is outrageous and an insult of Irishmen fighting with the Allied forces."

FIRE-SWEPT BERLIN—Incendiaries dropped by Allied airmen bring unchecked fires to Germany's capital city.

Taxi Drivers Strike In Midst of Storm

Demand Better Repair Service for Cabs —Rain Floods Streets, Causes Many Accidents

The heavy rain storm of last night and this morning provided a wonderful opportunity for 44 taxi drivers employed by the Queens Taxicab System to go on strike.

The drivers staged a walkout in an attempt to adjust differences over working conditions and wages, according to an announcement at the company's garage at Hillside Ave. and Metropolitan Ave., Queens.

The difference, according to an employe of the company, centers around the demands of the drivers for better repair service on their cabs and an adjustment in their "shape-up time." This latter, it was understood, comprises the arrival of drivers ahead of the time they are supposed to start work, in order that they may inspect their cabs, have last-minute repairs made, and prepare cabs for the day's work.

Two months ago the same employes, represented by a company union known as the Independent Drivers' Association, staged a walkout for more money. The matter was placed before the War Labor Board, but, it was announced, the appeal was turned down. The association is headed by William Dickerman and the ownership of the company is given as Katz Brothers, at the Hillside Ave. address.

The company owns 50 cabs, only six of which were operating this morning. It employs about a hundred drivers.

The weather forecast promised partly cloudy skies after the rain stops, with strong winds. The temperature was expected to rise to about 50 degrees from today's low of at one minute after midnight.

The driving rain was blamed by police for the accident this morning in which Patrolman Walter Lagrys, 48, of 1803 Beverly Road, attached to Traffic I, and Mary Jane Lent, 33, of 247 Garfield Place, whom he was assisting across the street, were struck by an automobile at Atlantic and Vanderbilt Aves.

Lagrys, with possible concussion of the brain, and Miss Lent, suffering from shock, were taken to Holy Family Hospital, where their condition today was said to be fair. No complaint was lodged against the motorist, Anthony Giandolvo of 259 Melrose St., who told the police he did not see the two in the path of his car until it was too late to stop.

Flood conditions were reported from scattered parts of the city. In the vicinity of W. 12th St. and Avenue T about four feet of water covered the street during the height of the storm, pouring into the cellars of homes and making wide lakes of adjoining vacant lots.

The storm also was believed to have been a factor in causing the death of Alfred F. Frank, 50, of 117-68 124th St., Richmond Hill, who was struck by a hit-and-run auto during the storm at 77th Ave. and Queens Boulevard, Kew Gardens.

U. S. 'Forts' Again Blast French Coast Targets

London, March 13 (U.P.)—American Flying Fortresses blasted again at mysterious military installations in northern France today, a few hours after the R. A. F.'s night-raiding Mosquito bombers stabbed at targets in western Germany.

Observers reported feverish daylight aerial activity over the Channel, but A. U. S. 8th Air Force communique reported only that a "small formation" of fighter-escorted fortresses attacked the French targets.

The Luftwaffe again made no attempt to interfere, but Nazi antiaircraft batteries shot down two Fortresses.

R. A. F. fighters shuttled back and forth across the Channel steadily after dawn.

Targets of the R. A. F.'s twin-engined Mosquitos in western Germany last night were not specified, but it was presumed they were war plants in the Ruhr or Rhineland.

An air alert was sounded in London last night but the all-clear followed soon afterward. No bombs were dropped.

B-24 Liberators of the 8th Air Force, flying without escort, attacked the French invasion coast without loss yesterday. No enemy fighters were encountered.

Roosevelt, Barkley Meet First Time Since Clash

Washington, March 13 (U.P.)—President Roosevelt and Senate Democratic Leader Alben W. Barkley of Kentucky met today for the first time since their dispute over Mr. Roosevelt's veto of the tax bill, which was assailed by Barkley and then overridden.

Barkley went to the White House for the President's regular Monday morning conference with his "Big Four" congressional advisers. Also present were Vice President Wallace, Speaker Sam Rayburn and House Democratic Leader John W. McCormack of Massachusetts.

SAVE WASTE PAPER—USE THE PHONE

If you are unable to dispose of your waste paper through your regular channel, telephone your borough CDVO-WPB salvage office.

Brooklyn—MAin 5-0061.
Manhattan—MUrray Hill 3-9660.
Bronx—FOrdham 5-1500.
Queens—CLeveland 3-0175.
Richmond—GIbraltar 7-1000.

REVEAL SHIP-TANKER CRASH COST 70 LIVES

A sea collision in a dense fog between the Liberty ship J. Pinckney Henderson and the tanker J. H. Senior cost more than 70 lives, it has just been revealed. Only three of the crew of 72 of the Henderson were saved and six men of the tanker were hauled out of the water.

The Henderson was loaded with combustibles and the tanker carried high octane gasoline. The impact set off a number of explosions and the resulting fire spread rapidly. The hulk of the Henderson was brought back to this port. The Todd Ship Yards Corporation engineers, after an examination, said the welding seams were intact in spite of the holocaust.

Vichy Says Stettinius Will Visit Moscow

London, March 13 (U.P.)—Radio Vichy reported today Edward R. Stettinius Jr., United States Undersecretary of State, due in London soon, will go to Moscow following the conversations in the British capital.

PREDICT CUT IN FOOD, OIL SHIPMENTS

Closing of Northern Ireland's Frontier Also Envisaged

London, March 13 (U.P.)—Drastic curtailment of shipments of food, oil and machinery to Eire and closure of the northern Ireland-Eire border were predicted today as the next Anglo-American steps in retaliation for southern Ireland's refusal to oust German and Japanese officials.

Britain took the first retaliatory move early today by banning virtually all travel between Britain on one hand and northern Ireland and Erie on the other because of military operations of "paramount importance"—an obvious reference to preparations for an invasion of western Europe.

Though northern Ireland was included in the travel embargo, it was aimed primarily at Eire, from where German and Japanese diplomatic and consular representatives have been keeping a close watch on western front preparations in Britain.

eManwhile, it was learned that Prof. D. L. Savory, Conservative member of Parliament from Northern Ireland, will ask Prime Minister Churchill to apply sanctions against Eire at the next sessiuon of Commons.

Eire's concern over the possible repercussions of her refusal of an American request for the removal of Axis officials was revealed by the fact that she asked Australia to intervene for the withdrawal of the American note.

Curtin Rejects Plea

At Canberra, Prime Minister John Curtin said Australia not only rejected Eire's plea, but notified Eire she was in accord with the American request and hoped the Irish Government would "see its way clear to agree thereto."

A sharp reduction in the shipments of wheat, oil, coal and machinery to Eire was expected momentarily in order to release every ton of United Nations shipping possible for the opening and maintenance of a western front.

With only a handful of ships of her own, Eire has been largely, probably almost wholly, dependent on British, American and other United Nations vessels to bring her vitally-needed supplies from abroad.

A London Daily Mail dispatch rom northern Ireland said cur-

Continued on Page 9

U. S. POSITION EXPLAINED

Washington, March 18 (U.P.) — Secretary of State Hull told his press conference today that the United States' firm position toward Eire was inspired by fear of future use of that country as a base for Axis espionage rather than by evidence of past leaks.

His comment was in awswer to statements by Prime Minister De Valera of Eire and the Irish Minister to the United States, Robert Brennan, both of whom have said that there have been no instances cited of information reaching Germany through ire.

'Shot' in Head Proves to Be Just Coincidence

Marcella Weeks, 16, of 450 Putnam Ave., and Earl Oliver, 16, of 585 Putnam Ave., were walking along Tompkins Ave. between Putnam Ave. and Madison St. last night when they heard a report which sounded like a gunshot. At the same time the girl felt a sting on the forehead, cried out that she had been shot, and collapsed on the sidewalk. Oliver notified police of the Gates Ave. station and three police cars and an ambulance from Beth Moses Hospital were rushed to the scene. Dr. Becker, the ambuland physician, found that the Weeks girl had only a laceration of the forehead.

Later, Detective David Zucker of Gates Ave. station said there had been no shooting but that a small stone, kicked up by a passing automobile, had struck the girl at the same time she heard the backfiring of an automobile motor. The girl was taken to the Kings County Hospital to be treated for the injury.

WHERE TO FIND IT

	Page		Page
Bridge	14	Patterns	14
Comics	17	Radio	17
Crossword	14	Ration Calendar	5
Dr. Brady	8	Real Estate	14
Editorial	8	Society	4
Financial	9	Sports	12-13
Grin and Bear It	8	Take My Word	8
Helen Worth	5	Theaters	7
Horoscope	18	These Women	
Movies	6	Tommy Holmes	
Music	6	Tucker	
Novel	14	Uncle Ray	
Obituaries	9	Want Ads	
Our Fighters — Precost	7	Wartime Best	
	8	Women	

They *Tell* Me

BY RALPH TROST

Pinehurst, March 18.

TRAVELING AND STEAKS—We were sitting in the billiard room of the Carolina minding our own business. What with the way that Eddie Burke, brother of the former National open champion, wielded a cue, it was a splendid idea, too. Willie Goggin, fresh in from the Winter tour, was being questioned about transportation difficulties met anywhere from here to San Francisco, the amazing success of Harold (Jug) McSpaden, the price of steaks and such oddities.

"Transportation?" sniffed Willie. "They had the S. R. O. sign out all the way. If it weren't for a happy accident somewhere the other side of Houston, Texas, we'd have made the New Orleans to Los Angeles trip standing up.

"Steaks? For $4 upward, plus a generous tip to a headwaiter, you could eat steak once in a while. It cost those who made the tour just about twice the ordinary expense.

"However, it was probably worth it. I discovered a new industry in California, a lucrative business, probably tax free and, certainly, without great pressure. It is called caddying. Toting a bag of clubs around a San Francisco or Los Angeles course brings a man $5 a round. Plus $1 per hour for any practicing. With reasonable luck and not too much effort, an enterprising caddie can earn $74 a week.

"Yes, $5 a round—not a day! Standard fees, no ifs or buts. Pay—or carry your own bag! We got so accustomed to that $5 a round, whether we won or lose, the mere $3 we paid in Phoenix, Ariz., looked like a bargain. When we hit Texas the $2 charge practically made us feel like thieves stealing something from the innocents."

"Any kickbacks?" I innocently inquired.

"Never heard the word kickback connected with caddying until I hit the deep South," interrupted a six-foot-four, brown-haired cue-wielder who, to judge from general appearance, finger-tip jacket, etc., might be one of the pros in from some secluded nine-hole course for a whack at the historic Pinehurst course.

"Get off the big circuit in Texas and they still try to pay caddies a buck a round—with a ten-cent kickback to the caddie master. How can a man live on that? Why, I've got to be making enough to support two pros I'm carrying along on this tour."

A caddie supporting two pros! That's how it goes these days. Sure, the caddie got his roll in the lush Frisco and Los Angeles caddie marts. The big point seems to be, that the racket today is caddying, not playing, Goggin pointed out.

ANENT JUG—That long-legged caddy put the finishing touch on any conversations along that line. So the talk switched to McSpaden, who plays behind those big, green goggles and who, if you've forgotten, not only managed to become THE man who beat Byron Nelson in a playoff (which Ben Hogan couldn't do) but won the big Victory tournament run by the Chicago District Golf Association, the L. A. Open, the Phoenix Open, the Gulfport Open, and was no farther back than second at San Francisco and New Orleans.

"Jug" has been a good golfer for nigh onto a dozen years, but no great winner. All of a sudden he burst into winning bloom and has shown no signs of withering. Had McSpaden, at last, found a driver he could trust? Last year he offered Ben Hogan $200 for his and made Nelson an "interesting offer." Or was his putting so phenomenal that he blazed a winning trail similar to those of Paul Runyan and Horton Smith when "Little Poison" and the Joplin kid seemingly couldn't miss?

A WALLOP—A BREAK—It turns out that McSpaden, who enters the current Charlotte Open the favorite, is riding a great break he got last Summer; riding it like a Hagen at his peak, a Mehlhorn at his best or like the man who broke the bank at Monte Carlo.

McSpaden got his break-of-breaks in that Victory Open last Summer. It came on the second hole of the last round. That's where "Jug" hit a shot that never should have been played. Using about twice the power club he needed, "Jug" let go with a second that soared over the green and even over the first of two lanes of tall trees that flank a road. That ball was riding for destruction—at least. It was due to pass the second lane of trees and leave "Jug" thoroughly stymied.

But instead of leaping on, it struck the hard road—and then bounded back toward the point from which it came. It leaped and it bounded. It crossed the road, went up the bank of the green. When it decided to stop, it was on the green.

"Jug" took two putts there, two putts for a par four, instead of a six or seven. Atop all this, he holed a goodly putt on the 18th to tie Buck White—and then he went on to beat him in the playoff.

The McSpaden tide changed with that shot. It was the great psychological break in his career, a morale boosting, pocketbook-filling break. He's been riding it ever since. As if that ball were a horse and McSpaden a Tod Sloan.

STATE PARK SECRETARY CALLS FOR LIFEGUARDS

Chester R. Blakelock, executive secretary of the Long Island State Park Commission, has sent out a hurry call for lifeguards.

"We need men badly this year in the State parks," he says. "We have lowered the minimum age to 17 and the maximum age is 40. Persons we 'ing glasses, or those less than five foot, seven inches, and weigh less than 140 pounds, need not apply," he declares.

The examinations include a physical and a water test in the surf at Jones Beach.

THE VOICE GIVES PEP TALK—Leo Durocher, right, gives his team a battle sermon before starting Spring training at the field house at West Point, N. Y. Boy, the season's ON!

CAGE FILBERTS SEE DE PAUL AS CHAMPIONS

By GEORGE COLEMAN

The basketball filberts have the National Invitation tournament all figured out. They see DePaul University beating Kentucky in the final. They contend the Demons of Chicago will reach the title match by a decision over Oklahoma A. and M., supposed winner over Canisius while the Wildcats from the Blue Grass State, after an expected triumph over Utah, are suppose to beat down St. John's U. Indians. That is the way the cage wizards along 50th St. have the entire competition diagramed on paper.

Now, all the teams must do is to follow the plans. Somehow, the cagers have their own ideas about these things and always seem to disagree with the experts as well as filberts, especially in tournament series.

Along Lewis Ave., where the De-Gray Indians of St. John's U. powwow, there is a more sensible trend. The Johnnies are taking the tournament one game at a time and only the contests in which they are performing. Right now, it's Kentucky and Utah that hold the stage along the curb.

Adolph Rupp's Wildcats from the Blue Grass country have a decision over the Redmen, but the Kentucky lads didn't down the Johnnies. The Redmen beat themselves. And when one recalls the Dec. 30 tilt he must agree on that opinion.

Missed Many Shots

If ever a team was "off" the Brooklyn Redskins were way off that night. They had 74 shots at the basket. At least 75 percent of them were easy layups and popshots while the Kentucky lads, grabbing the same number, scored on crazy one-handers.

Bill Kotsores flipped a dozen tries at the rim and missed on all, Hy Gotkin hit on two out of 17 and Ivy Summer accounted for a lone two-pointer. Dick McGuire did well, Ray Wertes, fair.

All this would make the chances of a St. John's victory seem certain. But after their Garden appearance, the Wildcats defeated Notre Dame, Ohio State, Ohio U., Georgia Tech, L. S. U. and Tulane in succession.

Yet the Johnnies are rooting for this Blue Grass team to win over the unknown Utah five. Joe Lapchick and his lads know what Kentucky can do but they know little about the Utes.

Sees Utah as Sleeper

However, the Westerners must be pretty good to chalk up a record of 18 wins and three setbacks. In fact, New Irish, the leader of Garden basketball, insists that Utah is the sleeper of the tournament. He tells of Frank Sheffield, a center, who scored 234 points to lead the squad that boasts of seven players who are six feet or over.

But, after seeing Bowling Green perform, the boys, especially the scribes, are nodding their heads in agreement with Irish but thinking of other things. Even in these days, one can yell "wolf" once too often.

Parks Boxing Dates Set by Committee

About 50 boxers will participate in the quarter-finals and the semi-finals of the boxing tournament conducted by the Department of Parks.

The schedule:

March 20—Quarter-finals: E. 54th St. Gymnasium, 343 E. 54th St., Manhattan.
March 22—Semi-finals (juniors): E. 4th St. Gymnasium, 343 E. 54th St., Manhattan.
March 24—Semi-finals (seniores): Lost Battalion Hall, 93-29 Queens Boulevard, Queens.

Handball Finals Sunday

The finals of the handball tournament of the New York Community Trust Winter Sports Championship will be conducted at North Meadow, Central Park, near 100th St. and the West Drive, tomorrow at 2 p.m.

TODAY'S SPORTS

BASKETBALL

Carmine St. Gymnpasium, Carmine and Varick Sts., Manhattan—N. Y. Community Trust Winter Sports Tournament: Queens vs. Richmond, 2 p.m.

BOXING

Ridgewood Grove Arena, St. Nicholas Ave. near Palmetto St.—Billy Grant vs. Herbie Katz, 8 rounds. Other bouts, 8:30 p.m.

FENCING

Washington Irving High School, Irving Place and 16th St.—P. S. A. L. tournament, 9:30 a.m.

SWIMMING

New York A. C., 120 Central Park South—Metropolitan championships, 8:30 p.m.

Evangeline House Pool, 123 W. 13th St. (Women)—N. Y. University vs. Penn Hall Junior College, 11 a.m.

WRESTLING

Broadway Arena, Broadway and Halsey St. — Joe (Dynamite) Cox vs. George Becker, finish, and other bouts, 8:30 p.m.

SAVED BY THE BELL—Al Davis is down for a count in fight with Beau Jack at Garden. Jack took the lead and never relinquished it by his speed and snappy punching.

Manual High's Infield Its Strong Point

By JAMES J. MURPHY

Now that baseball has gone into retirement, baseball has popped its noggin' into the schoolboy picture. Throughout the borough the various coaches have been taking advantage of Spring weather to get a line on candidates. It will take a lot of experimenting on the part of Murray Berk to acquaint himself with his prospects at Manual Training High. Berk, former mentor of the soccer eleven, has succeeded Artie Goldman, now connected with a White Plains school.

On paper it looks as if Berk has the makings of a strong combination, particularly in view of the fact that he has six seasoned veterans. The greatest task confronting him is the development of dependable pitchers and an outfield. The team is strongest in the infield, where veterans are available for every position. It is also well fortified behind the bat.

Sound Infield

Unless some of the newcomers see their challenge through to a successful conclusion, the infield will have a personnel of Pete Scorby, a converted outfielder, at first base; Ray Wasnieski of basketball fame at second; Joe McKee, shortstop, and Nick Miglio at third. Other infielders pressing the regulars include Charlie Jensen, first base; John Sgro, second base; Al Mirabile, shortstop, and Tom McKitty, third base. John Chino and Pete Inchautageur shouldn't be counted out.

Six lads are seeking outfield positions. They are Bob Schmidt, Bob Jones, George De Long, Joe Norton, Pete Costello and Bob Worst, one of the stars f football.

One Hurling Veteran

Of the six aspirants for the pitching staff, only one, Carl Carlson, has had previous experience with the varsity. The rest are newcomers. They are Bob Zeigler, Anthony Bello, Tony Franco, Ray Watson and George Georgas. The latter once managed the nine.

There is no need for concern about catching, not with a sturdy campaigner like Joe McGarry around. He is a handy handlre a heady player, has a strong arm and wields a potent bat. His understudies will be Rex Thomas and Pete Pichutto.

The schedule prepared by Manager Georgas contains 15 games, 10 of which are league encounters. The campaign will open with Poly Prep on Wednesday, March 29, and close with Fort Hamilton on May 23.

The schedule:

March 29—Poly Prep, away; 31, Brooklyn Academy, home; April 5—Cleveland, home; 18, Lincoln, away; 20, Seward Park, home; 21, Lafayette, home; 25, James Madison, home; 28, Erasmus Hall, away; May 2—Brooklyn Tech, home; 5, Boys High, away; 9, Samuel J. Tilden, home; 12, Midwood, away; 16, New Utrecht, away; 19, ushwick, home; 23, Fort Hamilton, home.

Cyclones Win Two

Central Cyclones won two games from Sail Loft in the Navy Yard League. Andy Spallina and Picture Perez weer high rollers.

Central Cyclones				Sail Loft			
Lan'rone	178	173	170	Dalbero	137	—	—
Taft	151	159	143	Reuter	179	137	190
Merrill	136	169	173	Volkens	165	166	182
Spallina	219	211	219	O'Do'nell	161	161	149
Perez	192	203	171	Corrica	169	199	171
				Smith	—	191	198
				Handicap	17	21	21
Totals	876	915	876	Totals	828	875	911

$132,823 Crowd Sees Davis Shackled by Beau's Speed

By CHARLEY VACKNER

"He fought like the old woman who lived in a shoe and seldom if ever he knew what to do." Thus did the poetical Lew Burston explain the defeat of Al Davis. Burston is Davis' manager and topnotch critic. Were the boys bowling, I would say Beau Jack scored a sweep. The Georgian won every one of the ten rounds.

Say what you will of Davis, but don't let any one tell you he lacks courage. The Brownsville left-hooker could have quit any time after round five without disgracing himself. Instead of taking a "powder," he took a trimming. The parade of punches which spattered all over Davis surpassed in numbers the marchers in the St. Patrick's Day meander. The only thing which would have netted Davis more clouts would have been the wearing of an orange tie yesterday.

Jack's Best Fight

Your agent thought Jack turned in the best fight of his career. Never did the young Negro punch as accurately. Jack actually beat Davis to left hooks. In only the first round was the Beau in trouble. Jack started this session by dribbling left jabs into the face of Al. A left hook to the head at the ten-second mark set Davis back, but the Brooklyn bangster returned the salute. Davis drove a solid portside swipe to Jack's head.

The Beau was badly shaken by the punch. Trying to bring his man down, Davis was wild with a series of lefts and rights. Jack fought back hard after being stung and tallied a left to the head after the bell sounded. The round and the manner in which Jack carried back the fighting was the tip-off on the result. In the second Davis scored hefty left hooks to the mid-section, but Jack forced the issue in the closing seconds.

Davis in Trouble

The third was Davis' worst session. After taking repeated left hooks to the head, Davis was sent spinning across the ring by a smashing right to the jaw. Jack tracked his reeling adversary and pounded Davis with short lefts to the face. The ropes saved Davis from hitting the canvas. Sensing a knockout, the gathering arose and cheered so loudly that neither the referee nor fighters heard the bell. Jack continued punching for fully three seconds as Davis hung against the strands in a semi-helpless condition.

Of course, such punching wasn't intentional, but can you imagine what would have happened were it Davis instead of Jack who punched after the round ended?

From there on Jack was the aggressor. Davis couldn't untrack himself. His theory of winning the fight on one punch was in hock. A long left hook spun Davis to his gloves tips in the sixth and he suffered a bulbed nose and a damaged left eye.

In ensuing stanzas Davis collected a badly bruised inner lower lip. As the bell clanged out the finish of the fight Davis was punched and slipped to the canvas.

The fight attracted a gate of $132,823, paid by 19,936 fans. This was balm for the badly mauled Brooklynite. Promoter Mike Jacobs visited Davis in his dressing room and said: "Don't worry about anything. You'll go right back."

Joe Agnello and Frank Forbes judged. The referee was Billy Cavanagh, who credited Davis with the first round. Agnello gave all ten to Jack and Forbes gave nine to Jack and termed the second round even. At 142½, Davis had a one-half pound advantage. It marked the first time in five fights that a Garden favorite booted his way home.

The Prelims

Johnny Dudley, 141, stopped Patsy Spataro, 138, in 1:09 of the sixth and final round. Dudley shapes up as a mighty promising welter.

In other sixes Solomon Stewart defeated Frankie Velez; Julie Kogan outpointed Ellis Phillips, and Ramon Alvarez took the measure of Pete Lelle. Felix Morales defeated Mayhew Smith in four-round opener.

SYMPHONY IN JABBING—Beau Jack, left, snapping a stiff left jab to Al Davis' face in the tenth round of their Garden fight last night. Jack's punch had all of his driving power behind it. If you study his torso, every muscle seems tense.

Dodger Trainer Recalls First Camp Setup in '07

Bear Mountain, March 18—This is Danny Comerford's 38th Spring training trip with the Dodgers. But the veteran clubhouse man remembers the first one in 1907 as if it were yesterday. Danny has grown gray in the service of the club. Keeping that long parade of ball players clothed and in bats, shoes and uniforms is a job that takes it out of a fellow. He has traveled 20,000 miles a year for the 38 years. That adds up to 760,000 miles. Abe Yeager, sports editor of the Eagle for 40 years, was the only reporter who covered the Dodgers when Danny broke into baseball.

"That first trip was different," mused Comerford from his rustic easy chair at the Bear Mountain Inn, staring into the wood fire in the huge fireplace. "We had one property trunk and one set of road suits. There were no showers. Six tin washtubs were nailed to the floor under a cold water faucet. The players used to steal my towels for sliding pads. We played with the same ball until it was black as licorice. We didn't have a coach to our name. Patsy Donovan was the manager."

The Dodgers trained at South Jacksonville, Fla., and had to take a ferry boat to get to their ball park. Those were the days when they had not more than 25 players in camp. Ten rookies was a big, awkward squad—a far cry from today. When Montreal gets here there will be a combined Dodger camp of approximately 100 athletes—big leaguers, minor leaguers and rookies. Danny doesn't know where he's going to dress 'em all.

On that first team were Nap Rucker, Tim Jordan, Silent John Hummell, Doc Scanlan, Harry Lumley, Bill Bergen, Jimmy Pastorious Doc Casey, Harry McIntyre, Eddie Lennox, Bill Bergen, Lou Ritter, Phil Lewis, Heinie Batch, Kaiser Wilhelm, Al Burch, Whitey Appleman—a long list of Brooklyn immortals. Casey, Lumley, Batch, Bergen, Wilhelm, Lennox, Burch and Pastorious are all gone. But Danny Comerford is still around and bragging that in his 38 years he never even mislaid a bandage.

BURR.

Frenchy, Snubbed by Army, Fails in Salary Talk, Too

By HAROLD C. BURR

Staff Writer of the Brooklyn Eagle

Bear Mountain, March 18—Frenchy Bordagaray had a cup of coffee with the Dodgers here yesterday. Rejected by the army doctors in New York in the morning, Frenchy caught the first train for camp, shot a game of pool with the press, hung around the lobby until President Branch Rickey finished a checker match with scout Tom Greenwade and went into a fruitless huddle with the Mahatma of Montague Street.

Half an hour later Frenchy was back tracking for the big city, still unsigned, without even doffing his fawn-colored overcoat. But he has undoubtedly strengthened his hold-out position. No ball club is going to let a ball player like the Unoccupied Frenchman stay out of baseball, considering that he's been classified 4-F in the draft.

"What, they did turn you down, Frenchy?" asked Rickey, shaking hands before the bell.

"Mental," said Frenchy, lightly.

"You've got at least 18 things wrong with you," contended the prexy of the Dodgers.

Mum on Diagnosis

Bordagaray looked a trifle bewildered and started to count on his fingers.

"There was the old football injury to my neck at Fresno State College in 1930 and in 1934 I dislocated my right kneecap. But the doctors wouldn't say why they passed me up. I can still play ball, Mr. Rickey," he added brightly.

"H'm," said Branch.

The Dodgers definitely lost title to their second string catcher with word coming from Birmingham that Bobby Bragan had entered the navy. But Rickey was expecting something of the sort after reading Thursday's news story on the change in the deferments of young men, 18 to 26, employed until now in war work.

It means that Brooklyn catching will be divided up among Mickey Owen, Ray Hayworth and, in all probability, Clyde Sukeforth. There won't be any one of the trio who will catch 100 games. Owen is to receive leave to return to his farm when the team is in Chicago and St. Louis and Hayworth and Sukeforth are too old for such heavy duty.

One of Rickey's bird dogs has caught up with Clay Jamieson Smith, the vanishing rookie pitcher from St. Paul. He was run to earth on a farm in Kansas. He promised to write to the Mahatma in a day or so. His draft status is somewhat confused. It's Rickey's opinion that you can include Smith out.

Three Remain Silent

Nothing has been heard from Black Bill Lohrman, Arky Vaughan or Rube Melton. The Rube is too busy figuring out where he stands with Uncle Sam to bother about following up his hold-out ultimatum —delivered several weeks ago—to stay on his farm. Negotiations are still on with Bob Chipman.

Manager Leo Durocher had all his young pitchers at the batting nets in the morning workout for members of the kindergarten class at West Point's Field House. Chick Hafey, George Sisler, Babe Ruth and Stan Musial all started as pitchers and the Lip doesn't want to take any chances of overlooking a future slugging star. Tommy Warren weighed in with four hits, switching from one side of the plate to the other. Tommy, unblushingly, predicts he's the man.

At the vesper practice the Dodgers first infield was composed of Steeple Schultz on first, Frank Drews on second, Bill Hart at short and Gil English on third. It's an inner defense that the fans may yet see on opening day.

RICKEY THANKS SCOUTS FOR YOUTH ROUNDUP

Special to the Brooklyn Eagle

Bear Mountain, March 18—"Don't overlook the Dodgers," said Branch Rickey, "if big league clubs have to depend on the kids to see them through."

It was the prexy's punch line to a tribute he had been paying to his bird dogs in rounding up youthful prospects in their nationwide search of the sandlots and high schools last Summer.

"It was one of the best jobs of the year in the whole Dodger organization," said Rickey, unstintingly. "And I want to thank them all, George Sisler, Tom Greenwade, Wid Mathews, Harold Roettger and my own son, Branch Jr. Only about one-fourth of the total reported. The other three-fourths are in the service. Roughly, there are 35 in camp, and Branch tells me he could have 25 more up here in a week.

"Of course, it's too early to go overboard on any of them yet. They must gain poise and adapt themselves. Some of them are still self-conscious. Here and there a boy may quit on himself. But as a class, I would venture to say that they are exceptional."

BURR.

CANADIEN WIN WOULD BE BALM FOR RANGERS

By RALPH TROST

Last hockey game of the year tomorrow night!

Yes, and the New York Rangers will have their last chance to inject a tiny ray of sunshine into a considerably sad season. Up to now the Rangers, even though they've won only six games, have managed to beat every team in the league at least once—except these fast-flying Canadiens, their opponents tomorrow night.

The Blueshirts have beaten the Boston Bruins twice, Chicago once, Detroit once—and, wonder of wonders, succeeded in beating Toronto twice ON Toronto ice. But all they've accomplished against the league-winning Canadiens has been a 2—2 tie. That tie interrupted the horrible monotony of that long, long string of 15 straight games in which they couldn't beat anyone; a string of defeats that set a record for big-league hockey—until the Rangers got off on the present winless string which started in mid-January and has been interrupted by only a couple of ties.

Though this is the last game of the season and the Rangers have been long washed out of any chance of Stanley Cup purses, they've been back laboring hard and long in practice sessions. As far as the Rangers are concerned, each game is practically the start of a new season. What happened before—and many dire things did occur—has been treated as water over the dam. So, back from their tough road trip, they started right in practicing again, and, this week put in two hard sessions.

After the 8—0 walloping handed 'em by Toronto in the last home game two weeks ago, the Rangers looked pitiful. But they went on the road and played good hockey. Their last game, against Chicago Sunday, was an inspired thing. Behind, 4—0, going into the final frame, they dug in and managed to come up with a tying goal with only 18 seconds left to play.

If they weren't convinced before, that Chicago game settled the issue. The Rangers now feel they can beat the Habitants. And, tomorrow night, theirs will be an all-out effort.

Pleasant as it would be for the Rangers to end the season with at least one victory over every club in the league and little it would cost the Canadiens to lose (they're so far ahead the second-place Detroiters can hardly see them) the Rangers expect no mercy from the visitors. There isn't much of that quality in hockey. There are too many goalies jealous of their records and too many, many, many even more eager for their goals and assists.

Mauriello Cleared

The District Attorney's office yesterday announced that a rape charge against heavyweight boxer Tami Mauriello has been dismissed.

General Sessions Judge John A. Mullin discharged the case, after the grand jury refused to indict on the basis of testimony by a 15-year-old girl who accused the 20-year-old boxer.

THE SPORTING THING

"For heaven's sake! Stop humming!"

McCarthy Eyes Buzas, Melton Pleases Ott

Atlantic City, N. J., March 18 (U.P.)—Manager Joe McCarthy of the Yankees paid special attention to the work of Joe Buzas, former athlete at Bucknell University who reported to the world champions as a possible shortstop candidate.

Facing a shortage of infielders, McCarthy said he had not signed Buzas, who played with the Newark farm last season, but that he would give the youngster a thorough trial.

McCarthy tried to be philosophical about the loss of his brilliant second baseman, Joe Gordon, to the armed forces, but coming on the heels of the induction of Catcher Bill Dickey, it was all that he could do to remain cheerful.

"I guess that we have to take these things as they come," Joe said, "Dickey and Gordon—that's a ball club, isn't it? Gordon was the best second baseman of recent years and Dickey the greatest catcher of all times."

Lakewood, N. J., March 18 (U.P.)—The Giant pitching staff is rounding into form in spite of adverse weather which has necessitated several days of indoor practice, Manager Mel Ott reported. Ott said he was especially pleased over the work of the veteran southpaw, Cliff Melton, who apparently has recovered from an elbow operation which made his arm lame through most of last season.

College Park, Md., March 18 (U.P.)—The Washington Nationals suffered their first 1944 injury when Pitcher Roger Wolff pulled up with a sore side and retired from practice. Wolff, who won 10 games and lost 15 with the Athletics last year; Alejandro Carrasquel, Dutch Leonard and Johnny Niggeling were impressive in the pitching drill shortened by heavy rain.

Boston, Mass., March 18 (U.P.)—Twelve Red Sox were in uniform in the club's opening drill at Tufts College, but only four are regarded as regulars for the 1944 season—Infielders Jim Tabor and Tony Lupien and Pitchers George Woods and Joe Wood Jr.

Hugh Duffy, who compiled a .438 batting average in the majors 50 years ago, was among those working out, but Manager Joe Cronin made it clear the old-timer is not a candidate for the team.

Wallingford, Conn., March 18 (U.P.)—The Braves had 11 holdovers from last year's team on hand for their opening Spring training season. Pitchers Al Javery and Ira Hutchinson, Infielders Eddie Joost and Connie Ryan and Outfielders Max Macon and Chet Ross, whom Manager Bob Coleman regards as his 1944 stars, were among the missing, but the new leader said they are awaiting permission from their draft boards to report for baseball.

Havana, Cuba, March 18 (U.P.) — Joe Cambria, baseball scout for the Senators, told the United Press that he had signed 15 additional Cuban ball players who plan to leave here next week for the club's Spring training site. Cambria previously had signed nearly 20 Cubans, some of whom are already in the Senators camp.

Bloomington, Ind., March 18 (U.P.)—Manager Bill McKechnie of the Reds sent his charges through a brisk two-hour workout indoors while awaiting word from six absentees.

Lafayette, Ind., March 18 (U.P.)—Russ Peters and Roy Roy Cullenbine arrived too late to take part in the Indians' outdoor training period, but their presence boosted the camp's roster to 18 players. Peters is successor to Ray Mack's second base spot, and Cullenbine again will be a regular outfielder.

SPORT SHORTS

BOXING—By Ben Gould

A CLEAN-CUT victory over Harry Jeffra next Monday in Baltimore will put Lou Salica a step nearer his goal—a shot at Manuel Ortiz's bantam title in the Garden in May . . . Jose Basora turned down a handsome offer from Panama promoters preferring to fight on the West Coast instead . . . He'll take on Holman Williams in San Francisco on April 10 . . . Petty Officer Tony Christoforidis, ex-world's lightweight champ, is a father.

Gould

Have you heard Aaron Perry's nickname? It's P-38. A champ in its own field . . . Recent 4-F's include heavyweight Lloyd Marshall and Irwin Rosee of Mike Jacobs' staff, while Jimmy Costello, ex-Yale ring ace, is 1-A . . . Larney Moore doesn't have to travel very far to do his training . . . He has a specially equipped gym in the rear of the gas station where he is employed.

Tippy Larkin worked out yesterday while Allie Stolz took it easy . . . Ticket sale is brisk . . . Beau Jack, having paid his wife and three kiddies another brief visit, returns this afternoon . . . The St. Nick reopens on April 3 with Larry Anzalone and Vic Dellicurti meeting in a rematch . . . The winner will get a shot at Jake LaMotta in the Garden . . . Incidentally, Jake paid a $28,000 income tax; do you still think your return was high?

You've heard of fighters being carried out of the ring feet first, but over in Algiers it rained so hard they had to carry the boxers into the ring to keep their shoes dry . . . Ensign Charlie Keller has blossomed into a first-rate boxing coach with the maritime service.

TURF—By Tapper Mills

ON THE lighter side in the turf world these days while waiting for the first at Jamaica on April 8, the boys and gals of the training fraternity are guffawing at the predicament in which grizzled veteran of the trade, Tom Smith, finds himself.

Tom, you may know, has just signed a contract to train for the stable of Mrs. E. Graham Lewis, the lady who dispenses beauty to the gals under the name of Elizabeth Arden.

Now it is bad enough that Mrs. Lewis has a reputation for changing her trainers as often as her—er—hair-do, but what is worse is the scene of operations she has selected for "Mr. Smith." It is a neat bungalow at Belmont Park and as one of the wags has said, "They'll either have to blindfold Tom or push him in backwards when he's shown the place."

The bungalow has a dining room and, so help me, a cocktail nook with walls of walnut veneer and diagonal panels of chromium. Then there is a foyer and two bedrooms and two baths, the bedrooms being done in pastel shades of blue and pinkish yellow with twin beds. And all of this grandeur is spanking new as the Lewis bungalow was damaged by fire last year and when it was repaired the interior decorators were permitted to run amuck.

And all this for a gent strictly from the "leaky roof" circuit, whose idea of heaven is to be permitted to slumber on a cot next to the stable of his "Big Horse."

HOMESTRETCHING—That medical discharge from the Army for Johnny Gilbert was first mentioned here . . . Tropical Park is enjoying such a big Spring meeting it is assuming vanning charges for horses quartered at Hialeah, retroactive to the meeting which opened in December . . . FECKLESS is ready to run for the sugar, only don't get reckless, folks . . . Jockey Ted Atkinson, who will pilot Pukka Gin in the Kentucky Derby, has been ordered by Trainer Andy Schuttinger to take a rest.

SOCCER—By Bill Graham

RICHARD Saffrath, who came up from local junior circles and guarded the nets for the former National Amateur champion, Brooklyn S. C. of the German-American League, is reported missing in action in Italy . . . Carl Weiss, a fan of the same club, which plays at Woodward Oval, is reported killed in action in the same theater.

Graham

Charlie Mellon of Brookhattan and Bob Laverty, captain of Brooklyn Wanderers, were ozoned Sunday at Starlight Park by Referee Fred Coggins for fisticuffs . . . The American League decided on the tariffs for Lewis Cup games some time ago and will not increase them after April 1 . . . George Bryndza, Kearny American goalie, has joined the navy . . . German prisoners-of-war at a Louisiana camp have been coloring their underwear for soccer uniforms . . . Yellow was derived from the malaria pills issued in North Africa, Red from mercurochrome and blue from boiling their outer garments.

Hans Maier of New York Americans has been wounded in the Italian campaign and is now in North Africa . . . An English all-star team will fly to Moscow soon to meet the best of the Red Army . . . St. Margaret's Guild dances Saturday night . . . Dennis Hughes, a full-back from Parklea of the Metropolitan League, has signed with Brooklyn Hispano . . . Henry Boener of Philadelphia Nationals has joined the navy . . . Jim Smith, an 18-year-old from the same lineup, is in the army.

ROUNDUP—By Joe Donovan

THE University of Utah, a member of the Rocky Mountain Conference, will replace Arkansas in the NCAA Western basketball playoffs in Kansas City Friday and Saturday . . . Utah was eliminated in the quarter-finals of the National Invitation by Kentucky . . . Arkansas U. withdrew from the tourney last Sunday after an assistant coach was killed and two star players were injured in an automobile accident. Utah meets Missouri in the opening game Friday night . . . Athletic officials of Syracuse University revealed that its two veteran coaches, Tom Keane and Lew Carr, will resign in June. Keane has been the track coach there for 37 years and Carr the baseball mentor for 32 years.

Donovan

Claude (Buddy), young Illinois freshman sprint star, will run in the Cleveland K. of C. meet Friday. On Saturday he will compete in the Purdue University Relays . . . Goody Rosen, veteran outfielder, will start his fifth season with the Syracuse Chiefs when they open training camp at Bedford, Ind., Friday. Rosen was once a member of the Dodgers.

Legation, a four-year-old, captured the featured Hallendale Purse at Tropical with Jockey Bobby Permane up. Legation paid $7.50, $3.90 and $3.40. Permane rode two winners, Edgemee in the fifth race, winning at $20.60, $6.50 and $2.80.

Jack Ogden, one-time Oriole general manager, is now a full-time football coach at Prospect Park, Pa. . . . Drew University of Madison, N. J., has carded 15 baseball games . . . Lt. Joe Stumm, former professional baseball and basketball player and coach, was appointed athletic director at Fort Meade, Md. . . . New Orleans promoters want Tami Mauriello to box Buddy Scott . . . Juan Zurita plans to retire after one title defense, he said in Mexico City . . . Len Merullo, shortstop, approved of the Cubs' 1944 terms at Wilmington, Mass. . . . Joe Glenn, slated to be the Yankees' No. 1 catcher to succeed Bill Dickey, was ordered to report for induction into the navy at Wilkes-Barre, Pa., April 1.

Catholic, PSAL Champs Paired for March 30 Tilt

For the first time in Metropolitan scholastic history the Catholic basketball champion and the P. S. A. L. titlist will oppose each other to determine the undisputed basketball ruler of New York City.

Dr. John E. Wade, Superintendent of Schools, and Ellsworth S. Buck, president of the Board of Education, have approved the March 30 contest for the benefit of the Red Cross Fund.

Ned Irish, president of the Garden, has donated Madison Square Garden for the game which pits Cardinal Hayes, C. H. S. A. A. Division A champ, against the winner of the Benjamin Franklin-Andrew Jackson game Saturday to determine the city P. S. A. L. champ.

Brother George, president of the Catholic High Schools Athletic Association, has approved the Catholic end of the game and Cardinal Hayes has consented to compete. A preliminary will be announced. Brother George has suggested that it bracket the Catholic B champion against the P. S. A. L. Vocational winner to be decided Saturday when Brooklyn Automotive and Samuel Gompers meet.

Tuesday and Wednesday, March 28 and 29, at the 13th Regiment Armory, has been set aside for the P. S. A. L. track championship. The meet was originally scheduled for March 18, but the three-alarm fire at the 13th Regiment prevented holding the meet. The meet will start at 3:30 p.m. Tuesday and all events not concluded on that day will be held Wednesday, commencing at 3:30 p.m.

Forman's 146 Tops Scoring In PSAL Play

Don Forman, Boys High captain, who registered 49 points against Manual Training for a new P. S. A. L. scoring record, clinched the Brooklyn P. S. A. L. individual scoring title with 146 points. Forman played eight games in the Brooklyn Division 1 race, scoring an average of 18½ points per game.

Al Gottlieb of New Utrecht decided the Brooklyn Division 2 crown with 137 points and finished second to Forman. Max Zaslofsky of Thomas Jefferson was third with 125, while Sheldon Fein of Midwood finished fourth with 118.

The scoring:

INDIVIDUAL SCORING DIVISION 1

	Games	Goals	Fouls	Total
Forman, Boys High	8	62	22	146
Zaslofsky, Jefferson	8	56	13	125
Verdi, Boys High	8	44	11	99
Warnieski, Manual	8	29	29	87
Svhwarz, Bklyn. Tech	8	34	16	84
Solomon, Eastern	8	31	14	76
Suchan, Tech	8	24	20	68
Rosenberg, Jefferson	8	29	6	64
Fox, Boys High	8	26	14	64
Malz, Tech	8	28	5	61
Schlossberg,, Tech	8	25	11	61
Inselberg, Eastern	6	21	10	52
Lee, Manuel	7	18	11	47
Garschag, Jefferson	6	15	12	42
Stone, Eastern	7	9	11	39
Simon, Boys High	8	15	8	38
Eisenberg, Eastern	8	12	13	37
Roach, Tech	8	14	6	36
Butterman, Tech	4	13	5	31
Berchofsky, Jefferson	4	8	11	27
Monasch, Boys High	8	11	5	27
Williky, Jefferson	4	11	3	25
Gordon, Jefferson	4	8	7	23
Havel, Tech	8	9	5	23
Urchenko, Eastern	8	7	7	21
Feldman, Eastern	4	7	6	20
Klammuth, Tech	5	6	8	20
Yoos, Manual	5	6	7	19
Kalish, Manual	4	7	4	18
Stone, Eastern	5	4	8	16
McGee, Manual	5	4	4	12
Weisman, Eastern	5	3	6	12
Goodman, Jefferson	5	4	3	11
Nadrich, Jefferson	5	5	1	11
Schweid, Tech	6	5	0	10
Banks, Boys High	5	4	2	10
Di Fronzo, Manual	7	3	4	10

TEAM SCORING DIVISION 1

	Won	Lost	Points For	Points Agst
Jefferson	7	1	375	262
Tech	6	2	392	296
Boys High	5	3	410	296
Eastern District	2	6	286	343
Manual	0	8	230	438

INDIVIDUAL SCORING DIVISION 2

	Games	Goals	Fouls	Total
Gottlieb, Utrecht	12	60	17	137
Fein, Midwood	12	48	22	118
Marshall, Erasmus	12	47	23	117
Cerra, Madison	11	45	26	116
Hutt, Lafayette	12	47	19	113
Rosenblatt, Midwood	12	43	18	104
Levy, Erasmus	12	42	19	103
Goodlerner, Utrecht	12	41	17	99
Wiener, Lincoln	12	37	23	97
Heller, Lincoln	12	42	13	97
Mogavero, Ft. Ham.	12	42	9	93
Lembo, Utrecht	12	34	23	91
Bywater, Ft. Ham.	12	31	22	84
Diesenhause, Lafay.	9	35	8	78
Fuertado, Madison	11	31	16	78
Harwood, Madison	12	31	14	76
Kaplan, Midwood	10	33	8	74
Bira, Lincoln	11	26	18	70
Remer, Lafayette	10	25	15	65
Singer, Midwood	6	29	6	64
Sharenow, Erasmus	12	20	21	61
Murphy, Lafayette	11	21	19	61
Olshin, Lafayette	6	19	18	56
Amascato, Ft. Ham.	10	22	4	48
Massa, Lincoln	7	18	12	48
Benson, Utrecht	7	19	9	47
Ehrlich, Midwood	11	18	9	45
D'Agostino, Lincoln	11	17	10	44
DeGregoria, Lafay'e	10	16	12	44
Schneider, Midwood	6	17	9	43
Benson, Erasmus	10	18	4	40
Adino, Ft. Ham.	7	16	8	40
Okin, Madison	10	18	4	40
Leibler, Eramus	12	12	11	35
Hoffman, Madison	11	15	5	35
B. Cohen, Utrecht	10	14	6	34
Strober, Madison	11	12	8	32
Reiser, Erasmus	12	10	8	28
Sturm, Madison	10	12	4	28
Rubin, Midwood	5	11	4	26
Weiner, Madison	11	11	4	26
Berntsein, Lafayette	6	11	2	24
Sahill, Ft. Ham.	6	8	8	24
Hilliard, Midwood	8	10	3	23
Morrison, Lincoln	6	8	6	22
Berner, Erasmus	11	5	10	20
Kaplan, Utrecht	12	7	6	20
Cole, Erasmus	8	7	5	19
Brasco, Lincoln	4	7	2	16
Hansen, Ft. Ham.	9	5	5	15
Kaufman, Erasmus	9	5	4	14
Belcastro, Erasmus	9	7	0	14
Sussman, Utrecht	9	5	3	13
Weissglass, Midwood	6	3	7	13
Goldstein, Madison	5	5	3	13
Weinstein, Lincoln	7	4	3	11
Franke, Ft. Ham.	6	4	3	11
Youngelman, Lafay.	5	4	3	11
Jetter, Lafayette	11	3	4	10

TEAM SCORING

	Won	Lost	Points For	Points Agst
Erasmus	10	2	455	401
Midwood	9	3	533	400
Madison	7	5	470	431
Lafayette	7	5	493	483
Utrecht	5	7	475	478
Lincoln	4	8	413	451
Fort Hamilton	0	12	330	523

Harrison's Putt Nips Jug McSpaden

Charlotte, N. C., March 22 (U.P.) — Sgt. E. J. (Dutch) Harrison, former Little Rock, Ark., professional, won the $7,500 Charlotte Open golf tournament with a 72-hole total of 275 yesterday, edging out Harold (Jug) McSpaden in the final round by one stroke.

Harrison, stationed at the Greensboro, N. C., Army Air Base, fired a one-over-par 73 on the final 18 holes, while McSpaden, playing with him, shot a 70 for a total of 276. Harrison had rounds of 66—70—66—73—275, while McSpaden scored 67—71—68—70—276.

Byron Nelson, who had been in and out of trouble since the tournament, started, fired a six-under-par 66 on the final round for 279 and third place. Craig Wood, Mamaroneck, N. Y., the national champion, was two under par for a 70 and took fourth money with 281. Sammy Byrd, Detroit, Mich., slipped to a 73 for 283.

Williams Scores Kayo In Jersey City Uproar

Jersey City, N. J., March 21 (U.P.)— Benny Williams, Newark, N. J., welterweight, was awarded a one-round knockout victory over Mickey Makar, Bayonne, N. J., last night more than an hour after the fight was declared no contest by Referee Joe Mangold of Atlantic City.

Williams felled his heavier opponent in one minute and 20 seconds of the first round and it was more than five minutes before Makar's seconds could revive him. Mangold, despite booing disapproval from the crowd of 2,000, would not award the victory to Williams, contending that Makar "was not hit." Later, he said Makar "was not hit hard enough."

In a semi-windup bout, Tony Riccio, 145, Bayonne, N. J., outpointed Julio Gallucci, 144, Hartford, Conn. (8).

Aid Red Cross Drive

St. Brendan's Girls School aided the Brooklyn Red Cross War Fund with a intermural basketball doubleheader. The Sophomore B class, paced by Margo Reilly's 12 points, defeated the Sophomore A class, 30—16.

Peggy Mantell and Mary Kirvin scored six points each for the Junior B team in defeating the Junior A's, 18—13.

Robins Are Caged By Bedford Team

By CHARLEY VACKNER

The Bedford Fishers caught Robins last night. On the Pearl Recreation alleys, the Robins suffered their first defeat of Spring. The birds lost all three to the team which now leads the Brooklyn Eagle D League, Boro Hall Division, by three tussles.

Unlike the horse Ideal Gift, which is an also ran, the Ideal Reds copped three games. They're on top in the Flatbush-Bay Ridge Division of the D's by three. Dave Roth zipped an even 200 as the Ideals swept a series from Quentin Red.

When news of the defeat of the Reds became known, the Quentin Blues went all out in their series against Elite. Nate Silver poked 210 for Quentin, which won all three.

Belloni Poles 230

Although the Vernons scored a 2—1 victory over Burkland, Ralph Belloni rapped 230 for the defeated quintet. Nick Englisis had a 203 for Burkland. Mike Derengo walloped 215, Charley Cabibi 208 and Artie James 203 and 204 for the conquering five.

Kopper's Coke snared three from Wabash Appliances. Strike Lamberti winged games of 224 and 203 for the Cokesmen. The sweep ushered Kopper's into second position in the Boro Hall Division. They supplanted the F. H. Levey rollers, who lost three to Oxford Filing Supply.

By winning two from Ovington, the Lafayette National Bankers are now tied for sixth place with the Brooklyn Eagle team. The Lafayettes won the first two tilts handily, but were set back in the final, 820—725.

The Eagles tallied a sweep over the Pratt team and the Knomarks lost three by forfeit to the Towns & James outfit.

BROOKLYN EAGLE D STANDINGS

Flatbush-Bay Ridge	W.	L.	Boro Hall	W.	L.
Ideal Red	47	22	Bedf'd Fishers	48	21
Burkland	44	25	Kopper's Koke	45	24
C. Quiz Kids	41	28	F. H. Levey	42	27
Vernons	40	29	Oxford Filing	40	29
Quentin Red	31	38	Lafay'te Bank	36	33
Ideal Blue	31	38	Bklyn. Eagle	36	33
Quentin Blue	27	42	Ovington	34	35
Elite	15	54	Wabash Appl.	29	40
			Knomarks	27	42
			Pratt	26	43
			Towns & James	26	43
			Robins	25	44

EAGLE D LEAGUE (Flatbush-Bay Ridge)

Quentin Red				Ideal Red (2)			
Freeman	140	137	133	Roth	200	148	150
Wenger	133	132	132	Goodman	182	148	157
Rubin	127	143	146	Russo	161	160	147
Ros'berg	145	158	171	Virga	167	172	155
Lonack	120	112	138	Swerdlow	127	157	157
Totals	655	682	710	Totals	837	785	766
Burkland				**Vernons (2)**			
Kopl'man	167	192	121	Derenzo	170	215	181
Slack'n	130	—	186	E.Martin	136	159	195
Bellino	186	230	161	W.Martin	127	151	186
Kolbe	138	161	—	James	171	203	204
Harms	151	177	147	Cabibi	208	156	154
Engl's	—	203	163				
Totals	792	963	778	Totals	812	884	940
Elite				**Quentin Blue (3)**			
Kaufman	87	129	116	Fusco	164	156	134
Hummel	123	101	—	Newman	154	146	150
Spall'j	99	135	119	Cohen	178	159	171
J.Chialli	165	144	153	Silver	210	188	180
Perrigo'e	121	126	126	Cinque	193	195	149
Murphy	—	—	96				
Totals	595	635	610	Totals	899	844	784
Ideal Blue				**Coll. Quiz Kids (3)**			
Lands'f	157	174	212	Hayes	134	—	158
Raia	145	131	111	Freeman	182	143	135
Gre'fo	114	181	150	Mangino	139	152	158
Krupn'k	149	143	147	Ekman'n	158	188	140
Samuels	136	135	135	Albert'n	144	179	186
				Horstein	—	156	—
Totals	701	764	755	Totals	758	820	777

Boro Hall D

Ovington				Lafayette N. B.			
Donohue	149	150	184	Volz	153	139	165
Fraser	129	141	159	Rabe	145	157	111
LeRay	91	—	144	Foy	159	175	179
Jablon	147	104	—	Smith	120	157	170
Buck'mer	159	—	183	Kitlitz	155	171	—
Buck	—	143	—	Harringt'n	—	—	100
Senuk	—	145	150				
Totals	675	683	820	Totals	732	799	725
Wabash App.				**Koppers Koke**			
Bellott	159	166	150	King	188	147	146
Wettlin	129	—	—	Ritchie	133	115	158
Iuzzolino	137	158	125	Santora	142	166	124
Garb'loto	142	107	—	Macint'h	158	137	176
Tucker	184	168	137	Lambe'ti	153	224	203
Shpiro	—	164	173				
Mangano	—	—	140				
Totals	751	763	725	Totals	774	789	807
Robins				**Bedford Fishers**			
Foley	124	130	167	Rella	164	159	154
Harmon	169	111	146	P.Fish'ti	150	167	164
Keegan	122	124	121	Oped'ano	147	133	—
Olson	133	133	142	A.Fish'ti	147	161	147
Bartsch	128	124	161	Balduc	113	166	174
				Jalmenro	—	—	157
Totals	676	622	737	Totals	721	786	796
Towns & James				**Knomarks**			
Yerkes	133	121	139				
Wiegmann	91	123	144				
Gisonna	137	145	207	Forfeit			
McG'kin	100	136	119				
Blind	100	100	100				
Totals	561	625	709				
Pratt				**Eagle (3)**			
Keane	116	114	112	Rabid'x	140	147	135
R. Ross	139	108	134	Eaton	123	150	160
Canonica	139	127	134	Parisi	112	141	135
Musto	160	124	—	Geiger	161	164	169
F. Ross	127	102	180	Watkins	164	165	160
Balvo	—	—	135				
Totals	681	575	695	Totals	700	767	759
F. H. Levey				**Oxford F Supply (3)**			
Schaef'r	127	117	—	Kruse	104	—	—
Gomez	136	144	125	West	156	119	151
Krolick	113	125	—	Xeller	137	132	122
Delisch	144	135	140	Luecher	157	157	143
Garcia	150	149	150	Beyer	134	163	164
Satchell	—	—	119	Schumm	—	107	152
Nastasi	—	—	132				
Totals	670	670	666	Totals	688	678	732

Bushwick Sign O'Neil,

Manager Joe Press of the Bushwicks, who sent 30 candidates through a three-hour drill at Dexter Park last Sunday, has scheduled Saturday and Sunday afternoon workouts.

Press announced taht he signed first baseman Jack O'Neil, formerly of New York University and who played with Little Rock of the Southern Association, to fill the spot left vacant by Gene Rodgers.

Xavier Still Redmen's Jinx In CHS Play

By JAMES J. MURPHY

Anyone knowing the whereabouts of a voodoo doctor please consult Herb Hess, athletic director of St. John's Prep. Ever since 1930, when his charges won the opening of the metropolitan Catholic high schools championship basketball tourney he has been trying to find the combination to a repeat performance. He has been jinxed since then.

The hoodoo dogged the steps of his well-groomed minions in the 15th edition of the competition in the Columbus Casey clubhouse last night. As a result the Redmen bowed to the club that seems to have a hex on them—Xavier High, 49—43. The elimination of the Redmen leaves the tourney a wide-open affair.

St. Dominic Bow

In other two games St. Nicholas of Tolentine, Bronx, repulsed a scrappy St. Dominic outfit from Oyster Bay, 49—30, and St. Peter's High of Staten Island, winner of the Brooklyn - Richmond - Lower Manhattan C. H. S. A. A. title, subdued Rice High of Manhattan, 50—28.

There will be a respite tonight, but when hostilities are resumed in the quarter-final round tomorrow night at 6:15 o'clock four games will be conducted. The show will open with St. Peter's Prep of Jersey City and St. Nicholas of Tolentine. Then, in order, games between St. Michael's High of Manhattan and All Hallows Institute, Power Memorial Academy and Xavier High, and Brooklyn Prep and St. Peter's High of Staten Island are scheduled.

St. John's started out as if it was going to hurdle the old jinx. The Redmen trailed by 11—9 at the quarter, but assumed command by 37—35 at the half, and maintained a 37—35 advantage at the three-quarter mark. The Hessmen went to pieces in the final quarter and were limited to six points.

Browne's Pops Decide

Jimmy Browne and his pop shots were a thorn in the side of the Redmen as evidenced by his 16 points, and George Kaftan's 11 tallies added insult to injury.

The St. Nicholas Tolentine attack was paced by Bill Crawford and Joe Liguori with 16 and 13 points, respectively. Bob Maguire had 14 for St. Dominic's, which trailed, 21—17, at intermission.

Joe Sinski and Aloysius registered 26 points between them for St. Peter's, which compiled a 22—11 part-time edge on Rice. Bill Rogers was outstanding for Rice.

St. Nicholas	G.	F.	P.	St. Dominic's	G.	F.	P.
Crawford	7	2	16	Maguire	5	4	14
Sullivan	1	0	2	Horan	1	2	4
Skea	2	0	4	De Bellis	1	1	3
Liguori	5	3	13	Suozzi	0	0	0
Hynes	0	0	0	Minicozzi	0	0	0
Kilgallon	1	1	3	Rodden	0	0	0
Martin	2	1	5	De Bellis	0	0	0
Chanfrau	1	1	3	Plimley	0	0	0
Cohane	1	1	3	Murphy	0	0	0
Cohn	0	0	0	Nicholson	4	0	8
				McGarr	0	0	0
				Addazzio	0	1	1
Totals	20	9	49	Totals	11	8	30

Xavier	G.	F.	P.	St. John's	G.	F.	P.
Sterrett	0	0	0	Kaiser	3	2	8
Keyes	1	0	2	Smyth	4	3	11
Byrnes	3	2	8	Powers	5	1	11
Novak	4	0	8	Della Monica	5	1	11
Kaftan	5	1	11	Haller	1	0	2
Butler	1	0	2	Griffin	0	0	0
Jackman	1	0	2	McGuire	0	0	0
Gilsenan	0	0	0				
Browne	7	2	16				
Carlin	0	0	0				
Totals	22	5	49	Totals	18	7	43

St. Peter's. S. I.	G.	F.	P.	Rice	G.	F.	P.
Corley	2	1	5	Schram	2	0	4
Barry	0	0	0	McCarron	0	0	0
Sinski	4	6	14	J. Duffy	0	0	0
Westcott	1	1	3	Levins	1	1	3
D. Naples	2	1	5	Casey	0	0	0
A. Naples	4	4	12	Liquorie	0	0	0
Miehe	1	0	2	Gettings	1	0	2
R. Duffy	3	0	6	Magee	0	0	0
Hicks	1	1	3	Rogers	5	0	10
				Guerci	1	3	5
				Foley	0	0	0
				Sullivan	1	1	3
				Lynch	0	1	1
				O'Connell	0	0	0
				Moylan	0	0	0
Totals	18	14	50	Totals	11	6	28

Three Teams Withdraw From Cup Soccer

By BILL GRAHAM

Three teams in the third round draw for the New York State Challenge Soccer Cup have forfeited to their opponents for various reasons. Recent heavy loss of players to the armed services is the reason advanced by the Prospect Unity, which had drawn the German-American A. C.

Maccabi F. C. of the Eastern District League, paired with the local Hakoah, demanded another draw after refusing to meet its obligation. The cup committee accepted its resignation from competition. Elizabeth F. C. was originally drawn at home to the Hota' of Astoria but the fact that the pitch in Elizabeth was not enclosed caused the game to be switched to Astoria. The Jersey ground was then declared qualified, but the committee refused to switch the engagement and the club withdrew.

Sunday's Pairings

The remainder of the draw Sunday is Eintracht vs. Swiss, Schlesier F. S. C. vs. New York, German-Hungarian vs. Kollsman, Brooklyn vs. Pfaelzer, Hoboken vs. Minerva.

Joe Novas of Brooklyn Hispano joined the navy and because of his efficiency in languages was sent to the U. S. Consulate at Costa Rica...He has now returned to Trinity College, Hartford, for a special language course...The last American League game of the season will be played at the Oval Sunday between the retiring champion, Hispano, and the new winners, Philadelphia Americans.

METROPOLITAN LEAGUE STANDING OF TEAMS

	W.	L.	T.	P.
Segura	12	1	3	27
Bronx Scots	10	0	5	25
Cork Celtic	9	1	4	22
Swedish	7	5	1	15
Parklea	6	7	3	15
Sada	3	7	5	11
Uhrik Truckers	5	10	1	11
White Plains	4	11	2	10
Peru	3	10	2	8
Wheeler	3	10	2	8

THE ASSEMBLY LINE

By BEN GOULD

Latest sport at Arma is, believe it or not, polo . . . Bill Carlson is preparing to have a team represent the plant in regular competition during the Summer months . . . Pete Sebekos, ex-Bendix hurler, now in the seabees at Joliet, Ill., was in town on an emergency weekend . . . His father-inlaw, Frank Lester was killed in a railroad accident . . . Lester was Pete's greatest admirer . . . Grumman's Larry Eckstein, a crack pro referee, has been rejected for military duty.

There are six war plant quintets represented in the Veterans of Foreign Wars basketball tourney, which starts tonight at the Jamaica Arena . . . They include the Martletes, Republic, Ranger, Colgate Aircraft, Ford Instrument and Pan-American Aircraft teams . . . 26 other clubs are also competing . . . Pete Reiher is directing the event . . . Aside to J. R.: Bobby McDermott's Zollner Pistons won the National basketball loop honors by beating Sheboygan in three straight playoff contests . . . Bendix's popular Ed Malone, now in the navy, has been transferred from the Newport Naval Training Station to a Manhattan post.

Maywood Recreation at Farmingdale is the scene of the annual Long Island Aircraft invitation team bowling tournament on Saturday . . . Bob Robideau, employed at Brewster, is the same chap who held the New England lightweight boxing title for four years . . . In competition in United States, England and France he showed he possessed an iron jaw . . . No one ever flattened him in 218 bouts . . . And, speaking of boxers, Columbia's French Loudoux once acted as Lou Ambers' trainer.

A protest lodged by Sperry against Grumman in the aircraft cage circuit has been rejected . . . The game was forfeited to the Wildcats when Sperry refused to finish the tilt with four minutes of play remaining . . . Jimmy McLarnin, one of the ring's greatest fighters, is now working for an airplane plant in Hollywood . . . His love right now is golf, and he never misses touring the links whenever his assembly line duties are over.

Dempsey to Referee Seamen's Bout Tonight

Lt. Comm. Jack Dempsey, U. S. C. G., will be honored by merchant seamen tonight at the United Seamen's Service Andrew Furuseth Club, 30 E. 37th St., Manhattan, when Dempsey Night is observed.

Dempsey will be third man in the ring when two seamen-in-training at the U. S. Maritime School, Sheepshead Bay, battle three rounds. The scrappers are welterweights Garland Parnell of Springfield, Ill., three-time champion of the Golden Gloves in 1938, 1940 and 1941, and Julius Rosenblum of Baltimore, two-time Maryland State amateur champion.

Former Police Commissioner Edward P. Mulrooney, U. S. S. port area chairman, will introduce Dempsey, who will also give a sports talk.

4 Empty Coal Pockets Damaged in Night Fire

Fire late last night caused considerable damage to four empty coal pockets in the yard of Soranno Brothers, coal and ice dealers, at Sackett St. and the Gowanus Canal.

Deputy Fire Chief Edward Conway was in charge of firemen who fought the blaze. The fireboat William J. Gaynor was at the scene, but had difficulty in getting there because of the low tide.

SPORT SHORTS

BASEBALL—By Harold C. Burr

SEVERAL National League clubs and one over in the American—presumably the Yankees—are after any Dodger surplus that happens to be on the market. . . . It's known that they have been making overtures toward securing Johnny Cooney, Paul Waner and Ray Hayworth. . . . There were eight pitchers with but a single mind at yesterday morning's workout at the West Point field house. . . . The pitching slab had been uprooted so the infield can be re-rolled. . . . Those eight hurlers measured off the proper distance with their eyes. . . . Then a steel tape was sent for and it was found that the hurlers had missed calculations by a quarter of an inch. . . . Manager Leo Durocher wishes they could be as deadly in locating the plate.

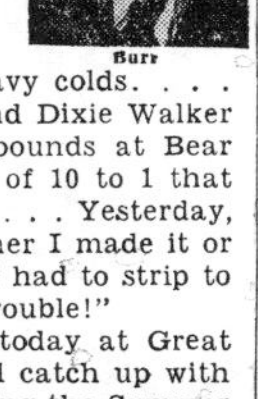
Burr

Luis Olmo and Augie Galan didn't work out. . . . The outfielders were nursing heavy colds. . . . Rube Melton lost his bets with Durocher and Dixie Walker that he would melt himself down to 205 pounds at Bear Mountain. . . . Leo gave the pitcher odds of 10 to 1 that he couldn't take off the requisite 20 pounds. . . . Yesterday, the Rube paid off . . . "I don't know whether I made it or not the last day," he said carelessly. "I'd of had to strip to get on the scales. Heck, it was too much trouble!"

Billy Herman began his boot training today at Great Lakes Naval Station. . . . The Dodgers will catch up with their former second baseman some time during the Summer when they play an exhibition game there. . . . Bill Sahlin, southpaw pitcher from the Bushwicks, is said to be going well with the Cubs. . . . Wallie Signer, who was on the Bushwick hurling corps with Bill and went up to the Cubs in 1943 only to be farmed to Nashville, is sticking to his Navy Yard [illegible] will return to pitching around Brooklyn this year.

TURF—By Tapper Mills

THE fourth season of New York racing under the pari-mutuel system of wagering opened at Jamaica today and, in marked contrast to other sports, the turf is anticipating the biggest year in its history.

Unless there is an actual shut-down of all sports—an occurrence most unlikely—racing will be at its very best, will handle the most money (at least $300,000,000, we figure) and make its greatest contribution to the war relief funds.

The $7,500 Paumonk, traditional Jamaica opener, will feature a battle of speed between Greentree Stable's Devil Diver and Belair Stud's coal black Apache, among others. Though the berth of favoritism will rest between one of these, a crack group of mizzlers will oppose them and it may well be that the stake will go to a long shot. We like Devil Diver, if that means anything to you.

Anyway, the main thing is that the horses are off and running in this neck o' the woods once more and will be with us until mid-November. Oh, for the co-makers' concession!

HOMESTRETCHING—We hate to toss cold water on the kid's sensational finish, but wasn't Bobby Permane's luck at Tropical Park the last ten days due as much to the absence of the "name" boys as it was to his riding skill? . . . GOOD THING may be just that at Jamaica . . . Seems to be ready and is in clever hands . . . Wayne Wright, a coast guardsman for the last couple of months, was able to arrange a furlough from Manhattan Beach to see the opener . . . The no parking edict will be a bonanza to the local house fraus and others who accommodate the turf fans who drive to the track, anyway . . . One chap made $11,000 last year as a result of owning a lot opposite Jamaica . . . Whom do you like in the double?

BOWLING—By Charles Vackner

The 26-year-old Bert Jacob is in North Camp Hood, Texas. . . . Bert used to manage the Quentin Bowling Center. . . . He's now with a tank destroyer battalion. . . . Sam Cohen of the Quentin D League champions, the Reds, enters the army a week from Friday. . . . Cohen, a consistent D bowler, averaged 147 in 87 games. . . . Last Wednesday Sam had a 537 series. . . . Cohen's 208 was individual high for the evening.

Wac Lt. Gertrude Goldberg rejoined her outfit yesterday. . . . The commissioned officer, who has completed 20 months as a member of the Wacs was home on a ten-day furlough. . . . Miss Goldberg bowled for the Destroyers of the Ocean Ladies' League last season and averaged 153. . . . In her most recent games in the E. 18th St. center she rolled 198 and 174. . . . Formerly stationed in Pine Bluff, Ark., Miss Goldberg has been summoned to serve with a unit in Oregon.

Vackner

Soldier Joe Aste, last of the Brooklyn individual champions for the duration, is now with an outfit in Lincoln, Neb. . . . Aste was stationed in Salt Lake City, Utah.

Joe Brown, who used to perform on local alleys, is now doing special police work in the Navy Yard. . . . Brown gets but little opportunity to bowl for he works the 4-12 trick. . . . Brownie tells us that Eddie (Kid) Whalen and Mickey White, former militia boxing champions, hook up in many torrid duckpin games. . . . Whalen and White work in the yard, too.

The St. Vincent Ferrer team won the Vanderveer C. Y. O. bowling title and is ready to compete against other sectional champs on the State alleys, April 19. . . . Ed Chatfield is chairman of the roll-offs. . . . Winners of this event will compete against the victors in the Nassau-Queens meet for the diocesan title. . . . Each section will also enter a team of stars to compete for the Diocesan All-Star championship.

ROUNDUP—By Joe Donovan

MICHIGAN STATE COLLEGE plans a 1944 football schedule, limiting games to colleges and universities where eligibility is confined to civilian students . . . Jockey Bobby Permane rode five straight winners yesterday at Tropical, bringing his winning series there to 44 in 29 days, 13 in the last three days . . . Dick Wakefield, former Detroit Tiger batting and outfield star, will be the mainstay of the Iowa Navy Pre-Flight team . . . Wakefield reported this week and is due to be stationed there three months.

Mervyn Dutton, hockey league prexy, says National Hockey League officials were empowered to forfeit to the visiting club any future Stanley Cup games which the fans delay by throwing debris on the ice . . . This action was prompted by a 20-minute demonstration at Chicago the other night . . . The Massachusetts Boxing Commission suspended Dannie Arditto for failing to fulfill a scheduled bout at the Fall River Casino, March 30.

Donovan

Lt. Ira Kepford, former Northwestern football star, is at his home in Muskegon, Mich., after shooting down 16 Jap planes in 75 days of combat in the Southwest Pacific . . . Al Barlick, major league ump now in the coast guard, may umpire Morgan Park, Conn., Twilight League games . . . Auburn appointed two new coaches, Arnold Umbach and Shorty Propst . . . Ray Flanagan of Staten Island may pitch for the Newark Bears against the Boston Braves at Plainfield tomorrow . . . George Trautman, American Association prexy, said a group of high school athletic czars have drafted a set of recommendations by which Organized Baseball might help promote the game in schools.

Sgt. Buddy Baer, now in Palm Beach, Fla., announced that he is engaged to marry Ruth Eleanor Phillips of Lake Worth, Fla. He said they would be married Sept. 9 when his divorce decree becomes final . . . Governor Dewey yesterday signed a bill legalizing the taking of both buck and doe deer with bow and arrow only in Westchester County . . . New Hampshire trails promise Eastern skiing . . . The Montclair, N. J., Golf Club has been awarded the N. J. State Open championship July 9 over 36 holes . . . War bonds will be prizes and the Red Cros will get admission fees.

UNITED PRESS SELECTIONS

Tropical Park

1—Great Albert, Smoky Snyder, Ever Flying.
2—Stitch Again, Liberty Pan, War Page.
3—The Captain, Nibble, Well entry.
4—Pigtails, Mintlock, Zaca Rosa.
5—Jamerica, Rosy Brand, Art of War.
6—Four Freedoms, Marriage, Grasshopper II.
7—Ski Lift, Santa Marie, Bell Call.
8—Liberty D., Belfry Chimes, Budded.
BEST—STITCH AGAIN.

"Sheppey," the W. Somerset Maughan comedy starring Edmund Gwenn, has been cordially received by reviewers in Boston, where the company is playing a two weeks' engagement at the Colonial Theater, with Sir Cedric Hardwicke supervising revisions and minor cast changes preparatory to the New York opening on Tuesday, April 18, at the Playhouse.

Jamaica Form

By TAPPER MILLS

(ONLY FIRST THREE HORSES ARE GRADED)

FOR SATURDAY

FIRST RACE—$1,800; claiming; four-year-olds and up; six furlongs.

P.P.	Horse	Jockey	Wt.	Prob. Odds
5	FLYING SON	Atkinson	119	4-1
7	HAPPY LARK	Parke	121	2-1
3	KING LEROY	Gonzalez	119	3-1
1	Wise Brave	Gonzalez	121	12-1
2	xxTatu	Pittarelli	116	10-1
4	Bygone Star	Westrope	121	10-1
6	Free Double	Guerin	121	6-1
8	Umbril	No boy	110	20-1

SECOND RACE—$2,100; maidens, three-year-olds and up; six furlongs.

P.P.	Horse	Jockey	Wt.	Prob. Odds
11	BULL DANDY	Lynch	113	7-2
1	BOUNDING BOW	Atkinson	113	5-2
9	GENERAL WAR	No boy	113	8-1
2	Blue Ridge	No boy	108	30-1
3	xxHeight O'Land	Pittarelli	108	20-1
4	All White	Rienzi	108	30-1
5	xxHockey	Phelps	108	20-1
6	Bric a Bac	No boy	113	8-1
7	xxQueens Reward	Gerlock	105	10-1
8	Songburst	Dodson	108	10-1
10	Jean Miracle	No boy	113	4-1

THIRD RACE—$2,500; the Worthmore; allowances; two-year-olds; five furlongs.

P.P.	Horse	Jockey	Wt.	Prob. Odds
1	REASON	Dodson	111	5-1
9	aFORUM	No boy	116	2-1
4	ANNIE LEA	No boy	108	10-1
2	Talmadge	No boy	116	2-1
3	Sel Cap	No boy	111	12-1
5	Motie Brand	Strange	116	15-1
6	He Got There	Atkinson	111	8-1
7	Nory	Jemas	108	20-1
8	aHillyer Court	Parke	111	2-1

aH. McL. Fenwick and V. Emanuel entry.

FOURTH RACE—$4,000; the Snark; allowances; three-year-olds; five and one-half furlongs.

P.P.	Horse	Jockey	Wt.	Prob. Odds
5	FOX BROWNIE	Guerin	117	12-1
11	aTambo	Atkinson	117	9-5
3	NAPOO	No boy	113	30-1
1	Tarpan	Loveridge	113	20-1
2	War Dressing	No boy	113	6-1
4	Say Sandy	Weidaman	108	30-1
6	Wild Rice	Dodson	113	10-1
7	Nursery Tale	No boy	113	12-1
8	aBroad Grin	Breen	117	9-5
9	Uncle Ace	No boy	113	10-1
10	xxWise Step	Gerlock	108	12-1
12	Smart Sheila	Atkinson	108	6-1
13	Bud Grey	Brooks	115	3-1

aGreentree Stable entry.

FIFTH RACE—$7,500 added; the Paumonock Handicap; three-year-olds and up; six furlongs.

P.P.	Horse	Jockey	Wt.	Prob. Odds
1	DEVIL DIVER	Atkinson	130	5-2
11	APACHE	No boy	130	3-1
10	aMETTLESOME	No boy	112	5-1
2	aFlak	No boy	106	5-1
3	bAlex Barth	No boy	110	20-1
4	Bill Sickle	No boy	108	30-1
5	bSwimmin Hole	No boy	105	20-1
6	Cassis	Brooks	120	6-1
7	Boysy	Westrope	112	10-1
8	Brownie	Guerin	112	8-1
9	cEurasian	Steffen	119	8-1
12	cEye For Eye	Lindberg	102	8-1
13	Go Gino	Dodson	110	20-1
14	Dartaway	No boy	102	15-1

aMrs. B Digiorgio entry.
bMillbrook Stable entry.
cHavahome Stable entry.

SIXTH RACE — $5,000; the King Saxon; allowances; four-year-olds and up; mile and one-sixteenth.

P.P.	Horse	Jockey	Wt.	Odds Prob.
5	ALEX BARTH	No boy	113	9-5
2	MOON MAIDEN	Atkinson	109	7-2
1	xxBIRCH ROD	No boy	109	5-1
2	Moon Maiden	Atkinson	109	7-2
3	Rascal	Schmidl	114	3-1
4	Happy Hunting	No boy	114	6-1
6	Rath Ronan	No boy	113	12-1

SEVENTH RACE — $1,800; claiming; four-year-olds and up; mile and one-sixteenth.

P.P.	Horse	Jockey	Wt.	Prob. Odds
6	SICKLE T	Gonzalez	120	2-1
7	xxLOST GOLD	Gerlock	112	5-1
10	xxTHRIFT	Haslett	110	20-1
1	xxBohemond	No boy	109	12-1
2	xxxOakford	Goggi	106	20-1
3	Lochness	Guerin	114	5-1
4	High Plaid	Murphy	120	7-2
5	Alca Gal	No boy	109	10-1
8	xxChickore	Pittarelli	109	15-1
9	Playfields	Jemas	109	10-1

BEST—FLYING SON, 1ST RACE.

xx5 pounds; xxx10 pounds; apprentice allowance claims listed.

Tropical Park Entries

FOR SATURDAY

FIRST RACE—$1,200; claiming; four-year-olds and up; six furlongs; chute.

P.P.	Wt.	P.P.	Wt.
1 xOrcus	112	7 Zacharias	109
2 Ever Flying	114	8 xPaladin	109
3 Lawyersville	109	9 Smoky Snyder	114
4 Balmy Spring	114	10 Illinois Star	112
5 xGreat Albert	107	11 xEpidown	101
6 Call to Colors	117		

SECOND RACE — $1,200; allowances; Grade D; four-year-olds and up; six furlongs; chute.

P.P.	Wt.	P.P.	Wt.
1 Equistar	111	5 Likeasnot	117
2 War Page	117	6 Liberty Pan	120
3 xStitch Again	112	7 Urge Me	106
4 xCyrus P.	106	8 Wishbone	111

THIRD RACE—$1,200; allowances; Grade D; three-year-olds; six furlongs; chute.

P.P.	Wt.	P.P.	Wt.
1 aCampion Hall	111	5 xThe Captain	106
2 aObserver	111	6 xChere Brandy	106
3 Celtics	111	7 Collar Ad	111
4 Lord Hairan	117	8 Nibble	117

aMrs. W. Weil and J. M. Hutchins entry.

FOURTH RACE—$1,200; the Easton; allowances; three-year-olds and up; six furlongs; chute.

P.P.	Wt.	P.P.	Wt.
1 Zaca Rosa	112	4 Blue Pom	111
2 xPig Tails	107	5 xMartian	112
3 Good Going	93	6 xMintlock	109

FIFTH RACE—$1,600; the Chesapeake; Grade D allowances; three-year-olds and up; mile and a sixteenth.

P.P.	Wt.	P.P.	Wt.
1 xJamerica	117	5 xHickory Head	109
2 xRosy Brand	109	6 Capt. Caution	113
3 Art of War	119	7 xRush Act	111
4 Port Harm'ny	108	8 xSpeedway	108

SIXTH RACE — $10,000 added; the Tropical Handicap; three-year-olds and up; mile and an eighth.

P.P.	Wt.	P.P.	Wt.
1 Sweep Singer	105	4 Marriage	126
2 Argon'e Wo'ds	108	5 Equinox	103
3 Gra'sho'per II	114	6 Four Freedoms	120

SEVENTH RACE — $1,200; claiming; three-year-olds; mile and a sixteenth.

P.P.	Wt.	P.P.	Wt.
1 xToo Much	107	5 xSki Lift	107
2 Bell Call	111	6 xSanta Marie	107
3 xBetty's Beau	106	7 Revive	111
4 Tib	106		

EIGHTH RACE—$1,200; claiming; four-year-olds and up; mile and one-half.

P.P.	Wt.	P.P.	Wt.
1 Farragut	111	5 xLiberty B	106
2 xRoyal Count	104	6 xJudfry	101
3 xBelfry Ch'es	101	7 xBudded	106
4 Calvert	111		

xApprentice allowance claimed.

Public Golf Links Open April 15

The 10 municipal golf courses operated by the Department of Parks will be opened for play for the season, April 15. All of the courses are readily accessible by transit facilities. The food and refreshment bars in the clubhouses will also open for the season. The same golf professionals will be on hand as last year. Golf pros will arrange for lessons and make repairs to golf equipment.

Golf permits for the season cost $5. An additional charge of 10c will be made to permit holders on weekdays and an additional charge of 50c on Saturdays, Sundays and holidays. Daily golf fees remain the same: 75c on weekdays and $1 on Saturdays, Sundays and holidays.

Complete listing of the golf courses can be found in the telephone directory.

Permits can be secured at any of the five borough offices.

Bowling League Averages

INDIVIDUAL AVERAGES of the BROOKLYN EAGLE LEAGUES

(Includes Games March 12)

Classic

BELL GRAY			
Johnson	75	13536	180.5
Lansing	75	13270	177
Bellman	72	13339	185.2
Cunningham	72	12923	179.5
Piazza	72	12714	176.7
PEARL RED			
Petito	64	12672	198
Bartos	68	11729	172.5
Soper	72	12924	179.5
Loufek	57	10419	182.8
Peluso	42	7428	177
Nastri	27	4561	169
Mang	22	3701	168.2
BURKLAND			
Burkland	75	14841	198
Fenimore	54	9624	178.2
Putney	75	13659	182
Wagner	75	13031	173.8
De Vito	74	13812	186.8
ELITE			
Corso	73	13980	191.5
Chamberlain	54	9988	185
Barnum	75	13586	181.2
Collins	69	12440	180.2
Ecks	54	10093	187
Hadley	41	6905	168.3
FARRAGUT			
Hadfield	74	13305	179.8
Snyder	70	12582	179.7
Gefry	47	7969	169.6
Schwarz	68	11767	173
Katz	55	9612	174.8
Peck	40	7018	175.6
KEYSTONE			
Deturris	75	14339	191.2
Al Caime	75	13721	183
Aldo Caime	72	12688	176
Amen	72	12655	175.7
De Simone	60	10754	179.2
LAWLER			
Saporita	72	13661	189.8
Lawler	75	13894	185.2
Rhodes	74	13841	187
Maddaloni	75	13914	185.6
De Phillips	36	6224	173
Roth	19	3037	160
SHORE VIEW			
Thoren	75	13405	178.8
Dicks	69	11479	166.2
O'Conner	66	11196	169.7
Fischer	51	9184	180
Johnson	27	4557	168.8
Hansen	45	7811	173.6
Ponella	23	3507	152.5
PEARL BLUE			
Bordiuk	73	13479	184.7
Nicolay	75	14074	187.7
Sarelakos	75	13833	184.4
Tonn	63	10707	170
Worsley	33	6076	184
BELL BLUE			
Aiello	75	13554	180.8
Platt	75	14377	191.7
Gerken	68	12396	182.3
Nicholas	69	12410	179.8
Harmon	75	13639	181.9

Class A

ALBEE SQUARE BLUE			
Falborn	72	12924	179.5
Suler	75	13833	184.7
Cipriano	66	11170	178.3
Gloisten	69	12068	175
Totten	63	10920	173.3
LAWLER BLUE			
Gemelaro	69	11855	172.2
Jacaruso	72	11502	159.8
Mirande	75	12718	169.6
Jamat	72	12380	172
Radke	51	8918	175
L. Shaw	24	4049	168.8
BURKLAND			
F. Nola	66	11512	174.4
Forte	72	12401	172.2
Vancel	75	13446	180
Keiser	72	12738	177
Alexander	69	11818	171.2
ELITE			
Meringolo	66	11298	171.2
Palmer	64	10585	165.4
Pasquenza	60	10147	169
McDonald	42	7562	180
Sims	42	7305	174
Buxbaum	30	5117	170.5
Durante	18	2847	158
FARRAGUT			
Jack Lucke	69	12225	177
Graham	72	12963	180
Joe Lucke	51	9146	179.4
Henriques	75	13431	179
Rosenquist	37	6497	175.6
Mula	60	9848	182.3
OCEAN			
Richmond	45	8119	180.4
Hograf	73	12626	173
Weidner	67	11639	173.7
Wilcox	26	4124	158.7
Lyons	62	10458	168.7
McAvoy	47	8048	171.2
Casazza	49	7940	162
PARKWAY			
De Leo	75	13369	178.2
Cohen	75	13512	180.2
Cipriano	75	13235	176.6
Herman	72	13000	180.6
Stefano	75	12993	173.2
KEYSTONE			
Dildarian	73	13031	178.5
Rogers	75	13311	177.5
Esposito	75	13067	174.2
Nocero	73	12376	169.6
Tomasi	30	5156	172
Rupp	24	4144	172.8
Treval	19	3232	170
LAWLER RED			
McLeod	72	12857	178.6
Coates	58	9661	166.7
Chattleton	66	11281	171
Saccardi	66	11357	172
N. Shaw	64	10990	171.8
Yockers	45	7508	167
SHORE VIEW			
Wendt	60	10267	171
Fayad	57	9287	163
Bracklein	45	7200	160
Eadeh	69	12139	176
Benford	29	4874	168
Strogarek	21	3383	161
COLLEGE			
Waller	72	12555	174.4
Humphrey	73	12450	170.6
Nelson	68	10670	157
Burati	55	9098	165.4
Strobel	61	9887	162
KINGSWAY			
Cucci	74	13539	183
Grape	75	13500	180
Williams	75	13302	177.4
Schroeder	60	10475	174.6
Garvin	57	10326	181
Kohl	19	3040	160
REGAL			
Petrizzo	75	13699	182.7
Sacer	75	12817	171
Tempera	67	11926	178
King	64	11281	176.2
Carrizzo	49	8475	173
Pesce	24	4230	176.2
ALBEE SQUARE RED			
Moore	72	12558	174.4
Fenniman	51	8793	172.4
Galetto	75	12416	165.6
Renda	69	12461	180.7
Lombardi	42	7743	184.3
Varone	24	4346	181
Weiler	36	6113	170

Brooklyn Eagle B

BURKLAND RED			
Ehrenberg	59	10322	175
Kraft	62	10468	169
Lipshutz	53	8162	154
Wesselhoft	51	8816	173
Keese	52	9130	175.6
KEYSTONE RED			
Leone	63	11130	176.7
Roberts	58	9599	165.5
Rankin	63	10928	173.5
Treval	60	10303	171.7
Rogers	63	11220	178
PARK SLOPE			
Acuri	52	8729	168
De Vito	57	9579	168
Molinelli	22	3548	161
Cossentino	58	10411	179.5
Falcone	53	9618	181.5
Rappa	57	10114	177.4
QUENTIN RED			
Slamowitz	62	9419	152
Moffie	5[illegible]	8380	161
Magnus	6[illegible]	[illegible]0421	165.4
Fusco	5[illegible]	[illegible]738	143.2
Friedman	[illegible]	[illegible]	158.5
Meyerson	36	[illegible]434	151
BORO			
Berinato	53	9008	170
Ricco	35	5817	166
Correnti	25	4139	165.6
Buddy	57	10288	180.5
Ramondetta	48	8363	174
Pisano	37	6606	178.5
Marghella	57	10420	182.8
QUENTIN BLUE			
Snyder	63	10713	170
Kunz	63	10059	159.7
Horn	63	10323	164
Shulman	60	9651	161
Sayre	45	7083	157.3
REGAL			
Cuthbertson	56	9789	174.8
Raitano	52	8787	169
Andersen	55	9257	168.3
Sosnowski	57	9610	168.6
Guady	54	9466	175.3
Sacer	34	6073	178.7
PEIL'S			
Stobitzer	61	9768	160
Mattel	63	10811	171.7
Tants	63	10637	169
Forest	20	2932	146.6
Meyer	60	10273	171.2
Hering	45	7741	172
MIQUES BAR and GRILL			
Haslinger	60	10435	174
Fantini	63	10625	168.7
Ancona	63	10703	170
Erickson	24	4440	185
Huff	40	6571	164.2
GROSS SHOES			
Schnepf	63	10382	164.8
Zwiercan	61	9736	159.6
Keegan	62	10306	166.2
Beare	54	9381	173.8
Seipel	59	9152	155
WONDER BREAD			
Spinard	63	10701	170
Zeimeister	52	7843	150.8
Meeteer	48	7142	148.8
Volpe	63	10189	161.7
Staar	60	9987	166.5
PORT ALBA			
T. Gigante	52	8743	168
Zurzola	48	7953	165.7
Pesce	58	10062	173.5
Barlow	47	7699	163.8
Lorenzo	46	7430	161.5
Cappiello	39	6576	168.7
KEYSTONE BLUE			
Pascale	63	10934	173.6
Di Pisa	62	9810	158.2
Abruzzo	61	10665	175
Nardone	53	8983	169.5
Molino	49	8066	164.7
BURKLAND BLUE			
Klein	59	9741	165
Labita	62	10209	164.8
Tenen	44	7424	168.8
Potter	58	10044	173
Heller	57	9647	169.2

Flatbush and Boro Hall C

BURKLAND RED			
Manzo	58	9753	168.9
N. Englisis	54	8499	157.4
T. Englisis	56	8942	159.7
Maida	62	10292	166
Jeanetti	60	10601	176.7
BUNNELL CO.			
Verniorey	60	9456	157.6
Minerva	52	8938	172
Rebele	32	4711	147.2
Finnegan	38	5822	153.2
Kulmacz'ski	23	3468	151
Pardo	27	3908	144.8
Horan	30	4810	160.3
Biondo	20	2781	139
BETHLEHEM BLUES			
Mathieson	53	8355	157.7
A. Bologna	50	7823	156.6
Lutz	60	9522	158.8
Ferrar	58	9003	155.2
Metzler	44	6986	158.8
Kircher	47	7669	163
REGENT			
Serrano	57	7707	135.2
Molinari	53	7908	149.2
Carboni	42	5505	131
O'Donnell	35	4733	135.2
Padgett	35	5021	143.4
Henry	30	3989	133
PEARL PICKUPS			
Fischer	51	8055	158
Medina	48	7165	149.2
Thomas	49	7093	144.8
Strub	59	9630	163.2
Detzel	52	8849	170.2
Mulhall	48	7425	154.7
HAUCK CO.			
Lackner	63	9780	155.2
Armstrong	59	9858	167
Windish	60	9565	159.2
Pearson	40	5739	143.5
Heinz	39	6131	157.2
ELITE			
Esler	60	9137	152.3
Lutjen	59	9275	157.2
Ayles	55	8525	155
Pfister	27	4249	157.3
Bono	63	10024	159.1
Combes	42	6751	160.7
Marsa			
Gulan	55	9127	166
O'Brien	63	9729	154.4
Franco	59	10059	170.5
Germano	58	8879	153
Farancz	50	8243	165
Saviano	29	4376	151
ALBEE SQUARE			
Lyons	63	10685	169.7
Avellina	63	10196	162
Robinson	54	8813	163.2
Sontag	53	8557	161.4
Dwyer	63	10371	164.7
BURKLAND BLUE			
Aron	25	3784	151.3
Chess	25	3621	145
Pantaleon	22	3135	142.6
Reitman	17	2252	132.3
Amendola	18	2553	142
Miller	11	1758	160

Bay Ridge C

BAY RIDGE OVALS			
Ponella	47	7175	152.8
Murtagh	37	5550	150
Johnston	41	6152	150
Senuk	63	10506	166.7
Rangold	31	4716	152
Cullen	31	5042	162.7
Chippardi	27	4596	170
EDGEWOOD CHURCH			
Bermas	49	7536	153.8
Anderson	61	9621	157.7
Dreyfus	31	4193	135.3
Grelia	45	6847	152.2
Beal	52	8726	168
Buck	24	3893	162
ST. FRANCIS			
Cafero	51	7767	152.2
Tomasulo	23	3444	149.8
Berinato	60	9953	166
Lategano	28	4168	149
Errichetti	18	2823	157
Ianaconi	35	5232	149.5
Ramondetta	28	4686	167.3
BEAUMONTS			
Thomsen	61	9584	157.1
Olsen	55	8663	157.5
Pedersen	60	10162	169.3
Wroldsen	63	10679	169.5
Dickson	39	6272	161
Hagopian	27	3962	147
HAMILTON GREYS			
Curtin	51	8318	163
James	53	8595	162.1
Ceglia	43	6952	161.7
Derenzo	48	7661	159.7
Shupback	59	10037	170
Burns	26	4068	156.4
McGill	35	5677	162
BORO C			
Geraci	63	10512	167
Correnti	34	5353	157.4
Pisano	53	9062	171
Riccio	34	5627	165.5
Laponzino	22	3403	155
Marghella	43	7453	173.3
D'Agostino	30	4655	155
BOWLERDOME			
Calandra	41	6786	165.5
Fish	34	5176	152.2
Hagenah	55	9271	168.6
Cabibi	57	9649	169.2
Johnson	29	5092	175.6
Lam	49	8005	163.3
Bischoff	29	4995	172
DIAMONDS			
Liccardi	55	8615	156.7
Donohue	59	9251	156.9
Wadsley	59	9174	155.5
Lundberg	42	6850	163
Beck	28	4348	155.2
Jensen	18	2864	159
Daly	21	3507	167
IDEAL			
Swerdlow	39	6278	161
Roth	42	7223	172
Agnello	21	3584	170.6
Russo	30	4912	163.8
Marlow	51	8377	164.2
Pappas	21	3196	152
D'Orazio	29	4465	154
SHOR BROOK			
Benson	60	9302	155
Johnson	54	8288	153.5
Noonan	58	9085	156.7
Hostetler	60	9916	165.2
Spanarelli	32	4946	154.6
Sabella	35	5510	157.4
ROYAL CAVE			
Furlain	51	8242	161.7
T. Vella	48	8006	167
Marzochi	58	9793	169
Zurzola	42	7049	168
T. Gigante	47	8176	174
Aquino	30	5081	169.3
FRITZ GRILL			
Reynolds	39	6687	171.6
Coscia	59	9759	165.4
Anderson	53	8101	153
Erickson	37	5844	158
John Shultz	47	7842	167
Joe Shultz	20	3186	159

Boro Hall D

PRATT			
Keane	53	7594	143
Musto	63	10257	163
Meyers	55	8209	149
F. Ross	47	6301	134
R. Ross	47	6263	133
LAFAYETTE NAT'L BANK			
Rabe	57	7929	139
Baum	48	7381	154
Ruppert	56	8407	150
Kitlitz	59	9651	164
Foy	47	6820	145
Reilly	18	2489	138
KOPPER'S KOKE			
Santora	42	5665	135
Bahman	62	9789	158
McIntosh	42	6422	153
Lamberti	63	10392	165
Pulcino	57	5732	155
Ritchie	40	5742	144
BEDFORD FISHERS			
Rella	60	9550	159
Jalermo	20	2616	131
A. Fischetti	59	9803	166
P. Fischetti	60	9079	151
Dellalonga	24	3177	132
Oppedisano	37	5310	144
Balduc	55	8449	154
OXFORD FILING SUPPLY			
Kruse	53	7936	150
Xeller	50	6677	134
Beyer	49	7350	150
Siesing	38	5210	137
West	44	6302	143
Luchner	46	7007	152
ROBINS			
Bartsch	59	8547	145
Keegan	55	7591	138
Harmon	56	7368	132
Foley	57	8290	145
Olson	59	8621	146
Misurella	26	3293	127
OVINGTON			
Donohue	61	9836	161
Liccardi	59	8765	149
Buckleitner	37	5852	158
Senuk	30	5019	167
Giacalone	46	6500	141
Tricarico	23	3422	149
TOWNE & JAMES			
Yerkes	54	7141	132
J. McGurkin	58	7630	132
Weigman	52	7105	137
Gisonna	37	5249	142
Uhlig	26	3859	148
Froum	21	2602	124
Harkins	34	4822	142
BROOKLYN EAGLE			
Rabidoux	60	8796	147
Watkins	60	9675	161
Geiger	60	8852	148
Niss	40	4993	125
Eaton	48	7238	151
Parisi	23	3382	147
WABASH APPLIANCES			
Belloff	52	8527	164
Tucker	60	8351	139
Moberg	42	5917	141
Garbeletto	57	8204	144
Mangino	24	2591	108
Shapiro	31	4270	138
Izzulino	26	3449	133
KNOMARK MFG.			
Abrams	38	5102	134
Balvo	54	8149	151
Mignone	60	9049	151
Poerio	57	8836	155
Bianco	47	6677	142
F. H. LEVEY			
Gomez	38	5778	152
Krolick	62	10146	164
Delistovich	61	9612	158
Garcia	63	10233	162
Schaeffer	22	2885	131
Nastasi	38	5552	146

Flatbush-Bay Ridge D

QUENTIN RED			
Freeman	60	8706	145
Lonack	62	9698	156
Wagner	52	7614	146
Rosenberg	60	8650	144
H. Newman	59	9325	158
QUENTIN BLUE			
N. Newman	56	8404	150
Cinque	63	9264	147
Fusco	60	8808	147
Hoffman	56	7874	141
Silver	39	5767	148
Brandfon	18	2561	142
COLLEGE QUIZ KIDS			
Hornstein	59	9709	165
Mangino	48	7563	158
Albertson	60	9592	160
Hayes	40	6189	155
Ekmanian	25	3995	160
S. Freeman	33	5243	159
BURKLAND			
Koppelman	53	8374	158
Harms	61	9436	155
N. Englisis	53	7909	149
Bellino	48	7184	150
Slackman	41	6721	164
Kolbe	34	5560	164
IDEAL RED			
Roth	63	10733	170
Virga	61	9460	155
Swerdlow	63	10415	165
Russo	44	6972	158
Goodman	33	5150	156
Lipari	15	2558	171
IDEAL BLUE			
Marlow	59	9467	160
Pappas	33	4696	142
D'Orazio	54	8740	162
Cipriano	56	8649	154
Silverman	24	3388	141
D'Alesandro	18	2718	151
Doweck	30	4732	158
ELITE			
Jas. Chirilli	41	5243	128
Joe Chirilli	60	8819	147
Duffy	40	5627	141
Langley	36	5293	147
Perricone	60	9009	150
Kaufman	18	2902	161
VERNONS			
James	58	9703	167
Dorenzo	61	9994	164
Tavalacci	20	2474	124
W. Martin	53	8011	151
E. Martin	45	6877	148
Cabibi	36	6242	173

IT'S ALL IN FUN! IT'S NATS, CARDS

By OSCAR FRALEY

Taking a rightful place in history alongside Rasputin, the "Mad Monk," we give you today a fantasy of 4Fs—the season's first prophecy of the outcome of the 1944 pennant races.

Content with having beaten the throw to first on the much-discussed question of our mental balance and demanding an assist for an ice-bound brain suffered in the "Spring" training camps, we see 'em this way:

AMERICAN LEAGUE

1. Washington Senators — A knuckleball tango.
2. Chicago White Sox—With a 4-F theme song.
3. Philadelphia Athletics—Connie says so.
4. St. Louis Browns—Jiving up the blues.
5. Cleveland Indians—On a pitch and a prayer.
6. New York Yankees—Gone are Dickey, Keller, Gordon, Chandler, Johnson—and the Yankees.
7. Detroit Tigers—2-B or not 2-B.
8. Boston Red Sox—The 1-A toboggan.

NATIONAL LEAGUE

1. St. Louis Cardinals—EE-I-EE-I-OH!
2. Cincinnati Reds—Holding their own.
3. Chicago Cubs—Good hit, fair pitch.
4. New York Giants—Could be better, and even worse.
5. Brooklyn Dodgers—Even Durocher might have to play.
6. Boston Braves—Fair pitch, no hit.
7. Pittsburgh Pirates—Good start, 1-A finishing.
8. Philadelphia Phillies—Still the Phillies.

The office boy informs me that there are only two divisions in a baseball league. The first division composed of the top four clubs and the second division composed of the bottom four teams. But from the looks of the various outfits the second division is going to have to be enlarged to accommodate a few more than usual. Yes, and maybe a third division added.

Our selections are made on the basis of the spread of 4-F's and antiques which are certain to be with, and possibly benefit, the clubs all season. That Cardinal farm system, along with a handy band from last year's pennant winners, seems certain to keep the Redbirds at the top of the National League heap.

The lads who form the Washington bean bag corps make up the strongest pitching staff in the American League and the Rhumba Beavers from South of the border should be enough to spark the Senators through a season of rough nightwork.

Boston's Red Sox may get an early foot, but they have only six sure to go the route and the armed forces probably won't be long blowing taps over their chances.

Bring on your psychiatrist!

STANLEY CUP DATA

April 4—Montreal, 5; Chicago, 1.
April 6—Montreal, 3; Chicago, 1.
April [illegible]—Montreal, [illegible]; Chicago, [illegible].
April 13—Chicago at Montreal.
April 15—Chicago at Montreal (if necessary.)
April 18—Chicago at Montreal (if necessary.)
April 20—Chicago at Montreal (if necessary.)

JAMAICA SELECTIONS

No. of Race	Tapper Mills, Brooklyn Eagle	Zev Daily Mirror	Cook, I. N. S.	Ortell World-Tele.	Consensus of Selections
1.	*Flying Son Happy Lark King Leroy	Happy Lark Free Double Wise Brave	Free Double Happy Lark Tatu	Happy Lark Flying Son King Leroy	Happy Lark Free Dougle Wise Brave
2.	Bull Dandy Bounding General War	Bounding Bow All White Jean Miracle	Bull Dandy General War Bric-a-Brac	Bounding Bow Bull Dandy Jean Miracle	Bull Dandy Bounding Bow All White
3.	Reason Forum Annie Lea	*Forum Talmadge He Got There	Forum Talmadge He Got There	Forum Talmadge Reason	Forum Talmadge He Got There
4.	Fox Brownie Tambo Napoo	Bud Grey Tambo Wild Rice	*Bud Grey Greentree Ent. Fox Brownie	Tambo Fox Brownie Smart Sheila	Greentree Ent. Bud Grey Smart Sheila
5.	Devil Diver Apache Mettelsome	Apache Mettlesome Devil Diver	Apache Boysy Cassis	Apache Devil Diver Cassis	Apache Devil Diver Mttlesome
6.	Alex Barth Moon Maiden Birch Rod	Moon Maiden Alex Barth Birch Rod	Alex Barth Moon Maden Rath Roman	*Alex Barth Moon Maiden Rascal	Alex Barth Moon Maiden Birch Rod
7.	Sickle T. Lost Gold Thrift	Playfields High Plaid Sickle T.	Loch Ness Sickle T.	Sickle T. Lost Gold High Plaid	Sickle T. High Plaid Playfields

*BEST BET.

COMES ACROSS—Samuel Faberman, who contributed liberally to the Red Cross Fund at the wrestling show at Broadway Arena. He is shown with his family. Left to right they are Mrs. Betty Faberman, Robert C., Pop and Rhoda Louise.

Ladies' Leaders Hit Bowling Road

By CHARLES VACKNER

With four-fifths of the season in the books, two teams are tied in the Eagle Ladies' League. With 47 victories each, the Lawler Red and Elite quintets are as even as the figure two. The Reds and Elite have been hammer and tonging it since March 11. On that occasion, Lil Williams and her chums invaded the Lawler lanes and won a pair of games. A week later at Elite the Reds scored a sweep and went into a one-game lead. Last Saturday while the Reds were losing one to the Albee Square Amazons the Elites swept a series from Burkland Blue.

This afternoon both leading teams will be on the road. Elite goes to Quentin and the Lawler Reds clash with Burkland Blue on the Utica Ave. paths. Quentin is batting a mere .153 average; Burkland Blue, having won 35 of 72 games, is bowling at a .486 clip.

Burk Reds Are Third

Forty-four victories against 28 defeats place the Burkland Reds in third place. Close on their heels are the Lawler Blues, who have copped 43 and lost 29 games. Today the Burkland unit goes to Albee Square to exchange strikes and spares with the Albee Amazons, led by Alfred De Feo.

The Bell White team will be the visitors at the Lawler Blues' alleys. Kay Mannion, who has been bowling consistently in the Red Cross games, rolls anchor for the Lawler team.

Today's Games

Brooklyn Eagle Ladies League—Lawler Red vs. Burkland Blue, at Burkland; Elite vs. Quentin, at Quentin; Burkland Red, vs. Albee Square Amazons, at Albee Square; Bell White vs. Lawler Blue, at Lawler's; Albee Square Blue vs. Bell Red, at Bell, and Bell Blue vs. Kingsway, at Kingsway.

Rod and Gun

By DANIEL LIONEL

NO SOONER did the flounder fishing method we proposed in yesterday's column hit print then the phone began ringing and flounder anglers from Brooklyn, Queens and adjacent parts told us their favorite methods.

"Do you mean to tell me," said Al Lambert, "that flounders can open their little mouths wide enough to swallow a killie? Did you ever see a flounder take a worm?"

John Phillips of the Metropolitan Rod and Gun Club also had his own ideas on how to catch flatties. His method calls for neither killies nor sandworms but mussels. It is a bait that they're a rather messy bait in cold weather, but on the hook they do what they should—catch fish.

CAPTAIN RAY SNYDER, skipper of the Dorothea, which sails out of Astoria on Sundays, announces the new sailing time of 7:45 a.m. Captain Snyder will make a second stop at Captain Bill's in Whitestone, leaving that point at 8:30 a.m. Captain Snyder had a swell day last Sunday with high hook man catching more than 40 fish. Low hook was 30. Every angler struck it rich and Ray is looking for similar fancy pickings.

CAPTAIN PAUL HAESSLER, genial veteran of the Peerless II, is in one boat that is on a daily sailing schedule, leaving from Sheepshead Bay. Captain Paul says he is getting numerous war workers aboard on their days off during the week and that the fresh air and sunshine are swell refreshers after long hours at the work bench.

GEORGE E. HOSCH of 133 Foster Ave. writes about the problem of getting Mrs. Hosch's coast guard identification card since she is a housewife and hence has no employer to vouch for her.

"I want her along. She is a good sport and besides she can row the boat." Both are good reasons, Mr. Hosch, and if your wife simply indicates that she is a housewife your vouching should suffice.

Joss Puts Okay On Mancini's Foe

In all his years as a matchmaker, Max Joss of the Broadway Arena has never made it a practice to personally endorse any fighter. Joss makes an exception and puts the stamp of approval on Tiger Nelson of Washington, D. C., who slugs with Lenny (Boom Boom) Mancini of Brooklyn in an eight-round welter scrap Tuesday night at the Halsey St. club.

Joss saw Nelson whip Aaron Perry, Washington, D. C., boy. He was so impressed by Nelson's style, similar to that of Henry Armstrong, Joss decided to use the Tiger at the first opportunity.

Santa Unbeaten

The meteoric rise of Santa Bucca has interested and amazed a number of fans will be on hand at the St. Nicholas Rink Monday night to see their idol engage in his 22d bout since he joined the pro ranks. Santa has never been beaten as a pro, engaging in 21 bouts to date and being held to but one draw, that in his last fight against Jackie Leamus.

But Santa's test comes on Monday when he faces the Chicago veteran, Pete Lello in an eight-round bout. Pete has met the best, even to engaging in title bouts and having a record of which any fighter might well be proud.

The bout is one of three all-star events. There is another eight in which Roman Alvarez will meet Doug Carter, Mayon Padlo, another Philadelphian, will meet Solomon Stewart of Harlem.

REPLACEMENTS MAKE CARDS CHOICE TO REPEAT IN N. L.

Chicago, April 8 (U.P.)—A spirited gang of St. Louis Cardinals, who have plugged the gaps left by service losses with high-caliber rookies, were odds-on favorites today to snare the 1944 National League pennant.

Owner Sam Breadon and Manager Billy Southworth are confident the Cards are pointed straight at their eighth flag in 18 years. With the farm system that Branch Rickey built still molding great neophyte players, the fighting St. Louis squad appears capable of upholding the brilliant form that has netted first division rules 15 times since 1926 and carried the Cardinals to four world's championships.

Despite such crushing losses as Harry Walker, Lou Klein, Alpha Brazle, Jimmy Brown, Howie Pollet, Frank Crespi, Terry Moore, Ernie White and Enos Slaughter, in the last two years, the Cards still have the following "big names" marking the 1944 roster: Mort and Walker Cooper, Harry Brecheen, Max Lanier, Johnny Hopp, Whitey Kurowski, Marty Marion, Ray Sanders, Stan Musial and Danny Litwhiler.

To fortify this nucleus of stars Southworth has at his disposal at least five rookies who have captured his attention.

Verban Is Impressive

Emil Verban—Fleet second baseman who played every inning of the season and through the Junior World Series for Columbus last season. "I believe Verban could win a regular spot even if Lou Klein still was with us," Southworth said.

Augie Bergamo—Walloping outfielder from Columbus who led the American Association in extracting bases on balls with 109 and tied for the lead in double-hitting.

Al Jurisich—Lanky right-handed pitcher discharged from the army. Southworth rates him good enough to gain a starter's role.

Blix Donnelly—No-hit specialist who won 17 games for Rochester last year and pitched the third no-hitter of his career. Won 21 for Sacramento in 1942 and 28 for Springfield in 1941.

Eldred Byerly—Tall Sacramento moundsman who held the Braves to one earned run in eight innings and defeated the Giants during one week with the Cards last season.

In addition to these rookies, Southworth has 40-year-old Pepper Martin trying to make a comeback for an outfield spot. And the "Wild Hoss" still has his notorious larceny tendencies on the base paths.

The fly in the Cardinal ointment comes in the number of stars who are 1-A — Hopp, Musial Litwhiler, Lanier and Harry Gumbert—and the limited service men—Walker Cooper and Slats Marion. If Marion can play out a good portion of the season, he no doubt will solidify an infield that otherwise is 4-F, but it also will give Southworth what he terms "the best second base combination I've ever had."

With this impressive infield combination, a strong pitching staff and Walker Cooper behind the bat, Southworth's chief worries are centered on the outfield, where he is depending upon Debs Garms and Martin to come through if Musial and Litwhiler are drafted.

Dunno What Sinatra's Got, But He's Got Plenty of It

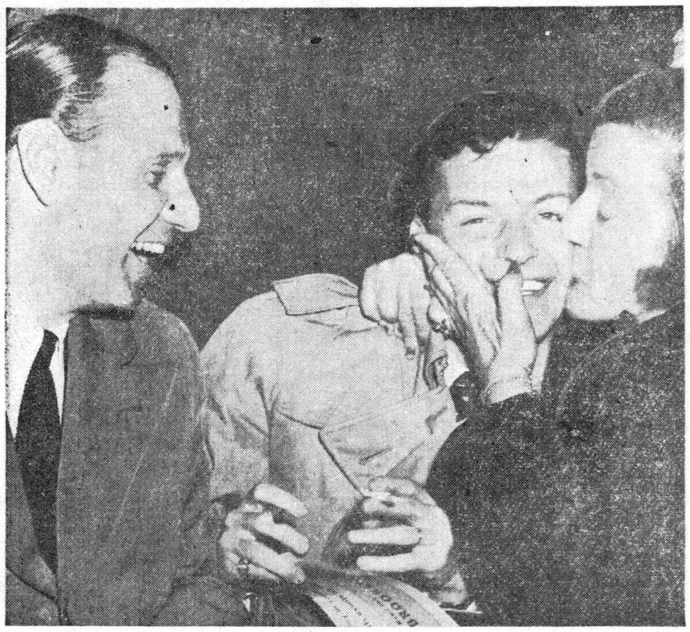

Eagle Staff photo by Lambert

SPEECHLESS—The Voice hadn't a word to say when Hilda, No. 1 Dodger fan, gave him a taste of real Brooklyn hospitality in the dugout. Yes, that's Durocher—and quiet.

By GERTRUDE McALLISTER

It was a little after 1 p.m. yesterday when the cabbie heard:

"Ebbets Field, please."

As the taxi shifted through Borough Hall traffic the driver remarked:

"Hope you're dressed warm. Gonna be cold out there."

"Guess it will but I'm not staying for the game," replied the fare.

Forgetting the trolley lumbering along just ahead of the front fender, the driver swung around, narrowed his eyes and spat:

"A Sinatra fan! Oi!"

He kept grumbling all the way to the field and every so often said loudly enough to be understood:

"I dunno what you dames see in that guy! I dunno!"

Well, now that this reporter has had the honor (in deference to Sinatra fans)—she dunno either! Whatever he has, it must be admitted that he has it in great quantities. Enough to make as one the seven to eight thousand bobby-sockers who gasped, sighed and all but died for him at the Red Cross rally yesterday. Or maybe there were even more than that in the crowd of 15,000—only some must have been there for a ball game.

It's a Mystery

Someday someone will delve deeply into the overpowering effect the youthful, even boyish, singer has on a whole parkful of high school girls and boys, as he did at Ebbets. No moon, no sun without Sinatra would sum up their feelings for him—and they'll take him Sunday, Monday and always.

To appreciate his superiority to all other men and crooners one has to get right in with his fans and stand there when he's in sight. To them, he isn't skinny—he's just so thin and frail. For them, he hasn't the best voice in the world—just the best in the world for them. You can say you don't like him and his young fans don't mind. They just feel sorry for you because you're so old and won't ever have any fun anymore.

"That's too bad," a perfectly beautiful 17-year-older from Erasmus will reply. "He's so awfully nice. He's just a darling—I mean he really is."

When his fans found out he was in the Dodger dugout yesterday they began that frantic surging forward in the stands. They didn't push so they hurt one another. And if one had a camera she was trying to focus for several rows ahead, young girls obligingly dipped their shoulders so Sinatra would be in clear view. They even tried to encourage him to look her way by waving hands and pointing fingers back over their shoulders.

Ah, That Sinatra Squeal!

When the commotion in the stands was at its height the Cause Of It All was sitting down in the dugout next to Leo Durocher. Sinatra kept pressing his thumbs together and tapping his feet. He was nervous as a witch but laughing all the time. Finally he popped from under the shed and the girls let out the Sinatra Squeal which has become internationally famous. He liked it. He laughed with them. He looked all up and down the stands at the thick clusters of girls waving and laughing. He seemed to enjoy them and appreciate them. He wasn't any hard-boiled celebrity. And the way some of the girls looked down at him you got the feeling that they were romantic about him but knew he had a wife and wasn't a wolf like so many stars were said to be. It might also be said that they liked looking at him quite as much as they did listening to him.

Even they don't call him handsome.

"Oh, no! He's just a darling," the little girl next to this reporter said when she was asked if she thought he was good looking.

And Then He Sings

Finally he sang—after the photographers had consumed an endless time with him down at the microphone. The anti-Sinatras expected him to break into some love melody right away and when he started with "Take Me Out to the Ball Game" they couldn't believe it. Then he sang "Let Me Call You Sweetheart." The fans went wild. When he asked them to join in, they did. But for his final number, they were quiet except for occasional Sinatra Squeals.

It was "People Will Say We're in Love."

They were in their trance. It was wonderful just to watch them.

In one of the boxes an army officer stood looking up at them. He had a broad smile.

"You know," he told this reporter, "down in the camp I'm at—in the South—the boys don't believe that shrieking and squealing is real. They think it's a machine. Well, now I can tell them it's real."

And it's real, all right. It's real!

SINGING IN BROOKLYN—Crooner Frank Sinatra and Coach Charlie Dressen warble for some 13,000 Dodger fans (all paying customers) for the benefit of the Red Cross.

LOCAL JITTERBUGS—Native women of Tarawa perform a tribal dance while Yanks watch in the background. Our men are not allowed to visit native villages, except when invited, and must respect all customs of the natives. Only shattered trees on the island serve as a reminder of the bloody battle staged there.

BENSON NAMES NEW YORK FUND AREA CHAIRMEN

Area chairmen for Brooklyn's effort in the Greater New York Fund campaign, which will be inaugurated at a dinner in the Towers Hotel next Thursday night, have been announced by Philip A. Benson, president of the Dime Savings Bank, who has accepted the chairmanship for the drive.

Among speakers at the opening dinner will be J. Stewart Baker, general chairman of the citywide appeal.

Brooklyn's quota of $500,000 will be raised among business and employe groups. William J. Fisher, general commercial representative of the New York Telephone Company, has been named chairman for the borough solicitation. Assisting as chairmen of the various areas are Carlo Agro, South Brooklyn; Harry J. Blank, Bush Terminal; Walter J. Brock, Flatbush-Mill Basin; Frederick W. Krueger, Williamsburg; Howard G. Launsbach, East New York-Brownsville, and Isidore Leviton, Greenpoint.

Goal Set at $4,500,000

The fund's citywide goal is $4,500,000. More than 2,000,000 New Yorkers, representing all races and creeds, were aided by hospitals and health and welfare agencies participating in the fund last year.

The city campaign will open at a dinner in the Hotel Astor on Tuesday. Boy Scouts are now distributing posters appealing for support of the drive, the first placards being presented yesterday to Norman Kennelly and Paul Perkins, Scouts of Troop 291, Brooklyn.

W. Roy Manny has been named employe gift chairman in the Brooklyn campaign. Everett M. Clark is in charge of public relations.

Section chairmen representing the industrial, commercial and professional life of Brooklyn and division chairmen who will serve under them were announced by Mr. Benson as follows:

Section Leaders Listed

Commerce Section—Walter Hammitt, vice president of Frederick Loeser & Co., as chairman; Harry Michaels, president of Michaels Brothers, as cochairman; Henry L. Holt, of Abraham & Straus, Inc., as employe gifts chairman; Fred J. Zeitz, president of Martin's, chairman of department and chain stores and specialty shops; George McCurrach, president of McCurrach Organization, Inc., chairman of men's shops and men's wear; Ernest J. Linka, vice president of Goodwin's, chairman of women's wear.

Industry Section — William T. Hunter, president of A. Schrader's Son, as chairman; Lorimer Rich, architect, chairman of building; L. Francis Case, president Central Paint & Varnish Company, chairman of chemicals and paints; Dr. William J. Dunne, assistant secretary of Intertype Corporation, chairman of machinery; Tracy Higgins, president of Higgins Ink Company, Inc., chairman of office equipment; Walter Weeks, executive manager of Affiliated Moving Van Owners, Inc., chairman of transportation.

Finance Section—George Whitlock, executive vice president of National City Bank, as chairman; Irvin S. Hawkins, executive secretary of Public Relations Bureau-Group V Savings Banks Association, chairman of employe gifts; Chester A. Allen, vice president of Kings County Trust Company, chairman of commercial banks and trust companies; John J. Hickey, vice president Greater New York Savings Bank, chairman of savings banks.

Utilities Section—Adelbert G. Wright, vice president of New York Telephone Company, as chairman and also chairman of communications; Edwin B. Wilson, chairman of advertising and newspapers; James Murphy, treasurer of Consolidated Lithographing Corporation, chairman of graphic arts; Hugh Cuthrell, vice president of Brooklyn Union Gas Company, as chairman of public utilities.

Professional Section—Joseph M. May, as chairman; Louis Schenkweiler, superintendent of Wyckoff Heights Hospital, chairman of hospitals; Jesse Krause, chairman of county, municipal and State employes; Hunter L. Delatour, of Delatour, Kennedy and Miller, chairman of legal, accountants and other professions; Dr. Paul A. Kennedy, assistant superintendent of schools, chairman of public schools; Frederick I. Daniels, general secretary of Brooklyn Bureau of Charities, chairman of welfare agencies.

Food Section—Carl Letsch, manager of Towers Hotel, as chairman; James Simms, of the Bossert Hotel, as co-chairman and also chairman of hotels and restaurants; Howard J. Cameron, treasurer of Rockwood & Co., chairman of confectionery; Nicholas A. Gesoalde, executive secretary of the New York State Pharmaceutical Association, chairman, and Abraham Sarason, of Consolidated Retail Pharmacists, Inc., co-chairman of cosmetics and drugs; Gerald J. Meany, general manager Dairymen's League Co-operative Association, Inc., chairman of dairy products; Joseph Weiss, of Consolidated Laundries, Inc., chairman of laundries, cleaners and dyers; Jack Kranis, attorney for Retail Food Industries, chairman of meats, poultry and fish; Max Mancher, Office Price Administration, and John J. Harrison, secretary of Retail Meat Dealers, Inc., co-chairmen of meats, poultry and fish; Arthur Horton, of Bulkley & Horton Company, chairman of real estate.

'Keeping Women on Job Is No. 1 Manpower Task'

Washington, April 14 (U.P.) — An Office of War Information report said today that the problem of keeping women in the wartime labor force has become the "No. 1 manpower task of 1944."

The report said the turnover rate among women had reached "alarming proportions," with large numbers quitting because of fatigue, a lack of community services or general difficulties in running two jobs—at home and in war plants.

Many women left because they felt their war service had been exaggerated or that the war was about over, the report said.

SALUTE TO THE VALIANT—Three doughboys in Michigan Central Railroad Station, Detroit, returning to camp after a furlough, freeze into a more than routine salute to a passing officer—1st Lt. John H. Brown of Ogdensburg, N. Y., on his way to Percy Jones Hospital to receive an artificial leg in place of the one he lost at Anzio.

'Hiya Brooklyn' Call Good News to Oil Man

Special to the Brooklyn Eagle

Washington, April 14 — When "Hiya, Brooklyn!" rings out over teh oil fields it's an even money bet it comes from or is aimed at blue-eyed Claude P. Parsons, who returns to his native Bay Ridge this Saturday from the Texas and Oklahoma oil lands by way of Washington, where he recently was appointed director of the Petroleum Administration for War's Division of Materials.

So far as he knows, Parsons has only one fellow Brooklynite in the oil industry, a "fellow named Crowley, who's vice president of an oil company in Texas.

"Whenever we meet he hollers, 'Hiya Brooklyn!' We never use names."

Parsons, whose family is part of Brooklyn's industrial traditions, was born in 1895 at 47th St. and 4th Ave. Although his branch of the Parsons family hasn't lived in Brooklyn since he was a child, he still considers himself a Brooklynite and has been back frequently to attend various family functions. This Saturday he will attend the wedding of Grace Volkman, daughter of his cousin, Mrs. Edward Volkman Jr. of 1059 81st St., Brooklyn.

The Parson saga, which includes aviation as well as oil, really begins in the middle of the last century, when grandfather Thomas Parsons came to Brooklyn from the city of Luton, English straw-bleaching center. The elder Parsons toured Massachusetts and Connecticut before finally settling in Brooklyn as a likely site in which to launch the industry in the United States.

Taking over the old De La Plain House at the foot of 39th St., Parsons established the first straw-bleaching plant in Brooklyn, turning the raw straw from the Orient into the fashionable skimmers of the gay nineties. In turn the five Parsons sons established the straw-manufacturing firm of Parsons Brothers at the foot of 19th St.

Served in World War I

Claude P. Parsons enlisted in the army air forces in World War I and became one of the first aviators from New York City. He was a lieutenant and chief test pilot at Love Field, Texas, when the war ended. A promising aviation career lay ahead.

"I was offered a chance to fly the first air mail run between Washington, Philadelphia and New York," Parsons recalls, "but the attraction of oil was stronger."

As a roustabout, Parsons learned the oil business and worked himself up to the post of district superintendent with the Magnolia Oil Company in Oklahoma. In 1929 he joined the Halliburton Oil Well Cementing Company of Tulsa, rising to chief field engineer that year. He was manager of sales by 1935 and became vice president in 1934.

Parsons has been on leave from the Halliburton firm since January, when he joined the P. A. W. as assistant director of the division he now heads. "I'm a duration bureaucrat," he declared.

Muzzle-Loader All Set

Daykin, Neb. (U.P.)—Grandfather's old muzzle-loading gun now is community concern. Alderman George Apking, who owns it, couldn't shoot it because he lacked some necessary parts. But Mayor Walter C. Parchow took care of that when he purchased a powder horn, shot pouch, percussion caps and gunwads at an auction. Daykinites are holding their ears in apprehension.

Today's Profile

Magistrate Nicholas H. Pinto believes in hard work and hard play. His favorite recreations are golf, swimming, detective stories and musical comedies.

Born May 17, 1890, he grew up in the Chelsea area of Manhattan, attended Public School 55, DeWitt Clinton and St. Francis Xavier High schools and Fordham Law School, passed his bar examination a few months before he graduated. He was made a magistrate in January, 1937.

Nicholas H. Pinto

His wife was Elizabeth Connolly. They were introduced by a priest, who later married them.

His three sons are all sea-minded. John, 23, is a petty officer 1st class in the coast guard; Francis, 18, is a seaman 3d class in the same service and Edward, 16, wants to go to Annapolis. Magistrate Pinto himself was a chief petty officer in the navy in World War I.

Fond of children, he gives them much of his time as president of the Italian Board of Guardians and is also active in the work of the Catholic Orphan Asylum. He is chairman of the East Flatbush CDVO and the 1944 Red Cross War Fund drive in Flatbush and has received the army-navy E award for his service in securing blood donors.

An inveterate smoker until he gave it up during Lent last year, he now smokes rarely but likes to chew on the end of a cigar. He is fond of chicken liver and shrimp and is trying to keep down his weight.

A dog lover, he owns an Irish setter. He wears conservative clothes, likes Milton Berle's acting. His friends call him Nick.

He still chuckles over an incident in the Coney Island Court some time ago. He came in one day to find an "old customer" there—a fellow repeatedly brought up on charges.

"Why do I keep seeing you here all the time?" he asked the defendant.

"Well, judge, is it my fault you're not promoted?" was the retort.

They're In It

If there's any question about the part the Smiths are playing in the war, take a look at these figures: According to a recent compilation, there are 21,476 men and women of that name in the navy alone. Next in numerical strength are the Johnsons with 15,045, while the Jones boys and girls are third with 11,035.

Dyker Heights May Top Red Cross Goal Tomorrow

Dyker Heights expects to complete its quota in the Brooklyn 1944 Red Cross War Fund appeal at a dance tomorrow night, thus joining several other borough areas which have gone over the top.

Several hundred Dyker Heights residents as well as Red Cross workers in the neighborhood will attend the event, which will be held at 8:30 p.m. in headquarters of John Hughes Council, K. of C., 86th St. and 13th Ave. A. F. Serocke, chairman of the local campaign, will be honored on the occasion of the successful conclusion of the drive.

David Marlow is chairman. Assisting are Edmund Scanio, Mrs. F. F. Stevens, M. M. Pizzi and Arthur R. Ryan.

Dyker Heights comes under Red Cross area headquarters No. 1, 549 86th St., of which Bernard Savage is co-ordinator.

The event is one of several in the borough intended to further Brooklyn's drive toward its quota of $3,331,000. At the last report, on April 3, 76 percent of the goal was reported. The city-wide drive lacks $2,200,000 of the $22,386,000 objective.

Citizens to Ask Governor Bar Jap Laborers

Great Meadows, N. J., April 14 (U.P.)—An independent township citizens committee planned to make a personal appeal to Governor Walter E. Edge today to avert future employment of Japanese-American laborers throughout New Jersey.

The pilgrimage to Trenton was an aftermath of the public indignation that arose when Edward Kowalick, 23-year-old local farmer, hired five Japanese as "sharecroppers" through the War Relocation Authority.

As result of insistent demands of the committee, the WRA yesterday removed the laborers to Philadelphia.

With Cream or Lemon?

The British merit their reputation as tea drinkers. According to U. S. Department of Agriculture figures, Britishers consume an average of 2,400 cups of tea year, or almost seven cups a day. In the United States the yearly average is only 140 cups.—*YOUR LIFE.*

Flier Tells of Flak 'So Thick You Could Walk Across on It'

A tremendous flak field "so thick you could walk across it," with enemy-occupied territory below alight "like Times Square on New Year's Eve," is described by a young Brooklyn flier in a letter to his father, Benjamin Albaum, an accountant with the Brooklyn division of Todd Shipyards Corporation.

The flier is Staff Sgt. Elvin Albaum, 20, of 2415 Newkirk Ave., rear gunner on the Flying Fortress Berlin First, one of a large formation of heavy bombers of the U. S. 8th Air Force which on March 4 made the first American air attack on Berlin.

How does it feel to come back from a bombing raid over Germany? "Most of it is a feeling of wanting to lie down in a corner and going to sleep forever," he wrote in a letter to his father after completing his seventh raid, the third in which he had participated in as many days. "You are glad to be back and alive and for the first time in 12 hours the tension is off. You feel sorry for the guys who went down, but you try not to think about that. They're gone—and tomorrow it might be you.

"Yesterday, although we didn't expect it, we ran into a tremendous flak field—youalways have flak, but yesterday you could step out of the ship and walk across it. It was terrifying. They shot the hell out of us. We were lucky.

"Just before we took off yesterday the Germans came over and bombed the area around us. When we took off we could see great patches of fire in several places. But it was puny—puny in comparison to our raid. The Continent looked like Times Square on New Year's Eve. I don't know how they stand up under our attacks — or where they get the fighter planes to attack us with. The last couple of raids our fighter protection has been excellent and we weren't hampered by fighters too much. It was mostly flak.

"It realy isn't worth mentioning, but our crew is going to be awarded the Air Medal (all 10 of us) for five combat missions over enemy territory."

Daffodils in Bloom

Visitors to the Brooklyn Botanic Garden today will find the daffodils on Boulder Hill in bloom.

Hospital Staffed By Negro Doctors Sought for Bedford

Plans for a new hospital in the Bedford-Stuyvesant area, to be staffed completely eventually by Negro physicians, were announced yesterday by Dr. Charles F. McCarty, executive secretary of the Kings County Medical Society.

A subcommittee of the society was disclosed Friday to have recommended hospital positions for 18 Negro doctors so that many Negroes in Brooklyn, who can afford it, could be admitted to private hospitals in Brooklyn.

Application for a charter for the new hospital has already been made to the State Department of Social Welfare, Dr. McCarty said, and it was the idea of the society's subcommittee that this institution should at first be staffed at the top by leading Brrklyn physicians who would train Negro physicians to take over.

The Comitia Minora of the society has approved the project, which is now before the State agency for approval as a postwar hospital project, Dr. McCarty said.

A large part of the funds needed for such a project could be raised within the Negro community, according to the subcommittee, headed by Dr. V. Leonard Williams, a Negro. Of the eight doctors on the subcommittee four are Negroes.

The Bedford-Stuyvesant area, from being a neighborhood made up largely of single-family houwses, has in recent years increased greatly in population, Dr. McCarty pointed out, creating the need for hospital facilities where none existed before.

Gusta Gale's Paintings To Be Shown in Library

An exhibition of oil and water-color paintings by Gusta Gale, Brooklyn artist, will be shown at the Brooklyn Public Library for two weeks beginning tomorrow, it was announced yesterday by Dr. Milton J. Ferguson, chief librarian.

Mrs. Gale, whose home is at 2801 Beverly Road, was a flower gardener before studying art under Maurice Gordon and Carl Nelson. She has exhibited in many cities, and her work hangs in the Executive Mansion in Harrisburg, Pa., and in other places.

WHEN OUT OF TOWN REGISTER FROM BROOKLYN

PRAYER FOR HEROIC UNDERGROUND FIGHTERS — During observance at City Hall of first anniversary of heroic resistance of Jews of Warsaw ghetto against Nazis, who finally exterminated them after suffering heavy losses. Max Greenberg, World War I veteran, stands in foreground under flag held by Pvt. Morris Luster, while Cantor Moishe Oysher chants a memorial prayer. Mayor LaGuardia is among those on City Hall steps.

2,000 HERE PAY TRIBUTE TO WARSAW DEAD

Honoring those who chose a fighting death instead of docile submission to Nazi "liquidation" in the Warsaw ghetto, more than 2,000 Jews packed New Lots Talmud Torah and overflowed into Pennsylvania and New Lots Aves. last night as part of a State-wide observance of the first anniversary of the pogrom's end.

It was a year ago yesterday that the last of 40,000 Jews, mostly the aged and children—those unfit for compulsory labor—were killed, ending six weeks of bare-fist resistance to the tough youths of the German army, armed with modern weapons and tanks.

Some of those who escaped from Warsaw were in last night's audience and most of the refugees wept as Rabbi Simon Grossbein intoned the Hebrew chant for honored dead, El Mole Rachmim (God, full of grace).

The impartial nature of the day's observance was stressed by former Magistrate Leo Healy, who spoke at the services. "When people fight for a common cause they know no creed," he said. "There is no line of demarcation between Catholic, Jew and Protestant, when all fight together as brothers. Their goal is liberty for all, under God."

Former Magistrate Joseph Goldstein hailed the Warsaw fighters as heroes in the ancient Hebrew tradition. Reminding his listeners that Spring is the Passover season, he recalled leaders such as Bar Kochba, who led a guerrilla band against the Persians in the time of Nebuchadnezzar, and Matthias, who headed the Maccabean struggle against the Greeks and is now celebrated in the Jewish "feast of lights."

"They fought for liberty, as we are fighting," Goldstein said, "and they shall not have died in vain."

Princess Royal Attends Theater on Birthday Eve

London, April 20 (U.P.)—The King and Queen took Princess Elizabeth to the theater last night on the eve of her 18th birthday anniversary to see the musical comedy "Something in the Air.".

The royal party was cheered when it appeared in the royal box, and the principals of the cast, including Jack Hulbert and Cicely Courtneidge, were received by the King, Queen and Princess during the intermission.

'A Losing Fight Is Truly Bitter' Says Jap's Diary

"Every day I am afraid . . . A losing fight is truly bitter." These excerpts from a dead Jap soldier's diary reveal how much the Japs want to die for the Emperor, said Lt. Col. Maxwell Rosenzweig. Speaking at a meeting of the Staff Society of the Jewish Hospital of Brooklyn in the Dr. Leon Louria Auditorium, 474 St. Mark's Ave., the colonel presented an account of his medical experiences in the Pacific war area.

In other entries the Jap mentioned that many dead and wounded were brought in daily; that no one had a cigarette; later, that he had contracted malaria, had no water, and that there were no doctors. The Jap wrote he had prayed and that in the afternoon his temperature dropped. From that time on he recorded the names of those with him who died; the last time he wrote in his diary he said, "I feel in a daze."

The army medical officer related stories of life during the Guadalcanal campaign and other Pacific battles. The duties of the doctors included not only surgical and medical care of the men, he pointed out, but also fly control, sanitation, ditching and draining swamps. "Marvelous progress has been made in the control of tropical diseases," he said, "but even at the height of a campaign it was rare that surgical cases exceeded medical ones."

Colonel Rosenzweig stated that, unlike the Japanese, the American soldier's sense of humor carries him through, more than anything else.

He closed by stating that "our progress in the Pacific is going ahead as scheduled" and praised the navy for its part in the Pacific war and in transporting the wounded.

The experiences of Commander Milton J. Matzner in the medical service in a naval hospital here in the States was the second part of the society's program.

He discussed the types of patients encountered in a naval hospital in this country and mentioned the importance of the psychogenic factors in the young fighting men sent to the hospitals.

Matzner commented on the number of malaria cases in this war and the use of atabrine as a suppressive therapy in its treatment.

Major Benjamin M. Bernstein, surgeon in the army reserve, spoke on the public health service and military medicine. He outlined the information taught to 118 medical men at a week's course held in Halloran General Hospital, Staten Island.

Among the subjects covered in this course were military decorum, aviation medicine, neuropsychology, uses of sulfa drugs and penicillin and the treatment of malaria, meningitis and tuberculosis.

Presiding was Dr. Irving Tran, president of the society.

Appeals Conviction In Spanking of Boy, 10

Lynbrook, April 20—Ira C. Mummert, principal of the Wheeler Avenue School in Valley Stream for 16 years, has filed an appeal in Nassau County Court to set aside an assault conviction for spanking a 10-year-old boy until the ruler broke.

Mummert was convicted of third degree assault by Judge Cyril J. Brown of District Court and sentenced was suspended. The judge found Mummert guilty of exceeding his statutory authority and failure to exercise restraint.

The principal admitted spanking the boy, Lester Hankinson of 289 Emerson Place, Valley Stream, for throwing a book from the balcony of the school on Jan. 27. He also admitted striking the boy with a 20-inch ruler several times and said the ruler broke.

The boy testified Mummert hit him 15 or 20 times with the ruler and that he pleaded with the principal to stop. He also said he washed his own face afterward to remove signs of tears.

Mrs. Nora Hankinson, Lester's mother, a Nassau County police sergeant and physicians testified they saw red welts and black and blue bruises on the boy's body.

Honey production in Mexico, greatly increased in recent years, reached over 12,000 tons in 1943; exports to the United States were nearly 8,000 tons.

Scrap Paper Yield Not Good Enough

Although salvage officials are still dissatisfied with scrap paper collections, it is evident today that Mayor LaGuardia's appeal to Brooklynites to keep the paper separate from garbage has had effect.

Yesterday's pickup by Sanitation Department trucks indicated that borough householders had been complying with the Mayor's plea and had been careful to remove all foreign matter from the paper as they placed it on sidewalks.

The collections resulted in a yield slightly greater than that of the previous week but officials of the drive have announced that the totals would be much higher if full co-operation were forthcoming.

The paper is rushed to mills, where it is converted into essential war materials such as food containers, shell casing, paper parachutes and plasma holders. Five pounds of salvaged paper makes 73 "K" field ration cartons.

Bucci Appointed To Family Court

Nicholas Bucci of 115 Henry St., assistant corporation counsel for the city in charge of education matters, has been appointed by Mayor LaGuardia as a temporary Domestic Relations Court Justice.

Bucci will serve in place of Justice Juvenal Marchisio, who has received a month's leave of absence to work for the Italian War Relief Committee, a National War Fund agency headed by Myron C. Taylor, President Roosevelt's special envoy to the Vatican.

Another assistant corporation counsel, Russell L. Tarbox, has been appointed a temporary member of the Municipal Service Commission to succeed Harry W. Marsh. Tarbox lives at 1165 5th Ave., Manhattan.

Marsh is now acting as commissioner of welfare in place of Commissioner Leo Arnstein, who is ill.

Today's Profile

Harold R. Moskovit, State president of the Affiliated Young Democrats, has the distinction of being one of the youngest men ever to crash "Who's Who in America." At 37 he is a politician, industrial, labor and public relations man.

Harold R. Moskovit

Born Dec. 1, 1906, he spent his younger days in New Hampshire and Massachusetts, attending Haverhill High School, Sanborn Seminary and Colby College. He left New England to study law here at St. John's where he edited the law yearbook and was president of the student council. He also served as athletic director and counselor for settlements and boys' clubs to defray the cost of his education.

At 26 he married Ruth Breitbart. They have an 8-year-old daughter, June, who attends Adelphi Academy. They live at 1900 Newkirk Ave.

His political career prospered with President Roosevelt and the New Deal in 1932 when he organized the Intercollegiate Democratic League of New York and the Intercollegiate Organizations of America. Both were later absorbed by the Affiliated Young Democrats. He also founded the First Voters of America and the Young Jeffersonians. His work as a Democrat was recognized by the President, who appointed him regional director of the Office of Government Reports for New York, Connecticut and Rhode Island.

The latest organization he is building is the Votes for Youth—which is an outgrowth of one of his strongest convictions: If you are old enough to fight, you are old enough to vote.

SMALL ARMS LAID DOWN AT ANZIO—But only in song. On a brief rest from the fighting lines, these boys on the beach at Anzio join in the strains of "Lay that pistol down, babe!" Sgt. Robert Lewis of Nassau County (front), Sgt. John Ferris of Brooklyn and Corp. Thomas Flynn of Manhattan, right, are the three men in a boat.

Borough ALP Demands Simpler Soldier Vote Law

The American Labor party in Kings County wired a demand to Governor Dewey today for an immediate special session of the Legislature to simplify the State soldier-vote law and to extend the law's provision to merchant marine and Red Cross personnel.

John Crawford, chairman, and Max Torchin, secretary, declared "the present law, passed by the Republican majority in the Legislature, is a cumbersome and ineffective procedure requiring a personal application by the soldier and three or four separate steps."

"This procedure," they added, "will prevent a large soldier vote. Our boys, who are fighting to maintain the right to vote for people all over the world, should not be disfranchised by their own Government. We urge an immediate special session of the Legislature to simplify soldier voting and to extend this right to merchant marine and Red Cross personnel."

A somewhat similar request last week by the Democratic minority leaders in the Legislature was rejected by Governor Dewey.

Crawford and Torchin announced 40 American Labor party clubs in Brooklyn were beginning a house-to-house canvass to distribute printed war ballot application cards to be sent to men in the armed forces by relatives and friends.

St. Francis Prep Lists 2 Scholarship Exams

Two high school scholarships will be offered at competitive examinations conducted by St. Francis Prep on April 29 at 9 a.m. in the school, 41 Butler Place. June candidates for graduation at parochial and elementary schools are eligible to compete, and no registration is necessary.

Dr. G. S. Avery to Direct Boro Botanic Garden

Dr. George S. Avery, professor of botany at Connecticut College, has been appointed director of the Brooklyn Botanic Garden to fill the vacancy caused by the death last year of Dr. C. Stuart Gager. The appointment is effective July 1.

Dr. George S. Avery

Dr. Avery was graduated from Tulane University and received graduate degrees from Dartmouth and the University of Wisconsin.

He served as assistant professor of botany at Duke University and during the past 13 years has been at Connecticut College. He held a national research fellowship and a foreign fellowship of the Rockefeller Foundation.

Dr. Avery served as secretary and also vice president of the Botanical Society of America and now is treasurer of the organization. He is a member of the American Society of Plant Physiologists, Torrey Botanical Club, Society for Growth and Development and Sigma Xi.

He is coauthor of a book, "Growth Hormones in Plants."

Thousands Trek To 'Potato' Whisky

Caravans of thirsty New Yorkers continued today to descend upon the newly-found oasis at Gimbel's Liquor Shop, 32d St. and Broadway, Manhattan, as word spread around the desert that "several thousand cases" of "potato" whisky at popular prices was available. The oasis will become a mirage by the end of the week, it was believed, as heavy demands showed no let-up.

The new concoction designed to satisfy parched throats is a domestically-blended whisky composed of 80 percent neutral spirits distilled from culled potatoes and 20 percent 4-year-old straight whisky. It is 86.6 proof.

Bottled under the label "Gold Coin," the stuff sells at $3.32 a fifth, and the limit is 12 bottles to each person. It is distilled on an experimental basis in Idaho Falls, Idaho, and the plant has been in operation between five and six weeks.

Northwest Airlines Show Big Increases

Northwest Airlines planes carried a total of 466,614 airmail pounds during March, as compared to 320,192 for the same month last year, Croil Hunter, president and general manager, announced today.

A total of 394,569,979 pound miles were flown during the month, an increase of 131,185,751 mail pound miles over totals in March, 1943.

Firemen's Fund Ordered Dissolved

Liquidation of the Firemen's Endowment Association of the city of New York, known as the Third Endowment, has been ordered by Justice Isador Wasservogel, who also has under advisement today in Manhattan Supreme Court the application of Attorney General Nathaniel Goldstein for liquidation of the Allied Endowment Association of the Fire Department of the city of New York.

These mutual disability insurance and retirement pension funds are two of the seven which the rank and file of the city's firemen have maintained over the past 50 years. Though never operated under the supervision of the Department of Insurance, their managements recently dumped all seven into the lap of that State regulatory agency with a request that it survey them and determine if they should be dissolved or financially rehabilitated.

While no detailed schedule of any of the funds' investments or debts was available today, the liquidation order disclosed that the Third Endowment has total assets of approximately $130,000, against total liabilities of "more than $240,000."

Orders for liquidation of two more of the seven funds are to be sought next week, it was learned.

Corp. Eugene T. Gillen of 225 94th St. and Pfc. Irwin I. Blackman of 37 Debevoise St. are aviation radiomen at Jacksonville, Fla.

Completing training at Edgewood Arsenal, Md., is 2d Lt. Nicholas S. Capasso of 8795 16th St.

Brooklynites who have completed the pilot's course at Sebring, Fla., are 2d Lts. Harvey S. Tarkan of 11 West End Ave., Irwin I. Shlansky of 2035 E. 3d St., and Harry L. Green of 1482 E. 2d St.

Taking pilot's training at Columbus, Ohio, is Lt. Charles H. Lustig of 1866 Ocean Ave.

Fireman 2d Class Clifford Dow of Brooklyn is on active duty in the South Pacific. A veteran of two world wars, Tech. Sgt. John J. Harding of 55 Hanson Place was honorably discharged recently in New Caledonia. His son, Corp. John J. Jr., is with the marines at Quantico, Va.

Pvt. William Sullivan of 174 13th St. took advantage of his last furlough from Fort Kearney, Newport, R. I., to get engaged to Audrey Munson of 729 55th St. His friend, Sgt. A. Mammone of 178A 13th St., is in a hospital in England.

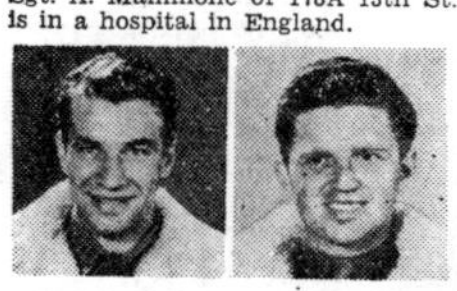

Transferred to Peterson Field, Col., for training as aerial engineers, are Corps. John Kobiernicki Jr. of 97 20th St. and Albert B. Coven of 1793 Sterling Place.

Charles G. Veitenmeimer of 365 78th St. has been commissioned second lieutenant at Jackson, Miss., where he was graduated from the army air forces pilot school.

New member of the Waves is Dorothy E. Friedland of 1616 85th Street.

The Expert Infantryman's Badge has been awarded to Pfc. Ignatzio Bonsignore of 991 Halsey St., stationed at Fort Bragg, N. C.

Corp. Salvatore Bassolino of Brooklyn, who spent his youth in Italy, is serving with the engineers at Camp Caliborne, La.

Advanced to sergeant technician fourth grade at Fort Mason, Cal., is Jerome Weintraub of 285 Grafton Street.

Recently graduated from Keesler Field, Miss., as a bomber mechanic, was Pvt. Jules L. Duval of 1162 75th St.

A laboratory technician in civilian life, Tech. 4th Grade Morris Schwartz of 194 Utica Ave. has completed the non-commissioned officers' course at Camp Beale, Cal.

Transferred to a navy blimp squadron, following training at Lakehurst, N. J., is Aviation Machinist's Mate 2d Class Walter E. Gunning of 173 Dahill Road.

Twin brothers serving Uncle Sam are Aviation Cadet Ray M. Brandstein of 4132 Bedford Ave., who recently completed basic flight training at Marana army air field, Ariz., and Marine Pvt. Irving Brandstein, stationed at Parris Island, S. C. Both brothers are graduates of James Madison High School and were attending St. John's Law School when they entered the services.

Seaman 1st Class William R. Hansen of 2364 E. 75th St. will be graduated April 29, from quartermaster school at Manhattan Beach. Assigned to active duty with the navy's amphibious forces is Radioman's Mate 3d Class Jack Horowitz of 403 Kosciusko St.

John G. McGinley of 374 87th St. was promoted to technician fourth grade at Camp Barkley, Texas.

Aviation Cadet Arthur Golumb of 1481 E. 8th St. has completed basic flight training at Gunter Field, Ala.

Jane Vernoica Mullens of 64 S. Oxford St., has joined the Waves.

From Overseas

EUROPE — Wounded the second time in eight months, Pvt. Maurice P. Enriquez, 34 Granite St., wrote in his last letter, Feb. 26: "Sicily, Salerno, Naples, Venefrio —I won't have enough room on my uniform to place all those service bars."

A paratrooper, the 23-year-old veteran received slight arm and leg wounds at still another battlefront, the Anzio beachhead, on March 20. "Well, I'm at it again," he wrote of the Anzio assignment. "But don't worry. This place is pretty rugged, but I'm an old soldier now and I know what it's all about."

First wounded in Sicily, July 11, Private Enriquez recovered in time to participate in the Salerno invasion. He entered the army 1942 and was sent overseas April, 1943. His younger brother, Billie, was recently shipped overseas, and an older brother, Vincent, is entering the army today.

Pfc. Frederick J. Fiederlein of 383 1st St. is stationed in England.

Serving with an antiaircraft unit on the Anzio beachhead is Corp. Thomas J. O'Brien of 508 81st St.

Tail-gunner on a B-24 Vincent Ganga of 786 Hart St. has been promoted to staff sergeant in 15th Army Air Force.

Finder of an unexpected American souvenir in a captured Italian city is Pvt. James J. Lewis of 175 15th St., who discovered an ancient single-barreled shotgun in the rubble, plainly marked with the name-plate of a Connecticut arms manufacturer.

Members of the only coast guard ship used in the raid on strategic Emirau Island were Ensign Clifford L. Benson of 3411 Clarendon Road, Coxswains Edward J. Muller of 793 Lexington Ave., Lawrence Birk of 540 St. John's Place, and Seaman Louis Stauber of 4220 15th Ave.

Joseph P. Maronna

Soldier Back Home; Absent 7 Years

Technician 4th Grade Joseph P. Maronna, back from Europe on a War Department "rotational plan" furlough, saw his parents, Mr. and Mrs. Charles Maronna of 6311 15th Ave., for the first time in more than seven years.

A former student at Georgetown University Dental School and once a ballet dancer, he left for Europe with the Philadelphia Ballet Company in 1936. He was in Paris when the Germans entered the city and spent a month in a Nazi prison.

Ultimately he got to England, drove an ambulance there during the air blitz and enlisted in the United States Army when the first American units arrived. He was an instructor of French and Italian to Wacs and army officers just before receiving his furlough.

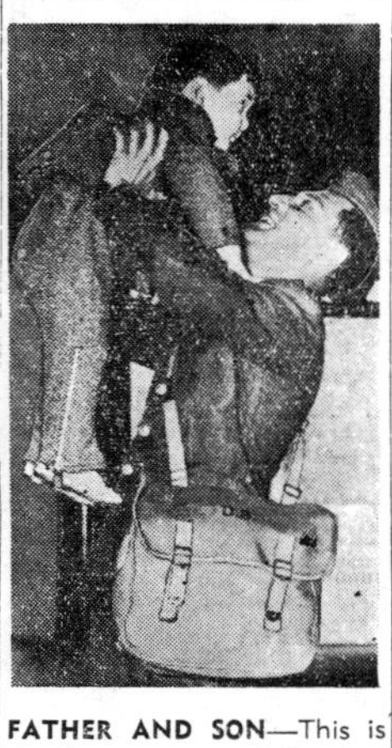

FATHER AND SON—This is the first meeting of Pvt. Leo Raskin of Brooklyn and his son, Marvin Franklin. Father was overseas two years, including seven and one-half months in a North Africa hospital.

Former Carrier For Eagle Missing In Romania Raid

Staff Sgt. Lawrence J. Tynan, a former carrier boy for the Brooklyn Eagle, has been reported missing in action, according to a telegram received recently by his parents, Mr. and Mrs. Launcelot Tynan of 8623 14th Ave. His brother, William, now is delivering the papers to Brooklyn homes.

The telegram said Sergeant Tynan was reported missing April 4 after a flight over Rumania, and the family is hoping he was picked up or is a prisoner of war.

Lawrence's 21st birthday fell on April 19. He was born in Brooklyn and as soon as he graduated from New Utrecht High School he enlisted. He was a radio operation on a bomber.

His last letter, sent from Foggia, Italy, told how he had taken part in the fight at Cassino and in raids over Bucharest and Vienna without getting a scratch.

The elder Tynan, who is employed in the Department of Sanitation, is a veteran of World War I and was a captain in the 5th Infantry. He was wounded in the Meuse-Argonne and is a member of the American Legion and the Veterans of Foreign Wars.

Your Wartime Problems

By RICHARD HART

Discharge Papers Should Be Guarded Closely

It is utterly amazing how careless some of the discharged veterans are about that precious and useful discharge certificate.

Only last night your columnist watched a chap showing his discharge at the corner drug store. Although he had just arrived from his last camp, it was dog-eared and frayed. He was carrying it around in his back pocket, not even enclosed by a wallet. At this rate of wear and tear it is doubtful whether the document will last out the week.

A discharge paper is something to guard with one's life. It is necessary to present the original in order to apply for the musterout pay because the disbursing officer has to stamp it on the back. The original should be shown to the draft board and most employers want to see a man's discharge before he goes on the payroll. The original is necessary for any pension claim, any claim for future bonuses, educational benefits, etc.

SAFE PLACE

It is mighty good policy to protect these discharge papers in some sore of durable cover and in some safe container. It is also good policy to have several true copies made of it (both sides) by a notary public and one of these will be sufficient to show or give to an employer who requests it. A still further safeguard is to have it registered at the county office just in case all the copies and the original are lost.

There is a common illusion that it is easy to get a copy of a discharge from the Adjutant General's Office in Washington. This is the most overworked office in the world and the same could be said of the Bureau of Naval Personnel and all the other record offices of the various services. It takes time to search for a man's records in their miles upon miles of record files containing over 10,000,000 cases. And there are bothersome regulations that must be satisfied.

When applying for any benefits, such as the musterout pay, a veteran should double-check whether he is sending his discharge papers to the proper office. As an extra precaution, attach a slip of paper which spells out in large block letters the correct return address. Print the return address clearly on the lefthand side of the envelope. It is the most valuable document that a veteran possesses and it is just as well to be fussy about it.

ASIDES TO READERS

To MRS. D. A. C. and others. An overseas soldier in a quiet sector is in line for a furlough home after 18 months of overseas service, but he has to wait his turn. The Navy and Marine Corps have about the same general policy. To S. E. E. The inductee is not entitled to be reimbursed for any moving expenses for his household effects as he enters the army.

If you have a problem, write to Richard Hart, care of this newspaper.

A stamped, addressed envelope will bring a personal reply.

32 Local Soldiers Listed With 539 As Nazi Captives

Washington, April 26 (U.P.) — The War Department made public today the names of 539 United States soldiers who are held as prisoners of war by Germany. They include the following 32 men from Brooklyn, Queens and Long Island:

ALINI, Pfc. Salvatore — Migliaro Alini, uncle, 44 Carroll St.

ANDERSON, Pfc Charles F.—Mrs. Loretta Anderson, mother, 215-13 Jamaica Ave., Queens Village.

BASSIN, Pvt. Philip — Mrs. Bessie Bassin, mother, 477 Hinsdale St.

BEALIN, Tech. Sgt. Frank A. — Mrs. Mamie Bealin, grandmother, 3810 Flatlands Ave.

CARNIE, Staff Sgt. Norman M.— Mrs. Ethel O. Carnie, wife, 224 E. Dean St., Freeport.

CORMANO, Pvt. Anthony M.—Mrs. Carmela Cormano, mother, 110-18 Sutphin Boulevard, Jamaica.

CRAWBUCK, Staff Sgt. John— Mrs. Florence Crawbuck, mother, 390 Rutland Road.

ENGEL, Pvt. John J. — Mrs. Ruth M. Engel, wife, 59-19 71st Ave.

FOULKES, Staff Sgt. Arthur F. Jr. —Arthur Foulkes, father, 523 12th Street.

FRANZO, Sgt. Anthony J.—Thomas A. Franzo, father, 227 Milford St.

FREEMAN, Pfc. Simon—Mrs. Mary Freeman, mother, 191 McKibbin Street.

GILIOTTI, Staff Sgt. Albert—Mrs. Rose Gilotti, mother, 127 Lynch Street.

GOLDSTEIN, Staff Sgt. Edward P. —Herman Goldstein, brother, 1601 Ocean Parkway.

GORDON, Pvt. Louis—Mrs. Mabel Gordon, wife, 520 Ocean View Ave.

GRATT, Staff Sgt. David—Mannie Gratt, father, 1532 50th St.

GREENBERG, 2d Lt. Murray S.— Mrs. Shirley Greenberg, wife, c/o Stern, 1466 St. Mark's Ave.

GREENFIELD, 2d Lt. Harvey B.— Mrs. Arline S. Greenfield, wife, 2601 Glenwood Road.

GRIFFITH, 2d Lt. Oliver J. — Mrs. Evelyn B. Griffith, wife, 2418 26th St., Astoria.

ITZIKOFF, Staff Sgt. Harry—Mrs. Ida Itzikoff, mother, 536 Montgomery St.

KAPLAN, 2d Lt. Jacob—Mrs. Evelyn S. Kaplan, wife, 235 Kingston Avenue.

KENNEDY, 2d Lt. Arthur J.— Thomas J. Kennedy. father, 454 Horton Highway, Williston Park.

KRYJAK, Tech. Sgt. Matthew S.— Mrs. Loretta Kryjak, mother, 909 Lorimer St.

LISSANDRELLO, Staff Sgt. George G.—Mrs. Nellie DeLuca, sister, 66-41 Burns St., Forest Hills.

McINTYRE, Staff Sgt. Kenneth J. —Mrs. Rebecca C. McIntyre, mother, 110-16 103d Ave., Richmond Hill.

PUGLIESE, Pfc. Anthony — Mrs. Rona Pugliese, wife, 10 Bergen St.

PUZINO, Pfc. Thomas—Mrs. Julia Puzino, mother, 53-43 98th St., Elmhurst.

RUTLEDGE, 2d Lt. Peter G.— James E. Rutledge, uncle, 37-17 93d St., Jackson Heights.

STRUETT, Sgt. Walter H. — Mrs. Ida Struett, mother, 76-05 58th Ave., Elmhurst.

VALENTINE, Pfc. John J.—Charles Valentine, father, 31-15 89th St., Jackson Heights.

VELO, Pfc. Anthony C. Jr. — Mrs. Anna L. Velo, mother, 188-34 Illion Ave., St. Albans.

VETRANO, Pvt. Tobio — Meo Menino, uncle, 101-18 102d St., Ozone Park.

VOLET, 2d Lt. Leonard—Dr. Max Volet, father, 570 Eastern Parkway.

THESE WOMEN!

By d'Alessio

"I don't mind asking for a raise, dear, if you promise I'll get something out of it if I succeed."

THEATERS UNITE TO SPUR DRIVE FOR 'G. I. JANES'

"G. I. Jane" will be the woman of the hour May 11 to 17, when motion picture theaters throughout Brooklyn will combine in putting over Wac Recruiting Week.

Plans for the drive were drawn up yesterday in the Albee Theater by Lt. Jean Conant, Wac officer in charge of Brooklyn recruiting, and representatives of the motion picture industry. Among the latter were Louis Goldberg, chairman of the drive; Al Zimbalist, publicist; John Hearns, Murray Greene, William A. Downs, Paul Binstock, Sol Handwerger, Edwin Gold, Sigurd Wexo, Ray Malone, Louis Levy, Edward Dowden and Murray Seedletz.

A special trailer in which Lionel Barrymore tells a Wac recruiting story will be shown in all theaters, followed by speeches by members of the corps. Fifty Wacs will participate in outdoor rallies at key spots in the borough and army bands will play. Brooklyn has been designated into small areas, captained by men in charge of organizing the theaters of the district.

Posters to Help

The American Legion, Hollywood stars, local color guards, wounded heroes and public officials will spur the campaign. Various slogans such as "Every gal that joins the Wac helps to make the Axis crack" will be posted throughout the borough.

Lieutenant Conant, discussing the urgent need for recruits, pointed out that in a few months "most of our men will be overseas preparing for the hardest job they have ever done. These men will be helpless, however," she added, "if the women back here don't work to get the necessary materials to them."

Declaring life in the Wacs was not "all play," Lieutenant Conant said, however, that most of the girls were enjoying the new experiences and many asserted they had never had such wondrful times. Most camps are near cities, she said, and new movies at nominal prices may be seen almost any night. She denounced as utterly false a rumor that Wacs aren't permitted to use makeup.

"Let us demonstrate once more that our industry stands ready to do its part," Mr. Goldberg, urged, pointing to the work done by the theaters in advancing the Red Cross and March of Dimes campaigns. He appealed to every man present to do "more than your best" in enlisting the aid of all available women.

Mr. Dowden pointed out that many women have left lucrative jobs to help the war effort.

The national chairman of the drive is Edward L. Alperson. Ned E. Sepinet is distributor chairman, E. Sepinet is distributor chairman; Harry Brandt and Charles B. McDonald, field directors.

Eagle Staff photo

CALL FOR "G. I. JANE"—Plans for Brooklyn's Wac Recruiting Week, to start May 11, are discussed by Al Zimbalist, left, publicist of the drive; Lt. Jean Conant, Wac officer heading campaign; Louis Goldberg, chairman.

Staff Sgt. Dawley Listed As Killed in Solomons

Shot down in combat over Vella La Vella in the Solomons, Staff Sgt. Willard J. Dawley of 1000 E. 19th St. has been listed by the Navy Department as killed in action. The 22-year-old marine was a radioman and gunner, spcecilaizing in night fighting with the Flight Echelon, Marine Air Wing. He had been overseas since September, 1943.

Sergeant Dawley left Fordham University to enlist shortly after Pearl Harbor. He attended Erasmus Hall High School.

WHEN OUT OF TOWN REGISTER FROM BROOKLYN

FIGHTING AGOGLIAS—Six sons of Mr. and Mrs. Vincent Agoglia, 310 19th St., are serving Uncle Sam. Left to right, Corp. John, former basketball star of St. Francis College, now in Italy; Pvt. Anthony, stationed in Texas; Pfc. Joseph, at Camp Butner, N. C.; Pvt. Frank and Pfc. Rocco, stationed in England, and Corp. James, serving in the Brooklyn army base.

WHEN OUT OF TOWN REGISTER FROM BROOKLYN

REAL ESTATE

FLATBUSH TRANSACTION—This one-family dwelling, 143 Buckingham Road, with double garage, has been purchased by Dr. I. S. Friedman from the Kings County Savings Bank through Chester H. Wainwright of the Flatbush office of M. C. O'Brien, Inc., as broker. Dr. Friedman will remodel the house for his residence and office.

PARK SLOPE TRANSACTION—This one-family dwelling, 234 8th Ave., corner of 3d St., built to order in 1911, has been sold by Rickard G. Mannheim to Dr. Stanley C. Hall for occupancy. The property is assessed at $25,000. The broker in the deal was L. L. Yearsley.

IN RECENT DEALS—This apartment house, 211 8th Ave., has been sold by Luther S. Bowman of the Charles Partridge Real Estate Company sales staff, for the Dime Savings Bank of Williamsburgh, to a client for investment.

OCEAN PARKWAY DEAL—This one-family dwelling, at the northwest corner of Ocean Parkway and Avenue T, has been purchased by Meyer Schwartz. The broker in the transaction was Henry J. Sacader.

Home Sales Reveal Active Queens Market

Butterly & Green of Jamaica, realty firm, sold the following houses for the HOLC and various other owners: 160-24 96th St., Howard Beach, to Walter Eden; 101-20 Liberty Ave., Ozone Park, to Frank A. Municion; 93-44 204th St., Hollis, to John H. Rogoseh; 175-30 127th Ave., Springfield, to Bernhard Fey; 130-14 176th Place, St. Albans, to Charles Conover; 115-34 198th St., St. Albans, to Catherine Deile; 86-19 240th St., Bellerose, to Dorothy V. Hamilton; 128-01 142d St., Ozone Park, to Frederick W. Ferber; 78-13 90th Ave., Woodhaven, to Otto Wiedmann, and 97-35 219th St., Queens Village, to George E. Anderson.

Says Real Estate Good Investment At Today's Prices

The real estate market of today is full of vast opportunities for the buyer according to Jack Helman of the real estate firm of Mecke and Helman. "Real estate as a commodity" he says, has not kept pace with the rising tide of prices that we see affecting commodities of every type, and needed in our every day life. However, the situation will correct itself, inasmuch as liquidation of institution-owned properties is almost completed. Entire areas in Brooklyn are without institution-owned properties, in the form of one or two family houses. Larger houses, of course, have long since been disposed of. The rate of liquidation on the remainder of the houses is increasing in tempo.

"It is a known fact that to go out and look for four, five, or six room apartments is an adventure indeed. Hardships are actually inflicted where sales are made and possession is required. This situation exists, remember, when approximately ten million or more men and women are in uniform. Imagine the condition when the war is over, and our people come marching home again. Take into consideration also the huge number of new marriages since Pearl Harbor or before, and the increase in the birthrate as a result thereof. These children by the end of the war, will need rooms of their own, especially those of families that can afford it.

"Foolish indeed is the man or woman who does not avail himself of the little time remaining in securing some of the properties still available. Some of the wiseacres amongst them say, "Well, I'll wait for new construction. The new buildings will have this, and that, and so on." Well, you and I know that there isn't anything in a new building that you cannot put into an old one, if the merchandise is available, such as colored tile, and other finishing touches, for which in new construction such high prices are paid. Larger apartments can easily be converted into two smaller apartments, and profits obtained as a result thereof, and with the completion of liquidation of institution-owned propertes, a real rise in price is sure to follow, when one takes into further consideration the amount of money in circulation."

Wide Interest Shown in Auction Of Herle Realty

Widespread interest among real estate investors and mortgage firms has been shown in the announcement that 12 well-located parcels of real estate and 61 mortgages are to be sold at auction by direction of the Lafayette National Bank as trustees for the estate of Louisa Herle, recluse and shrewd buyer of real estate, who died in 1934.

The bank has commissioned James A. Heaney Jr., auctioneer, to offer the real estate and mortgages at auction on Wednesday, May 3, at 1 p.m. in the Real Estate Exchange, 189 Montague St. Mr. Heaney said yesterday that, following the advertised announcements in the Brooklyn Eagle, hundreds of inquiries have come to his office in 189 Montague St. for additional information about the property. Owners of properties on which the mortgages to be sold are placed have expressed their intention of attending the sale to purchase the mortgage, the auctioneer stated.

The outstanding parcel in the list is the building, 755-763 Broadway in the Eastern District section, leased to F. W. Woolworth Company and assessed at $125,000 by the city. The building occupies a plot 96 feet on Broadway, 126 feet on Flushing Ave. and is 100 feet in depth.

Sale in Bensonhurst Area

Slomka Bros., Inc., sold the two-family frame house, 2143 84th St., for the Home Owners Loan Corporation to Leo Hassen. The co-operating broker was Clark Realty Company.

Insurance Firms Plan Postwar Home Projects

Several of the leading life insurance companies are making definite plans for large-scale housing projects, to be started as soon as war restrictions on construction are lifted, and it is possible that nearly $100,000,000 of such housing units will be under construction within six months of the war's end, it is reported by the Institute of Life Insurance.

"Life insurance funds will be put to work extensively in this new field in the early postwar period," the institute said. "This will serve the triple purpose of providing sound investment for policyholder reserve funds, aiding the urgent housing needs of the nation, and directly contributing to postwar employment."

Postwar Changes In Refrigerators Will Be Gradual

Philadelphia (U.P.)—The postwar refrigerator with its revolving shelves, transparent cabinets, automatic electric-eye doors and ice chutes will be the exception rather than the rule when civilian production is resumed.

W. Paul Jones, vice president in charge of refrigeration for Philco Corporation, told his company's dealers, "the first refrigerator to reach the consumer when production is resumed will not be radical or revolutionary in design." This prediction is based on the premise that manufacturers, distributors and dealers will be anxious to get back into civilian business quickly. Immediate production and transportation of materials will offer plenty of problems in the early months after the war, even without the complications of radical design changes and tooling up for new modes.

Jones said costly experience in other industries has proved that "the buying public reacts slowly and cautiously to radical design changes, and a period of transition between the prewar and real postwar models should be desirable from many angles." He pointed out that many designers and pseudo-designers indulging in the famous indoor sport of postwar speculation on the shape of products to come, picture the postwar refrigerator as a fantastic piece of equipment. Some vision doors that raise, doors that drop and many other dream features.

Jones agrees that a middle track is necessary to produce a practical piece of household equipment. Of one thing he is sure. There must be ample space for frozen food in the postwar refrigerator, since the trend toward that type of food is definitely here.

Sees Women Using War Plant Skill In Postwar Homes

Chicago (U.P.)—Production line efficiency which women are learning in war industry will be turned to use in theeir postwar homes, predicts Mrs. Julia Kiene, director of th Westinghouse Home Economics Institute.

"Even though the homemaker may only be assembling one little bolt," she declared, "sh has realized that it required planning and organization for her to assemble that bolt quickly. Undoubtedly these homemakers are beginning to wonder if they can't have something more akin to a production line in their own kitchens."

She advocated time and motion studies in order to increase the efficiency of kitchens in the future.

Experimental kitchens already are being built at the Westinghouse laboratories in Mansfield, O., Mrs. Kiene said, to conduct such tests.

The most spectacular change in household equipment, the home economist said, will be the automatic washer, which will eliminate heavy lifting and permit the housewife to do the washing "without any effort at any hour of any day."

Use of the average wringer-type washer today, she claims, involves lifting between 400 and 900 pounds of clothes and water, requiring energy equivalent to shoveling eight tone of coal into a furnace.

M. O. Atlass Joins Casey Office in Bay Ridge Section

Martin O. Atlass, widely known in Bay Ridge realty and financial circles, has joined the office staff of John J. Casey, whose real estate and law office is at 9437 5th Ave., corner of 95th St.

Mr. Atlass has been identified with the real estate business for the past 25 years. He was formerly associated with the real estate department of the Equitable Life Assurance Society and with Michael P. Curnin, Inc., and for several years maintained his own offices in Bay Ridge.

Mr. Casey recently purchased the building in which his office is located. He completely modernized the property and refurnished the office.

Recent sales made by the broker are One-family houses—268 78th St., 86 77th St., 1245 81st St., 433 Marine Ave., 206 Marine Ave., 25 89th St., 9935 Shore Road, 573 90th St., 357 76th St., 51 93d St., 1186 Schenectady Ave., 1165 80th St., 1145 80th St., 1017 77th St., 153 84th St., 127 97th St. 39 71st St., 88-65 108th St., Jamaica.

Two-family houses—8904 Colonial Road, 53 Marine Ave., 8312 7th Ave., 413 52d St., 7303 6th Ave., 526 54th St., and the three-family houses, 473 72d St. and 365 94th St.

Mr. Casey is a brother of Maj. Gen. Hugh John Casey, chief of engineers for the United Nations in the South Pacific area and a member of the staff of Gen. Douglas MacArthur.

Move Office to Queens

Gleeson and Donlon, Long Island developers identified with Garden City, Estates, Nassau Haven and Babylon Beach Estates, who recently took over 700 acres of the Deforrest estate at Huntington, have moved their offices from 42d St., Manhattan, to 167-09 Hillside Ave., Jamaica. The move, it was stated, was taken to be closed to the recently acquired property.

Brokers to Hold Monthly Meeting

The Realty Brokers of Bay Ridge, Inc., will hold a meeting Wednesday night, May 3, at the American Legion Post, 9002 4th Ave. Charles J. Bianco, president, will preside.

Paul H. Hempel, chairman of the educational committee, has arranged to have Harold J. McAuley, Assistant U. S. Attorney for the Southern District of New York, to give a talk on public speaking.

Buys 18th Ave. Home

Harry M. Lewis Company, Inc., sold for Lafayette National Bank of Brooklyn, as trustee, the two-story, semi-detached, duplex, two-family brick dwelling with two-car garage, on lot 20x100, at 1839 50th St., near 18th Ave., to Pasquale Patierno, for occupancy. This was an all-cash transaction.

Varied Parcels Of Real Estate To Be Auctioned

Fred Berger, auctioneer of the real estate firm of Fred Berger & Co., will offer at auction on May 2 at 2 p.m. in the Patio Room of the Hotel St. George 14 choice improved parcels located in the boroughs of Brooklyn and Queens.

The Brooklyn properties are: 2006 65th St., a store and apartment building; 725-7 Atlantic Ave., a business building; 8708 Bay Parkway, a three-family house; 10 Central Ave., a 4-story apartment building, and 246-8 Varet St.; a three-story six-family apartment building with an adjoining one-story store building. The Queens properties are 766-768 and 784 Empire Ave., Far Rockaway, each of which is a semi-detached two-family house; 816-824-826 Meehan Ave., Far Rockaway, consisting of one two-family and two one-family houses, and 78-19 90th Road, Woodhaven, a two-family detached house.

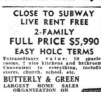

SCREEN By Jane Corby

George Cukor, Famous Film Director Of Many Hits, Directed New 'Gaslight'

After more than a year of intensified work with the motion picture division of the U. S. Army, George Cukor went back to Hollywood to take the directorial helm for "Gaslight," which opens at the Capitol Thursday. The new film presents Ingrid Bergman, Charles Boyer and Joseph Cotten in leading parts, is an adaptation of Patrick Hamilton's stage success known on Broadway as "Angel Street."

The fact that a writer once called Cukor "the greatest women's director in Hollywood" is a very incomplete indication of the success of this alumnus of the Broadway stage in all picture stories. He achieved remarkable results with such predominantly feminine stories as "Camille," "The Women," "A Woman's Face" and "The Philadelphia Story"; but he did equally well with stories in which the male performers were fully as dominant as their feminine colleagues, such productions as "David Copperfield," "Dinner at Eight," "The Royal Family" and "Holiday."

Before leaving Hollywood to make his contribution to Uncle Sam Cukor did "Keeper of the Flame," which co-starred Spencer Tracy and Katharine Hepburn. This dramatic story of present-day America was in contrast to "Gaslight," which is a psychological thriller, placed in London at the turn of the century.

Hollywood, Cukor thinks, has helped the Broadway stage rather than the reverse by introducing new ideas and by creating a new circle of playgoing interest among the ranks of those who become interested in drama through the films. He says that there isn't any great basic difference in directing an actor on the stage or in front of the movie camera, the essential thing being a telescoping of mood and confidence between the director and actor, both in themselves and in the story they are doing.

Billy Rose Will Do 'Nellie Bly'

Billy Rose has commissioned Sig Herzig and Jack Emmanuel, Hollywood writers, to write the book for a musical comedy tentatively titled "Nellie Bly." Mr. Rose is hoping for a first draft in ten weeks. The play, naturally, will have to do with the first lady reporter to circle the globe. The notion was suggested by Bert Lahr, who would be Nellie's rival reporter in the face when the script is completed. Mr. Rose is currently negotiating with a couple of song writers to write the tunes and lyrics but would not release any names as yet since contracts have not been negotiated.

Effective Sunday, May 7, "Allah Be Praised!" the Alfred Bloomingdale musical comedy at the Adelphi Theater, will add Sunday matinee and evening performances to its schedule. Tuesday evening and Wednesday matinee showings of the production will be omitted beginning from that date also.

"Junior Miss," the Jerome Chodorov-Joseph Fields comedy, enters its second and final week at the Flatbush Theater tonight.

Johnny Morgan, who appeared in "What's Up?" earlier this season, has been engaged for the leading comedy role in Sigmund Romberg's "The New Moon," which launches the festival of operettas at the New York City Center on Wednesday evening, May 17.

Following its current run in Philadelphia, "Porgy and Bess," the Gershwin-Heyward musical success, will return to Greater New York for a short tour of the subway circuit. Under the banner of Cheryl Crawford it opens at the Flatbush Theater May 9. The present cast and production will remain intact, with Alexander Smallens as conductor.

Dinah Halpern will return to the local Jewish stage in the stellar role of "The Refugee," a new Yiddish drama by William Siegel, which will have its premiere at the Hopkinson Theater in Brooklyn this Friday evening, May 5.

INGRID BERGMAN and Joseph Cotten, as they appear in "Gaslight," coming to the Capitol on Thursday. Charles Boyer is also starred.

THEATER By Arthur Pollock

Press Agent and Burlesque Producer Write a Play Full of Drama Critics

Charlie Washburn and Barney Gerard, press agent and ex-producer of burlesque shows, respectively, have written a play which may be along any time now. Some of the characters are going to be critics, so you can see, unless they merely appear in mob scenes, the dialogue will be brilliant. I don't know how a couple of writers ever worked up the courage to attempt such a thing, since it demands so much cleverness.

Shaw did it well enough in "Fanny's First Play," in which he brought on a number of English critics of the day and set them to contradicting each other in a remarkable satirical scene. But Shaw is a man quite special and used to be a critic himself. What Mr. Washburn and Mr. Gerard will do with the newspaper judges of the drama heaven only knows. Mr. Washburn will be writing under a handicap, being a press agent. He will want good notices for his play and is therefore sure to feel that he must sacrifice whatever he may consider the truth to whatever he may consider tact. No doubt he will kid each critic a little and then polish him off with a compliment of one sort or another to make him feel good.

Critics have seen themselves kidded in plays before Shaw and since. Sheridan wrote a famous comedy called "The Critic" in which the critics of his day took a beating. It is to be hoped that Messrs. Washburn and Gerard will not turn out to be a couple of twentieth-century Sheridans. It wouldn't be pleasant to have another Sheridan around. He was the dramatist who, when his theater was burning down and he stood watching the conflagration, replied, when asked by a friend why he showed no concern, "Surely a man may enjoy himself at his own fireside." Possibly the authors of "Public Genius No. 1," as the oncoming play is called, will curb their talents if they feel as witty as that.

"Arsenic and Old Lace" has, as everybody knows, a critic among its characters, a rather frivolous and romantic fellow who supplies one-half of the love interest in the play, indicating that critics are not the mere intellectual giants some may have mistakenly supposed. Possibly, since there is a vogue now for comedies about children, the authors of the new play will show New York's critics as Tarkington adolescents, though it isn't likely. That would be stretching the truth a little.

The most recent sober characterization of a critic was that of Samson Raphaelson in his play "Jason" of a few years ago. Mr. Raphaelson was not too kind. He pictured a bookish fellow in a state of mental conflict. Not only did he find himself faced with the necessity of getting a new idea or two into his head in order to be able adequately to measure the talent of a new and eccentric playwright but the young eccentric stole the critic's wife. Furthermore, the critic was such a stuffy gentleman that he dulled up the play considerably.

Probably Mr. Washburn will not be too realistic about making the critics of the new play perfect scholars, and, if he insists, no doubt Mr. Gerard, who used to produce burlesque shows in which Bozo Snyder was the star, will prevail upon him to lighten up the thing with a little colloquialism even at the expense of the critics' feelings.

Well, anyhow, soon we will see just what kind of people these critic guys are. It ought to be a marvelous play.

'Buffalo Bill' Begins Third Week at Roxy Tomorrow

The 20th Century-Fox Technicolor production "Buffalo Bill" begins its third week at the Roxy Theater starting tomorrow. Joel McCrea in the title role, Maureen O'Hara, Linda Darnell and Thomas Mitchell head the cast, which also features Edward Buchanan, Anthony Quinn, Moroni Olsen, Frank Fenton and Matt Briggs.

'Lady in the Dark' At Paramount Wednesday

The Paramount Theater will present as its feature attraction tomorrow Paramount's Technicolor picturization of the Broadway hit "Lady in the Dark." Seen in the starring roles are Ginger Rogers, Ray Milland, Warner Baxter and Jon Hall, while Mischa Auer tops the supporting cast. The associate feature will be "The Navy Way," with Robert Lowery, Jean Parker and Bill Henry.

The story of "Lady in the Dark" concerns the confusion and unhappiness of a successful fashion magazine editor (Ginger Rogers) who upon the advice of friends seeks help via a psychoanalyst.

'Jam Session' New Musical At the Palace Today

"Jam Session," newest of Columbia's Ann Miller musicals, which follows the general trend inaugurated with "Reveille With Beverly," opens for its first Broadway showing at the RKO Palace Theater today, featuring six of the nation's name bands.

Ann Miller is co-starred with Jess Barker, with Charlie Barnet, Louis Armstrong, Alvino Rey, Jan Garber, Glen Gray and Teddy Powell leading their respective bands in a story written for the screen by Manny Seff and directed by Charles Barton.

★★★★★★★ SPORTS Wall Street Financial News

BROOKLYN EAGLE

Weather—Partly cloudy tonight; increasing cloudiness, warmer tomorrow.

103d Year. No. 121. DAILY & SUNDAY • (Copyright 1944 The Brooklyn Eagle, Inc.) • BROOKLYN, N. Y., WEDNESDAY, MAY 3, 1944 • Entered at the Brooklyn Postoffice as 2d Class Mail Matter • 3 CENTS IN NEW YORK CITY ELSEWHERE 4 CENTS

MEAT RATION ENDS TONIGHT, CHOICE BEEF CUTS EXCEPTED

Bombs Cripple Nazi Rail Networks; Report 50 Enemy Divisions Shifted

100-MILE-DEEP COASTAL BELT IS DISRUPTED

Raids Threaten Berlin Plan to Shuttle Troops To Meet Invaders

London, May 3 (U.P.)—Allied bombing fleets have crippled every major German railroad yard in a 100-mile-deep coastal belt from Cologne to the Bay of Biscay, threatening to paralyze the movement of German reserves to the western "invasion front," the Ministry of Economic Warfare revealed today.

A Ministry spokesman said the terrific preinvasion bombing of the past month has had an "appalling" effect on the network of wetsern railroads over which the German high command planned to stuttle troops andequipment to meet the Anglo-American invasion armies.

The railways in northern France and Belgium, he said, are now unable to bear the peak load necessary to an effective defense of the Channel coast.

"No marshalling yards between Collogne and the Bay of Biscap for 100 miles inland are capable of forming trains," the spokesman said.

Germans Face Perils

He declared flatly that the Germans, faced with the possibility of an Allied invasion almost at any hour, have only these alternatives: To keep their reserves at dangerously-remote points more than 100 miles inland from the threatened coast, or to reinforce their coastal garrisons immediately, thereby running the risk of suffering great casualties.

The spokesman said his analysis of the German communications system was based on reliable information received by the ministry—presumably from the French underground.

Sabotage by French and Belgian patriots also has helped paralyze the Nazi-operated railway lines, and prevented reconstruction work, he added.

The spokesman said German railway lines in the Balkans also have been badly disrupted by sabotage and bombing.

Film Actor Held In Theft of $2,250 Ring

Hollywood, May 3 (U.P.)—Richard Allord, 24, film actor, has been ordered held for trial in Superior Court on a charge that he stole a $2,250 diamond ring from Mrs. Lou Dell Breese, divorced wife of Vance Breese, test pilot, last Jan. 4.

"I had decided to sell the ring because I was planning to enlist in the air corps," Mrs. Breese testified at the preliminary hearing before Municipal Judge Leroy Dawson, "and the defendant told me that he had a friend who would pay me more for the ring than I could get from an ordinary dealer. I let him have it to get it appraised. He never returned it."

BALKAN INVASION? — Arrows show route along which Allies would strike if they invade Balkans from Italy. Military mission of General Tito, Yugoslav Partisan leader, has just arrived in London for a series of conferences.

Liberators Hammer French 'Rocket Coast'

RAF Night Raiders Pound Ports, Rail Yards In France and Italy, Reich Poison Gas Plant

London, May 3 (U.P.)—U. S. bombers sent the great pre-invasion bombardment of Europe through its 17th day today after blockbuster attacks on railway yards and ports in France and Italy and a poison gas plant in Germany last night.

Liberators attacked the French "Rocket Coast" today, as Lt. Gen. James H. Doolittle sent a formation of his 8th Air Force Liberators against the mysterious German installations in the Pas de Calais area.

Fleets of swift Mosquito bombers struck by night at Leverkusen, the German site of poison gas and chemical works, and the French rail hub of Acheres, while Italy-based R. A. F. planes exploded a broadside against Italian harbors and rail yards.

Supply Trains Blasted

Hundreds of freight cars loaded with anti-invasion supplies were blown to bits as American and British bombers concentrated on rail bottlenecks in France, Belgium, Holland and western Germany.

The latest two-way night attacks

Continued on Page 11

Reds in Romania Start Offensive

London, May 3 (U.P.)—Strong Russian tank and infantry forces were reported by the German high command today to have opened a new offensive on both sides of the middle Siret River in northeastern Romania.

Lacking confirmation by non-Axis sources, the report of the attack indicated that Marshal Ivan S. Konev's 2d Army of the Ukraine was striking southward toward the 50-mile Galati Gap, the bottleneck of the Romanian defenses before Bucharest and the Ploesti oil fields.

In the first half of April the 2d Army of the Ukraine smashed across the Siret west of Iasi and seized aPscani, junction of the Bucharest-Cernauti trunk railway.

Planes Fire Troop Trains

Moscow, May 3 (U.P.)—Red air force bombers, paving the way for new Soviet offensives, kindled 30 huge fires in a heavy raid on Lwow, biggest communications hub in southeastern Europe, a Russian communique said today.

Farrell Names Ministers

Buenos Aires, May 3 (U.P.)—Appointment of Gen. Orlando Peluffo as Minister of Foreign Affairs and Dr. Alberto Baldrich as Minister of Justice and Education was announced by President Edelmiro Farrell last night.

REICH DROPS COMPROMISE PEACE HOPE

1,500,000 Massed In Western Europe, Stockholm Hears

London, May 3 (U.P.)—Germany warned her European satellites today that all hope for a compromise peace has been abandoned, and Swedish dispatches said the Nazi high command, gambling desperately for a victory in the west, has shifted 50 divisions from the Russian front to meet the impending Allied invasion.

The German Transocean News Agency declared in a broadcast to the continent that there no longer is any prospect of a break in the Anglo-American-Russian alliance and that Germany is braced for climactic land battles in the east and west.

"The invasion and the final battle in the east will take place shortly," Transocean said, quoting a dispatch written by Fritz Theil, Berlin correspondent for a Bucharest newspaper.

"Nobody in Berlin has the slightest illusions about a compromise peace," the broadcast added.

Nazis Split Armies

Simultaneously the German home radio warned its people that "we are on the eve of decisive military events."

"The German Reich is fully prepared for these decisions and no pre-invasion alarm can change even an iota of the measures that have been provided for the defense of the continent," the broadcast said.

Meanwhile the London Daily Telegraph's Stockholm correspondent reported that Germany has virtually split its armies in two through a huge transfer of men from the Russian front, massing 1,500,000 men in western Europe and 1,750,000 against the Soviet armies in the east.

The shift, which doubled Germany's western European forces, was made on the recommendation of Field Marshal Erwin Rommel, German anti-invasion commander, the dispatch said, characterizing the move as "the greatest military gamble ever made."

Await the Zero Hour

Radio Berlin disclosed that Rommel just had informed his battery commanders along the Atlantic Coast to expect an Allied air-borne landing "every day, every hour" and Capt. Ludwig Sertorious, Nazi military commentator, said the invasion "will not be long now."

At least seven other German commentators in the past 24 hours have broadcast warnings to the populations of Axis Europe that they must be prepared for heavy simultaneous blows from the east, west and south.

Kurt Dittmar, in a Berlin broadcast, acknowledged that the Allies held sea and air superiority in the west and said that "certain factors are extremely favorable to the Anglo-Americans."

Gandhi's Failing Health Alarming His Doctors

Bombay, India, May 3 (U.P.)—An official bulletin disclosed today a further decline in the condition of Mohandas K. Gandhi and his failing health was causing some anxiety.

The bulletin said Gandhi's anemic condition had become worse and his blood pressure had fallen further.

Yanks Blast Bridge In Northern China

Chungking, May 3 (U.P.)—Warhawk fighters of the 14th U. S. Air Force dive-bombed a bridge at Wan Laikam in northern Burma May 1, destroying one span, and strafed Japanese installations there, a communique announced today.

Pimlico Results

1—Telltale, 45.20, 16.80, 6.10; Molliann, 4.80, 2.90; Might Be, 2.60. Off time, 12:09½.

2—Andrew Palmer, 7.10, 4.10, 3.80; Walter Haight, 7.40, 5.90; Dark Danger, 19.70. Off time, 12:38.

DAILY DOUBLE PAID $229.10

3—Frederic II, 7.40, 4.40, 3.00; Eremon, 5.70, 3.20; Winged Hoofs, 2.90. Off time, 1:06½.

4—Alexis, 12.00, 5.30, 4.30; Neat Pleat, 4.30, 3.30; Sea Bees, 3.50. Off time, 1:39.

Justice Froessel

Masons Elect Justice Froessel Grand Lodge Head

Queens Jurist Elected New Grand Master of Organization in State

Supreme Court Justice Charles W. Froessel today was elected grand master of the Grand Lodge of Free and Accepted Masons, State of New York, at the annual communication of the Grand Lodge at Masonic Hall, 71 W. 23d St., Manhattan.

Justice Froessel is the fourth Supreme Court justice to hold that high office since the election of Justice Townsend Scudder in 1906. The other two are Justice S. Nelson Sawyer, who followed Justic eScudder, and Justice Arthur S. Tompkins, who was head of the organization in 1922 and 1923.

Brooklynites who were grand master since 1932 are Christopher C. Mollenhauer, president of the Dime Savings Bank of Williamsburgh; Jacob Charles Klinck, president of the Kings County Savings Bank, and Henry C. Turner.

Other Grand Lodge Officers

Other Grand Lodge officers elected were Gay H. Brown, Utica, N. Y., deputy grand master; Richard A. Rowlands, Schenectady, N. Y., senior warden; Ward B. Arbury, Buffalo, junior grand warden; Hamilton McInness, Manhattan, grand treasurer, and Charles H. Johnson, Manhattan, grand secretary.

Justice Froessel is a member of Tadmor Lodge 923 and during the 1942-43 term of Grand Master William F. Strang has been deputy grand master. He was born in Brooklyn Nov. 8, 1892, the son of Theodore and Barbara Froessel, and was graduated from New York Law School. On June 1, 1927, in Ridgewood he married Miss Elsie Stier.

He was counsel to the Queens

Continued on Page 11

Early End of War Seen After 1 Axis Partner Falls

London, May 3 (U.P.)—Rear Admiral George Barry Wilson of the U. S. Navy predicted today that defeat of one of the two major Axis partners would bring an early termination of the war.

"Success of the United Nations in one ocean immediately eases pressure in the other," Wilson said. "Our victory in either theater will be shortly followed by our final victory over the survivor of the Axis."

Wilson is chief of staff to Admiral Harold R. Stark, commander in chief of U. S. naval forces in European waters.

HEIGHTS ASS'N TO CO-OPERATE IN JAP HOSTEL

Resolves to Appoint Group to Meet Sponsors of Project

The Brooklyn Heights Association today announced it had adopted a resolution "viewing with interest" the proposed establishment of a Japanese-American hostel in Clinton St., and had appointed a committee of five to "co-operate with the authorities sponsoring the project."

At the same time, officials of the American Labor party in Kings County assailed discrimination stemming from war hysteria and defended the relocation center.

The Brooklyn Heights Association's board of governors adopted a resolution reading:

"Resolved, that the Brooklyn Heights Association views with interest the proposal to establish a Japanese-American relocation hostel on Brooklyn Heights, and that a committee of five be appointed as an advisory committee to co-operate with the authorities sponsoring the project."

Vote Secret

In a statement issued by Roy M. D. Richardson, president, it was announced that the vote of the board was not unanimous, although the actual number for and against it was not made known. Mr. Richardson said that the meeting held yesterday from five to seven p.m. was marked by a lively discussion. Sixteen of the Association's 23 governors attended.

Those present were, George N. Whittlesey, chairman of the board, Haughton Bell, James S. Brown, Jr., Walter Bruchhausen, William H. Cary, Russel V. Cruikshank, Guy Duval, Mrs. Edward Haynes, B. Meredith [illegible] the Rev. Dr. John Howl[illegible] Lathrop, the Rev. William H. Melish, Leonard P. Moore, Charles E. Rogers, Jr., Peter V. D. Voorhees, the Rev. Dr. Phillips Packer Elliott and Mr. Richardson.

Advisers Not Named

The advisory committee has not been named yet. Another advisory committee attended yesterday's meeting but absented itself when the vote was taken. This committee includes Sidney W. Davidson, Associate Justice of the Appellate Term William F. Hagarty, Robert A. Shaw and Gen. George Albert Win-

Continued on Page 11

Marine Roof, Hit By War, Won't Open

The famed Marine Roof of the Bossert Hotel for more than a quarter century a Brooklyn instiution, has had to give way to wartime rationing and the 30 percent cabaret tax.

David J. Martin, the hotel's managing director, announced to hotel guests today that at least for the current Summer the Marine Roof "will not function." In a letter to permanent guests, he explained:

"We struggled through the 1943 season—the help problem was acute then and has continued to increase during the past year.

'The rationing program is such that we will be unable to take care of the patrons who come from far and wide to patronize our famous roof. There are many other restrictions brought on by the war, and in the interest of the war effort we accept these inconveniences willingly.'

The Marine Roof has been a feature of Brooklyn's night life for 28 Summers. Here Brooklynites and visitors used to dance and dine amid cool breezes from the bay, with a full view of the skyscraper lights of lower Manhattan and New York Harbor.

Although he did not mention the tax situation in his leteer to guests, Mr. Martin today explained that it had played an "important part in my decision."

SURPRISE DECREE BY OPA FOLLOWS CANADIAN MOVE

Washington, May 3 (U.P.)—All meats will become ration-free at midnight except beef steaks and beek roasts.

The Office of Price Administration took them off the point list in a surprise announcement today, following recent action which removed many canned vegetables from rationing.

Administrator Chester Bowles said he could not say now "when or whether the meats we are [illegible] ing point free will again have to be given point values," but he promised that "point values will not be restored to these meats unless absolutely necessary."

The order means that after midnight consumers no longer will be required to surrender ration points to purchase any pork, veal, lamb, mutton, beef flank steak, beef hamburger, beef stew meats, variety meats, sausages, ready-to-eat meats or canned meat or fish.

Cut Red Point Allotment

The action was accompanied by an order halving the monthly red point allotment to individual consumers since so many points no longe wil be needed. After netx Monday 30 red points will be validated every four weeks intsead of 30 points every two weeks.

The move came only a few weeks after Canada stopped all meat rationing on grounds that storage facilities were filled to overflowing and much meat was in danger of spoiling. Canada's suspensioned rationing aroused considerable criticism in Congress of continued rationing of meats here.

Steak Points Unchanged

Points on all choice beefsteaks and roasts will not be changed from their present levels.

Bowles said the volume of these preferred meats now coming to market "is not large enough in relation to demand to warrant any point change at this time."

A record run of hogs has been coming to market and slaughter is near peak levels, he explained.

Lend-lease, which ordinarily takes up 35 percent of the pork production, he said, now had adequate

Continued on Page 11

WARD ELECTION POSTPONEMENT DENIED BY NLRB

Union Had Requested 21-Day Extension— Attorney Hits 'Speed'

BULLETIN

Chicago, May 3 (U.P.)—George J. Bott, regional director of the National Labor Relations Board, refused today a union request for postponement of a scheduled collective bargaining election among employes of the Chiago plants of Montgomery Ward and Company.

Chicago, May 3 (U.P.) — Union spokesmen protested today a National Labor Relations Board decision to conduct a collective bargaining election at Montgomery Ward & Co.'s Chicago plant within a week and said they would ask for a 21-day extension to prepare for it.

"It's obviously a trick," rFancis Heisler, union attorney said. "The board is hostile to the union because it is standing on its law-given rights. This unheard of speed disregards all rules of the Labor Board."

Leonard Levy, vice president of the United Retail, Wholesale and Department Store Employes Union (C. I. O.), said an extension of at least 21 days would be required.

"We are going to lodge a formal protest with the N. L. R. B. complaining that the company is firing our people and that company supervisors are preventing a fair and unbiased election by intimidating them and influencing them against the union.

Hit U. S. Grievance Set-up

"We are also going to demand that the grievance officer be more than a grievance officer in name only. The Government appointed John Goodloe grievance officer and he has refused to hear any grievances until the legal matters are settled. Now, even the Government won't co-operate with us."

The election was ordered by the NLRB in Washington yesterday, six days after troops weer called to take over the Chicago properties of the nation's second largest mail order house.

Meanwhile, Federal Judge William H. Holly weighed his decision on the Government's right to seize a retail store.

Hines Files Second Plea With Board of Parole

James J. Hines, who was a Tammany district leader until he was sentenced in 1939 for protecting the numbers racket of the late Arthur (Dutch Schultz) Flegenheimer, has filed his second application for a parole. The first application was denied last May. The hearing on the new application will be held in Sing Sing Prison on May 9.

Boro Youths to Get Chair; Lose Plea for New Trial

Winston Sealy and Gordon Cooke, Brooklyn youths reprieved from the electric chair two weeks ago, are scheduled to die this week following denial of motion for a new trial by County Judge Sobel.

Both were convicted of stabbing McKinley Kettles to death in front of his home at 678 Gates Ave. Yesterday's motion was based on alleged new evidence claiming that Cooke was not at the scene, but Judge Sobel relied on "uncontradicted testimony of four unimpeached eyewitnesses" in the denial.

Unlicensed Doctor Gets 60 Days in Jail

Alfred J. Johnerson, 53, of 7212 4th Ave., convicted by a jury in County Court of having practiced medicine without a license and also of having called himself a doctor of chiropractic, was sentenced by Judge Louis Goldstein today to a term of 60 days in jail. The court also imposed a fine of $250.

Judge Goldstein declared the sentence was intended as a warning to 1,800 practitioners of chiropractic in New York State, 100 of whom are in Brooklyn.

The court charged that medicine was being practiced openly and flagrantly in "brazen violation of the law."

Before the imposition of sentence on Johnerson, the court heard a statement by State Senator Louis B. Heller, Assemblyman Eugene Bannigan, counsel for Johnerson, and by Dr. C. B. Mangan, head of the medical grievance board of the Regents of the State of New York.

Reveal U. S. Planes Fly To Reds Via Siberia

Washington, May 3 (U.P.)—American planes have been flown directly to Russia during the past two years over a northern route—presumably via Alaska and Siberia—saving time and avoiding losses incurred in enemy U-boat attacks on plane-carrying convoys, the War Department revealed last night.

The planes, made available to Russia under lend-lease, were flown by Red Air Force pilots, the department said.

This time-and-plane saving achievement was revealed in a citation to Maj. Gen. Follett Bradley, Garden City, L. I., who was credited with effecting the arrangement with Soviet authorities "despite many obstacles."

Army Vans Crash, 6 Soldiers Hurt; Explosion Burns G. I. Mail in Street

Six soldiers and a civilian were injured and thousands of service men's letters were scattered along Lexington Ave., Manhattan, near E. 45th St., when two army trucks about to pass each other at that corner collided at 7:33 a.m. today. One of the trucks carried army mail and the other had prisoners.

A civilian automobile, which had been following one of the trucks, plowed into the trucks, and the driver, John Milton, 48, of 455 Ocean Ave., Cedarhurst, L. I., was among the injured.

One of the trucks burst into flames at the moment of the crash, and a fire truck, as well as 15 patrolmen from the E. 51st St. station, 25 postal employes from the Grand Central Postoffice station and a military police guard were summoned. While traffic remained halted for an hour, the scattered mail, some of it burned, was collected and stacked on the sidewalks.

Coming from Camp

The truck carrying prisoners, with three M. P. guards, was on its way from Camp Shanks, Orangeburg, N. Y., "en route to the proper authorities." The mail truck, with trailer, had started from the Hotel Breslin, Broadway and 29th St., which has been taken over by the army.

As the two vehicles collided the mail truck gasoline tank exploded and flames leaped 10 or 12 stories in the air. The flames burned the canvas cover of the prison truck. Prisoners and guards leaped off, while mail, including cigarettes and other gift packages, scattered over the street. The truck had carried 100 sacks of mail, and it was later reported that half of the mail was destroyed.

List of Injured

The injured, besides Milton, were: Pvt. Edward Brown, driver of prisoner truck, burned right hand, taken to Breslin Hotel dispensary; Pvt. Roland Merrill, 25, driver of mail truck, burns on face, Bellevue Hospital; M. P. Corp. Henry A. Jewell, 24, burns of face and hands, Breslin dispensary, and the following prisoners, all army privates:

Lindsey Duncan, 30, injured right leg, Bellevue; Sterling North Jr., 25, injured right leg, Breslin; Aaron Moore, 25, injured right leg, Breslin.

No prisoners escaped or apparently attempted to escape.

British Loan to China

London, May 3 (U.P.)—Britain signed a formal agreement today to loan £50,000,000 ($200,000,000) to China for war purchases and services in the British Empire area, Foreign Secretary Anthony Eden announced in Commons.

JAMAICA RESULTS

1—Sixteen Cents 5.80-3.20-2.40, Rita Jane 3.30-2.70, Paticia F 3.60. (1:20⅘)

Jeep Jockey's Home Stretch Ride Ends in 1-Man Roundup of 17 Japs

By DON CASWELL

Hollandia, Dutch New Guinea, May 3 (U.P.)—The telephone jingled at regimental headquarters and the signal sergeant almost dropped his mouthpiece from excitement.

"Sir," he called to the commanding major, "some guy just brought in 17 prisoners and he says he needs help."

And thereby hangs the tale of Pvt. Hurshal (Peewee) Wilson, a diminutive jeep-jockey, and his jeep, Helen, named after his girl friend, and how they brought in the 17 dejected Japanese. Peewee, who is 30, comes from Hawthorne, Cal.

Peewee is hardly the guy you'd expect to bring in what must be a record bag of prisoners by one man for this theater. He isn't a combat soldier but drives for Lt. Col. Arthur Anderson of the 41st Division. But he's always prowling around the front lines in his spare time hunting souvenirs.

17 Japs Surrender

At dusk yesterday he had driven Maj. Gen. Hugh J. Casey of Brooklyn, General MacArthur's engineering chief, and three colonels from the Cyclops airstrip to Lake Sentani. He was returning alone, about three miles from headquarters, when 17 Japanese jumped out of the marshy grass and swarmed across the road with their hands up.

Peewee takes over the story from here:

"First I thought they were Na-

Continued on Page 21

WHERE TO FIND IT

	Page		Page
Bridge	18	Radio	21
Comics	21	Real Estate	18
Crossword	18	Society	8
Dr. Brady	10	Sports	14-15
Editorial	10	Take My Word	10
Helen Worth	8	Theaters	16-17
Horoscope	21	These Women.	9
Movies	16-17	Tommy Holmes	14
Novel	18	Uncle Ray	21
Obituaries	11	Want Ads	18-19-20
Our Fighters	9	Wartime Problems	9
Patterns	16		
Prevost	10	Woman	9

★★★★★★★ SPORTS 7 Wall Street Financial News

BROOKLYN EAGLE

Weather—Clear, cool tonght; increasing cloudiness, warmer tomorrow

103d Year. No. 126. DAILY & SUNDAY • The Brooklyn Eagle, Inc. (Copyright 1944) • BROOKLYN, N. Y., MONDAY, MAY 8, 1944 • Entered at the Brooklyn Post-office as 2d Class Mail Matter • 3 CENTS IN NEW YORK CITY ELSEWHERE 5 CENTS

2,000 PLANES SMASH AIR FOES, RIP BERLIN

Those 20 Minutes Of Suspense Got Sergeant Really Mad

Brooklyn Flier Recounts How He Almost Fell From Plane During Raid on Berlin

It was on his 22d mission that Sgt. John E. Wood got really mad.

"That was the first time we bombed Berlin," he explained. "I was in the turret and just as we got over the target the door opened and I fell out. My feet caught in the turret and it was 20 minutes before I got the crew on the intercom and the waist-gunner pulled me back into the plane.

"I was sore," he continued. "I thought it was a pretty nasty thing to happen when I had only three more missions to go before getting my furlough. It wouldn't have been so bad if it happened on the first couple of trips—even if we don't have enough room to wear a 'chute in the turret."

Though he was anxious to return home when he was stationed in London, the sergeant is now just as eager to get back into combat.

"It's the doorbell," he said. "It keeps ringing all day long and people come in to make a fuss over you. I'll really need a rest after my furlough."

Wood is now spending a 20-day furlough with his family at 264 E. 43d St. He reports then to Atlantic City for further assignment which he hopes will put him back in action immediately.

The 21-year-old gunner holds the Distinguished Flying Cross and the Air Medal, with three oak leaf clusters. A graduate of Brooklyn Technical High School, he enlisted in the air corps two years ago. Last August he was shipped to England.

Wood was a crew member on the Tinkertoy when it flew on a bombing raid over Bremen last Oct. 8.

"We had to crash land in England on the return trip," he said. "One of the engines was out of commission and the nose of the plane was shot off. Though he was wounded in the shoulder, the copilot brought the plane back after our pilot was killed. Both the navigator and bombardier stuck to their positions though they were severely wounded too."

Bong's Record Is Tied By Flier Over Europe

Thunderbolt Pilot Chalks Up 26th, 27th Kills To Equal Score of the Pacific Champion

Eighth Air Force Fighter Base, England, May 8 (U.P.)—Capt. Robert Johnson, Lawton, Okla., Thunderbolt pilot, tied the American fighter ace record today by shooting down his 26th and 27th German planes.

Johnson, the European theater's leading American fighter pilot, who has made all his kills in the air, equaled the mark set last month by Maj. Richard I. Bong, Poplar, Wis., in the southwest Pacific.

Bong, who was proclaimed America's ace of aces by General MacArthur when he broke the record of 26 set by Capt. Eddie Rickenbacker in World War I, also shot down all his enemy planes in combat.

In the European theater, Johnson's closest rival is Capt. Don S. Gentile, Piqua, Ohio, who before starting a recent leave had destroyed 23 German planes in the air and seven others on the ground.

Two other southwest Pacific fliers have exceeded Gentile's combat record, Maj. Joe Foss, Sioux Falls, S. D., and Maj. Gregory Boyington, Okanogan, Wash., each with 26 planes to his credit. Boyington since has been reported missing.

Two British Pilots Rack Up 28 Planes Each

London, May 8 (U.P.)—Wing Commander J. R. D. Braham shot down his 28th enemy plane yesterday to move into a tie with Wing Commander J. E. Johnson for first place among R. A. F. pilots still flying. He shot down the 28th victim, a Junkers 88, while on an intruder patrol near Copenhagen. Braham is a vicar's son.

Negro Primary Decision Stands

Washington, May 2 (U.P.)—The Supreme Court today refused to reconsider its April 3 decision that Negroes are entitled under the Constitution to cast ballots in State primaries—a ruling which has provoked widespread criticism throughout the South.

The reconsideration was requested by Texas, the State involved in the original decision, and the two Houston election judges who were defendants in the suit. Democratic party leaders in Texas and several other Southern States have said publicly they plan to find some means of barring Negroes from voting in primaries.

The high court agreed to review lower court decisions in three other cases of general interest, and announced it will adjourn its 1943-44 term on May 29. It will sit on each of the next three Mondays, but only to hand down decisions.

The cases which the court agreed to review in the Fall:

1. The Southern New York Federal District Court decision in the Government's anti-trust suit against the Associated Press, holding the Associated Press must modify its bylaws with respect to admission of new members.

2. The Western Union Telegraph Company's appeal for reversal of a Southern New York Federal District Court decision that it must not employ messengers under 16.

Nazi Destroyer Wiped Out

London, May 8 (U.P.)—A German destroyer, which had been previously driven ashore after an engagement with the H. M. C. S. Haida off the northwest tip of France near Ouessant, was destroyed early today by light coastal forces of the Royal Navy, the Admiralty announced.

F. D. R., ON JOB AGAIN, CONFERS WITH LEADERS

Congressmen Say Ward Seizure Wasn't Taken Up at 1½-Hour Talk

Washington, May 8 (U.P.)—Congressional leaders today brought President Roosevelt up to date on the current legislative situation as he waded into a pile of official tasks accumulated during his four weeks' sunning and fishing vacation in South Carolina.

Mr. Roosevelt met for an hour and a half with Vice President Henry A. Wallace, Speaker Sam Rayburn, Senate Democratic leader Alben W. Barkley, and House Democratic leader John W. MvCormack.

Barkley said Mr. Roosevelt "recommended no new legislation." Under questioning, he added he saw "no indication" that any new legislation would be sought by the White House before Congress goes into recess this Summer for the national political conventions.

The Congressional leaders said they found the President "looking very fine indeed" after his month's rest at Hobcaw Barony Bernard M. Baruch's 23,000-acre coastal plantation near Georgetown, S. C. They added that there was no discussion at the conference of the Government's seizure of Montgomery Ward & Co. properties in Chicago.

Doctor Is Jubilant

Wallace, who will leave soon on a trip to China, remained behind for a few moments to chat with the President privately. Asked later whether he had discussed his trip, Wallace said, "Naturally it came up."

Mr. Roosevelt also scheduled conferences with Undersecretary of State Edward R. Stettinius Jr., recently returned from important conferences overseas, and with Secretary of State Hull. He also is expected to see W. Averell Harriman, U. S. Ambassador to Russia, who returned last week for a brief visit.

Mr. Roosevelt returned by train yesterday. Vice Admiral Ross T. McIntire, White House physician, was enthusiastic about his recuperation from the sinus and bronchial difficulties.

The President came home to a turbulent labor situation, and before the week is out he probably will have something to say on the complicated situation arising from Government seizure of Montgomery

Continued on Page 2

World-Telegram Joins Ranks of 5-Cent Papers

The New York World-Telegram increased its price from three to five cents per copy today, the newspaper announced in the first edition.

Numbers on the Hip

Police described Minnie Doliner of 1599 Bathgate Ave., Bronx, as a "walkie-talkie policy slip." They charged that she wrote policy numbere on her right thigh in indelible pencil.

BELMONT RESULTS

1—Flood Town 8.90-6.10-4.00, cAirflake 7.90-5.80, xFuture Hero 3.30. (1:37½) cBarrington Stable. xField.

2—So Risky 184.40-54.70-18.20, JeanMiracle 3.70-2.70, Magellan 3.40. (2:07½)

DAILY DOUBLE PAID $1,566.70

3—Navarin 3.10-2.30-out, aHimmel 2.30. out, Air Marshal out. (2:31½) aE. D. Wier entry.

Eagle Staff photo

ADVENTURE OVER BERLIN—Staff Sgt. John E. Wood tells his family all about his weird experience high over the German capital at his home, 264 E. 43d St. Left to right are Mrs. Mary J. Wood, his mother; two brothers, Joseph, 15, and Eugene, 17, and a sister, Agnes, 23.

Lost: One Reporter, in Vicinity Of a Very Black Coal Situation

A reporter for the Brooklyn Eagle trekked over to Manhattan today after fruitless hours trying to find any one who knew what to do about "orphan" coal consumers in Brooklyn.

His wanderings were in a good cause, to wit: a reasonable explanation of what should be done by a person in the dilemma of Mrs. Harriet Hoppe, landlord of a 40-family house at 107 Brooklyn Ave. Mrs. Hoppe revealed Saturday how she had sought vainly to get coal to supply hot water for her tenants and how equally in vain she sought advice on what to do about the OPA rent control, which says she must not take away essential services.

First stop in the reporter's trip was the office of Russell Ratcliffe, deputy rent control director for Brooklyn, at 26 Court St. Mr. Ratcliffe was clear on his understanding of the regulation, but had no comment to make on the Hoppe problem. He thought perhaps the fuel oil division, also OPA, might know something.

Sent to See Max

Charles Henry, chief clerk of the fuel oil division said that all such matters must be referred to Max Mencher, information director, OPA Regional Office, Empire State Building. At this office it was explained that:

1. The OPA has nothing to do with coal.

2. OPA rent control division could direct a reduction in rental at the Brooklyn Ave. address should Mrs. Hoppe fail in providing heat.

3. It might be action favoring the landlord, considering the fact that the lack of hot water was no fault of hers, or

4. After complaint and investigation a rent reduction might be ordered even though the withdrawal of an essential service was involuntary. "After all, she would be saving money."

At the office of the Brooklyn and Queens Fuel Merchants Association, 130 Clinton St., it was explained that no information was to be had here on Mrs. Hoppe's plight, and the reporter was referred to the office of Gen. Bryce P. Disue, U. S. A. (retired), who is president of the Coal Producers Protective Association.

Late advices had the reporter somewhere in Manhattan still seeking an answer to the problem presented by Mrs. Hoppe, one in which many a householder faced with contrary regulations, will have an interest.

Mayor LaGuardia, close on the heels of the disclosure of Miss Hoppe's dilemma, announced that solid fuels distribution committees will be set up in a week or two to handle the problems of new coal customers and those who cannot make satisfactory arrangements with dealers. He threatened that the names of violators of anthracite regulations will be made public.

Liquor Man Jailed, Is Fined $10,000

Morris Schoenfeld, president of Waldorf Liquors, Inc., of 575 Lexington Ave., Manhattan, was sentenced to six months in jail, and he and his firm were fined $10,000 for black market dealings in liquor.

Schoenfeld pleaded guilty after he was arrested by FBI agents while he was making a delivery to a hotel. He was the first liquor dealer to be sentenced since the Federal Government began an intensive drive to wipe out illegal liquor dealings in the New York area.

Air Alert in Alexandria

The German Transocean News Agency said today an air alert was sounded in Alexandria, Egypt, last night and that anti-aircraft guns went into action.

Pimlico Results

1—Connie's Girl, 5.00, 3.70, 3.10; Home Display, 5.10, 3.40; Zax, 4.60. Off time, 12:07½.

2—Tyrone, 9.10, 5.90, 4.00; Roman Matron, 14.00, 7.30; War Agent, 3.40. Off time, 12:38½.

DAILY DOUBLE PAID $27.50

3—Matsonia, 7.00, 3.30, 2.60; Tioga, 3.40, 2.70; Meeting House, 3.10. Off time, 1:06.

4—Tilting, 6.70, 4.30, 3.20; Indian Sun, 9.50, 6.00; Hialeah, 3.90. Off time, 1:37.

5—Spangled Game, 5.80, 3.40, 2.40; Edgemere, 4.10, 3.30; Hi Neighbor, 3.40. Off time, 2:11½.

6—Soilure, first; New Moon, second; Porter's Cap, third.

Narragansett Park Results

1—Bomb Berlin, 10.40, 4.80, 2.80; Gornil, 5.80, 3.60; Countess Play, 2.80. Off time, 2:34½.

Policeman in Training Held on Policy Charge

Despite reported instructions from Police Commissioner Valentine that no publicity was to be given the case, it was learned today that Stephen Dellegatti, 36, of 104-11 48th Ave., Queens, was arrested April 28 at the Police Academy in Manhattan and booked at the Long Island Precinct station house on two bench warrants, one of them dating back to 1935.

Dellegatti, at the time of his arrest on the warrants, was a probationary patrolman completing a 30-day training period, and was one of a group recently appointed to serve as provisionary policemen for the duration of the war and six months thereafter.

Dellegatti, since his arrest, is at liberty under $1,000 bail pending appearance June 1 in Court of Special Sessions, Queens, where he will face two charges, one accusing him of possessing policy slips and the other alleging secreting mortgaged property.

The first of two bench warrants on which Dellegatti was arrested was issued on May 6, 1935, when he failed to appear to answer a charge that on Jan. 19, 1935, he had 31 policy slips in his possession when arrested in Flushing, Queens. The other bench warrant, dated June 26, 1939, alleged that on June 1, 1937, he secreted an automobile against which there was a chattel mortgage.

Dellegatti, it was learned today, was certified for appointment as a provisional policeman the early part of this year while he was employed as a special policeman for a railroad. When he was arrested at the Police Academy, it was reported today, he was called upon to resign from his appointment with the New York Police Department.

L. I. R. R. TRESTLE BURNS, PASSENGERS IN HIKE

Firemen struggled for nearly an hour, stretching hose for more than 2,000 feet, to extinguish a stubborn blaze on the wooden Long Island Railroad trestle across Jamaica Bay to Rockaway this morning. Four trains, passengers on one of which had to walk nearly half a mile across the trestle to the Broad Channel station, were tied up from 10:45 to 11:30 a.m. Traffic was resumed at slow speed over the damaged part of the trestle.

Total Navy Casualties Are Now 44,753

Washington, May 8 (U.P.)—The Navy Department today announced 20 casualties of the U. S. naval forces (navy, marine corps and coast guard), including 10 dead, five wounded and five missing. The list brings to 44,753 the total casualties since Pearl Harbor. No local names are listed.

Commandos Wreck Nazis' Riviera Forts

Daring Raids Destroy Italy Coast Defenses As Invasion Tension of Both Sides Mounts

London, May 8 (U.P.)—Allied Commandos destroyed newly constructed coastal fortifications along the Italian Riviera in a series of daring weekend raids, Italian Fascist press dispatches said today as invasion tension mounted in both Britain and Axis Europe.

The British Broadcasting Corporation, meantime, again urged the French people to listen closely to their radios for instructions on what to do when the Allies invade western Europe, but to hide their sets immediately after they hear essential news every day.

Fascist newspapers reaching Switzerland acknowledged that some Allied Commandos, striking from Corsica and Sardinia, had succeeded in re-embarking after destroying coastal defenses only recently completed by the Italian branch of Germany's Todt Construction Agency.

Other Commandos were "quickly annihilated," however, the newspaper said.

Attacks Increasing

The Florence newspaper Nazione reported that while other commando raids had been carried out against the Italian coast in recent months, "never before have the attacks reached such a high number.

"Everything leads to the belief that if the Allies attempt a huge landing in western France it will be accompanied by numerous commando raids along the Italian Riviera and in southern France," Nazione said.

The newspaper also reported that Marshal Rommel, Germany's anti-invasion commander, had arrived in Italy for conferences with Marshal Albert Kesselring, commander in Italy, after inspecting defenses along the southern coast of France.

(The U. S. Office of War Information at Washington reported that Gestapo agents, dressed as Allied pilots, sometimes were dropped by parachute on occupied territory. Patriots who attempted to help them were arrested, the report said.)

Other Developments

Other developments contributing to the growing tension in Britain and Axis Europe with the obvious approach of the zero hour for invasion included:

1. Disclosure that American and British forces rehearsing for the invasion just thave completed the greatest airborne landings in history.

2. An article in the semi-official Russian publication, "War and the Working Class," warning that the "time has now run out and all preparations for co-ordinated blows from the East and West have been completed."

3. German propaganda threats of a counter invasion of Britain.

The practice landing exercises by glider and troop carrier forces were conducted with such secrecy that even accredited newspapermen were not permitted to witness them. It was learned, however, that American glider forces landed by day and British by night, similar to the bombing schedule now being carried out by the air forces of the two countries.

German threats of a counter-invasion of Britain were highlighted by the arrival of Nazi paratroops units on the Cherbourg peninsula of France opposite the English south coast and a boast by propaganda minster Goebbels that the Reich possesses "important glider formations" for a countermove.

JAPANESE OPEN FIERCE DRIVE ON KOHIMA FRONT

Suffer Heavy Losses As British Guns Pound Their Ranks

Advanced Allied Headquarters, Kandy, Ceylon, May 8 (U.P.)—Japanese troops, disregarding heavy losses, have opened a general counter offensive along the Kohima front in a desperate attempt to retake the positions captured by British forces last week, it was announced today.

Heavy Japanese attacks were reported in the hills north of Kohima which Allied armored forces penetrated several days ago, capturing several enemy strongpoints in a drive to clear the invaders from the area before the monsoon rains begin.

The Japanese assaults, which were said to be costing them disproportionate losses, came as Allied troops attempted to mop up the enemy pockets. Large numbers of enemy troops were killed as the British forces braced themselves against the drives and out-gunned the Japanese.

Fighting also continued around Kohima itself, a communique said, but the heaviest engagements were reported in the northern hills, where the Japanese artillery was entrenched firmly.

The Japanese held positions on difficult, rocky and bamboo-studded slopes north of Kohima, and it was pointed out at the beginning of the Allied offensive that stiff fighting was inevitable. There was no indication whether the Japanese were using tanks in the new counterattacks.

On the Arakan front in southwestern Burma the British maintained a firm hold on the high hills south of the Maungdaw-Buthidaung Road, following the voluntary withdrawal from Buthidaung.

A headquarters official said the withdrawal was not caused by enemy pressure and that the action was taken because it was not considered necessary to hold the battered village.

British Fliers Sink 2 Ships, Smash 3 In 2 Nazi Convoys

London, May 8 (U.P.)—Carrier planes of a British task force sank two enemy supply ship and damaged thre other vessels in a co-ordinated attack on two German convoys off the Norwegian coast early Saturday morning, an Admiralty communique disclose today.

Striking boldly within range of Nazi shore-based aircraft, the task force interceptted the enemy convoys running southward off Kristiansund.

Barracuda bombers, covered by naval fighters, struck one large, fully-loaded supply ship and broke it in two with direct bomb and torpedo hits. Another medium-sized supply vessel was sent to the bottom and a large tanker and another supply ship were damaged heavily. A German escort vessel also was damaged.

YOUTH, 18, SENTENCED FOR ROBBERIES TO TAKE OUT HIS GIRL

Ward Garcia, 18, who confessed that he committed robberies to get money to take his girl friend to night clubs, was sentenced today by County Judge Leibowitz to not less than ten nor more than 30 years in Sing Sing. Despite his youth Garcia is a graduate of Elmira Reformatory and has been arrested seven times. Police seized him as he slept in an automobile alleged to have been stolen.

He pleaded guilty to robbing two druggists, Sochor B. Tetz at 401 Church Ave. and Jacob Magenheim at 5223 13th Ave., getting $200 and a watch from Tetz and $300 from Magenheim. Garcia lived at 8019 10th Ave.

Trial Date Set for Pair In Fake Gas Coupon Case

Trial of two men, charged with conspiracy to possess and pass counterfeit gasoline coupons, was set for May 24 in Federal Court today. The defendants, Elkanan Cohen, 26, and Frank Bosco, 23, both of Newark, N. J., pleaded innocent.

They were arrested Feb. 26 at Hewlett, where, it is charged, they were found with counterfeit coupons representing 8,750 gallons of gasoline in their possession.

Bail for Cohen was continued at $5,000 and for Bosco, at $3,500.

15 Strip-Tease in Park To Protest Arrests

Vancouver, B. C., May 8 (U.P.)—While soldiers in the crowd yelled "Take it off," and "more, more," 15 members of the Doukhobor religious sect staged a strip-tease in crowded Stanley Park here yesterday before thousands of horrified Sunday strollers.

Police removed the demonstrators, still minus clothing, to the jail where they continued their chanting and singing.

The demonstration was staged in protest against imprisonment of other members of their sect for strippinig at Nelson, B. C.

NAZI FIGHTERS RAM SEVERAL YANK RAIDERS

Brunswick Also Hit As Invaders Pierce Reich Defense Shield

London, May 8 (UP)—A 2,000-plane American air fleet struck the second stunning blow at Berlin in 24 hours and hit Brunswick today after battling through massed German fighters which tried out all the tactics in the book, including ramming the U. S. bombers.

A thousand heavy bombers escorted by an equal number of fighters smashed through the blazing Nazi defense shield to drop 2,000 tons of explosives through clouds over Berlin, maintaining the unprecedented pitch of the pre-invasion bombardment on the first day of its fourth week.

Other big forces of Allied planes shuttled across the Channel to hammer the defenses of western Europe. By noon some 2,500 sorties had been flown, raising the total for 48 hours to around 11,500.

Scores of German fighters swarmed against the massive American formation sweeping against Berlin for the second straight day. Abandoning caution and the hoarding of planes for the invasion, the Nazi fighters barreled through the American formations, ignoring the rain of steel from the big bombers and their escorts.

Nazis Goaded to Action

Returning crewmen said Germans, goaded to desperation over the approaches to Berlin, rammed a number of Fortresses, steering an unwavering course through the torrent of gunfire.

The Nazis put up their stiffest opposition over the approaches to Berlin, especially in the region of Brunswick, 120 miles to the west, the main base of the forces defending the skyroads to the capital.

Over burning and cloud-covered Berlin itself fewer fighters challenged the Americans, and for the most part they were knocked aside by a tight defensive ring of escort planes.

Many groups over Berlin did not see a single German fighter, and reported their worst enemy was the weather. The temperature dropped to 45 degrees below zero as the bombers climbed more than four miles high, dropping their bombs through the overcast with special devices.

The forces which attacked Bruns-

Continued on Page 2

GIRL IS FOUND WADING INTO SURF AT MIDNIGHT WITH KITTEN IN HER ARMS

Police today were trying to establish the identity of a girl, about 17, who was found wading into the surf at Coney Island with a white kitten in her arms.

Two sailors saw her walk into the surf at the foot of E. 15th St. about midnight. They ran to her and led her back to shore. She would not answer any questions asked her by police at the Coney Island station.

The girl, described as about 17, weighing about 160 and about 5 feet 9 inches tall, was wearing a brown coat, red dress, brown and white shoes, no stockings. She had no handbag. She has brown eyes and brown hair.

She was taken to Bellevue Hospital for observation and the kitten was turned over to the S. P. C. A.

The sailors disappeared without identifying themselves.

WHERE TO FIND IT

	Page		Page
Bridge	12	Pattern	12
Comics	15	Radio	15
Crossword	12	Ration Calendar	4
Dr. Brady	6	Real Estate	12
Editorial	6	Society	4
Financial	7	Sports	10, 11
Helen Worth	4	Take My Word	6
Horoscope	15	Theaters	5
Movies	5	These Women	12
Music	5	Tommy Holmes	10
Novel	12	Uncle Ray	15
Obituaries	7	Want Ads	12-14
Our Fighters	8	Women	4

Dodgers Beaten, 8-4; Melton Fails in 5th

By HAROLD C. BURR
Staff Correspondent of the Brooklyn Eagle

St. Louis, May 13—If the Dodgers should ask that eminent authority on social usages, Emily Post, what to do about it the lady would unhesitatingly advise them to cut Sportsman's Park from their calling list. Not since 1941 have the Flatbushers won a series from the Cardinals in this home of champions. The Brooklyns made it three out of four on the wrong side of the baseball books here again today by taking it on their glass chin again, 8 to 4, in the presence of a squealing Ladies Day crowd of 7,609 assorted fans.

Manager Leo Durocher shook up his line-up once more. He sent Luis Olmo back to center field and little Pat Ankenman to the midway. Frenchy Bordagaray stayed in the game at third base and Gil English rode the bench splinters. Augie Galan shifted over to the left field pasture. Olmo gave his best at second base, but it just wasn't enough. Bordagaray's 10-game hitting streak came to an abrupt end.

Rube Melton started for the visitors. The Rube had appeared twice before on the mound, once as a starter against the Giants and again in a relief role against the same team, but he didn't figure in either decision. He was charged with today's defeat. Another unbeaten Cardinal pitcher was tossed at the Dodgers in Harry Brecheen. He notched his third straight triumph. At bat he wasn't so hot, leaving seven Cardinal runners marooned in his four trips to the plate.

MacLish Makes Debut

Melton was wild, passing six batters, three of 'em in a big fifth inning when the pesky Red Birds batted around when they weren't walking around. The Rube was requested to leave in the midst of the good, clean fun and young Calvin Coolidge MacLish made his big league debut. The 18-year-old schoolboy had a tough assignment, coming on with the bases full and one out. He was only charged with one run. He retired to let Bobby Bragan hit for him. Wes Flowers finished.

Catcher Mickey Owen received word from his Springfield, Mo., draft board that he has been placed in 1-A. The Dodgers left for Chicago on the midnight train where they expect the bedraggled tailend Cubs to give 'em a fresh start in life. There's a doubleheader tomorrow. Bob Chipman and Fred Ostermueller, a couple of southpaws will pitch for our side, and Hy Vanderburg, who once had a trial with the Giants, and Claude Passeau, will hurl for the Bruins.

The Dodgers broke through Brechen's service in the fourth. Bordagaray was safe on Marion's low throw. Walker dutifully laid it down. Olmo fetched Frenchy across with a single to center, but not before Bordagaray tumbled down rounding third. He picked himself up in time to beat Marion's listless peg home of the relay from the outfield.

Galan strolled and Schultz's skimmer through the left side of the infield tallied Olmo. But the revolt of the Flatbush fusileers was rudely put down then and there when Hart flied to Litwhiler and Owen forced Schultz.

Own Error Costly

Melton contrived to get by until the fifth. He might conceivably have escaped in that round, too, but for a muff of Hart's throw when the Rube had Verban hung up between bases, proving that you can't kid around with these Cardinals on the bases.

Verban opened up with a safety to left. Garms backed Walker up against the right field wall to gather in his hoist. Then came the comedy of trying to tag out Verban. Schultz finally lost him and the spry Columbus rookie skidded back to first in perfect safety. This amaturish work so upset Melton that he passed Musial, Walker, Cooper and Kurowski all in a row, forcing in Verban. Durocher was upset, no end too, and he sent in MacLish.

The Oklahoma Kid set Litwhiler down on strikes. But Sanders singled for two more markers and

Continued on Page 24

BROOKLYN EAGLE
SUNDAY, MAY 14, 1944 ★

Sports — Real Estate
Trend — Travel—Resorts
Theaters — Classified Ads

Betting Mark Set; Devil Diver Wins

By RALPH TROST

The track was fast, the races swift at Belmont yesterday, but quicker than Devil Diver, Bossuet or Aletern, the day's principal winners, were the customers in getting to the pari-mutuel machines.

There were only 39,239 of them, about 6,000 less than were at Jamaica on racing's biggest betting day. But they were active enough in getting $3,369,385 through the machines to top the old mark of $3,176,553 by plenty of bucks.

The racing honors were almost evenly divided. Though toting the goodly load of 134 pounds, Devil Diver won the 51st running of the Metropolitan Handicap in the admirable time of 1:35.4 to beat A. C. Ernst's Alquest. The winner of the Paumonok and Toboggan sprints won the mile race by about a length and a half.

Bossuet, though not out since last Summer, peeled off the fastest three-quarters run hereabouts this year, 1:10.3, as he whipped Adulator, Shut Out and Alsab by four good lengths of daylight.

Record Established

Altern, another Ernest horse, turned out to be a streak of almost black lightning as he rippled off a mile and a furlong in 1:48.4 after having covered the mile in 1:36.1, only two-fifths slower than Devil Diver's winning mile. Altern set a new mark for the Garden City Handicap and was only three-fifths off the track record.

After having backed, and unsuccessfully, four favorites in a row, including the 3-to-5 shot Grant Rice, the crowd poured it down heavy on the Metropolitan. Devil Diver and his stablemate Four Freedoms were backed so heavily there was only $1 profit for every $2 wagered.

It was Wait a Bit who broke fastest from the gate, with the light-weighted Porter's Cap and Pop's Pick alongside. In the .23 second first quarter Wait a Bit was out in front and winging, but by the time the first turn was reached Devil Diver was under way and bearing down fast. Once on the stretch there was little question as to the winner.

The Greentree Stable picked up a neat $10,350; $2,000 went to Alquest's owner, the Accountant A. C. Ernest; $1,000 to Tom Heard, owner of Boysy.

Shut Out Third

The Belair Stud's four-year-old colt Bossuet was tipped (with form to back it—he ran 1-2 in five out of six races last year) all over the lot—and ran away with the Voter Handicap. The crowd went, however, for the 1942 Derby winner Shut Out. But the six-furlong route was too short. Shut Out came on strongly to finish third, a neck behind Adulator, with Alsab right alongside. But while they passed Harvard Square and African Sun in the stretch, they didn't gain an inch on the leader, who won by four lengths.

The jumping race was a classic. Five horses started. The 4-to-5 shot Royal Archer threw Cruz at the second hedge. Harrison went off Lancastrian at the fifth, Seafight shelved Walker at the ninth—leaving Picture Prince and Our Sailor to fight it out. These two whacked

Continued on Page 24

NAVY OARSMEN SWEEP REGATTA ON SEVERN RIVER

Annapolis, Md., May 13—In one of the most eventful regattas ever staged on the Severn River, Naval Academy rowing crews triumphed over oarsmen of Massachusetts Institute of Technology, Cornell and Columbia today. The Middies varsity boat finished in front by a bare two feet after Tech had maintained a slight lead until the final stretch. Cornell finished third, trailing by six or seven lengths, while Columbia was a poor fourth.

In the junior varsity event the Middies won by little more than a length over the Bostonians, while Cornell was more than two lengths behind. Columbia failed to finish because of the collapse of Art Hausperg, No. 5.

Both races were rowed over a course of one and three-quarter miles. Navy's varsity negotiated the distance in 10:34 to Tech's 10:34.1. Cornell's time was 11:05 and Columbia's 11:09. The times in the jayvee brush was Navy 10:08.6, Tech 10:12.8 and Cornell 10:17.

That the times of the varsity crews were slower than the juniors was due to the fact that the varsity race was rowed against a stiff head wind that kicked up a choppy sea.

Navy Virtual Champ

The result of today's race placed Navy as the virtual champion of the East this year, sprint or otherwise, since the annual Poughkeepsie classic is off for the duration, and other colleges have abandoned aquatics for a like reason.

Today the middies were all out hosts, providing shells and other equipment for the visiting oarsmen.

The regatta was marked by false starts in each race, slight damage to rigging of the Cornell jayvee boat that caused nearly an hour's delay, and a mishap to the tiller ropes of Tech's varsity boat just after the getaway. The collapse of Hausperg caused the New York oarsmen to quit the race and paddle their shell to a nearby beach,

Continued on Page 24

Army Tops N. Y. U. In 10th Inning, 3-2

West Point, May 13—Pushing over a run in the 10th inning, the Army nine turned back N. Y. U., 3 to 2, here today, as Ralph Branca went down to defeat. Brayan Leeper's single with the bases full broke up the ball game.

		R.	H.	E.
N. Y. U.	0 0 0 0 2 0 0 0 0 1	3	9	5
Army	0 0 0 0 0 0 0 2 0 0	2	7	3

Batteries—Branca and Olsen; Kinney, Laboon and Janeczek.

Johnson 630 Tops In Spring Tourney

The third annual Spring bowling tournament got under way last night at Lawler's with Bell Grey of the Classic League just about grabbing off all the honors.

Dan Johnson's 630 series was tops for the night, he having rolled 216, 213 and 201. The team had a high series of 2627 while Johnson's teammate, Charlie Lansing was high individual man with 227.

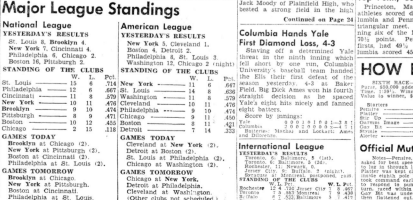

PRETTY CLOSE—But not close enough to nip Stuffy Stirnweiss of Yanks at second after he took a long lead in fourth inning of game with Indians yesterday. Catcher Rosar's throw to Manager Boudreau made Stuffy scramble back in a hurry. Yanks won, 5—1.

CUBS HUMBLED BY LEE OF PHILLIES, 6-2

Chicago, May 13 (U.P.)—The Philadelphia Phillies whipped the Cubs, 6 to 2, here today to take their first series of the year with the Chicagoans, 3 to 1. Bill Lee allowed his former Cub mates only seven hits for his second victory.

The Phillies broke a 2-to-2 deadlock with a four-run rally in the sixth that routed Henry Wyse and brought Bill Fleming in to finish the game. Ford Mullen led a nine-hit attack with three singles.

The box score:

Philadelphia	ab	r	h	o	a	Chicago	ab	r	h	o	a
Mullen.2b	5	1	3	3	3	Johnson.2b	3	0	0	3	2
cAdams.cf	4	0	0	6	1	Stanky	1	0	0	0	0
Wasdell.lf	5	1	2	3	0	Cav'tta.1b	4	0	2	10	0
Northey.rf	5	0	0	2	0	Novikoff.lf	4	0	0	2	0
Lupien.1b	3	2	1	10	1	Nichols'n.rf	3	1	0	1	0
Finley.c	4	2	1	1	0	Dal's'dro.cf	2	0	0	5	1
Cieslak.3b	2	0	1	0	1	York.3b	4	1	2	2	1
Hamr'k.ss	3	0	0	2	4	Merullo.ss	4	0	1	1	3
Lee.p	3	0	1	0	6	Holm.c	3	0	0	3	1
						aOstrowski	0	0	0	0	0
						Wyse	2	0	1	0	0
						Fleming.p	1	0	0	0	1
						bGoodman	1	0	1	0	0
Totals	34	6	9	27	16	Totals	32	2	7	27	9

aBatted for Holm in ninth.
bBatted for Fleming in ninth.
cBatted for Johnson in ninth.

Philadelphia	0 0 0 0 2 4 0 0 0	6
Chicago	0 0 0 2 0 0 0 0 0	2

Errors—Lee. Johnson. Holm. Runs batted in—Wasdell. Lupien. Finley. Cieslak. Hamrick. Lee. York. Two-base hits—Wasdell. Finley. Cieslak. Cavarretta. Sacrifices—Adams. Johnson. Double plays—Lee. Hamrick and Lupien; Merullo. Johnson and Cavarretta. Left on bases—Philadelphi 7. Chicago 8. Bases on balls—Off Lee 4. off Wyse 2. off Fleming 3. Struck out—By Lee 1. by Wyse 1. by Fleming 3. Hits—Off Wyse. 6 in 5 2-3 innings; off Fleming. 3 in 3 1-3 innings. Losing pitcher—Wyse. Umpires—Ballanfant. Boggess and Pinelli. Attendance (Actual)—3,469.

Braves Wallop Ball

Pittsburgh, May 13 (U.P.)—The Boston Braves continued to surprise every one including themselves as they staged a 23-hit batting spree here today to defeat the Pirates, 16—2 for the third straight game.

There never was any question about the outcome as the Braves teed off on Xavier Rescigno in the first for five hits and five runs and continued against Johnny Gee and Goden Wise.

Boston	ab	r	h	o	a	Pittsburgh	ab	r	h	o	a
Holmes.cf	6	1	1	1	0	J.Barrett.lf	4	1	0	5	0
Macon.1b	6	1	2	11	0	Russell.cf	2	0	0	3	0
Nieman.lf	5	1	3	4	0	Colman.rf	4	0	1	2	0
Work'n.rf	6	3	2	2	0	Elliott.3b	4	0	0	1	2
Hofferth.c	6	4	4	6	0	Custine.ss	4	0	0	1	1
Ryan.2b	5	2	2	1	1	Dahlgr'n.1b	4	0	1	10	1
Phillips.ss	6	3	4	1	3	Rubeli'g.2b	4	0	0	1	5
Gladu.3b	5	1	4	1	3	Lopez.c	2	0	0	3	0
C.Barret.p	6	0	1	0	1	Camilli.c	1	0	0	1	0
						Rescigno.p	0	0	0	0	0
						Gee.p	2	1	1	0	2
						zO'Brien	1	0	1	0	0
						Wise.p	0	0	0	0	0
Totals	50	16	23	27	8	Totals	32	2	4	27	11

Batted for Gee in 8th.

Boston	5 0 2 0 2 1 0 3 3	16
Pittsburgh	0 0 2 0 0 0 0 0 0	2

Errors — Colman. Rubeling. Macon. Phillips. Runs batted in—Hofferth 2. Phillips 5. Gladu 4. Colman. Elliott. C. Barret 3. Workman. Two-base hits—Phillips 2. Gladu. Dahlgren. C. Barrett. Workman. Hofferth. Three-base hits—Phillips. Nieman. Stolen bases—Macon. Sacrifice—Nieman. Double play—Ryan. Phillips and Macon. Left on bases—Boston 11. Pittsburgh 5. Bases on balls—Off C. Barrett 2. Gee 2. Wise 1. Struck out—By Gee 1. C. Barrett 4. Wise 1. Hits—Off Rescigno 5 in 2-3 innings. Gee 14 in 7 1-3. Wise 4 in 1. Losing pitcher—Rescigno. Umpires—Stewart and Magerkurth. Time—1:54.

Red Sox On Top, 4 to 2

Boston, May 13 (U.P.)—The Boston Red Sox scored three runs in a big fourth inning in which Rufus Gentry was tagged for five hits today, adding another in the sixth to beat Detroit, 4 to 2.

Detroit	ab	r	h	o	a	Boston	ab	r	h	o	a
Cramer.cf	3	1	1	2	0	Culb'son.cf	4	0	0	4	0
Hoover.ss	4	0	2	1	6	Doerr.2b	4	0	1	4	5
Mayo.2b	3	0	2	6	1	Cronin.1b	4	0	2	11	0
York.1b	3	1	1	9	1	Johnson.lf	2	1	1	1	1
Higgins.3b	4	0	1	0	3	Fox.rf	4	1	1	0	0
Ross.rf	4	0	0	1	0	Tabor.3b	3	1	2	2	1
Hos'tler.lf	4	0	1	3	1	Partee.c	4	1	2	5	0
Swift.c	4	0	0	2	0	News'me.ss	3	0	1	0	2
Gentry.p	2	0	0	0	1	O'Neil.p	3	0	1	0	2
aRichards	1	0	0	0	0						
Mooty.p	0	0	0	0	1						
bMetro	1	0	0	0	0						
Totals	33	2	8	24	14	Totals	31	4	11	27	11

aBatted for Gentry in seventh.
bBatted for Mooty in ninth.

Detroit	1 0 0 0 0 1 0 0 0	2
Boston	0 0 0 3 0 1 0 0 x	4

Error—Partee. Runs batted in—Mayo. Tabor. Partee. O'Neil. Newsome. (York scored in sixth on Partee error). Two-base hits—Tabor. Doerr. Partee. Double plays—Newsome. Doerr and Cronin: Hoover and Mayo; Higgins. Mayo and York. Left on bases—Detroit 7. Boston 6. Base on balls—Off O'Neil 3. Gentry 2. Mooty 1. Struck out—By Gentry 1. O'Neil 4. Hits—Off Gentry. 10 in 6 innings; Mooty. 1 in 2. Wild pitch—O'Neil. Losing pitcher—Gentry. Umpires—Summers, Boyer and Rue.

Philadelphia. May 13 (U.P.)—The St. Louis Browns' hopes of lengthening their first place lead at the expense of the Philadelphia Ath-

Continued on Page 24

Met. A. A. U. to Honor Downing at Dinner

The Metropolitan Association of the Amateur Athletic Union will honor its president, John J. Downing, at the traditional dinner to the president of that organization at the Hotel Capitol on Saturday evening, May 20.

An added feature at this year's dinner will be the presentation to Col. Charles J. Dieges of the Track Writers Association plaque awarded to him for his many years of activity in track athletics.

West Side T. C. Wins

The Yale tennis team lost by 5—4 to the West Side Club at Forest Hills yesterday. With the score tied at 3-all following singles play, the home forces took two of the three doubles matches. Clark and Courtney defeated Collins and De Bardeleben, 8—6, 6—4, and Burke and von Bernuth triumphed over Wendell and Weems, 6—4, 6—4.

Pensive Comes From Behind In Stretch to Win Preakness

Takes Record $60,710 Purse—Platter Second, Stir Up Third

By OSCAR FRALEY
United Press Staff Correspondent

Baltimore, Md., May 13—Pensive, a little brown horse with a big heart, and Conn McCreary, a fighting Irish lad from St. Louis, showed a doubting turf world that they were better than good today when they came out of a cluster of stragglers at old Pimlico to win the 54th running of the historic Preakness Stakes.

Pensive, the gallant chestnut colt the critics tabbed as "lucky," when he slipped through in the stretch to win the Kentucky Derby, was gently clucked to victory again today by McCreary, who had the heart to ride the same kind of a race as in the run for the Roses.

Despite the fact that the theme song this time was "Maryland My Maryland," instead of "My Old Kentucky Home," the result was the same. Once again they spotted the best of the opposition a commanding lead and then ran over them in the stretch to take the richest purse in the history of the Baltimore Classic.

Time Mediocre

They didn't set a record as they won top money of $60,710. For their time, when they flashed their Devil's red and blue silks under the wire, was a mediocre 1:59.1—two and four-fifths seconds over the track record.

But this under-rated pair did show the 33,011 fans crowded into the antique grandstands that although they might be rated just "good," they were better than the best that was sent against them.

They gave plenty of ground to their two leading rivals—Greentree Stable's Stir Up and George D. Widener's Platter, a colt never beaten over this wide, brown Maryland track. They gave them four and one-half lengths to the head of the stretch and then simply walked up alongside, looked them in the eye, laughed and ran right over them. That was the race—the same way they took the Derby.

'Had No Doubts'

"I never doubted that Pensive would do it," the smiling McCreary laughed as he reined the colt into the winner's circle. "This little old horse just laid back there

Continued on Page 24

SHOWING HIS HEELS TO THE FIELD—Pensive, scoring his second major victory, romps home the victor in the rich Preakness yesterday at Pimlico as Platter placed second and Stir Up third. Gramp's Image ran fourth. Pensive paid $5.30 to win.

Cohen, Tilden Ace, Blanks Bushwick With 3 Hits, 1-0

Behind the three-hit pitching of Bernard Cohen, Tilden notched its second loop win in six starts blanking Bushwick, 1—0, at Tilden yesterday. Tilden pushed across the winning run in the fifth inning when Herb Horowitz singled across Capt. Paul Gross, who had walked and stolen second.

Four jayvee hurlers from St. John's Prep combined their efforts to rout St. Finbar, 7—2, at Carey Field.

Bushwick	ab	r	h	o	a	Tilden	ab	r	h	o	a
Bonetti.rf	3	0	0	1	0	Boyers.2b	2	0	1	2	1
Hugue.1b	0	0	0	2	0	Gross.ss	2	1	0	1	2
Shea.cf	3	0	0	1	0	Hor'witz.1b	3	0	1	8	0
Rado.3b	2	0	0	0	0	Engelisis.cf	3	0	0	1	0
Santoro.ss	3	0	1	0	1	Chermak.lf	2	0	0	1	0
Br'dir'h.2b	3	0	1	1	2	Cohen.p	2	0	1	0	0
Berge.1b.p	2	0	0	3	1	Kazden.rf	2	0	0	0	0
K'mer.p.rf	2	0	0	0	2	Fink'st'n.rf	1	0	0	0	0
Cute.lf	3	0	1	0	0	Weiss.3b	3	0	0	0	5
Palmero.c	2	0	0	8	0	Tan'b'm.c	2	0	1	8	0
Foley.c	1	0	0	2	0						
Totals	24	0	3	18	6	Totals	22	1	4	21	8

Bushwick	0 0 0 0 0 0 0	0
Tilden	0 0 0 0 1 0 x	1

Errors—By Rado. Foley. Two-base hits—Bradirich. Three-base hit—Cohen. Stolen bases—Rado, Cute, Boyers, Gross, Horowitz. Bases on balls—Off Cohen 3. off Kramer 4. Struck out—By Cohen 8. by KWramer 8. by Berge 1. Wild pitch—Cohen. Passed ball—Palmero. Hits—Off Kramer, 4 in six innings. Umpire—Zifferblatt.

		R	H	E
St. Finbar	0 0 0 0 0 0 2 0 0	2	4	6
St. John's J.V.	2 0 0 1 0 0 0 4 x	7	8	4

Batteries—Yondola. DeMarco and Pentangello: DeBlavio: Heinbuckle, Mead, Russell, Smith and Murphy.

Nahem's Hitting Paces Fort Totten to Victory

Paced by Sammy Nahem, former Philly pitcher, who blasted two home runs and a single in four trips to the plate, Fort Totten scored its second straight win by defeating United States Navy Torpedo Range, 9—1, at Fort Totten yesterday.

The score by innings:

U. S. Torpedo	0 0 0 0 0 0 1 0	1	3	2
Fort Totten	1 0 5 1 1 0 1 x	9	12	0

Batteries—Johnson, Wood and Zepras; Todd and Batchelor Bednarz.

45,000 See Ascot Races

Ascot, England, May 13—Forty-five thousand people jammed the race track here today for a war-time record at the 1944 debut. $500,700 was wagered. Trains, and all possible means of transportation to the Ascot track were jammed.

Major League Standings

National League

YESTERDAY'S RESULTS

St. Louis 8, **Brooklyn** 4.
New York 7, Cincinnati 4.
Philadelphia 6, Chicago 2.
Boston 16, Pittsburgh 2.

STANDING OF THE CLUBS

	W.	L.	Pct.
St. Louis	15	6	.714
Philadelphia	12	6	.667
Cincinnati	11	8	.579
New York	10	11	.476
Brooklyn	9	10	.474
Pittsburgh	8	9	.471
Boston	10	12	.455
Chicago	2	15	.118

GAMES TODAY

Brooklyn at Chicago (2).
New York at Pittsburgh (2).
Boston at Cincinnati (2).
Philadelphia at St. Louis (2).

GAMES TOMORROW

Brooklyn at Chicago.
New York at Pittsburgh.
Boston at Cincinnati.
Philadelphia at St. Louis.

American League

YESTERDAY'S RESULTS

New York 5, Cleveland 1.
Boston 4, Detroit 2.
Philadelphia 8, St. Louis 3.
Washington 12, Chicago 2 (night)

STANDING OF THE CLUBS

	W.	L.	Pct.
New York	11	6	.647
St. Louis	14	8	.636
Washington	11	8	.579
Cleveland	10	11	.476
Philadelphia	9	10	.474
Chicago	9	11	.450
Boston	8	11	.421
Detroit	7	14	.333

GAMES TODAY

Cleveland at **New York** (2).
Detroit at Boston (2).
St. Louis at Philadelphia (2).
Chicago at Washington (2).

GAMES TOMORROW

Chicago at **New York**.
Detroit at Philadelphia.
Cleveland at Washington.
(Other clubs not scheduled.)

Buker Annexes Mile Novice Run—Loughlin Wins

By JAMES J. MURPHY

Training he acquired climbing the Chin hills of Burma into India to escape from the Japs two months before the arrival of Gen. Joseph Stillwell and his U. S. forces back in 1942. yesterday paid dividends for Ray Buker of Stony Brook School. The son of one of the greatest middle distance runners this country ever produced, making his initial start in major competition, captured the one-mile novice run in the sixth annual Boys High Eastern interscholastic championship meet at Randall's Island. Profiting by his war experience, Ray stepped the distance in 4:41.2 to account for one of the eight meet records in the largest schoolboy meet ever held in the Metropolitan area, the carnival drawing 1,400 entries from 53 schools.

Bishop Laughlin regained the open title from Mt. St. Michael's with 28 points, and Erasmus Hall's up and coming team annexed the novice point trophy with 14 points.

Ray, chip off the old block, as remarked by many who saw him, employed many of his dad's tricks in beating Poly Prep's sensational tennis star, Linton Baldwin, to the tape by 15 yards. Ray Sr., the pride of Bates College, now a missionary, who narrowly escaped having his ship torpedoed following his son out of the war area, is his boy's coach. He practically ran the race with the youngster as he circled the track in ideal atmospheric conditions. Ray Sr. was twice national mile champion, broke Abel Kiviat's American record for the 1.500 meters in 1928 and placed fifth to Paavo Nurmi, the wonderful Finn, in the 1924 Olympics in Paris. The boy has all the characteristics of his dad both facially and in his style of running. He paced himself nicely and there never was any doubt as to the outcome.

Eight Records Fall

While eight records were being bettered, four more were being established in new events, the 220-yard novice dash, 220-yard open dash, 440-yard novice run and 220-yard low hurdles.

If they ever get together, young Buker might make a worthy foe for Bill McGuire, George Washington's picture book miler, who copped the open race at the distance in 4:33.3 for another new meet record. The outcome was a repetition of the previous week in the P. S. A. L. Relays. McGuire let Walter Soltow, the national A. A. U. interscholastic indoor titlist, set the pace until the far turn was about to be approached, when he again gave his reserve power the gas and he went around the New Utrecht boy like a shot to win by a substantial margin. Armand Osterberg of Stuyvesant was again third.

McGuire, in stepping the fastest mile of the season, clipped five-tenths of a second from the mark of Frank Dixon made in 1941. Buker also erased Dixon's standard of 4:44.9 in the novice mile.

Phillips in Front

The other four open record shattering achievements were accomplished by Gil Phillips of George Washington, one of the greatest quarter-milers developed in the schoolboy ranks in a decade, who grabbed the two furlongs in 0:51.1; Jack Moody of Plainfield High, who bested a strong field in the high

Continued on Page 24

Columbia Hands Yale First Diamond Loss, 4-3

Staving off a determined Yale threat in the ninth inning which fell short by one run, Columbia University's baseball team handed the Elis their first defeat of the season yesterday, 4-3 at Baker Field. Big Dick Ames won his fourth straight decision as he spaced Yale's eight hits nicely and fanned eight batters.

Score by innings:

Yale	0 0 0 1 0 1 0 0 1	3	8	1
Columbia	2 0 0 2 0 0 0 0 x	4	7	1

Batteries: Machaj and Lockart; Ames and DiLorenzo.

International League

YESTERDAY'S RESULTS

Toronto, 6; Baltimore, 5 (1st).
Toronto, 6; Baltimore, 5 (2d).
Rochester, 11; Newark, 0.
Jersey City, 9; Buffalo, 2 (night).
Syracuse at Montreal, postponed, rain.

STANDING OF THE CLUBS

	W.	L.	Pct.		W.	L.	Pct.
Rochester	12	4	.750	Jersey City	7	8	.467
Toronto	7	5	.583	Montreal	7	9	.438
Buffalo	8	7	.533	Baltimore	5	7	.417
Syracuse	8	7	.533	Newark	5	12	.294

YANKS BEHIND PAGE TRIP INDIANS, 5-1

Rollie Hemsley may be a farmer out in Missouri in the off-seasons. But time was when he was a coal miner, and yesterday he caught the Yankees' Rookie Joe Page, who started his life as a wage earner in the pits of the Pittsburgh region, and between the two the visiting Indians had very little fun, losing the series opener, 5 to 1, at Yankee Stadium.

Hemsley knocked in the last two Bronx runs, and Page knocked in the first two, the other tally for the home side being forced in by a pass with the bases full.

Rookie Hal Kleine, who like Page is a southpaw, was the generous youth, his three passes in the sixth proving embarrassing to the visitors cause.

Equally embarrassing was a two base muff of Rolie Hemsley's fly in the fifth by shortstop-skipper Louis Rochambeau Boudreau, his bobble setting up the situation for Page to double two tallies over the plate. This Page chap, who won fourteen for Newark last season; has now notched two straight wins for the bunting-bombers, though yesterday was the first time he went the full distance.

Yields Five Hits

He romped the route in style, allowing but five hits, three of them made by Mickey Rosso.

Kleine, a mere child of 20, took his first major league loss after one victory. He gave seven hits in seven innings, before retiring for a pinch-hitter, with Charles (Red) Embree finishing.

Singles by Boudreau, Rocco and Herkett in the fourth accounted for the Cleveland run. Just before the game, the Indians received word from Cleveland that their strike-out king, Allie Reynolds, has passed his physical examination, and been accepted for the Navy.

To Play Until Called

Reynolds will rejoin the tribe at its next stop and will play until called to service.

The Yankees received word that their extra infielder, Oscar Grimes, had been changed from 3-A to 2-A classification by his Lakewood, Ohio, draft board. 2-A is understood to apply to men in essential civilian activities, and if that is correct, baseball might draw a pleasant inference.

Buddy Rosar, the Tribe's part-time catcher, will entrain right after tomorrows doubleheader to get back to his toolmaker's bench in a Cleveland defense plant. He has permission to work weekends, and in the Indians' games at home . . . The pitchers for the double-header will be Ernie Bonham and Atley Donald against Lefty Al Smith and Ray Poat.

Indians	ab	r	h	o	a	Yanks	ab	r	h	o	a
B'dreau.ss	4	1	1	0	2	St'nw'ss.2b	4	0	2	3	1
Rocco.1b	3	0	3	10	0	Metheny.rf	4	0	1	2	0
Cul'b'ne.rf	4	0	0	3	0	Levy.lf	4	0	1	5	0
Hockett.lf	3	0	1	3	0	Etten.1b	3	1	0	4	0
Keltner.3b	3	0	0	1	2	Savage.3b	4	1	1	2	1
Seerey.cf	3	0	0	1	0	Lindell.cf	3	1	0	4	0
Rosar.c	3	0	0	5	0	Mil'vich.ss	1	1	0	3	2
Peters.2b	3	0	0	1	4	Hemsley.c	4	1	1	4	1
Kleine.p	2	0	0	0	1	Page.p	3	0	1	0	1
xGromek	1	0	0	0	0						
Embreep	0	0	0	0	1						
Totals	29	1	5	24	10	Totals	30	5	7	27	6

aBatted for Kleine in eighth inning.

Cleveland	0 0 0 1 0 0 0 0 0	1
New York	0 0 0 0 2 3 0 0 x	5

Error—Boudreau. Runs batted in—Hockett. Page (2). Milosevich. Hemsley (2). Two-base hits—Page. Savage. Double plays—Milosevich, Stirnweiss and Etten; Boudreau, Peters and Rocco; Page, Milosevich and Etten. Left on bases—Yanks 6, Indians 2. Bases on balls—Off Page 1, Kleine 4, Embree 1. Strikeouts—By Page 4, Kleine 1, Embree 1. Hits—Off Kleine, 7 in 7 innings; Embree, 0 in 1. Losing pitcher—Kleine. Umpires—Jones, Grieve and Hubbard. Time—1:39.

GIANTS' EARLY SPREE BLASTS REDS BY 7-4

Special to the Brooklyn Eagle

Cincinnati, May 13—Deacon McKechnie dug down to the bottom of his pitching barrel today and before he could make a second dip into the hogshead, the Giants had defeated Rookie Bob Ferguson with a five-run shelling, and earned an even break in the four-game series with the Reds, through the ensuing 7-4 victory.

A single by Johnny Rucker, a triple by Mel Ott and colossal home run clout by Phil Weintraub for three runs in the second banished Ferguson, a youngster from Birmingham who started because Elmer Riddle and Ray Starr have ailing arms. The Giants went over Ferguson once lightly in the first, when Rucker singled, Ott was hit, Weintraub walked and two runs scored on a pop single by Ernie Lombardi and a long fly by Nap Reyes.

Reyes again played well in left in Joe Medwick's place, and lined a single in four tries. The Giants have won both games with Ducky benched, and will carry the budding streak in a double-header in Pittsburgh tomorrow.

Use Five Hurlers

McKechnie followed Ferguson with Bob Malloy, also from Birmingham. An error by Woody Williams let in two runs off Malloy in the third, for a 7-0 Giant lead, and although the Redleg boss tossed in three more twirlers—Lefty Arnold Carter from Syracuse, Army-dis-

Continued on Page 24

Grant and Goode Fight to a Draw

Bill Grant, 176, Orange, and Oscar Goode, 172½, Newark, fought a very interesting draw in the feature eight-round contest at Ridgewood Grove last night before 2,000 fans.

Goode proved effective in the early rounds with telling right and left hooks to the body. However, he seemed to weaken after the fourth and Grant won the next four rounds.

In the semi-final bout of six rounds Joe Curcio, 146½, Newark, scored a technical knockout over Johnny Harris, 155½, Newark, in 2:34 of the second round.

In two other six-rounders Charley Jones, 175, Harlem, defeated Brany Payne, 172, Detroit, and Ted Gordon, 161½, Bronx, defeated Harry Gary, 174¾.

In two scheduled four-rounders Dave Carver, 164, Bronx, beat Eddie Dutton, 159½, West Side, and Rocco Lescio, 142½, Brooklyn, decisioned John Attelly, 145, Harlem.

Princeton Runners Top Penn, Columbia

Princeton, May 13—Princeton's athletes scored decisively over Columbia and Penn here today in a triangular meet. Old Nassau winning six of the 15 events piled up 70½ points. Penn also won six firsts, had 49½ markers and Columbia scored 45 markers.

Antonio, Kringle Take Amateur-Pro Medal

Glen Ridge, N. J., May 13—The team of Alex Antonio and Frank Kringle captured the medal in the qualifying round of the annual amateur-pro club championship of the New Jersey State Golf Association today at Glen Ridge. The pair posted a 7-sup-par 65.

HOW PENSIVE WON

SIXTH RACE—Pimlico. For 3-year-olds; Preakness Stakes, 1 and 3-16 miles. Purse, $50,000 added. Post, 4:11; off, 4:12½. Start good, won driving, place same. Time, 1:59⅕. Winner, ch. c., 3, by Hyperion—Penicuik II. Trainer, B. A. Jones. Value to winner, $60,075.

Starters	Wt.	P.	St.	½	¾	1	Str.	Fin.	Jockeys	Equiv. Odds
				Running Positions						
Pensive	126	2	5	5^8	4^1	3^3	3^2	1¾	McCreary	1.65
Platter	126	3	4	2½	2^2	2^3	2^1	2^2	Longden	3.05
Stir Up	126	1	1	1 1½	1^2	1 1½	1½	3 1½	Arcaro	2.35
Garmps Image	126	7	2	4^3	5^3	5½	5^1	4^h	Bowers	15.90
Gay Bit	126	6	6	6^4	6^3	4^2	4^1	5^5	Westrope	14.80
Stymie	126	5	7	7	7	6^5	6^8	6	Roberts	23.30
Alorter	126	4	3	3^2	3 1½	7	7	eased up	Woolf	30.50

Official Mutuel Prices

	Straight	Place	Show
Pensive	5.30	3.10	2.20
Platter	—	4.10	2.70
Stir Up	—	—	2.50

Notes—Pensive, hard-held while following the early pace, saved ground until asked for best speed, was taken to outside for the challenge, appeared to be trying to lug in through last eighth but was well handled and went on to win in a drive. Platter was kept close to the early pace, appeared to have shown in front briefly inside eighth pole but could not stay with Pensive in the closing drive. Stir Up took command early without being extended, was rated to the stretch and failed to respond to punishment when challenged. Gramps Image, on outside at first turn, raced within striking distance of pace but had nothing left for the drive. Gay Bit was under restraint, early moved menacingly at the three furlong pole, then flattened out. Stymie was never a factor. Alorter raced in contention for three quarters, went lame and was eased up th last eighth mile.

Your Wartime Problems

By RICHARD HART

Letters From Doctors Are Helpful

Induction centers are busy spots and most of them are operated on a limited schedule of available doctors.

A man with some disability should save the doctors' time by bringing to the induction center a written statement of his condition. This statement should be written on the stationery of his attending physician and signed by the doctor. If the case has a history of hospitalization it is wise to state dates and diagnoses.

Some men are loath to bring such letters to the induction centers. Somehow, they get the notion that this is unpatriotic. Quite the opposite is true. None of the services wants to induct men who will break under the strain of basic training. And these induction center doctors need all the data available to guide them in their decisions.

SOME MEN IMPROVE

We are all aware that men are being accepted into service today who cannot stand the strain of the life in either the army or the navy. But, there is another side of this picture. Some men are borderline cases and some of them greatly improve their condition under the health regimes toward which they are headed. It may be tough going during the basic training period, especially for the office worker who has had some chronic ailment, but the outdoor life has been known to work wonders.

We strongly advise wives and mothers not to worry about how their men will stand up under the strain. Their worries will not help. Nor will their constant letters, harping on the subject, improve their men's morale. It is much better to adopt a "wait and see" attitude—difficult though often this may be.

On the other hand, a man is foolish to conceal his actual condition. It is all right to maintain a "stiff upper lip" but a man in pain should report at sick call and win the confidence of his medical officer by his sincere approach to the problem.

ASIDES TO READERS

To Mrs. W. O'B. He does not have to increase his allotment to you with his increase in rank. He gets an increase of 20 percent as soon as he goes overseas. To SONIA V. No, he cannot get a "military divorce"—there isn't such a thing. This is a matter for the civil courts. To Mrs. C. D. P. You may be very angry at your son's wife but don't fill your letters to him with bitterness and your tears.

If you have a problem, write to Richard Hart, care of this newspaper.

A stamped, addressed envelope will bring a personal reply.

Uncle Ray

Of all dogs in the world the Eskimo dog is closest to the wolf. Indeed we may say that is "largely wolf."

Often called a "husky" by white men, the Eskimo dog is strong and powerful. Eskimos in northern Canada and Alaska would find travel harder if it were not for animals of this kind.

Eskimos start training dogs when they are mere puppies. A little harness is put on, and the puppy strains hard to get back to its mother. By the time it is two or three months old it is placed in harness with one or more full-grown dogs, and in that way gets used to drawing a sledge.

An old, well-trained Eskimo dog is chosen as the leader for each team which draws a sledge. Where this dog goes the rest are supposed to follow.

The dogs, being savage by nature, bite at one another while they run along, but usually they follow the leader. This dog seems to understand the orders to turn right or left, or to halt. If he does not carry out an order at once the driver knows how to make him do so with his whip.

No bridles or reins are used to guide the huskies. The driver simply shouts to them, and uses his long whip. The whip has a short handle, only about a foot long, but the lash is very long sometimes measuring from 18 to 24 feet.

A sea captain who used Eskimo dogs while on land in the Arctic gives interesting notes on dog travel.

"Three of these dogs," he says, "could draw me on a 100-pound sledge at the rate of one mile in six minutes. My leader drew 196 pounds, singly, a mile in eight minutes.

"At another time seven of my dogs ran a mile in four minutes, drawing a sledge. Afterward, in carrying stores to the Fury nine of the dogs drew 1,611 pounds one mile in nine minutes."

Motor sleds have been used to carry mail in the Northland, but huskies still do a great deal for their Eskimo masters.

(For GENERAL INTEREST section of your scrapbook.)

Uncle Ray

Tomorrow: Story of the Violin.

To obtain a free copy of the illustrated leaflet on the "Seven Wonders of the World" send a self-addressed envelope bearing a three-cent stamp to Uncle Ray in care of this newspaper.

Sgt. Engebretsen Wins Decoration Posthumously

The Legion of Merit for "exceptionally meritorious conduct" has been posthumously awarded to Tech. Sgt. Andrew B. Engebretsen of 879 71st St., killed in action in New Guinea, June 6, 1943. The award was presented to the hero's mother, Mrs. Bertha Engebretsen, in ceremonies at Fort Jay, Governors Island.

Although the "small ships section had only a few boats and United States personnel for direction of activities was very limited," declared the citation, "Sergeant Engebretsen continued to keep the section functioning at maximum capacity, thus making an important contribution to the support of combat troops operating on the north coast of New Guinea."

For Service Men

The New York City Defense Recreation Committee, 99 Park Ave. (at 40th St.), member agency of the National War Fund through the generosity of the entertainment world, offers a partial list of free amusements available today. Afternoon tickets from 11 a.m., evening tickets after 4 p.m. Apply 99 Park Ave. for tickets.

The Brooklyn Defense Recreation Committee, Concord and Navy Sts., and the T. V. S. O. Information Center and Lounge, 191 Joralemon St., also distribute free tickets to leading Brooklyn motion picture theaters and various other amusements on special occasions.

STAGE PLAYS

Tickets available for matinee and evening performances of legitimate Broadway plays through the courtesy of the League of New York Theaters.

MOTION PICTURES

Albee.
Fox.
Metropolitan.
Paramount.
St. George Playhouse.
Tivoli.

PARTIES AND MISCELLANEOUS

Apply 99 Park Ave. for passes

Girls of the Research Institute—Dance, orchestra, refreshments, 8:15 p.m.

Simon Barere, pianist—Carnegie Hall, 8:30 p.m.

Junior Committee of the Town Hall Club—Dance, orchestra, refreshments, 8:30 p.m.

Chamber Orchestra, Sir Thomas Beecham, conductor—Town Hall, 8:30 p.m.

International Beauty Shop Owners—Dance with orchestra, 10:30 p.m.

Columbus Circle Rink—Roller-skating, 8-11:30 p.m.

NO PASSES REQUIRED

Navy Street Canteen, Navy and Concord Sts.—Tickets to Brooklyn movies and sports events, 9:30 a.m.-11 p.m.

Prospect Park Branch Y. M. C. A., 357 9th St.—Swimming, gym, entertainment, 9 a.m.-10 p.m.

The Brooklyn Defense Recreation Committee suggests that Brooklynites who have tickets for any kind of entertainment that they cannot attend send them to the committee at the Navy Street Canteen, Navy and Concord Sts.

Thomas Egan of 2024 E. 1st St. has been promoted to radioman third class in the naval air force.

PREPARING FOR ATTACK—Pvt. Max Rosenblum of Brooklyn digs a slit trench for himself on the Anzio-Nettuno beachhead while chatting with Ralph M. Chester, American Red Cross field director, during a lull in the air action.

With Our Fighters

Staff Sgt. Isidor Haitkin of 120 Willoughby St. recently won the Good Conduct Medal and three sharpshooter medals at Camp Edwards, Mass.

Seamen 1st Class Albert J. Zieminski of 191 32d St. and Albert G. Perna of 5611 17th Ave. were graduated from the naval air technical training center, Chicago, as aviation specialists.

E. Leslie Ross of 146-21 56th St., Flushing, field executive of Queens Council of Boy Scouts, has entered the army air corps.

New aircraft mechanic at Seymour Johnson Field, N. C., is Pvt. Salvatore G. B. Pandolfo of 115 Avenue S.

2d Lts. Herbert T. Altman of 213 E. 58th St. and Alfred Zudeck of 2137 E. 21st St. were recently graduated as navigators from Ellington Field, Texas.

Promoted to captain in the medical corps at Percy Jones General Hospital in Michigan is Dennis J. Florentino of 44 3d Place, a graduate of the Long Island Hospital of Medicine. He had completed one year of internship at Kings County Hospital when he entered the service. Pfc. Louis Singer of 1018 46th St. has completed training as an aerial gunner at Harlingen, Texas.

On leave from Sampson, N. Y., following completion of recruit training are Seamen 2d Class Raymond K. Hoffman of 540 Senator St., Sam Zarabet of 762 Miller Ave., Milton Shulman of 940 Dumont St., Morris Sobel of 146 Chester St. and Matthew J. Soccoa of 32 Spencer St.

The fourth member of her family to join the service, Pvt. Sally A. Leyland of 170 Woodruff Ave. is taking basic training at Fort Oglethorpe, Ga. Her brother, Howard, is a corporal with the 8th Air Force in England. Another brother, Pearce, is warrant officer in the navy overseas and her brother-in-law, Charles Terr, is with the 5th army in Italy.

Assigned to active duty with the amphibious forces, San Bruno, Cal., is Seaman 2d Class Joseph A. Franza of 239 8th St. Corp. William J. Miller of 478 6th St. is serving with an anti-aircraft unit in the Pacific.

The Good Conduct Medal has been awarded at Camp Atterbury, Ind., to Pfc. Edith L. Silbiger of 255 Hicks St.

Flight Officer Howard Scotcher of Flatbush is engaged to Lillian Aaron of 1583 E. 2d St. On leave from Sampson, N. Y., is Seaman 2d Class George F. Britton of 1769 E. 28th St.

Radio operator and gunner on a B-24, Staff Sgt. Lawrence J. Tynana of 8623 14th Ave. has arrived in Italy, where he was promoted to his present grade. Corp. Jack Fruchter of 628 Essex St. recently received his aerial gunner's wings at Harlingen, Texas.

Anthony Scarnati of 208 Franklin Ave. has been made staff sergeant at Fort Eustis, Va.

Navy Casualty List Names 4 From Area

Washington, March 15 (U.P.)—The Navy Department today announced 149 casualties of the navy, marine corps and coast guard. The list includes the following four men from Brooklyn and Queens:

CONNELLY, Pfc. James F., marine corps—wounded. James F. Connelly, father, 194-35 113th Road, St. Albans.

SORROCCO, Pfc. Charles, marine corps—wounded. Mrs. Charles Sorrocco, wife, 331 Knickerbocker Ave. Mrs. Julia Sorrocco, mother, 40 Clinton Ave.

TUFANO, Corp. Jack, marine corps—wounded. Jack Tufano, father, 9513 91st St., Ozone Park.

UEBERALL, Corp. Harold, marine corps—wounded. Mrs. Harold J. Ueberall, wife, 150 E. 18th St.

SOMETHING FOR THE BOYS—Glamorous singer Benay Venuta, who appeared at the U. S. O. show at Fort Hamilton, has a tete-a-tete with two admirers, Pfc. Richard Salik and Pvt. William Holbrook.

NO PHOTOS RETURNED

Photographs used in With Our Fighters cannot be returned to the sender. However, pictures and news of local men and women in the armed forces are welcome and should be addressed to Our Fighters Editor, Brooklyn Eagle, Brooklyn 1, N. Y.

Brother and sister serving Uncle Sam are Pharmacist's Mate 2d Class Betty R. Baskin of 78 Miller Ave., stationed in Boston, and Aviation Machinist's Mate 3d Class Jules A. Baskin, at the naval air station, Memphis, Tenn.

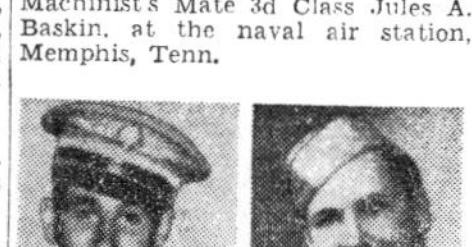

Sgt. Sidney Goodman of 836 Utica Ave. was recently married in North Africa. The bride is the former Mme. Lydia Levy of Oran. Home on leave from 19 months of duty in England, Ireland, Scotland, Africa and Corsica is Tech. Corp. August George Sartory of 147 Thames St.

John J. Fox of 217 Bay Ridge Ave. was commissioned an ensign in the naval reserve following completion of training at Pensacola, Fla. Serving with the 5th army, Italy, is Pvt. Charles Grasso of 486 Kosciusko St.

On double duty for Uncle Sam are these bombardier-navigators, recently graduated from Victorville, Cal.: 2d Lts. Frank E. De Borger of 1427 DeKalb Ave. and Herbert D. Friedlander of 2527 Cortelyou Road.

Completing training as crew members of a Liberator at Tucson, Ariz., are Lt. Leonard Peck of 1674 W. 5th St., navigator, and Lt. John J. Leonard of 718 Carroll St., bombardier.

REVENGE VIA RADAR—Martha Salvagione of 137 Guernsey St. is assembling radar tubes at Tungsol Electric Company plant, 51 Nassau Ave., Brooklyn—with good reason. It's her way of backing three brothers and her husband on the battlefront and of avenging the death of a fourth brother, Pfc. David McLean.

Aleutians, South Pacific Vet Home on Leave

Francis M. Hughes, quartermaster first class, U. S. navy, who has seen service in the Aleutians and the South Pacific, is home on leave. He is the son of Mr. and Mrs. Joseph Hughes of 542 Bergen St. and has been in the service six years. His mother is a member of the Brooklyn Chapter, Navy Mothers Club. A brother, Thomas, is at the U. S. Naval Air Station at Lakehurst, N. J.

From Overseas

EUROPE—Dissatisfied with the regulation army dental chair in use at his air force command base in Northern Ireland, 1st Lt. Herman Ivanhoe of 205 E. 17th St., Brooklyn dentist, put his ingenuity to use and assembled what he terms the "most modern army dental chair" in the country—built entirely from salvaged bomber parts by GI's.

The seat was formerly a Flying Fortress pilot seat, the head-rest came from a dissembled Marauder and the Royal Air Force pitched in with a dental cut-off.

The Silver Star for "gallantry in action" has been awarded to 2d Lt. Francis W. Scott of 1978 Fort St., who is credited with capturing several Germans single-handed. His citation reads

"While stationing outpost guards Lieutenant Scott was fired upon by the enemy. He boldly advanced and singlehandedly captured many prisoners with a jammed carbine as his only weapon. Lieutenant Scott's daring performance and fearless leadership were instrumental in obtaining information that led to the enemy's defeat."

PACIFIC—Robery William Hansen of 262 Wakeman Place has been promoted to chief pharmacist's mate in a marine air group.

Winner of the Air Medal with three Oak Leaf Clusters and the Distinguished Flying Cross, Capt. Dikran Hazirjian of 1 Roosevelt Court has been appointed assistant navigation officer of a Flying Fortress group in the 8th Air Force.

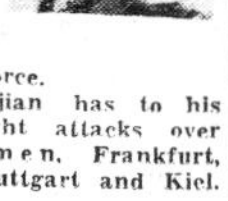

Captain Hazirjian has to his credit 25 daylight attacks over Hamburg, Bremen, Frankfurt, Wilhelshaven, Stuttgart and Kiel.

PACIFIC—Joseph J. Miller of 18 Cornelia St., who spent his recent furlough in Australia, has been promoted to staff sergeant in New Guinea.

Air Gunner Often Near Death Calls Raids 'Routine'

Staff Sgt. Martin A. Goldberg, who thinks air raid missions are rather routine things, missed death by a hair's breadth when a bullet from a German fighter plane was stopped by his parachute pack.

In another of his 25 raids on Europe the slim 21-year-old tail gunner virtually had his scalp singed by bullets whizzing past his head.

He had to be coaxed to talk. "There isn't anything to tell," he insisted. "Nothing much happened on those missions." He leaned back, frowning in an effort to concentrate, while he sat in his home at 1011 Clarkson St., enjoying a 21-day furlough before being reassigned.

Then he recalled the Schweinfurt attack, in which 60 American Flying Fortresses were lost. Some flak hit the plane, knocked one engine out, upset the control cables and disrupted the oxygen system. In addition there were holes in all four propellers.

Sgt. Martin A. Goldberg

Their plane fell out of formation with just about "a wing and a prayer" left and limping back ran into five German planes, Goldberg explained. "We drove them off," he said and then added regretfully, "Didn't get any, though."

His B17 Flying Fortress was in the first Yank raid over the Ruhr Valley.

Goldberg, who has the distinguished flying cross and the air medal with three oakleaf clusters, enlisted before Pearl Harbor. He came home unexpectedly yesterday, seeing his family for the first time in a year. His brother, Murray, 19, a private in Italy, was wounded.

He lauded the Red Cross, saying that "three-quarters of the fellows wouldn't know what to do most of the time if it weren't for the Red Cross clubs."

Lt. Caesar D. Todisco

Lt. C. D. Todisco Killed in China

"All of us are restless," wrote 1st Lt. Caesar D. Todisco from China to his family on Feb. 4. Soon after the letter arrived his wife, Julia, received a telegram from the War Department announcing he had been killed in action.

Todisco left Florida in February, 1943, and had been stationed in China since that time.

His mother, who lives at 960 68th St., is hopeful the report of his death is in error because last year he was incorrectly reported "missing in action." At that time he was able to bail out of his plane.

His wife, the former Julia La Penna, whom he married while in Georgia in November, 1942, however, has received a letter from his buddy, Lt. Bob Clapp, confirming the tragedy.

"His death was very quick and clean," wrote Clapp. "Flying is a dangerous game and a flier would rather die in his plane than any other way."

How You Can Help:

Here are home front organizations that can use your services in the war effort

AWVS — The American Women's Voluntary Services Brooklyn Unit, Inc., places volunteers with all organizations aiding the victory effort Girls from 13 to 18 may join the Junior Auxiliary. Call the AWVS at 147 Pierrepont St. TRiangle 5-8361.

VOLUNTEER BOND WORKERS—Volunteers to give time as speakers, typists and clerical workers at staff headquarters, etc., should telephone Mrs. Gray of the Kings County War Finance Committee at TRiangle 5-6295.

NAVY STREET CANTEEN — Mrs. Russell V. Cruikshank, chairman, asks for theater tickets, records, cakes, fruits, candies and cigarettes. Telephone TRiangle 5-6874.

FULTON-SUMNER CANTEEN — Service man's center at 1587 Fulton St. needs furnishings, games and other articles. Telephone TRiangle 5-8257.

AIR RAID WARDEN—Wardens are still needed. Register at the nearest police precinct or telephone Brooklyn CDVO, 131 Livingston St., TRiangle 5-9701.

BLOOD DONORS—Call in person or telephone Brooklyn Red Cross Blood Donor Center, 57 Willoughby St., TRiangle 5-8040. If you are a Legionnaire, call TRiangle 5-9140, 160 Pierrepont St.

NURSES' AIDES—Red Cross, 57 Willoughby St MAin 4-6001.

DIETITIAN AIDES—To relieve the shortage of hospital dietitians, Red Cross, 57 Willoughby St. MAin 4-6001.

CADET NURSES CORPS—Call Nurses' Registry for Long Island, 1 Hanson Place. STerling 3-4433.

ALL KINDS of home front war work, including training for volunteer work, telephone: Brooklyn CDVO, 131 Livingston St., TRiangle 5-9701.

NAVY Y. M. C. A. — Urgently needs pianos, all kinds of musical instruments, games, radios and electric victrolas, to be placed on ships that come to Brooklyn Navy Yard, Naval Barracks and Military Camps. Telephone TRiangle 5-2735.

THESE WOMEN!

By d'Alessio

"All I know—the net outcome of my net income is that I'm broke!"

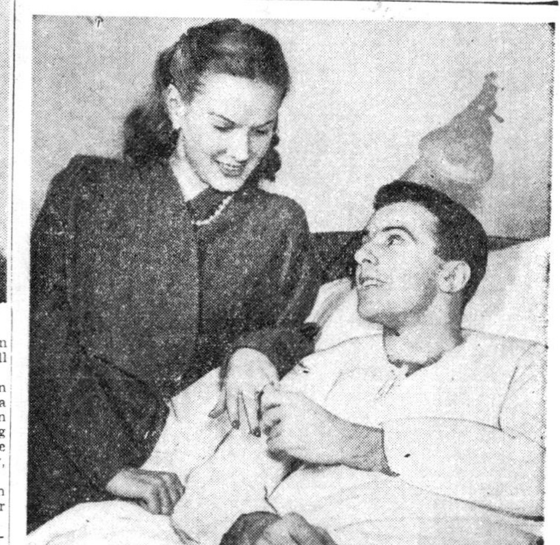

CUPID WINS THIS ONE—A patient at St. Albans Naval Hospital, Ensign William Sterling slips an engagement ring on the finger of June Vincent, Universal Pictures starlet.

FEUER VS. FUEHRER—Harry Feuer of Brooklyn, left, and Sgt. Milton Beasley check equipment on M-4 tank, newly arrived on Anzio beachhead. Feuer will drive the tank against the Nazis.

HERO OF 51 MISSIONS—Lt. Martin Biener of Flushing, who won the Air Medal with nine oak leaf clusters for piloting a B-25 Mitchell bomber in 51 missions over Africa, Greece, Bulgaria, Yugoslavia, Sardinia and Sicily, is shown in Boston with his fiancee, Phyllis Axelrod.

'Pineapples' for the Axis

Waterville, O. (U.P.) — More than 13 million "pineapple" hand grenades have ben produced by the Kilgore Manufacturing Company here. The gernades are small iron bombs about the size of a tennis ball.

★ ★ ★ ★ ★ ★ ★
SPORTS 7
Wall Street Financial News

BROOKLYN EAGLE

Weather—Cloudy tonight; cloudy, showers tomorrow.

103d Year. No. 141. DAILY & SUNDAY • (Copyright 1944 The Brooklyn Eagle, Inc.) • BROOKLYN, N. Y., TUESDAY, MAY 23, 1944 • Entered at the Brooklyn Post-office as 2d Class Mail Matter • 3 CENTS IN NEW YORK CITY ELSEWHERE 4 CENTS

ANZIO ALLIES ATTACK IN PINCER OFFENSIVE

A. L. P. NAMES UNION CHIEF FOR CONGRESS

Municipal Workers Head Chosen to Make Race in New 14th

James V. King, president of the C. I. O.-affiliated State, County and Municipal Workers, has become the first member of the American Labor party to be entered as a candidate in Brooklyn's 1944 Congressional race, it was learned today.

Petitions designating him to run in the new 14th Congressional District, as established under the State reapportionment act, have been placed in circulation with the leaders setting 10,000 signatures as their goal. The district is one of several in Brooklyn, where the Labor party outranks the Republicans as the runner-up to the Democrats in strength.

The new district has no Representative in Washington now and must elect one for the first time in November. This has produced a wide and open field to the Democratic, Republican and Labor parties, with the latter becoming the first to reach a definite agreement on its candidate. The district consists of the new 2d and 16th A. D.'s and includes Coney Island, much of the area which touches Gravesend Bay south of 16th Ave. and a large part of the Kings Highway section.

Ready to Fight

The Labor party's selection of King is regarded as the first confirmation of the party's determination to fight both the Democrats and Republicans, in certain districts, if necessary, in order to win a share of Brooklyn's legislative offices. Although the party in recent years indorsed numerous Democratic and a more limited number of Republicans, no A. L. P. member now holds an elective office from Brooklyn.

The only Democrats who have been assured to date of Labor party indorsements for re-election are Irwin Steingut, the Democratic minority leader in the Assembly at Albany, and Representative Emanuel Celler. A "limited number" of others will be indorsed, according to A. L. P. leaders, with such backing being based on the candidates' support of President Roosevelt's fourth term and his New Deal administration policies.

Rayfiel Mentioned

The Democratic leaders controlling their party's slate in the 14th Congressional District have reached no decision on their choice. They are Kenneth F. Sutherland, the Coney Island leader, and Joseph B. Whitty of the 2d A. D. However, the name of Assemblyman Leo F. Rayfiel has been prominently mentioned.

King is one of the Labor party's most experienced members in legislative procedure. He has gone frequently to Albany, where he has appeared at legislative hearings in support of progressive legislation. As legislative spokesman for the State, County and Municipal Workers he has been active particularly to obtain an adjustment in the wage standards of thousands of low-paid State hospital workers.

Detroit Truckers Call Off Strike

Detroit, May 23 (U.P.)—A wildcat strike caused by union rivalry over soft drink truckers which slowed production of vital war material at six Chrysler Corporation plants was called off today by local union leaders at the demand of United Automobile Workers (C. I. O.) international executives.

End of the week-long walkout was announced by U. A. W.-C. I. O. headquarters, which said the decision had been confirmed by William Jenkins, president of Local 490, U. A. W.-C. I. O., who had led a rebellion in which members employed at the Chrysler Highland Park plant defied International Union and War Labor Board orders to go back to work.

The strike was called off as the International Union's executive board prepare dto sit in judgment of Jenkins and other local officers acused of placing loyalty to union memb[illegible] before the war effort.

[illegible] Close Plants

[illegible] Wash., May 23 (U.P.)—The [illegible] strike of sawmill workers in [illegible] Oregon and Washington [illegible] caused the shutdown of [illegible] 40 plants in the heart of [illegible] Nations' principal wood [illegible] area.

O. K., Sergeant Rosila, Season Pass Is Yours

Branch Rickey Earmarks Precious Ducat For GI Who Says That's What He Fights For

By JAMES C. McGLINCY

With American Troops in England, May 23 (U.P.)—As soon as you heard them talk you knew that you'd found a little bit of Brooklyn 3,000 miles from home.

"You know what I'm fighting for," Sgt. Louis Rosila, 2688 E. 7th St., Brooklyn, was saying, "I'm fighting for a season ticket to Ebbets Field. I'm fighting for a chance to get back there and help Leo the Lip run that ball club. We'll make the Brooklyns proud of us when we go into action."

(At the offices of the Brooklyn Baseball Club, Branch Rickey, president, said today: "Sergeant Rosila's season pass is waiting for him here whenever he wants to pick it up.")

A bunch of the boys from Brooklyn, with a scattering of "foreigners" from other localities, were whooping it up over flowing flagons of "mild and bitter" early today after throwing a beer party for a busload of Waafs from a nearby R. A. F. establishment. Everybody had danced and drunk warm English beer until 11:30 and then the girls had gone home.

After that the boys had settled down to some serious singing and talking.

Most of the talk, of course, was about "when we get to the Continent."

"When we get to the Continent," said Pvt. Abe Levine, 2070 Union St., speaking for an assemblage of Ebbets Field alumni around him, "we're gonna knock hell out of the Bums. We're going to do to the Germans just what the Dodgers are doing to do to the other National League ball clubs. You'll see."

(Ah, such loyalty, such blind devotion.—Ed.)

Pvt. Philip Goldstein, 559 Hopkinson Ave., took a sip of beer and said:

Just to Even Matters

"Phooey, Brooklyn beer was never like this. I'm personally going to kill as many Germans as comes within my range because I figure it's on account of them I'm here drinking this here mild stuff."

"Them Jerries are supposed to be plenty tough," said Sgt. Waldron McElroy, who lived at the Pierrepont Hotel before he was drafted, "but they ain't any tougher than Brooklyns. We're ready for 'em."

The Brooklyn boys were members of a cannon company commanded by Capt. William Mathwig, Oshkosh, Wis. Officers and men stood around in a circle singing songs like "Auld Lang Syne," "Down by the Old Mill Stream," and "Sidewalks of New York." They also had a set of separate verses for "The Caissons Go Rolling Along" which made it their company song—and the way they roared it left no doubt that these men knew where they were going and whom they were going to "moider."

The party broke up with the singing of its company fighting song, which contains some language which would bring crimson to the cheeks of a bleacherite and will not be reproduced here.

"Yeah," said Lt. Kenneth Carr of Jersey City, "we'll moider 'em. Say ...what am I saying? I'm a Giant fan!"

SEDITION JURY IS TOLD 'STALIN CONTROLS F. D. R.'

Attorney Says He Will Prove U. S. Is on Verge Of Going Communist

Washington, May 23 (U.P.)—Henry H. Klein, attorney for Eugene N. Sanctuary in the mass sedition trial, told the jury today he would prove that President Roosevelt is "under the absolute control" of Josef Stalin "and his death ray."

He also promised to prove that "the United States is now on the verge of becoming a communist country" and that the trial was undertaken "to protect communism."

He said in his opening statement that Supreme Court Justice Felix Frankfurter, C. I. O. Leader Sidney Hillman and British Professor Harold Laski "are the chief instruments of communism in the United States."

Sanctuary has been accused of anti-Semitism, Klein said, but "he condemns the bad Jews and praises the good Jews." Klein, himself a Jew, said "the anti-Semitism charged in this indictment is a racket run by racketeers for graft purposes." He said that the flyleaf of one of Sanctuary's books bears this dedication: "To the good Jews of America."

"Note that 'good Jews,' Klein told the jury.

Calls Wise Political Rabbi

He depicted Rabbi Stephen S. Wise as a "political rabbi" who began anti-Nazi campaigns because he was "jealous" of the "personal glory" obtained by the late Samuel Untermeyer.

Klein, who was fined $200 for arguing with the judge yesterday, promised that Sanctuary would sing to the jury one of the patriotic songs he has composed.

Another defense attorney said the defendants "merely yielded to the spirit of the times" in an era when "we were all a little wacky," and "just shot off their bazooks."

Attorney J. H. Bilbrey, representin Franz K. Ferenz of Los Aneles, said in concluding an opening statement that the trial "is a hangover from that sorry period which we'd all like to forget."

The prosecution had described some of the defendants as anti-Semitic.

Nazis Say 2,000 Died In Raid on Belgrade

Stockholm, May 23 (U.P.)—The German-controlled Scandinavian Telegraph Bureau said in a dispatch from Belgrade today that more than 2,000 persons, including "many German officers and soldiers," were killed in Thursday's Allied raid on Belgrade.

It Costs 4F $25 to Ask Vet Why He's Fighting

Magistrate Hockert in Magistrate's Court, Long Island City, today declared that no service man needs to tell anybody for what he is fighting.

The magistrate then fined Richard Payne, 32, of 312 W. 116th St., Manhattan, $25 for disorderly conduct. The complaint was made by Peter Nulty, a U. S. Navy boatswain mate, 1st class, who is a patient at St. Albans Naval Hospital, St. Albans.

Nulty told Magistrate Hockert he and two other sailors were at the Queens Plaza, Long Island City, station of the Independent subway, yesterday, when Payne, who is in 4F, got into a discussion with them and exclaimed, "Why are you wearing that uniform and what are you fighting for when there is no democracy?"

Nulty, a veteran of two landings in the South Pacific theater of war with the Seabees, and also a veteran of World War I, declared the ensuing argument attracted a large crowd. Payne was arrested on Nulty's complaint.

He insisted in court he had not meant any insult to the armed forces, but that he questioned whether the war really is for "a true democracy and all that it means."

"This sailor does not have to tell anybody what he is fighting for," Hockert replied. "If he says he is fighting for democracy that's good enough for him, it's good enoukh for me and should be good enough for everybody else."

BELMONT RESULTS

1—June 4.00, 2.20, 2.50; Dinah Home 5.40, 3.30; Pharamonda 3.60. (6:36)

PINCERS IN ITALY—Allied drive from Anzio beachhead, opened today, if successful would trap 17 Nazi divisions assembled to fight off our forces along the broken Adolf Hitler line. Nazis' heaviest reinforcements were thrown against Americans at Terracina (1) while farther north they have to defend the crumbling line between Arce and Ceprano and South Giovanni (4). There is a string of spreading fortifications near Frosinone (3) and still nearer Rome is the last-stand line (2).

Simplified Tax Bill Goes to Roosevelt

Washington, May 23 (U.P.)—The House completed Congressional action today on the individual income tax simplication bill which will free approximately 30,000,000 Americans from the necessity of calculating their Federal taxes.

The measure, effective next Jan. 1, also would simplify the returns which must be filed by the remaining 20,000,000 taxpayers and would revise withholding schedules to make amounts withheld by employers cover, as nearly as possible, all Federal income taxes due.

Today's House action consisted of routine acceptance of technical amendments to the bill.

The bill has the Treasury's approval and is expected to be signed by President Roosevelt.

Solomon Libel Suit To Be Tried Here

The $1,400,000 libel suit of Milton Solomon, former deputy city controller, against Mayor LaGuardia was today placed on the Brooklyn Supreme Court non-jury "ready calendar" for call tomorrow before Charles C. Lockwood.

Unless the defense succeeds in having it shifted to the "military calendar" to await the war's end on the ground that one of the co-defendants is now in the armed service, trial may be had within a few days, court clerks said.

The absentee is Abraham Weinman, former investigator on the staff of William B. Herlands, former commissioner of investigations. Herlands and another of his investigators are also co-defendants. Weinman is at a training camp in the South.

The suit results from the criminal prosecution last Summer of Solomon on the charge that he sought an $8,000 fee on representation that he could control legislation pending before the City Council. Before the blue ribbon jury which acquitted him, Solomon claimed that he was the victim of a "conspiracy" to divert public attention from the "stiarrup pump scandal."

CLEAR SKY, HIGH TIDE REPORTED AT DOVER

London, May 23 (U.P.)—The weather over the Straits of Dover today:

The sun broke through and the sky became cloudless after an early morning haze. Moderately warmer with temperature going into 60's before 9 a.m.

Sea calm and unruffled. Barometer steady. High tides at Dover and Calais 1:20 a.m.

QUADS BORN TO WIFE OF OFFICER IN R. A. F.

Southend-on-Sea, England, May 23 (U.P.)—Quadruplets—three boys and one girl—were born today to Mrs. Daisy Moxham, wife of an R. A. F. flying officer.

The Moxham babies are Bryan, three pounds 10½ ounces; George, one pound 13½ ounces; Daisy, two pounds 14 ounces, and William, three pounds six ounces.

1,750 U. S. Planes Blast Dortmund, Brunswick

'Largest Air Fleet Ever Assembled' Reported Bombing Targets in Reich

London, May 23 (U.P.)—A 1,750-plane American task force lashed Germany and occupied France today after 1,000 British bombers dropped about 4,480 tons of explosives on Dortmund, Brunswick and other targets in three countries along and behind the invasion coast.

The resumed bombardment of western Europe soared to record or near-record heights on its fifth straight day. In the first 12 hours more than 3,000 Allied planes ranged over Germany and anti-invasion buffer areas, delivering at least 6,500 tons of bombs.

(The National Broadcasting Company reported from London that "the largest air fleets ever assembled are out over the Continent today, and before the day is over air history will be made.")

Escore of 1,000

About 750 Flying Fortresses and Liberators headed the daylight parade against the Continent, smashing at German airdromes and rail yards in France and targets in western Germany which were not identified immediately.

More than 1,000 U. S. Thunderbolts, Lightnings and Mustangs escorted the big bombers, which also were supported by R. A. F. Mustangs sweeping nearby areas. It was the greatest fighter fleet ever dispatched in any theater on a single operation.

The R. A. F. opened the day with its heaviest blows in a month soon after midnight. At a cost of 35 planes its heavy bombers hammered Germany's Ruhr steel center of Dortmund and the aircraft center of Brunswick, 120 miles west of Berlin.

Rail Centers Smashed

Other British bombers hit the French rail centers of Orleans and Le Mans, southwest of Paris, and speedly Mosquitoes jabbed at the German chemical center of Ludwigshafen and an airfield in Belgium.

The extra-large fighter escort apparently was dispatched over invasion-marked western Europe to draw the reluctant Luftwaffe into battle to thin further its already diminishing numbers in advance of the impending Allied invasion.

German broadcasts reported "heavy air battles" over southwest France and Belgium, an indication that the strategy may have succeeded.

Huge fires were left burning in Dortmund, whose railways radiate to Cologne, Munster, Bremen, Krefeld, Hamm, Hannover and Berlin. Clear weather enabled the bombers to pin-point their targets and the attack was concentrated, an Air Ministry communique said.

R. A. F. Mosquitoes rounded out the night's attacks with raids on the chemical center of Ludwigshafen in the Rhineland and an airfield in Belgium.

Tennis Star Mangin Is Awarded D. F. C. For Heroism in Air

Allied Headquarters, Naples, May 23 (U.P.)—Sgt. Gregory Mangin, former U. S. indoor tennis champion and now a tail-gunner on a Flying Fortress, has been awarded the distinguished Flying Cross for heroism, it was announced today.

He was cited for fighting off enemy planes over Wiener Neustadt, shooting down one plane, forcing a second to quit the fight and keeping others at a safe distance.

Previously Mangin had remained at his guns, although wounded by flak, in an attack on Treviso. He was wounded a second time when flak hit the tail turret over Toulon.

Mangin won the men's singles titles in 1932 and 1933 and was a member of the Davis Cup team.

NAZI FIELD GIVES R. A. F. GREEN LIGHT—BOOM!

London, May 23 (U.P.)—The control tower at a German night fighter station today flashed a green light, meaning "it's okay to come in," and R. A. F. Flying Officer B. I. Crofts went in—with the bomb bay doors of his Mosquito bomber wide open.

The embarrassed Nazi signalman realized his error and switched on his red lights, advising the British bomber to go away.

Crofts, a night intruder pilot, ignored the advice and laid his 500-pound bombs squarely across the intersection of the field's runways.

OWI Promises Spot News From the Invasion Theater

Washington, May 22 (U.P.)—Director George W. Healy Jr. of the Office of War Information's domestic branch, said today that "according to present plans" spot news of the invasion will come from the military theater.

Washington, as a rule, he said, will furnish only "complementary" military information. The OWI will be on a 24-hour schedule to provide "whatever assistance it can" to the pres, he added.

Red Skelton Reports For Induction Thursday

Hollywood, May 23 (U.P.)—Red Skelton, 31-year-old movie and radio comedian, was notified yesterday to report May 25 for army induction after an automatic review failed to show any reason for a deferment.

Charles Town Results

1—Buckeye, 19.60, 6.80, 2.40; Fast Light, 3.00, 2.20; June Pennant, 2.20. Off time, 1:06.

2—Pone, 10.40, 5.20, 4.80; Big Moose, 3.00, 2.40; Shailleen, 2.80. Off time, 1:36½.

DAILY DOUBLE PAID $261.60

Irene Manning Divorced

Hollywood, May 23 (U.P.)—Irene Manning, screen star, revealed today that she and H. E. T. Mannheim were divorced in Juarez, Mexico, two months ago.

U. S. BATTLESHIPS SHELL ENEMY IN SUPPORT OF DRIVE

By REYNOLDS PACKARD

Allied Headquarters, Naples, May 23 (U.P.)—Allied troops struck out from the Anzio beachhead today in an offensive co-ordinated with the campaign on the main Italian front in a bold bid to trap the 17 German divisions south of Rome.

The 5th Army forces in the long dormant beachhead attacked the German perimeter early this morning and were fighting under cover of a heavy bombardment by massed Allied planes pounding a 50-mile radius around Rome. American battleships supported the drive by shelling enemy positions.

An official announcement of the beachhead offensive said no details of the day's fighting were available yet.

Reports of airmen flying over the new battle zone indicated that the beachhead forces were pushing out southeastward toward the German "swing line" on the main front, squeezing the Nazis between their fire and Allied artillery in action to the south.

Twenty-three miles below the beachhead, American armored forces assaulted Terracina, coastal anchor of the German defenses, but were halted by explosives dropped from cliffs towering over the Appian Way. U. S. infantry, however, was closing in on the town from the north.

The announcement of the beachhead offensive said that with its launching the battle in Italy entered a new phase as the 5th and 8th Armies pressed their campaign designed to crush the German forces on the peninsula.

Lt. Gen. Mark W. Clark, commander of the 5th Army, watched the start of the Anzio offensive from an observation post overlooking the battlefront.

Nazis Getting Thrashed

British Information Minister Brendan Bracken, speaking at a meeting in London, said the Allies in Italy were giving the Germans "one of the greatest thrashings in their history."

The German DNB news agency reported today that German troops had evacuated Pico, middle hinge of the Nazi defenses on the main Italian front.

American battleships off Anzio shelled the German lines around the beachhead last night preliminary to the offensive, and also supported it throughout the early morning.

The battleships, air fleets and artillery joined in a three-way assault softening the German lines for land troops going into action 12 days after the 5th and 8th Armies drove forward on a main line.

Planes Support Drive

U. S. Flying Fortresses and Liberators with swarms of other Allied planes gave the new offensive powerful support with devastating assaults on German concentrations and strong points over a wide area.

Light fighter-bombers provided the aerial spearhead for the Anzio blow, smashing at a large force of German troops along an eight-mile stretch of a dry river bed near the trunk railway in the Cisterna area.

Inside an arc radiating 50 miles around Rome the Flying Fortresses and Liberators dropped their big loads of heavy fragmentation bombs on supply dumps and troop concentrations. They encountered no German air opposition and only slight anti-aircraft fire.

Low-flying Bostons showered the enemy with fragmentation and smoke bombs.

Warhawks and Thunderbolts struck at German guns and tanks in the Cisterna area outside the northeast corner of the beachhead and also attacked tanks and vehicles in the Froisone area.

Troop Concentrations

Fortresses hit the Avezzano road junction and various German troop concentrations, while Liberators attacked widespread targets, includ-

Continued on Page [illegible]

Nazi 'Spy' Planes Bomb English Invasion Bases

London, May 23 (U.P.)—German "spy" planes again searched the British coasts for invasion secrets during the night and a Nazi broadcast said the main force attacked Portsmouth, one of the principal ports at which the enemy has claimed Allied ships and troops were massing for the opening of a western front.

Bombs were dropped both along the south coast and in East Anglia, lying opposite the French, Belgian and Dutch invasion coasts. German planes also were over parts of east Scotland, from which the Germans believe an invasion of Denmark or Norway may be launched.

A German Transocean Agency commentator said 3,500,000 American and British troops already were concentrated in southern England for the impending invasion, and previous Axis broadcasts had said that Portsmouth and other ports in east, southeast, south and southwest England were "crammed to the bursting point' with invasion supplies.

King George VI, continuing his preinvasion inspectino of Allied forces, visited the headquarters of Gen. Sir Bernard L. Montgomery, commander of British invasion troops, "somewhere in the country," yesterday.

British travelers, meantime, were discovering that the Transport Ministry meant just what it said when it announced that trains henceforth were liable to be cancelled without notice because of "military needs." Five long-distance trains from Paddington Station in London were cancelled in two hours yesterday.

The Germans also were reported rushing their own preparations to meet the invasion. A neutral diplomat who has just arrived in Portugal told newsmen at Lisbon that the Germans were in the midst of large-

Friends to Testify For Killer of Doctor

Washington, May 23 (U.P.)—Friends and fellow attorneys of Robert I. Miller were expected to testify today in behalf of the 67-year-old criminal lawyer charged with first degree murder for shooting Dr. John E. Lind, allegedly to end the physician's attentions to Mrs. Miller.

Mrs. Marguerite Miller, 42, "probably' 'will take the stand, according to Defense Attorney H. Mason Welch. The buxom woman, Miller's second wife, was seated in Lind's automobile when Miller leaned across her and fired two shots into the doctor's chest and head.

Defense attorneys refused to disclose whether temporary insanity or self-defense will be the defendant's plea.

Taken Ill While Bowling, He Dies in Ambulance

George Grossman, 46, of 1418 Ferga Ave., the Bronx, became ill while bowling at the Queens Bowling Center, Queens Boulevard and 32d Place, Long Island City, last night and died in an ambulance.

WHERE TO FIND IT

	Page		Page
Bridge	14	Our Fighters	5
Comics	17	Radio	17
Crossword	14	Society	4
Dr. Brady	8	Sports	12, 13
Editorial	8	Take My Word	8
Financial	14	Theaters	6
Horoscope	17	These Women	14
Movies	6	Tommy Holmes	12
Music	6	Uncle Ray	17
[illegible]	14	Want Ads	14-18
Obituaries	9	Women	4

Eagle Staff photo

LEAVING FOR BIVOUAC—The 5th Regiment of Brooklyn of the State Guard went on an overnight bivouac yesterday. The photo shows members of Company F in a bus before they left. Capt. Leonard S. Carey and his staff inspected the troops.

Parade to Feature Tribute To War Dead Here Tuesday

Brooklyn and Queens residents will honor the memory of those who have given their lives for their country at parades and services on Memorial Day, highlighted by the appearance in the main Brooklyn parade of Daniel Harris, 99, of 231 Wodbine Ave., last borough Civil War veteran.

Mr. Harris will ride in an open car at the head of the procession as a representative of the G. A. R. The parade, which will start at Bedford and DeKalb Aves., at 9:30 a.m., will proceed along Bedford Ave., Eastern Parkway, past the reviewing stand opposite Brooklyn Museum and through the memorial arch.

Other Events Planned

Other events will be sponsored by four Knights of Columbus councils in South Brooklyn, St. Francis Prep, the Bellerose-Queens Honor Roll Association and the United Veterans Units of Richmond Hill and Woodhaven.

In the reviewing stand for the Brooklyn march will be Borough President Cashmore, reviewing officer; Brig. Gen. Emil M. Podeyn, commanding officer of the 5th Brigade of the New York Guard; Brig. Gen. Frederick W. Baldwin, Brig. Btyer H. Pendry, former Surrogate George Albert Wingate, Surrogate Francis D. McGarey, County Clerk Francis J. Sinnott, Police Commissioner Lewis J. Valentine, United States Commissioner Edward E. Fay and Representative John J. Delaney.

Col. William A. Dawkins

Harris, after riding in the automobile with Col. William A. Dawkins, grand marshal, will occupy a place of honor on the reviewing stand.

The order of march will be:

First Division—Army, Fort Hamilton; Marine Corps, Brooklyn Navy Yard, and the Navy, Brooklyn Navy Yard.

Second Division—New York Guard, 5th Brigade; 23d Regiment, 13th Regiment, 14th Regiment, 3d Battalion and Company F, 5th Regiment; 3d Separate Battalion, 1st Battalion, 5th Regiment and 5th Truck Company.

Third Division—Sons of Union Veterans of the Civil War.

Fourth Division—United Spanish War Veterans.

Fifth Division—Veterans of Foreign Wars.

Sixth Division—American Legion.

Seventh Division—Disabled American Veterans.

Eighth Division—Jewish War Veterans.

Ninth Division—Purple Heart Association.

Tenth Division — Catholic War Veterans.

Eleventh Division — Army and Navy Union.

Twelfth Division—Red Cross.

K. of C. to Parade

The Knights of Columbus will parade from the Thomas Dongan Council clubhouse, 76th St. and 4th Ave., to Our Lady of Perpetual Help R. C. Church, where a memorial mass for war dead will be celebrated at 11 a.m. Other councils participating are Gen. Phil H. Sheridan, Bishop John Hughes and Baron De Kalb.

It is expected that 1,500 members of the order and several bands will participate.

Before the parade conducted by the Richmond Hill and Woodhaven veteran groups, services will be conducted at the honor roll at Jamaica Ave. and Forest Parkway, where the procession will start, proceeding to the Buddy Monument in Forest Park at 109th St., where additional rites will be held.

St. Francis Prep will honor the memory of 18 men who have paid the supreme sacrifice at a solemn mass at 9 a.m. in St. Paul's Church, Court and Congress Sts. The Rev. Thomas Aquin Tyson, O.S.B., of the class of 1935, will be celebrant.

The Bellerose group will conduct services for five men killed in action in the churchyard of First Reformed Church, 247th St. and 91st Ave., Bellerose.

Truman, Here, Flays Corrigan

Senator Harry S. Truman (D., Mo.), repeated yesterday before leaving LaGuardia Field on a United Airlines plane for Chicago his declaration made in Washington Friday that Comm. John D. Corrigan should immediately be court martialed by the navy for disseminating "restricted" navy information for his own benefit.

Senator Truman, who is chairman of the Truman Defense investigating commitee, said:

"I think it is the most flagrant violation of the regulation, honesty and ethics of a public official I have ever run across in my whole investigating period. He took the same oath that I did."

The Senator said he was going to Chicago, en route to Grinnell, Iowa, where he will make a commencement address at Grinnell College today.

Corrigan Hopes to Prove Conduct 'Above Reproach'

Washington, May 27 (U.P.)—Comm. John D. Corrigan, suspended from duty as a production trouble-shooter for the navy after Truman investigating charges that he used his naval position to benefit his engineering firm, said today he was prepared to show that his conduct was "above reproach."

Meanwhile the navy was reported to be considering a demand by Chairman Harry S. Truman (D., Mo.) for Corrigan's immediate court-martial and a Federal grand jury in New York was expected to act.

Truman declared that information transmitted by Corrigan to the engineering firm of Corrigan, Osborne & Wells, Inc., as revealed before the committee, constituted "the most flagrant violation of the rules and regulations of the navy since this committee has been at work."

ROONEY, NOLAN PUSH CAMPAIGNS FOR CONGRESS

By JOSEPH H. SCHMALACKER

Rival candidates in the special election for Congress from Brooklyn's 4th Congressional district continued to step up their campaign activities yesterday against a background of doorbell-pulling and house-to-house canvassing to arouse voters for the balloting June 6.

William G. Nolan, the candidate nominated by the Republicans, came out with a statement through Republican county headquarters in which he asserted that "three terms of jitterbug government have convinced the electorate of the great need for more intelligent administration in Congress."

Meanwhile, John J. Rooney, the Democratic-American Labor Party candidate, who is an assistant district attorney, announced the personnel of his campaign committee. The chairman is M. Henry Martuscello, also an assistant district attorney.

'One Project to Another'

Defining "jitterbug government" as "the combined operation of the present Administration in hopping from one project to another, without rhyme or reason; unsuccessful conduct of hundreds of bureaus and agencies, and the socialization of the country's economic life," Nolan's statement added:

"My opponent carries the banner of 100 percent New Dealism to a frantic pitch, but I take pleasure in refuting many of his utterances which are distorted and misrepresented.

"Naturally, we are all interested in and wholeheartedly support all labor and social gains, but constructive government should come from the people by due process of legislation and congressional action, rather than by executive order and bureaucratic decree."

Serving for Rooney

Named to Rooney's campaign committee were the following:

Mrs. Christopher Barry, Bay Ridge civic worker; Louis C. Andreozzi, assistant district attorney and chairman of the 76th precinct C. D. V. O.; Mrs. Mary Tonry, past president of the Ladies Auxiliary, Division No. 1, of the Ancient Order of Hibernians; Mrs. George J. Joyce, wife of Justice Joyce of the City Court; Al Torre, sports promoter; Mrs. Mary McQuade, active in women's fraternal organizations; Joseph J. Glatzmayer, executive vice president of the Harbor Carriers of the Port of New York.

Also, Mrs. Katherine Neary, president of the women's unit of the Catholic Circle; Anthony F. Crissalli, Mrs. Mae Burns, past county president Kings County Ladies Auxiliary, Ancient Order of Hibernians; Walter T. Thomas, Mrs. Mary Sloan, president Women's Federal Jurors Association, Eastern District; Mrs. Mary B. Sessa, Michael J. Daly, Jacob Hertz, president of Congregation Baith Israel Anshei Emes, and Joseph P. Clavin, past president of the St. Patrick Society of Brooklyn. Mr. Daly becomes vice chairman of the committee and Mr. Hertz was named secretary.

Both the Republican and Democratic parties are concentrating their campaign activities on direct meetings with the voters. The campaign will conclude with a series of rallies during the current week.

Big City Appals Gentile, Ace Killer of Germans

Capt. Don S. Gentile, who destroyed 30 of Hitler's war planes in Europe, flew to New York from Washington yesterday and indicated pretty plainly that he was more appalled by the rush of the big city than the rush of Nazi planes in the sky around him.

At LaGuardia Field, where he arrived, and again at the Barbizon-Plaza Hotel, Manhattan, he said that the prospect of facing a radio microphone—in a broadcast today—was harder to face than any Messerschmitt he had yet met.

"A mike is a lot worse than going on a mission," he commented. "I'd rather go on a mission."

Reticent About Missions

Of the missions themselves he had little to say.

"I just like coming to the good old U. S. A.," he said when questioners pressed him. "I like seeing my family. I imagine after I see them I'll be ready to go back and do my job if they send me back." But that was up to the War Department.

About his flights and his air battles he didn't want to talk.

"There's just nothing to say except that a man goes out there to do his job. It's just something you don't want to talk about."

"Why?"

He thought a little about that.

"You want to forget it," he said. "You don't want to remember it."

Here With Uncle

Captain Gentile arrived with his uncle, Frank J. Cipriano, a Columbus lawyer. It was his first visit to New York except for passing through on the way to Europe and then on the way back, but he had no comments on the city—he hadn't seen it yet. There was a full schedule ahead—luncheon, then theater in the afternoon and another theater at night. The flier who, at 23, is a top American flying ace, found all that just a little too much for him.

"They certainly hustle you around here," he said.

(He used to hustle at 450 miles an hour over Germany.)

Captain Gentile and his uncle will leave for Columbus this afternoon.

Eagle Staff photo

Capt. Don Gentile

Lt. Rudy Vallee to Return To Home Front Band

Hollywood, May 27 (U.P.)—Lt. Rudy Vallee of the coast guard will fold his uniform this Summer and return, at his own request, to civilian tootling.

He will be placed on the inactive list, it was learned today, some time between July 15 and Aug. 22, after he and his non-seagoing jazz band make their final tour in the interest of the Fifth War Loan bond sale.

Vallee said he is 43, that he was more than 38 when he entered the coast guard, had biult up one of the finest service bands in the country, but now felt his work was finished.

'HEIL HITLER! SEIG HEIL!' SHOUTED IN RESTAURANT JAILS BORO MAN, 55

Shouts of "Heil Hitler! Seig Heil!" by Anthony Kojanckas, startled patrons in a restaurant at 353 Fulton St. yesterday, according to Patrolman Richard F. Sullivan of the Poplar St. station, who arrested Kojanckas on a charge of disorderly conduct.

Arraigned before Magistrate Sala in Brooklyn Weekend Court, Kojanckas said he had a few drinks and might have shouted "Heil!" a few times, but he did not remember saying "Heil Hitler." The policeman said he saw Kojanckas repeatedly give the Nazi salute and heard him shout "Heil Hitler."

The magistrate sentenced Kojanckas, 55, a Lithuanian, of 69 Gold St., to five days in jail or pay a $25 fine, and committed him to the Raymond Street Jail.

Draws 3 to 6 Years In Slaying of Wife

Alfred, Me., May 27 (U.P.)—George E. Ashworth, 60, was sentenced in Superior Court today to three to six years in State Prison after a jury convicted him of manslaughter in connectidon with the death of his wife, Sarah, last April 2.

Ashforth, who was convicted on Thursday, testified that he shot his wife in self-defense and that he fired a second shot to relieve her suffering. A son corroborated his father's testimony that Mrs. Ashworth threatened her husband with an axe.

Hit-Run Driver Gets Fine of $50

Joseph Modzelewski, 26, of 70 Greenpoint Ave., accused of leaving the scene of an accident without identifying himself, yesterday was fined $50 and his driver's license revoked by Magistrate Solomon after a hearing in Brooklyn Felony Court.

Modzelewski was arrested on complaint of Walter Greeves of 107 Greenpoint Ave. after Modzelewski's truck and an automobile driven by Greeve's daughter, Alice Greeves, collided.

Modzelewski said he had been discharged from the army six months ago due to a skin condition. The magistrate said: "I don't see why you couldn't drive a truck for the army."

Anti-Semitism Stand Urged

The Jewish Peoples Committee has urged both Democrats and Republicans to adopte stands at their coming national conventions condemning anti-Semitism, which it states is undermining morale on the home front and among armed forces.

BILLING, SANS COOING—Marlene Dietrich and Irving Berlin pause between assignments in Italy and compare short-snorter bills. The Dietrich glamorous gams are covered with GI-trousers.

Public Ignoring Pleas to Forego Holiday Travel

Col. J. Monroe Johnson, director of the Office of Defense Transportation, might just as well have saved himself the trouble of appealing to the public to avoid traveling during the holiday weekend. Railroads and bus lines serving the city will testify that his words apparently fell on deaf ears.

Practically every railroad reported last night that extra sections were added on long hauls, with all Pullman berths sold out early and standees in nearly all trains.

Beach traffic was particularly heavy, with the Pennsylvania, which serves the New Jersey resorts, and the Long Island, reporting heavy traffic to the Rockaways, bearing the brunt of the load.

Quiet on B. & O.

The Baltimore & Ohio was the only line not reporting record crowds, with its heaviest traffic on the run to Washington. A B. & O. spokesman said there was "nothing else much" out of the ordinary.

The New York Central and New York, New Haven and Hartford joined in issuing figures showing that up to early last night there was a 12 percent increase in traffic over last Memorial Day weekend, which in turn brought a 52 percent boost over 1942, establishing a record high. Thus, the spokesman pointed out, "It looks like some sort of new record this year."

Bus lines all said the same thing: merely a resigned, "Jammed."

Airlines had no such trouble, since most of them have been operating on priorities for months anyway. None of the airlines using LaGuardia Field had been in normal operation for the last three days because of bad weather, which meant a pile-up of priority traffic, eliminating virtually all hopes for an ordinary civilian seeking a reservation.

Good Weather Promised

Those who got out of town were promised good weather today, the Weather Bureau figuring it will be "partly cloudy" and continued warm, with a high of about 80 degrees. That high humidity which made things so sticky yesterday will be gone, too.

But the Weather Woman (it was a woman) would not go out on a limb about what might be expected for Monday and Tuesday. She said the original long-range forecast was changing, and she wouldn't say what might happen. Just what the original long-range forecast was, she also wouldn't say.

Lewyt Employes Mark Award of Army-Navy E

More than 800 employes of the Lewyt Corporation, 60 Broadway, and their guests, celebrated the award of the Army-Navy E to the plant at a dance held last night in the grand ballroom of the Hotel New Yorker, Manhattan. The company manufactures communications and ordnance equipment, and airplane parts for the army and navy.

It's Irish Night On Pacific Isle As Kellys Meet

It's nearly four years since Thomas and Andrew J. Kelly of 94-30 94th St., Ozone Park, said goodby and Tom went off with his National Guard unit to be be sworn into the army.

But the brothers are together again, somewhere on a Pacific island where marines and army men are living side by side.

Tom, wearing a sergeant's stripes, went to the island base with his army outfit a little more than two years ago. Andrew, who is better known as Buddy, then was still in Erasmus Hall High School and the family lived at 1236 Albany Ave.

Buddy reached his 17th birthday and promptly enlisted in the marines, completing his training at Parris Island and losing no time in being assigned overseas. When he went over he was a private, first class.

On May 12 he wrote to his parents, Mr. and Mrs. Michael J. Kelly, that he had arrived at a "nice" base in the Pacific.

Two days later Sergeant Tom wrote home to inform his parents that "Buddy walked right in on me. We're here together."

The services are pretty well represented in the Kelly family, for Papa Kelly served 18 months in the navy during World War I, and Nicholas E., now 16 and a student at John Adams High School in Ozone Park, is just itching to get into the merchant marine.

Utility Employes Get WLB Pay Rise

The Central New York Power Corporation, Niagara, Lockport and Ontario Power Company and the New York Power and Light Corporation of Syracuse were ordered yesterday by the Regional War Labor Board to increase rates for 1,700 employes four cents an hour retroactive to June 30, 1943.

The district WLB, headed by Thomas L. Norton, also directed the power companies to pay time and one-half for all holidays worked, regardless of the shift, in addition to the regular weekly rates retroactive to Jan. 13, 1944.

WHEN OUT OF TOWN REGISTER FROM BROOKLYN

★★★★★★★ SPORTS 7 Wall Street Financial News

BROOKLYN EAGLE

Weather—Fair, warm tonight and tomorrow.

103d Year. No. 148. DAILY & SUNDAY • (Copyright 1944 The Brooklyn Eagle, Inc.) • BROOKLYN, N. Y., WEDNESDAY, MAY 31, 1944 • Entered at the Brooklyn Post-office as 2d Class Mail Matter • 3 CENTS IN NEW YORK CITY ELSEWHERE 4 CENTS

YANKS AND GERMANS LOCKED IN DECISIVE BATTLE FOR ROME

2,750 U. S. Planes Hit Reich, Ploesti

German Rail Hubs, Air Base, Romanian Oil Center Bombed

London, May 31 (U.P.)—About 2,750 United States heavy bombers and fighters flew from Britain and Italy today against four rail hubs in northwest Germany, a Nazi air base in eastern France and the great Romanian oil center of Ploesti.

The U. S. 8th and 9th Air Forces sent 1,750 Flying Fortresses, Liberators and fighters against the Ruhr rail centers of Hamm, Osnabruck, Schwerte and Soest and the Luxduil airdrome near Mulhouse in northeastern France.

From Italy up to 750 Forts and Liberators, with a Lightning and Mustang escort, struck at oil refineries at Ploesti, reporting hits on at least one big refinery in the heart of the Romanian fields which supply the German war machine.

Battle Over Romania

A Naples announcement of the Ploesti attack said smoke visible for miles obscured the oil refinery area, preventing detailed observation.

The bombers encountered intense anti-aircraft fire over Romania and a number of fighters challenged them, but the results of the air battles were not made known immediately.

The massive escort of the bombers attacking Germany discouraged fighter resistance.

The yards at Hamm, Osnabruck, Schwerte, southeast of Dortmund, and Soest, southeast of Hamm, comprise key rail centers for the Ruhr industries contributing to the anti-invasion defenses of western Europe.

After two days of concentration on German aircraft plants, Lt. Gen. James H. Doolittle shifted the 8th Air Force bombing weight back to the Nazi transport system.

About 200 Marauder medium bombers, maintaining the pressure on German communications behind the west wall, hit three bridges across the Seine in an afternoon raid on northern France.

The new night and day bombardment followed a near-record day of attack during which an estimated 6,000 Allied warplanes from Britain and the Mediterranean dropped 5,000 tons of high explosives and fire bombs on five Nazi aircraft factories, 10 airdromes, at least 11 railway targets and other military objectives from the Channel coast to southern Austria.

Allied air forces blasting out a path for invasion have cut or disrupted all of Germany's railways and principal highways behind a 400-mile stretch of the Atlantic wall from the Dutch-Belgian border to the Bay of Biscay, the Air Ministry announced.

13,500 BREWSTER WORKERS AWAIT FEDERAL ACTION

Contract Board Meets Tomorrow to Consider New Work Possibilities

More than 5,300 "loyalty strikers" at the Brewster Aeronautical Corporation plant in Long Island City, their two-day sit-in demonstration against sudden cancellation of navy fighter plane (Corsair) contracts ended, today awaited results of the search for new contracts, as proposed by President Roosevelt.

It was that proposal which sent the sit-in demonstrators home, both those in the Long Island City plant and an additional 3,200 at the plant in Johnsville, Pa. A total of 13,500 Brewster employes in both plants face dismissal when the current navy contracts expire July 1.

Two hundred shop stewards from the Long Island City plants met today in the Brewster building at Northern Boulevard and Honeywell St. and received instructions from Marco Sicala, vice president of Local 365, United Automobile Workers of America, C. I. O., to have all the men who were laid off leave the building, so that there would be no interference with about 4,000 employes still at work.

All employes, both those still at

Continued on Page 11

Cabaret Tax Cut Voted by Senate

Washington, May 31 (U.P.)—The Senate voted today to cut the cabaret tax from 30 to 20 percent and to exempt uniformed service men and women from paying it altogether.

A few minutes later, the Senate passed the new national debt limit bill to permit the Government's outstanding obligations to rise from $210,000,000,000, the present limit, to $260,000,000,000.

The cabaret tax reduction, an amendment to this bill, was a compromise of the original amendment offered by Senator Sheridan Downey (D., Cal.), to reduce the levy to 10 percent.

Downey agreed to propose a 20 percent tax, coupled with the exemption for service personnel, after Finance Committee Chairman Walter F. George (D., Ga.), said he "could not accept" a 10 percent cabaret tax while theater admissions remain at 20 percent.

Ask U. S. to Preserve Sovereignty of Poland

Buffalo, May 31 (U.P.)—The Polish-American Congress ended its three-day constitutional convention yesterday with a "memorial' to President Roosevelt proclaiming "Poland's right to liberty."

The delegates ejected the lone dissenting member amid shouts of "Bolshevik" and called on the President to preserve the full sovereignty of Poland and "accept no compromise incompatible with the honor and tradition of America."

Union Promises Court To Act on Coal Gouger

A letter from a union declaring it had already denounced John L. Lewis "for his services to Hitler" and that it would "deal with our member who pleaded guilty in your court" was read today by Magistrate Surpless as Arthur Sherzer of 145 Thames St. came before him for the "bargain" sentence Surpless had promised him.

Sherzer had pleaded guilty to two accusations of overcharging on anthracite coal orders. Surpless had promised him a suspended sentence if he would introduce a resolution condemning Lewis before Local 455 of the International Association of Bridge, Structural and Ironworkers, A. F. of L. Sentence was suspended.

Undaunted by what he described as "a scurrilous letter" addressed by the United Mine Workers to Mayor LaGuardia, but directed at himself, Magistrate Surpless condemned Lewis. He also tossed verbal bricks at the Mayor and President Roosevelt.

The letter, by the United Mine Workers, the magistrate indicated, was aimed at his judicial head, but he said the Mayor should give it out as it was addressed to him.

"I received only a copy of it," he said.

Surpless Gets Union Letter

Surpless read a letter he received from William Colavito, president of Sherzer's local, saying the union in two resolutions had denounced Lewis "for his services to Hitler by two coal strikes," and: "Our indignant membership, opposed to black marketeering, will deal with our member who pleaded guilty in your court."

"Even in the face of this will you present this resolution to your local?" asked the magistrate.

Sherzer said he would do so and Magistrate Surpless asked him to present his union leaders with copies of the "fine American statement issued by R. J. Thomas, president

Continued on Page 11

BELMONT RESULTS

1—Gallantly 7.00-4.30-3.30, Houlgate 8.60-5.90, Cacho 9.10. (Off 1:34½)
2—Dark Maiden 14.70-7.40-6.40, First Gun 16.60-10.30, Nap 8.30. (2:06½)
DAILY DOUBLE PAID $78.40
3—Pamela C., 1st; Jamesina, 2d; Silver Smoke, 3d.

NATIONWIDE LIQUOR DEALS HOLD 3 HERE

Overcharge Profits Of $733,203 Alleged In Two Indictments

An indictment alleging what was said to be one of the most extensive black market liquor operations thus far disclosed was returned today by the Brooklyn Federal Grand Jury.

The indictment, handed up to Federal Judge Clarence G. Galston, charged that $661,755 was collected in black market profits on sales of liquor to distributing firms in various parts of the country from May, 1943, to last December.

Named as defendant in the indictment was Isidore Fried, 57, of the Essex House, Manhattan, general manager and sales agent of a Brooklyn wholesale liquor company. The indictment charges that, on sales for which invoices aggregated $1,624,338 Fried collected $661,755 in cash over and above the amount appearing on the bills.

Richmond Hill Men Named

The Federal Grand Jury returned a second indictment, also alleging black market deals, against Max Paul and his brother, Milton, and the Lamont Forbes Company, Inc., of 100-05 92d Ave., Richmond Hill. The two individuals and the corporation are accused of receiving $71,448 over and above the total of $156,533 appearing on invoices for shipments of liquor.

Assistant U. S. Attorney J. Wolfe Chassen, who has had charge of the five-month grand jury investigation resulting in the two indictments, said tha tthe probe will be continued. Defendants named in both indictments will be notified to appear for pleading in Brooklyn Federal Court next Monday.

The liquor distributors to which Fried is alleged to have made the sales, according to the first indictment, were:

The Houston Wholesale Liquor Company and the Tarrant Wholesale Drug Company, both of Houston, Texas; King Distributing Company, Jacksonville, Fla.; Tarrant Beverage Company, Beaumont, Texas; Max Ducov, Otho L. Nikles, Wolf C. Rimann and Ben Weinberg,

Continued on Page 11

Boro Theological Student Wins Fight For Navy Discharge

Providence, R. I., May 31 (U.P.)—A preinduction theological student won his fight today to be discharged from the navy when Federal Judge John P. Hartigan ruled that he had been inducted illegally.

Judge Hartigan sustained a writ of habeas corpus filed in behalf of Mortimer J. Rubin, 21, of 1627 53d St., Brooklyn, which claimed that the youth had been inducted illegally by Local Board 203 of Kings County last Nov. 17. The court also denied a petition to dismiss the habeas corpus filed by Capt. C. W. Magruder of the Newport Naval Training Station to which Rubin has been attached.

Rubin first was listed as 1-V-D, the classification for theological students, and then was classified 1-A while a student at the Beth Joseph Rabbinical Seminary in New York.

The judge said:

"I find that the registrant's change of class from 1-V-D to 1-A was an arbitrary, capricious and illegal act on the part of the local board. Basic principles of justice require that the respondent's motion to dismiss be denied and that the petition for habeas corpus be sustained."

Judge Hartigan said the boy's record showed clearly that he had been a serious student, preparing for the ministry, before Pearl Harbor. He will be released to resume his studies.

The Heat's on, Kids!

The Weather Man, reporting the mercury stood officially at 82 at 1 p.m., said it would probably go to 88 today. 'Nuff said.

Charles Town Results

1—Gallop A Mile, 11.40, 5.00, 2.40; Bettie Wynn, 5.80, 2.40; All Crystal, 2:20. Off time, 1:08½.

2—Famas Time, 2.80, 2.60, 2.60; Arch McDonald, 6.20, 4.80; Ginogret, 5.00. Off time, 1:40.

DAILY DOUBLE PAID $31.80

3—Precise, 7.20, 4.80, 3.20; Doctor's Nurse, 6.60, 5.80; Gradatim, 9.40. Off time, 2:09.

Suffolk Downs Results

1—Heel Call, 15.80, 7.20, 5.80; Subdeb, 7.80, 6.60; Flying Ned, 5.60. Off time, 2:31*.

THE ETERNAL CITY—Rome and the probable entrance (arrow) by which Allied armies, now battling Nazis some 15 miles south, will come to bring liberation.

100 Shipyard Workers Held by FBI in Fraud

Boston, May 31 (U.P.)—One hundred present or former employes of the Bethlehem Steel Company's Hingham shipyard were arrested by squads of FBI agents and U. S. deputy marshals today in what was described as one of the most widespread war frauds of its kind since the war began.

Those held were piece work welders and counters. No estimate of the total amount of money involved in the frauds was available immediately, but it was said to be large.

(Attorney General Francis Biddle in Washington said the amount of money involved was expected to amount to $500,000.)

E. A. Soucy, agent in charge of the FBI at Boston, said that those arrested had formed about 30 "clubs," each of which comprised one or two counters and from three to 30 welders.

According to Soucy, the counters in the "clubs" agreed with the welders to record false credits for extra production. In return for this "service" the welders would return to the counters a portion of their weekly salary checks which included payment for work not actually done.

According to the investigators, the counters received as much as $75 a week extra for their manipulation of the count.

Soucy said in one of the "clubs" which was operated jointly by two counters, false credits on tally slips were given to 21 different welders. Nineteen of the 21 welders paid the counters $5 weekly each and the counters split $100 a week in unlawfully obtained cash.

Long Distance U. S. Raid Makes It Hot for Peiping

A long-distance American air raid on Peiping, former capital of China, was reported by Tokyo radio today, which claimed one of two P-51 fighters participating in the raid was forced down and captured near Hotsin in Shansi province.

The Tokyo broadcast, heard by United Press at San Francisco, said the attack took place Tuesday morning.

Peiping, in Hopeh province, is well to the north of Tokyo, and the furtherest point reported reached by American planes based in southern and southwest China.

Body of Second Twin Recovered From River

The tragic history of the ill-fated Richie twins of 327 E. 89th St., Manhattan, drowned in the East River off 92d St., came to a close with the recovery of the body of 5-year-old Irene, found floating under Manhattan Bridge by a coast guard vessel. Michael's body had been found May 18, one day after the tragedy.

Barnard on ICC

Washington, May 31 (U.P.)—George M. Barnard of Indiana was nominated by President Roosevelt today to be a member of the Interstate Commerce Commission, succeeding the late Joseph B. Eastman.

Quiz 3d Suspect in Sale Of Alcohol Fatal to 14

A man suspected of having supplied to the candy store at 48 Hudson Ave. the wood alcohol which caused 14 deaths since last Saturday was picked up this afternoon by police and Federal alcohol control agents. Taken to the Poplar St. station, he was questioned there by Assistant District Attorney Louis Andreozzi and Paul Sullivan, in charge of the Federal agents of the Brooklyn-Long Island area.

The poisonous alcohol allegedly was bought by Sophie Krisuinas, 30, last Thursday night while her husband, George, 50, proprietor of the store, was at their country place, Sunnyside, near Flemington, N. J. Sophie was arrested late Saturday night and George surrendered Monday. The couple were remanded on a homicide charge yesterday in Felony Court to await grand jury action.

Dispensed From Kitchen

Mrs. Krisuinas, according to Andreozzi, paid $96 for 30 gallons of the wood alcohol, believing it was an inferior grade of potable alcohol such as she and her husband had been selling for some time to residents of the Navy Yard district for 50 cents a half pint. The alcohol was concealed between the ceiling and the kitchen, directly behind the store, and the floor of a bedroom above. It was dispensed from the kitchen by way of a pipe and seltzer bottle nozzle fitted into the wall behind a removable panel.

In an affidavit signed by Detective George Archer of the Poplar St. station, Krisuinas is specifically charged with having caused the death of Felix Ortowski by selling or giving him a quantity of wood alcohol at the candy store May 27.

Krisuinas surrendered at the office of Acting District Attorney Thomas Cradock Hughes in the custody of his counsel, former Magistrate Leo Healy. At the arraignment before Magistrate Masterson, Healy said he would not ask for bail at that time.

According to police, Krisuinas admitted having been arrested six times for selling liquor without a license.

FORRESTAL HITS TRIAL OF KIMMEL DURING THE WAR

Opposes Admiral's Request for Early Court-Martial

Washington, May 31 (U.P.)—Secretary of Navy James V. Forrestal said today that he was personally opposed to a court-martial for Rear Admiral Husband E. Kimmel in connection with the Japanese attack on Pearl Harbor so long as the war is in progress.

Forrestal was asked at his news conference to comment on Kimmel's request, in a letter to Senator Homer Ferguson (R., Mich.) for a trial "at the earliest practicable date."

The Secretary replied that "during this war—certainly during this phase of it—I would not be personally in favor of conducting such a trial."

The late Secretary of Navy Frank Knox also had indicated opposition to a wartime trial for Kimmel, who was commander-in-chief of the U. S. fleet and the Pacific fleet at the time of the Japanese attack.

Seek to Delay Trial

Legislation is pending in Congress to extend the statutory time period during which Kimmel and Maj. Gen. Walter C. Short, army commander at Pearl Harbor on Dec. 7, 1941, may be brought to trial on charges of dereliction of duty.

The U. S. Pacific Fleet is now engaged in a "permanent offensive" against the Japanese, Forrestal said.

"The tremendous mobility of our fleet has been imparted to our land and air forces, for by its use we have been able to reconquer territory and to establish airfields in all the forward areas," Forrestal declared.

Forrestal said the navy can now truly be called a world fleet, "with the might of our ships carrying the offensive on all oceans."

THUNDER OVER DOVER —BUT IT'S JUST WEATHER

London, May 31 (U.P.)—A thunderstorm broke over the Straits of Dover shortly after noon today.

Lightning and heavy thunderclaps accompanied the disturbance, which moved toward the English coast from well out toward the Boulogne area.

U. S. TANKS BY-PASS VELLETRI; FOE TAKES STAND AT LANUVIO

Allied Headquarters, Naples, May 31 (U.P.)—American tanks and troops slugging it out with the Germans in a showdown battle on the slopes of the Alban Hills, battered forward another hard mile today to within 15 miles or less of Rome.

United Press Correspondent Reynolds Packard in a dispatch from the 5th Army front reported the new United States gains along the Rome-Anzio highway. He said the Americans to the right and British to the left also had pressed forward in violent fighting all along 27-mile Valmontone-Jemini line athwart the approaches to Rome.

United States armored units by-passed Velletri, Appian Way bastion of the German defenses, Packard reported, and the Germans were making a fierce stand at Lanuvio, which the Americans also had passed in a thrust threatening Albano, 13 miles from Rome.

Tanks Battle in Hills

The great tank battle on the Alban slopes was in its fourth straight day, with Americans and Germans alike suffering casualties in men and machines.

At one point a tank spearhead thrust into Nazi territory, poured lead into dugouts and pillboxes of the permanent defenses in the hills, and returned to the American lines. On the way back the Americans picked up crewmen of our damaged tanks and put them on the outside of the machines along with German prisoners.

(A German communique claimed strong Allied attempts at a break-through below Rome were frustrated, with 78 of 200 attacking tanks being destroyed, mostly in close-quarter fighting, in the Lanuvio area alone.)

Warning by Alexander

The advances carried deep into the Valmontone-Campo Jemini line but Gen. Sir Harold R. L. G. Alexander, Allied commander in Italy, warned in his daily communique:

"It is now evident that the enemy intends to hold this line at all cost."

American tanks and tank destroyers made the deepest penetration of the enemy line when they rumbled "right up in front" of Genzano, 15 miles south of Rome, and Lanuvio, two miles farther south, and began pouring shells into the two towns on the southwest slopes of the Alban Hills, Reynolds Packard, United Press war correspondent, reported from the front.

Nazis May Quit Rome

Troops and tanks assaulting Lanuvio entered the outskirts of Villa Crocetta, a cluster of ruined buildings just outside the town.

(Radio Berlin said the battle had reached the "Gates of Rome" and a CBS broadcast from Madrid reported some Germans already were evacuating the capital after "cleaning out" all available food and merchandise in stores. A Berlin dispatch published in Stockholm told of "heavy fighting" raging inside both Velletri and Valmontone, two other strongholds in the German line.)

Claims Vatican Isolated

Stockholm, May 31 (U.P.)—A Rome dispatch of the Nazi-controlled Scandinavian Telegraph Bureau said today that the Vatican was isolated entirely, with all entry and exit passes canceled.

Telephone communications between Vatican City and Rome were suspended, the dispatch said, and even diplomats were subjected to the same restrictions as other residents of the Vatican.

A semi-official statement was quoted as saying that the measures were taken to enable the Vatican "to maintain strict neutrality in the present extremely complicated situation."

Changsha Civilians Flee As Japs Approach City

Enemy Force of 150,000 Pushes Near In Drive to Split China, Thwart Yanks

Chungking, May 31 (U.P.)—Civilians evacuated Changsha, capital of Hunan Province, as Japanese troops in a rapid advance along the Tungting Lake front approached within 30 miles of the city today in a full-scale attempt to split China and forestall an American landing on the southeast China coast.

The main column of an enemy force of approximately 150,000 troops reached the south shore of the Milo River, a tributary of Tungting Lake. The river crossing was made on naval barges.

Another column pushed southward from captured Tungcheng, while others advanced from Yangloushu, Yochow, Hwajung, Owchikou and Shihshilhshou, Central News Agency said.

Chinese Fall Back

Changsha, already a strafing target of low-flying Japanese planes, prepared for its fourth siege of the war.

Chinese forces north of the city resisted bitterly but fell back steadily under the enemy's aerial and ground blows. The Changsha garrison stored supplies in anticipation of a fierce defensive battle.

P. H. Chang, Councilor of the Chinese executive Yuan, told correspondents that the new offensive was aimed at dividing western and eastern China, regaining full control of the Canton-Hankow line and seizing the southeastern ports before American land, sea and air forces can bring them into operation against Japan.

"The situation is indeed very grave," Chang admitted.

Plea for Assistance

The Government spokesman expressed confidence, however, that the Chinese ground forces will be abel to halt the Japanese thrust if adequate air support can be brought into the battle.

"China will fight on," he said, adding in an appeal for greater Allied assistance, "Let the United Nations be united."

American fighter-bombers bombed and strafed enemy installations at Nanchang, on the Yangtze, and at the same time U. S. 14th Air Force Liberators dropped 28 tons of bombs on Japanese targets along the Burma Road in western Yunnan province, where Chinese ground troops gave ground at a number of points before heavy enemy counter-attacks.

Catholic Bishops Cable Hope Rome Will Be Spared

Washington, May 31 (U.P.)—Catholic bishops and archbishops of the United States cabled a joint message to Pope Pius XII today expressing confidence that the Allies will "discover a way" to gain their objectives in Italy without destroying Rome.

"The belligerents should for the sake of humanity make Rome an open city. Failing this for any reason, we confidently look for Allied ingenuity in strategy to prove itself and enrich our victory by saving Rome from destruction or further damage."

The message was signed by Archbishop Denis Cardinal Dougherty of Philadelphia, Archbishop Edward J. Mooney of Detroit, Archbishop Samuel A. Stritch of Chicago and Archbishop Francis J. Spellman of New York.

Building Workers Strike

Ten firemen and engineers working on the 11-story building at 628-644 11th Ave., Manhattan, walked out at 8 a.m. today in protest against a War Labor Board delay affecting pay raises. They returned to work at 11 a.m.

WHERE TO FIND IT

	Page		Page
Bridge	6	Ration Calendar	8
Comics	21	Society	8
Crossword	18	Sports	14, 15
Dr. Brady	10	Take My Word	10
Editorial	10	Theaters	16, 17
Events Calendar	6	These Women	16
Horoscope	21	Tommy Holmes	14
Movies	16, 17	Uncle Ray	6
Novel	18	Want Ads	18, 19, 20
Obituaries	11	Wartime	
Our Fighters	16	Women	8
Patterns	18	Problems	16
Radio	21		

HOW YANKS BLASTED JAPAN

★★★★ ★★★★ SPORTS · Wall Street Financial News

BROOKLYN EAGLE

Weather—Clear, warm tonight; clear, showers tomorrow.

103d Year. No. 164. DAILY & SUNDAY • (Copyright 1944 The Brooklyn Eagle, Inc.) • BROOKLYN, N. Y., FRIDAY, JUNE 16, 1944 • Entered at the Brooklyn Post-office as 2d Class Mail Matter • 3 CENTS IN NEW YORK CITY ELSEWHERE 4 CENTS

ROBOT BOMBERS BATTER BRITAIN

ONLY TWO LOST AS B-29s SET YAWATA AFIRE

U. S. Superfortresses Pour Destruction on Steel Center In Raid on Jap Homeland

By FRED SCHERFF

Washington, June 16 (U.P.)—United States Superfortresses from China inaugurated their war of destruction against the Japanese homealnd with precision bombing of targets at the steel center of Yawata which set off "large fires and explosions," the War Department announced today in a communique which listed American losses as two of the big bombers, both by accident.

The communique, first issued by the world-striding new 20th Air Force, said giant B-29s in "sizeable force" carried out yesterday's historic mission. The 100-word communique said the two planes that were lost did not go down as a result of enemy action. The crew of one was saved.

The communique, issued about 20 hours after the original announcement of the raid, was "based on preliminary incomplete reports from the combat zone" and lacked details as to the weight of bombs dropped and the damage done.

It did, however, disclose that "fliers who participated in the mission reported the bombing was accurate and that large fires and explosions were observed."

Flew From China

The communique said the huge bombers, carrying out their first major offensive operation, flew "from bases in China which were completed recently."

Japanese threw moderate to intense anti-aircraft fire at the Americans, the communique disclosed.

(Japanese radio reports of the bombing claimed that seven U. S. planes were shot down and three were damaged. A Japanese imperial headquarters communique said the industrial cities of Moji and Kokura were hit in addition to Yawata. All are on the home island of Kyushu, across from Korea on the Asiatic mainland.

(A dispatch from United Press staff correspondent Walter Rundle, at an advance echelon of the 20th Bomber Command in western China, said the B-29s, flying on history's longest raid, set the imperial iron and steel mills at Yawata on fire and that returning crew mem-

Continued on Page 8

Sees 'Longest Air Raid' As Good Start to Goal

General Wolfe Grins With Satisfaction As He Predicts End of Enemy's Empire

By WALTER RUNDLE

Advance Echelon, 20th U. S. Bomber Command, Western China, June 16 (U.P.)—A powerful force of B-29 Superfortresses flew the longest air raid in history to plaster explosives on the steel plants of Yawata, "the Pittsburgh of Japan," and officials today described the mission as a "good start" toward destruction of Nippon's industrial empire.

Watching the B-29s roll home, Brig. Gen. Kenneth B. Wolfe, commanding officer here of the new 20th Bomber Command, grinned with satisfaction today as he commented:

"I believe that Japan can be industrially weakened by proper application of strategic bombing and that she will rapidly lose the will to wage war when her industrial empire begins to disintegrate.

"No one in the 20th believes this task is a simple one. The logistics alone, under which the B-29s must carry their own fuel and bombs over the hump (the fliers' name for the Himalaya Mountain range between India and China), imposes a severe handicap.

"But my impression of today's raid is that the job can be done and the bombing of Yawata is a good start."

A communique issued by Lt. Gen. Joseph W. Stilwell, commander-in-chief of the China-Burma-India theater, said:

"In the longest round-trip mission in history, B-29 Superforts from the U. S. Army Air Forces Bomber Command, commanded by Brig. Gen. Kenneth B. Wolfe and operating from bases in China, attacked the Imperial Iron and Steel Works at Yawata, Japan, last night. Preliminary indications are that there was heavy damage to the targets, the largest steel mill in the Japanese Empire. Two of our aircraft were lost in operations."

Returning pilots said they went in over the sprawling steel works through an overcast sky, with occasional breaks over the target. Japanese flak was fairly heavy but inaccurate.

"It looked like we plastered hell out of the place," said Lt. Robert Winters, a co-pilot.

Capt. Roland A. Harte said flak

Continued on Page 8

Saw Bombs Rain Fire On Jap Steel Works

Reports Antiaircraft Blazing Below As 'Fort' Weaved and Dodged Way In

By United Press

A crewman on a B-29 Superfortress looked down as American bombs splashed fire and destruction on the Imperial Steel and Iron Works at Yawata, Japan, and exclaimed:

"Gosh, isn't it pretty down there!"

Roy Porter, who went on the flight for the combined American networks, said his plane weaved and dodged over the target for 10 minutes but "it seemed 10 times that long."

The broadcast was recorded by C. B. S. here.

"The searchlight batteries were full on us. The enemy anti-aircraft was blazing zelow. And even before we got near the target area we had to weave and dodge our way in. It got steadily worse as we flew steadily eastward toward the fine target of the Imperial Steel and Iron Works," Porter declared.

Flak Sprays Ship

"Flak began to spray the ship. The weaving searchlights picked us up time and again, only to lose us almost immediately. And then it happened.

"One field battery caught us in its fire. From that time on the whole cabin was lighted up like Madison Square Garden on hockey night..

"A whine and a sputter in the nose told us of a bullet hit; a thud on the right wing was a piece of shrapnel, as we found out later. We just turned and turned. Those faithful engines kept right on going without one moment's hesitation."

Porter said that after the bombs had been dropped on the target, seconds that had seemed hours before suddenly "became days in proportion of length."

"The ship pointed her nose upward, but still the searchlights held on. We climbed a bit, dropped a bit, and all this time cold steel

Continued on Page 8

Nazis Move 3 Belgian Princes Into Germany

London, June 16 (U.P.)—The Germans removed the three Belgian royal princes, Baudoin, Albert and Philip to Thuringer Wald, Germany, last Friday, thus separating them from King Leopold 3d, who was taken to Bavaria, the Belgian government announced today.

AQUEDUCT RESULTS

1—H. Smart 4.80-3.60-2.30, Star Song 11.80-4.50, One Evening 2.80. (1:21½)

2—Cousin Nan 5.70-3.70-3.50, Miss Sugar 4.60-4.10, Psychiatrist 9.00. (1:52)

DAILY DOUBLE PAID $27.10.

3—Pico Blanco II 12.60-5.80-4.00, Beneksar 19.80-8.60, Tioga 4.60. (2:25)

JAPS REPORT BONIN ISLES, KOREA BOMBED

Suggest Super-Forts Hit Defense Outpost After Blasting Nippon

By United Press

Japanese broadcasts reported American air attacks on Korea and the Bonin Islands, the latter 615 miles south of Tokyo, today, some 12 hours after disclosure that American B-29 Super-Fortresses had bombed Japan's home islands.

"Several enemy planes" bombed southern Korea, across Tsushima and Chosen Straits from Kyushu, Japanese home island which earlier broadcasts said had been the target of the Super-Fortresses, at 2 A.M. (Japanese Time) today, the official Domei Agency said.

Korea is across Tsushima and Chosen Straits from Kyushu, the Japanese homeland which the Tokyo radio said the B-29's hit.

Though the attacking planes were not identified, the hour of the attack suggested they may have been Superfortresses en route back to bases in China. Tokio said the industrial centers of Yawata, Moji and Kokura in northern Kyushu, were hit at 1:15 A. M. (Japanese time).

A Tokyo broadcast quoted an official communique that "some casualties had been sustained among ground units in northern Kyushu" but it claimed no damage had been done to air force or military installations. In a later broadcast, also recorded in San Francisco by United Press, Tokyo said air wardens had learned the American bombers were en route two hours before they appeared and "the enemy raiders have fallen an easy prey to our airtight defenses."

A Japanese imperial headquarters communique said an American task force had attacked the Bonin Islands Thursday afternoon (Japanese time) for the first time, raiding the islands of Chichi Jima and Iwo Jima.

"Our forces in that area intercepted the enemy and shot down more than 17 planes," the communique said. "Our losses were very slight."

The heavily-fortified Bonin group constitutes Japan's main defense outpost south of the home islands

Another Tokyo broadcast reported by government monitors said the Japanese cabinet met with Premier Gen. Hideeki Tojo today and heard reports that damage in the American raid on Kyushu was "very slight."

Bedroom Invader Is Outgeneraled By Service Wife

A young Manhattan matron whose husband is in the service talked fast at 2 a.m. today and outgeneraled a would-be assailant who had taken out a window screen and sneaked into her second-story bedroom.

Mrs. Florence Humphrey, 661 W. 222d St., was awakened by a light flashing in her eyes. When the intruder threatened harm, Mrs. Humphrey fought back with words. She spoke of her husband, of her four young children, the punishment he could expect when caught by police.

Finally she offered all the money she had. From a bureau drawer Mrs. Humphrey took $6 and handed it to the intruder.

"Lady," he said, "you need that money more than I do."

Mrs. Humphrey told police that he then bowed and walked out the front door.

Charles Town Results

1—Dashing Doe, 3.20, 2.60, 2.40; Mother Daisy, 9.00, 4.60; Wild Call, 4.60. Off time, 1:10.

2—Gun Bearer, 5.20, 2.80, 3.40; Crimson Lancer, 3.60, 3.20; Bellclapper, 16.40. Off time, 1:36½.

.. . DAILY DOUBLE PAID $14.20. . . ..

8 American Bundists Lose Citizenships

Boro Storm Trooper Leader Among Those Penalized by Court

Federal Judge Matthew T. Abruzzo today revoked the citizenship of eight notorious members of the German-American Bund, one of whom had ranked No. 2 nationally next to Fritz Kuhn.

The decision, which was filed in Brooklyn Federal Court, opens the way for Attorney General Francis Biddle to order the group before the Alien Enemy Hearing Board to determine whether they should be interned for the duration as alien enemies dangerous to the internal security of the United States. In the event of their internment, they will be deported to Germany after the war.

Judge Abruzzo's decision reflects on the current sedition trial at Washington, D. C., and touches specifically on the Baumgartner case which the U. S. Supreme Court overruled earlier this week.

19,000-Word Decision

The decision required 77 pages, encompassing 19,000 words, and capped the six-week trial of the Bundists who had been accused by U. S. Attorney Harold M. Kennedy with having obtained their citizenship fraudulently.

Kennedy issued the following statement to the Brooklyn Eagle:

"This decision should have a salutory effect. Too many persons accept the responsibilities of citizenship lightly and this case discloses that many apply for naturalization who have no real allegiance.

"This case indicates that tighter supervision is necessary before individuals are given the title of Americans. Furthermore, once a man becomes an American, he assumes a duty to act like one."

Long Resident in U. S.

The eight Bundists have resided in this country over long periods and several shuttled back and forth

Continued on Page 11

Henry Hauck · Carl Nicolay · Hugo Weiss · Karl Flick · F. W. Van den Bergh · Carl Bregler · Willy Seckel · Rudolph Markmann

Yank Forces Smashing Toward Saipan City

By WILLIAM F. TYREE

Pearl Harbor, June 16 (U.P.)—U. S. invasion troops, advancing under a curtain of shells and bombs from the biggest naval carrier task force in history, stormed inland from secure beachheads on the southwest coast of Saipan to day to within five miles of Garapan, the island's largest city.

(The Japanese Domei news agency, in a wireless transmission beamed to the United States, said the Americans landed "about one division," approximately 15,000 troops, on Saipan. The broadcast was recorded by U. S. Government monitors.)

(Another Domei dispatch said long-range Japanese guns on nearby Tinian island bombarded the naval force off Saipan and "heavily damaged and set afire" one American battleship.)

While the American warships stood offshore ready to meet any Japanese attempt to aid the island garrisons, the assault troops broke through the enemy defenses at Agingan point, turned back several armored counterattacks and struck into Charan Kanoa, where brisk fighting was reported.

Good Progress Reported

Admiral Chester W. Nimitz, in his second communique on the Marianas operations, said fighting was heavy but his troops were making "good progress" in their drive through Saipan, lying strategically in the middle of Japan's central Pacific island chain 1,449 miles southeast of Tokyo.

The Japanese were resisting fiercely with artillery, mortar and machine-gun fire in a desperate attempt to stop the American drive up the west coast of Saipan toward Garapan and Tanapag harbor, two miles farther north.

Possession of Tanapag, an almost land-locked harbor, would give the Pacific Fleet one of its best staging bases between Pearl Harbor and the China coast, the immediate goal set by Nimitz in his drive to Tokyo.

The invasion of Saipan, a volcanic peak island 15½ miles long and 4½ miles wide, outflanked the enemy's important Caroline Islands

Continued on Page 11

Insect Spray From Trees Killed 7 Cows, Owner Says

Islip, June 16—Insect spray that dripped from trees in Oakdale is blamed by a farmer for the death of seven cows.

The farmer, James Salvatore, has filed a complaint with the Islip town board in which he asks $1,500 from the tree-spraying company. It is the first case of the kind ever to come before the board.

British Planes Attack Convoy, Nazis Report

The German D. N. B. Agency reported today that British torpedo-carrying aircraft and bombers attacked a German convoy off the island of Borkum near the mouth of the German river Ems last night, scoring a hit on an escort vessel which later sank.

The dispatch, reported to United States Government monitors, said bombs also fell near some of the other ships, causing slight damage.

Show your pride in Brooklyn—buy all the War Bonds you can—and buy them in Brooklyn NOW—during the Fifth War Loan. Help YOUR borough meet its share of the $16,000,000,000 national quota.

U. S. FORCES SCORE GAINS IN NORMANDY

American Vanguards Menace Nazis' Escape Route From Cherbourg

By VIRGIL PINKLEY

Allied Supreme Headquarters, London, June 16 (U.P.) — American tank and infantry vanguards, spearheading a battering ram advance across the Normandy peninsula, drove to within a little more than two miles of the enemy's main escape highway and last railway from Cherbourg today.

On the other flank of the Normandy beachhead the Nazis reported they had blown up sluices and dikes at Caen, possibly foreshadowing abandonment of the ruined stronghold.

The weather turned the worst since D-Day and German resistance stiffened in a number of sectors, but Supreme Headquarters revealed that the Allies had hammered out gains, especially on the Cherbourg Peninsula where Lt. Gen. Omar N. Bradley's American troops were driving to cut off the great port.

Armored forces smashing across the waist of the peninsula on a 10-mile front were within two and one-half miles of St. Sauveur-Le Vicomte, rail and highway center vital to the maintenance or withdrawal of the German garrison in Cherbourg.

Allies Hold Caumont

To the northeast the Americans scored modest advances between Montebourg and Quineville, a four-mile coastal sector in which they were pushing toward Valognes and Cherbourg. Confused fighting still swirled through the ruins of Montebourg.

A headquarters spokesman revealed that the Allies were in firm possession of Caumont, hotly contested strong point at the center of the beachhead, and had pushed two miles southwest from it where British units met the enemy in strength and were fighting "superbly."

The German DNB news agency reported that Nazi engineers had blown up sluices and dikes at Caen,

Continued on Page 8

Ferry Coin-Tossing As Pastime Legal, Magistrate Rules

American citizens have a Constitutional right to flip coins on Staten Island-bound ferry boats, and they may, if they wish, even bet small amounts of change on the results, Magistrate Solomon said today in Staten Island Court. He castigated Patrolman Abe Martling who had arrested eight coin flippers.

The eight men, all longshoremen on a Staten Island army base, were whiling away the time while in transit from Brooklyn to work by flipping coins. Some were betting on the results.

They were arrested and hauled into court on disorderly conduct charges. Magistrate Solomon ruled that the arrest was an infringement on their legal rights and dismissed charges against them.

Bids Hungarion Envoys Disavow Pro-Nazi Rule

Vatican City, June 16 (U.P.)—Baron Gabriel Apor, Hungarian Minister to the Holy See, appealed to Hungarian diplomats in the neutral capitals of Europe today to disavow the present pro-Nazi government in Hungary.

His appeal, transmitted by the Vatican radio as a private message, went to Ministers in Bern, Stockholm, Lisbon, Madrid and Helsinki and to the Consul General in Istanbul. Helsinki was included "because Finland is not at war with the United States."

PILOTLESS PLANES ATTACK LONDON, SOUTH ENGLAND

By WALTER CRONKITE

London, June 16 (UP)—A fantastic stream of pilotless Nazi bombers rained fire and explosives across southern England all last night and throughout today, and radio Berlin said the robot fleet had smashed at London itself in "the beginning of vengeance" for the Allied attacks on Germany.

The Nazis, presumably still using the new mystery weapons, attacked on a smaller scale today than last night.

Adolf Hitler finally had launched his boasted secret weapon against Britain and the mighty invasion arsenal plied up on the island, and British official sources made no effort to minimize the gravity of the attack.

All southern England was alerted, and Home Secretary Herbert Morrison confirmed the existanee of the robot raiders and promised immediate counteraction in a statement to Commons.

A German high command communique said south England and the London City area were bombed last night with "new type explosives of very heavy caliber," and Berlin military commentators boasted that the mysterious raiders were "a new anti-invasion weapon of the greatest effect."

"The new weapon used against England is the beginning of vengeance" for the "barbaric" Allied bombing of the Nazi homeland, one enemy commentator said.

Reports from eyewitnesses who watched the Wellsian parade swoosh across southern England during the night poured into official London today, including one account that told of automatic machine guns raking the countryside.

Flashing across the night skies like a string of fiery comets, the mysterious projectiles whooshed down on scores of unidentified districts in southern England, exploding into gigantic balls of fire.

Eyewitness accounts of the raid varied, but all reports indicated that the missiles were either rocket-bombs or radio-controlled planes crammed with high explosives set to go off within a matter of seconds after striking the ground.

Challenged by RAF

Observers said the projectiles came over at terrific speeds, singly or in groups of two or three, some soaring 3,000 feet or more in the air and others slamming over the rooftops in level flight.

RAF night fighter pilots went up to challenge the robot raiders, diving recklessly through a terrific hail of flak thrown up by the British ground defenses in an effort to explode them in mid-air.

Many of the projectiles were believed to have been hit and eyewitnesses reported seeing tremendous explosions high overhead.

Many more fell with terrific impact on the countryside, and preliminary reports indicated that considerable damage and casualties resulted. Rescue squads still were digging through the wreckage for victims in a number of southern districts this afternoon.

Accounts of the bombing agreed on four major points:

1—The missiles traveled at tremendous speed.

2—All were equipped with bright tail and fuselage lights which flashed off just before the projectiles exploded.

3—They gave off a trail of fire and sparks, pparently from exhaust gases.

4—They traveled a remarkably straight course.

Pilots at one American air base

Continued on Page 8

Norris, Author, in Hospital

Charles G. Norris, author, was said to be "doing nicely" today in Doctors Hospital, Manhattan, after being reported to be in serious condition by his wife, Kathleen Norris, also a writer. He was stricken last Friday.

Robot Bomber Called Speedy 'Rocket Cigar'

Somewhere in Southern England, June 16 (U.P.)—American pilots who saw one of the Nazis' robot bombers pass over this area described it today as a stubby, cigar-shaped monoplane about 50 feet long that flew at high speed trailing flaming gases from its rocket exhaust.

If the rest of Britain reacts like the American fliers and their ground crews, the Nazis might as well keep their flying cigars home.

The Americans voiced the opinion that the Germans were using their robots mainly for propaganda purposes. The one sighted here, for example, came over at a very low altitude, and in broad laylight, as if the Nazis wanted to be certain everyone saw it.

Lt. Col. Leslie Bratton, deputy group commander at this base, said the plane was about as long the United States A-20 attack bomber and almost as big around as the Marauder.

Bratton said its wings were short and rounded and about one-third as long as the cylindrical fuselage.

The fliers got a "preview" when one of the mystery weapons passed about 4 o'clock Tuesday morning on a raid which was not announced until today.

Second Lt. Eugene J. Budrick said the projectiles made a "trampling, slamming sound," and Maj. Gordon W. Fowler said it resembled a twin-engined monoplane with a big white light amidships.

WHERE TO FIND IT

	Page		Page
Bridge	16	Real Estate	16
Comics	19	Society	6
Crossword	16	Sports	14, 15
Dr. Brady	10	Take My Word	10
Editorial	10	Theaters	8
Financial	9	These Women	16
Horoscope	16	Tommy Holmes	14
Movies	8	Uncle Ray	16
Novel	16	Want Ads	16, 17, 18
Obituaries	11	Wartime Problems	4
Our Fighters	4	Women	6

All-Out Drive Launched for Cherbourg

★ ★ ★ ★ ★ ★ ★
SPORTS 7
Wall Street Financial News

BROOKLYN EAGLE

WEATHER—Partly Cloudy, Humid Tonight; Cloudy, Thunderstorms Tomorrow.

103d Year. No. 170. DAILY & SUNDAY • (Copyright 1944 The Brooklyn Eagle, Inc.) • BROOKLYN, N. Y., THURSDAY, JUNE 22, 1944 • Entered at the Brooklyn Post-office as 2d Class Mail Matter • 3 CENTS IN NEW YORK CITY ELSEWHERE 4 CENTS

JAP FLEET DEFEATED BY U. S. CARRIER FORCE

AMERICANS OPEN ALL-OUT DRIVE TO SEIZE CHERBOURG

Hundreds of Planes Blast Nazis In One of Biggest Displays Since D-Day

By VIRGIL PINKLEY

Allied Supreme Headquarters, London, June 22 (U.P.)—American forces have launched an all-out attack on Cherbourg by land and air with hundreds of planes blasting the German fortifications in one of the greatest aerial displays since D-Day, while troops overwhelmed the suburban defense outpost of Martinvast.

Wave upon wave of United States light and medium bombers pounded and gunned German troops in the inner defenses of Cherbourg in a pulverizing bid to blast open the ring of fortifications for the siege army battering the burning city's defenses.

American siege forces probed the city fortifications and virtually isolated the doomed German garrison by driving almost to the sea on each side of it, a dispatch sent from the "vicinity of Cherbourg" at 10 a.m. reported.

"War correspondents are moving up for a box seat for the final battle of Cherbourg," Henry T. Gorrell of the United Press reported from outside the battered and burning French port.

"The enemy is manning his pillboxes of Festung Cherbourg, waiting for us, and stiff fighting for the seaport is anticipated."

Scores of towns and villages fell to Lt. Gen. Omar N. Bradley's troops closing in on Cherbourg, Gorrell reported, adding that the city's hours in German hands were believed numbered as the Allies prepared for a trip-hammer assault by land and air.

One prong of the steel arc clamped against Cherbourg had cut the coast highway to the east a short distance outside the city, and the other was within a few hundred yards of the one running west to Cap de la Hague.

The vanguard of the American column swinging east of Cherbourg hit the highway to St. Pierre-Eglise at several points, some of them southwest of Maupertus, five miles from the big port.

During the night advanced spearheads carried out intensive reconnaissance against the perimeter of the Cherbourg fortress area, drawing sharp German reaction, while main assault forces were driving through the suburbs for the final battle.

Find Dummy Minefields

American artillery hammered German positions and gun batteries throughout the night, with only occasional replies by the Nazi 88s. Some German minefields on the Cherbourg approaches turned out to be dummies when sappers investigated them.

The weather, unfavorable for flying for some days, was clearing, and there was every indication that Allied air forces were ready to join in the final assault on the Nazi garrison which ignored a surrender ultimatum and chose instead to make a fight of it.

Earlier front reports reaching Allied headquarters—admittedly 12 hours behind the actual fighting—placed the main American forces one to two miles below the city limits and two miles from the great harbor installations at the lower end of the inner basin.

Main Fight Not Joined

American patrols may have advanced even closer to the outskirts of the city, but an official spokesman said that up to noon yesterday the Americans had not pene-

Continued on Page 11

Boy, 16, Gets 10 Years In Rival Gang Shooting

County Judge Goldstein Subpenas Youths From Bedford Section to Witness Sentencing

At a practical symposium on juvenile delinquency, Kings County Judge Goldstein today gave 10 to 20 years imprisonment to a 16-year-old boy in a courtroom crowded with youths subpenaed from the Bedford-Stuyvesant section.

The object lesson submitted to the sullen witnesses was Joseph Parker of 12 Decatur St., who pleaded guilty May 31 to having shot and seriously wounded Joseph Foster, 16, of 354 Jefferson Ave., at Tompkins and Jefferson Aves. on March 28 at 10:30 p.m.

Last September Parker received a suspended sentence in Children's Court for carrying a dagger. He is currently under indictment in Manhattan for slashing another youth there across the face with a knife.

Reviewing the defendant's background, Judge Goldstein commented that he appeared destined to become a decent citizen until he joined the "Robins," one of the many gangs of youngsters from 13 to 17 who hang out on street corners, war upon

Continued on Page 3

Soldiers' Thirst Brings End to Brewery Strike

The 1,800 workers in eight Newark breweries who have been on strike for two weeks went back to work today, in compliance with a directive of the regional War Labor Board.

During the strike army and navy posts in the vicinity were short of beer. Officers had told the strikers the beer shortage was arousing the ire of soldiers and sailors and this is believed to have contributed greatly to calling off the strike.

Gun Dropped on Floor Shoots Cop in Jaw

Patrolman James O'Connor, 30, attached to the 135th St. precinct, Manhattan, was shot in the jaw today and is in serious condition at the Medical Center. O'Connor was injured when the service revolver of a fellow patrolman fell to the floor and accidentally was fired.

Dies at Night Club

Vincent Frith, Bermuda yachtsman, died shortly before midnight last night while at the 21 Club with a party of friends. The 42-year-old member of the Bermuda Commission suffered a heart attack. He lived in the Hotel Westbury, Manhattan.

PREDICTS FDR WILL ACCEPT 4TH TERM BID

President to Issue Statement Soon. Is Belief of Arnall

Washington, June 22 (U.P.)—Gov. Ellis Arnall of Georgia, after conferring with President Roosevelt, predicted today that the Chief Executive soon will issue a statement indicating his willingness to accept a fourth-term nomination if the Democratic Convention so desires.

Arnall told reporters as he left the Executive Office that he would "not be surprised" if Mr. Roosevelt makes "a big public statement" soon after the Republican Convention, but before the Democratic Convention. The Republicans meet next week; the Democrats July 19.

He said the President, in that statement, would be "taking the people of the country into his confidence" about his willingness — irrespecive of his personal desires—to abide by the party's decision, a willingness to submit to the mandates of the Democratic Convention."

Arnall then predicted that the President will be the Democratic nominee again, and defeat the Republican ticket—"particularly if it is headed by Governor Dewey—by a margin greater than he defeated Gov. Alf M. Landon in 1936."

Arnall also took sharp issue with the "attitude" of Democrats in Texas, Mississippi and South Carolina, where threats are being made that Democratic Presidential electors will cast their votes against Mr. Roosevelt.

Arnall told reporters that the President was "quite delighted to hear that Senator George is coming back to the Senate."

"He thinks quite highly of Senator George," Arnall said, "and was delighted to learn that the people were returning him."

Senator Walter F. George (D., Ga.), was one of Mr. Roosevelt's primary targets in his "purge" campaign of 1938.

Hear War Contract Termination Plan

Representatives of 200 war plant owners, at a meeting held under the auspices of the Brooklyn Chamber of Commerce in the St. George Hotel, today heard army and navy officers explain the mechanics of war contract termination, which will become a growing important issue as the end of the war draws near.

Robert F. Nelson, vice president of the Arma Corporation, who presided, outlined the problem at the outset and, as an example of the complexities involved, listed 12 cost items that could be legitimately included in billing the Government on a contract and five others that cannot.

Among speakers from the army and navy were Col. Curtis G. Pratt, Lt. Col. Charles E. Miller, Maj. E. Stratton, Lt. Comm. E. H. Eaton and Capt. Arthur Wadsworth.

600 Labor to Complete Landing Craft in 18 Hours

Boston, June 22 (U.P.)—Workmen at the George Lawley & Son Corporation's Neponsit Shipyard began work today on a 150-foot prefabricated landing craft that they hope to complete within 18 hours to set an all-time record.

Approximately 600 workers reported on the job at 7 a.m. to work straight through until the infantry landing craft is launched at about 1 a.m. tomorrow.

7th Day of Coma

Boston, June 22 (U.P.)—The condition of Mrs. Francis Lee Higginson Jr., 31, socialite wife of a navy officer, was unchanged today as she entered her seventh day of coma resulting from a mysterious beating in her West Cornwall, Conn., home Thursday night.

All That Fuss Over Nothing

A false alarm at 6 a.m. today at Penn Station brought 11 fire engines and four radio patrol cars to the scene. An extensive search of the station failed to disclose any signs of a fire.

Admiral Spruance

Admiral Maps Strategy As Symphonies Play

Spruance, Youngest of Rank, Doesn't Smoke And Rarely Drinks—Called Best Tactician

Washington, June 22 (U.P.) — The navy's high command was confident long before the American and Japanese fleet units tangled in the Pacific that the outcome would be as favorable as Admiral Nimitz reported today—and the reason for the optimism was Raymond Ames Spruance, who at 57 is the youngest full Admiral in the United States Navy.

Spruance, who commanded the 5th Fleet in its smashing air victory over a substantial portion of the imperial Jap navy, was virtually unknown to the public before the historic Marshall Islands invasion. But within the navy he has long been regarded as one of the greatest—if not the greatest—tacticians in the fleet.

High navy officials reposed such confidence in him because they know that he will capitalize on any break that comes his way. And they know, too, that he isn't one to wait for the breaks if he finds a chance for developing a tactical opportunity.

He doesn't smoke and rarely takes a drink. He is a lover of classical music. Sometimes, when he runs into a particularly tricky problem, he tries to think it out by retiring to his cabin to hear a symphonic recording on his phonograph.

Has Caught Japs Flat-Footed

Spruance, lean and gray-eyed, has been lucky so far. He has caught the Japanese flat-footed time and again. He was in command of a task force in the battle of Midway when the Japanese fleet was turned back in ignominious defeat.

He planned and commanded the Gilbert Islands and Marshalls campaigns and later the attacks on Palau, Yap and other enemy strong-

Continued on Page 11

Borough E Bond Sales Reach 18.9% of Quota

With Brooklyn residents buying more than $500,000 worth of E bonds yesterday, the borough total of E bond buying since the start of the 5th War Loan campaign, as of last night, was announced today at $9,055,773, or 1^.9 percent of quota.

Total sales to individuals in all bond denominations rose at the same time to $18,116,141.

While Brooklyn pushed ahead in far-flung efforts to achieve its quotas, Ted R. Gamble, national War Finance director, announced in Washington that sales to individuals through Tuesday had reached $1,081,000,000, or more than 18 percent of the $6,000,000,000 quota for individuals. The overall quota is $16,000,000,000.

At the same time one Brooklyn section, Bay Ridge, voluntarily assumed a quota five times that originally set for it.

Sylvester A. Miniter, recently appointed chairman of the war loan drive, made the announcement. Bay Ridge, he said, had increased its quota from $1,000,000 to $5,000,000, a sum far in excess of the quotas and the amounts raised in any of the previous war loans. The money is to be earmarked for erection and equipment of two hospitals for overseas wounded.

To keep track of the Bay Ridge

Continued on Page 11

Thrill of a Lifetime

Pittsurgh, June 22 (U.P.)—The highest bidder at a war bond auction Monday will be given a ride through downtown Pittsburgh on a hook and ladder fire truck with the siren screaming.

Show your pride in Brooklyn—buy all the War Bonds you can—and buy them in Brooklyn NOW—during the Fifth War Loan. Help YOUR borough meet its share of the $16,000,000,000 national quota.

AQUEDUCT RESULTS

1—Respire 11.60-6.10-5.00, Rec'd Crop 4.60-4.40, Scotch Mound 10.70. (1:21)
2—Lady Olga, first; Offenbach, second; One Look, third.

14 Ships Smashed In Battle Off Luzon

By WILLIAM F. TYREE

Pearl Harbor, June 22 (UP)—The United States fleet defeated a powerful unit of the Japanese Grand Fleet off the Philippines Monday, sinking or damaging 14 enemy warships, including four aircraft carriers and a battleship, to score one of America's greatest naval victories of the war.

An extraordinary announcement at Admiral Chester W. Nimitz' headquarters at 4 a.m. (9:30 a.m. Brooklyn time) today revealed that planes of the United States 5th Fleet pounced on the Japanese warships as they emerged from the channel between Luzon and Formosa.

In an air-sea battle reminiscent of Midway, the surface units never coming to grips, the Americans trounced the formidable Japanese force and sent its survivors limping back to the safety of their own waters.

The Americans lost 49 planes, today's communique said without mentioning loss of or damage to the ships of Admiral Raymond A. Spruance's 5th Fleet.

The Japanese force comprised four or more battleships, five or six carriers, five fleet tankers and attached cruisers and destroyers, the preliminary official accounting of the attack said.

One aircraft carrier, believed to be of the Syokaku class, received three 1,000-bomb hits.

One carrier of the Hayataka class was sunk.

One carrier of the same class was badly damaged and left burning furiously.

One light carrier of the Zuiho or Taiho class received at least one bomb hit.

One battleship of the Kongo class was damaged.

One cruiser was damaged.

Three destroyers were damaged and one of them believed sunk.

Three tankers were sunk and the two others badly damaged and left ablaze.

Continued on Page 2

VICTORY SPEEDS DRIVE FOR TOKYO, STIMSON AVERS

Calls It Mighty Impetus To Advance Into Inner Defenses of Japan

Washington, June 22 (U.P.)—The American naval victory off the Philippines "will be a mighty impetus to the speeding of our advance across the Pacific and into the inner defenses of Japan," Secretary of War Stimson declared today.

"The landings on the Island of Saipan in the Marianas and the first attack by B-29 Superfortresses on Japan already have called attention to the retrogressing lines of Japanese defense," Stimson said at a press conference.

He said the Superfortress attack "is only the first of many which will be directed with increasing strength and frequency against Japan."

Concerning the naval situation, the action off the Philippines was assessed as a sizable victory, but observers tempered this with the notation that the long-desired showdown battle with the enemy's fleet still remains to be fought.

Reveals Tough Opposition

Of the invasion of Saipan, Stimson said:

". . . The fighting as we advanced over the beaches was as bitter as any in the central Pacific."

Of the naval situation, observers emphasized that the Japanese formation encountered between the Philippines and the Marianas was strong, but hardly the whole or a major portion of the enemy's navy.

While greatly pleased by the results of the engagement in which four and possibly five Japanese ships were sunk and nine damaged, naval observers also noted some disappointment among those who had hoped that a large part of the enemy fleet could have been disposed of.

Still a Formidable Foe

They pointed out that of the ships definitely known to be sunk only one was a combat ship, a new-type Hayataka-class carrier. The other three sunk were tankers. And even if most of the other combat ships damaged—which included three carriers, a battleship, a cruiser and three destroyers—were to sink as a result of their wounds, the Japanese still would be left with a strong fleet.

In the opinion of some the Japanese fleet engaged was in reality a strong task force evidently bent on hitting the American task force covering the Saipan invasion.

Nazi General Hellmich Killed at Cherbourg

London, June 22 (U.P.)—A German communique, broadcast by D. N. B. News Agency, disclosed today the death of Lt. Gen Hellmich, commander of the German 243d Infantry Division, while fighting on the Cherbourg peninsula last Saturday. He was the second German general reported killed in two days.

Bad Check Jails Writer

Mario Amato, 41, son of the late opera baritone, Pasquale Amato, was sentenced to three months in the workhouse yesterday in Special Sessions Court, Manhattan, after pleading guilty to a charge of passing a worthless check. He is a writer.

Court Denies Appeal Of Nazi Spy's Associate

The appeal of Helmut Leiner, German-born Queens gardener, who was sentenced to 18 years imprisonment for dealing with the Nazi spy, Edward John Kerling, has been turned down by the United States Circuit Court of Appeals. Kerling, one of the German sabouteurs sent here by submarine, was executed.

In his appeal Leiner contended that the "trading with the enemy" statute was unconstitutional and failed to forbid the transactions of which he was accused. He had pleaded guilty to facts which the Government held were in violation of this law. The Circuit Court of Appeals upheld the statute in its decision.

Tokyo Bluff? Plans Salvage Of Superfortresses in Sea

By United Press

Tokyo Radio said today that operations had been started to salvage several B-29 Superfortresses which the Japanese claimed crashed into the sea during the raid on northern Kyushu last week.

The broadcast said that at least four of the huge planes, which hit Japan proper from Chinese bases, were known to have gone down at sea.

Japanese aviation experts hope to recover the planes intact, Tokyo said, in order to study their structure.

Superfortress Workers Protest Labor Board Delay

Orange, N. J., June 22 (U.P.)—Union officials said today they expected 1,500 workers soon would join the 100 who yesterday walked off the job at the Monroe Calculating Machine Company plant, which makes parts for B-29 Superfortresses.

The union, terming the walkout a "protest stoppage," said it was aimed at the War Labor Board's delay in giving a wage decision on a disputed contract which has been before the board since September.

Evelyn Ankers Expecting

Hollywood, June 22 (U.P.)—Actress Evelyn Ankers disclosed today she is expecting a baby in October. She is the wife of Richard Denning, actor, now in the navy.

WHERE TO FIND IT

	Page		Page
Bridge	16	Real Estate	19
Comics	19	Society	6
Crossword	16	Sports	14, 15
Dr. Brady	10	Take My Word	10
Editorial	10	Theaters	4, 5
Financial	16	These Women	20
Horoscope	16	Tommy Holmes	14
Movies	4, 5	Uncle Ray	16
Novel	16	Want Ads 16, 17, 18	
Obituaries	11	Wartime Problems	12
Our Fighters	12		
Radio	19	Women	8

SCREEN

Kid Star to Play in Film About Reformation of Nazi-Trained Dog

"Rusty," a new type of "boy-and-a-dog" tale, is being prepared by Al Martin to star Ted Donaldson when he returns to his home lot, Columbia. The ten-year-old player is currently completing the role of Neely in "A Tree Grows in Brooklyn" at 20th Century-Fox. The Columbia picture, to be produced by Sam Bischoff, treats of the reformation of a vicious Nazi-trained dog by a young boy. "Rusty," Donaldson's fourth film, will be the first solo starring vehicle for the youngster. He scored a personal triumph in "Once Upon a Time" with Cary Grant and Janet Blair, following which he played an important role in the soon to be released Edward G. Robinson starrer, "Mr. Winkle Goes to War."

In accordance with Paramount's pledge to the motion picture industry a year ago," "For Whom the Bell Tolls," the Ernest Hemingway film, will be withdrawn from release as a road show attraction on Aug. 1 and will not be shown again until Feb. 25, when it will be released for showing at popular prices.

Tom Neal and Ann Savage will play the leads in "A Nazi in the U. S. A.," Columbia drama of an escaped German war prisoner. One of the top featured roles has been given to Howard Freeman. Robert Wilmot will direct. This will be the first feature directorial assignment in the United States for Wilmot, once a noted Continental director. Abroad he directed such stars as S. Z. Sekall, Walter Slezak and Franciska Gael, while the 22 films for which he is responsible include "White Lilacs," "Rasputin," "The Little Cafe" and "Jealousy."

After completing his starring role in "Two Years Before the Mast," William Bendix will come to New York on his first visit here in two years. Accompanied by his wife, the actor will come East for the premiere of 20th Century-Fox's "Wilson." Bendix will leave Hollywood July 24 and will return shortly after Aug. 1.

Dietrich-Robinson-Raft At Strand Tomorrow

Edward G. Robinson, Marlene Dietrich and George Raft in "Manpower," the story of a couple of danger-loving linemen whose lives become inextricably bound up with an extravagantly luscious blond trouble-maker, will be the next attraction at the Brooklyn Strand Theater beginning tomorrow. The co-feature will be "They Made Me a Criminal," co-starring John Garfield, and Ann Sheridan with Claude Rains, the Dead End Kids, May Robson and Gloria Dickson. Both these pictures are Warner Bros. hits of a few seasons back.

'Christmas Holiday' Goes Into Second Week

Getting off to a flying start with record-breaking business since its opening, Universal's "Christmas Holiday," starring Deanna Durbin and Gene Kelly, will be held over at Loew's Criterion Theater for a second week beginning today. The picture is from W. Somerset Maugham's novel of the same title.

MOVIE TIME SCHEDULE

BROOKLYN

ALBEE—"Show Business," 11:00, 2:05, 4:50, 7:40, 10:30; "A Night of Adventure," 1:00, 3:50, 6:35, 9:25.
METROPOLITAN—"See Here, Pvt. Hargrove," 12:35, 3:55, 7:17, 10:39; "Voice in the Wind," 11:01, 2:23, 5:45, 9:07.
STRAND—"Man From Frisco," 11:00, 1:45, 4:40, 7:35, 10:30; "Follow the Leader," 12:40, 3:25, 6:20, 9:15.

MANHATTAN

CRITERION—"Christmas Holiday," 9:50, 11:40, 1:35, 3:25, 5:20, 7:10, 9:05, 11:00, 12:50.
MUSIC HALL—"Once Upon a Time," 9:05, 11:41, 2:17, 4:56, 7:50, 10:27. Stage, 10:51, 1:27, 4:03, 6:56, 9:36.
PARAMOUNT—"Going My Way," 10:18, 1:31, 4:51, 8:04, 10:29. Stage, 12:45, 4:05, 7:18, 10:31.
RIVOLI—"Story of Dr. Wassell," 10:00, 12:40, 3:20, 6:00, 8:40, 11:30.
ROXY—"Home in Indiana," 10:30, 1:30, 4:30, 7:30, 10:30. Stage, 12:30, 3:30, 6:30, 9:25.

MARLENE DIETRICH, with E. G. Robinson and George Raft in "Manpower," coming to the Strand tomorrow.

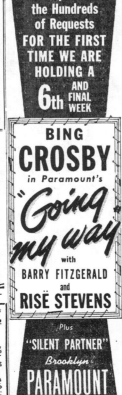

THEATER By Arthur Pollock

The Theater Takes a Vote and Picks Out the Best From Among Its People

The chosen people of the theater—chosen by the people of the theater themselves—have been stepping up to the mike at 5 o'clock for the last two days to accept awards for their achievements during the past season. The awards were the Donaldson Awards, given by The Billboard in the name of the founder of that publication, William H. Donaldson. The men and women who decided to whom they should go are the men and women of all branches of the theater.

So when on Monday afternoon Paul Robeson stood at a microphone in CBS' Radio Theater No. 4 on W. 54th St. to accept a parchment on which was inscribed a statement that he was adjudged the best actor of the year, it was his own people, the people of the theater, who had so judged him—actors, stage hands, press agents, treasurers, ticket sellers, producers, critics. Almost everybody gives awards to playwrights and actors these days, most of the donors having nothing to do with the stage save as admirers. Now at last those who live by the theater are choosing from among themselves the men and women they most esteem. It is very nice.

So, take it from the theater itself, Paul Robeson in "Othello" gave the finest performance of the year in a play without music. According to the stage hands, the ticket sellers, the producers, the playwrights, the critics, Margaret Sullavan in "The Voice of the Turtle" played better than any other woman star in what is called the legitimate.

In musical comedy it was Bobby Clark of "Mexican Hayride" whose fellow theater folk judged him the best male player, while the sunburned Mary Martin of "One Touch of Venus" came out ahead of all others as the most admired of the gals.

Jose Ferrer, for his performance in "Othello," was named as having distinguished himself more than any other actor in a supporting role in the more serious plays. For her work in "The Voice of the Turtle" Audrey Christie got the woman's award and brightened up the broadcast. June Havoc of "Mexican Hayride," present with a bum knee and on crutches, won the vote as best female supporting player in a musical, and Kenny Baker of "One Touch of Venus" as best among the male supporting roles.

Sona Osato of the same musical comedy, was adjudged the most proficient girl dancer, Paul Haakon of "Hayride" the most expert dancing man.

There were many other awards. "The Voice of the Turtle" won most hearts as the best play of the season. "Carmen Jones" triumphed as the best musical, bringing awards to Oscar Hammerstein 2d for both the best libretto and the best lyrics and to Hassard Short as best musical comedy director, to Howard Bay as best scenic designer, to Raoul Pene Du Bois as best costume designer.

Agnes de Mille, who has brought new grace and wit to the theater, was considered by her fellow folk of the stage the best choreographer for her dances in "One Touch of Venus." Moss Hart won the award for the best direction of a legitimate play, his own, "Winged Victory." Stewart Chaney was tapped for his settings in "The Voice of the Turtle."

WHEN OUT OF TOWN REGISTER FROM BROOKLYN

'Since You Went Away' Next at the Capitol

Capitol Theater will hold over for two more weeks "Two Girls and a Sailor." July 20 has been set for the concurrent world premieres of David O. Selznick's "Since You Went Away" and Gene Krupa's own new orchestra. "Two Girls and a Sailor," features Jimmy Durante, Lena Horne, Gracie Allen and the orchestras of Harry James and Xavier Cugat.

FEATURE FILMS SHOWING TODAY

BAY RIDGE
Electra, 75th St. and Third Ave. ... Wake Up and Live; also Four Men and a Prayer
Harbor, 92d St. and Fourth Ave. ... Trocadero; also Texas Masquerade
Stanley, Fifth Ave. and 75th St. ... Scarface; also Hell's Angels

BEDFORD
Lincoln, Bedford Ave.-Eastern P'kway ... Iceland; also Gentleman After Dark
National, 720 Washington Ave. ... Broadway Rhythm; also Her Primitive Man
Rogers, 333 Rogers Ave. PR. 4-2230 ... Northwest Passage; also Third Finger, Left Hand

BENSONHURST
Colony, 18th Ave.-65th St. BE. 6-2231. Stand By for Action; also Kiss the Boys Goodbye

BORO PARK
Elton, 43d St. and New Utrecht Ave. ... The Frisco Kid; also Get Hep to Love

BOROUGH HALL AND DOWNTOWN
Century's Tivoli, Fulton St., Boro Hall. Passion Island; also That Natzy Nuisance
Duffield, Duffield and Fulton Sts. ... Uncertain Glory; also Lady, Let's Dance
Momart, Fulton St. and Rockwell Pl. ... Flight Command; also Road Show
St. George Playhouse, 100 Pineapple St. Passage to Marseille; also Task Force
Terminal, Fourth Ave. and Dean St. ... Broadway Rhythm; also Her Primitive Man

BRIGHTON BEACH
Oceana, Brighton Beach Ave.-Hoff St. ... Hitler Dead or Alive; also Trocadero

BUSHWICK
Empire, Ralph Ave.-B'way. FO. 9-7940. Northwest Passage; also Third Finger, Left Hand

FLATBUSH
Flatbush, Flatbush and Church Aves. ... Tomorrow the World
Granada, Church and Nostrand Aves. ... Birth of the Blues; also Mr. Bug Goes to Town
Leader, Coney Island and Newkirk Aves. ... I Wake Up Screaming; Tall, Dark and Handsome

EAST FLATBUSH
Avenue D, Avenue D and E. 43d St. ... Northwest Passage; also Third Finger, Left Hand
Rugby, Utica and Church Aves. ... The Purple Heart; also Seven Days Ashore

GERRITSEN BEACH
Graham, 311 Whitney Ave. ... The Lodger; also Sailor's Holiday

PARK SLOPE
Carlton, Flatbush and Seventh Aves. ... Uncertain Glory; also Lady, Let's Dance
Plaza, Flatbush Ave. and Park Place ... Trocadero; Dizzy Pirates; Lady and the Monster
Sanders, Prospect Park West-14th St. ... Passage to Marseille; also Pardon My Rhythm
New Venus, 1224 Prospect Ave. ... This Is the Life; also The Impostor

KINGS HIGHWAY
Jewel, Kings Highway at Ocean P'kway ... Our Wife; also Three Faces West

AVENUE U SECTION
Avenue U, Avenue U and E. 16th St. ... Buffalo Bill; also Jam Session
Traymore, Avenue N and E. 46th St. ... The Purple Heart; also Seven Days Ashore

RIDGEWOOD
Colonial, Broadway and Chauncey ... Uncertain Glory; also Lady, Let's Dance
Ridgewood, 1673 Myrtle Ave. ... My Best Gal; also That Natzy Nuisance
Rivoli, Myrtle-Wilson Aves. GL. 5-0744. Lost Angel; also Rationing
Starr, Knickerbocker Ave. and Starr ... Buffalo Bill; also Jam Session

SHEEPSHEAD BAY
Sheepshead, Sheepshead Rd.-Voorhies ... Passage to Marseille; also My Best Gal

SOUTH BROOKLYN
Sanders Globe, 228 15th St. ... Northwest Passage; also That Natzy Nuisance

Mrs. Dewey, Fine Homemaker, Prefers the Background

Although Vitally Interested in Career Of Her Governor-Husband, Family Life Comes First With Her

By BETTY BAUER
United Press Staff Correspondent

Frances Eileen Hutt Dewey has a definite preference for the quiet of her farm home and the companionship of her family to any publicity and accord she might receive as wife of the Republican Presidential candidate.

Since 1931, her husband has either held public office or been in the public eye, and Mrs. Dewey has worked hard at remaining in the background as much as possible. However, she is a good campaigner and, although she would prefer not to, always travels with her husband on his political tours.

A thorough dislike for publicity often has resulted in her being termed "unassuming," "retiring" and "shy." But at home—the executive mansion or the farm, "Dapplemere," at Pawling—Mrs. Dewey is gay, vital and a sparkling hostess. She has an easy wit and laughs and jokes continually with her family.

Mrs. Dewey also is well-informed and has a mind of her own. When the Governor is preparing a speech, the next to the final draft is always submitted to her, and her suggestions and criticisms carry a lot of weight. Both are avid newspaper readers and keep up to the minute on community, national and world affairs.

Although vitally interested in her husband's career, Mrs. Dewey is above all else a homemaker and mother of the Dewey sons, Thomas E., 11, and John Martin, 8, whom both she and the Governor are determined to keep untouched by their official public life.

Takes Charge of Menus

Mrs. Dewey's days at the executive mansion are spent in keeping the huge building and grounds in smooth running order. She has a competent staff of servants and with the chef plans the menus, going to particular pains—just like any other housewife—when guests are expected.

When alone, the Governor and Mrs. Dewey dine with their sons about 6:30 o'clock and the boys then retire about 8. This happens generally at least twice a week, and sometimes more. If there are guests, Mrs. Dewey plans dinner for 8 or 8:30.

Although, since Mr. Dewey has been Governor, they have spent most of their time in Albany, the apple of all the Dewey eyes is "Dapplemere," where they live a quiet farm life with a few close friends. Their 150-year-old Dutch frame house is surrounded by spacious lawns, a variety of shade trees and a white picket fence. They bought the place in 1939, after renting it for two years. Besides the 12-room house, which Mrs. Dewey keeps going with but one or two help, there are two six-room houses on the property, used by the farmers who work their 486 acres of land.

Born in Texas

Mrs. Dewey is a quiet, soft-spoken Texan. She was born in Sherman, Tex., Feb. 17, 1903, the daughter of Orlo T. Hutt, a railroad man. Her great-great grand uncle was Jefferson Davis, president of the Confederacy.

The brown-eyed Mrs. Dewey dresses conservatively, tending to smart, tailored clothes. She wears black a great deal, but turns to colors for dinner and evening dresses. She likes to shop by herself and may be seen going in and out of Albany stores or window-shopping with the rest of the crowd.

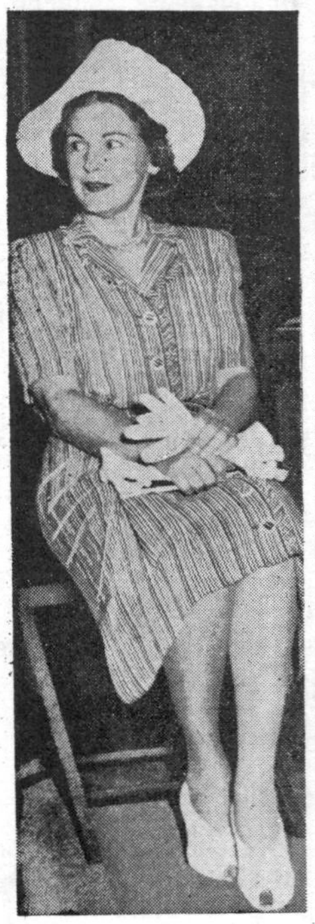

COOL . . . poised . . . impression Mrs. Dewey leaves.

MRS. DEWEY and her two boys chatting with the Rev. Ralph Lankler after Sunday services in Christ Church, Quaker Hills.

AT THE FARM—Governor and Mrs. Dewey.

Shop talk for Man Hunters:

Beauty Is a Complicated Business —Calls for a Definite Technique

Leave us talk about beauty . . . stuff about refrigerator complexions . . . starry eyes bright with eye wash . . . that Dalmatian look and how the camel can influence the Pink Garter . . .

Comes the ayem and either you are all peaches and cream and spit curls, have a tan, or look like a Dalmatian. If you're the peaches-and-cream type try putting yourself on ice. Well, anyway, run an ice cube over your face before you dash powder on it . . . then powder really stays on for hours, just like it says on the advertisements . . . .

If you're a Dalmatian type get up early—you've got lots to do . . . Freckles, as every owner knows, are a blight . . . They never confine themselves to the bridge of the nose, like they do on magazine story heroines . . . A good powder base is the ONLY way to play them down . . . Never a light one, but a good substantial mocha color, and just pat your friends on the head when they ask (and they will) why do you wear such dark make-up when you have such light skin . . .

Lucky people with tans can just apply soap and water, skip powder and look perfect . . .

The foundation laid, comes next the lipstick . . . Lipstick is best applied with a brush, and one of really good camel's hair is not too hard to find. Pink Garter is way over on the pastel side, but it isn't orangy and it isn't purplish . . . For deep tans, Bali, a dark red, rates more than a quick brush . . .

Nobody wants you to be glassy-eyed, but what's the point in rivaling a flounder just because it's **early???** To convince your eyes that they're supposed to shine, whip up a little boric acid and dunk them in it or try one of the commercial washes that come in nice fancy bottles . . .

Eye shadow or beady mascara looks pretty crumby in daylight, and besides, the Theda Bara age is all over now . . . However, liquid mascara does do a smooth job replacing eyebrow pencil on eyebrowless blondes and redheads . . .

Having supplied a thoroughly conservative background, you can now accent the job with a dash of peroxide and a comb. Hair-bleaching is not a job for semi-pros, even if you **happen** to be a chem major . . . but running a comb dipped in peroxide through the hair lights up brown hair and looks **completely** legit . . . Even the most conservative go for the very blond forelock that Conover blondes and brownettes have adopted . . . You know, the sun, my deah . . . S. McK.

Ceylon expects to produce at least 125,000 tons of copra this year.

Additional Society and Women's News on Page 12

The Menu

SATURDAY NIGHT SUPPER

Clear Consomme — *Cheese Crackers*
Salad Platter — *Sliced Tongue*
Plum Shortcake — *Iced Coffee*

SALAD PLATTER

4 medium tomatoes
1 cucumber
6 lettuce cups
6 slices whole wheat bread
1 cup cottage cheese
Radishes, Scallions
Dressing

Peel and slice the tomatoes and cucumber. Arrange slices in lettuce cups. Remove the crusts from the bread and spread the slices with soft butter and cottage cheese, then roll them into cones. Place a cone in each lettuce cup with the tomato and cucumber.. Garnish with radishes and scallions. Serve with mayonnaise or French dressing.

Local Women Attend Reunion in Mystic

Mrs. Frank H. Parcells, past president general of the Daughters of Founders and Patriots of America and Mrs. J. Richard Wiggins, Registrar general of the National Society New England Women, will attend the annual reunion of the Capt. George and Ann Borodel Society at the Denison Manor House at Mystic, Conn., tomorrow.

The Ration Calendar

PROCESSED FOODS—Blue stamps A8 through Z8, also blue stamp A5 in War Book 4 are now valid and good indefinitely. Four more blue stamps, B5, C5, D5 and F5, are valid Aug. 1 and will be good indefinitely. Each blue stamp is valid at ten points.

MEATS AND FATS—Many meats, also canned fish, have been reduced to zero point value. Red stamps A8 through Z8 in War Book 4 are good for five pounds indefinitely. Red Stamps A5, B5 and C5 are valid as of July 30. Each red stamp is valued at ten points.

SUGAR—Sugar stamps, 30, 31 and 32 in War Book 4 are good for five points of of sugar each and are good indefinitely. Sugar stamp 40 in War Book 4 is good for five pounds of sugar for home canning only and will be good through Feb 28, 1945. Applications may be made at rationing boards for additional maximum of ten pounds per person between July 16 and Oct. 31.

HELEN WORTH

Wife Finds Flying Fatigue Upsetting As Army Flyer Lets Hammer Fly at Home

Dear Helen Worth—My husband is an army flyer—takes bombers all over the world. When I married him four years ago, he had the sweetest, kindest nature you could imagine.

For a year now he has been acting so strangely. Sometimes kind, sometimes terrible. I never know which it will be. He drinks terribly at times. I'm no drinker and I hate it all.

The other day he blew up at me over nothing, or a very minor cause where he'd dare not take it out on any officers overranking him, or his buddies. Friends say for me to consider him mentally ill and to treat him as such, to talk with him but not let him know I feel any sympathy for him. The psychiatrist said I was the only one who could adjust him, so although I'd take the humiliating side, etc., it'd pay in the long run and we'd save our home.

Sent Red Roses

I felt I was strong enough mentally and I tackled the job. He melted at once and practically fell at my feet. He left last month on an overseas trip with the understanding I'd wait here for his return and talk to him again and if things didn't suit me I'd then leave him. He sent me a dozen red roses to be delivered after his departure. The same day came a card with "love and good health." So he has evidently thought a good bit and on this trip will think more.

He is a very odd person, somewhat an introvert, and the psychiatrist says he appears to have inferiority feeling with me, which must be corrected with my help.

However, I couldn't see what I had done and felt he was taking wrong slant but I couldn't correct things. However, the psychiatrist seems to have guided me in right direction to start ball rolling and I'm going to make myself big enough to give him another chance. The doctors claim many men in flying work are mentally upset, nervous and after a time have flying fatigue which affects each one differently.

All this was written before last night, when he threatened my life with a hammer. Screamed (he was drunk again), and the next door neighbors came in. What shall I do now? I can't stay here on an army post—I'm too humiliated. But if I leave, can I make him support me?

M. L.

No Happy Ending

My dear M. L.—Unless you are physically incapable of self-support, my advice is to find work in some other city. Today, there is a crying need for workers in every field. By your handwriting and manner of expression I am sure that you would be able to earn a living. For myself—I'd prefer bread and milk and peace— to "a stalled oxen and hatred therewith."

We shall pay more dearly than we can even now realize for the worldwide holocaust.

Drunkenness and emotional instability are unhappy companions. You have made a sincere effort to help him—let him do a little trying now for YOUR approval!

Truly—it is a sordid story that I fear can have no happy ending.

HELEN WORTH.

Ordinary Civility

Dear Helen Worth—Would it be possible for you to print, from time to time, a few pointers on manners? It seems to me that so many people today are lacking in the first principles of ordinary civility. Look about you in public places, and you will see what I mean.

P. A. S.

Need for Manners

My dear P. A. S.—Although I honestly think that many lessons in ordinary manners are needed, how much good do you think an occasional sermon would do?

Perhaps it is because of war nerves, but certainly one meets on all sides indifference or discourtesy. Today, I saw an older woman change her seat at a soda fountain so that a young couple might sit together. There was not one word of appreciation—no murmured thank you. Surely a few lessons to those two might be useful!

Just now, it's too hot to sermonize—but do remind me of your suggestion when it's cooler; please!

HELEN WORTH.

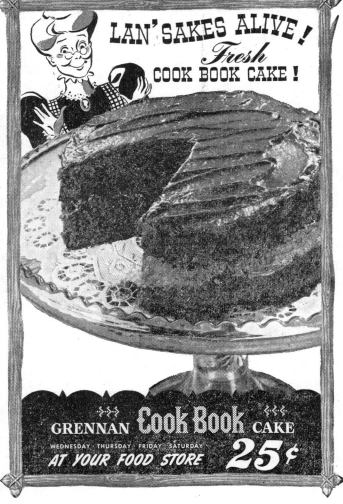

Mother's Diet Aids Health Of Newborn

Balanced Selection Of Food Helps Avoid Physical Deficiencies

By MARGARET PETTIGREW

As a result of food research conducted during the past two years, the Nutrition Foundation, Inc., has come out with a strong plea for better diets for mothers-to-be. Putting a punch into that plea is the Foundation's published report which says that malformations, such as missing toes, cleft palate and poorly formed jaws are "induced by moderately poor diets and are prevented by an improved diet based originally on supplementary liver or yeast."

Such findings as these emphasize the fact that wise diet plans are a must for the mother-to-be. Doctors stress the value of and the need for a well-rounded diet. But perhaps every mother will have a greater understanding of her need if we take that diet apart and see why each item is so important both to the mother and to the unborn child.

Consider first the importance of milk in the diet. A baby must have calcium for the formation of bones and teeth which grow before the baby is born. Milk or milk products (cheese), soy beans, oysters, clams, canned salmon (don't pick out the bones) and dark green leaves, such as turnip greens, mustard greens and kale must be prominent in the mother's diet if those bones and teeth are to be well formed and strong. If these calcium rich foods are not plentiful in the dietary, the mother's teeth will be the first to show the calcium drain on her system. Years ago, before we knew of this connection between calcium foods, teeth and bones, we used to say: "You lose a tooth with each child born."

Now we know that such a loss can be prevented.

Liver Once a Week

During the pre-natal period the baby stores up a great deal of iron. The mother must supply that iron from her dietary and thus help avoid severe anemia after the baby is born. She can help herself in that duty by including liver in her dietary at least once a week, an egg a day, dark green leaves, potatoes, whole grain breads and cereals every day and dark molasses frequently.

According to medical authorities, vitamins play a big role in the health of both mother and child. Your doctor may prescribe vitamin D in the form of fish liver oils and direct sunlight because he knows the importance of that vitamin in the formation of strong bones. All well known vitamins seem equally important so that the mother has yet another reason for drinking milk, eating dark green leaves and other vegetables, fresh fruits, eggs, liver, whole grain breads and cereals.

This listing supplemented by the doctor's advice on diet will point the way for the normal, healthy mother-to-be to see to it that she includes the foods so important to her health and to the health of her child.

SOCIETY

Barbara Busing Engaged to Student— Clinton Schelling Marries a Wave

Mr. and Mrs. Waldemar Busing of Scarsdale, N. Y., and Sayville announce the engagement of their daughter, Miss Barbara Anne Busing, to George Stiles Harris Jr., son of Mr. and Mrs. George S. Harris of Upper Montclair, N. J., and Walpole, N. H.

Miss Busing, a graduate of Scarsdale H. S. class of 1942, attended Middlebury College where she was a member of Delta Delta Delta. At present she is completing her college education at Barnard. She is the granddaughter of Mrs. Gustave W. Thompson and the late Dr. Gustave W. Thompson of Brooklyn.

Mr. Harris was also a student at Middlebury until his junior year and was a member of Delta Kappa Epsilon. He is at present in the A. S. T. P., finishing his premedical course at Temple University.

Schelling—Young

Ensign Eloise Young of the Waves, stationed at Newport, R. I., daughter of Mr. and Mrs. John Leslie Young of Maplewood, N. J., and Lt. Clinton Wolff Schelling, U. S. N. R., son of the late Mr. and Mrs. Louis Schelling of Brooklyn, were married Saturday at the Young home by the Rev. Howard Scharfe of the First Presbyterian and Trinity Church of South Orange. A reception for the families at the Maplewood Country Club followed the ceremony.

The bride was attended by her sisters, Mrs. Richard Bryant Gardner and Miss Marjorie Young.

Lieutenant Schelling's brother, George Schelling was best man. Mrs. Schelling was graduated from Principia College, Elsah, Ill., and received her commission at Northampton, Mass. The bridegroom is a graduate of Williams College. He was with the Central Hanover Bank & Trust Company of New York.

Rigg—Marcus

Mr. and Mrs. Lawrence Marcus of 1521 Ocean Ave. announce the marriage of their daughter, Miss Betty Fae Marcus, to Corp. Kenneth R. Rigg, son of Mr. and Mrs. Harold L. Rigg of 782 E. 18th St., on July 22 at Mountain Home, Idaho.

The bride attended Erasmus Hall High School and the Traphagen School of Art. Mr. Rigg is one of four brothers who are in the armed service.

Brown—O'Connor

Mrs. Florence Chase O'Connor, daughter of the late Mr. and Mrs. John B. Chase of Brooklyn, was married to William E. Brown, formerly of Manhattan. The ceremony was performed at the home of the bridegroom's uncle and aunt, Mr. and Mrs. John V. Kennedy, Pleasant Ridge, Cincinnati, Ohio. The Rev. Carl L. Kennedy of Circleville, Ohio, officiated.

Mr. and Mrs. J. William Kennedy of Champaign, Ill., attended the couple. A wedding supper followed. The couple will make their home in Cincinnati.

Mayer—Pfaff

Announcement is made of the engagement of Miss Edna M. Mayer, daughter of Mr. and Mrs. E. R. Mayer of 2911 Gerber Place, Bronx, to William J. Pfaff, son of Mr. and Mrs. William E. Pfaff of 450 49th St.

Miss Mayer is at present employed by the American Export Airlines. Mr. Pfaff, who was formerly employed at the Home Title Guaranty Company, 51 Willoughby St., has been serving in the U. S. Navy for the past two years and seven months, was home recently on a weekend leave.

Richter—Fine

Mr. and Mrs. Joseph L. Richter of Sea Gate announce the engagement of their daughter, Miss Gilda Millicent Richter, to Sidney Fine of Port Chester, N. Y.

Miss Richter attended Brooklyn Collage. She was one of the organizers of the Sea Gate Lighthouse Canteen, of which she has served as chairman since its opening two years ago. She is also president of Brooklyn and Long Island Judea and a member of the national board of Young Judaea and the Brooklyn board of Junior Hadassah.

Mr. Fine attended Iowa State University and is presently associated with Yale & Towne, Stamford, Conn.

7 ★★★★★★★ SPORTS
Wall Street Financial News

BROOKLYN EAGLE

WEATHER—Clear, warm tonight; sunny, warm tomorrow.

103d Year. No. 218. DAILY & SUNDAY • (Copyright 1944 The Brooklyn Eagle, Inc.) • BROOKLYN, N. Y., THURSDAY, AUGUST 10, 1944 • Entered at the Brooklyn Post-office as 2d Class Mail Matter • 3 CENTS IN NEW YORK CITY ELSEWHERE 4 CENTS

F. D. R. SEES M'ARTHUR AND NIMITZ IN HAWAII

General to Return to Philippines

PLANNING END OF JAPS—The President, General MacArthur and Admiral Nimitz gather at the spot where the Japs delivered their sneak punch Dec. 7, 1941.

Official Navy photo

U. S. TANK DRIVE THREATENS TO FLANK PARIS

First Air-Borne Army in History Formed by Allies—Set for Blows At Retreating Nazi Troops

By VIRGIL PINKLEY

Supreme Headquarters, A. E. F., Aug. 10 (U.P.) — Allied armies slashed through the riddled German defense arc covering the western and southwestern approaches to Paris today as General Eisenhower poised for a new threat to the Wehrmacht with the formation of the first entirely air-borne army in military history.

Creation of the new striking force, drawn from all Allied air-borne units in the European theater, came as American armored columns fanned out beyond captured Le Mans 100 miles or less from Paris in a drive that threatened to outflank the French capital from the south.

PATTON PARIS-BOUND?

London, Aug. 10 (U.P.)—The German DNB News Agency said today that Lt. Gen. George C. Patton "apparently has taken over the supreme command of the American 3d Army in France."

Allied headquarters has not identified an American "3d Army" as being in action in France, but DNB said it believed Patton was leading the tank forces moving on Paris from the southwest.

Unconfirmed reports said advanced American spearheads might already be only 40 or 50 miles west and southwest of Paris.

Headquarters spokesmen indicated that German rear guards were putting up increasingly stiff resistance against the Paris-bound Americans, although there was no sign that the doughboys had yet run into any major opposition.

The Nazis also were bracing desperately against three British and Canadian columns battering against their defenses below Caen in a full-scale attempt to turn the enemy's right flank and lay open the shortest road to Paris, 112 miles away.

On the isolated Breton peninsula small German garrisons were holding out bitterly in Brest, Lorient and Nantes, under heavy attack from American tanks and infantrymen,

Continued on Page 9

AMG ASKED TO NAB SUSPECT IN BORO MURDER

Genovese, Sought In 'Shadow' Slaying, Was Pal of Mussolini

The Brooklyn District Attorney's office has thrown out an international dragnet for Vito Genovese, notorious gangland overlord during the prohibition era, who is one of six men accused of killing Ferdinand (the Shadow) Boccia on Sept. 9, 1934. Genovese now is in Italy, where he is reported to be a banker.

While the prosecutor's office refused to comment on this development, the Brooklyn Eagle has learned that the transatlantic roundup operation already is under way. The Allied military government in Italy has been requested to use its facilities to locate Genovese and civil authorities in liberated areas also have been asked to aid in apprehending the 47-year-old one-time underworld boss of lower Manhattan during the 20's.

Fled to Italy in 1935

Genovese fled to Italy in 1935 when he was sought by Thomas E. Dewey, then at the height of his racket-busting activities. He was smuggled out of this country on orders from Benito Mussolini and took with him a considerable sum of money derived from gin, gambling and gunplay. During the palmy days of Fascism, he was seen on a number of occasions with Il Duce.

Whether or not Genovese will be

Continued on Page 9

Writer Describes Blum's Last Days

Moscow, Aug. 10 (U.P.)—The last days of Leon Blum, former popular front premier of France, in a German concentration camp near Lublin, were described in a dispatch by the Soviet writer Konstantin Simonov in the army newspaper Red Star today.

Blum allegedly was executed at the camp in May, 1943. Simonov said Blum was on a work detail with a Russian engineer, Peter Dennisov, who saw the 72-year-old ex-Premier carrying heavy construction planks and repeatedly collapsing under their weight.

A week later Dennisov asked another prisoner where Blum was and the man pointed to the sky, saying, "There, where I expect to be soon."

(In London, well-informed quarters said today that Blum was alive "a few days ago." They declined to elaborate for obvious reasons, remarking "The less said about the matter the better.")

Noise Crusader Plunges to Death

Williamsburg is a noisy section and Michael Kodoyka, 50, found it impossible to sleep in his home at 227 S. 1st St. last night. His wife was out and his two children were downstairs.

He yelled out the window to his neighbors to be quiet—but neighbors will be neighbors. Finally he filled a pail with water and splashed it out of the window at a few of the noisier ones. But his aim was bad.

He filled the pail again and leaned a little too far.

Kodoyka plunged two stories to the courtyard and struck a picket fence. An attendant from Greenpoint Hospital pronounced him dead.

45 LOCAL MEN LISTED AS WOUNDED IN BATTLE

The War Department today announced the names of 45 Brooklyn, Queens and Long Island men wounded in action in the Asiatic, Central Pacific, European, Mediterranean and Southwest Pacific areas.

The complete casualty lists for the Brooklyn area are on Page 10.

Mercury to Hit 90 Mark Today as Respite Ends

Hot sunny weather, with not a cloud in the sky, was forecast for today by the Weather Bureau. The short respite from the heat wave will end with the mercury reaching 90 this afternoon. Tomorrow will be hot with steadily increasing humidity.

'Saludos Amigos' in German

Hollywood, Aug. 10 (U.P.)—Walt Disney today began work on a German-language version of "Saludos Amigos." A similar version of "Fantasia" will follow, the film cartoonist said.

Hollywood Resort Admits Hiring Minors for Chorus

Hollywood, Aug. 10 (U.P.)—N. T. G.'s Florenaine Gardens will be sentenced today on a plea of guilty to having minors as chorus girls in violation of child labor laws.

Waiving sentence postponement, Earl Carrol's theater restaurant paid a $100 fine yesterday on a similar plea.

BELMONT RESULTS

(Saratoga Meeting)

1—F. Granted 52.20-18.70-5.40, Old Grad 5.70-3.00, M. Sugar 2.60. (1:22½)

2—Buymeabond, first; Pater, second; Ship Call, third.

CONFERS ON PLANS TO CRUSH JAPAN WITH NEW BLOWS

By MERRIMAN SMITH

Honolulu, July 29 (Delayed) (UP)—President Roosevelt completed three days of Hawaiian conferences today with Gen. Douglas MacArthur and Admiral Chester Nimitz on war plans to crush the Japanese with new offensives, and personally renewed his pledge that MacArthur would return to the Philippines with triumphant United States forces.

Mr. Roosevelt told a press conference at conclusion of his visit to this mighty Pacific base that his conferences with the top commanders and his first-hand inspection made him more confident than ever that the Japanese will be smashed into unconditional surrender.

The President came here by cruiser, and sailed today for an undisclosed destination.

(This dispatch was the first disclosure of Mr. Roosevelt's whereabouts since he made his fourth-term acceptance speech July 20 from a West Coast base, now revealed to have been the marine base at San Diego.

FIRST WORD OF MOVE BY M'ARTHUR

(It also was the first word that MacArthur, who disavowed efforts in this country to bring him forward as a possible Republican Presidential candidate, had left his headquarters in the Southwest Pacific to meet the President.)

Mr. Roosevelt said he had promised MacArthur, when the general was ordered to leave Corregidor, that he would go back. That promise still stands, the Chief Executive said.

We are going to get the Philippines back and give them their independence as soon as the Lord will allow, Mr. Roosevelt added, and there is no question as to MacArthur's part in the operation.

It was the first meeting between Mr. Roosevelt and MacArthur since the war started. The President said that while he had been corresponding with the general for years, it was much more satisfactory to talk with him directly.

It was Mr. Roosevelt's first wartime visit to the Pacific and his first here in exactly 10 years. He remarked on one occasion that he hoped "it won't be 10 years before I come back for the third time."

Amazed at Changes

In a luncheon talk at the Schofield Barracks Officers Club and mess on July 27 he commented on "the most amazing change" in the base since his last visit, and added:

"At that time Hawaii was one of our major outposts—the outpost. We weren't allowed to fortify Guam. Today it is no longer an

Other pictures on Page 11

outpost. It is one of our rear areas, in one sense of the word. From here we are conducting a campaign, one more advanced than any other campaign of the past."

To Pearl Harbor Navy Yard workers on July 29 he said: "We are going just about twice as fast today as ever before, and we are going to make it even faster." He added: "We've got, without question, the largest and best equipped navy in the world."

The President spent three days here, talking at length with the key military, air and naval leaders

Continued on Page 2

PARLEY MAY END WILDCAT STRIKE AT WRIGHT PLANT

Detroit, Aug. 10 (U.P.)—A walkout by 1,000 members of the United Automobile Workers (C. I. O.) Union today halted production of bomber sub-assemblies at the Ford Motor Company's Highland Park plant....

Paterson, N. J., Aug. 10—Hope was expressed for a quick settlement of the wildcat strike which has stopped production at several plants of the Wright Aeronautical Corporation in this area, as representatives of the company, the union and a Federal conciliation commissioner went into conference today in a effort to straighten out the tangle which has resulted from a dispute over contract provision interpretations.

The only Wright plant in the area operating, according to reports, was that at Woodbridge, where engines

Continued on Page 9

Kid Marine Grins From Stretcher As President Grips His Hand

By MERRIMAN SMITH

Honolulu, July 29 (Delayed) (U.P.)—The wounded kid in the stretcher shielded his eyes from the sun when they lifted him out of the hospital plane at Hickam Field.

He looked no more than 19 or 20 years old, but he was a marine lieutenant and had suffered a serious leg wound on Saipan. When the stretcher bearers carried him across the concrete runway to a waiting ambulance he was thinking only of a clean bed in a cool hospital.

The stretcher bearers stopped and the lieutenant uncovered his eyes to see why. There, leaning out of an automobile, was President Roosevelt.

"Hello, son," the President said, reaching to take the marine's hand. The young lieutenant didn't say a word. He just grinned.

"Well," the President said, "you're up here now. It is good to see you—I got here just in time.

Other litters passed by the President's car and he waved or talked to each of the men they bore. Most of the 17

Continued on Page 2

16 More Jap Ships Sunk by U. S. Subs

Washington, Aug. 10 (U.P.)—United States submarines have sunk 16 more enemy vessels i nthe Pacific, including one combatant ship, the navy announced today.

Their latest victims included five cargo transports, nine cargo vessels, one tanker and one escort vessel to bring the total number of enemy vessels hit by American undersea craft to 839.

The total included 687 sunk, 37 probably snnk and 115 damaged.

Jackie Cooper to Face Girl's Charges

South Bend, Ind., Aug. 10 (U.P.)—Jackie Cooper, film star and a naval V-12 student, has been turned over to civilian authorities by officers at the Notre Dame Naval Training School to face charges of contributing to the delinquency of a 15-year-old South Bend girl, authorities said today.

George Bender, 24, Sheffield, Ill., V-12 student who was charged with having immoral relations with the girl, also was turned over to Sheriff Steve Molnar. Cooper and Bender were released immediately under bonds.

The charges grew out of a hotel party July 22 at which the 15-year-old girl claimed that Cooper and a feminine companion plied her with liquor and helped Bender convince her that she should go with him to a room which Cooper had rented.

Union Head Sentenced For False Statement

A sentence of 30 days and a $500 fine were imposed today by Federal District Judge John McDuffie on Thomas V. de Lorenzo, 30, president of Local 365, United Automobile Workers of America, C. I. O., after he was found guilty of filing a false statement in an application with the U. S. Civil Service Commission. The application related to his appointment as a labor panel member of the War Labor Board.

Fala Gains Weight And Loses Hair

Honolulu, July 29 (Delayed) (U.P.)—Fala, the President's scottie and constant companion, had the doggondest trip to Hawaii, what with being shanghaied and losing much of his long black hair to souvenir-seeking sailors.

No sooner had the cruiser carrying the Presidential party left than a group of sailors shanghaied Fala and began clipping his hair. He finally got away from them but looking as if he'd gone to sleep in the barber's chair.

Then when the ship arrived at Pearl Harbor Fala could not go ashore with his master because of a local law requiring dogs to be quarantined for months before being allowed any freedom.

So Fala spent the time in Hawaii aboard the cruiser, getting fat on frequent feedings by the gobs and quietly suffering the loss of more of his hair.

Nazis Hurl Buzz Bombs After 24-Hour Lull

London, Aug. 10 (U.P.)—After a lull of nearly 24 hours, the Germans sent flying bombs into southern England and the London area for a short period after daybreak today.

A number of persons were injured and some damage was caused.

The lull was the longest since the robot attack started.

French Ace Missing

Algiers, Aug. 10 (U.P.)—Antoine de St. Exupery, famous French flier and author, is missing after a sortie over the Mediterranean, it was announced officially today.

F. D.'s Timetable

By United Press

The timetable of President Roosevelt's trip to Hawaii:

July 13—Left Washington.

July 14—Spent day at Hyde Park, leaving at night.

July 19—Arrived at Marine Base, San Diego, Cal.

July 20—Made fourth term nomination acceptance speech from San Diego.

July 21—Sailed for Hawaii.

July 26—Arrived at Pearl Harbor and took residence on Waikiki Beach section of Honolulu.

July 27—Visited Schofield barracks for review and lunch in officers club. Conferences in afternoon and evening.

July 28—Lengthy morning conference. Afternoon visit to jungle training center and Kanehoe Naval Air Station.

July 29—Visits to army and navy hospitals, lunch with Admiral Nimitz in Pearl Harbor, tea at home of Gov. Ingram Stainback and press-radio conference. Sailed for next destination.

WHERE TO FIND IT

	Page		Page
Comics	17	Radio	17
Crossword	13	Real Estate	17
Dr. Brady	8	Society	6
Editorial	8	Sports	12, 13
Financial	18	Take My Word	8
Helen Worth	7	Theaters	14
Horoscope	17	These Women	17
Mary Haworth	5	Tommy Holmes	12
Movies	14	Uncle Ray	17
Novel	15	Want Ads	15, 16
Obituaries	9	Women	4-7
Our Fighters	10		

OVER THEY GO—Entries in the fifth race, the Shillelah steeplechase of the Saratoga meeting at Belmont Park, are shown taking one of jumps. Elkridge, J. S. Harriman up, was winner, with Invader, second, and Floating Isle, third.

They *Tell* Me

BY RALPH TROST

FOR THE WOUNDED—There's a plot of about 22 acres near Halloran Hospital over on Staten Island. In the hospital are a large number of wounded, shell-shocked, etc., whose rehabilitation will be a lot of work. A real good aid toward soothing seared nerves, exercising torn muscles and, generally, making men keep occupied out in the open air, is golf. So golfers in the metropolitan area may be called upon for money to build a golf course and supply equipment with which to play. It all hinges on the availability of that piece of ground.

If the room can be had, golf can do the rest. And a nice job it would be for all concerned.

No one knows how many golf courses have been built at camps and hospitals. Not full courses. Some three holes, some nine, some 12. And they've been well used. These courses have bobbed up at the oddest places. On air field runways, (ash runways, not concrete), in deserts—in all sorts of places.

And, which is particularly pleasing, letters drift in from just as odd places thanking Long Islanders for the goodly quantity of balls and clubs that have been collected here for them. The most recent is from Augusta, Ga. One before that was from Trinidad. Still another from Panama.

Sgt. Jimmy Turnesa is over on Staten Island. With what little facilities he has, Sergeant Jimmy has done some excellent work. Golf has worked well on nerve cases, Jimmy told me. "However, I've also had some good luck on muscle cases, too. An officer, a dentist, with an arm well cut up got himself back into shape on golf. There wasn't exercise he could take that could make his arm move as fully and fast as swinging a golf club. If only we could get more room and equipment!"

Well, it looks as if he's going to get it.

THE ARMY-NAVY GAME—Reports have it that there's no doubt the Army-Navy football game will be played in a big city this year. We noted this in the papers this week. If you'd noticed these columns the day after the restricted, constricted game at West Point last Fall you'd have read the same news. Driving from Mitchie Stadium down to the Army gym we heard the higher-ups say, "Never again." Meaning that it just didn't make sense playing this game in private with only the Middies watching at Annapolis and only the Cadets at West Point. And with gobs and gobs of empty seats, no accommodations for players, bus rides to and from the stadium—and, generally, no zip to the thing at all.

There are only two logical spots for the game, Philadelphia or New York. Both can handle everything with the least possible strain on every one and everything. And Franklin Field, rather than the large Municipal Stadium way down South in Philly, is the best bet of all. Far better transportation.

A DAY OF DAYS—There were an awful lot of horses running at Belmont, Thursday; scads of them. But, believe it or not, you could have laid your little two bucks on every single entry, got yourself eight winners (which goes without saying)—and finished the day a neat 60-odd dollars winner.

You don't believe it? Well, go check up. It's de trut'.

On the subject of horses, there's a tall, slim, native-born Long Islander who's doing pretty well for himself. As both a trainer of horses and as sort of a super-specialist in getting horses to do their stuff when they've simply refused to do it for any one else. He's 31-year-old Billy Post, a very quiet, non-betting father of three who's finding himself with more and more horses to handle. Besides all those at Belmont, going through the ordinary courses of training and racing, he's got 29 back on the Post place at East Williston. Some are yearlings to be broken in, some bent and bowed to be repaired, some to be turned into jumpers and a couple just recalcitrants whose owners or trainers haven't been able to do much with them.

The rise of Billy Post, who, given half a break, looms about to become the best native trainer Long Island has known, brought up the question of how many natives of this Long Island have taken advantage of the tremendous amount of horse running to gain names and fame as trainers.

The list is probably as long as my arm—if I ever could get a history which listed the items I'm curious about. It must be. Horse racing in America started on this island. When it got to be a formal operation with grandstands, etc., Brooklyn was the national seat of horse racing. When I was considerably younger I could remember three tracks right on the street we called The Boulevard (they should have kept the name) but now called Ocean Parkway. There was one at Brighton Beach, there was the Gravesend track at Kings Highway. Across the street was another, the name of which I forget. And then there was that huge plant at Sheepshead Bay.

Those places gave up the ghost. But we're still operating at Belmont, Jamaica and Aqueduct—and are threatened with a bigger, better place on the site of the World's Fair.

There must have been a great number of natives who learned their horses and went on to make name and fortune. It had seemed to me that Maxie Hirsch was a Brooklynite. But no, he came from Texas.

How about Hirsch Jacobs? They say he came from Harlem. I must ask the little red head. The Dwyers came from Jersey. I asked Vince Mara to name some. Well, Bert Mulholland's father was a professor at St. John's. I guess he's a native. And Ed Haviland. Then there's George Clausen. The Odoms came from Georgia, Gaver and a lot of others from Maryland. Matt Brady shouts "Ireland" as his birthplace. Ben Jones is from the West, Cameron from California. The Coburns are from the same place.

Now that you brought this up, just how many Long Islanders, natives, have become trainers?

Guess I'll have to do a little research on this. Unless you readers really know.

Grays, Bushwicks Resume Their Feud

It will be an ambitious and aggressive Homestead Grays combination that will invade Dexter Park in Woodhaven tomorrow afternoon for a doubleheader. The World's Negro champions will make a determined bid to take both ends of the bargain bill and thus gain the edge in the season's series with the Bushwicks, who are currently setting a dizzy pace. The Bushwicks hold the advantage in the series at the present time with three victories against two losses. The opening fracas will get under way at 2:05 o'clock.

When the clubs first met this year the Grays captured a night game in 13 innings, 3 to 2. They came back again on June 30, and this time the Dexters won, 5—2. It was the Bushwicks' first victory over the Grays, to whom they had lost seven straight. Six of the Grays' triumphs dated back to the 1943 season. On July 9 the Grays came in for their first doubleheader of the campaign and lost both games, 3—2, 10—6. This gave the Bushwicks three straight. On Friday night, July 28, the Grays returned and shut out the Bushwicks, 7—0.

The meetings between the arch rivals' clubs have always been thrilling, hard-fought affairs. With so much at stake on this occasion, the Grays can be counted upon to muster their full strength for a perfect day. An even split will keep the Bushwicks in the driver's seat.

The Grays are expected to use Edsel Walker and Ray Brown, their ace hurlers. Gaston will do the catching.

Manager Joe Press of the Bushwicks has saved Bots Nekola, veteran lefty, who has twice beaten the Grays while losing one to the champs. Incidentally, it is the only loss checked against Bots this season. Either Wally Signer or Wally Holborow will toe the slab in the other game.

Provisions have been made to handle the biggest crowd of the season in Max Rosner's recreation yard.

Bushwicks Tame Stratford

Scoring 13 runs in the first three innings, the Bushwicks registered an easy win over the Stratford, Conn., club last night at Dexter Park by 13 to 2. Emil Moscowitz and Gene Philipps did the twirling for the victors, Moscowitz getting credit for his ninth win of the year and his fourth in a row.

It was the Bushwicks fifth straight and a record for the season of 39 wins, 9 losses and one tie.

Gene Walsh and Emil Gall were the leading batters for the Bushwicks with three hits each. Walsh again sparkled in the field with a one-hand catch in left field.

The box score:

Stratford	ab	r	h	o	a	Bushwicks	ab	r	h	o	a
C'gin'llo,2b	4	1	1	1	3	Adams,cf	4	3	1	1	0
Metoskie,ss	4	0	2	3	6	Contini,ss	5	2	2	2	5
Michaels,1b	4	0	1	11	0	Bell,rf	5	3	2	3	0
Peffer,cf	4	1	2	4	0	Walsh,lf	5	1	3	1	0
K'zm'zyk,rf	4	0	0	0	0	Detz,3b	5	1	0	1	1
Baker,lf	4	0	0	4	2	Gall,c	4	0	3	5	1
Noonon,c	4	0	1	1	1	O'Neill,1b	5	1	2	9	3
Devitt,3b	2	0	0	0	1	McBride,2b	4	1	1	2	3
Pezulia,p	0	0	0	0	0	Moscowitz,p	3	1	2	1	0
Quintard,p	3	0	0	0	1	Philipps,p	0	0	0	2	1
aH'rringt'n	1	0	0	0	0	cNekola	1	0	0	0	0
bNichols	1	0	0	0	0						
Totals	35	2	7	24	14	Totals	41	13	16	27	14

aBatted for Devitt in 9th.
bBatted for Quintard in 9th.
cBatted for Moscowitz in 6th.

Stratford	0	0	0	1	1	0	0	0	0	— 2
Bushwicks	3	8	2	0	0	0	0	0	x	—13

Errors—Metoskie 2, Devitt 2, McBride. Runs batted in—By Metoskie, Baker, Bell 3, Walsh 4, Gall, O'Neill, Moscowitz 2. Two-base hits — Metoskie, Moscowitz, Walsh 2. Three-base hits—Pepper, Caginello, Bell 2. Stolen base—Adams. Double plays — Baker, Metoskie and Michaels; Caginello, Metoskie and Michaels. Bases on balls—Off Pezulia 1, Quintard 1, Moscowitz 1. Struck out—By Quintard 1, Moscowitz 3, Philipps 2. Hits—Off Pezulia 6 in 1, none out in 2d; off Moscowith 7 in 6. Winning pitcher—Moscowitz. Losing pitcher—Pezulia. Umpires—Rauppius, Bergen and Urban.

LUIS OLMO — His hit won game for Dodgers.

Rickey Now Mourns Loss of Hal Peck On Hunt for Help

Chicago, Aug. 12—President Branch Rickey sat in a box behind the Dodger dugout at Wrigley Field yesterday and as is the Mahatma's conversational custom talked of many things. He was just making a stopover here on his homeward way to Brooklyn from St. Paul where he went in search of players.

"I think there's a pitcher with the Saints I can land,' he reported. "But we would have to give up a player in exchange. I wouldn't care to say anything more at this time." But he spoke freely—and with regret—on Hal Peck, the Milwaukee outfielder, once the property of the Dodgers. Peck was bought by Larry MacPhail after he had shot off a toe with a carelessly held hunting rifle, and was sent back to the American Asociation when it was found that he couldn't run.

"But I wasn't satisfied that an operation wouldn't cure the boy," said Rickey. "I remembered what it had done for Johnny Mize. I had four doctors look at Peck. All of 'e mshook their heads. 'If he has the operation,' they agreed, 'he will never play ball again.' So I cooled off on bringing Peck back. But he had the operation and now look at him. He can run, hit and field with the best of 'em. It was a blow."

Rickey further reported that the bidding for Frank Drewes, the St. Paul second baseman the Dodgers had at Bear Mountain on a $10,000 option, has become so brisk that Drewes is almost sure to be sold to some major league club for more than the 10 grand he would have cost Brooklyn.

"But we're still not interested in Drewes," concluded Branch. Rickey left for Brooklyn after the game.

Casey Stengel, former Dodger manager and now piloting Milwaukee to an American Association flag, was also a spectator. "It looks like a big year for us 'S' guys—Southworth, Sewell and Stengel," said Casey.

The Dodgers' new .391 hitting shortstop from the Iowa Pre-Flight team, Lou Rochelli, reported yesterday. But he's still ineligible to play until his draft status is readjusted.

Howie Schultz' father and mother are here from St. Paul to watch their boy hit a few.

Three Dodgers are limping through the West with bad legs—Dixie Walker, Jack Bolling and Tommy Warren. It's an old kickback from an ankle injury with Dixie. Bolling doesn't remember how or when he was hurt, but Tommy hurt his heel Thursday in trying to avoid spiking Phil Cavarretta while running out his game-winning hit.—**BURR.**

KEEP IT UP, GANG!

Brooklyn	ab	r	h	o	a	Chicago	ab	r	h	o	a
Rosen,cf	6	0	1	3	1	Hack,3b	4	1	0	1	3
Koch,2b	6	1	1	1	4	Hughes,ss	5	2	2	1	4
Galan,lf	5	2	2	2	0	Cav'r'tta,1b	5	0	1	13	0
Waner,rf	3	0	2	1	0	Nichols'n,rf	5	1	2	3	0
Bord'gary,rf	2	0	1	2	0	Dals'ndro,lf	5	1	2	3	0
Olmo,3b	6	0	2	2	2	Pafko,cf	5	0	2	2	0
Schultz,1b	5	2	1	12	1	Johnson,2b	4	0	0	4	3
Owen,c	4	1	1	7	0	Williams,c	3	0	0	6	0
Bragan,ss	1	0	0	1	1	bGoodman	1	0	0	0	0
aBolling	0	0	0	0	0	Kreitner,c	1	0	0	0	0
Stanky,ss	0	1	0	2	0	Fleming,p	1	0	0	0	2
Chapman,p	3	0	1	0	1	Erickson,p	2	1	1	0	2
McLish,p	1	0	0	0	0	cNovikoff	1	0	0	0	0
Webber,p	1	0	0	0	0	Chipman,p	1	0	1	0	1
Totals	43	7	12	33	11	Totals	43	6	11	33	15

aBatted for Bragan in sixth inning.
bBatted for Williams in eighth inning.
cBatted for Erickson in eighth inning.

Brooklyn	1	2	0	0	1	2	0	0	0	0	1	—7
Chicago	2	0	0	1	2	0	0	0	1	0	0	—6

Error—Hughes. Runs batted in—Rosen, Galan, Waner, Olmo, Chapman 2, Nicholson, Pafko 3, Erickson. Two-base hits—Galan, Waner, Olmo, Chapman. Three-base hit—Dallessandro. Home runs—Galan, Nicholson, Erickson. Stolen bases—Chapman, Hack, Hughes. Sacrifices—Galan, Owen, Bragan, Johnson. Left on bases—Brooklyn 11, Chicago 11. Bases on balls—Off Chapman 5, off Webber 1, off Erickson 4, off Chipman 1. Struck out—By Chapman 5, by Fleming 1, by Erickson 5. Hits—Off Chapman, 5 in 6⅔ innings; off McLish, 2 ni 1-3 (none out in eighth), off Webber 4 in 4; off Fleming 5 in 1⅔; off Erickson, 4 in 6⅓; off Chipman, 3 in 3. Wild pitches—Fleming, Erickson. Winning pitcher—Webber. Losing pitcher—Chipman. Umpires—Stewart, Dunn and Magerkruth. Time—3:00. Attendance—6,650.

INTERNATIONAL LEAGUE

YSTERDAY'S RESULTS

Newark 6, Montreal 1.
Rochester 9, **Jersey City** 3.
Toronto 3, Syracuse 0.
Baltimore 2, Buffalo 1 (1st).
Baltimore 9, Buffalo 5 (2d).

STANDING OF CLUBS

	W.	L.	Pct.		W.	L.	Pct.
Baltimore	69	47	.595	Montreal	53	61	.465
Newark	68	52	.567	Toronto	55	62	.470
Buffalo	61	58	.513	Syracuse	51	64	.443
Jersey City	58	56	.509	Rochester	52	68	.433

TODAY'S GAMES

Newark at Montreal.
Jersey City at Rochester.
Syracuse at Toronto, 2.
Baltimore at Buffalo, 2.

DODGERS HELP GIANTS KEEP FOURTH PLACE

Mel Ott May Recall Cliff Melton to Aid His Faltering Staff

Special to the Brooklyn Eagle

Pittsburgh, Aug. 12—Sounds like treason, but it's true nevertheless that the common foe from over the river in New York City—the Brooklyn Dodgers—have kept the Giants in fourth place. The Flatbushers saved the Ottmen's hide yesterday when they beat the Cubs for the third straight day while the invaders from Harlem were dropping three out of four to the Pirates in a nocturnal game here last night, 12—8.

In order to try and rescue the last combat of the five-game series here today, Manager Ott, who has aggravated his lame ankle, will send Bill Voiselle against Max Butcher, the feudists in the first game. The pitching staff has got Otte singing the blues again. To bolster the faltering mound corps, Cliff Melton, elongated southpaw, may be recalled from Jersey City, where he seems to nave recovered his curving composure.

Harry Feldman, who used to be the Giants main reliance under the arcs, but of late seems to have lost his magic, flivvered once more after his mates had given him a six-run lead in the first four innings. The Pirates put on the crusher with a seven-run outbreak in the fifth that sealed the Harlem contingent's doom.

Even the shaking up of the Giants' batting order didn't have the desired effect. Johnny Rucker, who has hit only for .158 since July 1, was dropped into seventh place and Joe Medwick was moved up to the third slot to let Phil Weintraub hit i nthe cleanup spot.

Before the Pirates got through with the feeble Giant chucking, Ewald Pyle, Jack Brewer and Ace Adams saw action. The loss was charged to Pyle, giving him an even break in 10 games. The winning chucker was Art Cuccurullo, a southpaw, who relieved starter Nick Strincevich during a four-run uprising in the fourth.

Ott, Kerr Chased

It was a weird exhibition with poor officiating that disgusted the 12,240 onlookers. The Giants collected a brace of tallies in the third. Errors by Bob Elliott and Strincevich paved the way on Feldman's bounder and Leon Treadway's scratch single. George Hausmann's hit scored both. Impetus was given the four-run splurge in the fourth when Al Lopez knocked Lombardi's easy pop out of Strincevich's mitt for a single. Singles by Hal Luby and Feldman drove in two of the runs and the other two resulted from an infield out and another from an error.

The Giant lead was cut in half in the last half of the fourth when Frank Colman delivered the first hit off Feldman, his third home run of the series and his fourth of the campaign, with two mates aboard.

In the fifth, Cuccurullo's double and Pete Coscarart's triple in rapid succession chased Feldman and Pyle failed to put out the fire. He was maced for a base-clearing double by Dahlgren, after Elliott's single had counted Coscarart. Brewer came on the scene and was spanked for two more runs as Gustine's single and Lopez's double wound up the seven-run splurge.

A Brewer wild pitch in the eighth gave the Pirates two more runs and brought such a squawk from Ott and Kerr that they were chased from hostilities by Lee Ballanfant.

The Giants went down fighting with two in the ninth.

DODGERS' BATTING

Player	g.	ab.	r.	h.	2b.	3b.	hr.	rbi.	Pct.
Chapman	2	7	3	3	2	0	0	5	.429
Bolling	39	118	21	43	13	1	1	21	.365
Walker	105	390	56	139	26	6	10	67	.356
Galan	111	395	68	124	28	7	9	61	.314
Warren	30	31	1	9	0	0	0	2	.290
Waner	69	101	14	29	3	1	0	15	.267
Bordagaray	95	375	65	101	19	4	4	38	.269
Olmo	97	377	50	101	12	5	7	61	.268
Rosen	61	207	32	55	6	1	0	19	.26[illegible]
Bragan	72	218	22	57	6	3	0	17	.2[illegible]
Schultz	90	338	39	85	16	2	8	56	.2[illegible]
Stanky	70	202	26	51	7	2	0	11	.2[illegible]
Owen	93	319	24	78	16	2	1	32	.2[illegible]
Brown	4	13	3	3	1	0	0	0	.2[illegible]
Webber	33	27	4	6	1	0	1	3	.2[illegible]
Gregg	33	50	5	11	0	0	0	2	.2[illegible]
McLish	29	32	6	7	1	0	0	1	.21[illegible]
Koch	15	52	6	11	1	0	0	0	.21[illegible]
Wyatt	10	12	1	2	1	0	0	1	.16[illegible]
Davis	23	45	1	6	1	0	0	3	.13[illegible]
Melton	25	39	1	3	1	0	0	2	.07[illegible]
Hayworth	6	6	1	0	0	0	0	0	.000

Major League Standings

NATIONAL LEAGUE

YESTERDAY'S RESULTS

Brooklyn 7, Chicago 6 (11innings)
Pittsburgh 12, **New York** 8
St. Louis 9, Philadelphia 4
Cincinnati 12, Boston 6

STANDING OF THE CLUBS

	W.	L.	Pct.	G.B.
St. Louis	75	27	.735	—
Cincinnati	56	45	.554	18
Pittsburgh	55	45	.550	19
New York	50	55	.476	26½
Chicago	46	52	.469	27
Boston	43	59	.422	32½
Brooklyn	43	62	.410	33½
Philadelphia	38	61	.384	35½

TODAY'S GAMES

Brooklyn (Webber 4-6) at Chicago (Lynn 1-1)—2:00 p.m.
New York (Voiselle 14-12) at Pittsburgh (Butcher 9-7)—3:00 p.m.
Boston (Hutchinson 7-5) at Cincinnati (Shoun 8-5)
Philadelphia (Lee 7-6) at St. Louis (Jurisich 7-8)

TOMORROW'S GAMES

Brooklyn at St. Louis (2)
New York at Cincinnati (2)
Boston at Pittsburgh (2)
Philadelphia at Chicago (2)

AMERICAN LEAGUE

YESTERDAY'S RESULTS

New York 6, St. Louis 1
Chicago 9, Boston 7
Detroit 11, Washington 4
Philadelphia 6, Cleveland 3

STANDING OF THE CLUBS

	W.	L.	Pct.	G.B.
St. Louis	64	43	.598	—
Boston	57	49	.538	6½
Detroit	55	50	.524	7½
New York	54	50	.519	8½
Cleveland	53	56	.486	11½
Chicago	51	55	.481	12½
Philadelphia	48	61	.440	16½
Washington	44	62	.415	19

TODAY'S GAMES

St. Louis (Potter 10-5) at **New York** Dubiel 7-9)2:30 p.m.
Detroit (Newhouser 18-6) at Washington (Wolff 3-7)
Cleveland (Klieman 8-6) at Philadelphia (Harris 9-8)
Chicago (Lopat 5-7) at Boston (Bowman 8-6)

TOMORROW'S GAMES

Chicago at **New York** (2)
St. Louis at Boston (2)
Detroit at Philadelphia (2)
Cleveland at Washington (2)

Leo May Have Found Right Combination

That Is Likely Answer to Reason For Form Reversal of Flatbushers

By **HAROLD C. BURR**
Staff Correspondent of the Eagle.

Chicago, Aug. 12—Nobody knew what to make of the Dodgers, not even themselves. This same ball club that couldn't win a game out West on its second invasion hasn't lost one yet on its third safari this side of the Alleghanies. For the third straight time yesterday at Wrigley Field it cooled off the Cubs, the hottest team in the league with the exception of the Cardinals, 7 to 6, in 11 innings. Their second overtime knockout in two days.

Either it's gone crazy from the heat that's hovering up around a torrid 100 out here or something has happened overnight to make it click. It has shown some preliminary symptoms of dementia. For instance, during all that long stretch when it won only three games in 30-odd it knocked out Al Javery, Bucky Walters and Rip Sewel for its trio of wins.

More recently the Cards came into Ebbets Field for a six-game series and the unpredictable Dodgers won two of the first five when they hadn't harmed a soul for weeks. Every so often the goats of the Gowanus fly into rage—probably at themselves—grab a bat and going around bashing in the crowned heads of the National League.

Veterans Deliver

But it might be that Manager Leo Durocher, after weeks and months of experimenting, has come up with the right combination at last. The kids have been pretty thoroughly weeded out of the lineup. It was experienced moundsmen who defeated the Cubs—Curt Davis, Rube Melton and Les Webber. There has been a rookie at second base through this dizzy winning spree in Barney Koch.

But the rest of the lineup has been tried and true veterans. Calvin Coolidge McLish was forcibly removed yesterday before he could gum up the ball game.

And, of course, the awakening bats of Howie Schultz and Luis Olmo have been a factor. The Puerto Rican perfecto shot a single to center yesterday in the 11th frame that beat Bob Chipman after the Dodger discard had hung it on 'em three times. But it still may be just the heat.

Except that he tried to slip a fast one past Swish Nicholson in the ninth, Webber pitched three gritty relief innings. He came to McLish's relief in the seventh after Buster had filled the bases with nobody out. The next three Cub batters couldn't get the ball out of the infield. Stan Hack, however, did make a bold bid for a hit through the box.

Webber had to chase the ball after deflecting it. A run was streaking home, the tying run. But Les caught up with the ball and with a low, desperate scoop got it to Schultz in time to retire the side runless.

Nick Smacks 26th

He had two out in the ninth and two strikes and no balls on Nicholson. That was when he should have played around with Swish. But instead he threw right down the gut and Bill hit it, behind a favoring wind, over the garden wall in right field for his 26th home run of the year. Nicholson came up again in the 11th, but by this time Webber had learned his lesson and not even the humid breeze that was blowing across Chicago off the par-boiled prairie could carry his fly beyond Frenchy Bordagaray's reach.

It was too bad that Webber didn't get Swish in the ninth. That would have been the out that would have returned Ben Chapman the victor in his second start as a Dodger. Ben, just arrived from Birmingham after a week's lay-off, didn't pitch so well. He saw a curve ball served up to Paul Erickson sail into the left-center bleachers, not only the relief pitcher's first home run of the year but his first hit of any kind in 22 games. And Chapman took a half windup, so that the alert Roy Hughes stole home in the fifth.

Yankees Triumph Improves Morale

By **HAROLD CONRAD**

It has been usual for the rest of the American League to find itself floundering around in the hot August dust kicked up by the Yankees as they majestically rode at the head of the junior circuit by anything from six to a dozen games. But August 1944 tells a different story. Just three days ago, before they opened their current series with the Browns, the Yanks were hoping that perhaps they had an outside chance of winning the flag. Two days later they were mired in fourth place and because of their low morale some of the Bronx worriers feared they were liable to wind up in the second division. But they've stopped worrying up in the Bronx today.

The Yanks finally stopped the Browns yesterday and have come to the conclusion that life isn't so bitter after all. But those first two setbacks at the hands of St. Louis really took the wind out of them. The realization that their pennant hopes had just about gone up in smoke was a bitter pill for the proud Yankees to swallow.

By the third inning of yesterday's game, they had completely shaken off this blue funk. They were skipping around merrily, talking it up and acting in general like a club that was ready to tackle anything. Those first two innings had netted them four runs and that was more than they were able to get in both of the games they blew to the Browns.

Now they're even talking about catching the Browns, who are 8½ game in front of them. This, of course, is a mathematical piece of wishful thinking, but when they talk about overtaking the second place Red Sox, who are only two games ahead of them, they're serious.

It was a happy change from the Yanks of two days ago and it was certainly reflected in their action on the field. In the fifth inning they routed Sig Jakucki, the fellow who beat them in the opener Wednesday. Hemsley and Derry hit homers, Donald was pitching masterfully in the pinches and they wound up on the long end of a 6—2 victory, snapping the Browns' 10-game winning streak.

The win was Atley's 12th, twice the number he won last year, and it was the 12th time he had beaten the Browns during his career. St. Louis kept getting men on base, but when the pressure was on, Donald tightened up. Nine Brownies were left stranded.

Luke Sewell took the defeat philosophically. "My boys can relax now and start building another streak. We've got to lose one once in a while and at that we've never lost more than two in a row.

Another good week-day crowd of 12,042 turned out for the third game of the series which is probably the best played engagement seen at the Stadium this year. Dubiel and Kramer are the mound choices for the fourth and final game today.

ROLLIE HEMSLEY — Blasted homer against Browns.

Grid Giants Sign Three Key Linemen

The New York Football Giants announce the signing of three veteran key linesmen. They are Frank Cope and Vic Carroll, tackles; Len Younce, guard. With this powerful trio back in the fold Coach Steve Owen figures the foundation is already set for his front line this season. Frank Cope's return is very important. The 6.3, 234-pound Californian has won National League tackle honors. Since 1939 Cope has been one of the mainstays of the rugged Polo Grounds first line. He has been with the team six years.

President John V. Mara announced that the last three to come to terms will participate in the first training practice Aug. 31 at Bear Mountain.

MAJOR LEAGUE LEADERS

AMERICAN LEAGUE

Player and Club	G.	AB.	R.	H.	Pct.
Doerr, Boston	107	401	83	134	.334
Siebert, Philadelphia	87	314	36	102	.325
Fox, Boston	84	347	54	111	.320
Boudreau, Cleveland	103	403	64	128	.318
Johnson, Boston	97	345	78	107	.310

NATIONAL LEAGUE

Player and Club	G.	AB.	R.	H.	Pct.
Walker, Brooklyn	105	390	56	139	.3564
Musial, St. Louis	103	405	83	144	.3556
Hopp, St. Louis	90	336	76	112	.333
Holmes, Boston	105	432	68	141	.327
Medwick, New York	94	367	56	119	.324

Runs Batted In		Home Runs	
Nicholson, Cubs	82	Nicholson, Cubs	26
Sanders, Cards	77	Ott, Giants	22
Stephens, Browns	73	Doerr, Red Sox	14
Elliott, Pirates	72	Weintraub, Giants	13
Weintraub, Giants	71	Johnson, Red Sox	13
		Kurowski, Cards	13

FORCED AT KEYSTONE BAG—Don Gutteridge, second baseman of the Browns, forced at his station on George McQuinn's grounder to Snuffy Stirnweiss, Yankees, who threw to Frank Crosetti, covering bag, in the first inning of yesterday's game at Yankee Stadium.

SPORTS

Old Timer Tells of Pitcher Who Mistook 2d Baseman for Batter, on Page 15.

BROOKLYN EAGLE

5c IN CITY AND LONG ISLAND

Weather—Sunny, not so warm today; fair tomorrow.

103d YEAR • No. 221 • DAILY AND SUNDAY — BROOKLYN, N. Y., SUNDAY, AUGUST 13, 1944 • • •

Entered at the Brooklyn Postoffice as 2d Class Mail Matter—(Copyright 1944 The Brooklyn Eagle, Inc.)

TRAP CLOSING ON 100,000 NAZIS

$500,000 Fire Sweeps Luna Park; Coney Threatened by 5-Alarm Blaze

THOUSANDS SEE FIGHT BY FIREMEN

Eight of Luna Park's 16½ acres were reduced to a mass of twisted, smoking wreckage late yesterday by a spectacular fire, which, though resulting

Other Pictures on Page 3

in an estimated total of $500,000 damage, was brought under control without causing a single fatality.

Flames shooting skyward as high as 400 feet roared and crackled across eight of the amusement park's 16½ acres, while thousands of spectators jammed Surf Ave.

Towers, rides and other recreation devices tumbled to the ground as the fire raged for two hours before being brought under control.

Panic Is Averted

But Coney Island, the playground of New York City's mililons, with an estimated 750,000 men, women and chilcren packing the beaches at the time, averted panic.

Late reports indicated the resort had come through one of its worst fi[illegible] in recent years with no more than 16 persons receiving minor injuries.

Last night Fire Marshal Thomas P. Brophy, after questioning witnesses and employes in an investigation of the fire, declared his inquiry had disclosed a delay in turning in the first of five alarms, which brought 42 engine companies, 16 truck companies and rescue squad into the battle to prevent a far more serious [illegible]

He sa[illegible] his inquiry showed that a period of at least 15 minutes had elapsed between the time the fire was first discovered and the time the first alarm was sounded. He declared that while the sounding of the first alarm was delayed, employes had sought to battle the flames with hand extinguishers.

Although Brophy estimated the total damage at $100,000, William Miller, one of the owners of the park, said it would reach $500,000.

The fire, beginning in a ride known as the Dragon's Gorge, was fanned by an ocean breeze that came up from the south and scattered sparks toward a huge gas tank belonging to the Brooklyn Borough Gas Company 400 feet north of the park.

The tank, the second largest of its kind in the city, was emptied at once; but while firemen were still battling Luna Park's flames four alarms were sounded for a fire in the B. M. T. car barns at Avenue X and McDonald Ave. Sparks believed to have been blown across from Luna Park ignited between 15 and 20 wooden cars which were destroyed, Fire Department officials reported.

The car barns are approximately

Continued on Page 3

FIRE AND SMOKE INSTEAD OF JOY AND LAUGHTER—Billows of black smoke and spurts of flame shoot above the Mile Sky Chaser, famous roller coaster, in historic Luna Park yesterday, where fire caused $500,000 damage.

MERCURY HITS 93 MARK WITH 85 AND SUNNY PREDICTED FOR TODAY

The man at the Weather Bureau yesterday looked at the stars and then figured out through his instruments that today will be a nice, sunny day. And what's more, tomorrow will be sunny, too.

The mercury yesterday commuted between 90 and 92 degrees, hitting 93 for a few minutes around 3:30 p.m.; and gave in only slightly as late as 10:30, when it stood at 85. The jrediction for today is that the temperature will hover around 85.

Longshoremen Arrested In Lend-Lease Ship Theft

Domonick Carmine Colasanto, 32, of 1549 81st St., a longeshoreman employed at the Brooklyn Army Base, was arraigned yesterday before United States Commissioner Jacob A. Visel in the Brooklyn Federal Building charged with the theft of Government property. He entered a plea of innocent to the charge and was released in $2,500 bail to await action of the Federal grand jury.

Colasanto was arrested Friday by FBI agents when, Commissioner Visel was told, they found him removing a case containing fountain pens, valued at $1,620, from a freighter being loaded with lend-lease goods bound for England.

BROOKLYN PUT BACK ON MAP AS WPB AREA

Court Street Branch Office to Be Restored As District Quarters

Brooklyn has won at least one battle with the non-Brooklyn minded Government agencies, it was revealed yesterday when Emile Zola Weinberg, who has headed the War Production oBard's Brooklyn office since its inception, announced that, effective Aug. 15, the branch at 16 Court St. will be reinstated as a district office.

This means that an order issued in June which reduced Weinberg's office to that of a mere offshoot to the Empire State Building WPB offices has been taken back and that final priorities may be cleared in Brooklyn without the added inconvenience and loss of time entailed in a trip to Manhattan.

Had Many Complaints

The previous order caused considerable dissatisfaction among Brooklyn manufacturers and business men. Many complaints were received by Weinberg, he admitted.

On the strength of these, he said, he had armed himself with the merits of the case and argued Brooklyn's rights in the matter through the regional office in Manhattan and finally to Washington. The staff, which was reduced drastically when the office ceased to

Continued on Page 10

Spellman Back in Rome

Rome, Aug. 12 (U.P.)—Archbishop Francis J. Spellman of New York returned to Rome by air today after a visit to the islands of Sardinia and Corsica, it was announced.

All Florence Occupied, AMG Functions in City

By ELEANOR PACKARD

Rome, Aug. 12 (U.P.)—Allied forces have occupied all of Florence, center of Italian Rennaisance art, and AMG officials already are taking over, it was announced today, but the Allies have been forced from the village of San Colombano, five miles to the west, by massed German fire from the Gothic Line.

The Germans, who for weeks took advantage of Allied hesitancy to shell Florence's art and architectual treasures, withdrew at 5 a.m. yesterday, and within an hour Allied military Government personnel had crossed the Arno and entered the heart of the city.

Greeted enthusiastically by Italians, the AMG men found that the Germans had blown up the railway station and buildings along the waterfront and the ancient Via Porta Santa Maria which intersects the river at the historic Vecchio Bridge.

Italians told AMG officers that Italian women and children were shot by snipers as they went through the streets, seeking food and water.

The Nazis, since the Allied entry into southern Florence, had imposed a 24-hour curfew on all males, front reports said, and in recent days had entered and searched private homes, confiscating watches, cameras and any other valuables attracting them.

Meanwhile, sharp fighting broke out west of Florence as the Germans battled furiously to hold the three shallow pockets south of the Arno in that sector.

Reports from Irun, Spain, quoting a German news agency dispatch in the French newspaper Petite Gironde, said an "assembly of transports and landing craft as well as the withdrawal of numerous paratroops from the Italian front indicates that the Anglo-Americans are preparing to disembark very soon on the Ligurian cost.

Son of Larchmont Doctor Disappears From Home

Larchmont, Aug. 12—Mrs. J. B. Proctor, wife of a physician here, today issued an appeal for the return of their 14-year-old son, Morgan, who disappeared from home July 31, she said, after quarreling with his father about the boy's golfing companions.

Mrs. Proctor asked that the boy communicate with her at 117 Rockland Ave., the Proctors' Summer home, or at their Bronx Home, 3155 Grand Concourse.

Mrs. Proctor said the boy is 5 feet 10 inches tall, weighs 134 pounds, has brown hair and eyes, and has surgical scars on the back of each ankle and on the top of each foot.

Orders Adding of Regents 'Must' Subjects Probed

Albany, Aug. 12 (U.P.)—State Education Commissioner George D. Stoddard has ordered a special investigation of the addition of two mandatory subjects to the Regents study program which must be followed by public school pupils throughout New York State, it was announced today.

The revised program, opposed by teachers, superintendents and vocational school heads as "restricting the pupil's choice and individual needs," makes social studies and health education compulsory. This move brings the number of "must" subjects to nine, two more than the number of elective subjects which students may choose to complete their curriculum.

Mother Sobs Over Empty Home; Tells of "Brother's Keeper" Killing

"Once there wasn't room enough for us all here. Now I've got an empty house."

Thus, succinctly, the mother of James and Joseph Good yesterday expressed the tragedy which brought bitter sorrow to herself and her family in the early dawn Friday.

Mrs. Anne Kuhlmann, a slender, graceful woman with blue eyes and high-swept light brown hair, sobbed, her hands over her face, as she remembered days before the war—when her greatest joy was to watch her four handsome sons from th window as they left for work or play.

Today Joseph, 17, her youngest son by her first husband, is dead. His brother, James, 19, is in Raymond St. Jail pending appearance in Brooklyn Felony Court tomorrow on the charge of slaying Joseph.

The elder boy, a war veteran, was arrested after a row with his brother during which the latter struck his head fatally against a sharp-edged bureau.

Mrs. Kuhlmann, interviewed in her modest, second floor, walk-up apartment at 439 Wilson Ave. in the Bushwick section, told of her love for her boys.

"When they walked out the door, I looked out the window—so proud of my big boys. Time went so quickly—they got so big for me," she said.

Then war came along with separations destined to bring tragedy.

While James was serving his country in the army, his twin brother, John, entered the air corps.

"John just got his rating as aviation machinist's mate, 3d class. He will be heartbroken when he hears of this," his mother related. John is believed to be in Bermuda.

Another brother, Anthony, 18, is

Continued on Page 10

REDS IN DRIVE TO SURROUND WARSAW NAZIS

Armies Link Forces Astride Vital Railway—Widen Estonia Break

By ROBERT MUSEL

London, Sunday, Aug. 13 (U.P.)—Two might Soviet armies yesterday began hammering a great wedge between East Prussia and embattled Warsaw, while other Russian troops smashed deeper into Estonia and Latvia in a drive to chop up Germany's trapped Baltic armies.

Hurling the Germans back from powerfully fortified defense lines, the 1st and 2d White Russian Armies, commanded by Marshal Konstantin K. Rokossovsky and Gen. Matvei Zakharov, linked forces astride the vital Bialystok-Warsaw Railroad and smashed forward in an attempt to outflank Warsaw to the north and East Prussia to the south.

At the same time three Soviet armies in Latvia and Estonia extended their breakthrough southwest of Lake Pskov, drove the grimly fighting Nazis back against the Dvina River southeast of Riga and struck out toward the Baltic port of Leipaja (Libau).

Marshal Rokossovsky's 1st White Russian Army, smashing northeast of Warsaw on a wide front against the German defense line along the Bialystok-Warsaw Railroad west of the Bug River, extended his front yesterday to 60 miles. He crossed to the east bank of the river, joining forces with Zakharov at the rail station of Szepetowo. Simultaneously, the northern wing of Zakharov's Army was driving toward the big East Prussian rail junction of Lyck, and advancing along the Bialystok-Lyck Railroad, captured Monki, 35 miles southeast of the German town.

Slicing through powerful German fortifications and throwing back German reserves, Gen. Ivan I. Maslennikov's 3d Baltic Army widened a 43-mile breakthrough into Southern Estonia and pushed along the southwestern shore of Lake Pskov to Molozhino.

20 Get Prison Terms In Michigan Conspiracy

Mason, Mich., Aug. 12 (U.P.)—An Ingham Circuit Court Jury, in less than six hours of deliberation, returned a verdict of guilty today against 20 of 22 defendants charged with conspiracy to corrupt the 1939 Michigan Legislature by unlawful action on two bills regulating automobile finance companies.

Special Judge John Simpson immediately sentenced the defendants to three-to-five-year terms in the State Penitentiary.

F. D. R. PROPOSES QUARANTINE OF JAPANESE EMPIRE

Describes Plan for Distant Bases To Protect U. S. Against Future Aggression

By MERRIMAN SMITH

Bremerton, Wash., Aug. 12 (U.P.)—President Roosevelt, reporting to the nation after a lengthy cruise to Pacific war bases, today proposed a virtual quarantine of Japan and said he was sure other United Nations would agree to a vast plan providing this nation with distant bases protecting all the Americas against future aggression.

"Years of proof" will be necessary, he said, to show that the Japanese will cooperate in maintaining permanent peace.

Speaking from the deck of a destroyer in the Puget Sound Navy Yard shortly after arriving from Alaskan waters, the Chief Executive told a nationwide radio audience that "the word and honor of Japan cannot be trusted," thus creating the need for an elaborate network of forward bases nearer to Japan in the years to come.

Fresh from a first-hand view of powerful bases at Pearl Harbor and Adak and Lodiak in the Aleutians, the President charted the need for "undisputed control" by this country of the "Great Circle course for sea and air navigation from Puget Sound to Siberia and Northern China.

Avoids Forecast of War's End

Mr. Roosevelt came home after an absence from Washington since July 13 more confident than ever of victory, but he declined to forecast or even hint at when an end to the war either in Europe or the Pacific would come.

He said, however, that his Pearl Harbor talks with "my old friend, Gen. Douglas MacArthur," and Admiral Chester W. Nimitz and other key figures in the Pacific commands had resulted in "complete accord" in understanding the problem presented in defeating Japan, as well as "to the best methods for its solution."

It was Mr. Roosevelt's first address since he accepted Democratic renomination in a speech from San Diego on July 20. His speech was made before a wartime back-drop of sailors and drydock workers at the huge Puget Sound Navy Yard.

He stood bareheaded and suntanned on the forward deck of the destroyer delivering his speech under the upraised forward gun, surrounded by members of his military and naval staffs who have been traveling with him.

After his speech the President went ashore for a brief tour of the installations here at the Navy Yard.

Reports War Well in Hand

Outspokenly impressed by his first-hand view of bases in Hawaii and the Aleutian Islands, the President said the war was "well in hand in the vast area" of the Pacific where, he said, "more than a million of our troops" are on duty."

But, he said, "I cannot tell you if I know when the war will be over either in Europe or in the Far East or the war against Japan."

He followed his reference to his inability to predict an end to the war by appealing for continued, full-strength public support of the war effort, saying the conflict would end sooner if the people maintained a continued production of "necessary supplies and ships and planes."

As to the future defense of the

Continued on Page 10

3,500 BOMBERS CLIMAX RAIDS BY SHUTTLE SWEEP

Blast Invasion-Jittery Nazis Along 320-Mile Mediterranean Front

Allied Supreme Headquarters, London, Aug. 12 (U.P.)—More than 3,500 Italy and British-based Allied bombers and fighters smashed at German targets in France today, climaxing their offensive with a powerful shuttle sweep against the invasion-jittery enemy along a 320-mile Mediterranean front.

While the Americans' 8th and 9th Air Forces and the R.A.F. throttled Nazi communications, airdromes, oil supplies and U-boat shelters in northern France, more than 1,500 shuttling 8th and 15th Air Force heavy bombers and fighters reared up from Italy to slash German airfields, transport and strong points from Toulouse to the Italian Riviera, where Berlin broadcasts hinted a possible new Allied landing.

Eighth Air Force fighter bombers, in one of their most successful days over northern France, flew more than 1,000 sorties up to 7 p.m. They were reported officially to have destroyed or damaged 325 locomotives and 2,860 railway cars, including 359 laden with fuel and 172 with ammunition.

(The German radio early Sunday announced that Allied planes were approaching Northwest and West Germany. The Belgrade radio said an Allied bomber formation was flying into eastern Croatia and Bulgarians were warned by the Sofia transmitter that "single enemy aircraft" were over that country's western border.)

Jap Ship Is Sunk, 34 Boats Damaged

Allied Headquarters, Southwest Pacific, Sunday, Aug. 13 (U.P.)—Medium Mitchell bombers, in a blitz bombing of the Japanese-held island of Halmahera, sank a 1,000-ton freighter and seriously damaged another of 3,000 tons, five coastal vessels and 28 barges, Gen. Douglas MacArthur announced today.

The Allied Air Force also sank 10 seaplanes and hit 31 parked Japanese planes, MacArthur's communique added.

Boston bombers, sweeping the Vogelkop Peninsula on Dutch New Guinea, sank three 1,000-ton freighters, seriously damaged another and destroyed or damaged five coastal vessels and eight barges, the communique said.

A single Liberator bombed the Davao waterfront on the Philippine Island of Mindanao, Friday night.

295 Australian War Brides Land, 74 Babies on Ship

San Francisco, Aug. 12 (U.P.)—While a military band blared out the stately strains of "Here Comes the Bride," 295 Australian war brides marched off a battle grey luxury liner today on to United States soil, where Red Cross nurses had thoughtfully arranged a lineup of baby carriages for the 74 babies who accompanied their mothers.

Every one seemed happy, and their thoughts concerned chiefly (1) their husbands and (2) a "good American steak," for which the girls were willing to pay $3.

For the first time since the start of the war, the press went out to board the ship as it entered the Golden Gate. Wives and babies lined the railings, seeking a glimpse of San Francisco Bay.

Jersey Shipbuilding Firm Needs More Workers

Kearny, N. J., Aug. 12—The need for more ship builders at both the Kearny and Port Newark yards of the U. S. Steel's Federal Shipbuilding and Dry Dock Company was revealed today in an announcement made here by Lynn H. Korndorff, company president.

The Port Newark yard, he said, has been given a "Swiss watch" assignment in ship building, with transfer to that yard from the Kearny yard of the work of building "pocket cruiser" type heavy destroyers.

2 Youths Arrested In Murder of News Vendor

Schenectady, Aug. 12 (U.P.)—State Police Chief Inspector Francis S. McGarvey today announced the arrest of two 19-year-old Schenectady youths, Frank Rossi and David Sender, for the brutal murder of Edward Reali, 36, a well-known downtown newspaper vendor.

McGarvey said the boys admitted picking up Reali Wednesday morning and taking him to nearby Niskayuna, where they beat and robbed him of $249.

ALLIED FLIERS SMASH AT ESCAPE PATH

Yank 'Ghost' Army And Canadians 15 Mi. From Junction

By EDWARD W. BEATTIE

Allied Supreme Headquarters, London (Sunday) Aug. 13 (U.P.)—An American "ghost" army and Anglo-Canadian column today were reported within 15 miles of a junction near Argentan that would snap shut a trap around possibly 100,000 Germans reeling back in retreat under a bewildering succession of Allied blows.

More than 200 American Marauder and Havoc bombers, answering a direct call for aid from the converging ground forces, drenched the last few miles of the escape gap with high explosives and fragmentation bombs late Saturday, concentrating on the area just west of Argentan.

MASSACRE FEARED

London, Sunday, Aug. 13 (U.P.)—The British Broadcasting Corporation, in a special announcement in French beamed to the continent early today, said that Gestapo officers were taking 1,500 political prisoners from Paris to Metz and it is "doubtful whether they will arrive at their destination."

"We believe it is the intention of these officers to masacre them en route," the BBC said. "The names of these officers are known and they will eventually be brought to justice for their crimes."

In the first official indication of the whereabouts of the American "Ghost Army" since it left Le Mans five days ago, 9th Air Force headquarters said that German forces were trying to withdraw in the Argentan area "under the pressure of American advances from the south."

This would represent another spectacular advance by the Yanks of 50 miles due north from Le Mans, bringing them within 15 miles of a junction with British and Canadian troops hammering south in the Falaise area.

Big Nazi Force Imperilled

Possibly 100,000 Germans, and most certainly the five panzer divisions which had just begun a belated retreat from the Vire area in the center of the front, were in imminent peril.

The Berlin radio asserted that the Yanks had smashed through Alençon in a 30-mile drive north from Le Mans, cutting the Germans' escape gap to 35 miles.

Doughboys cashing in on the withdrawal swept back into embattled Mortain and Sourdeval, anchors of the German salient below Vire. To the east, British and Canadian columns joined forces ten miles below Caen and wiped out another salient in the Forest of Cinglais—dubbed the "Forest of the Dead" for its heaps of German corpses.

Yank Battalion Rescued

Late dispatches said that the Yanks in their advance rescued an entire battalion of their comrades who had been isolated in the Mortain sector.

Gains up to five miles were scored on both sector sand indirectly responsible were the sweeping operations across the German rear by American flying columns which have not been officially pin-pointed since they left Le Mans five days ago.

The whereabouts of these Yanks, who, Berlin insists, are led by Lt. Gen. George S. Patton Jr., obviously is the key to the entire situation and for exactly that reason the situation beyond Le Mans "must remain ob-

Continued on Page 10

Germans Believed Set For One Major Stand

By REUEL S. MOORE

Washington, Aug. 12 (U.P.)—The Germans have left in western Europe sufficient resources for only one major stand against the Allies, and if that fails them they face disaster, observers here said tonight.

Moreover, the Germans are believed to have lost the option of making an effective stand west of Paris and the Seine.

Apparent German attemps to assemble a mobile striking force capable of offensive action against the Allies in Normandy and Brittany have all failed thus far.

Movement of German troops from east of the Seine and the south of France has been inadequate to create such a force. These troops have been committed to the present battle piecemeal, on an emergency basis.

The Germans apparently maintained offensive intentions in western France up to a few days ago, as indicated by the persistence of their efforts to slash through American supply lines between Mortain and Avranches.

These efforts proved futile, however, and now the Germans are deeply involved in a vulnerable salient where a number of divisions are threatened with encirclement by Canadian and British forces.

The Germans are believed to have employed more than 30 divisions thus far in Normandy and Brittany out of a maximum of about 70 available in all western Europe. German casualties in Normandy were estimated at nearly 200,000, equivalent of almost 20 divisions.

WHERE TO FIND IT

	Page		Page
Camera Club	14	Radio	22
Crossword	Comics	Real Estate	26
Dr. Brady	16	Schools	26
Editorial	16	Society	12, 13
Fighter's Digest	15	Sports	19, 20
Financial	25	Theaters	23, 24
Helen Worth	14	Trend	21
Horoscope	11	Want Ads	27, 28, 29
Mary Haworth	11	Wartime Problems	15
Movies	23, 24	Week Outdoors	22
Novel	8	Women	14
Obituaries	17		
Our Fighters	15		

Coney Threatened as $500,000 Fire Sweeps Luna Park

Official navy photo

CONEY LANDMARK GOING UP IN SMOKE—This airview shows the Luna Park blaze at its height. In the foreground is the Mile Sky Chaser, and just behind it in the lower center is the Dragon's Gorge, where the fire started. In right center is the 125-foot tower which crumpled in a mass of flame shortly after the photo was snapped.

Photo by A. Daldorf

GETTING UNDER WAY—Big blaze first showed up as one of Coney's topnotchers as photographer, standing behind airplane ride snapped this shot looking toward Dragon's Gorge, where fire started.

THOUSANDS WATCH FIGHT BY FIREMEN

Continued from Page 1

three-quarters of a mile from Luna Park.

According to the police, about 20 rides, games and amusement devices, in addition to two bar and grill establishments, were destroyed as the Luna Park fire raged across heat-dried wooden structures in the amusement center.

Mayor LaGuardia, reaching the scene while the scores of engine companies were pumping water into the flaming wreckage, discovered a group of firemen drinking bottled beer at the bar in the dance hall, according to an eyewitness account, and ordered the firemen out of the place.

The fire, gaining headway after originating in the Dragon's Gorge, ignited the Mile Sky Chaser and spread to the Victory Bar on Surf Avenue.

Other amusement devices falling victim to the spreading flames included the Boomerang, the Dodgem, Shoot the Chutes, Aqua Gal, Spook Street, Rollo-Plane, Mirror Maze, Harem Scarem and the shooting gallery.

One of the first indications of the blaze was smoke coming from the Dragon's Mouth. A barker, Bert Kaye, on duty chanting on the wonders of the headless girl and the human ostrich, had 175 inside his freak show when he first saw the smoke.

"There's nothing much to worry about," he said. "Just a small fire—in the dragon, no doubt. But come back later. I said come back later—and when I say don't come in I mean it."

A young boy, Michael Orsl, 14, was on top of the shoot the chutes when he saw the fire blazing in the nearby scenic railway.

"We're going to get killed," he yelled.

He attracted the attention of the dispatchers, who brought the ride to a sudden stop.

A 125-foot electric tower in the park's center, a landmark visible for miles around, was destroyed, together with the Luna Park circus, although park officials said all the animals in the circus, including dogs, ponies and monkeys, had been removed before the fire reached the structure.

Meanwhile, Coney's crowds remained orderly, although an estimated 10,000 jammed the south side of Surf Ave., as firemen pushed their battle against the flames.

Crowds jammed the resort as the fire broke. Their holiday mood changed swiftly to one of awe and consternation as they saw the park enveloped in smoke and flames and heard scores of engine and truck companies roaring into the seaside resort. Toward nightfall Coney's traditional evening crowd of merrymakers began to arrive.

William Lombard of 689 E. 49th St., the Luna Park promotion manager, told Fire Marshal Brophy he was standing on the sun deck of the park's swimming pool when he heard a six-bell signal sounded on the park's fire alarm system. He said the signal was from the Dragon's Gorge ride section.

Brophy questioned Irwin Jacobson, 18, of 3891 Neptune Ave., one of the Dragon's Gorge employes. Jacobson said he had gone into a wash room underneath the Gorge. There he said he heard sputtering and saw sparks and flames coming from an electrical fixture in the ceiling.

Jacobson told Brophy he seized a pan, ran to a sink and filled the

Eagle Staff photo

DISCOVERED FIRE — Irwin Jacobson, center, Dragon Gorge employe who first saw the flames, leaves the scene flanked by two other empolyes after being questioned by the Fire Marshal.

pan four or five times with water which he threw at the flames.

Robert Mulholland of 2963 W. 33d St., manager of the Dragon's Gorge, with Jacobson and other employes brought hand extinguishers into use. Mulholland told Brophy that just previously a car with seven or eight passengers had started out on a trip through the Gorge. The car was stopped at the first turn, where the passengers were discharged.

The fire's origin was traced eventually to a tool shed.

Brophy said it was almost impossible to determine who had sent in the first alarm, as several were turned in. The five alarms brought together 250 officers and men. Fire Commissioner Patrick Walsh and Police Commissioner Lewis Valentine hastened to the scene.

After the fifth alarm had been sounded, and still more apparatus was needed, a "simultaneous alarm" bringing a complement of men and equipment generally assembled for a five-alarm fire, was sounded from a box several miles away. This brought equipment from other sections of the city which had been untouched by the previous alarms. This call was turned in from 8th Ave. and Union St., and as firemen arrived there they were sent to Coney Island for duty at Luna Park.

The fire reached spectacular heights at about 4:30 p.m., when the 125-foot illuminated tower, with a huge electric sign at the top, became a blazing torch and crashed to the ground in a shower of sparks and embers.

Clouds of smoke meanwhile had become visible for miles around. The police were inundated with telephone calls and hundreds also reached the Brooklyn Eagle's switchboard.

Mayor LaGuardia reached the scene shortly before 5 p.m. Deputy Chief Police Inspector James J. Ryan and Deputy Chief Inspector Louis F. Schilling, in charge of police protection for Brooklyn, also had arrived. Deputy Chief John Waldron was among the Fire Department officials.

In the list of amusement places destroyed was the opera house, where a picture entitled "Hitler at

Eagle Staff photo

PARKED CAR — The fire reached this automobile before its unidentified owner could. Boatswain's Mate 2d class Mike Brereton surveys the result.

the End of a Rope" was playing.

Police said there was never any suggestion of panic despite the scope of the fire. They praised park employes for the efficiency and speed with which they had escorted spectators and merrymakers out of the park.

Thirteen of the 16 persons reported injured were civilian volunteer firemen. Dr. Rossman of Kings County Hospital said three firemen had received second degree burns and that two had collapsed from heat exhaustion.

Two employes of the park were unaccounted for, but police said they did not believe them to have been injured, and that, more likely, they had become lost in the crowds.

Luna Park was badly damaged on Dec. 11, 1911, by a fire which caused about $150,000 damage.

Within the past fortnight it was announced that Luna Park had been purchased by the three men who had been operating it since 1941. Theey are William Miller, the general manager; Capt. Edward J. Danziger, U. S. Army, and his brother, Lt. Harry Lee Danziger, U. S. Army. Contracts for the purchase were signed at the offices of the Prudence Bond Corporation, 10 E. 40th St., Manhattan, trustees for the Farmers Bank Trust Company, which had acquired the property some years ago under the foreclosure of a mortgage involving about $600,000.

Although the fire was under control at 5 p.m. firemen were still shooting water on the ruins at a late hour.

Miller said Luna park would be closed for the season and would open next year after the amusement places were rebuilt. The closing affects those places untouched by the flames.

Residents in teh vicinity of the B. M. T. fire were warned by the Fire Department to wet the grounds around their homes.

Latest Coney Island Fire Recalls Former Blazes Costing Millions

Brooklyn old-timers last night sadly reflected on the joker which life plays periodically at Coney Island at the expense of persons seeking pleasure and relief from the heat.

Yesterday's conflagration at the resort reminded old-timers of the Dreamland fire in 1911, when Coney Island was reduced to a shambles and the estimated damage was placed at more than $6,000,000. Five blocks were laid waste. Fifty amusement spots were leveled. Dreamland, the famous crown-towered feature, was lost permanently.

The more seriously injured of the eight firemen were Jeremiah McCann, 40, of 1446 E. 4th St., of Engine Company 247, second degree burns; David Sterling, 29, of 2116 76th St., Engine Company 228, eye injuries; Louis Bengi, 34, of 2064 W. 6th St., second degree burns, all sent to Coney Island Hospital, and Franklin Nelson, 31, of 3602 Avenue J, Engine Company 326, second degree burns, sent home.

Civilians injured included Louis Alfano, 17, of 850 Jefferson Ave., heat exhaustion, taken to Coney Island Hospital; Albert Allen, 36, of 2806 Mermaid Ave., sprained back; Francis Fox, 28, of 280 Ocean Parkway, sprained foot, and Rose Gormendia, 19, of 1901 Mermaid Ave., sprained ankle, all of whom were sent home.

Steeplechase Burns

Only four years before, Steeplechase Park was burned down and the loss was placed at $1,500,000. The fire ran along two blocks on Surf Ave., skirted two blocks of the Bowery and swept through to the ocean front.

The following year, on July 8, Pabst's Loop Hotel was destroyed in a four-alarm fire. The loss was estimated at $200,000.

Then, on the morning of May 27, 1911, Coney Island suffered its most spectacular fire when Dreamland was demolished.

On Aug. 20, 1917, a burning cigarette was flipped carelessly onto the "snow-capped" mountains of Luna Park, and the fire which resulted caused $10,000 in losses.

Parkway Baths Destroyed

Later that year, on Nov. 30, the Parkway Baths, Hubbs Hotel and a number of adjacent buildings were razed by fire. Property destruction was estimated at $500,000.

In 1923 Inman's Casino and neighboring buildings were swept by a blaze which caused damage of $75,000.

The Whitney Baths were wiped out in a $150,000 fire in April of 1924. The same year, four days before Christmas, the Boardwalk and a square block of unoccupied frame bath houses went up in a $200,000 blaze.

Three square blocks were leveled July 13, 1932, when fire swept up from the Boardwalk, and 2,000 persons were left homeless. The damage was placed at $5,000,000.

In October of 1939 a wind-swept blaze caused $100,000 damages to a number of dwellings facing the boardwalk.

Fire of undetermined origin destroyed the Mardi Gras motion picture house in a three-alarm fire Jan. 24, 1940.

On Oct. 5 of last year another Coney Island landmark burned down when Lane's Original Irish House was reduced by a two-alarm fire.

Patton Leads Tank Drive in the North

7 ★★★★★★★ SPORTS
Wall Street Financial News

BROOKLYN EAGLE

WEATHER—Hot, Humid Tonight; Hot Tomorrow

103d Year. No. 223. DAILY & SUNDAY • (Copyright 1944 The Brooklyn Eagle, Inc.) • BROOKLYN, N. Y., TUESDAY, AUGUST 15, 1944 • Entered at the Brooklyn Post-office as 2d Class Mail Matter • 3 CENTS IN NEW YORK CITY ELSEWHERE 4 CENTS

ALLIED ARMY LANDS IN SOUTHERN FRANCE

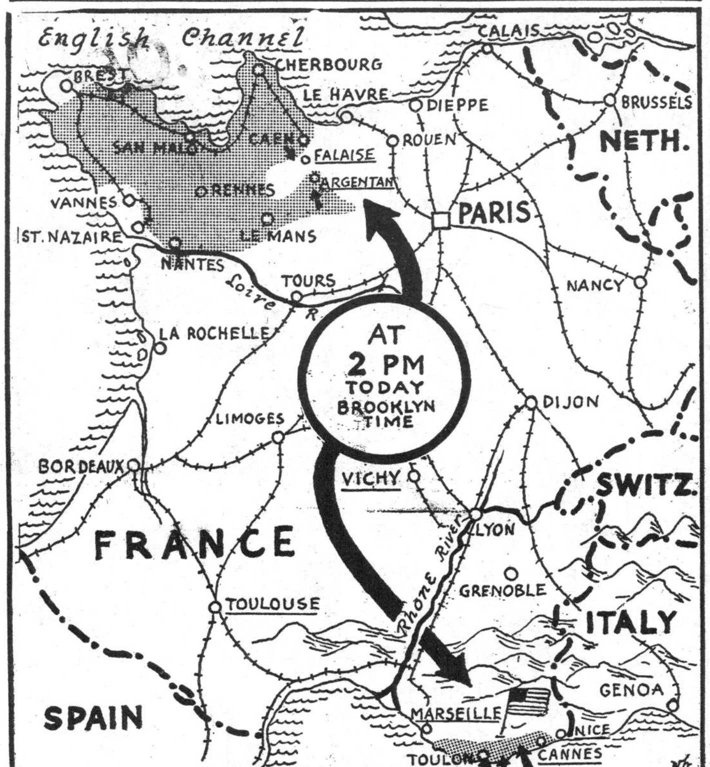

WE HIT SOUTH FRANCE—Shaded area between Marseille and Nice shows where Allies have established beachheads for the drive north. Shaded portion in north indicates liberated area and small arrows at Argentan and Falaise tell the story of the trap closing on 100,000 or more bewildered Nazis.

Firm Beachheads Carved Out; Foe in North Faces Annihilation

By ELEANOR PACKARD

Rome, Aug. 15 (UP)—A mighty Allied invasion force struck into southern France from sea and sky today and within a matter of hours overran the Germans' feeble shore defenses and established firm beachheads along a 100-mile strip of the Mediterrean coast between Nice and Marseille.

A miles-long sky train of gliders and transport planes swept in over the coast before dawn to shower thousands of American and British paratroopers across the rolling hills behind the Nazi coastal defenses, and the main assault force splashed ashore from landing craft at 8 a.m.

Between the two forces, the stunned Germans were rendered almost helpless and their once-formidable fortifications were breached almost without a struggle.

"By mid-morning all the landings were proceeding successfully according to schedule, against only light ground opposition and no air opposition," a headquarters communique announced.

"The supporting air-borne operation was also successfully executed."

First reports said American and French infantrymen, the pick of the veteran armies massing in the Mediterranean theater for months, made up the bulk of the assault force put ashore by an armada of some 800 warships and transport craft.

American and British paratroops and air-borne infantry spearheaded the attack, but it was indicated that the initial British army participation was limited to this phase of the invasion.

Reports trickling back from the thousands of Allied fliers who swept unchallenged over the beaches said the invading army was striking swiftly inland, in a drive aimed to the northwest of the Rhone Valley, less than 30 miles west of Marseille.

One observation plane flew 60 miles inland without sighting any large German troop concentration, but later reports said American Thunderbolts were dive-bombing Nazi tanks attempting to reach the coast.

Gen. Sir Henry Maitland Wilson, supreme Allied commander in the Mediterranean, declared that his forces would sweep the Germans from their path, march northward through the heart of France and join up with the Allied armies closing in on Paris from Normandy.

"Victory is certain," he proclaimed in a ringing message to the people of France. "Remember 1918."

The first special allied communique announcing the success of the landing carefully masked the principal assault points in an obvious

Continued on Page 2

ESCAPE ROAD IS SLICED BY PLANES, GUNS

By VIRGIL PINKLEY

Supreme Headquarters, A. E. F., Aug. 15 (U.P.)—Allied planes, tanks and infantrymen opened the battle of annihilation on some 100,000 cornered, fighting Germans in the Normandy pocket today as veteran Canadian troopers and the "Blood and Guts" armor of Lt. Gen. George S. Patton's American 3d Army virtually slammed shut the enemy's last escape route to the east.

Patton's slashing tank columns pounded up from Argentan to within eight miles or less of Falaise while the Canadian 1st Army stormed southward to within about two miles of that town and cut across one of the two main highways eastward to Lisieux.

Front reports suggested that the escape corridor might have been cut to less than ten miles and the flanking guns of the Canadian and American forces already had made that narrow life line impassable.

Burning Charnel House

Wave upon wave of Allied warplanes shuttled incessantly over the doomed Nazi Army, bombing and strafing every moving target and turning the entire area into a burning charnel house.

Headquarters reports indicated that Field Marshal Gunther von Kluge had abandoned all hope of extricating the remnants of his 12 divisious from the pocket and was reforming his battle-wearied troops for a death fight against the Allied armies pressing in from all sides.

The Germans appeared to be wheeling their remaining tanks into a stockade-type defense line similar to the covered wagon cordons once used by American pioneers, and massing their riflemen, machine gunners and artillery behind that barrier.

The bulk of the Nazi forces were

Continued on Page 7

Lt. Gen. George S. Patton

'Blood and Guts' In Tank Race To Trap Foe

By PHIL AULT

Supreme Headquarters, A. E. F., Aug. 15 (U.P.)—Old Blood and Guts is on the road back.

Gen. Dwight D. Eisenhower announced at his advanced command post today that Lt. Gen. George S. Patton, the blustery, rough-riding tank specialist with a gift for getting himself in the dog-house, is leading the American motorized spearheads in their race to trap the German army in western France.

The appointment, kept secret by the Allied command until Patton's troops had jammed the enemy into his present dilemma, showed Eisenhower's confidence that Old Blood and Guts is an inspired leader of motorized troops.

For days the German radio had

Continued on Page 7

MADE MAJOR GENERAL

Washington, Aug. 15 (U.P.)—The Senate Military Affairs Committee today unanimously approved the promotion of Lt. Gen. George S. Patton Jr. to the permanent rank of major general.

Senator A. B. (Happy) Chandler (D., Ky.) in announcing the committee's action said that members felt Patton had been "disciplined enough" for a soldier-slapping incident which occurred during the Sicilian campaign nearly a year ago.

Chandler said Patton's leadership of the 3d American Army had prompted the committee to confirm the promotion today.

Patton's name was originally sent to the full committee along with 13 others last October. Revelation of the slapping incidents caused the committee to table Patton's promotion while the others were approved.

3,000 PLANES POUND SCORE OF NAZI AIRFIELDS

Reich, Low Countries And Paris Area Hit To Support Invasions

London, Aug. 15 (U.P.)—Allied bombers and fighter forces totaling more than 3,000 planes attacked a score of German aircraft nests in the Reich, Low Countries and Paris area today as the RAF and USAAF continued their aerial campaign to neutralize the Luftwaffe over the twin invasion areas of France.

More than 1,100 aircraft of the RAF bomber command, with fighter cover, dropped 5,000 tons of high explosives on five airfields in Holland and four in Belgium used by enemy night fighters. All nine attacks were "very effective," the Air Ministry announced, listing two bombers as missing.

Meanwhile, a fleet of nearly 1,000 American heavy bombers, accompanied by upwards of 750 fighters, struck seven enemy air force bases and three airdromes in Germany, Belgium and Holland, while 9th Air Force medium bombers slashed at several other airdromes in the vicinity of the French capital.

The Allied campaign to smash enemy aircraft bases was coupled with widespread attacks by the 8th Air Force against German battlefront communications and an attack last night by the RAF coastal command on enemy warships in the Gironde River.

Smashing blows were delivered against Luftwaffe bases at Cologne-Ostheim, Wiesbaden - Erbenheim, Frankfort-Eschborn, Wittmund-Ardorf, Zwischenahm, Vechta and Handorf, the first three along the Rhine River and the others in northwest Germany.

Shipyard Union Votes To Strike if Pay Is Cut

Electricians' Walkout Would Hamper War Effort, Officials Say

Members of Local 277, International Brotherhood of Electrical Workers, A. F. L., have voted overwhelmingly to strike if the contractors for whom they work obey Government directive to cut their pay from $1.25 to $1.20 an hour.

The vote result was announced today by the Regional National Labor Relations Board. The NLRB held the strike ballot last night at the expiration of the 30-day intention to strike notice entered by the union.

Of 1,279 eligible voters, employed in a dozen New York and New Jersey shipyards, 758 cast ballots. Four were voided and the totals were: For interruption of work, 571; against, 183.

The men are working on merchant ships which are being converted into troopships, hospital ships and other war-vital categories and Government officials said the war effort would be hampered considerably if a strike is ordered.

The union members are at work today and John Gillen, president of the union said the next move was up to the Allied Marine Contractors Association, whose member firms

Continued on Page 7

Submarine Output Halted When 8,300 Quit Jobs at Groton

Groton, Conn., Aug. 15 (U.P.)—Production of submarines at the huge electric boat company yards was halted when "75 to 80 percent" of the 8,300 employes on the day shift failed to report for work, the company announced today.

Edward Darrow, personnel manager, said the company was waiting for the Independent Shipbuilding and Marine Engineers Union, which called the strike yesterday after workers had voted against it Saturday, to "make a move" toward arbitration.

The company is one of the world's largest producers of submarines.

Charles Suisman, counsel for the union, said that 90 percent of all workers, both on the day and night shift, have joined the strike.

More than 50 State policemen guarded approaches to the plant, but there were no reports of violence. Efforts to arbitrate the dispute yesterday ended in a stalemate.

WHERE TO FIND IT

	Page		Page
Comics	15	Patterns	12
Crossword	12	Radio	15
Dr. Brady	6	Society	4
Editorial	6	Sports	10, 11
Financial	9	Take My Word	6
Helen Worth	4	Theaters	12
Horoscope	15	These Women	15
Mary Haworth	5	Tommy Holmes	10
Movies	12	Uncle Ray	15
Novel	5	Want Ads	13, 14
Obituaries	7	Wartime Problems	9
Our Fighters	9	Women	4

Governor Dewey Busy On State Affairs

Albany, Aug. 15 (U.P.)—State affairs occupied Governor Dewey today following a weekend spent at his Pawling farm, where he worked on campaign speeches.

James C. Hagerty, his executive assistant, said the Governor had no political conferences scheduled, but would meet with newspaper reporters later in the day.

Germans Resume Robot Attacks on South England

London, Aug. 15 —The Germans sent flying bombs over southern England and the London area during the night, following a lull since early Monday. An unestimated number of casualties and some damage were caused.

NO RELIEF IN HEAT WAVE UNTIL FRIDAY

Another Record of 95 Forecast for Today—Crops in East Menaced

No relief is in sight from the heat wave until Friday, the Weather Bureau announced today. The bank of cold air, forming in the Dakota sections, has been delayed in its eastward sweep and the hoped for relief by tonight will not be forthcoming.

	Sun.	Mon.	Today
Midnight	80	82	80
2 a.m.	80	81	79
3 a.m.	78	79	76
4 a.m.	76	78	75
5 a.m.	76	78	75
6 a.m.	75	77	75
7 a.m.	75	77	75
8 a.m.	76	78	76
9 a.m.	77	79	77
10 a.m.	82	80	80
11 a.m.	84	85	83.67
Noon	80	86	86.63
1 p.m.	88	88	88

A blistering high reading of 95 was predicted for today which would be two degrees above the record for the date made in 1938.

Today's spell of torrid torture will mark the sixth consecutive day the city has been baked to a frazzle by higher than 90-degree temperatures.

Continued on Page 7

Plunges to Death On Facing Charge He Beat Daughters

Vincent Simmons' name was called in Special Sessions Court this morning as he faced a charged of beating his two children with a leather belt.

Vincent didn't anwser.

He was dead. He jumped or fell at 5:45 this morning from the roof of the home of a friend at 240 High St.

The 42-year-old Puerto Rican merchant seaman was arrested July 29 by Detective William Newbar after complaints that he had thrashed his daughters, Julia, 7, and Dorothy, 9, with his heavy belt. He was out on $1,500 bail for trial today.

His attorney, Morris Brettschneider, told the court his client was dead.

Tom Harmon to Wed Elyse Knox on Aug. 26

Ann Arbor, Mich., Aug. 15 (U.P.)—Lt. Tom Harmon and Elyse Knox, movie actress, will be married Aug. 25 in St. Mary's Student Chapel here, it was announced today.

Blames Heat, Tomatoes

Trenton, N. J., Aug. 15—The excessive heat and thousands of ripe tomatoes were too much for Willis V. Layton, 27, a convict at the Bordentown Prison Farm, so he just walked away from the huge tomato patch. Captured last night, he complained it was too hot to pick tomatoes.

BELMONT RESULTS
(Saratoga Meeting)

1—Epicure 134.40-67.50-33.10, Febridge 6.40-4.60, Refugee 7.10. (Off 1:21)
2—Gaytown, 1st; Hav U Heard, 2d; Little Flyer, 3d

Signal Corps Radio Telephoto to INS.

RECEIVING SPIRITUAL SUSTENANCE—Troops are given Holy Communion on the beach just before they board craft taking them to the point marking the second French invasion by American armed forces.

SCREEN

By Jane Corby

'Saga of Jenny' in 'Lady in Dark' Was Pre-Recorded by Ginger Rogers

The sound engineers at almost any Hollywood studio can work tricks of legerdemain at their dials and panels which would make most music critics gasp. If absolutely necessary they can, by a twist of a knob, turn a sour note into a true one by varying the vibration frequencies. If a phrase is too poorly delivered, the singer can repeat it until it is acceptable and the right "take" can be cut into the rest of the song, just as a retaken piece of film can be spliced into the rest of the continuity. When a Crosby or a Rise Stevens records, the musical director at the podium and the sound mixer at his panel usually prefer to go over the entire song again to obtain a perfect recording, but in the case of semi-amateurs such as Ray Milland, Warner Baxter and Jon Hall, headliners in "Lady in the Dark," at the N. Y. Paramount, it is usually preferable merely to repeat a certain phrase, because otherwise the number may go sour in another spot. In other words, the pastepot - and - shears method produces the best eventual results.

Songs are still pre-recorded for the most part, and then played back on the sound stage through a huge amplifier when the accompanying action is photographed, because it is easier for the actor to concentrate on one thing at a time. This was true of Ginger's provocative "Saga of Jenny" in the circus dream in "Lady in the Dark," because to coordinate a perfect recording with a dance which required innumerable rehearsals and "takes" for camera long-shots, medium shots and close-ups, would have required a patience and a perfection of execution almost unheard-of. Therefore, in addition to the recording of the song on sound film so that it may be eventually printed with the final photographic "take," a wax disc is cut for playback purposes.

All of which sounds very complicated. And Joe Lilley, Paramount music coach and supervisor, running back and forth from orchestra and piano to microphone and sound mixer, doesn't bother to explain the mechanics to his pupils. Where ignorance is vocal bliss, 'tis folly to scare a potential new singing star to death.

'Song of Russia' Due At the Met Tomorrow

M-G-M's "Song of Russia," starring Robert Taylor and Susan Peters, opening tomorrow at Loew's Metropolitan Theater, is the story of an American symphony conductor who falls in love with a lovely Russian girl while touring Russia prior to the Nazi invasion. War breaks out while they are on their honeymoon, and they are caught in the sweep of the initial Nazi success.

"The Woman of the Town," with Claire Trevor, Albert Dekker and Henry Hull is the companion feature having its first Brooklyn showing at the Met with M-G-M's "Song of Russia."

MOVIE TIME SCHEDULE

ALBEE—"North Star," 11:00, 1:50, 4:45, 7:35, 10:30; "Never a Dull Moment," 12:50, 3:45, 6:35, 9:30.
FOX—"Where Are Your Children," 12:14, 2:46, 5:28, 8:00, 10:32; "Timber Queen," 11:00, 1:32, 4:14, 6:56, 9:28.
METROPOLITAN—"A Guy Named Joe," 11:23, 2:03, 4:42, 7:22, 10:00.
STRAND—"The Uninvited," 11:00, 1:50, 4:40, 7:30, 10:20.

MANHATTAN

CAPITOL—"The Bridge of San Luis Rey," 10:15, 1:23, 4:24, 7:34, 10:53; stage, 12:21, 3:22, 6:32, 9:33.
CRITERION—"Ladies Courageous," 10:09, 12:15, 2:20, 4:25, 6:35, 8:40, 10:50, 12:55.
MUSIC HALL—"Up in Arms," 10:35, 1:25, 4:17, 7:28, 10:23; stage, 12:20, 3:13, 6:25, 9:30.
PARAMOUNT—"Lady in the Dark," 10:01, 12:54, 3:41, 6:56, 10:02, 12:47; stage, 11:57, 2:47, 6:02, 9:17, 11:45.
VICTORIA—"Voice in the Wind," 10:00, 11:50, 1:40, 3:30, 5:19, 7:09, 8:59, 10:49, 12:39.

"JANE EYRE," with Joan Fontaine and Orson Welles, opens tomorrow at the Albee, with the first New York showing of Charlie Chan in "The Chinese Cat."

'Up in Arms' Stays At the Music Hall

Establishing Danny Kaye as the screen's new comedy star, Goldwyn's hit film musical, "Up In Arms," in which he makes his hilarious debut, will enter its third big week at Radio City Music Hall tomorrow.

Goldwyn's first musical comedy in five years, "Up In Arms" is in Technicolor and features the popular songstress, Dinah Shore, Dana Andrews and Constance Dowling in a madcap story about Kaye's evolution from a love-sick civilian, obsessed with imaginary ills, to a dashing hero in the U. S. Army.

On the Music Hall stage is "Magazine Revue," featuring the Music Hall Rockettes, Corps de Ballet, Choral Ensemble and Music Hall Symphony Orchestra, with the famous ballerina, Patricia Bowman, and Ben Dova heading the list of guest artists.

'Purple Heart' Begins Its Second Roxy Week

Darryl F. Zanuck's "The Purple Heart" started its second week today at the Roxy Theater.

Produced by 20th Century-Fox and directed by Lewis Milestone, the new film features Dana Andrews, Richard Conte, Kevin O'Shea, Farley Granger, Donald Barry, Dave Willock, Charles Russell, Sam Levene and John Craven.

The special screening of "The Purple Heart," which was to be held at the Harkness Pavilion of the Presbyterian Hospital yesterday for J. B. Powell, former editor of the North China Review, was postponed to next Tuesday, March 21.

N. Y. Strand Continues Stage and Screen Show

The N. Y. Strand will hold its present stage show, headed by Russ Morgan and his famous orchestra, for a second week starting Friday. Featured with the orchestra is vocalist Sylvia Grey. As special attractions, the in-person show presents Borrah Minevitch's Original Harmonica Rascals, featuring Johnny, and dancing Barbara Blaine. The screen feature is the Warner Bros. picturization of the life of Nora Bayes. "Shine on Harvest Moon," starring Ann Sheridan, Dennis Morgan, Jack Carson and Irene Manning.

EXODUS OF 400 IDLEWILD FAMILIES BEGINS AS AIRPORT WORK STARTS

Eagle Staff photos

DOOMED BY PROGRESS—These houses lining canal are part of the 1,000 units to be torn down.

ALL HANDS HELP—Youngsters pitch in to get family belongings moved to a new home.

HE'S MOVING OUT—Louis Wehmert lived in the same house for 18 years.

PACKING UP—Mrs. James Willis and her son, Billy, get ready to move to their new home on Prospect Ave. The father is a trainee at the Sampson Naval Station.

Sept. 20 the Deadline; 30,000,000 Cu. Yds. Of Marsh Restored

Things are pretty much upset around Jamaica Creek nowadays. Jamaica Bay isn't what it used to be.

The largest airport in the world is under construction in that section on ground reclaimed from the bay and condemned from property owners by the city.

It is Idlewild Airport, and work has begun already on the first of the six runways which will launch the terminal as an international air depot.

Most of the 2,000 acres which make up the site were marshland. Officials of the engineering firm handling the contract say that 30,000,000 cubic yards of sand have been sucked from the bottom of Jamaica Bay and transported through pipes to fill the shallow pools. Hydraulic dredging is the technique being used.

Meantime, real estate appraisers who have helped Supreme Court Justice Lockwood settle the value of the land condemned to make room for the airport say that 1,000-family units living in the area must move.

By ordinary population standards this involves a community of 4,500 persons—the size of many a New York county seat. Many of these families have lived in the bay section for a score or more of years and now are faced with the problem of finding new homes.

Deadline for 400 Families

Sept. 20 is the deadline for 400 of these families. According to Thomas Malone, real estate agent and court-appointed appraiser, 300 of these are year-round residents of the district, the other 100 being Summer and weekend owners and tenants.

This exodus will make way for the first large-scale bulldozing detail which will begin its work when the frame dwellings involved are put to the torch—that's the way the city clears the land, setting fire to a few houses at a time until the entire area is leveled off.

Some May Stay a Year

On Nov. 1 another 25 families will be moved and on May 1, 1945, 150 more will go. After that 250 to 300 houses will remain pending construction progress and the decisions of engineers in charge. These families are on an indeterminate basis in their Jamaica homes but can feel fairly confident they won't be moved for another year.

Elmer E. Glanz, who has had a place down there for 30 years, is a letter carrier in the Brooklyn Postoffice. Glanz and his wife have a nice library, a cool porch and a desire to continue the way of life they have embraced.

Fishes From Porch

He fishes from the back stoop of his house—catches fluke and weakfish right out of Jamaica Creek. He had a couple of soft crabs in his icebox yesterday. He just picked them out of the creek.

Glanz' minnow trap was full of killies, the little minnows you fish with in those parts. He said they would be hard to find in Brooklyn. Clams were all over the flats and his rowboat was tied to his back steps. Nothing like it, he said.

Down the line was an elderly lady, living alone, who had not been able to find another place. She was going to court yesterday to see if there was any help for a person in her predicament.

Off at the end of the spit was a fisherman. For years he has made his living carrying parties to Jamaica Bay. He says he used to live in Canarsie and was moved out by a development.

He Makes Second Move

He is moving again. He sold his boats week before last and doesn't know what he will do next. He is rather piqued about the thing. To newspapermen he said, "I have a poster in my fishing shack which ought to make a swell picture. It's a Government picture. It says "This Is America."

Most of the residents do not share his feeling about moving—they just hate the inconvenience and they believe the city will leave their condemned property idle for many months before using it to make room for actual construction work.

Mrs. James C. Willis Jr. has lived on Jamaica Creek for years. She has three children and her husband is at the storekeeper school at the United States Naval Training Station at Sampson, N. Y. Mrs. Willis and her teen-aged youngsters moved out yesterday. They were lucky, Mrs. Willis said; they have found a place on Prospect Ave.

Farther along is the home of Mrs. Charles Hopkins who has lived on the Idlewild site for many Summers. With her are her daughter, Mrs. Everett Van Pelt, and four grandchildren. Mrs. Van Pelt's husband is a private in the army.

Mrs. Hopkins is moving to Prospect Ave., too. Her grandchildren hate to leave the section and no similar places are available.

Yet the appraisers have been lenient—with legal consistency—on evaulating the property before Justice Lockwood and no resident will lose money on the deal.

It's just a matter of "we've lived here all this time; they're moving us out; they better make a darned good airport or we'll squawk."

It's the pace of progress, some say. But any way you look at it, Queens will have the world's largest airport and 250 planes an hour is no small traffic.

The Question Is: Can Women Join The All-Male VFW?

Will women invade the strictly male precincts of the Veterans of Foreign Wars, a "stag" group since it was organized in 1899?

The 200 borough delegates to the national convention in Chicago this week, when the question will arise, are "evenly divided" on admission of the fair sex, according to John Gardella, Kings County commander. Resolutions making women in overseas service eligible for membership will be introduced by several States at the convention, which gets under way Tuesday.

"About half of the delegates remember that this organization has been stag from the start and want to exclude women," Gardella said last night. "The other half want them in. We will go along with whatever the convention decides."

The delegates are not instructed, he said, and will go into a caucus with the entire State body on the matter as soon as they arrive. New York State will vote as a unit.

Women nurses overseas in the Spanish-American War and in World War I have for years tried to get into the organization, only to be referred to the ladies' auxiliary. However, with the large number of women serving abroad today, pressure has increased for their admittance.

Conservative Judaism Unit Names Dr. Salit to Post

Dr. Norman Salit, vice president of the Far Rockaway Zionist District, and former rabbi of Congregation Shaaray Tefila of Far Rockaway, has been named executive director of the Wartime Emergency Committee for Conservative Judaism of the United States and Canada, it was announced yesterday.

Other members of the committee include Chaplain Bernard Segal, U. S. Army; Dr. Max Kadushin, Dr. Max Arzt, Rabbi Moshe Davis, Rabbi Max D. Davidson, Dr. Elias Solomon, Chaplain Philip R. Lipis, U. S. Army; Rabbi Arthur Neulander, Marvin Berger and Rabbi Samuel Cohen.

CHESLEY OUSTED AS OPA CHIEF—LAST BORO HEAD

Like Brooklyn before it, the Bronx yesterday became a borough without its own OPA office and OPA chairman.

Brooklyn's OPA interests were merged with the citywide office under Regional OPA Administrator Daniel P. Woolley last December, when the Kings County War Price and Rationing Board—the Brooklyn OPA—was abolished and William Jagger, its head, was, in effect, dismissed from the post.

Yesterday's action in the Bronx was more direct. It came with the announcement that Administrator Woolley had dismissed Adolph J. Chesley, president of the Bronx Board of Trade, as chairman of the Bronx County War Price and Rationing Board. In a letter of dismissal to Chesley, Woolley wrote that "we are in receipt of numerous serious written and verbal complaints from many sources of your lack of co-operation."

Chesley's dismissal left the city without any borough OPA ofices as such.

Among those listed as having complained of the Bronx OPA head's "lack of co-operation" were: James C. Quinn, secretary of the A. F. of L. Central Trades and Labor Council; Katherine Earnshaw, chairman, Cost of Living Committee of the New York C. I. O.; Louis Lufrano of Local 18205, Textile Examiners and Finishers, A. F. of L., and Mildred Gutwillig, representing the Bronx Consumers Co-ordinating Council.

Luna Fire Spurs New Building Code

Exactly one week after the $500,000 Luna Park fire, State Industrial Commissioner Edward Corsi, head of the State Labor Department, yesterday took steps to modernize the State Standard Building Code and widen his department's jurisdiction to prevent similar conflagrations in th efuture.

Headed by Deputy Commissioner Abraham Goodman of Brooklyn, a group of Labor Department officials will meet with a committee of experts named by Commissioner Corsi to discuss means of bringing the code up to date and recommend legislation. The combined committee will organize Sept 15 in the State Office Building, 80 Centre St., Manhattan.

Said Commissioner Corsi:

"At present we have no regulatory powers for places of public assembly within the City of New York, and had there been violations—and I am not suggesting that there were—at Luna Park, we would have been without power to act, either before or after the blaze."

PACIFIC FLIGHT TO COST LESS THAN BOAT FARE

Air travel from California to Hawaii in 300-mile-an-hour four-motored planes at less than cost of first-class steamer transportation is contemplated by United Air Lines in a post-war expansion proposal to the Civil Aeronautics Board.

The prewar cost for the air trip was $278.50. United would reduce it to $185 and the flying time from 17 to less than 11 hours.

Passengers carried would be 50 by day and 24 in night sleepers. Schedules would enable passengers, mail and express to leave California at 8 p.m. and arrive in Honolulu at 6:30 a.m. The day flight would be from California at 6:30 a.m.

Mail would be carried for three-tenths of a mill a pound, the same rate charged for mail transported within continental United States.

Officials of the company emphasized that United was not applying for an international route.

Bowling Alley Man Held In Seizure of Alcohol

Daniel Kettler, 310 Riverside Boulevard, Long Beach, was held in $500 bail for the grand jury by U. S. Commissioner Fay yesterday on a charge of possessing untaxed alcohol. He pleaded innocent.

Kettler was arrested by revenue agents, who alleged they found a half of a gallon of alcohol in a bowling alley he operated at 985 W. Beach St., Long Beach.

Kettler said the alcohol was left in the bowling allev by a sailor he had hired to do some painting there, and that the sailor had used some of the alcohol to thin the paint.

While You Enjoy the Breezes, Towermen Sizzle in 110° Heat

The weather, no doubt, was mild and even cool for you yesterday (highest official temperature, 76; lowest, 64)—but not for everybody

For instance, Henry Machold of 25 E. 25th St. and Louis Reder of 10 Morton St., B. M. T. subway switch tower operators, at the De Kalb Ave. station. The cooler weather had not arrived where they work.

At the entrance to their tower room, in the subway depths, the thermometer read 92—for in New York's subway tunnels the heat, which accumulated in eight successive plus-90-degree days, still lingered on and will remain for some time.

In the switch tower proper it was really hot. Machold and Reder labored at their jobs stripped to the waist, constantly mopping brows with damp handkerchiefs. The official temperature was 110.

Today, the Weather Bureau predicted, will be mild and tonight cool, with temperatures about the same as yesterday. That is, outdoors.

In the subway switch tower, according to confident predictions by Machold and Reder, it will be 110—with no relief in sight.

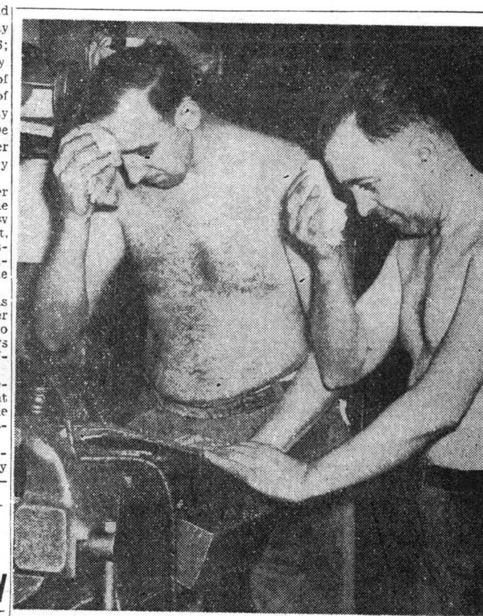

Eagle Staff photo

HOT SPOT—A switch tower room at the DeKalb Ave. B. M. T. subway station, where Henry Machold and Louis Reder, left to right, signal maintainers, work in 110-degree heat.

Prisoner Coddling Inquiry Under Way

Washington, Aug. 19 (U.P.)—Chairman Andrew J. May (D., Ky.) of the House Military Affairs Committee revealed tonight that committee investigators have been sent to prison camps in Pennsylvania and Kentucky to look into complaints "that Axis prisoners of war are being coddled and treated like heroes."

"We have received complaints that some prisoners are being treated like guests, are transported to movies and held up as great heroes," May said.

"It is one thing to treat them decently, but it is something else to give them a lot of privileges just because they happened to be captured while trying to kill our boys."

While receiving "many" reports of this nature, May said there have been numerous others of unworthy treatment of wounded American veterans who were returned to this country for hospitalization.

He referred to a report submitted by a committee member yesterday that the army's Bolling Field Station Hospital here is a "fire trap, inadequate and unworthy of the nation and those who are fighting its battles."

F. D. R., Halifax Confer On Security Conference

Washington, Aug. 19 (U.P.)—The Earl of Halifax, British Ambassador to the United States, conferred today with President Roosevelt and revealed upon leaving the White House that the President probably will receive British and Russian delegates to the Dumbarton Oaks security talks beginning Monday.

BROOKLYN

War Memorial

BOARD

Rules Governing

BROOKLYN EAGLE

PRIZE CONTEST

for the Best Idea or Plan for a

Brooklyn War Memorial

★ In order to consolidate public opinion upon a single dignified and appropriate Brooklyn Borough War Memorial honoring those who fought and died in World War II, the Brooklyn Eagle has announced the gift of $5,000 to be awarded as prizes for the best suggestions and designated the following persons to act as a Board of Judges to award these prizes:

JOHN CASHMORE
President, Borough of Brooklyn, Chairman

EDWARD C. BLUM
Chm., Board of Trustees, Brooklyn Institute of Arts and Sciences

MARY E. DILLON
President, Board of Education New York City

DR. HARRY S. ROGERS
President, Polytechnic Institute of Brooklyn

COL. JOHN J. BENNETT
Former Attorney General, State of New York

The primary purpose of this competition is to obtain ideas expressed in simple, straightforward English. It is not its aim to procure complete technical structural plans. It is unnecessary that contestants be architects, sculptors, engineers or technicians of any kind. It is also not essential that they be journalists or writers. The awards are to be made solely on the basis of the merit of the proposal as an appropriate memorial, not on the literary composition or the ability of the entrant to make accurate architectural or other technical plans to illustrate his proposal. After the names of the winners have been announced, copies of the winning proposals will be turned over to the responsible officials of the City Government for their consideration.

A first prize of $3,000, a second prize of $1,500 and a third prize of $500 will be awarded for the best suggestions, subject to the following rules formulated by the War Memorial Board:

1. Every suggestion shall be typewritten or legibly written on one side of every page, shall not be more than 600 words in length, and must be written in English. Illegible entries will be given no consideration. The suggestion must be made on paper that gives no indication of the entrant's identity or where he lives. With the suggestion is to be filed a sealed envelope containing the contestant's name and address. This envelope will be given a number and a like number will be placed upon the paper containing the suggestion or plan. In this way the identity of none of the contestants will be known until after the awards are made. If a suggestion is submitted jointly by more than one person, the name and home address of each of the persons must be enclosed in the sealed envelope just referred to, and if such suggestion wins a prize, the amount of the prize will be divided equally among those persons.

2. While no sketch or illustration is required, it would be desirable to have these submitted with the suggestion, but in no case should the suggestion be accompanied by more than two sketches, models or other graphic representations.

3. Every suggestion, plan or sketch shall include an estimate of cost.

4. Every contestant must be a legal resident of the City of New York, and must have maintained such residence since July 1, 1944. The Board may require any entrant to furnish proof satisfactory to it that said contestant is the real author of the suggestion.

5. Merely as a guide to contestants, two possible suggestions are made as to the nature of the Brooklyn Memorial. These suggestions are not exclusive and are merely offered by way of illustration:

a. A plaza or mall in the Civic Center at or near Cadman Plaza for meetings, parades, ceremonies, etc., with or without a triumphal arch or statuary group or groups similar to the Grand Army Plaza at the entrance to Prospect Park.

b. A memorial building in an appropriate setting at the Civic Center or elsewhere in Brooklyn with rooms for meetings of veterans and a reasonably large convention room. In this building provision could be made for the display of the flags of the various service divisions and for the installation of suitable memorial plaques listing the names of those killed in the war, etc.

6. In submitting an entry in this competition, the entrant agrees to be bound by all the provisions of these rules and further agrees to be bound by and accept the decision of the Board as conclusive and binding upon him or her.

7. Prizes will be awarded by the Brooklyn War Memorial Board, the members of which will act as Judges of the contest. All ideas, proposals and sketches submitted shall become the property of the Brooklyn War Memorial Board and may be used for whatever purpose the said Board may thereafter decide without accrual of any compensation to any entrant by reason of such use. No suggestion, plans or other data submitted will be returned.

8. No suggestion, plan or sketch will be published until after the prizes have been awarded and only the names of winners of prizes will be announced.

9. There shall be no communication relative to design or character of the memorial between any competitor and any member of the Board, which might be calculated to give one competitor an unfair advantage over others, but any answer the Board may see fit to give to any queries will be made solely by publication of such answer in the Brooklyn Eagle.

10. Entries to be eligible for consideration must be received at the Office of the Brooklyn War Memorial Board, Borough Hall, Brooklyn 2, N. Y., not later than noon of January 2, 1945. Neither the Brooklyn War Memorial Board nor anyone connected with the competition, will be responsible for entries delayed, damaged, undelivered or lost. Announcement of the winners will be made as soon as practicable after the close of the competition. Address and mail entries to the Brooklyn War Memorial Board, Borough Hall, Brooklyn 2, New York.

BROOKLYN WAR MEMORIAL BOARD
Joseph A. McNamara, Secretary, Room 21, Borough Hall, Brooklyn, N. Y.

$5,000 IN PRIZES

7 ★★★★★★★ SPORTS
Wall Street Financial News

BROOKLYN EAGLE

WEATHER—Partly cloudy, with moderate temperatures tonight and tomorrow.

103d Year. No. 231. DAILY & SUNDAY • (Copyright 1944 The Brooklyn Eagle, Inc.) • BROOKLYN, N. Y., WEDNESDAY, AUGUST 23, 1944 • Entered at the Brooklyn Post-office as 2d Class Mail Matter • 3 CENTS IN NEW YORK CITY ELSEWHERE 4 CENTS

PARIS FREED

We Push for Troyes; Enter Grenoble

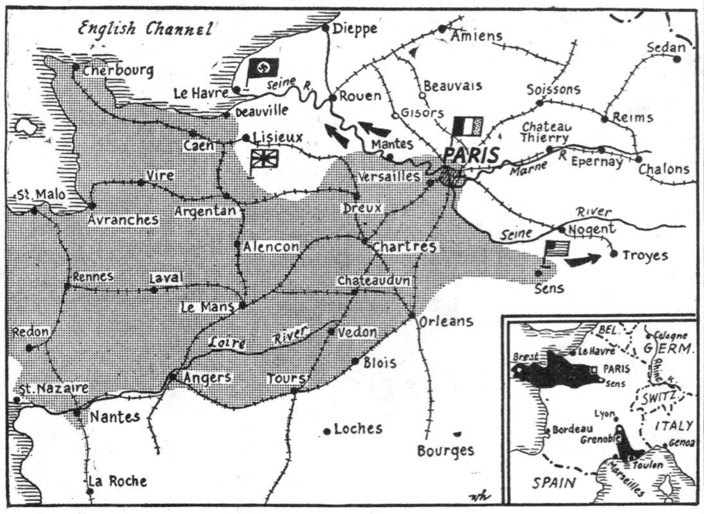

STORY OF AN HISTORIC DAY—The French flag was planted firmly in Paris today as Yank armored columns plunged for Troyes on the road to the German frontier. In the south we entered Grenoble, shown in inset. This map was prepared on the basis of information available at 2 p.m. Brooklyn time.

FRENCH PATRIOTS SMASH NAZIS AND HOIST TRICOLOR OVER CITY

By JOSEPH W. GRIGG

London, Aug. 23 (UP)—An angry army of French patriots rebelled against their Nazi conquerors and liberated their capital city of Paris today.

Striking for their own freedom even as a massive American tank army gathered at the city gates, hundreds of thousands of embattled Partisans stormed Nazi barricades, overwhelmed the enemy garrisons and hoisted the tri-color triumphantly over the city.

First word of the patriot blow came in a dramatic announcement from Gen. Pierre Koenig, commander in chief of the French Forces of the Interior, that insurrection had been raging through the capital since early Saturday morning when the call for a general uprising was flashed to the underground in Paris.

Five hours later, Allied headquarters had no comment on Koenig's statement. Headquarters press spokesmen said they had no knowledge of the announcement until after it was issued.

In four days of street fighting such as the ancient city had not seen since the storming of the Bastille 155 years ago, the ill-armed patriots routed the bulk of the German occupation forces from Paris and slaughtered the doomed rear guards left to cover the Nazi evacuation.

The reconquest of the city, the first of the Allied capitals to be wrested back from the Nazis, was the most spectacular blow struck by Europe's smoldering underground armies since the German hordes overran the Continent four years ago.

With the capture of Paris the patriots at a single stroke deprived the Germans of the main railway center in all France and cut off the main escape routes for the enemy troops

Continued on Page 2

AIM FOR RAIL HUB 130 MI. FROM REICH

Patton's Tanks Drive To Close Escape Route For Nazis in South

By VIRGIL PINKLEY

Supreme Headquarters, A. E. F., Aug. 23 (U.P.)—Powerful American tank columns pounded eastward within a day's ride of the German frontier today, striking for the key railway hub of Troyes in a bid to close the last direct escape route for all the Nazi armies of southern France.

Lt. Gen. George S. Patton's tanks and motorized infantrymen had broken contact with headquarters in their dramatic strike toward the frontiers of the Reich, and headquarters maintained strict secrecy on the whereabouts of the advanced American spearheads.

Front dispatches revealed, however, that the Yanks were driving at break-neck speed beyond the ancient fortified city of Sens, which they captured yesterday after a 65-mile thrust around the southern suburbs of Paris, and heading directly for Troyes, 130 miles west of Germany.

Battle of France Nears End

With the American break-through into eastern France headquarters permitted correspondents to state flatly that the battle of France is nearing its end and that the liberation of the entire country is not far off.

Far behind Patton's flying columns, a powerful American tank army massed around liberated Paris, while other American and Allied armies converged on the Seine River line, tightening a great noose around the broken remnants of the German 7th Army in Normandy.

One American column slashed deep into the southern flank of the corridor across which the Germans were fleeing, driving 28 miles northwest of Dreux to the Evreux area against light resistance. A second American force drove into the corridor along a parallel path more

Continued on Page 11

Telling It Briefly

PHONE WEATHER GIRL PLUGS WASTE PAPER

Weather-conscious Brooklynites who called telephone weather today were reassured that the mercury would hover in the comfortable lower 80's today, and, in addition, received a home front message.

"Save waste paper—it's needed for war," said the cute voice at the other end of the phone after a high of 85 today had been predicted. Breezes will ease moderate heat, with the temperature at noon being 79.

The weekend will again be cool, with the thermometer at about 80.

BABY WHO DELAYED BREATHING DOING WELL

Edwin Peter Apman, who waited for three and one-half hours after birth yesterday before drawing normal breath, was reported "doing well" today at Norwegian Hospital.

Although attaches despaired of his life, the infant responded after hours of artificial respiration, including injection of metrazole, the most powerful respiratory stimulant known.

GETS 90 DAYS FOR SMOKING ON PIER

Andrew Bothen, 58, of 254 49th St., today was given the alternative of a $200 fine or 90 days in county jail when arraigned before Police Court Justice Flaherty in Second Criminal Court, Jersey City, on a charge of smoking on a pier. Bothen took the 90 days in jail. The charge was made by the U. S. Coast Guard.

L. I. CITY 'DEAD' MAN REUNITED WITH KIN

New Haven, Conn., Aug. 23 (U.P.)—Henry Fenney, 50, of 3212 31st Ave., Long Island City, who was declared legally dead here in 1942, was reunited today with his brothers and sisters, whom he had not seen since 1925, and was attempting to straighten out his estate.

Declared dead when he was listed among the heirs to his sister's estate in 1942, Fenney's own estate was probated at that time, but had remained untouched under Connecticut's Enoch Arden law which requires a five-year wait under those circumstances.

MAN SLUMPS OVER DEAD IN AUTO

Matthew Mullen, 42, of 63-124 Fitchett St., Rego Park, who was superintendent of store yards for the Consolidated Telegraph and Electrical Subway Company, 54 Lafayette St., Manhattan, slumped over dead in his automobile at 101st Ave. and 94th St., Ozone Park, from a heart attack.

Mullen was on his way to the office of his physician, Dr. H. A. Fried, at 101-01 160th Ave., Howard Beach.

Continued on Page 11

BELMONT RESULTS
(Saratoga Meeting)

1—Wemite 30.50-13.40-8.60, Reason 7.40-5.00, Refugeegee 4.80. (1:24½)

2—Mondarah 10.20-5.00-3.50, Little Flyer 3.20-2.60, Pennyp'ker 5.10. (1:55)

DAILY DOUBLE PAID $702.80

3—Mateson 5.30-3.60-2.80, Muffled Drums 3.50-3.10, Fieldfare 3.50. (2:23½)

U. S. TANKS DRIVE INTO GRENOBLE, OUTFLANK NAZIS

Sensational Thrust Across French Alps Wins Lower Rhone

By ELEANOR PACKARD

Rome, Aug. 23 (U.P.)—American tanks and motorized infantry drove into Grenoble, only 58 miles southwest of the major city of Lyon, today after a spectacular 140-mile advance across the French Alps from the Mediterranean coast.

(A London broadcast said the Americans had "liberated" Grenoble and were 240 miles from Allied armies below Paris.)

(Radio France at Algiers said Allied patrols had reached the gates of Avigon, in the Rhone Valley, 52 miles northwest of Marseille. That would represent an advance of more than 14 miles west from the last Allied positions at Apt.)

The German DNB News Agency said a "small" force of American

Continued on Page 11

F. D. R., Churchill to Meet In France, Says Daily Mail

London, Aug. 23 (U.P.)—The London Daily Mail said today that President Roosevelt and Prime Minister Churchill will confer within a "matter of weeks on French soil."

Mr. Roosevelt already is packing his bags for the trip, which had been scheduled earlier but was postponed to permit his visit to the Pacific and because of Secret Service objections to his coming to London during the robot blitz, the Mail said.

PARATROOPER TELLS HOW 60 MEN HELD OFF 400 GERMANS

A force of 60 parachute infantrymen for two and a half days held off 400 Germans trying to push through their sector to retake the town of Ste. Mere Eglise during the Normandy invasion, Pfc. John E. Krostitz of 80 Sheridan Ave., Williston Park, disclosed today. Krostitz lost his left leg during the fracas and is now a patient in the Walter Reed General Hospital, Washington, D. C.

The 21-year-old paratrooper said his outfit jumped at 1:30 a.m. on D-Day and fought with knives and grenades until dawn to avoid hitting their own men with bullets in the darkness.

Hannegan Sinks Spurs Into Gallup Poll Count

By JOSEPH H. SCHMALACKER

Robert E. Hannegan, Democratic national chairman, took issue today with the first nation-wide returns in the Gallup poll which, while putting President Roosevelt in the lead over Governor Dewey, gave him only 20 more electoral votes than the majority of 266 which he needs to win his fourth term in the White House.

With Mayor Edward Kelly of Chicago at his side during a press conference in the Democratic national headquarters in the Hotel Biltmore, Chairman Hannegan specifically challenged the poll's figures on the States of Illinois, Indiana and Missouri which have a combined total of 56 electoral votes.

The poll, giving President Roosevelt 28 States, listed 17 with 151 electoral votes as "safe" for him today and 11, with 129 electoral votes, as "leaning" now in his favor. Thirteen States, with 141 electoral votes, were classed as safe today for Governor Dewey and seven with 104 electoral votes as leaning toward the Republican Presidential nominee.

The poll listed Illinois and Indiana as "safe" for Governor Dewey today and Missouri as leaning in his favor. Examining the returns, Chairman Hannegan remarked:

Points to Illinois

"The Mayor says Illinois is in the wrong column. I believe Indiana is in the wrong column and Missouri should be out of the column

Continued on Page 11

Narragansett Park Results

1—Daisy Lee, 8.20, 3.20, 2.60; New Boom, 2.60, 2.40; Little Foxy, 3.40. Off time, 2:35½.

Garden State Results

1—Hiccup, first; Second Love, second; Devon Cream, third.

NAZI COLLAPSE SHOULD NOT END LEND-LEASE—F.D.

President Sees Victory Over Japan Speeded By Plan's Extension

Washington, Aug. 23 (U.P.)—President Roosevelt informed Congress today that lend-lease shipments to the Allies reached a total of $28,270,000,000 on July 1 and urged the program be continued after the defeat of Germany to insure a speedier victory over Japan.

In apparent reference to recent discussions on whether lend-lease could not be halted after the war in Europe ends, Mr. Roosevelt warned in his 16th report to Congress:

"We should not permit any weakening of this system of combined war supply to delay final victory a single day or to cost unnecessarily the life of one American boy."

Says It Speeds Victory

Lend-lease has helped bring the prospect of complete victory "sooner than we had hoped," the Chief Ex-

Continued on Page 11

Equity Ratifies Contract

Actors Equity Association has ratified a year's extension of its minimum basic contract with the League of New York Theaters, which includes, producers, theater owners and operators, Alfred Harding, Equity spokesman, said today.

French Here Shed Tears of Joy Celebrating Long-Awaited Victory

In the office of France Forever, on the fifth floor of 587 5th Ave., Manhattan, there was an apparent calm today which proved to be only apparent. The group of office workers, volunteers and others who had worked for years for the freedom of France continued today at their routine jobs, but very little routine work was done and there was much talk of today's news, the news that Paris was again free.

"How did I hear the news?" asked Mrs. Raymond Kemper, Parisian born and a volunteer worker here. "I heard it early this morning over the shortwave radio. At first I couldn't believe it. I must have heard the Marseillaise at least 10 times. The French radio kept repeating 'French people, people of France, Paris is free again!' It was so wonderful."

What did she do on hearing the news?

"I'm afraid I cried."

Somebody looked up from an adjoining desk. "We all cried."

People kept coming in, stopping at passing desks, talking in French, chiefly about the events of the day.

A slim dark girl came in. She had been ill.

"But today I cannot be ill. I could not stay home. I had to come."

Said Mme. Louise Chevalaz: "There is no way to tell our joy. Actually it is hard to realize. Well,

Continued on Page 2

Perpignan, Gateway To Spain, Occupied

London, Aug. 23 (U.P.)—The Algiers radio said today that French Interior forces had occupied the ancient fortress city of Perpignan, on the Mediterranean just north of the Spanish frontier and across the southern tip of France from Arcachon, on the Bay of Biscay, where unconfirmed reports said Allied troops landed this morning.

The broadcast said the occupation of Perpignan, gateway from France to Spain, was completed after three Allied planes landed there with a mission which established liaison with French Forces of the Interior.

Frontier reports from Madrid, Algiers said, confirmed that the Germans had evacuated the Pyrenees after destroying a depot at the port of Vendres and the viaduct at Banyuls, both of which are between Perpignan and the Spanish border.

Coincidental with the reported evacuation, the Swiss radio said the German Lufthansa airline service between Berlin and Lisbon had been suspended.

American troops have landed also at St. Jean de Luz and Bordeaux, the German DNB news agency said.

Doubt Reported Landings

Washington, Aug. 23 (U.P.)—Informed military observers doubted today reports of Allied landings in the Bordeaux area and at other points on the French coast along the Bay of Biscay.

They said that neither Bordeaux nor any of the other ports on the Bay of Biscay were necessary to the operations now going on in France.

Town Closes Shop To Honor War Hero

Cleveland, Tenn., Aug. 23 (U.P.)—Business ceased today in this city of 10,000 as a hero's welcome was given to Sgt. Paul B. Huff, Tennessee's Alvin York of World War II.

The festivities will last until 1 a.m. Thursday. Huff won the Medal of Honor for leading an 18-man detail on the Anzio beachhead against 125 Germans. The Nazis were routed. Huff was credited with saving his small patrol by singlehandedly cleaning out a machine-gun nest.

On to Berlin!

By United Press

The shortest distances to Berlin from advanced Allied lines today:

Northern France—520 miles (gain of 75 miles in week).

Southern France—590 miles (gain of 71 miles in week).

Italy—602 miles (unchanged for week).

Russia—328 miles (unchanged for week).

Allied Planes Rake Fleeing Germans

London, Aug. 25 (U.P.)—Allied warplanes pounded fleeing German troops south of the Seine today while powerful raiding fleets from Italy slashed at the Vienna region for the second day in succession and at the Lyon area in France.

Military installations bombed by Lilberators in the Vienna region included the Markersdorf Airdrome, 35 miles west of the former Austrian capital. Heavy enemy opposition was encountered.

Mitchell bombers attacked a bridge and a railyard in the vicinity of Lyon, while others hit a second rail bridge near Montelimar, 90 miles northwest of Marseilles.

WHERE TO FIND IT

	Page		Page
Bridge	12	Patterns	9
Comics	19	Radio	19
Crossword	16	Society	6
Dr. Brady	10	Sports	14, 15
Editorial	10	Take My Word	10
Financial	16	Theaters	8
Helen Worth	6	These Women	19
Horoscope	19	Tommy Holmes	14
Mary Haworth	9	Uncle Ray	19
Movies	8	Want Ads	17, 18
Novel	16	Wartime Problems	20
Obituaries	11		
Our Fighters	16	Women	6

SCREEN By Jane Corby

'Kismet' Opens at the Astor Theater—Stars Colman and Marlene Dietrich

1944 Aug. 22 P.M. 4:52

JANE CORBY BROOKLYN EAGLE
THOUGHT YOU'D LIKE TO KNOW THAT UP TO THREE O'CLOCK TODAY "KISMET" HAS BROKEN EVERY RECORD IN THE OPENING DAY HISTORY OF THE ASTOR THEATER AND WITH LINES STILL RUNNING FOUR DEEP AROUND 45TH STREET CORNER THERE ARE NO SIGNS OF LET UP—HOWARD DIETZ, M-G-M.

Help yourself to a big chunk of forget-your-troubles—go see "Kismet" at the Astor Theater. Not since the address of Shangri-La was mislaid has there been such an opportunity to get away from it all, pamper the eye, soothe the ear and intrigue the imagination. "Kismet," you understand, is in Technicolor, and its cast is headed by Ronald Colman, Marlene Dietrich, James Craig, Edward Arnold and Joy Ann Page.

Metro-Goldwyn-Mayer was in an expansive mood when it made this one and William Dieterle, the director, was in no hurry to get it over with. In a swirl of color and a whirl of romance, "Kismet" wafts along for a languorous hour and 40 minutes, to its appointed end, which is to see Colman and Dietrich streaking off together to the far ends of some fabulous empire or other, and James Craig, as the young Caliph of Bagdad, bestowing the title of Mrs. Caliph on Joy Ann Page, the beggar's daughter.

This film "Kismet" is based upon the play by Edward Knoblock which was first produced on the New York stage several decades ago, with Otis Skinner. We haven't the least idea how it compares with the original version. It will doubtless be fun for those who saw it yesteryear to check up on this point, but for those who missed the first layout, the current setup is certainly one sockeroo way to make up for lost time.

The story? Oh, that . . . it has to do with how Edward Arnold, as the grafting Grand Vizier of Bagdad of 1,000 years ago, is holding captive or something this Mongolian princess of a Marlene Dietrich, and at the same time double-crossing Caliph James Craig, lately ascended to the throne. The Caliph has a yen to get acquainted with the plain people of Bagdad, and runs around nights, making like he's a son of a gardener, and meets Joy Ann Page, daughter of Beggar Ronald Colman. Colman, as the king of beggars, on the other hand, yearns for Bagdad cafe society, and he steals the right clothes (such turbans! such be-sashed, bejewelled and otherwise bedizened robes!) and goes wolfing around, and gets to meet Dietrich. They have a rendezvous in her own private tower, and all like that.

The film has a dancing interlude that would be well worth going to see, even if that's all there was to the picture. Scores of dancing girls in scarlet skirts offer a sort of preliminary bout until the main event comes on—Marlene veiled in black chiffon, with her legs gilded and her arms dripping bracelets, doing a strange Oriental dance.

The picture is punctuated with scenes in which Marlene slithers in and out from behind gauze portieres and reclines on divans and sings a little song, and the film could stand a lot more of her, and her singing, too. Chief complaint we have about the picture is the elusive quality of the Colman-Dietrich affair, while the less spectacular boy-meets-girl routine between Craig and Miss Page is played up. Craig is a hearty young man and Joy Ann Page is a bouncing young woman and they aren't entirely sold on the spirit of old Bagdad. Dietrich and Colman are tops at make-believe, however, and they almost, but not quite, succeed in counteracting the slightly jarring attitude of the other two principals.

But maybe that jolt is administered a-purpose, an M. G. M. reminder that the Bagdad of 1,000 years ago is gone forever, and that we ought to laugh at ourselves a little for enjoying so much this backward look. Could be.

'Kismet'

Metro-Goldwyn-Mayer picture, directed by William Dieterle from a screen play by John Meehan, based upon a play by Edward Knoblock. Presented at the Astor Theater.

The Cast

Hafiz	Ronald Colman
Jamilla	Marlene Dietrich
Caliph	James Craig
Grand Vizier	Edward Arnold
Feisal	Hugh Herbert
Marsinah	Joy Ann Page
Karsha	Florence Bates
Agha	Harry Davenport
Moolah	Hobart Cavanaugh

Marlene Dietrich

'Till We Meet Again' At Rivoli Aug. 29

"The Story of Dr. Wassell," Paramount's Technicolor saga of an heroic naval doctor and his valiant wards, is in its 12th and last week at the Rivoli Theater with Gary Cooper portraying Dr. Corydon M. Wassell.

"Till We Meet Again," another Paramount picture, will make its debut at the Rivoli on Tuesday, Aug. 29. Starring Ray Milland and Barbara Britton, this is a poignant story of an American flier forced down in occupied France, and his escape to England through the help of a beautiful young nun. Walter Slezak and Lucile Watson have important secondary roles.

'Wilson' Script To U. S. Archives

The script of the motion picture "Wilson," specially prepared and bound in leather, was presented by 20th Century-Fox to the National Archivist of the United States Archives as a permanent record of the important film which Darryl F. Zanuck produced. "Wilson," specifically prepared for the screen by ace scenarist Lamar Trotti, is now in its fourth record-breaking week at the Roxy Theater.

Ensign Jay Johnson, U. S. N., is winner of the $500 cash award in the nation-wide contest sponsored by Producer Frank Ross for the best conception of Salome by a living American artist. His portrait will be used in casting for the role of Salome in the Technicolor screen version of "The Robe," to be directed by Mervyn LeRoy at the RKO Radio Studio in Hollywood.

Gail Russell, a Santa Monica high school girl two years ago, has been assigned the co-starring role with Alan Ladd in "Salty O'Rourke," which Raoul Walsh will direct. Miss Russell will portray the school teacher who is wooed both by Ladd, the owner of a race horse, and Stanley Clements, a jockey. She soared to stardom by her performance in "The Uninvited."

Increased activity is reported by Producers Corporation of America, with four pictures being readied for production. "The Old West," a filmization in color of the life of Frederic Remington, American outdoor painter, will face the cameras as soon as casting is completed, with Harry Joe Brown as producer-director.

"BATHING BEAUTY" comes to Loew's Met tomorrow and has astounding happenings, to judge from the expressions of Red Skelton, Esther Williams and, aloft, Jean Porter. "They Live in Fear" will be the added attraction.

'Dragon Seed' Starting 6th Week at Music Hall

"Dragon Seed," beginning its sixth week at the Radio City Music Hall tomorrow, continues to set new all-time box office record at the big Rockefeller Center playhouse.

By the end of the fifth week tonight the Metro-Goldwyn-Mayer hit, starring Katharine Hepburn, will reach the unprecedented gross of $617,000, G. S. Eyssell, president and managing director of the Music Hall, estimated today, a new box office mark for the period.

Continuing with "Dragon Seed" at the Music Hall will be its elaborate stage revue "Sky High," produced by Leon Leonidoff.

"Mr. Winkle Goes to War' To Stay at Paramount

Edward G. Robinson is starred in Columbia's comedy "Mr. Winkle Goes to War," which is currently topping the program at the Paramount Theater and which remains for a second week beginning Friday. The associate feature "Kansas City Kitty," with Joan Davis, Jane Frazee and Bob Crosby, will also be held over.

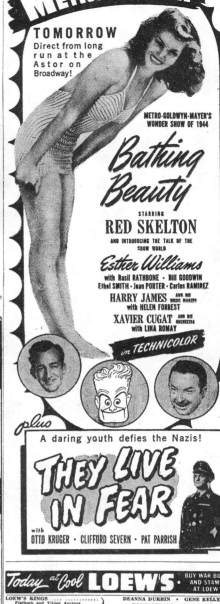

MOVIE TIME SCHEDULE

BROOKLYN

ALBEE—"Home in Indiana," 11, 1:55, 4:50, 7:45, 10:30; "Roger Touhy, Gangster," 12:50, 3:45, 6:40, 9:35.

FOX—"Mr. Skeffington," 11, 2:36, 6:14, 9:52; "Minstrel Man," 1:17, 4:55, 8:33.

METROPOLITAN—"Two Girls and a Sailor," 12:13, 3:37, 7:01, 10:25; "Secret of Scotland Yard," 11:01, 2:25, 5:49, 9:13.

PARAMOUNT—"Mr. Winkle Goes to War," 11:02, 2:04, 4:45, 7:26, 10:28; "Kansas City Kitty," 12:52, 3:33, 6:14, 9:16.

STRAND—"The Adventures of Mark Twain," 11, 2:37, 6:14, 9:50; "Louisiana Hayride," 1:30, 5:07, 8:44.

MANHATTAN

ASTOR—"Kismet," 10:45, 12:55, 3:15, 5:30, 7:45, 10, 12:10.

CAPITOL—"Since You Went Away," 9:10, 12:34, 4:02, 7:30, 11:01; stage, 12:05, 3:33, 7:01, 10:29.

CRITERION—"In Society," 10:10, 12, 1:55, 3:45, 5:40, 7:30, 9:25, 11:20, 1:10.

MUSIC HALL—"Dragon Seed," 9:30, 12:37, 3:42, 6:50, 9:58; stage, 11:58, 3:05, 6:10, 9:30.

PARAMOUNT—"Hail the Conquering Hero," 10:11, 12:59, 4:07, 7:15, 10:18, 12:10; stage, 12:03, 3:11, 6:19, 9:27.

RIVOLI—"Story of Dr. Wassell," 10, 12:43, 3:29, 6:15, 8:53, 11:31.

ROXY—"Wilson," 9:30, 12:35, 3:45, 6:55, 10:05; stage, 12:10, 3:15, 6:25, 9:40.

FEATURE FILMS SHOWING TODAY

BAY RIDGE
Electra, 75th St. and Third Ave. .... Lassie Come Home & I Married a Witch
Harbor, 92d St. and Fourth Ave. .... Buck Benny Rides Again & Forest Rangers
Stanley, Fifth Ave. and 75th St. .... Snow White & Falcon Out West

BEDFORD
Lincoln, Bedford Ave.-Eastern P'kway .... Gaslight & Casanova in Burlesque
National, 720 Washington Ave. .... Song of Bernadette
Rogers, 333 Rogers Ave. PR. 4-2230 ... My Favorite Wife & Pack Up Your Troubles

BENSONHURST
Colony, 18th Ave.-65th St. BE. 6-2231. Ball of Fire & Wagons Westward

BORO PARK
Elton, 43d St. and New Utrecht Ave. .. Great Man's Lady & Pied Piper

BOROUGH HALL AND DOWNTOWN
Century's Tivoli, Fulton St., Boro Hall .. Secret Command & The Hour Before the Dawn
Duffield, Duffield and Fulton Sts. ..... Secret Command & Hour Before the Dawn
Momart, Fulton St. and Rockwell Pl. ..... Mr. Lucky & Texas Rangers Ride Again
St. George Playhouse, 100 Pineapple St. White Cliffs of Dover & Short Subjects
Terminal, Fourth Ave. and Dean St. .... Up In Mabel's Room & Knickerbocker Holiday

BRIGHTON BEACH
Oceana, Brighton Beach Ave.-Hoff St. .... If I Had a Million & Follow the Leader

BUSHWICK
Empire, Ralph Ave.-B'way. FO. 9-7940 ... Girl in the Case & Stars on Parade

FLATBUSH
Granada, Church and Nostrand Aves. ... Show Business & Black Magic

EAST FLATBUSH
Avenue D, Avenue D and E. 43d St. ... See Here, Pvt. Hargrove & Man From Frisco
Rugby, Utica and Church Aves. .... Up In Mabel's Room & Knickerbocker Holiday

GERRITSEN BEACH
Graham, 311 Whitney Ave. .... Blues in the Night & Cowboy and the Senorita

PARK SLOPE
Carlton, Flatbush and Seventh Aves. .... Tender Comrade & Night of Adventure
Plaza, Flatbush Ave.-Park Place, Air-Cond. Andy Hardy's Double Life & Monster Maker
Sanders, Prospect Park West-14th St. .... Between Two Worlds & Make Your Own Bed
New Venus, 1224 Prospect Ave. .... The Lady Vanishes & Let 'Em Have It

KINGS HIGHWAY
Jewel, Kings Highway at Ocean P'kway . The Devil and Miss Jones & Arabian Nights

AVENUE U SECTION
Avenue U, Avenue U and E. 16th St. ...... See Here, Private Hargrove & Man From Frisco
Traymore, Avenue N and E. 46th St. ..... Pin Up Girl & Bermuda Mystery

RIDGEWOOD
Colonial, Broadway and Chauncey .... Secret Command & Hour Before the Dawn
Ridgewood, 1673 Myrtle Ave. .... Call of the South Seas & The Contender
Rivoli, Myrtle-Wilson Aves. GL. 5-0744 ... Gaslight & Casanova in Burlesque
Starr, Knickerbocker Ave. and Starr .... Show Business & Black Magic

SHEEPSHEAD BAY
Sheepshead, Sheepshead Rd.-Voorhies .... Between Two Worlds & Make Your Own Bed

SOUTH BROOKLYN
Sanders Globe, 228 15th St. .... Mr. Bug Goes to Town & Salute to the Marines

Yanks Trap 15,000 Nazis Along Rhone

7 ★★★★★★★ SPORTS
Wall Street Financial News

BROOKLYN EAGLE

WEATHER—Cloudy, occasional sprinkles tonight; partly cloudy, warm tomorrow.

103d Year. No. 236. DAILY & SUNDAY • (Copyright 1944 The Brooklyn Eagle, Inc.) • BROOKLYN, N. Y., MONDAY, AUGUST 28, 1944 • Entered at the Brooklyn Post-office as 2d Class Mail Matter • 3 CENTS IN NEW YORK CITY ELSEWHERE 4 CENTS

AMERICANS CROSS MARNE AS BRITISH OPEN TWIN DRIVES

Eagle Staff photo by Geller

HEY, MISTER!—Just because a fellow's only 4 is no reason why he can't get in and pitch. Bobby White, with a brother in the marines, another in the navy and one going into the merchant marine next week, passes the ammunition to Jerry Aragon, 76 Rogers Ave., of N. Y. Infantry Post 147, American Legion. Going around with a home-made wagon, Bobby and Jerry have collected 2,835 pounds of waste paper as a beginning for the Legion scrap drive, which begins Sept. 3.

Americans Trap 15,000 Nazis On Rhone Bank

Turn Murderous Fire On Pocketed Remnants Of German 19th Army

By ELEANOR PACKARD

Rome, Aug. 28 (U.P.)—American tanks and artillery, racing more than 50 miles overland into the Rhone Valley, closed behind the beaten remnants of the German 19th Army at Montelimar today and turned a murderous fire on some 15,000 Nazis trapped against the east bank of the Rhone.

With their bridges across the broad Rhone cut by Allied bombers, the survivors of the 19th Army faced imminent death or capture between the converging guns of the main American forces moving up from Avignon and the enveloping column at Montelimar, half-way between the Mediterranean coast and Lyon.

Headquarters spokesmen, who previously had issued an ambiguously worded statement indicating that 15,000 Germans were killed, wounded or captured in the new American stroke, explained that that figure referred to the number of Germans now pinned against the Rhone River.

The trap was sprung by a strong armored force that just swept into Montelimar after a secret force marched from the Sisterone-Grenoble highway more than 50 miles to the east.

The battered Nazis, fleeing up the east bank of the Rhone, raced into Montelimar to find the Americans ready and waiting.

Front dispatches said the startled Germans fell back to the river edge and braced for a death battle against the Americans closing around them. Throughout yesterday, United Press war correspondent Dana Adams Schmidt reported, American guns poured a deadly fire into the cornered enemy.

Nazi Casualties Enormous

American riflemen and hundreds of warplanes joined in the slaughter and casualties among the Nazis were described officially as "enormous."

Among the already-decimated German units brought to bay against the river banks were elements of the 11th Panzer and 198th Infantry Divisions, possibly reinforced by troops from three other divisions.

In addition, most of the German 242d and 244th infantry divisions were revealed to have been wiped out at Toulon, now completely lib-

Continued on Page 7

Germans Tortured Women During Paris 'Inquisition'

By RICHARD D. McMILLAN

Paris, Aug. 27 (Delayed). (U.P.)—Tortures inflicted by Germans upon Allied internees that "paralleled the Spanish Inquisition" were described today by escaped Allied women internees who have reached Paris for medical care.

"They were inhuman in their methods, but I never told them anything," the secretary to a Paris commercial attache said, smiling grimly.

She described an "electric bath" in torture chambers set up in the French Ministry of the Interior on the Rue de Saussaes. American, French and English women first were plunged into ice cold baths. If they refused to talk they then were forced to sit in a bath through which an electric current passed.

Another Nazi torture, the woman said, was to tear off the fingernails of men and women prisoners.

One English woman said she was suffering from an abscessed jaw when the Germans began to torture her. They deliberately opened the abscess by strangulation, she said. Seventy-five percent of the men subjected to similar tortures broke down and gave information to the Germans, she said.

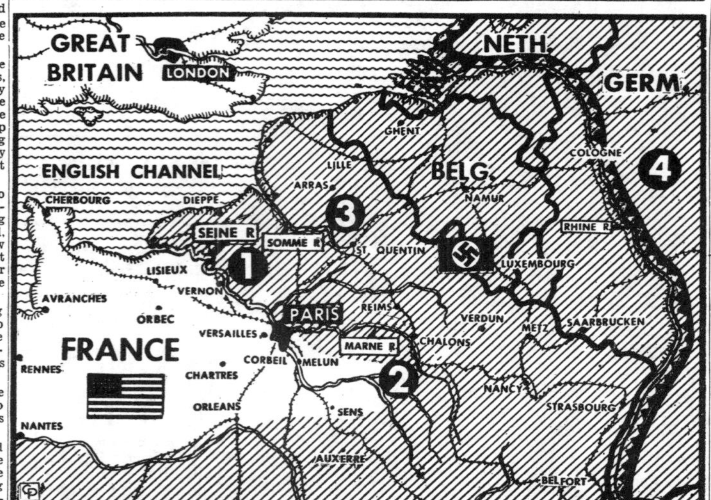

WACHT AM RHINE?—Military experts now believe the Germans will not be able to make a stand before their pell-mell retreat has carried them to the Siegfried Line and the Rhine River. General Patton's spearheads have crossed the Marne (2) and the Huns are falling back toward the Somme (3). North of Paris, Nazi units still are trying to cross the Seine (1).

PATTON'S MEN RIP FLEEING NAZI ARMIES

'Monty's' Units Peril Robot Coast and Aim For German Border

By VIRGIL PINKLEY

Supreme Headquarters, A. E. F., Aug. 28 (U.P.)—Triumphant American troops stormed through the valley of the Marne today, approaching the historic Battleground of Chateau-Thierry, while a powerful British armored force streamed across the Seine above Paris in a double-edged threat to the Nazis' robot bomb bases and the borders of Germany itself.

The battered German armies of northern France were in full retreat and Nazi reports said one American column had thrust on beyond captured Troyes to reach the Marne at Vitry-en-Francois, 100 miles southwest of Paris and barely 90 miles from the German frontier.

Meaux, 23 miles east of Paris, was captured by the advancing Americans and headquarters said Patton's men crossed to the north bank of the Marne and were approaching Chateau-Thierry, 23½ miles farther to the east.

As the Americans struck eastward, long lines of British tanks and mechanized infantry swarmed across the Seine River bridgehead at Vernon, 38 miles northwest of Paris, and struck out for Fluery, six miles beyond the Seine and 14 miles southeast of Rouen.

British Cross Seine

Other British columns swept across the Seine at Mantes, Elbeuf and a newly-won bridgehead at Louviers, almost midway between Vernon and Elbeuf.

Only feeble enemy opposition was encountered by the British spearheads, but headquarters spokesmen warned it was too early to determine whether Hitler had ordered his troops in the Pas de Calais to hold at all costs or to abandon their flying bomb bases to avoid encirclement.

Equally weak resistance met the American columns in their swift thrust up the Marne, and official reports placed the Yank spearheads on the approaches of Chateau-Thierry, barely 30 miles south-southeast of the forest of Compiegne where the armistice of 1918 was signed and where Germany imposed her harsh truce of 1940 on beaten France.

The third battle of the Marne was on, but official reports indicated that this time the Germans had nothing left to stem the khaki tide sweeping eastward on their frontiers.

Lt. Gen. George S. Patton's victory-flushed Yanks met sharp resistance at a number of places from enemy rear guards numbering up to

Continued on Page 7

SEES 33% CUT IN WAR OUTPUT ON REICH DEFEAT

Gen. Meyers Cites Figure at Meeting Of Aircraft Industry

Fully one-third of the nation's war production will be terminated at the conclusion of hostilities with Germany, Maj. Gen. Bennett E. Meyers, Deputy Director of the Army Air Forces Materiel and Services Division, today told 2,000 leaders of the aircraft industry at the Waldorf-Astoria.

Meeting to discuss the streamlining of reconversion and the problems brought about by the termination of war contracts, the industrialists were told by General Meyers that although Hitler's end was at hand it was not here yet.

Sees Hitler Defeat Soon

"We anticipate that one-third of our production program will be terminated at the end of the war with Germany," he said. "We are sure that Hitler's defeat will come soon, but it is not yet here. Twenty years after the last war we were

Continued on Page 7

Hart Gives $50,000 To Beautify Park

Hollywood, Aug. 28 (U.P.)—Two-gun William S. Hart, movie hero of two decades ago, has donated $50,000 to the City Park Commission to beautify his former West Hollywood estate as a public park, commissioners announced today.

Mystery 'Killer' of Blonde Agrees To Surrender in Times Square

'I'm the Man Who Did It,' Says Voice on Phone To Contact Man Named in Newmark Slaying

"I'm the man who did it. I'll surrender today in Times Square," a mysterious voice told Jet Mandel shortly before noon today. Mandel is the contact man named by Melville G. Newmark, husband of the woman whose battered body was found in the bushes near Hayden Planetarium, Manhattan, last Friday, with whom any one having information about his wife preceding her death could communicate without fear of police intervention.

Mandel said he thought the man speaking to him may have been the mysterious sailor mentioned as having been friendly with the slain woman and he made an appointment to meet the man in Times Square later in the day, then notified police.

Meanwhile, the police continued the search for the slayer. The bones in the woman's throat had been crushed by the strangler's fingers, her face was badly bruised and several teeth had been knocked out.

Police obtained information at the Clifton House, 127 W. 79th St., apartment where the Newmarks resided in a $120-a-month suite, that the woman had been seen in a sailor's company and that last Thursday night another woman, described at Clifton House as a "beautiful blonde," had left the house with Mrs. Newmark about 11:30.

Police reported that they have obtained information that a sailor mailed a letter to Mrs. Newmark last May in care of a woman residing on Riverside Drive. The woman, whose name is withheld, told police she had not seen Mrs. Newmark since delivering the letter to her last May.

Questioning of an unidentified man, wearing a khaki naval uniform, at the W. 68th St. police station by detectives at noon today aroused speculation as to his possible identification with the case. Deputy Chief Inspector John J. Gallagher, when asked about this angle, was silent.

Robot Raids Resumed After 31-Hour Respite

London, Aug. 28 (U.P.)—The Germans resumed their flying bomb attacks on London and the Southern Counties shortly after noon today, ending a 31-hour respite from the terror raids.

The missiles which hit the affected areas today were the first since before daylight Sunday and following big stories by London newspapers that the robot might be on the way out.

Headlines on the stories ranged from "Battle for Flybomb Sites has Begun" to "End of Flybomb Now in Sight."

The extent of today's attacks, however, was not disclosed.

Narragansett Results

1—Spare the Rod, 9.80, 4.40, 3.00; Fair Call, 5.40, 4.00; Cherriko, 3.20. Off time, 2:35.

BELMONT RESULTS
(Saratoga Meeting)

1—Cecrops 4.20-2.90-2.30, Stager 5.60-3.00, Lady Eccleston 2.30. (1:23½)
2—Pilates Heart 17.00-6.30-4.60, Light Reich 4.10-3.50, Raisin Bread 10.60
3—Longchamp II 9.40-6.10-4.30, Nordmeer 6.40-4.50, B'k Ned 4.10. (2:23)

DAILY DOUBLE PAID $86.40

Beg Allies Save 150,000 in Warsaw Slaughter Camp

Washington, Aug. 28 (U.P.)—The Polish government in exile today appealed to Allied and neutral governments and to the Vatican to prevent Germany from exterminating a large portion of the population of Warsaw "within the next few days."

Polish Ambassador Jan Ciechanowski delivered the appeal to the State Department.

"The German authorities aim at the extermination of the entire civilian population of Warsaw," the Ambassador said in a statement.

"According to authenticated information in the hands of the Polish government in London from the Polish underground civil administration, more than 150,000 persons, mostly women, children and older men are concentrated in a wholesale slaughter camp at Pruszkow. They are being starved, tortured, entirely deprived of food or water and facing inevitable death. Untold scenes of horror in the Pruszkow camp are beyond description."

67 FROM THIS AREA ON CASUALTY LISTS

The War Department today announced the names of 57 Brooklyn, Queens and Long Island men killed in action in the Asiatic, Central Pacific, European, Mediterranean and Southwest Pacific areas, and the Navy Department listed nine wounded and one dead. The complete latest casualty lists for the local area are on page 4.

SOVIET CAVALRY DRIVES ACROSS HUNGARY BORDER

2 Armies Pour Through Romania's Galati Gap, Aim at Ploesti Oilfields

By ROBERT MUSEL

London, Aug. 28 (U.P.)—Soviet cavalry forces drove over the eastern Carpathian mountains through Transylvania and crossed the Hungarian border today, a Berlin broadcoast admitted, while two other Russian armies poured through Galati Gap on Bucharest and Ploesti where German and Romanian troops, erstwhile allies, were reported fighting against each other.

The German DNB Agency admitted that Soviet cavalry units had penetrated the Hungarian border at an unidentified point, but claimed that Nazi and Hungarian troops had repelled them and that all the passes in the northern Carpathians still were firmly in German hands.

Although Moscow remained silent on the German announcement, the report indicated that Marshal Rodion Y. Malinovsky's 2d Ukrainian Army was making good progress toward a major breach into Transylvania, bone of contention between Romania and Hungary since its award to Hungary by German dictate in 1940.

DNB also reported that in northern Bucharest and in the Ploesti area fighting broke out when Romanian troops, "according to Soviet instructions," attempted to disarm the Germans. It asserted, however, that German troops were "holding out in their positions everywhere."

Malinovsky's mechanized Cossacks paced the drives down through the Galati Gap, which military observers believed would complete the liberation of the Balkans in a few weeks. They drove a spearhead through Ploesti's outer

Continued on Page 7

Big Manhunt Goes On For Paris Snipers

Nazis, Collaborationists to Be Shot on Sight After De Gaulle Escapes Assassination

By HENRY T. GORRELL

Paris, Aug. 28 (U.P.)—French partisans and police, aided by Allied troops, searched Paris today under orders to shoot on sight German snipers and armed collaborationists following the death of at least 15 persons in a series of abortive attempts to assassinate Gen. Charles de Gaulle during a "liberation parade" Saturday.

One attempt on De Gaulle's life touched off a miniature battle in Notre Dame Cathedral, where snipers hidden in the gallery exchanged shots with worshippers during a thanksgiving service climaxing the parade.

Other snipers entrenched on the roof of the American Embassy had fired into crowds on the Place de la Concorde, killing two persons and wounding 16. Still other shots came from buildings near the City Hall as the De Gaulle party approached.

Train Service Resumed

But even as authorities pressed their manhunt, Paris already was well on the road to normalcy after

Continued on Page 7

Nazis Attack Bucharest, Rush Agents to Sofia

London, Aug. 28 (U.P.)—Adolf Hitler, battling with guns and threats to hold his deserting Balkan satellites in line, launched a fullscale attack on Bucharest today and rushed his diplomatic trouble shooters to Sofia to block a Bulgarian declaration of war on the Reich.

The German Transocean News Agency said fierce fighting had broken out between Nazi troops and their erstwhile allies in Romania, where 11 German divisions were to have been killed, captured or trapped since Romania broke her ties with Berlin and went over to the Allies last week.

Transocean said German troops had completely encircled Bucharest, where Premier Marshal Constantin Senatescu and his new anti-Nazi Cabinet were holding the former Premier Ion Antonescu and members of a German military mission.

Bucharest has been cut off from all communication with the rest of the country, Transocean said, asserting that the Romanian Army itself has been divided into two camps, one supporting Senatescu and the other continuing the fight against Russia.

At the same time signs multiplied that Bulgaria, after breaking with Germany over the Romanian

Continued on Page 7

Mayer in Hospital After Riding Mishap

Hollywood, Aug. 28 (U.P.)—Louis B. Mayer, Metro-Goldwyn-Mayer chief, was doing "as well as could be expected" at Cedars of Lebanon Hospital today with a fractured pelvis and numerous bruises. He was injured at his ranch during an early morning horseback ride yesterday.

26 DIE AS U. S. PLANE CRASHES IN SCOTLAND

London, Aug. 28 (U.P.) — Twenty-six persons were killed today when a plane, believed an American Skymaster mail plane from the United States, crashed into a dwelling at Prestwick, Scotland.

The victims included seven crewmen, 14 passengers and five occupants of the demolished house.

The plane was understood to have circled twice before it crashed.

WHERE TO FIND IT

	Page		Page
Bridge	8	Real Estate	8
Comics	15	Sermons	8
Crossword	8	Society	5
Dr. Brady	6	Sports	10, 11
Editorial	6	Take My Word	6
Helen Worth	5	Theaters	20
Horoscope	15	These Women	15
Mary Haworth	9	Tommy Holmes	10
Movies	20	Uncle Ray	15
Novel	9	Want Ads	12-13-14
Obituaries	7	Wartime Problems	9
Our Fighters	4	Women	5
Patterns	9, 15		
Radio	15		

BOND SELLING CHAMPIONS—Six star War Bond salesmen from Brooklyn schools beam as Dodger Manager Leo Durocher autographs their programs at yesterday's Brooklyn-Philadelphia game. They and more than 1,000 other children who sold more than five E bonds were guests of Branch Rickey, president. The happy salesmen are Donald Collins of 1465 E. 53d St., Joan Guzowski of 152 Java St., Alvin Adamowski of 679 Winthrop St., Joseph McGloin of 448 E. 29th St., Richard Johnnsen of 71-12 Fort Hamilton Parkway and Edward Aziarz of 91 Java St.

Simplified Tax Plan Completed

Washington, Aug. 30 (U.P.) — The Treasury announced today that it has completed plans for putting into effect the new tax simplification law which will spare some 30,000,000 income taxpayers the trouble of figuring out their 1944 income taxes.

Joseph D. Nunan Jr., commissioner of internal revenue, said the Government is now distributing to employers withholding tax receipts which, when filled out, can be used by most employes in place of regular tax returns.

Under the new procedure, he explained, all taxpayers receiving less than $5,000 a year income, on which they paid withholding taxes, will receive from their employers by Jan. 31 a receipt showing their wages for the year and the total amount of taxes withheld from their pay checks.

On the receipt will be a few simple questions, together with brief instructions explaining just who is eligible to use the receipt instead of a return. The estimated 30,000,000 who will be eligible will simply forward the receipt to the Treasury before March 15, 1945, where experts will figure whether or not the correct amount of taxes has been withheld. If they find a difference, the taxpayer will get either a bill or a refund.

The new system gives each taxpayer an automatic deduction of about 10 percent for contributions to charity, taxes, medical expenses and other exemptions, thereby eliminating the need for him to figure his deductions. If, however, he has deductions of more than 10 percent of his income he must file the usual income tax form if he wishes to have them credited.

DEWEY'S DRIVE IS STEPPED UP BY 3 GOVERNORS

The Republican Presidential campaign stepped up a notch today, the speeches of three G. O. P. Governors on a nation-wide radio network having given it a substantial shove toward the November elections.

But while Governors Raymond E. Baldwin of Connecticut, Dwight Green of Illinois and Earl Warren of California were blasting President Roosevelt and the fourth-terms protagonists and praising Governor Dewey, the Republican nominee sat quietly in his Pawling, N. Y., farmhouse, where he is preparing a number of major talks he will deliver between Sept. 7 and 26.

The three Governors, speaking from their respective State capitals over the Blue Network, made drastic revisions in their speeches last night just before they went on the air for 15 minutes at 10:15. All the speeches were toned down considerably, but the only explanation from a G. O. P. spokesman was that they were brought "into conformity."

Governor Warren was the only one to refer to the C. I. O. Political Action Committee. He declared that the Republicans "do not intend to buy this election, and Sidney Hillman (director of the P. A. C.) and his committee shall not be permitted to do it either." The rules of fair play, he said, will govern the conduct of the G. O. P. drive.

"And the New Deal speeches," he added, "should not be designated as 'educational' while others of like character by Socialists and Republicans are suppressed from our fighting men as 'political.'"

'Tribute' to Dewey

Governor Baldwin expressed satisfaction that "Tammany Hall is against Governor Dewey; that Frank (I am the law) Hague is against Governor Dewey; that Boss Kelly in Chicago is against him, and that Boss Pendergast of Kansas City would be against him if Boss Pendergast were not so recently out of jail." He termed such opposition the greatest "tribute" to Dewey.

Governor Green charged that "ruthless heads of corrupt political machines" are carrying out New Deal edicts, while the Republicans, in contrast, are executing a program "drafted in consultation with the people."

The fourth-term candidate," he said, "will make his own issues in his occasional radio speeches by whatever name he may call them. Hannegan (Robert E., national Democratic chairman) and Hillman, and the rest of the bosses, will raise the fund, organize the workers and carry out the orders."

Priests End Visions Of 1,000 Chicken Feasts

Eagle Staff photo

ON THE WING—Here's where the chicken truck laid an egg.

Only an uncooked omelet on the pavement was left today of the vision of 1,000 free chicken dinners that went winging because the appearance of four priests nicked the conscience of the chicken-chasers.

Under a cloud of flying feathers the hunt started yesterday opposite the College of Arts and Sciences of St. John's University when a truck overturned at Willoughby and Lewis Aves., spilling its cargo of screeching, clucking Jersey Giants, Plymouth Rocks and Rhode Island Reds. Along with them went four crates of eggs, and to these were added many more by the frightened fowl.

As the chickens flapped their wings and attempted to escape hundreds of men, women and children, adding their yells to the bedlam, began a wild chase through the college grounds.

Scores of the pursuers grabbed luscious armfuls and pictured them in the oven or the pot. But then they spotted Father William J. Mahoney, president of the university, and three other priests, on the porch of the college. Not a word was said. It wasn't necessary. Nearly all the victors ruefully lined up to return their prizes.

A count of the casualties showed about 20 D. O. A. cases (police terminology for dead on arrival) and these were distributed among the crowd.

Six squad cars from the Gates Ave. Station and an emergency squad answered the alarm when the truck, driven by Harry Sidorsky, 50, of 5221 11th Ave., overturned as Sidorsky swerved to avoid a traffic stanchion.

Teamsters' Dinner Chosen for F. D. R. 'Political' Speech

Washington, Aug. 30 (U.P.)—President Roosevelt has chosen a dinner here on the night of Sept. 23 for his first self-labeled "political" speech in his fourth-term campaign.

The dinner is being given by Daniel Tobin, president of the International Brotherhood of Teamsters, A. F. L., for between 600 and 700 officers of State, district and local affiliates of the union.

David D. Beck, vice president of the union, pointed out that Mr. Roosevelt addressed the union's convention here in September, 1940, and he was invited to do so again this year as a matter of courtesy.

Asked whether the speech might be intended to cement the labor vote behind Mr. Roosevelt in November, Beck answered: "He's already got it."

The President told reporters late yesterday that, while his speech would not be very political, it would seem to have a tinge. He said he had not yet decided whether he would make other political speeches.

On the question of a nation-wide tour the Chief Executive was emphatic. He said he had too much to do to make one. The Democratic Vice Presidential candidate, Senator Harry S. Truman (D., Mo.) is expected to do most of the speechmaking for the party's national ticket.

Mr. Roosevelt conferred yesterday with Vice President Henry A. Wallace for the first time since the Democratic National Convention rebuffed Wallace's bid for renomination. Wallace said he would be active in the coming campaign.

41 to Get Nurses Caps At Jewish Hospital School

Forty-one students of the Jewish School of Nursing will be capped at ceremonies tonight in the Dr. Leon Louiria Auditorium, 567 Prospect Place, it was announced by Emma E. Heller, director of the School of Nursing and Nursing Service. Charles Jaffe, president of the school, will speak.

Others expected to be present include Isidor Leviton, president of the board of directors; Dr. Morris Hinenburg, executive director, and Max Abelman, secretary to the board of directors.

Babylon Seeks Control Of Sandpit Operations

Lindenhurst, Aug. 30—The first decisive step in a fight between the Town of Babylon and the Hughes-Kelly Corporation, operators of a sandpit in East Farmingdale, a short distance from the Republic Aircraft plant, will be taken today when a summons served on officials of the company will be returnable before Justice of the Peace William F. Wolter, here. The summons charges violation of ordinances and laws giving the town control over such operations.

If the town's contention is upheld by the courts, operators of every sandpit in Babylon will be obliged to obtain a permit.

'I REPENT,' SIGNALS DEAF MUTE—WINS MERCY IN THEFT

Proceedings in Judge Mullen's part in the Court of General Sessions were carried on in the sign language for several minutes today. Participants in the silent but animated conversation were Charles J. Peyton, personal attendant of Judge Mullen, and Otis Moseley, 24, of 88 W. 155th St., Manhattan, whom the court was ready to sentence on his plea of guilty to a charge of grand larceny. At the conclusion of the talk Peyton reported that Moseley, a deaf mute, had expressed repentance and a desire to make restitution of the $150 involved in the crime. Moseley was given a suspended sentence and placed on probation.

Seek to Honor City Wiped Out by Nazis

Formation of the committee for rebirth of Distomo, dedicated to having an American community renamed after the Greek town the Nazis destroyed, in revenge, on the second anniversary of the destruction of Czechoslovakia's Lidice, was announced today by Maxwell Anderson, playwright and committee chairman.

Distomo was wiped off the map and its 1,100 inhabitants slaughtered last June 10, first community to be thus dealt with after Hitler's threat to bathe Europe in blood before the Nazis go down to defeat. Thus the town's destruction constitutes a first public admission by the Nazis, Mr. Anderson said, that they were losing the war.

"There could be no more fitting monument to the heroism and the tradition of freedom of the people of Distomo," he added, than to carry on its name as that of an American town.

Included on the committee, besides Mr. Anderson, are: Representative Emanuel Celler of Brooklyn, Jo Davidson, sculptor; Senator Robert F. Wagner; Arthur Szyk, artist, and the Rt. Rev. Polyzoides, Bishop of Nyssa. The committee has set up headquarters at 140 W. 26th St., Manhattan.

CORRECTION

The words "since defunct" were inserted in error yesterday in a Brooklyn Eagle story mentioning the firm of Goldman, Sachs & Company and the former connection of Sidney J. Weinberg, resigned vice chairman of the War Production Board, with that firm. Actually, Goldman, Sachs & Company is a prominent brokerage firm with offices at 30 Pine St., Manhattan.

7 ★★★★★★★ SPORTS
Wall Street Financial News

BROOKLYN EAGLE

WEATHER—Clear, cool tonight; sunny, warmer tomorrow.

103d Year. No. 246. DAILY & SUNDAY • (Copyright 1944 The Brooklyn Eagle, Inc.) • BROOKLYN, N. Y., FRIDAY, SEPTEMBER 8, 1944 • Entered at the Brooklyn Postoffice as 2d Class Mail Matter • 3 CENTS IN NEW YORK CITY ELSEWHERE 4 CENTS

PATTON ARMY CLOSES ON METZ AND NANCY

Cashmore to Sift High Rates for Theft Insurance

Plans Conference Of Officials to Study Record Premiums

Borough President Cashmore jumped on Brooklyn's excessive theft insurance rate with both feet today with the announcement that he will call a meeting of insurance executives to sift charges that Brooklyn homeowners pay a far higher premium to protect their property than is paid anywhere else in the country.

"I do not know whether the higher rate is justified," Cashmore said, "but I am certain if there is any merit in claims that insurance is costing Brooklyn residents too much the proper rating officials will be quick to consider the opinion of the insurance group I plan to call together."

Pay $27.50 per $1,000

The Borough President was referring to the disclosures made Sunday by the Brooklyn Eagle that borough homeowners are paying $27.50 per $1,000 for theft insurance while the other boroughs are charged, respectively, $22 in the Bronx; $18 in Queens and $17 in Manhattan. The rest of New York State pays only $11.50.

Mr. Cashmore said he would set a date for the meeting of insurance men within a few days.

Meanwhile, the Brooklyn Chamber of Commerce has placed discussion of the borough's high theft insurance rate at the top of the agenda of the first Fall meeting Sept. 22 of its general insurance council.

Crime Srows Drop

The realization that Brooklynites are suckers on the insurance rate has become widespread in the borough since publication of the comparative figures. It was revealed that Brooklyn residents are paying premiums based on experience tables gathered in the five-year period ended in 1937 in spite of the fact that over-all crime statistics show a decrease in criminal activity in the last five years.

Buzzbomb Fails To Budge Audience Ogling Striptease

By ROBERT MUSEL

London, Sept. 8 (U.P.) — Phyllis Dixey, blond and demure, was doing a British strip tease on the stage of the Whitehall Theater in Trafalgar Square when a flying bomb came over.

What happened then was entirely in keeping with the British tradition for remaining imperturbable, and with Phyllis' own philosophy that buzzbombs or no, she intended to keep right on taking off her clothes.

Phyllis already had gone through the little preliminary song she does. Then she stepped up stage for her strip tease.

As I remember, Phyllis was fumbling with her dress catch this night the buzzbomb came over. The buzzbomb's noise grew to a mighty crescendo just as she whipped away her gown.

There was Phyllis on stage—there was a ton of terrible death overhead. The air-raid shelters were one way. Phyllis, lovely, unadorned, was the other.

For a long moment all life in the theater was stilled.

Then the bomb whistled down and the theater shook under the blast.

I realized then with a feeling of pride in our gallant Allies that, having a choice between the air-raid shelters and the beautiful tableaux on stage, every member of the audience had cheerfully taken the only chivalrous course.

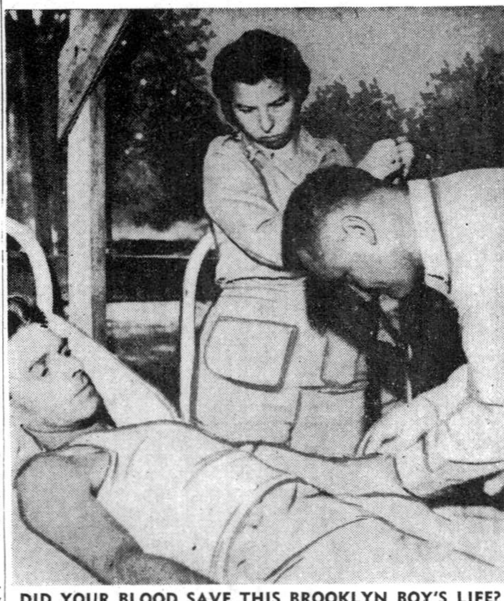

DID YOUR BLOOD SAVE THIS BROOKLYN BOY'S LIFE? —Pfc. Arthur E. Connelly of 56 Fane Court will live because some one gave a pint of blood. Badly burned during action in the South Pacific, he is here getting the lifesaving plasma from Army Nurse Lt. Grace I. Birris and Capt. Maurie B. Cree, Henderson, N. C. The Red Cross collects 4,000 pints of blood weekly for the armed forces.

Nurse Black Market Cited as Worst of All

Hospitals and Private Patients Blamed For Cutting Down Recruits for War

The army has sent out an urgent call in the nation for 4,000 more nurses in September, but the number recruited in Brooklyn so far this week has been—just eight, Brooklyn Red Cross headquarters at 57 Willoughby St. reported today.

Said Florance Unwin, chairman of the Brooklyn Chapter's army and navy nurse recruitment:

"Our quota for the first six months of the year, through June 30, was 214 nurses, but through August, which is two months later, we have recruited 152. Why?

"Well, there seems to be a genuine black market in nurses, which I would call the worst black market of all. Since Jan. 1, the War Manpower Commission has been classifying registered nurses according to their availability for service with the troops, and in Brooklyn, 1,144 nurses have been classified 1-A. But it is a 1-A which cannot be enforced, as with the men in Selective Service. Only 152 have taken the classification seriously. The rest, except perhaps where they have left the State and

Continued on Page 11

Telling It Briefly

FIGHT AMONG SAILORS CAUSES DEATH OF ONE

Police today are investigating the death of James Bell, 21, U. S. sailor who had been stationed at Floyd Bennett Field. Bell died at 3 a.m. today at Kings County Hospital from injuries received when he fell, striking the curbstone, during a fight among several sailors at Kingston Ave. and Fulton St.

MAN, 66, KILLED BY HIT-RUN AUTO

Christian Petersen, 66, of 267 68th St., died in Harbor Hospital today from injuries received when struck by a hit-run driver at Bay 8th St. and Belt Parkway.

63 NEW POLIO CASES REPORTED IN CITY

Sixty-three new cases of infantile paralysis in New York are reported today, bringing the Health Department total to 1,038 for the year. This compares with the 11,417 cases in the same period in 1935, the last epidemic year.

BOROUGH YOUTH CONVICTED IN SHOOTING

Brought back from Florida, where he was in the army, Cecil Clark, 20, reported to be the leader of a Bedford-Stuyvesant sidewalk gang, today faces 10 to 20 years in prison after being found guilty by a jury in ten minutes of attacking another youth with a gun. County Judge Leibowitz remanded Clark for sentence. He was charged with shooting Rufus Pegues of 899 Greene Ave. after a quarrel over stabbing of membes of Clark's mob, called the Black Shirts. Pegues spent five weeks in Kings County Hospital.

Continued on Page 11

AQUEDUCT RESULTS

1—Mountaineer 42.60-18.50-6.60, Herodotus 105.20 11.50, Hal 2.50. (1:21⅕) In the Wings won but disqualified.

Court Frees Veteran In Killing of Brother

Acting Prosecutor Declines to Press Charges Against Good as Mother Weeps

James Good, 19-year-old war veteran charged with killing his brother, Joseph, 17, in the "brother's keeper" case, stood in Brooklyn Supreme Court today and heard a district attorney decline to prosecute him for murder, an action in which the trial judge concurred.

Justice Rubenstein sustained a writ of habeas corpus obtained by defense attorney Hyman Barshay after Magistrate Surpless had held the youth on a homicide charge for action of the grand jury.

Later Acting District Attorney Hughes said he had "no intention of going any further in the case," although Judge Rubenstein's ruling did not bar the prosecutor from presenting charges to a grand jury for indictment.

"Considering all the circumstances," Mr. Hughes said, "it would not be the proper thing for the people's interest to prosecute further."

Given 'Benefit of Doubt'

The "circumstances" included those preceding and accompanying Joseph's death. James, recently discharged from the army and working on a war job, had assumed responsibility for his younger brother's conduct, quarreled with him when Joseph came home late on the night of Aug. 11 and knocked him down. His head struck the edge of a bureau and he died of a hemorrhage.

"After reading all the minutes of this case," Justice Rubenstein said, "I have a doubt that there is sufficient proof of felonious death,

Continued on Page 11

SAYS U. S. FIRMS GAVE JAPAN WAR 'KNOW HOW'

Official Testifies Foe Got Data on Oil For Pearl Harbor

Washington Sept. 8 (U.P.)—A Justice Department official disclosed today that as late as June, 1941, only six months before the Pearl Harbor attack, Japan was able to learn through American commercial channels the exact amounts of oil and gasoline shipped to the Hawaiian naval base from Los Angeles.

Testifying before the Senate Kilgore War Mobilization Committee, James S. Martin, chief of the department's Economic Warfare Division, also declared that:

1. Less than two years before Pearl Harbor a Japanese lieutenant commander visited the Boeing aircraft factories at Seattle, where he was shown plans and data on the Boeing 307 Stratoliner, and saw Boeing Flying Fortresses undergo tests outside the plant.

2. Japan was able to get technical "know-how" on some processes for production of 100 octane aviation gasoline before they were generally available to American firms.

Cartels Aided Japs

Martin emphasized that none of the methods employed by Japan were "illegal," but they showed how Japan used American business firms through cartel agreements to prepare for war.

Martin said Japan got its information on Pearl Harbor oil and gasoline shipments through the San Francisco branch of the Mitsubishi Trading Company. On June 7, 1941, he said, the branch wrote its home office that the export division of the

Continued on Page 11

Strike Halts Work On B-24 Bombers

Detroit, Sept. 8 (U.P.)—Production of B-24 bombers at the Ford Motor Company's Willow Run plant was halted today by a strike of crane operators and riveters.

A Ford company spokesman said the plant was shut at noon but would reopen for the 4 p.m. shift and work would resume then if a sufficient number of employes reported.

The spokesman said the walkout by members of the United Automobile Workers (C.I.O.) Union followed transfer of approximately 20 riveters from a department where they no longer were needed to another department at the same rate of pay.

A U. A. W.-C. I. O. International Union representative said that 1,500 workers were involved and that the walkout was in protest of "transfers and layoffs being made by the management without regard to seniority."

Taft Sees Cost of War Little Burden to Posterity

Washington, Sept. 8 (U.P.) — If thoughts of paying for the present war bother you, listen to Senator Robert A. Taft of Ohio.

He said in a brief interview today that he didn't think the war would ever be paid for. Moreover, he didn't seem bothered.

Instead, he cited the fact that the British still are paying for the War of 1812, adding that the debt now is of little burden to British subjects.

"As time goes on and wealth increases, people will find that a war debt of $300,000,000,000 which looks tremendous to us will mean little to our grandchildren," he declared.

Radio Circuit to Paris Open

London, Sept. 7 (U.P.)—The Cables and Wireless Company today announced the reopening of a radio circuit to Paris which had been closed since the German occupation in 1940.

Laurel Results

1—Rare, first; Pompous Fox, second; Frontier Jane, third.

Exiled Cabinet Flies to Belgium

By JOHN A. PARRIS

Aboard Belgian Premier's Plane, En Route to Brussels, Sept. 8 (U.P.)—The Belgian cabinet, first exiled government to return to its homeland, was on its way to Brussels today in a great transport plane, with Belgian flags painted on both sides.

I am riding in the plane with Premier Hubert Pierlot and other members of his government who escaped to France and later to England when the Germans drove into Belgium in May, 1940.

(Parris, only correspondent with the party, handed this dispatch from the plane just before it took off for Brussels.)

There were tears in Pierlot's eyes when he boarded the plane. When he waved goodby to the throng of well-wishers and came inside he said simply to me, "This is the happiest day of my life."

Before the party took off a hurried cabinet session was held and the Ministers were given last minute instructions as to their new duties in liberated Belgium.

Kaiser Learns to Fly Helicopter in 5 Minutes

Oakland, Cal., Sept. 8 (U.P.)—Henry J. Kaiser said today he had purchased patent rights to a revolutionary counter-robot helicopter, hired its 19-year-old inventor, and learned to fly the machine after five minutes instruction.

NEW CASUALTY LISTS NAME 89 LOCAL MEN

The War Department today announced the names of 78 Brooklyn, Queens and Long Island men wounded in action in the European, Mediterranean and Southwest Pacific areas and the Navy Department announced 11 local casualties. The latest casualty lists for this area are on page 9.

DEWEY SET TO OUTLINE PEACE VIEWS

Speeds to Louisville After Opening Blast At New Deal in Philly

By JOHN L. CUTTER

Aboard Dewey Campaign Train, Sept. 8 (U.P.)—Gov. Thomas E. Dewey sped toward Louisville, Ky., today to outline his views on how to prevent future wars in a speech to a convention of Republican women tonight.

Dewey formally opened his campaign in Philadelphia's Convention Hall last night. In the first of seven major speeches scheduled for his three-week swing to the West Coast he told a visual audience estimated at 12,500 and a nationwide radio audience that the Roosevelt Administration is "afraid to let men out of the army" because it lacks confidence in America's ability to return to a peacetime economy.

Quoting Selective Service Director Maj. Gen. Lewis B. Hershey as having announced recently that demobilization of the armed forces will be a gradual process because "we can keep people in the army about as cheaply as we could create an agency for them when they are out," Dewey declared:

"The New Deal prepares to keep men in the army because it is afraid of a resumption of its own depression. They can't think of anything for us to do once we stop building guns and tanks."

Wants Men Sent Home

Dewey said he believed that members of the armed forces should be brought home and released "at the earliest practical moment after victory.

"I believe that the occupation of Germany and Japan should very soon be confined to those who voluntarily choose to remain in the army when peace comes," he said.

"I am not afraid of the future of America—either immediate or distant. I am sure of our future, if

Continued on Page 11

BLUE RATION TOKENS TO BE DISCONTINUED

Washington, Sept. 8 (U.P.)—Price Chief Chester Bowles announced today that blue ration tokens, ordered by the Government to make change for blue ration stamps, will not be used after Oct. 1. He urged consumers to dispose of their supply as soon as possible.

Bowles said retailers were being instructed to discontinue issuing the tokens after Sept. 17, when 17 food items will be removed from the processed ration list.

De Gaulle Cabinet Orders Vichy Leaders Arrested

Paris, Sept. 8 (U.P.)—The De Gaulle cabinet has directed that every effort be made to arrest Marshal Philippe Petain and Pierre Laval, who are believed to be in Germany, and other Vichy leaders, it was learned today.

The newspaper Liberation said the biggest trial in French history would judge not only Petain and Laval but also "cabinet members of the 1940 capitulation to the Germans," ministers who favored the armistice and all who ruled in Vichy.

Willkie Resting in Hospital

Wendell L. Willkie was confined to a hospital today for "a rest and a checkup." His physician, Dr. Benjamin Salzer, said he suffered a "stomach attack" while in Indiana recently and needed rest.

German Cartels Must Be Ended, F.D.R. Warns

Washington, Sept. 8 (U.P.)—President Roosevelt said today that the defeat of the Nazi armies would have to be followed by the eradication of German cartels and stringent restrictions on cartel practices in international trade.

In a letter to Secretary of State Hull, the President asked Hull to "keep your eye" on the whole subject of international cartels "because we are approaching the time when discussions will almost certainly arise between us and other nations."

The President read the letter to his news conference and added the verbal comment that the subject of international cartels would become most important in the next six months.

The letter to Hull outlined the American traditional opposition to private monopolies and likewise the liberal American principles of free international trade for which Hull long has fought.

Mr. Roosevelt's discussion gave emphasis to a campaign which the Justice Department's anti-trust division has been waging to prevent postwar international cartel agreements.

BRITISH HURDLE ALBERT CANAL IN DRIVE NORTHEAST

By VIRGIL PINKLEY

Supreme Headquarters, A. E. F., Sept. 8 (U.P.)—Lt. Gen. George S. Patton's 3d Army closed against Metz and Nancy today in a Moselle valley drive carrying within 20 miles of Germany, and a spokesman predicted the fortress cities guarding the approaches to the Reich would fall or be neutralized within two days.

Four Allied armies—the American 1st, 3d and 7th and the British 2d—were driving the final miles up to the German frontier preparatory to a final offensive into the Reich, soon to be opened somewhere along the 500-mile border stretch between Switzerland and northern Holland.

The British Mediterranean radio reported that the American 3d and 7th Armies had joined in the area of Bel-

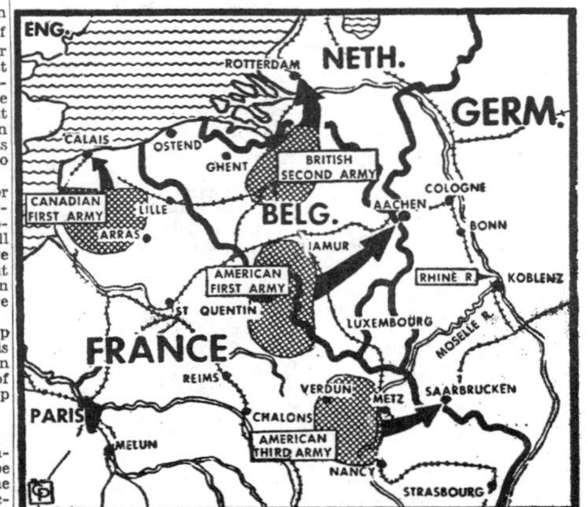

WAR TODAY—American 1st and 3d Armies press pincers drive (arrow) aimed at Siegfried Line, while British push north.

fort, establishing an unbroken Allied front from the North Sea to the Mediterranean, but there was no immediate confirmation.

A security blackout obscured most of the current operations. Front dispatches from the Moselle valley, however, revealed that the 3d Army was waging a general offensive from its bridgeheads across the river. The predicted capture of Metz and Nancy would collapse the Nazi defense line and open the way to Germany.

Planes Hit Rhineland

A 1,500-bomber fleet of American Flying Fortresses and Liberators swept in over the Rhineland and hammered German war plants at Ludwigshafen, Kastel and Gustavsburg.

The Canadians advanced steadily in the cleanup of the Channel ports. They were in the outskirts of Boulogne and Calais. A front dispatch said troops drawing an arc around

Continued on Page 2

Fuel Oil Authorized For Coal-Using Plants

Residual fuel oil supplies have increased to the point where the Petroleum Administration for War has authorized some apartment houses and small industrial plants which converted to coal two years ago to return to oil.

This is no help to homeowners, however, because the ruling applies only to the residual oil—a heavy industrial product.

Manchurian Mill Cities Ripped by Superforts

Washington, Sept. 8 (U.P.)—American B-29 Superfortresses struck today at "important industrial targets" in Japanese-dominated Manchuria, the War Department announced.

The Tokyo radio indicated the targets were the factory cities of Antung and Anshan.

The new assault by the mammoth bombers against Japan's war-making potential was announced by Gen. Henry H. Arnold, chief of the Army Air Forces and head of the 20th Bomber Command, that guides operations of the B-29s.

It was the eighth attack mission by the big four-engined bombers which operate from secret bases far back in the China-Burma-India theater.

Arnold did not disclose the number of planes taking part in the raid, nor did he identify the exact targets, but promised that "further details will be released as soon as additional information is available."

Report 100 Planes in Raid

Headquarters of the Japanese Kwangtung army announced that 100 American planes, presumably 8-29 Superfortresses, attacked Anshan an Pansipu in the industrial area of southern Manchuria.

Tokio radio boadcast a dispatch from Hsingking, Manchuria, quoting the communique which admitted damage to Japanese ground installations. The broadcast was recorded by United Press, San Francisco.

The target in one Japanese broadcast was identified as Anshan, an important iron and steel center 55 miles southwest of Mukden, but another Tokyo report said the Allied bombers were over Antung, 100 miles southeast of Anshan.

Antung, a city of 315,000 population on the Yalu River seven miles inland from Korea Bay, is the center of the Manchuria Light Metals Company, the Manchuria Electric Corporation and the Suiho Hydroelectric plant.

None of the broadcasts claimed that any planes were shot down, although two reports heard by FCC said the Allied formations were engaged by Japanese planes over both Antung and Anshan.

WHERE TO FIND IT

	Page		Page
Bridge	6	Our Fighters	8
Comics	21	Patterns	9-17
Crossword	15	Radio	21
Dr. Brady	10	Real Estate	15
Editorial	10	Society	13
Financial	15	Sports	14-15
Going Places	17	Take My Word	10
Helen Worth	9	Theaters	16
Horoscope	21	These Women	21
Mary Haworth	13	Tommy Holmes	14
Movies	16	Uncle Ray	21
Novel	18	Want Ads	18-19-20
Obituaries	11	Women	13

SCREEN

By Jane Corby

'Since You Went Away,' Now in 9th Week, Tribute to the Painstaking Selznick

David O. Selznick, whose home-front-of-America film story, "Since You Went Away," is now playing its ninth record-breaking week at the Capitol Theater, is probably not one bit surprised at the success of his latest film. There isn't a producer in Hollywood who is more determined than he that every picture that leaves his hands will be a hit.

"Perfectionist" is the term his co-workers apply to him, and he doesn't disclaim it. He devotes himself to polishing every inch of a Selznick offering, no matter what other people have to say about such meticulousness. Two outstanding films before the current offering are all-time tributes to his painstaking care: "Gone With the Wind" and "Rebecca."

The son of the late Lewis J. Selznick, a pioneer in the production and exhibition of movies, David Selznick got his first film training in the employ of his father. During his schooldays in New York, where the family had moved from Pittsburgh, he spent his vacations helping his father at theaters, film agencies and finally in the Selznick studios. He enrolled at Columbia, but quit early and headed for Hollywood, because he couldn't wait to get into the movie business for himself.

The first years were lean ones. Selznick made a quickie, "Will He Beat Dempsey?" (meaning Luis Angel Firpo), starring Firpo, who valued his time at $1,000 a day. Selznick employed him for half a day, paying him the $500 which represented his entire capital. The film made money and he got out another short, featuring Rudolph Valentino, again at a profit.

But Selznick wanted to get into the big time and got a job with Metro, where, as an associate producer, he distinguished himself chiefly by taking one "western" company out on location and returning with two pictures in the can, to the surprise of his bosses, who didn't know he had taken along two scripts with the one company.

In 1933, after working for several studios, he set up a motion picture company under the Selznick name. His first offering was "Little Lord Fauntleroy," followed by such successes as "A Star Is Born," "The Young In Heart" and "Intermezzo."

For "Since You Went Away" Selznick wrote the screen play, assembled a million-dollar cast (which lists Claudette Colbert, Joseph Cotten, Jennifer Jones, Shirley Temple, Lionel Barrymore, Monty Woolley and Robert Walker as its seven stars), engaged professional artists to build the sets, created the Hilton home, and gave his personal attention to photography and music. The musical score, penned by Max Steiner who scored "G W T W," was not dubbed into the film until Selznick passed on it.

'Janie' Stays for Third Paramount Hit Week

Warner Bros. comedy hit, "Janie," the story of a typical teen-age American girl, starring Joyce Reynolds, Robert Hutton and Edward Arnold, will be held over for a third week starting tomorrow at the Paramount. The co-feature, "Crime By Night," a mystery-drama with Jane Wyman and Jerome Cowan, will also be retained.

Twentieth Century-Fox has purchased the screen rights to "Fallen Angel," a murder mystery written by Marty Holland, which will soon be published by the E. P. Dutton Company. Otto Preminger is scheduled to produce the film.

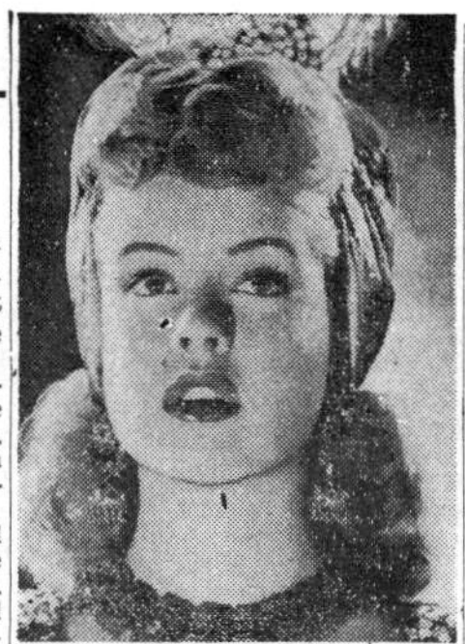

GLORIA DE HAVEN as she appears in one of the lavish numbers in "Step Lively," the headliner at the Albee, with Frank Sinatra. "The Falcon in Mexico" is added.

'Arsenic and Old Lace' BIG Hit

The record-breaking box office figures currently being registered by "Arsenic and Old Lace" at the N. Y. Strand Theater must come as no surprise to the many thousands who saw the Joseph Kesselring stage play, upon which the Strand's screen feature is based. The Warner Brothers screen treatment of the Brooklyn comedy has retained all of the laughs—and added new ones—which accounted for history-making attendance at the original play.

This comedy about delightfully mad people has been seen in play form by more than 3,000,000 persons. It grossed $2,000,000 in New York and more than that sum on three United States road tours, as well as an additional 144,327 pounds in London.

The play, which was produced by Howard Lindsay and Russel Crouse, opened on Broadway on Jan. 10, 1941, and played 1,444 consecutive performances at the Fulton and Hudson Theaters.

As of July 1, the play had given 637 consecutive performances at the Strand, London, and is still playing there. In addition, two road companies are touring the British Provinces. "Arsenic and Old Lace" has also been played in Rio de Janiero, Montevideo, Goteborg (Sweden), Honolulu, Buenos Aires and Lima (Peru).

"Arsenic and Old Lace" was the first play to be seen by General Montgomery when he returned incognito from the African campaign to London. It was the first play to been seen by Princess Elizabeth in London's West End. It has also been seen by Prime Minister Churchill, King George and Queen Elizabeth.

The play was the first to be presented by a Broadway cast in the great gymnasium at West Point, where it was witnessed by 3,000 future officers. It was also one of the first to be released to USO camp shows. Beginning its tour at Fort Sam Houston in Texas, "Arsenic and Old Lace" played 150 performances before 196,000 members of the armed forces.

The film, which was produced for Warner Brothers by Frank Capra, stars Cary Grant and features Raymond Massey, Jack Carson, Priscilla Lane, Peter Lorre, Edward Everett Horton, James Gleason, Josephine Hull, Jean Adair and John Alexander.

Lou Wills Jr., the 16-year dancer, has been signed for a featured role in the new Olson and Johnson show, "Laffing Room Only." This will mark the fourth Broadway show for the very youthful dancer, who has just left the cast of "One Touch of Venus."

KATINA PAXINOU, who will star in "Sophie Holenczik, American," new play to be produced by Meyer Davis and George Ross.

'Days of Glory' At RKO Theaters

"Roger Touhy, Gangster," starring Preston Foster, Victor McLaglen and Lois Andrews, started today at the RKO Brooklyn, Queens and Long Island theaters, sharing the bill with the romantic drama "Days of Glory," highlighting a cast of new screen personalities, with Tamara Toumanova, Gregory Peck, Alan Reed and Maria Palmer.

Paramount has started production of "Miss Susie Slagle's," the adaptation of Augusta Tucker's novel, with Sonny Tufts, Veronica Lake and Lillian Gish heading a large cast. This story of medical students and a boarding housekeeper is the first screen directorial assignment of John Berry, 26-year-old New York stage director, who did the powerful Negro drama "Native Son."

"An American Romance," M-G-M's Technicolor romantic saga of this country's industrial development, starring Brian Donlevy and Ann Richards, will have its world premiere simultaneously in 132 cities.

The first B. G. DeSylva production for Paramount will be a comedy starring Bob Hope, according to an announcement by DeSylva. The producer is seeking a story for Hope, and also is looking for a musical to star Bing Crosby for the second independent unit production.

Wally Brown and Alan Carney will start a coast-to-coast personal appearance tour on Nov. 11 following completion of their co-starring roles in RKO Radio's "Zombies on Broadway." Although both were vaudeville headliners, this will be their first tour in double harness.

Evelyn Keyes has been given the important role of the Genie-of-the-Lamp in "A Thousand and One Nights," Columbia's Technicolor musical extravaganza of Old Baghdad, in which Cornel Wilde plays the male romantic lead.

WHEN OUT OF TOWN REGISTER FROM BROOKLYN

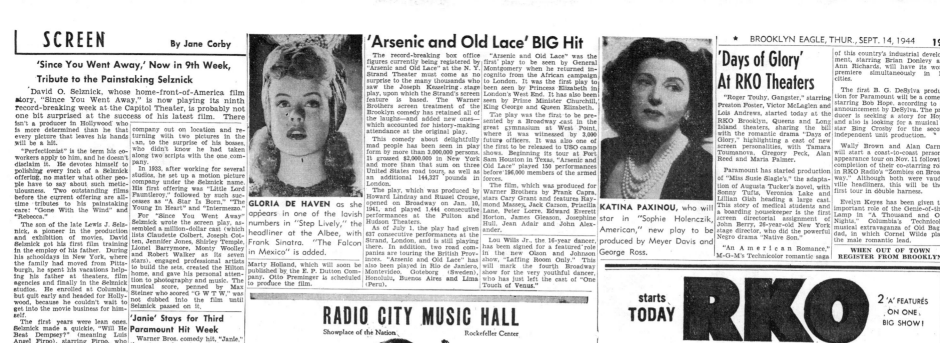

WHEN OUT OF TOWN REGISTER FROM BROOKLYN

Hurricane Kills 16 in Borough, Long Island

DAMAGE IS SET AT 2 MILLION

Continued from Page 1

mast pierced the pavilion roof. At least 20 sailboats were sunk—three showing upturned bottoms and 17 showing only masts above the surface of the water. Four small motor cruisers were beached.

Tilley's Pavilion, a private bathing establishment, was completely washed away, and the sea wall was badly damaged in several places. A grove of 100 old sycamore trees stood at an angle—all the trees being at a 45-degree slant.

Trains Halted

Long Island Railroad electric trains east of Jamaica were halted and steam trains ran hours late. Railroad officials said that service was back "almost to normal" at 7 a.m.

The storm battered some 750 miles of the Atlantic coast with winds of up to 80 miles and hour and torrential rains.

All day yesterday the Weather Bureau had sent out urgent storm warnings, and resulting precautions taken were given credit today for the relatively light loss of life and property damage.

Despite warnings and precautions, many small boats were torn from their moorings, ocean front properties were damaged and orchard and other unharvested crops were ruined. Much of the total damage, both on Long Island and elsewhere, consisted of crop spoilage.

Most dramatic of the storm precautions taken consisted of evacuating residents living in the path of the storm.

100 Families Evacuated

The coast guard evacuated more than 100 families from low-lying Fire Island, off Bay Shore, south of central Long Island. Several hundred year-round residents, however, remained on the island, which was half inundated by a persistently rising tide at the height of the storm last night. No injuries or casualties were reported today, however.

At Lindenhurst, 25 families were evacuated from Herr Park, on the South Shore of Long Island. Most of them were taken by local police to the St. John's Lutheran Church annex. Also at Lindenhurst, members of a military unit were evacuated after tents and wooden living quarters in which they were encamped were destroyed by the storm.

The storm passed out to sea near South Weymouth, Mass., early today. It had battered half a dozen cities and many towns and villages, from Beaufort, N. C., to Boston, on its way.

150 Are Injured

Besides the dead the number of injured was tentatively set at 150.

The storm was the worst since the one which killed 682 persons, mostly in New England, in 1938.

A land and sea area of about 500 miles in diameter was covered by the moving hurricane, which was most violent at the center and faded out at the fringes.

In the city the lash of the storm interrupted subway, bus and other transportation.

Police closed Prospect Park because of the danger from falling trees and flying tree branches.

Hundreds of telephone calls came in to Brooklyn police headquarters reporting trees felled and live wires down.

Some 10 miles of Belt Parkway was for a time under water and police closed it down for the night.

The Fire Department responded to 35 false fire alarms—touched off by short circuits in fire alarm boxes caused by the sloshing rain.

Army and other planes at LaGuardia Field for which hangar space could not be found were flown, as the storm approached nearer New York yesterday, to safer fields inland.

Even radio broadcasting was interrupted. Radio Station WEAF of the National Broadcasting Company was off the air from 7:49 to 8:12 p.m. because of transmission station failure. Station WHN was also forced off. The CBS (Columbia Broadcasting System) short-wave listening post was still not operating today.

Newport Beach Wrecked

Railway service between New York and Boston was restored today after a storm-caused interruption of 11 hours.

At Newport, R. I., excusive Bailey's Beach, which was wrecked by the 1938 hurricane and then rebuilt, was wrecked again last night. Tides flooded the bar where Newport's society used to foregather, destroyed eight tennis courts and scattered 62 cabanas along the beach sand.

The New York Telephone Company marshaled all available equipment and linemen to repair telephone lines. Utility companies of the Albany area sent their repair crews to the New York City-Long Island area for repair work here.

Westhampton Beach, which was the worst hit Long Island community in the 1938 hurricane, escaped with property damage of not more than $25,000 and no injuries.

Bay Ridge residents complained that their section of Brooklyn seemed to have taken the worst beating in the borough. Pavements were ripped up, and four out of five streets were blocked by fallen trees. It was the worst storm Bay Ridge has known within the memory of its oldest inhabitant.

Fire Commissioner Walsh today assigned every fireman with an elementary knowledge of electricity to the work of putting grounded fire alarm boxes back into working order. The entire fire alarm system in the city, with the exception only of Manhattan, was grounded by storm water last night and this morning 2,500 boxes were still out of order as against 1,500 that had been put back into service.

The Long Island Railroad reported that its chief difficulties, causing delays, were: Inundated tracks, trees blown across the tracks, power wires down.

War Plants Closed

Many war plants on Long Island, as well as in Connecticut, Massachusetts and Rhode Island, dispensed with night work last night, chiefly because of transportation difficulties facing employes.

At the Jamaica station of the Long Island yesterday afternoon a loudspeaker announcement was made again and again:

"Workers of Republic Aviation Corporation. The plant will be closed tonight. Report tomorrow as usual."

FIRE ISLAND REFUGEES—Residents of Fire Island, advised to evacuate to mainland before the hurricane hit, were transported to Bay Shore in ferries, private boats and coast guard vessels. They are shown boarding the Point o' Woods ferry.

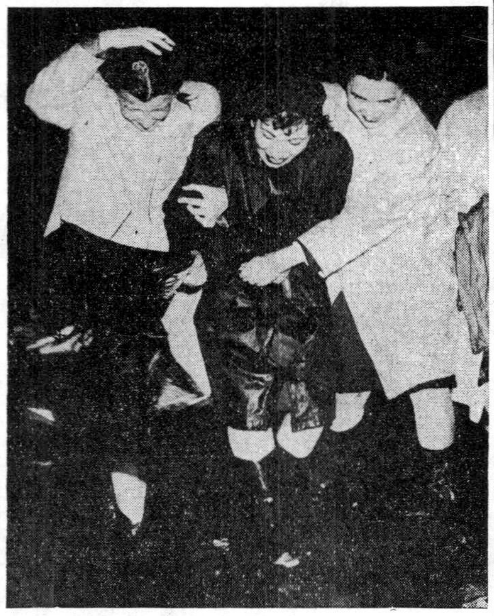

RAIN AND WIND IN THEIR HAIR—Three brave girls lean into teeth of torrential rain and gale as borough felt first whip of northward-rushing hurricane.

Rain-Soaked Cameraman's 'Pants Relief' Falls Short

Dan Fox, Brooklyn Eagle photographer, got his trousers so soaked, covering the storm in Canarsie, that he had to have dry replacements to carry on. He appealed to Brooklyn Red Cross workers for "pants relief." No man on the job had a spare pair.

But the Red Cross came to Fox's rescue—with women's slacks! The Eagle photographer put 'em on, but they were too tight. Undaunted, he kept working—with his shirt tail hanging out.

Work Around the Clock To Restore Electricity

With its augmented repair crews working on a continuous day and night basis, the Brooklyn Edison Company announced today that it will be tomorrow night or Sunday morning before electric service will be restored in the homes and business establishments of all its customers throughout Brooklyn and Queens.

"Literally thousands are right now without current and have been so since the storm struck here," said a company spokesman. "Felled trees which broke our lines also broke telephone wires, so that we don't know just how many places are out of service. Apace with the restoration of telephone service we are receiving a continuous stream of communications about no current for lights, radios, clocks and refrigerators."

List of Storm Dead

The death toll in the Brooklyn-Long Island area from the hurricane included:

LAUZON, JOSEPH, 55, of 1959 Troy Ave., electrocuted when he stepped off Bergen St. trolley and touched a live wire between Nostrand and Rogers Aves.

KOPPUS, ANTON, 54, of 1542 Gates Ave., electrocuted when he fell from Forest Ave. station of the B. M. T. and came in contact with the third rail.

BULLARO, CARL J., 30, of 7904 16th Ave., electrocuted outside his home.

BILOTTI, ALFRED, 23, of 107 60th St., electrocuted when he touched a live wire crossing 60th St.

RIZZO, CARMINE, 38, of Matawan, N. J., electrocuted trying to save Bilotti.

GRAFFIGINO, JACK, 60, of 104-62 107th St., Richmond Hill, electrocuted outside his home.

DORGAN, ALEXANDER, 58, of 178-11 91st Ave., Jamaica, electrocuted near his home.

CROUCHLEY, GEORGE, 52, of Fulton St., Westbury, electrocuted near his home.

McLAUGHLIN, BERNARD FRANCIS, 54, of 115-29 198th St., St. Albans, collapsed on the street near his home.

JACOBI, JOHN, 62, of 41-14 41st St., Thomson Hill, Queens, from fall down stairs.

MOEHRINGER, CHARLES, 77, of 77-80 88th Ave., Woodhaven, collapsed in street near his home.

VALENTINE, GEORGE, of West Shore Road, Roslyn, crushed between the side of a boat and a dock at Port Washington.

TORSIELLO, LOUIS, 55, of 169-21 104th Ave., Jamaica, electrocution or exhaustion at 170th St. south of the Jamaica Long Island Railroad station.

RICHARD ADDIS, 60, of Stony Brook, died of illuminating gas poisoning when gas pipe supplying his home was broken by falling tree.

SYLVESTER PURCELL, owner of a Brooklyn carpet cleaning establishment, asphyxiated in his home, 183 Maple Ave., Sea Cliff, by gas released through pipe-breakage caused by storm-uprooted tree.

A shipyard worker known only as "Williams," drowned at Port Washington.

Old Fire Bell Calls Aid to Pair Felled By Gas in Storm

Sea Cliff, Sept. 15. (U.P.)—An old fire bell, out of use for many years, summoned volunteer firemen today to the aid of a Sea Cliff couple overcome in their home by gas from a storm-broken pipe.

Authorities, notified by a neighbor that Mr. and Mrs. Sylvester Purcell were unconscious in their home at 183 Maple Ave., found the town's fire alarm system had been knocked out by the hurricane and summoned the emergency squad with the antiquated fire house bell. Purcell was pronounced dead after a pulmotor failed to revive him. His wife was said to have a chance of recovery.

The roots of two large trees, torn up by hurricane winds last night, were believed to have broken the gas pipe leading into the Purcell home. The couple apparently was overcome in their sleep.

Richard Addis, 60, of Stony Brook, died of illuminating gas poisoning when a gas pipe supplying his home was broken by a falling tree.

BORO SOLDIER AMUSED BY GAUDY UNIFORMS OF COPS IN INDIA

Policemen who wear bright blue uniforms with brilliant yellow trim and carry umbrellas as well as shiny yellow night sticks were described to Lt. William P. Young, Bergen St. Precinct, in a letter received from his nephew, Sgt. Charles Peterson, attached to a meteorological unit in Bombay, India.

Sergeant Peterson, 22, lived with his parents, Mr. and Mrs. Edmund Peterson, at 352 St. John's Place before he entered the army about two years ago. He writes his uncle that the Bombay cops walked their beats barefoot until they became sergeants, when they rate shoes.

The sergeant was also impressed with the highly polished postcard size brass buckles the Indian police force wore, and was intrigued with their trick of hooking their umbrellas under their coat collars when not in use. He passed this information on to his police lieutenant uncle for what it may be worth to the local force.

Boy Burned by Live Wire Blown Down in Storm

Raymond Rinfret, 10, of 972 74th St., today came in contact with a high voltage wire that had been blown down near his home by the storm. Knocked unconscious and severely burned on one hand, he was taken to Harbor Hospital.

WHEN OUT OF TOWN REGISTER FROM BROOKLYN

STORM-HIT LIRR GETTING BACK TO NORMAL SERVICE

With hundreds of crewmen of the Long Island Railroad working desperately to remove trees from the right of way, officials of the road announced that they are getting occasional trains through to the Rockaways and service has been restored to Long Beach, after being cut off last night.

Power, signal and wire trouble are still causing delays on some lines.

High waters in Jamaica Bay on the route to the Rockaways and over the Reynolds Channel Long Beach trestle accounted for the tieups. On other lines of the L. I. R. R., trains ran throughout the night but were hampered by trees that had fallen across tracks. The approaches to the Mill Creek bridge between Southold and Greenport were reported washed out.

Service on the Babylon line on the South Shore was interrupted after 9 p.m. when fallen trees on the power line between Babylon and Wantagh had to be removed to restore switch and signal operations. Three trains were sent out from Babylon between 10:58 and 5:56 a.m. Terrific winds caused intermittent delays.

Three regularly scheduled early-morning Long Island Railroad trains running between Riverhead and New York City were canceled. These trains are used mostly by war workers traveling to and from war plants in Farmingdale and East Farmingdale.

At Napeague, between Amagansett and Montauk, about two miles of track on the Montauk division were washed out by the high tide in Gardiner's Bay.

At Wainscott, a freight car on a siding blew over during the storm, on to the main line tracks of the Montauk division. At East Hampton, a tree fell across the tracks, completely holding up traffic from Bridgehampton to Montauk.

Brooklyn subways were not greatly affected during the storm, with the I. R. T. reporting normal service and the B. M. T. service suffering only slightly.

A ground insulator on the third rail over the Manhattan Bridge tied up West End, Sea Beach and B. M. T. bridge travel early today, and trains were rerouted through the Montague St. tunnel.

Traffic was suspended for some time on the 14th St. line between Atlantic Ave. and Canarsie.

Mead Says Dewey Draws War Into Campaign Fight

Washington, Sept. 15 (U.P.)—Senator James M. Mead, (D., N. Y.,) charged last night that Governor Dewey, in asking for more supplies for Gen. Douglas MacArthur, was drawing the conduct of the war into the Presidential campaign.

Mead said that Dewey previously had expressed confidence in the leadership of Army Chief of Staff Gen. George C. Marshall and Admiral Ernest J. King, conmmander-in-chief of the fleet.

Publisher Seek Divorce

Reno, Nev., Sept 15. (U.P.)—Pierrevont Isham Prentice, publisher of Time Magazine. has filed a divorce suit against his wife, Mildred Kathrpn Selcher Prentice, of New York, charging extreme mental cruelty.

Candidacy of Pinto Indorsed by Fawcett

Former Supreme Court Justice Lewis L. Fawcett today indorsed County Judge Nicholas H. Pinto, Republican and American Labor party nominee, to succeed himself. The retired jurist has agreed to serve as honorary chairman of the nonpartisan committee seeking the election of Judge Pinto.

Hold Former Queens Man In Fatal Stabbing

Christopher Pannone, 23, formerly of Queens, was held without bail in Felony Court on the charge of having fatally stabbed George Fatum, 49, of 297 Stagg St. Detective Salvatore Sisino said the stabbing followed a quarrel in front of 775 Grand St. on Sept. 19, 1943.

Missing Boro Flier Prisoner of Nazis

When the family of Sgt. Angelo Gambino of 277 Liberty Ave. were notified on Feb. 10 last that he was missing in action, they refused to give up hope. Each day they visited their parish church and prayed that the news was wrong.

Today these prayers were answered, for there came a telegram from the Red Cross announcing that the sergeant is a prisoner of war in Germany, and well.

It was on his 13th mission over Gefmany that he was captured.

Sergeant Gambino lived with his grandmother, Mrs. Angelino Lore at the above address. His father, Joseph, lives up-State. The Brooklyn fighter enlisted nearly two years ago and wears the Air Medal.

He has two brothers, Sgt. Sidney Gambino, and Sgt. Benjamin Gambino, both in this country, and a sister, Rose.

Red Cross District Office Handles Third of Cases

Opened only a year ago, the home service district office of the Brooklyn Red Cross now handles more than a third of the 30,000 active cases carried by the Red Cross home service department each month, it was announced today. The intake section of the Graham Ave. office is visited by between 1,000 and 2,000 persons every month.

Besides a large number of inquiries about service men reported wounded or missing or who have not written home for a long time, the unit gets many requests for help in planning domestic and marital readjustments, especially in cases where the families of service men are in financial difficulties until allotment checks begin to come in.

Party to Benefit Vets

Members of Our Lady of Loretta Council, K. of C., who are in the armed forces, will receive the proceeds of a card party to be held at the clubhouse, 117 1st Place, on Saturday, Sept. 30. Sal De Nave heads the committee of arrangements.

BUILT FIRST AIRFIELD—These four Brooklyn aviation engineers who landed in Southern France with the D-Day forces helped build the first Allied airfield on the beachhead. They are (left to right) Corp. Michael F. Alessi of 1353 61st St., Pfc. Desmond J. William Jr. of 151 W. 91st St., Sgt. Sam Baumel of 18 E. 21st St. and Pvt. Jack Steiner of 1576 Lincoln Place.

Dr. Shafer Greets Packer Students

Packer Collegiate Institute opened its school year today in the newly redecorated chapel at 170 Joralemon St. Students of the elementary and academic schools and the junior college were greeted by Dr. Paul D. Shafer, president of Packer. Graduates of last June were special guests.

"May I suggest," Dr. Shafer said, "that learning to think about personal and social, national and international problems, acting wisely in solving such problems as are within your provinces, using with intelligence the freedoms to speak and worship and work and choose which are among our goals in this war, and establishing in our minds and hearts high ideals and their attendant attitudes, are tasks of a student who would accept her responsibilities as she stands on the threshold of a school or college year in a world which reflects a tragic mixture of present war and hovering peace." He spoke also of the fact that Packer will celebrate its 100th anniversary this year.

Craft Textile Exhibit Will Open Next Monday

An exhibition of craft textiles, some of them dating back to before Christ and none of them later than the 18th century, will open at American House, 485 Madison Ave., Manhattan, next Monday.

The exhibition is sponsored by the American Craftsmen's Education Council. Mrs. Michelle Murphy of the Brooklyn Museum helped arrange it and some of the rare specimens from the museum will be shown.

State Drive Opened For Practical Nurses

A campaign to meet the needs of New York State for 5,000 additional practical nurses was announced yesterday at the first Fall meeting of the committee for the recruitment and education of practical nurses at its headquarters, 250 W. 57th St., Manhattan.

To stimulate registration in the 12 accredited nursing schools throughout the State, the committee has established a scholarship fund for tuition and maintenance of students on the basis of need.

To qualify for grants practical nurse applicants must be between 18 and 50, with an elementary school education or its equivalent, and be United States citizens or in possession of first papers. Mrs. Hazel Crandall, director of nurses at the Beth-El Hospital, Brooklyn, is a member of the committee.

Hibernians to Hold Service Men's Social

The third annual service men's social and dance benefiting members of the division who have gone to war will be held Saturday night under the auspices of Division 35 of the Ancient Order of Hibernians in the Midwood Grill, 1145 Flatbush Ave. Thomas A. Brennan and Denis P. O'Leary are chairman and vice chairman, respectively. P. J. Kelly is the division's president.

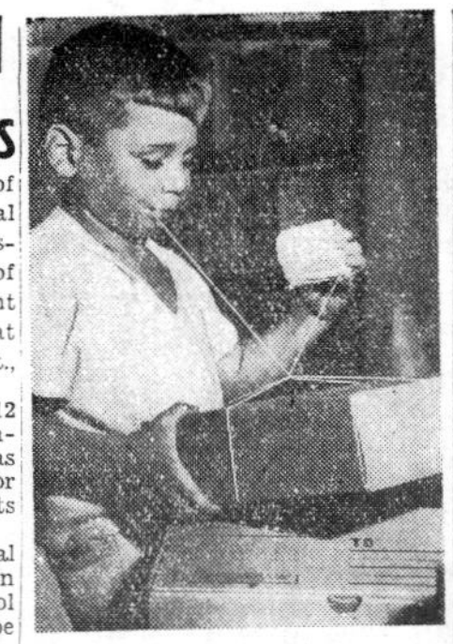

TO JOE, OVERSEAS — Six-year-old Harvey Bertan, like the rest of the 250 youngsters at Pride of Judea Children's Home of Brooklyn, is busy these evenings wrapping gift packages for former members of the institution fighting on foreign battlefronts.

Five Villages to Get National USO Awards

Cedarhurst, Sept. 20—On Saturday, Sept. 30, at the Lawrence High School, the National U. S. O. will award citations to the villages of Cedarhurst, Hewlett, Woodmere, Lawrence and Inwood, for the support given the organization by these communities. This is the first group of villages to be honored in this manner.

Chester Barnard, national president of the U. S. O., will make the presentation.

War Prisoners Aid is helping over 7,000,000 men behind barbed wire. It is one of the 31 member agencies of the New York War Fund. Give now!

7 ★★★★★★★ SPORTS
Wall Street Financial News

BROOKLYN EAGLE

WEATHER—Intermittent rain, cold tonight; cloudy, cold tomorrow.

104th Year. No. 320. DAILY & SUNDAY • (Copyright 1944 The Brooklyn Eagle, Inc.) • BROOKLYN, N. Y., TUESDAY, NOVEMBER 21, 1944 • Entered at the Brooklyn Post-office as 2d Class Mail Matter • 3 CENTS IN NEW YORK CITY ELSEWHERE 4 CENTS

GERMANS IN RETREAT ON 125-MILE FRONT

CIVIC CENTER PLAN FACES DRASTIC CUT

Report by Mayor's Unit Seen Asking Slash In Modernizing Cost

By JOSEPH H. SCHMALACKER

Definite indications arose in City Hall and civic circles today that Controller Joseph D. McGoldrick's widely approved plan to modernize 45 acres of run-down property, near the heart of the proposed Brooklyn Civic Center, is threatened with virtual emasculation when Mayor LaGuardia's City Planning Commission makes its report on the proposal.

Civic forces backing the Controller's plan were upset when word reached them the City Planning Commission, while not rejecting the proposal outright, was planning a compromise which, in effect, would practically reduce it to a skeleton of the original.

If the so-called compromise goes through, it was said, only about $1,400,000 of the $20,000,000 urged for the rehabilitation proposal by Controller McGoldrick and supported by bankers, real estate representatives and civic leaders would be allowed, although the $4,000,000 now recommended for the Brooklyn Civic Center in the pending capital budget would be increased.

$8,000,000 Top Seen

The word reaching the civic forces was that the City Planning Commission's report, as now prepared, would not favor allowing more than $8,000,000 for the combined Civic Center development and the property rehabilitation proposal.

About $2,900,000 of the total, it was stated, would be eaten up by costs for the proposed widening of Adams St. under the broad outlines of the Civic Center plan.

Controller McGoldrick's proposal was referred to the City Planning Commission last week for a report by a majority vote of the Board of

Continued on Page 7

FRENCH BLUEBEARD SAYS HIS 63 VICTIMS WERE COLLABORATORS

Paris, Nov. 21 (U.P.)—The fantastic Dr. Marcel Petiot, the Parisian "bluebeard" charged with mass murder on a scale unequalled in French criminal history, awaited a test of his sanity today after blandly admitting at a preliminary court hearing that he had killed at least 63 persons, some with a "secret weapon" of his own invention.

Petiot, who is accused of murdering and dismembering scores of men and women in an abandoned house at 21 Rue Lesueur during the German occupation of Paris last Summer, appeared before an examining magistrate for the first time since his arrest several weeks ago.

The heavily-bearded doctor assured the magistrate solemnly that all of his 63 admitted victims were collaborators. Thirty of them, he said, were Germans.

National Legion Head Spurs War Bond Drive

NOW HE'S A LIEUTENANT—Daniel Harris, 98, Brooklyn's sole survivor of the Civil War, in which he was a private, becomes a lieutenant—in the war bond drive Blue Star Brigade. By selling ten bonds he won the right to wear the lieutenant's pin, which is here awarded by Pvt. Alice Sheridan, 3, a neighbor, who sold a bond to her aunt.

'Don't Let Fighting Men Down on Home Front,' Scheiberling's Plea

The 6th War Loan drive swung into its second day today pushed by the challenge that there are still tremendous expenses ahead to finish the war and ease the return to peace.

For even when the war is won there will still be the overwhelming cost of caring for the nation's fighting men until they can be returned to their homes.

As Edward N. Scheiberling, national commander of the American Legion, said in a special war bond statement today, "Even if victory were to come tomorrow we would have to pay, feed, clothe and hospitalize our men for some time to come because demobilization cannot be instantaneous."

Warns Against Home Front Letdown

Scheiberling pointed out that service men had sidetracked their

Continued on Page 7

Sweden Ends Shipment Of Iron to Norway

Stockholm, Nov. 21 (U.P.)—The newspaper Dagens Nyheter reported today that Sweden had closed the last loophole for export of iron ore to Germany by discontinuing shipments from Kiruna to Narvik, Norway. The last iron ore shipment from Sweden reached Narvik Oct. 20, the newspaper said.

Nelson Appointed Personal Adviser To the President

Washington, Nov. 21 (U.P.)—President Roosevelt has named Donald M. Nelson as his personal representative and the former War Production Board chief will serve as adviser to the President in both domestic and foreign problems, the White House revealed today.

When Nelson is here he will sit in Cabinet meetings, as do heads of various special war agencies.

In a letter dated Nov. 2, the President asked Nelson to "assist and advise me in dealing with some of the most important problems now facing the American people and to undertake special missions..." The appointment was made effective Sept. 20.

First of the special missions was Nelson's second trip to Chungking to organize a "WPB" in China to aid in rejuvenation of the Chinese war effort. He is expected to return in mid-December and move into a White House office located in the State Department building.

Before leaving on his second trip to Chungking Nelson received a letter from the President stating that he was acting officially as Mr. Roosevelt's personal representative. The letter was necessary, apparently, because Nelson otherwise would have been operating without official status. On his first trip to China,, in September, he technically was still WPB chairman, a post he subsequently relinquished.

Nelson will leave in Chungking as his deputy Howard Coonley, former president of the National Association of Manufacturers, and a considerable staff of experts.

B-29s Rip Kyushu Isle, Jap Industrial Center

By FRED SCHERFF

Washington, Nov. 21 (U.P.)—A big task force of B-29 Superfortresses, perhaps 80 strong, bombed the Japanese home island of Kyushu for the second time this month today, and Tokyo reported the targets were the important industrial centers of Nagasaki and Omura.

Tokyo said Japanese fighters intercepted the four-engined bombers and engaged them above the clouds in "fierce air duels." Early claims that eight Superfortresses had been shot down and a ninth damaged subsequently were enlarged to 14 downed, 11 probably downed and seven others set afire. Four Japanese planes were missing, Tokyo said.

Industrial Targets Blasted

Japanese fighters previously had been reluctant to tangle with the heavily-armed Superfortresses and the enemy claims appeared to have been greatly exaggerated for the benefit of the Japanese home front, already jittery over the mounting American air offensive in the Pacific.

The China-based raid by Maj. Gen. Curtis Le May's 20th Bomber Command was disclosed by the War Department in a brief announcement which identified the objectives only as "industrial targets" on Kyushu.

Strike at Manila

While Superfortresses concentrated on the enemy homeland, other American bombers and carrier-based planes spread further ruin through Japan's shrinking, but still far-flung, Pacific empire.

Planes from a carrier task force of the Pacific fleet struck again at Manila, occupied capital of the Philippines, Sunday (Saturday, Pearl Harbor time), setting fire to two large cargo ships and a large tanker and destroying 118 enemy planes.

More than 100 Liberators from Gen. Douglas MacArthur's Southwest Pacific Command blasted oil installations and shipping Sunday at Tarakan, Borneo, with 121 tons of explosives. Huge fires were started, sending smoke towering 15,000 feet. Sixteen small vessels, including barges, were set afire in the harbor.

PETRILLO DEMANDS MARINE BANDSMEN QUIT TEACHING MUSIC

Washington, Nov. 21 (U.P.)—James C. Petrillo, president of the American Federation of Musicians (A. F. L.), has sent to the marine corps a letter demanding that members of the famous Marine Band cease giving music lessons in their off-duty hours, it was learned today.

Marine corps headquarters acknowledged receipt of the letter but declined comment pending a study by the legal department.

Petrillo, who last week concluded his long fight with two leading recording companies with an estimated $4,000,000 victory, was said to have dispatched the letter after a Washington musician and union member complained that Marine Band members were "gobbling up" his pupils.

'Got to Fight Like Hell,' Says Ike, Seeing Final Battle West of Rhine

By JAMES McGLINCY

Paris, Nov. 21 (U.P.)—Gen. Dwight D. Eisenhower said today the only sensible course open to the German Army is to fight to the bitter end west of the Rhine.

Eisenhower suggested inferentially that he expected the final battle of the European war to be fought west of the Rhine, where six Allied armies were waging the Allied grand offensive and hammering the Nazis back along a 400-mile front.

But the battle will not be easy, the supreme commander warned at a press conference. To win the victory and peace, he said, "we've got to fight like hell for it. Now let's do it."

Calls for Greater Effort

He called on his armies and the home fronts behind them for even greater effort, and warned that unless every element of the United Nations "keep on the job everlastingly and with mounting intensity we are only postponing the day of victory."

"We are keeping the pressure at maximum strength all along the front," Eisenhower said. "The German has to be hit with everything we've got—and finally the breaking point will come.

"The pressure must go up, both at home and on the front, and continue to increase so that the highest point is on the day Germany surrenders."

He said he wanted more supplies than he is getting, and "I think the soldier wants more than he is getting, both now and in the future."

Ike Is Optimistic

Eisenhower received 200 correspondents at supreme headquarters. He looked fresh and fit, and

Continued on Page 2

SHELL OUTPUT HALTED

Portsmouth, Ohio, Nov. 21 (U.P.)—Production of bomb and shell cases at the Portsmouth works of the Wheeling Steel Corporation was halted today by a sympathy strike of approximately 4,500 production workers in protest against the dismissal of a plant guard.

Officials of the United Steel Workers Union (C. I. O.) said the strike was not authorized and urged the men to return to their jobs.

The guard reportedly was discharged for "insubordination."

SNOW FLURRIES, RAIN TO GO ON ALL DAY—AIR TRAFFIC STOPPED

This morning's snow flurries will continue through the day but will become a mixture of snow and rain toward late afternoon, the Weather Bureau predicted. It will be cold, too, with temperatures remaining in the low 40s and dropping to the freezing level tonight.

Weather Bureau instruments recorded a 2.5-inch rainfall from 8 a.m. yesterday to noon today. Bad weather was responsible for the cancellation of 38 flights at LaGuardia Field today.

Roosevelt, Churchill Named to Academy

Paris, Nov. 21 (U.P.)—The Academy of Moral and Political Science has named President Roosevelt and Prime Minister Churchill as foreign associate members, filling the vacancies caused by the deaths of Nicolas Politis, former Greek minister to France, and Raoul Dandurand, Canadian politician.

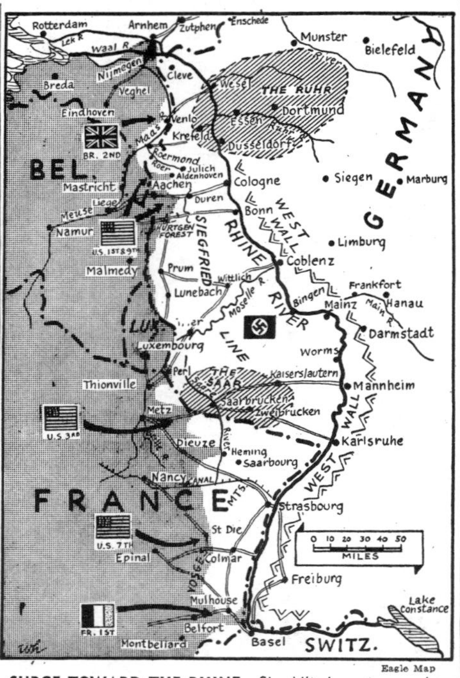

Eagle Map

SURGE TOWARD THE RHINE—Six Allied armies are beginning to roll up the Germans this side of the Rhine: the British 2d at Venlo on the Maas River; the U. S. 1st and 9th, east of Aachen; the U. S. 3d, which has driven three miles into the Saar east of conquered Metz; the U. S. 7th driving through the Vosges Mountains toward Saarebourg, and the French 1st Army, which has reached the Rhine after driving through the Belfort Gap, historic invasion road into Germany from the southwest.

By J. EDWARD MURRAY

Paris, Nov. 21 (U.P.)—French mobile forces rolling up the south end of a 125-mile front, along which the Germans appeared in full flight from eastern France, speared into the Mulhouse area today and a Swiss dispatch said they had captured Colmar, 23 miles farther north.

The German defenses of the upper Rhine valley west of the river fell apart and Gen. Jean de Lattre de Tassigny's forces were streaming northward at a lightning clip in the wake of the routed enemy.

Supreme headquarters reported advanced patrols of fast moving French 1st Army had reached the region of Mulhouse, fortress city 20 miles northwest of Basel, and the Berlin radio said French tanks already had reached the city itself.

The entire front angling across northeastern France swayed back under the driving impact of the French 1st, American 7th and American 3d armies. Lt Gen. George S. Patton's troops drove into the reversed forts of the Maginot Line at two points.

Dispatches from the Aachen front said indications increased that the Germans were pulling their general Rhineland defense line back to the east. U. S. 1st Army troops storming Eschweiler found resistance lighter than expected and the German garrison appeared to be pulling out.

The dispatches said it was possible that a defense line anchored on the stronghold of Duren, 20 miles southwest of Cologne, would give the Germans the advantage of a straightened front.

Clearing weather over the Aachen front gave the Allies stronger air support and fighter bombers swarmed in to make several strikes directly behind the fighting line.

The German retreat at the southern end of the front approached a rout as the French 1st Army seized a 10-mile stretch of the Rhine just north of the Swiss border and swung north behind the Vosges Mountains in a bold bid to encircle enemy forces withdrawing through the Vosges passes.

Break Into Sarrebourg

The Nazi DNB agency conceded the American 7th Army had broken into the industrial center of Sarrebourg, 50 miles southeast of Metz and an equal distance from the eastern tip of France, and was engaging the garrison in bloody street-to-street and house-to-house fighting.

Only in Germany itself was the enemy fighting for every yard, and even there he was driven steadily back. One American column penetrated to within a mile of the Saar River in the Saar basin and came under heavy fire from the main guns of the Siegfried Line, while others battled across the Rhineland to within 25½ miles of Cologne and 29 miles of Dusseldorf.

See 'Decisive Blow'

The German DNB agency, in a dispatch fraught with warning of impending doom, said the great battle array of six Allied armies confirmed that Gen. Dwight D. Eisenhower was attempting to deal the Reich a "last decisive blow."

"No doubt it will be difficult for the German defense to withstand this onslaught," Martin Hallensleben, DNB's military expert, conceded. "The Germans, however, possess the best preliminary conditions to wear down the enemy's offensive strength in a number of battles of attrition."

Latest successes, army by army,

Continued on Page 2

Nazi Oil Plants Blasted As 'Forts' Lash 3 Cities

London, Nov. 21 (U.P.)—An armada of more than 2,350 planes, more than half of them Flying Fortresses and Liberators, lashed at German synthetic oil plants at Hamburg, Merseburg and Harburg today.

First returning pilots reported heavy air battles over the three targets, with as many as 200 German planes, most of them FW-190s, attacking at one point over Merseburg. Early information indicated that at least 53 enemy planes were shot down in the three raids.

One group led jointly by Lt. Col. John Meyer of Forest Hills, L. I., and Maj. George Preddy of Greensboro, N. C., claimed 21 kills, of which Meyer got three and Preddy one.

The heavy blow at the fuel sources for the German war machine was delivered by more than 1,250 Liberators and Flying Fortresses of the 8th Air Force, covered by the greatest fighter protection force ever put into the air.

Record Fighting Cover

Approximately 1,100 8th and 9th Air Force Mustangs, Thunderbolts and Lightnings accompanied the bombers, far exceeding the previous record fighter cover of 950 planes.

The heavies concentrated on the Leuna plant at Merseburg, where almost three weeks ago the war's greatest air battle was fought against 500 enemy planes, of which 183 were shot down.

Clouds covered the targets at the three German cities, and the bombers dropped their heavy loads of explosives by instrument. Other scattered targets in western Germany also were hit.

The daylight assaults followed other attacks on Germany during the night by R. A. F. planes. More than 100 Mosquito bombers, carrying two-ton blockbusters, raided Hanover while a force of four-engined Lancasters hit Coblenz. Five planes were lost in the night raids.

Meantime, reconnaissance reports showed the bombing of fuel plants was paying dividends. It was announced the large plant at Bottrop, west of Gelsenkirchen, was put out of production and three others in the northern Ruhr damaged badly.

The Bottrop plant had a maximum annual yield of 100,000 tons of oil, enough to maintain four armored divisions in the field. Every major building was wrecked by instrument bombing.

King Receives Churchill

London, Nov. 21 (U.P.)—King George received Prime Minister Churchill in audience today. Churchill remained for luncheon.

PIMLICO RESULTS

1—Good Nite 11.20-6.50-4.40, Consignment 9.00-5.50, Say Miss 3.30. (12:32)
2—aSt'my Bill 13.60-5.20-3.20, Gal't Son 4.60-2.70, Morgil's Lad 2.70. (1:02)
aWoodward entry

DAILY DOUBLE PAID $74.10

3—Saxonian 6.20-4.00-3.30, Busy Man 7.60-6.40, Brother Dear 4.90. (1.32)
4—Houlgate 7.50-4.50-3.90, z-Pheecia 10.20-6.50, Cy Bart 4.90. (Off 2:01½)
z-Pheecia finished first but disqualified and placed second.
5—Surrogate 14.30-7.20-4.20, Heyorta 6.00-4.50, Art Brown 5.60. (2:36½)

84 From Area On Casualty Lists

The War Department today listed 77 Brooklyn, Queens and Long Island men wounded in action in the European area. The Navy Department listed five local men wounded and two missing. Lists of local casualties are on Page 5.

Call the Brooklyn Chapter American Red Cross and arrange to donate a pint of blood NOW, TRiangle 5-8040.

Chevalier Cleared Of Collaboration Charge

By United Press

Maurice Chevalier, French entertainer, has been cleared of charges of collaborating with the Germans during their occupation of France, the London radio said today.

"A statement issued in Paris says that Chevalier gave only one entertainment at a German prison camp," the broadcast said. "He was not paid and in exchange for his performans 10 prisoners were released."

Chevalier was among music hall entertainers whose activities during the occupation were investigated by a French committee.

Dust Blows 1,200 Miles To Blanket Auckland

Auckland, N. Z., Nov. 21 (U.P.)—The city of Auckland was blanketed today by a thick haze of reddish dust blown across the Tasman Sea from the dust bowl area of southeastern Australia, more than 1,200 miles away.

Motorists found dust settling heavily on their cars and many persons complained of sneezing and sore eyes caused by the phenomenon.

Pilots flying over the Tasman Sea reported that the dust limited visibility.

Yugo Chief in Moscow

London, Nov. 21 (U.P.)—Dr. Ivan Subasitch, premier of Yugoslavia, arrived in Moscow at the head of an official delegation for conferences with Russian leaders.

WHERE TO FIND IT

	Page		Page
Bridge	17	Our Fighters	4
Comics	17	Patterns	10
Crossword	14	Radio	17
Dr. Brady	6	Real Estate	14
Editorial	6	Society	9
Financial	18	Sports	11, 12
Helen Worth	10	Take My Word	6
Horoscope	10	Theaters	13, 14
Mary Haworth	9	These Women	17
Movies	13, 14	Tommy Holmes	11
Music	14	Uncle Ray	14
Novel	14	Want Ads	14-16
Obituaries	7	Women	9

WILBUR WACKEY — Evans Krehbiel

MARY WORTH'S FAMILY — By Dale Allen

DOTTY DRIPPLE

DR. BOBBS — Harry Tuthill

JANE ARDEN — By Monte Barrett and Russell Ross

INVISIBLE SCARLET O'NEIL — By Russell Stamm

BO — By Frank Beck

CHIEF WAHOO — By Saunders and Woggon

LEM AND OINIE — By Paul Fogarty

RADIO PROGRAMS

WMCA, 570. WEAF, 660. WOR, 710. WJZ, 770. WNYC, 830. WABC, 880. WAAT, 970. WINS, 1000. WHN, 1050. WNEW, 1130. WLIB, 1190. WFAS, 1240. WOV, 1280. WEVD, WBBR, 1330. WBNX, 1380. WBYN, 1430. WHOM, 1480. WQXR, 1560. WWRL 1600.

TODAY'S BEST BETS

2:05—Symphonic Matinee, WNYC.
3:30—Talk by Secretary of Agriculture Claude Wickard, WEAF.
6:15—New York City Symphony Orchestra, Leopold Stokowski, Conductor, WEAF.
7:00—Music Shop, Guest, WEAF; Masterwork Hour, WNYC.
7:30—Everything for the Boys, Dick Haymes, Jimmy Durante, Guest, WEAF.
8:00—Ginny Simms Show, WEAF.
8:30—Theater of Romance, Shirley Booth, Guest, WABC; "Roy Rogers Show," WOR; Alan Young Show, Diana Courtney, WJZ.
9:00—Gracie Fields Show, Fred Brady, WJZ; George Burns and Gracie Allen Program, Guest, WABC.
9:30—Spotlight Bands, Xavier Cugat Orchestra, WJZ; This Is My Best, Orson Welles, Guest, WABC; American Forum of the Air, WOR; Fibber McGee and Molly, WEAF.
10:00—Bob Hope Show, Skinnay Ennis Orchestra, Kay Kyser, Guest, WEAF.
10:15—Andy Russell Show, Anita Ellis, Mitchell Ayres Orchestra, WJZ.
10:30—Hildegarde Show, Billie Burke, Harry Savoy, Phil Brito, Guests, WEAF; Milton Berle Show, Elsa Maxwell, Guest, WJZ.

Where there is no listing for a station preceding program is on the air

2 P.M. TO 4 P.M.

2:00 WABC—Joyce Jordan.
WEAF—Guiding Light.
WJZ—Kiernan's Corner.
WOR—News, Foster.
WMCA—News; Love Songs
WHN—Dick Gilbert.
WNYC—News; Symphony.
WINS—News; Tune Factory.
2:15 WABC—Two On a Clue.
WEAF—Today's Children.
WJZ—Galan Drake.
WOR—Jane Cowl.
2:25 WHN—News.
2:30 WABC—Dr. Malone.
WEAF—Woman in White.
WOR—News, Egan.
WJZ—Ladies, Be Seated.
WHN—Dick Gilbert.
2:5 WABC—Perry Mason.
WEAF—Church Hymns.
WOR—Real Stories
3:00 WABC—Mary Marlin.
WEAF—Woman of America
WJZ—Morton Downey.
WOR—Martha Deane.
WMCA—News; LeRoy.
3:15 WABC—Tena and Tim.
WEAF—Ma Perkins.
WJZ—Star Time.
WMCA—Rollini Trio.
3:25 WHN—News.
3:30 WABC—High Places.
WEAF—Sec. Wickard.
WJZ—App't With Life.
WOR—Gambling.
WHN—Bandstand.
WMCA—News.
WNYC—Vikings Spirit.
3:45 WABC—News, Trout.
WEAF—Right Happiness.
WMCA—Three Qr. Time.
WNYC—News; Rationing.

4 P.M. TO 7 P.M.

4:00 WABC—Service Time.
WEAF—Backstage Wife.
WJZ—Correspondents.
WOR—News; Gambling.
WMCA—News; Ray Smith
WNYC—Four Strings.
4:15 WEAF—Stella Dallas.
WJZ—Don Norman Show.
WOR—Skylar, songs.
4:25 WHN—News.
4:30 WABC—Off the Record.
WEAF—Lorenzo Jones.
WJZ—News; Van Voorhis.
WOR—Food and Home.
WMCA—News; LeRoy.
WHN—Bandstand.
4:40 WABC—Promotion Spot.
4:45 WABC—R. Scott Show.
WEAF—Widder Brown.
WJZ—Hop Harrigan.
WMCA—Matinee.
WNYC—"Living and Learning."
5:00 WABC—Sing Along Club.
WEAF—A Girl Marries.
WJZ—Terry Pirates.
WOR—Uncle Don.
WHN—Dick Gilbert.
WMCA—News; Milt Greene
WNYC—Music for Young People.
5:15 WABC—Romance of Evelyn Winters.
WEAF—Portia Faces Life.
WJZ—Dick Tracy.
WOR—Chick Carter.
WMCA—Matinee.
WINS—Orch.
5:25 WHN—News.
5:30 WABC—Terry Allen with Ross Sisters.
WEAF—Just Plain Bill.
WJZ—Jack Armstrong.
WOR—Superman.
WMCA—News
WNYC—Shirley Sinclair.
WINS—News; Orch.
WHN—Weather; Gilbert.
5:45 WABC—Wilderness Road.
WEAF—Front Page Farrell
WJZ—Captain Midnight.
WOR—Tom Mix.
WMCA—Jerry Baker, Songs.
WNYC—Parents Series.
WINS—Racing Resume.
6:00 WABC—News, Howe.
WEAF—News.
WJZ—News; Kennedy.
WOR—Sydney Moseley.
WMCA—News; Help Wanted.
WNYC—United Nations Music.
WINS—News; Music.
WHN—Tod Williams.
6:13 WOR—Prayer.
6:15 WABC—Hill, news.
WJZ—Symphony Orch.
WJZ—Ethel and Albert.
WOR—Newsreel.
WMCA—Mr. Hollywood.
WHN—Clem McCarthy.
WINS—Cocktail Lounge.
6:25 WOR—Post Parade.
6:30 WABC—Ted Husing.
WJZ—Whose War; Sports.
WOR—Singiser, news.
WMCA—"Tropical Tunes."
WNYC—"Child Welfare."
WINS—News; Sports.
WHN—News, Lang.
6:40 WEAF—Sports, Stern.
WJZ—Band of the Week.
6:45 WABC—World Today.
WEAF—Lowell Thomas.
WJZ—Taylor, news.
WOR—Stan Lomax, sports.
WMCA—String Music.
WNYC—News.
WHN—Music.
WINS—Voice of Maritime.
6:55 WABC—News, Harsch.

7 P.M. TO 10 P.M.

7:00 WABC—I Love a Mystery
WEAF—Music Shop
WJZ—American Side Show
WOR—News, Lewis.
WMCA—News; Scott Or.
WNYC—Masterwork Hour.
WHN—News, Combs.
WINS—News; Music.
7:15 WABC—Music That Satisfies.
WEAF—News, Vandercook.
WOR—"Strange Doctor Weird."
WMCA—Five Star Final.
WHN—Sports Final.
7:30 WABC—American Melodies
WEAF—Dick Haymes.
WJZ—Jean Tighe, songs.
WOR—Arthur Hale.
WMCA—Steel, news.
WNYC—BBC News.
WHN—Adrienne Ames.
WINS—News; The Show.
7:45 WOR—The Answer Man.
WJZ—"Tell Me, Doctor."
WMCA—Sid Gary, songs.
WHN—Bob Howard.
WNYC—Masterwork Hour.
8:00 WABC—Big Town.
WEAF—Ginny Simms.
WJZ—Watch World Go By
WOR—News, Singiser.
WMCA—News; Lawrence.
WHN—Molly Picon.
WINS—News; Swing Parade.
WNYC—Queens College Forum.
8:15 WOR—Skylar Serenade.
WJZ—Lum and Abner.
WINS—Garrett Playviews.
8:30 WABC—Romance Theater.
WEAF—Date With Judy.
WJZ—Alan Young Show.
WOR—"Roy Rogers Show"
WHN—Bunkhouse Jamboree.
WINS—News; Swing Parade.
WNYC—"This Is Pawling"
8:45 WNYC—News.
8:55 WABC—News.
9:00 WABC—Burns and Allen.
WEAF—Mystery Theater.
WJZ—Gracie Fields Show.
WOR—Gabriel Heatter.
WHN—News, Gailmor.
WNYC—Concert Hall.
WMCA—News; Monroe Or.
WINS—News; Music.
9:15 WOR—Screen Test.
WMCA—Eaton.
WHN—Screen Test.
9:30 WABC—This Is My Best.
WEAF—Fibber McGee and Molly.
WJZ—Spotlight Bands.
WOR—American Forum.
WMCA—Lombardo Orch.
WHN—Bible of Air.
WINS—News; High Five.
9:45 WMCA—Spivak Orch.
9:55 WJZ—Story Teller.
WNYC—News.

10 P.M. TO 1 A.M.

10:00 WABC—Service Front.
WEAF—Bob Hope Show.
WJZ—News, Swing.
WHN—George Rosette.
WNYC—Sign off.
WMCA—News; Broadway.
WINS—News; Sports.
10:15 WOR—Paul Schubert.
WJZ—Andy Russell Show.
WHN—Punch Bowl.
WINS—Hep Cat Heaven.
10:25 WHN—Musical Interlude.
10:30 WABC—Congress Speaks.
WEAF—Hildegarde Show.
WOR—Symphonette.
WJZ—Berle Show.
WMCA—Frank Kingdon.
WHN—Commentary; Music
WINS—News; Veterans.
10:45 WABC—Behind the Scenes
WMCA—"Musical Encores"
WHN—Sidney Walton.
WINS—On Your Toes.
11:00 WABC—News, Daly.
WEAF—News, Van.
WJZ—News; Henle.
WOR—News, Vandeventer.
WMCA—News; Wayfarer.
WHN—Newsreel Theater.
WINS—News; Intermezzo.
11:15 WABC—Joan Brooks, songs
WEAF—Harkness.
WJZ—Piso Singers.
WOR—Fraser, news.
WMCA—Unity Viewpoint.
11:20 WJZ—Patti Clayton.
11:25 WOR—Weather Report.
11:30 WABC—Sixth War Loan Program.
WEAF—Words at War.
WJZ—Composers' Concerts.
WOR—Fields Orch.
WMCA—Drama Reviews.
WINS—News.
11:45 WINS—Slumbertime.
WMCA—Wagner Orch.
11:55 WJZ—To be announced.
12:00 WABC—News.
WEAF—News.
WJZ—Midnight Extra.
WOR—Madriguera Orch.
WMCA—News.
WHN—Music to Read By.
WINS—Sign off.
12:05 WABC—Buffalo Presents.
WEAF—Shield Orch.
WJZ—Olson's Room.
12:15 WMCA—Memory Lane.
WOR—Mann Orch.
12:30 WABC—Monroe Orch.
WJZ—Carle Orch.
WOR—Hudson Orch.
WMCA—Truths.
12:45 WOR—Trace Orch.
12:55 WJZ—Showcase.
WEAF—Prayers; News.
WHN—News.

Features On Other Stations

WEVD—
8:15—Jewish Philosopher.
9:00—Reports on Labor Front.
10:00—University Forum of Air
11:45—Theater Review.
12:00—Symphonic Hour.

WNEW—
4:45—Jersey Bounce.
5:35—Make Believe Ballroom
9:00—"Women of the World."
10:00—"Meet the Russians."
12:00—Milkman's Matinee.

WQXR—
4:00—Symphonic Matinee.
7:00—Lisa Sergio.
7:15—Operetta Scrapbook.
8:05—Symphony Hall.
11:00—Just Music.

TOMORROW

Morning

7:00 WABC—News; Godfrey.
WEAF—News; Manhattan.
WJZ—Breakfast Bedlam.
WOR—Havrilla, news.
WMCA—Gospel Church.
WHN—Eye Opener.
WNYC—News; Symphony.
WINS—News; Bob Burns
7:15 WOR—Musical Clock.
WMCA—Morning Herald.
WHN—News.
7:30 WEAF—News
WMCA—Rise and Shine.
WHN—Music Shop.
WINS—News.
7:40 WINS—Bub Burns.
7:45 WABC—News.
WEAF—Reveille Roundup.
WJZ—News; Kiernan.
WMCA—Help Wanted.
7:55 WHN—News.
8:00 WABC—World News.
WEAF—Chaplin, News.
WJZ—Agronsky, news.
WOR—Robinson, news.
WMCA—News; Herth Trio.
WNYC—News; Music Album.
WINS—News; Bub Burns.
WHN—Music Shop.
8:15 WABC—Cook 'n' Corn.
WEAF—Listen to Lewis.
WJZ—Your Life Today.
WOR—"Aunt Jennie"
WMCA—Unity Viewpoints.
8:20 WNYC—Music Moods.
8:25 WNYC—Consumers Guide.
8:30 WABC—Missus Shops.
WEAF—News.
WJZ—Nancy Craig.
WOR—Fitzgeralds.
WMCA—News.
WHN—Country Store.
WINS—News; Pied Piper
8:35 WNYC—Music Album.
8:40 WHN—Music Makers.
8:45 WABC—Margaret Arlen.
WEAF—Roy Hendrickson.
WMCA—Music.
WHN—News.
WNYC—News; Around New York.
8:55 WOR—News, Robinson.
WJZ—News.
9:00 WABC—News.
WEAF—Mirth and Madness.
WJZ—Breakfast Club.
WOR—Victor Lindlahr.
WHN—Gloom Dodgers.
WMCA—News; Alice Hughes.
WNYC—Masterwork Hour
WINS—News.
9:15 WABC—New Horizons.
WOR—Bing Crosby.
WMCA—Kitchen Window.
WINS—Food Magician.
9:25 WOR—Lanny and Ginger
9:30 WEAF—Adelaide Hawley
WOR—Pure Food Hour.
WINS—News; Music.
WMCA—Little Show.
9:45 WABC—Life Is Mine.
WEAF—Cornell, songs.
WHN—News.
WINS—French Chef.
10:00 WABC—Valiant Lady.
WEAF—Lora Lawton.
WJZ—True Story.
WOR—News; Gladstone.
WMCA—News; LeRoy.
WHN—Gloom Dodgers.
WNYC—Daniel P. Woolley
WINS—News, Music.
10:15 WABC—Light of World.
WEAF—News, St. John.
WOR—Bessie Beatty.
WNYC—Fredric March.
WMCA—Little Show.
WINS—Dorothy Day.
10:25 WJZ—Aunt Jemima.
10:30 WABC—Changing World.
WEAF—Finders Keepers.
WJZ—Cliff Edwards.
WNYC—BBC News.
WMCA—News; Little Show
WINS—News; Star Parade.
10:45 WABC—Bachelor's Child'n
WJZ—Listening Post.
WMCA—Little Show.
WHN—News.
WNYC—School Forum.
11:00 WABC—Amanda.
WEAF—Road of Life.
WJZ—Breakfast Interviews.
WOR—News, Robinson.
WMCA—News; Little Show
WHN—Gloom Dodgers.
WNYC—News.
WINS—News; Tune Factory.
11:15 WABC—Second Husband.
WEAF—Rosemary.
WOR—Music for You.
WNYC—Rations; Recipes.
11:20 WOR—Intermission Time.
11:25 WNYC—Musical Souvenirs.
11:30 WABC—Bright Horizon.
WEAF—Star Playhouse.
WJZ—News, Martyn.
WOR—Quiz Wizard.
WMCA—News.
11:40 WOR—Travelogue.
11:45 WABC—Aunt Jenny.
WEAF—David Harum.
WJZ—Jack Berch.
WOR—What's Your Idea?
WMCA—T. Dorsey Or.
WHN—News.
WNYC—Health Talk.
11:55 WOR—Lanny and Ginger.

12 M. TO 2 P.M.

12:00 WABC—Kate Smith.
WEAF—News, Goddard.
WJZ—Glamour Manor.
WOR—Moseley, News.
WMCA—News, J. Lawrence.
WHN—Weather; Dodgers.
WNYC—Music at Work.
WINS—Tobin, commentary
12:05 WINS—Tune Factory.
12:15 WABC—Big Sister.
WEAF—Maggie McNeills.
WOR—Music.
12:30 WABC—Helen Trent.
WEAF—Air Force Band.
WJZ—News; Story Drama.
WOR—News, Gladstone.
WINS—News; Tune Factory.
12:40 WJZ—Farm and Home.
12:45 WABC—Our Gal Sunday.
WOR—Album.
WHN—News.
1:00 WABC—Life Beautiful.
WEAF—Mary McBride.
WJZ—Baukhage Talking.
WOR—Consumer Quiz.
WMCA—News; Americana
WHN—For Women Only.
WNYC—Missing Persons.
1:05 WNYC—Wake Up N. Y.
1:15 WABC—Ma Perkins.
WJZ—Woman Exchange.
WOR—Terry's Party.
WMCA—Love Songs.
1:30 WABC—News, Flynn.
WOR—Lopez.
WHN—News; Gilbert.
WNYC—Change of Mood.
1:40 WJZ—Music for You.
1:45 WABC—Goldbergs.
WEAF—Morgan Beatty.
WJZ—Galen Drake.
WOR—American Woman's Jury
WNYC—"Story of New Amsterdam."

THESE WOMEN! — By d'Alessio

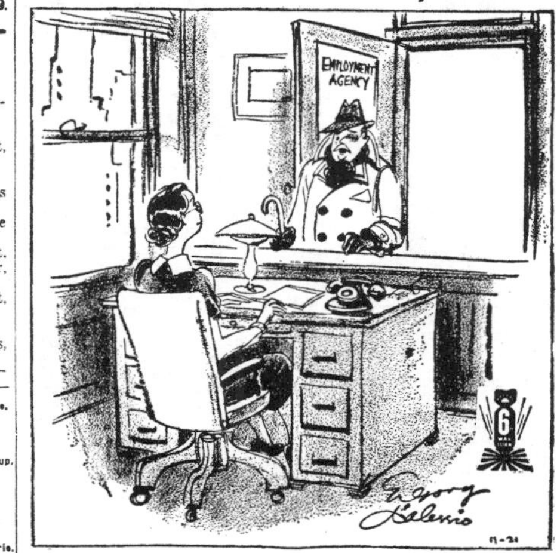

"——er, Ahem. . . . I want to hire a new secretary!"

HOLLYWOOD commentator, Paula Stone, will celebrate her second anniversary with WNEW next week. Ever been curious as to what a photograph of a fellow who photographs radio and screen folk would look like? Well, here's one of Bruno of Hollywood, who guested recently on WHN with Adrienne Ames.

BRIDGE — By Harry J. Roth

A slam contract may be bid if its success depends on a finesse. During the play of the hand, however, if two finesses must be taken then some other line of play must be developed if possible. When the dummy goes down the declarer should map out his entire line of play, but be prepared for a shift of tactics if anything goes wrong with his original plan.

On the hand shown today J. Hutton Hinch felt he absolutely had to make his slam contract. He had a run of hard luck, being in several contracts which had been set purely because of adverse distribution. When the dummy was laid down he saw that the success of his contract depended on either a diamond or club finesse, but he could not afford to risk both. He therefore planned his play on the assumption that West held the king of clubs since he did not lead a club.

The hand:
North dealer.
Neither side vulnerable.

North:
♠ A K Q 7 3
♡ A K 4
◇ A K J 6
♣ 2

West:
♠ 6 2
♡ 10 8 2
◇ 9 8 3
♣ K 10 9 7 5

East:
♠ 9 8 4
♡ Q 6 5
◇ Q 10 4
♣ 8 6 4 3

South (Hinch):
♠ J 10 5
♡ J 9 7 3
◇ 7 5 2
♣ A Q J

The bidding:

North	East	South	West
2♠	Pass	3♡	Pass
6♡	Pass	Pass	Pass

West opened the six of spades which Hinch won in his hand with the jack. He played the ace of clubs and then the queen. West covered with the king and Hinch ruffed in dummy with the four of hearts. The ace and king of hearts were cashed and Hinch returned to his hand with the ten of spades. He led a heart which East won with the queen, discarding a diamond from dummy. East returned a club which declarer took with the jack, discarding another diamond from dummy. The nine of spades was led to dummy and on the two good spades, Hinch discarded two diamonds from his hand.

RADIO — By William Juengst

RESEARCH (On a Sometimes-Sad Subject)—Recently Ol' Sour Ears began wondering what happens to Earlanders during the intervals when one sustaining program ends and another sustainer or commercial comes along...That bleak period comparable to an actor's "at liberty."...Recalling that the heavy purchasing of time by the politicos ended three of Songstress Elaine Howard's CBS shows at the end of October we decided to ask her about it...And radio being the wacky business it is, we found her the wrong person to ask...Although she knows the right answer...Because: "I'm the luckiest girl in the world...My dad's well-to-do... Where my bankroll ends, dad begins...But for lots of us, it's Heartbreak House...You have to live on what you've saved...Or take the kind of parts you don't quite want ...Or night club dates, when you want to stick exclusively to radio...I want to stick to radio exclusively because the hours are wonderful... In spite of what they say I don't believe you can work until the small hours of the morning and keep your voice...But lucky me—during these intervals I get a chance to study... And play benefits...And every Wednesday I have to give a performance for my Fan Club just as if my own song-show were still on the air."...That Fan Club, folks, is quite a proposition...Can you imagine 35 people, ranging from 11 to 26 years of age, getting their own show in a two-room hotel suite, and holding formal meetings there, too? ...Among the Brooklynites in this vigorous contingent are **Ruth and Muriel Lehman** of 952 Seneca Ave., **Jo Divalo** of 874 Greene Ave., and **Loretta Walther** of 1112 Putnam Ave....By way of bolstering her conviction that she's a mighty lucky girl, **Elaine's** manager is currently weighing two network jobs for her.

PATTER (Including Personalia) —**Ted Grover**, WBYN newscaster and **Mischa Auer** were chums at Ethical Culture School—where they voted **Mischa**: "Class Musician . . . **And Ted**: "Class Comedian"...Hey, Jeff 'n Leslie, and your kids, too, Mr. and Mrs. Brooklyn: Your beau ideal, **Cowboy Roy Rogers** premieres his WOR-show t'nite...**Dinah Shore** goes around asking people to guess how-come she became engaged to **Corp. George Montgomery** two days before he proposed...The answer: **George** wrote his "darling-will-you-be-mine" in the Aleutians...And beat that important epistle home by 48 hours...WNEW debuts its newest air-contest t'nite: "So You Want to Be a Radio Announcer?"... Brooklyn contestant on the inaugural b-cast: **Matthed A. Pavitt** . . . Look for a trick ending to **WEAF's** "Mystery Theater" tonight.

SCREEN

By Jane Corby

'Something for the Boys' at Roxy Theater. 'Bowery to Broadway' at Criterion Tomorrow

"Something for the Boys," one of the most elaborate Technicolor musicals on 20th Century-Fox's schedule for the current year, will have its New York opening at the Roxy Theater tomorrow. Based on the smash Broadway hit of the past year, the film version has undergone only a few minor changes. Carmen Miranda will be seen in the role made famous by Ethel Merman on the stage. Vivian Blaine and Michael O'Shea carry the romantic interest while crooner Perry Como will be heard singing "In the Middle of Nowhere," specially written by Jimmy McHugh and Harold Adamson for the production. Adding to the antics is comedian Phil Silvers as one of the trio of heirs who inherit a dilapidated Southern mansion and turn it into a much-needed residence for the wives of service men.

Concluding the engagement of "Lost in a Harem" today, the Criterion will get a new tenant tomorrow, Universal's "Bowery to Broadway." The film is a melodious, spectacular story of show business people from the 1890s to the early 1930s.

The cast boasts Maria Montez, Susanna Foster, Jack Oakie, Turhan Bey, Louise Allbritton, Ann Blyth, Frank McHugh, Donald Cook, Donald O'Connor, Peggy Ryan and many others. It was produced by John Grant, directed by Charles Lamont.

Present day activity of American fliers bombing Tokyo, as reported in current headlines, is having a signal effect on the Capitol Theater boxoffice, where "Thirty Seconds Over Tokyo," starring Spencer Tracy, Van Johnson, Phyllis Thaxter and Robert Walker, starts its third week Thursday, with Jimmy Dorsey's orchestra and Henny Youngman on the stage. Weekend holiday crowds were the largest in the Capitol's history, compelling the theater to open at 8:30 a.m. and run continuous performances until 3 a.m. The screen story is based on General Doolittle's famous exploit of two years ago.

The RKO Brooklyn, Queens and Long Island Theaters open on Thursday with the farce-comedy, "Doughgirls," starring Ann Sheridan, Jane Wyman and Jack Carson, and the poignant story of "My Pal, Wolf," featuring the new child star, Sharyn Moffett. Filmed from the recent Broadway stage success, "Doughgirls" highlights Alexis Smith, Eve Arden and Irene Manning in featured roles.

BETTINA ROSAY, ballerina, whose dancing is one of the attractions of the current stage show, "Spotlight Time," at Radio City Music Hall, where "Together Again" is on the screen.

LYNN BARI, as she appears in "Sweet and Lowdown," sharing the screen at the Albee with "Laura," mystery film. The entire bill will be held for a second week, starting Thursday.

"Sophie Halenczik, American," comedy by George Ross and Rose C. Feld starring Katina Paxinou, began a two-week engagement in Philadelphia last night. It opens in New York on Dec. 26.

MOVIE TIME SCHEDULE

BROOKLYN

ALBEE—"Laura," 11:00, 1:50, 4:45, 7:35, 10:30; "Sweet and Lowdown," 12:35, 3:30, 6:20, 9:20.

FOX—"Double Indemnity," 11:00, 2:15, 5:30, 8:45; "Meet Miss Bobby Socks," 12:16, 3:31, 6:46, 10:01.

METROPOLITAN—"The Mark of the Whistler," 11:01, 2:20, 5:39, 8:58; "American Romance," 12:09, 3:25, 6:44, 10:03.

PARAMOUNT—"Conspirators," 12:35, 3:49, 6:55, 10:09; "Henry Aldrich's Little Secret," 11:12, 2:26, 5:40, 8:46.

STRAND—"Barbary Coast Gent," 12:48, 4:03, 7:18, 10:33; "Strange Affair," 11:30, 2:45, 6:00, 9:15.

MANHATTAN

ASTOR—"Meet Me in St. Louis," 10:25, 12:41, 2:57, 5:13, 7:29, 9:45, 12:01.

CAPITOL—"Thirty Seconds Over Tokyo," 10:05, 1:23, 4:46, 8:09, 11:25. Stage, 12:39, 4:02, 7:25, 10:41.

CRITERION—"Lost in a Harem," 9:38, 11:30, 1:25, 3:20, 5:15, 7:00, 9:05, 11:00, 12:55.

MUSIC HALL—"Together Again," 11:00, 1:46, 4:36, 7:30, 10:19. Stage, 12:40, 3:26, 6:16, 9:30.

PARAMOUNT—"And Now Tomorrow," 9:01, 11:45, 2:29, 5:24, 8:17, 11:05, 12:30. Stage, 10:30, 1:14, 4:12, 7:07, 10:00.

RIVOLI—"Frenchman's Creek," 10:28, 12:28, 2:39, 4:53, 7:12, 9:32, 11:46.

ROXY—"Irish Eyes Are Smiling," 11:10, 1:50, 4:45, 7:30, 10:20. Stage, 1:00, 3:45, 6:35, 9:20.

'All-Winners' Night At Bedford Tomorrow

The second "All Winners" amateur night to be held at the Bedford Theater will take place tomorrow, when the former amateur night winners will compete for a first prize of a Pierce watch, awarded by the Pierce Watch Company.

Joe Martin, popular master of ceremonies, will conduct the contest, which promises to bring out some of the best talent in the borough. Each one of the contestants has won a previous amateur night at Loew's Bedford.

WHEN OUT OF TOWN REGISTER FROM BROOKLYN

A MUSICAL THAT'S
A Joy to Behold
WITH THE "CHERRY BLONDE" WHO'S A JOY TO BE HOLDING!
Carmen MIRANDA
Michael O'SHEA
Vivian BLAINE
(The Cherry Blonde)
SOMETHING FOR THE BOYS
IN TECHNICOLOR!
A 20th CENTURY-FOX PICTURE
with PHIL SILVERS
SHEILA RYAN
PERRY COMO
GLENN LANGAN
Directed by Lewis Seiler
Produced by Irving Starr
And ON THE STAGE
Cafe Society UPTOWN presents
JIMMY SAVO · MILDRED BAILEY
Plus CHUCK AND CHUCKLES · BIL AND CORA BAIRD
GAE FOSTER ROXYETTES · PAUL ASH AND ROXY THEATRE ORCHESTRA
Extra PEARL PRIMUS AND HER COMPANY
STARTS TOM'W
DOORS OPEN 11 A.M.
ROXY
7th AVE. at 50th ST.

MEET ME AT THE ASTOR THEATRE
You'll thrill to M-G-M's film delight in Technicolor! You'll take its glowing love story to your heart. Hear 7 hit tunes! You'll be sharing in a thrilling entertainment event!
"Clang-clang-clang Goes The Trolley"
Hear Judy Sing! "The Trolley Song"! No. 1 on Hit Parade!
STARRING
Judy Garland
WITH
Margaret O'Brien
in
MEET ME IN ST. LOUIS
M-G-M's TECHNICOLOR HIT!
MARY ASTOR · LUCILLE BREMER · TOM DRAKE · MARJORIE MAIN
Screen Play by Irving Brecher and Fred F. Finklehoffe · Based on the Book by Sally Benson
Directed by VINCENTE MINNELLI · Produced by ARTHUR FREED · An M-G-M Picture
STARTS TODAY
ASTOR
DOORS OPEN 10 A.M. CONTINUOUS POPULAR PRICES
B'way & 45th Street
The Smashing 6th War Loan is on! Buy an Extra Bond today!

Held Over! 2nd BIG WEEK!
A strange and dangerous experiment in love and murder! . . . "enormously exciting" —JOURNAL AMERICAN
GENE TIERNEY
DANA ANDREWS
CLIFTON WEBB
'Laura'
VINCENT PRICE · JUDITH ANDERSON
and
It's SWEET! It's HOT! It's HEAVENLY!
Benny GOODMAN AND BAND
LINDA DARNELL · LYNN BARI · JACK OAKIE
'Sweet and Low-Down'
BOTH ARE 20th Century Fox Hits!
RKO ALBEE
FULTON & DE KALB B'KLYN

The heart-to-heart PERSONAL story of New York's TWO great white ways!
BOWERY TO BROADWAY
Starring
MARIA MONTEZ
SUSANNA FOSTER
JACK OAKIE
TURHAN BEY
and a song-specialty by
DONALD O'CONNOR · PEGGY RYAN
A Universal Picture
TOM'W at 9 a.m.
LOEW'S CRITERION B'way & 45th St.
BUY WAR BONDS

"... tells of an illicit love" Cameron, News
George SANDERS
Linda DARNELL
"Summer Storm"
Brandt's GOTHAM
B'way and 47th St.

10th Week!
"Don't miss it!" Nick Kenny, Mirror
Joan Fontaine · Arturo de Cordova
"FRENCHMAN'S CREEK"
A MITCHELL LEISEN PRODUCTION
RIVOLI
B'way at 49th St.
DOORS OPEN 9:30 A.M.
Paramount's TECHNICOLOR Sensation

"... a must for thriller audiences" —Otis L. Guernsey, Jr., Tribune
Merle OBERON
Franchot TONE
Thomas MITCHELL
"Dark Waters"
BRANDT'S GLOBE
B'way & 46th St.

FEATURE FILMS SHOWING TODAY

BAY RIDGE AND SUNSET PARK
Electra, 75th St. and Third Ave........Wilson
Harbor, 92d St. and Fourth Ave........Wing and a Prayer; also Moonlight and Cactus
Stanley, Fifth Ave. and 75th St........Bride by Mistake; also The Big Noise
Park, 44th St. and Fifth Ave...........Cry of the Werewolf; also Soul of a Monster

BEDFORD
Lincoln, Bedford Ave.-Eastern P'kway..Sailor on Leave; also Lady in a Jam
National, 720 Washington Ave.........Palm Beach Story; also Night of January 16th
Rogers, 333 Rogers Ave. PR. 4-2230...Wilson

BENSONHURST
Colony, 18th Ave.-65th St. BE. 6-2231..Background to Danger; also Moon Over Las Vegas

BORO PARK
Elton, 43d St. and New Utrecht Ave....Moon and Sixpence; also I Met My Love Again

BOROUGH HALL AND DOWNTOWN
Century's Tivoli, Fulton St., Boro Hall Gypsy Wildcat; also Music in Manhattan
Duffield, Duffield and Fulton St.......Are These Our Parents?; also Singing Sheriff
Momart, Fulton St. and Rockwell Pl....Little Lord Fauntleroy; also Hari Kiri
St. George Playhouse, 100 Pineapple St. Wilson
Terminal, Fourth Ave. and Dean St....Weekend in Havana; also Quiet, Please, Murder!

BRIGHTON BEACH
Oceana, Brighton Beach Ave.-Huff St.. Gypsy Wildcat; also Are These Our Parents?

BUSHWICK
Empire, Ralph Ave.-B'way. FO. 9-7940.Action in the North Atlantic; Leave It to the Irish

FLATBUSH
Granada, Church and Nostrand Aves....Hail the Conquering Hero; also Take It Big
Kent, Coney Island Ave. & Ave. H.... Janie; also Crime by Night
Leader, Coney Island and Newkirk Aves.Wing and a Prayer; also Goin' to Town

EAST FLATBUSH
Avenue D, Avenue D and E. 43d St....Hail the Conquering Hero; also Take It Big
Rugby, Utica and Church Aves..........Wing and a Prayer; also Three Little Sisters

GERRITSEN BEACH
Graham, 311 Whitney Ave.............Janie; also Crime by Night

PARK SLOPE
Carlton, Flatbush and Seventh Aves.....Dragon Seed
Plaza, Flatbush Ave. and Park Place....Give Me a Sailor; also Song of Nevada
Sanders, Prospect Park West-14th St.....Greenwich Village; also Dangerous Journey
New Venus, 1224 Prospect Ave........Blues in the Night; also Cry of the Werewolf

KINGS HIGHWAY
Jewel, Kings Highway at Ocean P'kway..Primrose Path; also South of Tahiti

AVENUE U SECTION
Avenue U, Avenue U and E. 18th St.Arsenic and Old Lace; Johnny Doesn't Live Here Any More
Traymore, Avenue N and E. 46th St...Wing and a Prayer; also Three Little Sisters

RIDGEWOOD
Colonial, Broadway and Chauncey.......Dragon Seed; also Pearl of Death
Ridgewood, 1673 Myrtle Ave...........My Buddy; also Silver City Kid
Rivoli, Myrtle-Wilson Aves. GL. 5-0744.In Society; also Song of the Open Road

SHEEPSHEAD BAY
Sheepshead, Sheepshead Rd.-Voorhies..Wilson

SOUTH BROOKLYN
Sanders Globe, 226 15th St...........Roberta; also Pearl of Death

Eagle Staff photos

BROOKLYNITES ON THE U. S. S. BROOKLYN—These 30 officers and crew members of the cruiser Brooklyn are all residents of Brooklyn. In front row are: (left to right) Lt. Comm. William J. Valentine, Comm. Leil L. Young, Lt. George E. Grieb, Lt. Bruce L. Kubert, Lt. (j.g.) Walter A. Burch, Lt. William F. Coffield and Boatswain William P. Craft Jr.

Cruiser Brooklyn Is Back Home --Unscathed in Hottest Fights

The cruiser Brooklyn came back yesterday to the Brooklyn Navy Yard, where her keel was laid in 1936, after 15 months of battle duty without losing a man and without suffering any damage.

During that time, the Brooklyn, called on again and again for off-shore action in support of our landing troops, fought at Anzio, at Cassino, at Salerno, in the waters off Corsica, and off southern France.

Anzio was the "hottest," said her returning officers, because enemy bombers and shore batteries combined to pour hot lead on the cruiser. And southern France was bad, too, as the Brooklyn crept along offshore, knocking out Nazi strongpoints ahead of our advancing infantry. German 11-inch shore guns scored near hits—but only near—42 times.

Officers and crew, including 37 men from Brooklyn, brought back a whole museum of medals, citations, commendations. But, the Navy Department noted, there was no sensational heroism—the whole ship did a job so "well secured," or efficient, that the standard type of heroism in emergencies was not called for.

The Brooklyn, said her commanding officer, Capt. Frank R. Dodge, was a "workhorse ship and was never given a mission which she did not carry out successfully."

The Brooklyn, a light cruiser, was undergoing minor repairs in the Navy Yard here in September, 1943, when she received a hurry call to return to the Mediterranean theater of action, in which she had already had her baptism of fire. That came on Nov. 8, 1942, when she supported the landing at Casablanca. In the two years since then she was in four amphibious assaults in the Mediterranean area: North Africa, Sicily, Italy and France.

Hit Coast of Italy

The September, 1943, call came from Vice Admiral H. Kent Hewitt, then in charge of navy forces at Salerno. The Brooklyn whipped her way across the Atlantic in time to lend fire support to the advancing 5th Army troops. Until the following January the Brooklyn roamed up and down the Mediterranean coast of Italy, smashing enemy installations for miles inland.

At Anzio, the Brooklyn's guns helped clear the way for the beachhead landings, and for 29 days thereafter the cruiser remained in the vicinity, repelling enemy bombardments and counter-attacks. When the land troops broke out at Cassino, the Brooklyn raced back and forth between the two points, using her guns as off-shore artillery support for the break-through troops.

Fliers Score

While preparations were on for the invasion of southern France, the Brooklyn's aviators, flying P-51s and P-40s, flew numerous fighting missions with the army north of Rome. On D-Day of the southern France invasion, these pilots flew from fields on Corsica, spotted the targets, directed and co-ordinated naval gunfire on them.

The Brooklyn gave fire support to the army as it moved along inland after establishing the first beachhead.

"These landings are spectacular," said Captain Dodge (of Adrian, Mich.), "but don't let that fool you. The routine patroling for the next few days is what gets you. You are badly outgunned—you have six-inch guns against the enemy's 11-inchers—and all you can do is fire away and employ evasive tactics."

Captain Dodge was awarded the Silver Star for gallantry in action. He said it was the navy's way of decorating the entire crew. "We've never been given a mission we didn't complete and the Navy Department couldn't give a Silver Star to every man aboard," is the way he puts it.

The skipper thinks the finest accomplishment of his crew is the purchase of more than $144,000 worth of war bonds in the cash drive last July 4.

Average $111 a Man

"We paid for more rounds of ammunition than we fired," he said, "and we led the navy tally sheet. Next closest was a battle wagon and they carry a lot more men than we do. That averages $111 a man—and the crew did it on their own hook."

Among other awards were:

Gold star in lieu of a second Distinguished Flying Cross to Lt. Elmo L. Moss, 101 Willow St., and letters of commendation to Comm. William J. Valentine of 314 Clinton Ave., the ship's gunnery officer.

LIBERAL PARTY URGES REVIVAL OF CIVIC PLAN

By JOSEPH H. SCHMALACKER

Public sentiment favoring a continuation of the struggle for Controller McGoldrick's downtown Brooklyn property modernization proposal, despite its defeat in the Board of Estimate, began crystallizing yesterday when the public affairs council of the Liberal Party in Brooklyn served notice the plan must not be abandoned.

The council, acting at a special meeting in the party's Kings County headquarters at 66 Court St., adopted a three-point program highlighted by a recommendation calling for further study of the proposal by the Board of Estimate as a step toward reconsidering its rejection of the plan.

Votes for Committee

While declaring the fight for the plan should be continued and that further study should be made by the Board of Estimate, the public affairs council, in the third of its recommendations, voted for the appointment of a committee to consult Mayor LaGuardia, Controller McGoldrick, Council President Morris, the Borough Presidents who are members of the Board of Estimate as well as civic and other groups which have interested themselves in the project.

The subcommittee will be headed by Louis P. Goldberg, lawyer, author and former member of the City Council.

The stand taken by the public affairs council was the first formal one of its kind since the Board of Estimate at Thursday's meeting failed to adopt the Controller's proposal by a two-vote margin. The plan, requiring three-fourths of the Board of Estimate's 16 votes, was defeated when no more than 10 votes were cast in is favor.

Provided $20,000,000 Fund

McGoldrick's proposal urged an allocation of $20,000,000 in the city's 1945 capital budget to allow the city to acquire 45 acres of substandard downtown property in order to re-zone and resell it at public auction for redevelopment by private capital. He has contended this represents the most practical method open for handling the problem of blighted residential areas.

The program adopted by the Liberal party's council was the result of several hours of discussion. Individual members asked for its amplification in several directions. One of these specifies that provisions must be made for families now living in the area which would be dislocated by the modernization process and asserts they are entitled to priority in getting living accommodations if and when the area is rehabilitated.

The other provided that any land condemned must be dedicated to social use for housing or some other public project.

JAPANESE-AMERICANS WED—Midori Satomi, member of the first Japanese-American family to take up residence last may at the New York Relocation Hostel, 168 Clinton St., was married yesterday to Dr. Irving Isao Odo, dentist. The ceremony was performed in the First Presbyterian Church.

Ex-Convict Held In $25,000 Looting Of E. 22d St. Home

Paroled last Summer after serving a 3½-year jail term for assault and robbery in 1941, Frank Baglioro, 34, of 2626 Harway Ave., was held without bail by Magistrate Ramsgate in Brooklyn Felony Court yesterday on a charge of looting an apartment of $25,000 in jewelry and furs.

Baglioro, a machinist in a sewing machine factory at 67 Bleecker St., Manhattan, was arrested Friday night as he was leaving for home. Detective Joseph Kabelka of the Brooklyn Ave. station, who made the arrest, charged that Baglioro was one of four men who entered the topfloor apartment of Mrs. Yeta Boslow at 978 E. 22d St. last Wednesday night, tied up two housemaids and a partner and then ransacked the apartment. Mrs. Boslow's ten-year-old daughter, Joan, who entered while the robbery was in progress, was made to stand in the corner. She later released the trio after the burglars left.

Baglioro, who has a previous record of three arrests, was held for a hearing Friday. In 1933 he was held for assault and the charge was dropped. He received a suspended sentence in 1937 on a petty larceny charge.

A jail sentence of five to ten years was imposed in 1941 after he was convicted of robbing a laundry collector with three other men.

'STICK TO JOB,' ROOSEVELT ASKS WAR WORKERS

Washington, Dec. 2 (U.P.)—President Roosevelt, asserting that ultimate victory is inevitable, tonight called on the nation to dedicate "everything that we do" to achievement of lasting peace.

He voiced the plea in a letter to Col. John Callan O'Laughlin, editor of the Army and Navy Journal, for publication in the Journal's Dec. 7 "United States at War" edition. The President coupled his "ultimate victory is inevitable" assertion with a grim warning of the hard fighting and hard working which must precede victory.

"The weapons of war which America has turned out and which have given us superiority on land, on the sea, and in the air," Mr. Roosevelt said, "must continue to flow if we are to attain that victory. Everybody on a war job must stick to that job.

Co-operation Must Continue

"The effective co-operation among the United Nations which has done so much to insure final victory must continue after the war for building a structure of peace. All over the world peaceloving men and women are determined that this cannot occur again. Everything that we do must be dedicated to that objective."

He said 1944 "has been a year of outstanding accomplishment for the armed forces of the United States" —a year in which they "have taken part in 27 different D-Days—each one a triumphant success."

"We are now waging major offensive operations 13,000 miles apart from each other," the President wrote.

Strategy Determined at Start

"Although we were obliged to take the defense when the attack was first made upon us, it was our strategy from the beginning to move out to strike the enemy as soon as our power and resources were fully mobilized—to strike him on his own home grounds at points of our own choosing. That was the strategy from the beginning—that is the strategy today.

"As defensive fighters and as fighters on the offensive, the American soldiers and sailors and airmen have proven that they can slug it out victoriously with any armed forces our enemies may send against them.

"But in the midst of victorious battles we must never forget that the war is not yet won either in Europe or in Asia.

"The enemy in Europe is fighting on his own soil. The enemy in the Pacific is beginning to feel our attack in his own home waters and islands. With shortened supply lines, the Nazis and Japs are fighting with fanatical resistance."

Jewish Women to Hear Talk By U. S. Attorney

United States Attorney T. Vincent Quinn will speak at a meeting of the Women's Auxiliary of Congregation Best Elohim in the temple, 8th Ave. and Garfield Place, on Tuesday afternoon on "The Federal Prosecutor in Time of War."

Mrs. Grover M. Moscowitz, wife of a Federal judge, will introduce the speaker. Mrs. A. L. Marks will preside. A short Chanukah service will be conducted by Rabbi Isaac Landman and Cantor Reuben Rothman.

Officer to Address Club

The Men's Club of Bay Ridge will hear a talk tomorrow night by Col. Carlton S. Proctor of army overseas construction at the 42d birthday dinner in Union Parish House, 81st St. and Ridge Boulevard. Harold Bowie is dinner chairman.

Honor M. J. Solomon As 'Boro Citizen No. 1'

Honored as "Brooklyn Citizen No. 1" by the Men's League of Brooklyn, Morris J. Solomon, chairman of the Brooklyn Federation of Jewish Charities, received the league's annual award last night at a testimonial dinner at the Hotel St. George.

The civic and business leader, chosen as the man who has contributed most to borough civic and communal welfare during the year, was feted by the more than 1,000 members.

Borough President John Cashmore made the presentation on behalf of the award committee, headed by the former Supreme Court Justice Mitchell May as honorary chairman.

Dr. Abram Leon Sacher, national director of the B'nai B'rith Hillel Foundations, made the principal address. Other speakers were Justice May and Reuben R. Robinson, president of the league.

Among the guests were Supreme Court Justices Harry E. Lewis, Charles C. Lockwood, E. Ivan Rubinstein and John MacCrate, Brig. Gen. William O'Dwyer, Representative Emanuel Celler, Postmaster Frank J. Quayle Jr. and former Public Welfare Commissioner Frank J. Taylor.

The dinner committee was headed by Max Abrams, assisted by Irving Roaman, Samuel Sennet and Harry Zeitz.

Borough Soldier, Wounded in France, Returns

As a taxi rolled to a stop in front of 442 Bristol St. yesterday, it was immediately surrounded by a group of excited neighborhood people.

Out of the taxi, with the aid of crutches, came a young man in uniform. He greeted his friends with a grin as he noticed a banner unfurled across the front of his home, reading, "Welcome Home, Soldier."

He was Pfc. Jack Abolsky, 24, and he was home for the first time since he was wounded on a night reconnaisance patrol in St. Lo, France, July 27. It was a year to the day since he left for overseas. Abolsky suffered a broken hip and shrapnel wounds and is now at Tilton General Hospital at Fort Dix.

Joined by Wife

Waiting for him inside were his mother, Sarah, and a sister, Mrs. Lea Smith. Later, he was joined by his wife, Hilda, who has a war job, and another sister. He has a week-end pass.

Abolsky, a graduate of Samuel J. Tilden High School, was inducted Nov. 11, 1942, from a job as a machinist at the Brooklyn Navy Yard.

Another local fighting man, Arthur V. Metzger, 25, of 48-02 48th St., Woodside, arrived yesterday for his first Christmas at home since 1939. He is a navy radio operator with the rank of first-class petty officer. Metzger enlisted in November, 1940. After Pearl Harbor he saw action in the South Pacific.

Dinner Is Tendered St. Albans Monsignor

Mons. James A. Charters, pastor of the St. Catherine of Sienna Church, St. Albans, one of 15 priests in the diocese of Brooklyn just elevated by Pope Pius to the rank of domestic prelate, was the honored guest at a dinner in the rectory, 118-22 Riverton St., St. Albans, Thursday.

Among those attending were Lt. Com. Frederick A. Gallagher, S.J., and Lt. (S.G.) Thomas Dowd, Catholic chaplains stationed at the St. Albans Naval Hospital, and the three parish assistants at St. Catherine of Sienna, the Rev. Thomas J. Feeney, the Rev. Charles J. Murphy and the Rev. Charles W. McInenly. Dr. Wentworth Driscoll was toastmaster.

GIs Wield Artificial Hands to Eat Turkey

By MARJORIE COLLIER

Washington, Dec. 2 (U.P.)—Before them on the table was a turkey dinner but the four GIs weren't eating much; they hadn't quite got the hang of using their artificial hands.

They tried, though, and they wouldn't take help—except from each other. They weren't giving up because they knew from the experience of others that the time would come when their mechanical hands would do for them practically everything a flesh and bone hand can do.

These GIs were just four of 100,000 veterans of this war who are now in the United States receiving a new kind of training at army hospitals.

Reconditioning Isn't Easy

They call this training "reconditioning." Reconditioning, for these men who lost a hand or an arm, or leg on the D-Day beaches, or on some Pacific isle, or at St. Lo or Cassino, is not an easy thing that comes as you lie comfortably on your back on a hospital bed. It is a hard, serious business.

I was one of several news reporters who recently visited Lawson General Hospital at Atlanta, Ga., and other centers in the South. We saw reconditioning in operation.

In a physiotherapy ward at Lawson I talked with a boy from Brooklyn.

Wants to Come Home, Drive Car

"I've been on my back for three months," he said. "I want to go home for Christmas and drive my car again."

He'll do it. Lying there practicing toe-touching and other calisthenics in bed, he was getting himself in shape to be completely "on his own" when released from the hospital.

Reconditioning sometimes takes longer than in the case of the boy from Brooklyn. Some return to duty or get their discharge in four months. For others it takes as long as 13 months.

For some reason the men who have lost their arms or legs "have the highest morale," a nurse told me. I saw men with artificial legs taking dancing lessons from Arthur Murray instructors. Pvt. Werner Jean of New York, who had worn his artificial legs only 10 days, was giving dancing lessons to a buddy.

Stab Wounds Fatal To Two in Brawls

Three soldiers and a young woman, whose names were withheld, were questioned at the W. 152d St. police station, Manhattan, yesterday, following the fatal stabbing of Charles Duvall, 22, a garage worker of 745 Riverside Drive.

Police said Duvall resented a remark one of the soldiers made while Duvall and the woman were together in a tavern on Broadway near 163d St. He and the woman left but later encountered the soldiers on the street. A fight started and Duvall was stabbed in the abdomen, police said. He was dead when an ambulance arrived from Mother Cabrini Hospital.

In a second fatal Manhattan stabbing, Joseph Jackson, 28, of 138 W. 139th St., admitted slashing John Finch of 302 W. 114th St. when the latter attempted to stop an argument between Jackson and another man in a restaurant on 7th Ave. near 12[illegible]th St. Finch died in Sydenham Hospital.

Brooklyn Writers Club Hears Yule Program

A Christmas program was presented for 30 members of the Writers Club of Brooklyn at their monthly meeting in the Hotel Bossert yesterday. Participating were Mrs. Elmer E. O'Donnell, president of the Story Tellers Club of Brooklyn, who read a Christmas story, and Louise Mosgrove, who told of the Christmas observance in other lands. Several original poems were read. Mrs. Ida A. Anderson, president of the club, presided.

Poultry Sales Hit By U. S. Embargo

A long-pending Government order putting an embargo, for army purchase, on virtually all chickens raised and processed in the Delaware-Virginia-Pennsylvania peninsula and the Shenandoah Valley, will complete the virtual shutdown of north New Jersey poultry dealers, it was announced yesterday by Milton Schnoll, secretary of the New Jersey Live Poultry Dealers Association.

The region affected by the order, which is effective Dec. 11, Schnoll said, normally supplies 60 to 80 percent of the poultry needs of all east coast civilians.

He predicted the Government freeze will remain in effect for at least the first three months of 1945. During that time, he said, the army hopes to buy at least 2,000,000 pounds of poultry weekly.

Civil Employes Dine

More than 150 persons attended a luncheon of the Kings County Civil Service Employes Association yesterday in the Casablanca Restaurant, 74 Smith St. Joseph T. McGarry of the Surrogate's office is president of the group.

BROOKLYN EAGLE

BROOKLYN, N. Y., SUNDAY, DECEMBER 10, 1944

Eagle Staff photo

FREDERICK A. HELBY with his twilight scene. W. J. Bowdoin, director of the exhibit, looks on approvingly. Helby painted this picture after a brief visit, and was prompted by photographs taken in the area. Helby is a building superintendent.

Scratch Flatbush Housewife And You Discover an Artist

By MILDRED BEETMAN

Eight hours of the day Frederick A. Helby is superintendent of the Flatbush Chamber of Commerce building at 887 Flatbush Ave. In his blue work coat, he hires and fires the maintenance men, see that the elevators are in smooth working order and supervises the job of keeping the building clean.

At 5 p.m., however, he sheds the blue coat and the role of superintendent. He dons his own coat, says good night and goes to the door. By the time he steps on to Flatbush Ave., Helby the superintendent has disappeared and only Helby the artist remains.

One of the 26 artists whose works are now on display at the Chamber's tenth annual art exhibition, Helby is an illustration of the modern artist. Today's wielders of the brush no longer live in garrets and die of starvation. While waiting for their ships to come in, they don't disdain useful employment such as teaching, caring for a home—or acting as superintendents.

Helby, who believes artists should eat, spends only his evenings and days off producing landscapes, oil paintings of scenes in the Adirondacks.

With only the impressions of two weeks in the mountains, several photographs and three or four pencil sketches to go on, he produces detailed paintings in which every blade of grass and every shade of light speaks of realism. One of his landscapes of a stretch of countryside on Route A between Wells and Bakers Mills shows a typical country road at twilight with shadows in the foreground and light in the distance where the sun has just disappeared. It has been on exhibit at the Hall of Art at 5th Ave. near 36th St., Manhattan.

Eagle Staff photo

MRS. LOUISE H. NORBURY with her "The Lady of the Snows." Mrs. Norbury is one of twenty-six artists whose work is now on display.

Teacher Encouraged Him

Although Helby has never received formal art instruction, he has been interested in the subject since the time he dabbled in water colors at grammar school in Vienna. His teacher noticed his ability and encouraged him to continue with it. Since then he has been mixing art and maintenance work and finding out that the two don't conflict. His only contact with the art world has been through the National City Bank Art Club whose meetings he has been attending since 1936.

The exhibit, which will continue until Dec. 23, features oils, watercolors, black and white drawings and sculptures of Brooklyn artists. Each exhibitor is permitted to display two offerings not larger than 16x30 or one not larger than 30x36 which pass the inspection of a committee headed by W. G. Bowdoin, director of the exhibit, and three artists, Mr. Helby, Gustave Wiegand and Charles W. Townsend.

Jane Peterson, examples of whose art hang in the Brooklyn Athletic Club and the Society of Four Arts at Palm Beach, Fla., is the guest exhibitor this year. A one-time instructor for the Art Students League of New York, her portraits of a Wave, a Wac, a Spar and woman marine are at the City Center on W. 56th St., as a permanent war memorial.

Woman Sketches Botanic Garden

Art is a hobby for Mrs. Cornelia Durham, who has representations of scenes in the Botanic Garden at the exhibit. Like Helby, she is only a part-time painter, with housekeeping and a young son keeping her busy most of the time. When junior is in good hands, the petite, blonde artist goes off by herself to a secluded part of the Garden and sketches as long as the light is right.

For 50 years Charles W. Townsend, a tall, portly man, has been depicting everything from still life to portraits in everything from charcoal to oils. His first love, however, are landscape paintings, of which he has two, "Autumn in the Catskills" and "Winter Twilight," at the exhibit. Townsend devotes all his time to art and has sold more than 1,300 of his works.

Women are well represented at the exhibit, Mrs. Louise H. Norbury's "New Tenants" and "The Lady of the Snows" are two of the few watercolors on display. "New Tenants," a sunny painting depicting a family moving into a home in lower Flatbush, took two and a half hours to do and received honorable mention in an exhibit at the Argent Galleries, 42 W. 57th St., Manhattan. Now retired, Mrs. Norbury used to be an art supervisor in a New York grammar school.

Eagle Staff photo

MRS. CORNELIA DURHAM with her "October Gardens." Subjects chosen by the artists cover a wide range.

Eagle Staff photo

CHARLES W. TOWNSEND with his "Winter Twilight."

TEN BROOKLYNITES
And What They Think About Postwar Jobs

Availability of postwar jobs for returning GIs is one of the most pressing questions—and obligations—before the nation.

Should the Federal Government or private industry take the lead in providing jobs for veterans?

The answers of ten representative Brooklynites are published herewith.

BORO PRESIDENT CASHMORE

Taking the lead to provide jobs for the veterans is the responsibility of Government, private industry and organized labor.

The concurrent action of all these elements, so admirably effective in creating all-time production record, must be continued after the war. What we have accomplished to attain successes in battle will be needed to assure happiness for our returning service men. That means adequate work and fair compensation.

Borough President Cashmore

My office has been for many months preparing plans for extensive improvements in Brooklyn. These alone have an estimated cost of about $40,000,000.

HERBERT L. CARPENTER
Pres., Carpenter Container Corp.

If we are to win in America an enduring peace for which this terrible war has been fought, postwar jobs for our veterans must be provided in large part by private industry and business, whether it be as employe or the veteran establishing himself in his own business.

H. L. Carpenter

Upon the survival and healthy growth of American private enterprise depend the future happiness of our veterans and our nation and the gradual lifting of the heavy loads of taxation.

MARY E. DILLON
Pres., Brooklyn Borough Gas Co.

What is of prime importance is that the returning men get jobs and promptly.

Who gives the jobs is important, yes, but secondary.

How it can all best be done is a matter of administration. It requires masterly planning and close integration of private industry and Government resources. One should implement and sustain the other, and both should work indefatigably together in good faith to discharge with honor what becomes our number one obligation after the war—jobs for returning GI's.

Mary E. Dillon

JAMES V. KING
New York president, State, County and Municipal Workers of America.

We believe that the responsibility for insuring full employment and thereby insuring jobs for veterans rests with private industry but we also believe that the Federal Government has a responsibility to work with private industry to supplement its activities through Public works projects, etc.

James V. King

We are particularly concerned that the many thousands of small businesses should get from Government the necessary assistance and protection to guarantee that they will be able to make their contribution to production in the postwar world.

This would insure millions of additional jobs.

PHILIP A. BENSON
President, Dime Savings Bank

Private industry not only should, but will provide jobs for returning service men.

Naturally, they will take back all of the men and women formerly employed by the companies, but I believe there will be positions open for those veterans who left no jobs behind.

Without an undue interval between the war and revival of business, there will be a demand for every available person. I don't anticipate any economic slump, but rather a vast expansion of business with the great building needs and the postwar demand for new commodities.

Philip A. Benson

That depends a good deal on national policy governing foreign trade and taxation, but I believe that business will need the abilities of every man and woman willing and able to work.

MILTON SOLOMON
9 Prospect Park West

The Federal Government owes it to every returning veteran to do everything humanly possible to secure jobs for them immediately upon their return. With the Government's experience in control of industry during the war, it should be in a better position to handle the problem.

Milton Solomon

The Government has the machinery set up all ready and can accomplish the job of allocating veterans more quickly and efficiently than individual companies without such experience.

We don't want any time wasted in getting the veterans settled in the kind of work they want to do.

PFC. RALPH TEICHER
1420 Ocean Parkway

I don't think private industry is competent in itself to handle the job.

Just as the State would bungle a job like social security which has to be handled by the Federal Government private industry would be swamped by the tremendous amount of work involved in this task.

Pfc. R. Teicher

We need the Federal Government to co-ordinate the efforts of all industries. Through its over-all view, the Government could decide more readily where men are needed and see to it that they get jobs quickly.

MISS E. M. HUGHES
32 Court St.

There would be too much red tape with the Federal Government handling jobs for veterans. **Why, they wouldn't get their jobs until they were too old to need them.**

Miss E. M. Hughes

Private industry will want to build up their businesses after the war, and the new jobs they will have to create can go to the service men. They won't be held up by politics and legislation the way the Government would.

HARRY SANKIN
135 Eastern Parkway

Private industry should take the initiative in getting jobs for service men. Business, by expanding after the war, could absorb these men who in turn by their purchases would create jobs for more people.

Harry Sankin

I don't think the Government should be in business. It smacks too much of a permanent socialization of industry, which we don't want in this country.

Although the plan for Government control might start as a temporary proposition, it would be all too easy to relax and let the Government take over completely.

MRS. JOHN VILIAS
16 Court St.

Both should co-operate. **The job is too big for either business or the Government to handle alone.** The Government can't place people in industry without the consent of the company, and private industry can use the Government's help in determining where the men are most needed.

Mrs. John Vilias

I don't see that either one should take the lead, but both ought to work together now to prepare for the veterans' return.

Brooklyn's Man of the Week:

Solomon Is Wise to Ways Of Helping Worthy Causes

By VIOLET BROWN

By rights people should shudder when Moish shows up. (The name at his bar mitzvah was Morris Jonah Solomon, but even the New York Telephone Company lists him as "Moish.") He's always looking for a handout—for some one else. Doesn't matter what the cause—he collects with equally overpowering zeal for war bonds, Catholic seamen, the Salvation Army, Jewish orphans, the Red Cross or the Boy Scouts. He's been doing it for 35 years and by now his potential victims don't even bother arguing. They write the checks and cross their fingers that he won't raise the ante. And in symbol of their utter bondage, more than 1,000 of the most abundantly nicked the other day gave Moish a medal for being "Brooklyn's Citizen No. 1" and threw in a dinner complete with gefulte fish at the Hotel St. George besides.

Phenomenon that is Moish began in Williamsburg. Poor to begin with, the Solomons were poorer yet when the father died leaving four small children. Moish, then 16, became the breadwinner. He clerked in a law office and before and after work augmented his $6 a week serving summonses at $1 per head. Once he served a prize fighter right in the ring after a bout, pushing up front with the well-wishers. "I was four blocks away before he knew what I had hit him with," he explains.

It was while he was clerking for Judge William Rasquin that Moish began to do the first Solomon one better in regard to the lilies of the field. E. Berry Wall, Beau Brummell of his day, was one of Rasquin's frequent callers and the 19-year-old Moish fell, spats, vest and stickpin, for his wardrobe. Sported a combination of checked shirt, flashy vest and flamboyant tie from that time on until three years ago when he turned 50 and permitted himself to be convinced that it was time he looked a little less sharp. Now he wears white shirts but the ties are still the same—out of this world. He has about 300 (used to buy one every time he heard of a death but gave that up) and would have more except that if a man makes the mistake of admiring one of Moish's ties he has it in his mail the next morning. About the only man who could admire the Solomon ties with impunity was Father William Farrell, director of the Catholic Seaman's Institute, for which Moish raised some $50,000 this year. Obviously he wouldn't be able to use one.

Somewhere at the start of his organizational career, Moish founded the Elite Club, which has blossomed into one of the borough's more substantial institutions. Jack Davis, with whom he is now in the yarn business, was one of the co-founders and his best friend. They used to go up to Jack's house "for bagels and lox" and one evening Moish noticed that Jack's kid sister, Mollie, had grown up. And so they were married on June 10, 1922, the groom shaving off his mustache as a gift to the bride. They have one son, Irwin, who is a seaman first class on destroyer duty. Mrs. Solomon rarely sees her spouse but she sometimes runs into him at the Elite Club, where she is honorary president of the ladies auxiliary of the Morris J. Solomon Fund. This is a little idea of Moish's, supported out of his pocket largely, by which 1,500 Jewish families anonymously receive the wherewithal for their seders every Passover.

Obviously Moish has no time for rest or recreation in his schedule but a few years ago he bought a house at Wappingers Falls, N. Y. (His regular residence is at 510 Avenue T), where he goes whenever possible to relax. Here he puffs his dozen daily cigars, eats steaks, catches up on unread newspapers and sits. "I don't even pick up a leaf," says he. (He probably also duns his many guests for one of his causes, but they keep coming back anyhow.) With all this inactivity he has so endeared himself to the officials of Wappingers Falls that they throw him testimonial dinners, made him a deputy sheriff and gave him the freedom of the town, including the jail. Confidentially the inmates hope he never takes advantage of the offer. They're afraid their pockets will be picked—for charity, of course.

O'Loughlin Hears:

Big Bankroll To Win Brooklyn Favor for Coward

A good-sized bankroll is said to be in the making to back a movement to reinstate Noel Coward in the good graces of the people on this side of the river . . . Coward is the playwright who stirred a hornet's nest by an ill-timed slur against the soldiers from our borough. The Brooklyn Eagle spotted the obnoxious passage. Borough President John Cashmore, Congressman Dickstein and the Councilmen from Brooklyn went on record denouncing Coward.

The move to get Coward back in good standing is to be helped by specially spaced broadcasts, sugared pleas in certain columns and by other publicity.

Forty Years Ago—Forty years ago this month Supreme Court Justice Peter R. Smith was preparing to take office for the first time as an assistant D. A. under John Clarke. He made a distinguished record while serving as a prosecutor. He put in two terms under Clarke, until James C. Cropsey took office. After an interval ex-District Attorney Smith ascended the bench and has been there ever since . .

Who Were They, Jack?—Has Jack Gralla found out who were the two individuals in one of his election districts who voted for Dewey in the recent election? Every one else out there pulled the lever for Roosevelt. It upset the Brownsville leader because it marred an otherwise perfect score.

Peggy Bergen Still on Deck—A recent card of invitation from the 6th A. D. Republican Club, 44 Sumner Ave., to greet the new leader of the district, Assemblyman Robert J. Crews, reveals the fact that Marguerite B. Kuhn is still holding the fort as an associate executive member. It was as the popular Peggy Bergen that Mrs. Kuhn took hold years ago and helped materially to build up the women's half of the organization. I understand Peggy has lost none of her old-time charm and that her winning personality still has a lot to do with the regular vote that rolls around each election day to send a Republican Assemblyman to Albany in an otherwise heavy Democratic district . . .

The Nation
We Are Resuming the Grim Task of Winning the War

Returning to Brooklyn from various parts of the country, borough business men reported:

DETROIT
Walter Manning, president Atlantic Zinc Works, 210 Van Brunt St:

"I think the excessive optimism of three or four months ago is giving way to a realization that the war is going to last a little longer than had been expected this Summer. In Detroit especially, they don't see any immediate opportunity of starting on a postwar reconversion program but are settling down anew to a continuation of war production.

SOUTHWEST
Clinton W. Parker, assistant secretary Dime Savings Bank, 9 De Kalb Ave.:

"I found business conditions generally fine throughout Tennessee, Arizona, New Mexico, California and Texas. I stopped at various Rotary Clubs, talking to leading business men. **People seem to have a great deal of money and they are spending it.** Business conditions seem settled, there is a general feeling the good times are going to last."

CHICAGO AND DETROIT
Milton Dammann, president American Safety Razor Company, 315 Jay St.:

"I found business going at a very rapid pace in every phase of industry, wholesale and retail. While people recognize that there will be terrific problems of readjustment after the war is over, I think they are generally fairly optimistic."

FLORIDA
John H. Ungerland, vice president Quaker Maid Company, 68 39th Street:

"From present indications Florida is going to have a very busy tourist season; more than it can handle comfortably. Tourists, I should say, make up the State's biggest industry and that business is on the increase year after year. **This year people from the North have more money to spend and they will spend it.**"

Draft Ruling Chills Spirited Ball Trades

Dykes of Chisox Injects Some Life Into Meeting by Face-for-face Swaps

By HAROLD C. BURR

Big league owners are 16 frightened people today. Manager Jimmy Dykes of the White Sox has pumped the only sign of life into the Winter baseball meetings at a midtown hotel by figuring in all three deals made so far. Otherwise trading has been at a standstill, not a wheel turning except in the always busy rumor factory.

The biggest reason for the virtual shutdown is in the new draft ruling that calls for the mobilization of the 26 to 37-year-olds. Clubs are jealously clinging to what manpower they have left, not knowing who will go next. Baseball always scares easily.

Another reason why trading hasn't been as brisk as predicted is that six of the National and American League managers are overseas and a seventh is taking a vacation in California. Brooklyn's Leo Durocher, Mel Ott, Freddy Fitzsimmons, Frankie Frisch, Luke Sewell and Steve O'Neill are all on assignment by the USO to entertain our fighting men in France, the South Pacific, China and other theaters of war. The seventh is Connie Mack, who will eat his birthday cake with 82 candles on it in Los Angeles.

Face-for-Face Trades

Dykes' deals have all been what Joe Cronin calls face-for-face trades. Jimmy gave Whistling Jake Wade to the Yankees Monday for Johnny Johnson and yesterday swapped Skeeter Webb to the Tigers for Joe Orengo and gave up Eddie Carnett to the Indians for Oris Hockett—pitcher for pitcher, infielder for infielder and outfielder for outfielder, even up exchanges all, Cronin's new faces for old. Orengo and Hockett are former Dodgers. O'Neill will have his son-in-law playing for him. Webb is married to Steve's daughter.

The brass hats came through with the announcement of the committee that will rewrite the major and minor league agreement. The National Leaguers' personnel consists of Branch Rickey, Horace Stoneham, Sam Breadon, Warren Giles and Phil Wrigley. The Americans named Tom Yawkey, Alva Bradley, Jack Zeller, Don Barnes and their league lawyer, Joseph Hostetler. President Ford Frick will be the N. L.'s legal adviser. Breadon is the only selectee who signed the original 1921 pact.

The moguls check out today with a joint session of the two leagues. Night ball is still the big item to be cleared up. But it's expected that no restraint will be placed on the lavish arclight schedule that was adopted at Pittsburgh last Summer before the All-Star game. The American League has always been for leaving it up to the individual club owners and the National won't make a fight of it.

Four Support Minimum

Rickey will stick to his guns to have his Dodgers perform at Ebbets Field in a minimum of 14 combats, with the Reds, Giants and Pirates standing solidly behind the Mahatma of Montague Street. The Cardinals, Browns and Senators will again go in for heavy night work.

Meanwhile, the rumors of trades continued to fly far into the night. Manager Bob Coleman denied that the Dodgers had made any offer for Al Javery, his hard-luck Brave pitcher. The Cubs became competitors of Brooklyn for old Bear Tracks. But Owner Bob Quinn is said to have demanded Claude Passeau and a couple of other unnamed Bruins. Braves and Giants may yet get together . . . Phil Masi, the Hub catcher, for Doghouse Phil Weintraub.

Gus Mancuso, the veteran catcher recently released by the Giants, has been offered the job of managing the Richmond Colts in the Piedmont League, but Gus would prefer to coach in the big leagues. The Colts lost their pilot last year when Rickey brought in Ben Chapman to pitch winning ball for the Dodgers.

Yank-Bosox Deal On?

There was much dashing about the hotel lobby when it was learned that Cousin Egbert Barrow had gone into a huddle with Manager Joe McCarthy, Scout Paul Krichell and George Weiss, in charge of Yankee farm interests. Cronin joined the group behind locked doors and it was bruited around that the Yanks and Red Sox were going to make a deal. The Sox would ask for a first baseman and the Yanks an outfielder. Yanks and Indians are also said to have something on the fire.

The Giants are going to train at Baltimore if some final details can be arranged, passing up Lakewood, N. J., their northern base for the past two Springs, and the Braves are not going to return to the Choate School at Wallingford, Conn.

The Tigers are making no headway toward acquiring Shortstop Joe Sullivan from the Senators for their own shortstop, Joe Hoover, and Pitcher Johnny Gorsica.

Col. Larry MacPhail, gold eagles on his shoulders, received baseball's congratulations for his recent army promotion.

TOMMY HOLMES

Camilli Looks in At the Meetings

DOLPH — Those broad, square shoulders in the New Yorker lobby did look familiar and when the man turned around—well, darned if you didn't see the face of an old friend.

"The first time," said Dolph Camilli, "that I've ever been in New York in December. And I wouldn't be here now except that I couldn't get a reservation back to California until I hooked up with one on a train that leaves in just about an hour."

The rugged old first baseman, who was captain of Brooklyn's 1941 pennant winners and whose release to the Giants and temporary retirement in 1943 led to fan reaction that sizzled Branch Rickey's ears, looks fit.

But he smiled and shook his head when asked if he'd like to come back to the major leagues.

GOT "TIRED"—Camilli was player-manager at Oakland this past season.

"It was fine for a while," he said, "but toward the end of the season I got pretty tired. What's the use of kidding?

"I hit around .280 in about 120 games and had something like 15 home runs. Our park is pretty tough for home runs, you know. The right field fence isn't too distant but a strong wind blows steadily right over it and into home plate."

Dolph Camilli

Les Scarsella, formerly with the Reds and the Braves and recently drafted by the Phillies to play first base next season, was on Camilli's club. For most of the season, he and I were platooned at first base in the outfield while Dolph played first base. "But then," said Dolph, "I came up with a good kid first baseman and shifted to the outfield myself."

VAUGHAN DOUBTFUL—Mr. Vinegar Bill Essick, operative of the Yankees out on the Pacific Coast, vows, however, that Camilli was as fancy and as sure-footed around first base as ever.

"Just looking at him," said Vinegar Bill, "you couldn't see any reason why he ever dropped back from the majors."

Camilli was unable to bring any up-to-date news on Arky Vaughan, the Dodger shortstop who determinedly remained on his California ranch all through the late, lamented campaign.

"I saw Vaughan just once all Summer," said Dolph. "And that was only because he brought some cattle into town to sell. He looked fine, physically. At the time I thought there was a good chance that he'd play ball in 1945."

New draft regulations on the fire may reinfluence Vaughan to sit out another season. Another player with the Dodgers these developments may affect is Tom Seats, the left-handed pitcher drafted from the Coast a few weeks ago. Seats worked in a shipyard yet managed to get enough time away from his war job to win 26 games. Camilli, incidentally, thinks he is good.

YANKEE DEAL OFF — Col. Larry MacPhail buzzed hither and yon at the scene of the meetings. For weeks, the red-haired dynamo who never provided a dull moment in Flatbush, has been spearhead of a syndicate that aimed to buy the Yankees.

The underground says that this is now all off, that the Yankees have been withdrawn from the market.

The story is that the three ladies to whom the late Col. Jacob Ruppert willed his estate did wish to dispose of the ball club because they were staggered by the size of the inheritance tax.

The picture has changed because the Ruppert Brewery has made so much money that the tax is no longer a problem. And so the ladies, at least, are content to wait until the war is over and baseball picks up and the price of the Yankees will zoom.

That, at any rate, is the story I'm told.

CONCLUSION DEPARTMENT—On the ten-man joint committee named by the major leagues to draw up a new major-minor league agreement the name of Ed Barrow of the Yankees does not appear.

This is noteworthy because the man with the eyebrows is the only operator of an outstanding chain store baseball system who is not on the list, which includes such wholesale merchants in ivory as Sam Breadon, Warren Giles, our own Branch Rickey, Don Barnes, Jack Zeller and Tom Yawkey.

Not on the list are such celebrated elder statesmen as Connie Mack, Clark Griffith and Bob Quinn. They are real veterans of the game but they never have dipped intensively into chain store baseball.

The only conclusion to be drawn is that chain store baseball has won a victory over what its advocates undoubtedly would call the forces of reaction. No matter when or if a successor to the late Judge Landis is eventually selected, the chain store operators are bound to breathe more easily than they did in the last few years of old K. Mountain's reign. By that time, they will have formulated rules and regulations that will restrict the powers of the new commissioner.

THEY BATTLE UTAH IN GARDEN TONIGHT—The Redmen of St. John's have big job tonight in Garden—stopping lanky, speedy Utes of Utah. Left to right—Ivy Summers, Tom Larkin, Bill Kotsores, Murray Robinson, Vince Hurley, Roy Wertis, Joe Berreras and Hy Gotkin.

THE SPORTING THING

"The boss likes to know what's goin' on out in the plant!"

Cochran's Triumph In Billiards Earns Him $2,500, Bond

Welker Cochran of San Francisco won the world three-cushion billiard championship last night by defeating his old rival, Willie Hoppe of New York, 50 to 44, in 31 innings, completing his round robin of matches with nine straight triumphs, each against a different opponent.

Winning decisively over Hoppe, defending champion, whom he hadn't beaten in tournament competition since 1941, the San Francisco sharpshooter took an early lead in the third inning with his high run of seven billiards. Protecting his advantage of 11 to 4, he made it 17-8, 23-14, 31-25 and 32-29, the closest Hoppe got, before Cochran pulled away. Toward the finish he made it 43-35, 45-38, 47-41 and 48-42 and finished with two billiards to make the final count 50-44.

Cochran, by winning, gained first money of $2,500, plus a $500 war bond donated by an anonymous billiard fan. He also received a $300 trophy.

Rubin, who dropped his first four matches, finished with five straight victories, winning his final test against Joe Procita of Gloversville, N. Y., 50 to 45, in 41 innings.

He also distinguished himself with the only tournament victory over Hoppe, and by tying for the meet's high run of 12.

In the final match, Jay Bozeman of Vallejo, Cal., clinched third place by defeating Ralph Greenleaf of Detroit, 50 to 37, in 44 innings. Bozeman had a high run of six while Greenleaf's best was nine, his top effort.

Standing of the players:

	W.	L.	H.R.	B.G.
Welker Cochran, San. F.—	9	0	8	29
Willie Hoppe, New York—	7	2	8	20
Jay Bozeman, Vallejo, Cal.	7	2	9	36
Arthur Rubin, New York—	5	4	12	32
Ralph Greenleaf, Detroit—	4	5	9	28
John Fitzpatrick, Los Ang.	4	5	8	34
Joe Chamaco, Mexico City	4	5	9	41
Joe Procita, Glover'le N. Y.	3	6	9	32
Miguel Marquez, Mex. City	2	7	12	50
Andrew Ponzi, Philadelphia	0	2	9	—

Kingsmen Add to Slates

One contest each has been added to the Brooklyn College wrestling and swimming schedules, it was announced yesterday by Dr. Richard Boyce, faculty manager of athletics. The grapplers will entertain the Kings Point Merchant Marine Academy on Dec. 2, while the natators will be hosts to Rutgers University on Feb. 16.

Packer's Brock Ready for Big Jackpot Payoff

On Coach Steve Owen's admission, his big assignment this week will be to keep his Giants at their peak for Sunday's big jackpot game at the Polo Grounds with the Green Bay Packers for the pro football championship of the world. But that was before some bad news drifted in from Charlottesville, Va.

"We've been through four punishing encounters—and we've got to make it five in a row," said the still blissfully ignorant Stout Steve after yesterday's light preliminary workout. "It isn't easy to keep a team hot for a month at a solid stretch."

Owen, it develops, must realign his defenses. The Giants must stop a second scoring threat other than Don Hutson's deadly clutching hands. The Packers will have a ground punch, too. Word comes from the University of Virginia, where the Western champs are marking time, that Lou Brock is ready to resume his yard-eating romp over the chalkmarks.

Brock has been in drydock since midseason. He shakes a mean hip. For the first time in weeks Green Bay will have a dangerous running game to vary their overhead attack.

But the Giants themselves are straining their ears for the whistle and pawing, figuratively, of course, at the sideline turf to get at the Western Division champions. They are confident that they will meet the college All-Stars at Chicago in August, yearly reward of the National Football League titleholders.

Bill Paschal was excused from practice to give his sprained ankle another day of rest, but all the other cripples were out in uniform—Howie Livingston wearing his shoulder pad, Len Younce limbering up his stiff neck, Frank Liebel with his bruised fingers still not too sore to catch a pass, Carl Kinscherf stuttering through his split lip and Happy Sivell, his limp gone.

"This is my first playoff and I've been in the league six years," grinned Happy. "Just try and keep me out of it. That's all—just try," repeated the blood-thirsty creature.—**BURR.**

Sugar's Stout Shots Stop Sheik in 2d

Philadelphia, Dec. 13 (U.P.)—Ray (Sugar) Robinson, Harlem, 146½, stopped Richard (Sheik) Rangel, Fresno, Cal., 147, in the second round of a scheduled 10-round bout last night before 7,500 fans at Convention Hall.

Referee Charlie Daggert halted the contest at 2:50 of the round when Rangel came off the floor for the second time, helpless to defend himself.

Robinson dropped his Mexican opponent with a straight right to the jaw. Rangel got up at the count of nine and ran into a flurry of head punches which floored him for another nine count. Robinson was punching Rangel at will when the referee intervened.

White Plains, N. Y.—Pete Deruzza, 152½, Mamaroneck, N. Y., drew with J. C. Wilkins, New York, (8); Sal Amoroso, 125¼, New York, decisioned Bobby Henry, 131½, New York, (6); Bobby Brown, 160¼, Washington, D. C., knocked out Ralph Tiovelli, 160½, Poughkeepsie, N. Y., (3); Cosmo Ruggiero, 165, New York, knocked out Neal Stokes, 160¼, Detroit, (2); Earl Mintz, 127½, Newark, N. J., knocked out Percy Idlett, 123½, New York, (2).

Jersey City, N. J.—Joe Curcio, 148, Newark, stopped Oscar Suggs, 147, Providence, (2).

San Antonio, Tex.—Fritzie Zivic, Pittsburgh, and Camp Normoyle, here, decisioned Kid Azteca, Mexican welter, 10.

New Bedford, Mass.—Joey Gambar, 151, Newark, N. J., decisioned Mario Miceli, 155, Freeport, L. I., 10.

Private Schools Vie

The annual classic between St. Paul's School hockey club and Kent's School will be played in Madison Square Garden tomorrow afternoon. The game is scheduled to start at 3:15 o'clock. St. Paul's roster includes ten boys from New York City.

WHERE TO GET TICKETS FOR BOND SOCCER GAME

Tickets for the Sixth War Loan Indoor War Bond Soccer game may be obtained today and tomorrow until 3 p.m. at Bond's Department Store, 1530 Broadway. They are priced from $25 to $100 in war bonds.

After 3 p.m. tomorrow up until the start of the first game, at 8 p.m., tickets will be on sale at the 71st Regiment Armory, 34th St. and Park Ave., where the event will take place.

St. John's Needs Spirit To Cut Down Speedy Utes

By GEORGE COLEMAN

The St. John's Redmen aren't up to par. They know it, too. Nothing can be done about it for the Johnnies haven't anything too capable on the bench.

Garden customers will discover that tonight when the Tribe lines up against Utah University that also shows New York U. and the Oklahoma Aggies in another half of the doubleheader. Hy Gotkin, Bill Kotsores, Ray Wertis, Big Ivy Summer and Murray Robinson, either at par or below it, are scheduled to stay in the thick of it as long as they can stand.

"A couple of lickings may snap the boys into their National championship form, but that's an awful price to pay," said Coach Joe Lapchick yesterday. "And two beatings equals a poor season," he added.

The many freshmen on the squad haven't the experience while the few holdovers from last year can't seem to click with the regulars.

Larkin Coached

Lapchick has devoted much time to Tom Larkin, a tall, lean lad who is a fine shot, has speed and brains. He lacks only one thing—aggressiveness. Larkin is too easy-going.

The Johnnies could take a page out of Joe Byers' book. Seasons ago at Assumption Hall on Cranberry St., the Jersey Separates opened the campaign with a big, mild-mannered center. No other manager would use the big fellow because he lacked spirit. Yet, when he was rapped hard enough he was unbeatable. Smart opposing players would never rile the giant. But Byers took care of that. Usually in the first scrimmage, the teammate nearest the center hit, and hit him hard. That did the trick. Of course, collegians don't use that ruse, but then they might try it.

Lapchick, who scouted the Utes against St. Joseph's College last Saturday, says he's lucky in a way. The club is not as good as they were last season.

Ferrin Not Up to Par

Arnold Ferrin is the lone holdover from 'the nation's championship team and he isn't the scorer he was. Along with Ferrin, Coach Vadal Petersen has a group of long-limbed, speedy youngsters, but they are green as grass. If the St. John regulars can keep up with the Reindeer from Utah—and they can—it will be a smashing victory.

The Violets have a much more difficult problem than St. John's. They must stop the much-improved seven-foot Bob Kurland and the Oklahoma Aggies. Howard Cann and his cagers are going to use plenty of fight.

J. L. Parks

HOW GARDEN RIVALS LINEUP TONIGHT

First Game—8:15 o'Clock

Pos.	St. John's	Utah University
L.F.	Bill Kotsores	Lee Hamblin
R.F.	Ray Weris	Dave Howard
C.	Ivy Summer	Murray Satterfield
L.G.	Hy Gotkin	Arnold Ferrin
R.G.	Murray Robinson	George Keil

St. John's reserves—Frank Pare (5), Bill Shea (6), Joseph Barreras (7), Vince Hurley (8), Walter McCurdy (9), Jim Lennon (10), Ken Pressman (14), John Kaiser (15), Tom Larkin (17), Norman Ochs (19).

Utah reserves—George Smith (20), Wallace Jones (24), Ray Barnes (28), Don Dorton (29), Dwight Winslow (30), Anthony Tolich (32).

Officials—Hagan Andersen and Sam Schoenfeld.

Second Game

Pos.	N. Y. U.	Okla. Aggies
L.F.	Howard Sarath	Weldon Kern
R.F.	Al Grenert	Jack Lyons
C.	Herb Walsh	Bub Kurland
L.G.	Frank Mangiapane	J. L. Park
R.G.	Sid Tanenbaum	Gent Warren

N. Y. U. reserves—Fred Benanti (3), Jack Gordon (5), Donald Forman (8), John Derderian (9), Burton Monasch (10), Frank Alagia (12), Alvin Most (14), Marty Goldstein (17), Seymour Kravitz (18).

Oklahoma reserves—Harry Fennimore (22), Charles Crook (33), John Wylie (44), Doyle Johnson (75), Blake Williams (77), D. W. Jones (88), Joe Halbert (91).

Officials—Matty Begovich and William C. (Chuck) Solodare.

HOCKEY STANDING

LAST NIGHT'S RESULTS

Boston 7, Rangers 5.

	W.	L.	T.	Pts.
Montreal	11	4	1	23
Toronto	10	6	0	20
Detroit	9	4	2	20
Boston	8	9	1	17
Rangers	2	9	4	8
Chicago	2	10	2	4

TOMORROW'S GAME

Toronto at Montreal.

3-Goal Bruin Rally In Final Period Flattens Rangers

Boston, Dec. 13 (U.P.)—The Boston Bruins scored three goals in a fast final period last night to break a tie with the New York Rangers, who came from behind three times to tie the score and defeat the National Hockey League cellar dwellers, 7-5, before 10,000 fans at Boston Garden.

Rookie Winger Ken Smith led the Bruins with two goals and an assist while Herbie Cain collected two goals. Grant Warwick led the Rangers with a pair of tallies.

The Rangers' Wally Atanas and Defenseman Jack Shewchuk of the Bruins were knocked out when they collided 30 feet in front of the Boston net early in the second period. Shewchuk returned to the play but Atanas was carried off unconscious.

Bill Cupolo, assisted by Smith, broke the tie in the last period, and Smith and Cain scored again to build up the Bruins' margin. Warwick's second goal was the Rangers' final tally.

The lineup:

Pos.	New York	Boston
G.	McAuley	Bennett
R.W.	Warwick	Jennings
L.W.	MacDonald	Cain
C.	Watson	Cowley
R.D	Heller	Clapper
L.D.	Labrie	Crawford

New York Spares—Dill, Hunt, Atanas, Goldup, Thurier, De Marco, Shack, Moe.

Boston Spares—Shewchuk, Mario, Smith, Cupolo, Gaudreault, Calladine.

Referee—Bill Chadwick. Linesmen: Ag Smith, Bill Cleary.

SCORE BY PERIODS

Boston	2	2	3—7
New York	0	4	1—5

Scoring summary:

First Period—Boston: Smith (Crawford) 4:29; Cain (Cowley, Jennings) 8:20. Penalty: MacDonald.

Second Period—New York: Watson (unassisted) 12:04; Warwick (Shack) 13:56; Boston: Clapper (Jennings) 14:45; New York: Thurier (Goldup, Labrie) 17:07; Boston: Mario (Cupolo, Clapper) 18:17; New York: De Marco (MacDonald) 19:51. Penalties: Labrie, Mario.

Third Period—Boston: Cupolo (Smith) 3:42; Smith (Mario) 9:25; New York: Warwick (unassisted) 15:55. Boston: Cain (Cowley) 18:20. Penalties: None.

Dudley and Dobbs Duel Spices Randolph--Second Air Force Gam

By RALPH TROST

"I'll take Bill Dudley and ten chorus girls." That's the way Jack Lavalle sums up the coming Bond Bowl business in the Polo Grounds Saturday. The slightly stout Mr. Lavalle is sold on the Randolph Field Rambler's star back.

There is, of course, some chance that Jack, Notre Dame's scout extraordinary, is biased. He's been interested in Dudley ever since that potent ball carrier was an undergrad at Virginia. It wasn't Notre Dame interest, you understand. Lavalle was on the lookout for the New York Giants at the moment. Others were, too, notably some men from the Washington Redskins. But after a couple of looks at Dudley, Lavalle was certain that the boy had the stuff.

So, against that background, Jack picks the Randolph Field Ramblers to come out on top in that game against Lt. Glenn Dobbs and the rest of the Second Air Force team.

Warns About Dobbs

Lavalle, of course, has considerably more than bias to back him—and this no crack at Jack's svelte figure. The Ramblers have wrecked all opposition up to now. With poise, aplomb—and plenty of points. On the record, the Ramblers must be made favorite for they socked the Fourth Air Force team, best on the Pacific Coast. All the Second Air Force accomplished along these lines was to tie the Fourth.

"But don't overlook that Glenn Dobbs," Col. Don Storck warned Lavalle. Don is equally sold on the Randolph Field team, up to the hilt. But he's suspicious of the accomplishment of the Tulsa terror, Dobbs. Any man who could complete 14 out of 18 against the Chicago Bears, is not a man to be overlooked. Any one who saw Sid Luckman strut his stuff for the All-Army (meaning Camp Kilmer, mostly) team against the Brooklyn Tigers can understand this. Even dyed-in-the-wool sports writers of years standing—and, sometimes, boresome watching—would willingly have paid $2.40 for a view of Luckman that night in Ebbets Field. Dobbs, with a whole lot more in front of him that Sid had, can perform one or two minor miracles. It's well within reason.

Yes sir, there was a lot of gassing about the coming Bond Bowl game at the Lambert Trophy luncheon yesterday where Henry and Victor Lambert played host to a goodly crowd at the formal presentation of the Lambert Trophy to the Army (West Point) team. This presentation usually passes the Lambert Trophy to the team recognized as the best in the East. This year it went to the best in the nation. Collegiately speaking, at any rate.

Bill Dudley

Puff Two Cadets

Storck and Lt. Col. Andy Gustafson, who came from West Point to receive the trophy, had a bit of confab about this Army team. Storck was much interested in a youngster named Tucker. And a lad named Lombardo. Said Andy: "Don't worry a bit about that Tucker. He's got a lot of stuff. With half a break, he's not only our quarterback next year but even a possible All-America.

"Lombardo?" continued Andy. "There's the unsung hero of the Army team. It was more than poetic justice that he was running the team when we did our scoring against Navy. Tommy took on a heavy load. We put it up to him to operate our Plebe team in scrimmages. They made plenty of mistakes at first. But, well, you saw what a lot of these Plebes did to Navy. Tommy rates a lot of praise for that job."

This Bond Bowl game Saturday is definitely a success—from the Bond selling viewpoint. It'll top the Army-Navy total sure as shootin'. However, there are some tickets still available. At the established price of $2.40. And a bargain, at that figure.

WOMEN IN SPORTS

Abraham Lincoln High:

It happened in Oslo, Norway. Miss Bertha Ritchie, Lincoln's swimming coach, was visiting a school there, studying its outdoor pool. "The teacher was absent,' she recalls, "and I went to the dean and asked if I could take the class for the day." The dean gave his permission and Miss Ritchie took over. It seems that the girls had never heard of the back-stroke, but they had by the time the lesson was over.

"When I was finished, the girls asked me to be their teacher. There was another teacher absent that day—the one who played the piano for the gymnastics class, so, I took over for her, too. I teach piano after school."

That occurred on one of Miss Ritchie's many trips to Europe. There was one in 1933 when she taught life-saving and swimming in Sweden.

Miss Ritchie has been at Lincoln since 1930 and she has been teaching for 30 years. "Never late, never absent," she says proudly. Miss Ritchie estimates that she has put at least 5,000 girls through junior and senior life saving courses.

"My forte is life-saving," she adds. Life saving is her forte, for Miss Ritchie has been awarded a Croix de Guerre by the Red Cross for saving lives both on and off duty in pools and in the ocean.

The Swimming Club at Lincoln has approximately 120 members, with Hannah Strugatch, captain, and Vivian Sternbach, co-captain. Outstanding swimmers in the club are Hannah and Vivian, Roma Mittleman, Pearl Fink, Myra Shapiro, Lucille Cohen, Janis Levine, Caroline Schwint, Anita Schor, Paula Cohen ("one of the best," says Miss Ritchie), Renee Topol, Rita Silberlicht, Marilyn Fingerit and Louise Fernandez. Those girls can cover the length of the pool, 75 feet, in 20 seconds or less.

There aren't too many divers at Lincoln, but some of the better ones are Charlotte Rosmarin, Myra Shapiro, Hannah Strugatch, Paula Cohen and Vivian Sternbach. They each can do about six different dives, including the three compulsory ones, running dives, running jack and standing jack.

At the end of the term, there will be an intramural swimming meet.—JOAN CROSBY.

Racing Halted, Draft Reviews Ordered

SPORTS PROVIDED SOME THRILLS AS IT STAGGERED THROUGH THE YEAR

ACTION DURING ARMY-NAVY GAME WHICH WAS FINALLY PLAYED IN BALTIMORE. ARMY WON

ST. LOUIS CARDINALS HEADED FOR CLUBHOUSE CELEBRATION AFTER BEATING BROWNS IN WORLD SERIES

PENSIVE STEPPED OUT TO WIN PREAKNESS AFTER SCORING IN KENTUCKY DERBY, BUT COULD NOT WIN AGAIN AFTER THAT

DON HUTSON (LEFT) BEFORE HE GRABBED PASS AGAINST GIANTS AS GREEN BAY WON PRO CHAMPIONSHIP

ST. JOHN'S LOST TO UTAH IN NATIONAL FINALS AT GARDEN

Sports Staggered Along During Third Year of War

Pros Hit Hard By Manpower Losses in '44

By TOMMY HOLMES

Another year drifts toward its close and our fourth year of war has already begun. And sports keep staggering on.

If there is any lesson learned by this department in 1944 A. D., it is that the characteristic diversion of the American people is a rugged enough institution on this side of the waters to withstand almost anything.

That, if you please, is to the credit of the American people themselves.

There isn't any point in pretending that 1944 was a howling artistic success. It wasn't.

All professional sports suffered from the increasing losses of manpower to the armed forces or essential industry. The amateurs and the colleges were hit hard, too, and the uncertainty of wartime personnel made for frequent one-sided competition.

Turf Records Set

Horse racing, immune from most wartime troubles, set all kinds of attendance and betting records for the second successive year.

But the customers never complained about the caliber of competition in other sports. The public wanted sports, had the money to pay for sports and, by George, it got sports, even though an athletic purist sometimes shuddered.

I can't recall a more drab baseball season, but the major leagues drew well enough to make a profit. Most colleges which played football did not regret it. Professional football, like baseball, dipped close to the bottom of the barrel for material. It didn't seem to make much difference what, in the way of sports, was presented at New York's Madison Square Garden — the customers jammed the joint.

And so, if there is one outstanding sports figure of the year, he is old John Leonidas Public in person.

Among the other headliners you might include the St. Louis Cardinals, the Army and Navy football teams, Dixie Walker, St. John's and Utah on the basketball court, the Green Bay Packers and Steve Owen, Slats Marion and Hal Newhouser, Beau Jack and Bob Montgomery, Frankie Parker and Pauline Betz, the Montreal Canadiens, the St. Louis Browns, Carl Widdoes and Ohio State, Twilight Tear and Pavot, Joe Baksi, Byron Nelson, Felix Blanchard and Glen Dobbs.

They were among the best we had in 1944, and that seemed to be good enough for the fans.

MARTY MARION, Cardinals shortstop, was named most valuable in National League.

BATTING CHAMP—Dixie Walker, Brooklyn's popular outfielder, gained National League batting championship.

Baseball Scene Dominated by 2 St. Louis Entries

In baseball our big league picture was entirely dominated by the ball clubs from that old trading post on the west bank of the Mississippi. It was an old story for the St. Louis Cardinals, who romped to their third straight National League flag but a brand, new wonderful tale to the Browns, who won the very first American League pennant in their history.

Billy Southworth's Rapid Redbirds constituted the only thoroughly sound ball club left in the third year of war. They managed to retain such everyday stars as Slats Marion, Stan Musial, Ray Sanders, Whitey Kurowski, Johnny Hopp, Walker Cooper and Danny Litwhiler. Morton Cooper again was the ace of a pitching staff that possessed both quality and depth. They made a joke of the N. L. race. Despite a September letdown and a bad late slump they were 14½ games of the second place Pittsburgh Pirates at the finish line.

With the campaign in the National League a one-sided boat race, the American League furnished all of the drama after the first six weeks of the season. Pounding down the September stretch no fewer than four clubs wer in the running less than two weeks from the finish. Then Boston and New York faded, while St. Louis and Detroit fought it out. Three days and four games from the finish the Tigers led the Browns by a game. But St. Louis then swept a four-game series with the Yankees, while Detroit was losing two out of four to the tail-end Washington Senators.

Decided on Last Day

The pennant was decided on the very last day when Chet Laabs hit two home runs to spark the final Brownie victory over the Yanks while Washington's Emil Leonard's tight pitchin defeated Detroit.

Judged by any sort of pre-war standards, the victorious Browns were just another ball club. Luke Sewell's team did have the virtue of balance and a long line of good journeyman pitchers. Probably Detroit would have won if it had the services of Dick Wakefield, it's leading hitter all season. The Tigers picked up fast after Wakefield was released by the Naval Air Force in June. In Hal Newhouser and Dizzy Trout, Steve O'Neill had the two top pitchers in the league.

Class told in the St. Louis family circle World Series. After trailing at the end of the first three games, the Cardinals took three straight to win, four games to two. The annual All-Star game in Pittsburgh was also a National League victory by a score of 7 to 1.

For our Brooklyn Dodgers the second year of Branch Rickey's

PAVOT, unbeaten two-year-old, winning $76,000 Belmont Futurity.

reign in Flatbush proved a period of painful travail. Dixie Walker's capture of the batting championship was the one cheering note as the Dodgers floundered into seventh place only a game and a half above the tail-end Phillies. It was the first time in six years of Leo Durocher's management that Brooklyn finished in the second division, but Leo was re-engaged for 1945 nevertheless.

Most valuable players were Slats Marion and Hal Newhouser. The American League batting champ was Lou Beaudreau, shorstop-manager of the Indians.

Predominant baseball trend of the year was toward unlimited night games and, by all odds, the most important off-the-field occurence was the death of Kenesaw Mountain Landis, high commissioner of the game since 1921. The two league presidents and Leslie O'Connor, long-time secretary to Landis, were named to serve as high council of the game until committees from each league can draw up a new major league agreement.

Horse Racing Most Fortunate of All Wartime Sports

Most fortunate of all wartime sports is racing. Everything seems to play into the hands of track operators. Manpower losses have been negligible. There is no shortage of horses. And probably most important, all kinds of floating money is abroad in the land.

Racing plants broke all kinds of betting records in 1943. In the year drawing to a close they exceeded all the marks set in the previous season. In 1943, for example, a total of $285,000,000 was wagered at the three New York tracks alone. In 1944 betting at Belmont, Jamaica and Aqueduct approximated $400,000,000. It is estimated that horse players left $46,000,000 at the New York tracks in 1944.

Artistically, there were two standout horses. One was Twilight Tear. The other Pavot.

Won 14 Out of 17

Twilight Tear, black three-year-old filly from the Calumet Stables, rates comparison with the great lady horses of all time. She won 14 races in 17 starts, was recognized as the horse of the year after she impressively defeated Devil Diver and Megogo in the Pimlico Special.

Pavot, a brown two-year-old colt

But There's No Complaint From Customers

owned by Walter M. Jeffords, won all seven starts including the Hopeful and the Belmont Futurity. His claim to top honors in his division is not entirely clear because Free For All also was an undefeated two-year-old, winning three starts including the futurities at Arlington and Washington Park.

Pensive, Calumet stablemate of Twilight Tear, won both the Kentucky Derby and the Preakness, then failed to finish first in any race for the remainder of the year. The Belmont Stakes went to Bounding Home. When all the returns were in it is likely that the best three-year-old colt of the year was By Jimminy. He missed the classic races but won six sizable stakes including the Dwyer and the American Derby.

Devil Diver Stands Out

Among the handicap horses Devil Diver was generally considered the best despite his defeat at the hands of Twilight Tear and despite the fact that the five-year-old Greentree star encountered bad racing luck at several points of the season.

Finally, the racing associations are proud of the fact that they contributed something like $2,000,000 to charity. But there still has been no action regarding the "breakage" which, at New York tracks this year, amounted to more than $3,000,000 and was confiscated by the State and the various tracks.

Army Grid Forces In Class All By Themselves

To the satisfaction of most of us, the college football championship of the land was decided on Dec. 2. That cold, raw day in Baltimore, the Cadets of West Point trounced the Midshipmen of Annapolis, 37—7, in what some called the gridiron "game of the century."

It is entirely natural but comforting nevertheless that the Army and the Navy should present the most powerful football squads of all in a wartime year. And this season, Navy was good. But Army stood all by itself.

Doubtless, the team fashioned by Col. Red Blaik and his coaching aides up on the West Point plains was one of the top college football machines of all time. There was a whole regiment of good Army backs. The trio which earned the greatest recognition consisted of Glenn Davis, who racked up 20 touchdowns to become the nation's top scorer; Felix (Doc) Blanchard, a bruising plebe fullback who wrecked the opposition, and Doug Kenna, who quarterbacked brilliantly in Army's T attack. The West Point line was generally underestimated until the Navy game in which it outplayed the Annapolis forward wall, which had been considered the strongest in the country.

Scored 504 Points

This was the first Army victory over Navy in six years. Among the other Cadet triumphs was a smash-

DOC BLANCHARD supplied power in Army backfield as Cadets swept schedule.

MANAGER Billy Southworth led St. Louis Cardinals to National League pennant and World Series victory.

ing 59—0 victory over Notre Dame. Army had not beaten the Fighting Irish since 1931. All told, Army registered 504 points and yielded only 35 while racking up 10 victories.

The two servcice schools completely dominated Eastern football but one noteworthy achievement beyond their influence was registered by Eli Yale. Under Coach Howie Odell, the Bulldogs swept to an undefeated season. They were, however, held to a tie by Virginia in their final game.

In general, the better teams throughout the country were those owning squads generously loaded with navy and marine trainees in pre-combat courses. A notable exception was Ohio State, an all-civilian team which, coached by a competent newcomer named Carl Widdoes and spearheaded by a brilliant back named Les Horvath, won 10 straight and the Western conference title.

In other sections of the country, the final returns are not yet in due to the New Year's Day Bowl games.

Duke Bounced Back

In the South, the situation was considerably scrambled by Duke, which bounced back from a string of early defeats to beat Georgia Tech, conqueror of Navy, and to hand Wake Forest its first defeat. Although also beaten by Notre Dome, Georgia Tech probably has the most valid claim to the Dixie championship. In the Southwest, Oklahoma A. and M., by virtue of victories over Texas and Arkansas, looks best. Southern California was a standout on the Pacific slope.

Randolph Field's unbeaten and untied Ramblers, featuring Bill Dudley and eight other former professionals, took the honors among the service teams. Appearing at the Polo Grounds on Dec. 16, the Remblers had their closest call when they defeated the Superbombers of the Second Corps Area, 13—6, in a bond game to aid the 6th War Loan drive.

St. John's Again Suffered Setback In Red Cross Play

For the second successive year St. John's University of Brooklyn won the Madison Square Garden Invitation basketball tournament, only to fall before a team from the Rocky Mountain regions in the Red Cross struggle of champions.

Capably coached by Long Joe

Continued on Following Page

Racing Is Halted; All Pro Athletes Faced With Draft

Horse, Dog Tracks to Close By Jan. 3 Under Byrnes Request

Continued from Page 1

majority of whom are physically by-passed 4F's for their talent and even the loss of a small percentage of players would be likely to make it impossible for some teams to continue.

It appeared almost certain that the move, unless rescinded by the time that the season begins, would force suspension of numerous minor league circuits.

The same holds true for professional golf, football, and hockey, all of which have a large percentage of physically deferred athletes.

Racing Ban Announced

The racing and professional athletics orders were announced separately. The virtual ban on racing was announced in mid-afternoon, and was ascribed to the need of conserving manpower and transportation facilities. The action involving athletes was announced at 6 p.m.

Both came as a complete surprise. Racing was about to begin its Winter season. Professional sports officials this month have been discussing plans for 1945 and ways and means by which they could carry on in view of critical manpower shortages, but few believed their teams and leagues would be the object of such a pointed and sharp program as that announced by Byrnes.

The War Department early this month announced that henceforth no "name" athletes or other notables could be discharged from the army until after their cases had been reviewed in Washington. That order in itself was regarded as a blow to professional baseball and football—but it was nothing compared with Byrnes' announcement tonight.

Byrnes wrote Hershey he had been advised that in some cases professional athletes were not inducted because of "alleged physical unfitness," while in others they were inducted and later discharged.

Refers to Board Review

Byrnes disclosed that Hershey advised him on Dec. 15 that he was "directing that the local boards review the classification on men known to be engaged in professional athletics who have been deferred because of failure to meet the physical qualifications for service, or who have been in one of the services and have been discharged therefrom."

Byrnes said that Hershey also wrote him that Gen. George C. Marshall, on orders of the Secretary of War Henry L. Stimson last Nov. 29, issued a regulation which prohibited discharge from the army of any "big name" athletes or amusement stars without review of his case by the War Department.

Quoted by Byrnes in his statement, Marshall's regulation read in part:

"For example, to discharge a well-known professional football player for physical disability when that individual is able to participate in professional games immediately after discharge is obviously inconsistent.

"While it is not intended to discriminate against any group in the matter of opportunities for discharge, cases involving the discharge of nationally prominent athletes, stage, screen and radio stars, etc., which might occasion criticism of War Department discharge policies, will be referred to the War Department for final determination."

The order came as racing was about to begin its Winter season, Fair Grounds at New Orleans having opened today. Tropical Park was scheduled to open Monday and Santa Anita at Arcadia, Cal., was preparing to open Dec. 30. The order also followed what was racing's banner season in 1944 so far as attendance and betting was concerned.

Hope for Resumption in Spring

In disclosing that racing was willing to comply with the request because the "war comes first," hope was expressed that the war situation may be such to permit its resumption in the Spring in time to hold such features as the Kentucky Derby, the Preakness and the Belmont Stakes.

Byrnes issued his statement from the White House and revealed that his action had been approved by President Roosevelt.

He requisted the closing of horse race tracks only, but his office explained that it included dog racing tracks.

Charles S. Howard, one of America's leading turf men, said the request was "disappointing."

Agree War Effort Comes First

He added, however, that "all owners and track operators agree that the war effort is paramount."

Brynes' announcement caught most horse owners by surprise. They had shipped their horses to California, Louisiana and Florida for the Winter season and indications were that there would not be any transportation facilities available to shift the horses home.

Byrnes' statement did not formally order the tracks to close, but he made it clear that he would use the weapons at his disposal to prevent racing "until war conditions permit."

Byrnes said he had asked the

Contnued on Following Page

St. John's Wins As L. I. U. Bows— Gotkin Injured

By HAROLD PARROTT

St. John's and De Paul U. of Chicago were spectacular winners in Madison Square Garden doubleheader last night, although they did it different ways. Both were one-sided favorites in the gamblers' odds.

The Brooklyn Redmen, trailing for 16 minutes of the first half, played a brilliant 20 minutes after Hy Gotkin, their little sparkplug, was carried off the court, and sped off with a 41 to 35 victory as 18,196 yelled themselves hoarse. It was the biggest crowd of the court season that saw the Johnnies play a close first half, jump out to a 15-point lead in the second session, and then slump at the finish.

De Paul's Demons moving like something shot out of a gun, jumped out to an 18—3 lead in the first five minutes, and, although L. I. U. crept up to within 8 points (39—31) at the half, the Chicagoans swept to a 74—47 victory. Gene Stump, not the widely publicized Mikan, led De Paul with 21 points, 9 of them in swift succession in the first half.

Lose Gotkin Early

St. John's lost Gotkin after four minutes of the first half. It was thought the midget's collapsible knee had caved in as he was carried from the court, but his trouble was diagnosed as a sacroiliac condition. Oddly enough St. John's had only a 23—19 lead when Gotkin left, but Bill Kotsores stepped into othe leader's role and hopped the Redmen up so that they produced their best basketball of the season. The Johnnies jumped out in front, 38—23, and only a closing Puerto Rico rally with the Indian seconds in the game closed to gap to 41—35.

Although both Ivy Summer and Ray Wertis had 10 points each, and Kotsores scored only one field goal, it was the latter who played the outstanding ball for the Indians.

Although De Paul never was in any danger, L. I. U. crept up to

Continued on Following Page

Eagle Sports Photo

GETS POSSESSION—Bill Kotsores, No. 3, St. John's, retrieves ball off backboard, as Roque Diaz, No. 42, Puerto Rico, makes vain attempt to beat him to the snare in first game of Garden doubleheader last night. Ray Wertis, No. 4, St. John's, and Pedro Borras, No. 40, are also ready but have to assume the roles of onlookers.

BOUDREAU'S .327 LOWEST TITLE AVERAGE SINCE '08

By HAROLD C. BURR

Lou Boudreau didn't let the cares of managing the Cleveland Indians and locking the door of the doghouse on his rebel pitcher, Jim Bagby, get him down at bat. The Tribe's shortstop won the American League batting championship with .327, as revealed by the junior loop's official figures.

It's the lowest title average since Ty Cobb's .324 turned the trick in 1908 and the third lowest in league history. Elmer Flick, another Clevelander, hit the all-time low in 1905 with .306. Luke Appling last year was one point higher than Boudreau. Dick Wakefield hit .355 for the Detroit Tigers but wasn't around long enough to qualify.

The best of the Yankees was George Stirnweiss, who took part in every one of the Yankees' 154 games. He hammered out 205 hits, the only player to hit 200 or more. Snuffy knocked George Case from his base stealing five-year reign. The Yankee bas burglar purloined 55 sacks against 49 for the Washington Express. He scored the most runs and shared the triple-hitting honors with his Yankee buddy, Johnny Lindell, each slamming out 16 three-baggers. Stirnweiss was third in batting. Nine American League regulars hit .300 or better.

The only other Yankee to stay in there for every game was Nick Etten, and shades of Babe Ruth, led the home run hitters with 22 circuit clouts.

The Red Sox took the team batting title with .270, with the Yankees in the third slot with .264. The Browns, who won the pennant to the surprise of everybody were seventh, beating out the White Sox alone.

(Averages on Following Page)

O'Dwyer Wins John Doe Bribe Probe

7 ★★★★★★★ Complete

BROOKLYN EAGLE

WEATHER—Snow, sleet, rain tonight; clear, warmer tomorrow.

104th YEAR • No. 42 • DAILY AND SUNDAY • BROOKLYN, N. Y., TUESDAY, FEBRUARY 13, 1945 • • 3 CENTS IN NEW YORK CITY ELSEWHERE 4 CENTS

REDS CAPTURE BUDAPEST; NEW GAINS BY 3D ARMY

O'DWYER WINS JOHN DOE QUIZ IN CAGE BRIBE

Leibowitz Orders Public Hearings on Amateur Sports to Open Monday

A public John Doe investigation of bribery in amateur sports today was asked for by District Attorney William O'Dwyer and, on the prosecutor's petition, granted by County Judge Leibowitz.

Today's action is in line with an editorial in the Brooklyn Eagle of last Wednesday, headed "A Public John Doe Probe Is Needed in Basketball Case."

The investigation will start at 10 a.m. Monday, with Judge Leibowitz presiding as a committing magistrate.

In the words of the petition, the probe will go into "certain crimes, irregularities and conditions injurious to the public welfare in the matter of certain athletic contests"—meaning amateur sports such as the unplayed Brooklyn College basketball game which five college athletes admitted they intended to "throw" in return for a $1,000 bribe. The five were expelled from school.

Full Inquiry Ordered

General O'Dwyer called for—and the court ordered—"a full and complete investigation of the widest scope."

Not only the specific game involved will be taken up, but also such questions as the participation of colleges in professionally promoted college games, the effect on the student athletes of playing in an atmosphere lacking "the clean, wholesome safeguards of the campus" and why star players of military age are not in the armed forces.

The prosecutor stressed the point that the inquiry should be out in the open and not in the secrecy of the grand jury room.

Assistant District Attorney Charles N. Cohen, chief of the County Court division of the District Attorney's office, was placed in charge of the investigation.

O'Dwyer, in the statement read by Cohen, questioned the wisdom of permitting college teams to play in Madison Square Garden. He asked the court to determine "whether it is dangerous to the welfare of students and colleges . . . to be subjected to an atmosphere wherein the clean wholesome safeguards of the campus and faculty advisers are absent, and where they are replaced by professional exploitation of the exhibition."

O'Dwyer added that "men and women in the armed services and their relatives will be interested in knowing how men fit for strenuous athletic activities could have obtained release from the armed

Continued on Page 5

24 Dead in Crash Of Navy Plane

Alameda, Cal., Feb. 13 (U.P.)—A navy twin-engined transport plane crashed into San Francisco Bay today and 21 passengers and three crewmen were presumed to be killed.

At 12th Naval District headquarters at San Francisco, officers said one body had been recovered. The plane, a C-47 transport, took off from Oakland Airport and crashed 15 minutes later.

Numerous Alameda residents heard the crash.

The plane was about three-quarters of a mile off shore.

Truck, $700 in Meat Stolen as Driver Eats

A refrigerator truck loaded with one and a half tons of meat was stolen this morning while the driver sat in a restaurant at 64 Railroad Ave., Jersey City, having breakfast, according to police.

The load of assorted meats, valued at $700, belonged to the Western Trucking and Forwarding Company of Jersey City. The truck driver was Adam Kliniecki, 30, of Jersey City.

Four-Front War to Doom Nazis Believed Near as Parley Result

British Official photo

THEY ARRIVE AT HISTORIC AGREEMENT AT CRIMEAN CONFERENCE—On grounds of Livadia Palace at Yalta, during eight-day war-and-peace conference, are the "Big 3"—Prime Minister Churchill, left, President Roosevelt and Premier Stalin—and behind them, left to right, Field Marshal Sir Harold Alexander, Field Marshal Sir Henry Maitland Wilson, Field Marshal Sir Alan Brooke, Admiral of the Fleet Sir Andrew Cunningham, Gen. Sir Hastings Ismay, Marshal of the Air Force Sir Charles Portal, Admiral Leahy, General Marshall and Russian delegates.

BALTIC AREA INVASION IS EXPECTED

By W. R. HIGGINBOTHAM

London, Feb. 13 (U.P.)—Adolf Hitler's Germany today faced its doom in a four-front war with the knowledge that the Big Three were more closely united for victory than at any time in the World War II.

Already there were signs the epic decisions of the Crimea Conference were being implemented and that steps to seal Germany's fate and erect a new and permanent postwar peace structure were under way. Military observers believed the Big Three may have planned an invasion of southern Norway, Denmark or even the German Baltic coast.

Hints were present that decisions of consequence to the Pacific war rivaling those affecting Europe may also have been reached although all parties to the eight-day conference were significantly silent on this point.

Faces Attacks from All Sides

Today's developments included:

1—In Both London and Moscow military experts believed Germany must now face attacks from all sides of the fast-shrinking inner Nazi citadel; in addition to possible landings in Norway and Denmark, an all-out offensive in the west seemed likely; continuation of the crushing Red Army offensive in the east was seen with new attacks from the southern Allied spearheads in Italy and Hungary.

2—German propagandists, prepared for a Big Three peace bid along Wilsonian lines, were caught flat-footed by the unequivocal declaration that "Germany is doomed." For hours they offered no propaganda line to radio listeners within the Reich. To foreign audiences they inveighed uncertainly about

Continued on Page 5

PUNCHES 2 HOLES IN SIEGFRIED LINE PILLBOX DEFENSES

By JACK FLEISCHER

Paris, Feb. 13 (U.P.)—Lt. Gen. George S. Patton punched two new holes in the Siegfried pillbox belt north Echternach today, giving them three possible gateways to the Rhineland.

Canadian 1st Army units beat down brisk German counterattacks and suddenly stiffened resistance to score new gains in the offensive against the northern end of the Westwall.

Units of seven German divisions had been counted in the forces bracing against Gen. H. D. G. Crerar's push toward the Ruhr and Rhineland. The Germans appeared to be throwing in reinforcements at the expense of other portions of the Western Front.

Heavy Fighting Rages

Heavy fighting now was going on along an arc of 12 to 15 miles southwestward from the Rhine above the village of Griethausen, three miles northeast of Cleve. The village fell to Canadian troops who crossed the railway northeastward from Cleve.

The 80th and 5th Divisions of Patton's 3d Army shouldered past the concrete forts of the Siegfried

Map on Page 2

belt at points northwest of Echternach. Farther to the north Patton had a break through the West Wall in the Prum area.

The 4th Division rooted out the last sniper in Prum and repulsed two severe counterattacks across the Prum River northeast of the town.

Erase Ardennes Memory

To the south other 3d Army troops erased one of the last memories of the Ardennes bulge when they captured Vianden, lower anchor of the old St. Vith-Vianden line across the base of the salient.

The Germans, after losing more than 5,000 captives in the opening five days of the Ruhr-bound attack, were trying with partial success to establish a new defense line just east of the Reichswald, extending southward from the Rhine to the Goch area.

Fierce Battles Rage

Fierce tank and infantry battles were reported raging all along the makeshift Nazi defense line early today, although the flooded terrain prevented both sides from bringing their full armored strength to bear.

Farther south, the British 2d and American 1st and 9th armies were moving into position for a general offensive across the swollen Roer River into the Cologne plain.

The river still was running over its banks at a number of points as a result of the partial demolition of the Schwammaneul dam below Aachen, and there was no confirmation of an Atlantic Radio report that the three Allied armies already had opened their attack.

STALIN REVEALS REDS' CAPTURE OF BUDAPEST

Russians Shatter Nazi Defense Line On Bober River

BULLETIN

London, Feb. 13 (U.P.)—Marshal Stalin announced today that the Red Army had captured Budapest, capital of Hungary.

London, Feb. 13 (U.P.)—The German high command reported today that a Russian drive fanning out through Silesia toward Dresden and Berlin had carried to the Queis River, 7 to 10 miles beyond the breached Bober River line west of the Oder.

Both Moscow and Berlin said Marshal Konev's 1st Ukrainian Army was running rampant on a broad arc northwest of Breslau. His vanguard was beating into the Saxony border area some 70 miles from Dresden and swinging northwestward on the broad plain to Berlin.

The Berlin radio reported Soviet attacks toward Sommerfeld. This rail junction on the Luebst River is 72 miles southeast of Berlin and the same distance northeast of Dresden.

Say Front Is Crumbling

"There is every indication that the German front in Silesia is crumbling, and the roads to Dresden and Leipzig seem wide open to Konev's army," a Moscow dispatch said.

The Queis, a tributary of the Bober, flows seven miles west of it in the area of Soviet-captured Bunzlau and 10 miles separate the Rivers a little farther north.

Other Soviet forces to the north resumed their march toward the Baltic coast along a 200-mile front between the Vistula and Oder Riv-

Continued on Page 2

O'Toole in South for Health

Representative Donald J. O'Toole is in St. Petersburg, Fla., recovering from illness which struck him last week, his secretary, Richard J. Cantillion, announced today.

Foes of Anti-Bias Bill Force Public Hearing

Special to the Brooklyn Eagle

Albany, Feb. 13—The fight here over the Ives-Quinn bill to outlaw racial and religious discrimination in employment took an unexpected turn here today when foes of the measure won out in a demand for a public hearing on the bill before it goes to a final vote in the Legislature.

With only two negative votes being cast, the Republican-controlled Senate Finance Committee, at a meeting behind closed doors, agreed to order a public hearing when and if the bill is passed in the Assembly, where the measure is now on the calendar and is slated for a vote next week.

Senator Arthur H. Wicks, Kingston Republican and chairman of the Senate Finance Committee, and Senator Walter J. Mahoney, Buffalo Republican, were the only committee members voting against the hearing proposal.

The committee's action caught supporters of the measure by surprise.

The drive in the committee to force the hearing was led by Senator Frederic R. Coudert, Manhattan Republican.

The Senate committee's action followed the reading of a letter by Senator Coudert from Mark A. Daly, executive vice president of Associated Industries, Inc., who said he had received "word from various New York City groups to the effect that they believe the discrimination issue should be reopened and addi-

Continued on Page 5

6-Inch Snowfall Predicted as New Storm Hits City

Springlike weather, which gingerly entered on 40 degree temperatures early this morning, was given the bum's rush by rain, sleet and snow driven on a 25-to-35-mile-an-hour wind, which, the Weather Bureau said, might pile up six inches of snow before the day is over.

It was pointed that the heavy snow is a part of an Atlantic Coast storm and that "conditions today are almost identical to the combination of factors that produced last week's heavy snowfall."

The report emphasized that there is no relationship between the present storm and the tornadoes which have done considerable damage in the South Central States.

Warning flags were hoisted along the coastline to apprise small craft of the storm.

Corona Woman Seized On Charge of Bigamy

Mrs. Anna Moran, 22, of 55-25 96th St., Corona, will be arraigned today in Ridgewood Felony Court on a charge of bigamy.

Mrs. Moran was arrested last night on complaint of her husband, William J. Moran of 47-34 11th St., Long Island City, who, police said, charged his wife was married recently to Frank Cincotto of 24 Westmoreland Ave., White Plains.

65 From Area Killed in Action

The War Department, today announcing the names of 1,908 soldiers killed and 2,089 wounded in action, listed 65 Brooklyn, Queens and Long Island men killed in the Asiatic, European and Southwest Pacific areas, and 49 Brooklyn, Queens and Long Island men wounded in the European area. The navy listed two local men wounded and one missing. Local casualty lists are on Page 7.

Call the Brooklyn Chapter, American Red Cross, and arrange to donate a pint of blood NOW. TRiangle 5-8040.

Borough Man Gets Connecticut U. Post

Storrs, Conn., Feb. 13 (U.P.)—Dr. Fritz Semmler of 440 Lenox Road, Brooklyn, has been appointed to the department of foreign languages at the University of Connecticut. President A. N. Jorgensen announced today.

Dr. Semmler, a translator for the War Department since 1942, temporarily succeeds Dr. Theodor K. Siegel, who recently was convicted in Federal Court of "fraudulently and illegally" obtaining U. S. citizenship in 1936. Dr. Semmler, German-born, was naturalized in 1935 and served on the faculty of Hunter College and Long Island University.

CONGRESS HAILS BIG 3 PLEDGE OF POSTWAR UNITY

Treaty Framework Set for Conference Here on April 25

By LYLE C. WILSON
United Press Staff Correspondent

Washington, Feb. 13 (U.P.)—The Roosevelt-Stalin-Churchill conference report got an enthusiastic cheer from Congress today in its proposal that the United States, Russia and Great Britain be bound in postwar unity as a "sacred obligation" to the peoples of the world.

President Roosevelt, Marshal Josef V. Stalin and Prime Minister Winston Churchill made that postwar compact the foundation of their "report and statement" on the Crimean conversations.

To achieve it they announced they had summoned the United Nations to conference in San Francisco on April 25 to draft a world security treaty. It will be in the Dumbarton Oaks pattern. The Black Sea conferees announced they had reached final agreement on treaty framework, including voting methods.

Announcement yesterday of completion of the Roosevelt-Stalin-Churchill conversations and of the April conference call opens the administration campaign to present the security treaty to the Senate before hot weather begins to swelter this capital. Final Senate action is sought by mid-Summer.

Eight-Day Meeting

The conferees held their eight-day meeting in Yalta, a Crimean resort.

They said they had agreed on war and postwar plans for Germany. They passed on her a grim cleansing sentence, but assured the German people that they would survive and

Continued on Page 2

Tomorrow Is Waste Paper Day

Tomorrow is collection day for waste paper. Have all your old paper—newspaper, scraps, wrappings bundled and on the streets by 7 a.m.

Report Reds Captured Ex-Warsaw Governor

By United Press

Soviet troops "have captured the former Governor of Warsaw, Gustav Fischer, who was responsible for the liquidation of the Warsaw ghetto," the British radio said today.

The broadcast quoted reports from Moscow and was recorded by CBS shortwave listening post.

Royalty No Bar to Mumps

London, Feb. 13 (U.P.)—Princess Elizabeth was suffering from a light case of the mumps today.

Nazis Call Big 3 Report Work of 'Yalta Haters'

London, Feb. 13 (U.P.) — German propagandists today called the Crimean declaration the "program of the haters of Yalta."

Germany "will smash this Satanic plan, DNB, promised.

After a lengthy delay in informing the German public of the nature of the Crimean communique, an official DNB news agency dispatch was issued with instructions to German editors that it be headlined: "Germany Has to Be Exterminated."

The DNB dispatch charged President Roosevelt, Prime Minister Churchill and Marshal Stalin had decided upon "new crimes against humanity." It charged the Crimean conferees were imbued "with the spirit of Old Testament Jewish hatred" and were attempting the "greatest political murder of all time."

Apparently Propaganda Minister Paul Joseph Goebbels was caught off base as he had been busily warning the Reich to beware of a Wilsonian peace plea.

Ever since the Big Three conference had been rumored, Goebbels had turned loose the full propaganda facilities inside Germany to warn the Reich against a Big Three appeal to the German people.

But when the Big Three communique failed to bear out this buildup the Nazi propagandists apparently were at a loss how to present the grim news to the Nazi public. For hours after the news had been announced and Allied radios were blaring it into Germany on all available wave-lengths the domestic Nazi radio made no mention of the Crimea conference.

Calls It 'Political Crime'

The flat Big Three assertion that Germany is doomed appeared to have thrown a monkey-wrench into the usually well-oiled Nazi propaganda machinery.

One German commentator termed the Big Three agreement "the greatest political crime of all times," and a "super-Versailles that surpasses the old Versailles by 100 percent."

Woman With 8 Husbands Held on Fraud Charge

San Francisco, Feb. 13 (U.P.)—Mrs. Vilma Suberly, 25, who allegedly began a collection of eight or nine husbands in 1938, was held in Eugene, Ore., today on charges of defrauding service men.

Mrs. Suberly will be returned to Sacramento, where she was indicted last month on a charge of using the U. S. mails to defraud.

Operating as a blonde, red head and brunette, and under at least 28 different aliases, Mrs. Suberly was reported to have married five enlisted navy men, an army private and two civilians.

Eagle Gets 6-Ft. LST For Navy Yard Exhibit

They're clumsy-looking, box-like ships, with no pretense of the majestic bulk of a cruiser or battleship nor of the sleek lines of a destroyer. Yet they played one of the most vital roles in the invasion of France as their gaping bows disgorged on the bloody beaches of Normandy the Allied hordes which opened the second front. Every sailor—and soldier, too—has nothing but the deepest respect for the ungainly but so important vessels known as landing ship tank, or LST for short.

You can see at first hand a six-foot "mockup" or working model of one of these famed fighting craft, as well as many other absorbing displays, including sections of a Nazi V-2 bomb, at the Brooklyn Navy Yard Exhibit opening Monday, Feb. 19, at the Brooklyn Eagle, 24 Johnson St., and viewable free for the following three weeks.

Marking the 144th anniversary of

Continued on Page 5

WHERE TO FIND IT

	Page		Page
Comics	6	Obituaries	9
Crossword	6	Our Fighters	7
Currie	3	Pattern	12
Dr. Brady	8	Radio	6
Editorial	8	Sermons	10
Financial	15	Society	11, 12
Grin and Bear It	8	Sports	13, 14
Heffernan	8	Take My Word	8
Helen Worth	12	Theaters	4
Lindley	8	These Women	6
Mary Haworth	11	Tommy Holmes	13
Movies	4	Tucker	8
Music	4	Want Ads	15-17
Novel	12	Women	11, 12

WEATHER
Snow, colder tonight and tomorrow.

BROOKLYN EAGLE

COMPLETE NEWS ★★★★★

104th YEAR • No. 46 • DAILY AND SUNDAY • BROOKLYN, N. Y., SATURDAY, FEBRUARY 17, 1945 • Entered at the Brooklyn Postoffice as 2d Class Mail Matter—(Copyright 1945 The Brooklyn Eagle, Inc.) • 3 CENTS IN NEW YORK CITY ELSEWHERE 4 CENTS

IWO AND CORREGIDOR INVADED, JAPS REPORT

TIME OUT FOR A BREATHER—The ordeal of playing tag with death has left its mark on these Yanks, making their way back from the front lines for a 48-hour rest. Left to right, Pfc. Alfred Wiktor, Pfc. James Varvaro of Brooklyn, whose face is blackened by smoke from the fire in his covered foxhole, and Pvt. Leonard Russo.

REDS NEAR COTTBUS ON BERLIN ROAD

Break Through To Neisse River, 12 Mi. From Rail Hub

By ROBERT MUSEL

London, Feb. 17 (U.P.)—The Soviet newspaper Pravda said today that Russian armored vanguards broke through to the Neisse River on a broad front only 12 miles from bomb-battered Cottbus, one of the main strongholds guarding the southern approaches to Berlin.

The 12-mile advance crumbled German defense positions on the lower reaches of the Luebst River, a tributary of the Neisse, and put the Russians within easy artillery range of Cottbus, a big railway hub on the Spree River, 47 miles southeast of Berlin.

Northeast of Cottbus, other units of Marshal Ivan S. Konev's 1st Ukrainian Army sweeping along the west bank of the Oder River reached the outskirts of Crossen, 63 miles southeast of Berlin. This column was 17 miles from the first of the Oder bridgeheads which the Germans said the Red Army has established east of the capital.

Battle Encircled Troops

The southern wing of Konev's army, meantime, began a battle of annihilation against the encircled German garrison of Breslau, capital of Silesia. The encirclement was completed with the capture of Klettendorf, only a mile southwest of Breslau.

More than 200 other Silesian towns and villages were captured as the Soviets closed the ring about Breslau, the Soviet High Command announced.

Northeast of Berlin, the 2d White Russian Army drove forward on a 30-mile front to wthin 51 miles southwest of Danzig.

Pravda said Konev's spearheads reached the Neisse River, presumably directly opposite Forst on the Posen-Cottbus Railway, after a thrust from Sommerfeld, on the Luebst River. Cottbus itself has been bombed heavily by American Flying Fortresses directly supporting the Soviet drive.

Large Area Cleared

First Army forces northeast of Sommerfeld were arrayed along a 17-mile stretch of the Bober River running south from its confluence with the Oder at Crossen. Rusdorf, a mile and a half west of Crossen, and Deutsch Sagar, two miles southwest and 62 miles southeast of Berlin, were captured by the Soviets yesterday.

The advances cleared a 150-square-mile area in the Oder bend, between the Oder and the Bober River.

Tokyo Blasted for 2d Day By American Navy Planes

Washington, Feb. 17 (UP)—American troops invaded the fortress island of Corregidor at entrance to Manila Bay by air and sea today, radio Tokyo reported.

"Fierce battles now are raging on the southern shores of the island," a Tokyo domestic broadcast said.

Paratroops opened the assault, swarming down on the island from transport planes, and soon afterward seaborne forces stormed ashore from assault-landing barges, Tokyo said.

The reported combined operation followed by only a few hours Gen. Douglas MacArthur's announcement of the reconquest of Bataan in an amphibious landing on Thursday on the tip of the peninsula, five miles north of Corregidor.

Opens Drive's Final Phase

No further details of the Corregidor fighting were given in the broadcast, which was recorded by the FCC. However, it opened the final phase of an offensive to unlock Manila Bay to American shipping and to avenge the bloody defeats of 1941 and 1942.

Corregidor's giant batteries, which held off Japanese assaults on the island for months in 1942, had been all but neutralized by a terrific air and sea bombardment earlier this week.

They fired a few rounds at the convoy carrying troops to Bataan Thursday, but were silenced quickly by salvoes from American cruisers and destroyers, dispatches from Manila said. Tokyo said American minesweepers began clearing the channel between Bataan and Corregidor Tuesday, followed by 10 troop-jammed transports.

Makes Ship Movement Safe

After Corregidor has been captured, American shipping safely can enter the bay. Once inside the bay, American warships could lend their support to the annihilation of the last pockets of enemy troops holding out along the Manila waterfront. Newly captured Cavite naval base, south of Manila, also could be restored to use.

It was on May 6, 1942, that American forces on Corregidor surrendered to the Japanese, ending organized American resistance in the Philippines. Bataan had fallen a month earlier.

By WILLIAM B. DICKINSON

Manila, Feb. 17. (U.P.)—American troops have redeemed historic Bataan with a bold sea-borne landing on the southern shores of the peninsula under the guns of Japanese-held Corrigdor.

"We have captured Bataan," Gen. Douglas MacArthur announced in a triumphant communique.

Less than 48 hours after landing,

Continued on Page 3

Canadians Roll Ahead as Planes Blast the Path

Germans Driven From Rhine Pillboxes—British Hammer Out New Gain

By BOYD D. LEWIS

Paris, Feb. 17 (U.P.)—The Canadian 1st Army drive on the Ruhr rolled forward today against stunned German troops shaken out of their Rhineland forts and pillboxes by a tremendous Allied aerial bombardment.

Stalled for almost 48 hours by a flaming wall of German guns thrown across the 17-mile corridor between the Maas (Meuse) and Rhine Rivers, Gen. H. D. G. Crerar's troops were on the move again all along the front.

Hammering out gains of a mile or more, the British drove armored spearheads to within about two miles of the fortress towns of Goch and Calcar, barely 25 miles northwest of the Ruhr Valley.

Late reports from the front said the Canadian 1st Army gains were extended to as much as four miles early today as the Nazi lines began to buckle under the attack. Vanguards of the attacking force were reported within 1½ miles of Goch at a point near Asperden.

Nazi Resistance Softens

Field dispatches said Nazi resistance was softening under the shattering ground and air assault and the battle of the Rhineland appeared to be merging swiftly into the battle of the Ruhr.

More than 3,500 American and British warplanes set the offensive rolling yesterday afternoon, laying a terrible pattern of bombs and gunfire across the Maas-Rhine bottleneck. Elements of eight Nazi divisions were caught in the path of the aerial scythe and buried in the wreckage of their fortified villages and field fortificationn.

Every German strongpoint and battery in a five mile arc around Goch and Calcar was blasted with rockets, bombs and cannon-fire, and the nearby villages of Weeze, Hassum and Asperden rocked for hours under an almost continuous bombardment.

Other bombers ranged 20 miles east and 12 miles north of Goch to pound the Rhine crossings at Wesel and Rees.

Dazed Foe Rooted Out

Canadian, English and Scots infantrymen moved out of their muddy foxholes while the bombs still were falling up ahead and began rooting dazed Nazi troopers out of the wreckage of houses and earth-

Continued on Page 3

By WILLIAM F. TYREE

Admiral Nimitz' Headquarters, Guam, Feb. 17 (UP)—American troops stormed ashore early today on Iwo Island, only 750 miles south of Tokyo, enemy broadcasts reported, while carrier planes hit the burning Japanese capital itself for the second straight day of a diversionary assault.

Invasion forces swarmed over the southwest and southeast beaches of Iwo in twin landings only 10 minutes apart, a Tokyo Domei broadcast said. It added the customary claim that the troops had been "repulsed" after fierce fighting.

The report of the invasion came on the second day of an earth-shaking bombardment of Iwo by more than 30 American warships—ranging from battleships to destroyers—and scores of carrier and land-based bombers. Most shore batteries were knocked out yesterday.

A landing on Iwo would represent an amphibious jump of 750 miles—half-way to Tokyo—from the Marianas for the Americans and would give them at least three strategic air bases within Flying Fortress, Liberator and fighter-plane range of the enemy capital.

Wave after wave of American carrier planes sent hundreds more tons of bombs crashing down on smoking Tokyo today. A Japanese communique said the second day of the unprecedented assault got under way at 7 a.m. (6 p.m. Friday, Brooklyn time) and the raid still was continuing eight and a half hours later.

The enemy communique admitted that 61 Japanese planes had been lost in yesterday's 9 to 10-hour attack, but claimed 147 American planes were shot down and more than 50 damaged. Japanese planes counterattacking the American task force "heavily damaged and set afire" a large warship, believed an aircraft carrier, the communique said.

Fear Landing on Japan

Tokyo broadcasts freely interpreted the assault as a diversionary attack to cover an invesion of Iwo and one said an American landing on Japan itself may be near. Another warned without elaboration that American forces may "attempt to come near the homeland at two points, one of them the Boso peninsula," western arm of Tokyo Bay and site of the Yokosuka naval base.

Domei said American forces began landing operations on Futatsune Beach in southwest Iwo about 10:30 a.m (9:30 p.m. Friday, Brooklyn time), but were "completely smashed."

"Following the failure, all enemy troops withdrew far out to sea," the broadcast said.

Ten minutes later—10:40 a.m.—American troops began landing on Kamiyama Beach on the south eastern tip of the tiny eight-square-mile island, Domei said.

"Our garrison troops going into action to engage these enemy forces successfully repulsed them, with severe losses inflicted on the invaders," it asserted.

The broadcast, while saying that the second landing had been "repulsed," notably made no claim that these forces also had withdrawn.

Iwo, a gourd-shaped island in the Volcano group, is barren and rocky.

Continued on Page 3

WALLACE WON'T GET IN WITHOUT FIGHT—G. O. P.

However, Few Doubt He'll Be Confirmed in Senate Vote March 1

Washington, Feb. 17 (U.P.)—House passage of the George bill cleared the way today for Senate confirmation of Henry A. Wallace as Secretary of Commerce.

There appeared little doubt that Wallace would be confirmed after Presient Roosevelt signed the bill stripping the commerce job of control over the Reconstruction Finance Corporation and its subsidiaries. The President has said he will sign it.

Senate Republican leaders conceded that House acceptance of the measure without amendments improved Wallace's chances for confirmation. They served noitce, however, that he wouldn't get the post without a fight. The Senate vote on the Wallace nomination has been set for March 1.

Senator Robert A. Taft (R., Ohio), chairman of the Republican steering committee in the Senate, freely predicted that when that time comes "we'll have quite a battle."

Senator Kenneth S. Wherry (R., Neb.) Republican whip in the Senate, said he was going to vote against Wallace regardless of the legislation.

"I think that if the bill becomes law Wallace definitely will have a better chance for confirmation," Wherry said. "But I feel that regardless of the George bill the Senate has a definite responsibility to confirm only those whom we feel conform to our fundamental principles of government. Wallace doesn't fit that picture."

Senator Tom Connally (D., Tex.) a close personal friend of former Commerce Secretary Jesse Jones, said he now expects Wallace to be confirmed. So does Senate Democratic Leader Alben W. Barkley of Kentucky.

LaGuardia Boomed

Business Men for LaGuardia, a group organized to boom Mayor LaGuardia for a fourth term, was incorporated yesterday. Directors are Frank C. Taylor of 157 Monroe Place, C. Mathers Clark of 243-58 144th St., Rosedale, and William A. Hamlin of 3235 Parkside Place, the Bronx.

Eagle Show to Feature Navy Navigation Aids

An impressive array of navigation instruments will be part of the Brooklyn Navy Yard birthday exhibit which opens in the Brooklyn Eagle Building Monday.

The exhibit, saluting the Yard's 144th anniversary, will include unusual maritime exhibits.

The navigation section, for instance, includes everything from a picture of the first gyroscope installed on a United States warship to the actual presentation of the very latest thing in navigation—the "dead reckoning table,' on which is plotted the course of American warships.

Included also are a gyro compass repeater and the most modern types of gyro compasses. A gyro compass differs from a magnetic compass in that the gyro type isn't affected by the earth's magnetic poles or the metal i nthe ship's structure.

Byrd's Compass to Be Here

Also in the exhibit will be a magnesyn compass, the latest development in magnetic compasses.

Then, too, there is the gyro compass Admiral Byrd took with him on expeditions to the North and South Poles. This compass, which was also on the submarine Sir Hubert

Continued on Page 3

Sees Prejudice Stirred Up by Permanent FEPC

Washington, Feb. 17 (U.P.)—Representative P. Clark Fisher (D., Texas) said today that creation of a permanent Fair Employment Practices Commission would "stir up more racial and religious prejudice than this nation has seen in many a moon.

He assailed as "nefarious" the action of the House Labor Committee in approving a measure to establish a permanent five-man FEPC. Fisher and Representative Clare E. Hoffman (R., Mich.- opposed the bill in committee.

"We are in the middle of a war and should be united against the enemy," he said. "Yet this controversial bill will divide us more than any other bill to come before Congress in the past few years."

The bill would give the permanent board power to decide when a private employer has been guilty of racial or religious discrimination in hiring employes.

Fisher said he planned to ask the House Rules Committee not to allow the bill to reach the floor. He added that he expected the vast majority of Southern Congressmen to support him in his fight against its passage.

Navy Officer Charges His Marriage Was Coerced

Declaring his commanding officer in Atlanta threatened to "run him out of the navy" if he did not marry the woman who said she was to be the mother of his child, Lt. Clyde Monaghan, now stationed at Floyd Bennett Field, said he agreed to the ceremony.

Monaghan has filed suit in Superior Court, San Francisco, seeking an annulment of his marriage to Mrs. Nancy Monaghan of Washington on grounds that he was coerced into the wedding, the United Press reported. Through his attorney, Henry Jacobsen, Monaghan said, he will attempt to prove he was not the father of the child.

Vandenberg O. K. For Security Talks

Washington, Feb. 17 (U.P.)—Senate Republican leaders were reported today to have approved selection of Senator Arthur H. Vandenberg (R., Mich.) as a delegate to the United Nations security conference at San Francisco April 25.

The matter was discussed, it was learned, at a closed meeting yesterday of the Senate Republican steering committee.

Those who attended reported a general feeling prevalent that Vandenberg should attend. They took the position that it wouldn't necensarily be as an official representative of the Republican party. They were more interested in having a representative on the spot who could subsequently report to them the back-stage developments after the conference was over.

Vandenberg, who attended the steering committee meeting, refused to tell reporters whether he would accept the invitation.

LIGHT SNOW TODAY, TONIGHT, TOMORROW

Overcast skies with light snow this afternoon was forecast by the Weather Bureau. It will alno be colder today than yesterday, the bureau said, with a high of 40. Light snow again tonight and more snow tomorrow morning are on the weather menu.

Yesterday temperatures reached a maximum of 55 degrees at 1:30 p.m. It was the first time the temperature reached that level since New Year's day.

Truck Fire Delays War Prisoner Packages

More than 100 Red Cross volunteers, preparing packages for prisoners of war overseas left their tables yesterday when a fire alarm sounded through the building at 255 18th St. The fire was in a truck backed up to the loading platform, containing 50,000 items for the packages. The fire was put out after the 250 items of canned goods were ruined.

Cops Nab Boy Pistol Manufacturer in Bronx

Police arrested Ismael Cruz, 16, in his home at 768 Tinton Ave., the Bronx, for violation of the Sullivan law. They found revolvers in various stages of assembly in the boy's room. Cruz was doing a thriving business manufacturing .22-caliber pistols from pieces of wood, metal tubes and rubber bands. They found 61 rounds of ammunition, too.

List 5 Local Men As Navy Casualties

The Navy Department today, announcing the names of 124 casualties, listed five Brooklyn and Queens men killed, wounded or missing. The local casualty list is on Page 2.

Call the Brooklyn Chapter, American Red Cross, and arrange to donate a pint of blood NOW. TRiangle 5-8040.

DIAPER SHORTAGE IS REALLY BROUGHT HOME TO THE OPA

In its latest volunteer member, the Jamaica office of the OPA Rationing Board has signed up quite a problem, and a personal one, at that.

"Inspector" Barbara Joan Gannon of 90-13 Vanderveer St., Queens Village, is a full-fledged official, but there are certain stipulations the board itself must meet.

The most important is that "they change my diapers every so often, and be sure that I get my regular feedings and naps."

Miss Gannon was signed up through her secretary, in this case her mother, Mrs. Leonard D. Gannon, whe nshe received an invitation from Mrs. Vera Lobo, volunteer assistant supervisor. Her name was found in a list of Queens women asked to become price panel assistants. But there obviously was some mistake because—

Babs is just three and one-half months old.

Ex-Vichy Police Chief Yynched by French Mob

Paris, Feb. 17 (U.P.)—A French ppress dispatch from Dijon said today that former Vichyite police commissioner Jacques Marsac was lynched following a meeting to protest the Dijon court's postponement of his trial on collaborationist charges until the end of the war.

The crowd broke down prison doors, seized Marsac and hanged him from a sign post, after which the body was dragged through the streets and finally tied to a railing at the town hall, the dispatch said.

Clark Tells Italians Nazis May Withdraw

By United Press

Lt. Gen. Mark W. Clark, commander of Allied troops in Italy, told the people of northern Italy in a special message last night that German withdrawal from their country appeared "more and more likely."

The message, quoted by the Rome radio in a broadcast reported by the FCC, said the withdrawal might be planned in view of Allied advances on the Eastern and Western Fronts.

Szech Government-in-Exile Returning to Homeland

The Czechoslovak Government-in-exile, which has been functioning in London since July 29, 1941, is being transferred back to its homeland, President Edouard Benes said today.

"I am returning home. Our task here is completed," Benes announced in a broadcast beamed over the London radio to Czechoslovakia and recorded in New York by C. B. S.

Allied Invasion of Japan Predicted by Nip Paper

By United Press

The Tokyo newspaper Mainichi predicted "possible" Allied invasion of the Japanese homeland in commenting today on the carrier plane assault on the city, Tokyo Radio reported.

Both Mainichi and the Asahi Shimbun agreed the "latest air attacks on the homeland were diversional operations to cover the enemy's invasion of Iwo Jima," according to the broadcast, which was heard by the United Press in San Francisco.

Other newspapers viewed appearance of the mighty U. S. naval task force as "a golden opportunity for the Japanese to finish off the main strength of the American fleet at one stroke," the broadcast said.

The Yomuri Hochi was quoted as declaring "we must try and grasp this opportunity," and the Tokyo Shimbun "welcomed the enemy action as offering a chance for Japan to deal the enemy a lethal blow."

The broadcast continued with the Asami Shimbun's report of "breathless scenes" witnessed at Japanese army and naval bases in the Kanto district.

The newspaper said United States planes skimmed over one Japanese army base and then contradicted itself by declaring "our air defenses did not allow a single enemy raider to approach our base."

In one "daring chase when one enemy plane was shot down in a single stroke, a chorus of handclapping was heard from the many interested spectators," Asahi said.

"Naval air bases were also very busy," the newspaper added. "Over Hamamatsu many naval planes gave a hot reception to 30 carrier bombers and in a half-hour combat shot down 16 and damaged another."

‹e Hears Hitler Died of Brain Stroke

★★★★★★★ Complete

BROOKLYN EAGLE

WEATHER—Cloudy cool tonight cloudy rain tomorrow

YEAR • No. 119 • DAILY AND SUNDAY · BROOKLYN N Y WEDNESDAY MAY 2 1945 · 3 CENTS

NAZIS IN ITALY QUIT, TRUMAN ANNOUNCES

Surrender Unconditional; 600,000 Give Up to Allies

By HERBERT G. KING

Representing Combined U. S. Press

Royal Palace at Caserta, Near Naples, May 2 (UP)—The German armies of northern Italy and western Austria formally surrendered to the Allies today, effective at 8 A.M., EWT.

The surrender affects between 600,000 and 900,000 men commanded by Col. Gen. Heinrich von Vietinghoff and Gen. Karl Wolff, chief of police and security for northern Italy and western Austria.

Lt. Gen. W. D. Morgan of the British Army, who negotiated in behalf of Field Marshal Sir Harold R. L. G. Alexander, supreme commander in the Mediterranean theater, said the terms "in effect are complete and unconditional surrender."

The documents were signed in the Royal Palace here on Sunday by Morgan and two German officers, one of whom represented Von Vietinghoff and the other Wolff.

Move on Berchtesgaden

The surrender will permit the Allies to make an unhindered advance to within 10 miles of Adolf Hitler's former country home at Berchtesgaden. It also uncovers the flank of Col. Gen. Von Lehr, commanding enemy troops in the Trieste area.

The surrender documents were signed in the presence of a group of Allied officers which included Russians. Secret negotiations for the surrender have been going on for several days.

The terms are the immediate immobilization and disarmament of enemy ground, sea and air forces.

The surrender imposes upon the German commander in chief the obligation to carry out any further orders issued by Field Marshal Alexander.

Von Vietinghoff's command includes all of northern Italy to the Isonzo River and the Austrian provinces of Voralberg, Tyrol, Salzburg and parts of Corinthia and Styria.

Washington, May 2 (UP)—President Truman today announced the "unconditional surrender" of all German forces in Italy.

The President said that "the collapse of military tyranny in Italy, however, is no victory in Italy alone, but a part of the general triumph we are expectantly awaiting on the whole continent of Europe."

"Only folly and chaos can now delay the general capitulation of the everywhere defeated German armies," he said.

The President immediately sent messages to Field Marshal Sir Harold Alexander and Gen. Mark Clark, congratulating them for the "complete defeat of the Germans in Italy."

(A dispatch filed by Henry King, representing the combined American press, and datelined Royal Palace at Caserta, near Naples, said the German armies of northern Italy and western Austria formally surrendered to the Allies today, effective at 8 A.M., EWT.

(The surrender affects between 600,000 and 900,000 men.)

At the same time he warned Japan to understand the full meaning of these events.

"Unless they are lost in fanaticism or determined upon suicide," he said of the Japanese, as well as the Germans, "they must recognize the meaning of the increasing, swifter-moving power now ready for the capitulation or the destruction of the so-recently arrogant enemies of mankind."

In breaking the news of the complete victory over German forces in Italy, the President said, "The Allied armies in Italy have won the unconditional surrender of German forces on the first European soil on which, from the west, we carried our arms and our determination."

Praises Military Chiefs

In his message to Marshal Alexander and General Clark he congratulated them on their persistent, difficult campaign. He said no praise was adequate to tell of "the heroic achievements and magnificent courage of every individual under their command "during this long and trying campaign."

The President told this country that the Allied and American officers who led the victorious forces in Italy "deserve our praise for the victory—we have the right to be proud of the success of our armies."

Mr. Truman's announcement took Washington somewhat by surprise, despite the fact that it was known

Continued on Page 2

Here Are Terms Of Surrender

Naples, May 2 (U.P.)—The text of the surrender terms:

1. Unconditional surrender by the German commander in chief of the southwest of all forces under his command or control on land, sea or air to the Supreme Commander in Chief of the Mediterranean Theater.

2. Cessation of all hostilities on land, sea and air by enemy forces at 1200 hours GMT (8 a.m. EWT) May 2, 1945.

3. Immediate immobilization and disarmament of enemy ground, sea and air forces.

4. Obligation on the part of the German commander in chief of the southwest to carry out any further orders issued by the Supreme Allied Commander in the Mediterranean Theater.

5. Disobedience of orders or failure to comply with them to be dealt with in accordance with the accepted usages of war.

DOENITZ WAS INSANE ASYLUM INMATE AT END OF THE LAST WAR

London, May 2 (U.P.)—Grand Admiral Karl Doenitz, self-announced successor to Adolf Hitler as Nazi overlord of dying Germany, ended the last war as an inmate of a British insane asylum and emerged in this one with the fanatical credo "Kill! Kill! Kill!"

Doenitz scuttled and abandoned the submarine he commanded during a battle in the Mediterranean in October, 1918. Then he surrendered to the British.

Taken to England, he was committed to the Manchester insane asylum. Some who knew him said he feigned insanity. But he later was repatriated to Germany as insane.

In this war, Doenitz sent his U-boat crews into battle with the cry:

"Kill Kill! Kill! That is your duty to the Fatherland and Der Fuehrer. Have no humanity in your labor. Humanity means weakness."

WHERE TO FIND IT

	Page		Page
Bridge	14	Our Fighters	4
Brown	10	Patterns	14
Comics	2[illegible]	Radio	[illegible]
Crossword	18	Society	1[illegible]
Crime	3	Sports	15, 16
Dr. Brady	10	Take My Word	10
Editorial	10	Theaters	16, 17
Financial	18	These Women	21
Gen[illegible] Board	10	Tommy Holmes	15
Heffernan	10	Ticker	19
Horoscope	14	Uncle Ray	21
Mary Haworth	13	Veteran in Brooklyn	4
Movies	16, 17	Want Ads	[illegible]
Novel	18	Women	13
Obituaries	11		

Woman Kills Self With a Stocking

Police today listed as a suicide the death of Mrs. Edna Glassman, 37, of 2285 Ocean Ave., found with a stocking tied about her neck in her home yesterday. Relatives said she had been despondent and had been under psychiatric treatment.

Truman's Messages On Our Victory in Italy

Washington, May 2 (U.P.)—Text of the President's statement:

The Allied armies in Italy have won the unconditional surrender of German forces on the first European soil to which, from the west, we carried our arms and our determination. The collapse of military tyranny in Italy, however, is no victory in Italy alone but a part of the general triumph we are expectantly awaiting on the whole continent of Europe. Only folly and chaos can now delay the general capitulation of the everywhere defeated German armies.

I have dispatched congratulatory messages to the Allied and American officers who led our forces to complete defeat of the Germans in Italy. They deserve our praise for the victory. We have a right to be proud of the success of our armies.

Let Japan as well as Germany understand the meaning of these events. Unless they are lost in fanaticism or determined upon suicide, they must recognize the meaning of the increasing, swifter-moving power now ready for the capitulation or the destruction of

Continued on Page 2

…D TROOPS …ORM BERLIN …ANCELLERY

…sh Strongpoint …here Nazis Said …itler Met Death

…ETIN

…don, May 2 (U.P.)—Marshal Stalin …nounced tonight that the Red … had completed the liquidation …rman forces encircled south… …of Berlin, taking more than … prisoners.

…don, May 2 (U.P.)—The German …command admitted today that …survivors of Berlin's garrison …been splintered into isolated …ents in the government dis… …of the dying capital.

…t reports said Red Army … troops were storming the …ins of the German chancellery, … the Nazis said Adolf Hitler …at a command post yesterday.

… brevity and … of a German communique's report on Berlin …ted the Nazi command might …bout ready to write off the …l. It said:

…mnants of the brave garrison …rlin continue to fight doggedly …e government district, split up …lated battle groups."

…thwest of Berlin in Mecklen… … the German command said, … whirlwind sweep of Marshal …antin K. Rokossovsky's 2d … Russian Army had carried to …area of Rostock, last major … port short of the neck of the …h peninsula.

…cow dispatches said Russian … armies had driven many …es deep into Berlin's innermost …ibt, apparently splintering it

Continued on Page 11

…mans Still Hold …000 to 50,000 Yanks

…ashington, May 2 (U.P.)—The War …rtment said today that the …mans still hold 40,000 or 50,000 of …estimated 72,000 Americans they … taken as prisoners of war. …ied armies, however, have over… …64 of the 78 prisoner of war …ps and hospitals where Amer… …soldiers are known to be held, … War Department added.

…9 Local Men …mong Casualties

The War Department …day, announcing the …ames of 593 soldiers …illed in action, 2,904 …ounded, 360 missing …nd 426 prisoners of …ar, listed 20 Brooklyn, …ueens and Long Island …en dead, 50 wounded, …nd 11 missing in the …uropean and Pacific …reas, and nine prisoners of war held by Germany. The navy listed …ive dead and four …ounded. Local casualty …ts are on Page 5.

Call the Brooklyn Chapter, American Red Cross, and arrange to donate a pint of blood NOW—TRIangle 5-8040.

Yank Tank Men Seize Rundstedt at Dinner

Grab Nazi Who Battled Allies From Normandy To Rhine—Glad to Quit

By MALCOLM MUIR Jr.

With 7th Army in Germany, May 2 (U.P.)—An American tank crew surprised Field Marshal Karl von Rundstedt at his dinner table and captured the man who had battled the Allies from Normandy to the Rhine, it was announced today.

Von Rundstedt, twice commander of the German armies in the west since the Allied invasion, was taken at 10 p.m. last night at Bad Tolz, a resort town south of Munich.

He was having dinner with his wife and son, Hans Gerd, when a tank commanded by Lt. Joseph Burke rumbled into the hospital grounds at Bad Tolz. Von Rundstedt, who was taking a health treatment, was living in a house attached to the hospital.

Was Ready to Surrender

Von Rundstedt said he had not

Continued on Page …

Marshal Von Rundstedt

HITLER DIED OF STROKE, IKE HEARS

Nazi Claim Adolf Died Fighting Differs From Himmler Story

By PHIL AULT

London, May 2 (U.P.)—Gen. Dwight D. Eisenhower said today there was some evidence that Adolf Hitler had died of a brain hemorrhage instead of a hero's death in battle as the Nazis claimed.

The statement by Eisenhower was the first from any Allied official to shed light on the mystery of Hitler's reported death.

General Eisenhower said the enemy claim that Hitler died fighting the Russians in Berlin was "in contradiction of facts" given by Heinrich Himmler at a conference with Count Folke Bernadotte of Sweden at Luebeck eight days ago.

Himmler and a General Schillenburg, who accompanied him to the conference, said Hitler had a brain hemorrhage and might not live 48 hours, General Eisenhower said in a statement issued through supreme headquarters in France.

Get Data From Count

Even though this version of Hitler's death was based on Nazi information, it had the merit of coming to General Eisenhower through Bernadotte, a neutral. Observers were inclined to put more credence in the Himmler version than in the melodramatic account broadcast by the Hamburg radio yesterday.

Himmler admitted that Germany was finished, General Eisenhower said in the official confirmation of the Luebeck conference. Count Bernadotte said in Stockholm yesterday that he could make no disclosure of his activity as the reported intermediary in Nazi-Allied negotiations.

General Eisenhower said the radio statement by Admiral Karl Doenitz, announcing Hitler's death and proclaiming himself as his successor, represented an attempt to drive a wedge between the Russians and Anglo-Americans. The attempt

Continued on Page 11

Queens M. P. Rescues Pal In Nazi Camp

Pfc. Spencer Young Jr.

Pfc. Spencer C. Young Jr. of 114-73 178th Place, St. Albans, has been liberated from a German prisoner-of-war camp by a schoolboy friend "somewhere on the Elbe," after a "death march" of some 800 miles. His father, United States Marshal Spencer C. Young Sr., has learned this through a letter written by Pfc. Richard J. Buck of 100-19 205th St., Hollis, a military policeman who helped free the soldier.

"Imagine my surprise when I saw my friend, Cliff Young, walking toward me from the camp," Private Buck wrote his father, Louis P. Buck, an insurance executive. "My buddy had a rough time, and is not able to write, but he is safe in our hands."

As soon as Mr. Buck received the letter today, he phoned the marshal. Mr. Young is a former State vice commander of the American Legion and Mr. Buck has been the past commander of the Hollis-Bellaire Post of the Legion.

When Private Buck, who played basketball with Private Young on the Lindens, a team in Hollis, referred to Cliff, he was using his friend's nickname.

Private Young, who had been a German prisoner for more than a year, was forced to march from Stalag 3-B, near Neustettin, his father said, on Feb. 22, and the march continued until April 14, under "horrible" conditions.

Truman Orders Windup of OCD By End of June

President Stresses Continued Necessity For Volunteer Work

Washington, May 2 (U.P.)—President Truman today ordered the end of the Office of Civilian Defense by June 30.

Mr. Truman sent a letter to Congress withdrawing a $365,000 budget request for OCD for the next fiscal year.

He emphasized, however, the continued need for volunteer work in States and communities.

"Recent developments in the European war and the efficient operation of the volunteer forces in the communities made possible the decision that Federal supervision of civilian defense is no longer neces-

Continued on Page 2

British Irked Over Red Stand on Fate of Poles

London, May 2 (U.P.)—Minister of State Richard K. Law told Commons today that Foreign Secretary Anthony Eden had been unable to get from Soviet Foreign Commissar V. M. Molotov any hint of the fate of 14 Polish leaders reported to have disappeared in Poland in March. They were representatives of the Polish government in London.

In reply to angry questions in Commons, Law said the Soviet Government had ignored all British requests for information. He left the impression that the Russians had in effect taken the attitude that the matter was none of Britain's business.

Switch of Diplomats

The Polish government at Warsaw and the Italian government have signed an agreement for the exchange of diplomatic representatives, Radio Moscow said today.

TROOPS ON LIGHT DUTY TO HAVE RATIONS CUT

London, May 2 (U.P.)—The rations of United States troops in European theater who are engaged in "light duties" will be cut 10 percent because of a world food shortage, it was announced today by headquarters of the European theater of operations.

The basic military ration will be retained for troops performing moderately hard or hard work, including all combat units and hospital patients, it was announced.

The reduced ration will be approximately 3,650 calories per man daily, which is considered adequate for troops performing sedentary duties.

Pierre Laval, Deat Fly To Spain, Madrid Reports

Madrid, May 2 (U.P.)—Barcelona advices said Pierre Laval, Marcel Deat and four other Frenchmen arrived there by plane from Switzerland this afternoon.

Laval, the former premier in the Vichy regime, and his companions were at a hotel near the Barcelona airfield, the report said, while word was awaited from Madrid what to do about them.

British Sweep to Baltic Reported; Red Link Due

BULLETIN

Paris, May 2 (U.P.)—British 2d Army troops were reported to have slashed to the Baltic at Wismar today, isolating the great ports of Hamburg and Kiel and reaching within some 20 miles of a junction with Russian forces sweeping westward along the coast.

Paris, May 2 (U.P.)—Two American armies drove into the last 40-mile stretch before Berchtesgaden from the north and west today, meeting only sporadic opposition.

Gen. George S. Patton's 3d Army reached the Inn River barrier on a broad front east and west of Hitler's native city of Braunau, 43 miles north of Berchtesgaden.

London reports said the Yanks crossed the Inn, captured Braunau and struck southward into the mountain passes before Berchtesgaden.

Far to the west, the 7th Army drew abreast of Patton's men in

Continued on Page 11

★★★★★★★★ Complete

BROOKLYN EAGLE

WEATHER—Cloudy, cool tonight showers, cool tomorrow.

No. 124 • DAILY AND SUNDAY — BROOKLYN, N. Y., MONDAY, MAY 7, 1945 — 3 CENTS

Nazis Say:

WAR IS ENDED

Allied Leaders Withhold Confirmation

Eagle Staff photo

HOW DOWNTOWN BROOKLYN REACTED TO THE NEWS FROM EUROPE

By PHIL AULT

London, May 7 (UP)—A German broadcast said today that all remaining German forces in Europe have surrendered, and there were indications here that an Allied proclamation on the end of the war will be made today.

There was no confirmation from Allied sources that the Germans have surrendered, but every sign in London was that the end of the war is near.

Allied Supreme Headquarters in Paris, meanwhile, issued this statement:

"SHAEF authorizes correspondents at 4:45 p.m. Paris time (10:45 a.m. Brooklyn time) to state that SHAEF has made nowhere any official statement for publication up to that hour concerning complete surrender of all German armed forces in Europe and no story to that effect is authorized."

The British Ministry of Information said tonight that tomorrow "will be treated as Victory in Europe Day."

Prime Minister Churchill will broadcast at 3 p.m. double British Summer time (9 a.m. Brooklyn time), the Minister of Information said.

The text of the Ministry of Information announcement:

"It is understood that in accordance with arrangements between the three Great Powers an official announcement will be broadcast by Prime Minister Churchill at 3 p.m. tomorrow.

A speaker identified as German Foreign Minister Count Ludwig Schwerin von Krosigk announced over the Flensburg radio at 2:09 p.m. (8:09 a.m. Brooklyn time) that the high command of the German armed forces have surrendered unconditionally all "fighting German troops" today.

The order for surrender was given by Fuehrer Grand Admiral Karl Doenitz, the broadcast said. It came on the 2,074th day of the European war.

(The CBS short wave listening station heard the American Broadcasting Station in Europe) ABSIE say:

("Germany has surrendered unconditionally. American, British and Soviet representatives have accepted the surrender of the German armed forces at General Eisenhower's headquarters near Rheims, France, where the official announcement was made.

("Col. Gen. Gustav Jodl, the new German army chief of staff, signed for Germany. The war is officially over in Europe. The world now awaits the official proclama-

Continued on Page 3

A. P. SUSPENDED AFTER FLASHING SURRENDER NEWS

Supreme Allied HQ Cuts Off Europe Filing Facilities of Agency

The United Press Association, at 12:32 p.m. today, sent the following message to its clients:

Editors: Allied Supreme Headquarters in Paris authorised a statement today that the filing facilities of the Associated Press had been suspended throughout the entire European theater of operations.

At the New York headquarters of the A. P. it was said that no statement would be made immediately.

A radio flash, unqualified and unofficial, threw the world in general into a frenzy of excitement earlier at the news that Germany had surrendered unconditionally to the western Allies and Russia.

For the second time in little more than a week, the Associated Press had told of the fall of the Nazis. In the former case, the news turned out to be premature. In this case the country was still awaiting confirmation from any official source.

The bulletin which set the ticker tape flying and the whistles blowing was heard on the radio at 9:38 a.m. From that moment on, while the rest of the people celebrated, newsmen and city officials stuck to their jobs, awaiting confirmation.

No VE-Day News, Says White House

Washington, May 7 (U.P.)—Jonathan Daniels, White House press secretary, told reporters at 10:19 a.m. (Brooklyn time) today that the White House had nothing to announce at that time regarding the situation in Europe.

He said that President Truman planned, as was announced a week ago, to make a radio broadcast to the nation "in the event of the cessation of hostilities."

Shortly before Daniels talked with reporters, he conferred with Elmer Davis, director of the Office of War Information.

Mr. Davis said he had come to the White House "to get some documents that I will need in my business."

Mr. Davis would not identify the documents.

A Few Little Flakes Grow Into Vast 'VE' Paperstorm

By VIOLET BROWN

At first people were suspicious. It had been "over" so many times before. Even at 10:36 a.m., a quarter of an hour after the special VE signal that was to mobilize the city's 245,68? firemen, policemen, air-raid wardens and other volunteers was flashed, Borough Hall was quiet.

The only group discussing the as-yet-unconfirmed report that the end was at hand was a small group gathered in front of the key-making cubbyhole of Hyman Bass at 11 Myrtle Ave. He had a radio blaring forth the news, but people would listen and say, "Yeah, who knows? It's not official yet."

Then some one on the tenth floor of 32 Court St. tossed out some office-made confetti and suddenly the Borough Hall district was galvanized. The few flakes soon [illegible] into a paper snowstorm and in five minutes there seemed to be 5,000 people at least gathered in Borough Hall park.

Draft Records, Too?

The girls who work for the draft boards in the Temple Bar Building at 44 Court St.—Local Boards 150, 151, 178 and 192, whose greetings sent more than 50,000 Brooklyn men somewhere over the face of the globe—appeared on the third floor balcony and began to toss paper, scrap paper they were quick to shout to their audience below.

All morning long they threw out bits of paper and yelled, "It's over, it's over!" They were a little premature, of course, but they had reason to be happy—Mrs. Marjorie Jordon of 283 Jay St. has a sailor husband in Europe; Camilla Tristano of 636 4th Ave. has a sailor fiance in the Pacific; Josephine Natoli of 61 Douglas St. has a brother at Okinawa and another in Germany; Mrs. Bernice Medford of 19-17 132d St., St. Albans, has a brother in Germany.

Times Square Bars Autos

Meanwhile, the police were getting ready to take their posts on the borough's streets, 3,000 uniformed men and about 1,000 others, out of the 14,351 mobilized.

A large part of the force was concentrated in the city's most congested areas, with special attention to Times Square, which was closed to vehicular traffic from 42d to 48th St., and from 6th to 8th Ave.

Wall Street, staidest section in the city, at this period was the most unrestrained. Ticker tape and con-

Continued on Page 7

[illegible]thdrawal Mayor Helps [O']Dwyer Drive

[JO]SEPH H. SCHMALACKER

[illegible] all political camps thrown [into c]onfusion by Mayor LaGuardia's [w]ithdrawal from the municipal [electio]n campaign, Republican city [leaders] this afternoon abruptly can[celed] a scheduled conference to [consid]er their campaign slate.

[illegible]RIS HAT IN RING

[Cit]y Council President Newbold [Morr]is today threw his hat into [the r]ing for Mayor.

[Ask]ed if he were a candidate [to suc]ceed Mayor LaGuardia, Mr. [Morri]s told City Hall reporters: "[Of c]ourse, if I am asked. I have [alway]s stood for good government [and I] think that I could give New [York] City a good administration." [He] would not amplify his re[marks].

[The] decision of the leaders was [announ]ced by John R. Crews, Kings [Count]y G. O. P. chairman.

"[Wit]h VE-Day upon us," Mr. [Crew]s said, "we have decided not to [illegible]. We shall await further de[velopm]ents."

[The] cancellation of the G. O. P. [confe]rence deepened political un[certaint]ies unleashed by the Mayor's [illegible] decision which had the [effect] of throwing both major and [minor]ity party leaders into the worst [illegible] campaign dilemma of more [than] a decade.

[illegible] for causing a series of [illegible] developments, topped by a [illegible] rise in O'Dwyer-for-Mayor [illegible] a coalition proposal [illegible] Joseph D. McGold[rick] apparently coming to a [illegible] stand, the Mayor's sud-

Continued on Page 1[illegible]

[illegible]ION NAZI LEADER [illegible] AT UTRECHT

[illegible] Holland, May 7 (U.P.)— [illegible], leader of the Dutch [Nazi] party, was captured by Allied [illegible] at his headquarters here [illegible].

63 of Area's Men War Casualties

The War Department today, announcing the names of 469 soldiers killed in action, 182 wounded, 205 missing, 239 prisoners of war, and 297 liberated, listed 18 Brooklyn, Queens and Long Island men dead, two wounded, and eight missing in the European and Pacific regions, five prisoners of war held by Germany and ten released from German prison camps. The navy listed six dead, 23 wounded and one missing. Local casualty lists are on Page 5.

Call the Brooklyn Chapter, American Red Cross, and arrange to donate a pint of blood NOW. TRiangle 5-8040.

Erickson Questioned About Tax Returns

Frank Erickson, reputed big-time gambler, was questioned for several hours today by City Commissioner of Investigation [illegible], according to authoritative sources. He was asked about his [illegible] and gross income tax returns.

48-Hour Week to End In Many Areas After VE

Washington, May 7 (U.P.)—Soon after VE-Day the 48-hour week will be suspended in plants and areas where the labor market has "loosened up," WMC disclosed today.

At the same time WMC will probably lift controls on workers who are "frozen" to their present jobs. Already such controls have been lifted on women workers in scattered areas throughout the country. The labor market "is generally tending to loosen up as cutbacks occur," WMC said.

LOTS OF 'EM

RED SAYS GERMANS MUST REBUILD EUROPE

Moscow, May 7 (U.P.)—The semi-official Soviet publication War and the Working Class said today that German labor must be used after the war to rebuild Europe despite the opposition of "certain foreign elements."

By using German labor, an article by Alexander Trainin said, the Allies also will achieve the effective military and economic disarmament of Germany.

"The time has come to settle accounts," the article said. "The Crimean conference decided to make Germany repay damage in kind to the maximum possible degree."

"Naturally, Germany must submit all her resources to restore damage."

Burma Town Captured

Calcutta, May 7 (U.P.)—Troops of the British 14th Army, pushing southeast toward Rangoon from the Irrawaddy sector, have captured [illegible], 35 miles south of Prome, a communique said today.

Tokyo Press Calls For Break With Reich

The Tokyo press called today for a break in relations with Germany after Jap Foreign Minister Shigenoro Togo branded Gestapo Chief Himmler's reported peace offers a "flagrant violation of the Axis Tri-Partite Pact."

Domei said, in a dispatch reported by FCC, that diplomatic observers regard Togo's statement that Japan reserves the right to "re-examine all her relations with Germany" as the most important development on Japan's diplomatic front in years.

House to Act on War Criminal Measure

Washington, May 7 (U.P.)—The House planned to act today on a resolution to give the United Nations a free hand in dealing with neutral nations who harbor war criminals.

The measure would authorize the government to use "all the means available in addition to treaties of extradition" to root out war criminals.

PEACE SHARES ADVANCE AS WALL ST. OFFICES STEP OUT TO CELEBRATE

While Wall Street personnel quit offices and desks today to sally into the streets to celebrate, trading on the Stock Exchange proceeded at a brisk pace and prices advanced over a broad front after early hesitancy had brought about declines reaching to a point in industrials. Lack of demand rather than selling pressure caused the declines in steels and other heavy industry shares. Later, losses in these were replaced by good fractional gains.

Heaviest trading was in so-called "peace" shares, such as building, plumbing, air transport and paper shares. Hudson Motors jumped over a point, and other issues advancing sharply were American Radiator, Crane Co., Flintkote, Douglas, Eastern Air Lines and Pan American Airways. Railroads were quiet and firm.

Rain for Tomorrow

Today will be cool and cloudy followed by rain tomorrow, according to the Weather Bureau.

Polish Tanks Occupy Port of Wilhelmshaven

London, May 7 (U.P.)—Polish tank forces have occupied the German port of Wilhelmshaven, an Exchange Telegraph dispatch reported today from Field Marshal Sir Bernard L. Montgomery's headquarters.

The dispatch said the battered German cruiser Koeln was sunk in the harbor. The 8th Air Force had claimed the sinking of the Koeln during an attack on Wilhelmshaven.

The 3d Canadian Division entered Emden, German port and U-boat base, the dispatch added.

WHERE TO FIND IT

	Page		Page
Brown	6	Obituaries	7
Comics	15	Our Fighters	5
Crossword	10	Pattern	10
Currie	4	Radio	15
Dr. Brady	6	Society	9
Editorial	6	Sports	11
Financial	16	Take My Word	6
Grin and Bear It	6	Theaters	4
Helleman	6	These Women	15
Helen Worth	10	Tommy Holmes	11
Horoscope	15	Tucker	6
Mary Haworth	9	Uncle Ray	15
Movies	4	Want Ads	13-16
Music	4	Women	9
Novel	12		

VINSON LIFTS CURFEW, RACING BAN

★★★★★★★★ Complete

BROOKLYN EAGLE

WEATHER—Fair, mild tonight; cloudy, warmer tomorrow.

YEAR • No. 126 • DAILY AND SUNDAY (Copyright 1945 The Brooklyn Eagle, Inc.) BROOKLYN, N. Y., WEDNESDAY, MAY 9, 1945 Entered at the Brooklyn Postoffice as 2d Class Mail Matter 3 CENTS

YANKS SEIZE GOERING

VINSON LIFTS CURFEW AND BAN ON RACING

Promises Production Washing Machines, Refrigerators at Once

Washington, May 9 (U.P.)—Mobilization Director M. Vinson lifted the midnight curfew on amusement places today but said restrictions on transportation will continue.

He also revoked, effective at once, the Government ban on racing.

Vinson discussed almost every phase of home front activity at a press conference in which he said he was confident the American people would "keep their feet on the ground and not go haywire" during the coming months.

Vinson announced revocation of the midnight curfew with the remark "curfew will not ring tonight." He then went on to other phases of civilian life in wartime.

Reconversion

The production of electric refrigerators and washing machines will be started immediately in "medium quantities."

Reconversion, he continued, must proceed "vigorously." He warned, however, that complete change-over to a civilian economy must await the defeat of Japan.

Vinson also announced that: War plants will continue on the 48-hour work week.

The Little Steel wage formula and other stabilization policies will be continued.

The administration still favors legislation to put manpower ceilings on employment.

Strict manpower controls will continue to be necessary, especially in areas where war production remains at a high peak.

There will be an increase soon of about 16 percent in gasoline supplies available for civilian use. The increase will be distributed primarily to "B" and commercial card holders, with "A" card drivers possibly getting none of it.

Hold Price Level

Vinson said that generally speaking the objective will be to hold consumer goods back at the level of prices charged before they went up.

Concerning civilian food supplies, Vinson said he saw no prospect of early improvement.

Vinson not only said that present restrictions on travel would have to be continued but also that further curtailment "may be necessary." He added that "the shortage of tires, batteries and gasoline will

Continued on Page 15

Bribe Defendant Just A 'Dope,' Lawyer Says

Eagle Staff photo

AT BRIBERY TRIAL—Harvey Stemmer (left) and Henry Rosen in County Court at the wind-up of their trial.

Attorneys Ask Jury For Acquittal—Say No Crime Was Committed

Harvey Stemmer, the "big shot with the television radio set and the $100 bills," who with Henry Rosen is charged with conspiracy to bribe five Brooklyn College basketball players to throw a game so they could clean up on bets, "trafficked with the honesty and reputation of college boys," Assistant District Attorney Fred Loughran told a jury in Kings County Court today.

"That," he added in his summation, "is the lowest thing a man can do."

Answering the allegation of former Assistant District Attorney Edward Levine, counsel for 43-year-old Stemmer, and Bernard Pizzitola, counsel for 29-year-old Rosen, that no overt acts constituting a crime were committed, Mr. Loughran asserted that their meetings with the Brooklyn students and payment of $1,000 to them were "obvious overt acts." Any other interpretation, he said, was "ridiculous."

Both defense lawyers in their summations asked the jury to bring in a verdict of acquittal on the ground that no crime had been committed. The jury is expected to go out late this afternoon after summation by the court.

No Crime, Lawyer Says

"Shocking as it may seem to pay amateur basketball players to throw a game, it is not a crime," Mr.

Continued on Page 15

DEMOCRATIC CHIEFS COOL TO COALITION OFFER

Decision Pending On Proposal by A. L. P. And C. I. O.-P. A. C.

By JOSEPH H. SCHMALACKER

Democratic leaders adopted a cool and somewhat uncertain attitude today toward the proposal of the American Labor party and C. I. O.-Political Action Committee for coalition in the coming city election campaign.

Neither accepting nor rejecting the proposal immediately, the leaders indicated that before any action will be taken, they will await the outcome of a meeting tonight at which the Liberal Party's attitude is expected to be defined by the Liberal Party's administrative committee.

Democratic spokesmen indicated that if coalition negotiations are begun, the first approach will have to be made by the A. L. P. forces.

Secondly, they declared that if such discussions are opened, the A. L. P.-P. A. C. coalition proposal will have to be examined carefully, not only because there is, at present, no clear-cut sentiment in Democratic ranks on the question of adopting such a policy, but also because a deep-seated political cleavage exists between the Labor Party and the Liberal Party, the two principal minority party groups

Continued on Page 15

I. R. T. Fire Ties Up Rush Hour Crowds

Fire caused by a short circuit in underground cables leading from the I. R. T. generating station at 59th St. and 11th Ave., Manhattan, put a generator out of commission and tied up all traffic on the Broadway-7th Ave. line in Brooklyn and Manhattan for a half hour, just before the morning rush hour today.

Five manhole covers on W. 58th and W. 59th Sts. were blown out when gas fumes exploded at 6:17 a.m. Current on the subway line from W. 137th St., Manhattan, to New Lots immediately was cut off and trains stopped wherever they were. In all, 11 substations, three of them in Brooklyn, were put out of service, most of them for about 12 minutes.

1st Surrendered U-Boat To Reach England Today

London, May 9 (U.P.)—The first U-boat to surrender under Germany's capitulation agreement will put into Weymouth Harbor on the English coast late today, it was announced.

107 From Area On Casualty Lists

The War Department today, announcing the names of 1,044 soldiers killed in action, 2,303 wounded, 459 missing and 522 liberated, listed 28 Brooklyn, Queens and Long Island men dead, 60 wounded, and 12 missing in the European and Pacific areas, and 15 released from German prison camps. The navy listed three dead, one wounded and three missing. Local casualty lists are on Page 8.

Call the Brooklyn Chapter, American Red Cross, and arrange to donate a pint of blood NOW. TRiangle 5-8042.

Patton Praises Newsmen For Efficient Reporting

With the 3d Army, May 9 (U.P.)—Gen. George S. Patton held his final press conference yesterday with war correspondents attached to his army.

"This today marks the termination of combat in Europe," General Patton told the newsmen. "I desire to take this opportunity of expressing to all of you the thanks and appreciation of myself and all members of the 3d Army, past and present, not only for the generous and efficient manner in which you have reported our activities but also for your uncomplaining way in which you have shared our vicissitudes and accommodated yourselves to our way of life."

EUROPEAN AREA TROOPS ON WAY EAST

Service and Combat Outfits From Italy Have Left for Pacific

By J. EDWARD MURRAY

Rome, May 9 (U.P.)—The Allies already have begun shipping combat and service troops from Italy directly to the Pacific for the war against Japan, Gen. Joseph T. McNarney revealed today.

General McNarney, deputy supreme commander in the Mediterranean theater, said other troops would be sent from Italy to the Pacific by way of the United States.

It generally was known that engineering and other technical troops, as well as certain air force personnel, had been embarking for the Pacific for several weeks, but General McNarney's speech was the first confirmation that combat troops already were on the way.

General McNarney's speech was broadcast throughout the Mediterranean theater yesterday, but released for publication in the army newspaper Stars and Stripes and other newspapers only today.

Gives a Frank Answer

He said that his answer to persistent questions from Allied troops as to when they would be permitted to go home would be disappointing.

"But it would be unfair if I were not absolutely frank in answering that question even if it is unpleasant," he said.

The return to civilian life for the majority of troops in Italy would come only after Japan has been defeated, he said. All troops in the European and Mediterranean theaters had been divided into groups for future disposition, he declared.

"The first group will consist of men to be retained overseas and required for occupation, the tremendous job of re-establishing law

Continued on Page 2

Truman Signs Draft Extension

Washington, May 9 (U.P.)—President Truman today signed with reluctance a draft act extension measure which carries an amendment requiring that 18-year-old inductees be given six months training before being sent into combat.

The President said he signed the legislation only because immediate extension of the Selective Service act is necessary for continuing the war against Japan. The measure extends the act for one year after May 15.

"I am reluctantly giving my approval to this legislation," the President said in a statement. "I do not wish this approval to be interpreted as expressing my concurrence in section two of the bill, which places added restrictions on the War and Navy Departments in their management of the fighting forces.

"I signed the legislation only because the immediate extension of the Selective Service act is of compelling necessity in the continuance of military operations against Japan."

Caught in Bavaria Hideout; Kesselring Also Captured

Reichsmarshal Goering

By ELEANOR PACKARD

With 7th Army, May 9 (U.P.)—Reichsmarshal Hermann Goering has surrendered to the Americans, telling them that he had been in hiding since April 24 when Adolf Hitler condemned him to death for expressing a desire to take over control of the German Government.

An announcement today that Goering was in custody of the 7th Army also revealed the capture of Marshal Albert Kesselring, former commander of Germany's Western Front.

Goering was the first of the old guard Nazi triumvirate—Hitler, Goering, Goebbels—to be accounted for officially. He surrendered to the 36th Division, which was engaged in the 7th Army mop-up of the surrendered area on the southern wing of what was the Western Front.

(The Danish Kalundborg radio said it learned Heinrich Himmler, Gestapo chief and German Interior Minister, is in Sweden.)

Reichsmarshal Goering—the rank was his alone in the heyday of Nazism—gave up to Brig. Gen. Robert J. Stack, assistant divisional commander at Radstart, about 35 miles southeast of Salzburg.

He told General Stack that Hitler—who was reported by the Nazis to be dead in the ruins of Berlin—sentenced him to death on April 24, when the handwriting was on the wall for even the most near-sighted Nazi to read.

Rescued by Luftwaffe

Hitler's SS Elite Guards arrested him, Goering said. But members of the German air force, from the command of which he was ousted in the Nazi debacle, rescued him, he said.

He streaked for a hideout in the Bavarian Alps, the touted "national redoubt" in which the Nazi fanatics were going to hold out after the rest of Hitler's Reich was gone.

When the 36th Division approached his hideout, Goering sent his personal adjutant, Colonel Von Brauchitsch, a son of the commander in chief of the German Army in the early days of the war, to divisional headquarters with an offer to surrender to Gen. Dwight D. Eisenhower and Gen. Jacob L. Devers, commander of the 6th Army group.

Von Brauchitsch arrived at a command post at 9 a.m. yesterday. He explained his mission to General Stack and Maj. Gen. John E. Dahlquist, division commander.

General Stack went with Von Brauchitsch to the Radstadt hideout, meeting the Reichsmarshal on the road. Goering was accompanied by his wife, a child and several military aides and personal retainers.

Find Him in Castle

The entire party went to a castle near the famous ski resort of Kitzbuhl, which was occupied by friends of Goering. They arrived at 10:30 p.m. yesterday.

When General Stack and Goering met on the road, both clambered out of their cars and gave the military salute—Goering's, significantly, the Nazi salute.

"I am General Stack of the 36th Division," the officer told Goering.

Goering explained that he spoke some English but understood it better than he spoke it. On the drive to Kitzbuhl, Goering told Stack that he last spoke to Hitler on April 24.

Hitler Was at Redoubt

On that day—one day before the Red Army completed the encirclement of Berlin, where the Nazis

Continued on Page 2

Prague Falls to Reds; Nazis in Dunkirk Yield

BULLETIN

London, May 9 (U.P.)—The Red Army, fighting on against outlawed German diehards after the official end of the European war, today captured the Czechoslovak capital of Prague.

By PHIL AULT

London, May 9 (U.P.)—Outlawed German garrisons of historic Dunkirk, the French Atlantic ports and Bornholm in the Baltic have given up, but German planes bombed Prague in flagrant defiance of the unconditional surrender, it was reported today.

The Prague radio reported that German bombs crashed on the Czechoslovak capital and two other cities hours after the official end of the war in Europe. It added that Russian forces had entered Prague, and with Czechoslovak Patriots cleared the city of German troops.

Paris press dispatches reported that the Germans in Dunkirk, scene of the British evacuation from the continent in 1940, surrendered at 9 a.m. A French communique announced the German capitulations at St. Nazaire, La Rochelle and Lorient.

Telephone reports from Bornholm by way of Copenhagen said the German resistance on the Danish island off the tip of Sweden cracked during the night, and Russian warships put in after daylight.

The crumbling of the last nests of Nazi resistance followed word of the final formalizing of Germany's surrender in Berlin.

German planes began bombing

Continued on Page 15

Allied Chiefs at Work On Jap Invasion Plans

By FRANK TREMAINE

Guam, May 9 (U.P.)—The joint chiefs of staff now are working on plans for an invasion of Japan, Admiral Chester W. Nimitz disclosed today.

With the war spotlight now focused solely on the Pacific theater, Admiral Nimitz also told a press conference the United States immediately will step up "very materially" its air bombardment of the enemy homeland.

He spoke as adverse weather slowed ground operations on southern Okinawa, where five American divisions were hammering at the strongest Japanese defenses in the Pacific only a mile above Naha, capital of the island.

American battleships and cruisers knocked out enemy gun emplacements, artillery and mortars in a heavy bombardment.

Sink 14,000 Tons of Shipping

Navy patrol bombers sank 14,000 tons of shipping and damaged 2,100 in a series of attacks in Korean coastal waters Monday.

Other patrol bombers sank two small cargo ships, a large fishing craft and a coastal cargo ship in the fourth straight day of raids off southern Honshu yesterday.

Admiral Nimitz told his press conference that he was anticipating the shifting of large forces from Europe to the Pacific and added

Continued on Page 15

GI Mail Restricted

Individual copies of newspapers and magazines, offered for overseas mailing by publishers, will not be accepted unless the service man to whom the periodicals are addressed has requested them, Postmaster Frank J. Quayle announced today.

Pontiff Offers Prayer For 'Just End' to War

By HERBERT KING

Vatican City, May 9 (U.P.)—Pope Pius XII expressed gratitude today for the conclusion of the war in Europe and offered a prayer for a "just end" to the "bloody struggle" still under way in the Far East.

In a broadcast to the world he said the European war had left in its wake the greatest "material and moral ruin in the history of mankind."

"Cries of gratitude break forth ardently," he said in hailing the end of hostilities. "They rise from the depth of our hearts toward the Lord Father of mercy."

Prays for Full Peace

He implored "divine omnipotence and bounty for a just finish to the sanguinary struggle also under way in the Far East."

He said the world faces a difficult but holy enterprise to repair the innumerable disastrous effects of war.

Gigantic difficulties also confront the world in preparing for a "truthful and lasting peace," he said.

He asserted that those who have fallen in the war would say:

"May there arise from our bones and from our tombs workers and builders of a new and better Europe—a new and better world based . . . on the sacred principle of equality of rights of all nations, great and small, weak and strong."

The Pope declared the war had brought about discord, diffidence and hatred.

"If the world wants to gain peace it is necessary that lies and rancor disappear and be replaced with truth and charity," he asserted.

The Pope implored God to bring a quick end to the bloody struggle in the Far East. He said the war dead now were telling the survivors:

"May a new and better Europe, a new and better world arise from our bones and our graves, and from the earth where we have been given as grains of wheat."

VE Fails to Excite Typical Nazi Town

Somewhere in Germany, May 9 (U.P.)—The populace of this typical middle-sized German city took the news of the end of war quietly with only slight signs of relief cracking through generally deadpan expressions.

The city went about its dreary routine as usual. There were no special announcements posted, there were no newspapers and the news spread mainly by word of mouth after being picked up on radios.

There was no excitement. Smiles of relief showed mostly on the faces of women who, like in the majority of German towns, outnumber the men more than 10 to 1.

British Gain on Rangoon

Calcutta, May 9 (U.P.)—Two columns of the British 14th Army have scored new gains in a drive toward Rangoon from the north, a communique said today.

Report on Atrocities

Washington, May 9 (U.P.)—Twelve Congressmen who inspected Nazi concentration camps at the request of General Eisenhower prepared today to give a detailed report to Congress on the "pattern of death" they found.

Wilson Kin Says Hubby Tried to Choke Her

Hollywood, May 9 (U.P.)—Ellen Wilson McAdoo, granddaughter of the late President Woodrow Wilson, charged today that her ex-husband, Musician William A. Hinshaw, had slapped and tried to choke her.

Police said Hinshaw, held on an assault and battery complaint, admitted forcing his way into the home but denied striking her.

The plaintiff is the daughter of the late Senator William Gibbs McAdoo.

Sees VE as Time Lost To Pacific Supplies

V-Day was merely a "waste of time" in which the boys in the Pacific [illegible] lines might have been [illegible] a lot more supplies, [illegible] a Queens marine [illegible] at Iwo Jima and recuperating at St. Albans Naval Hospital.

Lieutenant King was wounded twice at Iwo. He suffered shell-shock on the fifth day of the invasion, returning to duty, and then was wounded by shrapnel in the [illegible] but back March 8.

He will be married this Summer to Gertrude King of [illegible] Road.

Other recuperating veterans interviewed included Pfc. Hyman [illegible] Ave. and Pfc. Thomas G. McMahon of 110 [illegible] Road, Douglaston. Private Kramer agreed with Lieutenant King in stating that he "got no bigger" [illegible] VE-Day.

WHERE TO FIND IT

	Page		Page
Bridge	20	Obituaries	15
Brown	14	Our Fighters	10
Comics	23	Patterns	18
Crossword	9	Radio	23
Curry	3	Real Estate	9
Dr Brady	[illegible]	Society	17
Editorial	14	Sports	19 20
Financial	8	Take My Word	4
Grin and Bear It	4	Theaters	3
Heffernan	13	These Women	23
Helen Worth	14	Tommy Holmes	19
Horoscope	19	Tucker	14
Mary Haworth	17	Uncle Ray	23
Movies	12, 13	Veteran in Bklyn	10
Music	13	Want Ads	21, 22
Novel	27	Women	17

Borough Flier Biked to Safety After Nazi Shoots Down Plane

Some German air ace, in the days when there was still a remnant of a Luftwaffe, was doubtless credited with a kill when Lt. Alfred Longo of 96-10 50th Ave., Elmhurst, resourceful P-47 Thunderbolt fighter-bomber pilot, was shot down near Leipzig.

The tale of how he escaped is told in a communication to his wife, Mrs. Gloria Longo, from the 9th Air Force public relations office.

Leader in Group

An element leader in the famed 365th Hell Hawk group, Lieutenant Longo was attacking rail lines east of Leipzig when a Messerschmitt poured shells into his left wing. With controls damaged and landing gear jammed, the Thunderbolt pilot brough his plane to a belly landing in a field and raced to a near by wood.

Shortly afterward the plane exploded and burned, but the pilot did not learn about this until many days later. By the time it happened he was well on his way along a road toward the American lines. He "borrowed" a bicycle from a German girl and rode until a tire blew out, then "borrowed" another and after a few miles ditched it to make a detour around a town.

Rode Tandem Style

Deciding those tactics were too slow, he waited until a boy appeared riding a bicycle.

Lt. Alfred Longo

"He was traveling in my direction," the pilot reported, "so I put him on the seat behind me and he held on to my waist while I pedaled off in a standing position. We came to one town and I pedaled like mad right through the place and the boy shouted in German as we passed, but I figured no snipers would dare take a shot for fear of hitting the lad. We passed through a second town in the same manner and half a mile beyond I saw a column of Sherman tanks and other American vehicles.

"It was a Ranger battalion getting ready to move into the town, and were they surprised to hear that I'd pedaled a bicycle with a passenger through the town and one beyond it!"

Manned Machine Gun

For the next three days the flyer manned a 50-caliber machine gun on one of the Ranger halftracks on patrols, on one occasion rounding up 30 German prisoners. He remained with the outfit as it advanced through the two villages and to the spot where the charred wreckage of his plane lay.

Lieutenant Longo has flown more than 45 dive bombing and strafing missions with the Hell Hawk group. He is 25, a graduate of Grover Cleveland High School and the Savage School for Physical Education and has completed a years post-graduate course at Ithaca College. His wife lives with his parents, Mr. and Mrs. Vincenzo Longo, at the Elmhurst address.

'Aid for Poland' Drive Opens With Appeal by Pastor

An appeal for remembrance of war-ravaged, starving Poland and Polish refugees everywhere has been made by the Rev. Joseph P. Tencza, pastor of St. Stanislaus R. C. Church, Ozone Park, on the eve of the opening of the "Aid for Poland" campaign, which will be in progress from today to June 17, inclusive.

Father Tencza is Brooklyn diocesan director of the campaign, which is sponsored nationally by the War Relief Services of the National Catholic Welfare Conference.

Housewives can help relieve the distress and sufferings of the Polish people by taking gifts of canned goods—fruits, vegetables or meats—from the kitchen shelf and delivering them to the collection depot at the nearest Polish Catholic Church. There are eight Polish Churches in the diocese. The hunger and misery of the destitute Polish people extends to millions, including countless numbers of slowly-starving children, it is pointed out.

In his plea for support of the campaign, Father Tencza stressed in particular the need of relief supplies for Polish refugees in Europe. Expatriated Poles in France, Belgium, the Netherlands as well as those released from Nazi prisoner-of war and slave-labor camps number millions, he said.

"The unfortunate refugees and liberated persons are unable to return to their homeland and are dependent upon the charity of others for their bare existence," Father Tencza said. "The appeal is primarily for canned good, foodstuffs, clothing, soap, vitamins and medicines, which will be collected at the nearest Polish Catholic church for packing and immediate shipment to Europe."

K. C. Extends Drive To Save Clubhouse

The drive to prevent loss of the Columbus Club, 1 Prospect Park West, through mortgage foreclosure will be extended for two weeks, Joseph P. Walsh, general chairman of the campaign, announced yesterday.

So far, a total of $124,220 has been raised through sale of mortgage participation certificates, he said. Club members are seeking to sell $400,000 worth of the certificates to acquire the first mortgage and pay city and Federal taxes.

Mr. Walsh said that although the drive got off to a slow start, it was gathering momentum. He expressed confidence that the full amount will be subscribed within two weeks.

Volunteer workers under William J. Woods reported a total of $11,675 in subscriptions Friday night. Second highest division was that led by P. S. DeMarco, with $10,985.

UNIVERSITY OF THE FUTURE—An architect's sketch of the proposed St. John's University campus to be built on a 100-acre site at Hillcrest, near Jamaica. The plan provides for a stadium and athletic field (shown in foreground), dormitories, a faculty residence and administration building, a classroom and library building, a hall of science and a combination auditorium and gymnasium.

Fine Educational Exhibit Planned For Oceanarium

Not since the World's Fair transformed the marshy Flushing Meadow into a magic wonderland has there been planned for this city such a resplendent educational exhibit as the Oceanarium which is coming to Coney Island

Fairfield Osborn, head of the New York Zoological Society, which drew up detailed plans and designs for the exhibit of marine life, said yesterday that "nothing like it will be has ever been seen in all the world."

To the best of Mr. Fairfield's knowledge, the marine life exhibits in European cities have either been bombed out or liquidated on account of lack of fuel. With human misery to be eliminated, and buildings to be erected first, it is doubtful whether Europeans will be able to get around to rebuilding their aquaria for many years.

To state that the oceanarium is a favorite project of Park Commissioner Moses is sufficient to make people realize that this will be no ordinary aquarium on two lots that the city has acquired opposite the famed boardwalk.

In typical Moses style, plus some excellent ideas by Borough President Cashmore, who fought side by side with the park commissioner to have the oceanarium located at Coney Island, a catwalk that goes inside an aquarium tauk and an old schooner anchored in a pond and containing exotic fish, will be features at the exhibit.

Preliminary Work Started

Preliminary work is being done in the area bounded by W. 8th St., Surf Ave., W. 5th St. and Seaside Park, the ultimate site of the exhibit, and lest you think that catwalk idea has been fashioned with mirrors, here is what is in store for you after the war.

You will proceed along the observation catwalk, right down with the big fish, but you won't be scared because your tank in a tank will be incased in glass.

Now that VE-Day has come and VJ-Day is on its way, the Park Commissioneer, Borough President Cashmore and Councilman Edward Vogel, who also has fought hard for the Coney Island site, are chafing at the bit to get the oceanarium built and give that Moses tone to Coney Island.

Friends to Honor Schorenstein

Former Commissioner of Records Hyman Schorenstein will be given a birthday dinner Wednesday night in the Hotel St. George.

Postmaster Frank J. Quayle, dinner chairman, announced yesterday that more than 1,000 reservations have already been made. The Postmaster is aided by Federal Jurors Commissioner Morris J. Solomon, Collector of Internal Revenue Joseph P. Marcelle, Aaron L. Jacoby and John J. Lynch of the Kings County Democratic organization.

Former Mayor James J. Walker will be toastmaster. Also on the dais will be ex-Governor Herbert H. Lehman, former Postmaster General James A. Farley, Kings County Democratic Leader Frank V. Kelly, Republican County Leader John R. Crews, former Presiding Justice of the Appellate Division Edward Lazansky, former Supreme Court Justice Mitchell May and District Attorney O'Dwyer.

Mr. Schorenstein, known to intimates as "Hymie," is reluctant to tell his age, although several years ago he was given a similar dinner, and announced at that time he was 60. He was Democratic leader of the 23d A. D. for many years.

The famous 10-in-1 army ration is packed in two sub units, each weighing 45 pounds, small enough to prevent careless dropping, but large enough to prevent its being tossed around and the packing damaged.

MEMORIAL DESIGNS—At top is sculpture group proposed for Prospect Park by Dr. Suzanne Silvercruys Stevenson and Clinton Loyd. The memorial tower was designed by David Miller Sr.

Museum Tower, Marine Statue Suggested for War Memorial

A dignified tower, housing an entrance hall, a memorial room and a museum at the top, was among the ideas submitted for a Brooklyn war memorial in the city-wide contest staged by the Brooklyn War Memorial Board.

Another suggestion, which received the favorable attention of the judges, proposed the execution of a bronze group representing the marines raising the flag on Mount Suribachi as immortalized in the famous news photograph.

The marine group was designed and submitted to the judges by Dr. Suzanne Silvercruys Stevenson of 1 W. 67th St., Manhattan, and Clinton Loyd of 2804 41st Ave., Long Island City.

The written explanation of the design suggested that the figures be half again over life size and that the flagpole be actually used each day for flag raising ceremonies serving as a tribute to the war dead. The site chosen was in Prospect Park opposite Eastern Boulevard, where there is now a flagstone terrace.

The total cost of the project was set by the designers at $50,500.

The memorial tower, for which no specific site was suggested, was submitted by David Miller Sr. of 952 Anderson Ave., the Bronx. Mr. Miller, an industrial draftsman, is a native of Glasgow, Scotland. He has a son in the armed forces overseas.

Mr. Miller proposed that the memorial room in the lower part of the tower be circular in construction with a domed ceiling. Names of the war dead would be inscribed on gilt metal strips running around the room.

Adjacent to the hall would be rooms for meetings of military and naval units. The cost of the tower was estimated at $2,000,000.

Mayor Discourses On Mistresses In Approving Opera

Having trouble with the womenfolk, mister? Want some hints on technique? Take it from the Mayor himself—there's only one way to handle the gals.

"Some men don't know how to treat a mistress," opined the Mayor yesterday. "That's when the trouble begins. You should treat a mistress just as you would a politician—use them when you want but never give them a break."

LaGuardia made known his views on the relationship between man and mistress during a conference in his office at City Hall with backers of "Troubled Island," an opera about a Frenchman who freed the slaves on a French island possession.

The group, headed by City Council President Newbold Morris, asked the Mayor's indorsement of a plan to present the opera, with an all-Negro cast and crew, in the New York City Center.

Commenting on the story of the opera, the Mayor revealed that the leading character, Jean Dessalines, had left his wife and taken a "very attractive mistress." It was then that he gave reporters and committee members his theories.

He said the opera had a "message of great merit" and would like to see it produced in the City Center.

Rites Held for Suicide And Daughter He Slew

Kansas City, Mo., July 2 (U.P.)—More than 1,000 persons overflowed a funeral chapel here today as double rites were held for Lulu Mae Davis, 21, and her father, Ray E. Davis, 42.

Lulu Mae was slain Tuesday night by her father in a fit of jealous insanity as she prepared for a date with a soldier. Davis shot himself fatally when cornered by police Thursday morning.

FINANCIAL NEWS

Sperry Arranges 75 Million Credit With Bank Group

A new regulation V Credit for $75,000,000 at 2½ percent interest on borrowings and running to Dec. 31, 1947, has been arranged by the Sperry Corporation with a group of 55 banks throughout the country, headed by the Bankers Trust Company of New York.

The new agreement replaces the credit arranged in 1943, which was for $125,000,000 at 2¾ percent and running to Dec. 31, 1946. Sperry's decision to reduce the amount of the credit is based on material reductions in the company's need for outside funds as a result of a reduced volume of war business, improved operating efficiencies and close control of commitments and inventories, according to Thomas A. Morgan, president. Another important factor, Mr. Morgan said, was the speeding up of settlements of terminated war contracts by the contract settlement act of 1944 and its administration to date by the Office of Contract Settlement and the services.

Bankers Trust Company of New York has been reappointed as agent for the participating banks. Other New York banks participating are Bank of the Manhattan Company, Bank of New York, The Chase National Bank of the City of New York, The Commercial National Bank and Trust Company of New York, The Continental Bank and Trust Company of New York, Guaranty Trust Company of New York, The New York Trust Company, United States Trust Company of New York and Brooklyn Trust Company.

Bowers Announces New Appointments

Appointment of Adam H. Oberheim and Edward J. McGaughan as assistant managers has been announced by LeRoy Bowers, manager of the Bowers Agency in New York City for the Mutual Life Insurance Company.

Mr. Oberheim, formerly agency organizer in charge of recruiting and training new representatives, and Mr. McGaughan, formerly supervising assistant, both will supervise the company's field organization in the New York counties of Suffolk, Kings, Nassau, Richmond, Queens, Westchester, Bronx and New York.

A native of Brooklyn, Mr. Oberheim joined the Mutual Life in 1926 as field representative in the Bowers Agency. On April 1, 1928, he was appointed agency organizer. Mr. Oberheim is a member of the Strathmore Civic Association, Rockville Centre, and is currently serving as treasurer.

Mr. McGaughan joined the Mutual Life as a field representative in the Bowers Agency in 1931. Ten years later he was appointed supervising assistant. He is a Fordham alumnus and a member of the Veterans of the 7th Regiment.

Strong Price Trends Develop On Exchanges

Stocks rose last week to the highest general level in more than seven years under the leadership of rails which hit eight-year peaks. Listed bonds advanced. Commodities generally improved with the exception of cotton futures which eased. Business activity held around its recent high level.

Demand for rail stocks was spurred by President Truman's forecast of heavy transportation of troops across country to the West Coast. American Telephone and Telegraph hit a new high since 1940 on announcement of a refunding program calculated to save $875,000 annually in interest charges. Stock sales averaged approximately 1,453,867 shares daily in the four full sessions compared with 1,140,000 shares in the previous week's full five sessions.

Activity in bonds centered in rail issues which led the market higher. Brazilian obligations featured the foreign dollar bond section on gains ranging to around eight points. United States Government funds firmed.

On the Chicago Board of Trade wheat futures rose several cents a bushel and corn was up fractionally. Oats and rye advanced. Barley improved over a cent. Cotton futures were unchanged to 10 points lower. Trade buying against Government textile contracts bolstered nearby months, and carried July to a 17-year high. Hedge selling developed in new crop positions. Wool tops futures rose around a cent a pound and wool futures were up more than a cent a pound.

Lumber Output Lower

Washington, June 2 (U.P.)—Nationwide lumber production in the first 1945 quarter fell 11 percent below last year to 6,861,116,000 board feet, the War Production Board reported today.

March production rose 15 percent over February, but was 9.2 percent under the 1944 month.

Sell Exchange Seats

The New York Cotton Exchange today reported the sale of two memberships, one for $6,750 and another for $7,000, up $750 and $1,000, respectively, compared with the last previous sale.

7★★★★★★★ Complete

BROOKLYN EAGLE

WEATHER—Clear, cool tonight; cloudy, warmer tomorrow.

104th YEAR • No. 153 • DAILY AND SUNDAY

BROOKLYN, N. Y., WEDNESDAY, JUNE 6, 1945

Entered at the Brooklyn Post-office as 2d Class Mail Matter

3 CENTS

FIND HITLER'S BODY IN BERLIN HIDEOUT

ONE OF FOUR CORPSES IN FORTRESS BENEATH CITY IDENTIFIED AS HIS

By JOSEPH W. GRIGG

Berlin, June 6 (U.P.)—Adolf Hitler's body has been found and identified with fair certainty, it was learned from a high Russian military source here today.

The body, smoke-blackened and charred, was one of four discovered in the ruins of the great underground fortress beneath the new Reichschancellery after the fall of Berlin.

These four bodies, any one of which answered pretty well to Hitler's description, were removed and carefully examined by Russian Army physicians. All were badly burned from the flame throwers with which the Red Army soldiers finally cleared out the underground command post where Hitler and his leading Nazis made their last-ditch stand.

After careful examination of teeth and other characteristics, the Russians singled out one body which they believe almost certainly is that of the Nazi Fuehrer.

Died of Poisoning

Asked why no official announcement of the discovery has been made yet by Moscow, this Russian source said as long as any element of uncertainty exists the Russians do not wish to state definitely that Hitler's body has been found.

The source added, however, that there seems little doubt that this actually is the corpse of Hitler.

Examination of the body showed that Hitler almost certainly died of poisoning. Whether this was self-administered or whether Hitler was killed by one of his henchmen there is no sure means of knowing.

It will be recalled, however, that Russian sources recently reported that Hitler died of an injection given him by his physician, Dr. Morel, after he had been insane and partly paralyzed for several days.

Death Reported May 1

According to a telegram sent by Propaganda Minister Paul Joseph Goebbels to Grand Admiral Karl Doenitz, Hitler died at 3:30 p.m. on May 1. Goebbels himself apparently committed suicide shortly afterward, just before the last stronghold of Nazidom in Berlin fell to the Russians.

Goebbels' own body was discovered by the Russians in the same underground shelter, together with those of his wife and children. All had died by poisoning. Goebbels apparently had administered poison to the members of his family and then committed suicide.

His body was found practically decapitated by a shell splinter or explosive charge which had caught him full in the neck, almost tearing his head from his body.

The bodies of Goebbels and his family also were badly burned, but were identified by the Russians without too much difficulty.

The Russians have given no hint as to how the bodies of Hitler, Goebbels and other Nazis found in Berlin have been disposed of. This probably will remain a secret for all time to guard against the possibility of Nazi fanatics trying to recover the bodies.

Lies Balking Solution Of Langford Murder, Police Head Charges

Second Loan Book of Victim's Widow Reveals $18,000 Advance to Unidentified Person

Police are stymied on the two-day-old Langford murder mystery because "somebody is not telling the truth."

That was the word today of a high police official who had just ended another interview with Mrs. Marion Langford, 70-year-old widow of Albert E. Langford, textile sales executive murdered in the foyer of his swank Park Ave. apartment.

The husky cafe society habitue was killed Monday night by one of two gunmen who gained access to the closely guarded Hotel Margüery suite in which he and his wife had resided since their marriage three years ago. He was 63.

Second Black Book Found

Subject of the latest interrogation of the volatile Mrs. Langford, patroness of stage and opera younglings who benefited by her largesse, was the disclosure of a second "little black book" which was uncovered by detectives of the 4th district.

Acting Deputy Chief Inspector Patrick Kenny, in charge of Manhattan, East, said the book contained the names of 30-odd persons who had received money from Mrs. Langford during the past three years.

According to police, Mrs. Langford had listed notations of money advanced. Opposite one of the names, which was not revealed to reporters, was the figure "$18,000."

Speculation Turns to Stage Star

Among the half-hundred newspapermen covering the baffling case from headquarters near the 51st St. station speculation was that the notation referred to a prominent young theatrical star who had been reported previously as having been helped by the wealthy socialite's widow.

Acting Capt. Vincent Kiernan, in charge of detectives at the 4th District, said the case was tougher than the Gideon, Lonergan and Titterton murders.

"These men did not come to the Margüery to shoot Mr. Langford," Captain Kiernan told reporters.

First Notebook Offers No Clue

Assistant District Attorney Jacob Grumet, in charge of the investigation, said the names in a first notebook found just after the murder had been culled with no results.

As the clueless mystery inquiry went into its third day conflicting stores were obtained at the scene of the crime and at Police Headquarters.

Reporters at headquarters were told that Mr. Grumet was basing his investigation on the near-certainty that thugs had shot Mr. Langford when he confronted them at the doorway. The murder, according to headquarters, was committed when the holdup men found somebody

Continued on Page 11

Turner Heads State Anti-Bias Commission

Henry C. Turner

Albany, June 6 (U.P.)—Governor Dewey today named a five-member commission to administer the Ives-Quinn law which outlaws discrimination in employment because of race, creed, color or national origin. Henry C. Turner of Brooklyn, former president of the New York City Board of Education, was named chairman.

Other members of the commission are: Elmer A. Carter, New York, member of the State War Council; Edward W. Edwards, Albany, secretary-treasurer of the State Federation of Labor; Julian J. Reiss, Lake Placid, director of the International Tailoring Company, New York, and Mrs. Leopold K. Simon, New York City, member of the State Workmen's Compensation Board. They will receive $10,000 a year.

The commission is given unprecedented powers until the new law, which Governor Dewey termed "New York State's employment bill of rights." It has power to investigate charges of discrimination by employers. Employers found guilty of discrimination are liable to fine of $500, a year in prison, or both.

Mr. Turner told reporters that the entire membership of the commis-

Continued on Page 11

DEMS' SLATE SPLITS RANKS FOR PRIMARY

Bosses' Fight Looms As Roe Balks Over O'Dwyer Ticket Mates

By JOSEPH H. SCHMALACKER

Embattled Democratic factions, although united in their support of District Attorney O'Dwyer's designation for Mayor, are moving steadily today toward a head-on primary collision over the nomination for Controller and president of the City Council.

Reliable sources disclosed there was no chance of a face-saving compromise.

United States Marshal Spencer C. Young, advanced by Queens Leader James A. Roe as his choice for Controller against Lawrence Gerosa of the Bronx Leader Edward J. Flynn's organization, indicated his readiness to run.

20 Years' Experience

Marshal Young, a former Brooklynite, now living in Queens, said: "After my 20 years of experience in the Controller's office I feel willing to let the voters of the City of New York decide. I have the greatest respect and admiration for the character and judgment of Representative James A. Roe and I am willing to stake my future in his hands, confident that we will be victorious. I was born and brought up in Brooklyn and represented the American Legion there, and I have many Brooklyn friends."

Henry Epstein, former State Solicitor General and also a former Brooklynite, maintained silence on the question of entering the primaries on the Roe slate for President of the City Council. He would make no statement beyond remarking he had not been consulted by Mr. Roe.

Denounces 'Bossism'

The Queens leader said yesterday Mr. Epstein or Judge Jonah J. Goldstein of the Court of General Sessions represented the type he hoped would run for this nomination.

Mr. Roe, denouncing "bossism" after Queens had been rejected for a place on the O'Dwyer ticket, served notice he would not support either Mr. Gerosa or Assemblyman Irwin Davidson, of Manhattan, who was chosen for president of the City Council. The Gerosa-Davidson designations were voted by Leaders Flynn, Frank V. Kelly, of Brooklyn; Tammany Leader Edward V. McLoughlin and Jeremiah Sullivan, of Richmond.

Friends of the leaders said there

Continued on Page 11

YANKS MOP UP BEATEN JAPS ON OKINAWA

Expect Nimitz Announcement That Battle Is Ended

By WILLIAM F. TYREE

Guam, June 6 (U.P.) — The battle of Okinawa entered the mop-up stage today and Tokyo predicted American invasion forces next will land in Japan itself in the "near future."

Admiral Chester W. Nimitz was expected momentarily to issue a communique announcing the end of all organized resistance on Okinawa, already being converted into a major base for the invasion of Japan.

For the first time since the 10th Army landed on Okinawa 66 days ago, Admiral Nimitz failed to mention ground action in his regular Pacific communique today. It was possible he was preparing a special "victory" communique.

Main Forces Destroyed

Admiral Nimitz announced yesterday that the principal enemy forces on Okinawa already had been destroyed.

Radio Tokyo, while regarding Okinawa as doomed, said Japanese troops were firmly entrenched in new positions and were "locked in fierce fighting with numerically superior enemy forces."

Field dispatches said the 7th Division overran Chinen Peninsula on the southeast coast of Okinawa to its easternmost and southeasternmost tips yesterday. Seventy-five to 100 Japanese soldiers were killed on the peninsula and more than 10,000 hungry, ragged civilians were taken into custody.

There have been no reports of American progress on the rest of the island since Monday, but it was likely that marines on the southwest coast had completed the capture of Naha airfield, biggest, best and last airfield on the island.

Japs Face Annihilation

Other units inland were believed to have squeezed the last survivors of the original garrison of perhaps 80,000 Japanese into the southern tip of the island for final mass annihilation.

The influential Tokyo newspaper Yomiuri Hochi bluntly told its readers that Okinawa had been reduced strategically to an "isolated island" and warned:

"The moment for the battle of decision on our own soil is rapidly approaching. It is high time for the entire nation of Japan completely burned all bridges and made the fullest, complete, all-out preparations for this imminent development, whose outcome will decide the rise or fall of our country for centuries to come. . . .

"The present course of military developments on Okinawa, coupled with recently intensified enemy air raids on Japanese cities, is considered an unmistakable sign of a direct invasion attempt against the Japanese mainland in the near future."

Tokyo broadcasts claimed American casualties in the Okinawa fighting totaled 150,000 dead. However, the last official American casualty total—for the period through May 24—was 35,116, including 9,602 killed or missing.

SURPRISE CALLER—Lt. Gen. Mark W. Clark popped into City Hall for a courtesy call on Mayor LaGuardia. They spent ten minutes chatting about the Italian campaign and present conditions in Italy.

BOWLES PLEA TO END FIGHT ON OPA IS REJECTED

Attempt to Extend Control Law Without Battle Turned Down

Washington, June 6 (U.P.)—Senator Elmer Thomas (D., Okla.) rejected today a last-minute plea from Price Administrator Chester Bowles that he call off a fight to amend the OPA-extention bill.

Senator Thomas told reporters Mr. Bowles had promised "practically eevrything" if he would withdraw his amendment.

The Senator's refusal squelched Administration efforts to get legislation extending OPA through the Senate without a floor battle.

Price control is due to expire June 30 under the current law. Legislation to continue it for another year is scheduled to come before the Senate late this afternoon.

Senator Thomas is chairman of the Senate Agriculture Committee. His amendment would direct OPA to allow meat packers—and processors of every other agricultural commodity — to make a "reasonable" margin of profit on their operations.

He told reporters that a former OPA official testifeid at a closed committee session today that OPA is keeping canned goods on the ration list "just so it can build up a bigger organization and fellows getting these fancy salaries can retain them."

He said the former official was William L. Dunn, Boston, who until May 26, headed the distribution section of the processed foods branch of OPA's food rationing division.

Senator Thomas said Mr. Dunn recommended last Fall that rationing of canned goods be discontinued immediately. The Senator cited his testimony as an example of a "fancy-salaried" man, a former $1,400-a-year school teacher who now makes $8,200 annually at OPA.

"Naturally," he added, "he doesn't want to give up his job to go back to teaching school at $1,400. I can't blame him. But it is not in the public interest."

Russians Would Free Japs in Europe Trap

Reds' Insistence on Deletion of Word 'Nationals' Delays Reich Control Pact, but It's Signed

By JOSEPH W. GRIGG Jr.

Berlin, June 5 (Delayed) (U.P.)—Russia's last-minute insistence on the deletion of a single word which she feared would compromise her neutrality with Japan delayed signature of the Big Four pact on Germany for nearly six hours today.

Marshal Gregory K. Zhukov, the Soviet delegate, also blocked immediate establishment of the Allied Control Council in Berlin and discussion of co-ordinated policies for the four occupation forces.

Marshal Zhukov said he had not been empowered by his Government to carry on further discussions until American troops had withdrawn from the zone of Germany assigned to the Red Army.

The Russians had prepared one of their now-famous banquets in celebration of the signing of the pact. However, both Gen. Dwight D. Eisenhower and Marshal Sir Bernard L. Montgomery, the American and British delegates, said they had to return to their headquarters tonight.

(Drew Middleton of the New York Times, in another dispatch for the combined press, said the day which "began with such high promise ended in frustration.")

The dispute which delayed the signing of the Big-Four pact from noon to 5:45 p.m. centered around the word "nationals" in Article 10:

Continued on Page 11

Hint Stalin Okays Meeting of Big 3

London, June 6 (U.P.) — A Soviet controlled broadcast and a hint in Commons indicated today that Marshal Stalin had agreed to meet with President Truman and Prime Minister Churchill and the place for the meeting had been picked.

Commons was told that Mr. Churchill regrets there is no chance of a Big Three meeting being held in London. Sir John Anderson, Chancellor of the Exchequer, passed the word to the House in answering a question for Mr. Churchill.

The negative report prompted speculation that London could not have been taken out of the picture without some other meeting place being selected. The British Government has made plain its feeling that London should have the next meeting of Big Three.

Sir John's report came on the heels of a broadcast from Soviet-controlled Austria quoting a Moscow report as saying Marshal Stalin had agreed to a conference of the Big Three.

Jackson to See Truman On War Crime Trials

Washington, June 6 (U.P.)—The White House announced today that Justice Robert H. Jackson, the American prosecutor for the forthcoming trials of European war criminals, will make a formal report to President Truman late today.

Justice Jackson recently returned from London where he arranged preliminary details.

U. S. Planes Shoot Down Japanese Bomb Balloons

Spokane, Wash., June 6 (U.P.)—The Spokane Chronicle disclosed today that U. S. planes have shot down some of the bomb-carrying balloons launched against this country by Japan.

New Cold Record Set Again Today; Sun Pays Brief Visit

Three-tenths of a point, Fahrenheit, early today set up another all-time record for cold on a specific date in June, following another all-time date record yesterday. At 6:30 a.m. today the temperature officially noted atop the Whitehall Building was 46.7 degrees, just under the 47-degree mark of June 6, 1878, previous lowest point in the Weather Bureau's 74-year history.

The Weather Man promised a more generous margin later. The forecast calls for partly cloudy and warmer this afternoon, highest temperature about 60, but tonight is expected to be mostly cloudy, with the lowest temperature between 45 and 50 in the city and 35 to 40 in the suburbs. Unofficial observers in Amityville reported a temperature there of 39 degrees at 5:30 a.m.

At noon the mercury was at 60 degrees.

For tomorrow the forecast offers partly cloudy and warmer, highest temperature between 65 and 70. Normal mean temperature for today is 67.

Yesterday's record low of 49 at 4:15 a.m. compared with the previous record for June 5 of 50 in 1878. On June 5, 1925, the temperature rose to 96 degrees.

The present long spell of unseasonable chill recalls the famous "year without a Summer," 1816, when birds froze to death. While the average temperature was only 4.3 degrees below normal, on some days the mercury dropped from 100 to the frost level, with the result that plants either froze or burned.

Elevator Falls 15 Feet, Riders Slightly Injured

William Berger, 52, of 150-29 20th Road, Whitestone, and three other employes of Parker-Kaylon, hardware dealers, suffered slight injuries when an elevator fell 15 feet yesterday to the basement of the Commercial Furniture Warehouse, 51 Downing St., Manhattan.

Plane Carrying 18 Wacs Disappears in Africa

Washington, June 6 (U.P.) — An army transport plane carrying 18 Wacs and a crew of three has been missing in Africa since May 30, the War Department announced today. The plane was lost on a 766-mile flight from Accra, on the Gold Coast of British West Africa, to Roberts Field, Liberia.

The Wacs, stationed at the Air Transport Command Base at Accra since last October, were being sent on a new assignment.

First Fabricated Houses Arrive in Britain

London, June 6 (U.P.)—The first batch of an expected total of 30,000 pre-fabricated houses en route here from the United States has arrived in Britain. Workmen will begin erecting them over the weekend in the London district of Tottenham.

Pope Sees Bishop McIntyre

Vatican City, June 6—Monsignor James McIntyre, auxiliary bishop of New York, was received in a private audience by Pope Pius XII today.

Reds to Back O'Dwyer, Daily Worker Asserts

Recent changes in the Communist line will not affect Leftist support of the Democratic party and its designated New York City candidate for Mayor, District Attorney William O'Dwyer.

Today's Daily Worker says it would be incorrect to draw a conclusion that:

The resumed battle against "monopoly capital" means that members of the Communist Political Association would "try to take the American Labor party away from Sidney Hillman and destroy that party's coalition with the Democrats."

In a political column by Max Gordon, the Communist position is slated as being in support of "the broadest national coalition of all anti-Fascist and democratic forces, including all supporters of Roosevelt's anti-Axis policies."

In or Out of Parties

This was interpreted in political circles as meaning that regardless of internecine Democratic struggles, Mr. O'Dwyer can count on the support of the A. L. P., Sidney Hillman's Political Action Committee and the Communists, in or out of either organization.

Meanwhile, the Liberal party, which appears pledged to coalition with the Republicans behind Controller Joseph D. McGoldrick faces opposition within its own ranks.

This opposition would come from those forces which supported President Roosevelt in the 1944 election and feel that the municipal elections cannot be separated from the 1946 State elections and that those, in turn, cannot be separated from the national political scene.

Mrs. Dorothy Norman, Liberal party vice president, is said to be one of those tending toward support of Mr. O'Dwyer on this basis.

Babe, Lippy, Lefty or Joe? Enter Contest!

The Baseball Contest now running in the Eagle is a lot of fun and provides $2,000 in War Bond prizes, plus hundreds of other prizes.

You can enter it today. See today's cartoon and rules on

PAGE 15

BELMONT RESULTS

FIRST RACE—Four-year-old and up; three-quarters mile.

Terse (D. Mills)	5.30	3.40	2.30
Minee-Mo (W. D. Wright)		11.30	7.50
Liquid Lunch (C. Leblanc)			3.20

Time, 1:14. Napoo, Rurales, Timgad, Esterita, Reaping Gem, Bubbling Image, Miss Puritan, Lawrinson, Proof Coil also ran. Off time, 1:32½.

Charles Town Results

FIRST RACE—Two-year-olds; four and one-half furlongs.

Old Jordan (R. Edens)	5.00	3.40	2.20
Lady Liconier (E. Carrillo)		4.40	2.80
Twilight Bay (G. Acosta)			3.40

Time, 0:51. Edar Bonnie, Mrs. Bomelady also ran. Off time, 1:19½.

POPULAR

Chinese Puzzle Solved; 10 Lees Find a Home

When the Lees of Woodside appeared in Long Island City Court last month to answer a Multiple Dwelling Law violation, there were nine of them crowded in one room at the rear of their Chinese laundry.

oday, however, it was reported to Magistrate Horn that the Lees at home number 10—Christopher having arrived May 27.

They will be moving out of their laundry home to a more spacious place in about two weeks though, the court was assured, thanks to a Catholic priest and a Jewish landlord.

It will be good news to send the two eldest of the dozen Lee children, too, both of whom are serving in the armed forces. One is in the army and the other is in the navy "with nine campaign stars."

Hong Lee, father of the family; Albert Engert, landlord of the building at 46-05 48th Ave., Woodside, in which the laundry is located; the Rev. Arthur Kane, a curate of St. Theresa's R. C. Church in Woodside, of which the Lees and parishioners, and Assistant Corporation Counsel James Hurley all were in court today to report progress.

Father Kane explained that he had some difficulty in obtaining a home for the family because it is Chinese but that "a man named Jacob Cohen" offered a place which will be ready as soon as plumbing and other repairs are made. An adjournment of the case to July 11 was granted in order to give the family time to move.

Soldier Thanks Eagle for New Vets' Handbook

Many touching letters have been received by the Eagle from servicemen and women and their families requesting the new Veterans Handbook.

This Handbook is a public service of the Eagle and is being distributed free. Details of the project and directions on how to get a copy for yourself or your serviceman will be found today on

PAGE 9

Windsors to Go Abroad

The Duke and Duchess of Windsor, touring the Salvation Army's Evangeline residence, Manhattan, revealed yesterday they intend to visit England and France in July.

55 Local Men On Casualty Lists

The War Department today, announcing the names of 169 soldiers killed in action, 1,834 wounded, 124 missing, and 3,655 liberated, listed two Brooklyn men dead, 33 Brooklyn, Queens and Long Island men wounded, three missing in the European and Pacific areas, and 131 released from German prison camps. The navy listed four dead, 12 wounded and one missing. Local casualty lists are on Page 17.

Call the Brooklyn Chapter, American Red Cross, and arrange to donate a pint of blood NOW. TRiangle 5-8040.

Chance at a Rib Steak --If You Buy War Bond

Brooklyn housewives feeling the pinch of the meat shortage will get a chance to replenish their larders Friday night with rib steaks—available only to purchasers of war bonds at Loew's Pitkin Theater.

Manager Al Weiss will produce 25 good-sized steaks at the 9 p.m. rally and hand them out to holders of lucky numbers. The numbers can be obtained in only one way—buy a bond.

Clifford E. Paige, chairman of the Kings County War Finance Committee, announced today that borough theaters still are in the lead in number of sales, having sold more than any other.

According to the latest figures, Brooklyn has sold $67,468,617 in individual bonds, or 64.6 percent of its quota. This represents a jump of $10,859,287 over yesterday, a percentage increase of 10.6.

In E bond sales, Brooklyn runs second to the Bronx, with sales of $29,893,865, or 48.6 percent of the quota. Nationally, the drive has passed the $4,000,000,000 mark.

At 6 p.m. today, before the Statue of Liberty in Times Square, a War Heroes bond rally will mark the anniversary of D-Day on the Normandy coast in France. Lt. Col. Timothy McInerny, a member of the personal staff of General Eisenhower, will address the meeting.

A week from Friday, a three-hour demonstration of battle technique by trained combat infantry teams will highlight the army bond show at Ebbets Field. Bond buyers—and admission is by war bond only—will get a first-hand picture of wire-laying, the setting of high explosives and methods employed in wiping out enemy patrols, snipers and road-blocks.

Members of Girl Scout Brownie Troop 2-366 will roll up nearly a quarter of the borough's entire $41,000 Girl Scout bond quota tomorrow when Julius N. Werk, president of a Manhattan fabrics concern, buys a $10,000 bond from the

WHERE TO FIND IT

	Page		Page
Bridge	18	Our Fighters	17
Brown	10	Patterns	14
Comics	21	Radio	21
Crossword	18	Real Estate	18
Currie	10	Society	14
Dr. Brady	10	Sports	15, 16
Editorial	10	Take My Word	10
Financial	16	Theaters	8
Grin and Bear It	10	These Women	21
Heffernan	10	Tommy Holmes	15
Helen Worth	14	Tucker	10
Horoscope	14	Uncle Ray	14
Mary Haworth	14	Vet. in B'klyn	19
Movies	8	Want Ads	18, 20
Novel	18	Women	12
Obituaries	11		

McGoldrick Pulls Out of Mayor Race

7 ★★★★★★★ Complete

BROOKLYN EAGLE

WEATHER—Clear, mild tonight; partly cloudy tomorrow.

104th YEAR • No. 154 • DAILY AND SUNDAY

BROOKLYN, N. Y., THURSDAY, JUNE 7, 1945

Entered at the Brooklyn Post-office as 2d Class Mail Matter

3 CENTS

McGOLDRICK PULLS OUT OF MAYOR RACE

Wants to Keep Job As Controller—Way Cleared for Goldstein

Republican and Liberal party leaders agreed this afternoon to offer the designation for Mayor to Judge Jonah J. Goldstein of the Court of General Sessions. It was believed he would accept, thus becoming the opponent of District Attorney William O'Dwyer, Democratic designee.

By JOSEPH H. SCHMALACKER

Controller Joseph D. McGoldrick threw a bombshell into New York City's municipal election campaign this afternoon by virtually eliminating his name from the race for Republican - Liberal - City Fusion nomination for Mayor.

Declaring he preferred not to be named for the Mayoralty designation, but that he was deeply concerned to have "honest, forward-looking, non-partisan government" preserved, Mr. McGoldrick announced he had told the leaders of the three parties he would consider being re-designated for his present post.

The announcement, which took political circles by surprise, was immediately interpreted as seemingly clearing the way for the independent, anti-Tammany forces to make Judge Jonah J. Goldstein of the Court of General Sessions in Manhattan their choice for Mayor if they so desired.

Before surprise over Mr. McGoldrick's announcement had subsided, the political campaign received another jolt when C. I. O.-PAC campaign planning board officials abruptly postponed a meeting which had been scheduled for this afternoon to recommend an American Labor party indorsement of the O'Dwyer candidacy for Mayor. The meeting had been scheduled also to recommend action on A. L. P. designations for Controller and President of the City Council.

Clarifies His Stand

Mr. McGoldrick's statement made it clear he was considering another race for Controller at the urging of the Republican, Liberal and Fusion party leaders.

"I am deeply concerned to see that honest, forward-looking, non-partisan government in this city is preserved," the Controller said.

"I am willing to do everything possible in the coming campaign, but I personally prefer not to head the ticket and so informed the Liberal, Republican and Fusion leaders Wednesday evening.

"At the urging I have agreed to consider being a candidate again for the Controllership."

Up to the moment of Mr. McGoldrick's announcement there was every indication that both Mr. McGoldrick and Judge Goldstein were

Continued on Page 11

Charles Town Results

FIRST RACE—Three-year-olds and up; four and one-half furlongs.

Famous Time (W. Kirk)	5.00	3.00	2.20
Maryland Morn (Dufford)	—	3.40	2.60
Gradea (E. Carrillo)	—	—	2.80

Time, 0:50 4-5. Secret Minerva, Sherrie Lee, Kiddie's Baby also ran. Off time, 1:18.

Wins Medal of Honor For K. O. of 40 Nazis

Eagle Staff photo

HE'S THEIR BOY — The family of Staff Sgt. Joseph E. Schaefer read about the infantryman's heroic deeds in Germany. Left to right are the father, Lawrence Schaefer of 86-17 102d St., Richmond Hill; Mrs. Schaefer, Pfc. Leonard, another son, and Virginia, the sergeant's sister. That's Joe in the picture.

Queens Soldier Defied Flame Throwers With His Rifle

A five-foot, four-inch infantryman from Queens who stopped an enemy breakthrough in Germany, put out of action 40 enemy soldiers singlehanded and then liberated an entire American squad, has been awarded the Medal of Honor, the War Department announced.

He is Staff Sgt. Joseph E. Schaefer, who already holds the Silver Star, the Bronze Star, the combat infantryman badge and the Purple Heart with two oak leaf clusters. The sixth New Yorker to win the highest award in the armed services, Schaefer is now in Czechoslovakia, the sixth country in which he has fought.

It all happened near Stolberg, Germany, last Sept. 24. Schaefer was commanding a rifle squad when the group of ten men was surrounded by two counterattacking companies of Germans.

The 26-year-old infantryman ordered his men into a house beside the road, crawling from one foxhole to another to give his commands. Then the Germans got ready to charge the house.

Aimed Deadly Fire

Stationing himself in the doorway, Sergeant Schaefer broke the first wave of infantry coming on. It was simple—he just killed the first five men with his rifle. When the Germans started coming in with grenades and flame throwers, he killed four more and wounded others.

The Germans regrouped, crawling

Continued on Page 11

SLAYING PROBERS HAVE 500 NAMES BUT NOT A CLUE

Mrs. Langford Says Marriage Was Kept Secret From Father

Four days after the murder of Albert E. Langford outside his suite in the luxurious Hotel Marguery a high police official admitted today: "All I know is that two men went to Langford's apartment and each had a gun. Then they left us with a dead body and a headache."

The only bromide for that "headache" was a series of "clues" in the hands of detectives, most of them stemming from four books containing about 500 names belonging to the wealthy cafe habitue who was the slain man's wife,

One of the men mentioned in that book is Reed Lawton, 30-year-old romantic baritone, who is on his way to New York from Chicago. Questioned about him, Mrs. Langford, it was disclosed, admitted giving him money amounting to $50,000 over a period of four years. She was reported infuriated by police queries designed to find out who else benefited from her check book.

"Are you trying to question me as to whom I should give my money?" she is reported to have said. "I can give my money to whomever I please."

She also revealed, it was disclosed, that her aged father, source of the greater part of her income, did not know she had been married to Langford for the last three years although he also had a suite at the exclusive Park Ave. apartment hotel in which they lived. The reason for that, she explained, was that he had warned her when her husband, Robert H. Grimes, died that any one who would marry her thereafter would do so only for her money.

Meanwhile, detectives again questioned George Riales, friend of the late Rafaelo Diaz, former Metropolitan Opera tenor and protege of Mrs. Marion Langford.

Carl Rood, Mrs. Langford's attorney and former law partner of

Continued on Page 11

Former Bund Leader Loses Citizenship

Gustave Karl Vogt, 44, of 35 Smith Terrace, Staten Island, was denaturalized in Brooklyn Federal Court by Judge Mortimer W. Byers, who ruled that Vogt, in his application for citizenship, filed in 1933, falsely swore that he knew a witness in his behalf for five years.

Vogt was born in Wertenberg, Germany, and came to the United States in 1926.

According to the Government, Vogt was the leader of the German-American Bund in Staten Island.

Gov. Dewey Reviews 85,000 Marchers Here

Governor Dewey and Borough President Cashmore, heading a party of army, navy and Government officials, reviewed 85,000 youthful marchers today in 28 divisional parades of the Brooklyn Sunday School Union.

Following a fast glimpse at the separate groups marching under church and national banners in the 116th annual observance of Anniversary Day, the party proceeded to Prospect Park, where 10,000 children converged at Long Meadow.

Youngsters stepped high and jauntily in the brisk air. They had the day off from school, they had on their best clothes and ice cream and cake were in the offing.

As usual, the parade was preceded by luncheon at the Montauk Club, 8th Ave. and Lincoln Place. Hosts were Supreme Court Justices Charles C. Lockwood and John MacCrate and Frederick J. H. Kracke, chairman of the city board of assessors.

At one point in the parades, the boys and girls stilled their waving flags and bowed their heads while taps played in memory of the 230 members of the 300 Sunday schools in the Union who died in service.

About 30,000 children marched in several sections of Queens. Proxy marchers in both boroughs, who, since the war, have paraded for member servicemen and women now scattered about the world, followed close behind the children.

Spotted among the adults were soldiers returned from fighting in Europe.

Among the reviewing party, which watched perambulators decorated in red, white and blue push past the stand and children in matching costumes wave gaily, were Chief Marshal Harold E. Meyer, Elmer E. Bullis, president of the Union; Lt. Gov. Joe R. Hanley, State Attorney General Nathaniel L. Goldstein and Controller Joseph D. McGoldrick.

Also included were City Council President Newbold Morris, Justice Lockwood, President Mary Dillon of the Board of Education, Superintendent of Schools John E. Wade, Capt. H. V. McKittrick, representing Rear Admiral Freeland A. Daubin, commandant of the Brooklyn Navy Yard, and Col. Arthur V. McDermott, city Selective Service director. Edwin B. Wilson, editor of the Brooklyn Eagle, and Mrs. Wilson reviewed the South District procession, consisting of Amersfort, Atlantic, Flatbush Central, Linden, Ocean Parkway, Rugby and Sheepshead Bay sections.

The theme of this year's procession was "Christ, Our Refuge and Strength."

BELMONT RESULTS

FIRST RACE—Two-year-olds; five-eighths mile.

Darby Darius (P. Roberts)	160.00	37.80	11.40
Stargazer (T. Atkinson)	—	3.30	2.40
Ruling Time (E. Arcaro)	—	—	2.90

Time, 1:00. Hasty Blue, Muy Triste, Schoolman, Svengali, Ellen Valjean, Stage Song, Kayscout also ran. Off time, 1:17.

SECOND RACE—Freddie's Game, 1st; Ecolire, 2d; Pharamonda, 3d.

YMCA Branches To Distribute Vets Handbook

Ten Brooklyn and three Queens offices of the YMCA will distribute the Brooklyn Veterans Handbook, just published by the Brooklyn Eagle and given free to veterans, men and women in the armed forces and families of servicemen.

Details of the offer and directions on how to get your copy appear today on PAGE 12.

SEE RED LINK IN ARREST OF SIX AS SPIES

Navy Officer, Editors, Writer, Officials Seized

Philip Jacob Jaffe, arrested yesterday by Federal Bureau of Investigation agents as a violator of the Espionage Act, was a heavy supporter of the Communist party in this country, it was disclosed today.

He was charged with four other men and a New York woman, co-editor of his Amerasia magazine, with stealing secret documents from a half-dozen United States Government departments and using the information in publications aimed at fostering Communistic propaganda efforts.

The magazine is recognized here as a Communist-front publication and Jaffa has been listed as a $5,000 annual contributor to the Communist political war chests.

Washington officials hinted that arrest of the six persons was part of a "whole series" of cases involving illicit use of Government information. Two others besides Jaffe were arraigned here last night and released in $10,000 bail.

Three of the arrests were made by FBI agents in Washington. They were a naval lieutenant and two State Department employes.

Grew Makes Statement

Acting Secretary of State Joseph C. Grew said the arrests were the result of a "comprehensive security program."

He said the program will be continued "unrelentingly in order to stop completely the illegal and disloyal conveyance of confidential and secret information to unauthorized persons."

FBI Director J. Edgar Hoover said the data from the Government's secret files usually were turned over to Jaffe and Kate Louise Mitchell, his magazine associate.

Jaffe and Miss Mitchell and Mark Julius Gayn, nationally known writer who allegedly used some of the material, were arraigned here.

Those apprehended in Washington were:

Lt. Andrew Roth, formerly assigned to the office of naval intelligence.

Emmanuel Sigurd Larsen, specialist in the State Department's China division.

John Stewart Service, State Department foreign service office employe who until recently was stationed in China.

Roth was arraigned last night and held in $10,000 bond. Larsen and Service were to be arraigned shortly.

If convicted all face maximum penalties of two years imprisonment and $10,000 fine.

Hoover said the arrests followed

Continued on Page 11

Ebbets Heirs Reject $650,000 for Stock

An offer to purchase the Ebbets estate holdings of 50 percent of the Brooklyn Baseball Club for $650,000 was rejected by all the Ebbets heirs in a conference in the chambers of Surrogate Francis D. McGarey today.

This bid was made by a group consisting of Branch Rickey, Andrew Schmitz, Walter O'Malley and John Smith through the Brooklyn Trust Company, one of the three executors of the estate. Although the Brooklyn Trust Company recommended the acceptance of the offer, it was emphatically rejected by the two other executors, Mrs. Grace Slade Ebbets and Joseph Gilleaudeau, as being ridiculously inadequate.

At the same time the Ebbets heirs, reports to the contrary, presented a united front against the sale of the Ebbets holdings unless a much larger bid is made.

Surrogate McGarey set June 20 as the date for a formal hearing, at which other bids may be considered and at which the application of the Brooklyn Trust Company to resign as an executor will be heard.

2d B-29 ATTACK BLASTS OSAKA

Boys on Carrier Off Okinawa Concerned About Folks in Boro

By FRANK D. SCHROTH

Mr. Schroth, publisher of the Brooklyn Eagle, is in the Pacific area from which he sends via navy radio the following account:

The real story of Okinawa is not ready to be told. It has yet to reach the decisive climax which will make the island available as the great strategic base for the activities that are now being planned by Admiral Nimitz and his staff. But it is timely to tell of the vast naval operations that have been conducted here in the Pacific in connection, not only with Okinawa, but the master plan that bodes ill for the Japs.

Reaching this spot not far from the mainland of Japan was an experience that will live forever. We were flown from Floyd Bennett Field to San Francisco, to Pearl Harbor, to Eniwetok, to Guam, to a fleet anchorage. This distance of about 12,000 miles was made in less than three days. From the anchorage I went by destroyer to catch up with the task force and to board this carrier.

This vast fleet of naval power is commanded by Admiral William F. Halsey. The carrier, aboard which I have been for more than a week, is a flagship of a task force. The ship's company is typical of that of every ship in the task force, perhaps the heaviest in firepower in the history of this or any other war.

Never a Gripe

So it is about the men of this task force that I think the people at home should know something. There has never been a finer group of young men aboard any ship in any fleet. And a good portion of them are from Brooklyn. I have lived with them. Talked with them by the hour. Have taken messages from them for their loved ones at home. They do so want to get home but not once have I heard a single gripe. Interested, they are, of course, in how things are in Brooklyn.

They were most unusually concerned about how the folks at home acted on VE-Day. They wanted to know if they went all out on an emotional debauch at the news from the European front and if they knew how difficult it was going to be here in the Pacific.

These boys know that the end of the European war does not mean that there will be any demobilization until Japan has been defeated. They know, and they worry, that reconversion plans in many instances are hurting the Pacific War effort.

Continued on Page 11

Meat on the Table For 2,000 Lucky Ones

3,000 Wait at Market—More Supplies Coming Up—Fruit Store Shutdown Looms

There will be meat for dinner tonight for the Brooklyn families of about 2,000 lucky customers of a crowd of more than 3,000 who today stormed the Fort Greene Retail Meat Market, 174 Fort Greene Place.

Gathering since 3 a.m., the line, five abreast, extended for more than a block when the market opened. Except for a momentary rush at the opening at 8, police reported the crowd orderly and showing marked restraint.

With a stock of 30,000 pounds of all meat items, Manager George Lazarus estimated that about 2,000 customers would get their orders. The disappointed will get another chance tomorrow, he said, when another 25,000 pounds will be on sale.

The favored customers were overseas veterans. Each customer was allowed to buy five items, the manager said, and the average sale was 12 pounds. The sale was strictly legal, he stressed, with red points required and ceiling prices prevailing.

Private Vincent Tondasco, 24, of 382 18th St., wounded in Europe, bought for a family of eight, and Aviation Metalsmith, 1st Class, Patrick Ruggierio, 24, of 690 5th Ave., for a family of four.

Though the supply was exhausted shortly after noon and the store closed, about 600 women continued to crowd the street. They refused to disperse despite the manager's insistence that the day's supply was gone and they would have to renew their meat quest by being on hand early tomorrow.

Fruit Shutdown Looms

Meanwhile, efforts of Mayor LaGuardia to prevent a shutdown of the city's retail fruit and vegetable stores appeared balked, at least temporarily, with the announcement that dealers had refused to submit sworn evidence against wholesalers whom they accuse of forced tie-in sales and general black market practices.

In an attempt to end the deadlock another meeting of city officials and retailers is scheduled for this afternoon. The organized dealers will vote on calling off the store strike at a mass meeting tomorrow night in the Manhattan Center. Unless voted down, the closing slated to begin Saturday will affect 1,500 member stores in Brooklyn and Queens and an equal number in Manhattan and the Bronx. Another 3,000 retailers are expected to join the protest closing.

Wholesalers have started reprisals against the complaining retailers, Mr. Hausman charged, by delaying delivery of non-perishable items to get higher prices later.

The City Council measure sponsored by Vice Chairman Joseph T. Sharkey of Brooklyn to set maximum penalties of 90 days in jail and $500 fines for price violations by food wholesalers today had the support of the New York City Consumer Council.

Yalta Not Secret, Says Churchill

London, June 7 (U.P.)—Prime Minister Churchill told Commons today no secret agreements were made at the Yalta conference except that giving Russia two extra votes in the Security Conference.

"The conversations of course proceeded in a very intimate manner, and I am not prepared to say that everything discussed at Yalta could be made the subject of a verbatim report," Mr. Churchill said.

Laborite Morgan Price raised the question of secret agreements at Yalta. If there were none, he asked, "why is it that the Russian Government has acted in the matter of broadening the Polish Government in a way usually at variance with the declared decisions of the conference?"

Mr. Churchill replied:

"There were no secret engagements entered into at all, except that we kept secret the addition of two members to Russia and the desire of the United States until the President could get home and make the necessary arrangements on the spot. Otherwise there are no secret engagements."

Yugoslavs Execute 6 Croatian Fascists

The Yugoslav telegraph agency reported today that six leaders of the former Croatian Fascist Government were executed after being convicted of high treason and war crimes by a Zagreb court martial. Among those shot were Premier Nikola Mandich.

Amsterdam, June 7 (U.P.)—Mathys Smets, a former United Press employe in Amsterdam and one of the few men to return from a Nazi death cell, said today that the Germans paralyzed the vocal chords of condemned prisoners before executing them.

Axis Sally Caught, Faces Treason Trial

Rome, June 7 (U.P.)—Allied headquarters announced today the arrest in Turin of "Axis Sally," whose honeyed voice dripped propaganda poison into the ears of radio listeners during the war in the Mediterranean.

Military police of the 4th Corps took Sally into custody. Authorities had said earlier that if she were caught she would be sent to the United States for trial on treason charges.

Sally is Rita Louisa Zucca, 33. She was born at 118 W. 49th St., New York City. Her father operates a restaurant in 49th St., officials said.

Miss Zucca began broadcasting for the Nazis in February, 1943, and soon became a star performer in the propaganda shows aimed at Allied military personnel in this theater.

Her well-modulated voice and often mysteriously accurate information about Allied prisoners and troop movements was supplemented by a "soldier sweetheart" patter. She always signed off with "Goodnight, boys, and a sweet kiss from Sally."

GIs dwelt at length on whether she was a glamorous pinup or an ugly duckling. After her capture she was described as 5-feet-4 and cross-eyed.

Think Girl Was Forced Into Propagandist Role

The family of Rita Louisa Zucca, arrested as "Axis Sally" in Turin, clung to the belief today that she had been forced into her role as a Fascist propagandist.

Timothy Zucca, a cousin, said the family had last heard from Miss Zucca in 1939, when she wrote from Italy that she wished to become an Italian citizen. She said she wanted Italian citizenship in order to get a job with the Italian radio.

TOKYO ADMITS OKINAWA DEFEAT IS IN SIGHT

Blames U. S. Air Fleet And Rocket Ships For Island Reverse

By WILLIAM F. TYREE

Guam, June 7 (U.P.)—The 10th Army hurled the last Japanese on southern Okinawa into a 25-square-mile pocket today and Radio Tokyo said their final defeat was in sight.

Tokyo conceded Okinawa's plight was due in part to the effectiveness of American rocket ships and planes in preventing Japanese suicide aircraft from crashing into American warships off the island.

Ragged remnants of the Japanese garrison were making their final stand from atop a 200-foot cliff shielding the southern tip of Okinawa and forming the backbone of their doomed pocket.

Strafe Okinawa Pocket

Waves of American planes bombed and strafed the Okinawa pocket.

Land-based tactical bombers, apparently scoring a lucky hit on an ammunition dump, blew up the side of a mountain at the edge of the

Continued on Page 11

Today Will Be Hot! Weather Man Sees 75

Doff your coat for a few hours this afternoon, if you want to—but keep it close at hand. While the Weather Man sees temperatures rising as high as 75 degrees this afternoon, tonight will be cool again. Around 50 degrees.

The lowest temperature this morning was recorded at 5:45—50.1 degrees. Tomorrow will be partly cloudy, mild in afternoon, cool again at night.

Casualties Include 32 From This Area

The War Department today, announcing the names of 221 soldiers killed in action, 379 wounded, 20 missing and 2,081 liberated, listed seven Brooklyn, Queens and Long Island men as dead, 14 wounded and one missing in the European and Pacific areas, and 85 released from German prison camps. The navy listed three local men dead, six wounded and one missing. Local casualty lists are on Page 9.

Call the Brooklyn Chapter, American Red Cross, and arrange to donate a pint of blood NOW. TRiangle 5-8040.

Miles of War Plants Razed By Fire Bombs

Guam, June 7 (U.P.) — Nearly 600 Superfortresses and fighters smashed mile after mile of war plants with 2,500 tons of fire and demolition bombs today in the second big raid in a week on Osaka, Japan's greatest industrial city.

Radio Tokyo said 40 other Thunderbolt, lightning, Mustang and Hellcat fighters, apparently from new American bases on Okinawa, almost simultaneously made a two-hour leaflet raid on the Kagoshima area of Kyushu in southern Japan.

The broadcast indicated the air war over Japan had entered a new phase with the completion of bases on Okinawa bringing the enemy homeland within range of all types of American planes from fighters to B-29s.

Tokyo admitted that Lightnings had not appeared over Japan proper before.

Bombs Blanket Target Area

Some 400 to 450 Superfortresses and 150 Mustangs struck shortly after noon at Osaka arsenal, the largest in Japan, and other major war plants in hitherto little-damabed eastern Osaka.

Heavy clouds prevented observation of results, returning pilots and crewmen said. But their fire bombs and high explosives, dropped with the aid of precision instruments, blanketed the target area.

The overcast prevented enemy fighter opposition and reduced the effect of anti-aircraft fire to a minimum.

Admit Fires Were Started

A Japanese Domei report admitted the B-29s started fires in the areas around Osaka castle which is near the Osaka arsenal, target of the attack.

A Japanese announcement said the raid lasted three hours. Fires were started in the northeastern and northern sections of the city, but were "steadily being brought under control," the announcement said.

The raid marked the third stage of the 21st Bomber Command's methodical destruction of Osaka, prewar Japan's second largest city with a population of 3,252,340.

Big Area Burned Out

Some 11½ square miles—18½ percent of the built-up area—of Osaka were burned out in the two previous heavy raids, the latest only last Thursday.

Today's attack boosted the total devastated area of Japan's main industrial cities well over the 90-square-mile mark, an area larger than Brooklyn.

Tokyo said 50,000 Japanese familiaes — 200,000 persons — rendered homeless by American air raids on Japanese cities will be moved to farms to help boost food production.

North of Japan, Liberators of the 11th Air Force bombed the Kataoka naval base on Shimushu and search aircraft of Fleet Airwing hit installations in the Hayake River area of Paramushiru.

To the south, a Pacific Fleet communique revealed, American planes have begun attacks on Japan proper and on the Ryukyu Islands from newly established airfields on Okinawa. Nearly 30 American smaller type planes from Okinawa attacked Japanese airfields on the southern home island of Kyushu, a Tokyo broadcast said.

Chaplin Given 10 Days To Appeal for New Trial

Hollywood, June 7 (U.P.)—Charlie Chaplin, wealthy 56-year-old comedian, today was given 10 days to appeal to a higher court a refusal of a third trial on Joan Barry's charges that he fathered her 20-month-old daughter.

Superior Judge Clarence Kincaid denied the white-haired actor a new trial on the grounds that, although the evidence was "highly conflicting," Miss Barry's story was sufficiently credible to warrant not overruling the jury.

WHERE TO FIND IT

	Page		Page
Bridge	6	Obituaries	11
Comics	21	Our Fighters	8
Crossword	6	Pattern	14
Currie	3	Radio	21
Dr. Brady	10	Real Estate	12
Editorial	10	Society	13, 14
Financial	18	Sports	15, 16
Grin and Bear It	10	Take My Word	10
Heffernan	10	Theaters	17
Helen Worth	14	These Women	21
Horoscope	14	Tommy Holmes	15
Lindley	10	Tucker	10
Mary Haworth	13	Uncle Ray	8
Movies	17	Want Ads	18-20
Novel	18	Women	13, 14

TOMMY HOLMES

A Greenberg Could Bust Race Wide Open

After the following column had been written, the Brooklyn Eagle learned this afternoon that Capt. Hank Greenberg is now at Fort Dix, N. J., being processed for discharge on points. He is expected to be a civilian—and eligible for baseball—within 48 hours.

HANK MAY BE OUT—Here is a pretty solid rumor that comes ticking over the baseball grapevine. Capt. Hank Greenberg, in the very near future (perhaps even sometime today) may be unconditionally released by the army and free to resume his civilian profession which involves belting pitched balls high and far for the Detroit Tigers.

The big boy from the Bronx has been among those absent in the major league picture for quite a spell. To be explicit he was first inducted by the army on May 7, 1941.

For the period of several days, he was a civilian again when, on Dec. 5, 1941, he was honorably discharged under a ruling which briefly was designed to release service men past the age of 28. You know what happened on Dec. 7, 1941. Within a week, Hank was back in khaki. He re-enlisted.

Hank Greenberg

RUSTY, NO DOUBT—Nor was Greenberg much of a ball-playing soldier. I don't know how much actual combat service he actually saw but he served overseas on special assignments in various parts of the world after being graduated from officers' training school.

Last time we saw him around was about two years ago when he played at the Polo Grounds with a service team in a War Bond baseball show. He hit nothing but the air that afternoon and explained it was the first time he had waved a bat that season.

Presumably, he has had little opportunity for bat-waving since and so right this minute, it is anybody's guess how much his return could help the Tigers, now in proud but jittery possession of a one-half game grip on first place.

NOT TOO OLD—Captain Hank isn't too old. He is 34. He is a long, lean fellow who never had any problem about weight. In the matter of speed, he always was mediocre so the chances are that he hasn't slowed up much.

There is only one thing. Four years and one month is an awful long time for a big league ball player to be away from the racket. Baseball inactivity dulls the edge of coordination so necessary to good hitting. How long will it take Greenberg to synchronize his batting eye and his batting swing? Will he ever come back all the way?

If he could come back all the way, he'd be so far the best ball player in the majors that it would be a laughing matter. In fact, it's hard to realize that once there were guys like Greenberg around.

He was in the American League for nine seasons and left with a lifetime batting average of .325. He hit 249 home runs, an average of better than 27 a season. One year, he hit 58. Babe Ruth was the only man who ever topped that. Twice—in 1935 and 1940—he received the American League most valuable player award.

MIGHT MEAN TIGER FLAG—One hesitates to think of how Hank would hit this season if, within a few weeks, he could get reasonably sharp. So much of our present wartime pitching is strictly on the sucker side.

Furthermore, it is entirely possible that this one man could tear what so far has been a completely unpredictable American League race wide open.

Something like that almost happened last year and in the same city, you may recall. It was almost the middle of July that Dick Wakefield, discharged as a naval air cadet, joined the Tigers, then below the .500 mark. From that point, the Tigers were far and away the best club in the league. Their long stretch run from far back caught them at the finish but Wakefield's bat was the reason for the great records of Trout and Newhouser. Make no mistake about that. Detroit leads the league at the moment, but they haven't looked anything like they did last Fall with Wakefield in the army.

MADHOUSE BASEBALL—It's possible that quite a few of the baseball guys will come drifting back here and there from time to time, a possibility that will further confuse two mad pennant races already dizzier than a hop-head's nightmare.

Take a look at the standings today. With one-third of the season gone, six clubs are within three and a half games of first place in the National League and the hottest team in the race is Boston, which has won eight straight. Cincinnati, in seventh place, is only six games out. Any club could win the pennant except Philadelphia, which now has lost 15 straight. In the American League, all eight clubs are telescoped within nine games.

If the baseball mob resembled horse handicappers, they'd simply size up the twin situations as a five-furlong sprint for two-year-old maiden fillies.

"No selections!"

Major League Records

NATIONAL LEAGUE

YESTERDAY'S RESULTS

Brooklyn 7, New York 4.
Boston 10, Philadelphia 0.
Pittsburgh 9, Chicago 3, night.
Cincinnati at St. Louis, rain.

STANDING OF THE CLUBS

	W.	L.	Pct.
New York	28	19	.596
Pittsburgh	27	20	.574
Brooklyn	26	20	.565
St. Louis	26	21	.553
Chicago	23	20	.535
Boston	23	21	.523
Cincinnati	21	24	.467
Philadelphia	10	39	.204

TODAY'S GAMES

New York (Feldman 5-3) at **Brooklyn** (Gregg 7-4), 8:30 p.m.
Cincinnati (Beck 2-4) at St. Louis (Creel 4-1), night.
Philadelphia (Lee 2-5 and D. Barrett 3-5) at Boston (Cooper 5-0 and Logan 3-1), 2 games.
Only games scheduled.

TOMORROW'S GAMES

New York at **Brooklyn,** 2:30 p.m.
Chicago at Pittsburgh, 2.
Philadelphia at Boston.
Only games scheduled.

AMERICAN LEAGUE

YESTERDAY'S RESULTS

Washington 5, **New York 3.**
Philadelphia 7, Boston 5, 12 inns.
Detroit 2, St. Louis 1, 11 inns. nite.
Chicago 1, Cleveland 0, night.

STANDING OF THE CLUBS

	W.	L.	Pct.
Detroit	26	17	.605
New York	27	19	.587
St. Louis	22	22	.500
Boston	23	23	.500
Chicago	22	24	.478
Washington	21	23	.477
Cleveland	20	23	.465
Philadelphia	17	27	.386

TODAY'S GAMES

Cleveland (Klieman 2-1) at Chicago (Haynes 3-5).
St. Louis (Shirley 3-3) at Detroit (Mueller 1-2).
Boston (Woods 2-1) at Philadelphia (Knerr 1-3), night.
(Only games scheduled).

TOMORROW'S GAMES

Boston at Philadelphia.
Cleveland at Chicago.
St. Louis at Detroit.
(Only games scheduled.)

Sam Mammone Proves He's Shrewd Boy

Refuses to Answer Bell for Fifth in Ruffin Contest

By CHARLES VACKNER

Viewing the handscribbling on the canvas and sensing he would soon be there himself, Sammy Mammone took a powder. In such manner did the Bobby Ruffin-Mammone squabble end in the fourth round last night. Slated for 10 sessions, the bout headlined the opening show in MacArthur Stadium. A gathering of 3,666 paid a gross gate of $4,693.50 to see Astoria's agile agent exhibit his bag o' tricks.

Advertised as Sammy Mammone and introduced as Sammy Mammone, Ruffin's adversary looked like a fat Conn. McCreary. Between rounds, I sort of expected old Pensive to provide the fighter with water and iodine, etc. However, I guess it was Sammy Mammone who fought Ruffin for Pensive never appeared. Maybe Mammone was two Eddie Arcaros?

Ruffin, billed for more fights than a free-style bartender, was more annoyed than hurt by his pudgy rival. After flailing Mammone about the ribs with sweeping right handers in the first round, Ruffin figured the gink from Cos Cob, Conn., would behave himself. Instead, Mammone came out in the second and clipped Ruffin with a long overhand right to the head. The punch made Ruffin wince and he lost the round by continually missing rights to the body.

The End Commences

At the start of round three, Ruffin took command. He spattered Mammone with sharp lefts to the face, smeared Sammy's nose and, at times, held him from tumbling. It looked as though Ruffin had no intention of trying to kayo his opponent. Manmone, too, sensed this. However, he fired overhand rights. The punches, of course, missed by feet and he was the chief receiving clerk during the remainder of the fight. Ruffin toyed with his man throughout the fourth round and hurt Mammone with powerful rights to the body.

Sitting in his corner, after the close of the fourth round, Mammone decided he wasn't going to give Ruffin the satisfaction of scoring a kayo and complained of injured ribs. The occasion marked the first time in several seasons the writer observed a beaten fighter display an ounce of common sense. Max Baer showed it against Joe Louis and Mammone revealed it against Ruffin. That's just about the story. At 143, Mammone held a five pound advantage. Jack Dorman refereed. The judges were Gus Galli and Mike Parisi. Stephen McDermott served as timekeeper.

Good Set of Prelims

The opening card found the winners of each fight coming out of the 85th St. corner. All the blokes who thundered out of the 86th St. side lost. In the semi-final six, after the main event, Tony DelGatto, 156¼, defeated the willing Dave Carver, 165¾. Del Gatto's smashing left hooks to the head won the verdict.

Lou Valles, 151, punched his way to a six round win over Jimmy Davis, 155. The fight proved to be the most interesting preliminary duel of the season. Davis was floored for a two in the second while Valles suffered a damaged right eye in the same reel.

Burl Charity, 150½, outscored the veteran Frankie Cavanna, 150½, over the six round route. Cavanna closed fast, but the youngster's early advantage earned him the decision.

Archie De Vino, 122, disposed of Bill Commodore, 122½, in 2:52 of the second and Helga Bakke, 173, defeated Dom Fussa, 165¼, in the four round opener.

Tony Janiro and Freddie Addeo meet in Tuesday night's feature bout.

YESTERDAY'S STAR

Emil (Dutch) Leonard, Washington knuckle-baller who beat the Yankees, 5 to 3, for the second time in a week, knocking them out of first place.

INTERNATIONAL LEAGUE

LAST NIGHT'S RESULTS

Newark 10, Montreal 9, 1st.
Montreal 6, Newark 3, 2d.
Buffalo 10, Baltimore 1, 1st.
Baltimore 17, Buffalo 5, 2d.
Toronto 7, Syracuse 4.
Jersey City 2, Rochester 1, 1st.
Jersey City 10, Rochester 3, 2d.

STANDING OF THE CLUBS

	W.	L.	Pct.		W.	L.	Pct.
Montreal	29	17	.630	Rochester	17	25	.405
Jersey C.	26	14	.650	Toronto	16	21	.432
Baltimore	25	19	.568	Syracuse	16	24	.400
Newark	23	18	.561	Buffalo	13	27	.325

TONIGHT'S GAMES

Montreal at Jersey City (8:30).
Rochester at Newark (8:30).
Toronto at Syracuse.
Buffalo at Baltimore.

Dodger Aces Poised to Boot Creaking Giants Off Perch

.BOSS IS BACK—On the coaching lines, braying and signaling, Leo Durocher led Dodgers to victory yesterday. Not a mark on him either.

Gregg, Davis Get Nod In Next Two Games —Lead at Stake

By TOMMY HOLMES

Major current mystery of the National League pennant race is how the New York Giants have managed to cling to first place as long as they have. When the Dodgers beat them, 7 to 4, before 13,017 cash customers at Ebbets Field yesterday, it marked the fourth straight defeat for Mel Ott's men of Manhattan, who also have lost 12 of their last 15 games.

"It won't be long now," is the cry around the rest of the league and "Look out below" the unvoiced slogan of the Giants, who display all the earmarks of a ball club that has more or less permanently shot its bolt.

Reasons for the Giant slump are obvious—a batting letdown and ineffective pitching—and their situation is bad because there are no strong reasons to look for immediate improvement The hot weather is coming on and Ott's attack depends too much upon old pappy guys to expect a hitting renaissance.

Cracking at Seams

The New York pitching is just plumb bad. Bill Voiselle, who burned up the league with eight straight victories at the start of the season, has since been knocked out in six straight starts over the course of which he suffered four defeats. Every hostile club in the league with the exception of the forlorn Phillies has taken a whack at the man from Ninety-six. Talk around the league now is that Voiselle suffers from lack of confidence.

Until yesterday, our old friend Van Mungo had the next best New York record. He had won six and lost one. But Van's arm hadn't been strong enough to enable him to go the route except on one occasion. Yesterday his appearance was briefer than usual. He departed, doubtless to kick his locker apart, when the Dodgers rocked him with four in the third.

Getting back to our puzzle department—where do the Dodgers rate anyway? Although they have won four straight games, our guys haven't been particularly impressive. The first three were at the expense of the Phillies, beaten by everybody these days. And I'll be hornswoggled if they were any redhot balls of fire as they committed four errors yesterday afternoon, yet won in handy fashion.

Leo's Ace All Set

Which leaves the Dodgers only a game and a half out of the league lead and pretty darned confident about increasing the discomfiture of the Giants in the remaining two games of the series. For one thing, Leo Durocher is in a far better spot for pitchers. He has his ace, Hal Gregg, ready to embarrass the enemy before a probable capacity crowd tonight, and can come in there with Curt Davis on Thursday aftrenoon. Hank Feldman tonight and the enigmatic Voiselle tomorrow form Ott's pitching program.

Durocher won his gamble at the start of the series when Vic Lombardi came up with the win. There's quite a little guy with a really marvelous pitching temperament. He hasn't too much stuff but there is a good reason why he wins. It's because the most important pitch in the game to him is the one which he is about to make. Bad breaks and errors leave him unruffled because he never loses sight of the main idea.

Like a Frigidaire

Errors jammed him up on several occasions yesterday but the lower case left hander kept plugging away, invariably coming up with the pitch the situation called for. It was a seven-hit effort and only one of the four New York runs were earned.

And so the most costly error of the day and the turning point of the game ruined the Giants. They led 2 to 0 in the third when Kerr and Hausmann gummed up a double play ball at second base, getting nobody. Whereupon the roof fell in on Mungo. Stanky sacrificed and Rosen singled to tie the score. A pass to Galan and Dixie Walker's resounding double completed Mungo's downfall.

Clean cut blasting fashioned the three final Dodger runs off Rube Fischer in the fifth. Doubles by Schultz and Dantonio, singles by Basinski and Stanky did the trick.

And that's about all except that Lombardi's pitching record is now 6 and 2 and Goody Rosen's hitting streak has extended through 11 games. And the Dodgers lead in their feud with the Giants, five games to four.

THE RIGHT STRETCH—Al Gardella makes long stretch to beat Howie Schultz in his dash to first base in second frame yesterday at Ebbets Field. Leo Durocher, the No. 1 man marked No. 2 in photo, is urging Schultz to hoof a little faster.

McCarthy Earns 2-Day Rest After Spotty Defeat

By GEORGE COLEMAN

"For the first time in my life I welcome a rest from baseball," said Manager Joe McCarthy after his Yankees bowed to the Senators, 5—3, at Yankee Stadium yesterday.

"It's only a two-day respite until Friday when we play in Philadelphia. By that time Hersh Martin should be back ready to play. We'll be a stronger club with him. Of course, we can't blame our emergency lineup that has Don Savage in left field for the loss. He did very well out there. It's a difficult job playing in the outfield after you have spent years in the infield," said Mac.

President Larry MacPhail is out of town. Perhaps he's searching for an outfielder.

This led Joe to reply: "No, I fear that Mr. MacPhail's trip to Montreal has nothing to do with our outfield situation. The Montreal club is playing in Newark. We know without looking that there is nothing there to help our outfield."

The scribes agreed with Joe on everything but Savage playing well. It was Fred Vaughn's triple in the seventh inning rally that netted three markers that put the game on ice for the Senators.

Most of the writers figured that the drive should have been caught. Savage went to left center for the ball. He was wary because Tuck Stainback had stepped on his foot while making a catch in the fifth frame.

In that big inning, Gil Torres doubled with one out in the seventh and scored on the ball Savage might have caught. Vaughn crossed the plate on Joe Kuhel's hit. Joe than tallied on Nick Etten's wild throw. That's reason enough for McCarthy welcoming the two-day rest.

Bing Crosby attended the game but had to leave before the end . . . Atley Donald has a sore arm. Dutch Leonard bruised his fingers catching a line drive off Crompton's bat in the fourth.

Erasmus Bats Way Into Tennis Final

The city P. S. A. L. tennis title will be decided when Erasmus Hall, Brooklyn titlist, meets Forest Hills, Queens champion, at a date yet not set. The Buff and Blue netmen qualified for the final round by defeating Bronx-Science, Manhattan-Bronx victor, 3—2, at the Mammoth Courts yesterday. It was the 10th win in 11 outings for Erasmus and the first setback in 11 starts.

The summaries:

Singles—Sid Schwartz, Erasmus, defeated Bert Wolfe, 6—2, 6—1; Bob Stichman, Erasmus, defeated Lionel Martin, 7—5, 4—6, 6—2; Phil Bennett, Bronx Science won by default; Mark Epstein, Bronx Science, defeated Geoffrey Kalmanson, 6—3, 8—6.

Doubles—Lary Laiks and Dick Siegel, Erasmus, defeated Fred Freund and Larry Gross, 6—2, 4—6, 6—1.

Fans Brush Off Lippy Incident; Claim Franchise Was Violated

By HAROLD CONRAD

The boss told us to go out to Ebbets Field yesterday to find out what the fans' reactions were to Leo Durocher since the law hung a felonious assault rap on him for allegedly belting a bellicose customer. We found out that although the legal aspect of L'Affaire Durocher may not yet be settled, the faithful followers of the Dodgers have written the incident off the books.

"Go out and sit among the fans," said the boss. "Don't tell 'em your a newspaperman. Just listen to what they have to say." So we went out and parked next to a rooting, red-faced gent in Section 8. After making some small talk about the game we worked around to the Durocher issue and asked slyly, "Do you think Leo belted that guy the other night?"

He took a hot-dog out of his kisser and bellowed, "if he didn't whack that bum, he coitainly should've. I've been comin' to this ball park for 25 years an' I've booed everybody from Ivy Olsen ta' Babe Hoiman when I thought they had it coming, but I never get poisonal with anybody. I listened to that guy scream at Bill Hart and Durocher fer three nights and if it wasn't that he was sitting upstairs and I was down here, I would'a belted him myself."

Doesn't Give a Hoot

Our next customer was a little tougher to get into conversation. The only answers we could get out of him were "yeh and naw." Then we finally worked around to the $64 question. "Do you think Durocher really belted that guy the other night?" we asked.

"Look buddy," he rasped. "I only come out here to see ball games. I don't care whether he slugged Durocher or Durocher slugged him. I don't care if they murdered each other. If Durocher can win the pennant for us, I wouldn't care if he had to slug 50 wise guys."

Leo Cheered by Fans

We canvassed a half-dozen more customers and not one seemed indignant over John Christian's charges. As a matter of fact, they regarded him as a traitor who took too much advantage of the fans' cherished franchise. Durocher, on the other hand, seems to have come out of this mess a veritable Dreyfuss. They showed they were 100 percent behind the Colorful Lip by giving him a rousing ovation when he first appeared on the field.

While most regarded the situation as unfortunate and said they didn't even think Leo hit the fellow, we couldn't help but sense a certain feeling of civic pride—as though they would have been hurt if this affair had happened in any other town but Brooklyn, which has a high priority on most of the zany incidents in baseball.

Dozens of witnesses have written the ball club. They want to testify to the abusive language and ungentlemanly-like conduct of the plaintiff. The story making the rounds yesterday was that he was seen in Flynn's Cabaret, which adjoins the field, after the game Saturday night. That he got into a fight at the bar and that an irate fan gave him a thorough going-over. If this is true, then, maybe, that's where he got those lacerations.

Hawks Keyed For Night Tilt With Bushwicks

The Bushwicks will be shooting for their eighth win out of nine games when they meet Jim Barton's Nighthawks in a floodlight game, starting at 8:45 o'clock tonight, at Dexter Park.

The Dexters are traveling at a fast pace after a slow start. They ran up a win streak of five straight until last Wednesday when the Black Yankees came in to score a 2—1 win. They came back on Friday night to whitewash the New York Cubans, 6—0, and on Saturday night they beat Arma, 9—8. Their season's record is 11 wins against five losses.

The Nighthawks will be making their first Dexter Park appearance since 1942 when they defeated the Bushwicks in a close game. Manager Mike Meola may decide to do the hurling tonight with Bill Weismeier catching. Bill Simmons, who hurled for Hollywood in the Pacific Coast League earlier this year, will also be ready to work for the visitors, if needed. Their line-up includes Jimmy Woods at first base. Fans will remember him for his antics when he covered the sack for the House of David nine. Joe Motto will be at second, Jack Moesch at short and Jack Winslow at third. George Dillingham, Frank Zachman and Bill Wengrowski will patrol the outfield.

Manager Joe Press will call on Emil Moscowicz to hurl for the Bushwicks, with Tony De Phillips or Emil Gall catching.

Tomorrow night the Bushwicks travel to the Polo Grounds to meet the New York Cubans in a return game. Friday night they return to Dexter Park for a floodlight game with the Newark Eagles.

FIGHT RESULTS

Philadelphia—Freddy Dawson, 136, Chicago, decisioned Dorsey Lay, 137, Philadelphia (12).

Buffalo—California Jackie Wilson, 150¾, Los Angeles, decisioned Al Jolson, 150¼, New Orleans (10); Wild Oscar Boyd, 161, Buffalo, decisioned Johnny Walker, 161¾, Philadelphia (8).

Hartford, Conn.—Bobby Pollowitzer, 128, East Hartford, Conn., knocked out Lou Rivers, 125½, Princeton, N. J. (4); Pat Brady, 133, New York, stopped Freddie Holmes, 130, Brooklyn (2); Ham Wiloby, 125½, Corona, N. Y., drew with Wilberto Osario, 125, San Juan, P. R. (6); Don Anderson, 158, New York, stopped Johnny Hall, 153½, Jersey City (5).

White Plains, N. Y.—Eddie Compo, 126½, New Haven, Conn., outpointed Rocco Progano, 128½, Stamford, Conn. (8).

New Bedford, Mass.—Freddie Camuso, 143, Fall River, Mass., outpointed Benny Singleton, 142, Waterbury, Conn. (10); Oscar St. Pierre, 138, Fall River, stopped Marcel Fournier, 138, Montreal (1).

Washington—Jimmy Bivins, 188, Cleveland, knocked out Buddy Scott, 186, Electra, Texas, (4).

Rochester—Eddie Smith, 140, Rochester, outpointed Bobby McIntire, 140½, Detroit (8); Johnny Virgo, 139½, Rochester, knocked out Joe Miller, 140, Buffalo (1).

San Antonio, Texas—Fritzie Zivic, 152, Pittsburgh, knocked out Baby Zavala, 147, Mexico City (4); Tommy Attra, 178, Austin, TKO'd Bud Thomas, 180, Washington (5).

Allentown, Pa. — Sante Bucca, 137, Philadelphia, outpointed Archie Wilmer, 132, Wilmington, Del. (10); Jimmy Smith, 186, Philadelphia, TKO'd Ray Scully, 186, Reading (3).

MUNGO NO GO

GIANTS

	ab	r	h	o	a
Rucker,cf	5	0	1	7	0
H'mann,2b	3	1	1	1	3
Ott,rf	5	0	0	1	0
Medwick,lf	3	1	2	2	0
E.L'bardi,c	3	0	0	3	0
D.G'ella,1b	3	0	0	9	0
Jurges,3b	4	1	3	0	3
Kerr, ss	4	1	1	1	4
Mungo,p	0	0	0	0	0
Fischer,p.	1	0	0	0	0
Em'rich,p	0	0	0	0	0
aFilipo'icz	1	0	0	0	0
Adams,p	0	0	0	0	0
bHudson	1	0	0	0	0
Totals	33	4	8	24	10

DODGERS

	ab	r	h	o	a
Stanky,2b	4	0	1	2	3
Rosen,cf	4	1	2	2	0
Galan,lf	2	1	0	2	0
Walker, rf	4	0	1	6	1
Bord'ray,rf	0	0	0	2	0
Olmo,3b	4	0	0	1	0
Schultz,1b	3	1	1	9	0
Dantonio,c	4	1	1	1	0
Basinksi,ss	4	2	3	2	2
V. L'bardi,p	3	1	0	0	1
Totals	32	7	9	27	7

aFlied out for Emmerich in seventh.
bFlied out for Adams in ninth.

Giants	0	1	1	0	0	0	2	0	0	—4
Dodgers	0	0	4	0	3	0	0	0	x	—7

Errors—Hausmann, Kerr, Stanky 2; Olmo Schultz. Runs batted in—Kerr, Filipowicz, Stanky, Rosen 2; Walker 2; Dantonio, V. Lombardi. Two-base hits—Walker, Schultz, Dantonio, Kerr. Stolen base—Schultz. Sacrifices—Stanky, V. Lombardi. Double plays—Dodgers 4 (Walker-Schultz; V. Lombardi-Basinski-Schultz; Schultz, unassisted; Stanky-Schultz). Left on bases—Giants 8, Dodgers 7. Bases on balls—Off Mungo 1, Fischer 3, V. Lombardi 5. Struck out—By Fischer 1 (Dantonio), Emmerich 1 (Olmo), Adams 1 (Schultz), V. Lombardi 1 (D. Gardella). Hits—Off Mungo, 4 and 4 runs in 21-3 innings; Fischer, 5 and 3 in 21-3; Emmerich, 0 and 0 in 11-3; Adams, 0 and 0 in 2. Hit by pitcher—By E. Lombardi (Mungo). Winning pitcher—V. Lombardi (4-2). Losing pitcher—Mungo (6-2). Time—2:16. Umpires—Henline, Goetz and Jorda. Attendance—15,013.

EAGLE BASEBALL CONTEST

IN CO-OPERATION WITH OLSEN AND JOHNSON AND BILL STERN ON NBC—WEAF

This Player Is______________
(Write Your Selection Here)

By OLSEN and JOHNSON
Stars of "Laffing Room Only"

I asked my Grandma the other day if Grandpa had played a lot of baseball. She said that in his day Grandpa had played lots of the sandlots. I said: "What's the matter, Grandma, did Grandpa get tired of the sandlots?" Granny said: "He didn't mind the sand-lots so much, son, but when they put in diving boards and life-guards —That was too much!"

RULES IN BRIEF—Thirty cartoons and limericks will comprise the Baseball Contest. Olsen and Johnson give a clue each day and Bill Stern broadcasts a clue each evening at 6:40 on WEAF. Contestants may use these clues if they wish. Deadline for mailing entries is MIDNIGHT, SUNDAY, July 1, 1945. No charge of any kind is levied on contestants. Facsimiles of the cartoons and limericks are acceptable. There is nothing to buy or sell, no coupons to clip, no subscriptions to obtain. Accuracy and simplicity are the main requisites. The decision of the judges in all matters is to be accepted as final by contestants. Each cartoon depicts ONE PLAYER and no player's name will be used more than once. Submit the 30 solved cartoons and the six worked-out limericks at one time—at the end of the contest. The limericks appear each Friday. You can obtain a set of the complete rules by writing the Contest Editor, Brooklyn Eagle, 24 Johnson St. You can call him at MAin 4-6200 to clarify any point you may have doubt about. This is a contest of skill and baseball knowledge.

BUY U. S. WAR BONDS AND SAVINGS STAMPS

PRIZE LIST
1945 Baseball Contest

FIRST PRIZE—
$1,000 war bond.
SECOND PRIZE
$500 war bond.
THIRD PRIZE
$250 war bond.
FOURTH TO EIGHTH PRIZES.
Five war bonds of $25 each.
CONSOLATION PRIZES
Fifty copies of "The Brooklyn Dodgers," new book by Frank Graham.
One hundred fifty pairs of tickets to Olsen and Johnson's "Laffing Room Only!"
One hundred fifty sets of reserved seats to regularly scheduled games at Ebbets Field, Polo Grounds, Yankee Stadium.
One hundred sets of seats to regularly scheduled big-time WEAF-N. B. C. broadcasts.

WOMEN IN SPORTS

So many awards were presented at the Brooklyn College awards dinner the other night that it was impossible to list all the recipients' names in one column. As a result, we are printing more today.

The non-varsity awards were as follows: dance — Major, Elaine Weiss; shields, Alma Abramson, Mildred Atliss, Eve Cohen, Rosalie Weintraub, Blanche Tischelman, Harriet Fourems, Phoebe Goldenberg, Shirley Golone, Helen Jalpern, Alma Hammer, Buna Kadish, Helen Koenigsberg, Sylvia Margolis, Thelma Milgrem, Rose Marie Rosa, Paula Prinz, Harriet Rypins, Harriet Schacter, Annette Strum, Mickey Wolf, Harriet Cohn, Irma Esner and Ruth Zinn.

Water ballet—Thelma Milgrem, Joan Zimmerman, Edith Kaufman, Dona Waldauer, Roslyn Kosseff, Anita (Butterscotch) Scheinman, Charlotte Levine, Muriel Holt, Miriam Rosen, Harriette Levy, Muriel Schaps, Sylvia Friedman, Joan Sugarman, Marcia Civin, Dorothy Bodner, Muriel Wexler, Audrey Dirnfeld, Jean Falvey, Margaret Davies, Adelaide Shapiro, Arline Peterson, Adelaide Paprin, Marilyn Podest and Lillian Mezette; minor, Elaine Gostel and Bernice Malkind.

Julia Kassell added two senior awards to the four major archery, basketball, fencing and hockey awards that she had previously collected. The first was a silver basketball denoting three years on the varsity, and the second was a gold, four-year fencing pin.

Other senior awards were: three-year basketball—Mildred McGrath; four-year dance—Rose Marie Rosa, Annette Strum and Blanche Tischelman; three-year hockey—Jacqueline Fieldman, Lyn Speyer and Pauline Weiner; swimming, four-year—Marguerite Blikken; three-year—Elaine Gostel; water ballet, four-year—Marguerite Blikken and Bernice Malkind; three-year—Elaine Gostel and Audrey Dirnfeld.

JOAN CROSBIE

7★★★★★★★ Complete

BROOKLYN EAGLE

WEATHER—Cloudy, cooler tonight; cloudy, mild tomorrow.

104th YEAR—No. 166—DAILY and SUNDAY (Copyright, 1945, The Brooklyn Eagle, Inc.) BROOKLYN, N. Y., TUESDAY, JUNE 19, 1945 Entered Brooklyn P. O. 2d Class Mail Matter 3 CENTS IN NEW YORK CITY ELSEWHERE 4 CENTS

CITY ROARS 'WELCOME, IKE'

Eagle Staff photo

NEW YORK CITY GREETS A HERO—Part of the vast crowd gathered in front of City Hall for the official reception to General Dwight D. Eisenhower is shown standing at attention during the singing of the national anthem at the beginning of the ceremonies.

CHEERING MILLIONS JOIN IN CITY'S GREATEST TRIBUTE

By VIOLET BROWN

New York City today gave General of the Army Dwight David Eisenhower a roaring, heartfelt welcome—greatest in its history.

From LaGuardia Field across the Triborough Bridge to the Battery and up along Lower Broadway, more than 6,000,000 grateful cheering men, women and children, twice as

HERE HE IS—Face wreathed in smiles and hands upraised, General Eisenhower responds to tumultuous welcome of New Yorkers as he drives through Central Park.

many as greeted Lindbergh, made a human victory road for the modest blue-eyed soldier from Kansas.

The skies were gray but not a drop of rain fell to mar the procession. It was as if the very clouds had gathered to shelter the nation's greatest living hero from the glare of the sun which yesterday in Washington blazed on his weather-beaten grinning face.

Except for war plants which continued turning out arms to finish the job the general had begun in the west, most of the city's work stood at a standstill. Schools remained open but 60,000 picked children watched the victory ride and thousands of others were taken briefly from their classrooms to watch as the 25-car cavalcade sped by.

Center of the city's homage was at City Hall Park, where 45,000 persons sat on specially erected benches in the triangular park in front of the Italian Renaissance City Hall.

"Welcome Ike" banners hung from buildings ringing the park and a huge red flag with five white stars, the flag of the general of the army, stretched horizontally across the top of City Hall.

A special reception stand had been built on the steps, with five silver stars arranged in front of the prow-like blue speaker's stand.

Wounded Attend Ceremony

There were 28 persons, including Borough Presidents Cashmore of Brooklyn and Burke of Queens, in the official box. Another 856 distinguished guests sat directly in front of the platform and in back of them, facing the steps, sat 530 wounded soldiers, sailors and marines, one whole row wearing the Distinguished Service Medal, all proud with their Purple Hearts.

At 12:13 p.m., while the crowd which had started gathering at 8 a.m.—equipped with lunches, field glasses and umbrellas, against all emergencies—was singing "God Bless America" lustily, the Eisenhower procession arrived.

There was a momentary pause.

Then the notables began to take their places on the platform and the officers and men in the General's party appeared. The 32d Army Service Forces Band of Fort Jay sounded ruffles and flourishes.

General Steps Into View

Meanwhile, Mayor LaGuardia, who had greeted the General just two hours before at the airport, and the city's guest began to walk slowly from the Mayor's office down the red carpeted corridor of City Hall. The carpet, last used when King George and Queen Elizabeth visited the United States, stretched all the way to the speakers' stand.

Onlookers reported that the General's face, free for the moment of the grin with which he had greeted New York, looked strained and that he paused for a moment as if gird-

Continued on Page 7

OKINAWA JAPS FLEE TOWARD SUICIDE SHORE

Abandon Foxholes As Yanks Dent Sides Of Tiny Death Pocket

By WILLIAM F. TYREE

Guam, June 19 (U.P.)—Tenth Army forces pushed within sight of the south Okinawa cliffs overlooking the east China Sea today in a converging drive against disorganized Japanese troops and panic-stricken civilians huddled in a tiny death pocket.

Admiral Chester W. Nimitz announced that the complete conquest of Okinawa was "imminent."

Front dispatches said Japanese soldiers, in groups of several hundred, abandoned foxholes and fled southward toward the deadend shoreline where they have been invited by Maj. Gen. John R. Hodge to commit suicide.

Two Miles From Sea

Avenging the death in action of their commander, Lt. Gen. Simon Bolivar Buckner, 10th Army troops swept to new positions ranging from a mile to two miles from the southern tip of Okinawa.

Witnesses reported that enemy

Continued on Page 7

Duke Studies U. S. Business

Cleveland, June 19 (U.P.)—The Duke of Windsor was in Cleveland today "studying American business methods."

Shock From Serum Kills Twins in Queens

Parents Had Sought to Protect Baby Boys From Diphtheria—Reaction Held Very Rare

Two young parents were plunged swiftly into grief today when their 10-month-old twin sons, whom they had sought to guard against diphtheria, died from the effects of diphtheria toxin-antitoxin.

Just yesterday Mr. and Mrs. Donald Miraglia of 37-38 84th St., Jackson Heights, Queens, were playing joyfully with their only children, Donald Jr. and Gary.

To keep their children in the fine health they had always enjoyed, the mother and father realized they must be immunized against disease. Despite yesterday's heat, therefore, the two babies were given a second injection of preventive serum by the family doctor, Dr. Edward Steingesser, 504 E. 5th St., Manhattan. It was just routine, part of a parent's responsibility. Nothing to worry about at all.

Goes to Performance

Mr. Miraglia, a dancer in "Follow the Girls," went to his performance last night secure in the knowledge that his little family was healthy and well.

This morning at 6 a.m. he took a peek in the crib where his sons were lying, but the tiny baby fists didn't wave him the glad good-morning he expected. Donald was strangely guiet. Gary was in pain. When Dr. Steingesser arrived, Donald was dead. Gary died at 10:40 a.m. in St. John's Hospital, Long Island City, where he had been taken in unconscious condition.

An autopsy performed by Dr. Jacob Werne, an assistant medical examiner, showed the deaths were due to anaphylactic shock, an extremely rare reaction to serum which cannot be determined before injection.

Cooler Weather Gives City Relief

	Yesterday	Today
6 a.m.	74	71
7 a.m.	76	70
8 a.m.	78	70
9 a.m.	78	70
10 a.m.	80	71
11 a.m.	81	72
12 noon	83	74
1 p.m.	88	75
2 p.m.	90	77

Cooler weather today brought relief to New Yorkers who have been sweltering for six days.

The highest temperature today was expected to be about 80. Yesterday's high of 90 was recorded at 3:05 p.m.

Tonight will be clear and cool with the mercury hovering between 60 and 65 but the sun gets another chance tomorrow with a forecast of sunny and warm with low humidity.

Expect Senate to Pass Truman's Tariff Bill Today

Washington, June 19 (U.P.)—President Truman was promised his first foreign policy victory in the Senate today.

The Senate scheduled a vote this afternoon on the tariff-cutting authority in the reciprocal trade extension bill.

Senate Democratic Leader Alben W. Barkley confidently predicted an administration victory over almost solid Republican opposition.

Charles Town Results

FIRST RACE—Three-year-olds and up; four and a half furlongs.

All Crystal (Edens)	3.60	2.20	2.20
Laugh and Play (Kelly)	—	2.60	2.40
Blue Beauty (Grant)	—	—	3.60

Time, :53 2-5. Lead Em All, Green Advice, Lady Doctor, Chillie Bubble also ran. Off time, 1:20.

Tomorrow Is Waste Paper Day

Tomorrow is collection day for waste paper. Have all your old paper—newspapers, scraps, wrappings—bundled and on the streets by 7 a.m.

TRUMAN STARTS ON PLANE TRIP TO WEST COAST

President Will Visit Olympia First, Then Go to San Francisco

Washington, June 19 (U.P.)—President Truman left today on a nonstop flight to the Pacific Coast—the first time a President ever has made an airplane trip in this country.

Mr. Truman's first destination was Olympia, Wash., some 2,450 miles away. There he will be the guest of Gov. Mon Wallgren.

After a few days' relaxation there the President will go to San Francisco to address the closing session of the United Nations Conference. Shortly after that he plans to visit his home town of Independence, Mo., and Kansas City.

The Presidential plane, a luxurious, especially-equipped C-54 of the Army Transport Command, took off at 8:21 a.m.

Ike Sees President Off

This is the four-engined plane that brought Gen. Dwight D. Eisenhower home from Europe. General Eisenhower, preparing to board

Continued on Page 2

Send U-Boats to Britain

Oslo, Norway, June 19 (U.P.)—Eighty-six German submarines, all the seaworthy U-boats found in Norway, have been sent to Britain pending a final decision on their disposition, Allied naval headquarters said today.

Boro Cobbler Gets 1st City Hall Seat at 4 A.M.

'It's Worth It to See Greatest Man on Earth,' He Says—Woman Who Greeted Pershing There

A Brooklyn shoe repair man, lunch in hand and quite excited at the prospect of seeing General Eisenhower, was first to enter the reception stand at City Hall, arriving there at 4 a.m.

He was Joseph Weissman of 1073 Blake Ave., who left his East New York home at 3 a.m. for the big event. Short and stocky, and wearing a fisherman' cap, Mr. Weissman, an amateur poet, had copies of his poem with him, and distributed them to anyone who would accept them.

"Why did I leave my home at 3 a.m.?" he stated "Well just to see the greatest man on earth."

Included among the spectators in the stands were two Congressional Medal of Honor winners in past wars—James Osborn of 854 St. John's Place, who was awarded the medal in the First World War, and Frederick Muller, 81, of Miami, Fla., who won the honor in the Spanish-

Continued on Page 7

Ike Gets Breakfast For Son as Wife Rushes for Train

Just like women all over the world, Brooklyn's first lady, Mrs. John Cashmore, today swapped breakfast gossip with General of the Army Dwight David Eisenhower's wife, Mamie.

"I left the general getting our son's breakfast this morning," Mrs. Eisenhower was overheard telling the Borough President's wife. "My train left before the general's plane, and I was worrying about breakfast.

"'Go ahead, Mamie,' he told me. 'I'll take care of breakfast.'"

Mrs. Cashmore smiled understandingly, recalling times when she, too, had been rushing for a train.

Scott Returns to Post As U. S. Court Clerk

John R. Scott Jr. was back on the job today as clerk of the criminal part of Brooklyn Federal Court after two years in the army as motor pool sergeant of the Base Unit 806, A. A. F., at Baer Field, Indiana.

A court clerk since January, 1915, Mr. Scott also took 22 months off during World War I to serve with the ammunition train of the 27th Division.

Now 48, Mr. Scott resides at the Pierrepont Hotel.

Man Is Killed By Brighton Line Train

A man who carried identification papers of Francis S. Smith, 41, 575 St. John's Place, was killed by a westbound train of the Brighton Beach line at Brighton Beach Ave. and Coney Island Ave. early today.

Police reported that no one at the St. John's Place address knew the victim.

8 Drown in Ontario

Youngstown, N. Y., June 19 (U.P.)—Eight Toronto, Ont., residents were drowned last night when their 44-foot schooner, the Siren, sank in Lake Ontario near here.

BELMONT RESULTS

FIRST RACE—Four-year-olds and up; six furlongs.

Col. Steve (Adams)	10.20	4.60	3.90
Star of Padula (Hansman)	—	4.50	3.60
Flying Son (Lindberg)	—	—	5.50

Off 1:15½. Time, 1:13 1-5. No scratches.

SECOND RACE—Orange Blossom, 1st; Little Alison 2d; Congo Song, 3d.

56 From Section On Casualty Lists

The War Department today, announcing the names of 468 soldiers killed in action, 883 wounded, 103 missing and 2,634 liberated, listed 17 Brooklyn, Queens and Long Island men dead, 28 wounded, and two missing in the European and Pacific areas, and 89 released from German prison camps. The navy listed four dead, three wounded and two missing. Local casualty lists are on Page 13.

Call the Brooklyn Chapter, American Red Cross, and arrange to donate a pint of blood NOW. TRiangle 5-8040.

COST OF ANTHRACITE IS HIKED $1 PER TON

Washington, June 19 (U.P.)—The Office of Price Administration said today that the four principal household sizes of anthracite—broken, egg, stove and chestnut—will cost an extra dollar a ton from now on.

The domestic pea size will be increased 85 cents a ton and buckwheat No. 1 and buckwheat No. 2 sizes will be hiked 50 cents a ton.

WHERE TO FIND IT

	Page		Page
Bridge	12	Music	5
Comics	4	Novel	13
Crossword	13	Obituaries	7
Currie	3	Our Fighters	8
Dr. Brady	6	Pattern	10
Editorial	6	Radio	4
Financial	12	Society	9, 10
Grin and Bear It	6	Sports	11, 12
Heffernan	6	Take My Word	6
Helen Worth	10	Theaters	5
Horoscope	10	Tommy Holmes	11
Lindley	6	Tucker	6
Mary Haworth	9	Want Ads	13-15
Movies	5	Women	[illegible]

TOMMY HOLMES

A Hero Goes to A Baseball Game

GENERAL IKE—It probably will be sometime today before the baseball people fully realize the enormity of the distinction conferred upon their business by General Dwight D. Eisenhower.

When the General of the Army—the army that broke the back of the German Wehrmacht—made the Polo Grounds the terminal of his triumphal tour of New York City, it was much more than the climax of a busy afternoon for him.

Shortly after Pearl Harbor, the late Franklin D. Roosevelt wrote in his celebrated "green light" letter that professional baseball, subject, of course, to wartime conditions, was, in his opinion, "thoroughly worthwhile."

General Eisenhower at game.

Yesterday the ranking hero of victory in Europe made a gesture that silently said the same thing. Silently—and yet so loudly that I do not think you'll hear any more about shutting down baseball for the duration of the war with Japan.

The baseball men applauded with the customers as General Ike entered the Harlem horseshoe in an open car with F. H. LaGuardia, the radio star. That wasn't enough. They should have got down on their knees and thanked him.

PLAYER "WILSON"—It is quite evident that the man from Kansas has a strong affection for the game. When he reached his box, Mel Ott of the Giants and Bob Coleman, manager of the Braves, gave him two autographed balls and an autographed bat.

The General thanked them with a smile, added that he had been a professional ball player briefly in his youth.

"One of the secrets of my past," he confided, "is that I played under the name of Wilson in the old Kansas State League."

BASEBALL CONSCIOUS—He wished to know the pitchers for the game. When Coleman mentioned Jim Tobin he added, "I'll bet you think you can take that bat and hit his soft stuff."

From time to time dispatches from Europe revealed General Eisenhower's baseball consciousness. In his order of the day on D-Day, he said something about landing in Normandy "to hit a home run." When there was some question about whether last Fall's World Series would be played, General Ike said that he hoped it would be and well broadcast "because my men want to listen to it." They say, too, that the General found time to listen to parts of it himself.

And then that last dispatch before his arrival in this country—that the General would be delighted to spend the afternoon at the Polo Grounds, that he'd love to see big league baseball again.

IT'S DIFFERENT—Pressbox dialogue:

"A fine thing. He expresses a desire to see big league baseball, so they show him Abbadabba Tobin throwing butterfly balls and Danny Gardella in the outfield.

"Maybe that's to teach him the meaning of total war."

HE WAS BUSY—Briefly, when the game began, General Eisenhower became John Q. Phan, in person. He opened his program and started to score the game. But there were too many interruptions to permit him continued concentration.

Mayor LaGuardia sat at his left at the start of the game. Thereafter, every half inning the seat was occupied by the various Borough Presidents. (Brooklyn's John Cashmore, incidentally, drew the top half of the third.)

Obviously, he shares the admiration most of us have for Melvin Ott. When the little manager of the Giants came to bat for the first time, General Ike was one of the spectators who applauded. Ott promptly was retired on a high pop fly. Later, Mel confessed that he was so nervous when he had been introduced to the General that he couldn't remember what had been said to him.

Eventually, it began to rain and the General with his party left their exposed boxes to watch the rest of the contest from the windows of Horace Stoneham's office behind the centerfield bleachers. Which wasn't bad place to be at that.

A FRIEND PASSES—It was not a day of unalloyed happiness so far as the Polo Grounds pressbox was concerned. There the boys were deeply affected by the news that Sid Mercer finally had succumbed to his long illness.

Mercer, who, as a boy, left a farm in Paxton, Ill., ultimately to become the dean of New York baseball writers, spent a portion of his long career covering the Dodgers. On several Spring training trips, he, Eddie Murphy and I shared a bungalow in Clearwater.

We had a Negress named Liza to cook for us and she was slightly wonderful even for those carefree, point-free days. Some of the most pleasant evenings of my life were spent on a porch down in Florida after Liza had filled us with fried chicken and hot biscuits. Sid would relax in a big chair, light a cigar and begin. He was the most entertaining raconteur I have ever heard.

A gracious gentleman, a great reporter and a gifted writer, Sid's death follows far too soon that of rollicking Jack Miley. They were fine men.

Major League Records

NATIONAL LEAGUE

YESTERDAY'S RESULTS

Brooklyn at Philadelphia, postponed, rain.

Boston 9, **New York** 2.

Cincinnati 1, St. Louis 0; 13 innings, night.

Only game scheduled.

STANDING OF THE CLUBS

	W.	L.	Pct.
Brooklyn	31	21	.596
Pittsburgh	30	23	.566
St. Louis	29	24	.547
New York	30	25	.545
Chicago	26	22	.542
Boston	26	25	.510
Cincinnati	23	27	.460
Philadelphia	14	42	.250

TODAY'S GAMES

Brooklyn (Davis 5-5 and Herring 0-0) at Philadelphia (Barrett 4-7 and Leone 0-0), Twilight 6:30 and night, 9 p.m.

Boston (Hutchings 3-2), at **New York** (Brewer 1-1); 8:45 p.m.

Pittsburgh (Butcher 6-2), at Chicago (Passeau 84).

(Only games scheduled.)

TOMORROW'S GAMES

Brooklyn at Philadelphia, 3:15 p.m.

St. Louis at Cincinnati.

Pittsburgh at Chicago.

(Only games scheduled.)

AMERICAN LEAGUE

YESTERDAY'S RESULTS

Boston 1, **New York** 0, (twilight).

Detroit 4, Cleveland 3, (twilight).

Washington 6, Philadelphia 0, 1st, twilight.

Washington 5, Philadelphia 3, 2d, night.

Chicago 5, St. Louis 4, night.

STANDING OF THE CLUBS

	W.	L.	Pct.
Detroit	30	21	.588
New York	28	23	.549
Boston	28	24	.538
Chicago	28	26	.519
St. Louis	24	25	.490
Washington	24	26	.480
Cleveland	21	27	.438
Philadelphia	20	31	.392

TODAY'S GAMES

New York at Boston (2), postponed, rain.

Philadelphia (Gerkin 0-4), at Washington (Niggeling 1-5), night.

Cleveland (Bagby 1-6), at Detroit (Newhouser 9-4).

Chicago (Humphries 2-4) at St. Louis (Jakucki 4-5), night.

TOMORROW'S GAMES

Cleveland at Detroit.

Philadelphia at Washington, night.

(Only game scheduled.)

Braves Give 5-Star Show Before Ike

Giants Awed by Eisenhower, Then Tobin to Blow 18th in Last 23

By GEORGE COLEMAN

General Dwight D. Eisenhower, surrounded by thousands of cheering fans at the Polo Grounds yesterday, may not have noticed but he received a tribute that seldom is extended to any human—the applause by professional athletes, especially from the almost-impossible-to-awe major league baseball players.

They were spellbound by the five-star General. Even Manager Mel Ott, who has kept his lightning brain going at top speed during those heart-breakers his Giants have been losing recently, went to pieces.

After Ott and Bob Coleman, the Braves' pilot, handed the General of the Army an autographed bat and two baseballs, the New York manager was asked: "What did the general say?"

"I don't know; I was too nervous," said Mel. "All I remember was his asking us 'who is going to pitch?' I don't know what I answered but I do remember Coleman asking the General if he thought he could hit his pitcher's 'soft stuff.'"

"What 'soft stuff' do you mean??" asked the General of Coleman. He said: "You'll see."

18th Defeat

Although the Giants did little with Butterfly Jim Tobin's soft stuff, losing the 18th game in their last 23, by 9—2 before 27,062 fans, the General didn't see much of the early innings. Mayor LaGuardia was presenting a steady flow of officials who kept moving into the General's box to be introduced.

From the Ottmen's angle there was much to watch. As early as the third, the Braves stormed Bill Emmerich for a homer by Dick Culler. After another run in the fourth, the Braves chased Emmerich with four runs in the sixth. Rube Fischer took over but gave way to a pinch hitter in the seventh when Bill Voiselle, the mound ace of the early season, appeared. The Braves added two more runs in the eighth and another in the ninth.

Likes New Club

Clyde Kluttz, who recently was traded by the Braves to the Giants, thinks New York is a wonderful place. "Why I haven't played before a crowd less than 30,000 yet." . . . Whitey Wietelmann gazed at the stands and said: "Boy, look at that mob—just here to see our red-hot Boston team." . . . The last half of the game was played in mud but General Eisenhower was watching from the centerfield clubhouse . . . Andy Hansen has a sore arm . . . Tommy Holmes' single extended his hitting streak to 16 straight games . . . The second game of the series is listed at the Polo Grounds tonight . . . In addition to four homers by Cullen, Tobin, Rucker and Hausmann, the General saw a plate umpire call a ball fair at the same moment a third-base bluecoat was waving it foul . . . Ziggy Sears, behind the plate, was the commander in chief of the arbiters. So the ball was fair.

THE SPORTING THING

"Worst case of gas I've ever seen!"

YANK CASTOFF TEACHES CLUB HUB LESSON

Hausmann Beats Borowy in 3-Hitter In Fenway Park

Special to the Brooklyn Eagle

Boston, June 20—The Yankees are becoming more and more bewildered as the days slip by. Manager Joe McCarthy was confident of opening with a triumph here yesterday. His victory-insurance, Pitcher Hank Borowy, was working while Manager Joe Cronin had a former Yankee farmhand, Clem Hausmann, opposing him.

But that's the reason for the confusion. Following nine innings of twilight ball, the McCarthymen were on the short end of a 1—0 score and pushed them within two games of dropping into third place.

Hausmann beat the Yanks at the Stadium and only recently whitewashed the Athletics.

Hausmann twirled well, allowing but three hits. The first was a double in the second by Stirnweiss, who was later caught stealing third base. The second came in the seventh by Hershel Martin, who was erased by a fast doubleplay. In the ninth, Frankie Crosetti singled only to be eliminated by another twin-killing. Hausmann certainly had the Bombers eating out of his hand. They only hit five balls hard and only eight out of the infield.

Hausmann had the 12,098 fans wondering why the Yankees ever allowed the former Kansas City moundsman to slip out of their system. Only once was Hausmann in trouble. That was in the second frame. The Yanks had two men on the base paths. Stirnweiss doubled and Oscar Grimes walked with one out. Both were on their way when Tuck Stainback drove a rifle-shot into left field. Bob Johnson made a running catch near the wall to force the Yanks to scamper back to their bases.

The Yanks, for the first time in 13 games, came through without an error . . . Dave Ferriss, whose winning streak was snapped by the Bombers, tries for his 10th victory in the twinbill today . . . If the Yanks lose both they'll drop to third place . . . Ferriss finally has been given a locker in the Boston clubhouse. It was once used by Lefty Grove . . . Bob Garbark, injured by a foul tip in the second, was replaced by Fred Walters . . . Brilliant catches by Stainback in the opening stanza and by Stirnweiss in the fifth kept the Sox from getting a few more runs.

Basinski and Rosen Making Flock Tick

Dressen Credited With Improving Their Stickwork

By HAROLD C. BURR

Staff Correspondent of the Eagle

Philadelphia, June 20—When the saga of the 1945 Dodgers has finally been written it's going to be difficult for the historians to brush off the part played in the amazing success story by Eddie Basinski, the ferocious violinist, and Goody Rosen, the Little Canuck.

Basinski's improved shortstop play and hitting and Rosen's hitting are the difference in this year's pennant contenders and last year's seventh-place humpty-dumpties.

"If we had a shortstop," said Leo Durocher in the early days of the race, "we'd be right up there with the leaders."

Nobody gave Basinski more than a regretful look as he made more discords at short than he had ever wheezed forth on his Buffalo Symphony Orchestra fiddle. There were ever-dreadful moments when he looked as if he was trying to field a ground ball with his violin under one arm.

Uses Special Signal

Eddie came out of Buffalo University last year with the sprigs of campus ivy still in his hair. He was the first shortstop of the half-dozen the desperate Lip had tried who could make a double play. But Basinski, the butinski, couldn't do anything else worthy of anything except a disparaging note.

"He was a dead left-field hitter," said Chuck Dressen, the astute gentleman who coaches at third base for the Dodgers. "Every pitcher in the league was making his hit off his fists. But this year we've got him to stand farther back from the plate and hit into right field. I've got a special sign when I want him to hit to right. It's good until he has two strikes on him. Then we let him hit any place.

"Eddie has been gaining confidence with experience. He's a good shortstop today. He gets the ball away very fast. I would say that he gets rid of it faster than Peewee Reese. He hasn't too strong an arm, but it's good enough to head batters on the long throw."

There are any number of high-grade shortstops in the National League—Slats Marion, the Cardinals' Mr. Shortstop; Eddie Miller of the Reds, Dick Culler of the Braves, Buddy Kerr of the Giants—and don't overlook Basinski in the reckoning. On attack, Eddie is hitting .305 and has an 11-game streak riding.

Dressen rates another assist on making a five-star hitter out of Rosen. Nobody thought anything of it when the little grass patrolman—in centerfield that April day at Ebbets Field solely because Red Durrett had reported with a stomachach—doubled off Ewald Pyle to beat the Giants out of a ball game. But Goody really made that hit up at Bear Mountain a month before.

Wanted to Quit

"Give Chuck all the credit in the world," says Rosen, smoking his cigar in the lobby and rolling his .355 batting average around his tongue. "I was ready to quit and go back home. I figured I was too young to become a confirmed utility outfielder. Chuck's my personal friend and when I talked about forgetting about baseball he would not listen."

"You keep on hanging in there, Goody," Dressen told me. "He had an idea what was wrong. 'Do you know what you're doing? You hold your arms too close to your body. You just push at the ball. Your swing is unnatural. It's all cramped up. Try it my way for a week; loosen up. Then if you still want to give up on yourself I won't say a word.' Well, I tried. The week was up and still I didn't seem to be getting any place."

Goody took the cigar out of his mouth, so that there would be no slurring of his next words.

Middle Strong Now

"Then I got that one off Pyle. Durocher used me only against right-handers for a while, benching me for Frenchy Bordagaray when a lefty was working against us. But when I saw that ball drop safely out of Mel Ott's reach I knew then that I would always hit. I still know that I always will. But if it hadn't been for Chuck—well, I'd be home in Toronto now 'sore at myself and the world."

It's an old baseball bromide that a team must be strong right down the middle to win a flag. The Dodgers have been steadily gathering strength at two of the vital positions—shortstop and centerfield, not forgetting Ed Stanky's yeoman service at the midway. Now Johnny Peacock gives them added strength behind the bat. The pitching is still on the knees of the gods, however.

MUTT AND JEFF COMBINATION with the Dodgers are Howie Schultz and Vic Lombardi, first sacker and pitcher, respectively. Howie stands 6 feet 6 inches while Vic is just 12 inches shorter any way you look at him.

JANIRO, ADDEO DO IT TONIGHT

By CHARLES VACKNER

Rain reigned supreme last night, postponing the boxing program at MacArthur Stadium until tonight.

Winner of 37 of his 38 fights, Tony Janiro, of Youngstown, Ohio, meets Freddie Addeo, Williamsburgher, in the feature event of eight rounds. The occasion will mark the Buckeye State boxer's debut in Brooklyn. Janiro, considered one of the standout lightweigths of the past season, is rapidly becoming a fullfledged welterweight. For tonight's knockout, the shifty and sharp punching blond battler will weigh 141¾ pounds. Janiro will have an advantage of one-quarter pound over the sturdy Addeo.

An experienced ringster, Addeo figures to force Janiro to step at top speed. Tiny Freddie has held his own with such headliners as Carmine Fatta, Johnny Price and Joey Bagnato. In the Ridgewood Grove earlier this season, Addeo, a 1-4 underpuppy, scored a technical knockout over the vaunted Benny Cartegena.

Del Gatto vs. Harvey

Middleweights will show in the six-round semi-final. At 161 pounds, Johnny Harvey will enjoy a pull of five pounds over the promising Tony Del Gatto. The latter possesses one of the best left hooks in the division and last week scored a thrilling verdict over the stiff-punching Dave Carver.

Matchmaker Al Torre has arranged two other sixes and a pair of fours to round out the program. In the six-round events, Ray Puig, 132½, will take on Joe Carkido, 131½, and Rocco Lescio, 141, meets Pete Maribello, 139. The fours will show Benny May, 123½, taking on Howard Monk, 124, and Pat Butler, 138½, mixing with the 139 Lou Saliveres, who has scored in a brace of bouts in Fort Hamilton this year.

Tonight, in Elizabeth, N. J., Jock Leslie will box the feature bout with Clint Miller.

INTERNATIONAL LEAGUE

LAST NIGHT'S RESULTS

Toronto 9, Newark 5, 1st.
Toronto 4, Newark 0, 2d.
Montreal 9, Syracuse 8.
Rochester 5, Baltimore 0, 1st
Baltimore 12, Rochester 5, 2d.
Buffalo 4, Jersey City 3, 1st
Buffalo 8, Jersey City 4, 2d.

STANDING OF THE CLUBS

	W.	L.	Pct.		W.	L.	Pct.
Montreal	36	19	.655	Toronto	21	26	.447
Jer. Cy.	31	18	.633	Syracuse	18	29	.383
Newark	28	21	.571	Rochester	19	32	.373
Baltimore	28	24	.538	Buffalo	16	29	.353

TONIGHT'S GAMES

Jersey City at Buffalo.
Newark at Toronto.
Baltimore at Rochester, twilight.
Syracuse at Montreal.

THE ASSEMBLY LINE

By BEN GOULD

Big Al Moschetti is back at his Arma post and showed his cage activities haven't interfered with his pitching. He's still the Knights' outstanding softball twirler . . . Joe Monahan, Bethlehem outfielder, was wounded three times, receiving the Purple Heart and two Oak Leaf Clusters. Other honorably discharged veterans on the team, which is bowling over all opposition, are Walter Flannery, a second sacker, and Pitcher Lefty Kosek . . . Al Abrams, who plays the infield with the Knomark Manufacturing Co. softball team, is one of the company's owners.

Republic's crack golf team overwhelmed Sperry, 51 to 3, in their challenge match . . . At Brooklyn Union Gas, Walter Clark picked up his golf clubs after four years (having been in the army three of them) and went on to win the company's Spring tournament at Bethpage with a sparkling 82 . . . Ted Merkt was close behind . . . And speaking of golf, at Grumman, the veteran Bob Brown paced the field of 60 linksmen with a score of 73 at Salisbury. . . . Second place went to Lou Dellavechia, while Tony Cisco, recently released from the navy, was third.

The Industrial Federation has mapped plans for a huge track meet on June 27, at Newtown Field . . . Team awards will be given in Classes A and B . . . Newtown's track coach, Lou Werner, will direct the games . . . Wayne Lemmon has joined the Industrial Recreation Association as national field consultant. He expects to travel throughout the land advising various athletic directors on program problems.

Alvin Shivley, former New York Stock Exchange catcher, is playing with Bendix . . . Two unbeaten softball teams meet tomorrow night when Grumman faces Liberty for the leadership of the Aircraft League . . . Russ Barber is no longer affiliated with Sperry . . . Fishing parties every Sunday at Leyt are gaining in popularity with 300 employes taking part trips . . . Carl Kneisch has joined the no-hit ranks in softball twirling circles, chalking up the feat against R. E. F.

EAGLE BASEBALL CONTEST

IN CO-OPERATION WITH OLSEN AND JOHNSON AND BILL STERN ON NBC—WEAF

(Cartoon No. 22)

This Player Is____________________

(Write Your Selection Here)

By OLSEN and JOHNSON
Stars of "Laffing Room Only"

Hitler wanted elbow room in Russia. Now the Reds have plenty of Elbe room in Germany!

RULES IN BRIEF—Thirty cartoons and limericks will comprise the Baseball Contest. Olsen and Johnson give a clue each day and Bill Stern broadcasts a clue each evening at 6:40 on WEAF. Contestants may use these clues if they wish. Deadline for mailing entries is MIDNIGHT, SUNDAY, July 1, 1945. No charge of any kind is levied on contestants. Facsimiles of the cartoons and limericks are acceptable. There is nothing to buy or sell, no coupons to clip, no subscriptions to obtain. Accuracy and simplicity are the main requisites. The decision of the judges in all matters is to be accepted as final by contestants. Each cartoon depicts ONE PLAYER and no player's name will be used more than once. Submit the 30 solved cartoons and the six worked-out limericks at one time—at the end of the contest. The limericks appear each Friday. You can obtain a set of the complete rules by writing the Contest Editor, Brooklyn Eagle, 24 Johnson St. You can call him at MAin 4-6200 to clarify any point you may have doubt about. This is a contest of skill and baseball knowledge. Editor's Note: Cartoons No. 29 and 30 will be published together on the final day of the contest.

PRIZE LIST 1945 Baseball Contest

FIRST PRIZE—
$1,000 war bond.
SECOND PRIZE
$500 war bond.
THIRD PRIZE
$250 war bond.
FOURTH TO EIGHTH PRIZES.
Five war bonds of $25 each.
CONSOLATION PRIZES
Fifty copies of "The Brooklyn Dodgers," new book by Frank Graham.
One hundred fifty pairs of tickets to Olsen and Johnson's "Laffing Room Only!"
One hundred fifty sets of reserved seats to regularly scheduled games at Ebbets Field, Polo Grounds, Yankee Stadium.
One hundred sets of seats to regularly scheduled big-time WEAF-N. B. C. broadcasts.

Seminole Club Clinches 6 of 7 Net Matches

The Seminole Club of Forest Hills took the lead in the Long Island Tennis League by defeating Bayside at Bayside, winning 6 of 7 matches.

Seminole won all of the singles as Carol defeated Cobleigh, 6—0, 6—2; Kilgus won from Lambert, 6—0, 7—5; Salichs defeated Sander, 7—5, 6—2, and Grunberg won from MacLean, 7—5, 3—6, 8—6.

In the only losing match in the doubles, Carol and Graziadei were defeated by Lambert and Christie, 2—6, 6—4, 6—4. Kilgus and Graziadei of Seminole won from Cobleigh and Sander, 6—4, 6—2, and Hochreiter and Johnson defeated Bacon and Rickards, 6—4, 6—3.

In the final of the club Class A singles, Ronald Carol defeated Frank Salichs, defending champion, 6—4, 8—6, 6—4.

ODT Cancels Exhibition Between Bucs, Tigers

Pittsburgh, June 20 (U.P.)—Due to increased troop movements, the Office of Defense Transportation has called off an exhibition game at Forbes Field between the Pirates and the Tigers in order to save transportation, it was announced today.

The game, to have been played July 10, was to have supplied money for the major leagues' baseball equipment fund for the army and navy.

YESTERDAY'S STAR

Roger Wolff, knuckle-ball ace of the Senators, who pitched a one-hit, 6-to-0 victory against his ex-mates, the Athletics.

Bushwicks' Hurling Staff Weakened For Stars' Game

The Bushwicks, with a record of 14 wins and seven losses, will be shooting for their 15th win of the season tonight when they face the Philadelphia Stars, members of the Negro National League, in a floodlight game at Dexter Park. It starts at 8:45 p.m. The Dexters have been traveling along at a fast clip, having won 10 out of their last 13 games.

Tonight's meeting will be their third of the year. Each club captured a game. The Stars have a crack staff of hurlers to make their selection for tonight's tilt. There is Barney Brown, Tom Sunkett, Roy Partlow, Will Ricks and Wilmer Harris. Bill Cash or Clarence Palm will do the catching. The visitors will have Jim West at first, Marvin Williams at second, Frank Austin, the N. N. L. batting at short, and Tom Duckett at third. Manager Curry, Gene Benson and Ed Stone will patrol the outfield. At this writing, the Stars are second in the N. N. L. race, behind the Homestead Grays.

Manager Joe Press is undecided on his Dexter Park hurling selection with the departure of Wally Signer to the Cubs. Bots Nekola, Bill Sahlin, Emil Moscowicz and Gene Philipps are available.

Friday night, the Kansas City Monarchs will come to Dexter Park for their first visit of the year.

FIGHT RESULTS

MILWAUKEE — Charles Parham, 149, Milwaukee, knocked out Bob Richardson, 152, Cleveland (8); Bill Parsons, 143, Chicago, knocked out Xavier Canadeo, 145, Chanute Field, Ill. (1); Charles Pope, 144, Milwaukee, knocked out Bob Lee, 137, Chicago (1); John Hubbard, 179, Milwaukee, stopped Jack Pumphrey, 100 (4); Bob Mills, 139, Gary, Ind., drew with Carmen Grecco, Milwaukee (4); Frank Gaudes, 135, Milwaukee, stopped Ed Rawlins, 129, Chicago (1).

BUFFALO, N. Y. — Harvey Mathe, 132, Sudbury, Ont., decisioned George Howard, 126, Lackawanna, N. Y. (4); Allan Faulkner, 151, Buffalo, decisioned Len Nelson, 151, Detroit (6); Mike Martyke, 132, St. Catherines, Ont., knocked out Chief Red Cloud, 132½, Flint, Mich. (2); Sunny Hampton, 140½, Buffalo, decisioned Stan Cleslik, 132, Detroit (6); Johnny Green, 147, Lackawanna, N. Y., technicaled Broadway Johnny Jones, 155½, New York (10).

UNION CITY, N. J.—Irish Jimmy Mulligan of Boston, and Ross Strickland of Philadelphia, will fight an eight-round bout at Roosevelt Stadium tonight. Their bout was postponed because of rain last night.

PHILADELPHIA — The ten-round bout, scheduled last night between Willie Joyce dGary, Ind., and Dave Freeman, Philadelphia, will be held tonight.

HARTFORD, Conn.—Tony Falco, 148, Middletown, Conn., outpointed George (Red) Doty, 148, Hartford (10). Bobby Pollowitzer, 127, East Hartford, drew with Gabriel Rios, 122, San Juan, P. R. (6). Pat Brady, 130, New York, knocked out Julio Vekesus, 134, San Juan (4).

WHITE PLAINS—Joe LaMotta, 153¼, New York, knocked out Jimmy Davis, 152½, Pittsburgh (4). Ballesando Carubia, 149, New York, knocked out Mayhew Smith, 146, Columbia, S. C. (3). Jimmy Rizzo, 136, outpointed Nick Primiani, 136, Montreal (6). Augie Lapara, 126, New Orleans, outpointed George Knox, 128½, Newark, N. J. (6). Louis Rousse, 152, New Orleans, knocked out Eddie Moore, 151½, Newark (1). Charley Lomski, 187, Paterson, N. J., knocked out Larry Shuck, 180, Mount Vernon, N. Y. (2).

NEW BEDFORD, Mass.—Johnny Cool, 134, Worcester, Mass., stopped Jerry Zullo, 133, Chelsea, Mass. (5). Basil Mazerak, 155, Cambridge, stopped John Harrington, 150, Boston (1). Walter Gomes, 140, New Beford, stopped Jose Fernandes, 140, Duxbury, Mass. (1). Joe Gomes, 135, Providence, outpointed John Mangar, 131, Boston (4). Gene La Blanc, 136, Providence, stopped Bud Gorman, 135, Boston (3).

BANGOR, Me. — Ralph Walton, 139, Montreal, drew with Rene Cantero, 137, Havana (8). Eden Germain, 132, Portland, Me., stopped Charley Sooster, 130, Frankfort, Me. (2). Young Gallant, 172, Skowhegan, Me., outpointed Eddie Turner, 173, Bangor (4).

OKLAHOMA CITY — Proctor Heinold, Oklahoma City, stopped Ted Christie, Chicago (5).

Harvard Grid Unchanged

Cambridge, Mass., June 20 (U.P.)—Harvard will continue to play football on an informal basis this Fall, despite the fact that head coach Richard C. (Dick) Harlow has been discharged from the navy and will return to take charge of the team.

MAJOR LEAGUE LEADERS

BATSMEN

NATIONAL LEAGUE

	G.	AB	R.	H.	PC.
Holmes, Boston	43	226	51	86	.381
Kurowski, St. Louis	48	171	35	61	.357
Rosen, Brooklyn	46	186	38	66	.355
Ott, New York	56	203	40	71	.350
Cavaretta, Chicago	49	185	34	64	.346

AMERICAN LEAGUE

	G.	AB	R.	H.	PC.
Cuccinello, Chicago	51	180	28	63	.350
Etten, New York	51	182	31	58	.319
Case, Washington	45	180	26	57	.317
Estalella, Phila.	51	191	24	60	.316
R. Johnson, Boston	53	205	28	63	.307

RUNS BATTED IN

NATIONAL LEAGUE

Elliott, Pitsburgh, 47; Olmo, Brooklyn, 42; Hlmes, Boston, 42.

AMERICAN LEAGUE

R. Johnson, Boston, 37; Etten, New York, 36; Schalk, Chicago, 29.

HOME RUN HITTERS

NATIONAL LEAGUE

Lombardi, New York, 13; DiMaggio, Philadelphia, 1; Ott, New York, 8; Weintraub, New York, 8; Adams, St. Louis, 8; Workman, Boston, 3.

AMERICAN LEAGUE

Stephens, St. Louis, 10; R. Johnson, Boston, 7; Hayes, Cleveland, 7.

WITH OUR FIGHTERS

Over There

Award of the Bronze Star Medal for heroic achievement April 8, near Budberg, Germany, has been made to Tech. 5th Grade William J. Newman Jr. of 237-20 93d Road, Bellerose.

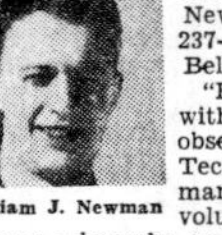

William J. Newman

"Radio operator with a forward observer team, Technician Newman fearlessly volunteered to serve as a bazooka ammunition carrier during a furious encounter with enemy tanks holding up an infantry attack on Budberg," declares his citation.

"Accompanying a bazooka gunner, Technician Newman went out into a road being shelled heavily by a German tank and courageously assisted in firing three rounds which destroyed the threatening hostile armor."

The 20-year-old hero, a graduate of Regis High School, was attending Fordham University when he entered service in March, 1943. He went overseas last July and wears four battle stars for the campaigns in Metz, the Moselle Valley, siege of the Rhine and the Ruhr. His sister, Anne E., is a cadet nurse at St. John's Hospital.

Milton and Oscar Shaller

Milton Shaller, 21, of 3099 Brighton 6th St., has been promoted to warrant officer in India, where is he serving in the legal department of an air force transport command headquarters. His brother, Warrant Officer Oscar, 27, is stationed with an anti-aircraft outfit in the Aleutians. Milton, a graduate of New York University, entered service in April, 1943, and has been overseas since January, 1944. Oscar is a C. C. N. Y. alumnus and has been overseas since October, 1943.

Carpenter's Mate 3d Class Edwin Severin, son of Mr. and Mrs. Julius Severin, 247 50th St., is rounding out 18 months of service in the Pacific with the Seabees. He enlisted in December, 1942, and was called to active duty the following April.

Award of the Air Medal has been made in the India-Burma theater to Staff Sgt. Edward W. Rosen, 24, of 513 Hegeman Ave.

Lt. Edward A. Johnson of 1361 E. 16th St., a special service officer with the 103d Infantry Division, has been awarded the Bronze Star Medal for meritorious service in combat against the enemy from Nov. 16, 1944, to May 7, 1945, in France, Germany and Austria.

Before entering service in July, 1942, Lieutenant Johnson was a member of the faculty of Bishop Loughlin Memorial High School. He is a graduate of St. Francis College and St. John's Graduate School.

Credited with shooting down two Jap planes during a B-29 raid over Japan, Sgt. Warren Lee Dettling, a Superfortress gunner of 396 Westminster Road, has received the Air Medal for "meritorious achievement and undaunted courage on his hazardous missions over the Japanese homeland."

Robert Collins of 300 Parkville Ave., has been advanced to motor machinist's mate third class in the Southwest Pacific. He is a graduate of St. Rose of Lima grammar school and Erasmus Hall.

George Ansloan John Kane

Infantry officers commissioned at Fort Benning, Ga., were 2d Lts. George E. Ansloan of 8022 5th Ave. and John J. Kane of 7306 3d Ave.

Pvt. Louis Freedman of 81 Covlain Place has returned to this country after ten months in the European theater. The Brooklyn infantryman wears the European campaign ribbon with four battle stars and the Good Conduct Medal.

James Reilly Marvin Mansberg

Cadet Midshipmen James V. Reilly of 6719 7th Ave. and Marvin Mansberg of 126 E. 53d St. will be graduated at the end of the month from the New York State Maritime Academy, Fort Schuyler, N. Y.

Stationed at Wakeman Convalescent Hospital, Camp Atterbury, Ind., as an instructor in reconditioning is Pvt. Herbert Flaum of 135 Prospect Park Southwest. Before entering service, Flaum was a business student at New York University and captain of the college basketball team.

Winner of the Distinguished Flying Cross, the Air Medal with three oak leaf clusters, the campaign ribbon with four battle stars and a Presidential citation, 1st Lt. Charles B. Gilfeather of 457 Park Place has returned to the United States after completing his tour of missions over Germany. He is a graduate of St. Teresa R. C. grammar school and St. Francis Prep.

Home on furlough from Kirtland Field, New Mexico, is Pvt. Hugh J. Maxwell of 175 14th St.

Over Here

Yeoman 3d Class Edward M. Timmins 3d of 192d St., Hollis, is home on 30-day leave after 14 months of service overseas aboard an LST. Timmins enlisted following graduation from Chaminade High School, Mineola, and is a veteran of the Normandy invasion. His parents are Mr. and Mrs. Edward M. Timmins 2d of the same address.

Marine Pvt. James J. Collins Jr. of 144 16th St. is home on furlough from Camp Lejeune, N. C.

Capt. Thomas W. Hamlen of 479 Washington Ave., was graduated from the officers department of the transportation corps school, New Orleans, La.

Advanced to corporal at the Atlantic overseas air technical service command, Newark, N. J., was Eva Osofsky of 515 Powell St.

Veteran of ten months in Europe, Capt. James J. La Penna of 21 Arthur St. has been assigned to the Spokane air technical service command, Wash.

Brooklyn GI Aids Rescue of 27 in Okinawa Ambush

Hell's Hollow, Pfc. Alex Yakolvic of 2352 Ocean Parkway and his marine platoon called the tiny valley on Okinawa where, caught in ambush, they struggled an entire day to free themselves from encircling Japs.

It was there that Private Yakolvic, stretcher bearer, dodged blasts of bullets to bring his wounded companions to safety.

Three men lay dead in the lush underbush and 27 others were injured before the unit fought its way out.

In order to work more quickly during the encounter, Private Yakolvic decided against the usual four-man stretcher team. He and another stretcher bearer found they could manage the rocks and boulders of the rough terrain more effectvely if only two of them worked together.

Time after time others who ran to the rescue of the wounded were themselves mowed down, but Private Yakolvic got through safely.

It was not until two days later that the valley and its surrounding hills were cleared of Japs.

2 in Race to Head County Legion

By CHARLES J. GRIFFIN

Louis F. Drago of Person Post will oppose John P. McGrath of 13th Post for Kings County American Legion commander at a convention which opens July 12 in the Columbus Club, 1 Prospect Park West, according to William Purcell, convention chairman.

Candidates for county vice commanders will be Mr. Purcell, Otto Lockhart, K. M. Nelson, Daniel Hall, Harold Woodhouse, James Walters and Edwin Duffy. Thomas Kilcourse is the sole candidate for adjutant and Henry J. Hoops the only one in the race for treasurer.

The 2d Division of the county Legion will honor its commander, Anthony Quattrone, at a reception next Saturday night at 8 o'clock in the headquarters of Boro Park Post, 4814 16th Ave. County Commander Lawrence Wiseman will attend.

Mr. Wiseman will preside over the last county committee meeting Wednesday at 8:30 in headquarters, 160 Pierrepont St.

SAVE FATS AND WASTEPAPER

VETERAN

In Brooklyn

By Sylvan Furman

Here's some more about those decorations and service ribbons you see on the chests of service men and veterans.

Ribbons stand for either of two types of award:

1—Special decorations or citations for valor or heroism. These generally refer to specific deeds, though not always.

2—Medals for services performed over a period of time in campaigns or wars, with different medal ribbons, according to the theater of operations where the services were performed.

Today we're talking about army decorations for valor.

While none of these decorations for valor get handed out on street corners and take a bit of earning, there is an order of precedence, as far as their value is concerned. They may cost anything from a gallon of sweat to one's very life.

War Department awards are rated in this order:

1—Medal of Honor
2—Distinguished Service Cross
3—Distinguished Service Medal
4—Legion of Merit
5—Silver Star
6—Distinguished Flying Cross
7—Sildier's Medal
8—Bronze Star
9—Purple Heart
10—Air Medal
11—Medal for Merit
12—Good Conduct Medal

These awards are made by the War Department or designated commanding officers, acting for the President. (And, lest you forget, the President is acting in *your* behalf.)

Some of these awards may be made to civilians, but never the Medal of Honor, Legion of Merit, Distinguished Flying Cross or Soldier's Medal.

On the other hand, American civilians such as war correspondents, Red Cross workers, and officers and members fo Merchant Marine crews, may be awarded the Purple Heart. The Army may also award the Distinguished Service Cross and the Silver Star to merchant seamen under appropriate circumstances.

Two medals may not be awarded for the same deed, except if the person was wounded while performing it. In such cases, he or she may also get the Purple Heart for the wound, in addition to the appropriate award.

If a person is awarded the same decoration more than once, he gets an Oak Leaf Cluster for each time after the first.

Here's an interesting point—enlisted men who win the Medal of Honor, Distinguished Service Cross, Distinguished Service Medal, Distinguished Flying Cross, or Soldier's Medal, are entitled to a $2.00 monthly raise in pay!

Later on, we're going to describe the ribbons which stand for these and other decorations. We'll also give a little of the history and background of these marks of distinction worn by brave men.

(Mr. Furman's column appears Sunday, Wednesday and Friday.)

Boro GI Wounded While Assisting Felled Comrade

Pfc. Peter J. Zebuda of 106 Engert Ave. has been awarded the Purple Heart for wounds received during the battle for Okinawa. He was hit while assisting a wounded comrade.

Pfc. Peter J. Zebuda

A member of the 10th Army, he entered the service Jan. 27, 1941 and has been overseas more than two years.

While participating in the battle for the Marshall Islands, Private Zebuda captured a Japanese flag which he sent home to his mother, Mrs. Agatha Zebuda.

He is a graduate of Public School 110 and Eastern District High School.

Military Training Urged By U. S. Legion Head

American Legion National Commander Edward N. Scheiberling, speaking last night before members of Gerald V. Carroll Post in Passaic, N. J., advocated the adoption of a universal military training program as a bulwark of peace.

He said it was the "let's wait tactics" which made the attack on Pearl Harbor possible.

Scheiberling also urged that steps be taken to give "satisfactory employment" to veterans without "red tape," and to trim a force of men and women in diplomacy as military leaders are trained.

Overseas Mail Flies Again

Postmaster Quayle announced that air mail service has been resumed to Belgium, Denmark, France, Luxembourg, Netherlands, Norway and Switzerland.

2 SOLDIERS ON LEAVE WED 2 SISTERS IN BORO CHURCH RITES

Both soldiers came home from camp on leave and both sisters exclaimed: "Now!" So the four were the principals in a double wedding ceremony, yesterday, at St. Anselm's Church, 82d St. and 4th Ave., where the Rev. Peter J. Flynn, assistant pastor, blinked twice and quadrupled on the "I do" questions.

Catherine and Rosalie Yeager, daughters of Mrs. Rose Yeager of 550 83d St., were the brides. Their bridegrooms were Corp. John McMahon of 250 73d St., stationed at Fort Miles, Del.—he married Catherine—and Staff Sgt. James Adams of 319 81st St., Rosalie's husband.

To keep everything family-like, both couples will live in Brooklyn, as near to each other as possible, when Hirohito decides to call it quits.

BORO OFFICER ABOARD FIRST U. S. WARSHIP TO ENTER OKINAWA AREA

Okinawa, June 23—With the costly battle for Okinawa over, a checkup today disclosed that Lt. (j. g.) William B. Walsh, 25, of 698 St. Mark's Ave., Brooklyn, was aboard the first warship to enter the waters around the embattled island.

Lieutenant Walsh's ship, a destroyer-minesweeper, led a squadron of others which probed the uncharted waters and braved the hazards of underwater explosions and Jap suicide planes. The flotilla cleared a path to the beach a week before the invasion.

A navy medical corps man, Lieutenant Walsh is a graduate of Brooklyn Preparatory School and the Georgetown School of Medicine, Washington, D. C. He interned at the Long Island College Hospital before entering service. His wife lives at Takoma Park, Md.

21st Bomber Command photo

BROOKLYN OVER TOKYO—The Superfortress City of Brooklyn and her crew, pictured here, have been acting as Brooklyn's representative in carrying the war to Japan. Kneeling at right is the lone Brooklynite aboard the ship, Sgt. Chester Moscicki of 377 5th St., tail gunner. Others, left to right, standing, are Lt. Harry M. Larned, commander; Lt. John W. Birthwhistle, navigator; Lt. Harold H. McTureous, bombadier; 2d Lt. John J. Anestis, instrument specialist, and Tech. Sgt. John T. Fleming, flight engineer, and kneeling, are Sgt. Harold D. Hindley, left gunner; Staff Sgt. Harry E. Ridings Jr., radio operator, and Sgt. John W. Weaver, right gunner. Two others in the crew are not in the photo.

Editor Old Timers:

Nearly 40 years ago there was a lumber yard on Broadway between Heyward and Lynch Sts. One night in 1906 it burned down. The next morning I stood across the street, on Boerum St., and drew a picture of it while the firemen were still pouring water on the lumber. This is a copy of that picture. This lumber yard was very close to a public school. Now what I would like to know: Is there an Old Timer who remembers if this fire was in 1906?

ANTHONY TREGLIA.

OLD TIMERS

9th St. Memories Presented Herein

Editor Old Timers:

I can add several names to Mr. Vackner's letter of Easter Sunday edition. My family (Smith) lived 45 years in South Brooklyn from 11th to 21st Streets, 6th to 8th Ave. When I was 5 years old we lived at 419 19th St. (Ganley's house). He was a motorman on the 7th Ave. trolley line. During that time the medicine factory at 8th Ave. and 19th St. burned down. (What a fire!) My father moved here from Philadelphia, Pa., when I was 4 years old. His name was James Hay Smith. He worked at Shewans and Todd's Erie Basin Ship Yards till his dath in 1933. Had a large delegation at his services in Herbst's, 75th St. Funeral Parlors as he belonged to Boilermaker and Ship Builders Unions. We lived in Burns' flats, 21st St. near 7th Ave. and he knew the Langton, Gilroy, Carey, Cosgrove, Lundy, Murphy, Pender, Green, Olsen, Oderhopt, Johnson Norman Cassidy, Malone, Borst, MacKenzie, Durgin and many more families. Also lived in Chadwick's houses, 237 17th St. with families of Gobel, Wolf, Van Syckle, McCarroll's, Slavin, Henderschott

How many recall the opening night of Prospect Theater? John McCormick did a lot of furnishings for it.

I worked for McCormick in his large department store which stood on the corner of 9th St. and 5th Ave. many years and was a landmark, really of South Brooklyn. Also Mr. Neergard's Drug Store next door is one of the real old timers and Avon Movie Theater on 9th St., not to forget Browning's Soda Shop, 9th St. and 5th Ave.

Would like to hear from some of our old-timer friends and neighbors.

Mrs. AGNES FITZPATRICK.
483 17th St.

Tom the Barber Writes a Letter

Editor Old Timers:

Read with great pleasure the letter from Mr. Vackner of the neighborhood of 19th St. and 6th Ave. I remember the Vackner family, if he was a brother of John and Marty, but he has left out a lot of the old neighbors. The ones he mentions I knew well, but I wonder why he has not mentioned the Browners, John and Willie; James Kearns, who had the saloon on 19th St. corner. The McDonough family, Michael, Helen, Joseph, Ann, Rich and two younger brothers. I wonder if he remembers Jackie, the hunchback grocer on 19th St. corner. Old Joe Van Vost, the mover up 19th St. and his helper, six-finger Bill Hockmeyer. Joe used to sell clams on Prospect and 5th Aves. on Saturday nights. How about the Galvins, Wilsons, Sanky Crowley, who pitched for the old Melrose; the McLoughlins, Mamie was a teacher in old St. John's; old fat Mary, who had the goats up 19th St.,; also the Cheeks, Websters, the Hamilton candy store near 18th St.; the Smith bakery (the son was called Quaker); the Driscolls in 20th St., Joe, Tim and John; the Barnetts in 18th St. (they were glaziers and used to go through the streets, one on each side, one calling out: "Glass put in" and the other answering: "Me too.") He mentioned Tom Clark, but not his brothers, Bull and a younger brother. His sister married Owen Cassidy who he mentioned. How about Dan Casey, the peddler; the Hennesseys, Frank and Bill; Jimmy Aikens, Ed Ward, Pat Lovely and his adopted son Harry. Well, I think I will quit for a while. Hoping some one else will carry on from here.

TOM THE BARBER.

Corrects Mr. Volk

In answer to Harry H. Volk. Well, Harry, in your article in the Old Timers section you stated that Terry McGovern won the bantamweight championship from Casper Leon at the old Greenwood Athletic Club. I am sorry that I have to say that Casper Leon never held the bantamweight title of the world. And you also say that Terry McGovern fought George Dixon at the Broadway Sporting Club at Waverly Place and Broadway, Manhattan. Terry McGovern met Dixon at the old Broadway A. C. in Brooklyn on Jan. 9, 1900, for the featherweight championship of the world, and Terry won the title in the eighth round when Tom O'Rourke, the manager of Dixon, threw the sponge in the ring, and the referee stopped the fight. So you see, Harry, you are wrong when you say they fought at the Broadway Sporting Club in Manhattan. And they did not fight 20 rounds as you stated.

THOMAS W. CASEY.
1562 Coleman St.

Professional Writer Scolds Contributors

Editor, Old Timers:

I have long been an interested reader of the Old Timers page. But as a professional writer I have been startled at times when some hazy contributor takes it upon himself to move Gowanus Canal over to Greenpoint. No real Brooklynite could do that.

Another thing. The North Side is always referred to as Greenpoint. This, too, is a gross error. The North Side has always been part of Williamsburg. It extends north from Grand St. (a dividing line) and ends at the junction of Manhattan, Bedford and Nassau Aves. From there on we are in Greenpoint. When we cross the Manhattan Ave. Bridge over Newtown Creek, we have left Greenpoint and are in Long Island City, formerly known as Hunter's Point. I trust this information will prevent some one moving Newtown Creek to Bensonhurst or Borough Park.

An article headed "N. 6th Streeter Answers N. 7th" made me call weakly for the smelling salts. I am still a bit shaken. In this article the writer states that he was born at N. 6th St. and Myrtle Ave.! This is utterly preposterous as any authentic map will prove. Myrtle Ave. is almost three miles from N. 6th St.!

The same writer says that he remembers the school at N. 7th and 38th Sts. With a school that size why did we bother to build others in Kings and Queens Counties? Please note that N. 7th St. is in Williamsburg, and 38th St. is part of Bay Ridge!

Does the writer stop there? No! He speaks of the old Dogherty mansion at N. 9th St. and Myrtle Ave. He's wrong again, for he means Wythe Ave. I clearly remember the old mansion, and as a boy I was acquainted with Mr. Dogherty, a perfect gentleman in every sense of the word. Back in the '80s Wythe Ave. was 2d St., but it was never Myrtle Ave.

The firehouse mentioned in the article still stands at the old spot, on the west side of Wythe Ave. near N. 11th St. Back about 1903 my cousin was an engineer in that company and I knew all the other men in the outfit. They had a parrot, a tame crow, a dog and a cat. The horses were trained to "shake hands," which was very thrilling to a youngster. At that time the company was known as "12 Engine." Then it became 112. Today it is 212. Collecting models of the old "steamers" is my hobby.

I respectfully suggest that contributors be a bit more accurate when writing of our honored but unjustly ridiculed borough. The Old Timers page is enjoyed by a host of sincere readers. (I'm sure the number would surprise you, Mr. Editor.)

So please let us keep it interesting and useful. Many old friendships have been revived through this page; many happy days have been lived once again, and many tired, lonesome hearts have been made gay by the exchange of pleasant reminiscences. Our youngsters like to hear us tell of our teen-age exploits. So let us show the real oldsters that we appreciate hearing of their adventures in the days when they could float lightly over the dance floor, pedal their high-wheeled bikes, sing solos at the church suppers, or swing a lusty baseball bat.

Some day I may write a book about Brooklyn. My trees won't be Ailanthus trees. They'll be the magnificent, towering specimens that matured in our rich, wholesome soil—the great clergymen, jurists, physicians, scientists, philanthropists, authors, artists, actors, musicians, inventors—of whom we may well be proud. Brooklyn has produced some of America's foremost and best-loved citizens. That it will continue to do so in the future we may rest assured.

A tree grows in Brooklyn. A tree invisible to the green eyes of those insignificant creatures who seek to hide their envy behind a barrage of vulgar jests. The tree is symbolic of past, present and future generations.

It is a mighty, majestic, invincible Oak.

ANTHONY S. HAVENWOOD.

Gaab Bakery Roundup—Plus Clincher!

Editor Old Timers:

In answer to Henry J. Hughes about Gaab's bakery: It was situated at the corner of Hicks and Degraw on the northwest side; I know quite well, as I went to P. S. 13, on Degraw above Hicks, and passed there four times daily.

Later on they moved to Woodhull St. above Hicks. About the bread he sold at one cent per loaf—that is all wrong. You mean your mother mixed the dough and then took a pan to the bakery which they charged one cent per loaf for baking.

G. F. S.

Editor Old Timers:

This is in reply to a request from Mr. Hughes as to the location of "Gaab's bakery." In the years I knew of it first it was on the corner of Woodhull St. and Hicks St., and then some time before the last World War it moved up to 69 Woodhull St., which was a few doors up from Hicks St. and next to Christy's saloon, in a double store under a house owned by John Mindermann. I do not remember the penny bread but maybe some one else will.

MARGARET EGAN MATHEWS.

Editor Old Timers:

H. J. Hughes, Fairfield, N. J., is a little wrong about buying a loaf of bread at Gaab's for a penny. He would cook you a loaf of bread for a penny. Mother would prepare the dough the night before. In the morning you would be handed the pan filled with the dough (on your way to school) and proceed to Hicks and Degraw Sts., go down the stairs on the Hicks St. side to the basement, deposit your pan and receive a metal disc with a number on it. At noon you would proceed to the basement, present the tag and get your pan back loaded with loaves of bread. They would charge you a penny a loaf. This was every day. I think, but Saturday. This job I had for three years. I should know.

OLD SIXTH WARDER.

Editor Old Timers:

Mr. Henry Hughes of Fairfield, N. J., inquires about the location of Gaab's bakery. It was on Hicks St. near Woodhull St. It is quite possible that a large loaf of home made bread could be bought for one cent but that is not within my recollection.

WILLIAM J. JACKSON.

Editor Old Timers:

We noted with great interest the query about the location of Gaab's bakery. The inquirer also asked if it were true that loaves of bread were sold there at one cent per loaf.

Charles Gaab operated the bakery in question at the corner of Hicks and DeGrew Sts., opening March 17, 1884. Many families in the neighborhood prepared their own dough at home and the children brought it to Gaab's on their way to school in the morning, carrying it in dishpans. At the bakery, the dough was kneaded and baked and when the children stopped in at noon the hot, crusty loaves were all ready to be taken home, at one cent a loaf. Over 30 families took advantage of this service every day.

Gaab's was especially well-known for a white bread priced at five and eight cents and called the "New England" loaf.

Charles Gaab died 18 years ago, but his widow is still living.

THE GAAB FAMILY.
344 Ovington Ave.

Charley Tells Em

Editor, Old Timers:

I would like to answer Thomas W. Casey, who asked, in your Old Timers column, who were the two boxers whom Terry McGovern knocked out in one night. They were, according to my records, Patsy Haley, who became a popular referee, and the other victim was "Turkey Point" Bill Smith.

The "battles" were staged in Chicago in, I believe, 1899. Terry wanted to make a train and so hurried up the job.

CHARLEY LAWSON.

Corrects Writer

Editor Old Timers:

Augustine C. Morris is wrong regarding the boundaries of Ambrose Park. He is also wrong about the 18th Precinct. This police station was removed two years before Ambrose Park was built, so that the drunks could not have been disturbed by shooting at the park.

OLD 39TH ST.

Anniversary Book Inspires Thoughts Of Sacred Heart's

Editor Old Timers:

While reading an old copy of a book commemorating the 25th anniversary of Sacred Heart Church in 1902, I got to wondering how many old timers could recall some of the facts concerning the Sacred Heart Parish.

Do you remember when the Rev. Thomas McGivern first said mass in a primary school on Vanderbilt Ave. near Park, and lived in a rented house at 35 Vanderbilt Ave.? In 1874 Bishop Loughlin laid the cornerstone for the present building on Clermont Ave. Later when the Rev. John Nash became the pastor of Sacred Heart. A short time thereafter he built and opened the Sacred Heart Institute, with boys' department conducted by the Franciscan Brothers and the girls' department under the supervision of the Sisters of Mercy. Remember the Christmas fairs conducted by the ladies of the parish, and the minstrel shows, where the younger set gave performances equal to Broadway shows? As a child I remember these affairs and how I enjoyed them.

How about it, old timers of Sacred Heart? Won't you write in and tell us about your memories and happy days at dear old Sacred Heart?

A SACRED HEART GRADUATE.

Fan Lists Players In Nickname Quiz

Editor Sunday Old Timers:

Off with the gun. Here is a list of answers (I hope) to Robert Ryder's baseball quiz. I'd like to name all of the fellows on the other end of those nicknames, and probably will, but I'm anxious to put my memory against some of the other "first guessers" at the moment.

From a Brooklyn point of view (I'm still very much Brooklyn even though away from it) Mr. Ryder left out what, at least to me, was the oddest nickname of all—"Hokey Pokey." Remember, Mr. Ryder? It was owned by a pitcher whom I saw (really did) pitch a no-hit game at Washington Park, with 15 strike-outs to boot, and to me the greatest Dodger pitcher of all. He has a nephew playing with the Giants—treason on the nephew's part!

The names:

Sultan of Swat—Ruth.
Wahoo Sam—Crawford.
Big Six—Mathewson.
Prince Hal—Chase.
Big Train—Johnson.
Bronx Thrush—Hassett.
Big City—Tim Jordan.
Jolting Joe—Jackson.
Jumping Joe—Dugan.
Flying Dutchman—Wagn
Jersey Joe—Medwick.
Fordham Flash—Frisch.
Smoky Joe—Wood.
The Adonis—"Handsome Harry" Intyre.
Roaring Bill—Kennedy.
Gray Eagle—Speaker.
Bad Bill—Dahlen.
Circus Solly—Hoffman.
Wild Bill—Donovan.
Wee Willie—Keeler.
Vinegar Bill—Klem.
The Mortician—Hoyt.
Steamer Al—Demaree.
Doctor—"Doc" Scanlon.
Tillie—Tillinghast.
Kentucky Colonel—Hornsby.
Hod—Ellis.
Colonel Bill—Huston.
Specks—Torporcer.
Country—Slaughter.
Boom Boom—Beck.
Old Stubble Beard—
Hooks—Wiltse.
Pistol Peter—Reiser.
The Mad Russian—Novikoff.
Duffy—Lewis.
Huska—Medwick.
Stuffy—McInnis (mentioned in Burr's column today.)
The Flea—Evers.
Bucky—Walters.
Rabbit—Maranville.
Wildfire—Schulte.
Little Poison—Lloyd Waner.
The Horse—Danning.
Big Poison—Paul Waner.
The Iron Horse—Gehrig.
The Dazzler—Vance.
Wild Horse of the Ozarks—Pepper Martin.
Jeff of the Ozarks—Tesreau.
Home Run—Baker.
Buster—Brown.
The People's Choice—"Dixie" Walker.
Moose—McCormick.
Silent John—Hummell.
Laughing Larry—Doyle.
Heine—Zimmerman.
Duke— ?
California Rancher—Camilli.
Goose—Goslin.
Zeke—Bonura.
King Kong—Keller.
Dummy—Taylor.
Steeple—Schultze.
Dutch—Leonard.
Frenchy—Bordagary.
Del—Bissonette.
Ki-Ki—Cuyler.
Jacques—Fournier.
Schoolboy—Rowe.
Cotton—Tierney.
Chief—Meyer.
Pinkey—Whitney.
Spud—Davis.
Rowdy—Bartell.
Rosey—Ryan.
Hank—Gowdy.
Wheezer—Dell.
Whitey—Kurowski.
Shuffling Phil—Douglas (News item in Eagle today about Douglas.)
Turkey Mike—Kelly.
Bump—Hadley.
Mickey—Owen.
Dolly—Stark.
Cookie—Lavagetto.
Chuck—Aleno.
The Iron Man—McGinnity.
Chet—Laabs.
Slats—Marion.
Tuck—Stainback.
Bugs—Raymond.
Tot— ?
Spike— ?
Rip—Collins.
Del—Delasandro.
Muddy—Ruel.
Kaiser—Wilhelm.
Truck— ?
Firpo Fred—Marberry.
Chick—Fewster.
The Crab—Evers.
The Giant Killer—Pfeister.
Deacon — McKetchie (Mentioned Burr's column today.)
Kid—Elberfeld.
Socks—Seybold.
Dode—Paskert.
The Schoolmaster—Leever.
EE-Yah—Jennings.
Swede—Risberg.
Goldie— ?
Mule—Haas.
Fat—Hogan.

A. F. A.
Pearl River, N. Y.

Knows All the Places

Editor Old Timers:

You had an item signed by Grandpa about several factories and stone yards, saying that there are very few persons knowing these places.

I knew every one of these places mentioned. I was born in the City of Brooklyn (Williamsburg), at 101 Meserole St., Oct. 2, 1868. My father kept a paint store at the same place for over 40 years. I am a reader of the Brooklyn Eagle over 60 years.

PHILIPP ALBOHN JR.
60-14 68th Ave., Ridgewood.

Remember Hurley Games?

Editor Old Timers:

Who remembers the hurley battles between teams representing the various counties in Ireland? They played in the Red Hook section and the champion team met at Celtic Park.

Many heads were cracked in these games. Stars just coming over from the old country were signed up immediately.

TOM GIBBONS.
Quentin Road.

DODGERS TAKE WILD GAME BY 14-12 SCORE

Rosen, Olmo, Nieman Hit Homers As Galan's Triple With Three On Brings Down the Braves

By HAROLD C. BURR

There were two mob scenes at Ebbets Field last night before the Dodgers finally beat the Braves for their seventh straight win, 14 to 12, after three hours and 10 minutes of bitter baseball. The see-saw fight kept the crowd of 27,031 on the edge of their seats. Some real fighting broke out in the eighth when Augie Galan's triple with the bases full broke up the ball game.

Pyle, Walker Wrestle

As the runs clattered over the plate, Ewald Pyle, only one of 11 pitchers used by both teams, came into back up and with a little time on his hands while the ball was being retrieved stuck out his foot to trip Ed Stanky, coming in to score. Dixie Walker, the next batter, rushed Pyle and wrestled him to the ground. In the twinkling of an eye the combatants were hidden under a pile of athletes, clawing away like mad.

When quiet was restored Walker and Pyle were put out of the game.

Home runs were hit by Goody Rosen, his sixth of the year, and Luis Olmo, his eighth. Butch Nieman, pinch-hitting in the ninth, also connected for the circuit. The Dodgers held a seven-to-four margin in the pitching parade. Leroy Pfund, Tom Seats, Art Herring, Ernie Rudolph, Cy Buker, Clyde King and Hal.

Manager Leo Durocher has Vic Lombardi (4-2) and Curt Davis (6-5) left for today's windup doubleheader with the Bostonians.

Bob Coleman used up Bob Logan, Ira Hutchinson, Pyle and Johnny Hutchings, which left him a comparative wide choice of Sunday workers. The Braves' manager is going to try and get an even break with Madame Butterfly Tobin (6-3) and the returned prodigal, Nate Andrews (3-4), but the Dodgers, aroused to fighting pitch by last night's rowdyism, have more than one method of knocking out an enemy.

Fan Heaves Bottle

Twice The Lip came storming up the dugout steps to dispute decisions by Umpires George Barr and Ziggy Sears and a fan tossed a pop bottle just to keep the Gowanus franchise open. Even Sears had words with Pyle before Ewald got in his crude footwork.

Each team collected 15 hits in their cruel pounding of the pitching. Included in the grist of the 30 safeties were nine doubles, three triples and as many homers.

The Dodgers put on two killing five-run rallies and a third of four tallies.

Frank Drews was benched and Whitey Weitelmann went to second for the Beaneaters, who were really full of beans last night.

Eddie Basinski ran his consecu-

Continued on Following Page

Adams' Slugging Paces Cards to 6-4 Triumph

Chicago, June 23 (U.P.)—Led by the home-run hitting of Buster Adams, the second-place Cardinals made it two in a row over the Cubs today by knocking out Hy Vandenberg to score a 6—4 victory.

Adams started Vandenberg's downfall when he hit his ninth homer of the year in the fourth inning to cut the Cubs' lead to one run. A three-run fifth inning finished Vandenberg. Red Schoendienst tripled, Vandenberg yielded a walk and then Adams singled to send the big Cub righthander to the showers and give the Cards a two-run lead.

Chicago	ab	r	h	o	a
Hack,3b	3	1	1	2	3
Johnson,2b	5	0	2	0	4
Nich's'n,rf	3	0	0	2	0
Cavar'ta,1b	5	0	1	10	2
Pafko,cf	4	1	2	4	0
Lowrey,lf	4	0	0	2	0
Williams,c	4	1	3	2	0
Merrulo,ss	3	0	0	2	1
bSecory	1	0	1	0	0
Scuster,ss	0	0	0	1	0
Vand'b'g,p	2	1	1	1	2
Erickson,p	0	0	0	0	0
aSauer	1	0	0	0	0
Signer,p	0	0	0	0	1
cLivingston	1	0	0	0	0
Warneke,p	0	0	0	1	0
Totals	36	4	11	27	13

St. Louis	ab	r	h	o	a
Sch'd'nst,lf	5	1	1	4	0
Hopp,rf	5	2	1	4	0
Adams,cf	5	1	2	3	0
Kur'wski,3b	5	1	2	1	0
Sanders,1b	4	0	0	9	0
O'Dean,c	3	0	2	2	0
Verban,2b	4	0	1	1	2
Marion,ss	4	0	1	3	5
Brecheen,p	1	0	0	0	1
Dockins,p	2	1	0	0	0
Totals	38	6	10	27	11

aSauer batted for Erickson in seventh.
bSecory batted for Merullo in eighth.
cLivingston batted for Singer in eighth.

St. Louis ——— 0 0 0 2 3 0 1 0 0—6
Chicago ——— 0 0 3 0 0 0 0 1 0—4

Error—Williams. Runs batted in—Adams (2), O'Dea, Schoendienst, Kurowski, Hack, Johnson, Cavarretta, Secory. Two-base hits—O'Dea, Williams, Kurowski. Three-base hit—Schoendienst. Home run—Adams. Stolen base—Hopp. Double plays—Verban to Marion to Sanders; Kurowski to Sanders. Left on base—St. Louis 7, Chicago 9. Bases on balls—Dockins 4, Vandenberg 1, Singer 1. Strikeouts—Brecheen 1, Vandenberg 1, Erickson 1. Hits—Off Brecheen, 6 in 2⅓ innings; Dockins, 5 in 6⅔ innings. Vandenberg, 6 in 4⅓; Erickson, 4 in 2⅔; Singer, 1 in 1; V. Warkene, 0 in 1. Winning pitcher—Dockins. Losing pitcher—Vendenberg. Umpires—Pinelli, Conlan and Boggess. Time of game—2:31.

Nats on Top, 6—5

Boston, June 23 (U.P.)—An error by Bob Johnson with two out in the seventh allowed two runs to score and gave Washington a 6-to-5 victory over the Red Sox. Rogert Wolff

Continued on Following Page

Giants Beaten In Slugfest by Phils in 11th, 9-8

Ott Refunds $500 Fine to Voiselle but Hurler Fails Again

Philadelphia, June 23—Mel Ott today refunded to Bill Voiselle the $500 fine which he slapped on the right-handed pitcher on June 1, but the manager's action served only to disconcert the former ace of the staff more than usual. Voiselle was batted out of the box in the first inning, under a six-run barrage, and while he escaped being charged with the defeat, the Giants didn't, as they outstaggered the Phillies to an 11-inning 9—8 loss in Shibe Park.

Ott explained he was satisfied Voiselle was sincere in trying to make a comeback, and that he didn't want the fine to stand as a possible deterrent of Bill's comeback. Mel made his pronouncement just before Voiselle went to the mound to be blasted by four Philadelphia singles, intermixed with two walks and a sacrifice.

Last year's 21-game winner failed to win for the ninth time since May 20, when he had a record of 8—0. He lost six of those nine starts.

Adams Tagged With Loss

Dick Coffman, the invulnerable Giant relief pitcher of 1936, won for the Phillies with two hitless innings, despite a two-base error by rightfielder Rene Monteagudo. Ace Adams, who worked the final four innings, lost his fifth game against four victories, and his fourth in succession.

But before these final two protagonists came on the scene, Ott had called on Loren Bain and Ray Harrell to check the Phils, and Fred Fitzsimmons had summoned Anton Karl, Oscar Judd and Isadore Leon to the aid of starter Bill Lee.

The Giants, with their usual profligacy, expended 16 hits and three walks to score only eight runs, and left 10 on base, which also is a New York custom. As Cuban to Cuban, Nap Reyes struck out in the ninth with two aboard, against Leon, and sundry opportunities to score were eliminated along the way as Dan Gardella, Phil Weintraub and even speedy Johnny Rucker hit double-play ground balls.

Bain in Debut

Rucker's triple set up one Giant run in the first. The Phils retaliated with six when Wally Flager, Jim Wasdell and Fred Daniels walked, John Antonelli, Vance Dinges, Vince DiMaggio and Gus Mancuso singled off Voiselle, and Lee's scratch single and a fly to Flager followed off Bain. The latter, who made his first appearance of the season, gave up two in the fifth on singles by Rene Monteagudo and Mancuso, a walk to Lee, a hit batsman, and a fly by Antonelli.

The Giants had picked up one more in the fourth on Gardella's walk and Ott's double, and two in the fifth, to chase Lee, on Buddy Kerr's single, Daniels 'error, and singles by George Hausmann, Gardella and Ott. Karl quelled the rally when Weintraub hit into his double play.

The Giants tied with two in the ninth on singles by Rucker and Gardella off Karl, and two more one-baggers off Judd by Ott and Kluttz.

Happy Chandler saw the game and had a confab with both owners, Horace Stoneham of the Giants, and Sgt. R. R. M. Carpenter Jr. of the Phillies . . . Bill De Koning, fourth catcher on the Giant roster, was optioned to Richmond of the Piedmont League . . . Bob Wooten, wounded in both legs in the Guadalcanal campaign, signed on today as an emergency first baseman. He was a Giant chattel at Jacksonville in the Sally League.

GIANTS BOX SCORE

Giants	ab	r	h	o	a
Rucker,cf	6	2	2	5	0
H'smann,2b	5	0	1	3	3
D.Gard'la,lf	4	1	2	2	0
Mallory,lf	1	1	0	0	0
Ott,rf	6	0	3	1	1
W'ntra'b,1b	5	0	0	13	2
Kluttz,c	6	1	3	2	1
Reyes,3b	5	1	1	1	3
Kerr,ss	5	1	2	2	5
Voiselle,p	0	0	0	0	0
Bain,p	2	1	1	0	0
bLombardi	1	0	1	0	0
cA.G'rdella	0	0	0	0	0
Harrell,p	0	0	0	2	0
dTreadway	1	0	0	0	0
Adams,p	1	0	0	0	2
Totals	48	8	16	31	17

Phillies	ab	r	h	o	a
Flager,ss	3	1	0	4	4
Antonelli,3b	5	1	1	2	1
Dinges,lf	5	1	1	5	0
Wasdell,1b	5	1	1	9	3
DiMaggio,cf	5	2	2	6	0
M'agudo,rf	3	1	2	1	0
Daniels,2b	2	1	0	0	2
Crawf'rd,2b	0	0	0	0	0
Mancuso,c	4	1	2	3	0
eTriplett	1	0	0	0	0
Seminick,c	1	0	1	1	0
Lee,p	2	0	1	0	0
Karl,p	1	0	1	2	5
Judd,p	0	0	0	0	0
Leon,p	0	0	0	0	0
fFoxx	1	0	0	0	0
Coffman,p	0	0	0	0	0
Totals	38	9	12	33	15

aOne out when winning run scored.
bBatted for Bain in sixth.
cRan for Lombardi in sixth.
dBatted for Harrell in eighth.
eBatted for Mancuso in ninth.
fBatted for Leon in ninth.

Giants ——— 1 0 0 1 2 2 0 0 2 0 0—8
Phillies ——— 6 0 0 0 2 0 0 0 0 0 1—9

Errors—Monteagudo, Daniels. Runs batted in—Ott (3), Hausmann, Lombardi, Kluttz, Dinges, Di Maggio (2), Mancuso (3), Flager, Antonelli, Seminick. Two-base hit—Ott. Three-base hit—Rucker. Sacrifices Daniels, Monteagudo (3). Double plays—Wasdell and Flager, Daniels, Flager and Wasdell; Wasdell, Flager and Karl. Left on bases—Giants 10, Phillies 12. Base on balls—Off Voiselle 3, Bain 2, Adams 2, Lee 2, Coffman 1. Struck out—By Adams 3, Karl 1, Leon 1, Coffman 1. Hits—Off Voiselle, 4 in one-third inning; Bain, 4 in 4 2-3 innings; Harrell, 1 in 2 innings; Adams, 3 in 3 1-3 innings; Lee, 8 in 4 1-3 innings; Karl, 6 in 4 innings; Judd, 2 in one-third inning; Leon, 0 in one-third; Coffman, 0 in 2 innings. Hit by pitcher—By Bain (Flager). Balk—Karl. Winning pitcher—Coffman. Losing pitcher—Adams. Umpires—Goetz, Jorda and Henline. Time of game—2:41.

Byrd Holds Edge Over Nelson in Detroit

Detroit, June 23 (U.P.)—Sam Byrd's eight-under-par 64 over his home course today gave him a one-stroke edge over Byron Nelson halfway in the 72-hole medal score match tournament and a new record for the layout.

Playing for the benefit of Percy Jones army convalescent patients, Byrd scored a 34-30 for his second 18-hole round, giving him a half-way total of 133.

Piccadilly, 25—1 Shot, Captures Irish Derby

Dublin, June 23—The Irish Derby over a mile and a half course at Curragh today was won by Piccadilly, a 25 to 1 shot. He won by a length from Coup De Myth, one of the favorites. The latter paid 3 to 1 for place. Redbay, a 50 to 1 shot, was third.

Major League Records

National League

YESTERDAY'S GAMES

Philadelphia 9, New York 8 (11 innings).
St. Louis 6, Chicago 4.
Brooklyn 14, Boston 12.
Only games scheduled.

STANDING OF THE CLUBS

	W.	L.	Pct.
Brooklyn	36	21	.632
St. Louis	32	24	.571
Pittsburgh	31	25	.554
Chicago	28	24	.538
New York	31	28	.525
Boston	27	27	.500
Cincinnati	23	29	.442
Philadelphia	16	46	.258

TODAY'S GAMES

Boston at Brooklyn, (2) 2:05 p.m.
New York at Philadelphia (2), 2 p.m.
St. Louis at Chicago, 2.
Pittsburgh at Cincinnati, 2.

TOMORROW'S GAMES

No games scheduled.

American League

YESTERDAY'S RESULTS

New York 7, Philadelphia 6.
Washington 6, Boston 5.
Detroit 5, St. Louis 1 (night).
Only games scheduled.

STANDING OF THE CLUBS

	W.	L.	Pct.
Detroit	33	22	.600
New York	31	23	.574
Boston	29	26	.527
Chicago	30	27	.526
Washington	26	27	.491
St. Louis	25	27	.481
Cleveland	22	30	.423
Philadelphia	20	34	.370

TODAY'S GAMES

Philadelphia at New York, 2, 2:05 p.m.
Washington at Boston, 2.
Detroit at St. Louis, 2.
Chicago at Cleveland, 2.

TOMORROW'S GAMES

No games scheduled.

Eagle Sports photo

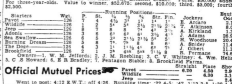

GOODY! GOODY! GOODY! Is what teammates say to Goodwin Rosen as he scores on home run hit in the second inning with two aboard. Ed Stanky and Augie Galan congratulate the little blaster as Ed Basinski and the Dodger mascot look on. The umpire is Ziggy Sears and the dejected looking catcher is Phil Masi of the Braves

Pavot, Arcaro Up, Takes Belmont By Five Lengths Before 42,832

BY HIMSELF—William Jeffords' Pavot made amends for previous disappointments as a three-year-old when he galloped home an easy winner in the Belmont Stakes in closing day of meeting at Belmont Park yesterday. Pavot was five lengths in front of Wildlife at the finish with Jeep coming up fast to take third place from Adonis. Eddie Arcaro rode the winner, who paid $6.20, 4.50 and 2.90 in the mutuels. Victory was worth $52,675 to Pavot's owner. A crowd of 42,832 saw the rich classic run and bet $543,207 on the feature.

YANKS HUMBLE A'S IN 9TH INNING, 7-6

There was a lot of baseball played at the Yankee Stadium yesterday, more of it bad than good, and it added up to a very exciting afternoon and another victory for the Yankees, 7 to 6, over the hapless Philadelphia Athletics.

This happy result was finally brought about in the ninth inning when Tut Stainback's long single to left allowed Bud Metheny to gallop home from second base, but what happened during the innings just before was what made this a most unusual ball game.

Definitely unusual, for instance, was the hitting of catcher Mike Garbark, known far and wide as the all-America "out" with a batting average of less than a hundred, he alone, with a triple and two singles, made it possible for the Yankees to win.

The three blows knocked in three runs and he scored two more himself. The triple, in the eighth, should have been the ball game, for it drove in two runs when the Yanks were one behind and became a third on George Stirnweiss ensuing fly.

Turner Yields Tallies

But the Yankees, whose pitcher, Joe Page, had previously wild-pitched home three of Philadelphia runs—the other was Charley Metro's homer that momentarily gave the visitors the lead in the eighth—refused to give Garbark the credit that was his due. Jim Turner, who had relieved Page in the seventh, promptly walked the first two Philly batters in the ninth, and both of them scored, the tieing run counting when Oscar Grimes fumbled what should have been Estalella's third out grounder.

The error was in the pattern of the Yankee play through most of the afternoon. The A's were in no mood to make trouble, but the Yanks insisted upon it.

Fortunately, Garbark's hitting was the compensating influence. He initiated a two-run attack in the third with a single, and his second blow drove home Stainback in the fourth.

Page was hauled out of there in the seventh after his second wild pitch had set up the tieing score. But it proved to be the one day when the heretofore impeccable Jim

Continued on Following Page

Charles (Red) Ruffing, ace New York Yankee pitcher who entered the army after the 1942 World Series and was honorably discharged recently, has signed a contract and will leave with the Yankees on their Western trip tonight.

Yankee President Larry McPhail did not disclose terms, but said that "in view of Ruffing's long service we did not haggle." Ruffing, who has been working out daily with the team, is still about 10 pounds overweight. He is 40 years old.

Harridge Fines Sewell, 3 Players Total of $550

Chicago, June 23 (U.P.)—President William Harridge of the American League today fined Manager Luke Sewell of the St. Louis Browns and three of his players an aggregate of $550 for their part in the dugout battle in St. Louis Wednesday night.

Harridge fined Sewell $250 for "failure to hold his players in restraint." He fined George Caster $100 for throwing the ball into the dugout in the eighth inning of the game, starting the fight.

Pitcher Sig Jakucki and Infielder Ellis Clary also were fined $100 each for their assault on Karl Scheel, batting practice pitcher for the White Sox.

The American League president stipulated that the fines must be paid within five days.

The free-for-all occurred in the eighth inning of the White Sox-Brown game when St. Louis players replied to the taunts of Scheel by swarming the Sox dugout and administering a severe beating to the former marine.

Women's Western To Babe Zaharias

Indianapolis, Ind., June 23 (U.P.)—Mrs. Babe Didrikson Zaharias of Los Angeles today won the 16th annual women's Western open golf championship by defeating Dorothy Germain of Philadelphia, 4 and 2 in 34 holes to become the only woman in history to win the title three times.

Mrs. Zaharias, defending champion, won the spectacular way. The former Olympic track star fired a record-breaking 72 over the first 18 holes of the Highland Country Club course to take a five-up lead which she never yielded as she defeated Miss Germain for the second year running.

In breaking the previous course record of 73 set by Dorothy Ellis, former Indiana State champion, Mrs. Zaharias shot one of the greatest back nines in the history of women's golf. She shattered par 76 by four strokes.

Rafferty Leads N.Y.A.C. To Another Met Title

The New York Athletic Club maintained it unbroken string of victories by capturing the Metropolitan senior track and field championships for the 29th consecutive year yesterday at Randalls Island. The Winged Footers garnered 72 points with the New York Pioneer Club receiving 48 points for second and the Columbia Midshipmen placed third with 35½.

Jim Rafferty, the N. Y. A. C.'s stellar performer, lived up to expectations in the tuneup mile stint. The smooth-striding runner captured the feature event of the afternoon in 4:17.9, nine yards in front of Thomas V. Quinn, a clubmate. The former Fordham flash held back until the backstretch. Then, moving from the inside, Rafferty cut to the outer lane and bagged Rudy Simms of the N. Y. Pioneer Club on the homeward turn.

Jim Herbert, the archaic ambler of the Grand Street Boys, showed his heels to the schoolboy speedster John Taylor of the N. Y. Pioneers, P. S. A. L. and Junior Met champion, in the quarter-mile dual. Herbert won by three yards and was clocked in 48.8.

The Clinton High School youth led all the way home until the last 50 yards. But the crafty Herbert then forged ahead and maintained his scant margin down to the tape.

Record by Bleifer

The lone record of the afternoon was hung up by Sam Bleifer of the Maccabi A. C. in the two-mile walk. Bleifer heeled and toed to victory in 15:55.1 to crack the mark of 15:58.7 held by Jim Wilson, a fellow club member.

Jack P. Morris and Henry Dreyer, Winged Foot representatives, annexed double wins. Morris, a navigation officer of the air transport command, took the 120-yard high

Continued on Following Page

One More Week To Go in Big Baseball Contest

Tomorrow begins the last week of the big Baseball Contest.

Cartoon No. 25 will appear tomorrow, and next Friday two cartoons —Nos. 29 and 30—will be published. On that day will also appear limerick No. 6.

The Baseball Contest, which is sponsored by the Brooklyn Eagle in co-operation with Olsen and Johnson, stars of "Laffing Room Only," and Bill Stern, noted sports commentator of NBC-WEAF, has been under way now for five weeks.

The competition involves recognition of a group of 30 players from 30 cartoons depicting their habits, methods of play or other characteristics. The competition also involves the completion of each of six limericks by providing a clever last line.

$1,000 Top Prize

The contestant recognizing the greatest number of players and providing the cleverest limerick lines will receive the first prize of a $1,000 War Bond. Other prizes are some $1,500 more in War Bonds, plus hundreds of tickets to ball games, broadcasts, shows and 50 copies of Frank Graham's book, "The Brooklyn Dodgers."

That's all there is to the competition. And it isn't too late to enter now—even though the end is only a week away.

Reprints of the first 14 cartoons (first three weeks) are available. You can get a set of them, plus the first four limericks, by sending an addressed, stamped envelope to the Contest Editor, Box GPO 99, Brooklyn 1, N. Y. Then you can obtain the back copies of the last two weeks of the Eagle and you will be right up to date!

You can enter now, so, if you want to get in on the fun and the profits, follow the above instructions immediately.

Clue Each Night

Each evening in the Eagle Olsen and Johnson provide a clue. Some of their writings have been real clues, others have been fun and confusion. Bill Stern gives a clue in his broadcast at 6:40 each evening over WEAF. Contestants may use these clues or discard them, whatever they wish.

There is nothing to buy or sell, no box tops to save, no subscriptions to get, to get into this contest. You do not even have to buy the Eagle. You can make facsimiles of the cartoons by copying them out of the files here at the Eagle Building, at 24 Johnson St., or at the public library.

Remember — tomorrow starts the last week. You gotta rush if you want to get in on the big deal.

N. Y. Beats Philly; Retains Sears Cup

Philadelphia, June 23—Sweeping the first five singles, New York's Eastern Association annexed its fourth straight triumph in the Sears Cup tennis championship here today at the Germantown Cricket Club. Mrs. Helen Pedersen Rihbany, national woman's indoor champion, started New York off on the right foot by beating Mrs. Laussat Clement, 6—3, 6—2.

International League

YESTERDAY'S RESULTS

Newark 8, Montreal 2.
Baltimore 12, Buffalo 11.
Rochester 3, Jersey City 1 (1st game).
Jersey City 8, Rochester 3 (2d game).
Toronto 6, Syracuse 1 (1st game).
Syracuse 1, Toronto 0 (2d game).

STANDING OF THE CLUBS

	W.	L.	Pct.		W.	L.	Pct.
Montreal	39	21	.650	Toronto	24	27	.481
Baltimore	33	24	.579	Rochester	22	34	.393
Newark	31	23	.574	Syracuse	19	32	.373
J. City	31	25	.554	Buffalo	16	35	.314

TODAY'S GAMES

Newark at Rochester (2).
Jersey City at Buffalo (2).
Baltimore at Montreal (2).
Toronto at Syracuse (2).

Wildlife Places 2d; $52,675 to Victor

By RALPH TROST

With racing's real time machine, Eddie Arcaro, to give him just the proper temper, Walter M. Jefford's Pavot, the flivver of the Withers and Preakness, came back to win the most important of all three-year-old stakes, the mile and a half Belmont, before a crowd of 42,832 yesterday. The man and the horse did it so smoothly that five other horses could have been fitted in a line between them and J. M. Roebling's Wildlife which finished second. Jeep, the favorite, landed in third place just ahead of Adonis.

With blinkers on, for a change, and Arcaro to do the thinking, Pavot again ran as he did last year when he finished the season unbeaten in eight starts, the acclaimed juvenile champion. How easy it was to win was best expressed by Arcaro after the race when he said, "I had to sit up on him like a park policeman to keep him from running right out in front at the start."

Arcaro came out of the race even more an outstanding figure than the colt for, in successive weeks Eddie won the Kentucky Derby on Hoop Jr., $50,000 added, won the Suburban on Devil Diver and yesterday collared the Belmont, $52,675 first money. Eddie also won on Hoop Jr. in the Wood Memorial.

The time, 2:30.1, wasn't not compared with Count Fleet's record of two years ago. But it didn't have to be. Besides, it was better than Whirlaway, Omaha and Gallant Fox ran in their victories. Pavot paid $6.20 to win, the biggest price he's ever paid.

In Front on Last Turn

There was really little to the race in retrospect. Arcaro contendedly let The Doge and Sea Swallow go whistling through a 22.4 first quarter and then a half .47. Eddie sat snugly in fifth and then fourth position. Eddie knew what his horse could do but there were plenty in the stands who thought he was burning him out. When The Doge and Sea Swallow began fading, Eddie kept his mount going smoothly and when they hit the last turn the green and white Jeffords colors were in front with nothing coming on to cause any worries.

When they hit the stretch Arcaro and Pavot had the situation well in hand and with nary a suggestion of the whip that George "The Iceman" Woolf had used unsuccessfully in the Withers, they practically slid right in to victory.

Where was Jeep? Last most of the way. In the stretch where the Wood Memorial winner (the first section) was supposed to run, he passed nothing but tiring horses. Pavot was uncatchable.

If horses know what it's all about,

Continued on Following Page

Tilden, Segura Take Net Matches

The tennis greats of past and present combined their efforts at the West Side Tennis Club yesterday to make the second of the three-day Red Cross Victory tennis exhibitions a success.

Big Bill Tilden, who won his first national singles crown in 1920, easily subdued Richard Skeen, 6—0, 6—0, in one of the six singles matches contested. Tilden, then teamed with Alice Marble in a doubles test against Vinnie Richards, former nationals doubles champion, and Welby Van Horn, North and South professional titleholder. Richards and Van Horn won, 6—3, 7—5.

Francisco Segura of Ecuador, employing the two-hand forehand shot that has made him a favorite of the spectators, won easily from Lt. Gardnar Mulloy of the navy, 6—4, 6—2. Welby Van Horn defeated John Nogrady, 1—6, 6—4, 7—5, in the only match to go more than two sets.

In the only feminine test, Mrs. Sarah Palfrey Cooke repeated her Friday defeat of Dorothy May Bundy, 6—1, 6—4.

Frank Shields, former captain in the Army Air Forces, and William Talbert won other singles matches. Shields turned back Lt. Seymour Greenberg, 6—4, 7—5, and Talbert overcame Elwood Cooke, 6—4, 6—4.

Mrs. Sarah Palfrey Cooke, Hollywood, Cal., defeated Miss Dorothy May Bundy, Santa Monica, Cal., 6—1, 6—4; Lieut. Seymour Greenberg, U. S. N., defeated Capt. Frank Shields, U. S. A., 6—4, 7—5; Welby Van Horn, Atlanta, Ga., defeated John Nogrady, Rockville Centre, N. Y., 1—6, 6—4, 7—5; William T. Tilden 2d, Philadelphia, defeated Richard Skeen, Los Angeles, Cal., 6—0, 6—0; William Talbert, Wilmington, Del., defeated Lt. Elwood Cooke, U. S. N., 6—4, 6—4; Francisco Segura, Ecuador, defeated Lt. Gardnar Mulloy, U. S. N., 6—4, 6—2; Van Horn and Vincent Richards, New York, defeated Miss Alice Marble, New York, and Tilden, 6—3, 7—5; Lt. Cooke and Talbert defeated Lt. Mulloy and Lt. Charles Mattmann, U. S. N., 11—9, 6—2. Mrs. Cook and Lt. Greenberg won first set 6—3 and Miss Bundy and Capt. Shields won second set 7—5, match called due to lateness.

Potsy Clark Named

Lincoln, Neb., June 23 (U.P.)—Lt. Com. George (Potsy) Clark, ex-football coach of the Dodgers, has been named head football coach at the University of Nebraska for the 1945 season, the Athletic Board announced today.

HOW PAVOT WON

The chart for the 77th running of the Belmont Stakes:

(Copyright, 1945, by Triangle Publications, Inc.)

SIXTH RACE—Mile and one-half. The Belmont Stakes. Purse, $50,000 added. For three-year-olds. Value to winner, $52,675; second, $10,000; third, $5,000; fourth, $2,500.

Starters	Wgt.	P.	St.	¼	½	¾	Str.	Fin.	Jockeys	Equiv. Odds
				Running Positions						
Pavot	126	7	4	4½	3³	1²	1⁴	1⁵	E. Arcaro	2.10
Wildlife	126	1	2	5⁴	5⁵	3½	2 1½	2 1¾	T. Atkinson	8.00
Jeep	126	8	7	8	8	7⁴	4³	3½	A. Kirkland	1.35
Adonis	126	3	6	6³	6²	6¹	3½	4¹⁰	J. Adams	26.95
Sea Swallow	126	6	5	3²	2 1½	2 1½	5⁵	5⁸	H. Woodhouse	20.40
Burning Dream	126	5	8	7⁵	7ʰ	8	8	6³	A. Snider	11.45
The Doge	126	4	3	1¹	1 1½	4¹	6²	7ʰ	J. Gilbert	11.15
Brookfield	126	2	1	2ʰ	4ⁿᵏ	5ⁿᵏ	7 1½	8	R. Permane	74.65

Owners—1, W. M. Jeffords; 2, J. M. Roebling; 3, C. V. Whitney; 4, Wm. Helis; 5, C. S. Howard; 6, E. R. Bradley; 7, Pentagon Stable; 8, Brookfield Farms.

Official Mutuel Prices

	Straight	Place	Show
Pavot	6.20	4.50	2.90
Wildlife	—	6.30	3.10
Jeep	—	—	2.40

Went to post: 4:12 E.W.T.; off 4:26. Running time: :22 4-5; :47, 1:12 2-5, 1:38 1-5; 2:04 1-5, 2:30 1-5. Weather clear, track fast. Start good, won driving, second same. Winner, br. c., by Case Ace-Coquelicot, by Man o' War. Trainer, Oscar White. Breeder's award $1,500. Mutuel handle on race, $543,207.

Pavot was kept forwardly from the start and under mild restraint to the stretch turn where he moved up with a rush, assumed command and drew away under pressure. Wildlife raced forwardly all the way, was blocked at the far turn, trying to go through, came again and finished well. Jeep dropped back at the start and raced choppy in the early stages, but made up some ground in the stretch run. Adonis was taken under restraint and kept forwardly, failed to gain when roused in the stretch run. Sea Swallow forced the early pace and then tired. Burning Dream stumbled at the start and almost went to his knees. The Doge had early speed. Brookfield tired badly and was not persevered with.

SPORTS

7★★★★★★★ Complete

BROOKLYN EAGLE

WEATHER—Showers, humid tonight; showers, warm tomorrow

104th YEAR—No. 213—DAILY and SUNDAY (Copyright, 1945, The Brooklyn Eagle, Inc.) BROOKLYN, N. Y., MONDAY, AUGUST 6, 1945 Entered Brooklyn P. O. 2d Class Mail Matter 3 CENTS IN NEW YORK CITY ELSEWHERE 4 CENTS

SECRET ATOMIC BOMB UNLEASHED ON JAPAN

Has Power Equal to 20,000 Tons of TNT

'Rain of Ruin' Faces Foe, Truman Warns, Unless They Quit

By CHILES COLEMAN

Washington, Aug. 6 (UP)—The United States has unleashed against Japan the terror of an atomic bomb 2,000 times more powerful than the biggest blockbusters ever used in warfare.

President Truman revealed this great scientific achievement today and warned the Japanese that they now face "a rain of ruin from the air the like of which has never been seen on this earth."

More and more of these devastating bombs, unlocking the vast hidden energy that lies within the atom, will tumble on Japan if they continue to reject the Potsdam surrender ultimatum, he said.

The new atomic bomb was used for the first time yesterday. An American plane dropped one on the Japanese army base at Hiroshima.

Its use marked victory for the Allies in the greatest scientific race in history. We put $2,000,000,000 and the work of 125,000 persons into the project.

A single bomb has more power than 20,000 tons of TNT. It has more than 2,000 times the blast power of the British "Grand Slam" bomb, the largest ever used previously in the history of warfare.

Secretary of War Stimson disclosed that an improved

More about the new atomic bomb on Page 2

bomb would be forthcoming shortly that would increase "by several fold" the present effectiveness of the new weapon.

The War Department said it was not yet able to make an accurate report of the damage caused by the first bomb.

"Reconnaissance planes state that an impenetrable cloud of dust and smoke covered the target area," an announcement said. "As soon as accurate details of the result of the bombing become available, they will be released by the Secretary of War."

Development of the bomb, a victory of American scientists in a desperate race with Germany, is "the greatest achievement of organized science in history," Mr. Truman said in a statement released at the White House.

The United States, he added, is now prepared "to obliterate more rapidly and completely every productive enterprise the Japanese have above ground in any city."

He revealed that the July 26 ultimatum issued to Japan at Potsdam was made "to spare the Japanese people from utter destruction."

When the ultimatum was rejected, the atomic bomb was sent into action.

"If they (the Japanese leaders) do not now accept our terms, they may expect a rain of ruin from the air, the like of which has never been seen on this earth," he said.

Mr. Truman revealed that "two great plants and many lesser works" employing more than 65,000 workers are pro-

Continued on Page 7

Eagle Staff photo

SOUVENIR-LADEN—This sextet came home today on the transport John Ericcson well equipped with mementoes. In the first row, left to right: Corp. Walter Burke of 602 E. 34th St.; Staff Sgt. Solomon E. Hirsh of 1967 Ocean Ave., and Corp. Joseph Fontana of 515 Avenue I. In the back, left to right: Sgt. Thomas Quinlan of 69-50 64th St., Glendale; Corp. Philip Pilats of 57 Himrod St. and Pfc. Bill Wilson of 866 E. 14th St.

Sen. Johnson, 78, Dies; Lifelong Isolationist

Veteran California Legislator Was Opponent Of League of Nations and World Charter

Washington, Aug. 6 (U.P.)—Senator Hiram Warren Johnson (R., Cal.), one of the few survivors of the "little band of willful men" who kept the United States out of the League of Nations in 1920, died today a few weeks after he had reaffirmed his lifelong isolationism by opposing the United Nations Charter.

Senator Hiram Johnson

The California elder statesman, dean of Senate Republicans, died in his sleep at Bethesda, Md., Naval Hospital at 6:45 a.m. He would have celebrated his 79th birthday on Sept. 2.

Mr. Johnson, who had been in ill health for several years, took little part in the Charter debate. He telephoned his "No" vote, the first recorded, to the Senate Foreign Affairs Committee when it approved the Charter. When the Senate itself voted, Johnson was unable to be on the floor but was paired against the Charter.

The other two survivors of the little isolationist group in the 1920 Senate credited with frustrating the dream of President Woodrow Wilson for U. S. leadership in the League of Nations both voted for the Charter this time. They were Senator Arthur Capper (R., Kan.) and Senator David I. Walsh (D., Mass.).

Johnson had been in the hospital since July 18, three days after he cast his committee vote on the Charter. During the past several years he had been absent from the Senate floor for long periods due to illness.

Wife at His Side

The immediate cause of death was given as cerebral thrombosis. His wife, the former Minnie L. McNeal, was with him when he died, and his only remaining son, Lt. Col. Hiram W. Johnson Jr., 55, was flying here from San Francisco.

Funeral arrangements were not announced immediately.

He was the second ranking member of the Senate in terms of continuous service. He had been a Sen-

Continued on Page 7

FIRE SWEEPS 4 JAP CITIES IN B-29 BLITZ

Flames Seen 150 Mi.; Fighter-Bombers Blast Tokyo Again

By WILLIAM F. TYREE

Guam, Aug. 6 (U.P.)—Towering fires visible 150 miles swept through four Japanese cities after a 580-plane Superfortress raid today and Tokyo reported that a "small number" of B-29s struck at Hiroshima, an important Japanese Army base 20 miles northwest of Kure.

(President Truman announced in Washington that the world's most powerful explosive—the new "atomic bomb," equal to 20,000 tons of TNT—was first used Sunday against Hiroshima. Tokyo said Hiroshima was raided at 8:20 a.m. Monday, Tokyo time, 7:20 p.m. Sunday (Brooklyn time).

(There was no immediate reaction from 20th U. S. Air Force headquarters to President Truman's

CANADIANS ARRIVE

Guam, Aug. 6 (U.P.) — The first contingents of Canadian troops, ships and planes have arrived in this area, marking Canada's all-out entry into the Pacific war, it was disclosed today.

disclosure of the existence of the atomic bomb, described as 2,000 times more powerful than the British "grand slam," largest bomb ever used in the history of warfare.

(Tokyo said both incendiary and explosive bombs were dropped on Hiroshima, but beyond President Truman's brief reference to it as the first atomic bomb target, there was no information available on the raid from official Allied sources.)

Veteran B-29 crewmen returning from their 3,850-ton pre-dawn raid said they started tremendous fires at the industrial centers of Maebashi and Nishinomiya-Mikabe on Honshu, Saga on Kyushu, Imbari on Shikoku and at the synthetic gasoline plant at Ube.

Tokyo reported U. S. fighter-bombers hit Tokyo and five surrounding prefectures a few hours after the Superfortress smash. Attackers included 130 Iwo-based Mustangs, which reportedly struck in two waves for an hour shortly before 9 a.m. Tokyo time, bombing

Continued on Page 7

COPS SHOOT 2 CAUGHT TRYING TO LOOT HOMES

Surprised by Housewife, Burglar Threatens Her With Carving Knife

Two would-be burglars occupy Brooklyn hospital beds today after being surprised by police in their nocturnal activities and shot in escape attempts.

Frank Cassin, 34, a dishwasher, who gave his address as the Mills Hotel, Manhattan, charged at Mrs. Martha Bernstein with a carving knife when she investigated footsteps in her living room at 1601 Ocean Parkway early this morning.

He was cornered on the roof of the six-story apartment house by police of the Sheepshead Bay precinct and dropped with two shots by Patrolman John Hatfield as he again charged with the knife. He was booked for felonious assault, possession of a dangerous weapon and burglary, at Coney Island Hospital.

Vincent Mondo, 29, of 2181 Pacific St., East New York, is in critical condition in Kings County Hospital after having been shot twice by Patrolman Edward Moore of the Empire Boulevard precinct, who charged that he found Mondo attempting to loot a two-family house at 149 E. 96th St. Neighbors in the Canarsie section knew that the house was temporarily vacant so they summoned police when they saw the beam of a flashlight bobbing about from room to room.

As police were trying the front door they heard a crash at the side of the house. Mondo had smashed a chair through a window, they said, had jumped out and was attempting to flee.

DEMS WIDEN ELIGIBLE LIST FOR D. A. POST

McDonald Is Latest To Be Considered—G.O.P. Awaits Dewey's Choice

By JOSEPH H. SCHMALACKER

The list of possible Democratic eligibles to succeed former District Attorney O'Dwyer in the Kings County prosecutor's office was being widened today as rival Republican forces awaited Governor Dewey's decision on the choice of a temporary appointee.

Kings County Republican Leader John R. Crews was sitting tight and refusing to admit whether or not he knew the identity of the likely appointee Governor Dewey has in mind to fill the vacancy caused by last week's resignation of Mr. O'Dwyer, Democratic and American Labor party candidate for Mayor.

Dark Horse Choice Seen

Talk in Republican circles began to veer toward a possible "dark horse" choice.

Meanwhile, it was learned that whether or not Governor Dewey has announced his appointee by Wednesday the Democrats will proceed at that time to choose their nominee in a county committee convention.

To a list of possible Democratic eligibles which includes the names

Continued on Page 7

WHERE TO FIND IT

	Page		Page
Bridge	13	Our Fighters	5
Brown	6	Patterns	10
Comics	17	Radio	17
Crossword	17	Real Estate	13
Currie	3	Society	9
Dr. Brady	6	Sports	11-12
Editorial	6	Take My Word	6
Financial	13	Theaters	4
Grin and Bear It	6	These Women	17
Heffernan	6	Tommy Holmes	11
Horoscope	10	Tucker	6
Lindley	6	Uncle Ray	17
Mary Haworth	9	Want Ads	13, 14, 15, 16
Movies	4		
Novel	17	Women	9-10
Obituaries	7		

GI Ducks War's Perils; Joyride His Undoing

Borough Corporal Is Among 11,859 Troops Returned From European Theater on Four Ships

Heavy fighting with the 20th Armored Division, including a narrow escape from a blazing tank, left Corp. Abraham Cheslow, 21, of 308 Sterling St., unscathed, but a joy ride a week after VE-Day sent him to the hospital.

Corporal Cheslow was one of 7,562 troops returned from Europe on the John Ericcson which landed at Pier 84, North River, at 8:45 a.m. In all, 11,854 soldiers came home aboard three transports.

The other troopships were the Sea Pike, with 2,761 soldiers, anchoring in the Hudson River off Piermont, N. Y., and the Santa Paula, with 1,531 troops, debarking at Pier 16, Staten Island. All troops were to be moved to Camp Shanks, N. Y., with the exception of 281 sent to Camp Kilmer, N. J.

Thrown From Peep

Corporal Cheslow was thrown from a peep at Berchtesgaden while he and his buddies were hunting for billets. Seventeen stitches were needed to close a head wound. He also suffered from concussion.

Also aboard the Ericcson was Lt. Mae Lopatin of 122 Bay 34th St., who trained at Cumberland Hospital and went overseas with the 130th Evacuation Hospital Unit. She helped care for Allied prisoners at the Moosburg camp and later treated political prisoners at the notorious Mauthausen concentration camp. She declared that all the stories about the horrors there were completely accurate and said she expected to get in touch with American relatives of persons whose names were given her as having died at Mauthausen.

Also returning were: Lt. Leif Hansen of 256 90th St., who has been in the army four years; Capt. Norman Gottlieb, M.C., of 1215

Continued on Page 7

Eagle Staff photo

MASCOT — Pfc. Edward F. Keller of 650 53d St., who returned on the John Ericcson today, brings with him his platoon mascot, a dachshund born VE-Day in South Austria. The pup's name is Semi because his GI pals think he resembles a semi-truck trailer.

Stalin, Molotov Home

London, Aug. 6 (U.P.) — Premier Stalin and Foreign Commissar V. M. Molotov returned to Moscow from the Potsdam Conference yesterday, Radio Moscow reported.

MAN ADMITS FATAL SHOOTING OF WIFE

Shipyard worker Horace Turmman, 30, of 1057 Prospect Ave., the Bronx, walked into the Charles St., Manhattan, police station at 11 today and said:

"I shot my wife."

Police, rushing to the scene of the shooting which resulted from an argument over a divorce, found Turman's wife, Ossie Mae, bleeding from a head wound in a car at Washington Ave. and 10th St., Manhattan. She was taken in an ambulance to Bellevue Hospital, where she was pronounced dead. Turman was held for booking on a homicide charge.

Attlee Cabinet to Map Five-Year Program

London, Aug. 6 (U.P.)—Prime Minister Attlee and his full cabinet will meet tomorrow to begin the draft of legislation for the first year of the Labor party's five-year plan.

National ownership of coal mines and a measure to bring the Bank of England under public ownership will be given priority, it was understood.

Japs Announce Loss Of Another Admiral

San Francisco, Aug. 6 (U.P.)—The Japanese Navy Ministry disclosed today in a dispatch reported by the FCC that Vice Admiral Seiichi Ito, a member of the naval general staff, was killed while leading a surface suicide attack against American ships off Okinawa last April.

Wounds Wife, Kills Self As They Dance Together

Chicago, Aug. 6 (U.P.)—While they danced cheek-to-cheek to the strains of "I'll Keep on Loving You," Edward Rzeszutko, 28, shot his pretty wife in the neck, then turned the gun on himself, police said today. Mrs. Rzeszutko, 27, was reported in critical condition. Rzeszutko, a clerk, died almost immediately.

Racing Results, Entries And Selections on Page 12

War Department Lists Casualties

The War Department today, announcing the names of 73 soldiers killed in action, 134 wounded, 22 missing and six liberated, listed one Brooklyn man wounded and one Queens man released from a German prison camp. The navy listed one local man dead, and 32 wounded. Local casualty lists are on Page 5.

Call the Brooklyn Chapter, American Red Cross, and arrange to donate a pint of blood NOW. TRiangle 5-8040.

The Hornet's Back for Repairs; Typhoon Hit Her—Not the Japs

Washington, Aug. 6 (U.P.)—The aircraft carrier Hornet, which has sunk or damaged about 1,270,000 tons of Japanese shipping and destroyed 1,410 enemy planes, is back home for repair—but it took a typhoon to bring her back. The Japanese never touched her.

The 27,000-ton Essex class carrier, named in honor of the ship which took the first American flyers to Tokyo in 1942, put in 14 months of battle-packed action in the Pacific before putting in at San Francisco for repairs and a rest.

During that period the Hornet and her fliers inflicted the following damage on the enemy: 668 planes shot down; 742 planes destroyed on the ground; one carrier, one cruiser, 10 destroyers and 42 cargo ships sunk, and an "assist" in the sinking of the battleship Yamato.

Bounced Like a Chip

The Hornet had been through one typhoon in the Philippines, but the typhoon of June 5—which damaged many other American warships—bounced her around like a chip. The 120-knot gale caught the Hornet 150 miles east of Okinawa at 2 a.m.

Suddenly her bow rose atop a tremendous wave and crashed downward with such force that the forward corners of the flight deck folded down along her sides. She was forced to retire from the battle area and head home.

As a part of the famed Task Force 58, and flagship of Rear Admiral J. J. (Jocko) Clark, the Hornet hammered the Japanese in every major action from the March, 1944, strikes on the Palaus through the Okinawa operation.

8 ★★★★★★★★★ Final Edition

BROOKLYN EAGLE

WEATHER—Cloudy, mild tonight and tomorrow.

104th YEAR—No. 214—DAILY and SUNDAY

BROOKLYN, N. Y., TUESDAY, AUGUST 7, 1945

Entered Brooklyn P. O. 2d Class Mail Matter

3 CENTS IN NEW YORK CITY ELSEWHERE 4 CENTS

Japs Admit:

GREAT DEVASTATION DONE BY ATOM BOMB

COL. POWERS BOOMED FOR O'DWYER JOB

Two G. O. P. District Leaders Urge Dewey To Appoint Him D. A.

By JOSEPH H. SCHMALACKER

While Governor Dewey continued his deliberations on the choice of a new Kings County District Attorney to fill the vacancy caused by last week's resignation of William O'Dwyer, Democratic - American Labor party candidate for Mayor, two Republican district leaders in Brooklyn took steps today to land the appointment for Lt. Col. William T. Powers.

Thomas G. Parisi, leader of the G. O. P. in the 16th A. D., and State Senator Joseph E. Parisi, his brother and leader in the adjacent 19th A. D., sent a telegram to the Governor citing the qualifications and war record of Colonel Powers and recommending his appointment.

Praise War Record

"His background and ability eminently qualify him for this appointment," their telegram said. "His record in World Wars I and II is outstanding. His appointment and nomination will be an asset to the city ticket. We sincerely think he will be elected and will reflect credit to our party."

The joint action of the two leaders tended to indicate a widening of sentiment in G. O. P. ranks over the appointment the Governor must make.

Kings County Republican Leader John R. Crews has not revealed his own personal choice, if any, for the post, although it is understood he has submitted a list of eligibles to the Governor, including the name of Mr. Powers.

Gave Up Law Practice

Mr. Powers, a West Pointer, served in World War I. After the outbreak of World War II he relinquished a lucrative law practice and returned to active duty. He was in the Pacific theater for many months, retiring with the rank of lieutenant colonel.

Mr. Powers himself is one of Brooklyn's Republican district leaders, heading the G. O. P. organization in the 2d A. D.

Tomorrow Is Waste Paper Day

Tomorrow is collection day for wastepaper. Have all your old paper—newspapers, scraps, wrappings—bundled and on the streets by 7 a.m.

Casualties Include 61 From This Area

The War Department today, announcing the names of 32 soldiers killed in action, 211 wounded, three missing and two liberated, listed one Long Island man dead, one Brooklyn man wounded and one Long Island man missing. The navy listed eight dead, 49 wounded and one missing. The local casualty lists are on Page 18.

Call the Brooklyn Chapter, American Red Cross, and arrange to donate a pint of blood NOW. TRiangle 5-8040.

Ex-Boro Police Chief Guards Bomb Plants

Took Over Job Soon After His Retirement in Fall

Former Deputy Chief Inspector Michael F. McDermott, in charge of all Brooklyn detectives before his retirement last Fall, was picked from among the nation's top police officials to take charge of protection at Oak Ridge, Tenn., the great atomic bomb city.

It was learned today that the former Brooklyn police officer, who lives at 34-06 81st St., Jackson Heights, took the job as soon as he retired. He rigidly concealed its real nature and mentioned only that he was going to work for "a small powder company."

He and his wife, Mary, have a son, Richard, in the navy, and a daughter, Marie, an admiralty attorney.

The former inspector was on the New York City force for 32 years during which time he won seven citations. He is 56.

Michael F. McDermott

Mayor to Define Attitude on Three Candidates Tonight

The Liberal party, which must nominate its candidates by petition, today filed with the Board of Elections 30,522 signatures of voters from Brooklyn and the Bronx as its first installment for the Goldstein-McGoldrick-Pette ticket. The Liberal party headquarters announced 20,000 of the signatures were from Brooklyn voters.

In the face of indications that new shifts were threatening established political lines in the city election campaign, Mayor LaGuardia prepared today to define publicly his attitude toward the three candidates battling to succeed him in City Hall.

Credited with much of the work behind the scenes which led to the formation of the No Deal ticket headed by Council President Newbold Morris for Mayor, Mr. LaGuardia was expected to declare his support of the slate in a speech on "good government" tonight at 8:15 over WOR.

The Mayor's speech was expected to be an extension of his remarks from the municipal broadcasting station, WNYC, on Sunday, May 6, when he announced he would not be a candidate for re-election and denounced what he termed a "'panorama of politicians" whom he accused of "scheming" and "conniving" to destroy a good administration.

Lull in Rival Camps

As the Mayor prepared to unlimber his campaign artillery a comparative lull settled over the opposing political camps after the flurry caused by the third ticket's entry in the city's election struggle.

Although the view has prevailed in political circles that the Morris ticket would inflict heavier damage upon the Republican-Liberal-City Fusion ticket headed by Judge Jonah J. Goldstein than upon the Democratic-American Labor party

Continued on Page 12

GOERING AUTO ARRIVES IN BOSTON, BUT NOT FOR U. S. TOUR BY FATSO

Boston, Aug. 7 (U.P.)—The automobile once owned by Hermann Goering arrived here today aboard the transport George Shiras, bringing GIs home from Europe. . . . .

The car, a Mercedes-Benz, was consigned to the "Commanding General of the 20th Armored Division" whom the army here believed was Maj. Gen. Orlando Ward. He was said to be on the high seas now en route home but was to dock at another unidentified port.

Continued Rain Ruining Fruit And Vegetables

The almost continuous rains have inundated acres of truck farm produce and spoiled many orchards on Long Island, threatening a serious food shortwtage, nearby farmers and fruit growers warned today.

The rain is not yet over, the Weather Bureau said. Today will be pleasanter, except for scattered afternoon showers, but for farmers it will be just another rainy day because any rain that falls now is too much for them.

Grain, which was cut before the heavy rains started, has begun to sprout and cannot be used as human food. Fruit has rotted on trees and growers have been unable to pick it. In one New Jersey area crop damage was estimated at $1,000,000, with most farmers not yet having reported new losses.

Some sections of Long Island and New Jersey report swarms of bigger, busier mosquitoes.

Many farms, which normally ship the bulk of their produce to New York, report their corn, peach, tomato and potato crops ruined. This condition has already reflected itself in higher prices. Tomatoes, which formerly sold for $1.50 a bushel, now bring $4 the half bushel.

The steady rains have filled the city's reservoirs to peak capacity. Croton and other water storage lakes were reported overflowing for the first time in August for many years.

20 Thought Killed In Grain Blast

Port Arthur, Ontario, Aug. 7 (U.P.)—Twenty persons were believed to have been killed and at least four were missing as a result of an explosion in No. 5 Saskatchewan wheat pool elevator today.

The explosion rocked police headquarters a mile distant. It was believed to have been caused by spontaneous combustion of dust in the big concrete structure.

Police said 40 to 50 employes normally were employed in the big terminal elevator unloading grain from incoming trains and onto lake boats.

How many workers actually were on the job at the time of the blast was not established immediately.

Stalin Quoted On Big 3 Conference

London, Aug. 7 (U.P.)—Premier Stalin was quoted by the Moscow radio today as saying that the Potsdam conference "proves the presence of incontestable justice."

"The crimes perpetrated by the Nazis will never be repeated," he said. "Germany and Fascist militarism are defeated."

JAPS BELIEVED FACING NEW ULTIMATUM

Order Seen Offering Surrender or Death By Atomic Power

Washington, Aug. 7 (U.P.)—Military observers believed today that the Allies were considering a new ultimatum calling on Japan to surrender or be annihilated with atomic power.

If it is decided to issue an ultimatum, the observers said, it probably would come within a few days, after President Truman arrives home from Potsdam.

The peroid until then will give the Japanese time to examine the effect of theatomic bombing of Hiroshima. This, and the threat of more to come, might tend to convert them to "rightful thinking," the sources said.

Any surrender brought about short of an invasion would, of course, save countless American lives, military men pointed out.

Cite Choice of City

The observers noted with interest that Tokyo was not picked as the target for the first atomic bomb. The purpose of this may have been to avoi ddetruction of the Japanese Government, the appropriate surrender authority. A second motive may have been to play on Japanese nerves by stirring fear of having the closely-packed capital blasted by atomic power.

Although still awaiting a detailed report of the effect of the bomb, observers doubted that it wiped out the entire city of Hiroshima. However, they thought it quite probable that the one explosive charge may have ruined the town's war-waging capacity for months to come.

The nation's highest strategists, meanwhile, held the secret as to how long the Japanese would be given to think it over before more and worse atom bombs are loosed upon them.

48-Hour Ultimatum Seen

London, Aug. 7 (U.P.) — James Brough, Daily Mail correspondent, reported from New York today that soon after the atomic bomb announcement "reliable sources" said a new ultimatum would be sent to Japan.

He reported the ultimatum will say:

"We will withhold the use of the atomic bomb for 48 hours, in which time you can surrender. Otherwise you face the prospect of the entire obliteration of the Japanese nation."

Nazi Names Banned

Frankfurt, Aug. 7 (U.P.) — The American Military Government directed all German civil governments today to remove Nazi names from streets, parks, public buildings, monuments and institutions.

British Planes Join Tokyo Raid, Japs Say

Guam, Aug. 7 (U.P.)—A fleet of 125 Superfortresses hit the Toyokawa naval arsenal with 880 tons of high explosive bombs today while smoke still belched from atom-bombed Hiroshima, 300 miles to the west.

Radio Tokyo said 40 Iwo-based American Mustang fighter-bombers led by a lone B-29 almost simultaneously bombed and strafed military installations and "cities" in the southwest section of the Tokyo-Yokohama area for an hour for the fourth time in five days.

Several British planes participated in the Tokyo raid, Tokyo said. It marked the first time Brit-

Continued on Page 7

REMEMBER, TOJO?

Fittingly enough, as dazed Japan looks with horror on the wreckage of Hiroshima, today marks the third anniversary of our first D-Day—the American landings on Guadalcanal, the beginning of the road back in the Pacific.

It was on Aug. 7, 1942, that U. S. Marines stormed ashore on the beaches of the steaming Solomon Island.

Guadalcanal, the "isle of heroes," lies serene in the South Pacific today, topped by the American graves attesting to the sacrifices of Americans.

Racing Results, Entries and Selections on Page 12

Damage Is So Widespread Full Extent Is Not Known

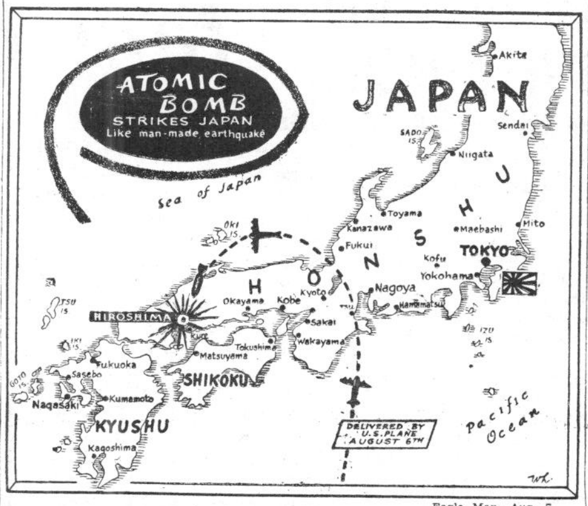

Eagle Map, Aug. 7

ATOMIC BOMB TARGET—Hiroshima, important industrial and communications center, was shattered by the new super-weapon.

By WILLIAM F. TYREE

Guam, Aug. 7 (UP)—Tokyo said today that American atomic bombs descended on Hiroshima by parachute yesterday, exploded before reaching the ground and caused such great devastation that authorities still have not ascertained its full extent.

Japanese propagandists said use of the new weapon was "sufficient to brand the enemy for ages to come as the destroyer of . . . mankind" and "public enemy number one of social justice."

An investigation was under way into the extent of the destruction in the world's first atomic bombing, Tokyo said. First reports showed a "considerable number" of houses had been demolished and fires broke out at several places, the broadcast added.

The broadcast, coming almost 36 hours after the raid, said the destructive power of the new weapon "cannot be slighted," but claimed that Japanese authorities already were working out "effective counter measures."

"The history of war shows that the new weapon, however effective, will eventually lose its power, as the opponent is bound to find methods to nullify its effects," Tokyo said hopefully.

The enemy version of the attack said a small number of American planes dropped a "few" of the new-type bombs. It was announced officially at Washington that only one bomb was dropped. It was apparent that the Japanese could not believe a single plane and a single bomb could cause so much destruction.

Tokyo attributed the American use of the atomic bomb to impatience over the "slow progress of the enemy's much-vaunted invasion of Japan's mainland."

"In view of the gallant resistance of the Japanese

Continued on Page 7

AtomBombCouldLevel Entire Flatbush Area

Exact Effect Seen Depending on Construction Of Buildings—Queens Would Be Hit Hard

An atomic bomb dropped at Flatbush and Church Aves. would probably level all of Flatbush and destroy many persons and property in neighborhoods as distant as Bay Ridge and East New York.

Since the exact effects of the bomb depend a great deal on the height and construction of buildings, the area destroyed in Brooklyn would be much greater than in Manhattan. In Queens, where many houses are made of wood, the waves of destruction would reach further yet—most likely all through the borough and part of Nassau County.

According to Dr. Harry S. Rogers, president of Brooklyn Polytechnic

Continued on Page 7

Now You Know

According to Webster's New International Dictionary, atom, derived from the roots "a" (meaning not) and "temnein" (to cut), literally means indivisible.

Yugo Censorship Ends

London, Aug. 7 (U.P.)—Radio Prague said today Yugoslavia has lifted censorship on outgoing dispatches.

BULLETINS

SOUTHWORTH RITES

Columbus, Aug. 7 (U.P.)—Military funeral services were held at Lockbourne Army Air Base today for Maj. Billy B. Southworth, 25, son of Manager Billy Southworth of the St. Louis Cardinals baseball team. Young Southworth's body was recovered Friday from Flushing Bay, N. Y., and brought to his father's home near here for burial. He was killed in the crash of a B-29 Superfortress Feb. 15.

UNDERSTANDS BOMB

Saranac Lake, Aug. 7 (U.P.)—Prof. Albert Einstein "thoroughly understands" how the atomic bomb works, his secretary said today, but he won't talk about it.

PETAIN DEAL TOLD

Paris, Aug. 7 (U.P.)—Marshal Petain was depicted in court today as negotiating a secret agreement with Great Britain while maintaining a pretense of complete collaboration with the Nazis in 1940-41. Jacques Chevalier, education minister at Vichy, testified that he himself was the go-between in the negotiations.

HITS NOMINATION

Thomas F. Cohalan, temporary chairman of the Democrats for Goldstein-McGoldrick-Pette, today denounced Tammany Hall's designation of former Alderman Morton Moses for City Council. Characterizing Mr. Moses as a "former James J. Hines lieutenant," Mr. Cohalan asserted William O'Dwyer, Democratic-A. L. P. candidate for Mayor, has "another choice running mate." Mr. Cohalan said the former Alderman's designation "shows Tammany is out to do business at the old stand."

See Fantastic World As Atom Is Leashed

Handfuls of Matter Seen Producing Energy to Run Cars, Ships, Heating Plants

By CHILES COLEMAN

Washington, Aug. 7 (U.P.)—The dawn of the age of atomic power brings with it visions of fantastic changes in our future civilization.

Not for tomorrow, probably not for our lifetime, but men of science can see reason now for believing that some time such things as these can be:

Automobiles, trains and airplanes that run for their lifetime on a single fueling of a bit of stuff from which atomic power can be released at will.

Furnaces of vest-pocket size.

Power for whole cities produced from a few handfuls of matter.

The experience of the past indicates that such achievements will come by very gradual steps. Stupendous problems in technical and practical science have to be overcome.

First Peak Surmounted

But the first great peak has been surmounted with discovery of how to use atomic energy as an explosive force.

Now, the atomic force will be applied to war. And like almost everything else about war, it is economically wasteful.

President Truman sounded such a warning in his announcement of the atomic bomb.

"Atomic energy may in the future supplement the power that now comes from coal, oil and falling water," he said. "But at present it cannot be produced on a basis to compete with them commercially.

"Before that comes, there must be a long period of research."

In simple terms, two fundamental problems face the postwar scientists:

Firstly, they must learn to govern

Continued on Page 7

Other stories and pictures about the atomic bomb on Pages 2, 3 and 12.

WHERE TO FIND IT

	Page		Page
Comics	17	Our Fighters	18
Crossword	17	Patterns	10
Currie	3	Radio	17
Dr. Brady	6	Society	9
Editorial	6	Sports	11, 12
Financial	13	Take My Word	6
Grin and Bear It	6	Theaters	4, 5
Heffernan	6	These Women	17
Horoscope	10	Tommy Holmes	11
Lindley	6	Tucker	6
Mary Haworth	9	Uncle Ray	17
Movies	4, 5	Want Ads	13-16
Novel	13	Women	9, 10
Obituaries	7		

Beldock Named Prosecutor by Dewey

7★★★★★★★ Complete

BROOKLYN EAGLE

WEATHER—Clear, mild tonight; sunny, warmer tomorrow. ★

104th YEAR—No. 216—DAILY and SUNDAY (Copyright, 1945, The Brooklyn Eagle, Inc.) BROOKLYN, N. Y., THURSDAY, AUGUST 9, 1945 Entered Brooklyn P. O. 2d Class Mail Matter 3 CENTS IN NEW YORK CITY ELSEWHERE 4 CENTS

NAGASAKI 'WIPED OUT': MANCHURIA REDS GAIN

DEWEY NAMES BELDOCK BORO PROSECUTOR

McDonald Chosen By Democrats for D. A. Race in the Fall

By CLARENCE GREENBAUM

George J. Beldock, a member of the State Mediation Board, was appointed temporary Kings County District Attorney by Governor Dewey today in Albany.

Meanwhile, United States Attorney Miles F. McDonald had the Democratic nomination for District Attorney in the November election by virtue of unanimous assent by the county committee of Frank V. Kelly's Brooklyn Democratic organization.

Mr. Beldock's appointment means he will serve at least until Dec. 31 in the post vacated by former District Attorney O'Dwyer, Democratic-A. L. P. nominee for Mayor. The Governor's appointee is expected to become the G. O. P. nominee in the November election for the prosecutor's post.

Republican County Leader John R. Crews has not yet fixed a date for that nomination.

Mr. McDonald, who was nominated for District Attorney last night in Jefferson Hall, 4-5 Court Square, announced that since holding a Federal job prevented his immediate acceptance, he would resign within ten days from the United States Attorneyship to make the race for prosecutor.

T. Vincent Quinn, former acting United States Attorney for the Eastern District, now in command of the Government's new, intensified anti-black market drive, and Frank J. Parker, chief of the civil division in the Federal Attorney's

Continued on Page 11

APPOINTED — George J. Beldock, named by Governor Dewey temporary Kings County prosecutor.

NOMINATED — Miles F. McDonald, selected by the Democratic County Committee for District Attorney.

WHO WILL BE BROOKLYN'S FIRST 'FIGHTING LADY'?

Radio Station WHN and the Brooklyn Eagle are co-operating in a program to honor Brooklyn's women in war work by naming four outstanding borough women as "Fighting Ladies."

The first will be announced Sunday. You can help pick her. For details turn to

Page 6

Boro Man Wins Medal

Coxswain Richard Schulman, U. S. N. R., of 91 Utica Ave., was awarded the Navy and Marine Corps Medal for saving the captain of his ship from death in heavy seas off Saipan on Feb. 14.

LEO DUROCHER HELD FOR JURY IN VET ATTACK

Dodger Fan Tells Of 'Blackjack' Assault After Game

His bruised jaw sufficiently healed for him to testify, John Christian, 21-year-old war veteran, today took the stand in Brooklyn Felony Court to accuse Leo (The Lip) Durocher of beating him after a night game at Ebbets Field on June 9.

At the conclusion of his testimony, Magistrate Abner C. Surpless continued bail at $1,000 for Durocher and his co-defendant, Joseph Moore, 50-year-old special patrolman at the field, and the case will go to the grand jury.

While the Dodger manager listened meekly, the Dodger fan declared that he had been summoned by Moore to the Dodger dugout on the ground that Durocher wanted to see him. At the end of the game, he said, he went to the dugout with one of the four servicemen with whom he had been sitting in the upper tier, Sgt. Jack Garfinkle.

They were met by Moore, Christian testified, and Garfinkle was not permitted to go any further. Moore pushed him into some kind of enclosure behind the dugout, he added, and some time later Durocher appeared.

"Listen, you, how would you like me to call your mother names?" Durocher asked him, according to Christian. "Those are my boys there and I don't like to have them insulted."

Hit With Blackjack

As he stood there, surprised at the verbal onslaught, he said, Moore struck him a glancing blow with something that looked like a "blackjack" and told him to pay attention to Durocher. Thereupon, Durocher grabbed the weapon and hit him,

Continued on Page 11

Poetry, Atomic Style

Oak Ridge, Tenn., Aug. 9 (U.P.)—The poetry at the home of atomic bomb also was extremely hush-hush. Here's a sample:

What you see here,
What you do here,
What you hear here,
When you leave here,
Let it stay here.

Giant Pincers Threaten Japs, Atom Bomb Blasts 2d Nip City

By PHIL AULT

London, Aug. 9 (U.P.)—A Red Army of 1,000,000 or more men crashed into Manchuria from the East and West at key points along a 2,000-mile front today and—Tokyo said—collided head-on in battle with Japan's crack Kwantung army.

Allied sources in Chungking said the Soviets already were several miles inside Manchuria at a number of points.

Radio Tokyo said Russian forces had crossed into Manchuria from the East along a 300-mile stretch of the Siberian border from Hunchun, 80 miles west of Vladivostok, to Hutou, 250 miles north of Vladivostok.

In the West, Tokyo said, the Russians forced the border at Manchouli, 50 miles east of the Outer Mongolian border.

"The garrison forces of Japan and Manchukuo (Manchuria) have engaged the invaders for self-defense and fighting is in progress," Japanese Imperial headquarters reported in another Tokyo broadcast.

Another enemy broadcast spoke of "sharp fighting" in all areas.

Tokyo said Red air force bombers, roaring out ahead of the advancing ground forces, bombed the communications centers of Hailan, Harbin, Chiamussu and Kirin in Manchuria and Rashin and Genzan in Northern Korea.

Giant Pincers in Action

Russia exploded her first Far Eastern offensive of World War II only a few minutes after her

Continued on Page 4

Eagle Map, April 9

PACIFIC PINCERS—Arrows show direction of Russian drive into Manchuria, reported to have crossed the Siberian border along a 300-mile stretch from Hunchun, 80 miles west of Vladivostok, to Hutou, 250 miles north of Vladivostok. Map also shows airline distances to Tokyo—660 miles from Vladivostok and 910 miles from Okinawa.

By WILLIAM F. TYREE

Guam, Aug. 9 (U.P.)—Preliminary reports indicated that the second atomic bomb dropped on Japan all but obliterated Nagasaki, a major naval base and Japan's 11th largest city, during the noon rush hour today.

Crew members of the Superfortress which loosed the terrifying bomb on Nagasaki watched the earth-shaking explosion and flashed back to Gen. Carl A. Spaatz, commander of the strategic air forces, that results were "good."

"No further details will be available until the mission returns," General Spaatz said in a brief communique.

But to all hands that brief report—"results good"—indicated that Nagasaki, a city of 252,630 persons, virtually had been blown off the map of Japan by an explosion equal to that which leveled four and one-tenth square miles of Hiroshima, target of the first atomic bombing raid last Monday.

Japs Silent on Attack

Radio Tokyo was silent on the results of the Nagasaki attack. Only yesterday, however, it told how searing flames and horrible concussion blasted and burned to death

Continued on Page 4

ARE YOU LISTENING, HUH?

San Francisco, Aug. 9 (U.P.)—Domei (Japanese) News Agency announced at 12:15 a.m. Friday, Tokyo time (11:15 a.m. Thursday, Brooklyn time), that its transmitters would remain open "throughout the night" for an expected special announcement.

Hours later, however, Domei had not transmitted any news of importance and there was no hint of the nature of the "special announcement."

Frequently in the past Domei has instructed its overseas editors and clients to stand by for transmission schedule changes. Today it admonished its listeners to "stand by." The broadcast was recorded by United Press, San Francisco.

Move to Make Steingut Talk Snarls Lawyers

By JOSEPH H. SCHMALACKER

Brooklyn Eagle Staff Correspondent

Albany, Aug. 9—Opposing counsel clashed before Supreme Court Justice Daniel F. Imrie in a two-and-one-half-hour secret hearing here today on an application to compel Irwin Steingut of Brooklyn, Democratic legislative leader, to answer certain undisclosed questions in the Todd Grand Jury investigation of legislative practices and spending.

Justice Imrie, presiding over the investigation by appointment of Governor Dewey, reserved decision.

Courtroom Closed

Courtroom spectators and a dozen newspapermen, converging on the Albany County Courthouse after learning that a surprise hearing had been called in the investigation, were excluded from the courtroom.

Mr. Steingut, flanked by attorneys, maintained silence as he emerged from the courtroom.

He was accompanied by former State Senator George R. Fearon of Syracuse, a leading up-State attorney; William Weisman, a New York City attorned and close personal friend of Mr. Steingut, and Saul

Continued on Page 11

VJ-Day May Not End Congressional Vacation

Washington, Aug. 9 (U.P.)—Reliable sources reported today that Congress may be permitted to continue its recess to Oct. 8, regardless of when the Japanese war ends.

The initiative rests with the White House. President Truman reportedly has no intention at this time of calling Congress to reconvene ahead of schedule.

Dodger Detail, Baseball, Racing Results, Entries and Selections on Page 16

Navy Lists 20 Local Casualties

The War Department today, announcing the names of 19 soldiers killed in action, 60 wounded, 11 missing and one released from a German prison camp, listed no local names. The navy listed seven dead, 12 wounded and one missing locally. Local casualty lists are on Page 22.

Call the Brooklyn Chapter, American Red Cross, and arrange to donate a pint of blood NOW. TRiangle 5-8040.

Gen. Casey Gets Oak Leaf Cluster For Pacific Job

Maj. Gen. Hugh J. Casey of Bay Ridge has added an oak leaf cluster to the Distinguished Service Medal, his mother, Mrs. John J. Casey, was informed today.

The latest award to General Casey came for handling of army construction operations from New Guinea to the Philippines. The Brooklyn army man is chief engineer in the Pacific.

He received his first Distinguished Service Medal in November, 1942, for organizing and completing construction in the Philippines.

Clear, Sunny Tomorrow After Today's Clouds

This will be an ordinary, partly cloudy, mild day, the Weather Bureau said, with highest temperature around 80 degrees, dropping tonight to about 60 degrees. Tomorrow, clear and sunny.

Yesterday mid-Manhattan was deluged with a black powderlike substance, but police said it was only soot from oil burners and incinerators.

Slaughter Japs in Burma

Calcutta, Aug. 9 (U.P.)—Allied troops operating north of Nyaunglebin, in southeastern Burma, today trapped a large number of Japanese and slaughtered the vast majority of them.

HALSEY HURLS CARRIER PLANE FLEET AT JAPS

Armada of 1,500 Smashes Home Isles —B-29s Hit Oil Center

Guam, Aug. 9 (U.P.)—Admiral William F. Halsey's 3d Fleet sailed into Japanese home waters today, unleashing 1,200 carrier planes against dwindling centers of enemy resistance and the Japanese reported that more than 80 struck at the Nippon oil refinery near Osaka.

Gen. Carl Spaatz, commander of the United States Strategic Air Force, announced that the most complete devastation ever brought to any Japanese city by high explosive bombs was visited on Tokama on northern Honshu a week ago.

Tokyo said a fleet of B-29s late this afternoon attacked industrial targets around the metropolitan area and that American warships earlier thrust within 10 to 20 miles

Continued on Page 11

Atomic Bomb Left U. S. Nine Days Before Use

Brig. Gen. Farrell Flew 1st 'Vial of Wrath' Weapon From Washington to Pacific Isle

Washington, Aug. 9 (U.P.)—The War Department disclosed today that Brig. Gen. Thomas F. Farrell, who supervised the handling and delivery of the first atomic bomb dropped on Japan, left Washington only nine days before the destructive new weapon was unleashed in the Pacific.

General Farrell acted as field representative for Maj. Gen. Leslie R. Groves, commander of the project.

General Farrell and General Groves never travel by air together, the War Department said, so that if "anything untoward" ever should happen to a plane, one of the men would be spared.

The War Department described General Farrell's part in the atomic project as follows:

"On July 27 General Farrell left Washington by air for a tiny island in the Pacific to supervise the delivery and care of the destructive 'vial of wrath' prior to its launching.

"There he acted as General

Continued on Page 11

STATIONS CARRYING TRUMAN'S SPEECH

President Truman will give a report on the Big Three Potsdam Conference tonight from 10 to 10:30 over WEAF, WJZ, WABC, WOR, WNEW, WMCA, WHN, WNYC, WQXR and WEVD.

WHERE TO FIND IT

	Page		Page
Comics	21	Our Fighters	22
Crossword	21	Patterns	14
Currie	3	Radio	21
Dr. Brady	10	Real Estate	9
Editorial	10	Society	13, 14
Financial	9	Sports	15, 16
Grin and Bear It	10	Take My Word	10
Heffernan	10	Theaters	8
Horoscope	14	These Women	21
Lindley	10	Tommy Holmes	15
Mary Haworth	13	Tucker	10
Movies	8	Uncle Ray	21
Novel	17	Want Ads	17-20
Obituaries	11	Women	13, 14

22 Feared Dead in Crash of Airliner

7 ★★★★★★★ Complete

BROOKLYN EAGLE

WEATHER—Clear tonight; sunny, warm tomorrow.

104th YEAR—No. 244—DAILY and SUNDAY (Copyright, 1945, The Brooklyn Eagle, Inc.) BROOKLYN, N. Y., FRIDAY, SEPTEMBER 7, 1945 Entered Brooklyn P. O. 2d Class Mail Matter 3 CENTS IN NEW YORK CITY ELSEWHERE 4 CENTS

MAC ENTERS TOKYO TONIGHT

BELDOCK HITS O'DWYER ON PAY 'SQUEEZE'

Accuses Predecessor Of Raising Moran at Expense of 'Deserving'

Republican District Attorney George J. Beldock today accused William O'Dwyer, his Democratic predecessor, of having instituted a "Tammany salary squeeze on the city pocketbook," by "overpaying political appointees like James J. Moran, his former chief clerk, "at the expense of competent, qualified but underpaid civil service employes."

"This Tammany salary squeeze on the city pocketbook came to light," Mr. Beldock said, "when I examined the office budget. I was amazed to find that under the Tammany regime here, competent, qualified civil service employes in this office have for years been discriminated against and underpaid."

Beldock: Is This Politics?

"Money intended for them," Mr. Beldock said, "has been directed to political appointees. Mr. O'Dwyer cannot dodge any responsibility here. He was District Attorney for years while this was going on. Both before and after he went on military leave he was busily engaged in increasing the salaries of and in elevating his political appointees.

"Is this politics, Mr. O'Dwyer?" the prosecutor asked. He went on: "Is it politics for me as District Attorney to endeavor to get returned to the city Treasury some $15,000 which Mr. O'Dwyer had caused to be paid to Mr. Moran over the course of some five years in violation of the law?" he asked.

Says He Cut Salaries

"This Tammany salary grab is defended," r. Beldock said, "on the ground that my efforts to restore the $15,000 is politics. Is it politics that caused Mr. Moran to resign his $3,250 job to which he returned last month in the County Court?"

Revealing that each of his new full assistants and deputies are receiving less than their predecessors in each particular job, Mr. Beldock

Continued on Page 11

Utilities Strike May Tie Up City

New York City was threatened today with a strike that would cripple its public utilities.

Joseph Fisher, president of the Brotherhood of Consolidated Edison Employes, C. I. O., announced that a mass meeting of 25,000 company workers will be held next week to discuss a strike vote.

At the same time an official of one of the four New York City locals of the union said "internal strife" existed in the union and that most of the workers did not favor a strike.

Joseph Curran, president of the National Maritime Union and president of the Greater New York C. I. O. Council, said the council's resolution backing the brotherhood pledged the support of 600,000 workers in the city.

Boro-Born Hero of Bataan To Reach U. S. on Tuesday

Brig. Gen. Clinton A. Pierce, Brooklyn-born hero who has just been released from the Jap prison camp at Hoten Mukden, Manchuria, will arrive in San Francisco on Tuesday, according to a telegram just received by his cousin, Walter E. Blythe of 91-23 112th St., Richmond Hill.

General Pierce's mother, Mrs. Nellie Pierce, has been living in California with her daughter-in-law since she heard the news of her son's capture on Bataan where he was leader of American and Filipino forces in their last-ditch stand.

AQUEDUCT RESULTS

FIRST RACE—Two-year-olds; five and one-half furlongs.

Home Spun (Guerin)	8.90	5.60	3.90
Stage Song (Bierman)	—	5.60	3.80
Little Action (Wright)	—	—	4.40

Off, 1:03. Time, 1:07 3-5.

Scratched—Hi Jo-Ann, Tetrafettle, Pete's Best, Queen of May, Good Pasture, Queen's Chance.

SECOND RACE—Three-year-olds and up; mile and one-sixteenth.

Volitant (Gilbert)	24.50	13.30	8.60
Bras (Permane)	—	21.10	11.00
Count Daunt (Guerin)	—	—	4.90

Off, 1:35½. Time, 1:48 1-5.

DAILY DOUBLE PAID $243.40

Leo Minus Lip in Court --Mumbles 'Not Guilty'

Eagle Staff photo

LEO LISTENS—The Dodger manager, right, takes in some advice from counsel as he awaits arraignment on an assault charge in Kings County Court.

Dodgers' Manager And Private Cop Deny Beating Fan

Leo Durocher, minus the lip, appeared in Kings County Court today to deny the charge of second degree assault in which he and an Ebbets Field patrolman are accused of beating a fan, an ex-soldier.

The Dodger manager and the patrolman, Joseph Moore, 50, of 132-09 82d St., Ozone Park, appeared before Judge Leibowitz and mumbled, "Not guilty," when the indictment was read. Bail for each was continued in $1,000.

In Cheerful Mood

In contrast to his last appearance in court, when he was belligerent enough to threaten a newspaper photographer, the manager was cheerful and dapper today. He was resplendent in a royal blue suit with suitable trimmings.

The ball player, whose tongue and temper have led him into many a storm, was required to wait an hour and a half before his case was called. During that time he sat in a filled courtroom and watched the appearance of other defendants with evident interest.

Prospects for an early trial appeared favorable when Walter O'Malley, who appeared in the man-

Continued on Page 11

LOVE'S IN BLOOM: GROOM, 83, BRIDE, 78, TAKE VOWS TOMORROW

The birds are on the wing and love's in bloom.

Frank Monahan, bachelor, of 631 Hancock St., and Elizabeth Higbid of Glen Rock, N. J., formerly head nurse at Bushwick Hospital, have taken out a license to wed. The marriage will be in the rectory of Our Lady of Good Counsel R. C. Church at 3:30 p.m. tomorrow.

The bridegroom is 83 and the bride 78. It's the first marriage for both.

TRUMAN GIVEN JAP SURRENDER DOCUMENTS

Washington, Sept. 7 (U.P.)—President Truman with obvious satisfaction received from an army courier today the formal Japanese surrender document, complete with authenticating letters and the official rescript by Emperor Hirohito proclaiming the defeat of Japan.

3 LEAD FIELD FOR SUCCESSOR TO VALENTINE

O'Connell, Williams, Wallander Considered —Appointment Due Soon

Chief Inspector John J. O'Connell, Assistant Chief Inspector Albert Williams and Deputy Chief Inspector Arthur W. Wallander today led the field as the possible successor to Police Commissioner Valentine.

Mayor LaGuardia is expected to name the new city police chief later today or possibly on his Sunday broadcast over WNYC.

Meanwhile the retirement today of Inspector Charles P. Dorschel, in charge of Brooklyn's 12th Division for 18 months, was understood to be the first resignation in a flood of retirements.

$50,000 Job for Valentine

Commissioner Valentine yesterday announced his resignation, effective Sept. 14, to take a $50,000-a-year job with a radio program to be spon-

Continued on Page 11

Held on $935,000 Tax Fraud Charge

A Brooklyn Federal grand jury today charged Thomas M. Gorman of Port Washington with evasion of more than $935,000 in income taxes for 1943.

The indictment alleged that Gorman filed tax returns understating his net income by more than $1,000,000. Conviction would carry a maximum penalty of five years' imprisonment, a $10,000 fine or both, in addition to liability for taxes, penalties and interest.

Attorney General Tom C. Clark said a criminal information was filed against Gorman on July 17, 1944, in Manhattan Federal Court, charging him with violating the Emergency Price Control Act by selling huge amounts of whisky at over-ceiling prices. According to the information, the liquor was sold in wholesale lots to dealers in East St. Louis, Ill.; Cairo, Ill.; St. Louis, Mo.; Kansas City, Mo., and Columbia, S. C.

Gorman was arrested last January in Atlanta, the announcement said. He has pleaded not guilty to the OPA charges. No date has been set for the trial.

Elevator Strike Settled In I. T. and T. Buildings

An elevator tieup caused by a strike in the International Telephone and Telegraph buildings in the Manhattan financial district was settled today after a dispute over the dismissal of a Queens porter, Robert Esposito, 50, of 109-27 142d St., Jamaica.

22 FEARED DEAD IN CRASH OF AIRLINER

New York-Bound Plane Found Demolished In South Carolina

Florence, S. C., Sept. 7 (U.P.)—An Eastern Airlines plane en route from Miami to New York with 22 persons aboard crashed a few miles west of here today near the Pee Dee River.

It could not be determined immediately whether any of the 19 passengers and three crew members survived. An army pilot who sighted the wreckage shortly before 10:30 a.m. said the ship was "totally demolished."

Before the tangled wreckage of the airliner was sighted the plane had been missing more than 10 hours. Two other Eastern Airlines planes, private airships and army planes had been searching a 100-mile area for the big passenger plane.

Rescue parties from Florence set out to find the wreckage after the army pilot's report was received here.

Ambulances Rush to Scene

Ambulances from Florence and from the Florence army air base set out in the general direction of the crash.

Airline officials did not know the cause of the crash which occurred in level country, dotted by woods and farms. The weather was clear, with a ceiling of more than 6,000 feet.

The plane had left Miami at 9 p.m. yesterday. It took off from Savannah, Ga., on schedule at 12:30 a.m. It had been due at Raleigh at 2:22 a.m.

At 2 a.m. the pilot, Capt. J. Olin King, reported by radio from the Florence area, presumably just a few moments before he crashed.

Captain King, at that time, gave no indication of any trouble. But a few minutes later, something happened which sent the big ship, a DC-3, plummeting downward.

List of Those Aboard

The plane carried 10 civilians and nine military personnel.

The crew members are Capt. J. Olin King; R. A. Kelley, co-pilot, and Gertrude Graham, flight attendant.

Civilian passengers are R. Shinefield; L. F. Cockburn, Miami; W. E. Gray, Standard Oil Company, Miami; Robert Stevenson and his mother, Mrs. G. G. R. Sharp, Kingston, Jamaica; Andres Gerard and Louisa Gerard, French citizens en route to New York; Mr. and Mrs. Oscar Figueredo, Caracas, Venezuela, and W. E. Pierce, who boarded the plane at Jacksonville, Fla.

Names of the military personnel were not disclosed.

Lana Turner Is Expected To Wed Turkish Actor

Hollywood, Sept. 7 (U.P.) — Lana Turner, sweater-girl movie star awarded a divorce from Joseph Stephen Crane, was expected today to marry Turhan Bey, Turkish actor, before the end of the month.

The curvaceous actress received her final decree yesterday. She charged cruelty.

Partial War Tax Relief Promised by Jan. 1

Washington, Sept. 7 (U.P.)—Chairman Walter F. George (D., Ga.) of the tax-writing Senate Finance Committee today promised at least partial relief from record high war taxes starting Jan. 1.

Spurred by President Truman's request for a transition tax bill to speed reconversion, Senator George promised relief for both corporations and individuals.

"I think that a tax bill applicable for 1946 will be enacted before the Christmas holidays," he told reporters. He said the joint tax committee of both Houses would get to work in new legislation within a week or two.

Leaders Indorse Plan

George and other Congressional tax leaders indorsed the President's suggestion of a transition tax bill. They felt that a bill for temporary relief could be enacted speedily and a long-range general tax readjustment taken up next year.

George said he thought the transition bill should eliminate entirely the wartime excess profits tax on corporations and include "corresponding reductions in the aggregate to individual income tax payers."

In addition, he proposed to eliminate the $5 Federal automobile use tax as further relief to individuals.

Senator Robert A. Taft (R., Ohio), a member of George's committee, said excess profits taxes should be repealed "immediately" and individual and excise taxes reduced "as soon as possible."

George estimated the transition tax bill would save corporate tax-payers $2,000,000,000 during 1946 and individuals fro $2,500,000,000 to $3,000,000,000.

The Finance Committee chairman said he thought the transition bill also should establish—as far as taxes are concerned—a definite date for termination of hostilities in the war. He thought that was necessary because many wartime taxes, including higher excise rates on luxury items, expire six months after the cessation of hostilities is proclaimed.

He declined to predict whether tax relief for individuals would be in the form of raising exemptions or a cut in the tax rate, but indicated a preference for a cut.

TOURISTS IN TOKYO—The first Coast Guardsmen to arrive in Tokyo use their jeep as a grandstand from which to view the damage done by our bombers to a main intersection of the capital. The consensus: plenty.

Elderly Couple Evicted By Son and His Wife

Court Battle Over Home Ownership, Dispute On Rent, Heat Blamed—Neighbor Gives Shelter

Frank Morris, 67, and his wife, Mary, 62, spent seven hours yesterday in front of their home at 104-12 216th St., Queens Village, after they had been evicted on a court order obtained by their own son and daughter-in-law, Mr. and Mrs. John Morris of the same address.

Finally Mrs. Helen Felaski of 99-16 216th St. took pity on the elderly couple sitting stunned among their household goods and took them to spend the night at her home.

It was the closing scene in a drama that began many years ago. In 1924 the couple bought the home on 216th St. During the depression the father took out a Home Owners Loan Corporation mortgage.

Four years ago John and his wife moved in to share the house. John contends his wife advanced the money for the monthly mortgage payments and his father refused to reimburse her. The son said his father finally deeded the property to the younger Mrs. Morris with the agreement that she continue making the mortgage payments while

Continued on Page 11

Winchell's Daughter's Sarge Sues for Alimony

Cambridge, Mass., Sept. 7 (U.P.)—Walda Winchell Lawless, 18-year-old actress daughter of gossip-columnist Walter Winchell, is being sued for divorce by her husband, who seeks alimony.

William F. Lawless, 29, of Cambridge, laboratory technician and part-time art student, said they never had lived together as man and wife since their surprise elopement last June 5.

U. S. Must Keep Lid On Japs for Years, Admiral Warns

By RICHARD W. JOHNSTON

Aboard Admiral Halsey's flagship, Yokosuka, Sept. 7 (U.P.)—The American people must be prepared to maintain the closest military pressure against Japan for years and perhaps generations to avoid wars in the Pacific, Rear Admiral Robert B. Carney said today.

Admiral Carney, chief of staff to Admiral William F. Halsey, also believes there is no indication that Japan is undergoing or contemplating any spiritual reform, he told me today.

"The terriers have got to stay at the rathole—since we didn't kill the rat," he said.

"We must have military pressure close at hand and continually exerted. These people think in terms of their grandchildren. And so must we."

He indicated that "maintenance of military pressure" should take the form either of garrisoning the Japanese mainland with Allied forces for an extended period or a tight air and sea encirclement.

Asked to comment on the "new democracy" now being hailed by the Japanese press, Admiral Carney said:

"The people who are going through this new process are exactly the same people who were guilty of atrocities during the last four years. There is no reason to think that under the same circumstances they wouldn't do it again.

"There is no reason to accept them until they have demonstrated over a long period of years their fitness to restore Japan to the community of nations."

He predicted our occupation forces would grow increasingly strict, so the Japanese "will not be permitted to forget they have been defeated and are being punished for aggression."

3 St. Louis Newspapers Resume Publication

St. Louis, Sept. 7 (U.P.)—Publication of St. Louis' three newspapers, serving 1,000,000 readers in the greater metropolitan area, was resumed today after settlement of a strike of carriers and an agreement between the publishers and the typographical union was reached.

The strike began Aug. 16 when the carriers union, A. F. L., walked out. They demanded that publishers consider them as employes. The publishers contended that since the carriers owned their routes they, in effect, were independent merchants.

The publishers agreed yesterday to purchase the carrier routes, estimated to be worth $2,225,000, and to consider the carriers as employes and to bargain collectively with them.

EIGHT INDICTED IN BLACK MARKET SUGAR DEALS

4 Persons, 4 Concerns Accused of Evading Taxes and Diversion

Federal grand juries in Manhattan and Newark, N. J., today charged four companies and four individuals with black market operations involving diversion of more than 25,000,000 pounds of sugar and attempted evasion of almost $1,000,000 in taxes.

The Manhattan indictment alleged that Murray Greenberg of 160 Irwin St. and Leo Greenberg, Passaic, N. J., attempted to avoid payment of $943,000 in taxes on unreported corporation income for the year ended May 31, 1944.

The New Jersey indictment named the corporation, the Greenbergs and the Royal Crown Bottling Company of Baltimore; Royal Crown Bottling Company of Washington, Inc.; William C. Franklyn, president of Royal Crown of Baltimore; Robert Sealfon, trading as Syro Syrup Company, Manhattan, and the S. J. Baron Corporation, Manhattan.

The second indictment charged that the defendants conspired to violate rationing controls by diverting huge quantities of sugar, ostensibly obtained for the manufacture of foodstuffs for the armed forces, into syrups sold to beverage manufacturers and other industrial users from 1942 to 1944.

Attorney General Tom C. Clark said in Washington that OPA operatives found evidence that the Fresh Fruit Preserve Corporation had obtained more than 25,000,000 pounds of sugar through fraudulent representations to the Rutherford, N. J., OPA Rationing Board. The company claimed the sugar was being used by army hospitals and other military installations, Clark said. The defendants counterfeited sugar ration certificates, according to the indictment.

Internal Revenue agents uncovered the tax evasion evidence against the Greenbergs, Clark said. He added that Treasury and OPA agents have been investigating the case for more than a year.

Wife Wins Divorce From Samuel S. Colt

Reno, Sept. 7 (U.P.)—Mrs. Margaret Mason Colt was divorced yesterday from Samuel Sloan Colt, New York banker, on grounds of cruelty. They were married in 1918 and have several children.

FLAG RAISING WILL CLIMAX TRIUMPH

Cavalry Spearhead Of the Occupation —Japs Repair Capital

By WILLIAM B. DICKINSON

General MacArthur's Headquarters, Yokohama, Sept. 7 (U.P.) — Plans were completed today for Gen. Douglas MacArthur's triumphal entry into bomb-ravaged Tokyo about 10 a.m. tomorrow (9 p.m. today, Brooklyn time).

The supreme commander is expected to raise the Stars and Stripes over the American Embassy across the street from Emperor Hirohito's palace at 10:30 a.m. (9:30 p.m. today, Brooklyn time).

The ceremony will symbolize the final act of Japan's capitulation. The flag is the same one which flew from the Capitol in Washington on Pearl Harbor day in 1941 and since has flown over Berlin and Rome and from the masthead of the U. S. S. Missouri during the signing of Japan's surrender last Sunday.

General MacArthur will return to his Yokohama headquarters after the flag-raising. He ultimately will establish headquarters in the Tokyo Embassy building, but not until sufficient office space and billets can be found in Tokyo for his staff.

Breakfast in Tokyo

The 7th and 8th Regiments of the 1st Cavalry Division, chosen by General MacArthur to spearhead the occupation of Tokyo, will roll into Tokyo in trucks and other vehicles about breakfast time tomorrow.

They will assemble at the main Tokyo railway station by 10 a.m. and then march 10 blocks to the Embassy for the flag-raising ceremony.

The 1st Cavalry band and the 7th Regiment, once commanded by Custer at Little Bighorn, will lead the parade with F Troop of the 3d Battalion providing a special honor guard for General MacArthur.

The Japanese people slowly have begun the task of repairing their bomb-pitted capital. Demobilized soldiers, clad partly in uniforms and partly in civilian clothes, slowly and painfully were filling in bomb craters and piling up rubble.

Take Over Jap Battleship

Tokyo was declared "in bounds" again for correspondents at noon today. The first car of each of the two trains operating daily between Yokosuka and Tokyo were reserved for American officers and correspondents.

Admiral William F. Halsey, meantime, disclosed that an American prize crew had taken over the Japanese battleship Fuji, presumably in Japan's inland sea. He also reported that five Japanese destroyers, two minelayers, two picket boats, four submarine chasers, six minesweepers, four submarines and 180 midget submarines have been seized.

Fleet dispatches said first units of Lt. Gen. John R. Hodge's United States 25th Corps will land at Jinsen on the west coast of Korea Sunday.

Japanese Governor General Abe, Lt. Gen. Yoshio Kozuki, commanding the Japanese 17th Army group, and Vice Admiral Gizaburo Yamaguchi, commander of naval forces in Korea, will surrender the southern Korean garrison of 185,000 troops Sunday.

Censorship Ends in Italy

Rome, Sept. 7 (U.P.)—Censorship ended in Italy today.

WHERE TO FIND IT

	Page		Page
Bridge	12	Our Champs	6
Comics	21	Pattern	14
Crossword	14	Radio	21
Currie	3	Real Estate	18
Dr. Brady	10	Society	13
Editorial	10	Sports	15, 16
Financial	17	Take My Word	10
Going Places	8	Theaters	9
Grin and Bear It	10	These Women	21
Heffernan	10	Tommy Holmes	15
Helen Worth	14	Tucker	10
Horoscope	14	Uncle Ray	21
Mary Haworth	13	Veterans in B'klyn	6
Movies	9	Want Ads	18, 19, 20
Novel	14	Women	13
Obituaries	11		

A list of Brooklyn, Queens and Long Island soldiers returning from Europe on the Marshall Elliott, docking today, and the Queen Mary, due Monday, will be found on page 5.

SCREEN

By Jane Corby

'Week-End at the Waldorf,' Starring Ginger Rogers, Opens at Music Hall

Quite an ad for the Waldorf-Astoria they're running at Radio City Music Hall. It's a film called "Week-End at the Waldorf," and besides the hotel itself, which proves highly photogenic, there is an impressive array of stars: Ginger Rogers, Walter Pidgeon, Lana Turner, Van Johnson at the top of the list, with Edward Arnold, Robert Benchley and Keenan Wynn in lesser roles. The Waldorf background really isn't—it was achieved by sets which duplicated the lobby, the Sert Room, the Starlight Roof, etc., but this only adds to the admiration due Metro-Goldwyn-Mayer's efforts, for the background is the Waldorf to the life.

'Week-End at the Waldorf'

M-G-M picture, directed by Robert Z. Leonard, from a screen play by Sam and Bella Spewack. Presented at Radio City Music Hall, with Ginger Rogers, Lana Turner, Walter Pidgeon, Van Johnson, Edward Arnold, Phyllis Thaxter, Keenan Wynn, Robert Benchley, Leon Ames, Lina Romay, Samuel S. Hinds, Xavier Cugat and his orchestra.

In a light-hearted way, "Week-End at the Waldorf" apes a little the famous Vicki Baum novel, "Grand Hotel." In fact the characters in this film kid each other about their Grand Hotel-like situation. But in spite of this sophisticated by-play, the film does tell the story of two quite serious romances, one between Miss Rogers and Pidgeon, the other with Miss Turner and Johnson as the principals.

The Rogers affair gets started when Ginger, playing a movie star named Irene Malvern, finds Walter Pidgeon in her suite and mistakes him for a burglar. He is a famous war correspondent, and he dived into Ginger's suite in the course of a little newspaper investigation of his own, having nothing to do with the star. Pidgeon promises to go straight, under urging by Miss Rogers, to her great resentment when she discovers his deceit. She finds it hard to get rid of him, however, and amusing complications develop. Meanwhile, Miss Turner, as a young public stenographer in the hotel, has met Van Johnson, an army flier, and is forced to choose between him and an elderly swindler, Edward Arnold, who is in the hotel for the purpose of fleecing a visiting Eastern Bey, complete with robes and headdress and a goat to supply milk.

Johnson offers marriage, the swindler offers Park Avenue with all the trimmings, but no wedding ring. In the end Pidgeon gets Ginger, Johnson gets Lana, just as you knew they would all along. But there are many interesting gay little excursions along various paths of this story, including entertainment on the Starlight Roof, featuring Xavier Cugat and his orchestra, which all add up to bright entertainment.

Miss Rogers plays a movie star with ease—as why shouldn't she?—and wears the screen's smartest clothes of the current season. Walter Pidgeon is as able an admirer of hers as he ever was of Greer Garson's. Van Johnson—charming young fellow—and a new Lana Turner, a wistful type, make an attractive twosome. The rest of the cast keep up the film's mood, which is radiant.

On the Music Hall stage is a new revue, "Golden Harvest," produced by Leonidoff, with settings by Bruno Maine, and featuring Patricia Bowman, ballerina; dancers, Fred and Sally Hartnell; Walter Graf, singer; Rudolf Kroeller and the Music Hall Corps de Ballet, in a spectacular ballet fantasy; the Glee Club with Edward Reichert, Bob Evans, ventriloquist, and Lucy Brown, concert pianist.

JOHN GARFIELD in 'Pride of the Marines,' which is starting a second week at the Fox, with 'Tell It to a Star.'

'Are You With It?' For the Century

After having its title changed several times, "Are You With It?" the musical comedy now being produced by Richard Kollmar and James W. Gardiner, has had its prospective New York home switched from the National Theater to the Century. The New York opening date still remains fixed for Saturday evening, Nov. 10. "Are You With It?" with Joan Roberts, Johnny Downs and Lew Parker in the leading roles, will open in Philadelphia from Oct. 17.

Opening tonight in Bridgeport is Oscar Serlin's production of Theodore Reeves' play "Beggars Are Coming to Town." The play features Paul Kelly, Luther Adler, and Dorothy Comingore in a cast of twenty. It goes to Boston Monday.

Zadel Skolovsky, concert pianst, will play the famous Chopin "Polonaise" for one week in the new musical of the same name that opens at the Alvin Theater tomorrow night.

With the signing of Vera Allen, Frank Tweddell, Juano Hernandez and Charlotte Keane for four of the key roles, Jose Ferrer has completed casting of his production of "Strange Fruit." Lillian Smith's dramatization of her best-selling novel, which Mr. Ferrer is directing, will begin its prior-to-Broadway tour on Saturday evening, Oct. 13, at His Majesty's Theater in Montreal.

Milton Lazarus, who wrote the libretto of "Song of Norway," has revised the original Henry Blossom book of "The Red Mill" for the new production of that 39-year-old musical comedy coming to the Zeigfield Theater Oct. 16.

Jerome Kern and Oscar Hammerstein 2d announce Carol Bruce for the role of Julie in the revival of "Show Boat."

NANETTE FABRAY in "Bloomer Girl," which starts its second year at the Shubert Theater tonight.

Additional Theater News On Page 10

Korean Liberation On Embassy Screens

First pictures of the liberation of Korea by American troops highlight the new program of late world wide news events at all Embassy Newsreel Theaters.

Yanks of the 7th Infantry Division occupy Korea, for 35 years the unwilling subjects of the Japanese Empire. All Jap troops and equipment in Korea are formally surrendered. Native Koreans give American soldiers a warm welcome.

MOVIE TIME SCHEDULE

BROOKLYN—

ALBEE—"Junior Miss," 12:49, 4:07, 7:25, 10:43; "True Glory," 11:25, 2:43, 6:01, 9:19

FOX—"Pride of the Marines," 12:15, 3:27, 6:39, 9:51; "Tell It to a Star," 11:08, 2:20, 5:32, 8:44

METROPOLITAN—"Anchors Aweigh," 9:45, 12:16, 2:47, 5:18, 7:49, 10:20.

PARAMOUNT—"Over 21," 12:25, 3:38, 6:51, 10:04; "Forever Yours," 11:02, 2:15, 5:28, 8:41.

STRAND—"This Gun for Hire," 10:37, 2:08, 5:39, 9:10; "Northwest Mounted Police," 11:56, 3:27, 6:58, 10:29.

MANHATTAN

AMBASSADOR — "The Fighting Guardsman," 10:44, 12:47, 2:50, 4:53, 6:56, 8:59, 11:00.

ASTOR—"Wonder Man," 10:33, 12:28, 2:23, 4:18, 6:13, 8:08, 10:03, 11:58.

CAPITOL—"Her Highness and the Bellboy," 10:15, 1:29, 4:46, 8:03, 11:26. Stage, 12:26, 3:43, 7:00, 10:17.

CRITERION — "Lady On a Train," 9:56, 11:55, 1:55, 3:55, 5:55, 7:55, 9:55, 11:55.

MUSIC HALL—"Weekend at the Waldorf," 10:05, 1:07, 4:10, 7:09, 10:13. Stage, 12:13, 3:15, 6:18, 9:20.

PARAMOUNT — "Duffy's Tavern," 10:31, 1:31, 4:41, 8:01, 11:16. Stage, 12:36, 3:46, 7:06, 10:16

RIVOLI—"Love Letters," 10:00, 12:00, 2:00, 4:00, 6:00, 8:00, 10:00, 12:00.

ROXY—"The House on 92d St.," 11:00, 1:45, 4:40, 7:35, 10:20. Stage, 12:50, 3:40, 6:40, 9:35

'Naughty Nineties' Now at the Kingsway

A new kind of Abbott and Costello comedy, their 13th, is now playing at Century's Kingsway Theater. "The Naughty Nineties" marks the first time that Abbott and Costello appear as individual characters. Abbott has the role of a showboat leading man. Costello is seen as the boat's chief roustabout and handy man. It is also the first time they have played in a period picture.

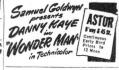

Alan Curtis, Rita Johnson, Henry Travers, Lois Collier and Joe Sawyer have prominent supporting roles.

FEATURE FILMS SHOWING TODAY

BAY RIDGE AND SUNSET PARK

Center, 6th Ave. and 56th St. .... The Phantom Speaks; Vampire's Ghost; Springtime in Texas
Electra, 75th St. and Third Ave. .... Tonight and Every Night; also Mummy's Curse
Harbor, 92d St. and Fourth Ave. .... Affairs of Susan; also Dangerous Passage
Stanley, Fifth Ave. and 75th St. .... This Man's Navy; also Counter-Attack
Park, 44th St. and Fifth Ave. .... Salty O'Rourke; also Man in Half Moon Street

BEDFORD

Lincoln, Bedford Ave.-Eastern Parkway ... Bring on the Girls; also Ministry of Fear
National, 720 Washington Ave. .... Slightly Dangerous; also Tall, Dark and Handsome
Rogers, 333 Rogers Ave. PR. 4-2230 ... The Corn Is Green; also Hitchhike to Happiness

BENSONHURST

Colony, 18th Ave.-65th St. BE. 6-2231 ... Something for the Boys; Roger Touhy, Gangster

BORO PARK

Elton, 43d St. and New Utrecht Ave. ... Salome, Where She Danced; also Within These Walls

BOROUGH HALL AND DOWNTOWN

Duffield, Duffield and Fulton St. .... Conflict; also Mama Loves Papa
Majestic, 651 Fulton St. .... Dracula; also Son of Dracula; also Three Stooges
Momart, Fulton St. and Rockwell Pl. ... Rainbow Island; also I Was Faithful
St. George Playhouse, 100 Pineapple St. Silver Fleet; also Gay Senorita
Terminal, Fourth Ave. and Dean St. ... Northwest Passage; also Pack Up Your Troubles
Tivoli, Fulton St. and Boro Hall .... Conflict; also Mama Loves Papa

BRIGHTON BEACH

Oceana, Brighton Beach Av.-Hoff St. ... Conflict; also Mama Loves Papa

BUSHWICK

Empire, Ralph Ave.-B'way. FO. 9-7940 .. Those Endearing Young Charms; also West of the Pecos
Monroe, Howard Ave. cor. Broadway ..... A Gentleman After Dark; also Reckless Age

FLATBUSH

Flatbush, Flatbush Ave. and Church .... Imitation of Life; also East Side of Heaven
Granada, Church and Nostrand Aves. .... Northwest Passage; also Blonde From Brooklyn
Kent, Coney Island Ave. and Avenue H .... Salome, Where She Danced; Within These Walls
Leader, Coney Island and Newkirk Aves. .. Conflict; also Mama Loves Papa

EAST FLATBUSH

Avenue D, Avenue D and E. 43d St. ..... Thrill of a Romance; also Woman in Green
Rugby, Utica and Church Avenues .... Imitation of Life; also East Side of Heaven

GERRITSEN BEACH

Graham, Gerritsen & Whitney Aves. .... Horn Blows at Midnight; also Escape in the Desert

PARK SLOPE

Atlantic, Flatbush Ave. and Dean St. .. The Sullivans; also The Gorilla
Carlton, Flatbush and Seventh Aves. ..... Conflict; also Mama Loves Papa
Plaza, Flatbush Ave. and Park Place .... Meet Me in St Louis; also Within These Walls
Sanders, Prospect Park West-14th St. .... Valley of Decision; also Gay Senorita
New Venus, 1224 Prospect Ave. .... Thrill of a Romance; also Woman in Green

KINGS HIGHWAY

Jewel, Kings Highway at Ocean Parkway Nothing Sacred; also Knickerbocker Holiday

AVENUE U SECTION

Avenue U, Avenue U and E. 16th St. .. Thrill of a Romance; also Woman in Green
Traymore, Avenue N and E. 46th St. ... Thrill of a Romance; also Woman in Green

RIDGEWOOD

Colonial, Broadway and Chauncey .... Stage Door; also Mr. Big
Ridgewood, 1673 Myrtle Avenue .... Salty O'Rourke; also Man in Half Moon St.
Rivoli, Myrtle-Wilson Aves. GI. 5-0744 . Oklahoma Kid; also Seven Sweethearts

SHEEPSHEAD BAY

Sheepshead, Sheepshead Rd.-Voorhies ... Valley of Decision; also Rustlers of the Badlands

SOUTH BROOKLYN

Sanders Globe, 226 15th St. .... Shanghai Gesture; Housekeeper's Daughter

VALLEY STREAM, L. I.

Sunrise Drive-In (Open-Air) .... Wing and a Prayer; also The Lodger

WILLIAMSBURG

[illegible], B'way at Wil'sburg Bridge Plaza. Street Scene; also Scarface

CENTURY THEATRES TODAY

BUY THAT VICTORY BOND TODAY AT ANY CENTURY THEATER

KINGSWAY Kings Highway, Coney Island Ave.	Abbott & Costello, "THE NAUGHTY NINETIES" "ON STAGE, EVERYBODY"
AVALON, Kings H'way and E. 18th St.	"CONEY ISLAND" and "JOHNNY APOLLO"
MARINE, Flatbush Ave.-Kings H'way	"Blood on the Sun" and "Delightfully Dangerous"
MAYFAIR, Avenue U-Coney Island Ave.; PATIO, Flatbush Ave. and Midwood St.; NOSTRAND, Kings H'way-Nostrand Av.; ALBEMARLE, Flatb'h Av.-Alb'm'le Rd.; ELM, Avenue M at East 17th St.; LINDEN, cor. Nostrand & Parkside Aves.; FARRAGUT, Flatbush Av.-Farragut Rd.; TIVOLI, Fulton St. and Boro Hall	HUMPHREY BOGART, ALEXIS SMITH, SYDNEY GREENSTREET "CONFLICT" and "MAMA LOVES PAPA" LEON ERROL
RIALTO, Flatbush Ave.-Cortelyou Rd.; VOGUE, Coney Isl. Ave. and Avenue K	"THE VALLEY OF DECISION" & "BOSTON BLACKIE'S RENDEZVOUS"
TRIANGLE, Kings H'way-E. 12th St.	"THRILL OF A ROMANCE" and Selected Short Subjects
QUENTIN, Quentin Rd. at E. 35th St.	Van Johnson, "Thrill of a Romance" & "Woman in Green"
MIDWOOD, Avenue J and E. 13th St.	"The Silver Fleet" and "The Gay Senorita"
PARKSIDE, Flatbush and Parkside Aves.; COLLEGE, Flatbush Ave.-Avenue H	"THOSE ENDEARING YOUNG CHARMS" & "WEST OF THE PECOS"

Laval Sentenced to Face Firing Squad

7★★★★★★★ Complete

BROOKLYN EAGLE

WEATHER—Cloudy, cold tonight; sunny, cool tomorrow.

104th YEAR—No. 276—DAILY and SUNDAY (Copyright, 1945, The Brooklyn Eagle, Inc.) BROOKLYN, N. Y., TUESDAY, OCTOBER 9, 1945 Entered Brooklyn P. O. 2d Class Mail Matter 3 CENTS IN NEW YORK CITY ELSEWHERE 4 CENTS

CITY HAILS ADMIRAL NIMITZ

Queen Elizabeth Unloaded by Troops

Strikers Hiss When Soldiers Work on Liner

The army today ordered Brooklyn-based troops to unload the Queen Elizabeth after striking longshoremen had refused to work on the big British liner.

In an unprecedented action officials at the New York Port of Embarkation directed 180 members of the 833rd Port Company, stationed at the Brooklyn Army Base, to proceed to Pier 90, North River, to replace the civilian dock workers. The action was taken "to prevent loss of even an hour's time" in sending the liner back to Europe.

Further delay in discharging the liner's cargo, a port official pointed out, would delay return to this country of 15,000 troops now waiting in Southampton. At the same time the official stated 32 army transports in the port area are being tied up by the longshoremen's strike.

Six Gangs Quit Jobs

Some of the dock men had continued to work on troop ships, but about 135 men in six gangs walked out in protest against the size of the sling loads used on the Queen Elizabeth. The army then announced troops would finish the job. Many of the strikers hissed and booed as the soldiers began to work.

The army's action was taken after export freight shipments into New York were frozen as shipping was completely tied up by the wildcat walkout. Striking longshoremen in Brooklyn will meet tomorrow night in Prospect Hall, Prospect Ave. near 5th Ave. to decide whether they will continue the paralyzing stoppage.

Elsewhere on the strike front violence flared in the walkout of drivers of the Consolidated Laundries Corporation, 400 were out at the Fairchild Camera and Instrument Corporation, Jamaica; bakery drivers in New Jersey ended their stoppage and strike votes against four city hospitals, three in Brooklyn, were withdrawn.

The official release in the Queen Elizabeth case, as distributed by the Port of Embarkation, read:

"To prevent loss of even an hour's time in effecting a turnabout of the giant liner, Queen Elizabeth, troops of the 833d Port Company at the

Continued on Page 9

Eagle Staff photo by John Kruh

A SON COMES HOME—Sgt. Irving Strobing, back from war and prison, sees his mother for the first time in five and a half years.

Corregidor Hero Home, But Only on Furlough

Sergeant Strobing Welcomed by Mother —Will Have Operation and Go Back to Army

Sgt. Irving Strobing, the Brooklyn boy whose last message out of Corregidor was the summary of the gallantry and the pain of that defeat, came home today after five and a half years.

He was 19 when he went away and he looked and acted much the

PUBLIC RECEPTION TODAY

Borough President Cashmore is to have a public reception for Sergeant Strobing on the steps of Borough Hall at 5 p.m. today.

same today, despite Bataan and his three-and-a-half years in a Japanese prison.

And when he ran up the steps of the little brick house at 605 Barbey St., straight into his mother's shaking arms, he was only a boy—

Continued on Page 9

LIGHTNING HITS RAILS, DELAYS L. I. R. R. TRAINS

Long Island Railroad trains from Babylon were 14 to 35 minutes late today because of signal trouble caused by an electrical storm shortly after 6 a.m.

Lightning struck third rail heaters, developing power trouble between Wantagh and Babylon. In turn, this power trouble caused the signal trouble. Power was back to normal at 7 a.m.

Reds Ask Time to Move A-Bomb Test Equipment

Stettin, Oct. 9 (U.P.)—Russia has asked Poland for a delay in turning over the Nazi atomic bomb and V-weapon experimental stations at Swinemuende and Peenemuende, it was revealed today.

The Russians, it was believed, desire additional time to remove equipment at Peenemuende, which was the center of German scientific research during the war.

It was expected the Soviet request will be granted, it was said.

Fire Lieutenant Hurt Battling 2-Alarm Blaze

Lt. Joseph Feger of Hook and Ladder 148 received a fractured left leg and contusions of the chest when the second floor of the Victory Food Market at 1326 38th St. collapsed under him during a two-alarm blaze early today. Damage to the building was listed as considerable. Lieutenant Peger, who lives at 68 McCabe Place, was taken to Israel Zion Hospital.

Fall's First Freeze Forecast for Tonight

The rain will be all over by afternoon, the Weather Bureau said, but it will remain cool and cloudy. Highest expected temperature for today is 55. Tonight the city will have its first taste of freezing weather this season. The mercury is expected to drop to 32 in the suburbs. Tomorrow will be fair and cool.

LAVAL DOOMED TO DIE BEFORE FIRING SQUAD

Jury Is Out One Hour As 'Most Hated Man' Sulks in His Cell

Paris, Oct. 9 (U.P.) — Pierre Laval, France's arch-collaborator with the Nazis, was convicted of treason in the High Court of Justice today and sentenced to death.

The jury which heard Laval's five-day trial received the case at 4:05 p.m. (10:05 a.m. Brooklyn time) and deliberated exactly an hour before returning its verdict.

Laval, who refused to attend the last two sessions of his trial, was found guilty on both counts of the indictment—plotting against the security of the state and intelligence with the enemy.

Now Laval's only hope lay in an appeal to Gen. Charles de Gaulle. If that fails—and by all signs it will—Laval will be executed by a firing squad, probably at the Montrouge fortress just outside Paris and possibly by the end of this week.

Laval took the news stolidly in his jail cell and announced that he would not ask Gen. Charles de Gaulle for clemency.

The former chief of government at Vichy was not in the courtroom when his fate was announced. He rebeled against the tumultuous court procedure and sulked in his cell while his fate was being sealed.

The conviction had not been left in doubt since the early sessions of his trial in the paneled courtroom of the Palace of Justice. There, two months ago, Marshal Henri Philippe Petain was convicted and sentenced to death, only to receive a commutation to life imprisonment.

When the jury trooped back to the courtroom after an hour's absence, Judge Pierre Mongibeaux read the verdict and the sentence in brusque formalities lasting only

Continued on Page 2

60,000 Navy Personnel Released in 6 Days

Washington, Oct. 9 (U.P.)—The navy said today that 60,000 navy men and women were released in the first six days of October. This raised the total demobilized by the navy to 208,000.

Merchant Marine Officer Guilty of Narcotics Charge

Albert Rosoff, 30, of 164 Linden Boulevard, a warrant officer in the merchant marine, pleaded guilty before Federal Judge Harold M. Kennedy yesterday to an indictment charging him with forging prescriptions for narcotics.

He will be sentenced Oct. 18.

Robbers Throw Ash Can in Window, Get $8,000 in Furs

Three husky thugs heaved an ash can through a plate glass window of the Elm Fur Shop at 1621 Avenue M early today and made away with 20 fur coats valued at $8,000. The thugs stripped seals, Perian lamb and beaver coats from eight mannequins.

A neighbor, who heard the burglar alarm, saw the men leap into a gray sedan and speed away.

The shop is owned by Henry Schloss and Jack Parness, both of 1280 E. 18th St.

Windsor Sees Attlee About Remaining Home

London, Oct. 9 (U.P.)—The Duke of Windsor conferred with Prime Minister Attlee at 10 Downing St. for 30 minutes yesterday, it was reported today.

An informed source said the decision whether the Duke should be permitted to remain in England and bring the Duchess, the former Wallis Simpson, to his homeland rests with the King, but the Prime Minister would be consulted.

Rockingham Results

FIRST RACE—$1,800; maiden two-year-olds; six furlongs

Old Mexico (Strange)	6.00	4.00	2.60
Babomac (Daniels)	—	8.60	3.80
Local Finance (Keene)	—	—	2.80

Time 1:17. Blanche Purcel, Oau Joods, Mescara, Storm Play, Grand Drive, High Water, Menace, Co-Lawyer, Mibil D. also ran. Off time, 1:16.

SECOND RACE—$1,800; claiming; four-year-olds and up; six furlongs.

Flaming High (B'z'etti)	17.20	7.40	4.40
Polly Lou (Strange)	—	7.60	4.40
Midluck (Layton)	—	—	4.20

Time, 1:16 4-5. Cananean Garza, Tell Me More, Saratoga Polly, Jane Hughes, Winecup, Selmalad, Two O'Clock also ran. Off 1:40½.

DAILY DOUBLE PAID $62

Laurel Results

FIRST RACE—Beauzar, 1st; Pharawell, 2d; Display Flight, 3d.

Eagle Staff photo

START OF A TRIUMPHAL PROCESSION—Fleet Admiral Chester W. Nimitz and Mayor LaGuardia as their official car left LaGuardia Field.

RED ISSUE VITAL, CATHOLIC ORGAN TELLS O'DWYER

Paper Contradicts His Claim of 'Fading Communist Problem

The position taken by William O'Dwyer in his campaign for Mayor on the Democratic and American Labor party tickets that the Communist issue has become a "faded red herring" was flatly contradicted today in a bulletin issued by the Crown Heights School of Catholic Workmen.

Emphatically denying that the issue is a "red herring," as Mr. O'Dwyer claimed in last week's speech repudiating Communist support, the bulletin declared:

"In the City of New York the Communist issue is one that is very vital, very acute and very important."

The contradiction of Mr. O'Dwyer's view was made in the Crown Heights Comment, a weekly bulletin issued to its members by the Crown Heights School of Catholic Workmen.

Continued on Page 2

Boro Hails Truman Okay of Vet Hospital

General Bradley Announces Presidential Approval of Fort Hamilton Institution

By CLARENCE GREENBAUM

Brooklyn veterans and their families today hailed, along with all other Brooklynites, the final green light given by President Truman in Washington to the long-awaited 1,000-bed veterans hospital which will soon be erected on 18 acres of the Fort Hamilton Army Reservation at a cost of more than $6,000,000.

Presidential approval of the ultra-modern project which, when completed, will overlook the attractive borough Narrows shoreline, was announced late yesterday in the capital by Gen. Omar N. Bradley, national head of the Veterans Administration. No construction date has been fixed as yet.

Members of Brooklyn's nine-man Congressional delegation, long-time proponents of the hospital, immediately greeted with joy the decision to erect the great medical and surgical institution here. On Sept. 27 last the Brooklyn Eagle revealed that the hospital would be located at Fort Hamilton.

For four long years Brooklyn veterans groups, civic and business as-

Continued on Page 9

Reject 120 Names, Restore 400 on Beldock Petition

Weary-eyed lawyers who had spent most of the night checking records in the office of the Board of Elections appeared before Supreme Court Justice Stoddart today and reported agreement on many points involved in the Democratic suit to nullify Liberal party petitions naming Republican District Attorney George J. Beldock as candidate for that office.

John P. McGrath, chief counsel for the Democrats, and Charles Pokorny, head of the Republican legal staff, told Justice Stoddart they carefully checked both sides' claims and that Mr. McGrath withdrew objections to some 40 pages of petitions. This restores about 400 names to the valid category. Mr. Pokorny agreed that about a dozen pages listed in the original objections are so defective as to be invalidated. He then relinquished more than 120 names. The proceeding will continute.

Bevin Blames Russia For Failure of Parley

London, Oct. 9 (U.P.)—British Foreign Secretary Ernest Bevin joined American spokesmen today in blaming Russia for the failure of the Foreign Ministers Council and revealed that the conference was called off only after a vain attempt to reach agreement through the Big Five government heads.

Former Prime Minister Winston Churchill arose at the close of Mr. Bevin's statement and demanded, as leader of the Conservative opposition, that the government debate its handling of the three-week conference.

Mr. Churchill branded the results of the three-week Foreign Ministers meeting as "disappointing," and made it clear that he would press for a fuller explanation of the government's position.

Mr. Bevin's statement was brief and revealed little that had not already been told to the world by U. S. Secretary of State James F. Byrnes.

He joined Mr. Byrnes in laying the blame for the conference failure on Russia and, inferentially, on Soviet Premier Stalin.

Mr. Bevin said Soviet Commissar V. M. Molotov at first consented to discussion of the Balkan treaties by all representatives of the Big Five. Then, mid-way through the meeting, Mr. Bevin said, Mr. Molotov received instructions from Moscow that France and China were to have no part in the Balkan settlements.

On that point, the conference broke up, despite a last-minute effort to keep it going by referring the dispute to the Big Three leaders in London, Washington and Moscow.

"The Big Three government heads, Mr. Bevin said, also "failed to agree."

The dynamic Laborite Minister said he was hopeful the discussions could be resumed and that a satisfactory solution could be worked out.

Mr. Bevin reiterated Mr. Byrnes' surprise that Molotov charged them with violating the Potsdam agreement by trying to include France and China in the Balkan discussions, asserting that the Soviet Foreign Commissar previously had agreed to that point.

Today's was the first session of the New House of Commons after its six-week Summer recess, and the galleries were packed with visitors and Allied diplomats.

JAMAICA RESULTS

FIRST RACE—$2,500; claiming; three-year-olds; six furlongs.

Helvetian (Atkinson)	16.00	6.40	3.60
a-Pyros (Arcaro)	—	4.60	3.30
Balladry (Lindberg)	—	—	2.70

Off time, 1:30½. Time, 1:13.

a-F. Foresterie entry.

Scratched—Hat Maker, Last Salute, Come East, Voloway, Tosajilla.

Butter for Civilians, 80 Million Lbs. of It

Washington, Oct. 9 (U.P.)—Eighty million pounds of butter, declared surplus by the army, are being turned over to the Department of Agriculture for disposal to civilian agencies, the War Department announced today.

The butter will increase civilian supplies greatly during the next few months during the normal short season in production. The butter will be released as soon as possible.

The army bought butter for all of the armed forces and the War Relocation Authority. It followed the practice of getting its supplies during the heaviest production season from April through August.

The sudden cessation of hostilities radically reduced requirements. The army quartermaster corps undertook to transfer surplus butter held in warehouses to the Department of Agriculture for disposal through civilian channels.

GI Shoots Self Fatally In Trying to Scare Girls

Buffalo, Oct. 9 (U.P.)—The death of Pfc. John B. Hassett, 21, who was killed by a .38-caliber bullet while "scaring" three girl companions, was termed accidental today by Medical Examiner Harold J. Welsh.

The shooting occurred when Hassett, a veteran of several European campaigns, walked into his brother's tavern yesterday with three members of the marine corps women's reserve. Discovering a revolver under the bar, he whispered to the bartender, "Watch me scare the girls," and placed the gun against his right temple.

Police said the soldier thought the gun was unloaded.

LONG ISLAND MAN GETS STATE TAX POST

Albany, Oct. 9 (U.P.)—Gov. Thomas E. Dewey appointed Spencer E. Bates, Hewlett, L. I., today as State Deputy Tax Commissioner to succeed Glenn R. Bedenkapp on the State Tax Commission.

Mr. Bedenkapp left the $10,000 a year post recently to devote his full time to the State Republican Committee chairmanship.

A native of East Rockaway, Bates had been Manhattan district supervisor of the State Taxation and Finance Department, heading the New York City offices. In 1938 Bates became Deputy Commissioner.

Postoffice to Be Open On Friday, Columbus Day

Postmaster Frank J. Quayle of Brooklyn announced today that on Columbus Day (Friday) the General Postoffice and all stations, including contract stations, will open and close at the regular weekday hours and the usual window service will be maintained. Foot delivery, parcel post delivery and collection trips will be made the same as on weekdays.

Admiral Byrd III On Ship at Yokohoma

Yokohama, Oct. 9 (U.P.)—The navy disclosed today that Rear Admiral Richard E. Byrd, 57, noted explorer, is ill aboard the Hospital Ship Marigold in Yokohama harbor. No details of his condition were revealed.

METROPOLIS GOES ALL OUT FOR NAVY HERO

Welcome Is 'Great,' He Declares as Mayor Greets Him

By VIOLET BROWN

Fleet Admiral Chester W. Nimitz, the white-haired grinning Texan who steered the Pacific fleet from the ruins of Pearl Harbor to the triumph of Tokyo Bay, took New York today in the most impressive reception awarded heroes of this war to date.

Given a tumultuous "well done" with him were 13 veterans who earned the Congressional Medal of Honor under his command during the three years it took to send the Japanese fleet to the bottom of the sea.

Climax of the reception, at which even the skies cleared for the man who was not afraid to ride typhoons to victory, was the stop at City Hall.

There, before massed thousands, after a triumphal parade led by 4,000 sailors, marines and coast guardsmen and seven proudly blaring bands through the traditional "heroes' canyon" of downtown Manhattan, Admiral Nimitz received the city's honorary citizenship and a specially struck gold medal.

Accepts for Men

Standing on the blue ship-like speakers' platform on the steps of City Hall, beneath a huge blue banner showing by jagged red lightning bolts the march across the "Nimitz Sea," the Admiral accepted the honors in the name of the men of his command.

"Any glory which may be attached to our series of sea, air and land victories in the Pacific Ocean areas belongs primarily to them," he said.

Then he made a plea that America remain prepared "to insure that we do not lose the peace" for which he and his men fought—with a bravery epitomized by the valiant 13 on the platform with him.

"Never again should we risk the threat which weakness invites," said he. "We owe this to the men who have fought and to the youngsters who are growing up today. Let us give our next generation a heritage of strength so that our citizens may live without having to spend their blood in battle."

Praises American Vigor

Admiral Nimitz praised American "vigor and vision, inventiveness and ingenuity," adding that the victory in the Pacific was the product of teamwork among the ground, air, sea, undersea and home-front forces.

The admiral arrived in the city by navy plane at LaGuardia Field at 11:05 a.m. As he stepped from

Continued on Page 2

German Cartels Expert Nabbed by Americans

Frankfurt, Germany, Oct. 9 (U.P.)—Gerhard Alois Westrick, 56, German cartels expert, was in an American military jail today.

Military authorities said Westrick was suspected of attempting to rebuild Germany's shattered cartels prior to his arrest in the French zone several days ago.

4-Power Court Set For War Criminal Trials

Berlin, Oct. 9 (U.P.)—The four-power court which will hear the Nuernberg trials of Axis war criminals met for the first time here today.

The meeting in effect comprised the formation of the court, which now was ready to receive indictments of major war criminals.

Returning GIs Listed

A list of Brooklyn, Queens and Long Island soldiers who returned today from Europe on the Queen Elizabeth will be found on page 10.

WHERE TO FIND IT

	Page		Page
Bridge	16	Novel	16
Comics	19	Obituaries	9
Crossword	16	Our Champs	4
Currie	3	Patterns	12
Dr. Brady	8	Radio	19
Editorial	8	Society	11
Financial	7	Sports	13-15
Grin and Bear It	8	Take My Word	8
Heffernan	8	Theaters	6, 7
Helen Worth	12	These Women	19
Horoscope	12	Tommy Holmes	13
Lindley	8	Tucker	8
Mary Haworth	11	Uncle Ray	19
Movies	6, 7	Want Ads	15-18
Music	7	Women	12

ELLA CINDERS

By Charles Plumb and Fred Fox

MARY WORTH'S FAMILY

By Dale Allen

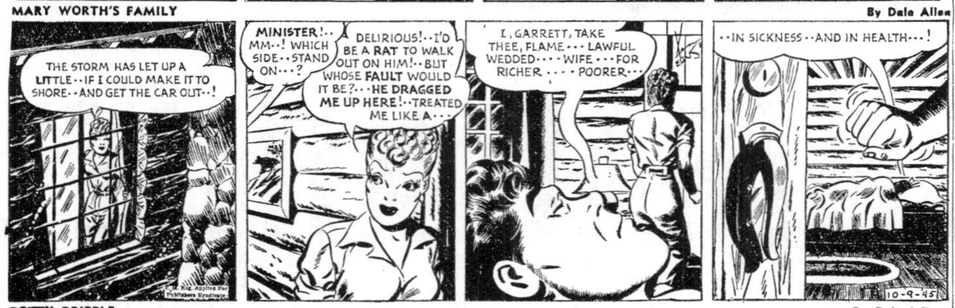

DOTTY DRIPPLE

By Buford Tune

DR. BOBBS

By Elliott and McArdle

JANE ARDEN

By Monte Barrett and Russell Ross

INVISIBLE SCARLET O'NEIL

By Russell Stamm

BO

By Frank Beck

CHIEF WAHOO

By Saunders and Woggon

LEM AND OINIE

By Paul Fogarty

RADIO PROGRAMS

WMCA, 570. WEAF, 660. WOR, 710. WJZ, 770. WNYC, 830. WABC, 880. WAAT, 970. WINS, 1000. WHN, 1050. WNEW, 1130. WLIB, 1190. WFAS, 1240. WOV, 1280. WEVD, 1330. WBBR, 1330. WBNX, 1380. WBYN, 1430. WHOM, 1480. WQXR, 1560. WWRL, 1600.

TODAY'S BEST BETS

12:15—Reception to Admiral Chester W. Nimitz, WABC.
7:00—Supper Club, WEAF; Masterwork Hour, WNYC; Jack Kirkwood Show, WABC.
7:15—Maria Kramer Serenade, WINS.
7:30—Everything for the Boys, Dick Haymes, WEAF.
8:00—Barry Wood Show, WEAF.
8:30—Theater of Romance, Anne Baxter, Vincent Price, Sir Cedric Hardwicke, Guests, WABC; Alan Young Show, WJZ.
9:00—Inner Sanctum, WABC; Guy Lombardo Show, WJZ; Amos 'n' Andy Program, WEAF.
9:30—Fibber McGee and Molly, WEAF; This Is My Best, Sylvia Sidney, Jean Pierre Aumont, Tom Conway, Guests, WABC; American Forum of the Air, WOR.,
10:00—Bob Hope Show, Frances Langford, Skinnay Ennis Orchestra, Billy Conn, Guest, WEAF; Jo Stafford-Lawrence Brooks Show, WABC; Dinner Honoring Admiral Chester Nimitz, WOR.
10:30—Hildegarde Show, Patsy Kelly, Burgess Meredith, Walter Abel, Guests, WEAF.

Where there is no listing for a station preceding program is on the air

2 P.M. TO 4 P.M.

2:00 WABC—Two on a Clue
WEAF—Guiding Light
WJZ—News, Kennedy.
WOR—News, Foster.
WMCA—News: Love Songs
WHN—Living Should Be Fun.
WNYC—News: Symphony.
WINS—News: Tune Factory.
2:15 WABC—Perry Mason.
WEAF—Today's Child'n.
WJZ—Ethel and Albert
WOR—Jane Cowl
WHN—Racing; News.
2:25 WOR—Cliff Edwards.
2:30 WABC—Rosemary.
WEAF—Woman in White.
WOR—"Queen for a Day."
WJZ—Fitzgeralds.
WHN—Racing; Music.
2:45 WABC—Tena and Tim
WEAF—Church Hymns
WHN—Music.
3:00 WABC—Time to Remember.
WEAF—Woman of America
WJZ—Best Sellers
WOR—Martha Deane.
WMCA—News; Americana.
WHN—Racing; Music.
3:15 WABC—Off the Record.
WEAF—Ma Perkins.
WMCA—Kirby Orch.
WHN—Music; News.
3:30 WEAF—Pepper Young.
WJZ—Ladies Be Seated
WHN—Racing; Music.
WOR—Gambling
WMCA—News.
WNYC—Vikings Spirit.
3:45 WABC—Sing Along Club.
WEAF—Right Happiness.
WMCA—Three Qt. Time.
WHN—Music.
WNYC—News; Rationing.

4 P.M. TO 7 P.M.

4:00 WABC—House Party.
WEAF—Backstage Wife.
WJZ—Berch Show.
WOR—News, Gambling.
WMCA—News; Ray Smith
WHN—Racing; Music.
WNYC—Four Strings.
4:15 WEAF—Stella Dallas.
WJZ—Van Voorhis, news.
WOR—Jay Johnson.
WHN—Music; News.
4:25 WABC—News.
4:30 WABC—National War Fund Program.
WEAF—Lorenzo Jones.
WJZ—David Wills.
WOR—Food and Home.
WMCA—News; Matinee.
WHN—Racing; Music.
4:45 WABC—Feature Story.
WEAF—Widder Brown.
WJZ—Hop Harrigan.
WINS—Battle Royal.
5:00 WABC—"Gateways to Music."
WEAF—A Girl Marries.
WJZ—Terry and Pirates.
WOR—Uncle Don.
WMCA—News; Matinee.
WNYC—Music for Young People.
WHN—Dick Gilbert.
WINS—News; Battle Royal.
5:15 WEAF—Portia Faces Life.
WJZ—Dick Tracy.
WOR—Superman.
WMCA—Listen to a Story.
WINS—Battle Royal.
5:30 WABC—Cimarron Tavern.
WEAF—Just Plain Bill.
WJZ—Jack Armstrong
WOR—Captain Midnight
WMCA—News
WNYC—Ruth Brall.
WHN—Weather; News.
5:38 WHN—Dick Gilbert.
5:45 WABC—Sparrow and the Hawk.
WEAF—Front Page Farrell.
WJZ—"Tennessee Jed."
WOR—Tom Mix.
WMCA—Jerry Baker, Songs.
WNYC—Youth Problems.
WINS—Music.
6:00 WABC—News, Howe.
WEAF—News.
WJZ—News; Kiernan's Corner.
WOR—Paul Schubert.
WMCA—News; Help Wanted.
WNYC—United Nations Music.
WHN—Sidney Walton.
WINS—News; Serenade.
6:15 WABC—Hill, news.
WEAF—Serenade.
WJZ—Here's Morgan.
WOR—Man on the Street.
WMCA—Mr Hollywood.
WHN—Racing Results.
6:20 WMCA—Sports, Ellis
6:30 WABC—Liberal Party Program.
WJZ—"News-Sports."
WOR—News, Van Deventer
WMCA—"Racing Results."
WNYC—N. Y. Overseas.
WHN—News, Lang.
WINS—Dunphy, sports.
6:40 WEAF—Sports, Stern.
6:45 WABC—World Today.
WEAF—Lowell Thomas
WJZ—Charlie Chan.
WOR—Stan Lomax, sports.
WMCA—"Tropical Tunes."
WNYC—News.
WHN—Bob Howard.
WINS—T. Dorsey Records.
6:55 WABC—News, Harsch.
WNYC—Help Wanted Column.

7 P.M. TO 10 P.M.

7:00 WABC—Kirkwood Show.
WEAF—Supper Club.
WJZ—Headline Edition.
WOR—News, Lewis.
WMCA—News; Sundown Serenade.
WHN—News, Combs.
WNYC—Masterwork Hour.
WINS—News; Serenade.
7:15 WABC—Smith Show.
WEAF—News; Vandercook.
WJZ—News, Swing.
WHN—Sports Final.
WOR—Answer Man.
WMCA—Five Star Final.
WINS—Kramer Serenade.
7:30 WABC—American Melodies.
WEAF—Everything for the Boys.
WJZ—"County Fair."
WOR—Arthur Hale.
WMCA—J. R. Walsh.
WHN—Shirley Palmer.
WINS—Blues in Night.
7:45 WOR—Brandt, sports.
WMCA—Political Talk.
WHN—Johannes Steel.
7:55 WINS—Sports Talk.
8:00 WABC—Big Town.
WMCA—News; Lawrence.
WJZ—Lum and Abner.
WEAF—Barry Wood Show.
WOR—News, Singiser.
WNYC—BBC News.
WHN—Music.
WINS—News: Overseas.
8:15 WOR—Kenny Baker.
WJZ—Radie Harris.
WNYC—"N. Y. Salutes."
WINS—Gould Records.
8:30 WABC—Romance Theater
WEAF—Date with Judy.
WJZ—Alan Young Show.
WOR—"The Falcon."
WINS—Kramer Music.
WNYC—Gloria Perkins.
WHN—Congressional Record.
8:45 WNYC—News.
WHN—Mooney Orch.
WINS—Name Band Show.
8:55 WABC—News. Henry
9:00 WABC—Inner Sanctum.
WEAF—Amos 'n' Andy.
WJZ—Lombardo Show.
WMCA—News; "Business Forum."
WOR—Gabriel Heatter.
WNYC—Concert Hall.
WHN—Dick Gilbert.
WINS—News; Music.
9:15 WOR—Real Stories.
WINS—Doctor Discovers.
9:30 WABC—"This Is My Best."
WEAF—Fibber McGee & Molly.
WJZ—"Doctor Talks it Over."
WOR—American Forum.
WMCA—Miller Orch.
WINS—Record Shop.
9:45 WMCA—Bing Crosby
WJZ—Citizens Committee.
9:55 WJZ—Story Teller.
WNYC—News.

10 P.M. TO 1 A.M.

10:00 WABC—Stafford-Brooks Show.
WEAF—Bob Hope Show.
WJZ—Transatlantic Quiz.
WMCA—News; Broadway.
WNYC—Signoff.
WHN—Boxing
WINS—News; Martin Records.
WOR—Admiral Nimitz.
10:15 WINS—Musicale.
WOR—Jonah Goldstein.
10:30 WABC—Congress Speaks.
WEAF—Hildegarde Show.
WOR—Symphonette.
WJZ—Choice of Week.
WMCA—Frank Kingdon.
WHN—Place in News.
WINS—Henry Milo.
10:35 WHN—Music.
10:45 WABC—Behind the Scenes.
WJZ—Concert Orch.
WMCA—Musical Encores.
WINS—Curtain Calls.
WHN—Punch Bowl.
11:00 WABC—News, Daly.
WEAF—News, Van.
WJZ—News; Gallmor.
WOR—News, Van Deventer
WMCA—News; Martin Or.
WHN—Newsreel Theater.
WINS—News
11:10 WINS—Concert Hall.
11:15 WABC—Joan Brooks, songs.
WEAF—Harkness.
WJZ—Hasel, sports.
WOR—News, Egan.
WMCA—Unity Viewpoint.
11:25 WOR—Financial Report.
11:28 WOR—Weather.
11:30 WABC—T. Dorsey Orch.
WEAF—Hits and Misses.
WJZ—Gems for Thought.
WOR—Monroe Orch.
WMCA—Drama Reviews.
11:35 WJZ—Russell Orch.
11:45 WMCA—"Crisis in Our Town."
WINS—News.
12:00 WABC—News; Buffalo Presents.
WEAF—News.
WJZ—News; Stan Shaw.
WOR—News; Bestor Orch.
WMCA—News.
WHN—Music to Read By.
WINS—Sign off.
12:05 WEAF—Shield Orch.
12:15 WMCA—"Music for Dreaming."
WOR—Aloma Orch.
12:30 WABC—Teddy Wilson
WOR—Keller Orch.
WJZ—Cross Presents.
WABC—Brooks Orch.
12:45 WOR—McCune Orch.
WHN—News.
12:55 WEAF—News.

Features On Other Stations

WEVD—
8:15—Jewish Philosopher.
9:45—Rev. Kernan.
11:30—On Wings of Song.
12:00—Symphonic Hour.
WNEW—
5:15—Hollywood Digest.
5:35—Make Believe Ballroom
7:45—Easy Aces.
12:00—Milkman's Matinee.
WQXR—
4:05—Symphonic Matinee.
7:30—Spotlight.
8:05—Symphony Hall
11:05—Hour of Symphony.

TOMORROW

Morning

7:00 WABC—Arthur Godfrey.
WEAF—Morning in Manhattan.
WJZ—News.
WOR—Elliott, news.
WMCA—"Seven o'Clock Special."
WHN—Art Brown.
WNYC—News; Symphony.
WINS—News; Musical Pet.
7:15 WOR—Musical Clock.
WMCA—Morning Herald.
WJZ—You Name It.
7:30 WEAF—News.
WMCA—"Rise and Shine"
WINS—News
7:40 WINS—Musical Pet.
7:45—WABC—Clark, news.
WEAF—Reveille Roundup
WMCA—Help Wanted.
7:50 WJZ—Fraser, news.
8:00 WABC—News Roundup.
WEAF—News, Stevenson.
WJZ—Fitzgeralds.
WOR—Robinson, news.
WMCA—News; Real Estate.
WNYC—News Music Album.
WINS—News Musical Pet
8:15 WABC—Phil Cook Show
WEAF—Jack Arthur.
WOR—Dorothy and Dick
WMCA—Unity Viewpoint
WNYC—Help Wanted Column.
8:20 WNYC—Music Album.
8:25 WNYC—Consumers Guide.
8:30 WABC—Missus Shops.
WEAF—News.
WJZ—Nancy Craig.
WMCA—News.
8:33 WNYC—Music Album.
8:45 WABC—Margaret Arlen.
WEAF—Rod Hendrickson
WMCA—Music of Moment.
WNYC—News: Around New York
8:55 WOR—News, Robinson
WJZ—Gems for Thought.
9:00 WABC—News.
WEAF—Ed East & Polly
WJZ—Breakfast Club.
WOR—Hunt, news.
WHN—Gloom Dodgers.
WMCA—News; Isabelle Beach.
WNYC—Masterwork Hour
WINS—News; Little Helper.
9:15 WABC—Arthur Godfrey
WOR—Love Notes.
9:20 WOR—Travelogue.
9:25 WHN—News; Gloom Dodgers.
9:30 WEAF—Adelaide Hawley
WOR—Alfred McCann.
WINS—News; Home Stylist.
WMCA—Music Box.
9:35 WINS—Little Helper.
9:45 WEAF—Daytime Classics.
10:00 WABC—Valiant Lady.
WEAF—News, St. John.
WJZ—True Story.
WOR—News, Gladstone.
WMCA—News; Music Box
WNYC—O. P. A. News.
WINS—News; Musical.
10:15 WABC—Light of World.
WEAF—Lora Lawton
WOR—Bessie Beatty.
WNYC—Treasury Salute.
WINS—Dorothy Day.
10:25 WJZ—News; Betty Crocker.
WHN—News; Gloom Dodgers.
10:30 WABC—Romance of Evelyn Winters.
WEAF—Road of Life.
WJZ—Church Hymns.
WNYC—BBC News.
WINS—Star Parade.
10:45 WABC—Bachelor's Child'n
WEAF—Joyce Jordan.
WJZ—Listening Post.
WNYC—Music Between News.
11:00 WABC—Amanda.
WEAF—Waring Show
WJZ—Breakfast Interviews
WOR—News, Robinson.
WNYC—News; Re-deployment Lists.
WINS—News; Tune Factory.
11:10 WINS—Home Stylist.
11:15 WABC—Second Husband.
WOR—Tello Test.
WNYC—Rations; Recipes.
WINS—Tune Factory.
11:25 WNYC—Musical Souvenirs.
WHN—News; Gloom Dodgers.
11:30 WABC—"A Woman's Life."
WEAF—Barry Cameron.
WJZ—News, Martyn.
WOR—Take It Easy.
WMCA—News.
WINS—Lady of Charm.
11:45 WABC—Aunt Jenny.
WEAF—David Harum.
WJZ—Ted Malone.
WOR—Letters to Lind Lahr.
WMCA—Bandstand.
WNYC—Health Talk.
WINS—Tune Factory.
11:57 WHN—Weather.

12 M. TO 2 P.M.

12:00 WABC—Kate Smith.
WEAF—News.
WJZ—Glamour Manor.
WOR—News, Lang
WMCA—News; Lawrence.
WHN—"World at Noon."
WNYC—Music at Work.
WINS—News; Commentary.
12:15 WABC—Big Sister.
WEAF—Maggi McNellis.
WOR—Richard Maxwell.
WHN—Gloom Dodgers.
WINS—Tune Factory.
12:30 WABC—Helen Trent.
WEAF—Merchant Marine Orch.
WJZ—News.
WOR—News, Gladstone.
12:35 WJZ—Women Exchange..
12:45 WABC—Our Gal Sunday
WEAF—Music Room.
WOR—Answer Man.
12:55 WEAF—Romance and You.
WHN—News.
1:00 WABC—Life Beautiful
WEAF—Mary McBride.
WJZ—Baukhage Talking.
WNYC—Missing Persons.
WOR—Mealtime Melodies.
WMCA—News; Holiday Rhythm.
WHN—For Women Only.
WINS—News; Tune Factory.
1:05 WNYC—CDVO Program.
1:15 WABC—Ma Perkins.
WJZ—Constance Bennett.
WOR—Bundy's Album.
1:30 WABC—MacDonald, news.
WJZ—Galen Drake.
WOR—Lopez Orch.
WHN—News; Music.
WNYC—Change of Mood.
WMCA—"Capt. Healys."
1:45 WABC—Young Dr. Malone.
WEAF—Beatty, news.
WOR—John J. Anthony.
WMCA—Vocal Varieties.
WHN—Living Should Be Fun.

War Fund Benefit

The Amy Mollison Chapter of the Wives, an organization of wives of service men and veterans, with headquarters at 8509 21st Ave., will hold a card party tomorrow night at the Savoy Mansion, 64th St. and 20th Ave. Proceeds will go to the National War Fund.

THESE WOMEN!

By d'Alessio

"I want to advertise for a lost husband, but I don't want to sound enthusiastic about finding him!"

RADIO

By William Juengst

PRESENTEE—Shirley Booth is the guest star who will be presented on WEAF's "Johnny Presents" tonight. And tonight Peter Donald debuts as emcee of "County Fair" Coast broadcast which WJZ has brought on to New York.

SHIFTS AND STARTS—With the effervescent **Peter Donald** taking over as master of ceremonies, WJZ's "County Fair" today shifts from Hollywood to N. Y. . . . The **Jerry Wald** orchestra this night inaugurates the 27th Fall season of Roseland Ballroom with five Jayzee wires a week . . . **Les Elgart** and his band tonight will reopen the Rustic Cabin in Englewood, N. J. . . . **WOR** is to be their radio outlet.

TRADE TALK—Capt. Eddie Rickenbacker has contracted to be narrator for "The World's Most Honored Flights," a series of 13 half-hour plays which a watch company will beam coast-to-coast early in 1946 . . The **Dick Haymes WEAFer** tonight will stage a three-way trans-oceanic interview, linking H-wood, Tokyo and Berlin . . . To be interviewed are a Brooklyn GI in Germany and a South Carolina lad in Japan . . . To help the World Christmas Festival movement, **Dave Elman,** on his WOR stanza, last night auctioned off the original **Rockwell Kent** drawing that is the talisman of the organization, which aims to provide Yuletide heart-warmth for the world's less fortunate small folk.

GUEST REGISTER—Visiting celebs on the **Hildegarde** program tonight will include **Burgess Meredith,** star of the "Story of GI Joe" flicker, **Walter Abel,** another well-known thespian, **Patsy Kelly,** the comedienne, and **Lee Sullivan,** singer from WOR's "Keep Ahead" . . . **Pearl Buck** will be quizzed by Martha Deane at WOR this matinee . . . That was **Bert Wheeler,** of the "Fresh Up Show," you heard with **Bessie Beatty** this ayem . . . Tomorrow **Bessie** draws **Roy Rogers,** the rodeo troubador.

DIRECT DISCOURSE—Memo to Brooklynites Who Like To Dance: During the "warmup" of the Jack Kirkwood WABCast (a "warmup" being that period in the life of a broadcast studio audience, when, a few minutes before broadcast time, stars like **Jack Benny** and **Fred Allen** come out and pull the same gags this Tuesday that they pulled for ticket-holders a year ago this Tuesday) **Kirkwood** and his supporting cast jump off the stage as soon as **Irving Miller's** orch gets going, select partners among the audience, and do alittle rug-cutting in the aisles . . . Memo to **Jim Hurley** and **Dave Newell,** who conduct that "Fishing and Hunting Club of the Air" for WJZ: So you're going to tell the folks, tomorrow, how fish live in a frozen pond, hah? . . . Well if Ol' Sour Ears were on the show with you he'd prove that goldfish in a bowl, at 3 a.m., are NOISY!

UNCLE RAY

Croesus Captured By Persian Leader

King Croesus lived 2,500 years ago. Lydia, the country which he ruled, is believed to have been the place where rounded coins were first minted.

The minting of Lydian coins started centuries before Croesus came to the throne. No doubt the father of this monarch left him a great deal of wealth, but Croesus kept on building the fortune until he was known as the richest man on earth.

Croesus also added to the size of his kingdom. Sending forth armies, he conquered one settlement after another around the borders. He was especially proud of the cavalrymen among his soldiers.

At that time, another empire was growing powerful. The Persians were winning control of one kingdom after another. Their leader was named Cyrus.

"Perhaps we should attack Cyrus before he spreads out too far," thought Croesus.

Hoping to learn in advance what would happen in case of such an attack, the monarch sent messengers to the Greek oracle at Delphi.

The reply of the oracle was this, in brief:

"If you make war on the Persians, you will destroy a mighty empire."

Feeling pleased that he was to destroy a mighty empire, Croesus opened war against Cyrus by invading a Persian colony in the area now known as Syria. The battle proved to be a hard one, with neither side winning the upper hand.

Croesus decided that he would wait until the next year before making another attack. Cyrus, however, ordered a surprise invasion of Lydia. Laying siege to the capital city, he captured it in 14 days.

An old record says that rich King Croesus was captured and was placed on a funeral pyre to be burned alive. As the flames started, he cried out, "Oh Solon, oh Solon!"

Cyrus then ordered his men to put out the fire. A sudden shower helped them in quenching the flames.

(For BIOGRAPHY section of your scrapbook.)

Uncle Ray

Tomorrow: More About Croesus.

O'Dwyer Visited Costello--Goldstein

7★★★★★★★ Complete

BROOKLYN EAGLE

WEATHER—Clear, mild tonight; sunny, warm tomorrow.

104th YEAR—No. 285—DAILY and SUNDAY (Copyright, 1945, The Brooklyn Eagle, Inc.) BROOKLYN, N. Y., THURSDAY, OCTOBER 18, 1945 Entered Brooklyn P. O. 2d Class Mail Matter 3 CENTS IN NEW YORK CITY ELSEWHERE 4 CENTS

24 NAZI LEADERS INDICTED FOR MASS MURDER, PLUNDER

O'DWYER SAW COSTELLO -GOLDSTEIN

Says Democrat Was Visitor at Gambler's Home

By JOSEPH H. SCHMALACKER

Judge Jonah J. Goldstein, Republican-Liberal-City Fusion party nominee for Mayor, supplementing his charge of a tie-up between the underworld and William O'Dwyer's candidacy for Mayor on the Democratic-ALP ticket, definitely named Mr. O'Dwyer today as a visitor to the home of Frank Costello, so-called slot machine king.

At a press conference in his Hotel Astor headquarters Judge Goldstein placed Mr. O'Dwyer in Costello's home by answering a question put to him for further details of his charge in a radio speech last night of a link between his opponent and Costello.

"Did Mr. O'Dwyer go to Costello's home?" the judge was asked by a reporter.

"Yes," was the reply.

"Do you care to say when?" he was asked.

"Let him (meaning Mr. O'Dwyer) answer that question first."

Judge Goldstein then said: "I am informed that the A. L. P. braintrusters are advising Mr. O'Dwyer to answer my questions about the visits and contacts by saying that they were either in connection with the war effort or foreign relief. They haven't decided yet which to use."

Just 'Trial Balloon'

Asked what he had to say concerning a reply to his charges by Wayne Johnson, chairman of the Independent Citizens Committee for Mr. O'Dwyer, Judge Goldstein said: "They sent that out as a trial balloon."

Mr. Johnson had stated: "The ghosts of Murder, Inc., are the answer to Jonah Goldstein's descent

Continued on Page 11

Forecast Warm Weather But No 'Indian Summer'

Officially there is no such thing as Indian Summer, the Weather Bureau reported today. However, the report continued, the temperature will fluctuate between 75 and 80 with moderate winds and the sky will be nice and blue.

Asked to explain why such a condition could now obtain without being Indian Summer, the Weather Bureau said: "There is no such official designation. It's just a poetic term—but it is pleasant."

Eagle Staff photos

NEARLY READY—Here's a striking picture, taken today, of our newest aircraft carrier, the Franklin D. Roosevelt, which will be commissioned at the Brooklyn Navy Yard in Navy Day ceremonies Oct. 27. Sister ship of the U. S. S. Midway, already in service, the 45,000-ton Roosevelt is one of the world's largest, strongest and most expensive warships. The inset shows Capt. Apollo Soucek, who will command the vessel.

BELDOCK WRAPS BROADCAST IN SECRECY CLOAK

Sensational Charges Against O'Dwyer Are 'ndicated

District Attorney George J. Beldock has placed a cloak of strict secrecy about his 15-minute broadcast starting at 8 o'clock tonight, over WOR, but there are indications that he will make hitherto unpublished, sensational charges about the office of his predecessor, William O'Dwyer. Mr. O'Dwyer is the Democratic-A. L. P. nominee for Mayor who was on military leave

Continued on Page 11

Jitterbug Halsey

Los Angeles, Oct. 18 (U.P.)—Admiral William F. (Bull) Halsey, 3d Fleet Commander, left today for Newark, N. J., after an evening of jitterbugging with movie stars.

City Armories Opened For Gobs to Sleep In

While the ten warships of the visiting victory fleet were being prepared for public inspection, Mayor LaGuardia announced that Lt. Hugh A. Drum, commander of the New York Guard, was throwing open the armories in the city for the use of sailors on shore leave who are unable to find other sleeping quarters. He said Douglas Elliman of the Red Cross was arranging to provide 1,000 cots.

The sailors meanwhile—both officers and men—took over the town.

Led by the 15,000-ton carrier Monterey, whose skipper, Capt. John B. Lyon, held seniority over the captains, the slate-blue warships whose battle feats humbled a powerful Jap navy sailed into New York Harbor with the dawn yesterday.

Designated in navy parlance as both Task Force 52 or the 1st Carrier Task Force, the flotilla, com-

Continued on Page 11

WHERE, WHEN TO SEE 'EM

Enterprise and Monterey—1:30 to 4 p.m., foot of Beach St., Hudson River.

Zellars, Douglas H. Fox, Young, Foote and Aulick—1:30 to 4 p.m., foot of Morton St., Hudson River.

Submarines and sub-tenders—1:30 to 4 p.m., Tompkinsville, S. I., naval base.

SENATORS O. K. ENDING TAX FOR 12,000,000

Approve House Plan Exempting Incomes of Low-Paid Workers

Washington, Oct. 18 (U.P.)—The Senate Finance Committee voted today to relieve 12,000,000 low-paid individuals from Federal income taxes next year.

The House last week passed a bill which would accomplish the same end and, although the Senate committee made some changes, the net effect would be the same for the low-income groups.

The Senate committee also voted to repeal, effective Jan. 1, the excess profits tax on corporations. That would save corporations next year approximately $2,555,000,000, it was estimated. The House had voted to cut the excess profits tax from 95 to 60 percent for 1946, saving corporations $1,088,000,000, and delay its elimination until Jan. 1, 1947.

In voting to end the excess profits tax this year the Senate committee struck out a House-approved 4 percent reduction of normal and surtax rates on corporations for 1946.

Committee Chairman Walter F. George (D., Ga.) estimated that the Senate committee revisions would save individual taxpayers next year the same amount recommended by the Treasury—$2,085,000,000.

The Senate committee followed House leadership, however, in rejecting the Treasury suggestion that this be accomplished by wiping out the 3 percent normal tax imposed on all income above $500 a year.

Senator George said he hoped to complete work on the bill late today—including reduction of excise taxes, repeal of the $5 automobile use tax, freezing the social security payroll tax and special benefits for small business and veterans.

New Hospitals O.K.'d

Washington, Oct. 18 (U.P.)—Gen. Omar N. Bradley, Veterans Administrator, announced today that President Truman has approved locations for 19 new hospitals and additions to 15 existing hospitals to be built at a total cost estimated at $125,000,000.

Cop Fires His Gun In Quarrel, Shoots Friend Accidentally

As the aftermath to a drinking session prompted by the death of his brother, a Queens fireman, Police Lt. Patrick Costello, 52, of 3054 Godwin Terrace, the Bronx, was suspended on departmental charges after accidentally shooting a friend today, police said.

The victim, Martin Morley, 48, of 78 W. 134th St., Manhattan, is in a serious condition with a bullet in his abdomen in the Columbia-Presbyterian Medical Center.

Police said Lieutenant Costello, who was off duty, went to see Morley at Logan's Tavern, 506 E. 181st St., the Bronx, where the latter is a bartender.

At about 3 a.m. today, police said, Lieutenant Costello had a row with a stranger over some change, took out his gun and pulled the trigger. The bullet ricocheted off the bar and struck Morley.

The officer's brother, James, 59, died Saturday in St. John's Hospital, Long Island City, a few hours after he fell from a fire pole. He was attached to Engine Company 263, 4206 Astoria Bouievard, Astoria, and lived at 49-11 21st Ave., Woodside.

Boston Bans Book, OK's Play

Boston, Oct. 18 (U.P.)—Though banned here in book form, "Strange Fruit" will open as a play at a Boston theater Oct. 29 after the city censor approved the play.

WEATHER MAN'S RECORD THREATENED BY STRIKE —SAVED BY TWO HOURS

The Weather Bureau would have missed its first forecast in 70 years today if a strike of workers who attend to boilers at 17 Battery Place had come two hours earlier. The boilers generate steam for operation of the building's electric system.

As it was, all weather reports, transmitted through teletype machines, were completed and in the office when the stoppage cut off electric current at 9:30 a.m. The strike, for higher wages, was quickly settled and service was resumed at 2 p.m.

If the walkout had continued, a Weather Bureau spokesman said, the forecast would have been made through data obtained at the bureau's LaGuardia Field office. Strikers were members of Locals 54 and 56 of the Brotherhood of Firemen, Oilers and Coal Passers.

8,000 Japs Released At Tule Lake Center

Tule Lake Japanese Center, Cal., Oct. 18 (U.P.)—More than half the 16,000 Japanese held here behind barbed wire for three and a half years were free to leave today but many remained.

Except for 4,200, who renounced U. S. citizenship and constitute a special case, most of the internees could walk out of the enclosure any time they wanted to.

Racing Results and Entries on Page 17

Sgt. Strobing's Story Starts in Eagle Monday

"My Last Days on the Rock," the thrilling and dramatic story of Sgt. Irving Strobing, the Brooklyn soldier who was the "last voice of Corregidor," will be published in the Brooklyn Eagle starting next Monday.

Sgt. Irving Strobing

Defeated, ill-equipped, disillusioned, the American troops in that Spring of 1942 held grimly to the rock that rose out of Manila Bay. But they, and their commanders, knew that their days were numbered. The Jap onslaughts grew more and more furious.

In those dismal, dreadful hours, Sgt. Irving Strobing of Brooklyn kept pounding at his wireless key.

Now Sgt. Irving Strobing has come home to Brooklyn. He has been hailed by his fellow citizens. And now, in the Brooklyn Eagle, he tells his own personal story of the last days on the Rock.

His story is not the story of Irving Strobing alone, for the sergeant is too modest for that. It is the story of the GI and the scared little nurse, of the ammunition carrier and the mess sergeant, of the handful of civilians and the remnants of spiritual leaders—in fact, the "little people" of the Rock.

Tells of Surrender

It is a story of real American heroism. He tells of General Wainwright's tearful and dramatic surrender. He tells of the "20-second smokers" and of the incessant air raids. He tells of the behavior of the children during the bombings and of the mysterious "singing bird of Omi."

Here is a Brooklyn boy's story of a dramatic chapter in our nation's military history.

Watch the Brooklyn Eagle for Monday, Oct. 22, when the series of articles, "My Last Days on the Rock," by Sgt. Irving Strobing, will begin.

Court Voids Names Of Many GOP Notables On Beldock Petition

Justice Stoddart today voided the signatures of many prominent Republicans on the Liberal party petitions designating Republican District Attorney George J. Beldock to succeed himself.

As the Brooklyn Supreme Court proceeding brought by the Democratic party got into its final phase he also voided many sheets of signatures gathered by well-known Republicans and reserved decision on Democratic requests to void others.

He also had before him this noon a compilation of 7,450 names of persons the Democrats say did not register last week, though their signatures are among the 11,788 on the Beldock Liberal party petition. A bona fide 5,000 signatures are required to sustain the petition.

Prior to submission of the alleged "not registered" list, Bernard Licht of the Democratic law committee tabulated the number of petition signatures already voided by the court at 4,380 and the number of disputed signatures on which the court had reserved decision at 2,133.

Signatures Ruled Out

Among signatures ruled out were the following:

Genevieve B. Earle, on the ground that a Republican Councilwoman did not mean what she stated in signing a petition that she would support a Liberal party candidate. (Abraham Roth had been the candidate when she signed; he withdrew in favor of Mr. Beldock.)

Transfer Tax Appraiser William S. Webb, Republican leader of the 17th A. D., and his wife, on the ground that the same hand had signed both signatures.

Assistant Attorney General Theodore Ostrow, an active Republican in the 18th A. D., on the ground that his signature appears on both lines 5 and 8 of sheet 806 of the petition.

Assistant District Attorney Irving Rollins and his wife on the ground that the same hand signed both names. Mr. Rollins resides at 225

Continued on Page 11

High Nazis Accused in Indictment

Berlin, Oct. 18 (U.P.)—The top 24 Nazis named in the indictment presented today by Allies four-Power tribunal were:

Reichsmarshal Hermann Goering—Former commander in chief of the German Air Force, a general in the Elite Guard and Storm Troops and former successor-designate to Hitler.

Goering Rudolf Hess

Rudolf Hess—Once designated as Hitler's seond choice for fuehrer and formerly deputy fuehrer until his flight to Britain in 1941.

Joachim von Ribbentrop—Former German Foreign Minister and a member of the secret cabinet council.

Von Ribbentrop Hjalmar Schacht

Franz von Papen—Former Ambassador to Austria at the time of the anschluss and later Turkey.

Walther Funk—Former Reichsminister of Economics and president of the Reichsbank.

Hjalmar Schacht—Former president of the Reichsbank and minister without portfolio.

Alfred Rosenberg—Official Nazi party philosopher and commissioner for occupied Russian territory.

Alfred Rosenberg Julius Streicher

Julius Streicher—Anti-Semitic leader.

Robert Ley—Leader of the Labor Front.

Hans Frank—Governor General of Poland.

Ernst Kaltenbrunner—Chief of the

Continued on Page 22

Dahl Pleads Innocent To Charge He Slew Dancer

Freshly shaved and dressed neatly in a tweed suit, Walter H. Dahl Jr., who, according to police, has confessed the brutal slaying of his roommate, Solon Burt Harger, internationally known dancer, pleaded not guilty today in General Sessions Court.

Dahl, who is 29, was arrested sometime after the torso of Harger had been found floating off Rockaway Point on Aug. 21.

The two men shared an apartment at 43 W. 46th St., Manhattan.

Remember Nazi Horrors, Veterans Are Told

Camp Cooke, Cal., Oct. 18 (U.P.)—Returned veterans of the European war should forget fancy German plumbing and scrubbed Teutonic faces and remember the horror camps, the 13th Armored Division's newspaper said editorially today.

In a special birthday ewition of The Black Cat, the division's paper, the editors warned veterans to be watchful to prevent Germany's return to militarism.

The paper is edited by Corp. Martin Abramson of Brooklyn.

London Dockers Still Out

London, Oct. 18 (U.P.)—Forty thousand dock workers continued their strike today in defiance of union leader's pleas to end the tieup.

Labor Group to Fly Home

Moscow, Oct. 18 (U.P.)—The first American Trade Union delegation to visit Soviet Russia in more than a score of years—representatives of the C. I. O.—will depart by air tomorrow for the United States.

Workers Flock to Piers --Tieup Seen Near End

The backbone of the port-paralyzing longshoremen's strike of insurgents in Brooklyn appeared to be broken today when 700 dock workers flocked back to Bush Terminal piers.

Shipping owners considered the number of men back on the job sufficient to reopen negotiations with union chiefs, headed by Joseph P. Ryan, president of the International Longshoremen's Association. There were additional reports of stevedores returning to work in Brooklyn. Police estimated the number working here at 2,300 and throughout the city at about 9,000.

A spokesman for the New York Port of Embarkation today said that in addition to the 700 workers reporting at Bush Terminal there were 300 men working at the Brooklyn Army Base and 1,000 at Staten

Continued on Page 11

10,000,000 BUTCHERED, ALLIES AVER

Loot and Destruction Set at 160 Billions in 4-Power Accusation

Washington, Oct. 18 (U.P.)—The Big Four Powers formally accused 24 top Nazi war criminals today of plotting and starting World War II, of murdering more than 10,000,000 civilians and prisoners of war and of plundering Europe on a scale unprecedented in history.

Exclusive of battle damage, they were charged with looting and destroying nearly $160,000,000,000 of property in Russia, France and Czechoslovakia.

In the killing of more than 10,000,000 innocent persons, including 5,700,000 Jews, they were charged with practicing systematic exterminations outside regular military operations.

Four-Nation Indictment

The formal charges were made by the joint international war crimes prosecutors of the United States, Britain, France and Russia in a 30,000-word indictment. The document was made public in Washington, London, Paris, Moscow and Berlin, and was handed to the Nazi criminals at Nuernberg.

The indictment is the first complete official record of Adolf Hitler's mad conspiracy to rule the world and of his era of Nazi terrorism.

It was divided into four counts. Twelve of the criminals, including Hermann Wilhelm Goering, Rudolf Hess and Joachim Ribbentrop, were accused on each count. The four counts:

1. Conspiracy—Formulation for execution of a common plan or conspiracy to commit crimes against peace, war crimes and crimes against humanity.

The Detailed Charges

2. Crimes Against Peace—Planning, preparing, initiating and waging wars of aggression in violation of

Continued on Page 22

5,700,000 SEEN SLAIN

Washington, Oct. 18 (U.P.)—Nazi Germany set out to exterminate the Jewish race in Europe—and nearly succeeded.

The war criminals indictment handed down today by the Big Four powers against 24 Nazi bigwigs painted a gruesome picture of that campaign of annihilation.

Of 9,600,000 Jews who lived in the parts of Europe dominated by the Nazis, the indictment said, "it is conservatively estimated that 5,700,000 have disappeared, most of them deliberately put to death by Nazi conspirators. Only remnants of the Jewish population of Europe remain."

WHERE TO FIND IT

	Page		Page
Bridge	18	Novel	18
Comics	21	Obituaries	11
Crossword	18	Our Champs	12
Currie	3	Pattern	14
Dr. Brady	10	Radio	21
Editorial	10	Real Estate	22
Financial	8	Society	13
Grin and Bear It	10	Sports	16, 17
Heffernan	10	Take My Word	10
Helen Worth	14	Theaters	8, 9
Horoscope	14	These Women	21
Leman	10	Tommy Holmes	16
Lindley	10	Uncle Ray	21
Mary Haworth	13	Want Ads	18-20
Movies	8, 9	Women	13
Music	9		

ERASMUS HALL SMOTHERED BY BOYS HIGH, 25-6

5,000 See Mullermen Carve Out 16th Victory of Traditional Series —Faske's Passes Yield Two Scores

By JAMES J. MURPHY

Getting the jump shortly after the echo of the whistle opening hostilities had died out, Boys High conquered Erasmus Hall in the 41st game of their 47-year-old traditional football series before 5,000 fans at Boys High Field yesterday afternoon, 25—6. Despite the setback, Erasmus Hall still holds an advantage, 21 triumphs to 16, four of the clashes terminating in stalemates.

ALAS FOR THIS PASS which Frank Sniadack of Columbia is batting down. The toss was made by Jim Cox of Colgate on the Lion's 15-yard stripe.

The Red and Black pushed over two of its touchdowns in the first quarter, Mel Walwyn cracking across from the one-yard line and Alex Baldwin taking Artie Haft's 20-yard pass in the end zone. Jerry (Skippy) Faske passed to Irv Rappaport for the other two scores, one in the third quarter, covering seven yards, and the other in the final chapter that was good for 15 yards.

Erasmus was saved from a shutout when it inaugurated a 90-yard march in the second quarter that was climaxed with Wally Gally bullying his way past the last white stripe from one yard out.

Boys' Drive Clicks

Forced to manipulate deep in its own territory after the game, starting kickoff and plagued by three offside penalties, Sandy Markowitz of Erasmus Hall was forced to kick out of danger from his 10-yard line to Haft, who ran it back five yards to midfield. Then the Wally Muller machine began to hit on all cylinders to reach its objective. The drive was sparked by Walwyn and Haft, who negotiated 36 yards between them. Faske and Walwyn advanced the oval to the 10, whereup two offside penalties were inflicted against Erasmus, resting the oval on the one-foot line, whence Walwyn scored. Danny Glassman made good on the conversion from placement.

Late in the quarter, Markowitz was again compelled to kick from his own goal line and Faske took it on the 30 and returned to the 15. After Walwyn picked up a yard, Haft skirted one of the flanks for 14 yards and an apparent second touchdown. The play was nullified and Boys penalized for a back in motion. It made no difference. On the subsequent play Haft fell back and dropped a perfect strike in Baldwin's arms in the end zone.

Erasmus Hall got back in the ball game with its second period score. Rappaport had put the Buff and Blue in the hole with a punt that went outside on the 10-yard line. Markowitz on three plays and Gally on one negotiated midfield. Markowitz then took to the air for four successive passes, connecting with Walt Noeri twice and Howie Beldock and Gally each once to make the 17-yard line. After getting to the one on two plays and failing on the third, Markowitz turned over the task to Gally, who plunged over.

Recover Fumble

Boys High sealed Erasmus Hall's doom in the third quarter. Captain Jimmy Ricca recovered an Erasmus fumble on the Flatbushers' 16-yard line. Walwyn and Rappaport lugged for nine yards and Faske then faded and aerialed into Rappaport's arms in the end zone.

In the final quarter, Boys High delivered the crusher. Haft carried back Markowitz's punt from midfield to the 33. Jack Payne moved the ball 18 yards nearer the goal line. The Faske and Rappaport combine repeated their act for the final touchdown and the second straight defeat of the season suffered by Erasmus Hall, the defending mythical champion of Brooklyn.

The lineup:

Pos.	Erasmus (6)	Boys High (25)
L.E.	Swayman	McDonough
L.T.	Harris	Radist
L.G.	Schneider	Melford
C.	Cohen	Welcome
R.G.	Donnelly	Hopewell
R.T.	Kane	Ricca
R.E.	Beldock	Rappaport
Q.B.	Boeri	Baldwin
L.H.	Sandy Markowitz	Haft
R.H.	Jones	Faske
F.B.	Gally	Walwyn

Score by periods:

Boys High	13	0	6	6	25
Erasmus	0	6	0	0	6

Touchdowns—Walwyn, Baldwin, Rappaport 2, Gally.
Point after touchdown—Glassman (placement).
Substitutes: Boys High—Fazio, Simonelli, Vogel, Hadad, Trafficante, Di Francisci, Husver, Pascarella, Glassman, Pisano, Barbaro, Payne, Horowitz, Kubiak, Seymour Markowitz. Erasmus Hall—Greshefsky, Sadowitz, Torre, Messana, Finkelstein, De Angelis, Washor and Gold.
Time of quarters—10 minutes.
Referee—Duke Wellington, Springfield. Umpire—Barney Cohen, N. Y. U. Head Linesman—Lew Drummond, Savage.

T. C. U. Wins, 13—12

Fort Worth, Texas, Oct. 20 (U.P.)—Texas Christian struck for 13 points in the first period today and then fought off desperate Texas A. & M. rallies for three quarters to sneak through with a 13-to-12 football victory before 25,000 spectators.

Brooklyn College Triumphs on Late Pass, 13 to 7

Special to the Brooklyn Eague

Amherst, Mass., Oct. 20—Halfback Herb Wilner returned to the Brooklyn College backfield after a two-week layoff and added enough power to the Kingsmen's T formation to give the unbeaten Maroon a 13—7 win over Massachusestts State College this afternoon before 2,000 onlookers. The Statesmen held on grimly to a 7—6 lead in the third quarter, but Wilner culminated a 62-yard fourth period Brooklyn march by heaving a 25-yard touchdown pass to Sherman Smith for the victory.

The Brooks drew first blood. After five minutes 205-pound fullback Sam Klein, alternating with Wilner and Morty Kunstler on running plays, sliced off his own right tackle from the two. Kalaka's attempted conversion was foiled by a poor pass from center.

Statesmen Gain Edge

A few minutes later the Kingsmen, paced by a 19-yard jaunt by Klein, drove to the State 15, but the offensive fizzled when a Len Mintzes-to-Kalaka aerial was dropped in the end zone.

The Statesmen came roaring back in the second stanza to carry down to the Brooklyn 17 on some flashy ball toting by halfback Dick Tomchick. The attack, however, went for naught when Kunstler chalked up the Brooks' fourth pass interception by snaring a Tomchick toss on the visitors' 10. Stan Struzziero and Ed Kosierek then led a 78-yard march in the third session for a score. Al Snyder's point from placement gave the New Englanders a 7—6 margin.

The lead was short-lived, however, as Brooklyn put on its clinching drive after an exchange of kicks. Kunstler and Wilner carried to a first down on the Flatbush 48. The latter cracked tackle for 24 yards. When the Kingsmen's attack stalled on the 25, the bespectacled Wilner passed to acting captain Smith,

Continued on Following Page

FELDMAN RUNS WILD AS TUFTS WINS, 70-0

Medford, Mass., Oct. 20 (U.P.)—George (Tubby) Feldman, a navy V-12 student from Erasmus Hall High School led the touchdown parade today as his Tufts College teammates massacred a makeshift Boston University football team 70 to 0 before 4,000 fans at the Tufts oval.

Feldman went around the end or ploughed through a war-veteran studded Boston line to score all four touchdowns of the first half.

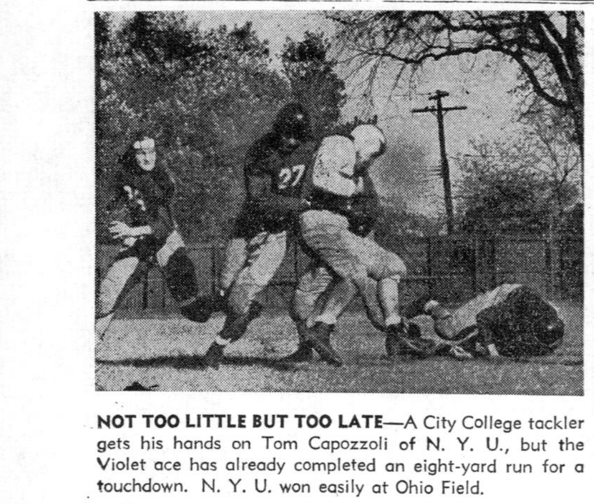

NOT TOO LITTLE BUT TOO LATE—A City College tackler gets his hands on Tom Capozzoli of N. Y. U., but the Violet ace has already completed an eight-yard run for a touchdown. N. Y. U. won easily at Ohio Field.

75,000 SEE PURDUE UPSET OHIO ST., 35-13

12-Game Buckeye Streak Shattered— DeMoss Paces Drive

Columbus, Ohio, Oct. 20 (U.P.) — Purdue's Boilermakers boiled over today, stunning Ohio State with a wide-open type of football they hadn't seen before to hand Carroll Widdoes the first defeat of his Big Ten coaching career, 35 to 13, before 75,000 fans.

The Ohioans, riding a 12-game victory streak, had been rated two-touchdown favorites, but Coach Cecil Isbeil's Indiana technicians lost no time in crossing up the odds-makers.

Hero of the game to Boilermaker fans—and the devil himself to Buckeye partisans—was Bob DeMoss a boy with an arm and an aim.

Professor's Son Scores

It was DeMoss to Bill Canfield on passes twice for touchdowns—one for 37 yards and another for eight—Canfield, son of a Purdue professor, filtering through the vaunted Buckeye line like a spook on a holiday.

Through the upset, Purdue and Ohio State switched roles in the Big Ten race, with the Boilermakers becoming title co-favorites with Minnesota.

The Purdue line, led by tackle Tom Hughes, stopped the Ohio State offense colder than a night watchman's lunch. With no blocking in front of them, neither Paul Sarringhaus nor Dick Fisher stood a chance.

The two touchdown passes from DeMoss to Canfield came in the first seven minutes of the period and State fans hardly had time to wring out their hankies before Robert Dove's kick was blocked and recovered in the end zone by Hughes for a safety to give Purdue a 22—0 lead at halftime.

Freshman Leads Rally

Harold Daugherty, third-string freshman halfback, entered in the final period for State and threw a touchdown pass that went to Bud Kessler on the two-yard line.

In three minutes, Captain Cody got that one back for Purdue, first going through center for 22 yards to the Ohio 43, then the rest of the way for the final Purdue touchdown.

Daugherty set up Ohio State's last touchdown with a pass which end, Tom Watson, caught on the Purdue 22 for a 32-yard gain. Third-stringer Chuck Gandee angled through tackle and scurried to the 7 where he brushed aside the tacklers and heaved a lateral to Alex Verdova, who carried it on over.

Pos.	OHIO STATE	PURDUE
L.E.	Kessler	Heck
L.T.	Thomas	O'Brien
L.G.	Amline	Crowe
C.	Lininger	Kodba
R.G.	Redd	Logan
R.T.	Dixon	Hughes
R.E.	Watson	Maloney
Q.	Priday	DeMoss
L.H.	Krall	Canfeild
R.H.	Fisher	Adams
F.B.	Cline	Cody

Ohio State	0	0	0	13	13
Purdue	6	16	6	7	35

Touchdowns—Cody 3, Canfield 2, Kessler, Verdova. Safety: Hughes. Points after touchdowns: Hughes 3, Schnjttker. Substitutions—Ohio State: Ends, Gorby, Steinberg, Wright; tackles, Winters, Hamilton, Schnittker, Fazio; guards, McGinnis, Roe; center, O'Dea, Baker; backs, Ehrsam, Dove, Fout, Sarringhaus, Daugherty, Verdova, Marshall, Biel, Gandee, Brown. Purdue—Ends: Fox, Gilbert; tackle, O'Bryan; guards, Clymer, Glaesner, Lenczyk; center, Lockwood; backs, Deem, Mihal, Dobrzykowski, Dale.

Officials—Referee, Mike Layden, Notre Dame; umpire, R. W. Finsterwald, Syracuse; field judge, William Orwig; head linesman, Roy Knipschild, Chicago.

Indiana's 'One-Two' Drubs Iowa, 52–20

Iowa City, Ia., Oct. 20 (U.P.)—Indiana's powerful Hoosiers used their famous one-two punch to wallop Iowa, 52 to 20, today and remain undefeated in the Big Ten football race.

Iowa, in dropping its third straight conference game, was helpless before the ruthless running of Freshman George Taliaferro, brilliant Negro halfback, and the riflelike passing of Ben Riamondi, veteran quarterback from Erasmus Hall.

Indiana piled up 40 points in the first half as Taliaferro, the Gray, Ind., galloper, sprinted 74 and 63 yards to touchdowns, Raimondi, directing Indiana's "cockeyed T" attack, called his own signals in the second half, pitching two touchdown passes in the third period.

Reddick Whips Zivic at Grove

Joe Reddick, Paterson, 153½, pounded out an impressive decision over former welterweight champion Corp. Fritzie Zivic, 152¾, in the feature 10-rounder before a capacity house at the Ridgewood Grove last night.

In the six-round semi-final Jimmy Davis, 158, Pittsburgh, defeated Johnny Smith, 155, Boston. In other sixes Marty Clark, 203, Astoria, stopped Jim Davenport, 187½, New York, 2:18 of the second round; Nick Primiani, 137, Montreal, defeated Julian Malaves, 141, New York.

In the two fours, Benny Davis, 159, Port Chester, N. Y., defeated Johnny King, 154, Harlem, and Ellie Simley, 138½, Harlem, defeated Jimmy Cagni, 136½, Brooklyn.

TRIPPI HANDCUFFED, GEORGIA BOWS, 32-0

Athens, Ga., Oct. 20 (U.P.)—Louisiana State bottled up Charlie Trippi today and scored a runaway 32 to 0 victory over Georgia before a homecoming crowd of 25,000 disappointed fans.

The contest that had been billed as a one-man show featuring Trippi, back from three years of military service, turned out to be just the opposite. LSU'S fine host of backs surged behind a sharp Tiger line and netted 336 yards rushing to Georgia's 30.

Lions' Late Spree Rips Colgate, 31-7; Rossides Scores on 72-Yard Run

'ALTER COWIE of Colgate goes through for first down in first quarter against Columbia.

Victors Trail In First Period, Tied at Half

By RALPH TROST

Columbia's rampant Lions did some more first-half stumbling and fumbling yesterday against Colgate but, as per 1945 custom, it all turned out okay as the young, occasionally erring but very dashing young 'uns mowed down the Red Raiders from the Chenango, 31 to 7, before just as many people as could possibly be jammed into Baker Field—about 35,000.

The Lions got into trouble real early, let Colgate pound 70 yards, mostly from the ancient double wing back formation, for a touchdown, committed some sorry bobbles and were thoroughly outpassed the whole game. Yet they won, and won handily.

Colgate Fumble Costly

After the sloppy start in which the 200-pound Colgate line ripped and tore Columbia to shreds, the Lions recovered their composure and with Brooklynite Gene Rossides at his dashing best, tied the score on his vivid 72-yard run, went ahead in the third period, 10 to 7, when Gene held the ball for Len Wills' 23-yard placement and put the game on ice by recovering Glen Treichler's dropped punt on the 20 and pushing on from there in three surges.

The latter score, at the opening of the last period, was concluded with Lou Kusserow's pile-driver smack off the Colgate right tackle. Don Bleasdale, replacement for the ailing Wal Kondratovich, who was rushed to the Presbyterian Hospital Friday night with an appendicitis attack—the very same thing that happened to lineman Joe Karas a week ago Friday—and Bill Olson came through with the other touchdowns.

With about three minutes to go, Bleasdale grabbed Jim Cox's booming punt and zoomed up the sideline for 65 yards and a score. A minute later Olson intercepted Pete Leyden's long pass and, with perfect aplomb, went zigging along 57 yards for a score.

Biggest Victory

Len Will, just back at Columbia after almost three years in service, converted after each touchdown—except Olson's. Bill took care of the extra point himself by bucking over as Colgate streamed in to block the kick Will was expected to attempt.

There were a lot of hands in Columbia's victory over Colgate—and only the second triumph over the Red Raiders in 13 tries. But the hand that was most forceful in keeping Columbia unbeaten and untied through four games was Rossides.

Columbia not only was trailing 7-0 after end Dick Birkins took Cox's pass on the one yard line and wiggled over for a touchdown, but was in trouble again when Andy Caruso fumbled right into Birkins' hands at midfield. Gene took a lot of the pressure off when Columbia finally forced a kick. After Kusserow peeled off about eight yards on a plunge, Rossides went for the whole piece, all 72 yards, for a touchdown on Columbia's pet play which looks like a latteral starting out but winds up with Gene crashing off tackle.

When this run started, Rossides didn't seem headed for any great run but with that slick change of pace of his, he wheedled his way through two, then three would-be tacklers—and then it was a chase with Rossides gone like the wind

Continued on Following Page

THERE HE GOES!—Gene Rossides, former Erasmus Hall star, on his way for 72 yards and a Columbia touchdown in first period of game with Colgate at Baker Field yesterday. Rossides was standout in Columbia's 31 to 7 victory.

54,875 Watch Navy Conquer Ga. Tech, 20-6

Baltimore, Oct. 20 (U.P.)—Opportunist Navy got all the breaks before a capacity crowd of 54,875 tonight and converted them into a 20-to-6 victory over outlucked but never out-fought Georgia Tech.

The battling Georgians had one consolation—a small one. They became the first team to score on unbeaten and untied Navy, which racked up its fourth straight victory. Navy's perfect defensive record was spoiled in the third period when fleet-footed Jack Peek raced 70 yards for a touchdown.

Navy needed the breaks to win, for the Georgians held supremacy over the Bluejackets on the ground and in the air.

Navy's first two touchdowns were luck-annointed and the third stemmed from a break. On the other hand, luck ran out completely against the Georgians who repeatedly threatened—once reaching the

Continued on Following Page

Grant, Cestone Set Golf Pace At North Hills

Malcolm Grant and Michael Cestone of Crestmont, medalists, led the field into the semi-final round of the North Hills member-guest golf tournament yesterday by defeating Charles Cornibert and Phillip Farley of Toronto, 4 and 3, in the morning play and Frank Cryan and Frank Strafaci of Shore View, 4 and 3, in the afternoon.

Grant and Cestone will meet Dr. J. Feminella and William Ballantyne of Hempstead in the upper half of the semi-finals today while Arthur Rudert Jr. and Dr. Ray Bowles of Cherry Valley will face C. E. Eble Jr. and Arnold Gray of Clearview in the lower half.

Dr. Feminella and Ballantyne defeated Marcel Corniber and Frank Paley of Woodmere, 1 up, and

Continued on Following Page

So. California Wallops College of Pacific, 52—0

Los Angeles, Oct. 20 (U.P.)—The University of Southern California, without throwing a single forward pass, rolled mercilessly over the College of Pacific 17-man football squad today, 52 to 0, before 10,000 chilled fans at the Los Angeles Coliseum.

Southern California scored before the game was three minutes old as a result of a bad pass from center. The Trojans paraded over the double stripe virtually at will after that.

Rangers Lose, 6—1

Winnipeg, Canada, Oct. 20 (U.P.)—The Chicago Black Hawks scored their second straight exhibition victory over the Rangers today by trouncing the New Yorkers, 6 to 1.

A. L. Hockey Results

Pittsburgh	3	2	2	7
Buffalo	0	4	1	5

A SAFETY PIN — Terry Brennan of Notre Dame is pinned behind his goal line for a safety in its game with Pitt yesterday. But the Irish won handily.

FOOTBALL RESULTS

Local

31	Columbia	Colgate	7
47	N. Y. U.	C. C. N. Y.	0

East

55	Army	Melville P. T. Base	13
13	Brooklyn College	Mass. State	7
18	Connecticut	Maine	12
19	Drexel	Haverford	0
25	Holy Cross	Brown	0
25	Kings Point M. M. A.	Lafayette	7
6	Lehigh	Muhlenberg	0
20	Navy	Georgia Tech	6
39	Notre Dame	Pittsburgh	9
46	Penn State	Bucknell	7
39	Rutgers	Rhode Island St.	7
70	Tufts	Boston U.	0
18	U. S. Sub Base	Harvard	7
21	V. P. I.	Maryland	13
46	Army J. V.	R. P. I.	0

South

25	Alabama	Tennessee	7
20	Auburn	Tulane	14
32	L. S. U.	Georgia	0
16	Mississippi St.	Maxwell Field	6
20	N. Carolina	Cherry Pt. Marines	14
21	Southern Methodist	Rice	18
49	Southern U.	Arkansas A. & M.	0
34	Texas	Arkansas	7
13	Texas Christian	Texas A. & M.	12
19	Vanderbilt	Kentucky	6
13	William & Mary	V. M. I.	9

West

56	Butler	Manchester	0
20	Case	Ohio Wesleyan	14
7	Central	Albion	0
6	Earlham	Franklin	0
52	Indiana	Iowa	20
27	Iowa State	Nebraska	7
27	Lawrence	Carroll	12
34	Miami	Ohio U.	0
27	Michigan State	Wayne	7
30	Minnesota	Northwestern	7
41	Missouri	Kansas State	7
26	Oberlin	De Pauw	14
39	Oklahoma	Kansas	7
35	Purdue	Ohio State	13
40	Tulsa	Nevada	0
7	Wisconsin	Illinois	7
39	Godman Field	Lincoln	7
13	Illinois Wes.	De Kalb Trs.	0
27	Lawrence	Carrol	12
20	N. Dakota	N. Dakota A. & M.	12
25	Springfield	Rockhurst	0

Far West

31	Colorado	Colorado College	0
46	Idaho	Montana State	0
13	Occidental	Pomono	12
46	Oklahoma A. & M.	Utah	6
26	Oregon	Washington St.	13
52	S. California	Col. of Pacific	0
13	Utah St.	Colorado St.	0
13	Washington	Oregon St.	0

SCHOLASTIC

6	Adams	Xavier	6
25	Boys High	Erasmus	6
27	Brooklyn Tech.	Lafayette	0
37	Curtis	Far Rockaway	0
20	Lincoln	Tilden	0
44	Manual	New Dorp	7
6	Poly Prep	Power Memorial	6
19	St. Francis J.V.	Chaminade J.V.	6
33	Brooklyn Prep	Fordham Prep	6

Betting Records Fall in Jamaica Getaway Card

Chief Barker of the B. F. Whitaker menage, and Lord Boswell, member of the Maine Chance Farm, carried off top honors yesterday on the closing day of the Jamaica meeting. Above the pair hovers Eric Guerin, who scored victories in the two feature events. Chief Barker accounted for the inaugural of the Roamer Handicap and he was driven out to the last ounce to beat Petrol Point and Buzfuz by three parts of a length. Lord Boswell had an easier time, for he skipped across the finish by an advantage of five lengths.

Two world's betting records and one track wagering mark were tumbled as 46,715 free-spending fans poured $4,349,835 through the mutuel machines.

The total handle was the highest ever registered for a seven-race card, topping the old standard of $4,-151,612 set at Jamaica last Saturday, though about $800,000 short of the eight-race card record. The world mark of $240,202 for a daily double pool was eclipsed by today's play of $251,682.

The handle on the fourth race, $760,112, set a new high for the Jamaica track. It was the second highest one-race play in New York, trailing only a figure of $763,127, hung up at Belmont.

The Roamer Handicap furnished fireworks throughout the trip of a mile and furlong. Buzfuz, as usual, cut out a sizzling pace and the light-weighted Bonfire was at his throat latch for a few furlongs. Right behind them was the doughty Chief Barker stepping along desperately to cut down the few lengths advantage of his leaders. Entering the final alley the scene grew intense in action. Chief Barker was a few strides behind Buzfuz with Petrol Point entering the arena.

Guerin never allowed the Chief to take a deep breath and hustled him along at a terrific gait. Buzfuz, which had regained its second wind, closed in on Chief Barker as did Petrol Point. The trio swept down the strip fighting out every stride. The Chief had his muzzle in front and kept that small space in his favor as he came closer and closer to the wire. The trio never gained or lost an inch and as they swept over the line the Chief was in front. Chief Barker paid $7.80, with Petrol Point $15.40 and Buzfuz $5.10. Chief Barker stepped over the nine furlongs in 1:58 1-5.

Mrs. Jake Freedman's Fire War-

Continued on Following Page

Brown Trampled By Crusaders, 25-0

Providence, R. I., Oct. 20 (U.P.)—Stan Koslowski and Holy Cross enhanced their ambitions together today for recognition as the best back and the best football team in New England, the brilliant hard-running war veteran sparking the Crusaders to a 25 to 0 victory over Brown at Brown Field. It was the fourth straight victory for Holy Cross.

Playing with an injured leg, ex-sailor Koslowski put on one of his greatest exhibitions of running and passing as he scored two touchdowns himself and passed to a third. A native Rhode Islander, the tow-headed triple-threat man got a tremendous ovation from the 25,000 fans when he left the game in the third period.

Sharing a little of the spotlight with Koslowski was left end Jim Dieckelman, a 17-year-old Holy Cross freshman, whose alert recovery of two Brown fumbles deep in scoring territory set up the Crusaders' early touchdowns. In the third period, Dieckelman raced downfield 33 yards to pull in Koslowski's tremendous pass on the Brown three yard line and then stepped across for the tally.

Byers Dashes 67 Yards

With the injured Koslowski resting in the final period, another freshman, Joe Byers, moved into the running spot and sprinted 67 yards on an off-tackle slant for the Purple's last marker.

The first two Holy Cross touchdown jaunts began on Brown's 30-yard line. Koslowski passed to the 10, and then went on the receiving end of Byers' aerial for the opening score. Shortly afterward, the

Continued on Following Page

Fighting Pitt Bows To Irish, 39-9

Pittsburgh, Oct. 20 (U.P.)—Notre Dame's undefeated Irish scored a 39 to 9 victory over a willing but inexperienced Pittsburgh eleven today before 66,000 fans at Pitt Stadium.

The Notre Dame attack jelled slowly and Pitt was in the game for the first two periods as the Panthers put up a stubborn defense. The Irish scored two touchdowns in the first half but had their hands full fighting off a determined but green Pitt Panther.

FRANK RUGGERIO of Notre Dame (arrow) stopped after six-yard gain against Pittsburgh. Notre Dame won, 39 to 9.

Notre Dame's defense gained momentum as the game went into the second half with Quarterback Francis Dancewicz showing the way. The Irish attack reached its full power in the final period when they put over three scores. Dancewicz definitely was the boss of Notre Dame's destiny as he passed for two touchdowns and set up a third.

Ruggerio Starts It Off

Notre Dame gained an early lead with Frank Ruggerio plunging for a touchdown after Dancewicz passed to Phil Colella to put the ball on the one-yard line in the first period. Pitt picked up two points on a safety in the second period when Jack Smodick put the Irish back on their four-yard line with a coffin-corner punt and Bill McPeak broke through to down Terry Brennan in his end zone.

Before the half ended a pass interference ruling gave Notre Dame the ball on Pitt's 10 and Dancewicz passed to End Bill Leonard for a score. In the third period, the Notre Dame field general flipped another touchdown pass with Elmer Angsman snaring the ball in the flat zone and running 28 yards.

The Pitt defense fell apart in the final period. Angsman plunged over from the one after Notre Dame recovered a Pitt fumble to start the parade. John Panelli cracked through tackle for 18 yards and another score. Then Ernest Virock intercepted a Pitt pass and sprinted 40 yards for a touchdown.

Pitt's parting shot was a 40-yard pass play, with Smodic passing to Herb Douglas for a score.

Pos.	PITT	NOTRE DAME
L.E.	Skladany	Skogland
L.T.	Chuffi	Miesczkowski
L.G.	Mattioli	Mastrangelo
C.	Koch	Walsh
R.G.	Ranii	Roval
R.T.	Johnson	Berezney
R.E.	McPeak	Cronin
Q.B.	Wolff	Dancewicz
L.H.	Robinson	Colella
R.H.	Wertman	Angsman
F.B.	Ralko	Ruggerio

Pitt	0	2	0	7	9
Notre Dame	6	6	7	20	39

Touchdowns—Ruggerio, Leonard, Angsman 2, Panelli, Virok, Douglas. Safety—Brennan. Points after touchdown—Krivik 3, Mattioli.

Substitutes—Pitt: Ends, Banasick, Nihm, Faoroni; tackles, Rozanski, Cerrone, De Frank; guards, Polach; center, Stopfard, Smith; backs, Roussos, Zimmovan, Temenoff, Smodic, Linelli, Douglas, Matthews; Notre Dame: Ends, Leonard, Burnett, Flynn, Bush, Opela; tackles, Fischer, Glaab, Russell, Vainisi; guards, Potter, Scott, Fallon, Fay, Lesko, Oracko; centers, Grothaus, Virok; backs, Zehler, Gompers, Gasparella, Panelli, Agnone, Yonto, Slovak, Ratterman, Brennan.

Officials — Referee, Dr. R. W. Hougel, Marquette; umpire, Ernie Vick, Michigan; field judge, Dr. David E. Reese, Dennison; linesman, Herbert S. Steger, Michigan.

Penn State Ahead

Lewisburg, Pa., Oct. 20 (U.P.)—Penn State's big and powerful Nittany Lions spoiled Bucknell University's homecoming today by clawing the Bisons, 46 to 7, before 7,500 fans at Memorial Stadium. It was State's first victory over Bucknell at Lewisburg since 1909.

Army Eleven Spots Melville 13 Points, Then Rolls Up 55

West Point, N. Y., Oct. 20 (U.P.)—In the manner made famous by the original "expendables"—the motor torpedo boats in the early days of the Philippine war—the Melville P. T. Base football team today stymied a more powerful opponent for a short time. Then Army rolled to a 55—13 victory.

The Torpedo Base boys wanted this game as a "going-away" present—the base closed today. A victory over national champion Army would have been the upset of the year. With Army's second team playing, John Welsh of Melville ran to two touchdowns in the first period, the first on a 30-yard run after Tom (Shorty) McWilliams fumbled for Army. His second was for 60 yards.

But the fun was over then for Melville. Army's first team came into the game and Glenn Davis and Felix Blanchard, called the best one-two punch in football, were just too much.

Army had the ball as the second period started and on the third play Davis went 41 yards to score. Dick Walterhouse missed the kick for goal but made six others. Davis, the speedster, and Blanchard, the power runner, collaborated for the next touchdown, the latter scoring. The same pattern worked for two more touchdowns—Davis, cutting, darting and driving, went 77 yards for a score and then Blanchard powered over from the six after Army recovered a fumble.

Coach Earl Blaik kept his first

Continued on Following Page

Kentucky Trails

Nashville, Tenn., Oct. 20 (U.P.)—Vanderbilt capitalized on the breaks today to defeat Kentucky, 19 to 6, before a crowd of 12,000.

NYU Trounces CCNY For First Victory, 47-0

By HAROLD CONRAD

After being belted around by Temple and Boston College the last two successive Saturdays, N. Y. U. got over its inferiority complex at the expense of City College at Ohio Field yesterday, where they whacked the wilting Beavers, 47—0, before a crowd of 7,000. Although there is a somewhat dubious distinction in beating City College, N. Y. U. was able to brag about its first victory of the season today. It was also the first game in which they had scored. Temple knocked them off, 59—0, and Boston College did it by 28—0.

It was the fourth loss of the year for City College, which is about par at this stage of the season, and it doesn't look as though they are going to mar their record of two years' standing by winning a game. It was a toss-up as to which was weaker, their offense of defense. City showed a deficit for total yardage gained. They made 19 yards on forward passing and lost 30 yards rushing, which left them 11 yards in the red.

N. Y. U. didn't take much time and it didn't seem too much effort as it rung up a touchdown in the first eight plays of the game. Two plays after the kick-off, Tom Capozzoli heaved a pass to Cy Kuppersmith in City's 46, who ripped off 42 yards to the Violet 12. After a few cracks at the line, Johnny Melone went over to score from the five.

City Line Folds Up

City's weight handicap started to show in the second quarter as their weak line collapsed. Kuppersmith took a kick on the Beaver 30 and ran to the 18. Two off-tackle plays carried them to the seven. Then N. Y. U. was penalized 15 yards for having a back in motion illegally but Melone run right back to the five yard line on the next play. Then Kuppersmith tossed a short pass to Melone that was good for a touchdown.

The Violets squeezed another touchdown just before the half

Continued on Following Page

TRUMAN PLEDGES U. S. MIGHT TO PRESERVE WORLD JUSTICE

7 ★★★★★★★ Complete

BROOKLYN EAGLE

WEATHER—Clear, cool tonight; sunny, warmer tomorrow.

105th YEAR—No. 294—DAILY and SUNDAY BROOKLYN, N. Y., SATURDAY, OCTOBER 27, 1945 — Entered Brooklyn P. O. 2d Class Mail Matter — 3 CENTS IN NEW YORK CITY ELSEWHERE 4 CENTS

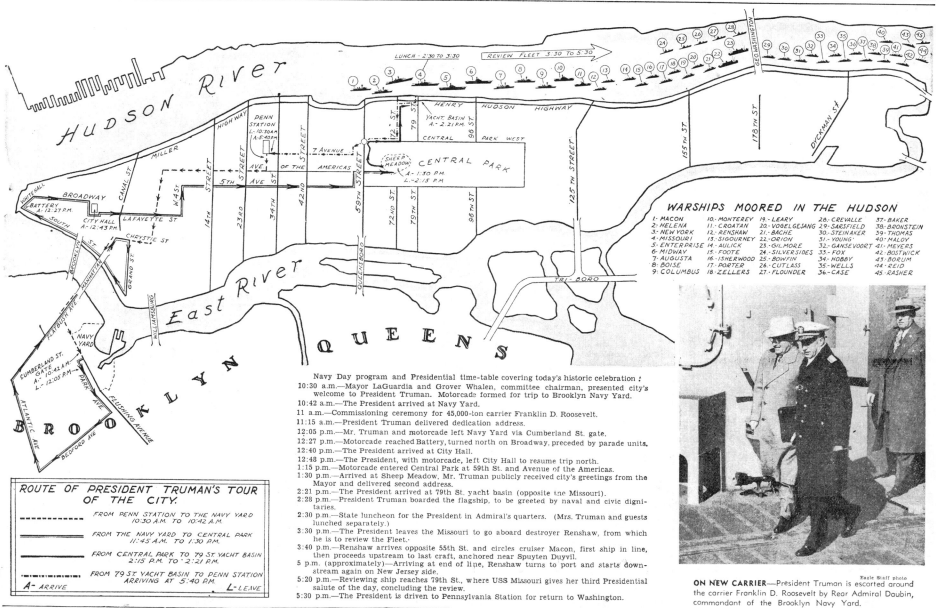

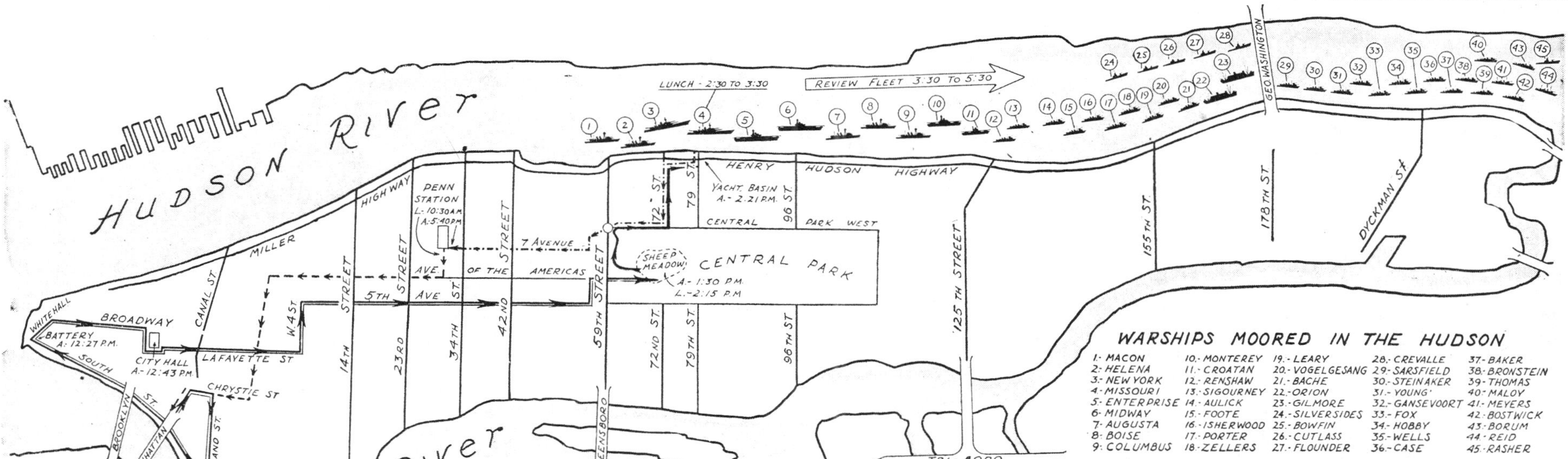
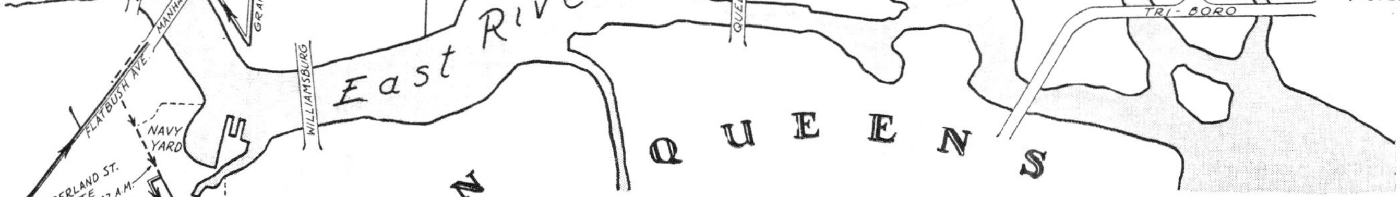
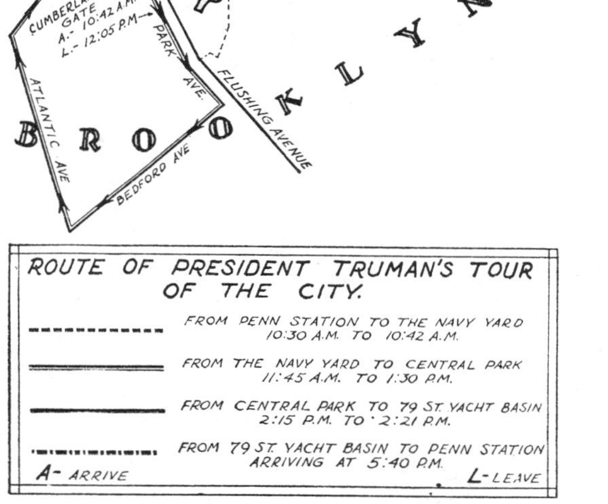

Navy Day program and Presidential time-table covering today's historic celebration:

10:30 a.m.—Mayor LaGuardia and Grover Whalen, committee chairman, presented city's welcome to President Truman. Motorcade formed for trip to Brooklyn Navy Yard.

10:42 a.m.—The President arrived at Navy Yard.

11 a.m.—Commissioning ceremony for 45,000-ton carrier Franklin D. Roosevelt.

11:15 a.m.—President Truman delivered dedication address.

12:05 p.m.—Mr. Truman and motorcade left Navy Yard via Cumberland St. gate.

12:27 p.m.—Motorcade reached Battery, turned north on Broadway, preceded by parade units.

12:40 p.m.—The President arrived at City Hall.

12:48 p.m.—The President, with motorcade, left City Hall to resume trip north.

1:15 p.m.—Motorcade entered Central Park at 59th St. and Avenue of the Americas.

1:30 p.m.—Arrived at Sheep Meadow, Mr. Truman publicly received city's greetings from the Mayor and delivered second address.

2:21 p.m.—The President arrived at 79th St. yacht basin (opposite the Missouri).

2:28 p.m.—President Truman boarded the flagship, to be greeted by naval and civic dignitaries.

2:30 p.m.—State luncheon for the President in Admiral's quarters. (Mrs. Truman and guests lunched separately.)

3:30 p.m.—The President leaves the Missouri to go aboard destroyer Renshaw, from which he is to review the Fleet.

3:40 p.m.—Renshaw arrives opposite 55th St. and circles cruiser Macon, first ship in line, then proceeds upstream to last craft, anchored near Spuyten Duyvil.

5 p.m. (approximately)—Arriving at end of line, Renshaw turns to port and starts downstream again on New Jersey side.

5:20 p.m.—Reviewing ship reaches 79th St., where USS Missouri gives her third Presidential salute of the day, concluding the review.

5:30 p.m.—The President is driven to Pennsylvania Station for return to Washington.

Eagle Staff photo

ON NEW CARRIER—President Truman is escorted around the carrier Franklin D. Roosevelt by Rear Admiral Daubin, commandant of the Brooklyn Navy Yard.

Army Scores on 1st Play Against Duke

McWilliams Cuts Through Tackle For 54 Yards—Navy, Penn Battle

ARMY—DUKE

Pos.	Army	Duke
L.E.	Pitzer	Mote
L.T.	Coulter	Sharkey
L.G.	Gerometta	Perini
C.	Fusion	Crowder
R.G.	Reen	Knotts
R.T.	Nemetz	Marshall
R.E.	Foldberg	Austin
Q.B.	Tucker	Krisza
L.H.	Davis	Clark
R.H.	McWilliams	Carver
F.	Blanchard	McCully

Referee—Harry Dayhoff, Bucknell. Umpire—A. Paul Menton, Loyola. Field Judge—Gabe Hill, Wofford. Linesman—Carl Reed, Springfield.

Army's football team, seeking its 14th consecutive victory over a two-year span, was favored to defeat a strong Duke team at the Polo Grounds today.

Both clubs were at peak strength with Army out to better Navy's showing over the Southerners. Navy turned back Duke, without the services of several star players, 21 to 0 earlier in the season.

The Blue Devils gave Army its second hardest game last year, finally succumbing 27 to 7 after holding a 7 to 6 half-time lead. crowd of 50,000 was present.

FIRST PERIOD—Army kicked off to Duke's 32 and the Blue Devils, losing six yards in two plays, punted to Army's 46. On the first play, McWilliams cut through left tackle and went 54 yards for a touchdown. Walterhouse added the point and after two and one-half minutes Army led, 7—0. Army kicked off to the 27 and Duke, failing to gain, punted to Army's 25. Three Army smashes netted nine yards and Blanchard punted to Duke's 28. Clark got two yards in two tries and Carver punted to Army's 33, Davis returning to the 44.

PENN—NAVY

Pos.	Penn	Navy
L.E.	Jenkins	Bramlett
L.T.	Savitsky	Coppedge
L.G.	Dickerson	Deramee
C.	Mostertz	R. Scott
R.G.	Adams	Carrington
R.T.	Reichenbach	N. Smith
R.E.	Sponaugle	Duden
Q.	Falcone	Hoernschemeyer
L.H.	Evans	Pettit
R.H.	Martin	Kelly
F.	Jones	Gerber

Referee—Albie J. Booth, Yale. Umpire—Frank Bergin, Princeton. Linesman—David B. Fawcett, Westminster. Field judge—J. Cooper French, Penn State.

Philadelphia, Oct. 27 (U.P.)—The undefeated football records of Pennsylvania and the Navy were at stake today as the teams met before a sell-out crowd of 73,000 at Franklin Field.

The kickoff was delayed until 2:05 p.m. for the conclusion of President Truman's Navy Day address.

Racing Results and Entries on Page 9

BULLETINS

STOPPAGE HITS HOSPITAL

About 200 maintenance and technical workers of the Israel Zion Hospital were staging a one-day work stoppage today, according to the Hospitals Employes Local of the State, County and Municipal Workers Union, C. I. O. They stopped work two hours yesterday in protest against the hospital's refusal to recognize the union.

TAX CONFEREES AGREE

Washington, Oct. 27 (U.P.)—Congressional tax conferees agreed today on the final form of a $5,920,000,000 tax reduction bill.

The prospective relief for taxpayers next year exceeds by almost $1,000,000,000 the limit asked by the Administration.

House conferees accepted the Senate proposal for individual income tax reductions totaling $2,644,000,000 on 1946 income.

The corporate tax dispute was compromised by adoption of features from both House and Senate proposals, including total repeal of the excess profits tax on Jan. 1.

5 DIE IN PLANE CRASH

Portland, Ind., Oct. 27 (U.P.)—Five service men were killed and 13 others were injured today when a C-47 army transport plane from Wright Field, Dayton, Ohio, crashed on a river bank near Pennville, Ind.

JAPAN-U. S. HOP DELAYED

Washington, Oct. 27 (U.P.)—The War Department said today that a projected non-stop flight from Japan to Washington had been delayed "for two or three days" by adverse weather.

Truman, at Navy Yard, Pledges U. S. 'Full Life'

10,000 Hear President Envision Era of Peace As Carrier Roosevelt Is Commissioned

Addressing two great Navy Day audiences, President Truman today called for an America in which a "full life" may be lived by all and for a world at peace, even if the peace must be maintained by force.

The President, who arrived in a special train from Washington which reached Pennsylvania Station just before 7 a.m., spoke first in Brooklyn, at the Navy Yard ceremonies commissioning the new aircraft carrier Franklin D. Roosevelt, largest and most powerful in the world.

Text of the President's speech at the Brooklyn Navy Yard is on Page 4.

To the audience of 10,000 navy people and invited civilians, the President pledged himself to work for the policies of his predecessor, the late President, for whom the carrier was named—"for our own people the full life which our resources make possible and for people everywhere an era of peace."

In the afternoon, speaking before a vast crowd on the Mall at Central Park, Manhattan, he returned to the subject of world peace and advocated self-government for all people who are prepared for it, such government to be attained "without interference from any foreign power." In some case, he explained, however, "it may be impossible to prevent forceful imposition" of a government by a foreign power, in which case "the United States will not recognize any such government."

The American navy, most powerful in the world, he declared, would be used on the side of "righteousness and justice," and the United States as a member of the United Nations Organization would "support a lasting peace by force if necessary."

After the Navy Yard ceremonies the President drove through miles of Brooklyn streets, where he was cheered by thousands lining the route, and then across the Manhattan Bridge for a brief official visit to City Hall. The Presidential cavalcade of automobiles doubled back, on the way, to the Battery, and then up Broadway through cheering crowds and clouds of ticker tape, descending in the spirit of Broadway's traditional reception to those it delights to honor.

The President, accompanied by Mayor LaGuardia, remained only a few minutes in City Hall, where he signed the distinguished visitors' book, and then proceeded north, to the accompaniment of cheers of a

Continued on Page 3

O'DWYER GUEST OF TRUMAN AT BREAKFAST HERE

President Truman, arriving in New York this morning, had breakfast on his train with a number of special guests, including William O'Dwyer, Democratic-American Labor candidate for Mayor.

The meeting was immediately hailed by Mr. O'Dwyer's supporters as a big boost in the election campaign, although the chortling was unofficial out of regard to the White House.

Other guests at the breakfast were Edward J. Flynn, Bronx leader; a number of other party leaders from this section and Paul E. Fitzpatrick of Buffalo, State chairman.

As the party left the train reporters who buttonholed guests had the utmost difficulty in obtaining information as to what was discussed. The closest to being communicative was Mr. Flynn, and he was smilingly evasive.

"We had a very fine breakfast," he blandly informed reporters who crowded around shooting questions.

"Did you discuss the campaign?"

"No," replied Mr. Flynn, smiling.

Continued on Page 4

Land Planes to Fly Ocean

Pan American World Airways will start its land plane clipper service to London this afternoon from LaGuardia Field. The service will operate on a biweekly basis.

U. S. Might to Preserve World Justice--Truman

Tells Navy Day Throng We Won't Recognize Any Rule Imposed by Force on Other Nations

President Truman in a 12-point enunciation of American foreign policy warned the world today that this country will "refuse to recognize" any government that is imposed on any nation by force of a foreign power.

Issuing a blunt "hands off" warning regarding the liberated and war-weakened countries, the President at the same time assured the world that our possession of the atomic bomb constituted "no threat to any nation."

"The possession in our hands of this new power of destruction we regard as a sacred trust," he said in an important Navy Day speech at Central Park. "Because of our love of peace, the thoughtful people of the world know that the trust will not be violated, that it will be faithfully executed."

The President used his Navy Day address to announce this country's intention to retain in peace the greatest naval power in the world. Together with our strong land and air forces, he said, it will be used to promote and protect a foreign policy of righteousness and justice.

In his most vigorous definition of this country's foreign policy, the President minced no words in saying that the United States advocated self-government for all people who are prepared for it and that their choice should be made without "interference from any foreign power."

"We shall," he said in a nationally broadcast address, "refuse to recognize any government imposed upon any nation by the force of any foreign power. In some cases it may be impossible to prevent forceful imposition of such a government. But the United States will not recognize any such government."

This position was the keystone of the foreign policy outlined by the President.

The Chief Executive admitted that "we are now passing through a difficult phase of international relations." But he said the current international differences among the victorious Allies were not "hopeless or irreconcilable."

"There are no conflicts of interest among the victorious powers so deeply rooted that they cannot be resolved," he said in apparent reference to current policy differences with Russia.

Devoting the latter portions of his 25-minute address to the atomic bomb, the President affirmed his prior declaration that this country will not reveal the industrial know-how of atomic bomb production.

He emphasized that the atomic

Continued on Page 4

ELLA CINDERS

By Charles Plumb and Fred Fox

MARY WORTH'S FAMILY

By Dale Allen

DOTTY DRIPPLE

By Buford Tune

DR. BOBBS

By Elliott and McArdle

JANE ARDEN

By Monte Barrett and Russell Rose

INVISIBLE SCARLET O'NEIL

By Russell Stamm

O

By Frank Beck

CHIEF WAHOO

By Saunders and Wogon

LEM AND OINIE

By Paul Fogarty

RADIO PROGRAMS

WMCA, 570. WEAF, 660. WOR, 710. WJZ, 770. WNYC, 830. WABC, 880. WAAT, 970. WINS, 1000. WHN, 1050. WNEW, 1130. WLIB, 1190. WFAS, 1240. WOV, 1280. WEVD, WBBR, 1330. WBNX, 1380. WBYN, 1430. WHOM, 1480. WQXR, 1560. WWRL, 1660.

TODAY'S BEST BETS

1:15—Football Harvard vs. Yale, WOR.
1:45—Football, Army vs. Navy, WEAF.
2:00—Metropolitan Opera Program, Mimi Benzell, Charles Kullman, Ezio Pinza, Nadine Conner, Bruno Walter, Conductor, WJZ.
2:45—Football, Notre Dame vs. Great Lakes, WABC.
5:30—Philadelphia Orchestra Eugene Ormandy, Conductor, WABC.
6:15—People's Platform, Guests, WABC.
7:00—"Our Foreign Policy," Senator Warren Austin, Senator Edwin Johnson, Representative Andrew J. May, Representative Dewey Short, Guests, WEAF; "Guess Who?" WOR; Texetron Theaater, Helen Hayes, WABC; Masterwork Hour, WNYC.
7:30—First Nighter, WABC.
8:00—Life of Riley William Bendix, WEAF; Dick Haymes Show, Helen Forrest, WABC; Woody Herman Show, WJZ.
8:30—Truth or Consequences, Ralph Edwards, WEAF; "Man From G-2," WJZ; Mayor of the Town, Lionel Barrymore, Agnes Moorehead, WABC.
9:00—Hit Parade, Dick Todd, Joan Edwards, Mark Warnow Orchestra, WABC; "Gang Busters," Lewis J. Valentine, WJZ.
9:30—"Can You Top This?" WEAF; Boston Symphony Orchestra Paul Paray Conductor, WJZ.
9:45—Serenade, Hollis Shaw, Bill Perry, WABC.
10:00—Judy Canova Show, WEAF.
10:30—Grand Ole Opry, WEAF.

Where there is no listing for a station preceding program is on the air

2 P.M. TO 4 P.M.

2:00 WABC—Of Men and Books.
WEAF—Football.
WJZ—Met. Opera Program.
WOR—Football.
WMCA—Tunes for Today.
WHN—Living Should Be Fun.
WNYC—News; Symphony.
WINS—News; Tune Factory.
2:15 WABC—Adventures in Science.
WHN—Racing; News.
2:30 WHN—Racing; Music.
WMCA—News; Three Suns.
WABC—Lawrence Orch.
2:45 WHN—Music.
WABC—Football.
WMCA—Latin Rhythms.
3:00 WHN—Racing; Music.
WMCA—News; Novena.
3:15 WHN—Music; News.
3:30 WHN—Racing; Music.
WMCA—News.
3:45 WHN—Music.
WNYC—News.
WMCA—Sylvia Karton, songs.
WOR—News; Sports.

4 P.M. TO 7 P.M.

4:00 WEAF—Autumn Afternoon.
WHN—Racing; Music.
WNYC—Four Strings.
WMCA—News; Ray Smith.
WOR—Win, Lose or Draw.
4:15 WEAF—Veterans Advisor.
WHN—Music; News.
4:30 WEAF—World of Melody.
WOR—Meet the Press.
WNYC—Pals of the P.A.L.
WHN—Racing; Music.
WMCA—News; Matinee.
4:45 WEAF—Radio Reporter.
5:00 WEAF—Music of Moment.
WMCA—News; Matinee.
WOR—Kaye Orch.
WNYC—Music for Young People.
WHN—Dick Gilbert.
5:30 WABC—Philadelphia Orch.
WEAF—News, Vandercook.
WMCA—News.
WHN—Weather; News.
5:35 WJZ—Stopak Orch.
5:38 WHN—Dick Gilbert.
5:45 WEAF—Tin Pan Alley.
WNYC—Songs People Sing.
WJZ—Cross Show.
WOR—Lanny and Ginger.
WMCA—Jerry Baker, songs
6:00 WABC—Howe, news.
WEAF—News.
WJZ—News; Fleisher.
WOR—Paul Schubert
WMCA—News; Cavallaro Orch.
WNYC—Global Neighbors.
WHN—Sidney Walton.
WINS—News; Music.
6:15 WABC—People's Platform.
WEAF—Steel Horizons.
WJZ—Christian Science Program.
WOR—Strictly Entre-Nous
WMCA—Steve Ellis.
WHN—Racing Results.
WINS—People's Voice Show.
6:30 WOR—News, Vandeventer.
WEAF—Music of Manhattan.
WJZ—Wismer, sports.
WMCA—"Racing Results."
WINS—Sports, Dunphy
WHN—News.
WNYC—People Make Music.
6:45 WABC—World Today.
WEAF—Religion in News.
WOR—Sports, Stan Lomax.
WJZ—"Labor-U.S.A."
WNYC—News.
WMCA—Interview with a Star.
WHN—Take Tip From Me.
WINS—T. Dorsey Records.
6:55 WABC—Trout, news.

7 P.M. TO 10 P.M.

7:00 WABC—Texatron Theater.
WJZ—"Jobs After Victory"
WOR—"Guess Who?"
WMCA—News; This Is Our Town.
WEAF—Our Foreign Policy.
WHN—News, Combs.
WNYC—Masterwork Hour.
WINS—News; Serenade.
7:15 WINS—Kramer Music.
WMCA—Let's Dance.
WJZ—Correspondents.
WHN—Sports Final.
7:30 WABC—First Nighter.
WEAF—Out of the Deep.
WJZ—Dick Tracy.
WMCA—News.
WOR—Arthur Hale
WHN—Bing Crosby.
WINS—Building Counselor.
7:45 WOR—Sports, Harmon.
WMCA—Dinah Shore.
WHN—Saturday Serenade.
WINS—Music.
8:00 WABC—Dick Haymes Show.
WEAF—Life of Riley.
WJZ—Woody Herman Show.
WOR—Answer Man.
WMCA—News; Barnet Or.
WNYC—BBC News.
WHN—Word of Life.
WINS—News; Music.
8:15 WOR—Eric Johnston.
WMCA—Brown Orch.
WNYC—Echoes of War.
8:30 WABC—Mayor of Town.
WEAF—Truth or Consequences.
WJZ—"Man From G-2."
WOR—Victory Bond Program.
WHN—So. American Sway.
WINS—Treasury Salute.
WMCA—Martin Orch.
8:45 WNYC—News.
WMCA—Bing Crosby.
WINS—Music.
8:55 WABC—News, Calmer.
9:00 WABC—Hit Parade.
WEAF—Barn Dance.
WJZ—Gang Busters.
WNYC—Concert Hall.
WOR—"Leave It To Girls."
WMCA—News; "Shoot the Works."
WINS—News; Music.
9:15 WINS—At Your Service.
WHN—Les Brown.
9:30 WEAF—Can You Top This?
WJZ—Boston Symphony.
WOR—"Break the Bank."
WMCA—Juke Box.
WHN—Jam Session.
WINS—Record Shop.
WNYC—Music of Theater.
9:45 WABC—Serenade.
WINS—Front Page Drama.
9:55 WJZ—Quick Quiz.
WNYC—News.

10 P.M. TO 1 A.M.

10:00 WEAF—Canova Show.
WOR—Chicago Theater.
WMCA—News; Juke Box.
WHN—Mooney Orch.
WNYC—Sign off.
WINS—News; Music.
10:15 WABC—Report to Nation.
WINS—Fashions in Jazz.
10:30 WEAF—Grand Ole Opry.
WJZ—Hayloft Hoedown.
WHN—Dance Time.
WMCA—Frank Kingdon
WINS—Mons. Fulton J. Sheen.
10:45 WABC—Talks.
WMCA—"Musical Encores"
WINS—Rhythm Room.
11:00 WABC—News, Calmer.
WEAF—News, Van.
WJZ—News; Hollenbeck.
WOR—News, Vandeventer
WMCA—News; Gypsy Caravan.
WHN—Newsreel Theater.
WINS—News.
11:10 WINS—Concert Hall.
11:15 WABC—Mooney Orch.
WEAF—News, Utley.
WOR—News; Financial Reports.
WJZ—Vera Massey, songs
11:28 WOR—Weather.
11:30 WABC—T. Dorsey Orch.
WEAF—Goodman Orch.
WJZ—Kaye Orch.
WOR—Spivak Orch.
WMCA—Bandbox.
11:45 WINS—Music.
WMCA—Treasury Salute.
12:00 WABC—News; Carle Orch.
WEAF—News.
WJZ—News; Tom Reddy.
WMCA—News.
WOR—News; Herman Or.
WHN—Music to Read By.
WINS—Sign off.
12:05 WEAF—Mooney Orch.
12:15 WMCA—Unity Viewpoint.
12:30 WABC—Long Orch.
WEAF—Three Suns Trio.
WJZ—Cross Presents.
WOR—Morris Orch.
WMCA—Music for Dreaming.
12:45 WOR—Gordon Orch.
12:55 WEAF—News.
WHN—News.

Features On Other Stations

WEVD—
10:00—Metropolitan Hour.
10:30—Music for Millions.
11:30—On Wings of Song.
12:00—Symphonic Hour.
WQXR—
6:05—Music to Remember.
8:05—Symphony Hall.
10:05—Record Album.
11:05—Hour of Symphony.
WNEW—
2:00—Music Hall.
5:00—"High School Hour."
5:35—Make Believe Ballroom.
9:00—Dance Parade.

BRIDGE By Harry J. Roth

The North player on the hand shown today really had a "gripe" when his partner insisted on playing the hand in notrump. He did everything in his power to steer him into a spade contract which could not be defeated, but South wanted to play the hand.

Neither side vulnerable.
South dealer.

	♠ K Q J 9 5 2 ♡ 5 4 3 ◇ A ♣ 7 6 3	
♠ 6 3 ♡ Q 9 6 ◇ Q J 10 8 7 4 ♣ 5 2	NORTH WEST EAST SOUTH	♠ A 8 7 ♡ 10 8 2 ◇ 9 6 5 ♣ K 10 9 8
	♠ 10 4 ♡ A K J 7 ◇ K 3 2 ♣ A Q J 4	

The bidding:

South	West	North	East
1 ♡	Pass	1 ♠	Pass
2 NT	Pass	4 ♠	Pass
4 NT	Pass	5 ◇	Pass
6 NT	Pass	Pass	Pass

Any bridge player knows that in bidding notrump you must be prepared for an opening lead in your weakest suit. With the North hand you could readily anticipate a diamond opening, and that would ruin the hand for notrump play. North tried to warn South against a notrump contract by jumping to game in spades on the second round, but south had to learn the hard way.

As expected, West opened the queen of diamonds and South was immediately confronted with a hopeless proposition. He must be given some credit for not giving up. Even if the ace of spades could be driven out on the first lead of that suit, three club tricks had to be won, so he took the club finesse immediately. The spade ten was next led and overtaken with the jack, but East refused to play the ace. Declarer took another club finesse and then played the four of spades. If the spade ace did not fall this time South planned to take the heart finesse. He saw a remote chance of making his contract—it was just barely possible that he might be able to run four heart tricks and two more club tricks.

But declarer did not deserve to be so fortunate. East took the second spade trick with his ace and returned a diamond to establish the suit for West.

"I WOULD get the killing opening lead," complained South. "Any other suit and it would have been a cinch." He made no reference to the fact that the hand should never have been played in a notrump contract. At the other tables the contract was played by North in spades.

Rabbi Gustave Falk Gives Sermon at Union Temple

Rabbi Gustave Falk, regional director of the Union of American Hebrew Congregation, spoke at the regular Friday evening services of Union Temple, 17 Eastern Parkway, last night.

The subject of Rabbi Falk's sermon was "Hanukkah for You and Me." He told the story of the Jewish hero Mattathais, declaring "he was filled with a constructive fear and anger against injustice for which he was ready to die."

Rabbi Falk emphasized that a "constructive anger" against injustice at home and abroad is needed today.

"Look, George—the attendant forgot to take the hose out of the gas tank."

THESE WOMEN!

By d'Alessio

"We probably should have paid more than a dollar a lesson!"

RADIO By William Juengst

BONDADIERING—As you'll notice, the Victory War Loan drive looms large in Your Earland Picture Gallery this week.

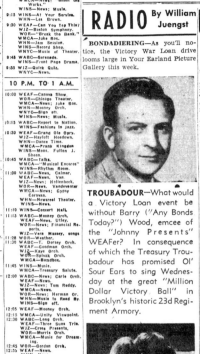

TROUBADOUR—What would a Victory Loan event be without Barry ("Any Bonds Today?") Wood, emcee of the "Johnny Presents" WEAFer? In consequence of which the Treasury Troubadour has promised Ol' Sour Ears to sing Wednesday at the great "Million Dollar Victory Ball" in Brooklyn's historic 23d Regiment Armory.

WELCOME VISITOR—Judy Canova and her show are in from the coast to broadcast here, do some visiting, and make some Bond drive appearances.

DOUBLING — Raymond Paige and his orchestra will play both classical and swing music to point up the arguments of Deems Taylor and Leonard Feather, in a series of longhair-versus-jive debates to be inaugurated on WEAF tomorrow.

UNCLE RAY

A Little Saturday Talk: 'Charming' of Birds

Sgt. Robert A. Brown has written me this letter:

"Your article on the possible power of a snake to 'charm' or hypnotize its victims was interesting. There is no doubt in my opinion of this matter, since it has been my privilege to witness it twice.

"The first time I watched a snake 'charm' a small sparrow to its doom. I sat very quietly and observed the whole procedure, since I was curious and had doubted the truth of the accounts I had read.

"The bird fluttered its wings and gave out a strange cry that one would never mistake if heard again. The snake was about three feet from the bird when I first saw it, and took about five minutes to work itself within the few inches needed for the final strike.

The bird's companions flitted from one nearby branch to another, also screaming, but the victim never changed its position, except to flutter its wings.

On the second occasion my wife was with me when I heard the scream of the birds, and I told her that a snake was nearby. After a bit of peering around we saw it. The situation was the same as the one described, with the snake slowly creeping up a branch to a bird. We promptly shot the snake."

A somewhat different kind of "charming" is reported by William A. Allen, who says:

"On a Spring day in 1904 I heard the distressful chirping of a bird. Looking out of a window I saw a robin on a tree branch about seven feet above the ground. Under the tree was a cat with its eyes fixed on the robin, and purring. All of a sudden the robin fell to the ground, as if shot, and the cat grabbed it. I yelled at the cat, but it was too late."

To these letters I should like to add this little note: It is possible for chickens to be "hypnotized" by human beings. I have seen this done several times, the head of the chicken being stroked in a certain way. Can it be that birds sometimes are put under a spell by the steady stare of snakes or other animals? Or is it simply that birds follow an instinct to defend their nests, and sometimes fall victims while doing so?

Uncle Ray

Dr. Brady Says:

I call tonsillectomy (the attempt to remove every bit of tonsil from the throat, whether by guillotine and snare or by dissection or by "enucleation" or by any other method) atrocious. By that I mean to say it is savagely brutal treatment when applied in the ordinary case of enlarged (hypertrophied) tonsils or infected (diseased) tonsils. In exceptional instances such radical surgery is not only justifiable but indispensable treatment—for example, malignancy (cancer).

If my tonsils or the tonsils of any one for whose well being I felt responsible were at stake, there probably wouldn't be any atrocity. If it were a child with hypertrophied or very large tonsils, a child too young to co-operate with the physician, I'd say okeh to clipping or slicing off a considerable portion of the enlarged tonsils with the tonsillotome, under general anesthesia.

For a child old enough to cooperate or for a youth or adult, with simple enlargement of the tonsils, I'd say wait a season or a year—unless obstruction of breathing were obviously handicapping health, and development or obstruction of Eustachian tubes (ventilating middle ear cavities) were impairing the hearing or contributing to earaches and middle ear inflammation or infection. In either event I'd say the patient should receive a series of X-ray treatments, especially if the hearing or ears are involved, or a series of diathermy (electro-coagulation) treatments by a physician skilled in this technique—which is far more difficult than any mere tonsil surgery.

QUESTIONS AND ANSWERS

Excess Acidity

I'll be grateful for your pamphlet dealing with excess acidity. Does smoking cause it? I smoke at least a pack a day, sometimes. A. S.

Answer—Smoking is one cause. Especially smoking before or during a meal. Send stamped envelope bearing your address and ask for the pamphlet "Yankee Stomach."

State Hospital Exhibit

Kings Park, Dec. 1—An exhibit and sale of the products of the occupational and re-educational classes of the Kings Park State Hospital will be held from Tuesday to Thursday, inclusive, at York Hall.

Hayworth Made Fort Worth Pilot; Nine Dodgers Ask for Release

TOMMY HOLMES

Topping's Jump May 'Make' New League

INEVITABLE—The decision of Major Dan Topping to pole-vault out of the National Football League into the All-America Conference scarcely can be startling news to readers of this corner. Several times in the past year I have pointed out that this development was inevitable if some drastic scheme were not employed to iron out apparently irreconcilable clashes of interest between Topping and the Maras, who operate the football Giants.

Dan Topping

As matters stood, Topping owned a ball club—the club that originally was the Brooklyn Dodgers, later became the Tigers and operated this waning season in conjunction with the Boston Yanks. He also owned the football rights in a stadium and a darned good stadium—that big thing in the Bronx.

But to operate he had to have a schedule and that was something he couldn't get in the NFL. Not as long as Tim and Jack Mara stood fast upon their vested territorial rights which gave them first call upon all the choice and juicy Sunday dates of the season.

HELPS OUR TOWN—Nobody can blame the Maras. They worked long and hard to build up a sturdy, money-making franchise. And under those circumstances, Topping could do nothing else but jump. He'd have been foolish to have stayed in the NFL with a grand franchise, a great ball park and a stepchild's schedule.

It is a long haul from our town to the Polo Grounds in Harlem or the Yankee Stadium in the Bronx. And yet Brooklyn is the borough most affected by this latest development in professional football. And I should say that our community gains the most from the crystallization of a decision that has been in the back of Topping's noggin for a long time.

The reason is evident. When William Drought Cox and Dr. Mal Stevens, a pair of old Yales, rented the football rights from Ebbets Field's Branch Rickey, the professional gridiron future of our town became definitely tied up with the new league. And, naturally, the success or failure of the All-America Conference is of prime importance to those of us who believe that Brooklyn potentially is one of the greatest sports towns in the world.

And, it seems to me, that the chances of success for the All-America Conference today are about five times greater than they were a week ago when the Topping tin was fighting a gallant but losing battle in the National Football League.

NO CRACKS, PLEASE—Until now there was real basis for some of the sarcastic cracks passed about the new loop headed by Sleepy Jim Crowley. It was worth a snicker when George Preston (Long Live Linen) Marshall called it the "All-Ameche League," in reference to the Hollywood citizen who is involved in backing the Los Angeles entry.

And when Elmer Layden, president of the NFL, scoffed, "Why, they haven't even got a football," he was both literally and figuratively correct.

The background of Layden's satire was an incident in Chicago when the president of that club in the new league signed Dick Hanley as his coach. Press photographers arrived to take pictures and do you know that the Chicago front office couldn't beg, borrow, buy or steal a football to lend gridiron atmosphere to the shots. If you tried to buy a football for your youngster last Christmas you'll know what they were up against.

But this isn't the "All-Ameche League" any longer. With the inclusion of Topping and a New York franchise as well as a Brooklyn franchise, it is an organization with a definite chance of success.

PROBLEMS—It has a lot of things in its flavor. It has stadiums—or, I guess, "stadia" is the word—that dwarf the places where the NFL teams play. Backing its clubs are men of vast means and a willful desire to make the venture a success. The mobilization of players will be no problem. The end of the war means a plethora of athletes and, so far, the new league has shown a disposition to pay more money for name talent than the established National League.

The fact that Topping has joined the AAC by no means guarantees the success of the new league, which faces a long and rugged fight. Topping, himself, won't find the going easy in the Yankee Stadium. He will be in there against the toughest competition there is—the well-run Giants with their devoted clientele.

SOMEHOW—And I still don't like the far-flung ramifications of the All-America circuit with teams as far away as Miami, Fla., and Los Angeles and San Francisco in what's the name of that State? In all ventures of this sort, geographical compactness is of great aid to success and the AAC is about as compact as a group of butterflies.

What the Topping decision does mean is that the league is geared for a long, hard fight toward success. And the chances are that it probably will succeed in some fashion although probably not in the form it assumes at the present time.

Eagle Sports picture

TAKES SHOT AT TARGET—Ronnie Nadell, Erasmus Hall, is jumping to drop in a field goal against Midwood in opening P. S. A. L. game of season yesterday on the former school's court. Al Cohen, No. 11, and Bill Baronblue, No. 7, Midwood desperately try to prevent the goal

REDMEN, LIU ON HARDWOOD AGAIN TONIGHT

Lapchick Hopes to Sit Quietly as Team Plays Cathedral

By GEORGE COLEMAN

There's plenty of basketball scheduled in Brooklyn tonight. Coach Joe Lapchick after sweating through the sloppy performance of his St. John's cagers against Western Michigan, hopes to sit comfortably through the game with Brooklyn Cathedral at the Lewis Ave. gymnasium. However, if the Johnnies give Jim Cavanaugh the least bit of encouragement, the Cathedral sharpshooter should score in double numbers just as he did in his team's upset of Manhattan College. Cavanaugh should test the Redmen's defense, their weakest link.

The game should also give Lapchick an opportunity to see just how fast his lads ane developing and whom he should use against Utah at Ned Irish's popshot palace on Wednesday.

Long Island U. meeting the Oklahoma Aggies on the same Garden program next week, also have a "tester." The Army Service Forces five visits the Long Island Pharmacy court. Bee is going to try two of his 6-foot-8 men along with Carl Meinhold, Jackie Goldsmith and Stan Waxman as a unit that he hopes will do well against the long stacks from Oklahoma.

St. Francis College cagers, with only the Alumni game under their belts, will try their high-scoring aces against Pratt Institute on the Artists' hardwood while Brooklyn College, another young club, is host to the Alumni team at the Bedford Ave. and Avenue H gymnasium.

Rams, Jaspers Busy

Over on the other side of the bridges, Fordham College opens its drillshed to Panzer College while Manhattan College, going along nicely since its first game setback by Brooklyn Cathedral College, tries for a victory over New York Cathedral.

Howard Cann, courtmaster at New York U, and Nat Holman, the wizard of City College, have been hard at work drilling their cagers for the second Garden twinbill tomorrow night. Every one in town figures that Cann has a wealth of material. There's Sid Tanenbaum, Adolph Schayes, Frank Mangiapane, Don Forman and Marty Goldstein ready to start against what is supposed to be Colgate's strongest team in years.

Veteran coaches expect the Violets to have no trouble with Colgate. But after the Western Michigan upset over St. John's, Cann knows anything can happen.

Holman is more confident. He figures his Beavers will beat Holy Cross. The former Celtic star rates his present quintet of Paul Schmones, Sonny Jameson, Bob Scheer, Marvin Hillman and Len Hassman, equal to any City five in the last ten years.

Cadets Sang Yule Carols on Eve of Clash With Navy

It takes an event of importance to make Col. Earl (Red) Blaik, the Army coach, overcome his natural shyness and stand up and talk. The red-head (auburn, really) spoke last night at the Sherry-Netherland—AFTER his aide, Andy Gustafson, had formally accepted the Lambert trophy that means the football championship of the East.

And Blaik can talk with conviction, too, in a deep bass.

Blaik had a little item on his mind that hadn't been touched upon by any speakers. Principally, because few besides Blaik knew about it.

"Aside from their football ability, I mean," Red said of his Army players, "they've got character. They're the kind of a team that needs no morale builder. They go out to play their best and nothing short of that will satisfy them. There was no telling them that any Army team that beats Navy by even a point has done its job. That's why, after the game against a great Navy team, there was no jubiliation in the locker room, no outbursts of enthusiasm. They simply felt they hadn't played their very best game.

"The number of touchdowns and points scored wasn't what they meant. It's as one of our tackles said to me, "Colonel, I'd like to get out there and play that game over."

"The night before the Navy game we took the boys to a movie. On the way back what do you thing they were doing? They were singing Christmas carols," he said.

Blaik got more kick out of that desire for perfection—and the boyish singing of carols—than all the touchdowns the Army made.

TROST

Senior Met Champs In Boro Armory Jan. 19

The senior metropolitan track and field championships will be held Saturday, Jan. 19, 1946, at the 23d Regiment Armory under the sponsorship of the Brooklyn Council Veterans of Foreign Wars, it was announced by Pincus Sober, chairman of the A. A. U. Championship Committee.

FIGHT RESULTS

FALL RIVER, Mass.—Gary Cooper, 137, Pittsburgh, knocked out Tommy Colton, 137, Boston (5); Oscar St. Pierre, 149, Fall River, stopped Dolly King, 147, Springfield (6); Joe Celletti, 138, Providence, R. I., stopped Pat Doyle, 143, Fall River (6); Freddie Fields, 164, Boston, stopped Jackson Clark, 159, Fall River (2).

PITTSBURGH—Art Robinson, 156, Pittsburgh tko'd Frank Serna, 151, New York (9).

LAWRENCE, MASS.—Blond Tiger, 129, Lowell, outpointed Joe Moneiro, 129, Wareham (10); Gene Howell, 130, Cincinnati, outpointed Jackie Pennington, 124, Alanta, Ga. (6).

PHILADELPHIA—Al Johnson, 164, Philadelphia, won a unanimous decision over Oscar Goode, 173, Newark (8). Willie Thomas, 221, Philadelphia, halted Ray Winbush, 200, Philadelphia (1). Lonnie Clark, 207, Philadelphia, knocked out Nat Hines, 182, Philadelphia (4). Joe Falco, 150, Philadelphia, decisioned Buster Hardy, 148½, Newark (8).

HIGHLAND PARK—Tom Monty, 129, Brooklyn, knocked out Al Cella, 131, Jamaica, N. Y., in 2:15 of the second round of a scheduled eight-rounder.

Skin Fans Regard Giants as Menace

See Oodles of Trouble Sunday —Owen Has Team in High Gear

By RALPH TROST

To judge from the Washington papers, Washingtonians seem to feel that the visit of the New York Giants on Sunday for a game with the Great White Washer's Redskins is going to be harder to take than the bus strikes, the telephone strike, the Management-Labor meeting and the Pearl Harbor investigation combined. The Giants are nothing less than a menace with a capital "M."

BOSTON FARM BOSS—Ted McGrew, former National League umpire and scout for the Phillies and Dodgers, was named head of the Braves expanded farm system to succeed Bob Quinn, who resigned.

What makes the Redskins—or Washingtonians—so fearful of Steve Owen's old men? The record, that's what. The Maramen not only have won 11, lost six and tied one in the National Football League battles with the Skins—an almost 2 to 1 average—since 1937, but they've done most of the winning in the late season. And this date on Sunday, one judges, is late enough.

Meanwhile, the Giants just go on practicing in that funny little hunk of mud left to them, just a small piece between home plate and second base, not yet touched by the men and machine that are reconstructing the Polo Grounds playing field. And Stout Steve says nothing more than that his team was great against the Eagles last Sunday and that he hopes they'll be greater this week-end.

Big Guns in Trim

If it weren't for Herber's pitching and Liebel's catching, this current crop of Giants wouldn't look like the team the Skins beat, 24—14, last October. Maybe, it won't be Sunday. Maybe Stout Steve will shelve his pitcher and catcher and depend upon the rocketing runners that have come to him since that game, including Junior Hovious, Bill Paschal, George Franck, Bill Petrillas and that ex-Redskin, Jack Doolen, who while at Georgetown, had a whole lot of the commodity Steven seemed to need most, speed. These, believe it or not, are just backs. Steve has accumulated linemen, too.

Come late November, Steve usually manages to blossom out with a sharp attack—and there's no depending on his laying all stress on the pass as he did last week. Particularly, with all the rain we've had.

Baugh Tuned Up

Those Skins also have freshened up a bit since that last meeting with the Giants. But not the way the Maramen have. Washington still leans heavily on the frame of Sammy, the Slinger, Baugh who, incidentally, has had some real good days against the Giants. One of his best was in that 24—14 session in New York.

There's going to be no rest for the Giants. They're headed for practice up to tomorrow morning. In fact, they'll just about have time after practice to shower and shove off for the 1:30 train. Yesterday was "skull day" with black board work. But Steve will get the boys back to the physical stuff today.

Owen Tells Tech Dads Boys Need Sports Fields

By JAMES J. MURPHY

"I have never seen a bad boy. It is the way he is handled," declared Coach Steve Owen, of the Giants, at the third annual Brooklyn Tech High School father and son football dinner last night at Michel's.

"Our authorities are not looking out for the welfare of the boy as they should," continued Steve. "A boy loves to play and to deny him that privelege is looking for trouble. Athletes in New York and Brooklyn practice under adverse conditions and when they should be entitled to the best. Once this situation is corrected juvenile delinquency will decline," concluded Owen.

Other speakers had the same thought and pleaded with the fathers to have their various organizations appeal to Mayor-elect William O'Dwyer and petition him to force the Board of Education to restore the athletic program it suspended for junior high and elementary students.

Van Rensslear Brookhahne was toastmaster. In addition to Owen, the gathering was also addressed by Principal William Pabst, Jimmy Jemail, the Inquiring Photographer of the Daily News, who played with Brown in the first Rose Bowl game against Washington State in 1915; Frank Downing Sr., chairman of the dinner; Coach Adam Cirillo, and the writer.

The writer presented to Co-Captain George Gerung, outstanding all-around member of the Tech team, the Robert Dznev Memorial Trophy. Cirillo introduced Gordon Fleming, leading scorer of the city this season. and George Salvino as the co-captains for 1946.

Frank Downing Jr., co-captain of 1945, on behalf of the team presented Christmas gifts to Cirillo and his assistants, John Simons, Phil Olivari, Phil Weis, former St. John's University grid star, and Harry Elbert, in charge of equipment; Vic Onorato, trainer, and Dr. Michael Veneziano, team physician.

Among former stars who served with distinction in the war and attended were former co-captains Joe Cassidy, Joe Certa and Skiffington, and Lou DiGiovani, Charley Engelhardt, Sal Feschiana, Billy Guidice, Edwin Rippier, Bill Simpson and Artie Stelljes.

Other guests included George Brenner, Joseph Fanning, Marcus Mayer, Joseph E. Peckham, Torquato Pisani, Harold Taylor, assistant administrator and Coach Jimmy McNamara of Manual Training.

Rutan's 68 Leaves Stars in Lurch

Miami, Fla., Dec. 7 (U.P.)—Chick Rutan, a little-known pro hoping to win his first tournament, clipped two strokes off par yesterday to finish with a 68 and a one-stroke lead in the first round of the $10,000 Miami open gold tournament.

Rutan, 37, of Grosse Pointe Wood, Mich., who has served as assistant pro to some of the best known golfers in the country, came up to the 18th tee needing a par four to take the lead.

He slapped out a 250-yard drive which split the center of the dog-leg 18th fairway. Then he shanked an iron shot badly into a rap. But he came back with a pitch shot which landed three feet from the cup, and his putt was good. Rutan, who has worked under Craig Wood and Ben Hogan, finished second in the Michigan P. G. A. this year but has never been on top.

Harold (Jug) McSpaden, Sanford, Maine, blew a chance to tie on the 18th when he overshot the green by 75 yards and ended up behind the bleachers. He chipped to withing 10 feet of the cup but missed his putt, finishing with a 69.

Bunched at 69 with McSpaden were veteran Henry Picard, Cleveland, Ohio; E. J. (Dutch) Harrison, Little Rock, Ark.; Tony Penna, Dayton, Ohio., and Ky Lafoon, Chicago. Dark horses in the same slot were Ben Yasko, West Orange, N. J.; Fred Annon, Old Greenwich, Conn., and George Paytone, Newport News, Virginia.

American League Hockey

Buffalo 6, Providence 5.
Indianapolis 6, New Haven 5.

U. S. Hockey League

Tulsa 6, St. Paul 4.

BASEBALL LAUGHS

By HAROLD C. BURR

Billy Evans was umpiring a game in the American League. That was years before he became a baseball executive. He was having his troubles pleasing the hitters on balls and strikes. This doesn't mean that he was umpiring a bad game. Some guys are hard to please when they are not getting their hits.

A batsman came up in bad humor. He had been in a slump for weeks. He couldn't hit a ball if it came up to him as big as a balloon and down the middle.

"Strike!" cried Billy, raising his right arm as the first offering cut the heart of the plate. The batter ignored it.

"You missed that one, Billy!" he snarled at the umpire over his shoulder.

"Maybe I did," retorted Evans sweetly, "but I wouldn't have if I'd a bat in my hand."

GETS HIS REWARD—James J. Murphy, scholastic sports editor of the Eagle (second from left), presenting the Robert Dznev Memorial Trophy to Co-Captain George Gerung of Brooklyn Tech's football team at the school's annual dinner last night at Michel's Restaurant.. He was the outstanding Tech player. Coach Steve Owen, Giants, extreme left; Gerung's father and Coach Adam Cirillo of Tech look on.

Eagle Sports picture

Garden Victor May Get Crack at Zale

By HAROLD CONRAD

Last August, Artie Levine, of Brooklyn, and Sonny Horne, of Valley Stream, got a chance to show their wares in a Madison Square Garden main event. Although Artie was the winner, the question of superiority between these two aspirants for middleweight honors was not decisively settled. The boys battled savagely for four rounds, but Sonny suffered a bad cut over his left eye in the fifth—so bad that Johnny Burns halted the contest. While this is a moot point, many of the experts at the ringside thought Horne would have won were it not for the unfortunate break.

As a result, Levine won himself a shot at the fabulous Rocky Graziano and they were supposed to meet in the ten-round Garden feature this evening. About two weeks ago, however, Graziano announced that he would not be able to go through with the bout because of a cold, which hadn't permitted him to train for the bout. So after one tough break, the fates smiled at Horne. He was called to sub for Rocky, giving him a chance to get even for that unfortunate incident last August.

Incidentally, the wound which cost Horne that first engagement is completely healed and a few weeks ago he resumed action with a convincing victory over Larry Fontana. He has now engaged in seven contests since receiving his discharge from the Navy early this year and has won six. The Levine bout was the only defeat and he expects to reverse that.

Levine, who was honorably discharged from the Marines the past Summer, of course, has other plans. As he pointed out after winding up his training campaign yesterday, "I whipped Horne once and right now I'm in even better shape than I was before so I can't see any reason why I won't repeat." Like Horne, Artie has his eye on Middleweight champion Tony Zale, who doffed his Navy uniform a few weeks ago.

In supporting six-rounders, Billy Walker is paired with Larry Fontana, Jimmy McDonough takes on Ralph Dougherty and Lou Vallee opposes Danny Martin. In the fours, Weyland Douglas faces Dough Ratford, and Clarence Wilkinson takes on Sam Barudi.

Madison Gridders Get Numerals at Annual Dinner

Football officially closed at James Madison High School with a dinner in the teachers' cafeteria there yesterday afternoon. In addition to having their efforts praised, the gridders were rewarded with major and minor letters.

The chief speakers numbered Samuel Shindler, head of the Health Education Department of the school; Lou Oshins, football coach of Brooklyn College; Coach Murray Gerenstein of the Golden Tornado, and James J. Murphy, Scholastic Sports Editor of the Eagle.

Captain Monroe Schussel, who took over as the leader when Fred Kimmel was injured, presented Gerenstein with a gold wrist watch on behalf of the team.

Those who came into possession of major letters follow: Nick Blend, Harold Elenz, Walter Grubman, Fred Kimmel, Monroe Schussel, Buddy Kahn, Leonard Steckler, Harold Siper, Chris Pappas, Henry Greenstein, Enrico Galli, William Malin, John Burke, Chris Kitsos, Richard Mogil, Arnold Schwartz, John Paver, Herman Wexler, John Panagakos, Levine; Rosenberg, "Pal" Palmeri, De Senag, Leonard Nelson and Holler.

Recipients of minor insignia included Richard Macaya, Tapoozian, Becks, Danziger, Pagero, Kammerman, Keating and Ken Olsen.

Temple Bags No. 7, Beats Mailmen

Union Temple posted its seventh basketball victory in beating the Fleet Post Office team of New York, 56—38, last night at the Temple court.

The winners led, 24—19, at the half with Carpien the high scorer of the game with 20 tallies.

The lineup:

Union Temple	G.	F.	P.	Fleet P. O., N. Y.	G.	F.	P.
Carpien	9	2	20	Sullivan	6	0	12
Cruz	1	1	3	Davis	3	0	6
Rosenblum	2	2	6	Kelly	0	0	0
Rubel	2	0	4	Keveny	1	1	3
Pauker	1	6	8	Rooney	0	0	0
Brocik	1	1	3	Bruini	5	4	14
Sills	1	0	2	Flynn	1	0	2
Feiner	1	2	4	Porter	0	1	1
Green	0	0	0				
Guss Off	0	0	0				
Walterson	3	0	6				
Totals	21	14	56	Totals	16	6	38

Mariners Start On Win Course

Schenectady, N. Y., Dec. 7—The Kings Point Mariner basketball team got off to a flying start last night by beating Union College, 42 to 31. The Mariners were never headed, holding a 28—15 edge at intermission.

Gil Zagelmieir was the big gun for the Mariners, dropping 17 points, including six field goals.

The lineups:

Union College	G.	F.	P.	Kings Point	G.	F.	P.
McCormick	1	1	3	Paflan	1	3	5
Stitts	1	0	2	Faris	3	0	6
Tauffer	2	4	8	Paterson	1	1	3
Redden	0	0	0	Zagelmie'r	6	5	17
Fisher	5	0	10	Burlingham	0	0	0
Ciss	0	0	0	Harless	3	1	7
Th[illegible]son	0	1	1	Viau	1	0	2
Young	0	0	0	Berger	1	0	2
Markes	2	1	5				
Wester	1	0	2				
Totals	12	7	31	Totals	16	10	42

BASKETBALL RESULTS

42	Kings Point	Union	31
53	Juniata	Carnegie Tech	31
58	Wyoming	Brigham Young	49
66	Arkansas	Western Kentucky	46
75	Texas Tech	Eastern New Mex. State	32
37	Concordia	Jamestown	32
74	Kent St	Heidelberg	42
56	Baldwin Wallace	John Carroll	36
41	Wooster	Crile Hosp.	31
39	Randolph Macon	Lynchburg	24
45	No. Dakota	Wahpeton Science	33
38	Ft. Bragg Rec. Cen.	Wake Forest	22
71	Wright Field	So. Ill. Norm.	56
30	Wheaton	Elmhurst	29
51	Valley Forge Hosp.	Aberdeen Torp.	35
74	Hutchinson NAS	Topeka AAF	35
40	Toledo	Findlay	32
46	TCU	No. Texas St. T.	37
37	Moorehead	Jamestown	32
42	Illinois Norm.	Concordia Sem.	24

Players Are Offered Manager's Posts—Reds Deal Collapses

By HAROLD C. BURR
Brooklyn Eagle Staff Correspondent

Columbus, Ohio, Dec. 7—Things became so desperate at the minor league Winter meetings here yesterday that the barren news hounds took to turning over rocks and watching the woodwork in the hope that a trade would pop out. President Branch Rickey remained in seclusion in his ivory tower a mile from baseball headquarters and those who sought players had to come to him

The Mahatma of Montague St. added a third farm manager when he appointed Ray Hayworth, veteran catcher, to pilot the newly-organized Fort Worth team in the Texas League. The Rickey breakfast was spoiled when nine of his ball players asked for their unconditional release to boss minor clubs. The names of such traitors to the Flatbush cause were not divulged.

Manager Ben Chapman of the Phillies was still eager to trade. But when he hinted that he might be interested in acquiring Johnny Rizzo from the Dodger organization nobody took him up to arrange an interview. Birmingham Benny did buy Johnny Humphries from the White Sox, the fast-ball pitcher who broke into the American League with the Indians. Jimmy Dykes receives Frank Martin, 25-year-old right-hander from Utica, the Phillies' Eastern League farm.

Snubbed By Giants

"I guess it's just a carry-over from my playing days," said Chapman morosely. "Whenever my name was mentioned at a meeting when I was an outfielder, the magnates would stare down their noses.

"We don't want to trade for Chapman," they would mumble and walk away. Now they don't want to trade with Chapman.

The Giants were not intrigued when he offered them Vince DiMaggio. Manager Ott wants a catcher and Chapman hasn't a catcher in captivity. Prexy Horace Stoneham and Master Melvin caught an early plane for Chicago and may swing a deal for a backstop when the convention cavalcade arrives this evening.

There was a rumor that Johnny Mize and Bill Voiselle had been offered to Chapman for Ron Northey and DiMaggio, but the Blue Jay pilot won't part with Northey and the Giants don't want the wrong DiMaggio.

The nearest thing to a swap was when the Indians and Athletics sought to turn over Sam Chapman for Jeff Heath, Peck's Bad Boy at Cleveland. The investigation proved that Sam injured his knee in service and on second thought it might not be polite to part with such a Shibe Park idol. Elephant fans don't forget either.

The bottom has fallen out of the proposed Olmo-Lamanno exchange. Rickey thinks that he's short of grass patrolmen and that he doesn't need catching badly enough to sacrifice an outfielder to get the Cincinnati star. Neither does Branch care to rebuild his pitching corps with Charley Schantz, Chapman's bait to get Howie Schultz and Olmo.

Betzel Jaycee Pilot

It didn't take the Giants 24 hours to grab Bruno Betzel to manage their Jersey City farm. Stoneham sent for Betzel, asked him what he wanted in the way of salary, Bruno told him and there was no hesitation on Horace's part. Betzel realizes that he isn't going to have as good a ball club as he had at Montreal last year, but he saw some good-looking, young players when the Royals engaged the Little Giants.

Tom Greenwade was another discharged Dodger who caught on quickly. The famous Ozark bird dog was signed by Laughing Larry MacPhail of the Yankees. MacPhail saw Tom work when they were both in Brooklyn, building up the Dodgers. The scout's best achievement was bringing in Rex Barney alive.

A couple of former Dodger neighbors went to the Braves. Jake Flowers was released from his Pirate obligations and became a coach with the Braves, and Ted McGrew, the man of many jobs, is now chief scout at Boston under Billy Southworth, who will need some scouting now that he hasn't the Cardinals' chain behind him to supply the missing links. There's a new coaching staff at Detroit, too, comprising Tommy Bridges and Frank Shellenbach.

The Columbus interlude comes to a close today. The big league meetings open Monday in Chicago, where it's confidently expected more deals will fall through.

Pea-Green Mariners In Cage Whirlpool

By BEN GOULD

One of the few coaches in the land who's equally at home on the basketball court and gridiron, Lt. Earl Brown literally had just about enough time to stow away his football charts and ideas to concentrate on Kings Point's Merchant Marine Academy hoopsters.

Though green, the Mariners have stuff on the ball, as was evidenced last night when they invaded Union College and won by 42 to 31. Their safari abroad will be continued this evening in the Tigers' lair at Princeton and if they get by this outfit Brown's charges will be well on their way to big-time achievements.

The lieutenant, who was assistant court coach at Brown before taking over coaching reins at both Harvard and Dartmouth, has a habit of molding winning teams. In 1943, he fashioned an Eastern Intercollegiate League champion at Dartmouth and given enough time he'll do the same at Great Neck.

It didn't take Earl long to pick his first five. At the forward posts, he has Si Taflan, a five, nine Bridgeporter, who is a tricky dribbler, and Bill Faris, six, one heaver from Bloomington, Ind., who dotes one-hand shots.

The squad's tallest man, Don Burlingham, who stands six, three, plays center. He played ball at Columbia Prep and hails from Salem, Ore.

Two newcomers are at guard posts. They are Paul Harless, who hails from San Francisco, and Louis Viau, who performed with Loyola University.

The Mariners will open their home campaign a week from tonight against formidable Villanova. Then they come back the next night on the same floor against City College.

Underprivileged Girls Find Happiness in Self-Government Borough Club —See Page 6

BROOKLYN EAGLE

5 CENTS EVERYWHERE

Weather—Partly cloudy, mild today.

105th YEAR—No. 335—DAILY and SUNDAY | BROOKLYN N. Y., SUNDAY, DECEMBER 9, 1945 | ★★★★

UAW Spurns Peace, Charges Truman's Use of 'Police Club'

Tells President He Strikes at Party Program

Detroit, Dec. 8 (U.P.)—Sharply rejecting a White House appeal for an end of the General Motors shutdown, the United Automobile Workers union (C.I.O.) tonight accused President Truman of using a "policeman's Club" to abrogate labor's right to strike.

U.A.W. President R. J. Thomas sternly warned the President that he was "striking at the heart" of the program which gave the Democratic party an election victory in 1944.

As the powerful union mobilized its 650,000 members for a fight against the Administration's labor legislation proposals, the wage dispute paralyzing General Motors appeared no nearer settlement than when 175,000 workers struck 93 G. M. plants 18 days ago.

10% Increase Again Rejected

A conference of 200 delegates representing G. M. local unions bitterly spurned the company's repeated offer to increase wages by 13½ cents an hour, or approximately 10 percent.

The conference said the strike would not end until the union's 30 percent wage demands had been "fully satisfied."

Then the delegates angrily rejected Mr. Truman's appeal for an immediate return to work as a "display of patriotism" to maintain reconversion production at wartime levels.

A resolution adopted by unanimous vote of the conference reiterated the charge of C. I. O. President Philip Murray that "the Federal Administration yields in abject cowardice" to the "arrogance of industry."

"Cooling Off Period" Condemned

"We are asked to retreat from economic democracy as furthered under the courageous leadership of Franklin D. Roosevelt," the resolution said.

Mr. Thomas keynoted the union attitude by condemning President Truman's request for compulsory fact-finding boards and a mandatory 30-day "cooling off" period before strikes can be called.

"It would tear from the hands of labor unions the major weapon es-

Continued on Page 2

TURNS HEAD AWAY—Rear Admiral Husband E. Kimmel, seated, Navy Pearl Harbor commander at the time of the sneak attack, averts his head as General of Army George C. Marshall strides by to testify before the Senate Committee investigating the disaster.

DEMS CLASH OVER NAMING U. S. ATTORNEY

Brooklyn and Queens Chiefs in Bitter War For Keogh, Quinn

By JOSEPH H. SCHMALACKER

A sharp political clash between the powerful Brooklyn Democratic organization and its counterpart in Queens over President Truman's choice of a new Federal Attorney for the Eastern U. S. District appeared last night to be reaching a critical stage.

Reports of increasingly bitter feeling between the two organizations were growing by leaps and bounds although the consensus in normally well-posted party circles, both at Washington and in New York City, strengthened a conviction among Brooklyn Democrats that their organization, with Leader Frank V. Kelly at its head, would come out on top.

Early Decision Seen

The belief was expressed that a decision on the appointment would be made in the near future after Democratic National Chairman Robert E. Hannegan's return from

Frank V. Kelly

James A. Roe

a flying trip to Europe. Mr. Hannegan, as chief patronage adviser to Mr. Truman, is known to be a strong exponent of orthodox organizational policies. In the 1944 Chicago convention struggle which Mr. Hannegan led for Mr. Truman's own nomination for the Vice Presidency his strongest supporters among the New York City chieftains were Mr. Kelly and Bronx Democratic Leader Edward J. Flynn, New York State's national committeeman.

In the current Brooklyn-Queens clash, J. Vincent Keogh, a wartime lieutenant commander in the navy, with an official citation for his service in the Normandy invasion, and a member of Mayor-elect William O'Dwyer's staff during his administration as District Attorney, has been recommended as the Brooklyn choice for the appointment.

Queens Leader James A. Roe, a member of the House at Washington, is reportedly insisting on the appointment of T. Vincent Quinn. Mr. Quinn has been discharging the duties of U. S. Attorney since the resignation of former Federal Attorney Miles F. McDonald, now Democratic District Attorney-elect of Kings County.

Behind-the-Scenes War

Against this background, according to well-informed reports, the struggle for the appointment between the two county organizations

Continued on Page 16

Rally to Mark Bible Sunday Program Today

Universal Bible Sunday, which is being widely marked in the churches of Brooklyn, as well as throughout the nation, today, will be especially observed this afternoon in a rally at the Academy of Music under the auspices of the Brooklyn Bible Society.

The chief speaker will be Robert G. LeTourneau, industrialist, who devotes his weekends to touring the nation in his private plane and addressing church groups.

The musical portion of the program will include selections by Mrs. Dorothy Streathearn, the vocalist who is featured in many of Mr. LeTourneau's evangelistic appearances, and selections by the Salvation Army Band.

Harold B. Pretlove, president of the Brooklyn Bible Society, will be chairman of the meeting. More than 200 clergymen, of various denominations are expected to attend, accompanied by delegations from their churches.

Special Desk Set Up To Speed Vet Discharges

An army and navy desk, manned 24 hours daily, has been set up in the LaGuardia Field Administration Building to arrange transportation to separation centers for the Pacific veterans who are retuning home to New York and vicinity for discharge. They were allocated 70 percent of space on commercial airlines flying from the West Coast to New York.

The project, known as Comm.-Air, short for Commercial Airlines, takes care of about 360 men daily, including 180 army and navy personnel.

With Today's Brooklyn Eagle

Staging Area--BROOKLYN Record of Borough at War

Secretary of War Robert P. Patterson congratulates the people of Brooklyn upon the borough's "magnificent" showing in the war as recorded today in Staging Area—BROOKLYN, a history of the community's wartime performance included with this issue of the Brooklyn Eagle. Mr. Patterson's letter is reproduced herewith:

WAR DEPARTMENT
WASHINGTON

The Editor,
The Brooklyn Eagle,
Brooklyn, N. Y.

November 19, 1945.

Dear Sir:

The great majority of the 327,000 Brooklyn men and women who served in the armed forces wore the colors of the Army or the Air Corps. The three million people of Brooklyn are justified in believing that the efforts of the community could not be surpassed by any place in the country. The contribution of those who served with the colors and those who fought on the home front was magnificent.

It is a happy idea to put on paper the history of the Borough from Pearl Harbor to the deck of the Missouri. For the Army, I want to congratulate the people of Brooklyn, those who served in the services as well as in war industry and allied activities, and express gratitude for their efforts.

Sincerely yours,

Robert P. Patterson,
Secretary of War.

Staging Area—BROOKLYN is a 64-page booklet, a copy of which is included without extra charge with this edition of the Brooklyn Eagle.

When you open your copy of Staging Area, BROOKLYN, you will see that you are projected through things of which every Brooklynite is proud, like its place as an Atlantic seaboard port, the Navy Yard, Fort Hamilton, etc., through the field of human experience, as told in "A Woman Will Remember," into stories of our men in uniform and of those who labored at home front occupations.

Additional copies will be on sale beginning tomorrow at ten cents each at the office of the Brooklyn Eagle, 24 Johnson St.

FARLEY FLAYS POLITICAL USE OF GRAND JURY

Ex-Postmaster General Warns Democrats of Responsibility to Voters

Misuse of grand jury powers to issue "vague charges," calious accusations and smears of the innocent in the midst of a political campaign was bitterly censured by former Postmaster General James A. Farley in a speech last night before the Bronx County Bar Association at a dinner in the Hotel Commodore.

At the same time, the former Democratic State and national chairman sounded a warning to his own party that the overwhelming victory for Mayor-elect William O'Dwyer and his running-mates in the city campaign confronts the party with a challenge and a great "obligation" to the voters which can be repaid only by good government, at the least possible cost and with the greatest efficinecy.

Failure to meet this responsibility properly, Mr. Farley predicted, will cause it to be thrown out of office, as before, with consequent "weeping and wailing and gnashing of teeth among the selfish and shortsighted ones."

Praises Bronx Official

Mr. Farley, speaking on "party responsibility," led into his main theme by lauding the administration of Bronx County District Attorney's office and predicting District Attorney Samuel J. Foley's "distinguished service" will eventually lead to his elevation to the Supreme Court.

"It is a profundly important thing to keep the administration of the law, especially the administration of the criminal law, on a non-political plane," Mr. Farley said. "We have all been distressed in the

Continued on Page 16

Seek Treaty Revision

Cairo, Dec. 8 (U.P.)—Arab press reports said today that a committee of Egyptian "elder statesmen" had decided to urge the Egyptian government to demand, immediately and formally, the opening of negotiations for revision of the Anglo-Egyptian treaty.

City Spots 1,000 Units Here for Apartments

A survey of one and two family dwellings in Brooklyn has disclosed more than 1,000 houses available for apartment units, City Housing Commissioner Joseph Platzker said yesterday.

The survey, which covered 1,970 houses, has been submitted to Mayor-elect O'Dwyer's Emergency Housing Committee, and is expected to be made public today by Mayor LaGuardia during his regular Sunday broadcast.

While the multiple-dwelling law is the main reason such houses are not turned into apartments for three or more families, Commissioner Platzker pointed out that due to the stringent housing shortage the law might be waived. The multiple-dwelling law, which does not cover one and two family houses would require certain expensive alterations.

Governor Dewey will go ahead with his program to convert surplus military and naval installations into emergency housing for veterans despite the sharp cleavage in Mr. O'Dwyer's committee over the question of whether such conversion is practicable, State Housing Commissioner Herman L. Stichman said last night.

Commissioner Stichman, who disclosed last week that Mr. O'Dwyer was in accord with him on the conversion program, stated: "Governor Dewey has his own program and will go ahead with it no matter what the committee decides."

The controversy over temporary housing versus renovation of old law tenements came out in the open Friday at a public hearing held by the City Housing Authority.

Backing Mayor LaGuardia in his renovation stand was Edward Weinfeld, State housing chief under Governor Lehman, while Thomas G. Grace, State director of the Federal Housing Administration, supported the Dewey plan.

Depends on Condition

Commissioner Stichman cast doubts on the proposal to turn untenanted one and two-family dwellings into three or more apartments. "It depends on what condition they're in," he said. "Some are in no condition to be lived in."

Conferences between Navy and

Continued on Page 16

Partly Cloudy and Mild Predicted for Today

Weather today will continue mild, with skies partly cloudy and temperatures in the low fifties. There will be "moderate to fresh" winds.

Citizen Group's Patrol Stops Prospect Park Area Holdups

Street patrolling by a committee of citizens banded together in a personal war on crime has stopped all outbreaks in the Prospect Park section for the last three weeks, it was learned yesterday.

"We got together after 22 cases of holdups and muggings occurred within eight days," Samuel Spector, of 901 Washington Ave., head of the Washington Avenue Citizens Committee, said. "We patrol the section from 8 p.m. until 1 a.m. every night, and have so far stopped all crime."

The committee includes 200 members, all of whom live in the neighborhood of Washington Ave. and Carroll St.

The section previously provided a happy hunting ground for lawbreakers, because wide open stretches of badly lighted streets were left unpatrolled in the police shortage. Robbers could escape along the B. M. T. tracks, through the Botanic Garden or through open school lots.

The civilian patrolmen work in pairs. They carry police whistles and wear armbands. Wives of the patrolmen provide a canteen where refreshments are served on cold nights.

The group operates with the co-operation of police of the 71st precinct, whom they call if they observe any incidents.

WIRES TAPPED BY NAZIS HELD UP PEARL TIP

Marshall Tells Probe Group Why Warning Failed to Reach Short

Washington, Dec. 8 (U.P.)—Gen. George C. Marshall disclosed today that the Germans intercepted prewar telephone conversations between the late President Roosevelt and former British Prime Minister Winston Churchill.

He told the Pearl Harbor investigating committee that knowledge of the German interceptions may have been one reason why he did not telephone a war warning to Hawaii on the morning of Dec. 7, 1941.

The message was dispatched by Western Union and Commercial Cable and did not reach Lt. Gen. Walter C. Short, Hawaiian army commander, until hours after the Japanese sneak attack.

Under questioning by committee members, General Marshall took a share of War Department responsibility for not realizing in late November that General Short's command was not properly alerted for a surprise attack. In response to a warning from Washington of possible hostilities, General Short sent a reply indicating his command was alerted for sabotage only.

Last week Lt. Gen. Leonard T. Gerow, former chief of the army's War Plans Division, told the committee he would take whatever blame there was for not noting that General Short's reply was inadequate.

Sen. Homer Ferguson (R., Mich.) asked General Marshall if he agreed that it was Gerow's "full responsibility."

"I would not say that was his full responsibility," General Marshall "It was his direct responsibility. But I had a responsibility as Chief of Staff, too."

General Marshall's first war warning, the one to which General Short replied, was sent Nov. 27, 1941. The second, which arrived too late, was sent a short time before the Dec. 7 attack.

Asked why he did not call General Short directly by telephone to de-

Continued on Page 16

O'DWYER NAMES W. J. DONOGHUE AS HIS SECRETARY

Former Newspaperman Was War Correspondent And Aide to Bennett

El Centro, Cal., Dec. 8 (U.P.)—William O'Dwyer, mayor-elect of New York, vacationing here, today named William J. Donoghue, 42-year-old former newspaperman, as Executive Secretary to take office January 1.

Mr. Donoghue, who has a long record in public relations and news writing, was one of the publicity managers in Mr. O'Dwyer's campaign, prior to that time "The Little Irishman" was West Coast publicity director for the Maritime Commission and War Shipping Administration in San Francisco. He was a war correspondent for the Maritime Commission in Europe, making beach landings at Anzio and Normandy.

He also served as civilian aide to then Brig. Gen. O'Dwyer, in 1942. His home is at 35-33 87th St., Jackson Heights, Queens.

Before the war, Mr. Donoghue was secretary to John J. Bennett, then New York's Attorney General, for seven years and worked on the copy desk of New York newspapers for 12 years.

Mr. O'Dwyer today awaited the arrival of Wayne Johnson, his campaign manager, before making any definite plans for the weekend. Mr. Johnson was reported to have stopped in Oceanside, Cal.

Mr. O'Dwyer previously planned to make a tour of Imperial Valley, Sunday, visiting the 25-million dollar all-American canal, the Imperial Dam on the Colorado River, as well as 30.000 acres of lettuce now being harvested here.

Flare Draws Hunt For Bombers to Swamp in Florida

Miami, Fla., Dec. 8 (U.P.)—Navy planes, a helicopter, jeeps, and an amphibious weasel converged tonight on a fog-shrouded swamp where a flare and a fire may have provided the first clue to the fate of five naval bombers and their 14 crewmen, mysteriously missing since Wednesday afternoon.

A low fog hanging over the marsh hampered the hunt.

The red flare in the swamp and a fire burning not far distant were reported by Capt. J. D. Morrison, airliner pilot bound from Miami to New York, after he passed over Melbourne in northcentral Florida. He said he saw the flare first, then a big fire whose glow outlined the solitary figure of a man. The scene was a desolate swamp.

19 Die in Crash

Billings, Mont., Dec. 8 (U.P.)—Seventeen soldiers and two civilians were killed and five soldiers were injured today when a C-47 army transport plane crashed and burned one mile south of the Billings airport during a blinding snowstorm.

Walsh Acts to Correct Firemen's Inequalities

216 Provisional Lieutenants Will Be Given Authority of Rank—8-Hour Day in Offing

By WALTER CROSBY

Fire Commissioner Patrick Walsh has ordered that 216 fire lieutenants who have not been given authority of their rank become regular lieutenants Jan. 1. The entire department's force of captains and lieutenants probably will go on an eight-hour day working schedule shortly after, it was learned yesterday.

The move was considered by fire officers to be a direct result of publicity given to internal workings of the department by the Uniformed Fire Officers Association and to stories carried exclusively in the Brooklyn Eagle about inequalities in working hours, the plight of the lieutenants who were not lieutenants and lowered morale among firemen and officers.

Officers Kept in Dark

The provisional lieutenants, appointed last December from civil service lists which were about to expire, had been kept in the dark ever since on their exact status. They were not given officers' supervisory duties, nor were they given firemen's routine jobs. They were, according to department orders, to be "obeyed and respected," but they were also, according to other orders, subject to regulations governing ordinary firemen and were supposed to wear officers' uniforms only when specifically assigned to officers' duties.

Fire officers said the new order, which will substantially strengthen the regular officer force, resulted from the newspaper stories and advertisements which, for the first time, presented to the public the story of what goes on in the department.

The gag rule imposed on the department, which prohibited firemen or officers from talking about the force, had been violated several times by firemen, who promptly were transferred to outlying stations far from their homes.

Officers Hire Civilian

The officers finally reached the point where they employed a civilian, designated him as secretary of the U. F. O. A. and permitted him to speak for the organization. Since he was not a member of the department, he could not be held on departmental charges for disclosing information about the department.

A week after the first Brooklyn

Continued on Page 16

Nazi Crematorium Found in Warsaw

A Polish press agency Warsaw dispatch said yesterday that a crematorium operated by the German Gestapo during the enemy occupation had been found in the cellar of a house on Szucha Ave., one of Warsaw's principal residential streets. Quantities of clothing, human ashes and bones were found, the dispatch said.

Bomber Zips Coast-to-Coast In 5 Hrs., 17 Min.

Washington, Dec. 8 (U.P.)—The army's new tail-propelled bomber —The Douglas XB-42 "Mixmaster" —arrived at Bolling Field tonight at 6:39 p.m. (Brooklyn time), to set a new transcontinental flight record of five hours, 17 minutes and 34 seconds.

The Mixmaster took off from Long Beach, Cal., at 1:22 p.m. It buzzed Bolling Field at 6:39 p.m. and landed at the army air base a few minutes later. It averaged better than 432 miles an hour for the 2,295 mile flight.

The previous unofficial transcontinental record was held by a Boeing C-97 transport which recently flew from Seattle to Washington, D. C., in six hours, three minutes.

The Mixmaster's record, however, was unofficial. It will not stand as an official record because its route was not plotted by the National Aeronautical Association.

The ship, propelled by counter-rotating twin propellers in its tail, will be used in commercial travel. As an airliner, it is capable of carrying 48 passengers.

Truman to Take Cruise On Presidential Yacht

Washington, Dec. 8 (U.P.)—President Truman will take a weekend cruise aboard the Presidential yacht Williamsburgh with a party of cabinet members, senators and friends, the White House announced today.

The Presidential party will leave from Washington Navy Yard and will sail the Potomac River tonight, all day Sunday and return to the White House about 8 a.m. Monday.

Town Ration Board To Get Fed-For Free

Cheshire, Conn., Dec. 8 (U.P.)—Turnabout is fair play.

Townspeople thought the ration board did a pretty good job of keeping everyone fed and warm during the war, so they're throwing a testimonial dinner for the board members Monday night.

More than that, they'll have their names inscribed on a town hall plaque.

Jap Sub Skipper To Testify at Trial Of Capt. McVay

Washington, Dec. 8 (U.P.)—Comm. Ike Hashimto, Japanese submarine captain who boasted he sank the U. S. cruiser Indianapolis, will testify at the court martial trial of Capt. Charles B. McVay III, the navy announced today.

The navy is flying Hashimoto from Japan to testify against Comm. McVay, captain of the Indianapolis who is charged with incompetence and neglect of duty. The cruiser sank in the Philippine sea last July 30 with the loss of 880 officers and men.

Comm. Hashimoto left Tokyo yesterday by naval air transport plane and is expected to arrive in Washington Monday or Tuesday.

The judge advocate of the court martial called the Jap submarine commander to strengthen the navy contention that the Indianapolis was torpedoed. Capt. McVay is charged with failing to zig-zag the warship in waters known to be infested with enemy submarines.

The court marital was in recess until Tuesday awaiting arrival of Hashimoto and 20 survivors of the Indianapolis summoned as witnesses.

Meanwhile, a new unofficial journal for service personnel, the Army and Navy Bulletin, charged that the navy was blaming Capt. McVay for heavy casualties in the loss of the Indianapolis when it was not his fault.

WHERE TO FIND IT

	Page		Page
Art	32	Obituaries	23
Better Housing	42	Old Timers	26
Bridge	37	Our Champs	26
Camera Club	21	Radio	32
Crossword Comics		Real Estate	37
Currie	3	Resorts	33-36
Dr. Brady	22	School News	29
Editorial	22	Society	18
Heffernan	22	Sports	27-29
Helen Worth	21	Take My Word	22
Horoscope	37	Theaters	30
Lindley	22	Travel	33-36
Mary Haworth	32	Veteran in Bklyn	26
Movies	30	Want Ads	38-41
Music	30	Week Outdoors	37
Novel	37	Women	21

GOING PLACES

By RUTH G. DAVIS

This is a reminder and a suggestion. The time to do your Christmas shopping is getting short, and also the time to see and hear the inimitable Hildegarde in the Persian Room of the **Hotel Plaza**, for she will leave there early next month. Probably nothing could please your wife or best gal more than an evening spent in this famous dining room. And we assure you it will be AN EVENING. Perhaps you wonder why that would be a special treat. Well, in slang, "you hain't

Continued on Following Page

BROOKLYN PUTS ON CHRISTMAS DRESS—Floodlights on the Soldiers and Sailors Arch at Grand Army Placa accentuate the beauty of the snow-covered structure. Maxine Kleinman, 8, of 75 Ocean Ave., tries to get the photographer into a snow fight in Prospect Park. One of the park's beauty spots gets Mother Nature's face-powdering at right.

Eagle Staff photos

Tropic Moon Inspires A Song About Brooklyn

The moon over Bali and other exotic lands he visited in the South Pacific at Uncle Sam's expense, couldn't hold a candle to Brooklyn's moon as far as Terry Shane, a former Brooklynite, is concerned. In fact, the Oriental moon gave him a big yen for a glimpse of the same moon which used to shine in the windows of his childhood home in Bensonhurst. And it brought memories of the times he squired Mazie, his childhood sweetheart, home from Ebbets Field; or when they went window-shopping along Flatbush Ave.

Since the same moon also shone on his debut as a pianist with Freddie Martin's orchestra in the Hotel Bossert, he naturally translated his feelings into music. Before many more moons had gone by the young GI found himself back in the United States with the words and music for "Moon Over Brooklyn" in his pocket.

While he was playing at the Bossert with Freddie Martin's band he became acquainted with Guy Lombardo, who, with his Royal Canadians, was featured at the Hotel St. George.

When he came up on a brief leave from Texas, dropped in on Lombardo at his Freeport, L. I., home to tell him about his song.

Band Leader Intrigued

Intrigued by the catchy tune, the orchestra leader immediately made arrangements to introduce it on his regular radio hour. Mr. Lombardo, whose orchestra plays in the grill of the Hotel Roosevelt, Manhattan, takes credit for introducing 16 of the 20 top tunes of this year, and feels certain that he has another hit on his hands.

"We'll give this song as a Christmas present to Brooklyn," he said. And so, on Christmas night, Mr. Lombardo will give his own "soft, sweet" arrangement of the Brooklynite's opus. Although he customarily dedicates his program over station WJZ to celebrities, he will provide a fitting background for the song by dedicating the whole program to Brooklyn.

The playing of his song will also be a big present for young Shane, who had to rush back to Texas, but who will be able to hear it on the nation-wide network.

Bus Line to Hire Strikebreakers; Men Hit Ruling

William Cooper, president of the struck Green Bus Lines in Queens, has announced intention to hire 250 drivers and maintenance men to replace strikers who walked out Saturday.

As the strike today went into its sixth day, Mr. Cooper declared that service was being maintained at 75 percent of normal through use of 120 stockholder-drivers and office personnel.

Milton E. Jacobowitz, attorney for the strikers, today declared the men are ready and willing to arbitrate the dispute and that "if the company wants arbitration, they can have it in five minutes." He said an impasse had been reached, with the company wanting the men to return to work before arbitration and the strikers insisting on arbitration first.

The strikers, meeting at the Woodhaven Democratic Club, 101-50 Woodhaven Boulevard, were highly critical of Justice Percy D. Stoddard of Queens Supreme Court for the "opinion" which aaccompanied his decision on the company application for a temporary injunction.

Justice Stoddard denied the company's plea but declared that "had the court the power to grant the relief it would do so."

Vincent Galasso, business agent for the drivers' union, Local 1179 of the Street, Electric Railway and Motor Coach Employes, A. F. L., declared that if the union is condemned for committing a breach of contract, "what has the judge to say about the company which has committed more than five breaches of contract?"

Britain Rebuffs Spain On UNO Membership

London, Dec. 20 (U.P.)—Great Britain flatly rejected a Spanish proposal that the British Foreign Office reconsider the Potsdam declaration barring Spain from membership in the United Nations Organization, a responsible diplomatic source disclosed today.

The informant said the rebuff was dealt Spain's new ambassador, Domingo De Las Barcenas, within 10 days after he had presented his credentials.

'Heartbroken Mother' Leaves Tot in Subway

There'll be another present under the Christmas tree at the New York Foundling Hospital next Monday night.

It will be placed there for a fat, round, fair-haired baby boy who was found on a Manhattan bound West End B.M.T train at about 10:30 last night.

A man passenger found the baby and after giving him to Isaac Goldberg, New Utrecht Ave. station agent, he disappeared. The infant was sent from there to the hospital.

Detective Thomas McCauley, of the Bath Beach station, was assigned to locate the baby's parents or relatives. He had nothing to work on today but a rather lengthy note, apparently signed by the baby's mother and pinned to his little cap.

The note, which was nervously scrawled on note paper, was signed "Heartbroken Mother" and told in short, jerky sentences the outline of a big city tragedy.

In any case the tragedy reached this climax only a few days before other children, and happier parents, prepare to celebrate the birth of Christ.

"Please take care of the baby for me," the note implored in part. "I am in no position to take care of it. He is a good boy. He is Irish-English. He is eight months old. I have no money to support or take care of him. His father is dead. Please do this, whoever finds him."

Police said the baby boy appeared to be in good health, weighed about 20 pounds and had a light complexion and fair hair.

He was comfortably dressed in a brown snow-suit, blue booties, white sweater and clean white baby clothes.

He didn't cry much at the station house, police said.

Ex-GI's 2 Wives Meet, Cook Up Bigamy Stew

Donald Gorsline, 25, of 39-07 Union St., Flushing, who had a wonderful double homecoming from the army, had his sad awakening today—in jail.

Mr. Gorsline was discharged from the army on Sept. 9 and went home to his wife, Mrs. Catherine Murray Gorsline, 24, at 149-09 Northern Boulevard, Flushing. That was welcome home No. 1.

According to her complaint in Queens Felony Court yesterday, they were married in the rectory of Our Lady of Pity Roman Catholic Church, the Bronx, on Jan. 14, 1944, while he was a private.

Private Gorsline did not send her an army allotment, but that, it seemed, was all right. He explained that his allotment was going to his mother. (Other married GIs who had dependent mothers were required to make allotments to mother and wife both.) From overseas he sent her $200, money he won at dice.

The second welcome home developed out of rumors young Catherine heard about another woman. She investigated and learned, according to the complaint, that there was a previous wife, Mrs. Virginia Arnold Gorsline, 25, of 252-21 4th Ave., Little Neck, whom he married at the Fort Totten chapel on June 21, 1942. They had a daughter, Caroline Ann, now two and a half years old.

The two welcomes were merged yesterday when both wives faced the veteran in Queens Felony Court, where he was arraigned on a bigamy charge. Magistrate Henry A. Soffer held him in $5,000 bail for action of the grand jury.

Retire 'Old Gray Mare,' Who Played Siren's Role

San Francisco, Dec. 20 (U.P.)—Belle, the plump "old gray mare," who lured more than 2,000 mules from boxcars to corrals for overseas processing during the war, was turned out to pasture today with a "well done" from Port of Embarkation officials.

Col. George J. Rife, chief of the Port Animal Depot, said Belle gave her bit for victory, but added he wasn't quite sure whether it was Belle, herself, or the bell he hung on Belle that really turned the trick.

George Currie's column will not appear in the Brooklyn Eagle this week. He is on vacation and will resume his musings upon the Brooklyn scene next Monday.

BAR TO TEACHER EVIDENCE HIT AT QUINN TRIAL

The three-man Board of Education committee, trying public school teacher Mary A. Quinn on charges of un-Americanism and intolerance, was under attack today by two Brooklyn organizations for excluding testimony of her colleagues.

The testimony relates to utterances made by Miss Quinn outside the classroom. The committee ruled the teacher's outside activities had no relevance to the charges.

Resolutions attacking the committee's ruling were passed last night by the Brooklyn chapter of the American Veterans Committee and the Brooklyn Committee Against Bigotry. Local 2 of the Teachers Guild, A. F. L., and Frederick T. Rope, education director of the Public Education Association, have made similar protests.

4 Librarians Testify

Meanwhile, as the trial continued yesterday, four librarians of the Bay Ridge branch of the Brooklyn Public Library testified they had neither seen nor lent Miss Quinn a book from which the suspended teacher said she obtained material for use in her civics class.

The four women, questioned by the committee prosecutor, Stuart C. Lucey, were Helen P. Bolman of 8 Clark St., Mildred E. Buente of 252 74th St., Catherine C. Blodgett of 89 Hicks St. and Elvira Stavenas of 267 Dahlgren Place.

Miss Quinn had previously testified during a pre-trial examination in an unsuccessful libel suit she brought against 14 fellow teachers that she obtained the material from the book "None More Courageous" by Stewart Holbrook.

Yesterday's first witness, Mary A. Kennedy, an assistant superintendent in the junior high division, who investigated Miss Quinn two years ago, said Miss Quinn had told her she lost the notes from the Holbrook book and accepted the same material from another teacher.

'First American' References

The material involves a series of sentences beginning with "The first American..." and naming persons of one nationality. It was brought out that the Holbrook book cites the war deeds of American heroes of all nationalities but does not use the "first American" outline.

The Brooklyn Committee Against Bigotry met last night in Savoy Mansion, 6322 20th Ave. Representatives of 26 organizations in the Bensonhurst and Borough Park sections voted to make the committee a permanent organization to combat intolerance in the schools.

The resolution passed by the veterans group which met at 381 Fulton St., accused the trial board of incompetency. It was sent to Dr. John E. Wade, superintendent of schools.

Text of Telegram

The Brooklyn committee voted to send the following telegram to the board members:

"Three hundred citizens of Brooklyn have voted to register their protest at the refusal of the committee hearing the case of May Quinn to permit the teachers to testify in the trial. Part of the superintendent's charges against May Quinn include her un-democratic utterances and activities in relation to her colleagues. Only her fellow teachers can bring testimony bearing on this charge. We call on the Board of Education to order that these teachers be allowed to testify."

Two guest speakers at the meeting were Samuel Wallach, president of the Teachers Union, C. I. O., and D., L. M. Birkhead, national director of the Friends of Democracy. Mr. Wallach criticized the Board of Education for having taken three years to bring Miss Quinn's case up for trial. His suggestion that the board be elected by the people received enthusiastic support.

Origin of Holiday Traditions Traced

The historical background of Christmas was discussed at the Academy of Music by Barbara Carper Lang, narrator, who told of several o fthe holiday customs borrowed from pagan religions.

Christmas feasting was taken from the old Yule festival of the Scandanavians, Miss Lang declared, and was part of their pagan faith. Misteltoe was once used by the Godless as a charm against evil and Christmas colors, red and green, come from the Roman's protection against harm, she said.

BUY U. S. VICTORY BONDS AND SAVINGS STAMPS

PSAL Group to Review Barring of Hoop Teams

A special meeting of the executive committee of the Public Schools Athletic League has been called for today at the Board of Education to reconsider and review the ban suspending Long Island City and Bryant High Schools from P. S. A. L. basketball competition.

The schools were dropped from the Queens P. S. A. L. North Shore loop at the monthly meeting of the High School Games Committee last Tuesday for playing an Oct. 30 basketball contest which raised more than $250 for the National War Fund. The P. S. A. L. law prohibits any competition before Nov. 15.

The suspension of the two quintets brought much unfavorable comment from city and State officials along with veteran and civic groups.

City Councilman Hugh Quinn of Queens released the following statement last night.

"Action of the P. S. A. L. was more than difficult on sports-minded Bryant and Long Island City, especially when you consider the athletes are now in the 'scholastic dog house" for playing for the National War Fund.

"This isn't the Christmas spirit or the welcome we guaranteed our returning service men. The P. S. A. L. may well reconsider its ruling and if it doesn't I propose a motion be brought up at the next City Council meeting asking the official body to rescind its ruling. I will do anything else possible to get the two schools reinstated in the league."

Another official, State Senator Seymour Halpern, declared that "the P. S. A. L.'s disregard for the public which threatens the very existence of interscholastic competition is becoming too great to be ignored. It is a disgrace. We in Queens will not stand by idly and see our boys so badly treated. I shall communicate at once with the State director of physical education and give him the facts of the case and urge immediate action."

Hope for Reinstatement

Meanwhile, Bill Lynch, Long Island City basketball coach and health education department chairman, and Charles J. Carpenter, gym department head, said both schools will continue to play out their schedule and are hopeful that today's meeting will bring the schools back in good standing.

At Long Island City High School the principal, Dr. Wallace A. Manheimer assumed full responsibility for the charity game. He said his school's team was approached with the idea of playing the contest and he sanctioned it because it was such a worthy cause.

"I didn't think we were disobeying any rules and I assume full responsibility for the move. I don't want any blame put on the pupils."

BUY U. S. VICTORY BONDS AND SAVINGS STAMPS

McQuillan to Retire As Tax Investigator

Hugh McQuillan, Government tax agent, who was in charge of the investigation of the Lindbergh ransom money and who was instrumental in tax evasion cases of many underworld characters, will retire Jan. 1 after 55 years of Government service, friends said today.

He was special agent in charge of the New York Division of the Intelligence Unit of the United States Internal Revenue Bureau.

Newspaper Condemned By Jewish War Vets

Accused of espousing an isolationist stand and publishing attacks on Jews, the Daily News was condemned in a resolution adopted last night by the Kings County Council of the Jewish War Veterans at a meeting in the Hotel Bossert.

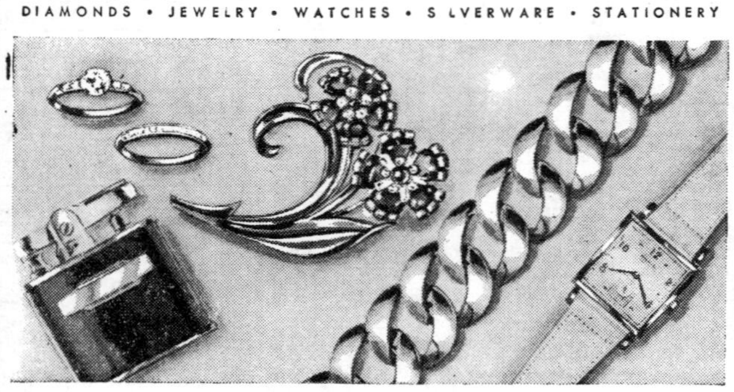

U. S. to Sift Firm Finances in Labor Rows

7★★★★★★★ Complete

BROOKLYN EAGLE

WEATHER—Clear, cold tonight; cloudy, cold tomorrow.

105th YEAR—No. 348—DAILY and SUNDAY (Copyright 1945, The Brooklyn Eagle, Inc.) BROOKLYN, N. Y., FRIDAY, DECEMBER 21, 1945 Entered Brooklyn P. O. 2d Class Mail Matter 3 CENTS IN NEW YORK CITY ELSEWHERE 4 CENTS

GENERAL PATTON DIES

Beldock Intensifies Probe of Anastasia

Seeks to Back Murder Charge Against 'Boss'

District Attorney George J. Beldock today intensified his probe into every angle of the activities of Albert Anastasia, reported waterfront rackets overlord.

Meanwhile, the Beldock special grand jury, having handed up a second presentment blasting the administration of Mayor-elect William O'Dwyer as Kings County prosecutor, fought for continuance of its official life beyond the Dec. 31 deadline, on the basis of its Anastasia revelations.

An abstract of the grand jury's second presentment will be found on Page 8.

Mr. Beldock said that County Judge Goldstein has not yet made known his decision on the jury's request for extension of its term.

Declaring that his office is "actively working" on the evidence in the Anastasia case, Mr. Beldock said, "We shall continue in our efforts to develop the evidence against him."

The jury repeated its accusation that Mr. O'Dwyer and his aides failed to carry out a "perfect murder case" prosecution.

The jury handed up the second presentment yesterday, quoting Mr. O'Dwyer as admitting during his eight appearances before it that its earlier presentment charging "gross laxity, inefficiency and mal-

Continued on Page 13

ANASTASIA—He's the boss.

FOX IS UPHELD IN HIS $95,000 L. I. U. CLAIM

Must Be Paid First In Any Liquidation, Appeals Court Rules

Frank Fox, president of Realty Associates, has a preferred claim of about $95,000 against Long Island University under a ruling handed down bv the United States Circuit Court of Appeals in Manhattan.

Last March, when the claim amounted to $5,000 less, Judge Matthew T. Abruzzo wrote in a Brooklyn Federal Court decision that if the priority advanced for the claim was sustained it would use up so much of the university's available cash that, "to all practical purposes, there could be no reorganization."

The university is seeking a court-supervised reorganization of its financial structure under Chapter 10 of the Bankruptcy Law. Its liabilities total some $250,000, its major creditor after Mr. Fox being the Manufacturers Trust Company.

The Circuit Court's ruling means that in any liquidation of the university Mr. Fox's claim must be paid in full before remaining assets are distributed pro rata among the other creditors.

Qualifying that disposition and still to be litigated, according to John McGrath, reorganization trustee, is an alleged agreement between Mr. Fox and the other creditors to accept settlement of their claims on a parity basis.

The Circuit Court's decision reversed a ruling by Judge Abruzzo that the recording by Mr. Fox of his judgment in January, 1943, had been technically defective and thereby reduced it to a general claim for pro rata settlement. If Judge Abruzzo now rules the alleged parity agreement valid, Mr. McGrath said, Mr. Fox's claim still would be reduced to only a general claim.

Might Be Paid Forthwith

"If the parity agreement is now ruled invalid, however," Mr. McGrath continued, "Mr. Fox will be paid in full forthwith. But that would mean no immediate likelihood now of the university going to the wall, though we might need some public contributions to put it on a sound financial basis. Enrollment has increased since VJ-Day from 250 to 750 and a 1,000

Continued on Page 5

ASKS PERMANENT HUMAN RELATION PLAN IN SCHOOLS

Yavner Recommends Bureau Be Added To Board of Education

Investigations Commissioner Louis E. Yavner today recommended to Mayor LaGuardia that a Bureau of Human Relations be set up as a permanent part of the Board of Education's administrative organization.

The recommendation came in the second part of the commissioner's 102-page report on administration of human relations programs in the city schools. The first part, released yesterday, strongly criticized Frank E. Karelsen Jr., resigned chairman of the Advisory Committee on Human Relations.

Mr. Yavner called recent public discussion of school problems "encouraging." It was principally through Mr. Karelsen's resignation and his charges of "administrative bankruptcy" in the school system that education problems were brought to the forefront.

Cites Other Programs

After reviewing the "causes of failure" of the advisory committee, from which 28 other members resigned after Mr. Karelsen quit, Mr. Yavner urged that "we learn the lesson and forget the fiasco."

The second part of the report cites human relations programs in various schools in the city, stressing the operation at Midwood High School in Brooklyn as an example of an "almost school-wide integrated human relations program."

It also gives substantial credit to the "East New York Activities" program in School Districts 43 and 44, under which Thomas Jefferson High School, Junior High School 149 and Public Schcols 174 and 182 have set up a broad intercultural education program.

Urges Fight on Prejudice

Commissioner Yavner urged a joint school-community drive to combat prejudice because, he said, "the schools alone, even if ideally staffed and administered, cannot create a complete environment in which the pupil may develop into an effective citizen."

He proposed that individual schools and areas be left to develop their own programs with the centarlized bureau integrating and co-ordinating their work.

Meanwhile, Mr. Karelsen attacked the first half of the report as a "vindication" of his stand that the Yavner probe was intended "to whitewash the criticisms that have been made" of the school system. He denied all "insinuations" in the report "of any religious bias or prejudice on my part whatsoever" and called the report "nothing but a compound of innuendo, reliance upon the rankest hearsay, without cross-examination, with unwarranted conclusions based upon selected portions of the testimony."

Rhatigan Named City Welfare Head

Mayor-elect William O'Dwyer today appointed Edward E. Rhatigan of Jackson Heights as City Welfare Commissioner.

Mr. Rhatigan, 36, who lived at 83-10 35th Ave., before going to Germany as a deputy director general of the European regional office of UNRRA, is in Washington resigning that post.

He returned recently from Germany.

Mr. Rhatigan was appointed director of public assistance by William Hodson of the Welfare Commission in March, 1941. When Mr. Hodson was killed in an airplane crash Mr. Rhatigan was serving as first deputy welfare commissioner. He then became acting commissioner in the department. A former administrator of the Home Relief Bureau, he also has served in the New York State Department of Social Welfare. He is a brother-in-law of Johnnie Rigney, White Sox baseball pitcher.

British Rocket Planes Pace Mopup in Java

Batavia, Dec. 21 (U.P.)—Rocket-firing R. A. F. planes broke up two strong Nationalist concentrations near Bandoeng today, clearing the way for British infantry forces mopping up on the outskirts of the Java Summer capital.

The planes were called in after advancing infantrymen ran into two strong Indonesian roadblocks.

U. S. TO SIFT FIRM PROFITS IN WAGE ROW

Authority Given Fact Finders—G. M., Union To Resume Talks

Washington, Dec. 21 (U.P.) — The Administration today gave Government fact-finding panels extensive authority to inquire into a company's ability to pay when recommending a wage increase for settlement of an industrial dispute.

The authority was granted in a directive to the oil industry fact-finding board for the Office of Reconversion, the Office of Price Administration and the Labor Department. The principles laid down will apply to other fact-finding boards.

The only limitation imposed was that a panel "ought not to recommend a wage increase which it believes will require the employer after six months to obtain price relief."

Meanwhile, General Motors Corporation and the United Automobile Workers (C. I. O.) agreed to meet in Detroit next Wednesday to discuss local plant union demands.

Vice President Harry W. Anderson of General Motors told reporters after a two and a half-hour meeting with union representatives that the union had agreed to submit its revised list of local plant demands at the Detroit meeting.

Both parties said they would appear at the 2:30 p.m. meeting scheduled by the President's fact-finding panel.

Applies to Other Cases

The directive in the oil case gave the panels no power to subpena books or to enforce their recommendations. It was drafted for the panel hearing the dispute over a demand by the Oil Workers Union (C. I. O.) for a 30 percent wage increase from 10 major oil refining companies.

It spelled out in detail the principles stated by President Truman late yesterday. It was intended to

Continued on Page 13

Palestine Hearings To Open Jan. 7

Washington, Dec. 21 (U.P.)—The Anglo-American commission set up to study the question of Jewish immigration into Palestine will begin hearings in Washington Jan. 7, it was announced today.

Jewish, Arab and Christian groups interested in the Palestine problem will be invited to appear.

Following initial hearings in Washington, members will go to London as the "best point of departure for the countries in which the problems arose," the commission said in an announcement issued simultaneously here and in London.

Surgeon Dares Death At Sea to Save GI

Three brief radio messages intercepted by the Air Sea Rescue Office of the Eastern Sea Frontier today told a dramatic story of a successful race for life at sea.

It began early yesterday when the 7,607-ton Frederick Victory, with 1,652 troops aboard, radioed from a point west of the Azores that a soldier aboard needed an immediate throat operation.

"Seriously ill soldier aboard. Possibly Ludwig's angina. Advise if qualified surgeon aboard. We are army troopship," read the message, addressed to the North Atlantic Patrol.

The U. S. S. Knoxville, a coast guard weather ship, sent the next message.

It was a simple report that she had transferred Surgeon Lieutenant Brodsky to the Frederick Victory "by breeches buoy in heavy seas," and was standing by. That was at 4:05 p.m.

Less than four hours later the Knoxville radioed that the doctor was back on board, and that he reported the operation was a success.

"We are resuming our station," the message concluded. "The Frederick Victory is proceeding to New York."

According to physicians, Ludwig's angina is a severe throat infection which may be caused by an abscess or a swelling. Either must be removed immediately.

Identity of the soldier was not revealed. Lieutenant Brodsky was believed to be a member of the Boston Public Health Service.

The Frederick Victory is due in New York Dec. 24.

GULFSTREAM RESULTS

FIRST RACE—$2,000; claiming; two-year-olds; seven furlongs.

Dale Maedic (Mattioli)	10.90	9.10	4.30
Fandango (Quattlebaum)	—	6.90	4.20
Bold Thrust (Jessop)	—	—	2.80

Off, 1:24. Time, 1:26 3-5. Scratched—Comaid, Mary Novick, Elbow Room, Twilight Boy.

2—James Acre, 1st; Fast Tempo, 2d; Cross B, 3d.

Gen. George S. Patton

Hart Charges Gamblers Thrive Under LaGuardia

Ring Has Operated 3 Years Under Cops' Noses, He Says, While Mayor Screamed at 'Tinhorns'

Councilman Walter R. Hart today charged that a gambling ring was operating undisturbed for three years under the noses of New York City police while Mayor LaGuardia was concentrating attention on "tinhorn gamblers and bookmakers."

The allegation was on eof a series of criticisms leveled by Mr. Hart at the outgoing administration at a meeting of the Kings County Grand Jurors Association last night in the Central Branch Y. M. C. A., 55 Hanson Place. Other charges were:

While a city appraiser was being indicted for income tax falsification he was appointed to another city post.

Hits Reds in Welfare Dept.

The Welfare Department was described as being "honeycombed with Communists."

The city placed high assessments on property, acquired this property on the owner's inability to pay taxes and then resold it at prices several thousand dollars below the assessed valuation.

"These are the things Mayor-elect O'Dwyer should have said during his recent campaign," Mr. Hart said, "instead of asking for consolidation of 'gains' made by the incumbent administration."

Officers elected by the County Grand Jurors are: Harry J. Smith, president; J. Howard Field and William F. Beck, vice presidents; Albert Janson, treasurer, and Joseph F. Cox and Lloyd L. Hockenbury, secretaries.

Committeemen Elected

Isaac Albert, Engelbert Bick, Henry W. Buehler, Jacob J. Dorman and John J. Magovern were elected executive committeemen for three-year terms and Francis Yacenda for a one-year term. Mr. Smith presided.

Leonard Collier, president of the Queens County Grand Jurors Association, was a guest at the meeting as were several other members of that borough's association.

Mr. Beck, chairman of the membership committee, announced that 23 new members joined the association in December. He placed the total membership at 646.

City School Students Start Christmas Vacation Today

The Christmas vacation for the city's public school pupils starts today as Monday will be a fuel conservation day. The children will return to their studies Jan. 2.

Marine Shot in China

Tientsin, Dec. 21 (U.P.)—An unidentified assailant shot a U. S. marine in the shoulder Dec. 17 near his station about 50 miles southwest of Chinwangtao, it was learned today.

KIMMEL BROKE AIR ALERT ORDER, ADMIRAL AVERS

Ignored High Command Warning by Failure to Use Planes, He Says

BULLETIN

Washington, Dec. 21 (U.P.)—Admiral Richmond Kelly Turner charged today that Admiral Husband E. Kimmel, commanding the Pacific fleet at Hawaii, violated a high command war warning by failing to have air reconnaissance in effect when Japan struck Pearl Harbor.

Washington, Dec. 21 (U.P.)—Admiral Richmond Kelly Turner said today that the United States fleet would have been safer on the west coast than at Pearl Harbor in 1941, but that its proper place was in Hawaii to defend "the security of the United States."

Admiral Turner, former chief of navy war plans, told the Pearl Harbor Investigating Committee that he believed as early as June, 1941, that war with Japan was inevitable. He criticized Admiral Husband E. Kimmel, Pearl Harbor commander, for not having the fleet deployed when the Japanese struck on Dec. 7, 1941.

If Admiral Kimmel had deployed the fleet, as he was ordered to do in war warnings sent from Washington in November, the Pearl Harbor disaster "would have been materially reduced," Admiral Turner said, "and I believe there would have been a good chance of inflict-

Continued on Page 13

British, French Confer On Levant Withdrawal

London, Dec. 21 (U.P.)—A joint Anglo-French statement revealed British and French military experts are meeting in Beirut today to work out details of the joint withdrawal of their troops from the Levant states.

Take Holiday Liquor

Linden, N. J., Dec. 21—Theft of a large stock of liquor accumulated for the holiday and $2,500 in cash from the rear room of a tavern here was reported to police today.

GOES PEACEFULLY AS HEART FAILS FROM INJURIES

Heidelberg, Dec. 21 (U.P.) — Gen. George S. Patton, "Old Blood and Guts," died in the army hospital here today.

Col. John M. Willems, chief of staff of the 7th Army, announced that General Patton died peacefully at 5:50 p.m. (11:50 a.m. Brooklyn time).

General Patton lost his fight against injuries suffered Dec. 9 when his car collided with an army truck as he was motoring to hunt pheasants not for from his headquarters.

The tough and stormy army veteran suffered a broken neck in the accident and was partially paralyzed. But a little more than 48 hours after being rushed to the hospital he was pronounced "out of danger" unless unforeseen complications set in.

Life Story of General Patton on Page 3.

Those complications, in the form of a bronchial infection, suddenly developed Wednesday night. Yesterday and last night his condition rapidly worsened. This morning his physicians said he was in "grave" danger.

General Patton's death was foreshadowed by an afternoon medical bulletin from the Heidelberg Army Hospital, disclosing that his heart had been affected by the strain and that secretions were accumulating in his lungs.

After the initial shock of the broken neck the tough soldier who led the 3d Army across Western Europe in the victorious drive against Germany rallied rapidly and began edging back from the shadow of death, into which he was cast by the collision of his automobile and an army truck a week ago Sunday.

Medical reports for the past 24 hours reported that 60-year-old General Patton's discomfort under a bronchial infection had resulted in constant coughing, placing further strain on his heart.

The morning's official report had said:

"Patton's condition is considered serious. There has been pulmonary complication which has resulted in accumulation of secretions in the lung thus embarrassing respiration.

Pulse, However, Is Strong

"The paralysis of one side of the diaphragm and intercostal muscles resulting from the spinal cord injury has made it difficult for him to get rid of the secretions by coughing.

"As a result of the pulmonary congestion the heart has become embarrassed. However, the pulse is strong and the temperature is only slightly above normal.

"The chief medical consultant for the theater has been in attendance."

His wife, Beatrice, was sitting at his bedside in the first-floor hospital room around which an almost deadly silence prevailed. Nurses tiptoed through the corridor, and white-helmeted military police kept visitors at a distance.

GROCER ROBBED OF $195 AS BORO STICKUPS RISE

2 Thugs Escape After 17th Holdup Here in Past Week

Two bandits, one armed, today held up Harry Schwartz, 60, of 651 Madison St., in his grocery store at 222 Stuyvesant Ave., and got away with $195 from the cash register.

The stickup was the 17th holdup in Brooklyn in the past week.

The thugs forced Schwartz to the rear of the store and warned him not to move for 15 minutes after they left. The victim could not furnish police with an accurate description of the bandits. They had caps pulled down over their eyes and their coat collars were turned up.

It was the second holdup experienced by Schwartz, he said. Fifteen years ago he was held up in a grocery store at Harrison Ave. and Walton St. The bandit was captured and received a 20-year prison term.

Two Thugs Rob Clerk

Shortly before midnight two armed bandits held up a lone clerk in the Community Pharmacy, 440 Bedford Ave., and got away with $75. The clerk, J. L. Backer of 1388 W. 6th St., gave police a good description of the pair.

In Manhattan police reported that a man in an army uniform, who attempted a mugging at Park Ave. and 41st St., was foiled by the arrival of a policeman. The victim was Russell H. Armstrong, 55, of 104 E. 40th St.

Patrolman James Reilly, who fired three shots at the fugitive, said he saw him stagger as though hit.

Also in Manhattan, a gunman approached the cashier of the Beverly Hill Theater, Broadway and 165th St., handed her a note, saying "Give me all your money," and escaped with $50.

Hurt in Auto Crash, Rider Gets $23,000

Isidore Davis, 49, of 2173 Pacific St., who was a "guest rider" in the automobile of Joseph De Robertis of 33-14 98th St., Corona, when injured as the car and a bus of the Queens-Nassau transit lines collided, will receive $23,000 in a settlement. This was announced by his attorney, John M. Wilson of 215 Montague St. before Supreme Court Justice Garvin today.

The settlement halted the trial of Mr. Davis' suit after Mr. Wilson drew testimony from both drivers that trees and bushes hid the intersection near Grand Central Parkway and 164th St., Queens, where the accident occurred, and that each assumed the road was clear. Mr. Davis received a fracture of the right leg. He and Mr. De Robertis were employed in the same fruit store in Mineola.

50,000 See Reds Hang 7 Nazi War Criminals

London, Dec. 21 (U.P.)—Radio Moscow said today more than 50,000 persons witnessed the public hanging of seven German war criminals in Smolensk's main square yesterday.

The seven had been convicted by a Russian court of committing atrocities in the Smolensk area during the war.

Returning GIs Listed

A list of Brooklyn, Queens and Long Island soldiers returning on nine troopships will be found on Page 6.

Hemingway Gets Divorce

Havana, Dec. 21 (U.P.) — Novelist Ernest Hemingway was granted an uncontested divorce today from his writer-wife, Martha Gellhorn, on grounds of desertion.

Man Fatally Stricken At Postoffice Window

George Konrath, 55, of 59-11 Catalpa Ave., Glendale, collapsed of a heart attack and died today while buying stamps at a postoffice window in the Brooklyn Federal Building, police reported. He was posting mail for the Allen D. Cardwell Manufacturing Corporation, Prospect and Pearl Sts., where he was employed.

19 Cops Work 1 Week To Nab Meter Thief

Newark, Dec. 21 (U.P.)—George F. Thall, 22, was in jail today for robbing parking meters of $10.50 and causing $800 worth of damage to the meters. A special squad of 19 detectives worked a week to catch Thall.

WHERE TO FIND IT

	Page		Page
Bridge	23	Obituaries	13
Brown	12	Our Champs	9
Comics	23	Patterns	16
Crossword	16	Radio	23
Dr. Brady	12	Real Estate	21
Editorial	12	Society	15
Financial	21	Sports	17, 18, 19
Going Places	10	Take My Word	12
Grin and Bear It	12	Theaters	20
Heffernan	12	These Women	23
Helen Worth	16	Tucker	12
Horoscope	16	Uncle Ray	23
Mary Haworth	15	Veteran in B'klyn	9
Movies	20	Want Ads	21, 22
Music	21	Women	15
Novel	21		

Patton, Master of Tank Warfare, Was Ruthless Fighter

PACED HIS OWN TROOPS INTO BATTLE

George S. Patton was a four-star general but never a brass hat.

Commanding as he did divisions and armies and hundreds of thousands of men, nobody ever pictured him as an officer sitting at a desk in an office or poring over maps in a headquarters.

He was no headquarters general. Instead, when you thought of Patton you thought of a rampaging, rip-snorting Patton blazing away with two guns at once, storming a beachhead with automatic rifle in hand going full blast, roaring out orders, sputtering profanity (and military good sense), thundering across enemy-held terrain, ahead of his infantry, astride his own tank.

They nicknamed him "Old Blood and Guts" and "Buck Rogers" and "The Green Hornet" and "The Man From Mars.'

They called him "cocksure," "fabulous," "boastful," "bloodthirsty," "daring," "swashbuckling," "spectacular" and a host of other biting, snarling adjectives aiming—without too great success—to describe the indescribable.

But Patton was much more than the picturesque, reckless, rough-and-ready soldier that such descriptive efforts sought to evoke.

Tank Specialist

He was also, behind all that and in addition to it, a great military leader who made himself a specialist in a new weapon—the armored tank—from the time it was first introduced in World War I; who talked tanks and fought for tanks while traditional army leaders were inclined to dismiss them as a novel auxiliary weapon but not more; who finally, under the pressure of a second World War, came into his own because he had prepared himself for it.

When the endless waves of tanks went rolling over the Nazi enemy in Sicily, in France, in Germany itself, that was in more than a fanciful sense Patton crushing the enemy.

Knew Nature of Foe

And he was, too, behind his sharp words and his indulgence in profanity, acutely aware of the nature of the enemy and how—and why—he must be fought. He sent his troops into action once with this battle order:

"We've got to kill Germans. That's the only way they'll understand. We've got to attack them, run our bayonet through them, and then take their blood and guts to grease the tracks of the tanks."

He became, in his lifetime, a legend. He was a driving, ruthless fighter, who drove himself as well as the men under him. Some men hated him but all gave him their respect.

He carried two pearl-handled revolvers, one on each hip. The legends about him are endless. The story is told that, after hanging the Congressional Medal of Honor on one of the men of his 3d Army, he remarked, "I would give my immortal soul to have one of these myself." He died with that goal unattained.

Born in California

He was born George Smith Patton Jr. on Nov. 11, 1885, on the ranch of his father at San Gabriel, Cal. His family was F. F. V.'s—aristocrats of aristocratic Virginia. His father was a wealthy operator in California real estate. Young George learned to ride and play polo at an early age. In later years he recalled that he made up his mind to be a soldier at the age of 7.

He attended Virginia Military Academy and entered West Point in 1904. There he played football but was never an outstanding player and proved to be far from a top-grade student. It took him five years to get through the normally four-year course—one of the few at West Point permitted to continue after flunking the first year. There was something about him which convinced the West Point faculty that, despite his marks, he would make a right officer.

He chose the cavalry as his branch of the service and, a new second lieutenant, took up his first post in Texas. He asked were there stable facilities for horses and the stables were pointed out to him—Patton produced a string of 26 polo ponies.

At West Point he developed into a fine pistol shot, swimmer and horseman. He came out fourth in the pentathlon competition in the 1912 Olympics at Stockholm — although in the pistol-shooting event he was credited with only nine shots out of ten. The tenth, some said, went clean through a hole previously made in the target, thus leaving no discernible mark and cutting down his score. He had set a new target-shooting record in the semi-finals, when all shots registered. In his late fifties he could still top all his junior officers at sharpshooting and most of them at handball, the 100-yard dash and polo.

Patton's interest in horsemanship, while he was still a young officer, flowered into romance and marriage. It was at a horse show in Massachusetts that he met — and then married—Beatrice Ayer of the family that owned the American Woollen Company.

Predicted His Fame

He was still a West Point student when he announced—hardly bettering his popularity thereby—that he would become a famous warrior.

It was not until 1916 that he had a chance to take the first step toward fulfilling that ambition. In that year of the Pancho Villa uprising in Mexico he became Gen. John J. Pershing's aide in the Mexican expedition and the general himself had to restrain him from exposing himself to the Villistas' fire power.

Despite everything the general could do, Patton set out with a specially selected squad after a "bandit" named Candelario Cervantes, cornered him personally in a hut—and found himself a target for Cervantes' shots while he himself was reloading.

However, Cervantes missed and Patton, when he finally was able to squeeze the trigger, didn't. Patton, the story tells, dumped Cervantes' body over the fender of his automobile like a carcass of a deer and thus drove back to Pershing headquarters.

Was Pershing's Aide

He was Pershing's aide again in World War I, and as the first timidly conceived tanks tentatively thrust their way into the war Patton was drawn toward them as with a kind of fascination. He attended French tank schools. He commanded such American tanks as there were and turned all his warrior eagerness toward tank warfare.

Less than two months before the war ended, on Sept. 26, 1918, he was wounded, and that war ended for him. He was decorated with the Distinguished Service Cross.

20 Dull Years

Patton was a colonel when the first World War ended but he found the two decades between the wars dull. He attended horse shows. He collected military books. He kept his eye on tank warfare, but there was no opportunity to do anything about it.

In 1935 he was assigned to Hawaii, and so he bought a second-hand schooner and, after a brief course in navigation, sailed with his wife the 9,000 miles to his new post via the Panama Canal.

Attains His First Star

In 1940 war was imminent again, and Patton was made a brigadier general and put in command of the 2d Armored Division. That meant tanks.

Patton used to say:

"An army without tanks is like a lobster without claws."

"The ideal tankman is a fellow who can drive 300 miles all day, then stay awake 72 hours after that."

"Dugout telephone days are over. You can't run a war from a desk. You run it from a tank or a motorcycle."

Rugged Desert Tactics

These and similar principles he now taught his armored division men. In 1942, in preparation for the North African invasion, he took his division down to the California desert, trained it with remorseless, ruthless driving discipline for desert warfare.

"Never tell a man to do anything that you wouldn't do yourself," he told his officers, and though that is a rule to which the whole army pays lip service Patton showed that he meant it.

Under the hottest burning desert sun Major General Patton—he had now become a two-star general—was out there in the thickest of the mock fighting.

Lands at Casablanca

On Nov. 8 of that year Patton's tanks went ashore at Casablanca. He was then corps commander with the 1st and 2d Armored Divisions under his leadership. He went ashore, actually, stepping out of a small boat into knee-deep water, firing an automatic rifle as he went.

French resistance was subdued in four days, and then his tanks, insufficient to keep Rommel from Von Arnim, nevertheless herded Rommel into Tunisia, a country not suitable for tank warfare.

Roars Across Sicily

The infantry under other commanders finished that job. Patton meanwhile trained the 7th Army and at the invasion of Sicily led it roaring across the Sicilian plains, speedily cleaning up the island.

It was in Italy that the unpredictable Patton, himself under terrific strain, slapped a hospitalized soldier in the belief that he was a malingerer—and when the story came out there was much righteous screaming and Eisenhower obtained and got a public apology from the swashbuckling Patton, and in Congress his scheduled promotion was held up. Eisenhower still knew that he had a good general, and said so.

Patton Quiet, Nazis Fret

For a time, however, Patton disappeared from the headlines—and the Germans began to worry. Radio Berlin went on fishing expeditions reporting that he had been seen here and there, including Corsica and Sardinia. Probably he was actually there, sent there so that the Germans would hear about it.

As invasion of France drew near, the Germans, more afraid of Patton than any other Anglo-American leader, became more and more convinced that it would be a Patton-led invasion by way of southern France.

Strikes From England

When D-Day finally came, Patton and his newly trained 3d Army were in England and invasion came by way of Normandy, with the Nazi forces divided and waiting for the Patton landing in the south.

Patton arrived a few days later—in Normandy—and after breaking through the German lines, sent his tanks thundering across France. That was in the Summer of 1944. When, that December, the Germans, having halted on their own borders, fought back in the Battle of the Bulge, Patton, who was facing east, turned north, harassed and clawed at Von Rundstedt until he was pushed back.

Rips Through Germany

Once again, this time after the crossing of the Rhine, Patton, the tank expert, had his chance. His 3d Army, led by Patton himself, roared across Europe in what proved the last days of World War II, from the Rhine to Czechoslovakia and into Austria and a junction with the Russians coming the other way.

That great drive was the climax of Patton's career. After V-E Day he was in command of occupation troops. Always outspoken and never too diplomatic in non-military affairs, he presently blundered into public statements which resulted in his removal from his command.

He was put in command of the 15th Army, a skeleton and largely paper organization, with the duty of writing the official history of World War II in Europe. He was still on that duty when the automobile accident came which led to his death.

PATTON PICTURES—Left, the general embraces Mrs. Patton as he arrives in Boston after cleaning up the war in Europe; middle, he gazes toward a battle in North Africa; right, just Patton, with his characteristic chuckle of victory.

George Currie's column will not appear in the Brooklyn Eagle this week. He is on vacation and will resume his musings upon the Brooklyn scene next Monday.

Patton a Master At Coining Phrase

Characteristic Patton sayings:

"Retreat is as cowardly as it is fatal."

"A pint of sweat will save a gallon of blood."

"Attack rapidly, ruthlessly, viciously, without rest."

To his troops after victory in Sicily:

"Born at sea, baptized in blood and crowned with victory, you have destroyed the prestige of the enemy. Your fame shall never die."

"An army without tanks is like a lobster without claws."

"A man can be ferocious as hell back home on three meals a day, but it takes guts to live in a fox-hole in the rain, eating cold rations."

"Goddammit, a soldier should salute even in the toilet."

"I've got to be dignified, goddammit."

"Eventually a battle gets down to blood and guts. That's when a commander is judged on what he can do.. That's where Georgie Patton will shine."

RISKS ALL FOR SIGHT OF GI SON BUT LOSES

Rochester, Dec. 21 (U.P.)—For four years Mrs. Bertha Ratke, 71, was blind.

This year she decided to risk a delicate operation so she might see her son, Corp. Henry Ratke, when he returned from overseas for his first Christmas at home in three years.

The bandages were removed from Mrs. Ratke's eyes. Her sight had been restored. She went home with her daughter and began preparations for a homecoming party for her son.

Two hours later she died without seeing him. The operation had proved too much for her weak heart.

Phony Bid for U. S. Food Laid to Jap Government

Tokyo, Dec. 21 (U.P.)—Col. Crawford F. Sams, chief of the public health and welfare section of Allied Supreme Headquarters, said today the Japanese Government had falsely represented the country's food situation in an effort to get the United States to furnish relief supplies. Colonel Sams said the Japanese are in no danger of starvation this Winter.

J. W. V. Post and Ladies Auxiliary Heads Installed

New officers of the Sgt. Stuart M. Adelman Post 277, Jewish War Veterans, and its Ladies Auxiliary, were installed last night in the Ocean Parkway Jewish Center, 550 Ocean Parkway.

The officers are Herman Stein, commander; Max Paitchell and Harry S. Wnuk, vice commanders; Robert Hitlin, adjutant, and Jack Siegel, quartermaster.

New auxiliary officers are Betty Adelman, president; Ray Berman and Ann Goldberg, vice presidents; Ruth Adelman, corresponding secretary, and Helen Hochberg, treasurer.

Window Cleaners Cited On Overcharge Claim

Callman Gottesman, chief enforcement attorney of the New York office of the OPA, announced today that 79 window cleaning firms in Brooklyn, Queens and Manhattan had been cited for alleged overcharges to customers in Federal Court treble-damage actions filed by the OPA.

Sports Enjoyed Tremendous Box-Office Appeal in '45 Despite Poor Competition

Attendance Records Smashed by Customers

By TOMMY HOLMES

The shooting part of World War II came to a close in 1945 and, as this old and toothless year staggers toward an end, it seems fashionable to predict that the piping times of peace ahead will usher in the most prosperous sports era ever.

That could be.

Certainly, the immediate future of sports shapes up as much more glamorous than the recent past. To some fields of athletic endeavor, like golf, tennis and polo, sharply curtailed or completely stopped for the last four years, there will be a renaissance. They'll come back. Indeed they will.

Improvement in Sports

And just as certainly the sports that have never been away in the past four years will be improved as thousands of returning athletes pour themselves back into civilian togs. That is, improved from the standpoint of competitive artistry.

But the most prosperous era of all time? I don't know. If the years ahead turn out to be that, we are truly moving into a fearful and wonderful age.

For prosperity never was a problem after Pearl Harbor to those sports industries which were able to carry on, more or less as usual. And this land of liberty is jumpin' with sports promoters who have been living in a dream world for four long years, the most startling of which was 1945 A.D.

The customers—millions of 'em—did it. They were equipped with large bundles of nervous take-home money. They wanted sports and were willing to pay for them. Mixed with the desire to spend was an utter lack of critical taste. That led to record gate receipts almost everywhere although competition in almost any sports you can name was never so mediocre in our time. The combination was a phenomenon that would have astonished the late Phineas T. Barnum even as it astonished Michael Strauss Jacobs.

A few examples:

New Baseball Figures

The over-all attendance for big league baseball exceeded all previous records. Five clubs, including our Dodgers, played to crowds totalling over a million. Yet veteran observers developed severe cases of the screaming meemies watching certain actions that passed for big league baseball.

The quality of horseflesh that galloped o'er the land was extremely ordinary. But long after any horse that raced this year has been forgotten, the attendance and betting marks established will be remembered. More people saw the horses run than ever before. Far more money was wagered than ever before. Some people deem this a scandal to the jaybirds—and they may be right.

In the boxing ring, championship competition was practically nonexistent. Ninety-nine boxing shows in 100 lacked any special significance. Yet the mob rushed for the doors of fight clubs with bills of large denominations clenched in each fist and wrote letters to the Mayor when fire department commissioners wouldn't let any more people in the joint.

College basketball, afflicted with its worse scandal since it became big-time stuff, didn't even stagger. Unless you know somebody it's as tough to get into Madison Square Garden on basketball nights as it is to crash the Army-Navy football game.

And so it went...

Yes, sir, this was a year. A great year for sports. Especially when you consider the conditions that prevailed 12 months ago. Then, racing already had been placed under ODT ban, effective Jan. 2. Baseball, facing a manpower shortage and possible ODT restrictions, wondered whether the pennant races could get off the ground. The possibility of a National Service Act hung heavily over all sports. The outlook was rugged.

But here's what happened—

CRASHED THE HEADLINES—Above are the men who made baseball history during the year of 1945. They are, top row (left to right), Branch Rickey, who, with a syndicate of friends bought control of the Dodgers; Albert (Happy) Chandler, who was named to succeed the late Judge Kenesaw Mountain Landis as High Commissioner of Baseball; Leland S. (Larry) MacPhail, who with Del Webb and Dan Topping, bought the Yankees. The bottom row (left to right) includes Bill Southworth, who quit as pilot of the Cardinals to manage the Braves; Judge Landis, who died during the year; Phil Cavarretta, Cubs, who led the National League in batting and was voted the senior loop's most valuable player, and Hal Newhouser, Tigers, who was similarly honored in the American League.

Turnstiles Clicked, Players Didn't

Financially, the 1945 baseball season was terrific. Artistically, it was terrible. Turnstiles spun and so did many of the spavined has-beens and awkward never-will-bes hopefully impersonating big league ball players. Competition was keen because all clubs were deficient in class.

The World Series sort of epitomized the final wartime season. Fans jam-packed Briggs Stadium in Detroit and Mr. Wrigley's lovely orchard on the North Side of Chicago and watched the Tigers falter and flounder, yet somehow manage to beat the Cubs in a limit series. Never do we expect to see another such World Series. Another world war alone could bring it on.

Perhaps the tip-off on the conditions that prevailed in 1945 is the fact that just about half a dozen members of Steve O'Neill's Detroit team—world's champions—are expected to be playing regularly in 1946. There will be Hank Greenberg, returned from the wars; Eddie Mayo, the second baseman, and three pitchers—Hal Newhouser, Dizzy Trout and Virgil Trucks, whose performances beat the Cubs.

Newhouser Starred

Newhouser, by the way, took the American League's most valuable player award for the second year in succession and rather neatly summed up wartime baseball conditions with a remarkably frank and modest statement. "In 1946," said he, "the good hitters will be back and I'll find out for myself if I'm a really good pitcher."

On form Charley Grimm's team of Chicago Cubs looked superior to the Tigers but Grimm ran out of pitching at the end and was forced to use Hank Borowy four times in the seven-game series. Borowy, starting the last game, was knocked out before he retired a man and the Tigers wearily pounded out a clinching 9-to-3 decision behind Newhouser.

It was this same Borowy who pitched the Cubs to the pennant. Probably the St. Louis Cardinals would have won for the fourth year in succession had not Larry MacPhail, new owner of the Yankees, come up with the fascinating theory that Borowy was constitutionally unable to win after mid-season. He secured American League waivers on the right-hander, sold him to Chicago, where he won 11 games and lost only two. Spurred by that performance, the Cubs drew away from the Cardinals and clinched the flag in the last week.

At that, the Cubs qualified for the World Series before the Tigers did. Detroit didn't scale the heights until the very last game on its schedule when the illustrious Greenberg hit a home run with the bases filled.

Dodgers Finished Third

An unprepossessing Washington team pressed Detroit to the wire. National League counterpart of the Senators was Leo Durocher's Dodgers. After looking indescribably bad in Spring training, the Dodgers actually led the league for a while and, though they ultimately faltered, finished a respectable third.

Phil Cavarretta, able first baseman of the Cubs, was N. L. batting champion and earned the most valuable player award. American League swat king was Snuffy Stirnweiss, Yankee second baseman, although his average of .309 was a new low for a batting champ. Tommy Holmes, outfielder of the Boston Braves, was home run boss of the year with 27 and also set a modern National League record by hitting safely in 37 consecutive games. Rookie of the year was Dave Ferriss, who came out of the army air forces to the Boston Red Sox. He pitched a shutout in his first big league appearance, won eight straight before he was beaten, wound up his freshman season with 21 victories and 11 defeats.

All kinds of baseball news crackled throughout the year. Quite the most startling innovation of all occurred in October when Brooklyn's Mr. Rickey signed Jack Robinson, a colored shortstop, for a trial with the Dodger farm at Montreal.

Three big league clubs changed hands. Larry MacPhail, Dan Topping and Del Webb bought the Yankees. A group headed by Branch Rickey gained control of the Dodgers. Don Barnes stepped out as boss of the Browns.

Chandler New Boss

The club owners selected Senator Happy Chandler as their new commissioner, then immediately started growling about their choice. The trend toward unlimited night baseball gained ground.

In the course of the season Del Bissonette succeeded Bob Coleman as manager of the Braves and Ben Chapman replaced Fred Fitzsimmons as boss of the Phillies. In November Billy Southworth, highly successful field marshal of the Cardinals, signed to manage the Braves because that club made him a better financial position than big-hearted Sam Breadon of St. Louis. Eddie Dyer, a journeyman pitcher 'way back, took over with the Cardinals.

Twelve minor league clubs started and finished the 1945 season. Many more than that should operate in 1946.

Postwar plans cloud the atmosphere but the scene is one of general confusion. Vast sources of man power relieving a condition which troubled the game so sorely after Pearl Harbor will be available. At present most of the clubs are likely to have more players than they'll know what to do with. If it isn't one thing it's another.

PENNANT WINNERS IN MINOR LEAGUES

The 1945 minor league baseball champions:

League	Pennant Winner	Playoff Winner
Am. Association	Milwaukee	Louisville
International	Montreal	Newark
Pacific Coast	Portland	S. Francisco
Southern	Atlanta	Mobile
Eastern	Utica	Albany
Inter-State	Lancaster	Lancaster
Piedmont	Norfolk	Portsmouth
Carolina	Danville	Danville
Appalachian	Kingsport	Kingsport
N. C. State	Hickory	Landis
Ohio State	Middlet'n	Zanesville
Pony	Batavia	Batavia

Army Gridders Led Sports Parade

So far this review of the 1945 sports season reads as though written by a critic suffering severely from dyspepsia. But now it is time to pay tribute to a team of champions that may be the equal of anything in its line we have ever seen.

The United States Military Academy's football team was the greatest thing in 1945 sports. For the second season in succession, Army swept undefeated, untied and unextended through a nine-game schedule to gain undisputed top rank in the college field.

Army had everything. It had a host of backfield stars spearheaded by a pair of super stars in Glenn Davis, an open field Mercury, and Felix Blanchard, a line smashing specialist. It had a stronger line than any one saw elsewhere anywhere in the East. It was superbly coached by Col. Red Blaik and his competent staff of assistants. It literally wowed the nation.

Army's 1945 team did not duplicate its record breaking 59—0 victory of the year before against Notre Dame. The Irish were stronger this year, strong enough to hold the Cadets to 0—48. Before 102,000 in Philadelphia's Municipal Stadium in the climax game of the season, Blaik's rollicking juggernaut crushed Navy by 32—13. And this Navy team probably was the second best in the land. It went into the Army game undefeated and tied only by Notre Dame.

Penn Ivy League Tops

There were other champions, of course, but the national picture was completely dominated by Army.

In the East, Pennsylvania topped the Ivy League. Holy Cross was

Continued on Following Page

GLENN DAVIS, Army, off for 49-yard touchdown run against Navy in one of season's most spectacular plays.

Turf Review Like Financial Report

Horse racing all over the country was eliminated by the O. D. T. from Jan. 2 until after VE-Day. Yet more people watched the horses run and more money was wagered on oat burners than in any other year in history. Personally, I feel that this year's review of racing belongs on the financial pages.

It is estimated that $1,400,000,000 was bet at horse tracks throughout the country. Various States received the record-breaking total in revenue of $66,000,000.

New York's racing season was 35 days shorter than in 1944 but $450,633,190 was wagered at New York tracks, slightly more than $48,500,000 in excess of the betting in '44. This State alone reaped more than $30,000,000 in taxes from the so-called sport of kings.

$5,016,745 Wagered

Until 1944 no pari-mutuel track had ever recorded a betting day of more than $3,000,000. On Sept. 22 at Belmont Park the public bet $5,016,745 through the machines. Eight other days in the New York season the handle topped $4,000,000. The average bet per person daily at New York tracks was $97.48. The total attendance at New York tracks was 4,622,927, a new record by plenty.

So much for figures. Artistically, the racing season wasn't so hot.

For the second year in succession the outstanding steed was a lady horse. She was Louis B. Mayer's three-year-old Busher, a daughter of War Admiral and a granddaughter of Man o' War. She won 10 races in 13 starts, finishing second twice and third once. She started out conquering racers of her own sex, then started running away from boy horses until she had increased her total earnings to $334,035, which places her seventh among the great money-winning horses on record, the highest ranking ever attained by a filly. In that respect she far outdistanced Twilight Tear, celebrated girl horse of 1944.

Derby to Hoop Jr.

Hoop Jr. won the Kentucky Derby. Polynesian won the Preakness. Pavot, former two-year-old champion, won the Belmont. This made hash of any attempt to establish supremacy among three-year-old colts. Leading two-year-old was Star Pilot of the Maine Chance Farm, winner of the Belmont and Pimlico Futurities and the Hopeful Stakes. Top handicap horse was Mrs. Ethel D. Jacobs' Stymie. He was slightly more consistent than his in-and-out fellows.

Leading jockey of the year was a 19-year-old lad named Job Dean Jessop, who booted home 275 winners up to Dec. 7. But the jock who led in money earned was Johnny Longden, who customarily rode Busher. By winning the Derby aboard Hoop Jr. Eddie Arcaro became the third jockey in history to pilot three winners of that race. The other saddlesmiths were Isaac Murphy and Earl Sande.

Only twice in the last 13 years has Hirsch Jacobs failed to finish first in saddling winners. This was one of those years. As of Dec. 7, comparatively unknown Stanley Lipiec, who trains Mrs. Lottie Wolf's racing string, had 113 winners, compared to 92 for Jacobs.

The Maine Chance Farm, operated by Elizabeth Arden, the cosmetic queen, was the greatest money-winning stable of the year with well over half a million dollars. And the same stable figured in the most sensational development of the year when its trainer, Tom Smith, was suspended for one year for allegedly "stimulating" a horse at Belmont Park. Smith denied any wrongdoing, appealed the case.

Gulfstream Feature To Twenty Thirty

Hallandale, Fla., Dec. 22 (U.P.)—Twenty Thirty, black two-year-old filly, scored her second consecutive victory today, winning the $5,000 Fountain of Youth Handicap at Gulfstream.

The daughter of Eight Thirty passed the tiring Flag Drill in the final furlong of the mile and 70 yards to win by a length and a quarter in 1:45 1-5. Flag Drill held on for the place by a half length over West Dress.

The victory was the third in 10 tries by the filly and raised her earnings to $9,072. The slight favorite, Twenty Thirty paid $7.10, $3.90, and $3.40.

WHO'S PLAYING WHOM IN FOOTBALL BOWLS

How they will line up for the football bowl games:

Rose Bowl, Pasadena, Cal., New Year's Day—Alabama vs. Southern California.

Sugar Bowl, New Orleans, La., New Year's Day — St. Mary's (Cal.) vs. Oklahoma A. & M.

Orange Bowl, Miami, Fla., New Year's Day—Miami vs. Holy Cross.

Cotton Bowl, Dallas, Texas, New Year's Day—Texas vs. Missouri.

Sun Bowl, El Paso, Texas, New Year's Day—New Mexico vs. Denver University.

Blue-Gray Game, Montgomery, Ala., Dec. 29 — Northern College All-Stars vs. Southern All-Stars.

Shrine Game, San Francisco, Cal., Dec. 25—East All Stars vs. West All-Stars.

Jacksonville Bowl, Jackson ville, Fla. — South Carolina vs. Wake Forest.

Beak-Bashing Business Boomed

In the bull-ring of Mexico City last April, Ike Williams, a sullen-visaged Negro, who fights out of Philadelphia, knocked out Juan Zurita of Vera Cruz in the second round. This was a notable event for 1945—the only occasion in the course of the year in which anything remotely resembling a world's boxing championship changed hands. Starching the Mexican gave Williams the right to call himself the N. B. A. lightweight boss.

And yet the beak-busting business surged forward to a rousing boom. Stimulated by the return of service men and expanding radio broadcasts, the ring industry flourished everywhere, especially around New York, where Mike Jacobs, the monopolist of maul, promoted no fewer than 82 shows at Madison Square Garden and the St. Nicholas Arena.

Most spectacular gladiator of the year was a square-shouldered, shaggy-maned young middleweight slugger born on Manhattan's East Side and now one of the neighbor's children out in Flatbush. His name is Rocky Graziano.

Flattened Cochrane

In the Garden one night back in March he was taking a pasting from a highly-touted young fellow named Billy Arnold. Rocky connected with a right thrown from the floor that led to a three-round knockout. In May he knocked out Al Davis in four. In June and again in August

Continued on Following Page

Sooner Aggies Cage Champions

Georgeous goons held the spotlight once more in college basketball. Consider what happened in the two major tournaments staged in Madison Square Garden.

Hank Iba's Oklahoma A. and M. team relied upon Bob (Foothills) Kurland, a doughty young man who is seven feet high. The Blue Demons of DePaul employed as their spearhead one, George Mikan, only six feet nine.

Well, the Sooner Aggies won the N. C. A. A. tournament promoted by the Garden's Ned Irish and DePaul won the Garden invitation tourney. The clash of the two teams for the so-called championship was heralded as the battle of the giants.

It didn't turn out that way because Mr. Mikan, who scored 487 points during the season and was generally rated the best all-around big fellow in basketball history, broke out in a rash of personal fouls and retired to the sidelines early. From that point Kureland & Co. went on to win rather handily by 52 to 44.

St. John's Topped Met Teams

Once again St. John's of Brooklyn topped the quintets of the metropolitan district, but Joe Lapchick's Redmen met disaster in the semi-finals of the invitation tourney.

As is well known, college basketball is roughly divided into two categories. There are schools that operate before large audiences in professionally promoted arenas like the Garden, more or less frankly commercializing the game. And then there are other schools that spurn the gold and exercise in the comparative solitude of their own gymnasiums and the gymnasiums of their opponents. Or should it be gymnasii?

Anyway, the best of these independent teams that we in the East know anything about was the outfit of the West Point Cadets, Army, paced by Dale Hall, was beaten by Pennsylvania in a surprising upset but swept through the remainder of a hard schedule. No one will ever know how the Cadets would have fared against the Irish-sponsored tournament teams.

Cagers Bribed

No basketball review would be complete without mention of the Brooklyn college scandal. Detectives, investigating a totally unrelated crime in our town, uncovered, to their surpise, evidence that five members of Brooklyn College had accepted bribes to "throw" a game with Akron University in the Boston Garden. A fascinating fillip was added to the story when, in the process of tossing the miscreants out of school, it was learned that one of them never attended school except to play basketball.

Of course there was the devil to pay. The situation was magnified

Continued on Following Page

GEORGE MIKAN and Jack Allen, De Paul, tried in vain to check Cecil Hawkins, Oklahoma A. & M., which won National title in Red Cross benefit, 52—44.

N. Y. U. Five Victor Over Rochester In Garden, 59-51

Victors Take Long Lead in Early Minutes of Play Before 18,000

By GEORGE COLEMAN

New York U. waltzed through the Rochester Rivermen to a 59—51 triumph before a packed Garden crowd of 18,000 fans last night. St. John's U. played Ohio U. in the second game.

Although the Upstaters completely outplayed the Cannmen throughout the second half they could not overcome the one-sided score of 27—7 the Violets built up in the opening struggle's 10 minutes.

During the rally the New Yorkers showed the best basketball played at Ned Irish's popshot palace this season. Frank Mangiapane and Al Schayes controlled the rebounds under the Rochester backboard and were passing up to the N. Y. U. sharpshooters, Marty Goldstein, Don Forman and Sid Tanenbaum, who connected on seven of their first 11 shots.

N. Y. U. Takes Quik Lead

New York U. clicked through the first half. Schayes and Managapane controlled the rebounds under the Rochester basket and passed to the Violet popshot artists, Tannebaum, Goldstein and Forman. Hutchins scored the opening double for Rochester but the next visitors' two-pointer arrived five minutes later. During that time the Cannmen connected on seven of their first 11 shots plus a pair of foul shots, enabling New York U. to lead, 16—5.

From there on the Violets eased up on their high rate of scoring but they had little trouble staying far ahead of the Upstaters. Leading, 25—7, at the 10-minute mark, Coach Howard Cann substituted Al Most and Frank Debonis for Marty Goldstein and Al Schayes. Don Forman was the only starter to finish the early half, as the Cannmen led, 40—29.

Rochester had much more fight in the late session. The Up-staters replaced their loose defense of the first half with each Riverman crowding his N. Y. U. rival. The performance enabled them to outscore the Violets for the opening 10 minutes.

The Rivermen, led by Hutchins with five markers, netted nine points to the Cannmen's four in the opening five minutes for an New York U. edge of 44—32.

For the next five minutes Coach Cann made a few substitutions but kept the bulk of his first team in action. Yet the Violets could net only fouls two by Herb Walsh, one by Goldstein and another by Forman while Hutchins came through with two baskets and a free throw to cut the New York U. lead to a 48—37 count.

A. L. Batting Honors Taken By Stirnweiss

By BEN GOLD

George (Snuffy) Stirnweiss, Joe Gordon's wartime replacement at second base for the New York Yankees, climaxed another fine season by nosing out the ancient Tony Cuccinello of Chicago for the American League batting championship with the unusually low mark of .309.

Stirnweiss' title-winning average is the lowest since 1905 when Elmer Flick of Cleveland took the crown with the all-time low of .306. In 1944 Stirnweiss batted .319 and was fourth in the circuit in batting.

Cuccinello, former Dodger infielder, lost the league lead the very last day of the season and wound up with an average of .308.

Stirnweiss, who took part in every one of the Yankees' 152 games, rapped out 195 base hits, the most in the league, and also was on top with 107 runs scored, 301 total bases, 22 triples and for the second straight year led the league in stolen bases with 33.

Stephens Tops in Homers

Wally Moses of the White Sox led in doubles with 35 while Vern Stephens of St. Louis dethroned Nick Etten of the Yanks as home run king with 24. Leroy Schalk of the Pale Hose was high man in sacrifice hits with 24.

James Seerey of Cleveland hit three home runs on July 13 to tie the major league record and with a triple in the same game tied the major league modern record for four long hits in a single game, held by many players.

Hank Greenberg, who returned from the armed service in time to participate in 78 games, aided materially in leading the Detroit Tigers into the World Series. He clouted 13 home runs and ended with a .311 batting average.

Chi Tops in Clubs Batting

The final wartime campaign took its toll in the team batting averages as Chicago, out of the pennant picture the greater part of the season, topped the league with .262.

The Boston Red Sox were second in club batting with .260 while the Yanks finished third with .259.

Stirnweiss was the only full-time member of the Yankees to bat over .300. Nick Etten was the second most potent New Yorker with an average of .285 and third was Herschel Martin with .267.

The Red Sox left the most men on base with 1,225 and the Bronx Bombers were runners up in this department with 1,197 runners stranded.

The Yanks as a team hit for the most total bases with 1,933, the most home runs with 93 and the most runs batted in with 639.

Barnhill to Arkansas

Little Rock, Ark., Dec. 22 (U.P.)—John Barnhill, Tennessee wartime head coach, today was named football coach at the University of Arkansas, succeeding Glen Rose.

34 Minor Leagues 3 of Them New, To Operate in '46

Durham, N. C., Dec. 22 (U.P.)—At least 34 minor leagues, 22 more than last season, will operate in 1946, President William H. Bramham of the National Association of Professional Baseball Leagues announced tonight.

Only three of the 22 leagues are new ones—the Florida-International, Georgia-Alabama and Kansas-Oklahoma-Missouri.

Active leagues which operated in 1945: Class AAA—American Association, Pacific Coast and International; Class AA—Southern Association; Class A—Eastern; Class B—Inter-State, Piedmont; Class C—Carolina; Class D—Appalachian, North Carolina State, Ohio State and Pony.

Suspended leagues restored to active status: Class AA—Texas; Class A—South Atlantic; Class B—Three-Eye, Western International; Class C—Canadian-American, Pioneer, Northern, Western Association; Class D—Georgia- Florida, Wisconsin State.

Disbanded leagues reorganized: Class B—Southeastern; Class C—California, East Texas, West Texas-New Mexico; Class D—Coastal Plain, Eastern Shore, Florida State, Evangeline, Kitty.

New leagues: Class C—Florida-International; Class D—Georgia-Alabama, Kansas-Oklahoma-Missouri.

Schwartz Advances In Junior Net Play

Top seeded Sidney Schwartz of Erasmus High School entered the quarter final round of the Eastern Junior Tennis championship tournament yesterday by defeating Kenneth M. Shimizu, 6—0, 6—1 at the 15th Armory. It was the first match Schwartz has had to play as he drew a first round bye and won by default in the second round.

James L. Bicknell of Garden City seeded fourth, and Walter Dockerill of Larchmont also entered the bracket of eight. Bicknell defeated Jerome Seifer, 6—3, 6—2 and Dockerill stopped Ashbel Green, 6—1, 6—3.

Robert M. Haft of Manhattan became the first to reach the semi-finals of the Eastern Boys championship tourney by upsetting Abraham M. Fabian in three sets, 6—3, 6—8, 6—2.

Arnold L. Ger of Erasmus scored an upset in the second round of the Junior play by beating Hans Eckardt of Forest Hills, 6—3, 3—6, 6—2. Eckardt, a student of Brooklyn Tech, had previously beaten Ger in love sets at the Brooklyn Junior championships last Summer.

Robert M. Luxenberg of Erasmus won his second round match from Richard M. Palmer, 6—2, 7—5. Luxenberg, Ger and Schwartz are all members of the Junior Davis Cup team of Brooklyn.

Richard C. Mouledous of New Orleans, top seeded in the Boys' tourney, breezed through his second round match with Kenneth D. Pearlman, 6—0, 6—2.

In the Junior Doubles competition four matches were played with Schwartz and Alan Hetzeck of Detroit defeating Richard Gassner and Richard Thompson, 6—4, 6—2. The illness of seven contestants raised havoc with the doubles draw sheet.

Competition in all classes continues this morning and afternoon and it is hoped the fials will be completed tomorrow.

JUNIOR SINGLES

Second Round—Arnold L. Ger defeated Hans Eckardt, 6—3, 3—6, 6—2; James L. Bicknell defeated Robert Eckstein, 5—7, 6—3, 6—4; Jerome Seifer won by default from Ira A. HawkinsIII; Richard B. Thompson defeated Richard Fine, 4—6, 6—4, 6—4; Ashbel Green III defeated Frank Hammond by default; Frederick Scribner defeated Ray Kaufman, 6—4, 6—3; John M. Williams defeated Richard Arnold, 6—1, 6—2; Alan Hetzeck defeated Arthur Broverman, 6—3, 6—0. John J. Simon defeated Leo Mabel, 6—3, 6—2; Robert M. Luxenberg defeated Richard M. Palmer, 6—2, 7—5.

Third Round—Sidney Schwartz defeated Kenneth M. Shimizu, 6—0, 6—1; Walter Dockenll defeated Ashbel Green, 6—1, 6—3; James L. Bucknell defeated Jerome Seifer, 6—3, 6—2.

Boys Singles

Second Round—Richard C. Mouledous defeated Kenneth D. Pearlman, 6—0, 6—2; Abraham M. Fabian won by default from Pablo S. Eisenberg; Thomas M. Lewyn defeated Don Dockenll, 6—3, 6—0; William Long defeated David Seifer, 6—0, 6—0; Alan J. Fischl won by default from Alan Seligson; Gilbert A. Bogley defeated Harold Lipton 6—2, 6—3.

Third Round—Robert M. Haft defeated Abraham M. Fabian, 6—3, 6—8, 6—2.

JUNIOR DOUBLES

Second Round—Hetzeck and Schwartz defeated Richard Gassner and Richard Thompson, 6—1, 6—2; Richard Palmer and Fred Feuerbach defeated Jay L. Funston and Wallace J. Ott, 6—4, 6—0; Marvin Mantin and Shimizu defeated James L. and Stewart D. Bucknell, 6—2, 6—2; Ashbed Green and John M. Williams defeated Arnold L. Ger and Ray Kaufman, 6—4, 6—3.